BRUDNEY AND CHIRELSTEIN'S

CASES AND MATERIALS

ON

CORPORATE FINANCE

FOURTH EDITION

By

VICTOR BRUDNEY

Weld Professor of Law Emeritus, Harvard Law School

and

WILLIAM W. BRATTON

Professor of Law, Rutgers University

Westbury, New York
THE FOUNDATION PRESS, INC.
1993

Library of Congress Cataloging-in-Publication Data
Brudney, Victor.
    Cases and materials on corporate finance / by Victor Brudney and
William W. Bratton. — 4th ed.
        p.   cm. — (University casebook series)
    Includes index.
    ISBN 1–56662–059–7
    1. Corporations—Finance—Law and legislation—United States—
Cases. I. Bratton, William W., 1951–   . II. Title.
III. Series.
KF1428.A7B78   1993
346.73'066—dc20
[347.30666]   93–3011

PREFACE TO THE FOURTH EDITION

We took the occasion of the preparation of this fourth edition to reexamine the book as a whole, as well as to update each of its parts. A number of segments have been reconstructed from the ground up in response to developments in economic theory or shifts in the law. Many have been reorganized or expanded for purposes of clarification. But the book's basic outline survives in substantially the same form.

The book still begins with valuation and the principles of financial economics. As before, the focus then shifts from the firm as a whole to the right side of its balance sheet. Working from the top to the bottom, the book describes the sources and parameters of the rights of the classes of securityholders that share in, and at times compete for, the firm's value. As the discussion moves down the balance sheet from debt to preferred, through convertible securities, and on to common stock, the economic causes of legal conflicts undergo a shift. With senior securities, struggles over value tend to occur when downside risks become realities. Contrariwise, the law of dividends, mergers, and takeovers comes to bear when possibilities for upside gain occasion allocational conflicts among the firm's common stockholders and managers. Sources of law also shift with the succession of topics. The law of senior securities is an exercise in advanced contract law that proceeds against the limit imposed by the legal institution of bankruptcy. As the interests in question become more junior and keyed to stakes in the firm's upside potential, legal intervention under corporate law's fiduciary rubric takes a more prominent place in the conflicts' resolution. Public trading and dispersed securityholding being a constant at all points on the balance sheet's right side, the book regularly makes reference over to federal and state requirements for disclosure of information in securities transactions. As in the previous editions, the book pauses at the break between senior securities and common stock to take up theoretical and practical questions about the role that the choice of capital structure plays in the maximization of the firm's overall value.

It is our hope that this structure provides a flexible base on which to shape an advanced corporations course. We anticipate that teachers come to this subject matter with differing pedagogical concerns and must respond to differing curricular demands. Depending on the number of hours allotted and the curricular fit, economics and policy may be emphasized over doctrine, or vice versa; senior securities may be emphasized over mergers and acquisitions, or vice versa; federal securities law questions may be given more or less emphasis.

One major structural change should be noted. We have eliminated the extended exposition of the policy content of the federal securities laws that concluded the third edition. Some of these materials have been relocated. Disclosure of projections and soft information is now taken up in the materials on mergers and acquisitions, along with a discussion of insider trading in tender offer contexts. In addition, a much condensed version of previous edition's general discussion of the federal statutes and their policy content now appears as the second segment of Appendix B. The condensation serves two functions. First, it provides the student unfamiliar with the outline of the mandatory disclosure system with background to support consideration of the units on disclosure problems that appear periodically in the book. Second, for those teachers inclined to get down to cases, it describes a context in which the economic theories set out in Part I plainly influence the development of an area of corporate law.

Part I contains a much expanded discussion of the efficient capital market hypothesis and the theories that now compete with it. In addition, textual material on valuation fundamentals has been added so as to make initial materials more accessible to the beginning student.

Part II, on senior securities, also has grown. The materials on debt securities are almost entirely new. They begin with a background presentation of debt contract provisions and contracting patterns. They go on to cover selected debt contract interpretation questions, the dislocations caused by the leveraged restructurings of the 1980s, the collective action problems of workouts, lender liability, and fraudulent conveyances. With this extended treatment, the book's section on debt now more closely parallels the section on preferred stock, duplicating some of the latter's themes. These themes can be given their due without both sets of materials being taken up in all particulars. We opted to include extensive treatments of both topics with the expectation that teachers will bring their own preferences to bear in emphasizing one chapter or the other.

The segment on chapter 11 reorganization in Part II has been expanded to cover recent debates on absolute priority and new value. It remains a unit that concentrates on theoretical questions rather than practical applications. Even so, the revision takes care to provide more in the way of supporting background materials, both historical and contemporary.

The preferred stock materials more closely resemble those of past editions. But here also we have trimmed and reorganized in order to accommodate recent cases. The segment on convertible securities also repeats the themes of the previous edition, but does so in reorganized form against a more extensive background presentation. The materials on state law regulation of capital, surplus, and dividends have been deleted in their entirety and replaced by a short textual description. We judged that the subject is in the process of becoming less complex in light of the movement to eliminate the old capital concepts from the law. While the matter still has some significance, the remaining questions simply are not worth the time of case by case treatment.

Parts III and IV, on capital structure and leverage and dividends and retained earnings, will look familiar to users of the previous editions. They have been updated and reorganized to accommodate the commentary and regulatory developments of the last six years. The cessation of leveraged restructuring leaves the themes in substantially the same alignment.

Part V, on mergers and acquisitions, has been completely revised on the economic side. Drawing on recent commentaries, we have enriched the book's development of the theme of valuation in a context of dispersed ownership as it bears on both the generation of mergers and the stakes in the regulation of takeovers. On the legal side, the most extensive revisions have been prompted by developments in the state law of appraisal rights and takeover defense and the application of federal antifraud provisions to mergers. Here also the new materials create opportunities for fresh consideration of the normative implications of the search for value. Significantly, all three of these topics show the insights of financial economics taking a forward role in the law's evolution.

Special thanks are due to the research assistants who helped with the project, Tara Barrett, Pete Malloy, Denis Segota, and Rich Shorten.

Finally, we recall an admonition attributed to William O. Douglas to those who tend to dwell on allocational problems among the firm's financial claimants. The struggle between the Class A stock and the Class B stock, he is said to have noted, is not the class struggle. Although mindful of this warning, we find that this book's organizational theme—the relation between the value of the firm and the legal structure of the competing claims of its securityholders—continues to engage and instruct as it comes to bear on new problems, new law and new ideas.

W.W.B.
V.B.

February 1993

University Casebook Series

ACKNOWLEDGMENTS

It is with appreciation that acknowledgment is made to the publishers and authors who gave permission for the reproduction of excerpts from the following materials:

American Accounting Association. Accounting Review

> Hong, Kaplan and Mandelker, Pooling v. Purchase: The Effects of Accounting for Mergers on Stock Prices © 1978

American Bar Association, Section of Corporation, Banking and Business Law. The Business Lawyer

> Campbell and Zack, Put a Bullet in the Poor Beast ... © 1977

> Greene and Freund, Substance over Form S–14: A Proposal to Reform SEC Regulation of Negotiated Acquisitions © 1981

> Schulman and Schenk, Shareholder's Voting and Appraisal Rights in Corporate Acquisition Transactions © 1983

American Economic Association. American Economic Review and Journal of Economic Perspectives

> Easterbrook, Two Agency–Cost Explanations of Dividends © 1984

> Jensen, Agency Costs of Free Cash Flow, Corporate Finance and Takeovers

> Lintner, Distributions of Incomes of Corporations Among Dividends, Retained Earnings and Taxes

> Lintner, Expectations, Mergers and Equilibrium in Purely Competitive Securities Markets

> Miller, The Modigliani–Miller Propositions After 30 Years © 1988

> Sheifer and Summers, The Noise Trading Approach to Finance © 1990

American Enterprise Institute for Public Policy Research, Manne (Ed.), Economic Policy and the Regulation of Corporate Securities © 1969

> Lintner, A Model of a Perfectly Functioning Securities Market

American Finance Association. Journal of Finance

> Miller, Leverage © 1991

California Law Review

> Eisenberg, The Legal Role of Shareholders and Management in Modern Corporate Decision Making © 1959

Columbia Law Review

> Kraakman, Taking Discounts Seriously: The Implications of "Discounted" Share Prices as an Acquisition Motive. This article originally appeared at 88 Colum.L.Rev. 891 (1988). Reprinted by permission.

Lowenstein, Management Buy–Outs. This article originally appeared at 85 Colum.L.Rev. 730 (1985). Reprinted by permission.

The Dryden Press, a division of Holt, Rinehart and Winston, Inc.

Brigham and Gapenski, Financial Management: Theory and Practice (6th ed. 1991) © 1991

Duke Law Journal

Bratton, Corporate Debt Relationships: Legal Theory in a Time of Restructuring © 1989

Yablon, Poison Pills and Litigation Uncertainty © 1989

Elsevier Science Publishers B.V. Journal of Financial Economics

Asquith and Mullins, Equity Issues and Offering Dilution © 1986

Smith and Warner, On Financial Contracting: An Analysis of Bond Covenants © 1979

Federal Reserve Bank of Philadelphia. Business Review of the Federal Reserve Bank of Philadelphia

Berlin, Bank Loans and Marketable Securities: How do Financial Contracts Control Borrowing Firms? © 1987

Financial Analysts Journal

Modigliani and Pogue, An Introduction to Risk and Return: Concepts and Evidence

Fordham University Press

Baumol, The Stock Market and Economic Efficiency © 1965

Harvard Business Review

Jensen, Michael C., Eclipse of the Public Corporation (September/October 1989) © 1989 by the President and Fellows of Harvard College; all rights reserved

Harvard Business School

Asquith and Mullins, Signalling with Dividends, Repurchases and Equity Issues. Research Paper 75th Anniversary Colloquium Series © (1984)

Harvard Law Review Association

Andrews, The Stockholder's Right to Equal Opportunity in the Sale of Shares © 1965

Henry Holt and Company, Inc. and CBS College Publishing

Buchanan, The Economics of Corporate Enterprise © 1940

Insights, a publication of Prentice Hall Law & Business

Steinwurtzel and Gardner, Super Poison Puts as a Protection Against Event Risk © 1989

Richard D. Irwin, Inc.

Hunt, Williams, and Donaldson, Basic Business Finance (4th Ed. 1971) © 1971

ACKNOWLEDGMENTS

Lorie, Dodd and Kimpton, The Stock Market: Theories and Evidence © 1985

Ross, Westerfield, and Jaffee, Corporate Finance (2d ed. 1990) © 1990

Ross, Westerfield, and Jordan, Fundamentals of Corporate Finance © 1991

Journal of Legal Studies

Bebchuk, The Sole Owner Standard for Takeover Policy © 1988

Schwartz, The Fairness of Tender Offer Prices in Utilitarian Theory © 1988

Law and Contemporary Problems, Duke University School of Law © 1958

Gibson, How Fixed are Class Shareholder Rights?

MacMillan Publishing Company

Bierman and Smidt, The Capital Budgeting Decision (1966) © 1966

McGraw–Hill, Inc.

Brealey and Myers, Principles of Corporate Finance (4th Ed.) © 1991

Cottle, Murray, and Block, Graham and Dodd's Security Analysis (Fifth ed. 1988) © 1988

Graham, Dodd and Cottle, Security Analysis (4th Ed.) © 1962

Sharpe, W.F., Portfolio Theory and Capital Markets © 1970

Michigan Law Review

Ayer, Rethinking Absolute Priority After *Ahlers* © 1989

MIT Press

Kolbe, Read and Hall, The Cost of Capital: Estimating the Rate of Return for Public Utilities © 1984

National Bureau of Economic Research

Durand, Costs of Debt and Equity Funds for Business: Trends and Problems of Measurement © (1952)

National Conference Board

F.A. Lees, Repurchasing Common Stock, Research Bulletin No. 147 © (1983)

New York Law School Review

Borden and Weiner, An Investment Decision Analysis of Cash Tender Offers

New York University Law Review

Note: The Courts and the Williams Act: Try a Little Tenderness © 1973

Oxford University Press, Coffee, Lowenstein and Rose–Ackerman, Editors (1987), Knights, Raiders, and Targets: The Impact of Hostile Takeovers © 1987 by Center for Law and Economic Studies, Columbia University

Coffee, Shareholders versus Managers: The Strain in the Corporate Web

Herman and Lowenstein, The Efficiency Effects of Hostile Takeovers

Quorum Books, an imprint of Greenwood Publishing Group, Inc., Westport, CT. Marc I. Steinberg, Editor, Tender Offers: Developments and Commentaries © 1985 by Marc I. Steinberg

Goelzer and Cohen, The Empire Strikes Back—Post Mite Developments in State Anti–Takeover Regulation

Sargent, Do the Second–Generation Takeover Statutes Violate the Commerce Clause?

Praeger Publishers, an imprint of Greenwood Publishing Group, Inc., Westport, CT

Donaldson, G., Managing Corporate Wealth: The Operation of a Comprehensive Financial Goals System © 1984 Gordon Donaldson

Prentice–Hall, Inc.

Farrar and Meyer, Managerial Economics © 1970

Van Horne, Financial Management and Policy (9th Ed. 1992) © 1992, (6th Ed. 1983) © 1983

Regents of the University of California, California Management Review © 1964

Brigham, The Profitability of a Firm's Repurchase of its Own Common Stock. By permission of the Regents

Rutgers Law Review

Hackney, Accounting for Mergers and Acquisitions Under the New Jersey Business Corporation Act

Standard and Poor's Corporation, The Review of Securities Regulation

Olson, Accounting for Mergers © 1970

University of Chicago Law Review

Blum and Katz, Depreciation and Enterprise Valuation

University of Pennsylvania Law Review

Blair–Smith and Helfenstein, A Death Sentence or a New Lease on Life: A Survey of Corporate Adjustments Under the Public Utility Holding Company Act © 1946

Klein, The Convertible Bond: A Peculiar Package © 1975

LoPucki and Whitford, Bargaining Over Equity's Share in the Bankruptcy Reorganization of Large Publicly Held Companies © 1990

ACKNOWLEDGMENTS

Virginia Law Review Association and Fred B. Rothman & Company

> Brudney, A Note on Materiality and Soft Information Under the Federal Securities Laws

> Coffee, Market Failure and the Economic Case for a Mandatory Disclosure System

> Easterbrook and Fischel, Mandatory Disclosure and the Protection of Investors

Wadsworth Publishing Company, Inc.

> Alchian and Allen, University Economics (3rd Ed., 1972) © 1972

> Lewellen, W.G., The Cost of Capital (1969) © 1969

John Wiley & Sons, Inc.

> Dewing, The Financial Policy of Corporations (5th Ed. 1953) © 1953

> Grayson, The Use of Statistical Techniques in Capital Budgeting, in Robichek, Editor, Financial Research and Management Decisions © 1967. Reprinted by permission of John Wiley & Sons, Inc.

Wisconsin Law Review

> Bratton, The Economics and Jurisprudence of Convertible Bonds © 1984

Yale Law Journal and Fred B. Rothman & Company

> Easterbrook and Fischel, Corporate Control Transactions

> Fischel, The Economics of Lender Liability, from *The Yale Journal*, Vol. 99, pp. 131–154

> Manning, The Shareholder's Appraisal Remedy: An Essay for Frank Coker

*

SUMMARY OF CONTENTS

APPENDICES

*

TABLE OF CONTENTS

PART V: MERGERS AND ACQUISITIONS

TABLE OF CONTENTS

TABLE OF CONTENTS

TABLE OF CASES

Principal cases are in italic type. Non-principal cases are in roman type. References are to Pages.

*

CASES AND MATERIALS

ON

CORPORATE FINANCE

*

Part I: ENTERPRISE AND SECURITIES VALUATION

INTRODUCTION

Valuation—of the corporate enterprise and of its securities—is a theme that pervades and loosely unifies the cases and readings collected in this volume, both those that are legal in character and those that are oriented to economics and business. From a legal standpoint, many of the most interesting issues in the field of corporate finance turn on questions of enterprise valuation. Thus, for example, the "fairness" of tender offers, mergers and other organic changes which alter the existing rights of security owners, the usefulness of appraisal as a remedy for dissenting stockholders, the right of junior security owners to participate in an insolvent enterprise undergoing reorganization, the "materiality" of information withheld by directors and officers who trade in the corporation's securities—all of these (and other) significant legal problems in some sense require an answer to the question of how much the corporate enterprise and its securities are worth. That this question is partly or even largely one of definition takes nothing away from its importance nor, certainly, from its complexity.

1. *Valuation and the Objective of the Firm.*

Valuation occurs in the first instance in business contexts. It is of central importance to the individuals who undertake the task of managing a corporation's financial affairs. The proper goals of the large, publicly held, professionally managed corporation have been debated by social theorists for many years, and institutional and other investors have been reported from time to time to be seriously reexamining their investment policies in the light of various social concerns. Nevertheless, it is difficult to entertain serious doubts about the dominant objectives of the investing public. The aim of ordinary equity investors—which they expect management to pursue in their behalf—is simply to enhance their economic welfare through stock ownership; for that reason the investor pays his money; for that reason he takes his chance; no other assumption is admissible as far as he is concerned. Accordingly, the objective of the firm from the equity investor's standpoint can be stated easily: it is to maximize the value of the corporation to its stockholders, subject to whatever constraints may be imposed by law and public policy. It is, of course, far from self-evident that corporate managers actually behave in accordance with this norm, and indeed a substantial body of opinion supports a contrary assumption, as later materials will suggest. Nevertheless, value-maximization is a useful organizing principle which serves well as a basis for further discussion of corporate goals and management behavior, and doubtless conforms reasonably closely to investors' expectations.

1

Even if adopted as a starting point, however, the above description of the firm's "objective" requires refinement. When we speak of "maximizing the value of the corporation", what measure of worth do we regard as relevant? Should our focus be on the firm's after-tax profits, or should it be on earnings per share, or dividends, or rate of return, or growth prospects, to name a few of the better known standards? For at least three reasons it appears that none of these measures is sufficiently comprehensive and unambiguous to serve our purpose in a wholly satisfactory way. First, if it is asserted that the goal of the firm should be (for example) to "maximize profits", there would still be the question of whether *current* or *future* profits is meant. Is a modest profit this year as good as, or worse or better than, a much larger profit at a later time? To answer, we must know exactly how much larger and how much later, since "profits" comprehends both possibilities. Second, given that the future is uncertain, what should be done to reflect the factor of investment risk? Is the expectation of a small but relatively safe profit as good as, or worse or better than, the expectation of a large but relatively risky one? Again, the question cannot be answered by reference only to a standard of profit-maximizing; something must also be known about investors' attitudes towards risk-taking. Finally, how is the term "profit" to be defined? Does it refer to the accounting definition of "income" (in all of its notorious variations), or to some other concept of annual accretion?

Taken by itself, therefore, the familiar profit-maximizing standard leaves open important questions about timing and risk, and lacks a clearly established definition of "profits" unless accounting practice is permitted, and is able, to supply one. As may be surmised, "earnings per share", "dividends", and other profit-related standards suffer from most or all of the same ambiguities and insufficiencies. The term "growth", in addition, lacks a clear referent; it might be taken to refer to growth in sales volume or asset size, for example, neither of which need always benefit the company's shareholders. And if expanded to mean "growth of profits," the same problems of timing, risk and definition are encountered once again.

How can these ambiguities be avoided? Let us return to our very first postulate about the proper objective of the firm; namely, that the firm's goal should be to maximize the economic welfare of its shareholders. Let us also ignore for the moment any question of social concerns and any conflicts of interest between stockholders and senior security-holders. What matters, on this view, is not profits, earnings, dividends or growth *as such*, but the ability of the company's shareholders, through the ownership of its shares, to acquire goods and services in the amounts and at the times that produce the largest measure of individual satisfaction. The important question is: How can the firm most directly aid its shareholders in achieving their personal wealth objectives?

Many financial writers would respond by saying that the aim of the firm should be to *maximize the market price per share of its stock*—that is, to achieve the highest sustainable market value for the company's common shares. If the market price of the company's stock is maximized, the stock owner's wealth is necessarily maximized as well—which means that his opportunity (whether through spending or saving) to acquire the satisfactions that wealth provides is likewise at an optimum. Of course, acceptance of this standard does not excuse management from being concerned with the timing and risk of expected returns, since those factors are presumably critical to investors whose decisions to buy or sell determine the market price of the company's shares. All that is meant is that when a given issue of financial policy is posed for decision, that issue should be resolved by reference to a single inclusive criterion, namely, the impact of management's action on the current market value of the owner's equity. See Van Horne, Financial Management and Policy (9th ed. 1992); Brealey and Myers, Principles of Corporate Finance (4th ed. 1991); Copeland and Weston, Financial Theory and Corporate Policy (2d ed. 1983).

But if maximum market price per share is accepted as the goal (or even as one important goal) of financial management, it is clear at once that the managers themselves require a valuation model for the shares of the corporation. The factors upon which share price depends must be known, or at least assumed, if the financial managers are to pursue the maximization objective in a rational manner. Thus, for example, if market price is a function of asset size, then the firm's managers should do all they can to increase assets; if it is a function of the firm's capital structure, or of its dividend or earnings patterns, different decision criteria might be relevant.

2. *Valuation, Capital Structure and Dividend Policies of the Firm.*

Presumably, if an enterprise has only common stock outstanding, the value of the enterprise should be equal to the aggregate value of the common stock on the market. Questions come up, however, respecting the value of enterprises having securities outstanding in addition to common stock. Consider two companies which are in all respects alike except that *A* has only common stock outstanding while *B* has long-term bonds and preferred stock outstanding as well as common shares. Even though *A* and *B* possess the same economic operating characteristics, is it possible that the market value of *B*'s shares might be higher or lower than that of *A*'s shares because of the presence of senior securities having a limited but prior claim on the income stream? Put otherwise, does the existence of the senior securities impose different risk-return characteristics on *B*'s common shares than those that relate directly to *B*'s business activities, with the possible consequence that the value of *B*'s shares will be penalized or enhanced, relative to *A*'s? Similarly, if *B* follows a more generous dividend policy than *A*, paying out a larger proportion of its annual earnings to stockholders, would this factor be likely to alter investors' outlooks and induce a preference for the securities of one firm over the other? In short, apart from the firm's business and investment policies, are there aspects of financial practice, whether in respect to capital structure or dividends, which independently affect the value of the firm or its securities? These issues are considered in Parts III and IV infra.

3. *Valuation and Trading Markets—The Relationship of Intrinsic Value and Market Value.*

Questions also come up about the import market prices have for valuation. Valuations occur when business actors trade producing assets as well as when they manage assets on a going concern basis. Whether the investment is in an entire firm, in a security, or in some other asset, a valuation will occur before a purchase and sale transaction is concluded. Where there exists an active and extensive market for securities or assets being bought and sold, the price set in the market by the many buyers and sellers comes to signal the value for the transacting parties.

When valuations occur in legal contexts, the same economic data that determine valuations in business transactions come to bear. But the legal valuations are undertaken to vindicate legal norms and, as a result, take on certain special characteristics. Legal valuation usually is conceived as the job of assimilating detailed economic data in sizable quantities and designing theoretical equipment with which the data can be reduced to a defensible value figure. The value figure, once derived, takes on objective significance as the "intrinsic value" of the firm, security, or asset.

Questions come up about the direction taken by this inquiry into "intrinsic value" whenever a trading market exists in the asset or security in question. Should the market price be taken as the best measure of intrinsic value? Much will depend on whether information flows between the enterprise and the financial community are adequate. If investors have been led to misperceive the risk-return attributes of the firm's real assets through insufficient or misleading data, then the market price of its securities may reflect that misperception as well, at least until corrected by voluntary action or under the compulsion of the securities laws. But, assuming that investors are fully and accurately informed, is it then likely, or indeed, inevitable, that enterprise and securities values will be identical?

Where judges search for "intrinsic" value even though an adequately informed "market value" derived from the market prices of the firm's securities is available, they assume that the value to which the law attaches certain consequences is not measured by the market accurately, or at least adequately for the purpose of vindicating the legal norm. It follows that inquiry into "intrinsic" value independent of market price of securities must be made in order to determine the existence or non-existence of a fact—value—which will trigger certain legal consequences. A significant body of commentary questions this approach. It draws on economic theory—particularly the capital asset pricing model and the efficient market hypothesis—to assert that market prices of the firm's securities are the best available indicators of value. But other, equally sophisticated economic theory can be drawn on to show that market prices and intrinsic values do not necessarily coincide.   Under this approach market prices and enterprise values persistently diverge because investors in securities act on different premises than purchasers of assets and in any event are unwise, uneducated, emotional and inclined to react to irrelevant variables.   As a result, investors must bear not only business, and possibly financial risks, but also the hazards of an unstable market in which real values are often disregarded.   Part I of this book describes both of these economic perspectives on market prices and intrinsic values.

4.   *Valuation and Financial Contracting.*

This book's exploration of value and the role of law in its maximization also includes consideration of financial contracts.   It is often asserted that where some institutional barrier prevents reliable market valuation, the appropriate solution to disputes over corporate value is not legal intervention but deregulation toward the end of getting the assets in question to the highest valuing user through the mechanism of free contract.   Thus, the study of valuation in matters of corporate finance requires consideration of contracts as value maximizing tools. The legal materials that follow frequently deal with conflicts among various classes of claimants within a given firm—common stockholders, preferred stockholders, bondholders and managers—where the stakes are the firm's value.   Resolution of these "pie splitting" contests in wholly equitable ways turns out to be quite difficult to achieve.   Traditionally, legal decisionmakers have brought a mix of contract and fairness concepts to bear on their resolution.   Throughout the materials that follow, "fairness" vies with "contract" as the basis for allocating slices of value among conflicting claimants.

5.   *Summary—Valuation and Law.*

Finally, let us assume that a sound theory of valuation of corporations and their securities can be derived.   A question arises.   Should the law and legal regulators employ the theory to encourage or require managers to produce higher market value for stock?   For the enterprise?   ·If the answer to either question is "yes," what is the cheapest and most effective mode of implementation and what are the allocative consequences of such regulation?   If the answer is "no," and such regulation turns out to be inappropriate, what factor is responsible?   Is regulation inappropriate because market forces suffice to encourage higher values?   Or is value maximization such a complex objective as to make effective legal regulation unachievable as a practical matter?   Or does our basic assumption that stock price maximization is the appropriate goal for corporate managers turn out to be too simplistic in some contexts because of conflicts of interest between the various constituents of the corporation—not only the shareholders and managers but also bondholders and other creditors?   Or, finally, do even the most soundly conceived theories of valuation, when applied in practical contexts, turn out to have serious shortcomings?   These questions recur in the materials collected in this book.

SECTION A. VALUATION OF
THE GOING CONCERN

The *Atlas Pipeline* case, which follows next, presents the valuation problem in the context of the two major interlocking themes of these materials.

Atlas Pipeline involves a failed business enterprise, one whose operating income has proved insufficient to meet the contractual claims of its creditors. Under Chapter X of the Bankruptcy Act, (which was replaced by Chapter 11 of the Bankruptcy Act of 1978) the federal court having approved the petition for reorganization, the company came under jurisdiction and authority of that court. The task of the court was to decide whether, and in what amounts, the claims of various individual and classes of creditors were valid, whether the enterprise was viable, and whether the value of the enterprise was sufficient to satisfy those claims. To make those decisions took time—sometimes several years—during which the enterprise's earnings-generating assets had to be preserved intact. Protection of the company's assets was afforded in a proceeding under Chapter X, (and still is, under the 1978 Bankruptcy Act) because once the jurisdiction of the court attached, the company's creditors were barred from immediately enforcing their claims—through ordinary foreclosure proceedings or otherwise. Instead, under Chapter X the enterprise was continued in operation, at least for the time being, while an effort was made to develop a plan of financial readjustment. The plan had to satisfy two legal standards. First, it had to be "feasible"—that is, a solvent future had to be a likely possibility for the reorganized firm. Second, it had to be "fair and equitable"—that is, it had to respect absolutely priorities of the securities in the firm's capital structure.

Having approved the petition, the court's duty in cases involving any sizeable amount was to appoint an independent trustee with responsibility for directing the continued operation of the business during the reorganization period. The trustee was authorized to investigate the conduct of the business by the prior management in order to recover assets they might have misapplied, and it was his task to formulate and file a reorganization plan. That plan was to provide (among other things) for the allocation of new participations in the enterprise among the various claimants. Claimants, usually organized in committees representing classes of creditors or stockholders, were authorized to submit their own competing reorganization plans. If one or more reorganization plans were approved by the court, it (or they) were then submitted to the corporation's security holders for their acceptance or rejection. Prior to judicial approval and submission to security holders, the reorganization plans were required to be referred to the Securities and Exchange Commission for an advisory report, to be sent to affected security holders and creditors, if the scheduled indebtedness exceeded $3,000,000; and the plans might be so referred in any event. The Commission's report was not binding on the court, and the Commission had no right to appeal the court's determination, though it might join in appeals taken by others.

The first question confronting the court in deciding on the nature of the reorganization was (and presumably still is under the 1978 Bankruptcy Act) whether the enterprise is worth more as a going concern than if it were liquidated and sold piecemeal. If it is worth more in liquidation, presumably its assets should be sold and the proceeds distributed to the creditors in accordance with their various entitlements. On the other hand, if the enterprise is worth more as a going concern, then, on the assumption that strangers will not pay as much for it as its current claimants will, new securities representing participations in the continuing enterprise should be distributed to the current claimants, again in accordance with their various entitlements. Valuation, of course, is a matter of estimate rather than certainty, and there will inevitably be disagreement among the parties about what value figure the court should finally accept. From the standpoint of their own self-interest, those creditors with prior ranking claims should urge a conservative valuation, since the lower the valuation (i.e., the less there seems to be to go around) the larger would be *their* percentage participation in the reorganized company. By the same token, junior claimants should urge a liberal valuation: the greater the appraised value of the company, the more "room" there would be for juniors to participate.

The foregoing is merely by way of background for the *Atlas Pipeline* case. In 1978 the Bankruptcy Act was substantially amended, and Chapter X was eliminated. Chapter 11 of the 1978 Act continues the "feasibility" requirement of Chapter X, in substance if not in form. But, under Chapter 11 the "fair and equitable" standard no longer prescribes the rights of all senior claimants vis-a-vis juniors. Furthermore, under the 1978 Act, the SEC has only a limited role to play in the proceeding; it no longer is to prepare advisory reports for security holders; and a trustee is no longer required to be appointed. (See pp. 309 to 312 infra.) Notwithstanding these changes in the law, the *Atlas Pipeline* case remains instructive. It is the first of a series of pie slicing contests among security holders that make up one theme of this book.

Atlas Pipeline must be read together with the economic materials in Section B of this Part. These set out the elements of valuation as presented in contemporary economic theory. Taken together, the case and the materials introduce the other main aspect of this work. Which of several alternative business decisions will maximize the value of the enterprise? Here the question is whether the Atlas Pipeline Company ought to be liquidated or reorganized; elsewhere we will deal with the question of the impact on enterprise values of the usual key financing decisions, e.g., the appropriate mix of stocks and bonds in the capital structure, the question of whether to finance through retained earnings or by going to the market for funds, the question of corporate dividend policy, etc. We will deal with questions of legal policy from the perspective of business practice and economic theory.

But again, whether the business or legal issue is how to increase the enterprise or how to split it, a theory of enterprise valuation is required, and it is with the development of such a theory that we will be concerned throughout. As indicated, the materials in this Part are intended to illustrate some of the more important economic variables relevant to that development.

In approaching the *Atlas Pipeline* case, it may be useful for some to read first the excerpt from Alchian and Allen, infra p. 33, on discounting expected future payments to present value. Calculation of present values is central to the valuation process, whether one's concern is with legal standards or with selection of investment projects and whether one is called upon to act as a lawyer or judge or as a participant in the day-to-day work of financial management. The mechanics of discounting, which are simple enough, should therefore be mastered at an early point.

IN THE MATTER OF ATLAS PIPELINE CORPORATION
9 S.E.C. 416 (1941).

[S.E.C. Advisory Report on Proposed Plan of Reorganization.]
HISTORY AND BUSINESS OF DEBTOR
DEBTOR'S BUSINESS AND PRINCIPAL ASSETS

The debtor is presently engaged in refining petroleum and marketing the products thereof. It owns an inland refinery located near Shreveport, La., and an oil pipe-line system connecting its refinery with oil fields in East Texas, Arkansas and Louisiana. In the past the debtor has operated as a pipe-line carrier transporting oil for other companies, but at the present time it is not carrying any oil through its East Texas line and is using its Arkansas–Louisiana line only to transport the crude oil requirements of its own refinery.

The debtor sells over half of its refined products to independent distributors and jobbers principally in the middle west area. The remainder of its output is sold locally, for the most part to major oil companies having retail distribution facilities in the Shreveport area; only about 3 percent of the debtor's output is sold through its own local retail subsidiary, Sparco Gasoline Company, Inc. In addition to its refinery and pipe-line properties the debtor owns an office building in Shreveport.

In November 1934 Atlas Pipeline Company, Inc., and its subsidiary, Spartan, both went into receivership. This was followed by a reorganization proceeding under Section 77B of the Bankruptcy Act. A plan was confirmed in that proceeding which provided, in brief, for a new $1,000,000 first mortgage bond issue, the proceeds of which were used to pay receiver's certificates ($225,000) and other cash requirements of the plan, and to provide increased working capital. The plan further provided for the issuance of $1,312,000 of second mortgage bonds, of which $712,000 went to Alco Products, Inc., a subsidiary of American Locomotive Company, in final settlement of the amount owing for cracking units which had been built in 1934. The remaining $600,000 of second mortgage bonds were issued to the holders of Shreveport–El Dorado bonds then outstanding in that amount.

The present debtor was organized in 1935 as a Delaware company to acquire the assets of Atlas and Spartan pursuant to the above plan, which went into effect on January 1, 1936. Thereafter the debtor defaulted on the interest payments due November 1, 1938 on both the first and second mortgage bonds, and a receivership proceeding was instituted on May 26, 1939 by the indenture trustee for the first mortgage bondholders. On August 17, 1939 the court directed a public sale of the mortgaged properties, and fixed an upset [i.e., minimum] price of $1,200,000. No bids were received and on September 20, 1939 the present proceeding was instituted by the filing of the debtor's petition for reorganization under Chapter X.

PRESENT CAPITALIZATION

The present capitalization of the debtor is as follows:

First mortgage 6% sinking-fund convertible bonds	$836,000	
Accrued interest to May 1, 1941	125,400	
		$961,400
Second mortgage 6% sinking-fund convertible bonds [a]	1,305,000	
Accrued interest to May 1, 1941	195,750	
		1,500,750
Common stock, par value $10 (shares)		268,800

[a] Exclusive of $7,000 face amount of bonds held by the debtor, which are to be canceled under the plan.

SUMMARY OF PLAN

A. DISTRIBUTION OF CASH AND SECURITIES

The proposed plan provides for the organization of a new company to take over the assets of the debtor. The new company will have the following capitalization:

4½% first mortgage bonds	$1,011,400
4% preferred stock	435,000
Common stock ($20 par value)	100,000

Under the plan federal tax claims aggregating approximately $43,000, as compromised, will be paid in cash. State ad valorem taxes in the amount of $56,669 and certain other state tax claims aggregating $5,710 will also be paid in cash in full. General unsecured claims aggregating approximately $400,000 will receive 10 percent in cash without interest. * * *

The first mortgage bondholders will receive $961,400 of the new 4½% first mortgage bonds, which corresponds to the principal amount of their claims plus accrued interest to May 1, 1941. The remaining $50,000 of new first mortgage bonds will be sold at par to the American Locomotive Company [3] subject to a purchase agreement with the Producers Group hereinafter described. The second mortgage bondholders will receive the new $435,000 issue of preferred stock, corresponding to one-third of the principal amount of their claims, "in exchange not only for the security of their mortgage but for their interest as ordinary creditors in the unmortgaged assets." In view of the debtor's insolvency, as found by the Court, its common stockholders are excluded from participation in the plan.

The common stock of the new company is to be purchased for $100,000 by a group of oil producers (hereinafter called "Producers Group" or "Group") who own or control substantial oil production in the Magnolia Oil Field, in Arkansas. As will be noted below, the common stock cannot be divested of control for at least the first 3 years of the company's existence because of failure to pay preferred stock dividends. The plan further provides that the new company shall enter into an oil purchase contract with the Producers Group under which it will agree to purchase all of its crude oil requirements from the group, up to a maximum of 8,000 barrels per day, for a period of 3 years. For such oil the contract provides that the company will pay the price posted in the Magnolia field by the major companies provided, however, that in no event shall the price payable under the contract be more than 5¢ above or more than 5¢ below $93/110$ths of the posted price for crude oil in the East Texas field. In other words, the price formula in the contract fixes a minimum and maximum price in terms of the price of East Texas crude. The contract provides that it may not be modified or extended during its life without the consent of those directors who are to represent the bondholders and preferred stockholders on the board.

In addition to their $100,000 payment for the common stock of the new company the Producers Group, in order to induce the American Locomotive Company to subscribe to $50,000 of new first mortgage bonds, agree to purchase such bonds from the latter at par plus accrued interest at the rate of $10,000 of bonds each year after consummation of the plan. The Producers Group further agree that during the life of the 3–year oil purchase contract they will advance the company short-term credit not to exceed $200,000 in the event that additional working capital is needed.[6]

---

3. This company holds $765,000 of the debtor's second mortgage bonds, including the $712,000 formerly held by Alco Products, Inc., its subsidiary.

6. Such credit may take the form of cash, commercial credit or crude oil and the Group:

"may require that the cash, credit or oil so furnished may be secured by an act of pledge, lien or chattel mortgage on the oil in storage and on the refined or manufactured products owned by the company on the basis of one hundred percent (100%) of the lower of cost or market value and together with the face amount of accounts receivable."

The plan further provides that such $200,000 loan or credit "may be declared due at any time that the company defaults in the payment for any oil purchased."

B. Terms and Voting Rights of New Securities

The new bonds will be dated May 1, 1941, and will mature in 15 years. They will bear interest at the rate of $4\frac{1}{2}\%$. Sinking-fund payments are required at the rate of $50,000 per year but it is provided that for the first 3 years this requirement may be met by expenditures for construction and deferred maintenance. It is also provided that the bonds may be purchased by the company in the open market (at not to exceed the call price of 105) and used at par in lieu of cash in meeting sinking-fund requirements. The lien securing the bonds will extend to the assets covered by the present first mortgage except for $150,600 in cash now held by the indenture trustee for the first mortgage bonds. This cash, representing the proceeds of the sale of certain mortgaged assets in 1938, will be transferred to the new company to be used for general purposes. The bondholders will be entitled to elect 1 out of 11 directors.

The preferred stock will carry a dividend rate of 4%. Dividends will be cumulative only if and to the extent earned for the first 33 months following consummation of the plan; thereafter dividends will be cumulative. The preferred stockholders are given the right to elect 1 director out of 11 at all times. If, after the first year eight successive quarterly preferred dividends are omitted, the entire voting rights pass to the preferred stock subject to the right of the common stockholders and the bondholders to elect two directors (one for each class). If, however, dividends are subsequently paid so as to reduce the arrears of unpaid preferred dividends to less than eight quarterly dividends (excluding the first year) control is to be revested in the common stock, subject again to the rights of the preferred stockholders and the bondholders to elect two directors.

The new common stock will have a par value of $20 per share. As noted above, the holders of the common stock will be entitled to elect 9 of the 11 directors subject only to the possibility of a shift of control to the preferred stockholders in the event of the omission of eight successive quarterly preferred dividends after the first year.

C. Summary

The plan, in brief, gives all the common stock and virtually complete control of the debtor to a group of oil producers who will have a 3–year contract to sell crude oil to the debtor, under which the latter is obligated to purchase all of its requirements. This group will pay $100,000 for the common stock of the company and will in effect guarantee the $50,000 investment in the new bonds by American Locomotive Company. In addition the group will to the extent required finance the sale of its crude to the new company up to $200,000 by secured short-term credit.

The first mortgage bondholders are required to take a reduction in interest from 6% to $4\frac{1}{2}\%$, to extend the maturity of their bonds for 15 years and to give up their lien on approximately $150,600 in cash held by the indenture trustee. The sinking-fund requirements in connection with their bonds are also reduced, and their conversion privilege is eliminated. The second mortgage bondholders are required to accept new 4% preferred stock having a par value equal to one-third of the principal amount of their claims.

EARNINGS

In order to pass on the fairness and feasibility of a plan of reorganization, it is necessary to determine the prospective earnings and value of the reorganized property. The capitalization of prospective earnings is the basic element in the latter determination. In estimating prospective earnings we may turn to the past earnings record of the debtor which, after adjustment for unusual conditions and reasonably foreseeable changes, here provides a guide to what may be anticipated in the future.

A. DEBTOR'S PAST EARNINGS

Table I * * * presents the debtor's net income by divisions before and after depreciation for the 5 years following the previous reorganization. In none of these years did the debtor earn a profit after depreciation, and losses even before depreciation were shown in 2 of the 5 years. It is to be noted also that the refining division reported a deficit before depreciation in every year and that such profits as were shown by the debtor were contributed by the pipe-line division.

It is against this background of unprofitable operations that the debtor's prospective earnings must be judged. However, a number of major changes have occurred during this 5–year period. Among the more significant of these is the loss of the debtor's former business in the transportation of crude oil for the account of others. This pipe-line business, which previously had contributed substantial revenues, ceased in September 1940 with the expiration of a contract with The Pure Oil Company. The debtor's system of gathering lines and the major part of its trunk line are not now in operation.

Since 1936 the debtor's source of crude oil supply has shifted frequently with the result that it has purchased oil from ten different fields at varying prices. This has involved changes in the type of oil processed, in the yield of refined products and in operating costs. The most important change that has occurred in this respect resulted from the bringing in of production in 1938 in the Magnolia and Schuler fields of southern Arkansas. Since these fields are located close to the debtor's pipe line and since Shreveport is now a natural outlet for some of this production large supplies of lower priced crude have become available to the debtor.

During the period refinery operations have also changed considerably both in volume and character. From 1936 to 1938 refining capacity was 9,000 barrels a day. Early in 1939 the refinery was shut down for a month and during the rest of 1939 and the greater part of 1940 one of the two cracking units was used for "topping" crude oil, thus lowering capacity to 6,000 barrels. However, from August to October 1940, certain rehabilitation work was completed which resulted in an increase in capacity to 8,000 barrels and in more efficient operation.

TABLE I

Earnings 1936–1940 by major divisions

	Net income before depreciation and nonoperating expenses	Depreciation	Net income after depreciation before nonoperating expenses
	Refinery division		
1936.............	($44,472.99)	$143,049.04	($187,522.03)
1937.............	(357,884.31)	143,524.58	(501,408.89)
1938.............	(240,776.12)	145,709.10	(386,485.22)
1939.............	(3,612.17)	148,090.94	(151,703.11)
1940.............	(60,714.98)	148,378.80	(209,093.78)
	Pipe-line division		
1936.............	183,778.05	85,092.23	98,685.82
1937.............	316,379.91	77,506.48	238,873.43
1938.............	175,692.42	80,553.70	95,136.72
1939.............	114,955.32	78,117.20	36,871.12
1940.............	108,846.53	73,957.25	34,889.28
	Other income (net)		
1936.............	32,184.40	27,131.23	5,053.17
1937.............	41,391.59	26,928.48	14,463.11
1938.............	1,450.00	—	1,450.00
1939.............	8,950.33	1,414.82	5,535.51
1940.............	(25,117.64)	1,414.80	(26,532.44)
	Total all divisions		
1936.............	171,489.46	255,272.50	(83,783.04)
1937.............	(112.81)	247,959.54	(248,072.35)
1938.............	(63,633.70)	226,262.80	(289,896.50)
1939.............	118,326.48	227,622.96	(109,296.48)
1940.............	23,013.91	223,750.85	(200,736.94)

( ) Loss

As a result of the significant changes in the character of the debtor's operations and in the conditions affecting them, it appears that the 5–year record of earnings as such does not constitute a satisfactory basis for the calculation of prospective earnings.

B. TRUSTEE'S ESTIMATE OF PROSPECTIVE EARNINGS

As the basis of his estimates the trustee has adopted the 5–month period from November 1940 through March 1941. To the debtor's earnings of this period he has applied various adjustments in arriving at his determination of prospective earnings. The use of this period as a base has certain advantages; it is a recent period, it follows the increase in refinery capacity and in operating efficiency which occurred in October 1940, it gives effect to the cessation of pipe-line transportation for the account of others and reflects the predominant use of Magnolia crude on which the refinery would operate during the life of the proposed purchase agreement. It appears therefore that although 5 months is a short record on which to predicate future earnings, the period selected by the trustee may here constitute an acceptable base period.

* * * [A]ctual earnings during the 5 months ended March 31, 1941, were $11,042 before depreciation, bond interest and discount. Without allowance for seasonal variation these earnings are at the rate of $26,500 for a full year. To these earnings the trustee has applied a number of adjustments as set forth in Table II.

We turn now to a consideration of the nature and reasonableness of the trustee's adjustments * * *.

TABLE II
Trustee's Estimate of Prospective Earnings
(Before bond interest, bond discount and depreciation)

Actual earnings (12 months' basis)		$26,500
Adjustments increasing earnings:		
Sales of refined products........................	$90,314	
Purchases: Crude oil *	78,733	
Purchases: Ethyl lead	45,444	
Refinery fuel.................................	29,798	
Total adjustments increasing earnings	244,289	
Adjustment decreasing earnings pipe-line operation	7,873	
Net adjustments increasing earnings		236,416
Trustee's estimated earnings (12 months' basis)		262,916

* [Ed.Note] The debtor contemplates savings by transporting some crude oil to its refinery over its own pipe-line, instead of paying third parties to transport the crude over their pipe-lines.

[The SEC disagreed with the Trustee's conclusion that owing to certain freight rate reductions ordered by the Interstate Commerce Commission for gasoline delivered in western territory, the debtor's net income from "Sales of refined products" would be increased by $90,314. The Commission accepted his assumption that competition would force refiners to absorb approximately 60 percent of the rate reduction by reducing prices to jobbers. However, the Commission questioned his assumption that the effect of the rate reduction would be to divert a substantial portion of the debtor's (and its local competitors') sales to the territory in which freight savings were to be realized by the shipper, and would result therefore in a decrease of local supplies and an increase in prices charged locally. It believed, because profits on local sales were so much higher than those in western territory, that even the retention of the amount of the rate reduction by shippers on western territory sales would not alter the relative profitability of local sales at prevailing prices, and therefore would not divert sales from the local market. Hence, it concluded that the effect of the rate reduction would extend to no more than a fraction of the debtor's gasoline sales, and reduced this item to $51,469, or $38,845 less than the Trustee's estimate.

The Commission found all other adjustments made by the Trustee to be acceptable, but it noted with respect to the adjustment for "Refinery fuel":]

During 1940 the debtor obtained a part of its natural gas requirements for refinery operation from a large gas company at a price of 9.167¢ per mcf. During the first 10 months of that year the debtor also purchased gas from a small supplier at a price of 5¢. However, this supply is apparently no longer available because none has been purchased from that source since October 1940. During the 5-month base period the price paid for gas was 9.167¢. It was testified that the debtor is considering an offer by an independent operator in the Sligo field to construct a pipe line to Shreveport, a distance of approximately 18 miles, and to sell gas to the debtor at 4¢ per mcf. delivered. There was also testimony regarding an alternative possibility of obtaining gas from the Waskom field, Texas, at 3¢ per mcf. at the field. This alternative would require the construction of a ¾ mile line by the debtor to connect its pipe line with the Waskom field and would entail the necessary operating cost incident to the operation of the line. However, in neither case has the operator made a commitment to supply gas nor has a showing been made as to reliability of either source of supply over a period of years. Nevertheless, the trustee has seen fit to make an adjustment to "Refinery fuel" to reflect the purchase of gas at the 4¢ rate. On the basis of gas purchases of 240,287 mcf. during the 5-month base period, the application of the 4¢ rate would result in a saving of $12,416 for 5 months, or $29,778 for a full year.

The evidence in the record is inconclusive with respect to the degree of probability attaching to the realization of this saving or the length of time for which it might be available. However, it is the trustee's opinion that recognition of this economy is reasonable. While we do not here take issue with the trustee on the inclusion of this adjustment, we point out that it involves a substantial element of uncertainty with respect to the realization and duration of the economy.

[The Commission then completed its review of the Trustee's projections with the following analysis of the debtor's "casing-head" operations:]

During the 5-month base period the debtor used 150,968 barrels of casing-head (natural) gasoline for blending purposes. This is at the rate of 362,323 barrels a year. The trustee's estimate of prospective earnings is predicated on the continuance of blending operations on this scale and at the rate of profit obtained during the base period. The record of the debtor's operations since the last reorganization indicates that the maximum amount of casing head used for blending purposes in any year prior to 1940 was 60,000 barrels. During 1940 the prices paid by the debtor for casing head were the lowest during the 5-year period. Furthermore, the blending margin in that year, the difference between the cost of casing head and the average netback on gasoline, was the highest of the entire period. The margin in 1940 was 58.42¢ per barrel, in 1939 17.01¢, in 1938 26.29¢, in 1937 24.23¢, and in 1936 7.60¢. As a result of the low prices and the high margin, the debtor in 1940 used 192,365 barrels of casing head for blending, or approximately three times the previous maximum. Although casing-head prices began to advance in the latter part of 1940, average prices during the base period remained low in relation to prices in earlier years and the average blending margin of 34.45¢ per barrel was substantially greater than in any year preceding 1940. Principally as the result of this wide margin, the debtor during the base period used abnormally large quantities of casing head for blending purposes, at the annual rate of 362,323 barrels or six times the maximum used in any year prior to 1940.

The testimony shows that price is the principal factor determining the quantity of casing-head used for blending. Casing-head prices were at uneconomically low levels prior to March 31, 1941. However, prices have subsequently risen and the testimony indicates that at the time of the hearing, May 5, 1941, the price of casing-head was high and that the debtor was "not buying very much." In view of the unusual price situation that prevailed during the base period and the extraordinary quantities of casing-head used for blending during that period, it is our opinion that the debtor's experience in blending operations during the 5 months to March 31, 1941 does not constitute a reasonable measure of prospective earnings from that source.

With the present plant facilities it appears that the debtor requires a certain amount of casing-head in order to meet customers' specifications. In determining prospective earnings we believe that the maximum blending operation to be assumed should not exceed the average of the 5 years 1936–1940 and that the assumed blending margin should not exceed a weighted average for this period. During these years the debtor blended an average of 78,159 barrels of casing-head a year at a weighted average blending margin of 38.47¢ per barrel, or an annual total of approximately $30,000. This compares with a blending profit of $125,000 based on the 5 months to March 31, 1941 which the trustee has included in his estimate of prospective earnings. In our opinion, therefore, the trustee's estimate of prospective earnings is overstated, with respect to casing-head operations, by $95,000.

    * * *

D. SUMMARY

In arriving at his estimate of prospective earnings the trustee has taken the actual earnings of the 5–month period which were at the annual rate of $26,500. To this he has added certain net adjustments in the amount of $236,416 representing estimated improvements which have not yet been realized. Total estimated earnings so arrived at amount to $262,916 before depreciation and bond interest. It is pertinent to note that these unrealized estimates represent 90 percent of the earnings forecast and only 10 percent consists of the actual earnings of the base period.

For the reasons indicated earlier, we believe that the trustee's adjustment to "Sales of refined products" is excessive by about $39,000 and that his estimate of prospective earnings should be reduced by

$95,000 to reflect the unusual situation in casing-head that prevailed during the base period. We have also pointed out the degree of uncertainty attaching to the trustee's estimated reduction of $29,798 in cost of refinery fuel. Taking into account these various factors, it is our opinion that the trustee's forecast is excessive by at least $135,000 and that the debtor's reasonably prospective earnings for reorganization purposes do not exceed $130,000 annually before depreciation and bond interest.

Even such an estimate, however, requires substantial qualification. Initially it is to be noted that the debtor's operation is a marginal one. Prospective earnings of $130,000 represent a profit of only 5.2¢ per barrel of crude processed before allowance for depreciation. Thus, a continued decline in refining margin equivalent to ³⁄₁₆¢ per gallon of gasoline sold would come near to eliminating all earnings, before depreciation, reducing them by $115,000. Because of the small margin of profit any such estimate of earnings is subject to a high degree of uncertainty.

It is also to be noted that the anticipated savings resulting from the reduction in price of ethyl lead and the lowering of freight rates are available to a great many other refiners. The history of competition in the refining industry indicates that economies have mainly been passed on in the form of lower prices. Therefore, even though the predicted savings may be reasonably anticipated over the short term, there is substantial question whether they would be available to the debtor over an extended period.

As a final matter, we point out that future earnings will be subject to the impact of major trends in the refining industry. Among these is the rapid improvement in the refining art which has reduced operating costs and resulted in a continued decline in the refining margin. Technological advances have likewise resulted in substantial improvement in the quality of gasoline. This improvement has been reflected in the advancing octane rating of regular grades of gasoline. Gasoline that sold as premium grade a few years ago is now regular grade and the continuation of this trend will result in lower prices for debtor's present production or will necessitate additional plant investment to meet the higher requirements.

It appears, therefore, that the estimate of prospective earnings in the amount of $130,000 if applied to an extended period of time is subject to substantial elements of uncertainty. This uncertainty may be only partially offset by such possibilities as may exist for obtaining pipe-line revenues. Therefore, in the light of the foregoing it appears that the estimate of prospective earnings of $130,000 before depreciation and bond interest must be regarded as a maximum.

VALUATION

In valuing this marginal enterprise it is necessary to consider what may be obtained from the debtor's assets on the basis of two alternative courses of action, (a) liquidation and sale of the property and (b) continuation of the debtor as an operating entity.

A. LIQUIDATING VALUE

(1) Fixed Assets

These assets consist primarily of pipe, tanks, pumping equipment and refining equipment. The only comprehensive testimony as to the liquidating value of these classes of assets indicated that they could be sold within 12 months at a net realization to the debtor of $628,000. With respect to the office building owned by the debtor, the trustee testified that a fair price would be $75,000 to $90,000. For our purposes we may take the average of these figures, or $83,000. On a similar basis the trustee testified that the refinery land was worth $250 per acre, or a total of $43,000. In addition to the above there are certain miscellaneous fixed assets such as telephone lines, vehicles, office equipment, etc., with a depreciated book value of approximately $123,000 as of December 31, 1940. No testimony was introduced as to the realizable value of these assets but it appears that they would bring but a fraction of their book value in liquidation, and for the purpose of this estimate the item has been disregarded. All of the fixed assets are pledged as security for the mortgage bond issues, except the Cotton Valley pipe line worth approximately $10,000.

(2) Current Assets

As of March 31, 1941, the debtor held cash in the amount of $211,000. In addition, the indenture trustee for the first mortgage bonds held $150,600 for the benefit of that issue, this sum representing the proceeds of sale of mortgaged assets. There was also $41,000 in special deposits which, however, are pledged and not available as general funds of the debtor. In addition to cash items the debtor had notes and accounts receivable in the amount of $137,000. The testimony showed that no losses on accounts receivable had been sustained during the past 2 years. In the light of this credit experience a 10 percent deduction would appear ample to cover any losses that might be incurred in liquidation.

As of March 31, 1941, the debtor held crude oil carried at $68,000 and refined products carried at $194,000. The testimony shows that in November 1940, a neighboring refinery in liquidation took a loss of about 20 percent below market in disposing of its crude oil inventory. We believe that a deduction at this rate should be ample for purposes of determining the liquidating value of the debtor's crude oil. Although there is no evidence as to the loss that might be incurred in the liquidation of the debtor's refined products inventory, we believe that the application of the 20% rate to this account would be reasonable.

As of March 31, 1941, the debtor carried its materials and supplies on its books at $185,000, including certain pledged assets with a book value of $41,573. However, as of the same date the trustee's books and also his pro forma balance sheet carry this account at $85,000. Although there is no testimony as to the amount that might be obtained in liquidation the trustee's write-down appears adequate to cover any losses that might be sustained.

(3) Other Assets

The only remaining asset to be considered here is the stock of Sparco Gasoline Co., Inc., which is pledged as security for the mortgage bond issues. As of March 31, 1941, the book value of this stock was $13,000 which may be accepted as its value.

(4) Summary of Liquidating Value

On the basis of the above data, the net liquidating value of the debtor's assets after allowance for $356,000 of trustee's liabilities as of March 31, 1941, is $1,189,600 and is summarized in Table III.

TABLE III
Estimated Liquidating Value of Debtor's Assets
(As of March 31, 1941)

(1) *Fixed assets*		
Pipe, tanks, pumping and refinery equipment	$628,000	
Office building	83,000	
Refinery land	43,000	
Total fixed assets		$754,000
(2) *Current assets*		
Cash on hand	211,000	
Cash on deposit with indenture trustee	150,600	
Notes and accounts receivable	123,000	
Inventories—crude	54,000	
Inventories—refined	155,000	
Inventories—materials and supplies	85,000	
Total current assets	778,600	
Less: Trustee's liabilities	356,000	
Net current assets		422,600
(3) *Other assets*		
Sparco Gasoline Company, Inc., stock		13,000
Total net liquidating value [a]		1,189,600

[a] The total net liquidating value of $1,189,600 is before allowance for reorganization expenses and prior tax claims.

B. Value as Operating Entity

The value derivable from this debtor as an operating entity is dependent in large part upon the amount of earnings to be obtained from the property as reorganized and the length of time for which such earnings will be available. The prospective earnings of the debtor have been discussed in a previous section. We turn now to a consideration of the remaining economic life of the enterprise.

(1) Economic Life

The trustee's estimate of the remaining life of the present plant facilities is indicated in note 8 to the trustee's pro forma balance sheet in which he computed annual depreciation for the reorganized company on the basis of a 10–year life for the present facilities.

Testimony at the TNEC hearings indicated that "a refinery built 5 years ago, is pretty well obsolete now." It was further testified that representative large refining companies charge depreciation at the rate of 15 percent, indicating a life of 7 years. These general estimates of the economic life of refining facilities appear to be borne out by the experience of the debtor and its predecessors which indicates that in the past substantial investment in plant has occurred at 7–year intervals. Thus the original tube-and-tank plant was built in 1920; in 1927 a 10,000 barrel shell plant was constructed; and in 1934–1935 two Gyro Process cracking units were completed at a cost of approximately $900,000. At the present time, therefore, the cracking units are 6 to 7 years old and most of the remaining equipment is 17 years old.

In view of the age of the equipment and the trend of technological advance in the industry it is our opinion that substantial investment in plant facilities will be required before the end of the 10–year period in order to keep the enterprise competitive. If this point is reached in 3 to 5 years as it very well may, the debtor's earnings would have provided for this purpose a total of $190,000 at the end of 3 years, and $328,000 at the end of 5 years. These figures are based on estimated earnings of $130,000 before depreciation and assume that no income taxes will be paid, no preferred dividends will be paid, and that the annual sinking-fund requirements will be met by the purchase of $50,000 face amount of bonds at $25,000.

Even though the debtor could continue to operate for the next 5 years there is substantial reason to doubt that $328,000 would be adequate to make competitive the cracking units, which cost $900,000 and which at that time will be 11–12 years old, and the other equipment most of which will be over 20 years old. If at the end of the economic life of the present facilities, the debtor has been unable to earn sufficient funds above its debt service requirements to re-equip its plant and maintain its competitive position, the debtor's existence as an operating entity will cease. Under these circumstances the proposed plan will in effect have provided for a deferred liquidation of the debtor's assets.

(2) Determination of Value

The trustee has estimated the going concern value of the reorganized debtor at approximately $1,700,000. This value gives effect to the proposed investment of $150,000 by the Producers Group and American Locomotive Company and reflects all payments of funds which are provided for in the plan except reorganization expenses. In arriving at this value the trustee deducted an annual depreciation charge of $90,000 from his estimated prospective earnings of $262,000. The balance of $170,000, representing his estimated prospective earnings before bond interest and income taxes, was capitalized at 10 percent.

In our opinion this value is predicated on an estimate of prospective earnings which is overstated by $135,000, the depreciation charge is calculated on the assumption of a 10–year remaining life for the present facilities which we believe excessive, and for the reasons set forth subsequently we believe 10 percent is too low a rate of capitalization in the light of the risks inherent in this enterprise.

We believe a more appropriate approach to the valuation of this debtor would be one which recognized the company's uncertain tenure of existence as an operating entity. In our opinion, it is improbable that this debtor will be able during the remaining economic life of its present properties to obtain sufficient funds from earnings to meet its debt service and to make the necessary plant replacements to maintain its competitive position. On this basis the elements of value derivable from the reorganized company consist of the present worth, at an appropriate discount rate, of the cash profits that may be produced during its remaining operating life and the present worth of the value realizable at the end of that life from the disposition of its assets.

The trustee has testified that in his opinion the proper rate of return to apply in valuing the debtor ranged from 8 to 20 percent. The general manager testified that in his opinion the rate should be 8 to 12 or possibly 14 percent. The rate used by them was 10 percent.

The determination of an appropriate rate must be predicated on the risks inherent in the enterprise.[44] The debtor is operating in a highly competitive field. Furthermore it has the weaknesses characteristic of a small inland refinery. In addition to the general risks arising from the nature of the industry and the debtor's position in it, there are numerous hazards affecting the realization by the debtor of the prospective earnings estimated herein. These have been set forth earlier in the report. In the light of the risks inherent in the enterprise it is our opinion that a proper rate of return to be applied to the debtor's prospective earnings before income taxes would be 15 percent, certainly not less than 12 percent.[47]

We have already indicated that in our opinion reasonably prospective earnings do not exceed $130,000 annually before depreciation and bond interest. There remain to be considered the values that may be realizable at the end of the debtor's operating life and the period over which this life may extend.

---

44. Dewing, Financial Policy of Corporations (3d ed. 6th reprinting 1939) at 145:

" * * * the rate at which a business shall be capitalized, to obtain its value, will depend on the relative uncertainty or certainty, the relative risk, of the continuation of the earnings. The greater the risk, the greater the doubt of continued earnings and the lower is the capitalized value of these earnings; and conversely, the lower the risk, the greater the value."

47. The only reference in the record to rates of return at which other companies are selling indicates that General Motors is selling (after taxes) on a 10 percent basis. Despite the distinction between selling price and value which was attempted in the testimony, the contrast between General Motors and the debtor points up the inadequacy of the trustee's rate.

In a previous section we have shown the liquidating value of the debtor's assets as indicated by the record. This value is applicable only to a liquidation undertaken by the debtor at the present time. The realization that may be obtained in a liquidation several years hence is a speculative and uncertain matter. The testimony is clear that present conditions provide an unusually favorable opportunity for the disposal of the debtor's fixed assets. There is a scarcity of new and used pipe, and prices advanced considerably in the 60 or 90 days preceding the hearing on the proposed plan. How long these unusual conditions may be expected to continue is a matter of speculation.

Although a precise determination cannot be made of values obtainable in a subsequent liquidation, there is ample ground for the belief that such values would not exceed those presently obtainable and may well be less because of changed market conditions and the continued aging of the equipment and pipe. We may therefore adopt the estimate of present liquidating value as a maximum measure of the realization available at the end of the debtor's operating life. However, because of the uncertainties of realization on the fixed assets we believe that the rate of discount to be applied in reducing this realization to present worth should be as high as the rate applicable to prospective earnings. With respect to current assets we believe a 6% rate is appropriate.

In our opinion, a reasonable estimate of the operating life of the reorganized company should be taken at approximately 5 years for purposes of valuation.[48] As indicated in Table IV the value of the

TABLE IV

Value of Reorganized Debtor as Operating Entity

	High		Low	
	Rate	Amount	Rate	Amount
	Percent		Percent	
Present worth				
Prospective earnings	12	$469,000	15	$436,000
Salvage value, fixed assets	12	428,000	15	375,000
Net current assets [a]	6	320,000	6	320,000
Sparco Gasoline Company stock	....	13,000	....	13,000
	....	1,230,000	....	1,144,000
Less—cost of capital improvements	....	110,000	....	110,000
Value of reorganized debtor as operating entity	....	1,120,000	....	1,034,000

[a] Based on trustee's pro forma balance sheet as of March 31, 1941, before deduction of reorganization expenses.

reorganized company as an operating entity, on the basis of a 5–year life and the other factors set forth above, ranges between $1,144,000 and $1,230,000 before allowance for capital improvements and reorganization expenses. From this must be deducted $110,000 representing

48. However, the value as an operating entity would not be materially altered even if the operating life were reduced to 3 years, or extended to 7 or 8. This is explained, briefly, by the fact that as the assumed operating life is extended, the present worth of future earnings is in-creased. However, at the same time the realization of the liquidating value of the assets is postponed and its present worth is correspondingly reduced. On the specific facts of this case these tendencies offset one another within fairly close limits.

the cost of necessary capital improvements. This sum include,
as the cost of the proposed 28–mile pipeline extension and $50,(
extended in connection with the rehabilitation program begun
gust 1940. The net value remaining after this deduction rang
tween $1,034,000 and $1,120,000 before reorganization expenses.

* * *

Since no adjustment for excessive or deficient working capital
seems necessary, it appears that the value of the reorganized debtor,
assuming continuation of operations and giving effect to the proposed
investment of $150,000 by the Producers Group and American Locomo-
tive Company, would be $1,100,000 before reorganization expenses,
provided that the property is managed in the best interests of its
security holders as such and that any renewal of the oil purchase
contract will be on equitable terms.

FEASIBILITY AND FAIRNESS

The soundness of any plan of reorganization for the debtor must be
weighed in light of the facts adduced in the preceding section of this
report. To recapitulate, the salient facts are that (a) the debtor's value
upon present liquidation may well equal, if not exceed, its value as a
continued operating entity; (b) its earnings prospects are subject to
substantial fluctuation, and as a going concern it would operate as a
marginal enterprise; (c) its remaining economic life is limited by reason
of advancing obsolescence of its refining facilities and its apparent
inability to earn the substantial investment to be required within a few
years if the enterprise is to be kept competitive.

Especially when viewed against this background, the terms of the
proposed plan do not meet the statutory requirement of feasibility. A
company emerging from reorganization as a going concern should
possess a sound capital structure. The amount and character of the
new securities proposed to be issued should be properly related to the
value of the property, and adequate provision must be made for working capital and the maintenance of a sound credit status. In a number
of respects the proposed plan violates these elementary requirements.

The plan provides for a total capitalization of $1,546,400, consisting
of $1,011,400 of 4½ first mortgage bonds, $435,000 of 4% preferred
stock and $100,000 par amount of common stock. It has been estimat-
ed in the preceding section of this report that the going-concern value
of the debtor does not exceed $1,100,000 before reorganization expenses.
The proposed new bond issue alone approximates that amount, and it is
obvious that the total capitalization proposed in the plan is excessive.
The new bond issue would represent 92 percent of the going-concern
value; the bonds and new preferred stock would represent 131 percent
of such value; and the total capitalization 140 percent.

Even if a valuation is assumed equal to the total capitalization
proposed in the plan, the capital structure would be unsound, with over
93 percent of the total capitalization in senior securities and approximately 65 percent in fixed-interest bearing debt. The plan sets up a
capital structure which would be unsound even for a company with a

long established record of stable earnings, and we have demonstrated that the debtor has not been and will not be such a company. In this connection, Mr. Boenning, chairman of the first mortgage bondholders' committee, testified that "if we were approaching this * * * on a basis of original financing we would certainly not set up the financing as it is set up in this proposed reorganization." [53]

We have emphasized in the preceding section that the company will have an uncertain tenure of existence as an operating unit. In our opinion, for the reasons set out above, it is improbable that the new company will be able during the remaining economic life of its present properties to obtain sufficient funds from earnings to meet its debt service and make the necessary plant replacements to maintain its competitive position. The effort to do so alternatively from the sale of securities would appear doomed to failure, in view of the nature of the proposed capitalization. With its property grossly overbonded and subject to the other deficiencies we have discussed, the plan thus contains the seeds of another early reorganization, or liquidation. In this connection it should be emphasized that the debtor was reorganized as recently as 1935 (when $880,000 of new money was brought into the enterprise). The present reorganization (the second within 5 years) was precipitated by the high fixed charges and heavy debt structure provided for in the previous reorganization plan. The present plan may well return the debtor to this court for a third reorganization, or liquidation, in the near future.

In view of the new company's relatively short prospective life and the marginal nature of its operations, it is important to the debtor's security holders that the terms and quality of the new securities they are to receive should constitute payment to them as certain and as much as liquidation would produce. In the event of present liquidation, whether or not it produces the estimates discussed earlier, the fact remains that all the fixed assets of the debtor, except the $10,000 Cotton Valley line, are subject to the lien of the first mortgage bonds. The proceeds derived from the sale of those assets would therefore be applied to the $961,400 claim of the first mortgage bondholders. The second mortgage bondholders would participate in the proceeds realized from the disposition of all the unpledged assets of the debtor, together with the first mortgage bondholders to the extent of their deficiency claim, and with general unsecured creditors.

The proposed plan purports to protect the first mortgage bondholders in the event of any early liquidation of the new company, by preserving their creditor position in the full face amount of their present claim. But the security behind the new bonds is diluted by the plan. Thus, the lien of the new bonds will not cover $150,000 in cash

53. The creation of an excessive and top-heavy capitalization for the new company (especially in view of its probable limited life) also involves the issuance of deceptive securities worth only a fraction of their face amount. There has been judicial recognition of the added responsibility which the exemption from the requirements of the Securities Act imposes upon the courts to reject any plan which provides for the issuance of unsound securities.

now held by the indenture trustee for the bondholders in the sinking fund, which sum the bondholders are required to relinquish to the new company. This represents the proceeds of the sale in 1938 of property subject to their lien. Under the plan, also, if the debtor's office building or any other property now subject to the lien of the first mortgage bonds were sold and the proceeds used, as apparently contemplated, to effect removal of a portion of the debtor's pipe line from the East Texas field to the Magnolia field, the liquidating value of the bondholders security will be lessened.[55]

Thus, under this plan the property which the first mortgage bondholders may look to at the end of the debtor's economic life would be less than the property to which they can look for satisfaction of their claims today, and the price which the property would bring at such future date might well be less than present prices. Furthermore, the new bonds which they are to receive upon consummation of the plan will be worth, as estimated by the chairman of the first mortgage bondholders committee, only about half their face amount. The second mortgage bondholders, who are to receive new preferred stock for only one-third of the face amount of their outstanding claims exclusive of accrued interest, give up their creditor position altogether, and on a subsequent liquidation they may well find that they have been deprived of the value of their presently realizable claim against the debtor's free assets.[56]

To summarize, the plan allocates to the first mortgage bondholders new bonds which, it was testified, will have a value materially less than their face amount, and their security is diluted. In addition, the bondholders' interest rate is reduced from 6% to 4½%, their annual fixed sinking-fund requirements are reduced from $100,000 to $50,000,[57] and they surrender the cash deposit of $150,600 now held by the indenture trustee for their benefit. If the operating life of the enterprise terminates in 3 years, the bondholders will have received in interest no more than the cash held by the indenture trustee which is presently available to them, and they will face the prospects of liquidation under circumstances which may be less favorable than those at present.[58] The bondholders, moreover, are to be made participants in

Summary

---

55. The plan also dilutes the bondholders' share in the security that is left to them to the extent that $50,000 of new bonds are to be issued which will participate in the security *pari passu* with the existing bondholders although the proceeds of the sale of the new bonds will not be subject to the lien.

56. Moreover, they are not to receive the cash payment to be made to other unsecured creditors with claims in the amount of $400,000. This variance in treatment provided for the deficiency claims of the second mortgage bondholders from the treatment granted the other unsecured claimants appears to violate the principle that all substantial claims having

the same legal status should receive the same treatment. Morgan & Co. v. Missouri Pacific R.R. Co., 85 F.2d 351 (C.C.A.8th, 1936).

57. In this respect, moreover, the plan provides, not that $50,000 a year must be applied in retiring bonds, but only that $50,000 *face amount* of bonds be retired yearly.

58. We do not suggest that a plan of reorganization dependent upon new contributions in order that the enterprise may be continued cannot require sacrifices from bondholders, if it is assumed that continuation as a going concern is in their interests, and new money must be raised by contri-

an excessive and top-heavy capital structure which plainly does not meet the requirements of the Act as to feasibility. In addition, as next discussed, they are to place the fate of their investment in the hands of the Producers Group despite the latter's conflicting interests, and the benefits, if any, which they are to obtain are not shown to be adequate to compensate them for the sacrifices and risks entailed by the plan, leading in our opinion to the conclusion that the plan cannot be considered fair.

As earlier described, the Group, which owns or controls substantial oil production in the Magnolia oil field, will purchase the common stock of the new company for $100,000 (with virtually complete control of the new company for at least the first 3 years after reorganization), and will agree to advance the new company credit if needed not to exceed $200,000, which may be secured by a lien on inventories and certain current assets. In addition, the new company will enter into a 3–year oil purchase contract with the Producers Group.

The contract obligates the debtor to purchase its crude oil requirements from the group up to a maximum of 8,000 barrels per day, for a period of 3 years. This makes the new company dependent upon the Producers Group exclusively for its entire supply of crude oil for that period, thereby depriving it of possible advantages accruing from use of diversified sources of supply. The debtor is so located that it has access to the crude oil production of many fields in addition to Magnolia, and as recently as March 1941 it obtained its crude oil from as many as five different fields. Certain of the fields which the debtor is in a position to tap, e.g., Cotton Valley, produce a higher grade crude than Magnolia. If it should prove advantageous for the debtor to use such higher grade crudes, that would be impossible under the terms of the contract which constitutes part of the proposed plan. If the comparable price to the debtor of crude oil in other fields should drop below the price of Magnolia crude, the debtor would be prevented by this contract from taking advantage of that fact. As recently as November 1940 the debtor found it possible to purchase a substantial quantity of distress crude oil at a price 20 percent below the prevailing market. * * *

Another feature of the contract which may operate to the detriment of the new company is the provision prescribing the price which the new company is to pay the Producers Group for its crude oil. This is fixed by the contract at the price posted in the Magnolia field unless the posted price of Magnolia crude is lower than $^{93}/_{110}$ of the East Texas posted price less 5¢, or is higher than $^{93}/_{110}$ of the East Texas posted price plus 5¢. In the first contingency the company would pay $^{93}/_{110}$ of

butions. But in turn the extent of the concessions they are called on to make in part determines whether such a plan is in their interests. From their viewpoint there is no virtue in the mere continuation of the enterprise at whatever cost. Stated in terms of legal requirements, for a plan to be "fair and equitable", as required by the statute, where junior or outside interests are permitted to participate on the basis of a contribution it must clearly appear that the contribution is necessary, and that the contribution is reasonably equivalent to the participation allocated to the contributors. Case v. Los Angeles Lumber Products Co., Ltd., 308 U.S. 106, 121–122 (1939).

the East Texas posted price less 5¢. This would be more than the Magnolia posted price and therefore to the disadvantage of the company. In the other contingency, however, the company would pay $^{93}/_{110}$ of the East Texas posted price plus 5¢. This would be less than the posted price and therefore to the advantage of the company * * *. [T]he operation of the price provisions of the contract throughout the 5 months ended March 31, 1941 would have been disadvantageous to the debtor * * *.

It is contended, however, that the contract does contain advantages for the new company in providing it with an assured supply of crude oil of uniform grade. Although there was testimony at the hearing on the plan to the effect that the debtor would benefit from having an assured supply of crude oil it does not appear from the record that the debtor has ever had any difficulty in obtaining as much crude oil as it needed and could pay for. The debtor's difficulties have not been with sources of supply, which appear to be ample.

The Producers Group, however, need the debtor because without the debtor they do not have sufficient outlet for their production. Thus, a spokesman for the Producers Group testified: "more or less we are buying a market for our crude which from time to time you have trouble in selling because of the pipe-line situation." The interest of the Producers Group in maintaining the outlet for their crude oil production will prompt continued operation of the refinery during the 3 years even if it is adverse to the interests of the other security holders of the new company. The problem will exist in aggravated form at the end of the 3–year period. During that time the Producers Group will have received what primarily they are now paying $100,000 for; namely, "a market for our crude." At the end of the period, if operations are to be continued, the position of the other security holders will be materially affected by the arrangements made for further purchases of crude from the Producers Group, which will have obvious conflicting interests. Although the present contract will have expired the Producers Group will still hold 100 percent of the stock of this corporation, and the decision as to whether the Producers Group will continue to sell crude oil to the company, and upon what terms, will be negotiated by the Producers Group, as vendors, with themselves as directors of the company.

The plan proposes that the Producers Group, who will own all the stock of the new corporation, will finance the latter's purchases of crude oil from the Producers Group to the extent of $200,000, and it is provided that this credit may be secured by a lien on the crude oil so purchased and on the refined products and accounts receivable. Because of the failure of the Producers Group to provide an adequate equity investment, the debtor must obtain a loan to supply necessary current assets. The Producers Group proposes to make this loan. Because this will constitute a creditor obligation of the debtor the proposal has a striking similarity to the situation condemned by the

Supreme Court in the so-called *Deep Rock* case,[64] involving as it does the operation of controlled corporations with inadequate equity investment, and the practice by controlling interests of making such investment as loans.

CONCLUSION

We believe that the proposed plan cannot be approved as feasible or fair. It has been suggested that the interests of the debtor's security holders require an agreement with the Producers Group, and that the plan embodies the most favorable terms which could be obtained from them. It is our view that the risks to the debtor's security holders entailed by disapproval of the plan are outweighed by the sacrifices they are asked to make under the plan, and by the probable existence of alternative courses of action which are not subject to these same objections.

(a) On the assumption that continuation of the debtor's operations would be in the interests of its security holders, and would rest on a sound capital structure, it does not appear that recent and prospective improvements in the debtor's earnings will not produce a substantial part of the funds needed for expenses and working capital within a short period as a result of the trustee's operations, and that the debtor could not borrow its remaining requirements directly from banks, or similar sources, or indeed borrow all of its requirements from such sources immediately. On that basis the Producers Group's contribution is not shown to be essential to continuation of operations,[65] i.e., "necessary" as required by Case v. Los Angeles Lumber Products Co., Ltd., 308 U.S. 106, 121–122.[66]

(b) The record contains evidence that there has been interest in the debtor's property on the part of producers other than the Producers Group as well as on the part of integrated companies.[67] If developed,

64. Taylor v. Standard Gas & Electric Co., 306 U.S. 307 (1939). The inadequacy of equity investment is here shown by the fact that the par value of the new common stock represents only 7 percent of the total face amount of the securities to be issued under the plan. And on the basis of the going concern value discussed earlier, the new senior securities to be issued (bonds and preferred stock) alone exceed the going concern value by 31 percent.

65. In any event, a device such as an underwriting instead of a subscription, by the Producers Group would at least permit the bondholders to retain an interest in the equity, if they so desire while permitting contribution of additional money required for operations.

66. The intangible benefits which might accrue to the debtor from the participation of the Producers Group are not sufficient to support the issuance of stock. They are not a "money's worth" contribu-

tion but are "illustrative of a host of intangibles which, if recognized as adequate consideration for issuance of stock * * *, would serve as easy evasions of the principle of full or absolute priority." Case v. Los Angeles Lumber Products Co., Ltd., 308 U.S. 106, 122–123 (1939). Indeed, under the plan the Producers Group expressly does not "obligate itself to perform any particular service in the management or control of the new corporation."

67. It appears that Lion Oil Company in December 1939 was "willing to negotiate an agreement for the purchase of the [debtor's] properties" on the basis involving issuance by Lion of its own obligations to the first mortgage bondholders of the debtor for the full amount of their claims, such obligations of Lion to be secured by all the assets now securing the debtor's first mortgage bonds. Other Lion obligations were to be allotted to the debtor's second mortgage bondholders for their claims. Mr.

such possibilities might actually achieve for the present bondholders the benefits of integration which this plan fails to give them.[68]   The fact that the record discloses negotiations, in most instances not described, with a number of different interests falls far short of demonstrating that the possibilities along these lines have been exhausted, particularly in view of indications that the parties have unduly restricted their efforts by attempting to work out a plan which would produce a maximum face amount of new fixed obligations for the bondholders.

(c) Finally, if it develops that no reorganization can be effected on a fair and feasible basis, a liquidation of the enterprise may be necessary.   In our opinion it is entirely possible that the debtor's bondholders will fare as well, if not better, in such event than they would under the present plan.   We have already considered at length the factors which point in that direction, such as the marginal nature of the enterprise, its necessarily limited life in view of the age of its equipment and the technological advances in the industry, the fact that liquidation will be probable in a relatively few years, and the indications that favorable liquidation possibilities exist at the present time which may not be present later.

APPENDIX A
ATLAS PIPELINE CORP.

Income Statement
(Five Months to March 31, 1941)

Income	
Sale of Refined Products	$1,577,264.81
Telephone Line Rentals	3,951.32
Office Building Rentals	3,392.14
Sundry Income	6,510.74
Total Income	$1,591,119.01
Cost of Products Sold	
Opening Inventory	210,433.91
Purchases: Crude Oil	934,069.49
Casinghead	284,491.09
Ethyl Lead	145,169.68
Freight	3,056.08
Total	$1,577,220.25
Less: Closing Inventory	262,173.56
Balance: Cost of Materials	$1,315,046.69
Refinery Fuel	23,203.69
Other Refinery Expense	176,869.22
Total: Cost of Sales	$1,515,119.60
Other Expense	
Pipeline Operating Expense	40,931.99
Office Building Operating Exp.	4,619.66
Gen. and Admin. Expense	13,472.56

Boenning described this plan as "a very satisfactory deal from the viewpoint of the bondholders."

68.   This plan is described by the trustee as "an attempt to tie in crude oil production * * * with the pipe line and refinery now owned and operated by the Debtor."

Obviously, however, the benefits of integration do not accrue to the debtor's bondholders under this plan, since an integrated business would enable them to share in the profits of production, which is not the fact here.

Interest Paid	4,133.68
Trustee's Expense	1,799.73
Total Other Expense	$ 64,957.62
Total Cost of Sales and Other Operating Expense	$1,580,077.22
Net Income before Bond Interest and Amortization and Depreciation	$ 11,041.79
Net Income as above (12 months basis)	$ 26,500.30

————

IN RE ATLAS PIPELINE CORPORATION

United States District Court, Western District of Louisiana, 1941.
39 F.Supp. 846.

DAWKINS, District Judge. The Trustee has presented to the court for tentative approval and submission to creditors a plan of reorganization for this corporation, which already has the approval of representatives of all classes of creditors. However, the Securities and Exchange Commission, to whom it was submitted under provisions of the Bankruptcy Act, * * * has filed a report to the effect that the plan is neither fair nor feasible.

* * *

The report of the Commission consisting of some sixty odd pages, criticized the figures of the Trustee in calculating or estimating the prospective earnings and consequent success of the new company in numerous respects, and of course, speaks for itself. I shall not undertake to discuss these in detail, but think it sufficient to say that while no one can be certain as to such matters, I believe that the Trustee has adopted a reasonable and conservative basis for his calculations, which are being borne out by his own experience over the period since certain improvements and changes in operations were instituted in the fall of 1940. The feasibility of the plan would seem to be further attested, if not assured, by the fact that the Purchasing Group, who will have charge of the new management, are men of large means with an assured supply of crude oil, which they agree to furnish upon a reasonable basis, so as to keep the refinery operating at something near capacity. Their investment of $100,000 in the common stock and willingness to extend additional credit or cash for another $200,000 is very tangible evidence of the faith of these experienced operators in the success of the undertaking. When this is considered, along with the fact that bankers and business men of wide experience acting for and interested with the present first and second mortgage bondholders, have unqualifiedly approved the plan,* the court would hesitate to turn

* [Ed. Note] Is it relevant in understanding the attitude toward the plan of the "bankers and business men" that Boenning & Co. (see p. 24 supra) had been underwriters of the defaulted First Mortgage Bonds and that American Locomotive Co. was the owner of a majority of the outstanding Second Mortgage Bonds? (See p. 10 supra.)

it down and adopt the suggestion of the Commission that the properties be scrapped and liquidated as junk.

I am impressed that the views of the Commission are somewhat cold blooded and are based on the theory that no new security should be issued which is not worth, at the time, its face value. If the organization of a new enterprise was involved that view might be justified, but when you have a situation such as is presented here, where it is the duty of the court to try to protect the interest of all creditors as far as the assets and circumstances of the debtor permit, a more practical view should be taken. Liquidation, according to the Commission's own calculation, would wipe out the second mortgage creditors entirely, except to the extent that they might participate along with the ordinary creditors in the free assets.

It seems to me that the proposal is fair in that it preserves the position of the first mortgage creditors to the full amount of their principal and accrued interest, and the only sacrifice they are making is in the reduction of the interest rate from 6 to $4\frac{1}{2}\%$ for the future. At the present time, the latter is more than can be obtained on a reasonably safe investment and the very spirit of the law which permits reorganization of embarrassed corporations appears to contemplate that there shall be some giving and taking by all concerned. If it is probable that the plan will realize a greater portion of the equity of any class of creditors in the assets of the corporation, then this is a sufficient consideration for the sacrifices that may be made to that end. The results of liquidation are highly speculative and uncertain. Under the plan the ordinary creditors will receive the equivalent of their share in the free assets and there will be substantial reduction in tax liability and other obligations which might have a preferred status in the event of liquidation.

Under all the circumstances, I think that the plan is both fair and feasible, and should be submitted to the creditors for their consideration.

Holding

———

NOTE: THE AFTERMATH OF THE ATLAS PIPELINE CASE

Atlas Pipeline Corporation emerged from reorganization as Atlas Oil and Refining Company in January 1942. The prices at which its bonds sold are as follows:

	1942	1943	1944	1945	1946	1947
High	88	95	100	$99\frac{1}{2}$	$103\frac{3}{4}$	$102\frac{1}{2}$
Low	62	80	$92\frac{1}{2}$	90	98	92

The enterprise apparently succeeded beyond all expectations. The following are its earnings before taxes and interest, after taxes and interest and per share of preferred stock and of common stock for the years ended November 30, 1943 and 1944, the only years for which figures are available:

	1943	1944
Before taxes & interest	$515,422	$966,955
After tax & interest	134,818	242,093
Per preferred	30.99	60.06
Per common	23.48	45.19

Atlas' common stock was purchased by Standard Oil (Ohio) periodically; by the end of 1945 Standard Oil owned 28% of the common stock, by the end of 1946 it owned 57% of the common stock, and in 1948 the bonds and the preferred stock were retired. As of the end of 1943 only $513,200 principal amount of the bonds was outstanding. The bonds in Atlas' treasury had been acquired by the company at a discount of approximately 11%.

SECTION B.   ELEMENTS OF VALUATION

1.   DISCOUNTING FUTURE RETURNS TO PRESENT VALUE

It should already be apparent that the concept of discounting is fundamental to the valuation process. To deal adequately with the analytic principles of valuation one must develop the intellectual habit of substituting present values for expectations about the future; indeed, it is precisely the act of substituting present for future values that is meant when one speaks of "valuing the corporate enterprise". While enterprise and securities valuation obviously involve much more than the mere mechanics of discounting, it is important that there be no confusion about how the latter process works. The discussion by Alchian and Allen, immediately following, should suffice to make clear both discounting and compounding, which are opposite sides of the same coin.

One knows intuitively that a dollar to be paid in the future is worth less than a dollar that is payable today, but it may be worthwhile to advance two related arguments which support that intuition. First, as long as investors or consumers are willing to borrow funds at a positive rate of interest, money has a time value. The owner of $1,000 today can, if he wishes, deposit that sum in a federally insured savings account at 5.5% and have $1,055 at the end of a year. It follows that an individual would not be indifferent if offered a choice of receiving $1,000 today and $1,000 a year from now; he would always prefer $1,000 today, since that amount, deposited at interest, will grow to be a larger sum by the end of the year's waiting period. This is true, moreover, even if receipt of the future payment is a guaranteed certainty, i.e., even when risk is wholly absent.

Secondly, even if an individual desires to expend his funds on consumption goods and is not interested in saving, it is reasonable to assume that he places greater value on present consumption than on future consumption. $1,000 worth of consumption today is better than $1,000 worth of consumption a year from now; satisfaction is pleasant, abstention less so. Hence an individual can be induced to forego current consumption only if he is paid for his forbearance by the promise of greater satisfaction at a future date. But if nothing can be gained by waiting, he may as well indulge. Again, therefore, an individual would not be indifferent as between $1,000 today and $1,000 a year from now; he would in almost every case prefer the former. For both of these reasons, amounts to be received in the future must be discounted by some factor (rate of interest) if one wishes to ascertain their present worth.

As the terms "discount", "capitalization" and "multiplier" appear frequently in the valuation literature, it may be helpful to say a word about their usage. As a matter of practice, the terms "discount" or "discounting" are commonly used in reference to a finite set of future payments, e.g., the rents to be received from a 10–year lease. When the future payments are expected to continue in perpetuity—e.g., dividends on a share of stock—the terms "capitalization" or "capitalizing" are generally employed. One would say, for example, that the present value of $1,000 a year for 10 years is determined by "discounting" the stream of payments at a given interest rate, while the present value of $1,000 a year forever is determined by "capitalizing" the stream of payments at a given rate. The term "multiplier", finally, refers to the reciprocal of the capitalization rate. Thus, if an 8% capitalization rate is assumed, the multiplier is 12.5 (i.e., $8/100 \times 12.5 = 1$); and the present value of $1,000 a year in perpetuity is $12.5 \times $1,000 or $12,500.

ALCHIAN AND ALLEN, UNIVERSITY ECONOMICS *

179–185 (3d ed. 1972).

The *more distant* the deferred service (or income, or goods), the *lower* its present price. At an interest rate of 6 percent, the current price of $1 deferred a year is 94 cents—the amount that will grow at 6 percent in one year to $1. This is given by the formula

$$p_1 = \frac{A}{(1 + r)} = \frac{\$1.00}{(1 + .06)} = \$.943.$$

[315a]

To get the present price for $1 deferred *two* years, simply repeat the above operation. If $1 deferred one year is now worth 94 cents, then deferring the dollar an additional year again reduces its present value by the same proportion. For two years, this is .943 × .943 = .890. A dollar due in two years is worth 89 cents today.

This can be expressed by noting that at 6 percent per year 89 cents will grow in one year to 94 cents, and then in the second year the 94 cents will grow to exactly $1. This can be written in algebraic form

$$p_2 (1 + r) (1 + r) = A.$$

where *p* represents the price now that will in two years grow at the 6

TABLE 11–1. Present Value of a Future $1: What a Dollar at End of Specified Future Year Is Worth Today

Year	3%	4%	5%	6%	7%	8%	10%	12%	15%	20%	Year
1	.971	.962	.952	.943	.935	.926	.909	.893	.870	.833	1
2	.943	.925	.907	.890	.873	.857	.826	.797	.756	.694	2
3	.915	.890	.864	.839	.816	.794	.751	.711	.658	.578	3
4	.889	.855	.823	.792	.763	.735	.683	.636	.572	.482	4
5	.863	.823	.784	.747	.713	.681	.620	.567	.497	.402	5
6	.838	.790	.746	.705	.666	.630	.564	.507	.432	.335	6
7	.813	.760	.711	.665	.623	.583	.513	.452	.376	.279	7
8	.789	.731	.677	.627	.582	.540	.466	.404	.326	.233	8
9	.766	.703	.645	.591	.544	.500	.424	.360	.284	.194	9
10	.744	.676	.614	.558	.508	.463	.385	.322	.247	.162	10
11	.722	.650	.585	.526	.475	.429	.350	.287	.215	.134	11
12	.701	.625	.557	.497	.444	.397	.318	.257	.187	.112	12
13	.681	.601	.530	.468	.415	.368	.289	.229	.162	.0935	13
14	.661	.577	.505	.442	.388	.340	.263	.204	.141	.0779	14
15	.642	.555	.481	.417	.362	.315	.239	.183	.122	.0649	15
16	.623	.534	.458	.393	.339	.292	.217	.163	.107	.0541	16
17	.605	.513	.436	.371	.317	.270	.197	.146	.093	.0451	17
18	.587	.494	.416	.350	.296	.250	.179	.130	.0808	.0376	18
19	.570	.475	.396	.330	.277	.232	.163	.116	.0703	.0313	19
20	.554	.456	.377	.311	.258	.215	.148	.104	.0611	.0261	20
25	.478	.375	.295	.232	.184	.146	.0923	.0588	.0304	.0105	25
30	.412	.308	.231	.174	.131	.0994	.0573	.0334	.0151	.00421	30
40	.307	.208	.142	.0972	.067	.0460	.0221	.0107	.00373	.000680	40
50	.228	.141	.087	.0543	.034	.0213	.00852	.00346	.000922	.000109	50

Each column lists how much a dollar received at the end of various years in the future is worth today. For example, at 6 percent per year a dollar to be received ten years hence is equivalent in value to $.558 now, in other words, $.558 invested now at 6 percent, with interest compounded annually, would grow to $1.00 in ten years. Note that $1.00 to be received at the end of fifty years is, at 6 percent, worth today just about a nickel. And at 10 percent it is worth only about .8 of one cent, which is to say that 8 mills (.8 of a cent) invested now would grow, at 10 percent interest compounded annually, to $1.00 in fifty years. Similarly $1,000 in fifty years is worth today $8.52, and $10,000 is worth today $85—all at 10 percent rate of interest. * * * Why not make that investment? Formula for entry in table is $1/(1 + r)^t$. (No inflation is involved in this table).

percent annual rate of interest to the amount A. Solvi

$$p_2 = \frac{A}{(1+r)\,(1+r)} = \frac{A}{(1+r)^2} = \frac{\$1.00}{(1.06)^2} =$$

Two years' discounting is measured by the factor $1/(1+.06)^2 = .890$; three years of discounting is obtained by multiplying the future amount due in three years by $1/(1.06)^3 = .839$. The present value of \$1 deferred t years from today is obtained by use of the "present value factor" $1/(1.06)^t$. Multiplying an amount due at the end of t years by this present-value factor gives the present value (or present price, or discounted value) of the deferred amount, A, due in t years. A set of these present-value factors is given in Table 11–1 for various rates of interest and years of deferment. The present-value factor decreases as t is larger: the farther into the future an amount is deferred, the lower is its *present* value. This is in no way dependent upon an assumption of inflation of prices.

FUTURE AMOUNTS CORRESPONDING TO GIVEN PRESENT VALUES

Instead of working from future amounts to present values, we can derive for any annual rate of interest the future amount that will be purchasable for any present value. How much will \$1 paid now purchase if the future amount is due in one year, or in two years, or in three years? At 15 percent per year, \$1 will be worth \$1.15 in one year. And at 15 percent for the next year, that \$1.15 will in turn grow to \$1.32. Hence, \$1 today is the present price or value of \$1.32 in two years. In terms of our formula, this can be expressed

$$p_2(1+r)(1+r) = A.$$

$$\$1(1.15)(1.15) = \$1(1.32) = \$1.32.$$

If the future amount is deferred three years, the term (1.15) enters three times, and if deferred t years, it enters t times. For three years, the quantity (1.15) is multiplied together three times, denoted $(1.15)^3$, and equals 1.52. Therefore, in three years \$1 will grow to \$1.52. In general, the formula is

$$p_t(1+r)^t = A$$

for any present payment, p_t that is paid for an amount A available t years later. The multiplicative factor $(1+r)^t$ is called the *future-value* (or *amount*) *factor*. Values of this future-amount factor for different combinations of t and r are given in Table 11–2. For example, at 6 percent in five years, the future-amount factor is 1.34, which means that a present payment of \$1 will buy, or grow to, the future amount \$1.34 at the end of five years. Notice that the entries in Table 11–2 are simply the reciprocals of the entries in Table 11–1.

BLE 11–2.   Compound Amount of $1: Amount to Which $1 Now Will Grow by End of
specified Year at Compounded Interest

Year	3%	4%	5%	6%	7%	8%	10%	12%	15%	20%	Year
1	1.03	1.04	1.05	1.06	1.07	1.08	1.10	1.12	1.15	1.20	1
2	1.06	1.08	1.10	1.12	1.14	1.17	1.21	1.25	1.32	1.44	2
3	1.09	1.12	1.16	1.19	1.23	1.26	1.33	1.40	1.52	1.73	3
4	1.13	1.17	1.22	1.26	1.31	1.36	1.46	1.57	1.74	2.07	4
5	1.16	1.22	1.28	1.34	1.40	1.47	1.61	1.76	2.01	2.49	5
6	1.19	1.27	1.34	1.41	1.50	1.59	1.77	1.97	2.31	2.99	6
7	1.23	1.32	1.41	1.50	1.61	1.71	1.94	2.21	2.66	3.58	7
8	1.27	1.37	1.48	1.59	1.72	1.85	2.14	2.48	3.05	4.30	8
9	1.30	1.42	1.55	1.68	1.84	2.00	2.35	2.77	3.52	5.16	9
10	1.34	1.48	1.63	1.79	1.97	2.16	2.59	3.11	4.05	6.19	10
11	1.38	1.54	1.71	1.89	2.10	2.33	2.85	3.48	4.66	7.43	11
12	1.43	1.60	1.80	2.01	2.25	2.52	3.13	3.90	5.30	8.92	12
13	1.47	1.67	1.89	2.13	2.41	2.72	3.45	4.36	6.10	10.7	13
14	1.51	1.73	1.98	2.26	2.58	2.94	3.79	4.89	7.00	12.8	14
15	1.56	1.80	2.08	2.39	2.76	3.17	4.17	5.47	8.13	15.4	15
16	1.60	1.87	2.18	2.54	2.95	3.43	4.59	6.13	9.40	18.5	16
17	1.65	1.95	2.29	2.69	3.16	3.70	5.05	6.87	10.6	22.2	17
18	1.70	2.03	2.41	2.85	3.38	4.00	5.55	7.70	12.5	26.6	18
19	1.75	2.11	2.53	3.02	3.62	4.32	6.11	8.61	14.0	31.9	19
20	1.81	2.19	2.65	3.20	3.87	4.66	6.72	9.65	16.1	38.3	20
25	2.09	2.67	3.39	4.29	5.43	6.85	10.8	17.0	32.9	95.4	25
30	2.43	3.24	4.32	5.74	7.61	10.0	17.4	30.0	66.2	237	30
40	3.26	4.80	7.04	10.3	15.0	21.7	45.3	93.1	267.0	1470	40
50	4.38	7.11	11.5	18.4	29.5	46.9	117	289	1080	9100	50

This table shows to what amounts $1.00 invested now will grow at the end of various
years, at different rates of growth compounded annually. For example, $1.00 invested
now will grow in thirty years to $5.74 at 6 percent. In other words, $5.74 due thirty
years hence is worth now exactly $1.00 at a 6 percent rate of interest per year. * * * The
entries in this table are the reciprocals of the entries in Table 11–1; that is, they are the
entries of Table 11–1 divided into 1. * * * Formula for entries in table is $1/(1 + r)^t$.

PRESENT CAPITAL VALUE FOR SERIES OF FUTURE AMOUNTS

For a sequence of amounts due at future times, we can find a
present value. Just as we add up the costs of individual items in a
market basket of groceries, we add the present values of each of the
future amounts due. That sum is the present value of the whole series
of amounts due at various future dates.

This series might be compared with an oil well that each year on
December 31 spurts out one gallon of oil that sells for $1. To simplify
the problem, let's first suppose that the series of dollars (spurts of oil)
continues for only two years. If the interest rate is 6 percent, the
present value of $1 deferred one year is 94 cents (see Table 11–1,
column of .06 rate of interest for one year); and the present value of $1
due in two years is 89.0 cents (see the same table, same column, but
now read the entry for year 2). The sum of the present capital values
of both amounts due is the sum of 94.3 cents and 89.0 cents, which is
$1.83. To say that the rate of interest is 6 percent per year is
equivalent to saying that you can exchange $1.83 today for the right to
receive $1 in one year *and* another dollar in two years.

Suppose the sequence is to last three years, with three $1 receipts.
The aggregate present value is augmented by the present value of the

dollar due in the third year. At a 6 percent rate of interest, this third dollar has a present value of 83.9 cents (see Table 11–1). Therefore, the present value of the three-year series is $2.67 (given in Table 11–3).

The present value of a series of amounts due is called the *capital value* of the future receipts. Capital value is the current *price* of the rights to the stream (series) of receipts.

Some technical jargon will be convenient for subsequent analyses. The sequence of future amounts due is called an *annuity,* a word that suggests *annual* amounts. A two-year sequence is a two-year annuity. A person who has purchased the right to a stream of future annuities or amounts due—for example, his pension benefits—is sometimes called an *annuitant.*

TABLE 11–3. Present Value of Annuity of $1, Received at End of Each Year

Year	3%	4%	5%	6%	7%	8%	10%	12%	15%	20%	Year
1	0.971	0.960	0.952	0.943	0.935	0.926	0.909	0.890	0.870	0.833	1
2	1.91	1.89	1.86	1.83	1.81	1.78	1.73	1.69	1.63	1.53	2
3	2.83	2.78	2.72	2.67	2.62	2.58	2.48	2.40	2.28	2.11	3
4	3.72	3.63	3.55	3.46	3.39	3.31	3.16	3.04	2.86	2.59	4
5	4.58	4.45	4.33	4.21	4.10	3.99	3.79	3.60	3.35	2.99	5
6	5.42	5.24	5.08	4.91	4.77	4.62	4.35	4.11	3.78	3.33	6
7	6.23	6.00	5.79	5.58	5.39	5.21	4.86	4.56	4.16	3.60	7
8	7.02	6.73	6.46	6.20	5.97	5.75	5.33	4.97	4.49	3.84	8
9	7.79	7.44	7.11	6.80	6.52	6.25	5.75	5.33	4.78	4.03	9
10	8.53	8.11	7.72	7.36	7.02	6.71	6.14	5.65	5.02	4.19	10
11	9.25	8.76	8.31	7.88	7.50	7.14	6.49	5.94	5.23	4.33	11
12	9.95	9.39	8.86	8.38	7.94	7.54	6.81	6.19	5.41	4.44	12
13	10.6	9.99	9.39	8.85	8.36	7.90	7.10	6.42	5.65	4.53	13
14	11.3	10.6	9.90	9.29	8.75	8.24	7.36	6.63	5.76	4.61	14
15	11.9	11.1	10.4	9.71	9.11	8.56	7.60	6.81	5.87	4.68	15
16	12.6	11.6	10.8	10.1	9.45	8.85	7.82	6.97	5.96	4.73	16
17	13.2	12.2	11.3	10.4	9.76	9.12	8.02	7.12	6.03	4.77	17
18	13.8	12.7	11.7	10.8	10.1	9.37	8.20	7.25	6.10	4.81	18
19	14.3	13.1	12.1	11.1	10.3	9.60	8.36	7.37	6.17	4.84	19
20	14.9	13.6	12.5	11.4	10.6	9.82	8.51	7.47	6.23	4.87	20
25	17.4	15.6	14.1	12.8	11.7	10.7	9.08	7.84	6.46	4.95	25
30	19.6	17.3	15.4	13.8	12.4	11.3	9.43	8.06	6.57	4.98	30
40	23.1	19.8	17.2	15.0	13.3	11.9	9.78	8.24	6.64	5.00	40
50	25.7	21.5	18.3	15.8	13.8	12.2	9.91	8.30	6.66	5.00	50

An annuity is a sequence of annual amounts received at annual intervals. This table shows with each entry how much it takes today to buy an annuity of $1 a year at the rates of interest indicated. For example, an annuity of $1 a year for twenty years at 6 percent interest could be purchased today with $11.40. This amount would, if invested at 6 percent, be sufficient to yield some interest which, along with some depletion of the principle in each year, would enable a payout of exactly $1 a year for twenty years, at which time the fund would be completely depleted. And $1,000 a year for twenty years would, at 6 percent compounded annually, cost today $11,400, which is obviously 1,000 times as much as for an annuity of just $1. Formula for entry is $[1-(1 + r)-^t]/r$.

What is the present capital value of a four-year annuity? The fourth year's $1 has a present value of 79.2 cents, which, when added to the present value of a three-year annuity of $1 a year, gives $3.46. A five-year annuity would have a present value of $4.21, because the dollar received at the end of the fifth year is now worth 74.7 cents. Proceed to the end of ten years, and you will find (in Table 11–3) that at 6 percent interest the present capital value of a ten-year annuity of $1 each year is $7.36.

If we extended the series to twenty years (still with $1 at the end of each year) at 6 percent per year, the present capital value would increase to $11.40. Notice that the *present* value of the *last half* of that series (the ten amounts due in the eleventh through the twentieth years) is only $4.04 (= 11.40 − 7.36). At a 6 percent interest rate. $4.04 *today* will buy you $1 a year for ten years, beginning at the end of the eleventh year.

Table 11–3 gives the present value of each separate future payment in the annuity. For convenience, Table 11–3 gives the present value of annuities of various lengths, where the payment *at the end* of each year is $1. Look at the entry for two years at 6 percent. It is the sum of .943 and .890, based on the data of Table 11–1. For an annuity lasting fifty years, the entry is 15.8—which says that a fifty-year annuity of $1 per year, with the first payment coming at the end of one year, has a present capital value of only $15.80 (at 6 percent).

Even an annuity that lasted forever (called a *perpetuity*), or for as long as you and your heirs desire, would have a finite capital value— namely, $16.67 (at 6 percent interest).

A second thought will remove the mystery from the fact that an infinitely long series of $1 amounts due yearly has a finite (limited) price today. To get a perpetual series of payments of $1 every year, all one has to do is keep $16.67 on deposit in a bank, if he can get 6 percent per year. Every year the interest payment of $1 can be taken out, and this can be done forever. In effect you pay $16.67 today to purchase an infinitely long sequence. But (from Table 11–3) you can also see that the first fifty years of receipts (a fifty-year annuity) has a present value of $15.80. Hence, the remaining infinitely long series of $1 receipts, beginning fifty years from now, is worth today only about 87 cents. Distant events have small present values!

NOTE: THE ROLE OF DISCOUNTING IN BOND VALUATION
BREALEY AND MYERS, PRINCIPLES OF CORPORATE FINANCE
47–48 (4th ed. 1991).

When you own a bond, you receive a fixed set of cash payoffs. Each year until the bond matures, you get an interest payment and then at maturity you also get back the face value of the bond.[1]

Suppose that in August 1989 you invest in a 12⅝ percent 1994 U.S. Treasury bond. The bond has a coupon rate of 12⅝ percent and a face value of $1000. This means that each year until 1994 you will receive an interest payment of .12625 × 1000 = $126.25. The bond matures in August 1994: At that time, the Treasury pays you the final $126.25 interest, plus the $1000 face value. So the cash flows from owning the bond are as follows:

1. The face value of the bond is known as the *principal*. Therefore, when the bond matures, the government pays you principal and interest.

CASH FLOWS, DOLLARS				
1990	1991	1992	1993	1994
126.25	126.25	126.25	126.25	1126.25

What is the 1989 market value of this stream of cash flows? To determine that, we need to look at the return provided by similar securities. Medium-term U.S. Treasury bonds in mid–1989 offered a return of about 7.6 percent. That is what investors were giving up when they bought the 12⅝ percent Treasury bonds. Therefore, to value the 12⅝ percent bonds, we need to discount the prospective stream of cash flows at 7.6 percent:

$$PV = \sum_{t=1}^{5} \frac{C_t}{(1+r)^t}$$

$$= \frac{126.25}{1+r} + \frac{126.25}{(1+r)^2} + \frac{126.25}{(1+r)^3} + \frac{126.25}{(1+r)^4} + \frac{1126.25}{(1+r)^5}$$

$$= \frac{126.25}{1.076} + \frac{126.25}{(1.076)^2} + \frac{126.25}{(1.076)^3} + \frac{126.25}{(1.076)^4} + \frac{1126.25}{(1.076)^5}$$

$$= \$1202.77$$

[317a]

Bond prices are usually expressed as a percentage of the face value. Thus, we can say that our 12⅝ percent Treasury bond is worth $1202.77, or 120.28 percent.

We could have phrased our question the other way around: If the price of the bond is $1202.77, what return do investors expect? In that case, we need to find the value of r that solves the following equation:

$$1202.77 = \frac{126.25}{1+r} + \frac{126.25}{(1+r)^2} + \frac{126.25}{(1+r)^3} + \frac{126.25}{(1+r)^4} + \frac{1126.25}{(1+r)^5}$$

[318a]

The rate r is often called the bond's **yield to maturity** or **internal rate of return.** In our case r is 7.6 percent. If you discount the cash flows at 7.6 percent, you arrive at the bond's price of $1202.77. * * * [T]he only *general* procedure for calculating r is trial and error. But specially programmed electronic calculators can be used to calculate r, or you can use a book of bond tables that show values of r for different coupon levels and different maturities.

In calculating the value of 12⅝ percent Treasury bonds, we made two approximations. First, we assumed that interest payments occurred annually. In practice, most U.S. bonds make coupon payments *semiannually.* Therefore, instead of receiving $126.25 every year, an investor holding 12⅝ percent bonds would receive $63.13 every *half* year.   Second, we treated the 7.6 percent yield as an annually compounded rate.   Bond yields are usually quoted as semiannually compounded rates.

* * *

NOTE: ROLE OF DISCOUNTING IN CAPITAL BUDGETING DECISIONS

The discounting process described by Alchian and Allen plays a central part not only in the valuation of the corporate enterprise as a whole, but in the development of a systematic approach to the firm's individual capital budgeting decisions.   The term "capital budgeting decision" is ordinarily used in reference to the evaluation of particular investment projects which are under consideration by the firm's management.   Such projects can, of course, range in size from the purchase of a single new machine to the acquisition of another company.   In every case, large or small, the question that necessarily confronts management is whether the project is worthwhile on an economic basis. What standards of evaluation should management employ in making this determination?

As in valuing the corporate enterprise itself, the capital budgeting decision entails (1) estimating the returns that can be expected to be realized from the investment over time, and (2) discounting those projected returns to present value.   The investment can be viewed as acceptable if the present value of the estimated returns equals or exceeds the cash outlay required to finance it, and on the same basis the investment can be compared with the available alternatives.   To illustrate simply, assume that a firm is considering the purchase of a new machine costing $18,000 with a useful life of 5 years, at the end of which time its value will be zero.   The new machine is expected to add $5,600 after taxes to the firm's annual income throughout the 5–year period.   Under the present-value method of evaluation, we first discount the expected cash inflows of $5,600 per year at an appropriate discount rate—say 10%—to establish the present value of those inflows. The result is then compared with the required outlay of $18,000 in order to determine whether the investment has a positive *net* present value.   Resorting to Table 11–3, supra, it turns out that the present value of the anticipated inflows is $21,224 (3.79 × $5,600).   Since the investment thus has a net present value of $3,224 ($21,224 − $18,000), it is acceptable and the outlay should be made.   In effect, if we are able to estimate the future returns of an investment project, if we know its out-of-pocket cost, and if an appropriate rate of discount is given (the word "if" being repeated for emphasis), management's decision problem can be resolved easily.   A management bent on maximizing the value of the enterprise should accept all investment projects having a positive net present value, because the effect of such acceptance is to replace cash assets with tangible assets of greater worth.   Obviously, management should reject all projects having a negative net present value. Finally, if two "acceptable" projects are for some reason mutually exclusive, a choice between them can be made by comparing their present values relative to their required cash outlays.

The decision rule just described can be presented in an alternative formulation, which is usually referred to as the internal-rate-of-return method of project evaluation, and which also involves discounting. Using the same illustration, under the internal-rate-of-return method we would first establish what rate of discount serves to equate the anticipated inflows of $5,600 per year for 5 years with the required cash outlay of $18,000. The result would then be compared with the required rate of return (10%) to determine whether the net yield on the investment is positive. The annuity tables tell us that the expected yield on the investment in the new machine is roughly 17% (i.e., $5,600 per year for 5 years discounted at 17% equals $18,000). Since this exceeds the 10% rate which the firm is assumed to require on investments of this character, the project is plainly acceptable.

The present-value and internal-rate-of-return methods differ in some respects. The principal difference involves the implied reinvestment rate on intermediate cash flows. The internal-rate-of-return method assumes that funds released by the project are reinvested at the same internal rate of return throughout the life of the project (17% in the above illustration), while the present-value method assumes a reinvestment rate equal to the company's existing or required rate of return (10%). The two methods will not necessarily produce the same accept-reject result—e.g. if the choice is between two mutually exclusive projects one of which involves a larger investment but a smaller rate of return than the other, or a project whose cash flows over time vary between positive and negative. Largely on grounds of conservatism and consistency, most writers prefer the latter procedure. For a fuller comparison see Van Horne, Financial Management and Policy (9th ed. 1992) 144–148; Brealey and Myers, Principles of Corporate Finance (4th ed. 1991) 79–88.

Despite these differences, the present-value and internal-rate-of-return methods of project evaluation frequently produce similar results, or, at least, the same "accept" or "reject" signal. The important thing to be noticed about both methods is that they take proper account of the *timing* of cash inflows and outflows over the entire life of the investment. Thus, the factor of delay (or anticipation) in the realization of expected inflows is given appropriate weight either through the determination of present value or, alternatively, through the calculation of internal rate of return.

By contrast, another very commonly used method of project evaluation—the so-called payback method—is usually thought to be inadequate just because it fails to take account of timing and ignores the need to discount all expected flows. Under the payback method, an investment is deemed acceptable if within a certain maximum period of time arbitrarily set by management the expected cash inflows produced by the investment equal the original cash outlay which the investment requires. If in the above illustration management sets the payback period at 3 years, the new machine would be rejected (3 × $5,500 < $18,000), even though the discounted cash flow methods show that the contrary decision is correct. Similarly, if the machine produced expected returns of $9,000 per year for only 2 years, automatic application of the payback method would lead to acceptance even though the net present value or the net yield of the investment is plainly negative. One would not expect the payback method to be employed so blindly, of course, but the examples do illustrate the point that a disregard of timing may result in error.

To avoid (or create) confusion at this point, it must be admitted that the 10% discount rate performs a double service in the above illustration. It reflects both the time-value of money and the operating risks involved in the proposed investment, and in the enterprise. While such duality of function does not affect the pure mechanics of discounting, it does raise the question of whether it is appropriate to merge the risk factor into the discount rate. This important problem is considered at pp. 57 to 80, infra, where alternative methods of allowing for risk are also briefly examined.

Do the decision rules outlined above have any application to the issue presented in the *Atlas Pipeline* case? The latter, of course, involved the valuation of an entire enterprise rather than a single piece of equipment. Are the decisional elements the same or different (conceptually)? What, for example, would be the analogue (in Atlas) of the $18,000 investment in the new machine?

2. THE FACTOR OF EXPECTED RETURNS

The mechanics of discounting describe the formal framework of valuation theory. The substantive content requires determining (1) the quantity and duration of the stream of expected returns to be discounted, and (2) the discount rate.

With respect to the determination of the quantity to be discounted—variously referred to as income, profits, earnings, returns, yield, etc.—two very general questions can be raised. First, what is (or ought to be) meant by the term "returns" (income, etc.) in the context of investment valuation? In the illustration used in the preceding Note, should the expectation of $5,600 per year be taken to refer to accounting income, or to some broader, or narrower, concept of enrichment? Second, is it appropriate for these purposes to utilize a single-valued estimate of expected returns, or should the investor or appraiser somehow attempt to take account of the full range of possible outcomes, insofar as they can be foreseen? Again, should $5,600 per year be assumed to represent the "best estimate" of probable returns, a conservative estimate, the absolute minimum that can be expected, or something else? These questions are taken up, in order, in the materials that follow.

(A) THE COMPOSITION OF "RETURNS"

BLUM AND KATZ, DEPRECIATION AND ENTERPRISE VALUATION

32 U.Chi.L.Rev. 236 (1965).

What function should prospective depreciation of assets serve in valuing an enterprise * * *?

The answer which in the past gained wide acceptance in legal literature can be stated rather simply. Value of an enterprise is to be arrived at by estimating its earnings in future years, on the basis of its assets and prospects * * * and capitalizing the projected earnings at an appropriate rate. If the firm is viewed as having an earnings capability for an unlimited time, the estimate of annual earnings is to be capitalized in perpetuity. The projection of earnings then must reflect the need to replace major operating assets where it is foreseen that they will lose value through use and that at some predictable date their retention by the firm will become uneconomic in the sense that in operation their worth to the firm will be less than their resale or scrap value. Replacement in this common situation has to be presumed in order to validate the basic assumption that the estimated annual earnings will continue undiminished in perpetuity. The projection of an annual charge for depreciation adjusts estimated earnings to accommodate such replacement in valuing an enterprise.

Under the generally accepted approach to valuation, the total of depreciation charges over the forecasted life of an asset reduces estimated earnings by the expected diminution in the value of that asset resulting from its consumption. The total usually has no connection with the foreseeable cost of replacing the asset with a new or better model. The main reason for tying depreciation to existing asset values is that earnings estimates are usually geared to assets of the firm as of the time of [valuation]. It would be incorrect to reduce such estimates by the anticipated cost of higher quality replacements inasmuch as, all other things being equal, these improvements can be expected to enhance the earnings picture.

In placing a value on a perpetual firm, the accepted approach usually entails calculating depreciation charges on the simple straight line annual basis—that is, dividing the total foreseeable charges for an asset by its estimated life. * * *

For purposes of valuing a perpetual enterprise, nothing turns on whether depreciation is thought of as reflecting anticipated declines in values or as reflecting costs which are to be amortized by charges against future operations. The two conceptions produce like results because in valuing an enterprise the total cost of depreciable assets to be amortized is, as previously stated, equal to the total anticipated deterioration in value.

Not all firms are viewed as perpetuities; in various situations it is anticipated that the enterprise will be liquidated at some foreseeable future date and it is not contemplated that major assets are to be replaced. In arriving at valuation in these cases, the prescription which has gained general acceptance is different. Estimated values obtainable on liquidation and estimated annual earnings for the finite period of predicted operation are to be discounted to present value without depreciation being taken into account in computing those earnings. Depreciation can be ignored because the prediction of earnings does not turn on replacing the existing assets of the enterprise. It is only necessary to take account of the estimated cost of maintaining and operating the existing assets until the date assumed for liquidation of the firm.

These principles for valuing perpetual and limited life enterprises were given official expression in corporate reorganization proceedings in the late thirties and early forties.[3] They appear still to receive general acceptance in reorganization literature. However, a reconsideration of the treatment of depreciation seems to be in order. More recent trends in financial analysis suggest that the old standard way of handling depreciation in valuing enterprises viewed as perpetuities is too simple and often leads to incorrect results.

The clue to the source of oversimplification is found in the accepted treatment of an enterprise of limited life. Assume for purposes of analysis that an enterprise is composed of a single asset, a commercial building, which was completed today at a total cost of $1,000,000; assume further that it is estimated to have a 40 year useful life and no scrap value thereafter, and that it is expected to produce an annual net cash inflow of $105,000 before depreciation; and finally assume that no working capital is required in running the enterprise, that there is no income tax, and that all agree that 8% is the appropriate rate for converting the projected net cash inflow into a statement of present value. If the venture is treated as a perpetuity—meaning that it is assumed that every 40 years the structure will be replaced by an identical building costing $1,000,000—the standard approach would operate as follows: Straight line depreciation of $1,000,000 spread over 40 years would call for an annual charge of $25,000; this would bring net cash inflow down to $80,000 a year; and capitalizing that amount in perpetuity at 8% would result in a valuation of $1,000,000. Suppose, however, it is assumed that the enterprise has a life limited to 40 years and that the building will not be replaced. Under the accepted approach, depreciation would not be taken into account, the $105,000 of estimated net cash inflow would be valued as a 40 year annuity on an 8% basis, and the result would be a present value of not $1,000,000 but $1,252,084.

Why, against all the dictates of common sense, is the same profitable enterprise found to be worth more as one of limited duration than

---

3. What is referred to as the generally accepted approach is well illustrated in Matter of Atlas Pipeline Corp., 9 S.E.C. 416 (1941).

as a perpetuity? A moment's reflection will point to the treatment of depreciation in the perpetuity calculation as the root of trouble. The straight line assumption produces an improper timing of earnings and therefore an understatement of value. Depreciation covered by earnings can be thought of as capital which has been disinvested from the depreciated asset and which is now available for other purposes: it can be left at risk generally in the operation of the enterprise; it can be accumulated in a savings account type of sinking fund for replacing the building; or it can be used to reduce outstanding indebtedness of the firm. Under any of these programs the value of the $25,000 a year taken as depreciation would at the end of 40 years exceed $1,000,000. If the savings account rate of interest were 4% per annum, the sinking fund would accumulate to $2,375,638 in 40 years; and if the business were to succeed in earning its rated 8% per annum, the added value attributable to the earnings retained by depreciation for general use in the business during that same period would be $6,476,413.[4] Obviously in either case the allowance for depreciation is far too generous. What is needed is not $1,000,000 in total charges over 40 years, but charges which, compounded at the proper earnings rate assigned to the disinvested amounts, will grow to a total of $1,000,000 in that time. Depreciation is thus like an annual annuity. At a 4% earnings rate on disinvested sums, the yearly depreciation annuity for the building would be $10,523; the net cash inflow after depreciation would then be $94,477, and the capitalized value of the enterprise, at 8% in perpetuity, would be $1,180,962. At 8% on disinvested sums the depreciation annuity would be $3,860, the net cash inflow after depreciation would be $101,140, and the capitalized value of the enterprise, at 8% in perpetuity, would be $1,264,250. It is to be noted that the value of the enterprise treated as an 8% perpetuity exceeds its value of $1,252,084 as an 8% venture with 40 years of life. This is an obviously correct relationship in view of the assumption that annual net cash inflow

4. If the disinvested capital is used to retire indebtedness, the appropriate computation might seem to be somewhat different. Assume, by way of illustration, that the firm had outstanding $1,000,000 principal sum of 4% debentures which could be called at any time at par plus accrued interest; assume further that the debentures always sell in the market at their call price. If the same amount of debentures is to be retired each year, and if the final retirement is to occur at the maturity date, the constant annual retirement would have to be $25,000 ($1,000,000 ÷ 40). In this situation, if debt retirement is thought of as being financed out of disinvestment by way of earned depreciation, the required amount of depreciation would appear to be $25,000 a year, or $1,000,000 in total—thus seeming to contradict the position taken in the text.

The contradiction, however, is only superficial. The effect of retiring the debt is to hold in the firm the amounts which otherwise would have been paid out in interest on the debt. The "savings" in the second year would be $1,000 (4% of $25,000); in the last year it would be $39,000 (4% of $975,000). The total savings is the sum to which the savings in the particular years ($1,000 in year two, and $1,000 plus $1,000 for each year after year two) will grow in 40 years when compounded at the appropriate rate. If the appropriate rate is 4%, the situation can be viewed as though the firm at the end of each year bought $25,000 of its own debt as an investment yielding 4% a year. The interest on the investment would cumulate to $1,375,638 in 40 years at 4%. (The similarity to putting $25,000 annually into a savings account sinking fund should be apparent.) If investment in the firm is rated at 8%, that rate, rather than the 4% interest rate on the debentures, is the proper one for compounding the investment attributable to the "savings" in interest payments.

after depreciation is positive and not negative. The excess of $12,166 is the present value of a deferred perpetual annuity of $101,140 starting 40 years from now.

It might now be asked whether the straight line approach to depreciation on the basis of existing values always results in an incorrect valuation of the firm. Further reflection on the commercial building example is helpful. The reason why the straight line approach is inappropriate is that it fails to take account of the time schedules for disinvestment and reinvestment. In the illustration, the $1,000,000 of anticipated disinvestment spread over 40 years through earned depreciation of course has a higher present value than anticipated reinvestment of $1,000,000 in a lump sum 40 years from date. A disparity of sufficient proportions between time of disinvestment and of reinvestment always causes straight line depreciation on existing values to produce distorted results; and this is equally true where reinvestment is expected to take place earlier than disinvestment through earned depreciation. Only where such disinvestment and reinvestment are expected to occur on substantially the same schedules—so that the two are in equilibrium—will straight line depreciation based on existing values produce a proper result in valuing the enterprise.

These reflections suggest that an enterprise can be valued without taking *annual* depreciation into account. It should be noted that the old generally accepted approach to depreciation imports a degree of circularity into the valuation process: value of the enterprise turns on earnings after depreciation, while the total amount of depreciation depends on the present value of certain existing assets of the firm. This circularity is especially troublesome where the present value of particular assets turns on their estimated earning power rather than on independent market data. Thus in the commercial building example, how can one estimate earnings after depreciation without knowing the current value of the building on which to base depreciation charges? And once that value has been determined, is not the whole problem of valuing the firm thereby solved? If these questions are answered in the affirmative, as they must be, it would seem advisable to find a route by which depreciation can be dispensed with entirely in the valuation of enterprises.

So long as elementary straight line depreciation continues to be applied in inappropriate situations—where the anticipated schedule of annual reinvestment does not match the anticipated schedule of annual disinvestment through earned depreciation—the omission of annual depreciation from the valuation computation would make a difference in the result reached. But such a difference reflects only the improper handling of depreciation. Were depreciation to be figured correctly, in accordance with the analysis presented earlier, an alternative approach would produce the same valuation of an enterprise without working through an accounting for annual depreciation. The alternative would treat the cost of anticipated asset replacements merely as cash outflows and would offset their negative present values against the valuation otherwise obtained by capitalizing anticipated positive annual net cash inflows. The commercial building case can be used as an illustration once again. The estimated annual net cash inflow of $105,000 (ignoring depreciation) would be capitalized in perpetuity at 8%, giving a present value of $1,312,500; the negative present value of $1,000,000 to be spent every 40 years to keep the enterprise operating in perpetuity is $48,250; combining the two components results in a valuation of $1,264,250—the same figure reached when depreciation is taken into account on a proper annuity basis in valuing the firm as a perpetuity.

NOTE: VALUATION AND ACCOUNTING EARNINGS

1. *Depreciation, Reinvestment, and Net Cash Flows.*

As Blum and Katz indicate, the conventional accounting process takes account of the progressive exhaustion of plant, equipment and other long-lived assets by annually offsetting a proportion of the original cost of such assets against the firm's operating income. Capital outlays are thus converted into current expense as fixed assets are used up in production. The familiar straight-line method of depreciation, which involves dividing the cost of the asset (less salvage value) by the number of years of its expected useful life, results in a level annual allowance regardless of the actual rate of physical exhaustion. Other methods, such as the declining-balance method, accelerate cost-recovery by requiring higher allowances in the earlier years and lower allowances in the later years of useful life.

While the accounting concept of depreciation is useful for a number of purposes, including the computation of federal income tax liability, its relevance to valuation is limited and indirect. Accounting depreciation *would* serve as a proxy for future replacement expenditures if an amount exactly equal to the depreciation allowance was annually reinvested to maintain the income-producing capacity of the firm, but such an outcome would occur only accidentally and certainly not in most cases. When it does not, as B & K show, the resulting "earnings" figure, however accurate as an accounting matter, is simply inadequate from the standpoint of valuation. As a consequence, it becomes necessary (at least in part) to disregard the results of the accounting process and to develop in lieu thereof an "earnings" concept which is specifically suited to the purposes of valuation. Such a concept, moreover, should be one which can be employed not only in appraising a company whose assets are kept at a constant level (like B & K's commercial building enterprise), but also in valuing a firm whose assets are expected to grow through the retention and reinvestment of some larger portion of its annual income.

B & K correctly suggest that the key to such a concept is the firm's annual cash flow expectations, including both positive flows in the form of net income from operations and negative flows in the form of replacement and expansion outlays. The amount and duration of these anticipated flows depend, in turn, on management's future investment plans—on whether management intends to contract, maintain, or expand the firm as time goes on. If (as would rarely be the case) management intends to operate the business for a limited period and then discontinue it, it may be unnecessary to set aside any amounts for replacing fixed assets; only positive cash flows need be taken into account. If, however, management intends to operate at existing levels for the indefinite future, then some allowance must be made (whether or not annually) for replacement costs. Finally, if in addition to the maintenance and replacement of existing assets management intends to *expand* the firm's operations by acquiring additional plant and equipment, allowance must also be made for anticipated expansion costs.

The first two situations are well illustrated in the B & K discussion. It will be recalled that the commercial building is expected to produce annual net cash inflows of $105,000 before depreciation. Under the assumption that the building will *not* be replaced at the end of its useful life, the value of the firm is determined by discounting to present value each of 40 annual payments of $105,000 at a rate of 8%. The firm's "earnings" are simply $105,000 annually for 40 years, and its value is $1,252,084. Under the second assumption—that the building *will* be replaced, and that the firm will maintain a constant income level in perpetuity—annual cash flows are reduced to $101,140 because of the need to fund replacement of the building at the end of 40 years. As a result, annual "earnings" are $101,140 in perpetuity, and the value of the enterprise is $1,264,250.

The expansion case can be handled through the same analysis, although a danger lies in overstating, rather than understating, the relevant "earnings" figure.

Assume management intends not merely to replace the original building when it wears out, but also to purchase a second smaller structure for $100,000 at the end of the first year of operations. The second building is expected to produce annual net cash flows of $10,114 after provision is made for *its* replacement. Since no further expansion is in view, net cash flows in the second year of operations, and in every year thereafter, are expected to be $111,254 (i.e., $101,140 plus $10,114).

Once again, the goals of valuation require that we define "earnings" as the anticipated *net* cash inflows of the firm. Since $100,000 is to be reinvested at the end of the first year, net flows must be reduced by that amount. The firm's "earnings" for the first year will therefore be only $1,140. With no further expansion intended, "earnings" for all subsequent years will be $111,254. The correct value is thus the present value of $1,140 ($101,140 at the end of the first year less the $100,000 that is retained) plus the present value of $111,254 starting in the second year and continuing in perpetuity. At an 8% capitalization rate, the value of the firm is $1,288,800.

Reduction of the first year's "earnings" by $100,000 is the critical point to observe. If the $100,000 that is reinvested by the firm *were* included in the first year's earnings, a double-counting error would result. The income to be earned *on* the $100,000 is fully reflected in the value of the enterprise when the expected cash flows of $10,114 are capitalized in perpetuity. To add in the *cost* of those expected flows as well would be to count the same quantity twice, and thus to overstate the firm's value. A similar error would arise if a bond were valued by adding its cost ($1,000) to the present value of future interest and principal payments (also $1,000), thus obviously doubling the correct valuation. See Bodenhorn, On the Problem of Capital Budgeting, 14 J.Fin. 473 (1959).

The above formulation holds true even when the company plans to retain and reinvest a fraction of its annual cash flows each year for an extended period or indefinitely. Here, too, for valuation purposes the term "earnings" should refer to the difference between the cash flows realized from operations and the amount retained by the company both to replace existing assets *and* to acquire new income-producing properties. To be sure, net cash flows can be expected to increase as the result of a decision to retain and reinvest a portion of the company's income annually; hence it now becomes appropriate to capitalize a growing, rather than a constant, stream of future returns. But because the company intends (for the foreseeable future) to reinvest a portion of those future returns in additional assets, it is necessary to reflect the "adverse value" of the intended outlays by deducting them from the larger anticipated inflows. See Bonbright, Valuation of Property, Ch. XII (1937).

It is worth noting that in all four of the cases dealt with above, the term "earnings" can also be described as the amount which is *not* required by the firm for plant replacement or reinvestment. As such, "earnings" should be viewed as excess capital, to be returned to shareholders in the form of periodic dividends. One may thus conclude that earnings (in the sense used here) and dividends are identical quantities, and that what we are really capitalizing when we value the enterprise is the amount that is annually available for distribution to shareholders. Bluntly stated, the value of the firm is equal to the present value of what the owners can expect to get out of it, neither more nor less.

2. *Valuation Practice and Accounting Results.*

In theory, net present value is calculated on the basis of "cash flow," rather than the so-called "accounting earnings" which are presented in a corporation's financial statements. The economic value of an investment project (e.g., in capital budgeting), an enterprise, or its securities is measured by the opportunity cost of alternative investments—i.e., the cash to be invested in an alternative. Hence in deriving present value, it is the expected return in cash or cash equivalents that is to be capitalized. Securities analysts using financial statements can generally adjust accounting earnings to arrive at an annual cash flow figure by adding back to accounting earnings non-cash charges incurred but not paid during the reporting period, e.g., depreciation and deferred taxes. These annual cash flow figures, netted for capital and other expenditures, can then be used in projecting expected annual net cash flows to be discounted in the present value calculation.

Computation in terms of cash flow is said to address measurement of economic value—which the accountant's discipline, focusing on recording and accounting for receipt and disbursement of assets, does not purport to measure. Kolbe, Read and Hall, The Cost of Capital (1984) points out (p. 47) that

> "the accounting rate of return for a company or an industry is a poor estimate of the true rate of return, particularly in an economy characterized by high and variable rates of inflation. No simple adjustment will eliminate this problem.
>
> "The source of difficulty is that the accounting concepts of income and value are not the same as the corresponding economic concepts. Accounting numbers derived from generally accepted accounting principles do not measure—nor do they purport to measure—income and value as defined by economic theory. It is not surprising, therefore, that accounting measures of return on investment do not coincide with economic measures.
>
> "Much of the confusion regarding the meaning of accounting numbers arises from the fact that the vocabulary of accounting contains many of the same terms as the vocabulary of economics. Accounting concepts are not unrelated to economic concepts, but the distinctions between accounting and economic definitions are crucial."

See also Benston, Accounting Numbers and Economic Values, 27 AntiTrust Bulletin 161 (1982).

Computation in terms of cash flow, even though no single definition of "net cash flow" prevails, is also said to avoid the accountant's difficulties in factoring into annual net returns costs that are incurred in one period for producing returns over several periods, and the resulting disparity between accounting earnings and economists' concepts of income. Accounting authorities have instituted cash flow reporting. A new "statement of cash flows" replaces the old "funds" statement. It sets out all cash receipts and cash payments during an accounting period, providing information about all investing and financing activities. See FASB Statement No. 95, "Statement of Cash Flows" (1987).

3. *Further Discussion.*

Appendix A, Section 1, Valuation and Accounting Earnings, discusses some additional difficulties that arise when accounting statements are used in valuation.

(B) EARNINGS ESTIMATES AND PROBABILITY
DISTRIBUTIONS

The discussion of expected returns has been carried on up to this point as if "returns" could be expressed as a single-valued estimate of future cash flows. Thus, in deciding (at page 42, supra) whether the firm should invest $18,000 in a new machine, we simply discounted the expected flows of $5,600 per year back to the present date and then compared the result with the required outlay in order to determine whether the investment possessed a positive net present value. The input data consisted of nothing more than the estimate of annual expected returns, the amount of the required outlay, and an appropriate rate of discount. With annuity tables, the necessary computation could be accomplished easily.

It is apparent, however, that a statement of investor expectations solely in the form of a single-valued estimate of future returns is incomplete. As the future is uncertain, investments will seldom yield an amount precisely equal to the anticipated return. Our single-valued estimate of returns should therefore not be taken to mean that no more nor less than $5,600 annually is actually expected to be realized from the investment. Yet if that is not the intention, just what do we mean by positing the $5,600 figure to the exclusion of all others?

The discussion that follows is again in terms of the individual capital budgeting decisions of the firm. However, it is no less relevant when one is concerned with valuing the enterprise as a whole or (as may be seen infra, page 65 with valuing its various securities.

GRAYSON, THE USE OF STATISTICAL TECHNIQUES
IN CAPITAL BUDGETING

Financial Research And Management Decisions, Robichek ed. 1967, pp. 98–107.

At the heart of any capital budgeting decision is a forecast of future events, regardless of whether that forecast is explicit or implicit. A typical forecast is a single figure, usually labeled "best estimate" or "most likely."

Let's take a closer look at this single figure. How confident is the forecaster of that figure? Is he very certain, very uncertain, or somewhere in between? And what does he really mean by the words, best estimate or most likely? Has he already reduced his "true" best estimate by some amount to reflect risk? Is he truly giving us the most likely figure, which is the *mode*? Is he really thinking through some internal calculus of a weighted average figure, the *mean*? Or, does he perhaps typically select the middle figure, the *median*? It's hard to say. Moreover, in some situations, which measure is inferred can make quite a difference in the investment decision.

Thus, the single forecasted figure limits the decision analysis in two ways. First, we do not know the uncertainty surrounding that figure, that is, we do not know the "probability distribution"—the range of the forecast and the probability estimates associated with figures within that range. Second, we do not know for sure whether his best estimate is really the mode, median, or mean. For both reasons, we would like, therefore, to have the forecaster give us not just one estimate, but a *range* of estimates and associated *probabilities*—a probability distribution.

A probability distribution, in its simplest form, could consist of only a few estimates. One popular form consists of three figures: the "optimistic, most likely, and pessimistic," or the "high, low, and best guess" estimates.

Forecast	Annual Sales (Units)
Optimistic	100,000
Most likely	75,000
Pessimistic	50,000

Some improvement has been made over the single forecast figure. More information has been obtained on the range of possible outcomes, but some information that may be critical is ignored. For example, *could* the firm sell less than 50,000 units? This might well mean a substantial loss for the firm, or bankruptcy for smaller firms, and a decision maker would undoubtedly want to know how likely this occurrence is. Moreover, how likely is the "most likely" estimate in the forecaster's mind? Is the optimistic forecast very improbable, or close to the most likely forecast? Or, are all three forecasts equally likely? It would be quite helpful, therefore, if the forecaster would describe for us more accurately his *degree of confidence* in his forecasts, or describe his feelings as to the probability of these estimates occurring.

Forecast	Units	Probability
Optimistic	100,000	.30
Most likely	75,000	.60
Pessimistic	50,000	.10

Clearly, more information is available now. This information may be used to advantage (1) in subsequent profitability calculations and (2) in assessing more clearly the effects of risk on the value of the investment to the decision maker. If attaching probabilities to this simple three-figure forecast is a gain in analysis, it is an appealing step to ask our forecaster to give us his estimates of the entire range of figures that might occur—the entire probability distribution as shown in Fig. 5.1.

Now, even more information is available for the decision maker. Granted that this may be valuable information, says a businessman, how can such probability distributions be obtained? This is a subject to which theorists have been devoting a great deal of attention in recent years, and with some success.

What has restrained the use of probability theory in business decision making for many years has been the classical "frequency"

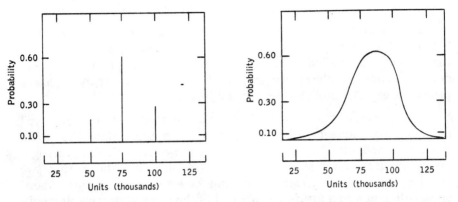

FIG. 5.1. *Left:* three-figure estimate; *right:* entire probability distribution.
[A5505]

concept of probability. Briefly, this concept indicates that no statement *whatsoever* can be made about the probability of any single event. In fact, the classical view holds that one can only talk about probability in a very long-run sense, given that the occurrence or nonoccurrence of the event can be repeatedly observed over a *very large number of times under independent identical conditions.*

Though this concept is a useful mathematical formulation for theoretical purposes, its use in business situations is severely restricted to a few applications—large-scale production runs, insurance, gambling—where the events to be forecasted are repeated again and again over a long run with "nearly constant" underlying probabilities. I submit that most business decisions are exactly the opposite—little (or no) prior experience on which to draw, lack of ability to repeat the event, and inability to create independent, identical conditions over time. Also, businessmen are interested quite often in predicting single events. Of what use, then, is probability theory for most business decisions?

Well, not all theorists agree with the point of view expressed above. In recent years another view of probability has revived, that is, the personalistic view, which holds that it makes a great deal of sense to talk about the probability of a *single event,* without reference to the repeatability, long-run frequency concept. It is perfectly valid, therefore, to talk about the probability of rain tomorrow, the probability of sales reaching a certain level next year, or the probability that earnings per share will exceed $2.50 next year, or five years hence. Such probability assignments are called *personal or subjective probabilities.*

" * * * on a personalistic view of probability, strictly interpreted, no probability is unknown to the person concerned, or, at any rate, he can determine probability only by interrogating himself * * * " *

* [Ed. Note] Savage, Foundations of Statistics (1954). And see, Farrar, The Invest-   ment Decision Under Uncertainty 1–7 (1967).

With this view, *uncertainty estimates can be made for every business decision, in an explicit fashion.* This is a powerful concept, and has tremendous implications for improving decision making procedures.

The usual first reaction of businessmen to this idea is that this procedure seems highly subjective, and they want *objective* probabilities. Though a detailed rebuttal of this objection takes quite a while to develop, a quick reply is that in real life there are no truly objective probabilities. All probabilities are subjective.

It is perfectly true that if there is a great amount of "objective" data, say on interest rates in the past, then these data should be considered and will *strongly influence* the subjective probability assignments to future interest rates. In fact, research has shown that two decision makers with roughly the same objective data or past experience, will assign to a future event roughly the same subjective probability if they believe the future will be similar to the past. *But,* if one forecaster thinks that there may be a structural shift in the economy, or has a direct pipeline to the Federal Reserve Board's thinking, *he may alter or throw away past data in making his probability assignment, and it is perfectly valid for him to do so.*

* * * Assuming for the purposes of this article that you accept this concept for the moment, a natural question is how can these probability assignments be obtained?

As stated previously, if there are large amounts of historical data, these should be strongly considered. This is where descriptive statistics and statistical inference become important. Past data can be organized in various ways to generate frequency distributions, index numbers, time series, regression, and correlation analysis. Certain central tendencies of the data can be described, such as the mean, median, or mode. And various measures can be used to describe the variation around these central tendencies and the shape of the distribution—standard deviation, variance, skewness, and kurtosis.

Such statistical analysis of past data may be extremely useful in making predictions of the future, for, under certain conditions, we may be willing to view the past data as a *sample* from an underlying process. And statistics have a lot to say about what the next sample in the future may look like. But, keep in mind, such past and present figures are only useful insofar as they are presumed to be representative of the future.

But what if the forecaster does not wish merely to project the past into the future? Or, even more compelling, what if there are *few or no data* relevant to the future. Perhaps the event to be predicted is almost unique—a completely new product. How can his probability assignments be obtained? There are several possible ways.

The simplest is by direct assessment. Ask the forecaster to write down or draw a probability distribution that describes *his* predictions. If he is very, very certain, then his distribution may look like Fig. 5.2.

If he is completely uncertain, if he thinks that all values are equally likely, then the distribution will look like Fig. 5.3.

In a typical situation, the forecaster will be neither very certain nor very uncertain, but somewhere in between as in Fig. 5.4. * * *

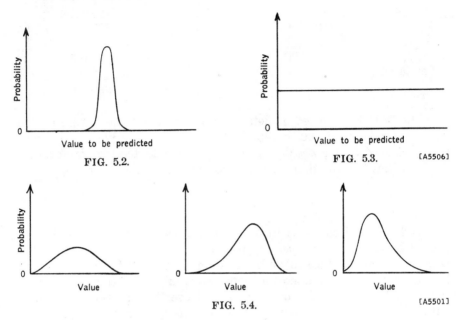

FIG. 5.2.

FIG. 5.3.   [A5506]

FIG. 5.4.   [A5501]

Some persons find it difficult to assess directly an entire numerical distribution, but can express their feelings more easily by using a mixture of language and numbers. For example, a typical statement might be:

"Well, I would guess there's about a 50–50 chance that the market share will be between 25% and 35%, and it could go as high as 40%, or even as low as 20%. Who knows? But I'd say that there's only a slight chance of that—oh, only about a 1 in 20 chance. When you get right down to it, my best guess is about 28%."

From this, a probability distribution can be described, using the quantitative estimates and making inferences about the intervening points. After it is drawn, the forecaster can examine the distribution and make any alterations he wishes before adopting it.

        * * *

Expected Monetary Value

Assuming that probability assignments are made to future events, what can be done with them? The next step typically is to multiply the probabilities times the monetary values of the possible events to get the "expected monetary value" of the investment.

Let us use the earlier simple illustration and assume for the moment that unit sales return a present monetary value of $1 each. In effect, we weight the value of the possible events by the probability that the events will be realized. The sum is the "weighted average" value of the investment.

Forecast	Profit	Probability	Expected Monetary Value
Optimistic	$100,000	.30	$30,000
Most like-ly	75,000	.60	45,000
Pessimistic	50,000	.10	5,000
			$80,000

The $80,000 expected monetary value figure becomes a figure with which we can work in our extended decision analysis. We can compare two decisions, and *generally speaking,* we would tend to prefer that decision that has the highest expected monetary value.

———

The above discussion can be compared with the SEC's method of prediction in the *Atlas Pipeline* case. It would be wrong no doubt (and certainly a cheap shot) to fault the Commission for failing to foresee how dramatically wartime conditions would affect the company's earnings (see "Aftermath," supra, p. 31). Nevertheless, one is at least entitled to wonder whether, in the Commission's contemplation, the predicted earnings figure of $130,000 was a "weighted average," or just the most pessimistic, of all foreseeable outcomes. If the latter, then it was clearly wrong to capitalize that figure at the conservative 12% rate (not to mention the even more conservative 15% rate). A much lower capitalization rate, and hence a higher estimated value for the firm, would have been appropriate if in reality $130,000 represented the Commission's minimum expectation.

What *did* the Commission intend? Initially (p. 17), the Commission states that "reasonably prospective earnings * * * do not exceed $130,-000." Further on (p. 19), the seemingly stronger assertion is made that "the estimate of prospective earnings of $130,000 * * * must be regarded as a maximum." In between, the point is urged that a drop in profit margin could virtually eliminate all earnings; and at another place the company's earnings prospects are said to be "subject to substantial fluctuation." Taking these several comments together, it appears that the figure of $130,000 came from the very *top* of the probability distribution as the Commission saw the matter * * * or did it? As stated infra, p. 79, the legal context in which the Commission's release was written leads one to suspect a bias in making estimates for the probability distribution. The capitalization rates chosen suggest that the Commission lacked faith that the estimated income would ever reach the $130,000 figure.

Speaking of cheap shots, Mr. Grayson (our author, supra) got a chance to put his theories into practice when, in 1971, he was appointed

Chairman of the Price Commission in "Phase II" of President Nixon's Economic Stabilization Program. He later reported that "management science" simply required too much data and too much time to be of any concrete value to a manager with "real" day-to-day responsibilities. In his words—

> "Although I thought about using management science tools on many occasions, I consistently decided against it because of the shortage of time * * *

> * * * A manager will ordinarily use data or a management science tool only if both are conveniently, speedily accessible. If he is told that the needed data are buried in another part of the organization, or that they must be compiled, or that the model must be created, nine times out of ten he will say, 'Skip it.' I did, ten times out of ten." Grayson, Management Science and Business Practice, Harv.Bus.Rev. (July–Aug. 1973) 41, 43–4.

For more counterpoint on the same theme, see Carter, What Are the Risks In Risk Analysis? Harv.Bus.Rev. (July–Aug. 1972) 72.

3. THE FACTOR OF RISK

As Grayson suggests in the discussion above, the factor of expected returns can be identified (at least theoretically!) as the arithmetic mean of the possible outcomes of an investment, with each such outcome being weighted by the probability of its occurrence. Given a choice among a number of investment projects, an investor will always prefer the one that offers the highest expected return, *provided* that the various projects under consideration are alike in degree of risk. The proviso is critically important. If Project A offers higher expected returns than Project B, but is also in some sense riskier, the investor may find that he fears the added risk even more than he likes the greater return and decide that B is the better choice from his standpoint. While investors no doubt react intuitively to such matters in most cases, financial managers and others serving in a capacity that calls for a formal appraisal would presumably wish to quantify, or at least to isolate, the risk factor in a systematic way, if possible. Accordingly, how should risk be measured? If probability distributions yield a statistical measure of the expected monetary value of future returns, do they also yield a statistical measure of risk? How should the adverse effect of risk be allowed for in the valuation process?

(A) RISK AS DEGREE OF DISPERSION
LEWELLEN, THE COST OF CAPITAL
Ch. 2 (1969).

THE UTILITY FUNCTION

A convenient vehicle for examining the nature of [investors'] attitudes is what an economist would term a "utility function". This is simply a representation of the satisfaction which investors can be thought of as deriving from different amounts of wealth. Although it could be described in mathematical terms, the graphical representation shown in Figure 2–1 will suffice for our purposes here. The various levels of wealth, in dollars, that an individual might conceivably experience are plotted on the horizontal axis and the enjoyment—the inner glow—he would feel at each level is plotted on the vertical scale. * * *

FIGURE 2–1. *An investor's utility function.*

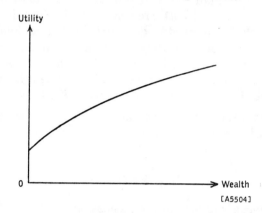

[A5504]

Despite its necessarily abstract nature, the utility function pictured above was not chosen at random. The fact that the curve, while steadily rising, falls away to the right at higher and higher levels of wealth conveys two important—and by now reasonably well accepted—features of the typical investor's attitudes: (1) the more money he has, the happier he is; (2) but equal successive increments to his wealth imply progressively smaller increments to his total utility.

The first of these is perhaps the easier to accept * * * Since in the business world, people attempt to make money, little more need be said to justify a rising utility function. Actually, the arguments to be made below do not require that the curve continually rise—just that it never turn downward. As long as additional wealth is no *dis*advantage to the investor, this will be a legitimate assumption.

The other point—i.e., that the curve is in fact a curve rather than a straight line—may have less logical appeal. As it turns out, this is merely an expression of the familiar economic principle of diminishing marginal returns. An individual eventually becomes somewhat satiated with his wealth. The second million he acquires, while still worth having, is not quite as valuable to him as the first million, since the latter has already provided him with most of the material satisfactions he wanted out of life. Three summer homes do not really generate half again the happiness of two.
        * * *

If such intuitive arguments are not wholly convincing, there is considerable empirical evidence to support them. Our discussion is leading up to the conclusion that a utility function of the type illustrated implies that investors dislike risk—and we have clear indications of risk aversion in the real world. We observe that people buy insurance; we see that they diversify their investment portfolios instead of putting all their funds into a single stock; we notice businessmen requiring larger prospective returns from ventures that are highly uncertain than they do from safer investments; and we see corporate bonds rated as grade "B" in terms of the ability of the issuer to meet the required payments selling at a lower price than those rated "Aaa." Thus, visible economic behavior is consistent with aversion to risk on the part of investors—and our curve, as we shall see, provides the underlying rationale for just such an attitude. In that respect, it is offered here as a rough, but valid, approximation of the wealth-utility responses of most security purchasers. * * *

RISK AND RETURN

Using this framework, then, let us examine the manner in which an individual would appraise the attractiveness of an investment opportunity whose outcome is uncertain. Since any such investment is basically a form of gambling, we may cast our analysis in a simple betting context for purposes of illustration. Consider the following circumstance: An individual whose total wealth amounts to $1,000 is offered the chance to bet $100 on the outcome of a coin toss. If the coin comes up heads, he wins $100; if it shows tails, he loses $100. The coin is "fair" so that the probabilities of winning and losing are both equal to one-half. The question therefore is: Will this be an attractive proposition?

We can answer that question by looking at his utility function in the region of $1,000 initial wealth. He perceives the possible results of the bet to be as shown in Figure 2–2. At the moment, he has a thousand dollars and enjoys the level of satisfaction denoted by U (1,000). That is, the goods and services he could purchase with those funds would provide him with that much "utility." If he accepts the bet and wins, his wealth rises to $1,100 and his satisfaction to $U(1,100)$. If he loses, his wealth declines to $900 and his satisfaction to $U(900)$. Should he gamble?

The answer clearly is no. Although the bet is fair in money terms, it is not fair with respect to what the money means to him. The additional satisfaction he would obtain by winning—the difference between $U(1,100)$ and $U(1,000)$—is less than the pain he would be subjected to in losing—the difference between $U(1,000)$ and $U(900)$. He will bet only if the amount he stands to win is sufficiently greater than his possible loss that the two increments on the *utility* scale are equal, as illustrated in Figure 2–3, where:

$$U(1,130) - U(1,000) = U(1,000) - U(930). \qquad (2–1)$$

A coin toss having the following outcomes *would* be acceptable: heads, he wins $130; tails, he loses $70. That situation could be achieved by making it a condition of the bet that the other party first pay our man $30 and then flip the coin. In this light, $30 can be interpreted as the "risk premium" necessary to induce participation. It measures the monetary equivalent of our investors "risk aversion" to the indicated set of uncertain outcomes. * * *

FIGURE 2–2. *Utility response to changes in wealth.*

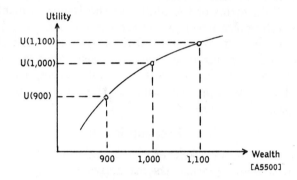

FIGURE 2–3. *An acceptable bet.*

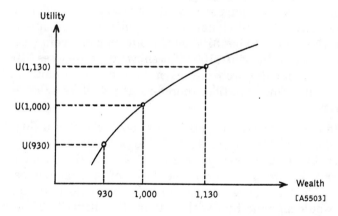

DISPERSION AND RISK PREMIUMS

If all this seems reasonable in the context of a single gamble, what can our utility function tell us about the relative attractiveness of different bets? Let us suppose our man with $1,000 is confronted with an additional opportunity. Someone else offers him a heads-or-tails bet in which the stakes now are $200 instead of only $100. We may characterize his reactions by Figure 2–4. If he accepts the first bet, the difference between the utility he stands to gain and that which he stands to lose is

$$\Delta U_1 = [\,U(1,100) - U(1,000)\,] - [\,U(1,000) - U(900)\,]. \qquad (2\text{--}2)$$

FIGURE 2–4. *Comparison of two gambles.*

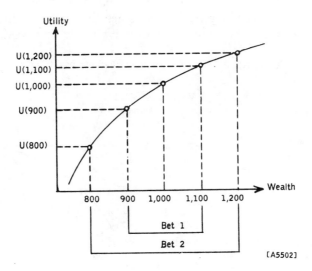

[A5502]

In the case of the second bet:

$$\Delta U_2 = [\,U(1,200)\ -\ U(1,000)\,] - [\,U(1,000) - U(800)\,]. \qquad (2\text{--}3)$$

Both of which, of course, are negative. By the nature of the curve, however, it will always be true that ΔU_2 exceeds (is more negative than) ΔU_1. The larger the bet—the greater the spread of its possible outcomes for a given monetary expected value—the less attractive it is.[1] An investor therefore must not only be "paid" something to take an even bet; he must be paid more the wider its range of consequences. Thus, he would be indifferent between the two bets if the terms were as in Figure 2–5, where the stipulation is that

$$U(1,130) - U(1,000) = U(1,000) - U(930) \qquad (2\text{--}4)$$
$$U(1,250) - U(1,000) = U(1,000) - U(850). \qquad (2\text{--}5)$$

His companions would have to pay him $30 to get him to take number 1, but $50 to take number 2 with its higher stakes.* In order to analyze the relative attractiveness of different investments, then, we must recognize not only the expected value of their outcomes but also the relative *dispersion* of the probability distribution associated with each. Fortunately, there is a convenient mathematical measure of that dispersion which we can make use of in our subsequent discussions of alternative financing decisions under uncertainty.

---

1. Put differently, the greater the spread of the dollar outcomes, the more negative is the expected *utility* value of the bet. Implicit in our discussion is the proposition that a "fair" gamble is one with an expected value of zero in utility terms.

* [Ed. Note] Logically, the risk premium associated with doubling the bet would have to be *more* than twice the risk premium for the initial bet—i.e. more than $60. Reference in the text to a $50 premium is simply an oversight.

WHY GAMBLE AND INVEST?

The objection might be raised at this point that something must be wrong with the preceding arguments, since they in effect imply that no one in the community would ever either gamble or invest. How can

FIGURE 2-5. *Comparison of two acceptable bets.*

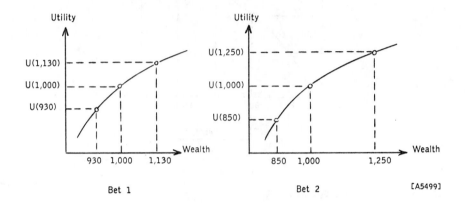

Bet 1   Bet 2   [A5499]

the existence of both activities be explained if we are really to believe that utility functions of the sort described adequately depict individual attitudes?

Take gambling first—in particular, the penny-ante poker game or similar small-stakes endeavors. We can fit these into our mold with only a minor stretching of the analysis. The rationale would be that the range of possible dollar wins and losses is so small in relation to the players' total wealth that they simply are not sufficiently sensitive to the utility implications to react adversely. The difference between the gain in utility from winning, say, $5 if you have a good night with the cards and the utility loss implied by ending up $5 in the hole on a bad night is just not great enough to notice, much less worry about. If you feel you are as likely to win as to lose such an amount—i.e., you play poker as well as anyone else in the game—you will play despite the minor utility consequences. Few of us, however, will stay in the game when the pots reach $500 per hand. By that time, the happiness connected with winning and the pain produced by losing are far enough out of balance that we abstain. The same phenomenon, of course, is observed where investments in common stocks are concerned. Most people are willing to put only a portion of their total wealth into equities, keeping some of their funds in savings accounts or similar secure investments.[2]

---

2. This continuing analogy between investing and gambling may not be entirely appreciated by the investment community. The following quotation attributed to the Dallas *Times–Herald* may be pertinent: "If you bet on a horse, that's gambling. If you bet you can make three spades, that's entertainment. If you bet AT & T will go up three points, that's business. See the difference?"

Another reason for gambling is that the process itself has some "utility." It's fun to get together with the boys and match wits. Poker is only the excuse for doing so. If you happen to lose a few dollars every once in a while, you regard that as merely the price of an evening's entertainment. Perhaps a better reason, however, is that you may in fact believe that your chances of winning are better than your chances of losing. You have faith in your ability at cards. You perceive yourself in the situation depicted in Figure 2–3 above where the potential win is $130 while the loss is only $70, so that in utility terms the gamble *is* sensible. This may be the attitude of most so-called "professional" gamblers. They think they know something that their adversaries do not and therefore are willing to participate in the game.

The same reasoning can be extended to investing. The expectation of the investor is that, on average, there *is* an opportunity to profit. The "bet" is weighted in his favor—its expected monetary value is positive. Empirical evidence, of course, supports that attitude. People *do* make money in the market if for no other reason than the fact that most firms whose shares are traded are themselves earning a profit from operations. Stock prices seem to be generally rising over time and, while the risks we are concerned with here are clearly present, so are attractive opportunities. The question for us, then, is the manner in which these two aspects of an investment are balanced in an investor's mind.

EXPECTED VALUE AND VARIANCE

The utility function approach described above suggests that the answer lies in an examination of the two features of the probability distribution of investment outcomes which measure "return" and "risk"—the expected monetary value of the investment and its degree of dispersion. The former, as was indicated, is defined simply as the average outcome of the opportunity: the sum of each possible result weighted by its probability of occurrence. Thus, an investment whose characteristics are as shown below has an expected value equal to $1,000.

Possible Outcome, x	Probability of Occurrence, Pr(x)	x • Pr(x)
$ 900	$\frac{1}{4}$	$ 225
1,000	$\frac{1}{2}$	500
1,100	$\frac{1}{4}$	275
		$1,000

This parameter, which is commonly called the "mean" of the distribution, will hereafter be denoted * * * by a bar over the pertinent variable, e.g., $\bar{x}$.

Similarly, the extent of the possible spread of a set of such outcomes is measured by a parameter termed its "variance" and defined as the [sum of the squares] of the deviations from the mean, also weighted by their respective probabilities:

Possible x	Pr(x)	$x - \bar{x}$	$(x-\bar{x})^2$	$[Pr(x)][(x-\bar{x})^2]$
$ 900	¼	-100	10,000	2,500
1,000	½	0	0	0
1,100	¼	$+100$	10,000	2,500

Variance = 5,000

The greater the potential variation in the results, the larger will be this parameter. Squaring any negative deviations ensures that relationship. * * *

The point of calculating the variance, it should be emphasized, is that the typical investor's utility function tells us that the greater the range of the consequences of a gamble, the less attractive it becomes. The utility disadvantages of the losses become progressively more severe in relation to the benefits of the profits. For that reason, variance is a convenient proxy measure of the size of the relevant "risk premiums."

———

The Lewellen discussion sets forth the alleged psychological roots of risk aversion and shows why economists and financial theorists generally express the idea of investment risk in terms of the dispersion of the expected outcomes about their mean or average value. The statistical concepts commonly used to measure the *degree* of dispersion, and hence of risk, are "variance" and (perhaps more often) "standard deviation." As indicated above, variance is defined with respect to a set of outcomes as the sum of the squares of the deviations from the mean, multiplied in each instance by the probability of occurrence. Standard deviation is merely the square root of variance. Thus, if variance is 5,000 in Lewellen's example above, standard deviation is the square root of 5,000, or 70.71.

It is important that the reader understand why risk is identified with the degree of dispersion in investment outcomes, since later discussion builds upon that understanding. The specific choice of a statistical measure of dispersion is somewhat less important.

———

The foregoing theoretical observations about the nature of risk and the relation of risk and investment returns are confirmed by historical record of the performance of securities with different risk characteristics.

BREALEY AND MYERS, PRINCIPLES
OF CORPORATE FINANCE

129–131, 135–136 (4th ed. 1991).

Financial analysts are blessed with an enormous quantity of data on security prices and returns. For example, the University of Chicago's Center for Research in Security Prices (CRSP) has developed a file of prices and dividends for each month since 1926 for every stock that has been listed on the New York Stock Exchange (NYSE). Other files give data for stocks that are traded on the American Stock Exchange and the over-the-counter market; data for bonds, for options, and so on. But this is supposed to be one easy lesson. We, therefore, concentrate on a study by Ibbotson Associates which measures the historical performance of four portfolios of securities:

1. A portfolio of Treasury bills, i.e., United States government debt securities maturing in less than 1 year

2. A portfolio of long-term United States government bonds

3. A portfolio of long-term corporate bonds [1]

4. Standard and Poor's Composite Index, which represents a portfolio of common stocks of 500 large firms

These portfolios offer different degrees of risk. Treasury bills are about as safe an investment as you can make. There is no risk of default, and their short maturity means that the prices of Treasury bills are relatively stable. In fact, an investor who wishes to lend money for, say, 3 months can achieve a perfectly certain payoff by purchasing a Treasury bill maturing in 3 months. However, the investor cannot lock in a *real* rate of return: There is still some uncertainty about inflation.

By switching to long-term government bonds, the investor acquires an asset whose prices fluctuate as interest rates vary. (Bond prices fall when interest rates rise and rise when interest rates fall.) An investor who switches from government to corporate bonds accepts an additional *default* risk. An investor who shifts from corporate bonds to common stocks has a direct share in the risks of the enterprise.

Ibbotson Associates calculated a rate of return for each of these portfolios for each year from 1926 to 1988. This rate of return reflects both cash receipts—dividends or interest—and the capital gain realized during the year. Averages of the 63 annual rates of return for each portfolio are shown in Table 7–1.[2] You can see that these returns coincide with our intuitive risk ranking. The safest investment, Treasury bills, also gave the lowest rate of return—3.6 percent a year in

---

1. The two bond portfolios were revised each year in order to maintain a constant maturity.

2. These are arithmetic averages. Ibbotson Associates simply added the 63 annual returns and divided by 63. The arithmetic average return is higher than the compound annual return over the period. For example, suppose the market doubles in value one year and halves the next. Since you are back where you started, the compound annual return is zero. But the arithmetic average return is $(+100 - 50)/2 = +25$ percent. When estimating discount rates, you are interested in the arithmetic average return.

nominal terms and .5 percent in *real* terms. In other words, the average rate of inflation over this period was just over 3 percent a year.

Long-term government bonds gave slightly higher returns than Treasury bills. Corporate bonds gave still higher returns. Common stocks were in a class by themselves. Investors who accepted the extra risk of common stocks received on average a premium of 8.4 percent a year over the return on Treasury bills.

You may ask why we look back over such a long period to measure average rates of return. The reason is that annual rates of return for common stocks fluctuate so much that averages taken over short periods are meaningless. Our only hope of gaining insights from historical rates of return is to look at a very long period.[3]

* * *

TABLE 7–1
Average rates of return on Treasury bills, government bonds, corporate bonds, and common stocks, 1926–1988 (figures in percent per year)

Portfolio	Average Annual Rate of Return (Nominal)	Average Annual Rate of Return (Real)	Average Risk Premium (Extra Return versus Treasury Bills)
Treasury bills	3.6	.5	0
Government bonds	4.7	1.7	1.1
Corporate bonds	5.3	2.4	1.7
Common stocks	12.1	8.8	8.4

Source: Ibbotson Associates, Inc., *Stocks, Bonds, Bills, and Inflation 1989 Yearbook,* Ibbotson Associates, Chicago, 1989.

* * *

The annual standard deviations and variances observed for our four portfolios over the period 1926–1988 were:[8]

3. Even with 63 years of data we cannot be sure that this period is truly representative and that the average is not distorted by a few unusually high or low returns. The reliability of an estimate of the average is usually measured by its *standard error.* For example, the standard error of our estimate of the average risk premium on common stocks is 2.6 percent. There is a 95 percent chance that the *true* average is within plus or minus 2 standard errors of the 12.1 percent estimate. In other words, if you said that the true average was between 6.9 and 17.3 percent, you would have a 95 percent chance of being right. (*Technical note:* The standard error of the mean is equal to the standard deviation divided by the square root of the number of observations. In our case the standard deviation is 20.9 percent, and therefore the standard error is $20.9/\sqrt{63} = 2.6$.)

8. Ibbotson Associates, op. cit. Notice that in discussing the riskiness of *bonds* we must be careful to specify the time period and whether we are speaking in real or nominal terms. The *nominal* return on a long-term government bond is absolutely certain to an investor who holds on until maturity; in other words, it is risk-free if you forget about inflation. After all, the government can always print money to pay off its debts. However, the real return on Treasury securities is uncertain because no one knows how much each future dollar will buy.

The bond returns reported by Ibbotson Associates were measured annually. The returns reflect year-to-year changes in bond prices as well as interest received. The *one-year* returns on long-term bonds are risky in *both* real and nominal terms.

TABLE 7–2

Portfolio	Standard Deviation σ	Variance σ^2
Treasury bills	3.3	10.9
Long-term government bonds	8.5	72.3
Corporate bonds	8.4	70.6
Common stocks	20.9	436.8

As expected, Treasury bills were the least variable security, and common stocks were the most variable. Government and corporate bonds hold the middle ground.[9]

You may find it interesting to compare the coin-tossing game and the stock market as alternative investments. The stock market generated an average annual return of 12.1 percent with a standard deviation of 20.9 percent. The game offers 10 and 21 percent, respectively—slightly lower return and about the same variability. Your gambling friends may have come up with a crude representation of the stock market.

Of course, there is no reason to believe that the market's variability should stay the same over more than 60 years. For example, it is

TABLE 7–3
Standard deviations for selected common stocks, 1984–1989 (figures in percent per year)

Stock	Standard Deviation	Stock	Standard Deviation
AT & T	24.2	Ford Motor Co.	28.7
Bristol Myers Squibb	19.8	Genentech	51.8
Capital Holding	26.4	McDonald's	21.7
Digital Equipment	38.4	McGraw–Hill	29.3
Exxon	19.8	Tandem Computer	50.7

Source: Merrill Lynch, Pierce, Fenner & Smith, Inc., "Security Risk Evaluation," January 1990.

clearly less now than in the Great Depression of the 1930s. Here are standard deviations of the returns on Ibbotson Associates' stockmarket portfolio for successive 10–year periods starting in 1926:

Period	Market Standard Deviation σ_m	Period	Market Standard Deviation σ_m
1926–1939	31.9	1960–1969	14.4
1940–1949	16.5	1970–1979	19.2
1950–1959	19.8	1980–1988	12.5

9. You may have noticed that corporate bonds come in just ahead of government bonds in terms of low variability. You shouldn't get excited about this. The problem is that it is difficult to get two sets of bonds that are alike in all other respects. For example, most corporate bonds are *callable* (i.e., the company has an option to repurchase them for their face value). Government bonds are not callable. Also interest payments are higher on corporate bonds. Therefore, investors in corporate bonds get their money sooner. * * * [T]his also reduces the bond's variability.

We should be cautious about reading too much into standard deviations calculated from 10 or so annual returns. However, these figures do not support the widespread impression of especially volatile stock prices during the 1980s. Overall the 1980s were below average on the volatility front.

However, there were brief episodes of extremely high volatility. On Black Monday, October 19, 1987, the market index fell by 23 percent *on a single day.* The standard deviation of the index for the week surrounding Black Monday was equivalent to 89 percent per year. Fortunately, volatility dropped back to normal levels within a few weeks after the crash.

(B) RISK AVERSION AND INVESTMENT DECISIONMAKING

The identification of the connection between risk and degree of dispersion leaves open an operational question. How should risk, once measured, be reflected or allowed for in the valuation process? Under any method of allowing for risk, there remains the problem of just *whose* utility function is relevant in making an investment decision. Are company managers in some sense "bound" by the risk-preferences of the company's stockholders, or even by those of the larger community of potential stockholders, to the extent that such composites can be ascertained? Or are managers free to exercise their own preferences, leaving it to investors to make suitable judgments about the policies of the companies whose shares they buy and sell? In the latter event, is it proper for management to expand, contract or otherwise alter the company's business objectives once those goals have been established in investor's minds, or should they seek to maintain a constant level of business risk so as to relieve investors of the need to make frequent reassessments? What mechanism enables—and what considerations should govern—the alignment of management's risk preferences in making corporate decisions with the risk preferences of dispersed investors in selecting investments in securities?

Consider the following from Bierman & Smidt, The Capital Budgeting Decision, 290–3 (1966):

"The point has been made that under conditions of uncertainty, subjective attitudes toward risk-bearing should play an important role in investment policy. However, the issue of whose risk attitudes are relevant for a corporation remains. Any ongoing business affects the interests of a variety of groups, among them the owners, the managers, the workers, the customers, and the suppliers. These groups may consist of separate individuals or there may be considerable overlap. In a small family store or farm, the owners, the managers, and the workers may all be members of the same family. In such a case it is clearly the family's attitude toward risk that will be considered. In a large corporation, there is typically less overlap.

"The traditional point of view is that where the owners are a distinct group, a business is run primarily in the interests of the owners, except insofar as their freedom to make decisions in their own interest has been limited by laws, custom, or by contractual arrangements with other interested parties.

"In many business situations it is not sufficient to refer simply to the owners. For example, we might distinguish three subgroups. First, there may be those of the owners who exercise a controlling interest in the business. The controlling owners may own a majority of the shares, or they may have a minority interest but a larger block than any other organized group of shareholders. In addition to those who have a controlling interest, there may be a much larger group of persons who have an ownership interest in the business, but do not attempt or cannot effectively control. This latter group has an interest in the financial results insofar as they affect stockholders. Finally, the concept of owners might usefully be expanded, for some purposes, to include not only the present stockholders but also potential stockholders—in effect, the entire financial community. For example, some investment or financial policies that a firm considers might reduce the appeal of the stock to at least some of its present owners but at the same time increase the stock market value by making it more attractive to persons who are not currently owners.

"If attitudes toward risk are to be considered in deciding what investments should be accepted, decision makers need a clear idea of whose attitudes toward risk are relevant and to what extent they should be considered. Suppose the group whose attitudes toward risk are relevant in selecting investments has been defined. There still remain important questions of how to implement the investment decision. One difficulty with the current procedures for making decisions under uncertainty is that where there are operating divisions it is likely that different criteria for evaluating (or incorporating) risk are being used. It may be that operating management is rejecting investments as being too risky that from the corporate standpoint would be very reasonable. One can imagine a credit officer of a bank rejecting a loan application, because of the risk, that from the point of view of the firm as a whole is a good investment. On the other hand, a second loan officer might be accepting loans that had too much risk from the point of view of the corporation. The element of personal judgment as to the likelihood of various events cannot be eliminated, but interpretation of the monetary consequences can at least be applied in a somewhat more consistent manner than is currently done.

"It is suggested that a utility function be obtained from individuals to be used by other individuals managing the corporation. The fact that persons rather than the corporate entity are used to obtain the function should not be surprising (the corporation entity is a fictional being existing only to satisfy the wants and needs of people). The utility function is by necessity subjective, because we are dealing with reactions to gains and losses. Rather than destroying the usefulness of the concept, the subjectivity of the measure enhances its usefulness.

We can take the monetary measures of the outcomes and transform them into utility measures that incorporate our attitudes toward the possible events. Another dimension is added to the available information to be used for making the decision.

"If the group whose risk attitudes the decision makers wish to take into account is a relatively small cohesive group with whom the decision makers can communicate directly (for example, if it were decided that investments should be selected in terms of the risk preferences of a small group of controlling stockholders or of an owner-manager or of the professional managers), the persons whose risk attitudes are relevant can be involved directly in the investment decision-making process. An attempt can be made to communicate the nature of the risk alternatives available and to obtain the reactions of the investors.

"A second set of circumstances would obtain if it were decided that the relevant risk preferences were those of the present stockholders, but the stockholders are a large and diverse group with whom direct communication is not easily possible. Given present techniques we know of no one who has effectively implemented such an attempt.

"A third possibility is that the relevant risk preferences would include those of all present or potential future owners. This is in some respects less difficult to implement than the second situation described. Assume that each stockholder has had ample opportunity to purchase the stock of other corporations (thus diversifying his portfolio, if he so wishes). In this situation, except for a very large investment that jeopardizes the existence of the firm or changes drastically its basic nature, it may be appropriate for the corporation to use the expected monetary value of the investment as the basis of the decision. The expected present value would be computed without taking risk into account other than the company's k. If the investment is a "fair" gamble (i.e., it has a positive monetary expectation), then the firm could follow a policy of accepting this investment. If the stockholder wanted less risk, he could change the risk characteristics of his investment by buying stock of other companies. The use of such an investment policy implies that the stockholder is reasonably well informed as to the nature of the risks of the firms he is investing in."

Would the risk aversion of the firm's shareholders ultimately be disregarded under an investment policy based on Bierman & Schmidt's third possibility, with the result that the firm selects riskier investments? For an analysis along these lines see Hu, Risk, Time, and Fiduciary Principles in Corporate Investment, 38 UCLA L.Rev. 277, 282–83 (1990):

" * * * Insofar as investment decisions should be dictated by shareholder considerations, managers of the typical, large, publicly held corporation should act consistently with 'blissful' shareholder wealth maximization, seeking to maximize what the share price would be in a stock market that is completely omniscient and fully efficient. That is, managers should make investment decisions consistent with the maximization of per share 'intrinsic value' thus defined, blissfully disregarding evidence that stock market pricing of shares is, to a disturbing extent, ill-informed and irrational. Such a standard has clearer operational meaning than classic fiduciary principles and avoids the biases introduced by an accounting-based framework. Moreover it leads away from an undue concern with the health of the particular corporate entity and toward concern with the value of a share of that corporation to a shareholder who holds stakes in many different corporations. More shareholder wealth-enhancing risk taking would be warranted."

Does management's decision as to the appropriate model of value maximization give rise to any *legal* policy questions? Is this matter too important to investors to permit the business judgment rule to operate? Or is the protection of management's discretion to make investment policy the central mission of the business judgment rule? If subsequent regulation is inappropriate here, should management be required to disclose policies respecting investments? For a suggestion to this effect, see infra p. 586.

(C) MEASURES OF RISK—COMPARABLE ENTERPRISES AND MARKET CAPITALIZATION RATES

FRANCIS I. DuPONT & CO. v. UNIVERSAL CITY STUDIOS, INC.

Court of Chancery of Delaware, 1973.
312 A.2d 344, affirmed 334 A.2d 216 (1975).

See p. 698, infra.

1. *Comparable Enterprises.*

In valuing an enterprise or its securities, the risk that the estimated stream of earnings will not be realized may be, and often is, quantified by reference to the risk which the market attributes to comparable enterprises or to comparable securities of comparable enterprises. Identifying comparable securities and enterprises may appear to entail less "subjectivity" than the other modes of measuring risk discussed previously, because it draws on market data rather than pure abstraction, but the process by no means eliminates reliance on subjective judgments, including most notably a judgment of what other company or companies are truly comparable. Francis I. DuPont & Co. v. Universal City Studios Inc., infra, p. 698, illustrates judicial attempts to deal with comparability. The problems are further illustrated in the following excerpt from the Advisory Report of the Securities and Exchange Commission in the insolvency reorganization under Chapter X of **Jade Oil & Gas Co.**, 44 S.E.C. 56 (1969):

* * * Jade is a small, independent oil company whose activities have been and probably will be largely speculative and promotional in character. Jade is more of an explorer and a developer than an established commercial producer. It looks for oil in unproven, unproductive areas that have been selected on the basis of preliminary geological or geophysical work. Since leases in such unproductive

areas can normally be acquired at relatively low cost, the actual expenditure on a particular prospect may not be very large, but the risk of loss is high. Commercial deposits of oil and gas are found on only a few of the many exploratory wells drilled by a "wildcatter" like Jade. The purchase of proven producing property, while less risky, is much more costly.

An investment in a small, independent oil company, like Jade, thus involves substantial risks, as Jade's own history demonstrates. An investment in such an enterprise also offers the possibility of large rewards in the event of a major discovery, and investors looking for such possibilities tend to be motivated by hope for large capital gains rather than by desire for dividend income.

A substantial discovery (if such is ever made) will normally be preceded by many unsuccessful ventures. The exploration and drilling costs incident to these ventures are charged against income. Yet the life of the enterprise depends upon continued exploration and drilling. Because of this factor small oil companies do not necessarily behave in a conventional profit-maximizing way. A vigorous exploration program may be regarded as more important than net income. According to the Trustee, a petroleum engineer, the historical record indicates that small oil producers that succeed in growing into large ones usually owe their good fortune to a few happy substantial discoveries rather than to normal, steady growth.

Since non-cash charges, such as depletion, bulk so large and because exploration and development costs are so significant, the reported net earnings of most small oil companies are nominal. Indeed, quite a few of them report consistent book losses, and Jade itself has sustained consistent and substantial losses over the years. Hence small, independent, exploratory oil companies are often valued on the basis of projected 'cash flow' rather than on the basis of probable 'earnings' computed in accordance with generally accepted accounting principles.*

* * *

The Trustee suggests that reorganized Jade's projected net cash flow (computed on his assumptions) be capitalized at 3%. In other words, he multiplies that projected average annual cash flow by 33 in

* [Ed. Abridgement]. Thus the Trustee projected the following cash flows:

	1970	1971	1972	1973	1974
Gross Income:					
Sales From Present Properties	$1,009,000	$ 907,000	$ 810,000	$ 737,000	$ 661,000
Sales From New Properties	66,600	240,900	429,000	575,300	678,100
Other Income	264,400	258,900	284,400	303,300	310,500
Total	1,340,000	1,406,800	1,523,400	1,615,600	1,649,600
Expenses	646,000	711,000	747,900	769,300	782,900
Interest Exp.	280,000	215,000	190,000	165,000	140,000
Net Cash Flow	414,000	460,800	585,500	681,300	726,700
Five–Year Aver.					$ 577,660

order to arrive at Jade's imputed value as a going concern. This capitalization rate is based on stock price data, i.e., on the multiples that the stock market has assigned the companies the Trustee considers comparable to Jade.[1]

We disagree with the Trustee's approach to the problem of valuation. For a small, wildcat oil company, a capitalized value bottomed on projected future cash flow, so much of which is to stem from unknown properties that the reorganized company hopes to be able to acquire or operate in the future, is far too conjectural for purposes of a plan of reorganization that is to bear the imprimatur of a court of equity. Basic to his projections * * * is the premise that the inescapable decline in Jade's income from its present properties will be considerably more than offset by a rise in receipts from new and as yet unacquired properties. He anticipates a growth of more than tenfold in gross receipts from these purely hypothetical properties from 1970 to 1974, expecting reorganized Jade to increase such receipts from $66,600 in 1970 to $678,100 in 1974.

In arriving at a capitalization rate, the Trustee notes that in his sample of 15 comparable companies the average cash flow is on the average capitalized at 37 times. He concludes therefore that 3% is the appropriate rate at which to capitalize Jade's prospective cash flow, or 33 times the anticipated average cash flow of $577,660 for 1970–1974. We think it impossible to derive a capitalization rate valid or acceptable for Chapter X purposes from a market in capitalized hope dominated by the pursuit of long shots. Market data based on investment values are highly significant and entitled to great weight. But market data that merely reflect composite assessments of the odds for or against lucky strikes and sensational finds—assessments shaped in large measure by extravagant intangibles—are much too shaky a foundation for judicial findings as to value and fairness.

Moreover, the Trustee's concept of striking and using some industrywide "average" is extremely dubious. One of the Trustee's sample of 15 companies sells for 10 times cash flow, and, at the other extreme, another sells for 450 times cash flow. There is not even the semblance of a clue as to which rate is appropriate, and "averaging" such disparate numbers contributes nothing to a rational resolution of the issue. The Trustee himself recognizes that there is something questionable about averaging the odds. He notes that small oil and gas companies tend to sell at multiples much higher than larger ones, and therefore begins by looking for small oil and gas companies comparable to Jade. He finds 15, four of which he considers unrepresentative because the multiples at which they sell seem too high. For those very high multiples he substitutes the arbitrarily chosen multiple of 50. Of those the Trustee regards as acceptable, one sells at 10 times cash flow while another sells at 41 times. In the face of the vast range of multipliers, we consider market prices an unreliable guide to value and fairness.

1. For this purpose the Trustee analyzed 15 small oil and gas companies each with an annual net cash flow of less than $1 million.

Is the SEC's rejection of the market capitalization rate "fair" to those who prefer to invest in the common shares of small exploratory oil companies? If the market really does capitalize the earnings (or cash flows) of such companies at a 3% rate, would not Jade's senior security holders receive a windfall as a result of the SEC's "under-appraisal" of the company's value? On the other hand, assuming that small wildcatters do sell in the market at 33 times their *current* cash flows, is the Trustee proceeding on a sound theoretical basis when he applies that multiplier to Jade's *prospective* cash flows—or, as implied below, is there a fallacy in applying current price/earnings ratios to anticipated future earnings? If Jade's net cash flows could be expected to grow at a rate of, say, 15% a year indefinitely, as the Trustee's projections appear to suggest, what would be the present value of those flows if capitalized at a rate of 3%? Finally, and in the same vein, why should small oil and gas companies tend to sell at higher multiples than larger ones? See Durand, Growth Stocks and the Petersburg Paradox, 12 J. of Finance 348 (1957).

2. *Inferred Capitalization Rates.*

In *Jade,* the S.E.C. rejected all attempts to establish a market rate of capitalization for the company's stock on the ground that the prospect of a "lucky strike" was simply too speculative to support a judicial finding. More commonly, however, the courts do resort to "comparable enterprises" in deriving capitalization rates for the earn-ings of companies which they are attempting to appraise. In any such process, one question which inevitably must be answered is how does one ascertain precisely (or even roughly) what capitalization rate the market is using in valuing a company's earnings? One once heard that so-called glamor stocks were selling at earnings multiples as high as 50. Did that mean that the market actually viewed such companies as a 2% risk? If not, how could the "true" rate of capitalization be in-ferred?

The answer is that since the market is engaged in capitalizing future (not past or even solely current) earnings, the capitalization rate cannot be observed directly or determined precisely. Thus the ratio of current earnings to the present price of a company's shares represents the market capitalization rate only if current earnings are expected to continue unchanged into the future. If earnings are expected to grow as time goes by, then the company's capitalization rate is necessarily greater than the current earnings-price ratio. In effect, the greater the anticipated rate of growth the higher also is the capitalization rate that equates future earnings with the present market price of the company's shares.

This point has been recognized in the literature, and a standard formula has been developed to reflect growth yields in capitalization rates. Under the formula, the capitalization rate applicable to the company's shares is obtained by adding the current dividend rate to the rate at which dividends are expected to grow in the indefinite future. To illustrate, assume that X Corporation has current and expected earnings of $5 a share after provision is made for the maintenance and replacement of existing assets. Assume further that X, having identified a profitable opportunity, decides to expand its capital each year for the foreseeable future by retaining and reinvesting 60% of its annual earnings in additional plant and equipment—as a result of which future earnings and dividends are expected to grow at a constant rate of 10%. Assume, finally, that the current market price of X shares is $100. The capitalization rate k would be:

$$k = \frac{Do}{Vo} + g$$

where Do/Vo is equal to the current dividend yield and g is the expected growth rate. In numerical terms:

$$k = \frac{\$2}{\$100} + 10\% = 12\%$$

Stated otherwise, if current dividends of $2 a share are expected to grow perpetually at a compound rate of 10%, the present value of the stream of future returns, discounted at a rate of 12%, is $100. Hence, to say merely that X stock is selling at 20 times current earnings ($100/$5), while it is a convenient shorthand expression and presumably implies that the market expects earnings and dividends to grow substantially in the future, is to conclude nothing directly about the rate of capitalization applicable to the company's shares.

The apparent precision of the above calculation should not disguise the very real difficulty of ascertaining what rate of growth the market actually anticipates for X. Information about the market's expectations is hard to come by. There is, however, no way to avoid the task of making an estimate if market capitalization rates of comparable companies are to be used for valuation purposes. In some instances, perhaps, historical earnings trends may furnish a fairly reliable indication of present investor expectations about the growth prospects of an industry or a firm, but in others there is no choice but to make a judgment about the market's outlook based on the published views of financial analysts, brokers, investment advisers and others who help form market opinion.

3. *Nonconstant Growth.*

It should be noted that the valuation model set out above assumes a constant and "perpetual" rate of growth for X. For most companies, it would seem much more realistic to assume that earnings will grow at a high rate for a few years and then level off. Even in that case, with some increase in arithmetical detail the above formula can be used to solve for the discount rate that equates the expected stream of future earnings with the present market price of the company's stock.

BRIGHAM & GAPENSKI, FINANCIAL MANAGEMENT: THEORY AND PRACTICE

241–246 (6th ed. 1991).

Firms typically go through *life cycles*. During the early part of their lives, their growth is much faster than that of the economy as a whole; then they match the economy's growth; and finally their growth is slower than that of the economy.[16] Automobile manufacturers in the 1920s and computer software firms such as Lotus in the 1980s are examples of firms in the early part of the cycle; these firms are called *supernormal growth* firms. Figure 7–8 illustrates supernormal growth and also compares it with normal growth, zero growth, and negative growth.[17]

16. The concept of life cycles could be broadened to *product cycle,* which would include both small, start-up companies and large companies like IBM, which periodically introduce new products that typically give sales and earnings a boost. We should also mention *business cycles,* which alternately depress and boost sales and profits. The growth rate just after a major new product has been introduced, or just after a firm emerges from the depths of a recession, is likely to be much higher than the "long-run average growth rate," which is the proper number for a constant growth analysis.

17. A negative growth rate indicates a declining company. A mining company whose profits are falling because of a de-clining ore body is an example. Someone buying such a company would expect its earnings, and consequently its dividends and stock price, to decline each year, and this would lead to capital losses rather than capital gains. Obviously, a declining company's stock price will be low, and its dividend yield must be high enough to off-set the expected capital loss and still produce a competitive total return. Students sometimes argue that they would not be willing to buy a stock whose price was expected to decline. However, if the annual dividends are large enough to *more than offset* the falling stock price, the stock still could provide a good return.

Figure 7-8   **Illustrative Dividend Growth Rates**

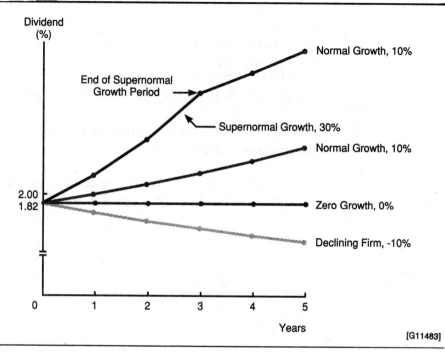

[G11483]

In the figure, the dividends of the supernormal growth firm are expected to grow at a 30 percent rate for 3 years, after which the growth rate is expected to fall to 10 percent, the assumed average for the economy. The value of this firm, like any other, is the present value of its expected future dividends as determined by Equation 7–4. In the case in which D_t is growing at a constant rate, we simplified Equation 7–4 to $\hat{P}_0 = D_1/(k_s - g)$. In the supernormal case, however, the expected growth rate is not a constant—it declines at the end of the period of supernormal growth. To find the value of such a stock, or any nonconstant growth stock when the growth rate will eventually stabilize, we proceed in three steps:

1. Find the PV of the dividends during the period of nonconstant growth.

2. Find the price of the stock at the end of the nonconstant growth period, at which point it has become a constant growth stock, and discount this price back to the present.

3. Add these two components to find the intrinsic value of the stock, $\hat{P}_0$.

To illustrate the process for valuing nonconstant growth stocks, suppose the following facts exist for Solar Laser Technology (SLT):

k_s = stockholders' required rate of return = 16%.

N = years of supernormal growth = 3.

g_s = rate of growth in both earnings and dividends during the super-normal growth period = 30%. (Note: The growth rate during the supernormal growth period could vary from year to year. Also, there could be several different supernormal growth periods; e.g., 30% for 3 years, then 20% for 3 years, and then a constant 10%.)

g_n = rate of constant growth after the supernormal period = 10%.

D_0 = last dividend the company paid = $1.82

The valuation process is diagrammed in Figure 7–9, and it is explained in the steps set forth below the time line. The value of SLT's stock is calculated to be $53.86.

* * *

Figure 7-9   Process for Finding the Value of a
                  Supernormal Growth Stock: Solar Laser Technology

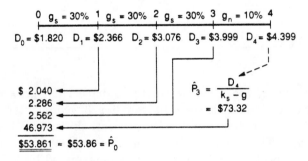

Step 1. Find the dividends paid (D_t) at the end of Years 1 to 3, and then find the present values of these dividends (PV D_t), using the following procedure:

D_0		$\times$	$(1 + g)^t$	$=$	D_t	$\times$	$\left(\dfrac{1}{1 + k}\right)^t$	$=$	PV D_t
D_1:	$1.82	$\times$	1.3000	=	$2.366;	$\times$	0.8621	=	$2.040
D_2:	1.82	$\times$	1.6900	=	3.076;	$\times$	0.7432	=	2.286
D_3:	1.82	$\times$	2.1970	=	3.999;	$\times$	0.6407	=	2.562
				Sum of PVs of supernormal period dividends				=	$6.888

Step 2. The stock price at the end of Year 3 is the PV of the dividends expected from Year 4 to infinity. To find this, we first (a) find the expected value of the stock at the end of Year 3 and then (b) find the present value of the Year 3 stock price:

a. $\hat{P}_3 = \dfrac{D_4}{k_s - g_n} = \dfrac{D_0(1 + g_s)^3 (1 + g_n)}{k_s - g_n} = \dfrac{D_3(1 + g_n)}{0.16 - 0.10}$

$= \dfrac{\$3.999(1.10)}{0.06} = \dfrac{\$4.399}{0.06} = \$73.32.$

b.   PV $\hat{P}_3 = \$73.32 \left(\dfrac{1}{1.16}\right)^3 = \$73.32(0.6407) = \$46.97.$

Step 3. Find $\hat{P}_0$, the value of the stock today:

$$\hat{P}_0 = \$6.89 + \$46.97 = \$53.86.$$

In recent years, courts deciding valuation questions have been employing the nonconstant growth approach described by Brigham and Gapenski. See Cede & Co. v. Technicolor, Inc., infra, p. 719 (appraisal rights); In re Pullman Construction Industries, 107 Bankr. 909 (Bkrtcy. N.D.Ill.1989) (bankruptcy reorganization), Appendix E infra; Wilson v. Great American Industries, 746 F.Supp. 251 (N.D.N.Y.1990) (calculation of damages for fraud under federal securities laws).

NOTE: VALUATION IN LEGAL CONTEXTS— THE PROBLEM OF NORMATIVE GOALS

Valuation is not an exact science and the available methods for determining the value of an enterprise and the value of its securities may produce different values for the same enterprise or security. Differences may result not only from the use of one method of valuation rather than another (e.g., capitalized earnings rather than asset appraisal) but also from differences among the factual and judgmental in-puts in the application of a particular method (e.g., the identification of facts deemed relevant in determining past earnings, or the judgment involved in determining an appropriate capitalization rate or an appropriate future earnings figure to capitalize). Whether or not there is any "correct" resolution of disagreements over the appropriate methods or in-puts in a purely voluntary transaction, the lawyer is concerned with the determination of which of the possible methods and in-puts are most appropriate for vindicating a particular legal norm. Hence, the value sought in legal proceedings is often defined in light of the consequences following from its determination, and is ascertained by the method which is most appropriate to the purpose for which it is sought.

In the insolvency reorganization context of *Atlas Pipeline,* for example, reliability of market prices as an index of value was affected because, *inter alia,* the very factors which led the firm to insolvency and to the uncertainties immediately thereafter operated to affect (i.e., make more uncertain) the value of its securities. Guesses by investors and potential investors as to the likely outcome of the reorganization bargaining also affected securities market prices by injecting factors which were irrelevant to the "intrinsic" value of the enterprise. But even apart from the question of disparity between market prices of securities and "intrinsic" value, the legal inquiry into enterprise value in *Atlas Pipeline* was concerned with dividing the value of assets (or participations) among claimants against the insolvent enterprise in satisfaction of their claims to cash payment. If valuing the assets on a liquidation basis produced a higher figure than valuing them as participations in a going concern, the legal norms dictated reliance on liquidation.

The legal context in which value is sought may affect estimates or judgments as to earnings and risk as well as the selection of a particular method of valuation. Thus, in the case of insolvency reorganization, the fact that the process contemplates realigning participations in an enterprise which has "failed" has an impact upon the estimates to be made about increased earnings in the future. It injects uncertainties about the future which would be lacking in the case of predictions with respect to similar businesses which have been continuously prosperous. Nor is it irrelevant, either in making the estimate of future earnings or determining the degree of risk, (1) that the legal context leaves the senior security holder unable to protect himself if errors in the process should produce a result which he deems over-valuation, or (2) that the junior security holder can protect himself against felt under-valuation by finding a bidder for the enterprise at a price higher than the value set in the reorganization proceeding. As a result, the legal norm (i.e., the vindication of senior security holders' rights) may well suggest the presence of a bias in favor of under-valuing, which means either lower estimates of future-earnings or higher capitalization rates.

What is (or should be) the impact on the valuation process in the *DuPont* case of the posture of the transaction as a unilateral merger freezing out a powerless minority?

(D) MEASURES OF RISK—THE CAPITAL ASSET PRICING MODEL AND BETA

A powerful, if increasingly disputed, theoretical analysis of asset pricing in the capital markets, known as the Capital Asset Pricing Model, has been developed by finance academics during the last quarter century. That model offers a different measure of the "risk" of an enterprise and its securities than that offered in theory by reliance essentially upon the standard deviation or variance of the particular firm's expected earnings, and in practice, by reliance upon comparison with the market's pricing of a comparable enterprise's stream of earnings. Instead of comparing the variance or standard deviation of the expected return on an asset (i.e., a particular firm or its securities) with that of comparable assets (i.e., comparable firms or securities) as reflected in their price earnings ratios (however adjusted for growth) the central notion is to measure risk by relating the return and variance of a particular firm or its securities to the return and variance of the market as a whole. Before turning to the model and the measure of risk it provides, it is necessary to consider the significance of portfolio theory and diversification of investment in explaining the risk-return trade-off that rational investors are said to make.

(1) Portfolio Theory

SHARPE, PORTFOLIO THEORY AND CAPITAL MARKETS
20–33 (1970).

* * *

Portfolio theory assumes that an investor is willing to choose among portfolios solely on the basis of these two measures [i.e., the expected value and the "spread" of the probability distribution]. Formally, it assumes that each pair summarizes a particular probability distribution. In practice such distributions need not be stated explicitly. The theory may be just as useful if predictions are provided directly and intuitively as if they are stated "scientifically."

To make clear the formal meanings, when referring to a portfolio, the two measures will be denoted:

E_p = expected (predicted) rate of return for a portfolio
σ_p = standard deviation (uncertainty) of rate of return for a portfolio.*

* * *

The desirability of a portfolio is expressed by the values of E_p and σ_p. * * * The theory assumes that any investor would consider [two portfolios with the same expected return and standard deviation] equivalent—he would just as soon have one as the other. This may not be strictly true in every instance. As always, abstraction may lead to error. But the chance of error may be small; and the error, if made, may not be serious.

Any portfolio can be represented by a point on a graph such as that shown in Fig. 2–4. Standard deviation of rate of return is plotted on the horizontal axis, and expected rate of return is plotted on the vertical axis.[2]

How does an investor choose among alternative portfolios? The following rules are assumed to apply for any investor:

---

* [Ed. Note] "The manner in which the standard deviation measures the 'spread' of a probability distribution is particularly accurate if the distribution is *normal;* i.e., follows the familiar bell-shaped curve. In such a case:

"The chances are roughly 2 out of 3 that the actual outcome will be between $(E - \sigma)$ and $(E + \sigma)$.

"The chances are roughly 95 out of 100 that the actual outcome will be between $(E - 2\sigma)$ and $(E + 2\sigma)$."

2. Some reverse the arrangement, plotting σ_p on the vertical axis and E_p on the horizontal. * * *

1. If two portfolios have the same standard deviation of return and different expected returns, the one with the larger expected return is preferred.

2. If two portfolios have the same expected return and different standard deviations of return, the one with the smaller standard deviation is preferred.

3. If one portfolio has a smaller standard deviation of return and a larger expected return than another, it is preferred.

The rules may be summarized succinctly:

4. E_p is *good:* other things equal, more is preferred to less.

5. σ_p is *bad:* other things equal, less is preferred to more.

FIGURE 2–4.

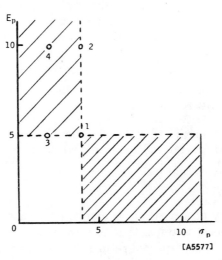

[A5577]

Assumption 5 is often termed *risk aversion.* A large body of evidence indicates that almost everyone is a risk averter when making important decisions. Clear counterexamples are rarely found. A day at the horse races provides something besides risk and probable loss, and even the ardent fan seldom takes his entire earnings to the track.

Figure 2–5 shows the distributions of rate of return for four portfolios; their E_p and σ_p values are plotted in Fig. 2–4. Among other things, the assumptions about investor preferences imply that:

Portfolio 2 is preferred to portfolio 1 (rules 1, 4).

Portfolio 3 is preferred to portfolio 1 (rules 2, 5).

Portfolio 4 is preferred to portfolio 1 (rules 3, 4, and 5).

Graphically, the rules assert that for any investor:

Portfolios represented by points lying to the northwest of the point representing a portfolio are better (i.e., preferred).

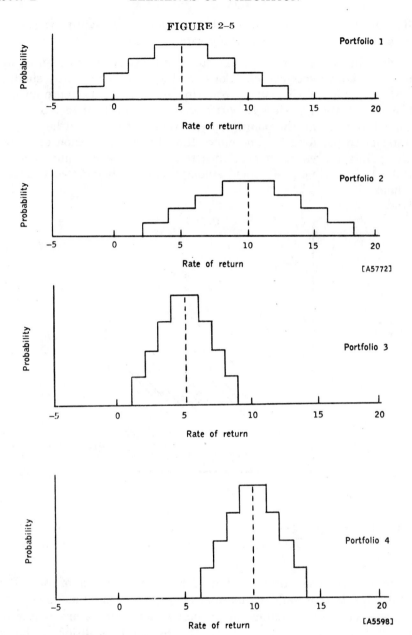

FIGURE 2-5

Portfolio 1

Portfolio 2

[A5772]

Portfolio 3

Portfolio 4

[A5598]

Portfolios represented by points lying to the southeast of the point representing a portfolio are worse (i.e., the original portfolio is preferred).

Portfolios represented by points lying in the lightly shaded area in Fig. 2–4 are preferred to portfolio 1, but portfolio 1 is preferred to all those represented by points lying in the darkly shaded area.

The major results of portfolio theory follow directly from the assumption that investors like E_p and dislike σ_p. Of course, more can be said about the preferences of any *given* investor. How strong is his dislike for σ_p vis-à-vis E_p?　How much uncertainty is he willing to accept to enhance his prospects for a likely rate of return?

The feelings of a particular investor can usefully be represented by a family of *indifference curves*.　Consider Fig. 2–6.　The lightly shaded area [to the left of the curve] contains all the points representing portfolios that Mr. *T* prefers to portfolio 1.　The darkly shaded area [to the right] contains all the points representing portfolios that he considers inferior to portfolio 1.　The curve that divides the region contains all the points representing portfolios that he considers equivalent to portfolio 1; he has no preferences among them—he is *indifferent* about the choice.

FIGURE 2–6

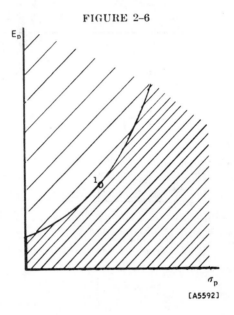

[A5592]

As long as E_p is desired and σ_p is not, every indifference curve will be upward-sloping.　Generally, each curve will become steeper as E_p and σ_p increase.

The indifference curve in Fig. 2–6 captures some of Mr. *T*'s feelings.　But to represent the manner in which he would make choices in a great variety of circumstances, many more curves are required. Figure 2–7 repeats the curve of Fig. 2–6 as I_1.　In addition it shows another curve derived by starting with portfolio 2.　Since portfolio 2 is preferred to portfolio 1, every point on I_2 must be preferred to every point on I_1.　This follows from the concept of indifference and minimal requirements for rational choice.　Indifference curves may not cross.

FIGURE 2-7

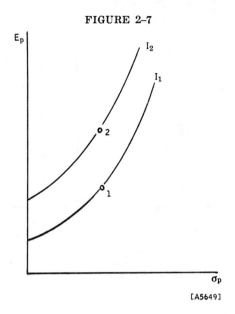

[A5649]

The number of indifference curves is almost limitless. Only a selected few are shown in graphical examples. It is conventional to label those shown in order of preference. Thus points on I_2 are preferred to those on I_1; points on I_3 are preferred to those on I_2, etc.

A set of indifference curves summarizes the preferences of a given individual. Figure 2-8 shows two extreme cases. Mr. Fearless is oblivious to risk; Mr. Chicken is oblivious to everything except risk.

Figure 2-9 shows more common cases. Mr. Birch is relatively conservative, requiring substantial increases in E_p to induce him to accept greater uncertainty (σ_p). Mr. Flynn is more adventuresome. Neither likes uncertainty, but Mr. Birch dislikes it more (relative to his preference for E_p).

FIGURE 2-8

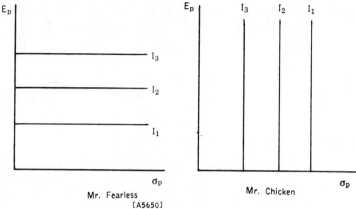

Mr. Fearless

[A5650]

Mr. Chicken

FIGURE 2-9

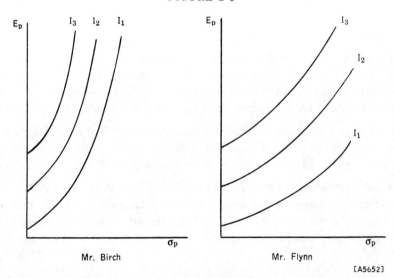

Mr. Birch

Mr. Flynn

[A5652]

Consider Mr. Z. His preferences are shown by the indifference curves in Fig. 2–10. Many portfolios are available to him. Their E_p and σ_p values may be shown by a group of points in the figure. Such points will entirely fill the shaded area. Which will Mr. Z prefer? Obviously the one shown by point B.

The decision illustrated in Fig. 2–10 can be broken into three separate phases: security analysis, portfolio analysis, and portfolio selection.

Security analysis is an art. It requires predictions about the future prospects of securities * * *. These predictions must take into account both uncertainty and interrelationships. In particular, they must be suitable for use in the next phase.

FIGURE 2-10

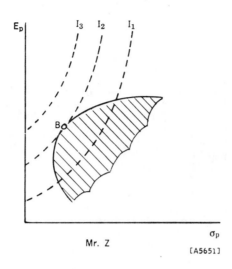

Mr. Z

[A5651]

Portfolio analysis produces predictions about portfolios. The predictions, in the form of E_p and σ_p estimates, are derived entirely from the predictions about securities produced in the first phase. No artistry is required, just computation.

Portfolio selection is the final phase. Given the available E_p, σ_p combinations, the investor, or someone knowing his preferences, selects the best.

The first phase requires the skills of a seer. The last requires knowledge of a specific investor's preferences. Portfolio analysis requires only technical skills. One person (e.g., the investor) can, of course, do the entire job. But comparative advantage may dictate a division of labor.

Portfolio theory is concerned primarily with the task of portfolio analysis. Given predictions about securities, what E_p, σ_p combinations can be obtained by the proper choice of a portfolio? The answer to such a question will be a large number of points (e.g., several million) entirely filling an area such as the shaded region of Fig. 2-10.

The portfolio analyst cannot normally choose the single best portfolio for a given investor. But he can reject certain possibilities. In particular, he can reject any portfolio not represented by a point on the upper border of the region. This is illustrated in Fig. 2-11. Portfolio *e* *dominates* portfolio *i*; it has a larger E_p and the same σ_p. Portfolio *e* is said to be an *efficient portfolio*; portfolio *i* is inefficient.

The upper border of the region of available E_p, σ_p combinations is called the *efficient frontier*. The portfolios whose E_p, σ_p values are plotted on the frontier comprise the set of efficient portfolios.

FIGURE 2–11

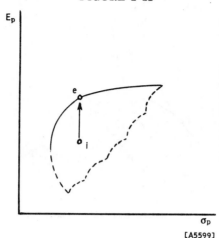

[A5599]

NOTE: DIVERSIFICATION AS A MEANS OF REDUCING RISK

Why is the Sharpe discussion, supra, carried on in terms of *portfolios* of securities rather than individual stocks? Indeed, why do most investors invest in combinations of securities—a little bit of this and a little bit of that—instead of putting everything they have into the single "best" security that is available in the market? The answer—as everyone knows intuitively—is that it is somehow dangerous to put all your eggs in one basket. As a result, investors usually prefer to hold securities of companies in different industries, or to accomplish the same end by owning shares of a mutual fund which affords participation in a widely varied portfolio. Can this preference be expressed in systematic terms?

The advantage of diversification (and of mutual funds) can be illustrated as follows. Suppose investors can purchase the stock of Warco, which manufactures weapons, and of Peaceco, which builds low-income housing. Both stocks sell at the same price. Performance of Warco depends on the size of the defense budget, as indicated in the following table:

Event	Probability of event	Warco Return
Large Defense Budget	1/3	12%
Medium–Size Defense Budget	1/3	8%
Small Defense Budget	1/3	4%

Performance of Peaceco depends on non-defense government expenditures, which are always inversely proportional to defense expenditures, e.g., a large defense budget means a small non-defense budget and low earnings for Peaceco. Peaceco's performance can be related directly to the size of the defense budget, as indicated in the following table:

Event	Probability of event	Peaceco Return
Large Defense Budget	⅓	4%
Medium–Size Defense Budget	⅓	8%
Small Defense Budget	⅓	12%

If an investor decides on a portfolio divided equally between Warco and Peaceco, he can expect the following results:

Event	Prob.	Warco Return	Peaceco Return	Average Return
Large Defense Budget	⅓	12%	4%	8%
Medium–Size Defense Budget	⅓	8%	8%	8%
Small Defense Budget	⅓	4%	12%	8%

Because Warco and Peaceco *always* react in *exactly* opposite ways to the same event, the return on a portfolio composed equally of both securities does not vary *at all*. Accordingly, if we assume that the size of the defense budget is the only event of significance to either company, an equal investment in both stocks produces an absolutely certain 8% return. By contrast, an investment in either company by itself, while it produces the same *expected* rate of return (8%), also produces the risk that the actual rate may fall substantially short of the expected rate. It will be recalled (see Lewellen, supra p. 58) that investors are assumed in general to be averse to risk, i.e., the loss of utility associated with a possible decline in their fortunes is never wholly compensated by the gain in utility associated with a possible rise in their fortunes, where the possible rise and possible decline are equal in dollar amount. Under this assumption, an investor will always prefer a stock (or portfolio of stocks) which offers a certain return of 8% to a stock which offers a ⅓ chance of 4%, a ⅓ chance of 8% and a ⅓ chance of 12%. It follows that the investor will feel himself to be better off if he divides his wealth equally between Warco and Peaceco than if he acquires either stock alone or even both stocks in a proportion other than the prescribed 50–50.

Another way of expressing this concept is to say that the expected return of a portfolio divided equally between two securities is equal to the average of the expected return from each security. The *risk* of such portfolio, however, is not necessarily the average of the individual risks. If individual securities react differently to the same future events, the risk of the portfolio as a whole will be less than the average of the individual risks. As shown, a portfolio that combines Warco and Peaceco in equal proportion is entirely *free* of risk; at the same time, expected dollar income is *unreduced*. Of course, the opportunity to get an 8% return on Warco and Peaceco would not last very long. Once the market became aware of the advantage of combining them, the prices of both stocks would be bid up until their expected yields approximated the yield on riskless securities such as government bonds. But the investor who first perceived the advantage would get the benefit of the rise.

In the real world, of course, a portfolio consisting of Warco and Peaceco would continue to have substantial risk, even if one accepts the "fact" that the net incomes of the two companies are negatively correlated. The reason is that, like most common stocks, the market prices of *both* Warco and Peaceco will rise and fall with the ups and downs of the market *as a whole*. The market, as everyone knows, reacts to all kinds of news having nothing directly to do with particular companies—indeed, it has been variously estimated that between one-third and one-half of the variability of most stocks listed on the New York Stock Exchange is attributable to events which occasion price changes in the entire market (i.e., political and economic developments of all sorts) or that a security's unsystematic risk ranges from 40% to 50% or more of its total risk.[a] Some stocks are highly responsive to market ups and downs, others less so. But it is a rare stock whose movements are inversely correlated with the market, or which is wholly unaffected by changes in the general level of market prices.

What this means, in effect, is that the risk, or variability, in the performance of a stock or a portfolio must be divided into two components. The first, called "independent" or "unsystematic" variability, relates to events that are unique to the firm itself—management strength, labor problems, research plans and so on. The second, called "market" or "systematic" variability, relates to price changes occasioned by movements in the market as a whole. Diversification—the act of combining Warco and Peaceco—is able to reduce the *independent* variability of a stock or portfolio, but it can do little to reduce the risk attributable to *market* variability.

It does not follow that diversification is unimportant. Quite the contrary: since independent variability can be reduced to (or near) zero by diversifying "efficiently," the only risk which an investor in stocks is actually obliged to take, and hence the only risk for which he can expect to be compensated by a high rate of return, is that of market variability—the one risk element that cannot be diversified away. Put another way, the existence of independent variability in a portfolio means that its owner is accepting a risk that he could avoid (through better diversification), and is doing so without any compensating increase in expected income. In summary, the object of diversification is to eliminate independent variability from the portfolio. Even when this is done, however, portfolios will still differ in degree of market risk, and hence will fall at different points on the efficient frontier. The

a. Sharpe, Factors in New York Stock Exchange Security Returns, 1931–1979, 5 J. of Portfolio Mgt. (Summer 1982) p. 19; Modigliani and Pogue, infra, p. 98.

distinction between "systematic" and "unsystematic" risks is important in this field and is taken up again at p. 98, infra.

As a final question of some importance, how *many* securities should an investor hold to achieve "efficient" diversification? While the average number of stocks owned by individual investors has been put at three or four, institutional investors such as mutual funds often maintain over 100 different stocks in their portfolios, as well as a variety of corporate and government bonds. Some financial writers have estimated that diversification beyond 15 or 20 securities cannot reduce risk by a meaningful amount, and that the quality of the diversification, i.e., the degree of interrelatedness among the securities selected, is significantly more important than the quantity. Noting that "one of the advantages claimed by investment institutions is that they provide the only opportunity for individuals to gain the full benefit of diversification", Brealey, An Introduction to Risk and Return From Common Stocks (1969) at 131, observes that, "While such an argument has much to recommend it, the number of holdings necessary to achieve an optimum amount of diversification may not be out of reach of many individual investors". In sum, a little diversification goes a long way. The point has practical implications since a portfolio containing 150 securities presumably costs more to manage than one containing 15. If relatively little reduction in risk is accomplished by holding the larger number, the additional management expense is simply not worthwhile.

In recent years index funds have developed as investment mechanisms offering to investors participation in a portfolio of a limited number of securities which will replicate the market portfolio or some other selected portfolio configurations of risk and return. Costs for such investments are said to be lower than those of more conventional investment funds.

Published work in the field of portfolio theory is highly technical. For the truly interested, major theoretical developments can be traced to (among others) Markowitz, Portfolio Selection, 7 J. Finance 1 (1952); Tobin, Liquidity Preference as Behavior Towards Risk, 27 Rev. of Econ. Studies 65 (1968); Hirshleifer, Efficient Allocation of Capital in an Uncertain World, 54 Am.Econ.Rev. 77 (1964); Sharpe, Capital Asset Prices: A Theory of Market Equilibrium Under Conditions of Risk, 19 J. Finance 425 (1964); Lintner, Security Prices, Risk, and Maximal Gains from Diversification, 19 J. Finance 589 (1965); Markowitz, Normative Portfolio Analysis: Past, Present and Future, 42 J. Econ. & Bus. 99 (1990); Sharpe, Capital Asset Prices With and Without Negative Holdings, 46 J. Finance 489 (1991). Finance textbooks discuss developments in the subject in summary fashion. See generally Van Horne, Financial Management and Policy (9th ed. 1992) Ch. 3; Brealey and Myers, Principles of Corporate Finance (4th ed. 1991) Chs. 7 and 9; Copeland and Weston, Financial Theory and Corporate Policy (3rd ed. 1988) Ch. 7.

* * *

NOTE: CHOOSING A "BEST" PORTFOLIO

Looking back at Sharpe's Figure 2–11 (supra, p. 88), it appears that only those portfolios which lie on the upper border of the shaded region (e.g., portfolio e) should be regarded by investors as acceptable. A portfolio represented by a point on what Sharpe terms the "efficient frontier" offers a greater return for a given level of risk than any portfolio not so represented and hence should be preferred by investors, just as portfolio e would be preferred to portfolio i in Figure 2–11.

Suppose, however, that we designate another point on the efficient frontier—call it portfolio n. By hypothesis, portfolios e and n are equally "efficient". Is there any basis for asserting that one is better than the other? Since each portfolio lies at a different point on the upper border in Figure 2–11, either e offers a greater return *but* is riskier than n, or n offers a greater return *but* is riskier than e. Neither has the advantage in both categories at once. Accordingly, it would seem that the choice between e and n is very much a matter of the individual investor's personal preference for greater return as opposed to greater risk, an idea which is portrayed in Figure 2–10 (supra, p. 87).

It has been argued, however, (indeed Sharpe himself later argues) that the availability of riskless assets (cash, U.S. treasury bills, insured savings accounts) makes it possible to name one of the two portfolios as "best"—that is, to regard portfolio e or n as superior to the other (and possibly to all other portfolios on the efficient frontier)—even recognizing that investors differ widely in their willingness to bear risk. Following are two essentially similar restatements of the analysis that lies behind this assertion:

LINTNER, A MODEL OF A PERFECTLY FUNCTIONING SECURITIES MARKET

Economic Policy and the Regulation of Corporate Securities (Manne, Ed.1969).
150–154.

Investor Response to a Given Set of Stock Prices

Consider then the individual investor facing *any* possible set of current prices for different stocks in the market which he might hold. The probability distribution of ending price-plus-dividend for each stock divided by the current price gives him an expected rate of return and risk-of-return for each stock and each percentage mix or portfolio of different stocks. Think of some one possible stock portfolio offering, say, an expected return of 8% with a risk of 12%. If the investor puts all his funds in this portfolio this would be his expected return and risk on all his assets. If the riskless rate is 5%, he *could* get 5% with no risk on all his assets. Splitting his funds equally between bonds and this portfolio would give him an overall expected return of $(8 + 5)/2 = 6\frac{1}{2}\%$ with an overall return risk of 6%. In general, even if this investor confines his attention to combining just this one stock portfolio with bills, he can vary his return and risk on his investable assets within wide limits by shifting the relative amount he holds in cash and the amount (including borrowing if he wishes, subject to margin limits) invested in this stock mix.

Suppose there is another stock portfolio offering an expected return of 10% with a risk of 15%. Would our investor prefer it? He clearly would. The reason is that a combination of *this* portfolio and government bonds (of appropriate maturity) which had the same expected return on his total investable funds would involve less risk, than the combination of this riskless asset with the first portfolio;[1] correspondingly, a combination of this second portfolio and the riskless asset which would show the same risk on all his investable funds would show a larger expected overall return.[2]

In general, the investor will always be able to duplicate the expected return on investable funds at lower overall risk by finding another stock portfolio which has a larger *"critical ratio"* of expected excess stock portfolio return to stock portfolio risk. (Excess portfolio return is the portfolio return less the return on the riskless asset). In our examples, the $(10-5)/15 = \frac{1}{3}$ for our second stock portfolio is preferred to the ratio $(8-5)/12 = \frac{1}{4}$ for the first. Under the conditions we are working with, this single ratio summarizes the desirability of alternative stock portfolios to the investor. But with any given joint probability distribution over a set of stocks, the investor can form a very large number of different possible stock portfolios by varying the subset of stocks he tentatively considers including, and even with each subset, by varying the percentage mix among the stocks. In principle, in his own self-interest he will search over all these possible stock portfolios (mixes) offered in the market and find the mix with the highest critical ratio.

After he has found the best stock mix, he can then determine *how much* (in dollars or as a percentage of his investable funds) he wants to invest in *this* stock portfolio, holding the remainder in the riskless asset (or borrowing). Analytically it turns out that risk averters (in the sense we used the term above) necessarily require larger and larger increments of expected return to feel as well off as they bear more and more risk. If an investor's return requirement per unit of added risk is

---

1. This investor could get an expected return of $6\frac{1}{2}\%$ by putting 70% of his funds in bills at 5% and 30% of his funds in this stock mix—the same expected return as the 50–50 split between bills and the first stock portfolio. But with the first stock mix, his corresponding risk was $.5(12\%) = 6\%$, while now he has a risk of only $.3(15\%) = 4.5\%$ on his total investable funds.

2. The investor had an overall return risk of 6% with a 50–50 investment in the first portfolio and bills; he would have the same overall risk of 6% on his entire investable funds by placing 40% of the funds in the second stock portfolio. His expected return on all his investable funds with the latter portfolio would be * * * [7%] which is greater than the 6% he had using the first portfolio.

greater than that offered by the best stock portfolio he sees in the market, he simply buys no stock. If the requirement is initially less than that offered by this portfolio, he buys some and continues to shift funds into this portfolio until his (increasing) return requirement as he bears more and more risk no longer is less than (and hence equals) the return-risk tradeoff offered by this best portfolio in the market.

LORIE, DODD AND KIMPTON, THE STOCKMARKET: THEORIES AND EVIDENCE

(2nd Ed.1985).
pp. 122–126.

* * *

A natural extension of the Markowitz analysis was to consider the problem of building portfolios which included riskless assets and port-folios purchased in part with borrowed funds, as well as portfolios of risky assets paid with the investor's equity.

Recall that the efficient frontier for portfolios made up of many risky assets is typically concave from below in the plane whose axes are risk (as measured by the standard deviation) and expected return. For any given period, there are assets whose rates of return can be predict-ed with virtual certainty—except for times of nuclear holocausts, natu-ral disasters, and revolution. Most investors have confidence that they can accurately predict the rate of return on federal government securi-ties for any period which is equal to their maturity. For example, Treasury bills maturing in one year have a precisely predictable rate of return for one year.*

The introduction of riskless assets into portfolios has interesting consequences. In the following diagrams, the return on a risk-free asset is designated by R_f on the vertical axis. Sharpe and Tobin stated that if this alternative exists, it is possible to select portfolios at any given point on line R_fB defined by the return on the riskless asset and the point of tangency with the efficient frontier of portfolios with risky assets (Figure 8–11.) This follows from the discussion of asset combina-tions.

* * *

Investing entirely in the risk-free asset is possible, investing entire-ly in the risky assets at the point of tangency is possible; and achieving portfolios at any point on a straight line between these points is also possible. Portfolios on this line are preferred to portfolios on curve AB, consisting solely of risky assets, since the former provide more return for given risk.

Sharpe further showed that one can hold efficient portfolios on line R_fB beyond the point of tangency if borrowing is allowed. If it is

---

* For government securities with period-ic interest payments, the prediction of the rate of return to maturity is somewhat less certain, since the rates that will exist when interest payments have to be reinvested cannot be known with certainty.

assumed that one can borrow to buy financial assets at a rate similar to what the investor receives on the risk-free assets, the efficient portfolios beyond the point of tangency lie on a linear extrapolation of the line to the point of tangency (Figure 8–12). Any point on line R_fBD is now attainable by combining the portfolio of risky assets at point B with the riskless asset, or by levering portfolio B by borrowing and investing the funds in B. Portfolios on R_fBD are preferred to portfolios between A and B and between B and C, since they offer greater return for a given level of risk or less risk for a given level of return. The efficient frontier is now entirely linear. R_fBD is Sharpe's capital market line. It relates the expected return on an efficient portfolio to its risk as measured by the standard deviation.

In Figure 8–12, there is only one portfolio of *risky* assets that is optimal, and it is the same for all investors. Since only one portfolio of risky assets is optimal, it must be the market portfolio. That is, it includes all assets in proportion to their market value.

* * *

FIGURE 8-11   **The efficient frontier with lending**

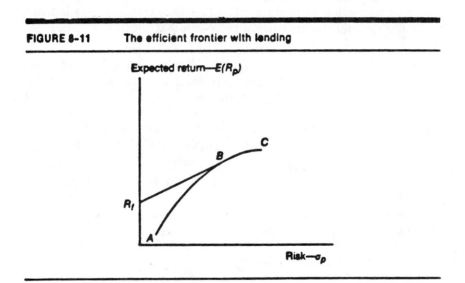

FIGURE 8-12   **The efficient frontier with lending and borrowing**

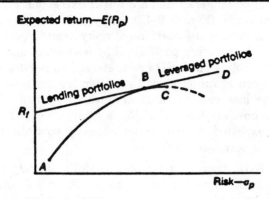

In Sharpe's model, individual preferences will determine only the amount of borrowing or lending. The fact that this choice is independent of the optimal combination of risky assets is called the "separation theorem."

Two qualifications should be noted. If only lending is allowed, the separation theorem will not hold. For example, in Figure 8–14, the efficient set of portfolios is not limited to those on line R_fM. It also includes portfolios of risky assets between M and C. A particular investor might prefer one of the latter to portfolios on R_fM. In other words, there is no single optimum combination of risky assets.

The second qualification is that the efficient frontier for portfolios of risky assets can have linear segments. If the frontier is linear at the

FIGURE 8-14   **The efficient frontier with no borrowing**

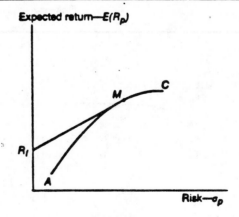

point of tangency, once again there is more than one optimum portfolio of risky assets. This is illustrated in Figure 8–15. Portfolios *B* and *C,* and all those on the line between them, are efficient portfolios of risky assets. Their returns are perfectly correlated.

FIGURE 8-15   The efficient frontier with a linear segment

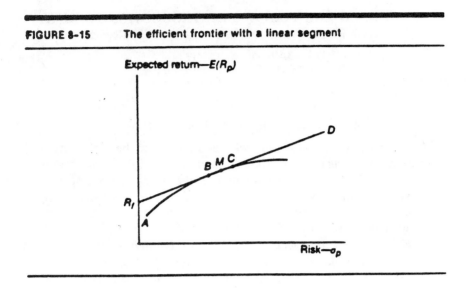

(2) The Capital Asset Pricing Model

As suggested above, financial theory makes an important distinction between the "systematic" and the "unsystematic" risk that inheres in every security. Unsystematic risk—the tendency of a stock to react to events that particularly affect the company, such as strikes, new inventions, management changes or new legal regulations—can be largely "washed away" by mixing the security with other securities in a diversified portfolio. Warco and Peaceco (supra, p. 88) each depends for its profitability on the size of the defense budget, but since each reacts oppositely to the same event, the risk that the defense budget will be high (disfavoring Peaceco) or low (disfavoring Warco) can be wholly eliminated by combining both securities in a single portfolio. This can be done, moreover, without any sacrifice in expected return.

But even if a Warco–Peaceco portfolio existed in the market, the fact is that the portfolio would *still* contain risk. This would be true because of the tendency of *all* stocks to fluctuate with changes in the overall level of the stock market. The important point is that this element of systematic risk is *unaffected* by diversification. Thus, the systematic risk of a portfolio is simply the average of the systematic risks of all the securities included in that portfolio.

The distinction between systematic and unsystematic risk is of great importance in portfolio theory and leads directly to the formulation of a "benchmark" against which the performance of a portfolio can be measured. This benchmark is referred to as the Capital Asset Pricing Model, a concept that is explained in the excerpt following.

MODIGLIANI AND POGUE, AN INTRODUCTION TO RISK AND RETURN: CONCEPTS AND EVIDENCE

30 Fin.Anal.J. 68 (March/April, 1974).

30 Fin.Anal.J. 69 (May/June, 1974).

* * *

5. The Risk of Individual Securities

* * * In the previous section we concluded that the systematic risk of an individual security is that portion of its total risk (standard deviation of return) which cannot be eliminated by combining it with other securities in a well diversified portfolio. We now need a way of quantifying the systematic risk of a security and relating the systematic risk of a portfolio to that of its component securities. This can be accomplished by dividing security return into two parts: one dependent (i.e., perfectly correlated), and a second independent (i.e., uncorrelated) of market return. The first component of return is usually referred to as "systematic", the second as "unsystematic" return. Thus we have

$$\text{Security Return} = \text{Systematic Return} + \text{Unsystematic Return.} \tag{4}$$

Since the systematic return is perfectly correlated with the market return, it can be expressed as a factor, designated beta (β), times the market return, R_m. The beta factor is a market sensitivity index, indicating how sensitive the security return is to changes in the market level. The unsystematic return, which is independent of market returns, is usually represented by a factor epsilon (ε'). Thus the security return, R, may be expressed

$$R = \beta R_m + \varepsilon'. \tag{5}$$

For example, if a security had a β factor of 2.0 (e.g., an airline stock), then a 10 per cent market return would generate a systematic return for the stock of 20 per cent. The security return for the period would be the 20 per cent plus the unsystematic component. The unsystematic component depends on factors unique to the company, such as labor difficulties, higher than expected sales, etc.

The security returns model given by Equation (5) is usually written in a way such that the average value of the residual term, ε', is zero. This is accomplished by adding a factor, alpha (α), to the model to represent the average value of the unsystematic returns over time. That is, we set $\varepsilon' = \alpha + \varepsilon$ so that

$$R = \alpha + \beta R_m + \varepsilon, \tag{6}$$

where the average ε over time is equal to zero.

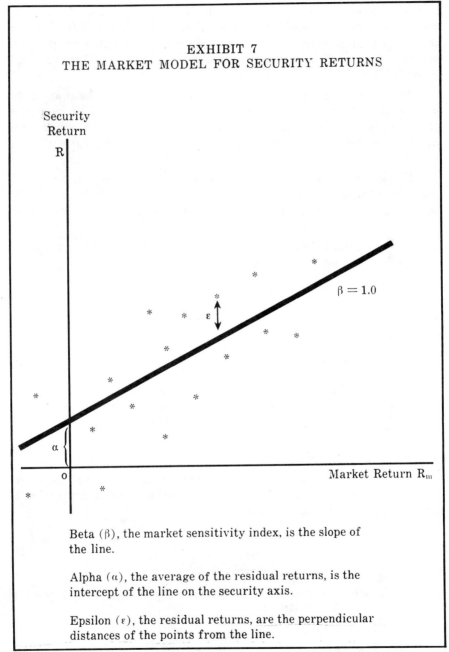

EXHIBIT 7
THE MARKET MODEL FOR SECURITY RETURNS

Beta (β), the market sensitivity index, is the slope of the line.

Alpha (α), the average of the residual returns, is the intercept of the line on the security axis.

Epsilon (ε), the residual returns, are the perpendicular distances of the points from the line.

[B9959]

The model for security returns given by Equation (6) is usually referred to as the "market model". Graphically, the model can be depicted as a line fitted to a plot of security returns against rates of return on the market index. This is shown in Exhibit 7 for a hypothetical security.

The beta factor can be thought of as the slope of the line. It gives the expected increase in security return for a one per cent increase in market return. In Exhibit 7, the security has a beta of 1.0. Thus, a ten per cent market return will result, on the average, in a ten per cent security return. The market-weighted average beta for all stocks is 1.0 by definition.

The alpha factor is represented by the intercept of the line on the vertical security return axis. It is equal to the average value over time of the unsystematic returns (ε') on the stock. For most stocks, the alpha factor tends to be small and unstable. (We shall return to alpha later.)

Using the definition of security return given by the market model, the specification of systematic and unsystematic risk is straighforward—they are simply the standard deviations of the two return components.

The systematic risk of a security is equal to β times the standard deviation of the market return:

$$\text{Systematic Risk} = \beta\sigma_m. \tag{7}$$

The unsystematic risk equals the standard deviation of the residual return factor ε:

$$\text{Unsystematic Risk} = \sigma_e. \tag{8}$$

Given measures of individual security systematic risk, we can now compute the systematic risk of portfolio. It is equal to the beta factor for the portfolio, β_p, times the risk of the market index, σ_m:

$$\text{Portfolio Systematic Risk} = \beta_p\sigma_m. \tag{9}$$

The portfolio beta factor in turn can be shown to be simply an average of the individual security betas, weighted by the proportion of each security in the portfolio, or

$$\beta_p = \sum_{j=1}^{N} X_j\beta_j, \tag{10}$$

where
  X_j = the proportion of portfolio market value represented by security j
  N = the number of securities.

Thus the systematic risk of the portfolio is simply a weighted average of the systematic risk of the individual securities. If the portfolio is composed of an equal dollar investment in each stock * * * the β_p is simply an unweighted average of the component security betas.

The unsystematic risk of the portfolio is also a function of the unsystematic security risks, but the form is more complex. The important point is that with increasing diversification this risk can be reduced toward zero.*

The main results of this section can be summarized as follows: First, * * * roughly 40 to 50 per cent of total security risk can be eliminated by diversification. Second, the remaining systematic risk is equal to the security β times market risk. Third, portfolio systematic risk is a weighted average of security systematic risks.

The implications of these results are substantial. First, we would expect realized rates of return over substantial periods of time to be related to the systematic as opposed to total risk of securities. Since the unsystematic risk is relatively easily eliminated, we should not expect the market to offer a risk premium for bearing it. Second, since security systematic risk is equal to the security beta times σ_m (which is common to all securities), beta is useful as a *relative* risk measure. The β gives the systematic risk of a security (or portfolio) relative to the risk of the market index. * * * †

* [Ed. Note] The phenomenon may be illustrated graphically as follows:

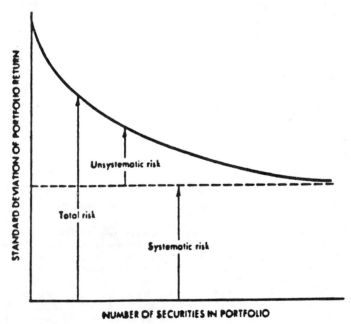

NUMBER OF SECURITIES IN PORTFOLIO

As the number of securities (randomly selected) increases, unsystematic risk and pro tanto total risk, are reduced—rapidly at first, but at a decreasing rate.

† [Ed. Note] A. Kolbe, J. Read, Jr., and G. Hall, The Cost of Capital: Estimating the Rate of Return for Public Utilities (1984) at 68–69 points out: "An asset's beta combines the volatility of the asset's returns and the correlation of those returns with other assets into a single measure.

The first factor in beta is the width of the average swing in the asset's value relative to the average swing in the portfolio's value. This can be measured by the standard deviation of the asset's returns divided by the standard deviation of the portfolio's returns.

* * *

6. The Relationship Between Expected Return and Risk: The Capital Asset Pricing Model

The first part of this article developed two measures of risk: one is a measure of total risk (standard deviation), the other a relative index of systematic or nondiversifiable risk (beta). The beta measure would appear to be the more relevant for the pricing of securities. Returns expected by investors should logically be related to systematic as opposed to total risk. Securities with higher systematic risk should have higher expected returns.

The question to be considered now is the form of the relationship between risk and return. In this section we describe a relationship called the "Capital Asset Pricing Model" (CAPM), which is based on elementary logic and simple economic principles. The basic postulate underlying finance theory is that assets with the same risk should have the same expected rate of return. That is, the prices of assets in the capital markets should adjust until equivalent risk assets have identical expected returns.

To see the implications of this postulate, let us consider an investor who holds a risky portfolio with the same risk as the market portfolio (beta equal to 1.0). What return should he expect? Logically, he should expect the same return as that of the market portfolio.

Let us consider another investor who holds a riskless portfolio (beta equal to zero). The investor in this case should expect to earn the rate of return on riskless assets such as treasury bills. By taking no risk, he earns the riskless rate of return.

Now let us consider the case of an investor who holds a mixture of these two portfolios. Assuming he invests a proportion X of his money in the risky portfolio and $(1 - X)$ in the riskless portfolio, what risk does he bear and what return should he expect? The risk of the composite portfolio is easily computed when we recall that the beta of a portfolio is simply a weighted average of the component security betas,

The second factor in beta is the correlation between the asset's moves and the portfolio's moves. A correlation of -1 implies the asset's returns *always* move up when the portfolio's returns move up. A correlation of 1 implies the asset's returns always move *down* when the portfolio's return moves *up*. A correlation of 0 implies the asset and the portfolio move independently of each other.

The product of the correlation and the ratio of the standard deviations is the asset's beta *with respect to that portfolio.*

An important conclusion of the CAPM is that all investors hold the 'market portfolio,' a portfolio consisting of shares of all stocks. One way to understand this conclusion is to note that such a portfolio would provide maximum diversification. Investors would calculate each asset's beta with respect to 'the market.' Few investors literally hold the market. However, the returns of well-diversified portfolios are highly correlated with market movements. Thus asset betas measured relative to the market are attractive general measures of asset risk. Betas measured with respect to the market are also the sole measure of asset risk in the CAPM.

* * *

Thus an asset's beta depends on the correlation of its rate of return with the market's rate of return and on the size of its standard deviation (its variability) relative to the market's."

where the weights are the portfolio proportions. Thus the portfolio beta, β_p, is a weighted average of the beta of the market portfolio and the beta of the risk-free rate. However, the market beta is 1.0, and that of the risk-free rate is zero. Therefore

$$\beta_p = (1 - X) \bullet 0 + X \bullet 1,$$
$$= X. \tag{11}$$

Thus β_p is equal to the fraction of his money invested in the risky portfolio. If 100 per cent or less of the investor's funds is invested in the risky portfolio, his portfolio beta will be between zero and 1.0. If he borrows at the risk-free rate and invests the proceeds in the risky portfolio, his portfolio beta will be greater than 1.0.

The expected return of the composite portfolio is also a weighted average of the expected returns on the two-component portfolios; that is,

$$E(R_p) = (1 - X) \bullet R_f + X \bullet E(R_m), \tag{12}$$

where $E(R_p)$, $E(R_m)$, and R_r are the expected returns on the portfolio, the market index, and the risk-free rate. Now, from Equation (11) we know that X is equal to β_p. Substituting into Equation (12), we have

$$E(R_p) = (1 - \beta_p) \bullet R_F + \beta_p \bullet E(R_m),$$
or
$$E(R_p) = R_F + \beta_p \bullet (E(R_m) - R_F). \tag{13}$$

Equation (13) is the Capital Asset Pricing Model (CAPM), an extremely important theoretical result. It says that the expected return on a portfolio should exceed the riskless rate of return by an amount which is proportional to the portfolio beta. That is, the relationship between return and risk should be linear.

The model is often stated in "risk-premium" form. Risk premiums are obtained by subtracting the risk-free rate from the rates of return. The expected portfolio and market risk premiums (designated $E(r_p)$ and $E(r_m)$ respectively) are given by

$$E(r_p) = E(R_P) - R_F \tag{14a}$$

$$E(r_m) = E(R_m) - R_F. \tag{14b}$$

Substituting these risk premiums into Equation (13), we obtain

$$E(r_p) = \beta_P \bullet E(r_m). \tag{15}$$

In this form, the CAPM states that the expected risk premium for the investor's portfolio is equal to its beta value times the expected market risk premium.

We can illustrate the model by assuming that short-term (risk-free) interest rate is 6 per cent and the expected return on the market is 10 per cent. The expected risk premium for holding the market portfolio is just the difference between the 10 per cent and the short-term interest rate of 6 per cent, or 4 per cent. Investors who hold the market portfolio expect to earn 10 per cent, which is 4 per cent greater than they could earn on a short-term market instrument for certain. In order to satisfy Equation (13), the expected return on securities or portfolios with different levels of risk must be:

Expected Return for Different Levels of Portfolio Beta

Beta	Expected Return
0.0	6%
0.5	8%
1.0	10%
1.5	12%
2.0	14%

The predictions of the model are inherently sensible. For safe investments ($\beta = 0$), the model predicts that investors would expect to earn the risk-free rate of interest. For a risky investment ($\beta > 0$) investors would expect a rate of return proportional to the market sensitivity (β) of the investment. Thus, stocks with lower than average market sensitivities (such as most utilities) would offer expected returns less than the expected market return. Stocks with above average values of beta (such as most airline securities) would offer expected returns in excess of the market.*

* [Ed. Note] In practice, the risk premium may be calculated by reference to historical returns with an adjustment for inflation. But care must be taken in the exercise, as Brealey and Myers, Principles of Corporate Finance (4th ed. 1991) 130–131 points out:

Suppose there is a capital investment project which you *know* —don't ask how— has the same risk as Standard and Poor's Composite Index. We will say that it has the same degree of risk as the *market portfolio,* although this is speaking loosely, because the index does not include all risky securities. What rate should you use to discount this project's forecasted cash flows?

Clearly you should use the currently expected rate of return on the market portfolio; that is, the return investors would forgo by investing in the proposed project. Let us call it r_m. One way to estimate r_m is to assume that the future will be like the past and that today investors expect to receive the same "normal" rates of return revealed by the averages shown in [the table reproduced supra p. 67] * * *. In this case you would set r_m at 12.1 percent, the average of past market returns.

Unfortunately, this is *not* the way to do it. The normal value of r_m is not likely to be stable over time. Remember that it is the sum of the risk-free interest rate r_f and a premium for risk. We know r_f varies over time. For example, as we write this chapter in early 1990, Treasury bills yield about 8 percent, more than 4 percentage points above the 3.6 percent average return of Ibbotson and Sinquefield's Treasury bill portfolio.

What if you were called upon to estimate r_m in 1990? Would you have said 12.1 percent? That would have squeezed the risk premium by 4.3 percentage points. A more sensible procedure would have been to take the current interest rate on Treasury bills plus 8.4 percent, the average *risk premium* shown in [the above] Table * * *. With a rate of 8 percent for Treasury bills, that would have given

$$r_m (1990) = r_f{}^1(1990) + \text{normal risk premium} = .08 + .084 = .164 \text{ or } 16.4\%$$

The crucial assumption here is that there is a normal, stable risk premium on the market portfolio, so that the expected *future* risk premium can be measured by the average past risk premium. One could

* * *

In our development of CAPM we have made a number of assumptions that are required if the model is to be established on a rigorous basis. These assumptions involve investor behavior and conditions in the capital markets. The following is a set of assumptions that will allow a simple derivation of the model.

(a) The market is composed of risk-averse investors who measure risk in terms of standard deviation of portfolio return. This assumption provides a basis for the use of beta-type risk measures.

(b) All investors have a common time horizon for investment decision making (e.g., one month, one year, etc.). This assumption allows us to measure investor expectations over some common interval, thus making comparisons meaningful.

(c) All investors are assumed to have the same expectations about future security returns and risks. Without this assumption, the analysis would become much more complicated.

(d) Capital markets are perfect in the sense that all assets are completely divisible, there are no transactions costs or differential taxes, and borrowing and lending rates are equal to each other and the same for all investors. Without these conditions, frictional barriers would exist to the equilibrium conditions on which the model is based.

While these assumptions are sufficient to derive the model, it is not clear that all are necessary in their current form. It may well be that several of the assumptions can be substantially relaxed without major change in the form of the model. A good deal of research is currently being conducted toward this end.

While the CAPM is indeed simple and elegant, these qualities do not in themselves guarantee that it will be useful in explaining observed risk-return patterns. In Section 8 we will review the empirical literature on attempts to verify the model.

* * *

8. Tests of The Capital Asset Pricing Model

The major difficulty in testing the CAPM is that the model is stated in terms of investors' expectations and not in terms of realized returns. The fact that expectations are not always realized introduces an error term, which from a statistical point of view should be zero *on the average*, but not necessarily zero for any single stock or single period of time.

* * *

Summary of Test Results

We will briefly summarize the major results of the empirical tests.

quarrel with this assumption, but at least
it yields estimates of r_m that seem sensible.

1. The evidence shows a significant positive relationship between realized returns and systematic risk. However, the slope of the relationship (γ_1) is usually less than predicted by the CAPM.

2. The relationship between risk and return appears to be linear. The studies give no evidence of significant curvature in the risk-return relationship.

3. Tests that attempt to discriminate between the effects of systematic and unsystematic risk do not yield definitive results. Both kinds of risk appear to be positively related to security returns. However, there is substantial support for the proposition that the relationship between return and unsystematic risk is at least partly spurious— that is, it partly reflects statistical problems rather than the true nature of capital markets.

Obviously, we cannot claim that the CAPM is absolutely right. On the other hand, the empirical tests do support the view that beta is a useful risk measure and that high beta stocks tend to be priced so as to yield correspondingly high rates of return.

VAN HORNE, FINANCIAL MANAGEMENT AND POLICY

(9th Edition 1992).
pp. 75–78, 89–90.

In keeping with the capital asset pricing model and the separation theorem, we are able to make certain generalizations about the valuation of a firm, without having to determine directly the risk preferences of investors. If management wishes to act in the best interests of the owners, it will attempt to maximize the market value of the stock. Recall * * * that the market value per share can be expressed as the present value of the stream of expected future dividends:

$$P_O = \sum_{t=1}^{\infty \alpha} \frac{D_t}{(1 + k)^t}$$

where P_o is the market price per share at time O; D_t is the expected dividend at the end of period t; and k is the required rate of return. The CAPM approach allows us to determine the appropriate discount rate to employ in discounting expected dividends to their present value. That rate will be the risk-free rate plus a premium sufficient to compensate for the systematic risk associated with the expected dividend stream. The greater the systematic risk, of course, the greater the risk premium and the return required, and the lower the value of the stock, all other things being the same. Thus, we are pointed toward determining required rates of return for individual securities.

Seemingly, all decisions of the firm should be judged in a market context, using the capital asset pricing model. Recall, however, that the model presented has a number of simplifying assumptions, some of them untenable in the real world. To the extent that they do not hold, unique or unsystematic risk may become a factor affecting valuation. Indeed, * * * [possible] market imperfections [may] make unique risk a factor of importance.

Nonetheless, the CAPM serves as a useful framework for evaluating financial decisions. The basic tenets of the model hold even when assumptions are relaxed to reflect real-world conditions. Given that investors tend to be risk-averse, a positive tradeoff exists between risk and expected return for efficient portfolios. Moreover, expected returns for individual securities should bear a positive relationship to their marginal contributions of risk to the market portfolio (i.e., systematic risk).

　　　* * *

ZERO BETA VERSION OF THE CAPM

One of the assumptions of the CAPM is that the investor can both borrow and lend at the risk-free rate. Obviously, the investor can lend at this rate. If the borrowing rate is higher, however, an imperfection is introduced, and the [capital market line] is no longer linear throughout. In Fig. 3–12, it is straight for the segment originating from the risk-free lending rate on the vertical axis to portfolio L on the efficient frontier. Because the borrowing rate is higher, however, another tangency point on the efficient frontier, B, is introduced. The relevant portion of this line is from point B to the right; it represents borrowing to invest in portfolio B. The segment of the line between L and B is curved and is simply a portion of the efficient frontier of the opportunity set of risky securities. As is evident from the figure, the greater the spread between the borrowing and the lending rates, the greater the curved segment.

If the market portfolio lies between points L and B, it is possible to use a *zero beta portfolio* in place of the risk-free asset in the capital asset pricing model.[16] Drawing a dashed line tangent to the efficient frontier at market portfolio M, we see that it intercepts the vertical axis between the borrowing rate, R_{fb}, and the lending rate, R_{fl}. The intercept z represents the return on a zero beta portfolio. This simply means a portfolio with no covariability with the market portfolio, which may be created by short selling.[17] Depending on their utility preferences, investors will hold some combination of the zero-beta portfolio and the market portfolio, m. The same general picture emerges as if investors could both borrow and lend at the risk-free rate, except the

16. Fischer Black, "Capital Market Equilibrium with Restricted Borrowing," *Journal of Business,* 45 (July 1972), 444–54. See also Richard Roll, "Orthogonal Portfolios," *Journal of Financial and Quantitative Analysis,* 15 (December 1980), 1005–11.

17. In a short sale, the investor borrows securities and sells them in the market.

Eventually the securities must be replaced, and this is done by purchasing them in the market. Often a short sale is in anticipation of a decline in price so that the securities borrowed can be replaced at a price lower than that for which they were sold. However, the motivation can be simply to create a hedge.

dashed line in the figure has a different slope. The expected return for the individual security, j, becomes

$$\overline{R}_j = z + (\overline{R}_m - z)\beta_j \tag{3-11}$$

where z is the expected return associated with a zero beta asset, and the other symbols are the same as before.

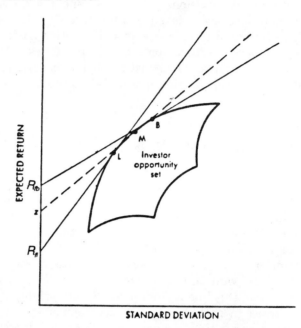

Figure 3-12
Effect of differing borrowing
and lending rates

It is important to note that the z intercept in Fig. 3–12 is inferred from return information on stocks; we cannot look up the zero-beta return in a newspaper, as we can the return on Treasury securities. However, one can estimate the zero beta security market line and from that the zero beta return.

The procedure frequently employed is to estimate future dividends for a large sample of companies, which is representative of the market portfolio. Solving for the discount rate that equates the present value of the dividend stream with the market price of the stock, one obtains the expected return for each of the companies in the sample. These expected returns, together with their respective betas, are then plotted on a scatter diagram. A line is fitted to the observations. This line represents the zero beta security market line, sometimes known as the "empirical" SML.

The intercept of the zero beta SML on the vertical axis is the estimated zero-beta return. As the intercept typically exceeds the risk-free lending rate, the zero-beta security line is flatter than the security market line based on the risk free rate * * *. However, all securities presumably will lie along the zero-beta security market line, and essentially the same risk-return conclusions are possible whether we use a zero-beta portfolio or the risk-free lending rate in the capital asset pricing model.

HETEROGENEOUS EXPECTATIONS, TRANSACTION AND INFORMATION COSTS

Relaxation of another major assumption, homogeneous expectations, complicates the problem in a different way. With heterogeneous expectations, a complex blending of expectations, wealth, and utility preferences of individual investors emerges in the equilibrating process. This complex equilibrating process has been examined by the author elsewhere and will not be presented here.[18] The principal implication is that precise generalizations are not possible. With only moderate heterogeneity in expectations, however, the basic tenets of the capital asset pricing model still hold, and rough estimates of the expected return-risk tradeoffs for portfolios and individual securities are possible.* Still, the lack of precise description must be recognized.[19]

Transaction costs also affect market equilibrium. The greater these costs, the less investors will undertake transactions to make their portfolios truly efficient. Rather than all portfolios being on the efficient frontier or capital market line, some may be on one side or the other because transaction costs more than offset the advantages of being right on the line. In other words, there may be bands on either side of the capital market line within which portfolios would lie. The greater the transaction costs, the wider the bands might be. Similarly, when securities are not infinitely divisible, as is the case in the real world, investors are able to achieve an efficient portfolio only up to the nearest share of stock or the nearest bond. Recall that another assumption of perfect capital markets is that all information about a firm is instantaneously available, free, to all investors. To the extent that there are delays and costs, there will be differing expectations among investors for these reasons alone. The effect here is the same as that for heterogeneous expectations. In general, the greater the imperfections, the more important the unique, or unsystematic, risk of the firm. Remember that the CAPM assumes that this risk can be diversified away. If it cannot, certain implications of the model do not entirely hold.

* * *

THE PRESENCE OF INFLATION

In our presentation of valuation principles we implicitly assumed that market equilibration occurred in nominal terms; however, we

---

18. James C. Van Horne, Financial Market Rates and Flows, 3d ed. (Englewood Cliffs, N.J.: Prentice–Hall, 1990), chap. 3.

*[Ed. Note] Lintner suggested that heterogeneous investor expectations need not critically flaw CAPM. Lintner, The Aggregation of Investors' Diverse Judgments and Preferences in Purely Competitive Securities Markets, J. of Fin. and Quan. Analysis (Dec.1969) 347–400.

19. Another assumption is that the probability distributions of possible returns on all portfolios are normal. As long as the distributions are nearly symmetric, however, this condition is met in a practical sense.

know that investors are concerned with inflation, and they factor this into account when making an investment decision. The realized real return for a security can be expressed as:

$$R_j^r = R_j - p \qquad (4\text{-}13)$$

$$\text{where } R_j^r = \text{the return for security } j \text{ in real terms}$$
$$R_j = \text{the return for security } j \text{ in nominal terms}$$
$$p = \text{inflation during the period}$$

If inflation is highly predictable, investors simply will add an inflation premium onto the real return they require, and markets will equilibrate in the manner described earlier in the chapter. As long as inflation is predictable, it is not a source of uncertainty. Therefore, the risk of a security can be described by its systematic and unsystematic risk, regardless of whether these risks are measured in real or nominal terms.

* * *

When inflation is uncertain, however, things are different. By uncertainty, we mean that the market does not anticipate changes that occur in the rate of inflation. Whether uncertain inflation is good or bad for a stock depends on the covariance of this uncertainty with that of the stock. If the return on a stock increases with unanticipated increases in inflation, this desirable property reduces the systematic risk of the stock in real terms and provides a hedge. Contrarily, if the stock's return goes down when unanticipated inflation occurs, this is undesirable because it increases the systematic risk of the stock in real terms.

We would expect that the greater the covariance of the return of a stock with unanticipated changes in inflation, the lower the expected nominal return the market will require. If this is so, one could express the expected nominal return of a stock as a positive function of its beta and a negative function of its covariance with unanticipated inflation.
* * *

NOTE: EMPIRICAL TESTING—THE CAPM IN CRISIS

The CAPM also has encountered difficulties in meeting empirical tests. In the first place, CAPM is expressed in terms that do not permit rigorous empirical testing. Thus, Roll early raised the question whether, if CAPM measures the value of an asset by relating its return and volatility to those of a true market portfolio (consisting of all assets, including securities, real estate, contracts, human capital, etc.), CAPM's validity can ever be tested by measuring only the returns on a security held by an investor against a market portfolio of securities, such as the NYSE index (Roll, A Critique of the Asset Pricing Theory's Tests, Part I: On Past and Potential Testability of the Theory, 4 J. of Fin.Econ.

129–176 (1977); cf. Roll, Performance Evaluation and Benchmark Errors, 6 J. of Portfolio Mgt. 5 (Summer, 1980); Gordon and Kornhauser, Efficient Markets, Costly Information, and Securities Research 60 N.Y.U.L.Rev. 761, 784–786 (1985)). This limitation may not be fatal to practical testing and application of beta, but it dilutes the full power of the concept. In the second place, investors' expectations of returns (on the security and on the market) are not observable. In order to test their validity, the model proceeds on the assumptions of investors' "rational expectations" about risk and return and the market as a "fair game," assumptions which finance economists consider sufficient to overcome effectively the hurdle of non-observability. (See Brealey and Myers, supra, at 166–168; Copeland and Weston, Financial Theory and Corporate Policy (3d ed. 1988), pp. 212–213).

As Modigliani and Pogue point out, the empirical evidence does not support the view that "CAPM is absolutely right." The linearity predicted between risk and return has not materialized in the testing studies of the model. See Copeland and Weston, supra, at 214–215. And the results of other studies pose a more than trivial challenge to the validity of the notion that price relates *solely* to a security's market risk or beta. Thus, Copeland and Weston indicate (supra, at 215) that factors other than beta are successful in explaining that portion of security returns not captured by beta. They cite studies that suggest that low price earnings portfolios have rates of return higher than could be explained by the CAPM, that smaller firms tend to have high abnormal rates of return, and that the market requires higher rates of return on equities with high dividend yields. Gordon and Kornhauser, supra, (at pp. 782–783) make the further point: "Many researchers have claimed superior results with asset pricing models that considered variables in addition to market risk—for example, industry risk, asset size, the skewness of expected ventures, the effect of taxes, or investor time horizons."

In recent years, the cumulation of awkward empirical results has accelerated to such a degree as to create a crisis for the CAPM. Not only do small firms (that is, firms with a low product of stock price times shares outstanding) have high abnormal rates of return, but

(1) a positive relation between leverage and average stock return has been shown, see Bhandari, Debt/Equity Ratio and Expected Common Stock Returns: Empirical Evidence, 43 J. Finance 507 (1988);

(2) a positive relation has been shown between average stock return and the ratio of the book value of the firm's equity to its market value, see, e.g., Rosenberg, Reid and Lanstein, Persuasive Evidence of Market Inefficiency, 11 J. Portfolio Mgt. 9 (1985);

(3) earnings-to-price ratios (E/P) have been found useful in explaining average returns on stocks: whatever the source of risk, E/P tends to be higher for riskier stocks, see Basu, The Relationship Between Earnings Yield, Market Value, and Return for NYSE Common Stocks: Further Evidence, 12 J. Financial Econs. 129 (1983); and

(4) the studies that confirmed the positive correlation of beta with average stock returns turn out to cover only the period through 1969; studies of the more recent period of 1963 to 1990 show that the relation between beta and average return *disappears*. See Fama and French, The Cross–Section of Expected Stock Returns, 47 J. Finance 427 (1992); Lakonishok and Shapiro, Systematic Risk, Total Risk and Size as Determinants of Stock Market Returns, 10 J. Banking & Finance 115 (1986).

Fama and French, supra, at p. 428, conclude:

" * * * [O]ur tests do not support the most basic prediction of the [CAPM], that average stock returns are positively related to market [betas].

"Unlike the simple relation between [beta] and average return, the univariate relations between average return and size, leverage, E/P, and book-to-market equity are strong. In multivariate tests, the negative relation between size and average return is robust to the inclusion of other variables. The positive relation between book-to-market equity and average return also persists in competition with other variables. Moreover, although the size effect has attracted more attention, book-to-market equity has a consistently stronger role in average returns. Our bottom-line results are: (a) [beta] does not seem to help explain the cross-section of average stock returns, and (b) the combination of size and book-to-market equity seems to absorb the roles of leverage and E/P in average stock returns * * *.

"If securities are priced rationally, our results suggest that stock risks are multidimensional. One dimension of risk is proxied by size * * *. Another dimension of risk is proxied by * * * the ratio of the book value of common equity to market value."

Might another conclusion be drawn from the apparent failure of systematic risk to prove out as the determinant of market pricing—that securities are not priced rationally? For exploration of this possibility, see infra pp. 136–146.

NOTE: ARBITRAGE PRICING THEORY

If systematic risk is not the sole or dominant determinant of a security's price, then it becomes important to identify the factors in addition to systematic risk that more or less systematically affect security pricing, and to seek to establish the proportionate impact on price of systematic risk and these other factors. Models to facilitate this analysis have appeared. These offer complex variations on the "simple" CAPM. The most powerful of these is the Arbitrage Pricing Theory (APT). Van Horne, Financial Management and Policy 95–96 (9th ed. 1992), explains the role of arbitrage:

"Like the CAPM, arbitrage pricing theory (APT) is an equilibrium model as to how security prices are determined. Originally developed by Stephen A. Ross, this theory is based on the idea that in competitive financial markets arbitrage will ensure that riskless assets provide the same expected return.[4] Arbitrage simply means finding two things that are essentially the same and buying the cheaper and selling, or selling short, the more expensive. The model is based on the simple notion that security prices adjust as investors form portfolios in search of arbitrage profits. When such profit opportunities have been exhausted, security prices are said to be in equilibrium. In this context, a definition of market efficiency is the absence of arbitrage opportunities, their having been eliminated by arbitragers.

"The APT suggests that the market equilibration process is driven by individuals eliminating arbitrage profits across these multiple factors. The model does not tell us what the factors are or why they are economically or behaviorally relevant. It merely states that there is a relationship between security returns and a limited number of factors. That is, security returns move together because of some common attributes. One of the factors might be the market return, as in the CAPM, but this need not be the case."

Ross, Westerfield and Jaffe, Corporate Finance 310–311 (2d ed. 1988) sets out the differences between the CAPM and the APT:

Differences in Pedagogy

We feel that the CAPM has at least one strong advantage from the student's point of view. The derivation of the CAPM necessarily brings the reader through a discussion of efficient sets. This treatment— beginning with the case of two risky assets, moving to the case of many risky assets, and finishing when a riskless asset is added to the many risky ones—is of great intuitive value. This sort of presentation is not as easily accomplished with the APT.

However, the APT has an offsetting advantage. The model adds factors until the unsystematic risk of any security is uncorrelated with the unsystematic risk of every other security. Under this formulation, it is easily shown that (1) unsystematic risk steadily falls (and ultimately vanishes) as the number of securities in the portfolio increases but (2) the systematic risks do not decrease. This result was also shown in the CAPM, though the intuition was cloudier because the unsystematic risks could be correlated across securities.

Differences in Application

One advantage of the APT is that it can handle multiple factors while the CAPM ignores them. Although the bulk of our presentation in this chapter focused on the one-factor model, a multi-factor model is probably more reflective of reality. That is, one must abstract from many market-wide and industry-wide factors before the unsystematic

---

4. Stephen A. Ross, "The Arbitrage Theory of Capital Asset Pricing," Journal of Economic Theory, 13 (December 1976), pp. 341–60.

risk of one security becomes uncorrelated with the unsystematic risks of other securities. Under this multi-factor version of the APT, the relationship between risk and return can be expressed as:

$$\overline{R} = R_F + (\overline{R_1} - R_F)\beta_1 + (\overline{R_2} - R_F)\beta_2 +$$
$$(\overline{R_3} - R_F)\beta_3 + \ldots + (R_K - R_F)\beta_K \quad (10.6)$$

In this equation, β_1 stands for the security's beta with respect to the first factor, β_2 stands for the security's beta with respect to the second factor, and so on. For example, if the first factor is GNP, β_1 is the security's GNP beta. The term $\overline{R_1}$ is the expected return on a security (or portfolio) whose beta with respect to the first factor is 1 and whose beta with respect to all other factors is zero. Because the market compensates for risk, $(\overline{R_1} - R_F)$ will be positive in the normal case.[10] (An analogous interpretation can be given to $\overline{R_2}$, $\overline{R_3}$, and so on.)

The equation states that the security's expected return is related to the security's factor betas. The intuition in equation (10.6) is straight-forward. Each factor represents risk that cannot be diversified away. The higher a security's beta with regard to a particular factor is, the higher is the risk that the security bears. In a rational world, the expected return on the security should compensate for this risk. The above equation states that the expected return is a summation of the risk-free rate plus the compensation for each type of risk that the security bears.

As an example, consider a study where the factors were monthly growth in industrial production (IP), change in expected inflation (ΔEI), unanticipated inflation (UI), unanticipated change in the risk-premium between risky bonds and default-free bonds (URP), and unanticipated change in the difference between the return on long-term government bonds and the return on short-term government bonds (UBR). Using the period 1958–1984, the empirical results of the study indicated that the expected monthly return on any stock, R_S, can be described as

$$\overline{R_S} = 0.0041 + 0.0136\beta_{IP} - 0.0001\,\beta_{\Delta EI} - 0.0006\beta_{UI} + 0.0072\beta_{URP} - 0.0052\beta_{UBR}$$

Suppose a particular stock had the following betas: $\beta_{IP} = 1.1$, $\beta_{\Delta EI} = 2$, $\beta_{UI} = 3$, $\beta_{URP} = 0.1$, $\beta_{UBR} = 1.6$. The expected monthly return on that security would be

$$R_S = 0.0041 + 0.0136 \times 1.1 - 0.0001 \times 2 -$$
$$0.0006 \times 3 + 0.0072 \times 0.1 - 0.0052 \times 1.6 = 0.0095$$

Assuming that a firm is unlevered and that one of the firm's projects has risk equivalent to that of the firm, this value of 0.0095 can be used as the monthly discount rate for the project. (Because annual data is often supplied for capital budgeting purposes, the annual rate of 0.120 ($[1.0095]^{12} - 1$) might be used instead.)

---

10. Actually $(\overline{R_1} - \overline{R_F})$ could be nega-tive in the case where factor i is perceived as a hedge of some sort.

Because many factors appear on the right hand side of equation * * *, the APT formulation has the potential to measure expected returns more accurately than does the CAPM. However, as we mentioned earlier, one cannot easily determine which are the appropriate factors. The factors in the above study were included for reasons of both common sense and convenience. They were not derived from theory.

(3) The Usefulness of Beta in Valuation

Notwithstanding increasing doubts about the theoretical validity of CAPM, beta is put to increasing use in valuing firms, securities, and portfolios, and in capital budgeting. Does beta turn out to be good practical tool despite its theoretical shortcomings?

IN RE PULLMAN CONSTRUCTION INDUSTRIES INC.

United States Bankruptcy Court,

Northern District of Illinois, 1989.

107 B.R. 909

Appendix E, infra

Pullman Construction demonstrates the application of the CAPM (and the APT) in connection with the valuation of the collateral securing a claim in a proceeding under chapter 11 of the Bankruptcy Code. For an application of the CAPM in the context of an appraisal rights proceeding under section 262 of the Delaware Corporation Law, see **Cede & Co. v. Technicolor,** 1990 WL 161084 (Del.Ch.1990), excerpted infra p. 719.

BREALEY AND MYERS, PRINCIPLES OF CORPORATE FINANCE

181–189 (4th ed. 1991)

Long before the development of modern theories linking risk and expected return, smart financial managers adjusted for risk in capital budgeting. They realized intuitively that, other things being equal, risky projects are less desirable than safe ones. Therefore financial managers demanded a higher rate of return from risky projects, or they based their decisions on conservative estimates of the cash flows.

Various rules of thumb are often used to make these risk adjustments. For example, many companies estimate the rate of return required by investors in their securities and use the **company cost of capital** to discount the cash flows on all new projects. Since investors require a higher rate of return from a very risky company, such a firm will have a higher company cost of capital and will set a higher discount rate for its new investment opportunities. [Assume that investors expect] a rate of return of .189 or about 19 percent from the stock of Digital Equipment Corporation (DEC). Therefore, according to the company cost of capital rule, DEC should have been using a 19 percent discount rate to compute project net present values.

This is a step in the right direction. Even though we can't measure risk or the expected return on risky securities with absolute precision, it is still reasonable to assert that DEC faced more risk than the average firm and, therefore, should have demanded a higher rate of return from its capital investments.

But the company cost of capital rule can also get a firm into trouble if the new projects are more or less risky than its existing business. Each project should be evaluated at its *own* opportunity cost of capital. * * * For a firm composed of assets A and B, the firm value is

Firm value = PV(AB) = PV(A) + PV(B) = sum of separate asset values

Here PV(A) and PV(B) are valued just as if they were mini-firms in which stockholders could invest directly. *Note:* Investors would value A by discounting its forecasted cash flows at a rate reflecting the risk of A. They would value B by discounting at a rate reflecting the risk of B. The two discount rates will, in general, be different.

If the firm considers investing in a third project C, it should also value C as if C were a mini-firm. That is, the firm should discount the cash flows of C at the expected rate of return that investors would demand to make a separate investment in C. *The true cost of capital depends on the use to which the capital is put.*

This means that DEC should accept any project that more than compensates for the *project's beta*. In other words, DEC should accept any project lying above the upward-sloping line that links expected return to risk in Figure 9–1. If the project has a high risk, DEC needs a higher prospective return than if the project has a low risk. Now contrast this with the company cost of capital rule, which is to accept any project *regardless of its risk* as long as it offers a higher return than the *company's* cost of capital. In terms of Figure 9–1, the rule tells DEC to accept any project above the horizontal cost-of-capital line, i.e., any project offering a return of more than 19 percent.

FIGURE 9-1

A comparison between the company cost of capital rule and the required return under the capital asset pricing model. DEC's company cost of capital is about 19 percent. This is the correct discount rate only if the project beta is 1.30. In general, the correct discount rate increases as project beta increases. DEC should accept projects with rates of return above the security market line relating required return to beta.

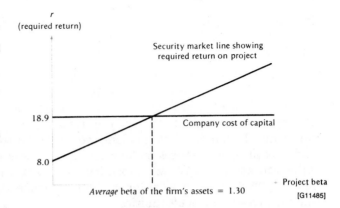

It is clearly silly to suggest that DEC should demand the same rate of return from a very safe project as from a very risky one. If DEC used the company cost of capital rule, it would reject many good low-risk projects and accept many poor high-risk projects. It is also silly to suggest that just because AT & T has a low company cost of capital, it is justified in accepting projects that DEC would reject. If you followed such a rule to its seemingly logical conclusion, you would think it possible to enlarge the company's investment opportunities by investing a large sum in Treasury bills. That would make the common stock safe and create a low company cost of capital.[2]

The notion that each company has some individual discount rate or cost of capital is widespread, but far from universal. Many firms require different returns from different categories of investment. Discount rates might be set, e.g., as follows:

Category	Discount Rate, %
Speculative ventures	30
New products	20
Expansion of existing business	15 (company cost of capital)
Cost improvement, known technology	10

The capital asset pricing model is widely used by large corporations to estimate the discount rate. It states

$$\text{Expected project return} = r = r_f + (\text{project beta})\,(r_m - r_f)$$

To calculate this, you have to figure out the project beta. Before thinking about the betas of individual projects, we will look at some problems you would encounter in using beta to estimate a company's cost of capital. It turns out that beta is difficult to measure accurately for an individual firm: Much greater accuracy can be achieved by looking at an average of similar companies. But then we have to define *similar*. Among other things, we will find that a firm's borrow-

2. If the present value of an asset depended on the identity of the company that bought it, present values would not add up.

Remember that a good project is a good project is a good project.

ing policy affects its stock beta. It would be misleading, e.g., to average the betas of Chrysler, which is a heavy borrower, and General Motors, which is not.

The company cost of capital is the correct discount rate for projects that have the same risk as the company's existing business but *not* for those projects that are safer or riskier than the company's average. The problem is to judge the relative risks of the projects available to the firm. To handle that problem, we will need to dig a little deeper and look at what features make some investments riskier than others. After you know *why* AT & T stock has less market risk than, say, Ford Motor, you will be in a better position to judge the relative risks of capital investment opportunities.

There is still another complication: Project betas can shift over time. Some projects are safer in youth than in old age; others are riskier. In this case, what do we mean by *the* project beta? There may be a separate beta for each year of the project's life. To put it another way, can we jump from the capital asset pricing model, which looks out one period into the future, to the discounted-cash-flow formula * * * for valuing long-lived assets? Most of the time it is safe to do so, but you should be able to recognize and deal with the exceptions.

MEASURING BETAS

* * *

* * * [B]etas appear to be reasonably stable. An extensive study of stability was provided by Sharpe and Cooper.[3] They divided stocks into 10 classes according to the estimated beta in that period. Each class contained one-tenth of the stocks in the sample. The stocks with the lowest betas went into class 1. Class 2 contained stocks with slightly higher betas, and so on. Sharpe and Cooper then looked at the frequency with which stocks jumped from one class to another. The more jumps, the less stability. You can see from Table 9–1 * that there is a marked tendency for stocks with very high or very low betas to stay

3. W.F. Sharpe and G.M. Cooper, "Risk–Return Classes of New York Stock Exchange Common Stocks, 1931–1967," Financial Analysts Journal, 28:46–54, 81 (March–April 1972).

Sharpe and Cooper divided stocks into risk classes according to their betas in one 5-year period (class 10 contains high betas, class 1 contains low betas). They then looked at how many of these stocks were in the same risk class 5 years later.

* [Ed. Note] Table 9–1 appears as follows in Brealey and Myers, p. 186:

Risk Class	Percent in Same Risk Class 5 Years Later	Percent Within One Risk Class 5 Years Later
10	35	69
9	18	54
8	16	45
7	13	41
6	14	39
5	14	42
4	13	40
3	16	45
2	21	61
1	40	62

that way. If you are willing to stretch the definition of stable to include a jump to an adjacent risk class, then from 40 to 70 percent of the betas were stable over the subsequent 5 years.

One reason that these estimates of beta are only imperfect guides to the future is that the stocks may genuinely change their market risk. However, a more important reason is that the betas in any one period are just estimates based on a limited number of observations. If good company news coincides by chance with high market returns, the stock's beta will appear higher than if the news coincides with low market returns. We can twist this the other way around. If a stock appears to have a high beta, it may be because it genuinely does have a high beta, or it may be because we have overestimated it.

This explains some of the fluctuation in betas. Suppose a company's true beta really is stable. Its apparent (estimated) beta will fluctuate from period to period due to random measurement errors. So the stability of true betas is probably better than Sharpe and Cooper's results seem to imply.**

* * *

In Table 9–3 we set out some estimates of industry betas. They range from a high of 1.49 for electronic components to a low of 0.46 for electric utilities. You can see why diversified companies should set different discount rates for their different activities.

————

NOTES

1. Brealey and Myers also point out, in discussing the uses of beta in capital budgeting, that the problem is not merely that of relying on past data with respect to a firm's stock price to estimate the future. There is also the problem, encountered in insolvency reorganization and mergers, of being unable to use past betas based on the firm's past performance because of changes being effected in the enterprise. This requires looking elsewhere—i.e., to similar firms or to averages of performances of similar firms. But that throws us back to the problem of defining and identifying similar companies with public records of stock price performance.

2. Brealey and Myers employ the CAPM in capital budgeting to distinguish different projects in accordance with their different risk levels. But they also remind us that "a good project is a good project is a good project." Does this imply that a firm's managers should invest in all "good projects" regardless of their betas? The implication of the "capital market line" is that given the right return, the firm's stockholders will be indifferent if management takes on riskier projects.

** [Ed. Note] For a collection of citations suggesting that betas of individual securities are not stable over time see Wang, Some Arguments That The Stock Market is Not Efficient, 19 U.C.Davis L.Rev. 341, 369 n. 78 (1986).

Should managers disregard the implications of the capital market line and distinguish among the pool of good projects, selecting those that fit into a preexisting risk profile understood by investors in the market-place on the theory that it thereby protect the "expectations" of those investors? In considering these questions, consult again the material at p. 68, supra.

4. EFFICIENT MARKETS

Thus far we have discussed operational techniques for measuring the value of a particular firm or its securities if there is no market directly available. The assumptions underlying each of the techniques require some reliance on the market's pricing of other assets in order to translate the particular firm's expected return into present value. That reliance implicates the question whether the market is an accurate, or at least adequate, pricer of the other assets for our purposes—in particular of the securities of publicly held corporations. Relevant to that question is the notion of the securities markets as "efficient," a notion described in the excerpt that follows.

Appendix B, Section 1 contains a brief overview of the operation of the capital markets.

(A) THE EFFICIENT MARKET HYPOTHESIS
BREALEY AND MYERS, PRINCIPLES
OF CORPORATE FINANCE
(4th Ed. 1991), pp. 290–297.

13–2 WHAT IS AN EFFICIENT MARKET?

When economists say that the security market is efficient, they are not talking about whether the filing is up-to-date or whether desktops are tidy. They mean that information is widely and cheaply available to investors and that all relevant and ascertainable information is already reflected in security prices. That is why purchases or sales in an efficient market cannot be positive–NPV transactions.

A Startling Discovery: Price Changes Are Random

As is so often the case with important ideas, this concept of efficient markets was a by-product of a chance discovery. In 1953 the Royal Statistical Society met in London to discuss a rather unusual paper.[2] Its author, Maurice Kendall, was a distinguished statistician, and the subject was the behavior of stock and commodity prices. Kendall had been looking for regular price cycles, but to his surprise he could not find them. Each series appeared to be "a 'wandering' one,

---

2. See M.G. Kendall, "The Analysis of   *Journal of the Royal Statistical Society,* 96:
Economic Time–Series, Part I. Prices,"   11–25 (1953).

almost as if once a week the Demon of Chance drew a random number
* * * and added it to the current price to determine the next week's
price." In other words, prices seemed to follow a *random walk.*

If you are not sure what we mean by *random walk,* you might like
to think of the following example. You are given $100 to play a game.
At the end of each week a coin is tossed. If it comes up heads, you win
3 percent of your investment; if it is tails, you lose 2.5 percent.
Therefore your capital at the end of the first week is either $103.00 or
$97.50. At the end of the second week the coin is tossed again. Now
the possible outcomes are:

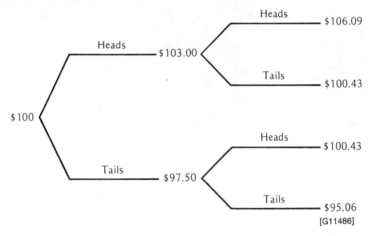

[G11486]

This process is a random walk with a positive drift of .25 percent
per week.[3] It is a random walk because successive changes in value are
independent. That is, the odds each week are 50 percent, regardless of
the value at the start of the week or of the pattern of heads and tails in
the previous weeks.

If you find it difficult to believe that there are no patterns in share
price changes, look at the two charts in Figure 13–1. One of these
charts shows the outcome from playing our game for 5 years; the other
shows the actual performance of the Standard and Poor's Index for a 5–
year period. Can you tell which one is which? [4]

When Maurice Kendall suggested that stock prices follow a random
walk, he was implying that the price changes are as independent of one

---

3. The drift is equal to the expected
outcome:

$$\tfrac{1}{2}(3) + \tfrac{1}{2}(-2.5) = .25\%$$

4. The top chart in Figure 13–1 shows
the real Standard and Poor's Index for the
years 1980 through 1984; the lower chart
is a series of cumulated random numbers.

Of course, 50 percent of you will have
guessed right, but we bet it was just a
guess. A similar comparison between cumulated random numbers and actual price
series was first suggested by H.V. Roberts,
"Stock Market 'Patterns' and Financial
Analysis: Methodological Suggestions,"
Journal of Finance, 14: 1–10 (March 1959).

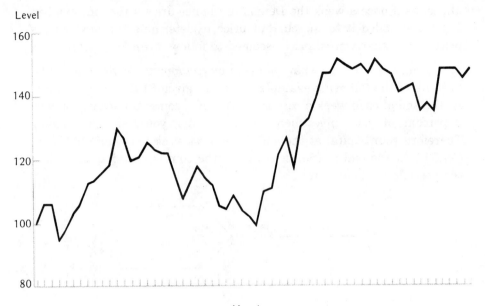

Months

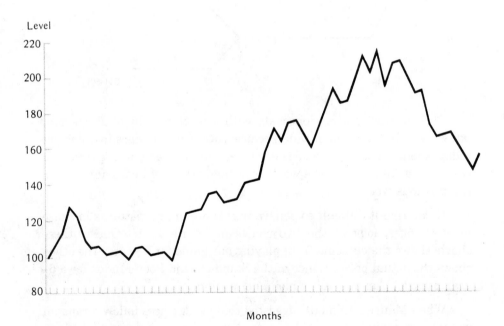

Months

FIGURE 13-1
One of these charts shows the Standard and Poor's Index for a 5-year period. The other shows the results of playing our coin-tossing game for 5 years. Can you tell which is which?

[G11487]

another as the gains and losses in our game. To most economists this was a startling and bizarre idea. In fact the idea was *not* completely novel. It had been proposed in an almost forgotten doctoral thesis written 53 years earlier by a Frenchman, Louis Bachelier.[5] Bachelier's suggestion was original enough, but his accompanying development of the mathematical theory of random processes anticipated by 5 years Einstein's famous work on the random motion of colliding gas molecules.

Kendall's work did not suffer the neglect of Bachelier's. As computers and data became more readily available, economists and statisticians rapidly amassed a large volume of supporting evidence. Let us look very briefly at the kinds of tests that they have used.

Suppose that you wished to assess whether there is any tendency for price changes to persist from one day to the next. You might begin by drawing a scatter diagram of changes on successive days. Figure 13–2 is an example of such a diagram. Each cross shows the change in the price of Weyerhaeuser stock on successive days. The circled cross in the southeast quadrant refers to a pair of days in which a 1 percent increase was followed by a 5 percent decrease. If there had been a systematic tendency for increases to be followed by decreases, there would be many crosses in the southeast quadrant and few in the northeast quadrant. It is obvious from a glance that there is very little pattern in these price movements, but we can test this more precisely by calculating the coefficient of correlation between each day's price change and the next. If price movements persisted, the correlation would be significantly positive; if there was no relationship, it would be 0. In our example, the correlation was + .03—there was a negligible tendency for price rises to be followed by further rises.

Figure 13–2 showed the behavior of only one stock, but our finding is typical. Researchers have looked at daily changes, weekly changes, monthly changes; they have looked at many different stocks in many different countries and for many different periods; they have calculated the coefficient of correlation between these price changes; they have looked for runs of positive or negative price changes; they have examined some of the *technical rules* that have been used by some investors to exploit the "patterns" they claim to see in past stock prices. With remarkable unanimity researchers have concluded that there is no useful information in the sequence of past changes in stock price. As a result, many of the researchers have become famous. None has become rich.

5. See L. Bachelier, Theorie de la Spec- ulation, Gauthier–Villars, Paris, 1900. Re- printed in English (A.J. Boness, trans.) in P.H. Cootner (ed.), *The Random Character of Stock Market Prices,* M.I.T. Press, Cam- bridge, Mass., 1964, pp. 17–78. During the 1930s the food economist Holbrook Work- ing had also noticed the random behavior of commodity prices. See H. Working, "A Random Difference Series for Use in the Analysis of Time Series," Journal of the American Statistical Association, 29: 11– 24 (March 1934).

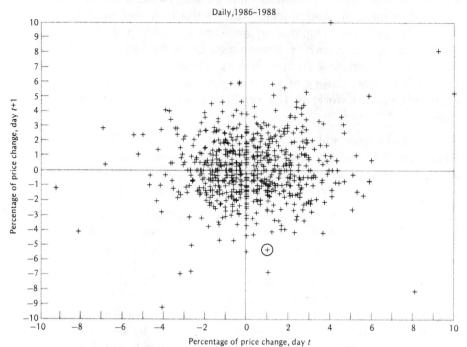

FIGURE 13-2
Each point shows a pair of returns for Weyerhaeuser stock on two successive days in 1986, 1987, and 1988. (The points reflecting the stock market crash of October 19, 1987, are off-scale and thus not shown.) The circled point records a daily return of +1 percent and then −5 percent on the next day. The scatter diagram shows no significant relationship between returns on successive days.

[G11488]

A Theory to Fit the Facts

We have mentioned that the initial reaction to the random-walk finding was surprise. It was several years before economists appreciated that this price behavior is exactly what one should expect in any competitive market.

Suppose, e.g., that you wish to sell an antique painting at an auction but you have no idea of its value. Can you be sure of receiving a fair price? The answer is that you can if the auction is sufficiently competitive. In other words, you need to satisfy yourself that it is to be properly conducted,[6] that there is no substantial cost involved in submitting a bid, and that the auction is attended by a reasonable number of skilled potential bidders, each of whom has access to the available information. In this case, no matter how ignorant *you* may be, competition among experts will ensure that the price you realize fully reflects the value of the painting.

In just the same way, competition among investment analysts will lead to a stock market in which prices at all times reflect true value.

6. That includes no collusion among bidders.

But what do we mean by *true value?* It is a potentially slippery phrase. True value does not mean ultimate *future* value—we do not expect investors to be fortune-tellers. It means an equilibrium price which incorporates *all* the information available to investors at that time. That was our definition of an efficient market.

Now you can begin to see why price changes in an efficient market are random. If prices always reflect all relevant information, then they will change only when new information arrives. But new information *by definition* cannot be predicted ahead of time (otherwise it would not be new information). Therefore price changes cannot be predicted ahead of time. To put it another way, if stock prices already reflect all that is predictable, then stock price *changes* must reflect only the unpredictable. The series of price changes must be random.[7]

Suppose, however, that competition among research analysts was not so strong and that there were predictable cycles in stock prices. Investors could then make superior profits by trading on the basis of these cycles. Figure 13–3, for example, shows a 2–month upswing for Establishment Industries (EI). The upswing started last month, when EI's stock price was $40, and it is expected to carry the stock price to $60 next month. What will happen when investors perceive this bonanza? It will self-destruct. Since EI stock is a bargain at $50, investors will rush to buy. They will stop buying only when the stock offers a normal rate of return. Therefore, as soon as a cycle becomes apparent to investors, they immediately eliminate it by their trading.

FIGURE 13-3

Cycles self-destruct as soon as they are recognized by investors. The stock price instantaneously jumps to the present value of the expected future price.

Two types of investment analyst help to make price changes random. Many analysts study the company's business and try to uncover information about its profitability that will shed new light on the value of the stock. These analysts are often called *fundamental*

----

7. When economists speak of stock prices as following a random walk, they are being a little imprecise. A statistician reserves the term *random walk* to describe a series that has a constant expected change each period and a constant degree of variability. But market efficiency does not imply that expected risks and expected returns cannot shift over time.

analysts. Competition in fundamental research will tend to ensure that prices reflect *all* relevant information and that price changes are unpredictable. The other analysts study the past price record and look for cycles. These analysts are called *technical analysts.* Competition in technical research will tend to ensure that current prices reflect all information in the past sequence of prices and that future price changes cannot be predicted from past prices.

Three Forms of the Efficient–Market Theory

Harry Roberts has defined three levels of market efficiency.[8] The first is the case in which prices reflect all information contained in the record of past prices. Roberts called this a *weak* form of efficiency. The random-walk research shows that the market is *at least* efficient in this weak sense.

The second level of efficiency is the case in which prices reflect not only past prices but all other published information. Roberts called this a *semistrong* form of efficiency. Researchers have tested this by looking at specific items of news such as announcements of earnings and dividends, forecasts of company earnings, changes in accounting practices, and mergers.[9] Most of this information was rapidly and accurately impounded in the price of the stock.[10]

Finally, Harry Roberts envisaged a *strong* form of efficiency in which prices reflect not just public information but *all* the information that can be acquired by painstaking fundamental analysis of the company and the economy. In such a case, the stock market would be like our ideal auction house: Prices would *always* be fair and *no* investor would be able to make consistently superior forecasts of stock prices. Most tests of this view have involved an analysis of the performance of professionally managed portfolios. These studies have concluded that, after taking account of differences in risk, no group of institutions has been able to out-perform the market consistently and

8. See H.V. Roberts, "Statistical versus Clinical Prediction of the Stock Market." Unpublished paper presented to the Seminar on the Analysis of Security Prices, University of Chicago, May 1967.

9. See, for example, R. Ball and P. Brown, "An Empirical Evaluation of Accounting Income Numbers," Journal of Accounting Research, 6: 159–178 (Autumn 1968); R.R. Pettit, "Dividend Announcements, Security Performance, and Capital Market Efficiency," Journal of Finance, 27: 993–1007 (December 1972); G. Foster, "Stock Market Reaction to Estimates of Earnings per Share by Company Officials," Journal of Accounting Research, 11: 25–37 (Spring 1973); R.S. Kaplan and R. Roll, "Investor Evaluation of Accounting Information: Some Empirical Evidence," Journal of Business, 45: 225–257 (April 1972); G. Mandelker, "Risk and Return: The

Case of Merging Firms," Journal of Financial Economics, 1: 303–335 (December 1974).

10. The price reaction to news appears to be almost immediate. For example, within 5 to 10 minutes of earnings or dividend announcements appearing on the broad tape, most of the price adjustment has occurred and any remaining gain from acting on the news is less than the transaction costs. See J.M. Patell and M.A. Wolfson, "The Intraday Speed of Adjustment of Stock Prices to Earnings and Dividend Announcements," Journal of Financial Economics, 13: 223–252 (June 1984). The price reaction to the sale of a large block of stock seems to be equally rapid. See L. Dann, D. Mayers, and R. Raab, "Trading Rules, Large Blocks, and the Speed of Adjustment," Journal of Financial Economics, 4: 3–22 (January 1977).

that even the differences between the performance of individual funds are no greater than you would expect from chance.[11]

The efficient-market hypothesis is frequently misinterpreted. One common error is to think it implies perfect forecasting ability. In fact it implies only that prices reflect all available information. In the same vein, some have suggested that prices cannot represent fair value because they go up and down. The answer, however, is that they would not represent fair value *unless* they went up and down. It is because the future is so uncertain and people are so often surprised that prices fluctuate. (Of course, when we look *back,* nothing seems quite so surprising: It is easy to convince ourselves that we really knew all along how prices were going to change.) A rather different temptation is to believe that the inability of institutions to achieve superior portfolio performance is an indication that their portfolio managers are incompetent. This is incorrect. Market efficiency exists only because competition is keen and managers are doing their job.

Another error is to think that the random behavior of stock prices implies that the stock market is irrational. *Randomness* and *irrationality* are not synonymous. Stock price changes are random because investors are rational and competitive.

No Theory Is Perfect

Although few simple economic ideas are as well supported by the evidence as the efficient-market theory, it would be wrong to pretend that there are no puzzles or apparent exceptions. * * *

We believe that there is now widespread agreement that capital markets function well.[14] So nowadays when economists come across instances where this apparently isn't true, they don't throw the efficient-market hypothesis onto the economic garbage heap. Instead they ask whether there isn't some missing ingredient that their theories ignore. Thus, despite the apparent superior performance of small company stocks, no economist has to our knowledge been tempted to

---

11. The classic study was M.C. Jensen, "The Performance of Mutual Funds in the Period 1945–64," Journal of Finance, 23: 389–416 (May 1968). More recent studies include J.C. Bogle and J.M. Twardowski, "Institutional Investment Performance Compared: Banks, Investment Counselors, Insurance Companies, and Mutual Funds," Financial Analysts Journal, 36: 33–41 (January–February 1980); M. Grinblatt and S. Titman, "Mutual Fund Performance: An Analysis of Quarterly Portfolio Holdings," Journal of Business, 62: 393–416 (July 1989); and R.A. Ippolito, "Efficiency with Costly Information: A Study of Mutual Fund Performance, 1965–84," Quarterly Journal of Economics, 104: 1–23 (February 1989).

14. Everyone thinks they know a duck when they see one, but it is hard to come up with a satisfactory definition. It is rather like that with efficient markets. We have talked about "well-functioning" markets and "fair" markets without ever saying what this means. Fama defined efficient markets in terms of the difference between the actual price and the price that investors expected given a particular set of information. An efficient market, Fama argues, is one in which the expected value of this difference is zero. See E.F. Fama, "Efficient Capital Markets: A Review of Theory and Empirical Work," Journal of Finance, 25: 383–417 (May 1970). Rubinstein defines an efficient market as one in which prices would not be altered if everyone revealed all that they knew. See M. Rubinstein, "Securities Market Efficiency in an Arrow–Debreu Economy," American Economic Review, 65: 812–824 (December 1975).

make a king-size investment in such stocks. Instead economists have assumed that investors aren't stupid and have looked at whether small firm stocks suffer from some other defect, such as a lack of easy marketability, that is not allowed for in our theories or tests.

NOTE: QUESTIONS ABOUT THE EFFICIENT MARKET HYPOTHESIS

1. *The Weak, Strong and Semi–Strong Versions.*

Most of the questions that follow concern the validity of the semi-strong version of the efficient market hypothesis. This is because the weak form is widely, although not uniformly accepted, and the strong form hardly accepted at all.

The weak form of the hypothesis has the strongest empirical support. The random walk point has been generally upheld, although studies do isolate some predictable patterns in stock prices (see the discussion of "anomalies" below), and to that extent qualify it. But, according to Malkiel, Is the Stock Market Efficient? 243 Science 1313, 1314 (1989), "the departures from randomness that have occurred do not appear large enough to leave unexploited investment opportunities, leaving in place the weak form assertion that unexploited investment opportunities should not persist in any efficient market."

The strong form of the hypothesis presupposes that information and trading costs are zero. "Since there are surely positive information and trading costs, the extreme version of the * * * hypothesis is surely false." Fama, Efficient Capital Markets: II, 46 J.Finance 1575 (1991). The strong version also is flatly contradicted by the persistence of insider trading for high profits. An extensive empirical literature on insider trading confirms that insiders can, in fact, earn extranormal trading profits. Seyhun, Insiders' Profits, Costs of Trading, and Market Efficiency, 16 J.Financial Econ. 189 (1986); Lorie & Niederhoffer, Predictive and Statistical Properties of Insider Trading, 11 J.L. & Econs. 35 (1968). And as noted in Ausubel, Insider Trading in a Rational Expectations Economy, 80 Amer.Econ.Rev. 1022, 1026 (1990): "Extensive (unpublished, but widely publicized) experimental work on insider trading was conducted in the mid–1980's by R. Foster Winans, Dennis Levine, Ivan Boesky, Drexel Burnham Lambert Inc. and others. The experimental studies were able to replicate the conclusions that had been reached by the earlier empirical articles."

2. *The Efficiency Paradox and Its Solution.*

The process by which the relevant information reaches the "efficient" market manifests an anomaly. If the mechanism for effecting discovery and "instantaneous" absorption of information by the market is the eager search by thousands of aggressively competing investors and analysts, the hypothesis contemplates systematic expenditure of funds by such persons to discover information with which, by the hypothesis, a profit cannot be made systematically. A paradox arises. Why would anyone who believes the market is efficient incur these expenses? But, then, if no one incurs these expenses, how will the relevant information become "promptly" available so as to make the market efficient?

The efficient markets hypothesis had to be modified to avoid this implicit paradox. Unmodified, the EMH ultimately seemed implausible. As pointed out in Gordon and Kornhauser, Efficient Markets, Costly Information and Securities Research, 60 N.Y.U.L.Rev. 761, 771 (1985):

> "It is not difficult to specify conditions under which capital markets will inevitably be speculatively efficient: no transactions costs in trading securities, costless access by all market participants to available information, and agreement by market participants as to implications of such information for the current price and distributions of future prices of each security (i.e., homogenous expectations.) Prices that prevail under these conditions by definition 'fully reflect' all available information. The efficient market hypothesis, however, purports to make a strong statement where some of these conditions are not present. It states that despite transaction costs, the lack of universal access to available information, and differing assessments of information, prevailing prices fully reflect available information." [b]

The assertion that the market price reflects the information level of the best informed trader was abandoned in due course. Market efficiency was recast as a matter of degree. The pathbreaking article was Grossman and Stiglitz, On the Impossibility of Informationally Efficient Markets, 70 Am.Econ.Rev. 393 (1980). The Grossman and Stiglitz model drops the assumption of competitive equilibrium and substitutes a picture of an "equilibrium degree of disequilibrium." In this model, prices only partially reflect the information level of the most sophisticated trader. The price becomes more informative as the number of well-informed individuals trading the security increases. The price is completely accurate only if all traders have full information. Id. at 393–395. Given this model, there is nothing inconsistent about having efficient markets and security analysis at the same time. Gilson and Kraakman, The Mechanisms of Market Efficiency, 70 Va. L.Rev. 549, 622–626 (1984), expand on this approach. Their analysis focuses on the market for information and the differential costs (and prices) of different kinds of information. They suggest that the securities market has varying degrees of efficiency in reflecting information in price, depending on differences in the cost of discovery and speed of absorption of different kinds of information. They also relate those

---

b. [Ed. note] Of course, proponents of the hypothesis never asserted that all "available" information is in fact instantaneously and costlessly available to all investors. Two assumptions lay beneath their assertion that the price "fully reflects" all information: that the price is set at the margin, and that the market behaves "as if" the information were in fact available to all investors.

differences to the operation of different identified market mechanisms—(1) universally informed trading, most closely approximated
with respect to old price information and big news stories like presidential election results, (2) professionally informed trading, (3) derivatively
informed trading, which occurs when traders without information act
in response to the observed behavior of those with information, and (4)
uninformed trading.

3. *Speculative Efficiency and Allocative Efficiency.*

Different claims are made respecting the meaning of the market
efficiency assertion. The more modest claim confines the hypothesis to
a statement about the promptness with which information thought by
investors to be relevant in pricing shares of stock (including information which does not necessarily relate to the "intrinsic value" of the
particular enterprise) is reflected in prices—and the resultant inability
of investors to make advantageous purchases or sales systematically by
acquiring information before it is reflected in prices. This is the
"speculative" or "no bargains" version of the hypothesis. There is a
stronger, separate claim that has a much weaker basis in the body of
empirical work that supports the hypothesis. This asserts a definite
relationship between the market prices of securities and the "intrinsic"
or "true" value of the enterprise (i.e., the capitalized value of the
expected cash flow). This is the "intrinsic value" or "allocative efficiency" version of the hypothesis. This version goes substantially beyond
the claim that market prices promptly reflect all available information
so as to negate the possibility of profitable trading strategies or arbitrage opportunities. From the basic observation that market prices
promptly reflect all available information, it draws the inference that
the resulting market prices "correctly" reflect the "true" value of the
firm. This entails the assertion that the price reflects not only full
information, but rational treatment of that information by market
actors. In other words, only information about expected cash flows
shows up in the price. Tobin points out that the validity of the
intrinsic value version "is by no means implied by" the validity of the
"no-bargains" version. Tobin, On the Efficiency of the Financial System, 153 Lloyd's Bank Review 1, 5 (July 1984). See also Summers, Does
the Stock Market Rationally Reflect Fundamental Values? 41 J.Fin.
591 (1986).

The two versions of the hypothesis have different ramifications in
legal contexts. To the extent that speculative efficiency is found to
obtain, views about the need for regulation to protect disadvantaged
investors against advantaged professionals and others may change.
See Appendix B, Section 2, infra. The implications of the allocative
efficiency claim reach more broadly. Some of these implications are
deregulatory. If market prices in fact reflect fundamental value, then
any cause of action that results in judicial revaluation of a publicly
traded security appears to be substantively unsound. On the other
hand, the allocative efficiency assertion arguably justifies heightened

legal intervention to protect the market pricing process from misinformation, insufficient information or manipulation.

Finally, does the allocative efficiency assertion imply operating efficiency in the conduct of the business whose securities are thus "efficiently" priced? See Mullins, Managerial Discretion and Corporate Financial Management (1984). The connection between efficient markets and efficient allocation of capital requires that investors be able to see whether the current stock price reflects operating inefficiency in the firm, and be able—presumably by voting or buying and selling stock—to cure the defect by replacing management or otherwise.

4. *Pricing Differentials Between the Market for Shares and the Market for Firms.*

As noted above, one seriously mooted question is whether the price of a share reflects its pro-rata claim against the stream of earnings or whether the whole stream may be more (or less) valuable, i.e., ultimately priced higher (or lower) than the sum of its parts. If so, the market may still be efficient (i.e., it fully reflects all available information), but it is a market for shares not for firms, and is pricing something that is not quite the same as the whole stream of earnings. Lowenstein, Management Buy–Outs, 85 Colum.L.Rev. 730, 751–754 (1985) argues as follows:

> " * * * Markets are made by specific buyers and sellers, and assuming that they have the homogeneous expectations that * * * theory requires, their expectations, and the time horizons implicit in them, are those of the persons doing the trading and not of others who remain on the sidelines and enter the market on rare occasions and then only on a firm-as-a-whole basis.

> "The evidence is that more and more these two groups—the buyers of shares and the buyers of firms—have different time horizons and that they look, therefore, at rather different variables or measures of value. The market in shares of firms has become more short-term focused, as reflected in the increasing volume of transactions and turnover rates.

> * * *

> "At some point, a high turnover makes sense only if investors are paying a high degree of attention to what their fellow investors are about to do and to the short term expectations that motivate them, and paying less attention to asset values and other measures that would influence a buyer (or seller) of the business as a whole. The stock market investor's position is not necessarily inferior. As a purely passive investor who generally deals only with other, equally passive folk, he may be correct to pay little attention to asset values. * * *

> * * *

" * * * [But] the market does not seem to reflect well these longer terms or contingent values. Instead the market tends to mirror the near-term expectations of institutional investors who turn over their entire portfolios annually and, by accounting for the great bulk of the trading, determine the prices. Whatever the efficiency of a stock market in which values are determined by those who function with such a short fuse, that efficiency is not the same for all purposes or purchasers."

See also Kraakman, Taking Discounts Seriously: The Implications of Discounted Share Prices as an Acquisitions Motive, 88 Colum.L.Rev. 891 (1988); Lowenstein, Pruning Deadwood in Hostile Take–Overs: A Proposal for Legislation, 83 Colum.L.Rev. 249, 268–306 (1983); Gordon and Kornhauser, supra p. 129 at pp. 825–830; Shubik, Corporate Control, Efficient Markets, The Public Good, the Law and Economic Theory and Advice, in Coffee, Lowenstein and Rose–Ackerman (editors), Knights, Raiders and Targets: The Impact of the Hostile Takeover (1988).

––––––––

NOTE: EMPIRICAL TESTING OF THE HYPOTHESIS

1. *The Empirical Case in Favor of the EMH.*

The EMH is the object of a large body of empirical study. As we have seen, the weak form of the hypothesis has the strongest empirical support and the strong form little support. The question is whether the semi-strong version proves out.

There is said to be considerable support for the semi-strong form's prediction of speculative efficiency—the assertions that relevant fundamental information is indeed "available," and that prices reflect it quickly enough to make it nearly impossible for most investors systematically to acquire bargains. These studies confirm the hypothesis by relying on inquiries for data that could confirm or negate, and then find that the data are consistent with the hypothesis. Thus, tests of the speed with which the market price adjusts to new information (such as announcements of stock splits, dividends or earnings reports) indicate that individuals cannot systematically acquire and use the information before the price reflects it. Other studies reveal the market's acute, if not just as speedy, perception of ambiguous or misleading information in statements permitted by generally accepted accounting principles (e.g., by reflecting the "actual" rather than the higher or lower reported earnings made possible by changed accounting methods). Other studies claim to establish that if risk is held constant, mutual funds, presumed to be the most sophisticated and diligent investors, do not outperform each other or the market. These studies have been criticized both in respect of their methods and their claimed import. For summaries, see Gilson and Kraakman, supra at 555, Gordon and

Kornhauser, supra;   Note, The Efficient Capital Market Hypothesis, Economic Theory and the Regulation of the Securities Industry, 29 Stan.L.Rev. 1031, 1044–48 (1979).

2. *An Underlying Theoretical Limit.*

A significant theoretical objection has been lodged against the claim that the hypothesis has been verified.   Fama terms this the "joint-hypothesis problem."   Fama, supra at 1575–1576.   According to Gordon and Kornhauser, supra at 771–772:

> "[U]nfortunately the efficient market hypothesis cannot be tested in a straightforward way.   It is not a hypothesis subject to relatively simple observation, such as 'all the balls in the urn are white.'   The basic data, prices and price changes, are interpretable only through the lens of a larger model of investor behavior and market processes.   Thus we cannot test the validity of the efficient market hypothesis alone; every test of EMH also assumes some particular theory of what the 'right' price for an asset is.   These asset pricing models establish the benchmark of 'normal' returns in order to determine the efficiency of the market.   Consequently, every empirical test of the efficient market hypothesis is a 'joint test' of both the hypothesis and an asset pricing model.   If the test yields evidence consistent with market efficiency, it also yields evidence consistent with the asset pricing model.   If however, the test yields anomalous evidence, either the market is inefficient or the asset pricing model used is incorrect (or possibly both EMH and the pricing model are wrong).   Understanding EMH therefore requires that we consider the asset pricing models that have been used to test it." [c]

3. *The Empirical Case Against the Hypothesis.*

(a) *Anomalies.*

The markets themselves resist the EMH.   They persist in behaving in "anomalous" ways not conforming to its predictions.   These intensively studied phenomena include the following:

Small Firms and Low P/E Firms.   Smaller corporations tend to have high abnormal rates of return.   It also has been found that stocks issued by firms with low Price/Earnings ratios have higher risk adjusted returns than stocks of high P/E firms.   See Symposium, 12 J.Fin. Econ. 3 (1983).

The Closed–End Fund Discount.   As noted above, fundamental value is difficult to measure.   But, in the case of closed-end funds holding portfolios of publicly traded securities, fundamental value can be measured easily.   "Closed-end" funds, like "open-end" or "mutual" funds, are investment companies.   The difference is that closed-end

---

c. Of course, the EMH may be a valid analysis even if the particular asset pricing models by which it is tested are invalid.

funds issue shares of common stock in respect of equity capital, just as do industrial corporations. The equity capital is thus locked in. Investments in mutual funds, in contrast, can be redeemed. The fundamental value of a closed-end fund that pays dividends equal to the dividends on the stocks in its portfolio is the value of its portfolio. Yet, securities issued by these funds persistently trade at variance with their net asset values—usually at a discount but sometimes at a premium. The consensus view is that these discounts cannot be explained in terms of fundamental value factors, despite attempts to account for them in terms of the agency costs of fund management or in terms of tax liabilities. See De Long, Shleifer, Summers and Waldmann, Noise Trader Risk in Financial Markets, 98 J.Pol.Econ. 703, 728 (1990). See also Kraakman, Taking Discounts Seriously: The Implications of Discounted Share Prices as an Acquisition Motive, 88 Colum.L.Rev. 891, 902–06 (1988); Malkiel, The Valuation of Closed–End Investment Company Shares, 32 J.Fin. 847 (1977).

The Magellan Fund. Fidelity's Magellan Fund outperformed the Standard & Poor's 500 in eleven of the thirteen years ending in 1989.

Timing. There are a number of documented patterns in stock returns over weekends, holidays and different calendar periods. One is the "week-end effect": a pattern of systematic negative returns on Mondays. See Keim and Stanbaugh, A Further Investigation of the Week End Effect on Stock Returns, 39 J.Finance 819 (1984); Schatzberg and Datta, The Weekend Effect and Corporate Dividend Announcements, 15 J.Fin.Research 69 (1992). There also is a "holiday effect." Ariel, High Stock Returns before Holidays: Existence and Evidence on Possible Causes, 45 J.Finance 1611 (1990), shows that over one third of the total return accruing to the market portfolio from 1963 to 1982 was earned on the eight yearly trading days falling before holiday closings. Then there is the "January effect:" a pattern of abnormally high returns in early January, primarily for small firms. Some of these studies are summarized in Thaler, Anomalies: Weekend, Holiday, Turn of the Month and Intraday Effects, 1 J.Econ.Perspectives 169 (1987); Thaler, Anomalies: The January Effect, 1 J.Econ.Perspectives 197 (1987).

Timing also figures into the finding that return volatility is greater when the market is open than when it is closed. French and Roll, Stock Return Variances: The Arrival of Information and the Reaction of Traders, 17 J.Financial Economics 17 (1986). This finding gives rise to the inference that the market makes its own news—news not keyed to fundamental value points. See Malkiel, supra at 1316.

Stock Splits and Stock Dividends. Shareholders make abnormal gains both when a stock split or stock dividend is declared and when it takes place. See Grinblatt, Masulis and Titman, The Valuation Effects of Stock Splits and Stock Dividends, 13 J.Financial Econs. 461 (1984).

The Super Bowl Stock Market Predictor. Through 1992, if the Super Bowl is won by a team from the old National Football League,

the stock market finishes the year higher than it began; i
lower if a team from the old American Football League w
discussion, see Krueger and Kennedy, An Examination of t
Bowl Stock Market Predictor, 45 J.Fin. 691 (1990). The tl
implications of this anomaly are left for the reader to develop.

(b) *Return Predictability.*

A body of studies shows positive and negative serial correlations of
stock prices over different periods of time. Over short periods of time,
like a week or a month, price changes tend to persist. Over longer
periods of time, like a year or more, stock returns display a negative
serial correlation. Together these findings suggest a contrarian investment strategy. See Cutler, Poterba and Summers, Speculative Dynamics (unpublished) (1989); Malkiel, supra at 1314. For a critical summary of this work, see Fama, Efficient Capital Markets: II, 46 J.Fi-
nance 1575, 1609 (1991).

Note that findings of patterns in stock prices over time stand in
opposition not only to the semi-strong version of the EMH, but also to
the random walk model in the EMH's weak form.

(c) *Empirical Challenges to the Allocative Efficiency Assertion.*

A number of empirical studies purport to show allocative inefficiencies in stock price behavior. This body of research isolates cases where
stock prices depart from fundamental value. Some of these cases are
claimed to be significant and long lasting. For example, several studies
show that stock prices overreact to changes in fundamentals. Cutler,
Poterba and Summers, What Moves Stock Prices? 15 J.Portfolio Management 4, 9 (1989), suggests the "difficulty of explaining as much as
half the variance in aggregate stock prices on the basis of publicly
available news bearing on fundamental values." Jacobs and Levy, On
the Value of "Value," Financial Analysts J. 47, 48 (1988), finds that
value as measured by a dividend discount model is "but a small part of
the security pricing story." Shiller, Do Stock Prices Move Too Much to
be Justified by Subsequent Dividends? 71 Amer.Econ.Rev. 421, 432–33
(1981), suggests that "stock price volatility over the past century
appears to be far too high to be attributed to new information about
future real dividends if uncertainty about future dividends is measured
by the sample standard deviations of real dividends around their long
run exponential growth path." See also Shiller, Fashions, Fads, and
Bubbles in Financial Markets, in Knights, Raiders and Targets 56–68
(Coffee, Lowenstein, Rose–Ackerman, eds. 1988); Roll, R2, 42 J.Finance
541 (1988).

(d) *Other Challenges.*

Even core EMH assertions respecting fundamental analysis and
the rapidity of price changes are being questioned. Stice, The Market
Reaction to 10–K and 10–Q Filings and to Subsequent *The Wall Street
Journal* Earnings Announcements, 66 Accounting Rev. 42 (1991) shows
that in cases where earnings results are reported first in an SEC filing

with the press announcement coming several days later, the market reaction comes only upon the subsequent announcement to the media. Ou and Penman, Financial Statement Analysis and the Prediction of Stock Returns, 11 J.Accounting & Econs. 295 (1989), sets up a model of traditional fundamental analysis, and analyzes corporations at moments in past. The results of this reconstructed analysis are then checked against subsequent returns on the corporations' stock. The study finds that the fundamental analysis gives a "robust" prediction of future stock returns.

––––––

(B) THE NOISE TRADING APPROACH AND OTHER ALTERNATIVES TO THE EFFICIENT MARKET HYPOTHESIS

The empirical work discussed in the preceding Note has prompted many economic observers to abandon the allocative efficiency assertion. The assertion's failure to prove out has, moreover, implied problems for the "rational investor" assumption on which the hypothesis is based. See Merton, On the Current State of the Stock Market Rationality Hypothesis, in S. Fisher (Ed.); Macroeconomics and Finance: Essays in Honor of Franco Modigliani (1986). Compare Arrow, Risk Perception in Psychology and Economics, 20 Economic Inquiry 1–9 (Jan. 1982).

Given this, a question arises: If competition among diverse investors and arbitrage does not keep stock prices close to fundamental value, conceived in terms of discounted flows of future dividends, what factors *do* determine stock prices? A new body of stock pricing theory responds to this question. Drawing on the empirical findings, this work focuses on psychological factors, "noise" trading and fads in investment styles.

Such speculation is not new. There were insightful conjectures about the behavior of market actors long before the current interest in the nature and import of efficient markets. The most famous of these is a metaphor set out in Keynes, General Theory of Employment, Interest and Money 156 (1936):

" * * * professional investment may be likened to those newspaper competitions in which the competitors have to pick out the six prettiest faces from a hundred photographs, the prize being awarded to the competitor whose choice most nearly corresponds to the average preferences of the competitors as a whole; so that each competitor has to pick, not those faces which he himself finds prettiest, but those which he thinks likeliest to catch the fancy of the other competitors, all of whom are looking at the problem from the same point of view. It is not a case of choosing those which, to the best of one's judgment, are really the prettiest, nor even those which average opinion genuinely thinks the prettiest. We have reached the third degree where we devote our intelligences to anticipating what average opinion expects the average opinion to be. And there are some, I believe, who practice the fourth, fifth and higher degrees."

**SHLEIFER AND SUMMERS, THE NOISE
TRADER APPROACH TO FINANCE**

4 J.Economic Perspectives 19, 19–22, 23–26 (1990).

* * * Our approach rests on two assumptions. First, some investors are not fully rational and their demand for risky assets is affected by their beliefs and sentiments that are not fully justified by fundamental news. Second, arbitrage—defined as trading by fully rational investors not subject to such sentiment—is risky and therefore limited. The two assumptions together imply that changes in investor sentiment are not fully countered by arbitrageurs and so affect security returns. We argue that this approach to financial markets is in many ways superior to the efficient markets paradigm.

* * * The efficient markets hypothesis obtains only as an extreme case of perfect riskless arbitrage that is unlikely to apply in practice. * * * [T]he investor sentiment/limited arbitrage approach yields a more accurate description of the financial markets * * *.

* * *

The Limits of Arbitrage

We think of the market as consisting of two types of investors: "arbitrageurs"—also called "smart money" and "rational speculators"—and other investors. Arbitrageurs are defined as investors who form fully rational expectations about security returns. In contrast, the opinions and trading patterns of other investors—also known as "noise traders" and "liquidity traders"—may be subject to systematic biases. In practice, the line between arbitrageurs and other investors may be blurred, but for our argument it helps to draw a sharp distinction between them, since the arbitrageurs do the work of bringing prices toward fundamentals.

Arbitrageurs play a central role in standard finance. They trade to ensure that if a security has a perfect substitute—a portfolio of other securities that yields the same returns—then the price of the security equals the price of that substitute portfolio. If the price of the security falls below that of the substitute portfolio, arbitrageurs sell the portfolio and buy the security until the prices are equalized, and vice versa if the price of a security rises above that of the substitute portfolio. When the substitute is indeed perfect, this arbitrage is riskless. As a result, arbitrageurs have perfectly elastic demand for the security at the price of its substitute portfolio. Arbitrage thus assures that relative prices of securities must be in line for there to be no riskless arbitrage opportunities. Such riskless arbitrage is very effective for derivative securities, such as futures and options, but also for individual stocks and bonds where reasonably close substitutes are usually available.

Although riskless arbitrage ensures that relative prices are in line, it does not help to pin price levels of, say, stocks or bonds as a whole. These classes of securities do not have close substitute portfolios, and therefore if for some reason they are mispriced, there is no riskless hedge for the arbitrageur. For example, an arbitrageur who thinks that stocks are underpriced cannot buy stocks and sell the substitute portfolio, since such a portfolio does not exist. The arbitrageur can instead simply buy stocks in hopes of an above-normal return, but this arbitrage is no longer riskless. If the arbitrageur is risk-averse, his demand for underpriced stocks will be limited. With a finite number of arbitrageurs, their combined demand curve is no longer perfectly elastic.

Two types of risk limit arbitrage. The first is fundamental risk. Suppose that stocks are selling above the expected value of future dividends and an arbitrageur is selling them short. The arbitrageur then bears the risk that the realization of dividends—or of the news about dividends—is better than expected, in which case he loses on his trade. Selling "overvalued" stocks is risky because there is always a chance that the market will do very well. Fear of such a loss limits the arbitrageur's original position, and keeps his short-selling from driving prices all the way down to fundamentals.

The second source of risk that limits arbitrage comes from unpredictability of the future resale price * * *. Suppose again that stocks are overpriced and an arbitrageur is selling them short. As long as the arbitrageur is thinking of liquidating his position in the future, he must bear the risk that at that time stocks will be even more overpriced than they are today. If future mispricing is more extreme than when the arbitrage trade is put on, the arbitrageur suffers a loss on his position. Again, fear of this loss limits the size of the arbitrageur's initial position, and so keeps him from driving the price all the way down to fundamentals.

Clearly, this resale price risk depends on the arbitrageur having a finite horizon. If the arbitrageur's horizon is infinite, he simply sells the stock short and pays dividends on it in all the future periods, recognizing that the present value of those is lower than his proceeds from the short sale. But there are several reasons that it makes sense to assume that arbitrageurs have short horizons. Most importantly, arbitrageurs have to borrow cash or securities to implement their trades, and as a result must pay the lenders per period fees. These fees cumulate over the period that the position remains open, and can add up to large amounts for long term arbitrage. The structure of transaction costs thus induces a strong bias toward short horizons * * *. In addition, the performance of most money managers is evaluated at least one year and usually once every few months, also limiting the horizon of arbitrage. As a result of these problems, resources dedicated to long-term arbitrage against fundamental mispricing are very scarce.

* * *

These arguments that risk makes arbitrage ineffective actually understate the limits of arbitrage. After all, they presume that the arbitrageur knows the fundamental value of the security. In fact, the arbitrageur might not exactly know what this value is, or be able to detect price changes that reflect deviations from fundamentals. In this case, arbitrage is even riskier than before.

* * *

Substantial evidence shows that, contrary to the efficient markets hypothesis, arbitrage does not completely counter responses of prices to fluctuations in uninformed demand. Of course, identifying such fluctuations in demand is tricky, since price changes may reflect new market information which changes the equilibrium price at which arbitrageurs trade. Several recent studies do, however, avoid this objection by looking at responses of prices to changes in demand that do not plausibly reflect any new fundamental information because they have institutional or tax motives.

* * *

Investor Sentiment

Some shifts in investor demand for securities are completely rational. Such changes could reflect, for example, reactions to public announcements that affect future growth rate of dividends, risk, or risk aversion. Rational demand changes can also reflect adjustment to news conveyed through the trading process itself. Finally, rational demand changes can reflect tax trading or trading done for institutional reasons of the types discussed above.

But not all demand changes appear to be so rational; some seem to be a response to changes in expectations or sentiment that are not fully justified by information. Such changes can be a response to pseudo-signals that investors believe convey information about future returns but that would not convey such information in a fully rational model * * *. An example of such pseudo-signals is advice of brokers or financial gurus. We use the term "noise traders" to describe such investors * * *. Changes in demand can also reflect investors' use of inflexible trading strategies or of "popular models" * * *. One such strategy is trend chasing. Although these changes in demand are unwarranted by fundamentals, they can be related to fundamentals, as in the case of overreaction to news.

These demand shifts will only matter if they are correlated across noise traders. If all investors trade randomly, their trades cancel out and there are no aggregate shifts in demand. Undoubtedly, some trading in the market brings together noise traders with different models who cancel each other out. However, many trading strategies based on pseudo-signals, noise, and popular models are correlated, leading to aggregate demand shifts. The reason for this is that judgment biases afflicting investors in processing information tend to be the same. Subjects in psychological experiments tend to make the same mistake; they do not make random mistakes.

Many of these persistent mistakes are relevant for financial markets. For example, experimental subjects tend to be overconfident * * * which makes them take on more risk. Experimental subjects also tend to extrapolate past time series, which can lead them to chase trends * * *. Finally, in making inferences experimental subjects put too little weight on base rates and too much weight on new information * * *, which might lead them to overreact to news.

* * *

A look at how market participants behave provides perhaps the most convincing evidence that noise rather than information drives many of their decisions. Investors follow market gurus and forecasters, such as Joe Granville and "Wall Street Week." Charging bulls, Jimmy Connors and John Houseman all affect where and how people entrust their money.

* * *

So-called "technical analysis" is another example of demand shifts without a fundamental rationalization. Technical analysis typically calls for buying more stocks when stocks have risen (broke through a barrier), and selling stocks when they fall through a floor.

* * *

There can be little doubt that these sorts of factors influence demand for securities, but can they be big enough to make a difference? The standard economist's reason for doubting the size of these effects has been to posit that investors trading on noise might lose their money to arbitrageurs, leading to a diminution of their wealth and effect on demand * * *. Noise traders might also learn the error of their ways and reform into rational arbitrageurs.

However, the argument that noise traders lose money and eventually disappear is not self-evident. First, noise traders might be on average more aggressive than the arbitrageurs—either because they are overoptimistic or because they are overconfident—and so bear more risk. If risk-taking is rewarded in the market, noise traders can earn higher expected returns even despite buying high and selling low on average. The risk rewarded by the market need not even be fundamental; it can be the resale price risk arising from the unpredictability of future noise traders' opinions. With higher expected returns, noise traders as a group do not disappear from the market rapidly, if at all.

Of course, higher expected returns because of higher risk come together with a greater variance of returns. Noise traders might end up very rich with a trivial probability, and poor almost for sure. Almost for sure, then, they fail to affect demand in the long run. But in principle, either the expected return or the variance effect can dominate.

Learning and imitation may not adversely affect noise traders either. When noise traders earn high average returns, many other investors might imitate them, ignoring the fact that they took more risk and just got lucky. Such imitation brings more money to follow noise traders strategies. Noise traders themselves might become even more cocky, attributing their investment success to skill rather than luck. As noise traders who do well become more aggressive, their effect on demand increases.

The case against the importance of noise traders also ignores the fact that new investors enter the market all the time, and old investors who have lost money come back. These investors are subject to the same judgment biases as the current survivors in the market and so add to the effect of judgment biases on demand.

These arguments suggest that the case for long run unimportance of noise traders is at best premature. In other words, shifts in the demand for stocks that do not depend on news or fundamental factors are likely to affect prices even in the long run.

Explaining the Puzzles

When arbitrage is limited, and investor demand for securities responds to noise and to predictions of popular models, security prices move in response to these changes in demand as well as to changes in fundamentals. Arbitrageurs counter the shifts in demand prompted by changes in investor sentiment, but do not eliminate the effects of such shifts on the price completely.

* * *

The effects of demand shifts on prices are larger when most investors follow the finance textbooks and passively hold the market portfolio. In this case, a switch in the sentiment of some investors is not countered by a change of position of all the market participants, but only of a few arbitrageurs. The smaller the risk bearing capacity of arbitrageurs, the bigger the effect of a sentiment shift on the price. A simple example highlights this point. Suppose that all investors are sure that the market is efficient and hold the market portfolio. Now suppose that one investor decides to hold additional shares of a particular security. Its price is driven to infinity.

This approach fits very neatly with the conventional nonacademic view of financial markets. On that view, the key to investment success is not just predicting future fundamentals, but also predicting the movement of other active investors. Market professionals spend considerable resources tracking price trends, volume, short interest, odd lot volume, investor sentiment indexes and numerous other gauges of demand for equities. Tracking these possible indicators of demand makes no sense if prices responded only to fundamental news and not to investor demand. They make perfect sense, in contrast, in a world where investor sentiment moves prices and so predicting changes in this sentiment pays. The prevalence of investment strategies based on indicators of demand in financial markets suggests the recognition by arbitrageurs of the role of demand.

Not only do arbitrageurs spend time and money to predict noise trader moves, they also make active attempts to take advantage of these moves. When noise traders are optimistic about particular securities, it pays arbitrageurs to create more of them. These securities might be mutual funds, new share issues, penny oil stocks, or junk bonds: anything that is overpriced at the moment.

* * *

When they bet against noise traders, arbitrageurs begin to look like noise traders themselves. They pick stocks instead of diversifying, because that is what betting against noise traders requires. They time the market to take advantage of noise trader mood swings. If these swings are temporary, arbitrageurs who cannot predict noise trader moves simply follow contrarian strategies. It becomes hard to tell the noise traders from the arbitrageurs.

NOTES

1. DeLong, Shleifer, Summers & Waldmann, The Survival of Noise Traders in Financial Markets, 64 J.Bus. 1 (1991) extends the model with an attack on the proposition that all noise traders must fail in the long run. They assert that individual noise traders may fail, but noise traders as a whole may survive, without reference having to be made to an outside pool of new noise traders. In this model of market evolution and survival of the fittest, we get an ever shrinking army of ever richer fools who collectively dominate the market. Id. at 4, 14, 18. Meanwhile, the proposition that smart money pushes the market in rational directions is under empirical attack. De Bondt, What do Economists Know about the Stock Market?, 17 J.Portfolio Management, Winter 1991 at 84, presents an empirical survey of the record of expert economic forecasters. Citing the "overreaction hypothesis" of Kahneman and Tversky, On the Psychology of Prediction, 80 Psychological Rev. 237 (1973), De Bondt finds that the experts overreact and that their forecast errors are systematic.

For further reading, see Summers, Does the Stock Market Rationally Reflect Fundamental Values? 41 J.Finance 591 (1986); Black, Noise, 41 J.Finance 529 (1986).

2. Under the noise trader approach, arbitrage is limited because noise traders driven by sentiment affect stock prices and sentiment is unpredictable. These points have been applied (1) to suggest that stocks will have higher returns than their fundamentals warrant because stocks will be subject to larger fluctuations of investor sentiment than bonds and thus will command enlarged risk premiums, and (2) to explain the persistence of closed-end fund discounts. See De Long,

Shleifer, Summers & Waldmann, Noise Trader Risk in Financial Markets, 98 J.Pol.Econ. 703, 724–730 (1990); Lee, Schleifer & Thaler, Investor Sentiment and the Closed–End Fund Puzzle, 46 J.Finance 75 (1991).

3. What are the implications of the noise trading approach for legal policy making? For discussion, see Langevoort, Theories, Assumptions, and Securities Regulation: Market Efficiency Revisited, 140 U.Pa.L.Rev. 851 (1992).

Given noise trading and a market price that need not reflect fundamental values—how should the law characterize the duties of corporate managers to shareholders? Should they maximize the stock price, or maximize the value of the firm, taken as the discounted value of future cash flows? Given the absence of a generally accepted theory of asset pricing and noise trading, maximum stock price and maximum firm value will not necessarily be identical. For discussion of this question in the context of mandatory disclosure rules, see Ayres, Back to *Basics:* Regulating How Corporations Speak to the Market, 77 Va.L.Rev. 945, 993–994 (1991):

> " * * * [I]n moving away from profit maximization as the unitary objective of management, we interject the possibility of disparate objectives for different shareholders. Shareholders of corporations with palace guards having earlier access to fundamental information are likely to demand more corporate speech, as are shareholders who are likely to sell their stock for liquidity reasons.
>
> "If different types of shareholders hold a given corporate stock, whose objectives should management pursue?   * * * [C]orporations should, at their inception, announce their planned quantity and quality of corporate speech then allow shareholders to sort themselves by voting with their feet— investing in those corporations that provide their preferred package of speech and divesting their holdings in corporations that do not. * * * "

For a contrasting approach, see Hu, Risk, Time, and Fiduciary Principles in Corporate Investment, 38 UCLA L.Rev. 277, 290–291 (1990).

NOTE: THE CRASH OF 1987

In early October 1987, the Dow Jones average was at approximately 2600. Then, on October 19, the Dow Jones fell by more than 500 points on unprecedented trading volume. Before the end of the month, the Dow was trading under 1800—a drop of about one third during the course of the month.

In the aftermath of the crash, most observers did not look to changes in economic fundamentals for explanations. Instead of drawing on the EMH, they pointed to technical factors. Thus the reputation of the EMH suffered along with the fortunes of equity investors. The October 23, 1987 *Wall Street Journal* dismissed the EMH as "the most remarkable error in the history of economic theory." Unsympathetic economists took the occasion to pronounce its death. Jacobs and Levy, The Complexity of the Stock Market, 15 J.Portfolio Management 19, 22 (1989).

Three factors dominated these discussions. See generally, Report of the Presidential Task Force on Market Mechanisms (1988) (the "Brady Report"):

(1) It was noted that an imbalance of sell orders had exhausted market liquidity. Once the exchange hit its capacity, prices fell drastically. The problem with this as a complete explanation for the crash was that prices did not rebound once liquidity was restored. See Harris, The Dangers of Regulatory Overreaction to the October 1987 Crash, 74 Cornell L.Rev. 927, 933 (1989).

(2) Observers blamed arbitrage between index futures and the stock market, and the "program trading" mechanism for executing the orders of arbitrageurs. But, according to Harris, supra, this explanation also was unpersuasive: "[T]he two markets provide markets for essentially the same underlying risk. All strategies that can be executed in one market also can be * * * executed in the other market. Their main difference is that the futures market, under some circumstances, provides lower transactions costs than the cash market. Arbitrage only serves to link the two markets together. * * * [It] cannot explain the sell order submitted in the first place." To address these problems, the principal exchanges have instituted "circuit breaker" rules. These halt trading for set periods in response to sharp price drops. See S.Rep. No. 300, 101st Congress, 2d Sess., at 37–38 (1990). For criticisms of this and other regulatory responses to the crash, see Haddock, An Economic Analysis of the Brady Report: Public Interest, Special Interest, or Rent Extraction? 74 Cornell L.Rev. 841 (1989).

(3) Observers blamed the use of a "price insensitive" strategy called "portfolio insurance." Portfolio insurance is a dynamic hedging strategy pursuant to which an investor tries to maintain a synthetic put option on a portfolio. A put option is an option to sell a security at a stated exercise price. If one buys a stock and a put on the stock simultaneously, down-side risk on the stock holding is reduced—if the stock drops below the exercise price on the put, one exercises the put and thus receives the difference between the exercise price and the depressed stock price less the cost of the put. See Ayres, supra at 979 n. 143. Under the synthetic option strategy, one buys stock or stock index futures when the market is rising and sells stock when the market falls. Specifically, one gets down-side protection by short-selling a proportion of the shares held and placing the proceeds, plus the cost of the put in a safe security. The idea is that the portfolio's value does not fall below a fixed value called the "strike price," and that the portfolio also does not perform worse than the market as a

whole. To maintain the synthetic option, the strike price must constantly change with the market. Thus the strike price goes up with the market, locking in the holders' gains. But, with a market drop, the owner of the insurance has to sell more shares short (or more index risk). Id. at 979–980. These orders add to selling pressure in the market. See Harris, supra at 934. On the day of the crash, portfolio insurance schemes caused waves of institutional selling.

The Brady Report placed particular emphasis on portfolio insurance related sales in accounting for the crash. But subsequent studies cast doubt on this conclusion. See Brennan and Schwartz, Portfolio Insurance and Financial Market Equilibrium," 62 J.Bus. 455 (1989). The $6 billion of portfolio insurance outstanding amounted to less than 0.2 percent of the $3.5 trillion of equity value in existence at dawn on October 19. Sales pressure of this magnitude does not, taken alone, account for a 20% loss of value. See Gennotte and Leland, Market Liquidity, Hedging and Crashes, 80 Amer.Econ.Rev. 99 (1990).

Gennotte and Leland, supra, couple illiquidity and hedging sales with other factors in a model of crashes. The model combines investors with different information levels, information changes, illiquidity, and the presence of undisclosed hedging strategies. They show that information differentials can cause markets to be relatively illiquid, and that a small, unobserved supply shock can result in a large price decline. This is because uninformed investors do not know whether the sellers are selling for liquidity reasons or because they have undisclosed negative fundamental information. As a result, they balk at buying when prices suddenly drop. Given these uninformed investors who overestimate the market's liquidity, additional sales because of hedging programs can have a destabilizing effect. See also Ayres, supra at 978–979.

Under the EMH, we should, presumably, disregard illiquidity and undisclosed hedging strategies and look to changes in underlying economic fundamentals to explain the 1987 crash. The crash can, indeed, be explained in terms of fundamental value. Malkiel, Is the Stock Market Efficient? 243 Science 1313, 1317 (1989), points to three rational explanations for a sharp change in market valuations during the fall of 1987: a substantial increase in interest rates during the summer and early fall, with yields on long-term treasuries increasing from 9 to 10½ percent; risks that merger activity might be curtailed as the result of the imposition of a proposed federal "merger tax;" and threats by the Secretary of the Treasury to encourage a further fall in the price of the dollar. Malkiel invokes the dividend model of stock pricing to point out that small changes in fundamentals can produce large price changes. He hypothesizes a stock that pays a dividend of $5, is priced at $100, and has an expected growth rate of 6 percent, given a market discount rate of 11 percent. Under these assumptions, he shows that the combination of a 1½ percent increase in the riskless rate of return plus a ½ percent increase in the risk premium demanded by stockholders will cause the discount rate for stocks to increase from 11 to 13 percent. The result is a 29.5 percent drop in the hypothetical stock's present value from $100 to $71.43. See also Smith, Market Volatility: Causes and Consequences, 74 Cornell L.Rev. 953, 957 (1989); Fama, Perspectives on October 1987, or What did we learn from the Crash?, in R. Kamphuis, R. Kormendi, and J. Watson, eds., Black Monday and the Future of the Financial Markets (1989).

Shleifer and Summers, supra at 29, criticize such attempts to explain the 1987 crash. There is, they say, no evidence that risk increased tremendously or that dividend growth in fact was revised sharply downward on October 19. In fact, long-term forecasts were not revised downward even after the crash, and insiders bought stock in record numbers during and after the crash. They explain the crash in terms of "positive feedback trading"—the tendency to chase the trend. The dramatic rise in the 1987 market to a peak in August as investors chased the trend; then downside positive feedback trading caused the crash, once it started, to go deep. Id. at 28–30. This, in effect, returns us to the Keynesian beauty contest, but with a contemporary title. Seyhun, Overreaction or Fundamentals: Some Lessons from Insiders' Response to the Market Crash of 1987, 45 J. Finance 1363 (1990), provides support for this conclusion with a study of insider stock purchases before and after the crash. Before the crash there was no increase in insider selling activity. But after the crash insiders bought their own firms' stocks in record numbers. This implies that fundamentals were not driving the market and that "overreaction" contributed to the crash.

Note that there was a second, smaller crash on Friday, October 13, 1989. The Dow Jones lost 190 points that day, raising fears of a repeat of the 1987 experience. According to a poll of 101 market professionals conducted the following Monday and Tuesday, this crash was caused by fear of a crash. Shiller and Feltus, Fear of a Crash Caused the Crash, The New York Times, Sunday, October 29, 1989, sec. F, p. 3.

CLOSING NOTE

1. There is a body of economic studies that isolates three factors as the causes of variation in stock returns. These are shocks to expected cash flows, predictable variation over time in the discount rates that price expected cash flows, and shocks to discount rates. To the extent that variation in stock prices can be attributed to these factors, the efficiency of stock prices in a fundamental value sense has been demonstrated. The economist Eugene Fama recently produced a study of the combined explanatory power of the three factors, and found that about 58 percent of the variance of annual real returns on the value-weighted portfolio of NYSE stocks could be attributed to the factors. Fama, Stock Returns, Expected Returns and Real Activity, 45 J. Finance 1089 (1990). He concluded, id. p. 1090: "are these results good or bad news about market efficiency? One can argue that vari-

ance explained is understated because the explanatory variables do not capture all rational variance in returns. One can, on the other hand, argue that variance explained is overstated because the explanatory variables are chosen largely on the basis of goodness to fit. As always, then, the answer to the basic market-rationality question must be left to the reader."

2. Given all of the foregoing materials, is the functioning of the securities markets something we need to worry about in legal contexts? Commentators, opinion writers and policy makers in the field of securities regulation tend to share a common assumption about information, trading markets and economic efficiency. Specifically, the sooner that information related to the assets or expected performance of an enterprise is found by actors in the marketplace, the more accurately the enterprise is appraised; furthermore, the more quickly the information figures into a purchase or sale, the more precisely will the market price of the securities correspond to the value of the enterprise. The market thereby will function efficiently to allocate savings to enterprises which are more profitable and divert them from enterprises that are less profitable. The well-functioning market therefore makes us all better off.

How safe is this assumption? It is questioned in Stout, The Unimportance of Being Efficient: An Economic Analysis of Stock Market Pricing and Securities Regulation, 87 Mich.L.Rev. 613 (1988). For a contrasting discussion, see Kahan, Securities Laws and the Social Costs of "Inaccurate" Stock Prices, 41 Duke L.J. 977 (1992).

Part II: SENIOR SECURITIES
INTRODUCTION

This Part presents and examines the rules, contractual and otherwise, that govern the distribution of risks and rewards between senior and junior security holders.

What makes a senior claim "senior"? The valuation materials suggest that the enterprise should be regarded as a potential stream of earnings, with the possibility (generally remote) of a distribution of its assets in liquidation. The security holder's investment contract may, in turn, be viewed as describing (1) his claim to share in that earnings stream and in any liquidating distribution, and (2) his right to affect the conduct of the enterprise so as to protect and enhance the value of that claim. The claims of the various investment securities upon the earnings and assets of the enterprise are defined in the portion of the investment contract which sets forth the amount of such claims and prescribes their priority vis-a-vis other claimants. Thus, typically, a senior debt claim (e.g., principal or interest on a bond) has a right to payment which must be satisfied before the next most junior claim (e.g., preferred stock liquidating distributions or dividends) may be paid, and the preferred stock has a comparable prior claim to dividends and in liquidation over the common stock. Technically the claim of the debt is an obligation, since generally it represents a promise to pay principal and interest, which on default may be enforced by the creditor. In contrast, the preferred stock's claim is only a priority against the claims of other stockholders. It is embodied in a negative covenant, which becomes enforceable only if the commons or other juniors seek to distribute earnings or assets to themselves. In operation, the difference between the obligation to pay the principal amount of the debt and the priority of the preferred stock—although not the difference between the seniority of the two kinds of claims—tends to become blurred as a result of the insolvency reorganization process, as the materials that follow will show.

A necessary corollary to the priority of a claim is the existence of a ceiling or limit on its amount. It is with respect to that maximum amount that the claim on earnings or assets must be met before the next claim in the hierarchy is entitled to any portion of the earnings or assets. No more than that amount need (or may) be diverted from the stream of earnings or from the assets in payment of the prior claim, no matter how greatly the stream or assets expand; no less than the prescribed amount is legally payable before the other, more junior, claimants against the earnings or assets may share, no matter how

148

severely the earnings or assets contract.[a] The limited character of the "senior" claims contrasts with the open ended residual character of the common stock claim. The common stock is exposed to the greatest risk because it is entitled to receive distributions only after all other claims are satisfied, but it also has the opportunity to reap the greatest rewards because it is entitled to all amounts available in excess of the prior limited claim of the seniors.

Accompanying the common stock's greater exposure to risk and greater opportunity for benefit is its control of the enterprise. While the "control" of dispersed common stock over management is problematic, compared to the power of voteless senior securities it can be significant. That control gives the common stock the possibility of affecting the levels of risk and the growth or contraction of earnings and assets by electing management which makes decisions about operations and investments; it also offers the opportunity to affect determination about which portions, if any, of the earnings or assets shall be distributed to security holders; and, finally, it enables the common stock's management representatives to determine what kinds of other claims on those earnings and assets may be created prior to itself (e.g., new bonds or preferred stock) and possibly prior to existing claims, as well as the risk-return characteristics of the business undertaken by the firm. In a distress situation it enables the management representatives of the common to determine what alterations may be sought in existing claims by refinancing or recapitalizing. Its power to seek such alterations, even where subject to the consent of the class of outstanding senior securities, often is tantamount to the power to compel them.

The legal issues with which we will be concerned derive from the efforts of junior security holders, generally common stockholders, to exercise these powers so as to benefit themselves at the expense of senior claimants. Since the seniors' and juniors' legal rights are embodied in an investment contract (which, in the case of stock, imports various statutory provisions) the issues in the first instance involve the interpretation of contracts and statutes. Sometimes, the junior security holders wield their power to injure the interests of senior security holders during prosperous times, as where additional senior capital is borrowed to invest in riskier projects or to fund a return of capital to the common stockholders. Here, if the senior claimants have not reserved contract rights against the injurious course of conduct, the legal question will be whether such a right should be implied in fact or in law. More often, the setting for senior-junior conflict is one of economic adversity; the company has experienced operating losses over an extended period, and default on senior obli-

a. There may be prior claims to amounts which are contingent or uncertain, subject to a ceiling. Thus, an income bond will entitle the holder to interest up to a certain amount only if earned, and a preferred stock may entitle a holder only to such amounts as may be declared but not in excess of a specified ceiling. It is also possible for prior claims to have, in addition to their priority rights, rights to participate with the common stock in the residual amounts. Such rights to participate are not, of course, priorities, unless they too are fixed in maximum amount and stated to be prior.

gations is imminent or may already have occurred. In this context the common stockholders, through their management representatives, may seek to rebargain their relationship with the senior security owners in order to preserve for themselves an economic interest in the enterprise at a minimum sacrifice. The seniors, on the other hand, will prefer a strict enforcement of their contract rights, even if that entails the extinguishment of the common stockholders' interest and possibly a liquidation of the corporation. In the tug-of-war that follows, the common stockholders have the advantage both of having drafted (through their representatives, and generally without serious or direct bargaining by the seniors) the original investment contract and, by comparison with the seniors, of being in control of the enterprise at all critical dates thereafter. As a consequence, when class interests come in conflict, the seniors often appear to occupy a weaker negotiating position than the common, and sometimes even to be subject to the dictates of the latter group. In addition, therefore, to conventional issues of contract interpretation, a question of major concern is whether the law should impose limitations on the rebargaining process to reflect this apparent inequality.

SECTION A.　BONDHOLDERS' RIGHTS

————

1.　DEBT FINANCING

————

(A) OVERVIEW

There follows an introduction to some principal terms, forms, and practices respecting debt financing.

1. *Bonds, Debentures, and Notes.*

All of these are long term promissory notes. No inherent or legally recognized definition distinguishes one from the other. As a matter of historical practice, bonds and debentures are long term obligations issued under indentures, bonds generally being secured obligations and debentures being unsecured obligations. Under the historical practice, notes may be long term or short term obligations, but in either case are not issued pursuant to an indenture. Recent practice has changed this. Today, "notes" often are issued pursuant to indentures as unsecured long term obligations. But they tend to be intermediate term securities, coming due in ten years or less, where "debentures" tend to mature in ten years or more.

A bond, debenture or note is simply a promise by the borrower to pay a specified amount on a specified date, together with interest at specified times, on the terms and subject to the conditions spelled out in a governing indenture or note agreement. Bonds, debentures and notes are, then, promissory notes issued pursuant to and governed by longer contracts. Some of the governing terms and conditions will be set out on the face of the promissory note itself. Most terms, however, will be in the contract that governs the instrument and will be merely referred to on its face. The note incorporates the contract by reference.[b]

It is the practice in both financial and legal writing to use "bond" as a generic term for all long term debt securities. The practice will be followed here, although "debenture" and "note" will be used where particular contexts require.

Some concepts basic to bond valuation are set out at pp. 38–40.

2. *Indentures.*

An indenture is a contract entered into between the borrowing corporation and a trustee. The trustee administers the payments of interest and principal, and monitors and enforces compliance with other obligations on behalf of the bondholders as a group. The indenture defines the assorted obligations of the borrower, the rights and remedies of the holders of the bonds, and the role of the trustee.

The borrower contracts with a trustee rather than directly with the holders of the bonds so as to permit the bonds to be sold in small denominations to large numbers of scattered investors. Given widespread ownership in small amounts, unilateral monitoring and enforcement by each holder is not cost effective. The device of the trust solves this problem.

Trust indentures date back to financing of 19th century railroads, the earliest large scale, long term debt financings. Railroad entrepreneurs were forced to sell mortgage notes to many persons, since no one person was willing or able to furnish all of the funds to be raised. These bonds had to be made marketable and tradable while simultaneously carrying a lien against the mortgaged property. Each of the widely disbursed holders of the bonds had to be given the security of a mortgage on the railroad's assets without at the same time being granted an individual fractional interest in the collateral. The solution was to convey the mortgaged assets, under a trust indenture, to someone as trustee for the equal and ratable benefit of each of the holders.

b. Historically, bonds were issued in bearer form. Coupons giving the holder the right to each scheduled interest payment literally were attached to the bond to be clipped and turned into the issuer for payment. The benefit of a bearer instrument is anonymity, but it carries a concomitant risk of loss or theft. In the post war era, the practice in this country changed, and registered bonds became the dominant form. Registered bonds, like common stock, are issued in the name of the owner. The issuer, or its agent (usually the trustee), keeps a registry of the owners of the issue, and remits interest, sinking fund and redemption payments to the registered owner. Registered bonds are negotiable and transferable, with the concomitant recordation of the transfer on the books of the issuer. Under the Tax Equity and Fiscal Responsibility Act of 1982, Internal Revenue Code, § 163(f), issuers are denied interest deductions for bearer securities issued after 1982. As a result, new bearer bonds are not issued in this country. Anonymity is still the rule in the Euromarkets, and the Code contains an exception for Eurobond issues of American firms.

By the turn of the century, the device of the trust indenture was extended to cover unsecured borrowing by large industrial corporations.

The student should keep in mind a distinction between the "bonds" and the "indenture." The bonds set out a promise to pay that runs to the holders of the bonds. The indenture is a bundle of additional promises (including a backup promise to pay) that run to the trustee. The holders of the bonds are third party beneficiaries of the promises in the indenture. Even though the promises in the bonds run directly to the holders, the bonds are subject to the indenture, and therefore may be enforced directly by the holders only to the extent that the indenture allows. Indentures generally constrain the unilateral enforcement rights of small holders, channelling enforcement through the central agency of the trustee. The device of the trust indenture, then, not only facilitates enforcement by the widely scattered holders, but also restrains such enforcement. It facilitates borrowing in small amounts from large numbers of widely scattered lenders not only by constraining the issuer as against the holders, but by protecting the issuer from the holders.

Where, as in a private placement of notes to an insurance company or pension fund or a long term loan by a bank, the loan is large enough to make direct monitoring and enforcement cost effective, the trust device is not employed. Such a note is issued pursuant to a "note agreement" or "loan agreement" entered into between the borrower and lender directly.

3. *Terms of Indentures.*

In many respects, trust indentures do not change much from decade to decade. The following summary of their contents from 1 A. Dewing, The Financial Policy of Corporations 173–174 (5th ed. 1953), remains accurate so far as it goes:

" * * * This rather elaborate document has, ordinarily, six important sets of provisions, some of which are mere recapitulations or elaborations of statements made in the primary contract, the bond, and some are provisions only indirectly referred to in the bond. There is, first, the set of provisions summarizing the amounts of money and the future date of payment, the interest rate and the time of interest payment—provisions which acknowledge that the bondholder is a creditor of the corporation entitled to the payment of his loan with interest. Furthermore, if the payment of the debt may be anticipated by the corporation, the fact will be clearly stated, together with the specific mechanism of prepayment which shall insure fairness to all the scattered bondholders. The second set of provisions describes the character and the extent of the property against which the bondholder may levy in order to satisfy his debt. If there is no such property, the agreement will categorically state that fact. Thirdly, there is a set of provisions which represents the special covenants accepted by the corporation which insure the preservation of the value of the corporate property, during the long period while the debt shall endure. The corporation will pay its taxes, make the necessary repairs, set aside adequate reserves for depreciation, replace worn-out or obsolete equipment, protect its franchises or patent rights; it will not give a prior lien to the property reserved for the bondholders. The corporation agrees not to permit the wastage or destruction of the property covered by the agreement. Fourthly, there is a set of provisions which defines with a high degree of precision the exact course the bondholders, acting individually or together, must pursue in order to levy on the corporation, as general creditors, or to levy on the specific property, if any, set aside for the security of the bonds issued under the indenture. Again, fifthly, there are provisions describing the duties and the obligations of the trustee. These clauses define with precision what he can and what he cannot do, on behalf both of the corporation and of the individual and collective bondholders. Finally—as a matter of tradition because the trustee could not legally do otherwise—there is a covenant on the part of the bondholders, acting through the trustee, that when the corporation has paid back the original loans—the face of the bonds—and has met the successive payments of interest, the lien or claims of the bondholders will cease and the corporation will no longer be bound by any of the promises of the bonds or the supplementary agreement."

Traditionally, the third item on Dewing's list—protective provisions—appear in stronger, more complex versions in indentures governing debentures than in indentures governing bonds (narrow definition). The holder of a bond relies on the security of pledged assets in addition to the earning power of the going concern. The holder of a debenture has no mortgage on particular property and relies only on the going concern. Provisions of indentures, the so-called "business covenants," protect this reliance, and thereby protect the debenture's value. The most important of these provisions limit the issuer's power (a) to pledge its free assets to other creditors, (b) to incur additional debt on a parity with, or superior to, the debentures, and (c) to make dividends or other payments to holders of its stock.

The terms and protective provisions in indentures accreted over a long period, reflecting the accumulated fears of generations of lawyers. The history of this development is briefly discussed in Rodgers, The Corporate Trust Indenture Project, 20 Bus.Law. 551 (1965). For some two decades the American Bar Foundation sponsored a Corporate Debt Financing Project for the purpose of reforming the complex and convoluted terms of indentures and offering a standardized form of the most conventional covenants and provisions. Its efforts have produced model incorporating forms of indentures, standard or "model" indenture provisions (sometimes with alternatives), and "negotiable" provisions for terms most likely to vary with particular borrowings. See Model Debenture Indenture (1965) and related Sample Incorporating Indenture; Model Debenture Indenture Provisions—All Registered Issues (1967) and related Sample Incorporating Indenture; Commentaries on both the 1965 and 1967 products. A more recent Model Simplified Indenture (text and accompanying notes in 38 Bus.Law. 741 (1983)), based on a form originally prepared by Morey W. McDaniel, seeks to simplify the language of frequently used provisions.

Sections of the Model Simplified Indenture are set out in Appendix C. Protective provisions of indentures are treated in more detail infra pp. 187–193.

4. *Duration.*

The bond's face states a due date. But the ascertainment of bond's maturity often is a complicated matter that cannot be settled by a simple reference to the face of the bond. Most bond issuers must make "sinking fund" payments—prepayments of principal in advance of the due date. A bond subject to such mandatory prepayments has, in substance, serial maturities.

Complicating matters, most bonds are redeemable, in whole or in part, at the option of the borrowing corporation. The redeeming issuer is said to "call" the bond. In other words, the indenture provides for prepayments of principal at the option of the issuer in addition to the prepayments of principal that the issuer is required to make. Sinking fund payments disadvantage the borrower, while redemption payments disadvantage the lender. Sinking fund and redemption provisions are treated at greater length infra pp. 174–186.

5. *Public Offerings and Private Placements.*

When bonds are offered to the public, the issuer and underwriters must comply with the registration requirements of the Securities Act of 1933. In addition, the execution of a trust indenture conforming with the requirements of the Trust Indenture Act of 1939 is mandatory for public offerings. The compliance process requires substantial lead time, although large issuers can shortcut the registration process through the shelf registration device provided for in Rule 415 under the 1933 Act. The company registers a large quantity of securities for future issue—up to two years in advance. When it wishes to offer and sell some of these preregistered securities, it files an amendment with the SEC containing details about the securities on offer. Under this system, new debt securities can be publicly marketed in a matter of days. Transaction costs are lowered and the issuer gains timing flexibility. See Kadapakkam & Kon, The Value of Shelf Registration for New Debt Issues, 62 J. Business 271 (1989).

Issuers too small to gain access to the public debt markets and issuers too small to qualify for shelf registrations have the alternative of issuing long term debt in the private placement market. Both the 1933 Act, in section 4(2) and Rule 144 thereunder, and the 1939 Act, in section 304, contain exemptions for securities that are not offered to the general public. Under these sections, registration of the issue and the qualification of a trust indenture can be avoided if the offer and sale of the bonds is limited to a small number of sophisticated institutional investors.

"Private placements," transactions taking advantage of these exemptions, constitute a substantial portion of all issues of long term debt. In 1988, $200 billion of new private placement securities were issued and sold, amounting to 42 percent of the total of new debt

financing. Broka, Private Placements: So Far, So Fast, 91 Best's
Review 44 (1990). Private placements involve face to face negotiations
between the issuer and an institutional purchaser or group of purchasers. The process can be concluded quickly and relatively cheaply. The
compliance and incidental expenses of public offerings are avoided.
Terms can be tailored to meet the situation and needs of the borrower.
Funds can be disbursed at intervals to meet the borrower's specific
financing needs.

Before the development of the junk bond market, described in
Appendix C, Section 1, infra, private placements, along with long term
loans from banks, were the only available source of long term debt
financing for small and medium sized issuers whose debt was rated Ba,
B or below.[c] These issuers continue to dominate the private placement
market. As a result, the face amount of each issue of debt sold in a
private placement transaction tends to be smaller than that sold in a
public offering. Large corporate borrowers do enter the private placement market on occasion, however—when the available terms are as
favorable as those on offer in the public market. The largest lenders in
the private placement market are life insurance companies. Pension
funds also participate.

Private placement note agreements tend to contain tighter, more
complex business covenants than do trust indentures governing public
issue debentures and notes. This can be explained both from the
lender's and the borrower's point of view. From the lender's point of
view, a private placement represents a long term commitment of
capital to a smaller issuer—a less secure investment than those on offer
in the public trading market. Such a loan imports high risk; strict
covenants lessen the risk. See generally, Malitz, On Financial Contracting: The Determinants of Bond Covenants, Fin. Management,
Summer 1986; Smith & Warner, On Financial Contracting: An Analysis of Bond Covenants, 7 J. Financial Economics 117 (1979). Tighter
monitoring does so also. Thus, the private placement lender can be
expected to do its own careful study of the borrower before committing
to lend. The absence of public disclosure requirements creates an
environment conducive to frank discussion of the borrower's prospects.
The monitoring continues during the life of the loan: private placement
note agreements tend to provide for more extensive periodic reports
than do public indentures.

From the borrower's point of view, strict business covenants are not
only inconvenient, they also create the possibility of a contractual
barrier to beneficial new investment activity. In the case of publicly
traded debentures, this contractual barrier could be insurmountable as
a practical matter. The costs of collecting the consents requisite for the

---

c. Issuers pay two firms, Moody's and
Standard & Poor's to rate their debt for
creditworthiness. The firms assess the
likelihood of default. The ratings do not
cover risk due to changes in interest rates.
Under Moody's rating system "high grade"
is Aaa and Aa; "medium grade" is A and
Baa; "low grade," or "junk" is Ba and B;
Caa and Ca is lower still; C is in default.
A 1, 2 or 3, added to a Moody's rating
functions like a plus or a minus, with a 1
being a plus. See Ross, Westerfield & Jordan, Fundamentals of Corporate Finance
373 (1991).

waiver of such a covenant may be prohibitive. In contrast, with a single or small group of institutional investors it is mechanically feasible to obtain the lender's waiver. Indeed, periodic renegotiation of terms according with the changing circumstances of the borrower is not uncommon in private placement relationships. Private placement noteholders are likely to be responsive to changes that the borrower perceives will enhance its economic well being. With publicly held debentures, the scattered holders are less likely to be able or willing to make the judgment that concessions are advantageous to themselves as well as to the debtor. See Zinbarg, The Private Placement Loan Agreement, Fin. Analysts J., July–Aug. 1975, p. 33.

The total initial cost of a private placement tends to be much less than that of a public offering. But some contend that the total cost to the borrower is higher. According to Van Horne, Financial Management and Policy 597–598 (8th ed. 1989), "[f]ragmentary evidence here indicates that the yield on private placements is above that on public offerings. In addition to interest costs, institutional investors sometimes will request an equity "sweetener," such as warrants, to entice them to invest in the debt issue of a company." Blackwell & Kidwell, An Investigation of Cost Differences Between Public Sales and Private Placements of Debt, 22 J. Financial Econs. 253 (1988), reaches a different conclusion. Blackwell and Kidwell find that (1) small firms that tend to finance exclusively with private placements would pay an additional 132 basis points (that is, 1.32 percent) interest to sell debt publicly, and (2) as to larger firms that switch back and forth between the public and private markets, there is no difference in average yield to net proceeds.

Rule 144A, promulgated under the 1933 Act in 1990, permits trading of private placement notes among institutional investors that meet stated qualifications. It also serves the purpose of providing foreign issuers an inexpensive means of access to United States debt markets. This new trading market is not as yet extensive. See McQuiston, Rule 144A, Regulation S and Amending the Glass–Steagall Act: A New Look at Foreign Banks and Foreign Issuers Participating in the United States Securities Market, 17 Syracuse J. Int'l L. & Com. 171 (1991). Cooper, Private Placements Under Rule 144A: A Rose by Another Name, New York Law Journal, Jan. 27, 1992, p. 1, suggests that the development of the market has taken an unexpected turn. New Rule 144A issues tend to come from investment grade firms that take advantage of the Rule 144A market as a cheaper venue for making what in substance amount to public offerings.

6. *Junk Bonds.*

Twenty years ago the private placement market was the only alternative to bank borrowing for small and medium sized issuers looking for long term debt capital. The public markets were foreclosed to these lower grade companies. This changed with the development of a "junk bond" market constituted of publicly traded low-grade debt. For a detailed description, see Appendix C, Section 1, infra.

7. *Convertible Bonds.*

These are debentures or notes that can be changed at the holder's option into a specified number of shares of the issuer's common stock. These "hybrid" securities combine the downside protection of senior status with the upside potential of common stock. For further discussion, see pp. 397–439 infra.

8. *Mortgage Bonds.*

With rare exceptions, corporate bonds and debentures constitute unconditional promises to pay principal at a fixed time, and interest on fixed dates. However, not all bonds and debentures rank equally as claims upon the enterprise. Two frequently encountered variations affecting the priority of the bondholders' claims are the mortgage bond and the subordinated debenture, discussed below. Holders of the former are secured as to the payment of principal and interest by a pledge or mortgage of described assets of the debtor, and thus have a prior claim to payment against other creditors with respect to the mortgaged assets or their proceeds. On the other hand, the subordinated debenture has precisely the opposite effect for its holders—it effectively prescribes repayment of principal in the event of liquidation or reorganization (or occasionally, in all events) only after all other creditors to whom it purports to be subordinated are repaid in full.

The mortgage bond is an obligation secured by specified property which either is made subject to the obligee's lien by the mortgage (although technically title continues to be held by the obligor) or, in some states, is technically transferred to the obligee to be held solely as security for the repayment of the debt. In theory, the mortgagee of a corporate mortgage, like the mortgagee of a simple home mortgage, applies the security in payment of the defaulted debt by foreclosure on the mortgaged property in a proceeding which results in a sale. The mortgagee may purchase the property at the sale, which ideally is an auction at which competitive bidding is designed, at least formally, to assure a fair price. Whether the property is sold to the obligee or otherwise, its proceeds are applied in payment of the obligation. The inadequacy of the foreclosure procedure to protect the corporate bondholders has been the subject of considerable literature and has resulted in the development of bankruptcy reorganization procedure under federal legislation.

To the extent that the property subject to a corporate mortgage is an integral part of a going concern, it generally has a higher monetary value if it continues to be a part of the going concern than if it is sold for cash, piecemeal or *in toto.* Hence, even when mortgage foreclosure was technically an available remedy of the bondholders, it functioned to enable them to acquire new participations in the continuing enterprise (i.e., the securities of a newly formed corporation, in exchange for which the insolvent's assets were "sold"), rather than to force the sale of the liened property to third persons for cash. When reorganizations thus were consummated through the process of mortgage foreclosure—principally in the case of railroads—the value of the property subject to the mortgage was theoretically available to pay the debt it secured to the extent thereof. If the pledged property was "worth" more than the amount of the debt, the surplus was available to second or even more junior mortgagees or to general creditors. On the other hand, if the property was not "worth" enough to pay the debt, the unpaid balance became an unsecured claim against the borrower, and the mortgage bondholders shared with other general creditors in the borrower's unsecured assets. The principle of allocating the full "value" of the mortgaged property to satisfy the mortgage bondholder before any other creditor could receive any part of the proceeds was imported into the statutory procedure for bankruptcy reorganization, as will be seen.

A corporation's mortgage bonds may be issued in different classes having different liens and terms, such as maturity dates, interest rates, call premiums; each class may be secured by specific property dedicated exclusively to it, or by a lesser—i.e., junior—lien on the same property that secures other bonds, or, as has often happened with railroads, by a combination of the two security arrangements. In the case of different liens on the same property, the rank of its lien in the hierarchy determines the order of the bond's priority in payment from the proceeds of the mortgaged property.

Mortgages may be closed-end, in which case no bonds in addition to those initially issued against the mortgaged property may be created with that property as the subject of a first mortgage. Any subsequent mortgage on that property must be only a secondary lien on it, subject to the primary claim of the closed mortgage. If the borrowing corporation wishes to borrow additional funds on first mortgage, it must pledge other property. A closed-end mortgage thus assures the lender that no other lender can acquire a primary lien on the pledged property, but by the same token it deprives the borrower of the opportunity to borrow additional amounts on that property at the relatively low interest rates available for a first mortgage. That deprivation is not trivial if improvements or additions have been made during the period of the mortgage or the property can support a larger first mortgage than it carries. The open-end mortgage is a device to permit additional bonds to be issued as a first lien on property already subject to a first lien securing outstanding bonds. The additional bonds may be issued from time to time, in different series and at different interest rates. Since an open-end mortgage permits creation of larger debt on property which is already mortgaged, an existing lender may subsequently find its security diluted. In order to avoid undue dilution of the security, protective limits are set on the quantity of new first mortgage bonds that may be issued against the security of already mortgaged property. Generally, the limits are defined in terms of the proportions which property and earnings shall bear respectively to total amount of bonds and interest. Thus, the open-end mortgage may provide that additional bonds may only be issued up to 60% of the cost of unencumbered property additions, or with interest charges which, when taken together with all other mortgage bond interest charges, are covered at least two times by the borrower's operating earnings.[d]

When lenders require not only the security of presently pledged property but also of after-acquired property, provision must be made to subject newly acquired property to the lien of the mortgage. When such a clause is contained in a mortgage, the debtor may be hard-pressed to obtain additional credit, notwithstanding its acquisition of additional property. To avoid the restrictive effect of an after-acquired property clause, the issuer may resort to a variety of devices, the cleanest, if most expensive, of which is to redeem the outstanding bond issue. It may also be possible for the issuer to induce an exchange of outstanding bonds for new bonds or to persuade the bondholders to modify the restrictions. More elaborate avoidance devices (which more sophisticated creditors proscribe), entail the acquisition of additional property through subsidiaries, or the leasing, rather than the purchase, of additional property or the use of a purchase money mortgage. Occasionally merger or consolidation with another corporation may permit avoidance of after-acquired property clauses.

The mortgage may be secured not only by a pledge of the property but also by a pledge of the income from the property. Since, however, the debtor imperatively requires the use of that income, the pledge is subject to a retraction or defeasance clause which authorizes application of the income for the operation of the property. Since the income is generated after the date of the mortgage, it constitutes a form of after-acquired property, and is theoretically subject to application for the benefit of the mortgagee in the event of default. The conceptual and practical difficulties attending efforts to resolve the conflicting claims to ownership of the income (as it actually comes into the debtor's possession) by the debtor and its general creditors, on the one hand, and on the other hand by the mortgagee who has not yet foreclosed, are legion. See generally Israels and Kramer, The Significance of the Income Clause in a Corporate Mortgage, 30 Colum.L.Rev. 488 (1930); Cohen and Gerber, The After Acquired Property Clause, 89 U.Pa.L.Rev. 635 (1939); Note, After Acquired Property Security Interests in Bankruptcy: A Substitution of Collateral Defense of the U.C.C., 77 Yale L.J. 139 (1967); Hillman, Non–Bankruptcy Problems of Future Advances and After–Acquired Property, PLI, The Secured Creditor in Court (1984), p. 21.

In addition to the security aspects of a mortgage bond, there usually are, as we have seen, elaborate covenants designed to protect the property, and to insure its appropriate maintenance or replacement in order to preserve its value as security.

When the property securing a mortgage bond is itself an investment security such as bonds or stocks the instrument is called a collateral trust bond. Generally the pledge takes the form of a transfer

---

d. See e.g., the limitations prescribed by the S.E.C. in its Statement of Policy Regarding First Mortgage Bonds subject to the Public Utility Holding Company Act of 1935 (PUHCA Rel. No. 13, 105, Feb. 16, 1956), CCH Fed.Sec.L.Rep. 36,675–36,687.

of title to a trustee but the obligor corporation retains substantial control over the pledged property and enjoys the income from it so long as there is no default on the bonds themselves. Another form of security—for either debt or equity—issued to public investors in increasing amounts by operating companies and financial institutions during the past few years is a participation in a specific pool of the firm's assets. To the extent that the securing assets are of a higher quality than the credit of the issuer, the package enables the issuer to raise funds at a lower cost than by way of standard financing.

The questions why or in what circumstances lenders should require security rather than, for example, increased interest rates or other protective covenants—in perfect markets, and in the less than perfect markets of the "real" world,—are subjects of considerable debate. A variety of considerations have been explored in the literature, such as the fact that some kinds of property are more fungible (less firm-specific) and therefore less costly for debtors and creditors to secure than others; some kinds of business are more costly to monitor than others, so that security is sought in lieu of explicit monitoring obligations; or some enterprises are so risky that any rational interest demand to compensate for the risk would be too high, and therefore the lender reduces risk by taking security.

For debate over the economic rationale of secured debt, in light particularly of the Modigliani–Miller hypothesis see Scott, Bankruptcy, Secured Debt and Optimal Capital Structure, 32 J.Finance 1 (1979); Smith and Warner, Bankruptcy, Secured Debt, and Optimal Capital Structure; Comment, 34 J.Finance 247 (1979); Ross, Reply, 34 J.Finance 252 (1979); Schwartz, Security Interests and Bankruptcy Priorities: A Review of Current Theories, 10 J. Legal Stud. 1 (1981); Levmore, Monitors and Freeriders in Commercial and Corporate Settings, 92 Yale L.J. 49 (1982); White, Efficiency Justifications for Personal Property Security, 37 Vanderbilt L.Rev. 473 (1984); Schwartz, The Continuing Puzzle of Secured Debt, 37 Vanderbilt L.Rev. 1051 (1984); Buckley, The Bankruptcy Priority Puzzle, 72 Va.L.Rev. 1393 (1986); Shupack, Solving the Puzzle of Secured Transactions, 41 Rutgers L.Rev. 1067 (1989).

9. *Leasing.*

Entering into a "financial lease" has many of the elements of secured borrowing. The lessee takes the position of the borrower. The lessor, which may be a financial institution, takes the place of the lender. Large items of equipment, such as railroad rolling stock, airplanes, and machines used in mining are financed through financial leases.

The lessee, which gets the use of the leased asset, promises to make rental payments under the lease. The lease extends over most of the economic life of the asset and will either be noncancelable or cancelable only upon reimbursement of any losses incurred by the lessor. It also probably will be a "net" lease—the lessee promises to maintain and insure the property and pay the property taxes. The lease payments are tax deductible as business expenses. But the lessee does not get the tax benefits of the depreciation on the property—these go to the lessor. The lessor not only takes the tax benefits of depreciation, but has the security that having title to the property brings. From the lessor's point of view, the lease is profitable if the stream of rental payments, discounted on an after tax basis, are greater than the present cost of the leased property. See Brealey & Myers, Principles of Corporate Finance 653–654 (4th ed. 1991).

There are many variants on the theme of financial leasing. Under a "leveraged lease," the lessor borrows part of the purchase price of the leased property, using the leased property and the stream of payments under the lease as security for the loan. To achieve a nonrecourse basis for the loan, the financial institution will have an "owner trust" established to take title to the property and take the position of lessor. The financial institution is the beneficiary of the trust.

Another form of leasing entails the use of equipment trust certificates. This form is used primarily by railroads and airlines to finance their acquisition of rolling stock and airplanes. Typically the equipment is bought by the trustee, a financial institution, from the manufacturer who builds it in accordance with the specifications of the using railroad or airline. The trustee pays for the equipment with funds it receives in small part from the user, but in large part from the proceeds of its issuance of equipment trust certificates to public investors. The trustee leases the equipment to the railroad or airline at a rental calculated to pay the investors an annual return plus repayment of a portion of the principal each year. The equipment secures the obligation to repay the certificate holders. When the last principal payment is made, which is to occur with the last rental payment, the certificates are retired and the equipment belongs to the railroad or airline. The duration of these leases varies according to the equipment involved. Since the equipment is essential, and is for the operations of all enterprises in the industry, it has a ready market value, and is therefore financeable at relatively favorable terms to the user.

"Sale and leaseback" transactions tend occur when a business wishes to realize cash on a piece of real estate but continue to operate the facility located thereon. The property is sold to a financial purchaser simultaneously with the execution of a long-term lease from the purchaser to the seller. See Slovin, Sushka, Polonchek, Corporate Sale-and-Leasebacks and Shareholder Wealth, 45 J. Finance 289 (1990) (empirical study indicating that these transactions enhance the wealth of the shareholders of the lessee).

Finally, "operating leases" should be distinguished from financial leases. Operating leases are short term, cancelable leases where the lessor services the equipment. Office equipment such as computers and photocopiers often is obtained on this basis.

10. *Subordination.*

Not infrequently, the debt structure of an enterprise needing additional funds may be inadequate to support further senior or "prime" debt, but the corporation may be unable or may find it too costly to secure additional equity capital. Its need for additional long-term capital may be met by issuing an intermediate type of instrument known as a subordinated debenture which has appropriately been characterized as "debt that serves as equity". Subordinated obligations are unconditional promises to pay principal and interest at specified dates, and in that sense, do not differ from conventional debentures. However, by the subordination agreement, payment of principal is effectively deferred, either until senior debt has been paid (called complete subordination) or only in the event of liquidation, dissolution, bankruptcy or reorganization (sometimes called inchoate or insolvency subordination). Complete subordination is found more often in private subordination agreements than in publicly issued subordinated debt, which is more likely to be of the insolvency or inchoate variety. Both subordinated debt and senior debt are proved on a parity with each other. But, the subordination agreement entitles the senior creditor to receive the assets of the debtor which are distributable to the subordinated creditor, to the extent that the distributable assets otherwise fail to satisfy the senior claim.

Typically, the debentures will be made subordinate to existing or future "borrowed" funds from financial institutions or from public investors. However, if the obligation is an otherwise unconditional promise to pay at a fixed time, the inchoate subordinated debenture may be due (or pre-paid) at a point of time prior to the maturity date of senior debt, which may later find itself not fully paid off. Notwithstanding the possibility of such temporally prior payment, the subordinated debenture is effectively junior to "borrowed" funds, and therefore commands a higher interest rate. On the other hand it is debt, which ranks ahead of preferred stocks, and therefore will carry a lower interest rate than the dividend required for a preferred stock. Moreover, since the interest is deductible for federal income tax purposes, it may enjoy a substantial economic advantage over preferred stock as a means of obtaining long-term capital, as indicated infra, pp. 335 et seq.

For discussion of subordinated debt, see Calligar, Subordination Agreements, 70 Yale L.J. 376 (1961); Carlson, A Theory of Contractual Debt Subordination and Lien Priority, 38 Vand.L.Rev. 975 (1985); Everett, Subordinated Debt—Nature, Objectives and Enforcement, 44 Bost.U.L.Rev. 487 (1964); Johnson, Subordinated Debentures: Debt That Serves As Equity, 10 J.Fin. 1 (1955); Coogan, Kripke and Weiss, The Outer Fringes of Article 9: Subordination Agreements, Security Interests in Money and Deposits, Negative Pledge Clauses and Participation Agreements, 79 Harv.L.Rev. 229 (1965).

Subordination provisions are contained in Article 11 of the Model Simplified Indenture in Appendix C.

11. *Short Term Borrowing.*

Many firms require outside financing to handle short intervals in which cash inflows fall short of cash outflows. For example, a manufacturer may incur cash costs of production in advance of its principal selling season, causing a time lag between the time the expenses have to be paid and the time the sales revenues that cover them are realized. Short term borrowing, that is, borrowing for a term of less than one year, is the financial solution to the problem.

There are many modes of short term borrowing. The firm can arrange for a line of credit with a bank. This may involve a formal commitment of up to one year and commitment fee. The interest rate probably will float at a percentage over the prime rate. The borrower may have to keep a "compensating balance" at the bank. This is literally an account at the bank in which the borrower deposits cash flow. It will be a low interest or non interest bearing account, and thus will provide the bank additional return on the loan.

The line of credit may be secured by a "floating lien" on the borrower's accounts receivables or inventories. With a receivables financing arrangement, the bank will lend up to a stated percentage of the firm's receivables. On default, the bank collects the proceeds of the receivables, but has a deficiency claim against the borrower if the proceeds of the receivables fall short of the principal amount of the loan. Under a "factoring" arrangement, the receivable is discounted and sold to the lender. The lender collects the proceeds and has no recourse against the borrower. Other techniques are employed when inventory is used as security. See Brealey & Myers, Principals of Corporate Finance 801–806 (4th ed. 1991); Ross, Westerfield & Jordan, Fundamentals of Corporate Finance 556–559 (1991).

Large, highly rated firms requiring short term financing can issue commercial paper. This consists of promissory notes maturing within 270 days. Some commercial paper is issued through a handful of major dealers, who purchase it and resell it in a market dominated by institutional investors. The largest issuers bypass the dealers and sell to the institutions directly. Rates are lower than those prevailing on bank lines of credit. See Van Horne, Financial Management and Policy 477–478 (8th ed. 1989).

(B) INNOVATION

Substantial changes have occurred in the markets for debt securities during the last twenty years. These include the appearance of original issue junk bonds, floating rate debt, interest rate swaps, zero coupon bonds, and interest rate futures. For descriptions of these developments, see Appendix C, Section 1, infra.

(C) THE LAW OF CORPORATE TRUST AND
THE TRUST INDENTURE ACT OF 1939

(1) Corporate Trust

ELLIOTT ASSOCIATES v. J. HENRY SCHRODER
BANK & TRUST CO.

United States Court of Appeals, Second Circuit, 1988.
838 F.2d 66.

[The case involved an indenture which required the issuer to give
50 days notice to the Trustee of an issue of convertible debentures
before redeeming the debentures, "unless a shorter notice shall be
satisfactory to the [t]rustee." The provision was designed to give the
Trustee enough time to handle the mechanics of sending notice of
redemption to the debenture holders within the time prescribed for
such notice to them. If the Trustee required less time for the mechanics, it was authorized to waive—that is, shorten—the 50 day period
within which the issuer was to inform the Trustee of its proposed
redemption; the notice period for the bondholders would not be affected
by the waiver. In this case, if the Trustee did not shorten the 50 day
period, the redemption would have occurred on a date *after* an interest
payment was due on the debentures; on the other hand, if the Trustee
shortened the 50 day period, the issuer could redeem *before* the interest
payment date, and thus save itself one quarter's interest payment. The
Trustee shortened the notice period because the mechanics of the
particular redemption were simple and could easily be handled within a
shorter period. The notice provision, including the waiver clause, was
modeled on the American Bar Foundation Model Indenture, and it
apparently was the regular practice of Trustees to shorten the notice
period in circumstances in which they did not need the full period to
handle the mechanics. In a debenture holder's class action against the
Trustee for shortening the notice period, the Court of Appeals affirmed
the holding of the District Court that "the trustee's waiver did not
constitute a breach of any duty owed to the debenture holders—under
the indenture or otherwise—because a trustee's pre-default duties are
limited to those duties expressly provided in the indenture." The court
of Appeals (Altimari, J.) went on as follows.]

Thus, it is clear from the express terms of the Act and its legislative history that no implicit duties, such as those suggested by Elliott,
are imposed on the trustee to limit its pre-default conduct.

It is equally well-established under state common law that the
duties of an indenture trustee are strictly defined and limited to the
terms of the indenture, see, e.g., Green v. Title Guarantee & Trust Co.,
223 A.D. 12, 227 N.Y.S. 252 (1st Dep't), aff'd, 248 N.Y. 627, 162 N.E. 552
(1928); Hazzard v. Chase National Bank, 159 Misc. 57, 287 N.Y.S. 541
(Sup.Ct.N.Y.County 1936), aff'd, 257 A.D. 950, 14 N.Y.S.2d 147 (1st
Dep't), aff'd, 282 N.Y. 652, 26 N.E.2d 801, cert. denied, 311 U.S. 708
(1940), although the trustee must nevertheless refrain from engaging in

conflicts of interest. See United States Trust Co. v. First National City Bank, 57 A.D. 285, 394 N.Y.S.2d 653 (1st Dep't 1977), aff'd, 45 N.Y.2d 869, 410 N.Y.S.2d 680 (1978).

In view of the foregoing, it is no surprise that we have consistently rejected the imposition of additional duties on the trustee in light of the special relationship that the trustee already has with both the issuer and the debenture holders under the indenture. See Meckel v. Continental Resources Co., 758 F.2d 811, 816 (2d Cir.1985); In Re W.T. Grant Co., 699 F.2d 599, 612 (2d Cir.), cert. denied, 464 U.S. 822 (1983); Browning Debenture Holders' Comm. v. DASA Corp., 560 F.2d 1078, 1083 (2d Cir.1977). As we recognized in *Meckel,*

> [a]n indenture trustee is not subject to the ordinary trustee's duty of undivided loyalty. Unlike the ordinary trustee, who has historic common-law duties imposed beyond those in the trust agreement, *an indenture trustee is more like a stakeholder whose duties and obligations are exclusively defined by the terms of the indenture agreement.*

758 F.2d at 816 (citing Hazzard v. Chase National Bank, supra) (emphasis added). We therefore conclude that, so long as the trustee fulfills its obligations under the express terms of the indenture, it owes the debenture holders no additional, implicit pre-default duties or obligations except to avoid conflicts of interest.

* * *

* * * It is clear that Schroder complied with the letter and spirit of the indenture when it waived compliance with the full 50–day notice. Schroder was given the discretion to waive full notice under appropriate circumstances, and we find that it reasonably exercised that discretion.

To support its argument that Schroder was obligated to consider the impact of the waiver on the interest of the debenture holders, Elliott relies on our decision in Dabney v. Chase National Bank, 196 F.2d 668 (2d Cir.1952), as suppl'd, 201 F.2d 635 (2d Cir.), cert. dismissed per stipulation, 346 U.S. 863 (1953). *Dabney* provided that

> the duty of a trustee, not to profit at the possible expense of his beneficiary, is the most fundamental of the duties which he accepts when he becomes a trustee. It is part of his obligation to give his beneficiary his undivided loyalty, free from any conflicting personal interest; an obligation that has been nowhere more jealously and rigidly enforced than in New York where these indentures were executed. "The most fundamental duty owed by the trustee to the beneficiaries of the trust is the duty of loyalty. * * * In some relations the fiduciary element is more intense than in others; it is peculiarly intense in the case of a trust." We should be even disposed to say that without this duty there could be no trust at all.

196 F.2d at 670 (footnotes omitted) (citations omitted); see United States Trust Co. v. First National City Bank, 57 A.D.2d 285, 394 N.Y.S.2d 653, 660–61 (1st Dept.1977), aff'd 45 N.Y.2d 869, 410 N.Y.S.2d 680 (1978) (adopting *Dabney*). *Dabney* arose, however, in an entirely different factual context than the instant case.

The *Dabney* court examined the conduct of a trustee who knew or should have known that the company for whose bonds it served as trustee was insolvent. While possessing knowledge of the company's insolvency, the trustee proceeded to collect loan obligations from the company. The court held that the trustee's conduct in this regard constituted a breach of its obligation not to take an action which might disadvantage the debenture holders while providing itself with a financial advantage, i.e., the trustee engaged in a conflict of interest. See 196 F.2d at 673. Thus, while *Dabney* stands for the proposition that a trustee must refrain from engaging in conflicts of interest, it simply does not support the broader proposition that an implied fiduciary duty is imposed on a trustee to advance the financial interests of the debenture holders during the period prior to default. Because no evidence was offered in the instant case to suggest that Schroder benefitted, directly or indirectly, from its decision to waive the 50–day notice, and thus did not engage in a conflict of interest, it is clear that *Dabney* is inapposite to the instant appeal.

Model Simplified Indenture, Appendix C, Section 3
Article 7 (Duties of the trustee)

NOTE: CORPORATE TRUST

Notwithstanding the title "trustee," the norms determining the care and fidelity to which indenture trustees were held prior to enactment of the Trust Indenture Act of 1939 derived more from the terms of the Indenture (and its exculpatory clauses) than from any legally imposed fiduciary obligations. The dominance of the "contract" over the "trust" aspects of the indenture trustee's duties at common law, which is reflected in *Elliott Associates,* has not been uniformly accepted. Since Sturges v. Knapp, 31 Vt. 1 (1858), the leading early case, the decisions reveal wide variations in the conception of the trustee's role. Commentators have summarized the case law as follows:

> "Some courts have held that relationships between Trustees and investors are fiduciary. York v. Guaranty Trust Co. of New York, 143 F.2d 503 (2d Cir.1944), reversed on other grounds, 326 U.S. 99 (1945). Others have resolved controversies by drawing principles from the law of agency, regarding Trustees as agents for investors. First Trust Co. of Lincoln v. Carlsen, 129 Neb. 118, 261 N.W. 333 (1935). A third line of cases sees the indenture as essentially a contract, the terms of which exclusively define the rights and duties of Trustees. Hazzard v. Chase Nat. Bank of the City of New York, 159 Misc. 57, 287 N.Y.S. 541 (Sup.Ct.1936). The fourth approach is to regard Trustees as partaking of the characteristics of more than one relationship, such as those of both depositary and ordinary Trustees. Dunn v. Reading Trust Co., 121 F.2d 854 (3d Cir.1941).

"An examination of authorities in the corporate trust field reveals a similar divergence of opinion. Some regard Trustees solely as a fiduciary, subject to the rules of trust law in general. G.G. Bogert & G.T. Bogert, The Law of Trust and Trustee, 64–65 (2d ed. 1968); Palmer, Trusteeship under the Trust Indenture, 41 Colum.L.Rev. 193 (1941). Others see the indenture as an instrument *sui generis,* combining elements of various legal relationships, particularly contract and trust, but being identical with none. Kennedy, Corporate Trust Administration 1, note 9, at 18–25; Posner, The Trustee and the Trust Indenture: A Further Study, 46 Yale L.J. 737, 794 (1937).

"All Trustees may intend to act prudently and without negligence. Under the model provisions of the American Bar Foundation, however, these intentions are set forth in a contract even as to indentures not required to be qualified under the 1939 Act. Under the model provisions it becomes a moot question whether the nature of Trustees is defined by fiduciary principles or by the terms of the contract; the two are synonymous. * * * [American Bar Foundation, Sample Incorporating Indenture and Model Debenture Indenture Provisions, All Registered Issues (1967), American Bar Foundation, Commentaries on Indentures (1971); see also Model Simplified Indenture, 38 Bus.Law. 741 (1983)]. For a discussion of the history and purposes of the model provisions, see Rodgers, The Corporate Trust Indenture Project, 20 Bus.Law. 551 (1965); and Myers, The Model Indenture, 104 Trusts and Estates 690 (1965).

"Where any compromises of investors rights are undertaken to cure a default condition, Trustees are the recognized agents for the investors who are entitled to their informed judgment as to the fairness and feasibility of the proposed plan. Not infrequently such a plan originated from the obligor who is likely to attempt to enlist the support, or at least the acquiescence, of Trustees in the presentation of its proposal to investors. Such a situation poses a test to Trustees' prudence."

Campbell and Zack, Put a Bullet in the Poor Beast * * *. 32 Bus.Law. 1705, 1723, note 56 (1977).

For discussion of the operation of trust indentures, see R. Landau's 4th Edition of J. Kennedy and R. Landau, Corporate Trust Administration and Management (1992); Johnson, Default Administration of Corporate Trust Indentures, 15 St. Louis Union L.J. 203, 374, 509 (1970–71).

---

(2) The Trust Indenture Act of 1939

The Trust Indenture Act of 1939 (15 U.S.C. § 77aaa, et seq.) protects the bondholders by requiring that publicly issued bonds be issued pursuant to a trust indenture conforming to specific standards.

In addition to regulating the terms of trust indentures, the Act sets standards for the eligibility and qualification of trustees, including conflict of interest standards.

The manner in which the trustee's duties were defined and performed prior to the Act is described in the following excerpt from the Securities and Exchange Commission Report on the Study and Investigation of the Work, Activities, Personnel and Functions of Protective and Reorganization Committees, (hereinafter called the SEC Protective Committee Report) Part VI (1936) 2–6:

"Under modern trust indentures securing issues of corporate bonds, debentures and notes, important powers are vested in the trustee. The security holders themselves are generally widely scattered and their individual interest in the issue is likely to be small. The trustee, on the other hand, is usually a single bank. By virtue of the broad discretionary powers vested in it under the typical trust indenture it is in a position to take immediate action in a variety of ways to protect or enforce the security underlying the bonds, debentures and notes. But the security holders are rarely given any voice in formulation of policies which the trustee pursues; the trust indenture ordinarily does not require that they be consulted before the trustee acts. Hence the trustee generally need not be delayed or embarrassed by the necessity of consulting the security holders or of reconciling their divergent opinions and policies. Theoretically, the result should be beneficial to all concerned: to the security holder because of increased efficiency, expedition and economy; to the issuer because a trustee is a convenient legal device for conveying title, and because the presence of the trustee relieves the issuer of possible suits and supervision by many individual security holders.

* * *

"Both in law and in practice, this reliance of the security holder upon the trustee for protection of his investment is complete. * * *

* * *

"* * * But an examination of the provisions of modern trust indentures and their administration by trustees will show that this reliance is unfounded. It will show that typically the trustees do not exercise the elaborate powers which are the bondholders' only protection; that they have taken virtually all of the powers designed to protect the bondholders, but have rejected any duty to exercise them; and that they have shorn themselves of all responsibilities which normally trusteeship imports. The 'so-called trustee' which is left is merely a clerical agency and a formal instrument which can be used by the bondholders when and if enough of them combine as specified in the indenture.

* * *

"Nevertheless one basic, fundamental fact cannot be overlooked: the trustee is the only agency avowedly designed for the protection of security holders during the entire life of the security. Furthermore, under the modern trust indenture it alone is capable of effective action. The individual security holder is impotent when acting alone and can get together with his fellow security holders only at great labor and expense. It is likewise true that the common understanding of the lay investor is that the trustee is his *alter ego* in safeguarding his rights. On these facts the trustee should not be allowed, through indenture provisions never seen by the beneficiary, and which would not be understood if they were seen, to whittle away at the number of his express duties until they are practically non-existent, and to surround itself with exculpatory clauses which leave it harmless, despite inactivity or negligence.

"Bankers, lawyers and courts who have contributed to the evolution of the trustee under these indentures have given almost exclusive consideration and weight to the intent of the parties to the indenture. Accordingly, it has been assumed that the trustee could take or refuse to take practically any right or duty, power or privilege, which was agreeable to him and the issuer. It has also been assumed that this contract between trustee and issuer is binding on security holders on the theory that they acquire only such rights as the contract which these parties have made gives them. That is to say, the supposition is that the indenture evidences the intent of the security holders whose loans it secures. But that mutuality of intent which is assumed is in fact non-existent. To the extent that the indenture is the product of the borrower, the underwriter or the trustee, only their respective intents are reflected therein. It is no refutation of this to say that by voluntary purchase of his bonds, debentures or notes, the security holder accepts just so much as is given and no more. The individual purchaser of such security cannot normally bargain for special provisions. Nor can prospective buyers normally unite in anticipation of an issue, to exact desired terms. Inequality of bargaining power between investor and issuer is inherent in the very technique of security distribution. Yet the courts in their treatment of the trust indenture have proceeded on the same basis as the draftsmen and have concluded that the indenture is a contract which binds the security holders even though they had no part in its making. * * *

* * *

"The basic problem is to refashion the trust indenture for the purpose of according greater protection to investors. That entails prescribing certain minimum standard specifications for the conduct of trustee and issuer thereunder. As in the case of other contracts involving persons not capable nor in a position to protect themselves, the contents of the trust indenture can no longer be left to the conventions of the issuer, the trustee or the underwriter.

"This means that a more proper balance between the interests of investors and requirements of issuers can be had only by enlarging the definition of the trustee's duties in those cases where its failure to take swift and positive action leaves the investors without effective protection of their interests. The contrary desires of issuer, trustee and underwriter must be made to bow to the insistent demands of investors and of the public interest in such cases."

TRUST INDENTURE ACT OF 1939 AS AMENDED 1990

Section 315

(a) The indenture to be qualified shall automatically be deemed (unless it is expressly provided therein that any such provision is excluded) to provide that, prior to default (as such term is defined in such indenture)—

(1) the indenture trustee shall not be liable except for the performance of such duties as are specifically set out in such indenture; and

(2) the indenture trustee may conclusively rely, as to the truth of the statements and the correctness of the opinions expressed therein, in the absence of bad faith on the part of such trustee, upon certificates or opinions conforming to the requirements of the indenture;

but the indenture trustee shall examine the evidence furnished to it pursuant to section 314 to determine whether or not such evidence conforms to the requirements of the indenture.

(b) The indenture trustee shall give to the indenture security holders, in the manner and to the extent provided in subsection (c) of section 313, notice of all defaults known to the trustee, within ninety days after the occurrence thereof: Provided, That such indenture shall automatically be deemed (unless it is expressly provided therein that such provision is excluded) to provide that, except in the case of default in the payment of the principal of or interest on any indenture security, or in the payment of any sinking or purchase fund installment, the trustee shall be protected in withholding such notice if and so long as the board of directors, the executive committee, or a trust committee of directors and/or responsible officers, of the trustee in good faith determine that the withholding of such notice is in the interests of the indenture security holders.

(c) The indenture trustee shall exercise in case of default (as such term is defined in such indenture) such of the rights and powers vested in it by such indenture, and to use the same degree of care and skill in their exercise, as a prudent man would exercise or use under the circumstances in the conduct of his own affairs.

(d) The indenture to be qualified shall not contain any provisions relieving the indenture trustee from liability for its own negligent action, its own negligent failure to act, or its own willful misconduct, except that—

(1) such indenture shall automatically be deemed (unless it is expressly provided therein that any such provision is excluded) to contain the provisions authorized by paragraphs (1) and (2) of subsection (a) of this section;

(2) such indenture shall automatically be deemed (unless it is expressly provided therein that any such provision is excluded) to contain provisions protecting the indenture trustee from liability for any error of judgment made in good faith by a responsible officer or officers of such trustee, unless it shall be proved that such trustee was negligent in ascertaining the pertinent facts; and

(3) such indenture shall automatically be deemed (unless it is expressly provided therein that any such provision is excluded) to contain provisions protecting the indenture trustee with respect to any action taken or omitted to be taken by it in good faith in accordance with the direction of the holders of not less than a majority in principal amount of the indenture securities at the time outstanding (determined as provided in subsection (a) of section 316) relating to the time, method, and place of conducting any proceeding for any remedy available to such trustee, or exercising any trust or power conferred upon such trustee, under such indenture.

SENATE REPORT NO. 101–155

101st Congress, 1st Session, 1989.

TITLE IV—TRUST INDENTURE REFORM ACT OF 1939

C. *Conflicts of interest*

Title IV would make significant changes to the Act's method for determining conflict of interest. In the Act's present form, the existence of any of the nine relationships described in section 310(b) at any time indenture securities are outstanding requires the trustee either to remove the conflict or to resign within 90 days. This requirement is an outgrowth of the 1936 Report and reflected Congress' concern about instances of abuses involving relationship between the obligor and the trustee. However, each of the instances of abuse cited in the 1936 Report arose in situations in which there had been a default on the bonds. In the cases described in the Report, the trustees took steps to protect their own financial interests, instead of protecting the interests of the bondholders. There is no indication in the legislation history of the TIA that Congress was concerned about abuses by trustees prior to a default. In its memorandum in support of the legislation, the Commission has stated that, in the absence of default, the indenture trustee's duties are essentially ministerial, consisting largely of maintaining security holders' lists and transmitting interest payments to holders. The Commission has said that prior to default, there is no incentive for a trustee, even one with a technical conflict of interest, to withhold these services. Furthermore, there is no historical evidence showing a trustee in dereliction of its duties in the absence of default.

At the time of default, however, the character of the trustee's duties becomes critically different. At that time, inconsistent loyalties in the trustee, whether to holders of other securities of the obligor, to the obligor or to an underwriter, are unacceptable. Insistence on independence after a default is necessary to permit the indenture trustee to take vigorous action for the enforcement of rights under the indenture.

The Act's current conflicts standard, disqualifying a trustee from service if a conflict exists without regard to default or the character of the trustee's duties, may unnecessarily restrict an institutional trustee's ability both to act as trustee and to engage in other legitimate business activities. The most inhibiting example of this restriction is the Act's prohibition against qualifying a trustee if the proposed trustee or an affiliate has served as an underwriter of securities issued by the obligor within the previous three years. * * *

Title IV would recognize the differences in a trustee's duties before and after default by removing these and other restrictions on trustees pre-default conduct. This would be accomplished by making the event of default the time at which conflicts defined by section 310(b) become disabling relationships. To prevent evasion, grace and notice provisions within the indenture would be disregarded for the purpose of determining when a default occurs. In view of the added significance of the existence of a default, the legislation would require the obligor to certify annually whether a default exists under the indenture.

In a significant change from the existing statutory scheme, a creditor relationship would become a prohibited conflict of interest. The omission of the creditor relationship as a disqualification to serve as an indenture trustee has been the source of the criticism under the existing statute. No conflict could be clearer than that between the interests of a trustee with significant loans to a corporate borrower, for example, and that corporation's bondholders. On default, a trustee/creditor may become a competitor for funds of the corporation and, thus, in a relation adverse to the rights of the bondholders. Because most institutional trustees are commercial banks, a creditor relationship with the obligor is an ordinary occurrence. Under current practice, trustee-creditors customarily resign their offices at the time of default, even though resignation is not now compelled by the Act, in recognition that they may no longer be able to represent fairly both the claims of security holders under the indenture and their claims. This Title would accommodate all of these factors by making the creditor relationship a statutory conflict, but, as with other proposed conflict provisions, one that would disqualify the trustee until a default.

NOTES

1. The 1990 amendment of the Trust Indenture Act's conflict of interest provisions followed two decades of commentary. The commen-

tators challenged the political compromise made by Congress in 1939 for failure to include among the automatically prohibited conflicts of interest the occupancy of a dual role by a bank-Trustee—as indenture Trustee and as a direct lender to the corporation which is the obligor under the indenture. Proposed remedies for the conflict included suggestions of categorical prohibition of a dual role as well as less drastic suggestions such as forced subordination of the Trustee-lender's claims to the claims of the bondholders under the indenture. See Friedman, Updating the Trust Indenture Act, 7 Mich.J. of L.Ref. 329 (1974); Note, 24 UCLA L.Rev. 131 (1976); Johnson, The Forgotten Securities Statute: Problems in the Trust Indenture Act, 13 U.Tol. L.Rev. 92–114 (1981); Campbell and Zack, supra, pp. 149–150. For the view that no such remedies were needed see Smith, Case and Morison, The Trust Indenture Act of 1939 Needs No Conflict of Interest Revision, 35 Bus.Law. 161 (1979).

2. In addition to the requirements of the Trust Indenture Act, an indenture also may be governed by the listing requirements of a stock exchange. See New York Stock Exchange, Listed Company Manual § 603. There also may be additional proscriptions of state law. See, e.g., Coogan and Bok, The Impact of Article 9 of The Uniform Commercial Code on the Corporate Indenture, 69 Yale L.J. 203 (1959).

2. THE BONDHOLDER AND THE GOING CONCERN

(A) THE PROMISE TO PAY
1 DEWING, THE FINANCIAL POLICY OF CORPORATIONS
(5th Ed.1953) 172–174.

Attitude Toward Bonded Debt.—The intent of bonds is that they should be paid. The difference between bonded debt and bank loans is merely the period during which the loan shall remain outstanding. The bank expects the loan to be paid when due; the investor expects the bond to be paid when due. Yet, in view of the longer life of the bond, there has [sic] developed, through the years, two distinctly different attitudes which a corporation management may take with reference to long-term debt. In the one case the management may look upon corporate debt, and the bonds issued to represent it, as the evidence of borrowed capital; and inherent in the nature of borrowed capital is the obvious fact that the equivalent in money, once borrowed, must be returned at a later time. Debt, however distant its due date, must be paid. The other point of view ignores the strict legal implication of debt. A corporate management regards the issue of bonds as a device to give investors a favored participation in the fortunes of the enterprise in return for the willingness, on the part of investors, to accept a low fixed return. The explicit implications of the debt can be ignored; in the continuing success of the corporation, new debt can be incurred to refund the old and if the corporation is not a success, the debt holders can be paid only out of the dying body of the corporation. In the event of failure, the debt holders must take their fortunes along with the stockholders, except that they will be paid first out of the proceeds of liquidation or be given prior rights in any attempt to rehabilitate the business. The one point of view looks upon the bondholders as creditors beyond the pale of the corporation—outsiders who have lent capital which must be returned; the other point of view looks upon bondholders as joint heirs in the corporate fortunes— participants in the success or failure who have been given preferential rights in the common hazard.

* * *

* * * [I]n spite of much legislation intended to imperil the legal rights of the bondholder, the corporation manager must face the legal obligation that bonds should be paid at maturity unless the business is to become bankrupt or at best forced into a program of compulsory readjustments. Whether or not under recent ameliorative statutes, anything can be salvaged for the stockholder is an entirely different matter. This is true, whatever attitude a management may take toward its funded debt. The presence of funded debt implies, from the point of view of the corporation, either the finding of means to pay the maturing bonds or else a financial crisis with results inevitably inimical to the stockholders.

Model Simplified Indenture, Appendix C, Section 3
Exhibit A (Debenture form)

Section 1 of the debenture form sets out the issuer's promise to repay at interest. This promise is modified in sections 5, 6, 7 and 8. Section 6 is the provision for sinking fund payments—mandatory prepayments of principal by the issuer. Sections 5 and 7 provide for redemption rights—prepayments of principal at the issuer's option.

The following materials describe the dynamics of redemption and sinking fund provisions.

VAN HORNE, FINANCIAL MANAGEMENT AND POLICY
(9th ed. 1992) pp. 573–575.

CALL PROVISION AND REFUNDING

Most corporate bond issues provide for a call feature, which gives the corporation the option to buy back the bonds at a stated price before their maturity. Not all bond issues are callable; in times of low interest rates in particular, some corporations issue noncallable or "noncall-life" bonds as they are known. When a bond is callable, the call price usually is above the par value of the bond and decreases over time. A bond with 20 years to maturity might be callable at $110 ($1,100 per $1,000 face value bond) the next 2 years, $109 the following 2 years, and so on until the final 2 years, when it is callable at $101. Frequently, the call price in the first year is established at 1 year's interest above the face value of the bond. If the coupon rate is 14 percent, the initial call price may be $114 ($1,140 per $1,000 face value).

There are two types of call provision, according to when they can be exercised. The security may be immediately callable, which simply means that the instrument may be bought back by the issuer at the call price at any time. Rather than being immediately callable, the call provision may be deferred for a period of time. The most widely used deferred call periods are 5 years for public utility bonds and 10 years for industrial bonds. During this deferment period, the investor is protected from a call by the issuer. In recent years, virtually all issues of corporate bonds have involved a deferred call as opposed to an immediate call feature.

The call provision gives the company flexibility in its financing. If interest rates should decline significantly, it can call the bonds and refinance the issue at a lower interest cost. Thus, the company does not have to wait until the final maturity to refinance. In addition, the provision may be advantageous to the company if it finds any of the protective covenants in the bond indenture to be unduly restrictive. By calling the bonds before maturity, the company can eliminate these restrictions. Of course, if the issue is refinanced with bonds, similar restrictions may be imposed.

The deferment period protects the investor from early call. * * *

However, many bond issues can be redeemed provided the source of the redemption is not a refunding. It may be the issuer has excess liquidity, or it could sell assets. It might issue common stock or be acquired in a merger. As long as the funds used to redeem the bond issue do not come from a new one, the investor has no deferred call protection. * * * Investors had best read the fine print before investing to see the conditions under which redemption is possible. Many are surprised.

VALUE OF CALL PRIVILEGE

Although the call privilege is beneficial to the issuing corporation, it works to the detriment of investors. If interest rates fall and the bond issue is called, they can invest in other bonds only at a sacrifice in yield to maturity. Consequently, the call privilege usually does not come free to the borrower. Its cost, or value, is measured at the time of issuance by the difference in yield on the callable bond and the yield that would be necessary if the security were noncallable. This value is determined by supply and demand forces in the market for callable securities. In equilibrium, the value of the call feature will be just sufficient to bring the demand for callable securities by investors into balance with the supply of callable securities by borrowers. In the equilibrating process, both borrowers and investors are influenced by expectations of the future course of interest rates.

When interest rates are high and expected to fall, the call feature is likely to have significant value. Investors are unwilling to invest in callable bonds unless such bonds yield more than bonds that are noncallable, all other things the same. In other words, they must be compensated for assuming the risk that the bonds might be called. On the other hand, borrowers are willing to pay a premium in yield for the call privilege in the belief that yields will fall and that it will be advantageous to refund the bonds. In equilibrium, both the marginal borrower and the marginal investor will be indifferent to whether the bond issue is callable or noncallable.

When interest rates are low and expected to rise, the call privilege may have a negligible value in that the company might pay the same yield if there were no call privilege. For the privilege to have value, interest-rate expectations must make it seem possible that the issue will be called. If interest rates are very low and not expected to fall further, there is little probability that the bonds will be called. The key factor is that the borrower has to be able to refund the issue at a profit and that cannot be done unless interest rates drop significantly, for the issuer must pay the call price—which is usually at a premium above par value—as well as the flotation costs involved in refinancing. If there is no probability that the borrower can refund the issue at a profit, the call privilege is unlikely to have a value.

The announcement of a call may convey information to investors about the future of the company. If the call changes the capital structure of the company, for example, investors may react to the leverage change apart from whether or not the bond issue is refunded at a lower interest cost. * * * [T]he leverage change may convey information about an unanticipated change in the earnings prospects of the company—positive for increases in leverage and negative for decreases.

BRIGHAM AND GAPENSKI, FINANCIAL MANAGEMENT: THEORY AND PRACTICE
(6th Ed.1991), pp. 626–627.

A *sinking fund* is a provision that provides for the systematic retirement of a bond issue (or an issue of preferred stock). Typically, the sinking fund provision requires a firm to retire a portion of its bonds each year. On some occasions, the firm may be required to deposit money with a trustee, who invests the funds and then uses the accumulated sum to retire the entire bond issue when it matures. Sometimes the stipulated sinking fund payment is tied to sales or earnings of the current year, but usually it is a mandatory fixed amount. If it is mandatory, a failure to meet the sinking fund requirement causes the bond issue to be thrown into default, which may force the company into bankruptcy.

In most cases, the firm is given the right to handle the sinking fund in either of two ways:

     1. It may call in for redemption (at par value) a certain percentage of the bonds each year—for example, it might be able to call 2 percent of the total original amount of the issue at a price of $1,000 per bond. The bonds are numbered serially, and the ones called for redemption are determined by a lottery. * * *

     2. It may buy the required amount of bonds on the open market.

The firm will choose the least cost method. Therefore, if interest rates have risen, causing bond prices to fall, the company will elect to use the option of buying bonds in the open market at a discount. Otherwise, it will call them. Note that a call for sinking fund purposes is quite different from a refunding call * * *. A sinking fund call requires no call premium, but only a small percentage of the issue is callable in any one year.

Although the sinking fund is designed to protect the bondholders by assuring that the issue is retired in an orderly fashion, it must be recognized that the sinking fund will at times work to the detriment of bondholders. If, for example, the bond carries a 13 percent interest rate, and if yields on similar bonds have fallen to 9 percent, then the bond will sell above par. A sinking fund call at par would thus greatly disadvantage those bondholders whose bonds were called. On balance, however, securities that provide for a sinking fund and continuing redemption are regarded as being safer than bonds without sinking funds, so adding a sinking fund provision to a bond issue will lower the interest rate on the bond.

It has been suggested that call and sinking fund provisions help to solve the agency costs problems of debt—information asymmetry as between issuer and bondholder, and the issuer's incentive to invest in riskier projects or not to invest at all. See Kao and Wu, Sinking Funds and the Agency Costs of Corporate Debt, 25 Financial Rev. 95 (1990); Barnea, Haugen & Senbet, A Rationale for Debt Maturing Structure and Call Provisions in the Agency Theoretic Framework, 35 J. Finance 1223 (1980).

But, as the following case shows, these provisions also create agency costs of their own.

MORGAN STANLEY & CO., INC. v. ARCHER DANIELS MIDLAND CO.

United States District Court, Southern District of New York, 1983.
570 F.Supp. 1529.

SAND, District Judge.

This action * * * arises out of the planned redemption of $125 million in 16% Sinking Fund Debentures ("the Debentures") by the defendant ADM Midland Company ("ADM") scheduled to take place on Monday, August 1st, 1983. Morgan Stanley & Company, Inc. ("Morgan Stanley") brings this suit under § 10(b) of the Securities Exchange Act of 1934, * * * and other state and federal laws * * *. Morgan Stanley seeks a preliminary injunction enjoining ADM from consummating the redemption as planned * * *. Both parties * * * now cross-move for summary judgment.

FACTS

In May, 1981, Archer Daniels issued $125,000,000 of 16% Sinking Fund Debentures due May 15, 2011. * * * The Debentures state in relevant part:

The Debentures are subject to redemption upon not less than 30 nor more than 60 days' notice by mail, at any time, in whole or in part, at the election of the Company, at the following optional Redemption Price (expressed in percentages of the principal amount), together with accrued interest to the Redemption Date * * *, all as provided in the Indenture: If redeemed during the twelve-month period beginning May 15 of the years indicated:

Year	Percentage	Year	Percentage
1981	115.500%	1991	107.750%
1982	114.725	1992	106.975
1983	113.950	1993	106.200
1984	113.175	1994	105.425
1985	112.400	1995	104.650
1986	111.625	1996	103.875
1987	110.850	1997	103.100
1988	110.075	1998	102.325
1989	109.300	1999	101.550
1990	108.525	2000	100.775

and thereafter at 100%; provided, however, that prior to May 15, 1991, the Company may not redeem any of the Debentures pursuant to such option from the proceeds, or in anticipation, of the issuance of any indebtedness for money borrowed by or for the account of the Company or any Subsidiary (as defined in the Indenture) or from the proceeds, or in anticipation of a sale and leaseback transaction (as defined in Section 1008 of the Indenture), if, in either case, the interest cost or interest factor applicable thereto (calculated in accordance with generally accepted financial practice) shall be less than 16.08% per annum.

The May 12, 1981 Prospectus and the Indenture pursuant to which the Debentures were issued contain substantially similar language. The Moody's Bond Survey of April 27, 1981, in reviewing its rating of the Debentures, described the redemption provision in the following manner:

> "The 16% sinking fund debentures are nonrefundable with lower cost interest debt before April 15, 1991. Otherwise, they are callable in whole or in part at prices to be determined."

The proceeds of the Debenture offering were applied to the purchase of long-term government securities bearing rates of interest below 16.089%.

ADM raised money through public borrowing at interest rates less than 16.08% on at least two occasions subsequent to the issuance of the Debentures. On May 7, 1982, over a year before the announcement of the planned redemption, ADM borrowed $50,555,500 by the issuance of $400,000,000 face amount zero coupon debentures due 2002 and $100,-000,000 face amount zero coupon notes due 1992 (the "Zeroes"). The Zeroes bore an effective interest rate of less than 16.08%. On March 10, 1983, ADM raised an additional $86,400,000 by the issuance of $263,232,500 face amount Secured Trust Accrual Receipts, known as "Stars," through a wholly-owned subsidiary, Midland Stars Inc. The Stars carry an effective interest rate of less than 16.08%. The Stars were in the form of notes with varying maturities secured by government securities deposited by ADM with a trustee established for that purpose. There is significant dispute between the parties as to whether the Stars transaction should be treated as an issuance of debt or as a sale of government securities. We assume, for purposes of this motion, that the transaction resulted in the incurring of debt.

In the period since the issuance of the Debentures, ADM also raised money through two common stock offerings. Six million shares of common stock were issued by prospectus dated January 28, 1983, resulting in proceeds of $131,370,000. And by a prospectus supplement dated June 1, 1983, ADM raised an additional $15,450,000 by issuing 600,000 shares of common stock.

Morgan Stanley, the plaintiff in this action, bought $15,518,000 principal amount of the Debentures at $1,252.50 per $1,000 face amount on May 5, 1983, and $500,000 principal amount at $1,200 per $1,000 face amount on May 31, 1983. The next day, June 1, ADM announced that it was calling for the redemption of the 16% Sinking Fund Debentures, effective August 1, 1983. The direct source of funds was to be the two ADM common stock offerings of January and June, 1983. The proceeds of these offerings were delivered to the Indenture Trustee, Morgan Guaranty Trust Company, and deposited in a special account to be applied to the redemption. * * *

Prior to the announcement of the call for redemption, the Debentures were trading at a price in excess of the $1,139.50 call price. * * *

* * * [P]laintiff contends that the proposed redemption is barred by the express terms of the call provisions of the Debenture and the Indenture Agreement * * *. The plaintiff's claim is founded on the language contained in the Debenture and Trust Indenture that states that the company may not redeem the Debentures "from the proceeds, or in anticipation, of the issuance of any indebtedness * * * if * * * the interest cost or interest factor * * * [is] less than 16.08% per annum." Plaintiff points to the $86,400,000 raised by the Stars transaction within 90 days of the June 1 redemption announcement, and the $50,555,500 raised by the Zeroes transaction in May, 1982—both at interest rates below 16.08%—as proof that the redemption is being funded, at least indirectly, from the proceeds of borrowing in violation of the Debentures and Indenture agreement. The fact that ADM raised sufficient funds to redeem the Debentures entirely through the issuance of common stock is, according to the plaintiffs, an irrelevant "juggling of funds" used to circumvent the protections afforded investors by the redemption provisions of the Debenture. Plaintiff would have the Court interpret the provision as barring redemption during any period when the issuer has borrowing [sic] at a rate lower than that prescribed by the Debentures, regardless of whether the direct source of the funds is the issuance of equity, the sale of assets, or merely cash on hand.

* * *

DISCUSSION

* * *

* * * Even if we were to assume, *arguendo,* that Morgan Stanley had made out a claim for irreparable harm, it has failed to meet the additional criteria necessary for the issuance of a preliminary injunction.

With respect to the likelihood of success on the merits, defendant's interpretation of the redemption provision seems at least as likely to be in accord with the language of the Debentures, the Indenture, and the available authorities than is the view proffered by the plaintiff. We first note that the one court to directly address this issue chose to construe the language in the manner set forth in this action by the defendant. Franklin Life Insurance Co. v. Commonwealth Edison Co., 451 F.Supp. 602 (S.D.Ill.1978), aff'd per curiam on the opinion below, 598 F.2d 1109 (7th Cir.), rehearing and rehearing en banc denied, id., cert. denied, 444 U.S. 900 (1979). While plaintiff is correct in noting that this Circuit is not bound by this decision, and while this case can no doubt be distinguished factually on a number of grounds, none of which we deem to be of major significance, *Franklin* is nevertheless persuasive authority in support of defendant's position.

Defendant's view of the redemption language is also arguably supported by The American Bar Foundation's Commentaries on Model Debenture Indenture Provisions (1977), from which the boilerplate language in question was apparently taken verbatim. In discussing the various types of available redemption provisions, the Commentaries state:

> [I]nstead of an absolute restriction [on redemption], the parties may agree that the borrower may not redeem with funds borrowed at an interest rate lower than the interest rate in the debentures. *Such an arrangement recognizes that funds for redemption may become available from other than borrowing,* but correspondingly recognizes that the debenture holder is entitled to be protected for a while against redemption if interest rates fall and the borrower can borrow funds at a lower rate to pay off the debentures.

Id. at 477 (emphasis added). We read this comment as pointing to the *source* of funds as the dispositive factor in determining the availability of redemption to the issuer—the position advanced by defendant ADM.

Finally, we view the redemption language itself as supporting defendant's position. The redemption provision in the Indenture and the Debentures begins with the broad statement that the Debentures are "subject to redemption * * * at any time, in whole or in part, at the election of the company, at the following optional Redemption Price * * *." Following this language is a table of decreasing redemption percentages keyed to the year in which the redemption occurs. This broad language is then followed by the narrowing provision "provided, however * * * the Company may not redeem any of the Debentures pursuant to such option from the proceeds, or in anticipation, of the issuance of any indebtedness" borrowed at rates less than that paid on the Debentures.

While the "plain meaning" of this language is not entirely clear with respect to the question presented in this case, we think the restrictive phrasing of the redemption provision, together with its placement after broad language allowing redemption in all other cases at the election of the company, supports defendant's more restrictive reading.

Morgan Stanley asserts that defendant's view would afford bondholders no protection against redemption through lower-cost borrowing and would result in great uncertainty among holders of bonds containing similar provisions. In its view, the "plain meaning" of the redemption bondholders of these bonds and the investment community generally, is that the issuer may not redeem when it is contemporaneously engaging in lower-cost borrowing, regardless of the source of the funds for redemption. At the same time, however, the plaintiff does not contend that redemption through equity funding is prohibited for the life of the redemption restriction once the issuer borrows funds at a lower interest rate subsequent to the Debenture's issuance. On the contrary, plaintiff concedes that the legality of the redemption transaction would depend on a factual inquiry into the magnitude of the borrowing relative to the size of the contemplated equity-funded redemption and its proximity in time relative to the date the redemption was to take place. Thus, a $100 million redemption two years after a $1 million short-term debt issue might be allowable, while the same redemption six months after a $20 million long-term debt issue might not be allowable.

This case-by-case approach is problematic in a number of respects. First, it appears keyed to the subjective expectations of the bondholders; if it *appears* that the redemption is funded through lower-cost borrowing, based on the Company's recent or prospective borrowing history, the redemption is deemed unlawful. The approach thus reads a subjective element into what presumably should be an objective determination based on the language appearing in the bond agreement. Second, and most important, this approach would likely cause greater uncertainty among bondholders than a strict "source" rule such as that adopted in *Franklin,* supra.

Plaintiff's fear that bondholders would be left "unprotected" by adoption of the "source" rule also appears rather overstated. The rule proposed by defendant does not, as plaintiff suggests, entail a virtual emasculation of the refunding restrictions. An issuer contemplating redemption would still be required to fund such redemption from a source other than lower-cost borrowing, such as reserves, the sale of assets, or the proceeds of a common stock issue. Bondholders would thus be protected against the type of continuous short-term refunding of debt in times of plummeting interest rates that the language was apparently intended to prohibit. See *Franklin,* supra, 451 F.Supp. at 609. Moreover, this is not an instance where protections against premature redemption are wholly absent from the Debenture. On the contrary, the Debentures and the Indenture explicitly provide for early redemption expressed in declining percentages of the principal amount, depending on the year the redemption is effected.

* * *

For all of the above reasons, and on the record now before us, plaintiff's application for preliminary injunctive relief is hereby denied.

ON MOTION FOR SUMMARY JUDGMENT

SAND, District Judge.

* * * [W]e now grant the motion of [ADM] for partial summary judgment on the contract claims * * *.

Contract Claims

The plaintiff's contract claims arise out of alleged violations of state contract law. Section 113 of the Indenture provides that the Indenture and the Debentures shall be governed by New York law. Under New York law, the terms of the Debentures constitute a contract between ADM and the holders of the Debentures, including Morgan Stanley. * * * The relevant contract terms are printed on the Debentures and, by incorporation, in the Indenture.[2]

---

2. ADM argues that, because Morgan Stanley holds less than 25% of the outstanding Debentures, it has no standing under § 507(2) of the Indenture to maintain its contract claims. Section 507(2) provides that no Debenture holder shall

We note as an initial matter that where, as here, the contract language in dispute is a "boilerplate" provision found in numerous debentures and indenture agreements, the desire to give such language a consistent, uniform interpretation requires that the Court construe the language as a matter of law. See Sharon Steel Corp. v. Chase Manhattan Bank, N.A., 691 F.2d 1039, 1048–49 (2d Cir.1982) (applying New York law), cert. denied, ___ U.S. ___, 103 S.Ct. 1253, 75 L.Ed.2d 482 (1983). * * *

In Franklin Life Insurance Co. v. Commonwealth Edison Co., 451 F.Supp. 602 (S.D.Ill.1978), aff'd per curiam on the opinion below, 598 F.2d 1109 (7th Cir.), rehearing and rehearing en banc denied, id., cert. denied, 444 U.S. 900 (1979), the district court found, with respect to language nearly identical to that now before us, that an early redemption of preferred stock was lawful where funded directly from the proceeds of a common stock offering.

Morgan Stanley argues, however, that *Franklin* was incorrectly decided and should therefore be limited to its facts. We find any attempt to distinguish *Franklin* on its facts to be wholly unpersuasive. * * *

* * *

Morgan Stanley contends * * * that *Franklin* was wrongly decided, as a matter of law, and that a fresh examination of the redemption language in light of the applicable New York cases would lead us to reject the "source" rule. In this regard, Morgan Stanley suggests a number of universal axioms of contract construction intended to guide us in construing the redemption language as a matter of first impression. * * *

We find these well-accepted and universal principles of contract construction singularly unhelpful in construing the contract language before us. * * *

Not only do the rules of contract construction provide little aid on the facts before us, but we find the equities in this action to be more or less in equilibrium. Morgan Stanley now argues, no doubt in good faith, that the redemption is unlawful under the Indenture. Nevertheless, as we noted in our prior opinion, Morgan Stanley employees were fully aware of the uncertain legal status of an early call at the time they purchased the ADM Debentures. To speak of upsetting Morgan's "settled expectations" would thus be rather misleading under the circumstances. By the same token, however, it is also clear that ADM

have the right to institute suit with respect to the Indenture unless the holders of not less than 25% of the outstanding Debentures first request the Trustee to institute proceedings in its own name. Such limitations on the rights of bondholders to seek legal relief are not enforceable, however, where the face of the bond does not give adequate notice of the restriction. Fried- man v. Airlift International, Inc., 44 A.D.2d 459, 355 N.Y.S.2d 613 (1st Dep't 1974). The ADM Debentures do not explicitly mention the restrictions contained in § 507. In any event, we view the intervention in this action by the Indenture Trustee, Morgan Guaranty, as a waiver of § 507 to the extent applicable.

had no expectations with respect to the availability of an early redemption call until the idea was first suggested by Merrill Lynch.

Because we find equitable rules of contract construction so unhelpful on the facts of this case, the decision in *Franklin* takes on added importance. * * * Moreover, we note that the decision in *Franklin* preceded the drafting of the ADM Indenture by several years. We must assume, therefore, that the decision was readily available to bond counsel for all parties. * * * While *Franklin* was decided under Illinois law and is therefore not binding on the New York courts, we cannot ignore the fact that it was the single existing authority on this issue, and was decided on the basis of universal contract principles. Under these circumstances, it was predictable that *Franklin* would affect any subsequent decision under New York law. * * *

Finally, we note that to cast aside the holding in *Franklin* would, in effect, result in the very situation the Second Circuit sought to avoid in *Sharon Steel, supra.* In that case, the Court warned that allowing juries to construe boilerplate language as they saw fit would likely result in intolerable uncertainty in the capital markets. To avoid such an outcome, the Court found that the interpretation of boilerplate should be left to the Court as a matter of law. *Sharon Steel,* supra, 691 F.2d at 1048. While the Court in *Sharon Steel* was addressing the issue of varying interpretations by juries rather than by the courts, this distinction does not diminish the uncertainty that would result were we to reject the holding in *Franklin.* Given the paramount interest in uniformly construing boilerplate provisions, and for all the other reasons stated above and in our prior Opinion, we chose to follow the holding in *Franklin.*[4]

4. We note in this regard that the "source" rule adopted in *Franklin* in no sense constitutes a license to violate the refunding provision. The court is still required to make a finding of the true source of the proceeds for redemption. Where the facts indicate that the proposed redemption was indirectly funded by the proceeds of anticipated debt borrowed at a prohibited interest rate, such redemption would be barred regardless of the name of the account from which the funds were withdrawn. Thus, a different case would be before us if ADM, contemporaneously with the redemption, issued new, lower-cost debt and used the proceeds of such debt to repurchase the stock issued in the first instance to finance the original redemption. On those facts, the redemption could arguably be said to have been indirectly funded through the proceeds of anticipated lower-cost debt, since ADM would be in virtually the same financial posture after the transaction as it was before the redemption— except that the new debt would be carried at a lower interest rate. Here, by contrast, there is no allegation that ADM intends to repurchase the common stock it issued to fund the redemption. The issuance of stock, with its concomitant effect on the company's debt/equity ratio, is exactly the type of substantive financial transaction the proceeds of which may be used for early redemption.

Moreover, we fail to see how, on the facts of this case, the redemption could be argued to be a refunding from the proceeds of lower-cost debt. The Zeroes transaction occurred over a year before the redemption and appears completely unrelated to it. The proceeds of that transaction were used to purchase government securities that remain in ADM's portfolio. The Stars transaction, while closer in time, similarly is not fairly viewed as the source of the redemption, given that the proceeds of that transaction were applied directly to reducing ADM's short-term debt. To view the redemption as having been funded *indirectly* "from the proceeds" of the Stars transaction would require us to ignore the *direct* source of the refunding, the two ADM common stock issues.

NOTE: REFUNDING CASES

Harris v. Union Electric Co., 622 S.W.2d 239 (Mo.Ct.App.1981), concerned a refunding limitation similar to that in *Morgan Stanley v. Archer Daniels Midland.* Here the refunding limitation was set out in the supplemental indenture governing an issue of bonds, and contained a parenthetical excepting redemptions from a "maintenance fund." This maintenance fund had been set up under earlier supplemental indentures and was intended to force a partial redemption to the extent that the issuer failed to devote fifteen percent of any year's earnings to property maintenance. Unfortunately for the bondholders, the earlier supplemental indentures limited neither the source of the money that went into the maintenance fund nor the occasion for its use. The issuer sold a new issue of bonds at a lower coupon rate, put the proceeds in the maintenance fund and redeemed the original bonds at face value out of the maintenance fund. It thereby avoided not only the refunding limitation but a redemption premium also provided for in the supplemental indenture. The court found the language in the supplemental indenture to be unambiguous on its face and ruled for the issuer. The court made this ruling despite the fact that contextual evidence, including the subjective understanding of officers of the issuer, showed that no one involved with the transactions foresaw that the maintenance fund could be used to circumvent the refunding limitation.

John Hancock Mutual Life Insurance Co. v. Carolina Power & Light Co., 717 F.2d 664 (2d Cir.1983) presented a different version of the same question raised in *Harris* and reached the same result as the Missouri court.

Shenandoah Life Insurance Co. v. Valero Energy Corp., 1988 WL 63491 (Del.Ch.), took up another variation on the theme. There the issuer did a debt financing at a lower rate simultaneously with an equity financing. The proceeds of the equity financing were segregated and applied to the redemption of an issue of $16\frac{3}{4}\%$ debt subject to a six year bar of refunding "by the application * * * indirectly of [borrowed] moneys." The court held that the fact that the new equity was integrated with an equally large debt financing did not cause the redemption "indirectly" to be funded with cheaper debt. Chancellor Allen read the word "indirectly" narrowly: "the inclusion of that phrase is intended to reach situations in which the underlying economic reality of the completed transaction is the functional equivalent of a direct loan for the purposes of effectuating a redemption and nothing more."

The Union Electric bondholders did successfully pursue a federal antifraud remedy. In **Harris v. Union Electric Co.,** 787 F.2d 355 (8th Cir.1986), failure to make the fragility of call protection clear in a prospectus was held to underpin liability for a violation of Rule 10b–5. The prospectus was materially misleading, said the court, because it gave the impression that the bonds were noncallable at a lower rate for 10 years. Even the list of redemption premiums in the prospectus was misleading—since the issuer always could pay down the issue without premium through the maintenance fund the list represented prices that never would be paid.

———

NOTE: BONDHOLDER REMEDIES UPON DEFAULT

Model Simplified Indenture, Appendix C, Section 3

Article 6 (Defaults and remedies)

These provisions determine the bondholders' rights in the event of the issuer's failure to perform one or more of its promises to pay.

These provisions make distinctions between payment defaults, section 6.01(1) and (2), and failure to perform other promises in the indenture, such as business covenants, section 6.01(3). First, under section 6.02, in order for acceleration of the bonds to follow as the result of the "default," the default must be an "event of default," and, under the last paragraph of section 6.01, covenant defaults are not events of default unless the issuer has failed to cure the default 60 days after receipt of notice from the trustee.

Second, payment defaults may be the subject of a direct lawsuit by the bondholder, pursuant to section 6.07. This section is declaratory of a bondholder right provided for in section 316(b) of the Trust Indenture Act. See infra p. 236. But this unwaivable provision for a direct bondholder action goes only to separate skipped payments of interest. It does not carry into a unilateral bondholder right to accelerate in respect of a payment default and sue for the entire principal amount of the bond. See section 6.02. Direct bondholder actions in respect of defaults other than payment defaults are subject to the "no action" clause in section 6.06. This requires that, as a prerequisite to a direct action, the plaintiff bondholder (1) assemble a group of the holders of 25 percent of the outstanding bonds, (2) make a group demand on the trustee that the trustee pursue the action, and (3) that the trustee fail to comply with the bondholders' demand. Such "no action" clauses are enforceable, although they are strictly construed. See Cruden v. Bank of New York, 957 F.2d 961 (2d Cir.1992); Morgan Stanley v. Archer Daniels Midland, supra p. 182 n. 2. Courts also excuse compliance with the provision in the rare case where the bondholder can make out a showing of trustee incompetence, whether by virtue of negligence or a conflict of interest. See, e.g., Rabinowitz v. Kaiser–Frazer Corp., 111 N.Y.S.2d 539 (Supr.Ct.1952) (compliance excused where trustee loans to issuer facilitated the transaction that caused the event of default). In addition, no action clauses do not block bondholder suits against the trustee itself. Cruden v. Bank of New York, supra.

(B) PROMISES THAT PROTECT THE VALUE OF THE PROMISE TO PAY

(1) Business Covenants

(a) Debt Contracts and Debtor Misbehavior

Once a loan closes, the borrower's expectations are substantially fulfilled. It has possession of the capital and the discretion to invest it. The lender expects repayment at interest and has a contract right to this effect. But, having parted with the capital, it ultimately must rely on the borrower's conduct of its business for the fulfillment of its expectations. Much can happen to impair the lender's position during the life of the loan. Business reverses can diminish the borrower's ability to pay. In addition, the borrower can make business decisions that have the effect of making payment of the loan less likely even as they have the effect of enhancing the positions of its stockholders and managers. Obviously, the best protection against these risks is full security. The unsecured long term lender foregoes this protection, exchanging a higher rate of return for additional risks of nonperformance. These additional risks can be made more manageable if provisions respecting the course and conduct of the borrower's business are included in the debt contract. Such promises cannot assure business success. But they can give the lender the option of calling a default in the event of business reverses or opportunistic conduct by the borrower.

The option of calling a default does not assure payment either. But, as the cases that follow in this part will show, it has a value nevertheless. The borrower in default has a choice—it can cure the default, seek the protection of a bankruptcy proceeding, or make the lender an offer of a substitute performance in exchange for a waiver. If the default occurs when the borrower is not in a situation of extreme distress, the borrower will not necessarily see a bankruptcy proceeding as in its best interests. Accordingly, in the right case, the right to call a default can be a substantial guarantee of performance. In distress situations, performance of the contract will not be a practical possibility. But, depending on the circumstances, contract rights can enhance the lender's position in the event of a recapitalization outside of bankruptcy.

Fischel, The Economics of Lender Liability, 99 Yale L.J. 131, 134–135 (1989), describes the interrelated problems of business failure and debtor misbehavior:

"The effect of exogenous events such as dramatic changes in market or industry conditions (i.e., a recession or a sharp decline in the price of oil) is clear. These events can significantly affect the probability of default and the likely recovery if a default occurs.

"The effect of debtor misbehavior is also straightforward. Debtors have an incentive to engage in several types of misbehavior once a loan has been made.

"(1) *Asset withdrawal.* Once a lender contributes capital to a firm, the borrower has an incentive to withdraw assets from the firm by, for example, declaring a dividend for the amount of the loan. This harmful incentive structure is exacerbated in situations involving extensions of credit to firms with limited liability;

"(2) *Risky investment policy.* The existence of debt creates an incentive for borrowers to invest in riskier projects. This incentive arises because the lender bears the downside risk if the project turns out poorly, but he does not share in the upside potential if the project turns out well. In other words, before the loan was made, the borrower bore the costs of risky investments that failed; now these costs are shared with the lender. Before and after the extension of credit, however, the borrower alone obtains the benefit from risky investments that succeed.

"This incentive to invest in risky projects is a direct function of the amount the borrower has at risk—the size of the equity cushion. In the extreme case in which the value of the firm equals the value of outstanding debt, the firm has nothing to lose and everything to gain by adopting a 'shoot the moon' investment strategy;

"(3) *Claim dilution.* The value of debt is a function, *inter alia,* of the amount of other debt. The greater the amount of debt of the same or higher seniority, the lower the value of debt. Thus a borrower can reduce the value of outstanding debt by issuing more debt and thereby diluting the claims of existing creditors; and

"(4) *Underinvestment.* The creation of debt imposes an additional claimant on the firm's income stream. This additional claim can result in the borrower failing to invest in a profitable investment project if too much of the benefit from the project will accrue to the lender. In this event, the value of outstanding debt will again be reduced because of the borrower's actions.

"At first blush, the two types of events that can adversely affect lenders after credit has been extended—exogenous events and debtor misbehavior—seem completely unrelated. In reality, however, there is a close relationship between the two. As exogenous events adversely affect the borrower, the probability of debtor misbehavior increases. This point can best be illustrated by a simple numerical example: Consider a hypothetical company with capital of $200, consisting of equal $100 contributions of debt and equity. Now assume that the company suffers a $100 decline in value as a result of a recession. The remaining $100 of value is just enough to pay off the lender.

"Although debtor misbehavior did not cause the $100 decline in value, this decline will have a profound effect on the borrower's incentives. For example, as discussed above, the borrower's incentive to invest in risky projects increases as the value of the debt falls, because the borrower now has less of its own funds at risk. Returning to the example, the borrower would not have been likely to have accepted a project with a negative net present value of less than $100 when the firm was worth $200 because the borrower would bear the loss. However, once the value of the firm has fallen to $100, the borrower might be willing to invest in a project with some upside potential even if its expected value is negative because the loss is borne by the lender. Furthermore, if the value of the firm falls below $100, the borrower may even reject some positive net present value projects due to the underinvestment problem. Because the benefits of the investment in this situation go to the lender, the borrower has no incentive to proceed.

"Similarly, the probability that the declaration of a dividend or an increase in the amount of outstanding debt will hurt existing creditors is a function of the value of the borrower not represented by debt. The lower the equity cushion, the greater the probability that these actions will harm existing creditors. Thus, if the equity cushion is eroded or eliminated entirely, as in the above example by adverse market or industry developments, actions such as withdrawal of assets will impose greater harm on existing creditors."

See also Gertner and Scharfstein, A Theory of Workouts and the Effects of Reorganization Law, 46 J. Finance 1189 (1991); Smith and Warner, On Financial Contracting, An Analysis of Bond Covenants, 7 J. Financial Econ. 117 (1979). For a game theoretic analysis of debt contracting under the threat of debtor misbehavior see Ayres, The Possibility of Inefficient Corporate Contracts, 60 U.Cinn.L.Rev. 387 (1991).

———

As Fischel states, the unsecured lender finds its ultimate protection in the borrower's "equity cushion." Business covenants are designed to keep the equity cushion in place and make it available to generate payments on the loan. In so doing, they regulate, directly and indirectly, each of the several types of borrower misbehavior Fischel describes. There follows a description of the principal business covenants.

(1) *Restriction on dividends and other payments to shareholders*

This covenant is directed both to the problems of "asset withdrawal" and "underinvestment" identified by Fischel. It restricts transfers of corporate assets to shareholders, whether by way of a dividend or by redemption or repurchase of outstanding stock. The restriction typically operates by reference to the borrower's level of profits: It sets a base date, and permits dividends and redemptions only to the extent of cumulative earnings after that date, and then only up to a given percentage or amount. Credit might be given for the proceeds of the sale of new equity.

(2) *Restriction on additional debt*

This covenant is one of the two principal means of protecting the lender against claim dilution. Lenders are best served neither by a blanket permission for new debt nor a categorical prohibition of new debt. On the one hand, to the extent that additional debt is issued, the number of claims on the equity cushion increase. The risk of insolvency likewise increases, and the lender's position in a bankruptcy proceeding is proportionately impaired. On other hand, additional debt can benefit existing lenders by providing the borrower with additional capital that permits its business to grow and thereby make existing lenders more secure. Debt covenants, therefore, tend to regulate rather than prohibit the incurrence of new debt, allowing it when justified by the economic state of the enterprise. These covenants tend to set out ratios of total debt to net assets and ratios of earnings available to pay debt to debt service costs, and permit new debt to be incurred to the extent that the tests are met.

Debt covenants also tend to restrict transactions that lenders view as the functional equivalent of borrowing, such as financial leases and the guaranties of the obligations of others. Debt covenants also can make distinctions between short term borrowing and long term debt and between subordinated and unsubordinated debt. For example, the borrowing window can be made larger for new debt issues subordinated to the issue covered by the covenant. The cumulation of factors and precise regulations can result in a very complicated exercise in contract drafting.

Note that by regulating the conditions in which the borrower can incur additional debt, the lender indirectly discourages risky investment policy—risky debt and risky investments tend to be concomitants. Note also that the greater the covenant's complication and the tighter its restriction, the more likely that the borrower may request a waiver of the covenant so as to be able to pursue a legitimate investment opportunity. Accordingly, strict debt covenants tend to appear only where a later waiver is feasible, as in a private placement.

(3) *Restriction on mortgages and liens*

This covenant is the other principal barrier to claim dilution. Unsecured creditors look only to the borrower's unencumbered property—if the property is subject to mortgages, security interests and other liens, it is not available to pay their claims on a liquidation scenario. Secured creditors, moreover, are accorded priority in a bankruptcy reorganization to the extent of the value of the property covered by their liens. Contracts governing unsecured debt, accordingly, tend to restrict the creation of new liens. There are two modes of drafting such a restriction. The first is a direct and sweeping prohibition, subject to negotiated exceptions. Exceptions are most likely to be granted for purchase money security interests. This rigid drafting technique is more likely to be employed in a private placement than in a public offering. The second is the "negative pledge" covenant. This comparatively simple provision states that no lien will be created unless that lien also equally and ratably secures the debentures or notes covered by the provision. This version tends to show up in indentures covering public issues.

Sale and leaseback transactions, which take assets presently owned by the borrower and available to pay the lender and transfer title to them to a third party, are the functional equivalents of liens from the lender's point of view. Separate sale and leaseback prohibitions are common in all debt contracts.

(4) *Restriction on mergers and sales of assets*

A merger with another operating company can work to the detriment of the lender, even though the surviving corporation is a larger firm. Claim dilution can follow if the merger partner is highly leveraged. If the partner has a riskier line of business, the merger accomplishes a detrimental shift to a risky investment policy. Similar problems can follow from the sale of all or substantially all of the borrower's assets. In contrast, a merger into or sale of assets to a shell acquisition subsidiary organized by a conservatively managed firm may be a matter of indifference or benefit to the lender. Covenants dealing with prospective mergers and acquisitions range from very loose to very strict. With public issues, mergers and sales of all or substantially all assets may be permitted subject to the assumption of the debt by the surviving or purchasing corporation. Private placements are likely to impose tighter constraints—a transaction will be permitted only so long as the survivor or purchaser can demonstrate compliance with every covenant and test in the debt contract. There are other available modes of regulating these transactions. For example, they may be permitted subject to a right of redemption in the bondholders.

Piecemeal sales of assets present problems of asset withdrawal and risky investment policy. Any sale of producing assets raises a question respecting the adequacy and reinvestment of the proceeds. Moreover, a firm that sells off pieces of itself over a period of time and reinvests the proceeds in a different line of business can effect a change to a riskier asset base. Covenants regulating these transactions may put a book value or fair value cap on the aggregate annual permissible amount of assets sold, along with a fair value standard to govern the terms of permitted sales.

(5) *Restriction on investments*

There does not appear to be such a thing as a meaningful affirmative promise to invest capital competitively at an acceptable risk level. But a lender can impose a prohibition against some varieties of risky investment. Investment covenants prohibit liquid investments (for example, portfolios of common stocks or futures contracts) other than safe, short term investments such as treasury securities or certificates of deposit. They thereby indirectly require the borrower to devote its capital to its going concern or to new going concerns. Note that such a covenant, taken together with a dividend covenant, also indirectly addresses the underinvestment problem. The investment covenant restricts the set of available investments for the borrower's free cash flow, while the dividend covenant blocks the payment of the free cash flow to the shareholders. Given spare cash and no attractive reinvestment opportunities in the going concern, the prepayment of the bonds is left as the best use of the free capital.

Managers are especially likely to resist restriction of their discretion to make investments. Accordingly, these covenants are likely to appear only in private placement transactions in which the lender has substantial bargaining power.

(6) *Maintenance of financial condition*

Some lenders impose financial maintenance tests. These tend to set a minimum level of net worth (assets minus liabilities), either as a dollar amount or a ratio. A net worth test establishes the smallest equity cushion that the lender must tolerate, and functions as an early warning of distress. If the borrower fails to meet the test, it must either raise equity capital or go into default. Tests of working capital (current assets minus current liabilities) also appear, either as dollar amounts or ratios. Here failure to meet the test gives the lender an early warning of a possible liquidity crisis.

(7) *Maintenance of business and property*

These covenants contain affirmative promises to stay in the same line of business and keep property insured and in good repair.

(8) *Reporting provisions*

Recall that, but for the mandatory disclosure system of the federal securities laws, a holder of common stock seeking basic financial information respecting the issuer has the burden under state law to make an inspection demand, and then perfect in court a right to go to the firm's offices to extract information. In contrast, debt contracts customarily facilitate ongoing monitoring by the holders by requiring the borrower to provide periodic financial reports to the lender, along with certification that the borrower is complying with the contract's terms. This provision also may stipulate that the borrower follow generally accepted accounting principles, have an annual audit conducted by a national accounting firm and, in the case of a private placement, send the lender a copy of the annual auditor's letter. In a private placement, an inspection right also may be included.

Smith and Warner, On Financial Contracting: An Analysis of Bond Covenants, 7 J. Financial Econ. 117 (1979), views the range of business covenants through the lens of agency cost analysis. They conclude (p. 153):

"Our analysis * * * sheds some light on the relative costs of the alternative types of restrictions which can be written into the debt contract. We conclude that production/investment policy is very expensive to monitor. Stockholder use (or misuse) of production/investment policy frequently involves not some explicit act, but the failure to take a certain action (e.g., failure to accept a positive net present value project). It is expensive even to ascertain when the firm's production/investment policy is not optimal, since such a determination depends on magnitudes which are difficult to observe. The high monitoring costs which would be associated with restrictive production/investment covenants, including the potential legal costs associated with bondholder control, dictate that few production/investment decisions will be contractually proscribed. For the firm's owners to go very far in directly restricting the firm's production/investment policy would be inefficient.

"On the other hand, we conclude that dividend policy and financing policy involve lower monitoring costs. Stockholder use of these policies to 'hurt' bondholders involves acts (e.g., the sale of a large bond issue) which are readily observable. Because they are cheaper to monitor, it is efficient to restrict production/investment policy by writing dividend and financing policy covenants in a way which helps assure that stockholders will act to maximize the value of the firm."

For further reading on business covenants, see American Bar Foundation, Commentaries on the Model Debenture Indenture Provisions (1971); R. Nassberg, The Lender's Handbook (1986); Lloyd, Financial Covenants in Commercial Loan Documentation: Uses and Limitations, 58 Tenn.L.Rev. 335 (1991); Berlin and Loeys, Bond Covenants and Delegated Monitoring, 43 J.Finance 397 (1988); McDaniel, Are Negative Pledge Clauses in Public Debt Issues Obsolete? 39 Bus.Law. 867 (1983); Smith and Warner, supra; Simpson, The Drafting of Loan Agreements: A Borrower's Viewpoint, 28 Bus.Law. 1161 (1973).

———

(b) Judicial Interpretation of Covenants

SHARON STEEL CORP. v. THE CHASE MANHATTAN BANK, N.A.

United States Court of Appeals for the Second Circuit, 1982.
691 F.2d 1039, cert. denied, 460 U.S. 1012, 103 S.Ct. 1253, 75 L.Ed.2d 482 (1983).

Before FEINBERG, Chief Judge, and NEWMAN and WINTER, Circuit Judges.

RALPH K. WINTER, Circuit Judge:

[UV Industries, Inc. ("UV") had around $155 million of long term debt outstanding pursuant to five separate indentures. Each indenture provided for redemption at a premium prior to maturity, and contained a "successor obligor" provision allowing UV to assign its debt to a corporate successor which purchased "all or substantially all" of UV's assets.

[UV operated three lines of business: (1) Federal Electric, which generated 61 percent of UV's operating revenues and 81 percent of its profits, and constituted 44 percent of the book value of UV's assets; (2) oil and gas properties, which generated 2 percent of its revenues and 6 percent of its profits, and constituted 5 percent of its book value; and (3) Mueller Brass, which generated 38 percent of its revenues and 13 percent of its profits and constituted 34 percent of the book value of its assets.

[In early 1979 UV submitted to its shareholders a plan to sell Federal for $345 million cash and then, within 12 months, sell the rest of its assets and liquidate. UV's shareholders approved the plan and the sale of federal was consummated by the end of March. UV contracted to sell the oil and gas properties for $135 million cash in July. UV made an $18 per share dividend to its shareholders in April, after agreeing with the trustees of the bonds to set aside $155 million to pay down the bonds. Then, in November, UV changed course. It entered into an asset purchase agreement with Sharon Steel Corp. pursuant to which Sharon would purchase the rest of UV's assets, which by then constituted Mueller Brass and $322 million in cash, in exchange for $107 million cash and $411 million face amount of Sharon's subordinated debentures.

[The sale to Sharon included an agreement that Sharon assume all of UV's liabilities *including* the obligations outstanding under the five indentures. Sharon and UV took the position that Sharon was purchasing "all or substantially all" of UV's assets within the meaning of the successor obligor clauses. Sharon and UV executed the supplemental indentures provided for in the successor obligor clauses and tendered them to the indenture trustees. The trustees refused to sign, and instead issued notices of default and brought actions for redemption of the debentures.]

1. *The Successor Obligor Clauses*

Sharon Steel argues that Judge Werker erred in not submitting to the jury issues going to the meaning of the successor obligor clauses. We disagree.

Successor obligor clauses are "boilerplate" or contractual provisions which are standard in a certain genre of contracts. Successor obligor clauses are thus found in virtually all indentures. Such boilerplate must be distinguished from contractual provisions which are peculiar to a particular indenture and must be given a consistent, uniform interpretation. As the American Bar Foundation Commentaries on Indentures (1971) ("*Commentaries*") state:

Since there is seldom any difference in the intended meaning [boilerplate] provisions are susceptible of standardized expression. The use of standardized language can result in a better and quicker understanding of those provisions and a substantial saving of time not only for the draftsman but also for the parties and all others who must comply with or refer to the indenture, including governmental bodies whose approval or authorization of the issuance of the securities is required by law.

Id.

Boilerplate provisions are thus not the consequence of the relationship of particular borrowers and lenders and do not depend upon particularized intentions of the parties to an indenture. There are no adjudicative facts relating to the parties to the litigation for a jury to find and the meaning of boilerplate provisions is, therefore, a matter of law rather than fact.

Moreover, uniformity in interpretation is important to the efficiency of capital markets. As the Fifth Circuit has stated:

A large degree of uniformity in the language of debenture indentures is essential to the effective functioning of the financial markets: uniformity of the indentures that govern competing debenture issues is what makes it possible meaningfully to compare one debenture issue with another, focusing only on the business provisions of the issue (such as the interest rate, the maturity date, the redemption and sinking fund provisions in the conversion rate) and the economic conditions of the issuer, without being misled by peculiarities in the underlying instruments.

Broad v. Rockwell International Corp., 642 F.2d 929, 943 (5th Cir.), cert. denied, 454 U.S. 965 (1981). Whereas participants in the capital market can adjust their affairs according to a uniform interpretation, whether it be correct or not as an initial proposition, the creation of enduring uncertainties as to the meaning of boilerplate provisions would decrease the value of all debenture issues and greatly impair the efficient working of capital markets. Such uncertainties would vastly increase the risks and, therefore, the costs of borrowing with no offsetting benefits either in the capital market or in the administration of justice. Just such uncertainties would be created if interpretation of boilerplate provisions were submitted to juries sitting in every judicial district in the nation.

Sharon also argues that Judge Werker erred in rejecting evidence of custom and usage and practical construction as to the meaning of the successor obligor clauses. While custom or usage might in some circumstances create a fact question as to the interpretation of boilerplate provisions, the evidence actually offered by Sharon simply did not tend to prove a relevant custom or usage. * * *

We turn now to the meaning of the successor obligor clauses. Interpretation of indenture provisions is a matter of basic contract law. As the *Commentaries* at 2 state:

The second fundamental characteristic of long term debt financing is that the rights of holders of the debt securities are largely a matter of contract. There is no governing body of statutory or common law that protects the holder of unsecured debt securities against harmful acts by the debtor except in the most extreme situations * * * [T]he debt securityholder can do nothing to protect himself against actions of the borrower which jeopardize its ability to pay the debt unless he * * * establishes his rights through contractual provisions set forth in the * * * indenture.

Contract language is thus the starting point in the search for meaning and Sharon argues strenuously that the language of the successor obligor clauses clearly permits its assumption of UV's public debt. Sharon's argument is a masterpiece of simplicity: on November 26, 1979, it bought everything UV owned; therefore, the transaction was a "sale" of "all" UV's "assets." * * *

Sharon's literalist approach simply proves too much. If proceeds from earlier piecemeal sales are "assets," then UV continued to own "all" its "assets" even after the Sharon transaction since the proceeds of that transaction, including the $107 million cash for cash "sale," went into the UV treasury. If the language is to be given the "literal" meaning attributed to it by Sharon, therefore, UV's "assets" were not "sold" on November 26 and the ensuing liquidation requires the redemption of the debentures by UV. Sharon's literal approach is thus self-defeating.

* * *

Sharon argues that the sole purpose of successor obligor clauses is to leave the borrower free to merge, liquidate or to sell its assets in order to enter a wholly new business free of public debt and that they are not intended to offer any protection to lenders. On their face, however, they seem designed to protect lenders as well by assuring a degree of continuity of assets. Thus, a borrower which sells all its assets does not have an option to continue holding the debt. It must either assign the debt or pay it off. * * * The single reported decision construing a successor obligor clause, B.S.F. Company v. Philadelphia National Bank, 42 Del.Ch. 106, 204 A.2d 746 (1964), clearly held that one purpose of the clause was to insure that the principal operating assets of a borrower are available for satisfaction of the debt.

Sharon seeks to rebut such inferences by arguing that a number of transactions which seriously dilute the assets of a company are perfectly permissible under such clauses. For example, UV might merge with, or sell its assets to, a company which has a miniscule equity base and is debt heavy. They argue from these examples that the successor obligor clause was not intended to protect borrowers from the kind of transaction in which UV and Sharon engaged.

We disagree. In fact, a substantial degree of protection against diluting transactions exists for the lender. Lenders can rely, for example, on the self-interest of equityholders for protection against mergers which result in a firm with a substantially greater danger of insolvency. So far as the sale of assets to such a firm is concerned, that can occur but substantial protection exists even there since the more debt heavy the purchaser, the less likely it is that the seller's equityholders would accept anything but cash for the assets. A sale to a truly crippled firm is thus unlikely given the self-interest of the equityholders. After a sale, moreover, the lenders would continue to have the protection of the original assets. * * *

Sharon poses hypotheticals closer to home in the hope of demonstrating that successor obligor clauses protect only borrowers: *e.g.*, a transaction involving a sale of Federal and the oil and gas properties in the regular course of UV's business followed by an $18 per share distribution to shareholders after which the assets are sold to Sharon and Sharon assumes the indenture obligations. To the extent that a decision to sell off some properties is not part of an overall scheme to liquidate and is made in the regular course of business it is considerably different from a plan of piecemeal liquidation, whether or not followed by independent and subsequent decisions to sell off the rest. A sale in the absence of a plan to liquidate is undertaken because the directors expect the sale to strengthen the corporation as a going concern. A plan of liquidation, however, may be undertaken solely because of the financial needs and opportunities or the tax status of the major shareholders. In the latter case, relatively quick sales may be at low prices or may break up profitable asset combinations, thus drastically increasing the lender's risks if the last sale assigns the public debt. In this case, for example, tax considerations compelled completion of the liquidation within 12 months. The fact that piecemeal sales in the regular course of business are permitted thus does not demonstrate that successor obligor clauses apply to piecemeal liquidations, allowing the buyer last in time to assume the entire public debt.

We hold, therefore, that protection for borrowers as well as for lenders may be fairly inferred from the nature of successor obligor clauses. The former are enabled to sell entire businesses and liquidate, to consolidate or merge with another corporation, or to liquidate their operating assets and enter a new field free of the public debt. Lenders, on the other hand, are assured a degree of continuity of assets.

Where contractual language seems designed to protect the interests of both parties and where conflicting interpretations are argued, the contract should be construed to sacrifice the principal interests of each party as little as possible. An interpretation which sacrifices a major interest of one of the parties while furthering only a marginal interest of the other should be rejected in favor of an interpretation which sacrifices marginal interests of both parties in order to protect their major concerns.

Of the contending positions, we believe that of the Indenture Trustees and Debentureholders best accommodates the principal interests of corporate borrowers and their lenders. Even if the UV/Sharon transaction is held not to be covered by the successor obligor clauses, borrowers are free to merge, consolidate or dispose of the operating assets of the business. Accepting Sharon's position, however, would severely impair the interests of lenders. Sharon's view would allow a borrowing corporation to engage in a piecemeal sale of assets, with concurrent liquidating dividends to that point at which the asset restrictions of an indenture prohibited further distribution. A sale of "all or substantially all" of the remaining assets could then be consummated, a new debtor substituted, and the liquidation of the borrower completed. * * * We hold, therefore, that boilerplate successor obligor clauses do not permit assignment of the public debt to another party in the course of a liquidation unless "all or substantially all" of the assets of the company at the time the plan of liquidation is determined upon are transferred to a single purchaser.

* * *

Since we do not regard the question in this case as even close, we need not determine how the substantiality of corporate assets is to be measured, what percentage meets the "all or substantially all" test or what role a jury might play in determining those issues. Even when the liquid assets (other than proceeds from the sale of Federal and the oil and gas properties) are aggregated with the operating properties, the transfer to Sharon accounted for only 51% of the total book value of UV's assets. In no sense, therefore, are they "all or substantially all" of those assets. The successor obligor clauses are, therefore, not applicable. UV is thus in default on the indentures and the debentures are due and payable. For that reason, we need not reach the question whether the April Document was breached by UV.

* * *

3. *The Redemption Premium*

Judge Werker held that the redemption premium under the indentures need not be paid by UV. His reasoning was essentially that UV defaulted under the indenture agreement and that the default provisions provide for acceleration rather than a redemption premium. We do not agree. The acceleration provisions of the indentures are explicitly permissive and not exclusive of other remedies. We see no bar, therefore, to the Indenture Trustees seeking specific performance of the redemption provisions where the debtor causes the debentures to become due and payable by its voluntary actions.

This is not a case in which a debtor finds itself unable to make required payments. The default here stemmed from the plan of voluntary liquidation approved on March 26, 1979, followed by the unsuccessful attempt to invoke the successor obligor clauses. The purpose of a redemption premium is to put a price upon the voluntary satisfaction of a debt before the date of maturity. While such premiums may seem largely irrelevant for commercial purposes in times of high interest rates, they nevertheless are part of the contract and would apply in a voluntary liquidation which included plans for payment and satisfaction of the public debt. We believe it undermines the plain purpose of the redemption provisions to allow a liquidating debtor to avoid their terms simply by failing to take the steps necessary to redeem the debentures, thereby creating a default. We hold, therefore, that the redemption premium must be paid. See Harnickell v. Omaha Water

Co., 146 A.D. 693, 131 N.Y.S. 489 (1st Dep't 1911), aff'd, 208 N.Y. 520, 101 N.E. 1104 (1913).

* * *

CONCLUSION

We affirm Judge Werker's dismissal of Sharon's amended complaint and award of judgment to the Indenture Trustees and Debentureholders on their claim that the debentures are due and payable. We reverse his dismissal of the claim for payment of the redemption premium * * *.

NOTE: CONTRACT INTERPRETATION

1. *Sharon Steel* is one of a number of recent cases in which indenture trustees brought covenants to bear in attempting to protect bondholders against rapid-fire transactions in the market for corporate assets. The courts' approaches to interpretation in these cases have varied. Compare Alleco, Inc. v. IBJ Schroder Bank & Trust Co., 745 F.Supp. 1467 (D.Minn.1989) (shell corporation organized by party controlling target (that had sold off all its operating assets and held only liquid assets) incurs debt to finance successful tender offer for stock of target and merges shell into target causing target to assume shell's debt; dividend covenant in target debt contract held to apply to subsequent repayment of shell's debt even though as a formal matter the target had not paid a dividend or redeemed any stock), with Harris Trust and Savings Bank v. E–II Holdings, Inc., 722 F.Supp. 429 (N.D.Ill. 1989) (literal reading of indenture reporting provisions blocks trustee demand for additional information necessary to determine whether dividend paid to new control party to provide funds to repay acquisition indebtedness amounted to event of default).

2. Consider each of the following "rules" or "maxims" of contract interpretation. How does each come to bear in the context of the interpretation of a trust indenture? Is the interpretation of a note agreement governing a private placement between a single borrower and a single lender a substantively different exercise?

*The court should protect the expectations of the parties.

*The court should interpret contract language in accordance with its generally prevailing meaning. Restatement (Second) Contracts, § 203(3)(a).

*An interpretation giving effect to all terms of an agreement should prevail over an interpretation leaving a part with an unreasonable or ineffective meaning. Restatement (Second) Contracts, § 202(1)– (2).

*The contract should be interpreted against the drafter.

*The court should give effect to the plain meaning of the provision.

*Contract provisions should be interpreted in light of all the circumstances.

*Where the parties attach different meanings to a provision, it is interpreted in accordance with the meaning attached by one of them, if at the time the contract was entered into, that party had no reason to know of a different meaning attached by the other party, and the other had reason to know of the meaning attached by the first party. Restatement (Second) Contracts, § 201(2)(b).

For discussion, see Riger, The Trust Indenture as Bargained Contract: The Persistence of Myth, 16 J.Corp.L. 211 (1991); Bratton, The Interpretation of Contracts Governing Corporate Debt Relationships, 5 Cardozo L.Rev. 371 (1984).

————

(2) Bonds Without Covenants and High Leverage Restructuring

(a) The Disappearance and Reappearance of Covenants

BRATTON, CORPORATE DEBT RELATIONSHIPS: LEGAL THEORY IN A TIME OF RESTRUCTURING
1989 Duke.L.J. 135–142.*

Restructurings disrupt the postwar pattern of relations among management, equity, and long-term debt interests. They realign power, causing management and debt to suffer while equity gains.

Recapitalizations are the means to the end of restructuring. They come in several transactional modes: friendly mergers, hostile tender offers followed by mergers, leveraged buyouts, and defensive recapitalizations. Whatever the mode, recapitalizations entail the payment of a bonus to equityholders, financed by substantial borrowing. The new borrowing injures existing bondholders: in effect, it transfers value from their securities to the equity's premium. Beginning in 1985, when large corporations began to undergo restructurings, these wealth transfers made bondholder protection a prominent legal policy question for the first time since the Depression era. Another aspect of the restructuring movement, the incidence of higher corporate debt-equity ratios, also has prompted new policy discussions. * * *

A. *Bondholder Wealth Transfers*

* * *

* [Ed. Note] Some footnotes are omitted. References in the footnotes to McDaniel, Bondholders I and McDaniel, Bondholders II are, respectively, to McDaniel, Bondholders and Corporate Governance, 41 Bus. Law. 413 (1986) and McDaniel, Bondholders and Stockholders, 13 J.Corp.L. 205 (1988). These pathbreaking articles urge fiduciary protection for bondholders against strategic behavior by management or equity.

1. *Restructuring and Bondholder Wealth Transfers.*

a. Incidence and magnitude. Restructurings began when players in the capital markets lost their tolerance for corporate investment policies keyed to management's preferences.[187] Restructuring transactions undo the effects of suboptimal investment practices, returning suboptimally invested capital to equityholders.

High debt-equity ratios serve the restructuring objective in several ways. New borrowing finances the initial return of capital to the equity. Given an antecedent capital structure shaped by risk-averse managers, new borrowing also raises the debt-equity ratio and lowers the corporation's overall cost of capital because of savings from the tax deductibility of interest payments.[189] The higher debt-equity ratio encourages management discipline in the future, because interest payments on debt are mandatory, while dividends on stock are discretionary. The heavy debt load forces management periodically to return substantial capital to the investment community. No extra capital is left for suboptimal investment.[190]

The "wealth transfers," therefore, are incident to a wider shift in corporate debt-equity relations. The transfers occur prior to or at the start of a restructuring. They victimize the holders of the restructured corporation's long-term, unsecured debt securities. To use agency language, leverage incident to restructuring increases these debtholders' agency costs. To use plainer language, the preexisting debt becomes riskier and falls in price as the issuer's debt-equity ratio rises.

Restructuring first jeopardized the bonds of large corporations in 1985. It brought sudden price drops and concomitant downgradings of formerly high grade bonds. The Unocal and Phillips Petroleum transactions were the most notorious. In each case, the restructured company's bond rating fell from AA to BBB. In another famous case, an issuer's announcement of a one time special dividend as a defensive

---

187. Restructurings dissolve the implicit agreement between management and the capital markets concerning corporate investment power. The investment community used to accept management's pursuit of corporate "growth" passively. Managers were left alone because they had special expertise in investment policy. This idea held despite the fact that managers' personal needs for institutional security often led to investments at risk levels lower than stockholders' interests would dictate. Even if a corporation's management made manifestly suboptimal investments, the cost-effective stockholder response was to sell, rather than to attempt to challenge management directly in order to force changed policies.

189. See I.R.C. § 163(a) (West 1988).

190. * * * In Jensen's parlance, the substitution of interest payments for dividends "bonds" the promise to pay out future cash flows. Of course, the higher debt-equity ratio results in higher agency costs for debt. * * *

Ironically, heavy indebtedness might make management less risk-averse. Managers anxious to lessen risk by paying down debt may be enticed by the big pay off held out by a risky investment. Coffee, Stockholders Versus Managers: The Strain in the Corporate Web, 85 Mich.L.Rev. 1, 62, 65–66 (1986) [hereinafter Coffee, Corporate Web]. In Coffee's parlance, a higher debt-equity ratio pushes up managers' "aspiration level." Id. at 65.

The "management-disciplinary" explanation of the restructuring movement is a reduction. It suffices for present purposes, subject to the caveat that the real world is more complex. See Coffee, The Uncertain Case for Takeover Reform: An Essay on Stockholders, Stakeholders and Bust–Ups, 1988 Wis.L.Rev. 435, 441–43 [hereinafter Coffee, Takeover Reform].

move caused its bonds to drop $200 in value.[192] Even rumors of a tender offer can cause bonds to fall. The phenomenon continues unabated, as the food company restructurings of fall 1988 demonstrate.

Since 1985, downgradings because of the risk of restructuring—called "event risk" by the bond-rating agencies—have become commonplace. Bond analysis no longer considers only corporate fundamentals and the business cycle. In 1986, downgrades at Standard & Poor's exceeded upgrades by a two-to-one ratio; one-third of these downgrades related to restructurings. In the same year the record number of industrial bond downgrades exceeded upgrades by 4.2 to 1. By mid–1987, the median grade for an industrial bond was a speculative BB; in 1982 the median grade had been A.

Different observers make different assessments of the wealth transfers' magnitude. If one focuses only on the bonds affected and their prices before and after the events in question, the amounts transferred seem impressive. Bond analysts point out that a one-grade drop from AA to A causes a 5% to 6% drop in market value; a drop from A to B causes a 15% to 20% drop in market value. The Unocal bondholders alone lost the substantial sum of $170 million. If one shifts perspective to look at each restructuring transaction as a whole, however, the quantum of bondholder injury seems less impressive. The face value of two issues of Unocal bonds declined only 4.2% and 3% respectively. At the same time, the Unocal stockholders received $2.8 billion. Economic studies generalize on this lesson. [They recognize significant bondholder losses in individual cases, but stress that the losses are on average so small that stockholder gains outstrip them.] The studies conclude that the wealth transfer effect, while a real benefit to equityholders in restructurings, is not enough of a boon to drive the wider restructuring movement.[204]

---

192. McDaniel, Bondholders II, supra note 10, at 209 (Colt Industries). The wealth transfer effect occurs as an incident of each of the major modes of restructuring: leveraged buyouts (Macy's announcement of a leveraged buyout caused its stock to go up $16 and its notes to drop 3 points), hostile tender offers followed by mergers (Unocal's and Phillips Petroleum's bond ratings fell from AA to BBB after firms took on debt to deter corporate raiders), defensive restructurings (CBS's AA-rated bonds dropped 4 points upon the announcement of an exchange of new debt for old equity in response to Ted Turner's tender offer), friendly mergers (the merger of ABC and Capital Cities caused the credit ratings of both to drop; 11.75% debentures of Capital Cities traded at 85 basis points above Treasury bills prior to the merger and traded at 125 basis points above Treasury bills after the merger). See Farrell, supra note 191, at 113; Prokesch, Merger Wave: How Stock and Bonds Fare, N.Y. Times, Jan. 7, 1986, at A1, col. 1. * * *

204. * * *

The financial economics literature includes a large number of studies on the wealth effects of mergers and tender offers. So far as bondholder-to-stockholder wealth transfers are concerned, these studies test two opposing models. One is the agency-costs model. Under this model, the stockholders of an acquiring firm have an incentive to increase the variability of their own firm's cash flow in ways that injure its bondholders. * * * The opposing model, the "coinsurance" theory, holds that the merger of two firms could create a portfolio effect that would reduce the variability of the firms' combined cash flows, transferring wealth to the bondholders. See Dennis & McConnell, Corporate Mergers and Security Returns, 16 J.Fin.Econ. 143, 179 (1986). The studies show that stockholders of both acquired and acquiring corporations tend to gain in mergers, but that bondholders of both types of corporations tend neither to gain nor to lose. See, e.g.,

b. The facilitating conditions: the disappearance of business covenants and the limited force of reputation. Bondholders would not have suffered wealth transfers if the contracts governing their bonds had contained restrictions against additional debt. With covenants prohibiting the transactions, those in control would have had to "take out" the bondholders by prepaying the old debt in order to take on new debt. Unfortunately for bondholders, by 1985 trust indentures governing the long-term unsecured debt of large corporations usually did not contain these restrictions.

This practice reflected a change from earlier contracting patterns, a change unnoticed in legal and economic commentary on debt contracts until the wealth transfers highlighted it.[206] For most of this century, contracts governing long-term debt restricted subsequent substantial indebtedness, along with subsequent dividends and liens.[207] Until recently, investors considered these provisions central to the bargain. They served as a substitute for security, protecting debtholders' interest in issuer earning streams from issuer misbehavior. In financial economic terms, the provisions insulated holders from agency costs. The degree of constraint depended on each issuer's credit standing. Better credits with access to public bond markets faced fewer restraints than smaller issuers making private placements. The best credits issued debt with no restraints other than a debt covenant.[209]

This pattern continued until the mid–1970s. Since then, new public, unsecured debt of large industrials has tended to contain only a "negative pledge" against additional secured debt and a covenant prohibiting the sale and leaseback of issuer assets. Debt and dividend covenants have disappeared, surviving to restrain only smaller issuers.[211]

---

id. at 184–85 (study showing that preferred stockholders of acquiring companies and preferred stockholders and senior securityholders of acquired companies benefit, with minimal effect on other equity interests). Because these studies cover merger activity only through 1980, they should not be read to contradict the conclusions of empirical studies of the restructuring movement that began in 1985. * * *

206. Morey McDaniel has pointed out this change in Bondholders I, supra note 10, at 424–26.

207. See, e.g., ABF Commentaries, * * * at 369–71, 402–04 (debt contracts nearly always contain debt and dividend covenants); * * * cf. A. Berle & G. Means, The Modern Corporation and Private Property 122–23 (rev. ed. 1968) (discussing dividend covenants).

209. Simpson, The Drafting of Loan Agreements: A Borrower's Viewpoint, 28 Bus.Law. 1161, 1161–62 (1973). Smith and Warner's study of 87 public issues registered between January 1974 and December 1975 shows that 90.8% had some prohibi-

tion on the issuance of additional debt. Interestingly, only 23% of the issues contained dividend restrictions. Smith & Warner, * * *, at 122–23. Evidently, the standard picture had already begun to change in 1974–1975.

211. McDaniel surveyed the debt contracts of Fortune's 100 largest industrials in 1984. He found that negative pledge and sale-leaseback covenants were ubiquitous. Of the 92 companies reported as having one or more senior issues, one or more subordinated issues, or both, only 28% of the issues continued debt covenants. Of the newer issues, only 16% contained a debt covenant. Dividend restrictions appeared in 35% of the issues, but in only 20% of the newer issues. McDaniel, Bondholders I, supra note 10, at 425–26.

Malitz surveyed all long-term senior nonconvertible debentures issued between 1960 and 1980 and described in Moody's Bond Survey or Moody's Industrial Manual. Of these, 49% contained no debt covenant. Malitz found a negative correlation

When large restructurings commenced, the affected bondholders lacked defenses, but did not seem to know their exposure. Apparently everyone, except for the handful of lawyers and underwriters directly involved and perhaps a few traders and portfolio managers, thought that debt contracts still took the traditional form, or at least supplied some minimal protection.

The covenants had disappeared because they seemed unnecessary. Before 1985, economic prosperity combined with management's dominant governance position to make large corporations look reliable as unsecured borrowers.[213] Whatever the turns of the business cycle, management seemed unlikely to seek to benefit stockholders by abusing bondholders. Management wanted growth and security—goals best realized with conservative leverage and retained-earnings financing. Moreover, managers had passed up opportunities to injure bondholders even when debt contracts posed no obstacle. According to the conventional wisdom, such opportunistic conduct would lead creditors in future financings to impose unfavorable terms, the costs of which would outweigh the benefits of present wealth transfers.[214]

The assumption that management held an unassailable position[215] ultimately led to questions about the need for covenants. Covenants became a subject of bargaining.[216] Management characterized covenants as an unnecessary and costly backstop for the bondholders' position.[217] Since the costs were real and the bondholders confident, management won the point.

between the presence of debt covenants and the size of the issuer. Malitz, * * * at 21–24.

213. Between the Depression and the late 1970s, very little law relating to bonds was made, presumably because bond contracting patterns, investors' expectations, and institutional practices interrelated harmoniously. Reported cases tended to concern the conversion privilege, and even these cases did not arise often until the merger movement heated up in the late 1970s and early 1980s. See generally Bratton, Convertible Bonds, * * * at 671, 693–98. The other factor that led to friction—and gave management incentives for opportunism—was the rise in interest rates after 1978. See, e.g., Morgan Stanley & Co. v. Archer Daniels Midland Co., 570 F.Supp. 1529 (S.D.N.Y.1983) (dispute stemming from redemption of high coupon debt); cf. Sharon Steel Corp. v. Chase Manhattan Bank, N.A., 691 F.2d 1039 (2d Cir. 1982), cert. denied, 460 U.S. 1012 (1983) (low coupon rate explains management disincentive to redeem plaintiffs' bonds).

214. * * * John and Nachman have modeled reputation as a force that curtails agency costs. Under this model, management reduces underinvestment without needing the constraint of an explicit covenant; the authors call reputation an "implied contract." John & Nachman, Risky Debt, Investment Incentives, and Reputation in a Sequential Equilibrium, 40 J.Fin. 863, 870–76 (1985).

215. Coffee associates the disappearance of restrictive covenants with reliance on management's position. Coffee, Corporate Web, supra note 190, at 68–69.

216. Tight, close-to-perfect sets of covenants, while easy enough to draft (private placement and term loan forms contain them) never appeared in public debt contracts. The rigor of such covenants might easily cause management to forgo a value-increasing transaction, while conferring no material benefit on the bondholders. And, given a dispersed body of bondholders, managers and bondholders would find it hard to loosen tight covenants by contract amendment. Furthermore, the difficulty of executing a binding amendment has created a holdout problem in times of financial stress. * * *

217. McDaniel accounts in part for the disappearance of covenants by noting that their value has become dubious—a decline attributable to the reality that loopholes exploitable by good lawyers or creative managers are inevitable. See McDaniel, Bondholders II, supra note 10, at 236–38;

The restructuring movement has shattered the managerialist assumptions behind the covenantless debt contract. The financial markets have proved that the manager-emperors had no clothes. Power over investment and financing has shifted to the capital markets. Corporate reputation—the unprotected bondholders' backstop—has proved ineffective. Managers' and stockholders' incentives to maintain good reputations in the capital markets do not have the staying power of contract promises; they shift along with power and money. Exiting stockholders and managers care nothing about a corporate entity's future financing costs. Managers battling to stay on might indeed care, but have more immediate problems. As Jensen and Meckling noted in 1976, and bondholders discovered in 1985, sainthood does not have infinite benefits, and agency costs do not reduce to zero.

* * *

Succeeding instances of restructuring injury caused bondholders to insist on covenants to protect against event risk. These came in two generations—"poison puts," followed by "super poison puts." They are described by Steinwurtzel and Gardner, Super Poison Puts as a Protection Against Event Risks, Insights, vol. 3, no. 10 (October, 1989):

> The first generation of poison put provisions gave bondholders the right to demand that the issuer repurchase the debt securities at the initial offering price upon the occurrence of certain events, generally limited to unfriendly takeovers. The principal shortcoming of these provisions, however, was that most hostile takeover attempts became "friendly" in the end and therefore did not trigger the poison put. Moreover, the poison put provisions were not triggered by recapitalizations that often were undertaken by issuers in response to hostile bids or other unfriendly actions. Because substantial new debt is frequently incurred in recapitalizations, such transactions subject the bondholders to the same economic consequences that the poison put provisions were designed to prevent.

see also Coffee, Corporate Web, supra note 190, at 69 (theorizing that use of covenants has declined because no covenant could cover all of the ways that management can increase bondholders' risk). But this contracting problem, often obscured in the discussion, is not impossible to address effectively, even though contract perfection is unattainable. Any junior associate can draft a set of showstopping covenants. The basic elements of restructuring—borrowing, security, dividends and other payments to stockholders, and mergers and sales of assets—are the bread and butter of traditional business covenants. The problem stems from drafters' inability to foresee the future. If drafters could overcome this problem, they could impede precise injurious potential transactions without constraining management in other legitimate activity. Since the drafters cannot foresee the future, effective protections are necessarily overinclusive. This overinclusiveness has costs.

Today, given several years of experience with restructuring-related wealth transfers, one could easily draft a covenant that would permit a restructuring to go forward and would not injure bondholders. Such a covenant would tie a change in the interest rate to stated increases in the issuer's debt-equity ratio. * * *

In response to institutional investors' demands for new safeguards, issuers began to utilize indentures with an enhanced bondholder protection which has become known as a "super poison put" or, less colloquially, an "event risk" provision. The terms of event risk provisions vary from issuer to issuer. They differ from their predecessors in that the trigger events include recapitalizations and leveraged buy-outs, other major dividend distributions that substantially affect the underlying value of the company, purchases of a controlling interest, and stock repurchase programs.* In addition, the event risk provision often is contingent upon a trigger event resulting in a downgrading of the credit rating of the debt securities.

The purpose of these provisions is to "shift to the issuer the 'event risk' of the investment." These provisions, however, have proved beneficial to issuers from a financing standpoint as well. In addition to improving the general receptivity of investors to offerings of debt securities, event risk provisions arguably have resulted in lower borrowing costs and better credit ratings.

From the point of view of bondholders, the "designated events," or triggers, that activate the protective provisions are far from perfect. Apart from the limitations on the number or kinds of events that any given borrower may be able to insist upon in the bargaining process,** the definition of the "event" inevitably contains ambiguities that require judicial interpretation. No contract that is feasible can anticipate all possible strategic behavior.***

The consequences of triggering the protective provision may be to give the bondholder a right to "put" the bond back to the issuer at principal plus accrued interest or they may be to alter the coupon rate of the bonds either to a higher fixed rate (designated in advance) or to a varying rate that will keep the market price of the bonds at par.

According to Crabbe, Event Risk: An Analysis of Losses to Bondholders and "Super Poison Put" Bond Covenants, 46 J. Finance 689 (1991), 40 percent of recently issued investment grade industrial bonds contain super poison put covenants. Kahan and Klausner, Anti-Takeover Provisions in Bonds: Bondholder Protection or Management Retrenchment? 40 UCLA L.Rev.931 (1993), add that a "dual trigger" provision appeared most frequently. Under this, the bondholder protective provision (usually a put at par, but in a few instances an

* [Ed. Note] Designated events often include (1) mergers and acquisitions and (2) significant changes in the composition of the board of directors. Could the insertion of the latter provisions or other control change "puts", be held to constitute a violation of the controllers' or officers' or directors' fiduciary duties to stockholders? See Airline Pilots Assn. v. U.A.L. Corp., CCH para. 95,209 (7th Cir.1990).

** [Ed. Note] On the other hand, some borrowers may be forced to accept a trigger that consists merely in a lowering of the bond rating by a designated bond rating agency.

*** [Ed. Note] The risk covenants often fail to protect against behavior like the sale of crown jewels or the acquisition by the issuer of a substantial new business on a highly leveraged basis.

interest rate adjustment tied to a change in credit rating) is triggered by the combination of a defined takeover related event and a fall in the bonds' rating from investment grade to below investment grade.

The restructuring wave subsided when Federated Department Stores, a large restructured firm, defaulted and went into bankruptcy during the fourth quarter of 1989. Thereafter, default, recession, tight credit, and a smaller pool of appropriate targets, among other factors, caused a drastically diminished flow of restructuring transactions. Bond contract protection against event risk also began to disappear. Kahan and Klausner report that dual trigger antitakeover provisions (along with other forms of antitakeover covenant protection) appeared with substantially diminished frequency beginning in 1991. Does the cessation of restructuring activity imply the cessation of event risk? If not, how can this second disappearance of effective contract protection in bond contracts be explained?

Appendix C, Section 2 contains background materials on the leveraged restructurings of the 1980s.

(b) Fiduciary and Good Faith Duties in the Absence of Covenants

METROPOLITAN LIFE INSURANCE COMPANY v. RJR NABISCO, INC.

United States District Court, Southern District of New York, 1989.
716 F.Supp. 1504.

WALKER, District Judge:

I. INTRODUCTION

The corporate parties to this action are among the country's most sophisticated financial institutions, as familiar with the Wall Street investment community and the securities market as American consumers are with the Oreo cookies and Winston cigarettes made by defendant RJR Nabisco, Inc. (sometimes "the company" or "RJR Nabisco"). The present action traces its origins to October 20, 1988, when F. Ross Johnson, then the Chief Executive Officer of RJR Nabisco, proposed a $17 billion leveraged buy-out ("LBO") of the company's shareholders, at $75 per share.[1] Within a few days, a bidding war developed among the investment group led by Johnson and the investment firm of Kohlberg Kravis Roberts & Co. ("KKR"), and others. On December 1, 1988, a special committee of RJR Nabisco directors, established by the company

----

1. A leveraged buy-out occurs when a group of investors, usually including members of a company's management team, buy the company under financial arrangements that include little equity and significant new debt. The necessary debt financing typically includes mortgages or high risk/high yield bonds, popularly known as "junk bonds." Additionally, a portion of this debt is generally secured by the company's assets. Some of the acquired company's assets are usually sold after the transaction is completed in order to reduce the debt incurred in the acquisition.

specifically to consider the competing proposals, recommended that the company accept the KKR proposal, a $24 billion LBO that called for the purchase of the company's outstanding stock at roughly $109 per share.*

* * * The Court agreed to hear the present action—filed even before the company accepted the KKR proposal—on an expedited basis, with an eye toward March 1, 1989, when RJR Nabisco was expected to merge with the KKR holding entities created to facilitate the LBO. On that date, RJR Nabisco was also scheduled to assume roughly $19 billion of new debt. After a delay unrelated to the present action, the merger was ultimately completed during the week of April 24, 1989.

Plaintiffs now allege, in short, that RJR Nabisco's actions have drastically impaired the value of bonds previously issued to plaintiffs by, in effect, misappropriating the value of those bonds to help finance the LBO and to distribute an enormous windfall to the company's shareholders. As a result, plaintiffs argue, they have unfairly suffered a multimillion dollar loss in the value of their bonds.[4]

* * *

For the reasons set forth below, this Court agrees with defendants. There being no express covenant between the parties that would restrict the incurrence of new debt, and no perceived direction to that end from covenants that are express, this Court will not imply a covenant to prevent the recent LBO and thereby create an indenture term that, while bargained for in other contexts, was not bargained for here and was not even within the mutual contemplation of the parties.

II. BACKGROUND

* * *

A. The Parties:

Metropolitan Life Insurance Co. ("MetLife"), incorporated in New York, is a life insurance company that provides pension benefits for 42 million individuals. According to its most recent annual report, Met-Life's assets exceed $88 billion and its debt securities holdings exceed $49 billion. * * * MetLife is a mutual company and therefore has no

---

* [Ed. Note. The Court's footnote 8:] On February 9, 1989, KKR completed its tender offer for roughly 74 percent of RJR Nabisco's common stock (of which approximately 97% of the outstanding shares were tendered) and all of its Series B Cumulative Preferred Stock (of which approximately 95% of the outstanding shares were tendered). Approximately $18 billion in cash was paid out to those stockholders. KKR acquired the remaining stock in the late April merger through the issuance of roughly $4.1 billion of pay-in-kind exchangeable preferred stock and roughly $1.8 billion in face amount of convertible debentures. See Bradley Reply Aff. ¶ 2.

4. Agencies like Standard & Poor's and Moody's generally rate bonds in two broad categories: investment grade and speculative grade. Standard & Poor's rates investment grade bonds from "AAA" to "BBB." Moody's rates those bonds from "AAA" to "Baa3." Speculative grade bonds are rated either "BB" and lower, or "Ba1" and lower, by Standard & Poor's and Moody's, respectively. See, e.g., Standard and Poor's Debt Rating Criteria at 10–11. No one disputes that, subsequent to the announcement of the LBO, the RJR Nabisco bonds lost their "A" ratings.

stockholders and is instead operated for the benefit of its policyholders. * * * MetLife alleges that it owns $340,542,000 in principal amount of six separate RJR Nabisco debt issues, bonds allegedly purchased between July 1975 and July 1988. Some bonds become due as early as this year, others will not become due until 2017. The bonds bear interest rates of anywhere from 8 to 10.25 percent. MetLife also owned 186,000 shares of RJR Nabisco common stock at the time this suit was filed. * * *

Jefferson–Pilot Life Insurance Co. ("Jefferson–Pilot") is a North Carolina company that has more than $3 billion in total assets, $1.5 billion of which are invested in debt securities. * * * Jefferson–Pilot alleges that it owns $9.34 million in principal amount of three separate RJR Nabisco debt issues, allegedly purchased between June 1978 and June 1988. Those bonds, bearing interest rates of anywhere from 8.45 to 10.75 percent, become due in 1993 and 1998. * * *

RJR Nabisco, a Delaware corporation, is a consumer products holding company that owns some of the country's best known product lines, including LifeSavers candy, Oreo cookies, and Winston cigarettes. The company was formed in 1985, when R.J. Reynolds Industries, Inc. ("R.J. Reynolds") merged with Nabisco Brands, Inc. ("Nabisco Brands"). In 1979, and thus before the R.J. Reynolds–Nabisco Brands merger, R.J. Reynolds acquired the Del Monte Corporation ("Del Monte"), which distributes canned fruits and vegetables. From January 1987 until February 1989, co-defendant Johnson served as the company's CEO. KKR, a private investment firm, organizes funds through which investors provide pools of equity to finance LBOs. * * *

B. The Indentures:

The bonds implicated by this suit are governed by long, detailed indentures, which in turn are governed by New York contract law.[10] * * * [U]nderwriters ordinarily negotiate the terms of the indentures with the issuers. Since the underwriters must then sell or place the bonds, they necessarily negotiate in part with the interests of the buyers in mind. Moreover, these indentures were not secret agreements foisted upon unwitting participants in the bond market. No successive holder is required to accept or to continue to hold the bonds, * * * indeed, plaintiffs readily admit that they could have sold their bonds right up until the announcement of the LBO. * * * Instead, sophisticated investors like plaintiffs are well aware of the indenture terms and, presumably, review them carefully before lending hundreds of millions of dollars to any company.

Indeed, the prospectuses for the indentures contain a statement relevant to this action:

> The Indenture contains no restrictions on the creation of unsecured short-term debt by [RJR Nabisco] or its subsidiaries, no restriction on the creation of unsecured Funded Debt by [RJR

---

10. Both sides agree that New York law controls this Court's interpretation of the indentures, which contain explicit designations to that effect. * * *

Nabisco] or its subsidiaries which are not Restricted Subsidiaries, and no restriction on the payment of dividends by [RJR Nabisco].

* * * Further, as plaintiffs themselves note, the contracts at issue "[do] not impose debt limits, since debt is assumed to be used for productive purposes." * * *

[The court noted that two of the issues of RJR Nabisco debt held by MetLife had originally been governed by debt covenants that would have been violated by the debt to be issued in connection with the LBO, but that MetLife had agreed to amend the contracts to remove the covenants. One issue was a private placement entered into between Del Monte and MetLife in 1975, the other was a private placement entered into between Reynolds and MetLife in 1976. The Del Monte notes had been assumed by Reynolds in 1979. In 1983, MetLife agreed to amend the note agreement to delete its business covenants in exchange for a guaranty of the debt by the parent corporation. Met-Life gave up the protection of the business covenants in the 1976 Reynolds notes at Reynolds' request in 1985. Reynolds needed to incur additional debt in connection with the consummation of its merger with Nabisco, and offered to exchange debentures issued under a public indenture for the private placement notes. MetLife agreed to the exchange despite the fact that the new notes had the same interest rate but no business covenant protection because (1) it was participating in a new financing in connection with the merger, and (2) the "debenturized" notes offered in exchange could be sold to the public.

[The court also noted that the problem of the LBOs' effects on bond value had been discussed in internal MetLife memoranda circulated in 1982 and 1985. The 1982 memorandum discussed an LBO in which MetLife had participated and also had held existing bonds which had been downgraded. Said the memorandum:

"Questions have * * * been raised about our ability to force pay-outs in similar future situations, particularly when we would not be participating in the buyout financing. * * * A method of closing this apparent 'loophole' * * * would be through a covenant dealing with a change in ownership. Such a covenant is standard in financings with privately-held companies. * * * It provides the lender with * * * some type of special redemption."

The 1985 memorandum discussed the general absence of business covenants in public indentures, noted that the lack of covenants had caused MetLife holdings to lose value in 10 or 15 takeover or LBO situations, predicted that the problem would continue, and suggested that "appropriate language" be included in new indentures.

[The court stressed that the documents "highlight the risks" inherent in the market and that sophisticated investors such as MetLife (and Jefferson–Pilot) "would be hard-pressed to plead ignorance of these market risks."]

These documents must be read in conjunction with plaintiffs' Amended Complaint. That document asserts that the LBO "undermines the foundation of the investment grade debt market * * *," that, although "the indentures do not purport to limit dividends or debt * * * [s]uch covenants were believed unnecessary with blue chip companies * * *", * * * that "the transaction contradicts the premise of the investment grade market * * *", * * * and, finally, that "[t]his buy-out was not contemplated at the time the debt was issued, contradicts the premise of the investment grade ratings that RJR Nabisco actively solicited and received, and is inconsistent with the understandings of the market * * * which [p]laintiffs relied upon." * * *

Solely for the purposes of these motions, the Court accepts various factual assertions advanced by plaintiffs: first, that RJR Nabisco actively solicited "investment grade" ratings for its debt; second, that it relied on descriptions of its strong capital structure and earnings record which included prominent display of its ability to pay the interest obligations on its long-term debt several times over, * * * and third, that the company made express or implied representations not contained in the relevant indentures concerning its future creditworthiness. * * * In support of those allegations, plaintiffs have marshaled a number of speeches made by co-defendant Johnson and other executives of RJR Nabisco.[18] In addition, plaintiffs rely on an affidavit sworn to by John Dowdle, the former Treasurer and then Senior Vice President of RJR Nabisco from 1970 until 1987. In his opinion, the LBO "clearly undermines the fundamental premise of the [c]ompany's bargain with the bondholders, and the commitment that I believe the [c]ompany made to the bondholders * * * I firmly believe that the company made commitments * * * that require it to redeem [these bonds and notes] before paying out the value to the shareholders." * * *

III. DISCUSSION

At the outset, the Court notes that nothing in its evaluation is substantively altered by the speeches given or remarks made by RJR Nabisco executives, or the opinions of various individuals—what, for instance, former RJR Nabisco Treasurer Dowdle personally did or did not "firmly believe" the indentures meant. * * * The parol evidence rule bars plaintiffs from arguing that the speeches made by company executives prove defendants agreed or acquiesced to a term that does not appear in the indentures. See West, Weir & Bartel, Inc. v. Mary Carter Paint Co., 25 N.Y.2d 535, 540, 307 N.Y.S.2d 449, 452, 255 N.E.2d 709, 712 (1969) * * *.

---

18. See, e.g., Address by F. Ross Johnson, November 12, 1987, * * * ("Our strong balance sheet is a cornerstone of our strategies. It gives us the resources to modernize facilities, develop new technologies, bring on new products, and support our leading brands around the world."); Remarks of Edward J. Robinson, Executive Vice President and Chief Financial Officer, February 15, 1988, * * * at 1 ("RJR Nabisco's financial strategy is * * * to enhance the strength of the balance sheet by reducing the level of debt as well as lowering the cost of existing debt."); Remarks by Dr. Robert J. Carbonell, Vice Chairman of RJR Nabisco, June 3, 1987, * * * ("We will not sacrifice our longer-term health for the sake of short term heroics.").

The indentures at issue clearly address the eventuality of a merger. They impose certain related restrictions not at issue in this suit, but no restriction that would prevent the recent RJR Nabisco merger transaction. * * * The indentures also explicitly set forth provisions for the adoption of new covenants, if such a course is deemed appropriate. * * * While it may be true that no explicit provision either permits or prohibits an LBO, such contractual silence itself cannot create ambiguity to avoid the dictates of the parol evidence rule, particularly where the indentures impose no debt limitations.

Under certain circumstances, however, courts will, as plaintiffs note, consider extrinsic evidence to evaluate the scope of an implied covenant of good faith. * * * However, [in *Sharon Steel*] the Second Circuit has established a different rule for customary, or boilerplate, provisions of detailed indentures used and relied upon throughout the securities market, such as those at issue.[20] * * *

A. Plaintiffs' Case Against the RJR Nabisco LBO:

1. Count One: The implied covenant:

* * *

A plaintiff always can allege a violation of an express covenant. If there has been such a violation, of course, the court need not reach the question of whether or not an *implied* covenant has been violated. That inquiry surfaces where, while the express terms may not have been technically breached, one party has nonetheless effectively deprived the other of those express, explicitly bargained-for benefits. In such a case, a court will read an implied covenant of good faith and fair dealing into a contract to ensure that neither party deprives the other of "the fruits of the agreement." See, e.g., Greenwich Village Assoc. v. Salle, 110 A.D.2d 111, 115, 493 N.Y.S.2d 461, 464 (1st Dep't 1985). See also Van Gemert v. Boeing Co., 553 F.2d 812, 815 ("*Van Gemert II*") (2d.Cir.1977). Such a covenant is implied only where the implied term "is consistent with other mutually agreed upon terms in the contract." Sabetay v. Sterling Drug, Inc., 69 N.Y.2d 329, 335, 514 N.Y.S.2d 209, 212, 506 N.E.2d 919, 922 (1987). * * * Viewed another way, the implied covenant of good faith is breached only when one party seeks to prevent the contract's performance or to withhold its benefits. See Collard v. Incorporated Village of Flower Hill, 75 A.D.2d 631, 632, 427 N.Y.S.2d 301, 302 (2d Dep't 1980). As a result, it thus ensures that parties to a contract perform the substantive, bargained-for terms of their agreement. See, e.g., Wakefield v. Northern Telecom, Inc., 769 F.2d 109, 112 (2d Cir.1985) (Winter, J.)

---

20. To a certain extent, this discussion is academic. Even if the Court did consider the extrinsic evidence offered by plaintiffs, its ultimate decision would be no different. * * * More important, those representations are improperly raised under the rubric of an implied covenant of good faith when they cannot properly or reasonably be construed as evidencing a binding agreement or acquiescence by defendants to substantive restrictive covenants. * * *

The parole evidence rule of course does not bar descriptions of either the background of this suit or market realities consistent with the contracts at issue.

In contracts like bond indentures, "an implied covenant * * * derives its substance directly from the language of the Indenture, and 'cannot give the holders of Debentures any rights inconsistent with those set out in the Indenture.' *[Where] plaintiffs' contractual rights [have not been] violated, there can have been no breach of an implied covenant.*" Gardner & Florence Call Cowles Foundation v. Empire Inc., 589 F.Supp. 669, 673 (S.D.N.Y.1984), vacated on procedural grounds, 754 F.2d 478 (2d Cir.1985) (quoting Broad v. Rockwell, 642 F.2d 929, 957 (5th Cir.) (en banc), cert. denied, 454 U.S. 965, 102 S.Ct. 506, 70 L.Ed.2d 380 (1981)) (emphasis added).

Thus, in cases like Van Gemert v. Boeing Co., 520 F.2d 1373 (2d Cir.), cert. denied, 423 U.S. 947 (1975) ("*Van Gemert I*"), and Pittsburgh Terminal Corp. v. Baltimore & Ohio Ry. Co., 680 F.2d 933 (3d Cir.), cert. denied, 459 U.S. 1056 (1982)—both relied upon by plaintiffs—the courts used the implied covenant of good faith and fair dealing to ensure that the bondholders received the benefit of their bargain as determined from the face of the contracts at issue. In *Van Gemert I*, the plaintiff bondholders alleged inadequate notice to them of defendant's intention to redeem the debentures in question and hence an inability to exercise their conversion rights before the applicable deadline. The contract itself provided that notice would be given in the first place. * * * Faced with those provisions, defendants in that case unsurprisingly admitted that the indentures specifically required the company to provide the bondholders with notice. See id. at 1379. While defendant there issued a press release that mentioned the possible redemption of outstanding convertible debentures, that limited release did not "mention even the tentative dates for redemption and expiration of the conversion rights of debenture holders." Id. at 1375. Moreover, defendant did not issue any general publicity or news release. Through an implied covenant, then, the court fleshed out the full extent of the more skeletal right that appeared in the contract itself, and thus protected plaintiff's bargained-for right of conversion.[21]

I also note, in passing, that *Van Gemert I* presented the Second Circuit with "less sophisticated investors." Id. at 1383. Similarly, the court in *Pittsburgh Terminal* applied an implied covenant to the indentures at issue because defendants there "took steps to prevent the Bondholders from receiving information which they needed *in order to receive the fruits of their conversion option should they choose to exercise it.*" *Pittsburgh Terminal*, 680 F.2d at 941 (emphasis added).

The appropriate analysis, then, is first to examine the indentures to determine "the fruits of the agreement" between the parties, and then to decide whether those "fruits" have been spoiled—which is to say, whether plaintiffs' contractual rights have been violated by defendants.

---

21. Since newspaper notice, for instance, was promised in the indenture, the court used an implied covenant to ensure that meaningful, reasonable newspaper notice was provided. See id. at 1383.

The American Bar Foundation's *Commentaries on Indentures* ("the *Commentaries* "), relied upon and respected by both plaintiffs and defendants, describes the rights and risks generally found in bond indentures like those at issue:

> The most obvious and important characteristic of long-term debt financing is that the holder ordinarily has not bargained for and does not expect any substantial gain in the value of the security to compensate for the risk of loss * * * [T]he significant fact, *which accounts in part for the detailed protective provisions of the typical long-term debt financing instrument,* is that *the lender (the purchaser of the debt security) can expect only interest at the prescribed rate plus the eventual return of the principal.* * * * Short of bankruptcy, *the debt security holder can do nothing to protect himself against actions of the borrower which jeopardize its ability to pay the debt unless he * * * establishes his rights through contractual provisions set forth in the debt agreement or indenture.*

Id. at 1–2 (1971) (emphasis added).

A review of the parties' submissions and the indentures themselves satisfies the Court that the substantive "fruits" guaranteed by those contracts and relevant to the present motions include the periodic and regular payment of interest and the eventual repayment of principal. * * * According to a typical indenture, a default shall occur if the company either (1) fails to pay principal when due; (2) fails to make a timely sinking fund payment; (3) fails to pay within 30 days of the due date thereof any interest on the date; or (4) fails duly to observe or perform any of the express covenants or agreements set forth in the agreement. * * *[23] Plaintiffs' Amended Complaint nowhere alleges that RJR Nabisco has breached these contractual obligations; interest payments continue and there is no reason to believe that the principal will not be paid when due.

[T]his Court holds that the "fruits" of these indentures do not include an implied restrictive covenant that would prevent the incurrence of new debt to facilitate the recent LBO. To hold otherwise would permit these plaintiffs to straightjacket the company in order to guarantee their investment. These plaintiffs do not invoke an implied covenant of good faith to protect a legitimate, mutually contemplated benefit of the indentures; rather, they seek to have this Court create an additional benefit for which they did not bargain.

---

23. Plaintiffs originally indicated that, depending on the Court's disposition of the instant motions, they might seek to amend their complaint to allege that "they are not equally and ratably secured under the [express terms of the] 'negative pledge' clause of the indentures." * * * On May 26, 1989, shortly before this Opinion was filed, the Court granted defendants' request to assert a counterclaim for a declaratory judgment that those "negative pledge" covenants have not been violated by the post-LBO financial structure of RJR Nabisco.

This counterclaim was advanced in response to notices of default by plaintiffs based on matters not raised in the Amended Complaint.

The Court of course will not now determine whether an alleged implied covenant flowing from a "negative pledge" provision has been breached. That inquiry necessarily must follow the Court's determination of whether or not the "negative pledge" provision has been expressly breached.

Although the indentures generally permit mergers and the incurrence of new debt, there admittedly is not an explicit indenture provision to the contrary of what plaintiffs now claim the implied covenant requires. That absence, however, does *not* mean that the Court should imply into those very same indentures a covenant of good faith so broad that it imposes a new, substantive term of enormous scope. This is so particularly where, as here, that very term—a limitation on the incurrence of additional debt—has in other past contexts been expressly bargained for; particularly where the indentures grant the company broad discretion in the management of its affairs, as plaintiffs admit, * * * particularly where the indentures explicitly set forth specific provisions for the adoption of new covenants and restrictions, * * * and *especially* where there has been no breach of the parties' bargained-for contractual rights on which the implied covenant necessarily is based. While the Court stands ready to employ an implied covenant of good faith to ensure that such bargained-for rights are performed and upheld, it will not, however, permit an implied covenant to shoehorn into an indenture additional terms plaintiffs now wish had been included. See also Broad v. Rockwell International Corp., 642 F.2d 929 (5th Cir.) (en banc) (applying New York law), cert. denied, 454 U.S. 965 (1981) (finding no liability pursuant to an implied covenant where the terms of the indenture, as bargained for, were enforced).[25]

Plaintiffs argue in the most general terms that the fundamental basis of all these indentures was that an LBO along the lines of the recent RJR Nabisco transaction would never be undertaken, that indeed *no* action would be taken, intentionally or not, that would significantly deplete the company's assets. Accepting plaintiffs' theory, their fundamental bargain with defendants dictated that nothing would be done to jeopardize the extremely high probability that the company would remain able to make interest payments and repay principal over the 20 to 30 year indenture term—and perhaps by logical extension even included the right to ask a court "to make sure that plaintiffs had made a good investment." *Gardner*, 589 F.Supp. at 674. But as Judge Knapp aptly concluded in *Gardner*, "Defendants * * * were under a duty to carry out the terms of the contract, but not to make sure that plaintiffs had made a good investment. The former they have done;

25. The cases relied on by plaintiffs are not to the contrary. They invoke an implied covenant where it proves necessary to fulfill the explicit terms of an agreement, or to give meaning to ambiguous terms. See, e.g., Grad v. Roberts, 14 N.Y.2d 70, 248 N.Y.S.2d 633, 636, 198 N.E.2d 26, 28 (1964) (court relied on implied covenant to effect "performance of [an] option agreement according to its terms"); Zilg v. Prentice–Hall, Inc., 717 F.2d 671 (2d Cir.1983), cert. denied, 466 U.S. 938, 104 S.Ct. 1911, 80 L.Ed.2d 460 (1984). In *Zilg*, the Second Circuit first described a contract which, on its face, established the publisher's obligation to publish, advertise and publicize the book at issue. The court then determined that "the contract in question establishes a relationship between the publisher and author which implies an obligation upon the former to make certain [good faith] efforts in publishing a book it has accepted notwithstanding the clause which leaves the number of volumes to be printed and the advertising budget to the publisher's discretion." 717 F.2d at 679. In other words, the court there sought to ensure a meaningful fulfillment of the contract's express terms. See also *Van Gemert I,* supra; *Pittsburgh Terminal,* supra. In the latter two cases, the courts sought to protect the bondholders' express, bargained-for rights.

the latter we have no jurisdiction over." Id. Plaintiffs' submissions and MetLife's previous undisputed internal memoranda remind the Court that a "fundamental basis" or a "fruit of an agreement" is often in the eye of the beholder, whose vision may well change along with the market, and who may, with hindsight, imagine a different bargain than the one he actually and initially accepted with open eyes.

The sort of unbounded and one-sided elasticity urged by plaintiffs would interfere with and destabilize the market. And this Court, like the parties to these contracts, cannot ignore or disavow the market-place in which the contract is performed. Nor can it ignore the expectations of that market—expectations, for instance, that the terms of an indenture will be upheld, and that a court will not, *sua sponte*, add new substantive terms to that indenture as it sees fit. The Court has no reason to believe that the market, in evaluating bonds such as those at issue here, did not discount for the possibility that any company, even one the size of RJR Nabisco, might engage in an LBO heavily financed by debt. That the bonds did not lose any of their value until the October 20, 1988 announcement of a possible RJR Nabisco LBO only suggests that the market had theretofore evaluated the risks of such a transaction as slight.

* * * To support their argument that defendants have violated an implied covenant, plaintiffs contend that, since the October 20, 1988 announcement, the bond market has "stopped functioning." * * * They argue that if they had "sold and abandoned the market [before October 20, 1988], the market, if everyone had the same attitude, would have disappeared." * * * What plaintiffs term "stopped functioning" or "disappeared," however, are properly seen as natural responses and adjustments to market realities. Plaintiffs of course do not contend that no new issues are being sold, or that existing issues are no longer being traded or have become worthless.

To respond to changed market forces, new indenture provisions can be negotiated, such as provisions that were in fact once included in the 8.9 percent and 10.25 percent debentures implicated by this action. New provisions could include special debt restrictions or change-of-control covenants. There is no guarantee, of course, that companies like RJR Nabisco would accept such new covenants; parties retain the freedom to enter into contracts as they choose. But presumably, multi-billion dollar investors like plaintiffs have some say in the terms of the investments they make and continue to hold. And, presumably, companies like RJR Nabisco need the infusions of capital such investors are capable of providing.

Whatever else may be true about this case, it certainly does not present an example of the classic sort of form contract or contract of adhesion often frowned upon by courts. In those cases, what motivates a court is the strikingly inequitable nature of the parties' respective bargaining positions. See generally, Rakoff, Contracts of Adhesion: An Essay in Reconstruction, 96 Harv.L.Rev. 1173 (1982). Plaintiffs here entered this "liquid trading market," * * * with their eyes open and were free to leave at any time. Instead they remained there notwithstanding its well understood risks.

Ultimately, plaintiffs cannot escape the inherent illogic of their argument. On the one hand, it is undisputed that investors like plaintiffs recognized that companies like RJR Nabisco strenuously opposed additional restrictive covenants that might limit the incurrence of new debt or the company's ability to engage in a merger. Furthermore, plaintiffs argue that they had no choice other than to accept the indentures as written, without additional restrictive covenants, or to "abandon" the market. * * *

Yet on the other hand, plaintiffs ask this Court to imply a covenant that would have just that restrictive effect because, they contend, it reflects precisely the fundamental assumption of the market and the fundamental basis of their bargain with defendants. If that truly were the case here, it is difficult to imagine why an insistence on that term would have forced the plaintiffs to abandon the market. The Second Circuit has offered a better explanation: "[a] promise by the defendant should be implied only if the court may rightfully assume that the parties would have included it in their written agreement had their attention been called to it * * * *Any such assumption in this case would be completely unwarranted.*" Neuman v. Pike, 591 F.2d 191, 195 (2d Cir.1979) (emphasis added, citations omitted).

In the final analysis, plaintiffs offer no objective or reasonable standard for a court to use in its effort to define the sort of actions their "implied covenant" would permit a corporation to take, and those it would not.[28] Plaintiffs say only that investors like themselves rely upon the "skill" and "good faith" of a company's board and management, * * * and that their covenant would prevent the company from "destroy[ing] * * * the legitimate expectations of its long-term bondholders." * * * As is clear from the preceding discussion, however, plaintiffs have failed to convince the Court that by upholding the explicit, bargained-for terms of the indenture, RJR Nabisco has either exhibited bad faith or destroyed plaintiffs' *legitimate,* protected expectations.

* * * [This court] concludes that courts are properly reluctant to imply into an integrated agreement terms that have been and remain subject to specific, explicit provisions, where the parties are sophisticated investors, well versed in the market's assumptions, and do not stand in a fiduciary relationship with one another.

2. Count Five: In Equity:

Count Five substantially restates and realleges the contract claims advanced in Count I. * * * [These] equity claims cannot survive defendants' motion for summary judgment.

---

28. Under plaintiffs' theory, bondholders might ask a court to prohibit a company like RJR Nabisco not only from engaging in an LBO, but also from entering a new line of business—with the attendant costs of building new physical plants and hiring new workers—or from acquiring new businesses such as RJR Nabisco did when it acquired Del Monte.

In their papers, plaintiffs variously attempt to justify Count V as being based on unjust enrichment, frustration of purpose [or] an alleged breach of something approaching a fiduciary duty * * *. Each claim fails. * * *

* * * [P]laintiffs advance a claim that remains based, their assertions to the contrary notwithstanding, on an alleged breach of a fiduciary duty.[33] Defendants go to great lengths to prove that the law of Delaware, and not New York, governs this question. Defendants' attempt to rely on Delaware law is readily explained by even a cursory reading of Simons v. Cogan, 549 A.2d 300, 303 (Del.1988), the recent Delaware Supreme Court ruling which held, *inter alia*, that a corporate bond "represents a contractual entitlement to the repayment of a debt and does not represent an equitable interest in the issuing corporation necessary for the imposition of a trust relationship with concomitant fiduciary duties." Before such a fiduciary duty arises, "an existing property right or equitable interest supporting such a duty must exist." Id. at 304. A bondholder, that court concluded, "acquires no equitable interest, and remains a creditor of the corporation whose interests are protected by the contractual terms of the indenture." Id. Defendants argue that New York law is not to the contrary, but the single Supreme Court case they cite—a case decided over fifty years ago that was not squarely presented with the issue addressed by the *Simons* court— provides something less than dispositive support. See Marx v. Merchants' National Properties, Inc., 148 Misc. 6, 7, 265 N.Y.S. 163, 165 (1933). For their part, plaintiffs more convincingly demonstrate that New York law applies than that New York law recognizes their claim.[34]

---

33. * * * [C]ases relied upon by plaintiffs to support their "In Equity" Count focus on fraudulent schemes or conveyances. See, e.g., United States v. Tabor Court Realty Corp., 803 F.2d 1288, 1295 (3d Cir. 1986) (explaining lower court's findings in United States v. Gleneagles Investment Co., 565 F.Supp. 556 (M.D.Pa.1983)); Pepper v. Litton, 308 U.S. 295, 296, 60 S.Ct. 238, 84 L.Ed. 281 (1939) ("The findings by the District Court, amply supported by the evidence, reveal a scheme to defraud creditors * * *"); Harff v. Kerkorian, 347 A.2d 133, 134 (Del.1975) (bondholders limited to contract claims in absence of " 'fraud, insolvency, or a violation of a statute.' ") (citation omitted). Moreover, if the Court here were confronted with an insolvent corporation, which is not the case, the company's officers and directors might become trustees of its assets for the protection of its creditors, among others. See, e.g., New York Credit Men's Adjustment Bureau v. Weiss, 278 A.D. 501, 503, 105 N.Y.S.2d 604, 606 (1st Dep't 1951), aff'd, 305 N.Y. 1, 110 N.E.2d 397 (1953).

If not based on a fiduciary duty and the other equitable principles addressed by the Court, plaintiffs' claim, in effect, asks this Court to use its broad equitable powers to fashion a new cause of action that would adopt precisely the same arguments the Court rejected in Count I.

34. The indenture provision designating New York law as controlling,* * * would, one might assume, resolve at least the issue of the applicable law. In quoting the relevant indenture provision, however, plaintiffs omit the proviso "except as may otherwise be required by mandatory provisions of law." P.Mem. at 52, n. 46. Defendants, however, fail to argue that the internal affairs doctrine, which they assert dictates that Delaware law controls this question, is such a "mandatory provision of law." Nor do defendants respond to plaintiffs' reliance on First National City Bank v. Banco Para El Comercio, 462 U.S. 611, 621, 103 S.Ct. 2591, 2597, 77 L.Ed.2d 46 (1983) ("Different conflicts principles apply, however, where the rights of third parties *external* to the corporation are at issue.") (emphasis in original, citation omitted). Ultimately, the point is academic; as explained below, the Court would grant defendants summary judgment on this Count under either New York or Delaware law.

Regardless, this Court finds *Simons* persuasive, and believes that a New York court would agree with that conclusion. In the venerable case of Meinhard v. Salmon, 249 N.Y. 458, 164 N.E. 545 (1928), then Chief Judge Cardozo explained the obligations imposed on a fiduciary, and why those obligations are so special and rare:

> Many forms of conduct permissible in a workaday world for those acting at arm's length, are forbidden to those bound by fiduciary ties. A trustee is held to something stricter than the morals of the market place. Not honesty alone, but the punctilio of an honor the most sensitive, is then the standard of behavior.

Id. at 464 (citation omitted). Before a court recognizes the duty of a "punctilio of an honor the most sensitive," it must be certain that the complainant is entitled to more than the "morals of the market place," and the protections offered by actions based on fraud, state statutes or the panoply of available federal securities laws. This Court has concluded that the plaintiffs presently before it—sophisticated investors who are unsecured creditors—are not entitled to such additional protections.

Equally important, plaintiffs' position on this issue * * * provides no reasonable or workable limits, and is thus reminiscent of their implied covenant of good faith. Indeed, many indisputably legitimate corporate transactions would not survive plaintiffs' theory. With no workable limits, plaintiffs' envisioned duty would extend equally to trade creditors, employees, and every other person to whom the defendants are liable in any way. Of all such parties, these informed plaintiffs least require a Court's equitable protection; not only are they willing participants in a largely impersonal market, but they also possess the financial sophistication and size to secure their own protection.

* * *

NOTE: THE AFTERMATH OF THE RJR
NABISCO RESTRUCTURING

In March 1990 RJR Nabisco had $29 billion of debt and a debt-equity ratio of 23:1. According to G. Anders, Merchants of Debt: KKR and the Mortgaging of American Business 263–271 (1992), KKR came to a realization in April and May 1990 that RJR Nabisco would default on its debt absent a recapitalization. A multi-phase deleveraging of the firm began in July 1990. Several junk bond issues were repurchased at discounted prices on the open market. This buying program reduced an outstanding $4.8 billion of junk bonds to $1.7 billion over eight months. Another issue of debt was the object of an exchange offer for a package of cash and new preferred stock. The cash for this debt reduction was provided by the $5.7 billion proceeds of the sale of the

Del Monte subsidiary. RJR also redeemed an issue of increasing rate notes held by institutions with the proceeds of a new loan. In addition, KKR invested $1.5 billion in new common stock. By the end of 1990, RJR Nabisco had $18.7 billion of debt outstanding.

In March 1991 KKR commenced a new $1.5 billion junk bond retirement program. Half of the $1.5 billion came from a public common stock offering; the other half came from new debt financing. There followed, in October 1991, an exchange offer of common stock for outstanding convertible preferred and preferred issued in the earlier debt retirement program.

The completion of these programs left RJR's debt below $15 billion and raised its equity to $8 billion. In December 1991, RJR lost its junk bond rating. The reduction in interest costs resulted in positive accounting earnings for the year.

An issue in the bondholder litigation remained unresolved for some time. The debt contracts contained negative pledge clauses, and the plaintiffs contended that these had been violated by the terms of the restructuring. Settlement of these claims was announced in January 1991.

NOTE: SPIN OFFS

High leverage restructurings are not the only form of event risk. Consider a plan announced by the Marriott Corp. in October 1992. Marriott, which both owned hotels and managed hotels owned by others, proposed to split the two lines of business into two separately owned corporations. It would shift the management business to a new entity called Marriott International ("International") and declare a one-to-one dividend of the International shares (a "spin off"). Its real estate and almost all of its debt would remain behind in a corporation to be renamed Host Marriott ("Host"). Under the proposed separation, pro forma based on 1992 figures for the company as a whole, International would have annual sales of $7.4 billion and operating cash flow of $500 million; Host would have annual sales of $1.7 billion and operating cash flow of $350 million, much of which would have to be devoted to annual interest payments of $225 million per year. McDowell, Will Marriott ever Stand Divided? New York Times, sec. D, p. 1, col. 3., Feb. 4, 1993. See PPM America, Inc. v. Marriott Corp., 1993 WL 135295 (D.Md.1993).

The announcement of the spin off caused Marriott's stock price to rise from $17\frac{1}{8}$ to $21\frac{7}{8}$. But the bond market got nervous. Marriott's bonds immediately lost $360 million in market value; its twenty year bond lost 30 percent of its value. One investment banking house estimated market-wide losses in the wake of the Marriott announcement at $11 billion.

By early 1993 twenty-two such spin offs were pending. Marriott bondholders, meanwhile, were attempting to prevent the accomplishment of its spin off with lawsuits. How might one draft a covenant to protect a debt issue from this species of event risk? Assuming the Marriott bondholders did not have the benefit of such a covenant, can this spin off be distinguished from RJR Nabisco's leveraged restructuring for purposes of a claim of breach of a good faith duty? If the remaining corporation becomes insolvent where the combined corporation would not have been, can the creditors pursue the assets of the spun off company? On what theory?

NOTE: FIDUCIARY THEORY, GOOD FAITH DUTIES, AND OTHER BASES FOR JUDICIAL PROTECTION OF PUBLIC BONDHOLDERS

Notwithstanding the efforts to re-insert protective provisions addressed to "event risks", it is impossible to draft express protection against the open horizon of risky contingencies that are necessarily entailed in long term relational contracts, and, at the same time, to leave management free to get on with the job of maximizing value. The possibilities of opportunistic behavior by management to the advantage of the equity and the disadvantage of the debt inevitably remain substantial. Those possibilities could be narrowed by judicially imputed covenants of good faith to govern the parties in their ongoing contractual relationship, or by judicially imposed fiduciary restrictions on the behavior of management and the equity holders vis-a-vis the debt holders.

As the *Metropolitan Life* case indicates, even if adumbrations from received contract doctrine are the source of such judicial power, difficult problems remain in determining the substance of good faith obligations. What, for example, are the limits of opportunistic behavior by the management and the equity that good faith permits? Where should the judge look to find those limits, apart from the language of the contract, which is the beginning of the inquiry—in the institutional circumstances of the bargain? In the particular circumstances of the parties' particular agreement? In economic theory? In psychology? In moral reasoning? In all of the above?

If the fiduciary notion is to be invoked to protect the bondholders, then similar problems arise. If the "fiduciary" is identified as the equity holders as a group, then one group of dispersed investors is being asked to serve as a fiduciary for another group with respect to their conflicting claims under relational contracts which do not specify all the circumstances in which conflict may arise. If management is identified as the "fiduciary," an agent selected by one group to work for it is being asked to resolve conflicting claims of that group against another group which had no role in the agent's selection. Is fiduciary theory responsive to resolution of these conflicts? What should the courts use as the measure of the extent to which the designated fiduciary may adversely affect the beneficiary if the fiduciary represents each of the two conflicting claimants? Do managers engaged in self dealing or other self aggrandizing conduct owe a duty to bondholders with respect to such behavior?

There is also the question of how the "fiduciary" obligation differs from the "good faith" obligation. At the poles, the differences seem clear enough. The fiduciary obligation, in its purest version, not only prohibits the fiduciary from dealing with the beneficiary's property so as to effect benefits for itself at the expense of the beneficiary (whether by way of causing loss or denying gain to the beneficiary), but also forbids the fiduciary from thus benefitting itself even if the beneficiary is not injured thereby. The "good faith" restrictions on behavior of parties to a contract start from the conception that each party is expected to derive some gains and some sacrifices in the course of their contractual relationship. As the fiduciary obligation is diluted to permit the fiduciary not only to derive some gains from use of the beneficiary's property, but thereby to deprive the beneficiary of the full gain from the transaction, the court is obliged to define the limits on the gain-sharing. And as the duty of good faith is detached from the rigid connection to an express provision of the contract, the court becomes obliged to set limits on the extent to which bondholders may be injured consistently with "good faith." In many cases, the two criteria will produce the same result.

Plainly, fiduciary restrictions demand more restraint from the fiduciary than do good faith obligations from a contracting party. The breadth of fiduciary restrictions suggests that imposing them must rest on some different justification in the parties' relationship than obtains for contract obligations. What is there about the relationship among common stockholders (that is, between a controlling shareholder and a dispersed minority), or between common stockholders and management that underpins the accepted notion of a fiduciary obligation that is missing in the relationship among bondholders, or between them and the corporation, its stockholders, and its management?

Fiduciary theory contemplates a dependent relationship in which the fiduciary serves only the interest of the beneficiary, as opposed to its own interests, when dealing with the beneficiary's assets. In contrast, the relationship of common stockholders to bondholders (and to preferred stockholders), although consensual, is adversarial in origin and operation. It lacks the essential import of a fiduciary or agency relationship: one party acting primarily, if not solely for the other under the other's nominal direction or control. It contemplates open-ended discretion and self-dealing with the common assets by the common stockholder without any need for bondholder consent or any bondholder entitlement to share in control or gains other than those provided by the terms of the contract. Neither the fiduciary's expected self-denial nor its obligation to preserve the value of the assets for the beneficiary fits the legitimate aspirations of the common stockholder, who is given the discretion to and is expected to take the risks involved in seeking to maximize the value of the common assets for its own benefit, subject only to the restrictions of the contract (and of "law"). Bondholders are entitled to return only of a limited amount: principal at a fixed date and interest in the interim. Common stockholders have no such entitlement to either a fixed sum or a fixed date, but no limits are placed on their potential return. However, they must leave their funds at risk for an indefinite period. Arguably, the obligation to return a fixed amount at a fixed date (along with interest in the interim) itself limits the stockholder's use of the bondholder's investment. Hence, for the bargain between them to be productive during the period of the loan, the stockholders must be free, at least in their regular operations, from the indeterminate restrictions that are implicit in a fiduciary relationship. That interest must be paid and the loan must be renewed or repaid may act as sufficient constraints on stockholder strategic behavior to reduce the need for fiduciary—albeit not contractual—restraints during the loan's term.[e] In any event, to the extent that the fiduciary concept has come to permit self-aggrandizing conduct, it offers no special clue beyond the notion of "fairness" regarding how to share gains or losses of such behavior.

Can the gain-sharing problem be avoided by offering bondholders in the *Metropolitan Life* situation an exit door as their sole remedy? In other words, the transaction would be deemed to create an implied redemption right. Could such a rule result in a bondholder windfall? What would be the effect of such a rule on the cost of the transaction?

About the only obligation that separates a fiduciary from an arms-length contracting party that generally may be imposed on the common stock vis-a-vis the bondholders (or preferred stockholders) is the obligation to disclose when seeking a change in the contract. And it is not clear how or why that obligation differs from the "good faith" obligation of contracting parties to each other.[f]

In any event, is the problem of protecting holders of bonds different when the creditor is a private or institutional lender than when the lenders are public investors? In view of the difference between the bargaining incentives of private lenders and the underwriter who is the only bargainer for the public investor, it is likely that a private loan agreement will have more protective provisions than the looser provi-

---

e. The Delaware Supreme Court, discussing an issue of convertible debentures in Simons v. Cogan, 549 A.2d 300, 303–304 (1988), stated that "a mere expectancy interest does not create a fiduciary relationship. Before a fiduciary duty arises, an existing property right or an equitable interest supporting that duty must exist. The obvious example is stock ownership." If the stockholder can waive its entitlement to fiduciary protection by contract in advance, see, e.g., Del.Corp.L. sec. 102(b)(7); Matter of Reading Co., 711 F.2d 509 (3d Cir.1983), why should the difference between "property" and "contract" or "expectancy" be treated as so significant?

f. Do any or all the considerations that underpin the imposition of fiduciary restrictions on management or controllers for the benefit of common stockholders jus-

tify imposition of such restrictions on common stock or management in order to protect preferred stockholders? If the justification that validates invoking fiduciary constraints varies, depending on whether the beneficiaries are holders of bonds, convertible bonds, preferred stock or common stock, should the content of the restrictions vary? For example, if disclosure, rather than regulatory allocation or prohibition of gains, is the restraining behavior required by fiduciary considerations, may the fiduciary concept be invoked for a relationship that does not otherwise require or justify its invocations? See Zahn v. Transamerica Corp., 162 F.2d 36 (3d Cir.1947). How can a court define that content in terms that leave planners or litigators with meaningful guidelines?

sions that are contained in an equivalently priced public loan agreement.[g] The bond market is said to be a continuum that permits borrowers to go to the public for loans if they are not satisfied with the protective provisions that private lenders insist upon. However, if the public investor is likely to be less well protected than the private lender (because of the difference between his institutional bargaining position with that of the private lender) the competition thus generated for the borrower's business between private and public lenders is not that envisioned in an economist's model. Is there a market defect which might require different protective remedies for public bondholders than are needed by private investors? Should that protection be afforded by a more sympathetic judicial reading of the protective covenant (particularly the "notice" provisions) in an indenture governing public issue of debt than of similar provisions in a private loan agreement? Would such an interpretive tilt be contrary to the admonition of the court in *Sharon Steel*? Or do public bondholders require legislative or administrative prescription of protective provisions?

Quite apart from offering bondholders fiduciary or expanded contractual protection against strategic behavior by the equity or its management, there are two other possibilities for restraining strategic behavior that disadvantages them. One is to resort to antifraud strictures under the securities laws to require *ex ante* disclosure of risks of strategic behavior to which the bondholders are exposed. That path presents substantial obstacles, illustrated by the *McMahan* case and others discussed infra pp. 226–231.[h] Another possibility is to give bondholders voting power over any changes in corporate structure that might adversely affect them. Is the hold up potential of such a remedy more costly than its benefits? Would the voting power remedy be too costly if required for holders of public bonds but not for private lenders?

Finally, it should be noted that, in both law and economics, the nature of the bondholder's relationship to the borrower, its common stockholders, and its managers undergoes a change when the borrower becomes insolvent, or insolvency becomes immediately foreseeable. At this point, business judgments that maximize value from the common stockholder's point of view may not maximize value if viewed in the abstract. See the discussion of the agency costs of debt supra p. 188. In theory, the corporate law system of stockholder-directed fiduciary duties collapses at this point, and the directors make decisions that maximize the value of the corporate entity, and thus benefit the bondholders. See Credit Lyonnais Bank Nederland, N.V. v. MGM Pathe Communications Co., 1991 WL 277613 at 42 & n. 55 (Del.Ch.1991)

---

g. It has been suggested as a basis for denying fiduciary protection to bondholders that the contracts negotiated with the debtor by underwriters and indenture trustees offer dispersed public bondholders more or better protection against strategic behavior during the life of the bonds than do the contracts negotiated for equally dispersed public common stockholders by underwriters. Simons v. Cogan, 542 A.2d 785 (Del.Ch.1987), aff'd, 549 A.2d 300 (Del. 1988). Is the difference enough to justify denying to the former the fiduciary protection offered to the latter?

h. These are occasionally overcome. See Harris v. Union Electric Co., 787 F.2d 355 (8th Cir.1986).

(Allen, C.); Geyer v. Ingersoll Publications Co., 1992 WL 136473 (Del. Ch.1992). This creditor-directed duty has been brought to bear to protect bondholders injured by high leverage restructurings under the rubric of fraudulent conveyance avoidance. But, as the materials infra pp. 254–269 show, this occurs only in extreme situations. Many questions arise as to when an enterprise is insolvent or so foreseeably insolvent as to trigger these obligations, the exact scope of these obligations, and their integration with directors' obligations to stockholders. Some of these questions are discussed in LoPucki and Whitford, Corporate Governance in the Bankruptcy of Large Publicly Held Companies, 141 U.Pa.L.Rev. 669, 767–96 (1992), and Davis, McCullogh, McNulty and Schuler, Corporate Reorganization in the 1990s, 47 Bus. Law. 1 (1991).

Recent commentary on bondholder protection takes a range of positions on the questions set out above. Fiduciary duties to bondholders are advocated in McDaniel, Bondholders and Stockholders, 1988 J.Corp.Law 205, McDaniel, Bondholders and Corporate Governance, 41 Bus.Law. 413 (1986), Mitchell, The Fairness Rights of Corporate Bondholders, 65 N.Y.U.L.Rev. 1165 (1990), and, Barkey, The Financial Articulation of a Fiduciary Duty to Bondholders with Fiduciary Duties to the Stockholders of the Corporation, 20 Creighton L.Rev. 47 (1986). A contractual good faith duty with power to substitute for covenants and constrain opportunism in respect of bonds issued prior to the appearance of new event risks is advocated in Brudney, Corporate Bondholders and Debtor Opportunism: In Bad Times and Good, 105 Harv.L.Rev. 1821 (1992), Bratton, Corporate Debt Relationships: Legal Theory in a Time of Restructuring, 1989 Duke L.J. 92, and Bratton, The Economics and Jurisprudence of Convertible Bonds, 1984 Wis.L.Rev. 667. A contractual good faith duty without the power to substitute for covenants is recognized in Coffee, Unstable Coalitions: Corporate Governance As a Multi–Player Game, 78 Geo.L.J. 1495 (1990), and Tauke, Should Bonds Have More Fun? A Reexamination of the Debate Over Corporate Bondholder Rights, 1989 Colum.Bus.Rev. 1. Hurst and McGuinness, The Corporation, the Bondholder and Fiduciary Duties, 10 J.L. & Commerce 187 (1991), also argues against judicial intervention, recommending that bondholders get stricter covenants, keep themselves informed and, in extreme cases, invoke the fraudulent conveyance laws. Economic analysts have tended to argue against judicial intervention. See Kanda, Debtholders and Equityholders, 21 J. Legal Stud. 431 (1992); Lehn and Poulsen, The Economics of Event Risk: The Case of Bondholders in Leveraged Buyouts, 15 J.Corp.L. 197 (1990); Lehn and Poulsen, Contractual Resolution of Bondholder–Stockholder Conflicts in Leveraged Buyouts, 34 J.L. & Econ. 645 (1991).

(3) The Unprotected Bond and the Antifraud
Rules of the Federal Securities Laws.
McMAHAN & CO. v. WHEREHOUSE ENTERTAINMENT, INC.
United States Court of Appeals, Second Circuit, 1990.

900 F.2d 576, cert. denied, __ U.S. __, 111 S.Ct. 2887, 115 L.Ed.2d 1052 (1991).

Before: OAKES, PRATT, Circuit Judges, and LEONARD B. SAND, United States District Judge for the Southern District of New York, sitting by designation.

Opinion of PRATT, Circuit Judge.

* * *

BACKGROUND

Defendant Wherehouse Entertainment, Inc. offered 6¼% convertible subordinated debentures whose key selling feature was a right of holders to tender the debentures to Wherehouse in the case of certain triggering events which might endanger the value of the debentures. The tender right was to arise if:

(a) A person or group * * * shall attain the beneficial ownership * * * of an equity interest representing at least 80% of the voting power * * * unless such attainment has been approved by a majority of the Independent Directors;

(b) The Company * * * consolidates or merges * * * unless approved by a majority of the Independent Directors;

(c) The Company * * * incurs * * * any Debt * * * excluding * * * Debt which is authorized or ratified by a majority of the Independent Directors, immediately after the incurrence of which the ratio of the Company's Consolidated Total Debt to its Consolidated Capitalization exceeds .65 to 1.0.

* * *

The offering materials defined an "Independent Director" as "a director of the Company" who was not a recent employee but who was a member of the board of directors on the date of the offering or who was subsequently elected to the board by the then-Independent Directors. * * * The reason offered for this unusual right to tender was that it would be a protection against certain forms of take-over attempts, including leveraged buy-outs. Prospectus Description of Debentures, "Effect on Certain Takeovers", 27. At the heart of this appeal is the meaning of the limitation placed on the right to tender by the role of "Independent Directors".

Plaintiffs are financial institutions that purchased 34% of the convertible debentures. Eighteen months after the purchase, Wherehouse entered into a merger agreement with defendants WEI Holdings, Inc. and its subsidiary WEI Acquisition Corp. The practical effect of the merger, accomplished through a leveraged buyout, left Wherehouse with a debt approaching 90% of its capitalization and left plaintiffs' debentures valued at only approximately 50% of par. Plaintiffs attempted to exercise their right to tender, but the company refused to redeem the debentures on the ground that the "board of directors" had approved the merger. Plaintiffs then commenced this suit for damages and an injunction to prevent the merger. * * * Plaintiffs claimed that the descriptions of the debentures in the registration materials, as well as representations made during conversations, were materially misleading. Specifically, they claimed that, even though the defendants knew that the right to tender was illusory, their representations of the right as valuable and protected had misled investors into buying the debentures and therefore violated federal securities laws. * * *

Defendants argued that all the relevant provisions were clear and unambiguous and that no false statements were made; thus the offering was not materially misleading or in violation of the securities laws.

The district court found nothing misleading. * * * The district court held that defendants were not required to speculate about the likelihood of a waiver of debentureholders' right by the Independent Directors and that, even if the right were worthless, defendants were not required to use pejorative terms describing it as such. Moreover, it found the tender option was not illusory, because it (was possible that it) might provide a benefit to debentureholders in the case of a takeover hostile to shareholders which management chose to fight. * * *

We disagree with the district court's atomistic consideration of the presentation of the debentureholders' right to tender. The district court concluded that defendants had not misled plaintiffs because the information they included in the written and oral representations was "literally true". We think, however, that when read as a whole, the defendants' representations connoted a richer message than that conveyed by a literal reading of the statements. The central issue on all three claims is not whether the particular statements, taken separately, were literally true, but whether defendants' representations, taken together and in context, would have mislead a reasonable investor about the nature of the debentures.

Some statements, although literally accurate, can become, through their context and manner of presentation, devices which mislead investors. For that reason, the disclosure required by the securities laws is measured not by literal truth, but by the ability of the material to accurately inform rather than mislead prospective buyers. Greenapple v. Detroit Edison Co., 618 F.2d 198, 205 (2d Cir.1980) (where method of presentation or "gloss" placed on information obscures or distorts significance of material facts, it is misleading). Even " 'a statement which is literally true, if susceptible to quite another interpretation by the reasonable investor * * * may properly * * * be considered a material misrepresentation.' " Beecher v. Able, 374 F.Supp. 341, 347 (S.D.N.Y.1974) quoting SEC v. First American Bank & Trust Co., 481 F.2d 673 (8th Cir.1973).

We hold that * * * plaintiffs have raised a triable issue as to whether the written and oral representations about the right to tender these debentures were materially misleading to a reasonable investor in violation of § 11 and § 12 of the 1933 Securities Act and also of § 10(b) of the 1934 Securities Exchange Act. Since the analysis for all three securities claims is similar, we will first consider it in some detail under § 11, and then review it only briefly under §§ 12 and 10(b).

A. *Section 11 of the Securities Act of 1933*

Section 11 states that any signer, officer of the issuer, and underwriter may be held liable for a registration statement which "contained an untrue statement of a material fact or omitted to state a material fact * * * necessary to make the statements therein not misleading". Plaintiffs claim that these offering materials misstated the right to tender and omitted important information about it in violation of § 11. They argue that a reasonable investor would have believed that the right to tender was valuable because it was presented as a right to be exercised at the holder's option and as a protection against takeovers that might affect the security of the debentures. In truth, however, the right to tender was illusory, they argue, because it was designed to be exercised only at the option of management and therefore was intended to protect the interest of shareholders, not of debentureholders.

Plaintiffs are correct that the offering materials can reasonably be read to present the option to tender as a valuable right. The language used was invariably language of entitlement:

> *Holder's Right to Tender.* The Holder of any Security or Securities shall have the right, at his option, * * * to tender for redemption any such Security or Securities.

Indenture § 5.01, 10 (emphasis added). The prospectus summary provided that:

> "Each holder of Debentures has the option to require the Company to redeem the holder's Debentures."

And the prospectus itself stated:

> "Holders of the Debentures *will have the option * * * to require* the Company to redeem such Debentures."

Further, a jury could reasonably view the presentation of the right to tender as a special feature to protect investors, for the offering materials stressed the purported value of the right in any takeover transaction which would threaten the value of the debentures.

> Since the events which give rise to such right of redemption could be expected to occur in connection with certain forms of takeover attempts, the optional tender provisions could deter takeovers where the person attempting the takeover views itself as unable to finance the redemption of the principal amount of Debentures which may be tendered * * * To the extent that Debentures may be tendered * * * the Company would be unable to use the financing provided by the sale of the Debentures offered hereby. In addition, the ability of the Company to obtain additional Senior Debt based on the existence of the Debentures would be similarly adversely affected.

Prospectus Description of Debentures, "Effect on Certain Takeovers", 27; see also id. "Optional Debenture Tender", 26.

Finally, the right was restricted only in that it was subject to action by "the Independent Directors". Similar language describing the restriction—the right to tender occurs upon a triggering event, "*unless* [the event is] approved by a majority of the Independent Directors" (emphasis added)—is found in the Indenture—* * * A jury could reasonably find that this repeated use of the word "unless" encouraged the inference that exercise of the right would be the norm and that waiver would be the exception.

Although the offering materials explain that the Independent Directors would be chosen from the company's board of directors, the term "Independent Director" implies a special status, some distinction from an "ordinary" director. The term suggests that these directors would be "independent" of management and the normal obligations of board members to act in the interests of shareholders. Thus the restriction could reasonably be understood to mean that in the case of a triggering event, the right to tender would arise *unless* the Independent Directors find the event to be in the interests of the debentureholders. In short, as plaintiffs argue, a reasonable investor could have regarded the right to tender as a valuable right, protected by Independent Directors who would, in situations endangering the security of the debentures, consider debentureholders' interest before approving any waiver of their right.

By thus representing that in a takeover context the Independent Directors would be considering the interests of debentureholders, the defendants implied that the Independent Directors had a duty to protect the debentureholders' interests. Defendants, however, have shown nothing in their corporate charter or by-laws that would have permitted, much less required, these Independent Directors to favor debentureholders over shareholders. Moreover, at the time of the approval of this merger, the Independent Directors constituted all but one of the "ordinary" directors on the board. As ordinary directors, they had a fiduciary duty to protect the interest of shareholders in any takeover situation, regardless of debentureholders' interests or rights. It is inevitable, then, that the so-called Independent Directors had no independence; they would never protect the interest of debentureholders except by coincidence because, as ordinary directors, they were required by law to protect the interests of the shareholders. From this perspective, there is merit in plaintiffs' contentions that the right to tender was illusory and that the representations of it in the offering materials were misleading.

In sum, on a fair reading of the offering materials, despite their literal meaning, an investor could have reasonably believed that the tender option was presented as a valuable right for debentureholders; that it provided a special feature of protection for their interests; and that Independent Directors were to render independent votes on the right to tender based on the impact of a merger and on the interests of debentureholders. But if, as plaintiffs claim, the right to tender was illusory because the Independent Directors were tied to management, served its needs, protected shareholders' interests, and would inevitably waive the right in any merger beneficial to management regardless of debentureholders' interests, then the offering materials could be found by a rational trier of fact to be materially misleading in violation of § 11 of the Securities Act of 1933. * * *

B. *Section 12 of the Securities Act of 1933*

    * * *

C. *Section 10(b) of the Securities Exchange Act of 1934*

    * * *

The district court, having dismissed the claims under § 11, found it was therefore impossible to state a § 10(b) claim. Since we have concluded that a question of fact is presented as to whether the offering materials and the oral communications, taken together, could have misled a reasonable investor, it follows that a jury should also determine whether the defendants violated of § 10(b).

    * * *

Reversed and remanded.

[Dissenting opinion of Sand, District Judge].

The reasons why I am constrained to dissent may be briefly stated.

The question whether an anti-takeover provision provides a "special protection" to debentureholders cannot be answered in the negative merely because the "Independent Directors" decided to waive its provisions and approve a particular transaction. These directors were explicitly empowered to act in this fashion by virtue of the fully disclosed terms of the provision. A significant function of an anti-takeover provision is to serve as a deterrent to hostile takeovers, including takeovers which would be contrary to the interests of both shareholders and debenture holders. One cannot, I believe, fairly characterize such a provision as being "worthless" to the debentureholders, even though as a matter of Delaware law directors owe a fiduciary duty solely to shareholders. The anti-takeover provision was therefore a "special protection" to debentureholders, albeit a limited one.

Federal securities laws do not impose an obligation to advise investors of the fundamentals of corporate governance. The disclosure required by the federal securities laws is not a "rite of confession or exercise in common law pleading. What is required is the disclosure of material objective factual matters." Data Probe Acquisition Corp. v. Data Lab, Inc., 722 F.2d 1, 5–6 (2d Cir.1983), cert. denied, 415 U.S. 1052 (1984). Especially is this so where, as here, the investor-complainants are sophisticated financial institutions making major investments. The role of the federal securities laws is not to remedy all perceived injustices in securities transactions. Rather, as invoked in this case, it proscribes only the making of false and misleading statements or material omissions.

* * *

Believing no valid federal claim to be present, I would affirm essentially for the reasons set forth in the Opinions of the Magistrate and District Court.

(C) ALTERING THE BOND CONTRACT—
COERCED VOTES AND HOLD OUTS

Promises in bond contracts, like promises in all contracts, can be amended, or their performance can be waived. Sometimes debt issuers request amendments or waivers during good times. For instance, an issuer subject to a tight set of business covenants might need a waiver to do a financing or make an investment outside of the framework permitted by the debt contract. As noted above, the process of collecting bondholder consents to such waivers is much less onerous with private placements than with public issues.

Amendments and waivers are particularly likely to be requested by issuers in financial difficulty. When a bond issuer encounters serious distress, lessening its debt obligations is the most obvious means of alleviating the problem. If the bondholders can be induced to lower the interest rate, forgive a payment default, waive a prepayment or prepayments, waive or amend one or more business covenants, consent to some combination of the foregoing, or exchange their bonds for some less onerous package of securities, the "distress" is diminished or even eliminated without the expense and uncertainty of a bankruptcy proceeding.

Various terms describe the process of revising debt obligations to avoid distress—"workout," "composition," "restructuring," "recapitalization." Whatever the term, the distressed issuer takes advantage of the fact that its debt obligations sell at a deep discount from face value. There are a number of standard techniques. If the debt is publicly traded and the issuer has some free cash flow, it can take the simple step of repurchasing the bonds on the market at the discounted price, thereby reducing its debt carrying cost. Such a cash repurchase also might be done by means of a public tender offer, or in the case of privately held debt, by face to face negotiation. More often, the issuer does not have the spare cash to repurchase the debt, and must deal with publicly traded debt by means of an "exchange offer." This is a public offer to the holders of the debt, the consideration for which is new debt securities with scaled down rights, equity securities, cash, or a mix of the three. With privately held debt, an equivalent offer would be the subject of a face to face negotiation. Either way, the issuer must offer the bondholders a package with a value higher than the current trading value of the bonds. In exchange for the increase in present value, the bondholders give up their contract right to full payment, and possibly other contract rights. The process may or may not involve a direct amendment of outstanding debt contracts.

Two problems recur in workout situations. First, particularly in the case of exchange offers, questions arise as to whether the context allows the bondholders to make an effective choice. As the materials that follow show, issuers can work elements of coercion into exchange offers and bond amendment processes, whether or not they control a voting majority of the bonds. And, in any event, the issuer's power to determine the timing of the restructuring or amendment and to over-state the gloomy consequences of a failure to acquiesce in it offers dispersed bondholders a distorted choice and puts them at a substantial bargaining disadvantage.

Second, if a bargaining arrangement that entails aggregative action (e.g., an exchange or repurchase offer) or collective action (e.g., a majority vote that binds a minority) by bondholders to approve a proposed readjustment is vulnerable to debtor opportunism, a bargain-ing arrangement that permits holdouts creates an added possibility of failure of the readjustment, even though it may increase the debtor's offering price to bondholders. If the necessary majority exchanges its bonds or consents to the amendment a benefit may flow to the non-consenting minority. By refusing to consent, these holders will be left holding bonds carrying rights to full principal and coupon—although they incur the risk that they will not be paid until later and may be paid less than the amount offered in the proposed readjustment. They therefore have an incentive to hold out, but at a risk. If too many hold out, a bargaining impasse results, and the recapitalization fails to garner sufficient consents. The issuer proceeds to a more costly bank-ruptcy, having lost the chance to substitute an advantageous revised capital structure.

Widespread debtor distress following on the restructuring move-ment of the 1980s, has made the problems of recapitalizations a topic of concern. With substantial numbers of junk bond issues in or near default, see supra p. 207, recapitalization proposals have become every-day business in recent years.

ALADDIN HOTEL CO. v. BLOOM
United States Court of Appeals, Eighth Circuit, 1953.
200 F.2d 627.

GARDNER, Chief Judge. As originally brought this was in form a class action in which Josephine Loeb Bloom as plaintiff sought for herself and other minority bondholders of the Aladdin Hotel Company similarly situated equitable relief. She named as defendants Aladdin Hotel Company, a corporation, Charles O. Jones, Inez M. Jones, Charles R. Jones, Kathryn Dorothea Jones, Barbara Ann Jones and Mississippi Valley Trust Company, a corporation. She alleged that the class whom she purported to represent consisted of approximately 130 members who were the owners of a minority in value of certain bonds issued by the Aladdin Hotel Company, and that the object of the action was to obtain an adjudication of claims which affected specific property involved in the action and that common questions of law and fact affecting the rights of the parties constituting the class were involved; that on September 1, 1938, the Aladdin Hotel Company executed and delivered a series of 647 bonds aggregating in principal amount the sum of $250,000.00. The bonds on their face were made payable September 1, 1948, with interest to that date at 5 per cent per annum payable only out of net earnings and with interest at the rate of 8 per cent per annum from maturity until paid; that the Hotel Company to secure payment of said bond issue executed its deed of trust by which it mortgaged certain real estate owned by it in Kansas City, Missouri; that the mortgage also covered furnishings and fixtures in the hotel property owned by the Aladdin Hotel Company; that the Mississippi Valley Trust Company was named as trustee in said deed of trust; that the bonds and deed of trust contained provision empowering the bondholders of not less than two-thirds principal amount of the bonds, by agreement with the Hotel Company to modify and extend the date of payment of said bonds provided such extension affected all bonds alike. She then alleged that she was the owner of some of said bonds of the total principal amount of $3500; that the defendants, other than the Hotel Company and the Mississippi Valley Trust Company, were all members of the so-called Jones family and during the period from May 1, 1948 to the time of the commencement of this action they were the owners of a majority of the stock of the Hotel Company and controlling members of its Board of Directors and dominated and controlled all acts and policies of the Hotel Company; that they were also the owners and holders of more than two-thirds of the principal amount of said bonds, being the owners of more than 72 per cent thereof; that they entered into an agreement with the Hotel Company June 1, 1948 to extend the maturity date of said bonds from September 1, 1948 to September 1, 1958. It was also alleged that other changes were similarly made, on various dates, in the provisions of the trust deed but as the trial court deemed them immaterial we pretermit reciting them here in detail. It was alleged that the defendant Mississippi Valley Trust Company certified the modifications as provided in the trust deed; that the purported changes were made on application of the Hotel Company and with the consent of the holders of two-thirds in principal value of the outstanding bonds; that no notice of said application for change in the due date of the bonds was given to the mortgage bondholders and that plaintiff did not consent nor agree to the modification. She then alleged that the modifications were invalid because not made in good faith and were not for the equal benefit of all bondholders but were made corruptly for the benefit of the defendants and such modification deprived plaintiff and the other mortgage bondholders of their rights and property; that said modification extended for ten additional years the powers and compensation of the Mississippi Valley Trust Company as trustee; that the Mississippi Valley Trust Company is made defendant because it is a party to the aforesaid modifications and waivers and participated in effecting them and because it benefitted by aforesaid modifications, waivers and certifications. * * * Plaintiff prayed for a declaratory judgment declaring and holding that the purported modifications, waivers and certifications are illegal, inequitable and void; that she and all other bondholders of the defendant Aladdin Hotel Company have judgment against defendant Aladdin Hotel Company for the principal amount of the bonds held by each of them with interest thereon at 8 per cent per annum (allowing said defendant credit thereon, however, for the 5 per cent per annum interest paid thereon) from September 1, 1948 until the payment of such principal and interest.

On trial the court dismissed as to all individual defendants, including the Mississippi Valley Trust Company, and made findings that the amendments benefitted the Hotel Company and the Joneses but did not benefit the bondholders; that all bondholders were entitled to notice of any proposed amendments; that the Joneses acting as the Hotel Company's officers and as majority bondholders, had a legal duty to exercise an honest discretion in extending the bonds; that the power to postpone the maturity date of the bonds could not be legally recognized in the majority bondholders under the facts of this case; that the decree, however, should be limited to a money judgment because that would grant plaintiff full relief. * * *

In seeking reversal the Hotel Company in substance contends * * * that the modification of the provisions of the trust deed extending the time of maturity of the bonds was effected in strict compliance with the provisions of the contract of the parties and hence was binding on all the bondholders * * *.

The trust deed contained provision that,

"In the event the Company shall propose any change, modification, alteration or extension of the bonds issued hereunder or of this Indenture, such change, if approved by the holders of not less than two-thirds in face amount of the bonds at the time outstanding, shall be binding and effective upon all of the holders of the then outstanding bonds, provided, however, that such modification, change, alteration or extension shall affect all of the outstanding bonds similarly."

The bonds, including those held by plaintiff, contained the following:

"The terms of this bond or of the Indenture securing the same may be modified, extended, changed or altered by agreement between the Company and the holders of two-thirds or more in face amount of bonds of this issue at the time outstanding. Any default under the Indenture may be waived by the holders of two-thirds or more in face amount of the bonds at the time outstanding."

The bonds also contained the following provision:

"For a more particular description of the covenants of the
Company as well as a description of the mortgaged property, of the
nature and extent of the security, of the rights of the holders of the
bonds and of the terms and conditions upon which the bonds are
issued and secured, reference is made to said General Mortgage
Deed of Trust."

It appears without dispute that the modification here under consideration was made in strict compliance with the provisions contained in
the trust deed and by reference embodied in the bonds. The Hotel
Company made the application to the trustee and it was approved by
the holders of more than two-thirds in face amount of the bonds at the
time outstanding. When this application for modification was made to
the trustee he was guided in his action by the terms of the contract
between the parties. That contract made no provision for notice. It
required that such application have the approval of those holding two-
thirds or more in face value of the bonds. The only other limitation
contained in the contract with reference to the power to modify its
terms was to the effect that "such modification, change, alteration or
extension shall affect all of the outstanding bonds similarly." The
modification did affect all outstanding *bonds* similarly and it is important, we think, to observe that the contract does not require that such
modification affect all *bondholders* similarly. What effect this change
might have on various bondholders might depend upon various circumstances and conditions with which the trustee was not required to
concern itself. The so-called Joneses were the controlling stockholders
of the Hotel Company and were its officers and the court found that the
alteration was advantageous to the Hotel Company. It was doubtless
effected primarily to benefit the financial standing and operating
efficiency of the hotel. It does not follow, however, that such modification was prejudicial to the bondholders. Their security was greatly
improved in value by the management and it is inconceivable that the
Joneses should deliberately act to the prejudice or detriment of the
bondholders when they held and owned some 72 per cent of the entire
outstanding bond issue. It is urged that because the Joneses were
acting in a dual capacity they became trustees for the other bondholders and that as such it was incumbent upon them to do no act
detrimental to the rights of the bondholders. The rights of the bondholders, however, are to be determined by their contract and courts will
not make or remake a contract merely because one of the parties
thereto may become dissatisfied with its provisions, but if legal will
interpret and enforce it. Monticello Bldg. Corp. v. Monticello Inv. Co.,
330 Mo. 1128, 52 S.W.2d 545; Minneapolis–Moline Co. v. Chicago M. St.
P. & P.R. Co., 8 Cir., 199 F.2d 725. There is no question that the
provision in the trust deed and bonds was a legal provision which
violated no principle of public policy nor private right. The sole ground
for holding the modification extending the time for payment void is
that no notice was given the minority bondholders. If the Joneses had
not been acting in a dual capacity, then, we assume, the modification,
effected as it was with the approval of the holders of two-thirds of the

face value of the outstanding bonds, would have been held good. It is conceded that under such circumstances no notice would have been necessary. We think the situation must be viewed realistically. No notice was required so far as the parties to the contract were concerned. Their rights must be determined by their contract and not by any equitable doctrine, and notice to the other bondholders could have served no possible purpose. Litigants have no standing in a court of equity where a remedy at law is available. The holders of more than two-thirds of the face value of the bonds could not have been prevented from approving the proposed change even had notice been given and the acts of the parties must be determined in relation to the terms of their contract. It follows that no prejudice could have been suffered by plaintiff or her grantors by the fact that notice of the proposed change or modification was not given them.

We have searched the record with great care and find no substantial evidence warranting a finding of bad faith, fraud, corruption or conspiracy of the Joneses. When Charles O. Jones became manager of the hotel properties in 1944 no interest had been paid on the bonds prior to that date. The Hotel Company paid the interest to all bondholders in 1944 and the interest has been paid each year since. Numerous improvements were made in the hotel property at an expense of over $300,000. At the time the Joneses took over the management in 1944 the Company had a deficit of $70,000 and a balance due of $24,000 on the first mortgage of $50,000, all of which has been paid off, and the gross income of the hotel has increased from $219,000 in 1944 to $600,000 in 1951, and the book value of the stock has increased from $384,000 in 1944 to $916,000 in 1951. The properties covered by the trust deed were at the time of the trial of the proximate value of $1,000,000.

* * *

The judgment appealed from is * * * reversed and the cause is remanded to the trial court with directions to dismiss plaintiff's complaint.

NOTE: AMENDMENT UNDER THE TRUST INDENTURE ACT

Model Simplified Indenture, Appendix C, Section 1
Article 9 (Amendments)

Trust Indenture Act of 1939, as amended 1990
Section 316

(a) The indenture to be qualified

(1) shall automatically be deemed (unless it is expressly provided therein that any such provision is excluded) to contain provi-

sions authorizing the holders of not less than a majority in principal amount of the indenture securities or if expressly specified in such indenture, of any series of securities at the time outstanding (A) to direct the time, method, and place of conducting any proceeding for any remedy available to such trustee, or exercising any trust or power conferred upon such trustee, under such indenture, or (B) on behalf of the holders of all such indenture securities, to consent to the waiver of any past default and its consequences; or

(2) may contain provisions authorizing the holders of not less than 75 per centum in principal amount of the indenture securities or if expressly specified in such indenture, of any series of securities at the time outstanding to consent on behalf of the holders of all such indenture securities to the postponement of any interest payment for a period not exceeding three years from its due date.

For the purposes of this subsection and paragraph (3) of subsection (d) of section 315, in determining whether the holders of the required principal amount of indenture securities have concurred in any such direction or consent, indenture securities owned by any obligor upon the indenture securities, or by any person directly or indirectly controlling or controlled by or under direct or indirect common control with any such obligor, shall be disregarded, except that for the purposes of determining whether the indenture trustee shall be protected in relying on any such direction or consent, only indenture securities which such trustee knows are so owned shall be so disregarded.

(b) Notwithstanding any other provision of the indenture to be qualified, the right of any holder of any indenture security to receive payment of the principal of and interest on such indenture security, on or after the respective due dates expressed in such indenture security, or to institute suit for the enforcement of any such payment on or after such respective dates, shall not be impaired or affected without the consent of such holder, except as to a postponement of an interest payment consented to as provided in paragraph (2) of subsection (a), and except that such indenture may contain provisions limiting or denying the right of any such holder to institute any such suit, if and to the extent that the institution or prosecution thereof or the entry of judgment therein would, under applicable law, result in the surrender, impairment, waiver, or loss of the lien of such indenture upon any property subject to such lien.

Section 316 of the Trust Indenture Act restricts the power of majorities of bondholders to defer or forgive principal and interest payments. It was enacted as a response to process abuses that occurred in Depression-era recapitalizations. The trust indentures of the era did not tend to limit majoritarian amendment power. Under those clauses, majorities often were induced to make modifications which were seriously detrimental to all the bondholders, without a comparable sacrifice being made by the debtor's stockholders, and sometimes without there even being any necessity for the particular concession extracted. In some cases the vote of the bondholders for the modification was obtained by misinformation or inadequate information from biased sources. In other cases, as in *Aladdin Hotel v. Bloom,* votes were cast by bondholders with interests adverse to others of their class.

How does section 316(a) of the Act affect the structure of the workout in *Oak Industries,* which follows? Does section 316 assure bondholders an opportunity to maximize the value of their bonds in distress situations? If not, what problem do the bondholders face, and how should the problem be solved?

KATZ v. OAK INDUSTRIES INC.

Court of Chancery of Delaware, 1986.
508 A.2d 873.

ALLEN, Chancellor.

* * *

Plaintiff is the owner of long-term debt securities issued by Oak Industries, Inc. ("Oak"), a Delaware corporation; in this class action he seeks to enjoin the consummation of an exchange offer and consent solicitation made by Oak to holders of various classes of its long-term debt. As detailed below that offer is an integral part of a series of transactions that together would effect a major reorganization and recapitalization of Oak. The claim asserted is in essence, that the exchange offer is a coercive device and, in the circumstances, consti-tutes a breach of contract. This is the Court's opinion on plaintiff's pending application for a preliminary injunction.

I.

The background facts are involved even when set forth in the abbreviated form the decision within the time period currently avail-able requires.

Through its domestic and foreign subsidiaries and affiliated enti-ties, Oak manufactures and markets component equipments used in consumer, industrial and military products (the "Components Seg-ment"); produces communications equipment for use in cable television systems and satellite television systems (the "Communications Seg-ment") and manufactures and markets laminates and other materials used in printed circuit board applications (the "Materials Segment"). During 1985, the Company has terminated certain other unrelated businesses. As detailed below, it has now entered into an agreement with Allied–Signal, Inc. for the sale of the Materials Segment of its business and is currently seeking a buyer for its Communications Segment.

Even a casual review of Oak's financial results over the last several years shows it unmistakably to be a company in deep trouble. During the period from January 1, 1982 through September 30, 1985, the

Company has experienced unremitting losses from operations; on net sales of approximately $1.26 billion during that period * * * it has lost over $335 million * * *. As a result its total stockholders' equity has first shriveled (from $260 million on 12/31/81 to $85 million on 12/31/83) and then disappeared completely (as of 9/30/85 there was a $62 million deficit in its stockholders' equity accounts) * * *. Financial markets, of course, reflected this gloomy history.[2]

Unless Oak can be made profitable within some reasonably short time it will not continue as an operating company. Oak's board of directors, comprised almost entirely of outside directors, has authorized steps to buy the company time. In February, 1985, in order to reduce a burdensome annual cash interest obligation on its $230 million of then outstanding debentures, the Company offered to exchange such debentures for a combination of notes, common stock and warrants. As a result, approximately $180 million principal amount of the then outstanding debentures were exchanged. Since interest on certain of the notes issued in that exchange offer is payable in common stock, the effect of the 1985 exchange offer was to reduce to some extent the cash drain on the Company caused by its significant debt.

About the same time that the 1985 exchange offer was made, the Company announced its intention to discontinue certain of its operations and sell certain of its properties. Taking these steps, while effective to stave off a default and to reduce to some extent the immediate cash drain, did not address Oak's longer-range problems. Therefore, also during 1985 representatives of the Company held informal discussions with several interested parties exploring the possibility of an investment from, combination with or acquisition by another company. As a result of these discussions, the Company and Allied–Signal, Inc. entered into two agreements. The first, the Acquisition Agreement, contemplates the sale to Allied–Signal of the Materials Segment for $160 million in cash. The second agreement, the Stock Purchase Agreement, provides for the purchase by Allied–Signal for $15 million cash of 10 million shares of the Company's common stock together with warrants to purchase additional common stock.

The Stock Purchase Agreement provides as a condition to Allied–Signal's obligation that at least 85% of the aggregate principal amount of all of the Company's debt securities shall have tendered and accepted the exchange offers that are the subject of this lawsuit. Oak has six classes of such long term debt.[3] If less than 85% of the aggregate principal amount of such debt accepts the offer, Allied–Signal has an

2. The price of the company's common stock has fallen from over $30 per share on December 31, 1981 to approximately $2 per share recently. * * * The debt securities that are the subject of the exchange offer here involved (see note 3 for identification) have traded at substantial discounts.

3. The three classes of debentures are: 13.65% debentures due April 1, 2001, 10½% convertible subordinated debentures due February 1, 2002, and 11⅞% subordi-

nated debentures due May 15, 1998. In addition, as a result of the 1985 exchange offer the company has three classes of notes which were issued in exchange for debentures that were tendered in that offer. Those are: 13.5% senior notes due May 15, 1990, 9⅝% convertible notes due September 15, 1991 and 11⅝% notes due September 15, 1990.

option, but no obligation, to purchase the common stock and warrants contemplated by the Stock Purchase Agreement. An additional condition for the closing of the Stock Purchase Agreement is that the sale of the Company's Materials Segment contemplated by the Acquisition Agreement shall have been concluded.

Thus, as part of the restructuring and recapitalization contemplated by the Acquisition Agreement and the Stock Purchase Agreement, the Company has extended an exchange offer to each of the holders of the six classes of its long-term debt securities. These pending exchange offers include a Common Stock Exchange Offer (available only to holders of the 9⅝% convertible notes) and the Payment Certificate Exchange Offers (available to holders of all six classes of Oak's long-term debt securities). The Common Stock Exchange Offer currently provides for the payment to each tendering noteholder of 407 shares of the Company's common stock in exchange for each $1,000 9⅝% note accepted. The offer is limited to $38.6 million principal amount of notes (out of approximately $83.9 million outstanding).

The Payment Certificate Exchange Offer is an any and all offer. Under its terms, a payment certificate, payable in cash five days after the closing of the sale of the Materials Segment to Allied–Signal, is offered in exchange for debt securities. The cash value of the Payment Certificate will vary depending upon the particular security tendered. In each instance, however, that payment will be less than the face amount of the obligation. The cash payments range in amount, per $1,000 of principal, from $918 to $655. These cash values however appear to represent a premium over the market prices for the Company's debentures as of the time the terms of the transaction were set.

The Payment Certificate Exchange Offer is subject to certain important conditions before Oak has an obligation to accept tenders under it. First, it is necessary that a minimum amount ($38.6 million principal amount out of $83.9 total outstanding principal amount) of the 9⅝% notes be tendered pursuant to the Common Stock Exchange Offer. Secondly, it is necessary that certain minimum amounts of each class of debt securities be tendered, together with consents to amendments to the underlying indentures.[4] Indeed, under the offer one may not tender securities unless at the same time one consents to the proposed amendments to the relevant indentures.

The condition of the offer that tendering security holders must consent to amendments in the indentures governing the securities gives rise to plaintiff's claim of breach of contract in this case. Those amendments would, if implemented, have the effect of removing significant negotiated protections to holders of the Company's long-term debt including the deletion of all financial covenants. Such modification

---

4. The holders of more than 50% of the principal amount of each of the 13.5% notes, the 9⅝% notes and the 11⅝% notes and at least 66⅔% of the principal amount of the 13.65% debentures, 10½% debentures, and 11⅞% debentures, must validly tender such securities and consent to certain proposed amendments to the indentures governing those securities.

may have adverse consequences to debt holders who elect not to tender pursuant to either exchange offer.

Allied–Signal apparently was unwilling to commit to the $15 million cash infusion contemplated by the Stock Purchase Agreement, unless Oak's long-term debt is reduced by 85% (at least that is a condition of their obligation to close on that contract). Mathematically, such a reduction may not occur without the Company reducing the principal amount of outstanding debentures (that is the three classes outstanding notes constitute less than 85% of all long-term debt). But existing indenture covenants * * * prohibit the Company, so long as any of its long-term notes are outstanding, from issuing any obligation (including the Payment Certificates) in exchange for any of the debentures. Thus, in this respect, amendment to the indentures is required in order to close the Stock Purchase Agreement as presently structured.

Restrictive covenants in the indentures would appear to interfere with effectuation of the recapitalization in another way. Section 4.07 of the 13.50% Indenture provides that the Company may not "acquire" for value any of the $9\frac{5}{8}\%$ Notes or $11\frac{5}{8}\%$ Notes unless it concurrently "redeems" a proportionate amount of the 13.50% Notes. This covenant, if unamended, would prohibit the disproportionate acquisition of the $9\frac{5}{8}\%$ Notes that may well occur as a result of the Exchange Offers; in addition, it would appear to require the payment of the "redemption" price for the 13.50% Notes rather than the lower, market price offered in the exchange offer.

In sum, the failure to obtain the requisite consents to the proposed amendments would permit Allied–Signal to decline to consummate both the Acquisition Agreement and the Stock Purchase Agreement.

* * *

II.

* * *

As amplified in briefing on the pending motion, plaintiff's claim is that no free choice is provided to bondholders by the exchange offer and consent solicitation. Under its terms, a rational bondholder is "forced" to tender and consent. Failure to do so would face a bondholder with the risk of owning a security stripped of all financial covenant protections and for which it is likely that there would be no ready market. A reasonable bondholder, it is suggested, cannot possibly accept those risks and thus such a bondholder is coerced to tender and thus to consent to the proposed indenture amendments.

It is urged this linking of the offer and the consent solicitation constitutes a breach of a contractual obligation that Oak owes to its bondholders to act in good faith. Specifically, plaintiff points to three contractual provisions from which it can be seen that the structuring of the current offer constitutes a breach of good faith. Those provisions (1) establish a requirement that no modification in the term of the various indentures may be effectuated without the consent of a stated percentage of bondholders; (2) restrict Oak from exercising the power to grant such consent with respect to any securities it may hold in its treasury; and (3) establish the price at which and manner in which Oak may force bondholders to submit their securities for redemption. * * * 6

III.

* * *

I turn first to an evaluation of the probability of plaintiff's ultimate success on the merits of his claim. I begin that analysis with two preliminary points. The first concerns what is not involved in this case. To focus briefly on this clears away much of the corporation law case law of this jurisdiction upon which plaintiff in part relies. This case does not involve the measurement of corporate or directorial conduct against that high standard of fidelity required of fiduciaries when they act with respect to the interests of the beneficiaries of their trust. Under our law—and the law generally—the relationship between a corporation and the holders of its debt securities, even convertible debt securities, is contractual in nature.

* * *

Arrangements among a corporation, the underwriters of its debt, trustees under its indentures and sometimes ultimate investors are typically thoroughly negotiated and massively documented. The rights and obligations of the various parties are or should be spelled out in that documentation. The terms of the contractual relationship agreed to and not broad concepts such as fairness define the corporation's obligation to its bondholders.[7]

Thus, the first aspect of the pending Exchange Offers about which plaintiff complains—that "the purpose and effect of the Exchange Offers is to benefit Oak's common stockholders at the expense of the Holders of its debt"—does not itself appear to allege a cognizable legal wrong. It is the obligation of directors to attempt, within the law, to maximize the long-run interests of the corporation's stockholders; that they may sometimes do so "at the expense" of others (even assuming that a transaction which one may refuse to enter into can meaningfully

6. It is worthy of note that a very high percentage of the principal value of Oak's debt securities are owned in substantial amounts by a handful of large financial institutions. Almost 85% of the value of the 13.50% Notes is owned by four such institutions (one investment banker owns 55% of that issue); 69.1% of the 9⅜% Notes are owned by four financial institutions (the same investment banker owning 25% of that issue) and 85% of the 11⅜% Notes are owned by five such institutions. Of the debentures, 89% of the 13.65% debentures are owned by four large banks; and approximately 45% of the two remaining issues is owned by two banks.

7. To say that the broad duty of loyalty that a director owes to his corporation and ultimately its shareholders is not implicated in this case is not to say, as the discussion below reflects, that as a matter of contract law a corporation owes no duty to bondholders of good faith and fair dealing. See, Restatement of Law, Contracts 2d, § 205 (1979). Such a duty, however, is quite different from the congeries of duties that are assumed by a fiduciary. See generally, Bratton, The Economics and Jurisprudence of Convertible Bonds, 1984 Wis. L.Rev. 667.

be said to be at his expense does not for that reason constitute a breach of duty. It seems likely that corporate restructurings designed to maximize shareholder values may in some instances have the effect of requiring bondholders to bear greater risk of loss and thus in effect transfer economic value from bondholders to stockholders. See generally, Prokesch, Merger Wave: How Stocks and Bonds Fare, N.Y. Times, Jan. 7, 1986, at A1, col. 1; McDaniel, Bondholders and Corporate Governance, 41 Bus.Law. 413, 418–423 (1986). But if courts are to provide protection against such enhanced risk, they will require either legislative direction to do so or the negotiation of indenture provisions designed to afford such protection.

The second preliminary point concerns the limited analytical utility, at least in this context, of the word "coercive" which is central to plaintiff's own articulation of his theory of recovery. If, *pro arguendo,* we are to extend the meaning of the word coercion beyond its core meaning—dealing with the utilization of physical force to overcome the will of another—to reach instances in which the claimed coercion arises from an act designed to affect the will of another party by offering inducements to the act sought to be encouraged or by arranging unpleasant consequences for an alternative sought to be discouraged, then—in order to make the term legally meaningful at all—we must acknowledge that some further refinement is essential. Clearly some "coercion" of this kind is legally unproblematic. Parents may "coerce" a child to study with the threat of withholding an allowance; employers may "coerce" regular attendance at work by either docking wages for time absent or by rewarding with a bonus such regular attendance. Other "coercion" so defined clearly would be legally relevant (to encourage regular attendance by corporal punishment, for example). Thus, for purposes of legal analysis, the term "coercion" itself—covering a multitude of situations—is not very meaningful. For the word to have much meaning for purposes of legal analysis, it is necessary in each case that a normative judgment be attached to the concept ("inappropriately coercive" or "wrongfully coercive", etc.). But, it is then readily seen that what is legally relevant is not the conclusory term "coercion" itself but rather the norm that leads to the adverb modifying it.

In this instance, assuming that the Exchange Offers and Consent Solicitation can meaningfully be regarded as "coercive" (in the sense that Oak has structured it in a way designed—and I assume effectively so—to "force" rational bondholders to tender), the relevant legal norm that will support the judgment whether such "coercion" is wrongful or not will, for the reasons mentioned above, be derived from the law of contracts. I turn then to that subject to determine the appropriate legal test or rule.

Modern contract law has generally recognized an implied covenant to the effect that each party to a contract will act with good faith towards the other with respect to the subject matter of the contract. See, Restatement of Law, Contracts 2d, § 205 (1981); Rowe v. Great Atlantic and Pacific Tea Company, N.Y.Ct.Apps., 46 N.Y.2d 62, 412

N.Y.S.2d 827, 830, 385 N.E.2d 566, 569 (1978). The contractual theory for this implied obligation is well stated in a leading treatise:

> If the purpose of contract law is to enforce the reasonable expectations of parties induced by promises, then at some point it becomes necessary for courts to look to the substance rather than to the form of the agreement, and to hold that substance controls over form. What courts are doing here, whether calling the process "implication" of promises, or interpreting the requirements of "good faith", as the current fashion may be, is but a recognition that the parties occasionally have understandings or expectations that were so fundamental that they did not need to negotiate about those expectations. When the court "implies a promise" or holds that "good faith" requires a party not to violate those expectations, it is recognizing that sometimes silence says more than words, and it is understanding its duty to the spirit of the bargain is higher than its duty to the technicalities of the language. Corbin on Contracts (Kaufman Supp.1984), § 570.

It is this obligation to act in good faith and to deal fairly that plaintiff claims is breached by the structure of Oak's coercive exchange offer. Because it is an implied *contractual* obligation that is asserted as the basis for the relief sought, the appropriate legal test is not difficult to deduce. It is this: is it clear from what was expressly agreed upon that the parties who negotiated the express terms of the contract would have agreed to proscribe the act later complained of as a breach of the implied covenant of good faith—had they thought to negotiate with respect to that matter. If the answer to this question is yes, then, in my opinion, a court is justified in concluding that such act constitutes a breach of the implied covenant of good faith.

* * *

With this test in mind, I turn now to a review of the specific provisions of the various indentures from which one may be best able to infer whether it is apparent that the contracting parties—had they negotiated with the exchange offer and consent solicitation in mind—would have expressly agreed to prohibit contractually the linking of the giving of consent with the purchase and sale of the security.

IV.

Applying the foregoing standard to the exchange offer and consent solicitation, I find first that there is nothing in the indenture provisions granting bondholders power to veto proposed modifications in the relevant indenture that implies that Oak may not offer an inducement to bondholders to consent to such amendments. Such an implication, at least where, as here, the inducement is offered on the same terms to each holder of an affected security, would be wholly inconsistent with the strictly commercial nature of the relationship.

Nor does the second pertinent contractual provision supply a ground to conclude that defendant's conduct violates the reasonable expectations of those who negotiated the indentures on behalf of the bondholders. Under that provision Oak may not vote debt securities held in its treasury. Plaintiff urges that Oak's conditioning of its offer to purchase debt on the giving of consents has the effect of subverting the purpose of that provision; it permits Oak to "dictate" the vote on securities which it could not itself vote.

The evident purpose of the restriction on the voting of treasury securities is to afford protection against the issuer voting as a bondholder in favor of modifications that would benefit it as issuer, even though such changes would be detrimental to bondholders. But the linking of the exchange offer and the consent solicitation does not involve the risk that bondholder interests will be affected by a vote involving anyone with a financial interest in the subject of the vote other than a bondholder's interest. That the consent is to be given concurrently with the transfer of the bond to the issuer does not in any sense create the kind of conflict of interest that the indenture's prohibition on voting treasury securities contemplates. Not only will the proposed consents be granted or withheld only by those with a financial interest to maximize the return on their investment in Oak's bonds, but the incentive to consent is equally available to all members of each class of bondholders. Thus the "vote" implied by the consent solicitation is not affected in any sense by those with a financial conflict of interest.

In these circumstances, while it is clear that Oak has fashioned the exchange offer and consent solicitation in a way designed to encourage consents, I cannot conclude that the offer violates the intendment of any of the express contractual provisions considered or, applying the test set out above, that its structure and timing breaches an implied obligation of good faith and fair dealing.

One further set of contractual provisions should be touched upon: Those granting to Oak a power to redeem the securities here treated at a price set by the relevant indentures. Plaintiff asserts that the attempt to force all bondholders to tender their securities at less than the redemption price constitutes, if not a breach of the redemption provision itself, at least a breach of an implied covenant of good faith and fair dealing associated with it. The flaw, or at least one fatal flaw, in this argument is that the present offer is not the functional equivalent of a redemption which is, of course, an act that the issuer may take unilaterally. In this instance it may happen that Oak will get tenders of a large percentage of its outstanding long-term debt securities. If it does, that fact will, in my judgment, be in major part a function of the merits of the offer (i.e., the price offered in light of the Company's financial position and the market value of its debt). To answer plaintiff's contention that the structure of the offer "forces" debt holders to tender, one only has to imagine what response this offer would receive if the price offered did not reflect a premium over market but rather was, for example, ten percent of market value. The exchange offer's success ultimately depends upon the ability and willingness of the issuer to extend an offer that will be a financially attractive alternative to holders. This process is hardly the functional equivalent of the unilateral election of redemption and thus cannot be said in any sense to constitute a subversion by Oak of the negotiated provisions dealing with redemption of its debt.

Accordingly, I conclude that plaintiff has failed to demonstrate a probability of ultimate success on the theory of liability asserted.

V.

An independent ground for the decision to deny the pending motion is supplied by the requirement that a court of equity will not issue the extraordinary remedy of preliminary injunction where to do so threatens the party sought to be enjoined with irreparable injury that, in the circumstances, seems greater than the injury that plaintiff seeks to avoid. Eastern Shore Natural Gas Co. v. Stauffer Chemical Co., Del.Supr., 298 A.2d 322 (1972). That principal has application here.

Oak is in a weak state financially. Its board, comprised of persons of experience and, in some instances, distinction, have approved the complex and interrelated transactions outlined above. It is not unreasonable to accord weight to the claims of Oak that the reorganization and recapitalization of which the exchange offer is a part may present the last good chance to regain vitality for this enterprise. I have not discussed plaintiff's claim of irreparable injury, although I have considered it. I am satisfied simply to note my conclusion that it is far outweighed by the harm that an improvidently granted injunction would threaten to Oak.

For the foregoing reasons plaintiff's application for a preliminary injunction shall be denied.

It is so ordered.

––––––––

Would the recapitalization process in *Katz v. Oak Industries* have gone differently if all the issues of debt had been held by a single lender? Compare the process of amendment and substantive result in *Katz v. Oak Industries,* with that in the following case.

RIEVMAN v. BURLINGTON NORTHERN RAILROAD CO.

United States District Court, Southern District of New York, 1987.
118 F.R.D. 29.

ROBERT L. CARTER, District Judge.

This matter is before the court on the parties' petition for approval of a class settlement pursuant to Rule 23(e), F.R.Civ.P. Plaintiffs, a class comprising the holders of bonds issued in 1896 by the predecessor of defendant Burlington Northern Railroad Company ("the Railroad"), brought suit in 1985 to enjoin the Railroad from substituting other collateral for certain realty ("the Resource Properties") by which the bond mortgages are secured. The Railroad now proposes to make a one-time cash payment on each outstanding bond in return for the release of the Resource Properties. Objecting to the proposal are institutions holding some three percent of the outstanding indebtedness who claim to represent holders of an additional eighteen percent, as well as various individuals.

BACKGROUND

Two series of bonds are involved in this litigation. One series, issued pursuant to a mortgage and yielding four percent annual interest, will mature in 1997 ("the Prior Lien Bonds"). The other series, issued pursuant to a second mortgage on the same properties and yielding three percent, will mature in 2047 ("the General Lien Bonds."). Roughly $117.7 million par value of the Prior and General Lien Bonds (collectively, "the Bonds") are outstanding.

Among other collateral, several million acres of land and mineral rights in six Midwestern and Northwestern states secure the underlying mortgages. By virtue of the extensive natural resources they contain, these lands are referred to as the Resource Properties. While the current market value of the Resource Properties may be in the billions of dollars, the terms of the bond mortgages severely inhibit the sale and development of the Resource Properties. Nor do the mortgages provide for the withdrawal of excess collateral.

On June 21, 1985, this court preliminarily enjoined the Railroad from effecting agreements with the Bonds' trustees [2] ("the Letter Agreements") by which the Railroad would deposit United States securities in place of the Resource Properties and tender then-current market prices for all outstanding bonds. Rievman v. Burlington Northern R. Co., 618 F.Supp. 592 (S.D.N.Y.1985) (Carter, J.) ("*Rievman I* "). The court found irreparable harm in that,

> [i]f the Letter Agreements are implemented, it will be difficult, if not impossible, to determine what price the bondholders and the Railroad would have finally agreed on in a buy-back to release the properties.

Rievman I, 618 F.Supp. at 597. The Railroad subsequently abandoned its deposit plan, but refrained from assuring the court that it would not attempt a similar transaction in the future. Rievman v. Burlington Northern R. Co., 644 F.Supp. 168, 171 (S.D.N.Y.1986) (Carter, J.) ("*Rievman II* "). As a result, on plaintiffs' motion to make the injunction permanent, the court ruled, on September 5, 1986, that

> [w]e cannot issue an injunction absent a specific proposal to release the [Resource] [P]roperties * * *. However, we must protect plaintiffs' right to a judicial declaration of their rights prior to any defeasance.

2. The trustees of the Prior Lien Bonds and the General Lien Bonds, Bankers Trust Company and Citibank, N.A., respectively, are the remaining parties defendant to this action.

Rievman II, supra, 644 F.Supp. at 172. The court similarly rejected the Railroad's argument that the case be dismissed as moot, id. at 171–72, and retained jurisdiction "to enable plaintiffs to contest * * * any plan to release the Resource Properties." Id. at 172.

Following oral argument of appeals by the Railroad and one of the trustees from this court's September 5 order, the parties engaged in negotiations which culminated in the announcement of a proposed agreement of settlement on April 3, 1987. Under the terms of the agreement, the Railroad has placed $35.5 million in escrow to earn interest pending distribution. Upon approval, the escrow balance (less an allowance for plaintiffs' attorneys' fees and litigation costs) would be paid out among the outstanding Bonds in an amount of $14.75 plus interest per $100 face amount of the Prior Lien Bonds, and $45.625 plus interest per $100 face amount of the General Lien Bonds. Outstanding bonds would remain in the hands of their holders, and continue to be secured by assets having a present value of approximately $778,400,-000,[4] but not by the Resource Properties.

* * *

[Opposition to the proposed settlement was expressed by Metropolitan Acquisition Partners I.L.P. and several individuals purporting to represent, in the aggregate, some $20,000,000 principal amount of debt.]

DISCUSSION

The proponents of a class settlement bear the burden, under Rule 23(e), F.R.Civ.P., of showing that the proposed agreement is fair, reasonable and adequate with respect to the absent class members. The proponents, while they have raised serious questions about the true numerical strength of the opposition, have not made a clear showing on this score.

The court must measure the fairness, reasonableness and adequacy of the proposal against a number of factors. Those relevant to the settlement of an action seeking purely injunctive relief are the reaction of class members to the settlement, the stage of the proceedings and the amount of discovery completed, the terms of the settlement, the costs and risks of continued litigation and the likelihood of recovery. * * * The "most significant" of these factors is "the strength of plaintiffs' case balanced against the settlement offer." * * * It is with these latter considerations, then—the terms of the compromise and the costs and likely rewards of further litigation—, that the court begins its analysis.

The critical fact that must be appreciated in assessing the risks and benefits of litigating this action to a conclusion is that this court cannot award monetary damages to the class. Apart from the fact that plaintiffs have sought purely injunctive relief and not damages in their complaint, the bondholders "do not have any direct interest in the

---

4. In connection with this proposal, both Moody's Investors Service and Standard & Poor's have advised the Railroad that they will maintain their present high ratings of the Bonds should the Resource Properties be released.

[Resource Properties]," but have only a lien on them. *Rievman I,* supra, 618 F.Supp. at 596. Should defendants be permanently enjoined from prematurely releasing the Resource Properties from the lien—the most favorable relief plaintiffs could possibly obtain—that lien would cease to confer any "hold-up" value on the bonds. In short, only by settling can plaintiffs realize their goals. Litigation *per se* holds out no rewards, likely or remote.

On the other hand, while this court has neither "the right [n]or the duty to reach any ultimate conclusions on the issues of fact and law which underlie the merits of the dispute," City of Detroit v. Grinnell, 495 F.2d 448, 456 (2d Cir.1974), it must take account of the "complexity, difficulty and uncertainty" of those issues. *Wellman,* supra, 497 F.Supp. at 831. In granting the motion for a preliminary injunction, the court noted that "this is a difficult, complex case," *Rievman I,* supra, 618 F.Supp. at 601, and "nothing adduced in relation to [the] motion [for permanent injunctive relief] diminishe[d] our uncertainty." *Rievman II,* supra, 644 F.Supp. at 172.[9] The conclusion is inescapable that the risks of continued litigation far outweigh the potential rewards.

When the terms of the compromise are set against the expected results of litigation, they appear eminently reasonable. The proposed settlement agreement, without impairing the security of the bonds as debt instruments, provides for an immediate cash payment to the bondholders, a result which no amount of litigation could produce.

Metropolitan and several of the individual objectors, however, challenge the *adequacy* of the amount offered in settlement. Metropolitan urges that the adequacy of the $35.5 million fund must be determined in comparison to the value that the Railroad is to realize in return, which may amount to billions of dollars. This objection misses the mark. The bondholders' lien does not entitle them to an equitable share of the worth of the Resource Properties, but simply permits them to insist on receiving the "hold-up" premium to which that lien has given rise.

As this court noted earlier, there is "no objective way" to value that "hold-up" premium except through negotiation in light of the market for the Bonds. *Rievman I,* supra, 618 F.Supp. at 597. In the court's view, the parties have evaluated the "hold-up" premium legitimately. The parties first agreed to utilize the market values of the Bonds as of the first week of February 1987, as the basis of their calculations.

* * *

The Prior Lien Bonds brought an average of $79.20 per $100 face value that week, while the General Lien Bonds averaged $70.30.   * * *

---

9. The Court of Appeals apparently found the issues of law equally difficult and uncertain. Although the Court heard argument on January 22, 1987, no decision had been rendered when the appeals were withdrawn more than three months later, on April 27.

The parties' experts concurred, moreover, in their calculations of the values of the Bonds as debt instruments alone; absent any "hold-up" premium, the Prior Lien Bonds would have traded at about $74.50, and the General Lien Bonds at about $36.75 as of February 1987. * * *

Based on these figures, the Railroad offered to pay the difference between the then-current market value of the Bonds and their estimated market value as debt instruments alone, a sum totalling $20 million. Plaintiffs' counsel, claiming that the market was undervaluing the "hold-up" premium, suggested that the Prior Lien Bonds were more accurately valued at $90 and the General Lien Bonds at $85 each, and sought the difference between those amounts and the estimated value of the Bonds as debt instruments alone, for a total of $39 million. The parties finally settled on $35.5 million.

While Metropolitan offers alternative assessments of the "hold-up" value of the Bonds, none of these shows the proposed sum to be inadequate. Indeed, even accepting the view of Metropolitan's expert that, as of June 1987, the value of the Prior and General Lien Bonds as debt instruments alone was only $67 and $30, respectively, * * * the total "hold-up" value of the Bonds would amount to less than $28 million, or well under eighty percent of the proposed principal payment.[10]

The remaining factors pose no barrier to the approval of this settlement agreement. Ample discovery was conducted, albeit on an expedited basis, prior to the hearing on plaintiffs' motion for a preliminary injunction, and the proceedings are now at an advanced stage. Finally, the opposition of the holders of even a majority of the outstanding bonds

> cannot serve as an automatic bar to a settlement that a district judge, after weighing all the strengths and weaknesses of a case and the risks of litigation, determines to be manifestly reasonable.

TBK Partners, Ltd. v. Western Union Corp., 675 F.2d 456, 462 (2d Cir.1982) (settlement properly approved over opposition by 54–58% of outstanding shares); accord Bryan v. Pittsburgh Plate Glass Co., 494 F.2d 799, 803 (3d Cir.), cert. denied, 419 U.S. 900 (1974) (20% of class opposed). The instant compromise has the support of at least 53% of the outstanding Bonds, with possibly fewer than 5% opposed. Even if those additional bondholders are included that Metropolitan claims to be authorized to represent, the objectors have failed to persuade the court that the proposal is anything but fair, reasonable and adequate. The settlement agreement will accordingly be approved.

Plaintiffs' counsel also petition the court for a joint award, from the common fund, of attorneys' fees in the amount of $3,388,243 and of expenses in the amount of $231,669.17. * * *

---

10. It should also be noted that the objection raised at the July 15, 1987 hearing, on behalf of plaintiffs Garfield and Geseg, Inc., that the proposal would injure the class by precipitating a drop in the market value of the Bonds, Tr. at 38, is not persuasive. A decree permanently enjoining the substitution of collateral, which those same plaintiffs sought earlier in this litigation, would have produced an identical effect, with none of the compensating benefits of this proposed compromise.

The benefits that counsel obtained for the class are also substantial. Had no action been filed, the class would have been essentially compelled to accept a tender of $53.50 per Prior Lien Bond and $39 per General Lien Bond. *Rievman I,* supra, 618 F.Supp. at 595. Instead, the class now will receive at least $14.75 and $45.62 respectively, per Bond, in addition to retaining Bonds which will subsequently be valued at $67–75 and $30–37, respectively, per Bond. The total benefit obtained for the class is thus worth some $45 million dollars, of which the requested fee constitutes only 7%.

* * *

The class settlement is approved.

NOTE: COERCED VOTES AND HOLD OUTS

1. *Identifying the Bondholders' Problem.*

Roe, The Voting Prohibition in Bond Workouts, 97 Yale L.J. 232 (1987), asks (1) whether section 316(b) of the Trust Indenture Act should be repealed because denial of the sufficiency of majority action to alter core terms of indenture provisions is unnecessarily costly in contemporary markets dominated by institutional intermediaries, and (2) whether the evils at which the unanimity requirement is addressed—inadequate information, insider control of the bond issue, and largely unsophisticated individuals as investors in bonds—any longer exist in sufficient force to be worth the cost of precluding inexpensive pre-bankruptcy workouts by majority action without judicial supervision.

Roe suggests that section 316 exacerbates the bondholder's problem by creating holdout potential.

But the bondholder's problem can occur even where, as in *Katz v. Oak Industries,* the issuer side-steps section 316 by structuring the payment terms of the offer as an exchange and limiting amendment of the indenture to promises other than payment terms. Assume a distressed issuer and an issue of bonds trading for $500. The issuer offers these holders a package worth $550, and, as in *Oak Industries,* attaches an exit consent. The bondholders believe the intrinsic value of the bonds to be $600, and could obtain that figure in a workout given a small number of holders and a face to face negotiation. If a given bondholder does not exchange, but the requisite majority does exchange, the stripped bond will be worth $450. Here, Coffee and Klein, Bondholder Coercion: The Problem of Constrained Choice in Debt Tender Offers and Recapitalizations, 58 U.Chi.L.Rev. 1207 (1991), notes that the rational bondholder, unable to negotiate for more than $550, will tender for less than it believes the bonds to be worth. On these facts, the coercing party is not the holdout, but the issuer.

On the other hand, the potential holdout does create a problem for bondholders if the debtor's condition is so precarious that failure of the proposed workout will result in insolvency reorganization. To a greater or lesser extent, insolvency reorganization adds costs to the enterprise and therefore diminishes the amounts distributable to pre-bankruptcy claimants. If the power to hold out (that is, to decline to accept the proposed readjustment) is exercised by holders of a large portion of the debt so as to preclude the readjustment and the debtor is forced into bankruptcy reorganization, presumably all bondholders are worse off than if the proposed readjustment had been accepted.

Under what circumstances are potential holdouts likely to become actual holdouts, so as to endanger, or indeed preclude, the readjustment? Consider the three scenarios. Under the first, some bondholders simply believe that the readjustment price is too low, and seek to raise it for all bondholders by declining the tendered price. A second scenario involves a holdout who owns enough bonds to seek a voice in, or control of, the reorganized enterprise and thereby achieve a greater return than the other bondholders receive. A third scenario also involves a holdout seeking a greater return than the other bondholders receive. This actor expects the vast bulk of the bondholders to accept the readjustment, and thereafter himself to be bought off by the issuer on the market, or to have a larger claim (e.g., for $1,000) than those who accepted the $550 claim in any ensuing bankruptcy. The first scenario requires the assistance of section 316(b) of the Trust Indenture Act. The second scenario does not; it is the inevitable concomitant of a trading market in bonds. The third is indeed aided by section 316(b), and creates a larger possibility of failure of the workout because of the holdout's willingness to gamble with his, and the others,' money. The question is whether the cost of allowing such holdouts is greater than the benefits section 316(b) offers to those dispersed investors who are otherwise obliged to act collectively, and therefore are likely to be offered lower payouts in the proposed readjustment than if the section were repealed.

For differing analyses of, and proposed solutions for, the bondholders' problem, see—in addition to Roe, supra—Coffee and Klein, supra, Brudney, Corporate Bondholders and Debtor Opportunism: In Bad Times and Good, 105 Harv.L.Rev. 1821 (1992), and Gertner and Scharfstein, A Theory of Workouts and the Effects of Reorganization Law, 46 J.Finance 1189 (1991). For an empirical picture, see Gilson, John and Lang, Troubled Debt Restructurings: An Empirical Study of Private Reorganizations of Firms in Default, 27 J.Financial Econ. 315 (1990).

2. *Cash Payments.*

If instead of a tender offer at a premium to induce the bondholders to consent to elimination of protective covenants, the issuer offers simple cash payments (and retention of their bonds) to all who consent to such amendments and a bondholder challenges the offer, how will *Katz v. Oak Industries* apply? Does the cash offer make this case distinguishable, by analogy to the prohibition against the purchase and sale of the votes of stockholders? Kass v. Eastern Airlines, Inc., 1986 WL 13008, 12 Del.J.Corp.L. 1074 (Del.Ch.1986), aff'd, 518 A.2d 583 (Del.1986), sanctions vote buying in the context of an offer made publicly to all bondholders on the same terms, but suggests that a paid solicitation to a limited number of bondholders might violate a good faith duty.

NOTE: PREPACKAGED BANKRUPTCY

The Bankruptcy Act of 1978 contemplates the "prepackaged bankruptcy," a hybrid procedure that begins as a workout and ends as a chapter 11 reorganization. Section 1126(b) of the Bankruptcy Act of 1978, 11 U.S.C. § 1126(b), permits an issuer to conduct a binding vote on a plan of reorganization prior to filing for bankruptcy. In addition, section 1102(b)(1) allows a prepetition creditors committee to act as the committee in bankruptcy if it is representative of the claims and interests in the case, and section 1121(a) allows the debtor to file a plan with its chapter 11 petition. See Trost, Business Reorganization Under Chapter 11 of the New Bankruptcy Code, 34 Bus.Law. 1309, 1325 (1979). The statutory "prepackaged" bankruptcy, duly recognized by the courts, see In re TS Industries, Inc., 117 B.R. 682 (Bkrtcy.D.Utah 1990); In re Colonial Ford, Inc., 24 B.R. 1014 (Bkrtcy.D.Utah 1982), has influenced recapitalization practice in recent years. It allows a corporation in distress to take advantage of the chapter 11 creditor consent standard of two thirds in amount and one half in number. The debtor collects the consents to the plan before it files under chapter 11. When it files, it presents the preapproved reorganization plan for quick confirmation. With luck, the process is completed in a few months, or even more quickly.

This technique has the obvious advantage of circumventing the holdout problem. The Bankruptcy Act not only reduces the number of necessary consents, it provides that plans that meet its legal standards can be "crammed down" on nonconsenting creditors and classes of creditors. For discussion of the standards, see pp. 312–318 infra. There also is a tax advantage. An exchange of old debt for new debt outside of bankruptcy results in the realization of cancellation of indebtedness income, where under Internal Revenue Code § 108(a), an economically equivalent recapitalization conducted in the bankruptcy context does not realize this income. Berg, The Budget Package and Debt Restructurings, Insights, vol. 5, no. 2 p. 9 (February 1991).

Prepackaged bankruptcies have been employed in recent years by a number of well known corporations in distress—most prominently, Donald Trump's Taj Mahal casino and Carl Icahn's Trans World Airlines. See generally Case and Harwood, Current Issues in Prepackaged Chapter 11 Plans of Reorganization, 1991 Ann.Surv.Amer.L. 75. But the practice is by no means universal among serious distress cases. Most debtors still attempt to recapitalize privately. Coffee and Klein, supra, suggest that debtors are deterred by litigation uncertainties and possibilities of business impairment that remain intrinsic to the chapter 11 process.

3.   FRAUDULENT CONVEYANCE LAW

UNIFORM FRAUDULENT TRANSFER ACT, 7A U.L.A. (1985)

§ 4.   Transfers Fraudulent as to Present and Future Creditors

(a) A transfer made or obligation incurred by a debtor is fraudulent as to a creditor, whether the creditor's claim arose before or after the transfer was made or the obligation was incurred, if the debtor made the transfer or incurred the obligation:

(1) with actual intent to hinder, delay, or defraud any creditor of the debtor; or

(2) without receiving a reasonably equivalent value in exchange for the transfer or obligation, and the debtor:

(i) was engaged or was about to engage in a business or a transaction for which the remaining assets of the debtor were unreasonably small in relation to the business or transaction; or

(ii) intended to incur, or believed or reasonably should have believed that he would incur, debts beyond his ability to pay as they became due.

WIEBOLDT STORES, INC. v. SCHOTTENSTEIN

United States District Court, Northern District of Illinois, 1988.
94 B.R. 488.

HOLDERMAN, District Judge:

Wieboldt Stores, Inc. ("Wieboldt") filed this action on September 18, 1987 under the federal bankruptcy laws, 11 U.S.C. §§ 101 et seq., the state fraudulent conveyance laws, Ill.Rev.Stat. ch. 59, ¶ 4, and the Illinois Business Corporation Act, Ill.Rev.Stat. ch. 32, ¶ 1.01 et seq. Pending before the court are numerous motions to dismiss this action under Rules 9(b), 12(b)(2), 12(b)(6) and 19 of the Federal Rules of Civil Procedure.

* * *

Wieboldt's complaint against the defendants concerns the events and transactions surrounding a leveraged buyout ("LBO") of Wieboldt by WSI Acquisition Corporation ("WSI"). WSI, a corporation formed solely for the purpose of acquiring Wieboldt, borrowed funds from third-party lenders and delivered the proceeds to the shareholders in return for their shares. Wieboldt thereafter pledged certain of its assets to the LBO lenders to secure repayment of the loan.

* * *

[Wieboldt operated a chain of twelve department stores in the Chicago area. In 1982 it had 4,000 employees and annual sales of

$190,000,000. Its stock was listed on the New York Stock Exchange. But, after 1979, Wieboldt showed no profit and continued operations only by periodically selling assets to generate working capital.

[After 1982, Wieboldt was controlled by Julius and Edmond Trump, holding through a vehicle called MBT Corporation (collectively, the "Trump interests"), and Jerome Schottenstein and affiliates (collectively, the "Schottenstein interests"). The Trump and Schottenstein interests (collectively, the "controlling shareholders") each held approximately 15% of Wieboldt's outstanding shares.

[In January 1985, WSI proposed a tender offer for all outstanding Wieboldt shares for $13.50 per share. Wieboldt's Board of Directors agreed to cooperate. WSI then spent most of 1985 arranging debt financing for the transaction.

[By October 1985 WSI had funding commitments from three lenders: Household Commercial Financial Services ("HCFS"), BA Mortgage and International Realty Corporation ("BAMIRCO"), and General Electric Credit Corporation ("GECC"). The lenders knew that WSI intended to use the proceeds of the financing to (1) purchase tendered shares of Wieboldt stock; (2) pay surrender prices for Wieboldt stock options; and (3) eliminate preexisting debt of Wieboldt owed to Continental Illinois National Bank ("CINB") and secured by Wieboldt real estate.

[WSI needed approximately $38,000,000 to purchase the Wieboldt stock in the tender offer. The HCFS loan to WSI was to provide these funds. This loan was to be secured by all of Wieboldt's real estate other than its main store property at One North State Street, Chicago.

[WSI needed an additional sum in excess of $30,000,000 to pay off CINB and lift the mortgage on the One North State Street property. The BAMIRCO loan was to provide most of this. This loan was to be secured by a first mortgage on One North State Street. WSI structured this transaction through an intermediary limited partnership ("ONSSLP") set up between WSI and a real estate broker. Specifically, One North State Street was to be conveyed to ONSSLP by Wieboldt for $30,000,000, the purchase money to be loaned by BAMIRCO and a mortgage given back. The $30,000,000 would then be applied to pay down Wieboldt's obligations to CINB.

[Unfortunately, the $30,000,000 sale of One North State Street did not generate sufficient funds to pay off all the CINB obligations. The GECC commitment of a line of credit not to exceed $35,000,000 provided these additional funds. This transaction was structured as a sale of Wieboldt's customer charge card accounts. In addition to the sale of the charge card accounts, this "accounts purchase agreement" required Wieboldt to pledge all of its accounts receivable as additional security.]

The Board of Directors was fully aware of the progress of WSI's negotiations. The Board understood that WSI intended to finance the tender offer by pledging a substantial portion of Wieboldt's assets to its lenders, and that WSI did not intend to use any of its own funds or the funds of its shareholders to finance the acquisition. Moreover, although the Board initially believed that the tender offer would produce $10 million in working capital for the company, the members knew that the proceeds from the LBO lenders would not result in this additional working capital.

Nevertheless, in October, 1985 the Board directed Mr. Darrow *
and Wieboldt's lawyers to work with WSI to effect the acquisition. During these negotiations, the Board learned that HCFS would provide financing for the tender offer only if Wieboldt would provide a statement from a nationally recognized accounting firm stating that Wieboldt was solvent and a going concern prior to the planned acquisition and would be solvent and a going concern after the acquisition. Mr. Darrow informed WSI that Wieboldt would only continue cooperating in the LBO if HCFS agreed not to require this solvency certificate. HCFS acceded to Wieboldt's demand and no solvency certificate was ever provided to HCFS on Wieboldt's behalf.

On November 18, 1985 Wieboldt's Board of Directors voted to approve WSI's tender offer, and on November 20, 1985 WSI announced its offer to purchase Wieboldt stock for $13.50 per share. By December 20, 1985 the tender offer was complete and WSI had acquired ownership of Wieboldt through its purchase of 99% of Wieboldt's stock at a total price of $38,462,164.00. All of the funds WSI used to purchase the tendered shares were provided by HCFS and were secured by the assets which BAMIRCO and GECC loan proceeds had freed from CINB obligations.

[Certain of Wieboldt's creditors commenced an involuntary liquidation proceeding against Wieboldt under chapter 7 of the Bankruptcy Code (the "Code") in September 1986. On the same day, Wieboldt filed a voluntary reorganization proceeding pursuant to chapter 11.

[Thereafter Wieboldt brought this action against (1) the controlling shareholders and Wieboldt's officers and directors, (2) other Wieboldt shareholders who owned and tendered more than 1,000 shares in response to the tender offer (the "Schedule A shareholders"), and (3) the lenders who funded the tender offer and associated purchase of One North State Street. In its complaint, Wieboldt alleged that WSI's tender offer and the resulting LBO was a fraudulent conveyance under the federal bankruptcy statute and the Illinois fraudulent conveyance laws. The various defendants move to dismiss the complaint under Rule 12(b)(6) on the grounds that Wieboldt has failed to state a claim.]

1. *Applicability of Fraudulent Conveyance Law.*

Both the federal Bankruptcy Code and Illinois law protect creditors from transfers of property that are intended to impair a creditor's ability to enforce its rights to payment or that deplete a debtor's assets at a time when its financial condition is precarious. Modern fraudulent conveyance law derives from the English Statute of Elizabeth enacted in 1570, the substance of which has been either enacted in American statutes prohibiting such transactions or has been incorpo-

---

* [Ed. Note] A Wieboldt director.

rated into American law as a part of the English common law heritage. See Sherwin, "Creditors' Rights Against Participants in a Leveraged Buy-out," 72 Minn.L.Rev. 449, 465–66 (1988).

The controlling shareholders, insider shareholders, and some of the Schedule A shareholders argue that fraudulent conveyance laws do not apply to leveraged buy-outs. These defendants argue (1) that applying fraudulent conveyance laws to public tender offers effectively allows creditors to insure themselves against subsequent mismanagement of the company; (2) that applying fraudulent conveyance laws to LBO transactions and thereby rendering them void severely restricts the usefulness of LBOs and results in great unfairness; and (3) that fraudulent conveyance laws were never intended to be used to prohibit or restrict public tender offers.

Although some support exists for defendants' arguments,[13] this court cannot hold at this stage in this litigation that the LBO in question here is entirely exempt from fraudulent conveyance laws. Neither Section 548 of the Code nor the Illinois statute exempt such transactions from their statutory coverage. Section 548 invalidates fraudulent "transfers" of a debtor's property. Section 101(50) defines such a transfer very broadly to include "every mode, direct or indirect, absolute or conditional, voluntary or involuntary, of disposing of or parting with property or with an interest in property, including retention of title as a security interest." 11 U.S.C. § 101(50). Likewise, the Illinois statute applies to gifts, grants, conveyances, assignments and transfers. Ill.Rev.Stat. ch. 59, ¶ 4. The language of these statutes in no way limits their application so as to exclude LBOs.

In addition, those courts which have addressed this issue have concluded that LBOs in some circumstances may constitute a fraudulent conveyance. See e.g., Kupetz v. Continental Illinois National Bank and Trust, 77 B.R. 754 (Bankr.C.D.Cal.1987), aff'd Kupetz v. Wolf, 845 F.2d 842 (9th Cir.1988) (applying Section 548 and the California statute, West's Ann.Cal.Civ.Code ¶¶ 3439–3439.12); In re Ohio Corrugating Company, 70 B.R. 920 (Bankr.N.D.Ohio 1987) (applying Section 548 and the Ohio statute, Ohio Rev.Code, Sect. 1336.01 et seq.); In re Anderson Industries, Inc., 55 B.R. 922 (Bankr.W.D.Mich.1985) (applying Michigan law, M.C.L.A. § 566.11); and United States v. Gleneagles Investment Co., Inc., 565 F.Supp. 556 (M.D.Pa.1983), aff'd in part and remanded in part United States v. Tabor Court Realty, 803 F.2d 1288 (3rd Cir.1986), cert. denied, McClellan Realty Co. v. United States, ___ U.S. ___ (1987) (applying the Pennsylvania Uniform Fraudulent Conveyances Act, 39 P.S. § 351). See also Sherwin, "Creditor's Rights Against Participants in a Leveraged Buyout," 72 Minn.L.Rev. 449 (1988). Defendants have presented no case law which holds to the contrary.[14]

---

13. See, e.g., Baird & Jackson, "Fraudulent Conveyance Law and Its Proper Domain," 38 Vand.L.Rev. 829 (1985).

14. Cf. Credit Managers Ass'n of Southern California v. Federal Company, 629 F.Supp. 175, 179 (C.D.Cal.1985), in which a California court expressed reservations about extending fraudulent conveyance law to leveraged buyouts but specifically reserved the issue in its decision.

The court is aware that permitting debtors to avoid all LBO transfers through the fraudulent conveyance laws could have the effect of insuring against a corporation's subsequent insolvency and failure. *Anderson Industries, Inc.* 55 B.R. at 926; see also Baird & Jackson, supra n. 11 at 839. In light of the case law and the broad statutory language, however, this court sees no reason to hold as a general rule that LBOs are exempt from the fraudulent conveyance laws. As the court stated in *Anderson,* "[i]f this holding is too broad in the light of the present marketplace, it is the legislature, not the courts, that must narrow the statute." 55 B.R. at 926.

2. *The Structure of the Transaction.*

Although the court finds that the fraudulent conveyance laws generally are applicable to LBO transactions, a debtor cannot use these laws to avoid any and all LBO transfers. In this case, certain defendants argue that they are entitled to dismissal because the LBO transfers at issue do not fall within the parameters of the laws. These defendants argue that they are protected by the literal language of Section 548 of the Code and the "good faith transferee for value" rule in Section 550.[15] They contend, initially, that they did not receive Wieboldt property during the tender offer and, secondarily, that, even if they received Wieboldt property, they tendered their shares in good faith, for value, and without the requisite knowledge and therefore cannot be held liable under Section 550.

The merit of this assertion turns on the court's interpretation of the tender offer and LBO transactions. Defendants contend that the tender offer and LBO were composed of a series of interrelated but independent transactions. They assert, for example, that the transfer of property from HCFS to WSI and ultimately to the shareholders constituted one series of several transactions while the pledge of Wieboldt assets to HCFS to secure the financing constituted a second series of transactions. Under this view, defendants did not receive the *debtor*'s property during the tender offer but rather received *WSI*'s property in exchange for their shares.

Wieboldt, on the other hand, urges the court to "collapse" the interrelated transactions into one aggregate transaction which had the overall effect of conveying Wieboldt property to the tendering shareholders and LBO lenders. This approach requires the court to find that

---

15. While Section 548 defines the nature of the transactions that are avoidable by the debtor, Section 550 places limits on Section 548 by defining the kind of transferee from whom a debtor may recover transferred property. Section 550(a) permits a trustee to recover fraudulently transferred property from

1. the initial transferee;

2. the entity for whose benefit such transfer was made; or

3. an immediate or mediate transferee of such initial transferee (a "subsequent transferee").

11 U.S.C. § 550(a). Section 550(b) states that a trustee may *not* recover from

1. a subsequent transferee who takes the property for value, in good faith, and without knowledge of the voidability of the transfer; or

2. an immediate or mediate good faith transferee of such a transferee.

the persons and entities receiving the conveyance were direct transferrees who received "an interest of the debtor in property" during the tender offer/buyout, and that WSI and any other parties to the transactions were "mere conduits" of Wieboldt's property. If the court finds that all the transfers constituted one transaction, then defendants received property from Wieboldt and Wieboldt has stated a claim against them.

Few courts have considered whether complicated LBO transfers should be evaluated separately or collapsed into one integrated transaction. However, two United States Courts of Appeals opinions provide some illumination on this issue. See Kupetz v. Wolf, 845 F.2d 842 (9th Cir.1988); United States v. Tabor Court Realty, 803 F.2d 1288 (3rd Cir.1986), cert. denied McClellan Realty Co. v. United States, ___ U.S. ___ (1987).

* * *

Neither of these two cases involved transactions which were identical to the WSI–Wieboldt buyout. However, the *Kupetz* and *Tabor Court* opinions are nonetheless significant because the courts in both cases expressed the view that an LBO transfer—in whatever form—was a fraudulent conveyance if the circumstances of the transaction were not "above board." *Kupetz,* 845 F.2d at 847. Thus, even though the court in *Kupetz* declined to hold the selling shareholders liable, there was no showing in *Kupetz* that the shareholders intended to defraud [the debtor company's] creditors nor even that the purchaser intended to finance the takeover by leveraging the company's assets. On the other hand, the court in *Tabor Court* found the LBO lender liable because it participated in the negotiations surrounding the LBO transactions and knew that the proceeds of its loan to [the corporation effecting the LBO] would deplete the debtor's assets to the point at which it was functionally insolvent under the fraudulent conveyance and bankruptcy laws. These cases indicate that a court should focus not on the formal structure of the transaction but rather on the knowledge and intent of the parties involved in the transaction.

Applying this principle to defendants' assertions, it is clear that, at least as regards the liability of the controlling shareholders, the LBO lenders, and the insider shareholders, the LBO transfers must be collapsed into one transaction. The complaint alleges clearly that these participants in the LBO negotiations attempted to structure the LBO with the requisite knowledge and contemplation that the full transaction, tender offer and LBO, be completed.[20] The Board and the insider shareholders knew that WSI intended to finance its acquisition of Wieboldt through an LBO * * * and not with any of its own funds * * *. They knew that Wieboldt was insolvent before the LBO and

11 U.S.C. § 550(b).

20. Although many of the allegations in the complaint refer to the state of mind and activities of the Board of Directors, these allegations may fairly be imputed to the controlling shareholders. The controlling shareholders nominated a majority of the directors to their positions on the Board. In addition, many of the individuals who served on the Board were "insiders" to Schottenstein Stores, Inc. or MBT Corporation.

that the LBO would result in further encumbrance of Wieboldt's already encumbered assets. * * * Attorneys for Schottenstein Stores apprised the Board of the fraudulent conveyance laws and suggested that they structure the LBO so as to avoid liability. * * * Nonetheless, these shareholders recommended that Wieboldt accept the tender offer and themselves tendered their shares to WSI. * * *

Wieboldt's complaint also alleges sufficient facts to implicate the LBO lenders in the scheme. HCFS, BAMIRCO and GECC were well aware of each other's loan or credit commitments to WSI and knew that WSI intended to use the proceeds of their financing commitments to purchase Wieboldt shares or options and to release certain Wieboldt assets from prior encumbrances. * * * Representatives of the lenders received the same information concerning the fraudulent conveyance laws as did the Board of Directors. (Complaint ¶ 80). These LBO lenders agreed with WSI and the Board of Directors to structure the LBO so as to avoid fraudulent conveyance liability. * * *

The court, however, is not willing to "collapse" the transaction in order to find that the Schedule A shareholders also received the debtor's property in the transfer. While Wieboldt directs specific allegations of fraud against the controlling and insider shareholders and LBO lenders, Wieboldt does not allege that the Schedule A shareholders were aware that WSI's acquisition encumbered virtually all of Wieboldt's assets. Nor is there an allegation that these shareholders were aware that the consideration they received for their tendered shares was Wieboldt property. In fact, the complaint does not suggest that the Schedule A shareholders had any part in the LBO except as innocent pawns in the scheme. They were aware only that WSI made a public tender offer for shares of Wieboldt stock. * * * Viewing the transactions from the perspective of the Schedule A shareholders and considering their knowledge and intent, therefore, the asset transfers to the LBO lenders were indeed independent of the tender offer to the Schedule A shareholders.

This conclusion is in accord with the purpose of the fraudulent conveyance laws. The drafters of the Code, while attempting to protect parties harmed by fraudulent conveyances, also intended to shield innocent recipients of fraudulently conveyed property from liability. Thus, although Subsection (a) of Section 550 permits a trustee to avoid a transfer to an initial transferee or its subsequent transferee, Subsection (b) of that Section limits recovery from a subsequent transferee by providing that a trustee may not recover fraudulently conveyed property from a subsequent transferee who takes the property in good faith, for value, and without knowledge that the original transfer was voidable. Subsection (b) applies, however, only to subsequent transferees.

Similarly, the LBO lenders and the controlling and insider shareholders of Wieboldt are direct transferees of Wieboldt property. Although WSI participated in effecting the transactions, Wieboldt's complaint alleges that WSI was a corporation formed solely for the purpose of acquiring Wieboldt stock. The court can reasonably infer from the complaint, therefore, that WSI served mainly as a conduit for the exchange of assets and loan proceeds between LBO lenders and Wieboldt and for the exchange of loan proceeds and shares of stock between the LBO lenders and the insider and controlling shareholders. On the other hand, the Schedule A shareholders are not direct transferees of Wieboldt property. From their perspective, WSI was the direct transferee of Wieboldt property and the shareholders were merely indirect transferees because WSI was an independent entity in the transaction.

* * *

3. *The Elements of a Fraudulent Conveyance.*

As discussed above, the transfers to and between the debtor and the LBO lenders, controlling shareholders, and insider shareholders are subject to the provisions in Section 548(a) of the Code and Section 4 of the Illinois statute. The court now must determine whether Wieboldt's complaint states sufficient facts to allege the elements of these causes of action.

a. Section 548(a)(1)

In order to state a claim for relief under Section 548(a)(1) of the Code, a debtor or trustee must allege (1) that the transfer was made within one year before the debtor filed a petition in bankruptcy, and (2) that the transfer was made with the actual intent to hinder, delay or defraud the debtor's creditors. 11 U.S.C. § 548(a)(1). See In re F & C Services, Inc., 44 B.R. 863, 871–72 (Bankr.S.D.Fla.1984). Although defendants do not dispute that the LBO transfers occurred within a year of the date on which Wieboldt filed for bankruptcy, they vigorously assert that Wieboldt has failed to properly allege "intent to defraud" as required by Section 548(a)(1).

"Actual intent" in the context of fraudulent transfers of property is rarely susceptible to proof and "must be gleaned from inferences drawn from a course of conduct." In re Vecchione, 407 F.Supp. 609, 615 (E.D.N.Y.1976). A general scheme or plan to strip the debtor of its assets without regard to the needs of its creditors can support a finding of actual intent. In re F & C Services, 44 B.R. at 872. In addition, certain "badges of fraud" can form the basis for a finding of actual intent to hinder, delay or defraud. 4 Collier on Bankruptcy ¶ 548.02[5] (15th ed. 1987).[24]

Counts I and III of Wieboldt's complaint state a claim under Section 548(a)(1). Count I, which Wieboldt brings against the controlling and insider shareholders, states that these defendants exchanged their shares with the actual intent to hinder, delay or defraud Wieboldt's unsecured creditors. * * * Count III states that the State Street defendants received Wieboldt's interest in One North State Street

---

24. For example, when a debtor conceals a fact or makes false pretenses, reserves rights in the property which is transferred, or creates a closely held corporation to receive the transfer, or when the value of the transfer is unconscionably greater than the consideration received for it, the transaction is said to bear the "badge of fraud." 4 Collier on Bankruptcy ¶ 548.02[4] (15th ed. 1987).

property with the actual intent to defraud Wieboldt's unsecured creditors. * * * The complaint also states generally that the LBO Lenders and the controlling and insider shareholders structured the LBO transfers in such a way as to attempt to evade fraudulent conveyance liability. * * * These allegations are a sufficient assertion of actual fraud. Defendants' motions to dismiss Counts I and III are therefore denied.

b. Section 548(a)(2)

Unlike Section 548(a)(1), which requires a plaintiff to allege "actual fraud," Section 548(a)(2) requires a plaintiff to allege only constructive fraud. A plaintiff states a claim under Section 548(a)(2) by alleging that the debtor (1) transferred property within a year of filing a petition in bankruptcy; (2) received less than the reasonably equivalent value for the property transferred; and (3) either (a) was insolvent or became insolvent as a result of the transfer, (b) retained unreasonably small capital after the transfer, or (c) made the transfer with the intent to incur debts beyond its ability to pay. 11 U.S.C. § 548(a)(2).

Defendants argue that Wieboldt's allegation of insolvency is insufficient as a matter of law to satisfy the insolvency requirement in Section 548(a)(2)(B)(i). Section 101(31)(A) of the Code defines "insolvency" as a condition which occurs when the sum of an entity's debts exceeds the sum of its property "at a fair valuation." 11 U.S.C. § 101(31)(A). Wieboldt's complaint alleges that the corporation was insolvent in November, 1985 "in that the fair saleable value of its assets was exceeded by its liabilities when the illiquidity of those assets is taken into account." * * *

Wieboldt's allegations satisfy the "insolvency" requirement of Section 548(a)(2)(B)(i). Defendants' attempt to distinguish Wieboldt's phrase "fair saleable value" from Section 101(31)(A)'s "fair valuation" is, as Wieboldt suggests, "hyper-technical." (Mem. in Opp. at 66). "Fair valuation" is near enough in meaning to "fair value of saleable assets" to defeat defendants' motion to dismiss. See In re A. Fassnacht & Sons, Inc., 45 B.R. 209, 217 (Bkrtcy.E.D.Tenn.1984). In addition, Wieboldt did not destroy its claim of insolvency by characterizing its assets as "illiquid" at the time of the transfer. In determining "fair valuation," a court must consider the property's intrinsic value, selling value, and the earning power of the property. Black's Law Dictionary, 538 (5th Ed.1979). Assets may be reduced by the value of the assets that cannot be readily liquidated. Briden v. Foley, 776 F.2d 379, 382 (1st Cir.1985). The complaint meets the financial condition test of Section 548(a)(2)(B)(i).

Finally, defendants claim that Wieboldt cannot state a claim under Section 548(a)(2) because it received "reasonably equivalent value" in the transfer to the shareholders and the conveyance of the One North State Street property. Wieboldt granted a security interest in substantially all of its real estate assets to HCFS and received from the shareholders in return 99% of its outstanding shares of stock.[25] * * * This stock was virtually worthless to Wieboldt. In re Roco Corp., 701 F.2d 978, 982 (1st Cir.1983); In re Ipswich Bituminous Concrete Products, Inc., 79 B.R. 511, 517 (Bkrtcy.D.Mass.1987); In re Corporate Jet Aviation, Inc., 45 B.R. 629, 634 (Bkrtcy.N.D.Ga.1985). See also Hyde Properties v. McCoy, 507 F.2d 301, 307 (6th Cir.1974) (decided under the Tennessee fraudulent conveyance statute, T.C.A. § 64–311, 64–312). Wieboldt received less than a reasonably equivalent value in exchange for an encumbrance on virtually all of its non-inventory assets, and therefore has stated a claim against the controlling and insider shareholders.

Likewise, the court need not dismiss Wieboldt's Section 548(a)(2) claim against the State Street defendants on the grounds that Wieboldt received reasonably equivalent value in exchange for its One North State Street property. The effect and intention of the parties to the One North State Street conveyance was to generate funds to purchase outstanding shares of Wieboldt stock. Although Wieboldt sold the property to ONSSLP for $30 million,[26] and used the proceeds to pay off part of the $35 million it owed CINB, Wieboldt did not receive a benefit from this transfer. * * * See *Tabor Court,* 803 F.2d at 1300. Defendants knew that the conveyance would neither increase Wieboldt's assets nor result in a net reduction of its liabilities. In fact, all parties to the conveyance were aware that the newly unencumbered assets would be immediately remortgaged to HCFS to finance the acquisition. * * * According to the complaint, therefore, Wieboldt received less than reasonably equivalent value for the conveyance of the One North State Street property and has stated a claim against the State Street defendants under Section 548(a)(2).

In sum, Counts II and IV of Wieboldt's complaint state a claim under Section 548(a)(2). Defendants' motions to dismiss these counts are denied.

c. Illinois Fraudulent Conveyance Law

Under Section 544(b) of the Code, a trustee may avoid transfers that are avoidable under state law if there is at least one creditor at the time who has standing under state law to challenge the transfer. 11 U.S.C. § 544(b). Wieboldt utilizes this section to pursue a claim under the Illinois fraudulent conveyance statute, Ill.Rev.Stat. ch. 59, § 4.

The Illinois fraudulent conveyance statute is similar to Section 548 of the Code. The statute provides that:

25. Defendants argue that WSI (and not Wieboldt) received the outstanding shares of Wieboldt stock. However, a court analyzing an allegedly fraudulent transfer must direct its attention to "what the Debtor surrendered and what the Debtor received, irrespective of what any third party may have gained or lost." In re Ohio Corrugating Co., 70 B.R. 920, 927 (Bkrtcy.N.D.Ohio 1987). As discussed in Section C.2. of this opinion, the court considers the tender offer and buyout transfers as one transaction for the purposes of this motion.

26. In reality, Wieboldt conveyed the property to ONSSLP as beneficiary of a land trust with Boulevard Bank as trustee. (Complaint ¶ 103(a)).

> Every gift, grant, conveyance, assignment or transfer of, or charge
> upon any estate, real or personal, * * * made with the intent to
> disturb, delay, hinder or defraud creditors or other persons, * * *
> shall be void as against the creditors, purchasers and other persons.

Ill.Rev.Stat. ch. 59, § 4 (1976). Illinois courts divide fraudulent conveyances into two categories: fraud in law and fraud in fact. Tcherepnin
v. Franz, 475 F.Supp. 92, 96 (N.D.Ill.1979). In fraud in fact cases, a
court must find a specific intent to defraud creditors; in fraud in law
cases, fraud is presumed from the circumstances. Id.

[The court ruled that Count VIII of Wieboldt's complaint stated a
claim for fraud in law and denied defendants' motion to dismiss.]

NOTE: FRAUDULENT CONVEYANCE AVOIDANCE
OF LEVERAGED BUYOUTS

1. *Constructive Fraud and Form versus Substance.*

The LBOs and other high leverage restructurings of the late 1980s
proceeded against a cognizable legal risk of subsequent fraudulent
conveyance attack. No controversy surrounds the proposition that
avoidance should follow upon a finding of actual intent to defraud—the
first ground pursued in *Wieboldt Stores.* Controversy does surround
the second ground pursued in the case—constructive fraud on the
theory that payments to the equity holders taken out are transfers for
inadequate consideration leaving the corporation either insolvent or
with unreasonably small capital. Despite the controversy, the risk of
subsequent challenge on this theory was well known as restructuring
movement went forward. The first constructive fraud case came down
in 1983. United States v. Gleneagles Investment Co., 565 F.Supp. 556
(M.D.Pa.1983), aff'd United States v. Tabor Court Realty Corp., 803 F.2d
1288 (3d Cir.1986), cert. denied, 483 U.S. 1005 (1987).

Courts have differed on the constructive fraud proposition. The
essential "transfer for inadequate consideration" emerges only if, as in
Wieboldt Stores, the court applies a "substance over form" analysis.
The constituent transactions are collapsed into a whole. The shell
corporation that purchases the stock is disregarded so that the LBO
debt is viewed as incurred by the target for the purpose of repurchasing
its own stock. A second analytical step then must be taken: the
payment to the target stockholders must be deemed to have no value to
the target and its creditors. In effect, the payment is characterized as
a dividend rather than as a purchase of stock for value. See In re
Vadnais Lumber Supply, Inc., 100 B.R. 127, 136 (Bkrtcy.D.Mass.1989).
See also Moody v. Security Pacific Business Credit, Inc., 127 B.R. 958,
992 (W.D.Pa.1991), aff'd, 971 F.2d 1056 (3d Cir.1992).

C–T of Virginia, Inc. v. Euroshoe Associates Ltd. Partnership,
953 F.2d 637 (4th Cir.1992), takes a view much more favorable to LBOs.
The court construed the Virginia fraudulent conveyance statute (which
requires receipt by the debtor of "consideration deemed valuable" in

order to justify a conveyance of assets) to be satisfied if "anything of value" is received. The acquiring company invested $4 million and borrowed approximately $26 million (which was assumed by the target) to pay off the target's stockholders a total of approximately $30 million. The court concluded that the $4 million of new investment met the test of "anything of value."[i] See also Kupetz v. Wolf, 845 F.2d 842 (9th Cir.1988) and Credit Managers Association of Southern California v. Federal Co., 629 F.Supp. 175 (C.D.Cal.1985) both of which question whether LBOs should be subject to attack as constructive frauds under section 4(a)(2) of the Uniform Fraudulent Transfer Act.

Would it be necessary for a court to employ a "substance over form" analysis in order to hold the spin off described supra p. 220 to be a constructive fraud? Could such a transaction be restructured so as to create a formal barrier to fraudulent conveyance scrutiny?

2. Constructive Fraud and Public Policy.

What policy gloss should be applied to high leveraged restructurings for purposes of determining the application of fraudulent conveyance law? To what extent should the analysis be influenced by the fact that restructured companies started going into bankruptcy in substantial numbers in 1989?

Under the optimistic description articulated in the 1980s, leveraged restructurings are efficiency driven transactions that provide corporate governance benefits. The payment to the equity holders amounts to a remedy for past suboptimal reinvestment of earnings by entrenched managers. The fixed coupon on the debt prevents future suboptimal capital investment. Meanwhile, tax benefits accrue to the restructured corporation. The high leverage presents no problem because the capital markets will make sure that only corporations well suited to high leverage are selected: mature, noncyclical industries are best. Although some bankruptcies inevitably will occur, they will not be as costly as some fear: the interested actors will work out low cost contract solutions to the problem of defaulted loans.

Under a more pessimistic description, the governance justification for LBOs is dismissed as a rationalization for a classic case of market speculation. The market is that for corporate assets, bought and sold on a going concern basis. The story is that speculators in the late 1980s took advantage of loose lending practices to bid up the prices of corporate assets and turn quick profits. Analogies are made to the public utility pyramids of the 1920s, described infra pp. 506–513. Furthermore, no particular governance benefits accrue from the speculative replay during the 1980s: it does not take a business genius to shut down a factory and lay off employees. Nor have actors in the financial markets acted with acuity: many LBOs occurred in weak,

i. In re C–T of Virginia, Inc., 958 F.2d 606 (4th Cir.1992), involved a claim against the directors based on the assertion that the LBO distribution violated the Virginia Corporation Code's limitations on dividends and other distributions. The Court took a form over substance approach—since the cash payout in the LBO was in form effected by a merger, it could not be a "distribution."

cyclical segments where default was inevitable, as *Wieboldt Stores* demonstrates.

Baird & Jackson, Fraudulent Conveyance Law and its Proper Domain, 38 Vand.L.Rev. 829 (1985), takes an optimistic view of LBOs. The article argues that LBOs should not be subject to attack as constructive fraud. First, LBOs hold out potential benefits for the economy as a whole. Second, the preexisting creditors are not seriously injured. Even though they sustain a short run injury, in the long run they benefit from improved management. Third, because "the debtor-creditor relationship is essentially contractual," id. at 835, creditors can protect themselves by adjusting the terms of their contracts. Carlson, Leveraged Buyouts in Bankruptcy, 20 Ga.L.Rev. 73 (1985), takes a similar approach, arguing that fraudulent conveyance liability should attach only if the LBO lender "anticipates an upcoming liquidation." Id. at 76–77. See also White, Leveraged Buyouts and Fraudulent Conveyance Laws Under the Bankruptcy Code—Like Oil and Water, They Just Don't Mix, 1991 Ann.Surv.Amer.L. 359.

Professor Baird takes a more equivocal position in a more recent article. See Baird, Fraudulent Conveyances, Agency Costs, and Leveraged Buyouts, 20 J. Legal Studies 1 (1991). This article explores the problematics of constructive fraud actions, but leaves open the ultimate policy question respecting the costs and benefits of a creditor protective rule. This, says Baird, depends on "an understanding of why leveraged buyouts take place." As yet we do not know, but "useful answers to these empirical questions may be forthcoming." Id. at 3. Nor need LBOs necessarily redound to the interests of creditors: "The practical problem facing the creditors * * * lies in their inability to distinguish in advance those transactions that increase the total wealth of creditors and shareholders from those that enrich shareholders at the creditors' expense and make the creditors and shareholders as a group worse off. This problem, however, is not at all peculiar to changing a firm's capital structure but permeates corporate law whenever ownership interests are arranged hierarchically." Id. at 10.

3. *The Scope of Constructive Fraud Avoidance.*

Does the theory of constructive fraud articulated in *Wieboldt Stores* presumptively apply to every highly leveraged restructuring that leads to a bankruptcy reorganization? Case law under section 4(a)(2) of the Uniform Fraudulent Transfer Act, and its substantive equivalents, section 5 of the earlier Uniform Fraudulent Conveyance Act and section 548(a)(2) of the Bankruptcy Code, provides only rough guidance.

(a) *Valuation.* Determining whether a transaction leaves a debtor insolvent or with unreasonably small capital entails a valuation of the debtor. The cases look at the debtor as a going concern at the time of the transaction and take a flexible approach. Balance sheet tests are avoided; cash flow projections are employed. See Moody v. Security Pacific Business Credit, 127 B.R. 958, 995 (W.D.Pa.1991); In re Vadnais Lumber Supply, Inc., 100 B.R. 127, 131–32 (Bkrtcy.D.Mass.1989); Credit

Managers Association of Southern California v. Federal Co., 629 F.Supp. 175, 184 (C.D.Cal.1985).

(b) *The meaning of "unreasonably small capital."* There is no fixed test. The cases treat inadequate capitalization as a fact question for determination in the particular context of the challenged transaction. According to the court in In re Vadnais Lumber Supply, Inc., supra at 137, the court looks "to the ability of the debtor to generate enough cash from operations or asset sales to pay its debts and sustain itself." The standard "encompasses difficulties which are short of insolvency in any sense but are likely to lead to insolvency at some time in the future."

(c) *Causation.* Implicitly, the transfer, and the denuded capitalization that results from it, must lead to default, and default must be a reasonably foreseeable result of the transfer. Supervening business reverses can break the nexus to the business circumstances at the time of the transfer under scrutiny. Moody v. Security Pacific Business Credit, supra,; Credit Managers, supra; Jacobson v. First State Bank, 48 Bankr. 497 (Bkrtcy.D.Minn.1985); Jenney v. Vining, 120 N.H. 377, 415 A.2d 681 (1980).

(d) *Remedies.* Fraudulent conveyance law calls for the "avoidance of the transfer." It is not yet clear what sort of a decree this should lead to in the context of an LBO bankruptcy. Difficult questions come up respecting recoupment of payments made to holders of publicly traded shares and cancellation of the LBO debt. The Preliminary Report of Examiner Professor Barry Zaretsky in **In re Revco,** 118 B.R. 468 (Bkrtcy.N.D.Ohio 1990) recommends that, as in *Wieboldt Stores,* the selling shareholders of the target not be pursued. **In re Kaiser Steel Corp.,** 952 F.2d 1230 (10th Cir.1991), imposes a statutory barrier. Kaiser Steel Resources, Inc., formerly known as Kaiser Steel Corp., sought to retrieve amounts paid out to former Kaiser Steel shareholders in connection with a leveraged buyout of the company in 1984. Kaiser claimed that these payments constituted a fraudulent conveyance. The defense was that a Bankruptcy Code exemption, section 546(e), precluded the trustee from avoiding "settlement payments" made by or to stockbrokers, financial institutions, and clearing agencies. The court held that the section 546(e) exemption encompassed amounts paid to the shareholders in the LBO, and accordingly prevented Kaiser from unwinding the transaction. For discussion of the case, see Cook, Axelrod, and Frankel, The Judicially Created "Innocent Shareholder" Defense to Constructive Fraudulent Transfer Liability in Failed Leveraged Buyouts, 43 S.C.L.Rev. 777 (1992).

Professor Zaretsky's *Revco* report suggests that the interests of the LBO participants be dealt with through the analytical device of a constructive unwind of the merger of the target and the LBO promoters' shell corporation. Under this approach, the LBO lenders' claims in bankruptcy are reconstructed as claims of creditors to the LBO shell corporation; the bankruptcy claims of the LBO promoters are treated as claims of the stockholders of the shell; and the reconstructed shell is treated as the owner of all the stock of the bankrupt corporation. This treatment detaches the LBO debt from the bankrupt corporation. The analysis in effect returns the bankrupt corporation to solvency and permits its preexisting creditors to be paid in full. Any value left over goes to interest holders in the constructive shell, first to the lenders, and then to the equity participants. In substance this amounts to equitable subordination of the LBO participants' claims.

4. *Problem.*

Imagine a leveraged buyout structured along the lines of the *Wieboldt Stores* transaction, but in respect of a chain of department stores with a stronger financial condition and brighter future prospects. The business has been declining but not to the point where asset liquidations are necessary to keep the going concern afloat. The business is not insolvent at the time the LBO closes.

After the incurrence of the LBO debt, the corporation's debt to equity ratio is 9 to 1. But the acquisition group projects that available cash flows will exceed interest costs by 1.4 times during the five year period following the closing. This figure is a reduction of the following projection:

Coverage	Probability
3 ×	.05
2 ×	.10
1.50 ×	.30
1.25 ×	.30
1 ×	.15
.75 × (default)	.10

The projection is made in good faith after exhaustive analysis.

The corporation makes a voluntary Chapter 11 filing one year after the closing. The failure of the business is due to a combination of (a) an unexpectedly early and severe recession, (b) unexpected price competition in its market, (c) unexpected management problems, and (d) expected high cost of debt.

What result when the bankrupt attacks the LBO as a fraudulent conveyance?

How should a court go about determining whether, on the facts stated, the corporation was left with unreasonably small capital? Must this determination depend on an assumed level of risk aversion? What level of risk aversion should the court bring to bear—that of a financial promoter, that of a small investor, that of an institutional lender, or some other level?

Who are the appropriate defendants in the proceeding—the cashed out shareholders, the LBO lenders, or the promoters who hold the equity in the shell corporation that acquires the target? Holders of the shares? What remedies are appropriate?

Would the following figures change your analysis? A projected ratio of cash flows to interest costs was 1.175 based on the following projection:

2 ×	.05
1.5 ×	.20
1.25 ×	.30
1 ×	.25
.75 × (default)	.20

4. INSOLVENCY REORGANIZATION

(A) INTRODUCTION: THE REORGANIZATION BARGAIN AND THE LIMITS OF THE PARTIES' BARGAINING FREEDOM

(1) Reorganization by Judicial Proceedings

We have seen that private, out-of-court reorganizations tend to offer the best returns to the holders of the distressed firm's equity. But we also have seen that the distressed firms do not always propose private compositions that command the assent of a sufficient number of creditors. In the latter event, a chapter 11 reorganization becomes the maximizing choice for the firm's equity holders and managers.

The filing of the chapter 11 petition brings immediate benefits to the debtor. Bankruptcy carries an automatic stay of creditor enforcement proceedings. The stay halts a "race to the courthouse" by individual creditors pursuing contractual remedies for default. Left unstayed, the race results in foreclosures in the case of secured debt, and money judgments followed by levy of execution in the case of unsecured debt. Liquidation of the debtor follows as a practical matter.

In theory, the reorganization proceeding also has advantages for the firm's creditors. As we saw in *Atlas Pipeline*, bankruptcy proceedings turn on the determination whether the realization of maximum distributable value for the creditors and best use of the debtors' assets calls for holding the assets together (in whole or in substantial part) as a going concern or calls for liquidating them. The decision to preserve the going concern by means of reorganization implies a creditor-beneficial determination that going concern value exceeds liquidation value.

Under the traditional bankruptcy scheme, liquidation entails an actual sale to third parties, while preservation of the going concern entails a constructive sale of the enterprise to the present creditors. This approach assumes that markets for the assets of distressed firms are imperfect to a substantial degree. If these markets were perfect, and the debtors' assets costlessly and instantly could be transferred to

the highest valuing user or users in exchange for cash, corporate
reorganization as we know it would not have to exist. All claimants
could be paid off in cash in order of priority. There would still be a
need for a proceeding—creditors presumably would litigate and bargain
over distributional matters, such as the validity, scope and priority of
their claims. There would be no need, however, to argue over the value
of the assets or the capital structure of the reorganized enterprise.

But, since transfers in markets for the assets of distressed firms
have not, historically, been considered a reliable means of value maximization, the reorganization process has evolved so as to leave the assets
in the hands of the present claimants and avoid their sale for cash to
third parties. This requires that the creditors' claims be satisfied in a
form other than cash, specifically, in new participations in the going
concern. The claimants receive varied forms of securities in the
reorganized enterprise—mortgage debt, unsecured debt, subordinated
debt, convertible debt or preferred stock, common stock and warrants.
The bundle of pre-bankruptcy claims is transformed into participations
in the post-bankruptcy entity. The process of allocating new participations in accordance with old priorities requires a determination of
the value of the enterprise. The reorganization system, both under
pre–1978 bankruptcy law and under chapter 11 of the Bankruptcy
Reform Act of 1978 (the "Bankruptcy Code"), provides for this valuation without reference to market measures of the value of the firm or
its separate assets. The most recent generation of commentary questions this approach. As we will see, it suggests that the system would
provide a better means to the end of maximum value in the context of
distress if it were revised to rely on market sales of the firm's assets or,
in the alternative, to rely on means of setting value based on the
behavior of transacting parties rather than on judicial determinations
or structured negotiations.

Putting the system's critics to one side for the moment, we see that
the bankruptcy reorganization process contemplates that the dispersed
claimants will bargain at one level over the scope, validity and priority
of their claims, and at another level over the value of the enterprise
and its assets and the value and composition of the packages of new
securities offered in satisfaction of the old claims. The resulting
negotiations, as we saw in the case of out-of-court recapitalizations,
generally produce strategic behavior, often at the expense of public
investors. But strategic behavior is treated differently in the bankruptcy context. In bankruptcy, unlike in the private reorganization, the
negotiation process leads to and culminates in a legal proceeding. The
court approves, or requires modification of, the proposed bargain, and
orders its implementation. This system of court supervised recapitalization entails two types of rules: (a) rules which prescribe and set
limits on the bargaining processes in which the dispersed claimants are
permitted to engage [e.g. who may speak, and how to determine who
may speak, for which groups of claimants? How are the bargains
reached by representatives to be communicated and approved by the
members of each group?] and, (b) rules which set limits on the substan-

tive bargains the parties may reach [e.g. how much participation may a senior class be permitted to yield (for *all* the seniors) over the protest of some of its members to an opportunistically behaving junior class?]

(2) The Parameters of the Bankruptcy Bargain

The bankruptcy "claims" of creditors are determined in fair part by the terms of their bond contracts. These, as we have seen, generally provide that when the debtor defaults in the payment of interest or principal, the bondholder has a right to demand and receive principal and accrued interest in cash. It follows that in bankruptcy the quantitative measure of a claim's priority in the distribution of the available assets is its principal and accrued interest, as if matured.

The process of satisfying the claim, thus defined, is complicated by the system's allowance of payment in units other than cash. This gives rise to issues of equivalence: whether the security, or package of securities, being accepted in satisfaction of the claim is equivalent to the cash award called for by the matured claim. The appearance of these issues opens room for disagreement among claimants on the question whether the proposed new participations in fact meet their claims. Disagreement also tends to come up over the matter of the value of the enterprise. The more value that appears, the more room opens for participation by junior claimants. Thus, disputes over matters of value in bankruptcy tend to be made as moves in larger allocative contests in which junior claimants seek recoveries at the expense of seniors.

The bondholders' bargaining posture tends to suffer in these contests. Delay favors juniors, particularly shareholders and their management representatives. By delaying, they continue the enterprise with the bondholders' capital, subjecting the bondholders to the risks of the enterprise (which during reorganization are, in effect, equity or junior debt risks). This may be seen as an extreme deprivation of the seniors' expectations. The seniors presumably invested for a cash return, accepting a limited return in exchange for priorities to income and principal. Prompt completion of the readjustment and resumption of cash flow best fulfills their expectations. In contrast, the juniors are willing to speculate on residual values over time. Time costs the juniors nothing—they face partial or total elimination if the seniors' claims are honored at face amounts. Hence the juniors use delay (both to stave off initiation of reorganization and to hold up its completion) both as a bargaining lever and in hope that the enterprise's values will increase with time and the turn of the business cycle.

The senior's awkward bargaining position gives rise to an additional source of possible disagreement in the proceeding—disagreement among members of a senior class as to whether, notwithstanding their entitlement to full payment, they should waive that claim and accept less. Many members of a senior class may be willing to settle for less than is their legal right in order to settle quickly.[j] There is no doubt that 100 percent of a class of creditors can make such a settlement, even though the concession is prompted by the juniors' nuisance power. But, as we have seen, public bond contracts are regulated by section 316(b) of the Trust Indenture Act, and will not permit a majority of the bondholders to approve an amendment that reduces the principal amount payable, or alters more than trivially the payment of interest.

Should bankruptcy law give a majority of a senior class the power to bind a minority to accept less than payment in full? Until 1978, when chapter X of the Bankruptcy Act of 1938 was repealed, both courts and Congress nominally declined to allow such majoritarian settlements. The reasons for thus imposing a rule of "absolute priority" in lieu of requiring unanimous acceptance of the bargain (and thus nominally refusing to allow a majority to bind a minority to accept less in "value" than the amount of its claim) were to be found in the conditions under which bargaining between classes of security holders occurred in the reorganization process. Historically, the bargaining process in insolvency reorganization effected through the receivership procedure was corrupted by conflicts of interest among representatives of the bargaining groups, as well as by arrangements between senior creditors and stockholders which circumvented the legal rights and economic expectations of intermediate claimants.[k] No less important, the strategic position of juniors in the bargaining gave them such substantial negotiating advantages over seniors that, as a class, the latter were generally induced to enter into reorganization bargains

---

j. A recent economic study describes the juniors' ability to delay reorganization as a call option. The seniors have to pay for the forfeiture of the option—that is, the juniors' agreement to a reorganization plan sooner rather than later. The payment is value distributed in violation of the seniors' priorities. Franks & Torous, An Empirical Investigation of U.S. Firms in Reorganization, 44 J. Finance 747 (1989).

k. The unrestricted freedom of banking houses and other financial intermediaries, or of designees of management, to assume roles on bondholders' committees created substantial conflicts of interest—e.g., (a) a member of the committee representing, and bargaining for, senior bonds might also, for his own account and accounts of his customers, be trading in those securities or be interested in securities of other classes whose values might be affected by the reorganization bargaining; (b) he might have an interest (in future underwritings or other emoluments) not shared by other bondholders of the class, in acquiring or preserving control of the enterprise emerging from reorganization, and therefore be willing to trade off the class's rights for personal advantages from the locus of control; (c) he might have an in-

terest in concealing wrongdoing by, or not ousting, those previously in control of the debtor; or (d) he might have a personal interest in fees and emoluments from the reorganization process, for which he will sacrifice his class's interests. The existence of such conflicts impeded effective bargaining on behalf of seniors. Moreover, the significance of such conflicts of interest was magnified by the fact that the authorization to committees to act for them given by depositing bondholders had many of the characteristics of blank checks—and were generally effectively irrevocable. Hence, the reorganization plans were often formulated by persons either representing the juniors or having an interest in the junior position; and the information purveyed to bondholders to induce their proxies often was, if not misleading, at least not complete. See Securities and Exchange Commission, Report on the Study and Investigation of the Work, Activities, Personnel and Functions of Protective and Reorganization Committees, Part II.

For an illustration of the squeeze on intermediate creditors see Northern Pacific Ry. v. Boyd, 228 U.S. 482 (1913).

which were more forced upon them than "free", in the classic market sense of a bargain between willing and able buyers and sellers.[1]

Absolute priority survives under the present Bankruptcy Code, but not as an absolute proposition. The Code, as amended in 1978, provides increased room for majorities of senior classes to make concessions to juniors, subject to modest disclosure rules. Absolute priority remains in background as the legal standard governing the confirmation of reorganization plans that fail to garner the requisite consents and are judicially ordered to be crammed down on nonconsenting classes.

The materials that follow take up the reorganization bargain in two modules. The first concentrates on policy, tracing the ongoing development of the absolute priority concept in bankruptcy law. The second concentrates on doctrine, showing the influence of absolute priority policy in the decision of selected valuation questions under the present Bankruptcy Code.

(B) THE RISE, DECLINE AND RESURGENCE OF ABSOLUTE PRIORITY

The law of corporate reorganization has been described in terms of a tension between the need to respect the pre-bankruptcy bargain, and the harshness of the bargain's after the fact vindication. Baird and Jackson, Bargaining After the Fall and the Contours of the Absolute Priority Rule, 55 U.Chi.L.Rev. 738, 738 (1988), citing Blum, The Law and Language of Corporate Reorganizations, 17 U.Chi.L.Rev. 565 (1950). Different resolutions of this tension have been set during the history of

---

1. In addition, at least prior to the insolvency reorganization legislation of the 1930's, there were procedural obstacles to effective exercise of seniors' power in, and to effective judicial supervision of, the bargaining process. Senior organizing power was often handicapped by the geographic and social dispersion (and relatively small stake in the outcome) of individual bondholders, and the limited access to bondholders' lists, and by the restrictive clauses in bond indentures, which had been drafted by the debtor's representatives. In sharp contrast, common stock, through management, was likely to function as a coherent interest group, with ready (and effectively exclusive) access to the means of communication with security holders. Moreover, the equity foreclosure form which the reorganization process took hampered, if it did not entirely paralyze, judicial supervision of the bargaining process and the propriety of the bargain—on which the court was asked to rule only *after* expenditure of time and money in securing bondholder approval, which the court was understandably reluctant to overturn. Hence, it is not surprising that unnecessary concessions were made to juniors by overwhelming numbers of bondholders, even under the early form of statutory reorganization embodied in Section 77B of the Bankruptcy Act. See, e.g. Case v. Los Angeles Lumber Products Co., 308 U.S. 106 (1939) where 92% of the bondholders consented to stockholders participation on the basis primarily of their nuisance value, and the lower court declined to find the Plan unfair. See generally SEC Protective Committee Report, Part VIII, Section V. Many of the disadvantages of the bargaining process were eliminated by the reorganization and securities legislation of the 1930s, which not only imposed broad disclosure requirements, but created a more equitable bargaining process (by encouraging creation of committees for each class of security holder with easy, if not inexpensive, access to all members of the class: by seeking to prohibit conflicts of interest on committees; and by placing a Trustee in control of the debtor and directing him to submit a plan of reorganization) and involved the court (and the SEC) in every crucial step in the process *before* security holders are asked to vote. Several of those investor protections were diluted by the Bankruptcy Act of 1978.

bankruptcy law. The materials that follow draw on this historical evolution in presenting the absolute priority concept. The evolution continues. As we will see, contemporary commentary on the bankruptcy reorganization takes a range of positions on the appropriate resolution of the tension between respecting priorities and ameliorating the harshness of their imposition.

––––––

(1) The Evolution of Absolute Priority Under the Bankruptcy Act of 1938

AYER, RETHINKING ABSOLUTE PRIORITY AFTER *AHLERS*

87 Mich.L.Rev. 963, 969–977 (1989).

* * * The [absolute priority] rule arose in the context of the equity receivership. The equity receivership, in turn, is bound up with the building of the railroads. From the Civil War until World War II, investors repeatedly built railroads that could not generate operating revenues sufficient to service their debt.[28] Picture a railroad that borrows $100 to lay down rail lines and build stations, selling $100 worth of bonds and giving the creditor-bondholder a senior mortgage on all the plant and equipment. Suppose the interest rate is 5%: Thus, the road needs $5 of revenue per year just for debt service. Suppose the railroad also owes an additional $20 to junior, unsecured trade creditors. Suppose the railroad generates only $4 a year of income above operating costs. One way of interpreting these numbers is to say that the plant and equipment are "worth" no more than $80—$4 per year capitalized at 5%. One solution to the problem would be simply to "give" the railroad to the bondholders. They lose $20 on their $100 investment, but they capture the whole value of the enterprise, and junior interests, including trade creditors and stockholders, are extinguished.

But the equity receivership didn't work that way. Instead, a "creditor," often in collusion with management, would file a proceeding in federal court, alleging that the debtor was unable to pay its debts as they matured. He would ask the court to use its equity power to administer the property for the satisfaction of claims, and to appoint a receiver to keep the business going in the meantime: hence, "equity receivership." The debtor would consent. Eventually, the receiver would "sell" the assets to a "new" entity—typically a reshuffling of the old investors. The price would be lower than the amount of the senior debt—in the current example, the buyers might agree to pay $30 for a railroad "worth" $80. The money would go to senior bondholders, but

---

28. A leading reorganization lawyer noted in 1927 that as of March, 1916, 16% of the nation's total rail mileage (80 railroads, 42,000 miles) was in receivership, at the end of 1925 these figures were 48 railroads with 18,000 miles of track. Swaine, Reorganization of Corporations: Certain Developments of the Last Decade, 27 Colum.L.Rev. 901, 901 (1927).

they would receive less than the total of their claim ($100) and less even than the nominal worth of the road ($80). Unsecured creditors would be eliminated, but the "new" entity, controlled by stockholders of the "old," would emerge with a company worth $80, for which they had paid only $30.

One may well ask why creditors would ever assent to such a deal, let alone collude in it. There are two reasons. One is the price of justice: old shareholders found out that they could always raise objections which, however invalid, might cost time and money to litigate. So seniors often found it cheaper to buy them off than to insist on their rights.[30] A far more important reason is that the typical reorganization was controlled by "managers"—insiders who had an interest both in bonds and in stock. For the insider-managers, it didn't matter if they lost on bonds if they gained on stock. This approach is innocent enough for those who hold both bonds and stock, but it is devastating to those who do not. In particular, this approach damages two groups. One is the unsecured trade creditors. The other group is the noninsider bondholders, not part of the management ring, who don't hold stock and who don't have the inducement of the managers to trade away their bond interest.[31]

This *modus vivendi* collapsed during the Great Depression under the weight of the investor protective legislation implemented by the New Deal.[32] Those regulatory changes have become so pervasive that they are almost part of the air we breathe. To understand the absolute priority rule, it is necessary to recognize that it emerged first as a primitive pre-statutory effort to regulate receiverships in the judicial process.

In the chronicle of case law, the critical juncture is *Northern Pacific Railway Co. v. Boyd,* decided 5–4 by the Supreme Court in 1913.[33] Boyd was a general creditor of the Northern Pacific Rail*road*. The "Road" asserted that it was not liable, in that all of its property had been transferred (via receivership) to the Northern Pacific Rail*way*.[34] Boyd then sued the Railway, which, of course, claimed that it

---

30. The classic case seeking to restrict the debtor's power to litigate creditors into submission is Fleischmann & Devine, Inc. v. Saul Wolfson Dry Goods Co., 299 F. 15 (5th Cir.1924) * * *

31. For a dramatic instance of court-sanctioned minority victimization, see Aladdin Hotel Co. v. Bloom, 200 F.2d 627 (8th Cir.1953).

32. See, e.g., Glass–Steagall Act of 1933, ch. 89, 48 Stat. 162 (1933) (codified as amended at 12 U.S.C. § 378 (1982)); Public Utility Holding Company Act of 1935, ch. 687, tit. I, 49 Stat. 803 (1935) (codified as amended at 15 U.S.C. § 79k (1982 & Supp. IV 1986)); Investment Company Act of 1940, ch. 686, tit. I, 54 Stat. 789 (1940) (codified as amended at 15 U.S.C. § 80a–1 to –64 (1982 & Supp. IV 1986)); Chapter X

of the old Bankruptcy Act, codified in former 11 U.S.C. §§ 501–676 (repealed 1978); Trust Indenture Act of 1939, ch. 411, 53 Stat. 1149 (1939) (codified as amended at 15 U.S.C. § 77aaa–yyy (1982)). See Memorandum of Homer Kripke, Report of the Commission on the Bankruptcy Laws of the United States, H.R. Doc. No. 137, 93d Cong., 1st Sess. 359–61 (1973). * * *

33. 228 U.S. 482 (1913). * * *

34. The flummery over name changes in equity receiverships may account for one of the more cherished arcana in the Bluebook—the distinction between the abbreviation used in citing the name of a Railroad (R.R.) and that used in citing the name of a Railway (Ry.). A Uniform System of Citation R. 10.2.2(a) (14th ed. 1986).

was insulated in that it had purchased the assets via a bona fide receivership. But by the Court's account, the receivership sale was in fact a transfer engineered by the old bondholders and stockholders from themselves and to themselves, "squeezing out" the intermediate unsecured debt. The Court held that such a sale cannot defeat the claim of a nonassenting creditor. As against him the sale is void in equity, regardless of the motive with which it is made.[35] As the Court put it: "[I]f purposely or unintentionally a single creditor was not paid, or provided for in the reorganization, he could assert his superior rights against the subordinate interests of the old stockholders in the property transferred to the new company."[36]

* * *

The decision sent chills of terror down the spines of the corporate reorganization bar.[37] * * *

In any event, absolute priority thereafter passed into the language and lore of the corporate lawyer.[42] But ingrained practice seems to have proved stronger than writ, as reorganization lawyers developed elaborate schemes to circumvent or emasculate the rule. Thus, counsel developed the practice of getting the reorganization court to bless the deal, with the intent of barring later objections.[43] Some courts seem to have assumed (in the teeth of *Boyd*) that acceptance by a substantial majority of senior creditors gave evidence of the fairness of the plan.[44] And reorganization managers learned how to engineer the process so as to discourage dissent.[45] Fifteen years after *Boyd*, two scholars were able to argue that corporate practice recognized two priority rules—a rule of absolute priority, à la *Boyd*, and a rule of "relative" priority, functioning in practice much like the informal "share" scheme that obtained before *Boyd*.[46] * * * Moreover, Congress complicated matters during the Great Depression by adopting legislation to supplant the

---

35. *Boyd*, 228 U.S. at 502.

36. 228 U.S. at 504.

37. "The *Boyd* case was received by the reorganization bar and bankers with something akin to horror. It has been a nightmare to the lawyer who presents a decree for the sale of property to a reorganization committee." Rosenberg, Reorganization—The Next Step, 22 Colum.L.Rev. 14 (1922). See generally Cravath, The Reorganization of Corporations; Bondholders' and Stockholders' Protective Committees; Reorganization Committees, and the Voluntary Recapitalization of Corporations, in Some Legal Phases of Corporate Financing, Reorganization and Regulation 191–98 (The Association of the Bar of the City of New York ed. 1917).

42. The first important use of the term seems to have occurred in Bonbright & Bergerman, Two Rival Theories of Priority Rights of Security Holders in a Corporate

Reorganization, 28 Colum.L.Rev. 127, 130 (1928).

43. See Swaine, supra note 28, at 907–11.

44. Jameson v. Guaranty Trust Co., 20 F.2d 808, 815 (7th Cir.1927); Samuels v. Northeastern Pub. Serv. Co., 20 Del.Ch. 204, 211, 174 A. 127, 130 (Del.Ch.1934).

45. Weiner, The Conflicting Functions of the Upset Price in a Corporate Reorganization, 27 Colum.L.Rev. 132 (1927), outlines the process by which the upset price, designed as a method for protecting debtors, evolved into a device for scotching dissent.

46. Bonbright & Bergerman, supra note 42. Bonbright, who first embraced the relative-priority alternative, later repented and called for "the strictest feasible enforcement of the absolute-priority idea." 2 J. Bonbright, The Valuation of Property 868 n. 64 (1937).

equity receivership * * * [47]

That was the situation as it stood when the Supreme Court decided *Case v. Los Angeles Lumber Products Co.* in 1939.[48] The facts of *Case* are simple: the debtor holding company had liabilities of $3.8 million and held a subsidiary that owned the Los Angeles Shipyard and Drydock—an asset valued at $830,000. The plan was to cancel old securities and issue new ones in their place. Some twenty-three percent of the new securities would go to the former stockholders.[49] Both lower courts confirmed the plan, but a unanimous Supreme Court reversed.

The case is both historically and doctrinally important. In terms of political history, the case marks a milestone in the career of Justice William O. Douglas, who wrote the opinion for the unanimous Court. Douglas had served on the Court less than a year at the time of the decision, having come from the chairmanship of the Securities and Exchange Commission. At the SEC, he was one of the principal architects of the New Deal corporate law reforms, and one of the authors of Chapter X of the Bankruptcy Act. His opinion adopts much of the substance of an *amicus* brief filed by the SEC.

As an instance of decisionmaking strategy, the case is noteworthy because it is the first major absolute priority case in which the Court interprets a statute. And indeed, Justice Douglas' interpretation has become so rooted in the culture of the law that it is a surprise to note just how attenuated it is. For the statute—Bankruptcy Act, section 77B, the precursor of Chapter X—nowhere states that claims must be paid by a principle of absolute priority.[54] Instead, Justice Douglas deploys a provision in subsection (f), which provides that a plan must be "fair and equitable." These words, Justice Douglas writes, "are words of art which prior to the advent of Section 77B had acquired a fixed meaning through judicial interpretations in the field of equity receivership reorganizations." [55] Strictly speaking, this is poppycock, and Justice Douglas knew it. None of the Supreme Court's absolute priority cases used that particular phrase in that particular way. Indeed, Justice Douglas himself cites only one prior use of the term in case law, and that is in an appellate opinion which the Supreme Court later overturned.[56] On the other hand, the question was at least open, and it was reasonable to infer that the drafters intended to import at least some kind of absolute priority rule into Section 77B.

---

47. Particularly, Act of March 3, 1933, ch. 204 § 77, 47 Stat. 1467, 1474 (repealed 1978); Act of June 7, 1934, ch. 424, § 77B, 48 Stat. 911 (repealed 1938) (corporate reorganizations).

* * *

48. 308 U.S. 106, rehg. denied, 308 U.S. 637 (1939).

49. 308 U.S. at 112. * * *

54. Pub.L. No. 73–296, 48 Stat. 912 (1933) (repealed 1978).

55. 308 U.S. at 115.

56. Flershem v. National Radiator Corp., 64 F.2d 847, 852 (3d Cir.1933), modified sub nom. First Natl. Bank of Cincinnati v. Flershem, 290 U.S. 504 (1934) (cited in 308 U.S. at 118 n. 9). Justice Douglas also cited a number of variants of the phrase. See 308 U.S. at 118.

But what kind of rule? Substantively, the remarkable fact about *Case* is that over ninety percent of all bondholders had accepted the plan. Justice Douglas held that this fact was "immaterial on the basic issue of its fairness." [59] The only possible inference was that this time, the Supreme Court meant business.

Case interpreted old Section 77B, already superseded before the Supreme Court issued its opinion.[60] But the Court soon made clear that the "fair and equitable" language also applied under the superseding Chapter X.[61] * * *

The Court [in *Case* and *Consolidated Rock Products Co.*, which follows] thus established absolute priority as the ruling principle in Chapter X. That would have finished the story (until the coming of the Bankruptcy Act of 1978) except that Chapter X was not the only pre–1978 source of reorganization law. Rather, there were—indeed there long had been—two separate strains of reorganization law, existing side-by-side in uneasy harness. One evolved from the law of equity receivership and crystallized in Chapter X, as just described. The other grew out of the common law remedy of composition, whereby creditors and debtor together agree to "compose"—or scale down—the debtor's debts. A common law composition might be binding on all creditors who agreed to it, but it was not binding on dissenters. As early as 1874, American bankruptcy law provided a scheme whereby a compromise accepted by a majority of creditors might be binding on all, including dissenters. In 1938, Congress acknowledged this tradition by embodying it in Chapter XI of the Chandler Act.[68]

The line between "compositions" and equity receiverships had never been clear, but a vulgar oversimplification, adequate for present purposes, is that the composition cases involved small businesses and face-to-face dealings between owner-managers, on the one hand, and vendor-creditors, on the other. The receivership cases, by contrast, involved publicly-traded, mortgage-backed debt and limited-liability corporations. Perhaps more important, the cases emerged from different cultures, each habituated to its own way of going about its task. No one can be certain of the influence that the competing principles of equity receivership and common law composition had upon the development of absolute priority doctrine. It is safe to conclude, however, that each laid an independent foundation for the ultimate bankruptcy structure.

Under the Bankruptcy Act, the Court encountered recurrent difficulties over the years in determining just which chapter was appropri-

59. 308 U.S. at 115.

60. *Case* was argued October 18, 1939, and decided on November 6, 1939. The Chandler Act, repealing § 77B and replacing it with Chapter X, was adopted June 22, 1938. See Chandler Act, ch. 575, 52 Stat. 883 (1938).

61. See Marine Harbor Properties, Inc. v. Manufacturers Trust Co., 317 U.S. 78, 85 (1942).

68. Ch. 575, 52 Stat. 840, 912 (1938).

ate for any particular case.[70] For our purposes, the important point is this: The absolute priority rule had never been a principle of composition law. Quite the contrary, the point was that a creditor might be bound to anything he agreed to in a composition.

This was part and parcel of the theory of composition: if you had to pay the full going concern value of the enterprise to your creditors, even though they might agree to accept less, composition was never possible. This might have been acceptable public policy to an enterprise like a publicly-held corporation, where the equity ownership might come and go. It was less palatable in the case of the typical Chapter 11 debtor—a sole proprietorship or a closely-held "family" corporation.

CONSOLIDATED ROCK PRODUCTS CO. v. DU BOIS

Supreme Court of the United States, 1941.
312 U.S. 510, 61 S.Ct. 675, 85 L.Ed. 982.

Mr. Justice DOUGLAS delivered the opinion of the Court.

This case involves questions as to the fairness under § 77B of the Bankruptcy Act * * * of a plan of reorganization for a parent corporation (Consolidated Rock Products Co.) and its two wholly owned subsidiaries—Union Rock Co. and Consumers Rock and Gravel Co., Inc. The District Court confirmed the plan; the Circuit Court of Appeals reversed. 114 F.2d 102. We granted the petitions for certiorari because of the importance in the administration of the reorganization provisions of the Act of certain principles enunciated by the Circuit Court of Appeals.

The stock of Union and Consumers is held by Consolidated. Union has outstanding in the hands of the public $1,877,000 of 6% bonds secured by an indenture on its property, with accrued and unpaid interest thereon of $403,555—a total mortgage indebtedness of $2,280,-555. Consumers has outstanding in the hands of the public $1,137,000 of 6% bonds secured by an indenture on its property, with accrued and unpaid interest thereon of $221,715—a total mortgage indebtedness of $1,358,715. Consolidated has outstanding 285,947 shares of no par value preferred stock and 397,455 shares of no par common stock.

The plan of reorganization calls for the formation of a new corporation to which will be transferred all of the assets of Consolidated Union, and Consumers free of all claims. The securities of the new corporation are to be distributed as follows:

Union and Consumers bonds held by the public will be exchanged for income bonds and preferred stock of the new company. For 50 per cent of the principal amounts of their claims, those bondholders will receive income bonds secured by a mortgage on all of the property of

70. See SEC v. United States Realty & Improvement Co., 310 U.S. 434 (1940); General Stores Corp. v. Shlensky, 350 U.S. 462 (1956); SEC v. American Trailer Rentals, 379 U.S. 594 (1965).

the new company; for the balance they will receive an equal amount of par value preferred stock. Their claims to accrued interest are to be extinguished, no new securities being issued therefor. Thus Union bondholders for their claims of $2,280,555 will receive income bonds and preferred stock in the face amount of $1,877,000; Consumers bondholders for their claims of $1,358,715 will receive income bonds and preferred stock in the face amount of $1,137,000. Each share of new preferred stock will have a warrant for the purchase of two shares of new $2 par value common stock at prices ranging from $2 per share within six months of issuance, to $6 per share during the fifth year after issuance.

Preferred stockholders of Consolidated will receive one share of new common stock ($2 par value) for each share of old preferred or an aggregate of 285,947 shares of new common.

A warrant to purchase one share of new common for $1 within three months of issuance will be given to the common stockholders of Consolidated for each five shares of old common.   * * *

　　* * *

The bonds of Union and Consumers held by Consolidated, the stock of those companies held by Consolidated, and the intercompany claims (discussed hereafter) will be cancelled.   * * *

　　* * * The District Court did not find specific values for the separate properties of Consolidated, Union, or Consumers, or for the properties of the enterprise as a unit. The average of the valuations (apparently based on physical factors) given by three witnesses at the hearing before the master were $2,202,733 for Union as against a mortgage indebtedness of $2,280,555; $1,151,033 for Consumers as against a mortgage indebtedness of $1,358,715. Relying on similar testimony, Consolidated argues that the value of its property, to be contributed to the new company, is over $1,359,000, or exclusive of an alleged good will of $500,000, $859,784. These estimated values somewhat conflict with the consolidated balance sheet (as at June 30, 1938) which shows assets of $3,723,738.15 and liabilities (exclusive of capital and surplus) of $4,253,224.41. More important, the earnings record of the enterprise casts grave doubts on the soundness of the estimated values. No dividends were ever paid on Consolidated's common stock; and except for five quarterly dividends in 1929 and 1931, none on its preferred stock. For the eight and a half years from April 1, 1929, to September 30, 1937, Consolidated had a loss of about $1,200,000 before bond interest but after depreciation and depletion. And except for the year 1929, Consolidated had no net operating profit, after bond interest and amortization, depreciation and depletion, in any year down to September 30, 1937. Yet on this record the District Court found that the present fair value of all the assets of the several companies, exclusive of good will and going concern value, was in excess of the total bonded indebtedness, plus accrued and unpaid interest. And it also found that such value, including good will and going concern value, was insufficient to pay the bonded indebtedness plus accrued and unpaid interest

and the liquidation preferences and accrued dividends on Consolidated preferred stock. It further found that the present fair value of the assets admittedly subject to the trust indentures of Union and Consumers was insufficient to pay the face amount, plus accrued and unpaid interest of the respective bond issues. In spite of that finding, the District Court also found that "it would be physically impossible to determine and segregate with any degree of accuracy or fairness properties which originally belong to the companies separately"; that as a result of unified operation properties of every character "have been commingled and are now in the main held by Consolidated without any way of ascertaining what part, if any thereof, belongs to each or any of the companies separately"; and that, as a consequence, an appraisal "would be of such an indefinite and unsatisfactory nature as to produce further confusion."

The unified operation which resulted in that commingling of assets was pursuant to an operating agreement which Consolidated caused its wholly owned subsidiaries to execute in 1929. Under that agreement the subsidiaries ceased all operating functions and the entire management, operation and financing of the business and properties of the subsidiaries were undertaken by Consolidated. The corporate existence of the subsidiaries, however, was maintained and certain separate accounts were kept. Under this agreement Consolidated undertook, *inter alia,* to pay the subsidiaries the amounts necessary for the interest and sinking fund provisions of the indentures and to credit their current accounts with items of depreciation, depletion, amortization and obsolescence. Upon termination of the agreement the properties were to be returned and a final settlement of accounts made, Consolidated meanwhile to retain all net revenues after its obligations thereunder to the subsidiaries had been met. It was specifically provided that the agreement was made for the benefit of the parties, not "for the benefit of any third person." Consolidated's books as at June 30, 1938, showed a net indebtedness under that agreement to Union and Consumers of somewhat over $5,000,000. That claim was cancelled by the plan of reorganization, no securities being issued to the creditors of the subsidiaries therefor. The District Court made no findings as respects the amount or validity of that intercompany claim; it summarily disposed of it by concluding that any liability under the operating agreement was "not made for the benefit of any third parties and the bondholders are included in that category."

We agree with the Circuit Court of Appeals that it was error to confirm this plan of reorganization.

I. On this record no determination of the fairness of any plan of reorganization could be made. Absent the requisite valuation data, the court was in no position to exercise the "informed, independent judgment" (National Surety Co. v. Coriell, 289 U.S. 426, 436) which appraisal of the fairness of a plan of reorganization entails. Case v. Los Angeles Lumber Products Co., 308 U.S. 106. * * * There are two aspects of that valuation problem.

In the first place, there must be a determination of what assets are subject to the payment of the respective claims. This obvious requirement was not met. The status of the Union and Consumers bondholders emphasizes its necessity and importance. According to the District Court the mortgaged assets are insufficient to pay the mortgage debt. There is no finding, however, as to the extent of the deficiency or the amount of unmortgaged assets and their value. It is plain that the bondholders would have, as against Consolidated and its stockholders, prior recourse against any unmortgaged assets of Union and Consumers. The full and absolute priority rule of Northern Pacific Ry. Co. v. Boyd, 228 U.S. 482, and Case v. Los Angeles Lumber Products Co., supra, would preclude participation by the equity interests in any of those assets until the bondholders had been made whole. Here there are some unmortgaged assets, for there is a claim of Union and Consumers against Consolidated—a claim which according to the books of Consolidated is over $5,000,000 in amount. If that claim is valid, or even if it were allowed only to the extent of 25% of its face amount, then the entire assets of Consolidated would be drawn down into the estates of the subsidiaries. In that event Union and Consumers might or might not be solvent in the bankruptcy sense. But certainly it would render untenable the present contention of Consolidated and the preferred stockholders that they are contributing all of the assets of Consolidated to the new company in exchange for which they are entitled to new securities. On that theory of the case they would be making a contribution of only such assets of Consolidated, if any, as remained after any deficiency of the bondholders had been wholly satisfied.

* * * Consolidated makes some point of the difficulty and expense of determining the extent of its liability under the operating agreement and of the necessity to abide by the technical terms of that agreement in ascertaining that liability. But equity will not permit a holding company, which has dominated and controlled its subsidiaries, to escape or reduce its liability to those subsidiaries by reliance upon self-serving contracts which it has imposed on them. A holding company, as well as others in dominating or controlling positions (Pepper v. Litton, 308 U.S. 295), has fiduciary duties to security holders of its system which will be strictly enforced. See Taylor v. Standard Gas & Electric Co., 306 U.S. 307. * * *

So far as the ability of the bondholders of Union and Consumers to reach the assets of Consolidated on claims of the kind covered by the operation agreement is concerned, there is another and more direct route which reaches the same end. There has been a unified operation of those several properties by Consolidated pursuant to the operating agreement. That operation not only resulted in extensive commingling of assets. All management functions of the several companies were assumed by Consolidated. The subsidiaries abdicated. Consolidated operated them as mere departments of its own business. Not even the formalities of separate corporate organizations were observed, except in minor particulars such as the maintenance of certain separate accounts. In view of these facts, Consolidated is in no position to claim that its assets are insulated from such claims of creditors of the subsidiaries. To the contrary, it is well settled that where a holding company directly intervenes in the management of its subsidiaries so as to treat them as mere departments of its own enterprise, it is responsible for the obligations of those subsidiaries incurred or arising during its management. * * * We are not dealing here with a situation where other creditors of a parent company are competing with creditors of its subsidiaries. If meticulous regard to corporate forms, which Consolidated has long ignored, is now observed, the stockholders of Consolidated may be the direct beneficiaries. Equity will not countenance such a result. A holding company which assumes to treat the properties of its subsidiaries as its own cannot take the benefits of direct management without the burdens.

We have already noted that no adequate finding was made as to the value of the assets of Consolidated. In view of what we have said, it is apparent that a determination of that value must be made so that criteria will be available to determine an appropriate allocation of new securities between bondholders and stockholders in case there is an equity remaining after the bondholders have been made whole.

There is another reason why the failure to ascertain what assets are subject to the payment of the Union and Consumers bonds is fatal. There is a question raised as to the fairness of the plan as respects the bondholders *inter sese.* While the total mortgage debt of Consumers is less than that of Union, the net income of the new company, as we have seen, is to be divided into two equal parts, one to service the new securities issued to Consumers bondholders, the other to service those issued to Union bondholders. That allocation is attacked here by respondent as discriminatory against Union, on the ground that the assets of Union are much greater in volume and in value than those of Consumers. It does not appear from this record that Union and Consumers have individual earnings records. If they do not, some appropriate formula for at least an approximate ascertainment of their respective assets must be designed in spite of the difficulties occasioned by the commingling. Otherwise the issue of fairness of any plan of reorganization as between Union and Consumers bondholders cannot be intelligently resolved.

In the second place, there is the question of the method of valuation. From this record it is apparent that little, if any, effort was made to value the whole enterprise by a capitalization of prospective earnings. The necessity for such an inquiry is emphasized by the poor earnings record of this enterprise in the past. Findings as to the earning capacity of an enterprise are essential to a determination of the feasibility as well as the fairness of a plan of reorganization. Whether or not the earnings may reasonably be expected to meet the interest and dividend requirements of the new securities is a *sine qua non* to a determination of the integrity and practicability of the new capital structure. It is also essential for satisfaction of the absolute priority rule of Case v. Los Angeles Lumber Products Co., supra. Unless

meticulous regard for earning capacity be had, indefensible participation of junior securities in plans of reorganization may result. * * *

* * * It is plain that valuations for other purposes are not relevant
to or helpful in a determination of that issue, except as they may
indirectly bear on earning capacity. * * * The criterion of earning
capacity is the essential one if the enterprise is to be freed from the
heavy hand of past errors, miscalculations or disaster, and if the
allocation of securities among the various claimants is to be fair and
equitable. * * * Since its application requires a prediction as to what
will occur in the future, an estimate, as distinguished from mathematical certitude, is all that can be made. But that estimate must be based
on an informed judgment which embraces all facts relevant to future
earning capacity and hence to present worth, including, of course, the
nature and condition of the properties, the past earnings record, and all
circumstances which indicate whether or not that record is a reliable
criterion of future performance. A sum of values based on physical
factors and assigned to separate units of the property without regard to
the earning capacity of the whole enterprise is plainly inadequate.
* * * But hardly more than that was done here. The Circuit Court of
Appeals correctly left the matter of a formal appraisal to the discretion
of the District Court. The extent and method of inquiry necessary for a
valuation based on earning capacity are necessarily dependent on the
facts of each case.

II. The Circuit Court of Appeals held that the absolute priority
rule of Northern Pacific Ry. Co. v. Boyd, supra, and Case v. Los Angeles
Lumber Products Co., supra, applied to reorganizations of solvent as
well as insolvent companies. That is true. Whether a company is
solvent or insolvent in either the equity or the bankruptcy sense, "any
arrangement of the parties by which the subordinate rights and interests of the stockholders are attempted to be secured at the expense of
the prior rights" of creditors "comes within judicial denunciation."
Louisville Trust Co. v. Louisville, N.A. & C. Ry. Co., 174 U.S. 674, 684.
And we indicated in Case v. Los Angeles Lumber Products Co., supra,
that that rule was not satisfied even though the "relative priorities" of
creditors and stockholders were maintained (pp. 119–120).

The instant plan runs afoul of that principle. In the first place, no
provision is made for the accrued interest on the bonds. This interest
is entitled to the same priority as the principal. * * * In the second
place, and apart from the cancellation of interest, the plan does not
satisfy the fixed principle of the *Boyd* case even on the assumption that
the enterprise as a whole is solvent in the bankruptcy sense. The
bondholders for the principal amount of their 6% bonds receive an
equal face amount of new 5% income bonds and preferred stock, while
the preferred stockholders receive new common stock. True, the relative priorities are maintained. But the bondholders have not been
made whole. They have received an inferior grade of securities, inferi-
or in the sense that the interest rate has been reduced, a contingent
return has been substituted for a fixed one, the maturities have been in
part extended and in part eliminated by the substitution of preferred

stock, and their former strategic position has been weakened. Those lost rights are of value. Full compensatory provision must be made for the entire bundle of rights which the creditors surrender.

The absolute priority rule does not mean that bondholders cannot be given inferior grades of securities, or even securities of the same grade as are received by junior interests. Requirements of feasibility of reorganization plans frequently necessitate it in the interests of simpler and more conservative capital structures. And standards of fairness permit it. * * * Thus it is plain that while creditors may be given inferior grades of securities, their "superior rights" must be recognized. Clearly, those prior rights are not recognized, in cases where stockholders are participating in the plan, if creditors are given only a face amount of inferior securities equal to the face amount of their claims. They must receive, in addition, compensation for the senior rights which they are to surrender. If they receive less than that full compensatory treatment, some of their property rights will be appropriated for the benefit of stockholders without compensation. That is not permissible. The plan then comes within judicial denunciation because it does not recognize the creditors' "equitable right to be preferred to stockholders against the full value of all property belonging to the debtor corporation." * * *

Practical adjustments, rather than a rigid formula, are necessary. The method of effecting full compensation for senior claimants will vary from case to case. As indicated in the *Boyd* case (228 U.S. at p. 508) the creditors are entitled to have the full value of the property, whether "present or prospective, for dividends or only for purposes of control," first appropriated to payment of their claims. But whether in case of a solvent company the creditors should be made whole for the change in or loss of their seniority by an increased participation in assets, in earnings or in control, or in any combination thereof, will be dependent on the facts and requirements of each case.[1] So long as the new securities offered are of a value equal to the creditors' claims, the appropriateness of the formula employed rests in the informed discretion of the court.

---

1. In view of the condition of the record relative to the value of the properties and the fact that the accrued interest is cancelled by the plan, it is not profitable to attempt a detailed discussion of the deficiencies in the alleged compensatory treatment of the bondholders. It should, however, be noted as respects the warrants issued to the old common stockholders that they admittedly have no equity in the enterprise. Accordingly, it should have been shown that there was a necessity of seeking new money from them and that the participation accorded them was not more than reasonably equivalent to their contribution. Kansas City Terminal Ry. Co. v. Central Union Trust Co., supra; Case v. Los Angeles Lumber Products Co., * * * In the latter case we warned against the dilution of creditors' rights by inadequate contributions by stockholders. Here that dilution takes a rather obvious form in view of the lower price at which the stockholders may exercise the warrants. Warrants exercised by them would dilute the value of common stock purchased by bondholders during the same period. Furthermore, on Consolidated's estimate of the equity in the enterprise, the values of the new common would have to increase many fold to reach a value which exceeds the warrant price by the amount of the accrued interest.

The Circuit Court of Appeals, however, made certain statements which if taken literally do not comport with the requirements of the absolute priority rule. It apparently ruled that a class of claimants with a lien on specific properties must receive full compensation out of those properties, and that a plan of reorganization is *per se* unfair and inequitable if it substitutes for several old bond issues, separately secured, new securities constituting an interest in all of the properties. That does not follow from Case v. Los Angeles Lumber Products Co., supra. If the creditors are adequately compensated for the loss of their prior claims, it is not material out of what assets they are paid. So long as they receive full compensatory treatment and so long as each group shares in the securities of the whole enterprise on an equitable basis, the requirements of "fair and equitable" are satisfied.

Any other standard might well place insuperable obstacles in the way of feasible plans of reorganization. Certainly where unified operations of separate properties are deemed advisable and essential, as they were in this case, the elimination of divisional mortgages may be necessary as well as wise. Moreover, the substitution of a simple, conservative capital structure for a highly complicated one may be a primary requirement of any reorganization plan. There is no necessity to construct the new capital structure on the framework of the old.

Affirmed.

NOTE: THE AFTERMATH OF THE CONSOLIDATED ROCK PRODUCTS COMPANY CASE

Under the amended plan of reorganization which became effective February 23, 1945, each Union Rock bondholder received $1,000 principal amount in new bonds and 892 shares of new common stock for each $1,000 principal amount of Union Rock bonds and all accumulated interest; Consumers Rock bondholders received $1,000 principal amount in new bonds and 832 shares of new common stock for each $1,000 principal amount of Consumers Rock bonds and all accumulated interest. Consolidated Rock's preferred stockholders received 2.236 shares of new common for each share of old preferred, and its common stockholders were wiped out. A total of $2,944,000 principal amount of new bonds and 3,196,091 shares of common stock (par value $1 per share) were issued in the reorganization. How does the value reflected by the principal amount of bonds and par value of stock thus issued compare with the value of the enterprise discussed in the Court's opinion?

The new common stock was denied the right to receive dividends until after the principal amount of new bonds outstanding was reduced to $1,250,000.

The $2,944,000 principal amount of new bonds bearing annual interest at 3%, plus 2% if earned, were retired through sinking fund operations over the period between 1945 and 1951.

The prices of the bonds and of the stock of the reorganized company from the time the latter was first quoted, and the earnings per share applicable to the common stock, were as follows:

| | BONDS | | COMMON STOCK | | EARNINGS PER SHARE |
	High	Low	High	Low	
1944					.05
1945	89½	81			.02
1946	90	74			.12
1947	83	75			.21
1948	88	78			.24
1949	91	86	1	⅝	.08
1950			1⅛	¾	.20
1951			1⅝	1⅛	.18
1952			1.73	1.20	.13
1953			1.92	1.21	.26

NOTE: ABSOLUTE PRIORITY AND THE DEFINITION OF THE CLAIM

1. *Principal and Accrued Interest.*

The major premise of the absolute priority rule is that the trade-off of risk and return embodied in the bond contract reflects—quite apart from any acceleration clauses—the risk of failure to receive payment of all or any part of principal and accrued interest from the debtor's assets when adverse economic contingencies materialize. But nothing in the bond contract or the circumstances of its issuance is thought to embody the additional risk of a reduction in the amount of the claim when economic failure makes the amount of the claim most relevant. For a general discussion of priority theory in insolvency reorganization, see Blum, The Law and the Language of Corporate Reorganization, supra; Blum, Full Priority and Full Compensation in Corporate Reorganization: A Reappraisal, 25 U.Chi.L.Rev. 417 (1958); Warner, Bankruptcy, Absolute Priority and the Pricing of Risky Debt Claims, 4 J. Financial Econ. 23 (1977); Baird and Jackson, Bargaining After the Fall and the Contours of the Absolute Priority Rule, supra.

Assuming the priority status of a claim has been duly recognized, how is the precise amount of the claim calculated? Under both the Bankruptcy Act of 1938 and the present Bankruptcy Code, the quantitative measure of a claim's priority is its principal and accrued interest as if matured. The maturing of the claim is said to result either from the express terms of the investment contract, which typically accelerate maturity on default (see e.g., In The Matter of Chicago, Milwaukee, St. Paul and Pacific Railroad Company, 784 F.2d 831 (7th Cir.1986)), or from the formal "sale" of the debtor's property and liquidation of the debtor, on which the older form of equity receivership proceedings was predicated.

There have, however, been many suggestions for measuring claims of senior securities and the limits of permissible settlements of those claims, by criteria other than principal plus accrued interest in determining the fairness of a reorganization bargain in insolvency. On one theory, the claims of investors in a particular class of securities might be measured by reference to the market values of the outstanding securities of the class prior to approval of the petition for reorganization.

It is also possible to affect the measure of the claim of a bond by reference to its due date or to "pure" interest rates at the time of reorganization. For example, a $1000 bond due in 2016 might have a lesser claim in an insolvency reorganization in 1991 than an equivalent $1000 bond (with the same interest rate and security) due in 1992. Or a 6% debenture might have a larger claim than a 4% debenture, or the claim of each debenture might be less when the prime rate is 10% than when it is 5%, without regard to the financial condition of the particular debtor and the degree of risk of the particular debenture. The theory, with regard to interest rates, would be that insolvency and the reorganization process should not improve the position of the 4% debenture holder vis-a-vis the 6% debenture holder, or, if money rates have risen, of both of them vis-a-vis the stockholders, over what those positions would have been had the enterprise prospered and the debt remained outstanding. The 4% and 6% debenture holders should not be entitled to the principal amounts of their debentures, with which they can buy 8% bonds at current money rates. By the same token, if money rates have fallen (e.g., to 3%), insolvency should not injure the debenture holder by reducing his 6% claim to its principal amount, which can purchase only a 3% debenture. (cf. In re Childs Co., infra, p. 389). In short, those changes in the value of the outstanding debentures attributable solely to factors external to the risks of the particular enterprise (e.g., changes in money rates) should not be altered or offset in a reorganization process which is occurring by reason of the materialization of the risks of the enterprise. See Bonbright and Bergerman, Two Rival Theories of Priority Rights of Security Holders in a Corporate Reorganization, 28 Col.L.Rev. 127, 156–157 (1928).

It also has been suggested that the measure of a senior's claim and settlement possibility in insolvency should be determined by its investment value, as in reorganizations of solvent enterprises under the Public Utility Holding Company Act of 1935. See Billyou, Priority Rights of Security Holders in Bankruptcy Reorganization: New Directions, 67 Harv.L.Rev. 553 (1954); Blum, The "New Directions" For Priority Rights in Bankruptcy Reorganization, 67 Harv.L.Rev. 1367 (1954); Billyou, New Directions: A Further Comment, 67 Harv.L.Rev. 1379 (1954); Brudney, The Investment–Value Doctrine and Corporate Readjustments, 72 Harv.L.Rev. 645 (1959).

2. *Postpetition Interest.*

The extent to which interest on debt securities and dividends on preferred stock continue to accrue and augment the claim after the filing of the petition is not entirely clear. Under the current Bankruptcy Code, which continues the earlier treatment, the general rule is that accrual of interest stops upon filing. 11 U.S.C. § 502(b)(2). But, as between some classes of security holders, (e.g., between secured and junior or unsecured to the extent of the security), accrual appears to be required. See 11 U.S.C. § 506(b); United Savings Ass'n v. Timbers of Inwood Forest, 484 U.S. 365 (1988), discussed in Appendix E infra. In addition, in straight bankruptcy liquidations, accrual is required for the benefit of unsecured creditors where the debtor is solvent. 11 U.S.C. § 726(a)(5). Is there any valid rationale for making distinctions in the accrual of postpetition interest, (a) depending upon whether the context is a straight bankruptcy liquidation or a reorganization, (b) between intra-class and inter-class claims, or (c) between various kinds of inter-class claims (e.g., tax claims)? See generally Collier on Bankruptcy, vol. 3, pp. 502.02; 506.06; vol. 4, pp. 726.02[5]; 726.03. See also Blum, Treatment of Interest on Debtor Obligations in Reorganization under the Bankruptcy Code, 59 U.Chi.L.Rev. 430 (1983).

NOTE: "FULL SATISFACTION" IN INSOLVENCY REORGANIZATION UNDER CHAPTER X

1. *Cash equivalent or reasonable prospect.*

(a) As is apparent from the *Atlas Pipeline* case, supra, p. 8, and as may be inferred from the *Consolidated Rock Products Co.* case, even if under the rule of absolute priority the claim of the senior security holders could not be reduced without the unanimous consent of the class, questions arose as to whether the payoff in securities of the reorganized enterprise was required to consist of immediate cash equivalents in the amount of the claim in order for the bargain to meet the standard. Occasional commentators and even less occasional decisions suggested that full satisfaction under the absolute priority rule should require payment in immediate cash equivalents, not merely in securities having a face amount which equals the cash claim. Friendly, Some Comments on the Corporate Reorganizations Act, 48 Harv.L.Rev. 39, 77–78 (1934). Indeed in one case, state courts held senior creditors not to have been fully satisfied by new securities (which although approved by the Supreme Court as full satisfaction had never sold at face amount) and allowed them to acquire an asset on which concededly unsatisfied junior creditors had a claim. See Guaranty Trust Co. v. Chase Nat. Bank, 302 N.Y. 658, 98 N.E.2d 474 (1951).

On the other hand, the prevailing view seems to have been that "full satisfaction" was given if the surrendering senior security holders "receive, for their total claim, a par amount of the claims for which they were exchanged. * * * " even though not immediately equal to that amount in cash. Missouri Pacific R.R. Reorganization, 290 I.C.C. 477, 555 (1954), plan approved 129 F.Supp. 392 (E.D.Mo.1955), aff'd 225 F.2d 761 (8th Cir.1955), cert. denied 350 U.S. 959 (1956). Consider also the following comment from Frank, Epithetical Jurisprudence and the

Work of the Securities and Exchange Commission in the Administration of Chapter X of the Bankruptcy Act, 18 N.Y.U.L.Q.Rev. 317, 340 (1941):

" * * * We believe that senior security holders are entitled to receive more than mere paper securities of a face amount equal to their claims; and that the securities they receive should be such as to give them really compensatory treatment for their claims. In other words, the new securities should be intrinsically sound, so that there is a reasonable prospect that they will have values equal to their face amounts, or in the case of stocks, equal to the values put upon them for reorganization purposes. If the securities seem not likely to meet this test, in our opinion, a greater amount must be issued to the senior security holders than would be warranted if the test were met, so that the value of the new securities will equal the claims of the bondholders."

Estimates of expected value are matters about which reasonable people may disagree, even though they agree, or seem to agree on the target—i.e. that the dollar amount of the matured claim should be paid in a package of securities which will, within the near future, have a cash value equal to the amount of the claim. However, to the extent that reorganization plans approved by administrative agencies and courts over a period of years embody almost consistent overestimate of the expected value of the payout, and therefore almost consistent underpayment of the claim, the question may fairly be asked whether such an approach to the determination of the expected value of the package of new securities reflects actual disagreement as to the target.

(b) The reorganization of the New York, New Haven and Hartford Railroad Company (New Haven) under Section 77 of the Bankruptcy Act, 11 U.S.C. § 205, was effected in conjunction with a merger of the New Haven into the Penn Central Company (Penn Central), a merger which was required to be "just and reasonable" under Section 5 of the Interstate Commerce Act, 49 U.S.C. § 5. The merger contemplated that the New Haven would receive in exchange for its net assets, inter alia, common stock of Penn Central, the value of which would be allocated among those bondholders of the New Haven for payment of whose claims sufficient distributable assets were found. The plan of reorganization was required under § 77(e) to be "fair and equitable"; under § 77(b), if the plan provided for sale of the debtor's assets, such sale had to be at "not less than a fair upset price." In reviewing the reorganization court's determination of the adequacy of the portion of the purchase price represented by Penn Central stock (304 F.Supp. 793, 808–810 (D.Conn.)), the Supreme Court (**New Haven Inclusion Cases,** 399 U.S. 392, 483–489 (1969)) shared that court's vision of the proper measure of the payment to New Haven as being cash value. New Haven's "give-up" (i.e., its assets) was valued on a liquidation basis, because its assets were plainly worth more on that basis than as a going concern. Although it would have taken years to liquidate New Haven's properties, the court apparently proceeded on the assumption that the testimonially estimated liquidation value of those properties was the equivalent of cash in hand. While the stock of Penn Central which New Haven was to receive in the merger in partial exchange for those properties was found to have a reorganization or intrinsic value equal to the value of the "give-up", it had a considerably lower cash value on the effective date of the merger. The court announced a new principle in accommodating to that disparity between the imputed cash value of the "give-up" and the actual cash value of the payment therefor. It stated that the "fairness" of the transaction was to be measured over a period of approximately ten years after the merger, and required Penn Central to pay New Haven the difference between the value the lower court had "found" for New Haven's properties and the highest market price quoted for the Penn Central stock on the New York Stock Exchange during that period, but did not require New Haven to repay anything if the price of the Penn Central stock rose higher than that value.

Is this technique of "a second look" at the value of the pay-out a rational solution for resolving uncertainties about the value at the time of the payment in insolvency reorganization—or in a merger of solvent enterprises?

If the package of securities to be distributed is designed to reflect not present cash equivalents but estimates of future earnings discounted to present value by reason of estimated risk factors, is there room in the reorganization process for offering those for whose claims there are no "present" values a participation which will have value only if the most optimistic earnings estimates are realized? Why did the Court reject the issuance of warrants to Consolidated's common stock?

2. *Loss of senior status.*

In the Consolidated Rock Products case, Justice Douglas indicated that senior creditors were permitted to receive securities of the same quality as those awarded to junior creditors in satisfaction of their claims, but in that event, seniors were to be "adequately compensated for the loss of their prior claims. * * * " The present Bankruptcy Code, § 1129(b), seems to perpetuate the same mandate for unsecured creditors (while requiring secured creditors to receive debt securities to the extent of their secured claims, at least when the secured class dissents from the plan). How is such adequate compensation to be effected?

If the payoff of claims were required to be made in immediate cash equivalents, would there be any need for (or right to) such compensation? Thus, if the holder of a defaulted 8% secured bond in the amount of $1000 receives in full satisfaction of his claim a new 6% unsecured $1000 debenture at a time when the prime money rate is at the 5% level, and the new bond sells for $1000 or more, is there any need to "compensate" for the loss of secured position and the diminution of the coupon rate, since the bondholder could sell his new debenture at once for at least $1000?

On the other hand, if the payoff is to be made in securities which are not the immediate cash equivalent of the claim, the question arises as to how, in the forced sharing of the risks of the continuing enterprise, the seniors should be compensated for loss of a preferred position. An effort can be made to quantify the value of the seniors' loss (of a secured position or a sinking fund or a fixed interest obligation) and to compensate them by a corresponding increase in the value of new participations. Presumably, compensation for assuming a relatively riskier position vis-a-vis the participating juniors implies a higher return, either in the form of a higher coupon or dividend rate or in the form of a larger share of the new securities being awarded.

Thus, assume that an enterprise with outstanding debt of $1 million in 5% secured bonds and $1 million in 4% unsecured debentures is to be reorganized, and that it is valued in going concern terms at $1,500,000. If only common stock were to be issued in the reorganization, compensatory treatment would require the bondholders to receive proportionately more than the debenture holders, owing to the loss of their pledged security and higher interest claim. The problem is how to quantify the value of the loss and the value of the appropriate compensation therefor.

If the pledged security were found to have a "value" of $800,000, the seniors would be entitled to $8/15$ of the common stock plus some added portion of the common stock for the loss of their secured position. In any event, even if $8/15$ of the common stock had an immediate cash value of $800,000 and were allocated to the 5% bonds, the bondholders would have an unsatisfied claim of $200,000 and the unsecured 4% debentures would have a claim of $1,000,000. Would the remaining $7/15$ of the common stock be divided in the ratio of 2 to 10, or (by reason of the seniors' lost interest superiority) 1 to 4? Would the latter be compensatory for the loss of a higher interest rate? Or would the seniors be entitled to still more compensation because they are being exposed to the same risk and return as the juniors?

However difficult may be the problems of compensatory adjustment of the pay-outs to juniors and seniors when they each receive securities carrying the same risk and return (e.g., common stock), an added set of problems is presented when they receive securities with lesser protection than those surrendered, but each receives a security with different risk and return characteristics. If the seniors receive 4% debentures and the juniors receive common stock, should the seniors receive more than $1,000,000 face amount of new debentures? Should they receive some common stock? How should one determine how much of each?

Finally, apart from questions with respect to compensation of seniors by reason of payment to them of inferior securities, there is the question whether they may be entitled to some compensation even when they receive securities with the same terms as those they surrender. Thus, assume an enterprise with the following expected values:

Estimated Value	Associated Probability	Expected Value
$100	10%	$10.00
$ 70	15%	10.50
$ 50	50%	25.00
$ 30	15%	4.50
$ 10	10%	1.00
		$51.00

Suppose the enterprise has outstanding $30 principal amount, 5% first mortgage bonds and $30 principal amount, 4% second mortgage bonds (on the same assets). Under the plan of reorganization, the seniors are to receive new 5% first mortgage bonds with the same terms in the amount of $30 and the juniors only common stock. Is a compensatory adjustment required, and how should it be made? The new bonds, with a 90% chance of realizing at least $30 and a 10% chance of realizing only $10, would have an expected value of $28, at least if they carried a more or less conventional interest coupon. The new common, with a 50% chance of $20, a 15% chance of $40, and a 10% chance of $70, would have an expected value of $23. Are the seniors entitled to $2/23$ (or more) of the stock by way of compensation? Would they be better off with $20 in new bonds and one-third of the common stock?

An innovative rationale for, and formula for determining appropriate, "compensatory treatment" are offered in, Note, Giving Substance to the Bonus Rule in Corporate Reorganizations: The Investment Value Doctrine Analogy, 84 Yale L.J. 932 (1975). See also Blum, Corporate Reorganization Doctrine As Recently Applied by the Securities and Exchange Commission, 40 U.Chi.L.Rev. 96, 107 et seq. (1972).

3. *New Value.*

If uncertainty as to the value found for the business of the enterprise and the preference of old seniors for new senior securities create difficulties for effecting full satisfaction of their claims, the insistence of the old equity that it is entitled to participate in the new enterprise if it contributes "new value" creates additional problems. What kind of new value must the old equity contribute and what quantity of new participation should it receive?

The learning under the absolute priority doctrine prior to the 1978 Bankruptcy Act was hostile to new value contributions that consisted of intangibles (such as experience with the enterprise, financial standing in the community and continuity of management), presumably because such contributions were too ephemeral and too easily misvalued to permit them to underpin the participations proposed. Cf. Case v. Los Angeles Lumber Products Co., 308 U.S. 106 (1939). The notion was expressed, however, that new participations could be offered to the old equity if the enterprise required capital and the contributors offered cash or cash equivalents. The problem was how to determine the appropriate amount of such new participations if the absolute priority formula permitted the contributors of cash to receive a participation "reasonably equivalent to their contribution" (Los Angeles Lumber, 308 U.S. at 121), but also required the old creditors to be paid "in full" before the old equity could participate.

The solution to the problem depends on whether payment "in full" under absolute priority means "in full" from the value of the enterprise in its reorganized form or only from the value of the old business. To illustrate, assume that the old business is valued on a going concern basis in a reorganization proceeding at $100 before taking account of an infusion of new capital, that the old creditors have a claim of $110, and that the old equity proposes to contribute $20 in cash for all of the common stock of the reorganized firm. If a new contribution by the old equity will raise the value of the firm to at least $120, should not the requirement of payment "in full" result in $10 of the $20 going to the old creditors? But why would any one make an equity contribution on such terms? If the equity contributors proceed despite the allocation of $10 of the $20 to the old creditors, they must be making their $20 contribution in the belief that the reorganizers' calculation of a going concern value of $100 is too low and that, given an infusion of $20, the firm has a present value of at least $130. Will this reading of payment "in full"—which as a practical matter opens a door to old equity contributions only in cases where the contributor values the enterprise at more than $120, and indeed more than $130—mean that some reorganizations will fail that would not have failed under a less rigorous rule allowing the old equity to receive *all* the value of the new enterprise in excess of $100?

Consider the possibility that the old enterprise is not "undervalued" at $100 and that at the same time the $20 new value transaction can succeed with the old creditors taking $10 of the $20. This result could obtain because, in the language of the cases, "control" has a value. That value is purchased here by the $20 contributor. Does the "control" embodied in ownership of all the equity in a highly leveraged enterprise add a value that is not apparent in the imputed going concern value of the old assets? If so, when the cash contributions are made to acquire the equity in the new enterprise the contributors should not be unwilling to share some of that value (possibly up to the extent of the creditors' unmet claims) with the creditors who are selling them control.

Assume that all the debt claims in the above example are held by a single claimant. In that case there is little doubt that upon the sale of control of the firm to the contributors of new equity capital, the sole lender would seek to get, and probably would get, a share of the value of that control at least equal to the amount of its unmet claim. Should the result be different in the case of a dispersed class of bondholders who are unable effectively to generate an informed and volitional consent to their concession in a bargaining process in which the representatives of the old equity have structural and informational advantages?

If absolute priority means that the contributor of "new value" is entitled to receive "the equivalent of the value contributed," how is such equivalence to be measured? How, under such a rule, can the old creditors be paid "in full" for the control they surrender? For discussion of these problems, see Ayer, Rethinking Absolute Priority After *Ahlers,* 87 Mich.L.Rev. 940 (1989); Markell, Owners, Auctions and Absolute Priority in Bankruptcy Reorganizations, 44 Stan.L.Rev. 69 (1991).

Would the difficulty be mitigated if the old creditors were willing to accept all or some of the equity in the new enterprise? If so, should the law attempt to encourage such willingness by determining an allocation of such new equity between old creditors and old stockholders by means of an auction? Should the law encourage old creditors to take sufficiently little new debt and all the equity so that any needed capital infusion can come from new borrowing?

A somewhat different problem is presented if the new value comes from a stranger who seeks to acquire the enterprise in an arms length bargain. The stranger, by definition, lacks the informational advantages and power to overreach that is possessed by representatives of the old equity. But it still has a structural advantage in bargaining with the dispersed bondholders. Arguably a sole lender standard imposed by law should govern the propriety of the resulting bargain, or the bargaining should be structured so as to give the dispersed bondholders a comparable chance to get full value. The transaction might be viewed as the effort by the newcomer to make a tender offer for the dispersed owners of the enterprise. Under this view the newcomer would have less of an obligation to the old creditors and fewer limits would be imposed on the new capital transaction than would obtain in the case of a new contribution by old equityholders or insiders. Would an auction for "the business" with outside bids being solicited be an appropriate process for realizing the maximum return? Who would conduct the auction, and on behalf of which claimants? See LoPucki and Whitford, Corporate Governance in the Bankruptcy Reorganization of Large, Publicly Held Companies, 141 U.Pa.L.Rev. 669, 753–767 (1992).

Quite apart from ascription of value to "control," is it possible that the aggregate "value" of the new participations to be awarded to old security-holders exceeds the going concern "value" of the assets of the enterprise, notwithstanding reliance upon the same estimate of future earnings and over-all risk? (See discussion of leverage, taxes, and feasibility infra, pp. 499–506). If so, can the junior securityholders of the debtor be excluded from new participations in the reorganized enterprise without first determining its capital structure? Does this imply a process of reorganizing which first determines the new capital structure (i.e., creates a hierarchy of claims on segments of estimated earnings in order of risk of realization of each segment) and fits it to the old claims, with the most certain segment of estimated earnings being allocated to old seniors and the most risky segment (expected to be realized only on the most optimistic assumptions) being allocated to those old juniors for whom there is any participation available? Does this process in turn imply, in practice if not also in logic, a total value of the enterprise which is higher than one which would be reached in determining the going concern value of the old business? See Blum, Full Priority and Full Compensation in Corporate Reorganizations, A Reappraisal, 25 U. of Chi.L.Rev. 417 (1958).

NOTE: THE COMPOSITION TRADITION AND THE BEST INTEREST OF CREDITORS STANDARD

There is a tradition of composition in bankruptcy proceedings which was continued in Chapter XI of the Bankruptcy Act until its repeal by the 1978 Act. Under Section 12 of the Bankruptcy Act (52 Stat. 840, which was repealed in 1938) a majority in number and interest of the creditors of an enterprise were authorized to force a minority to accept a composition proposed by the debtor which resulted in the creditors receiving less than full payment, even though the debtor retained otherwise distributable assets. The limits on the power of the majority thus to force a minority to accept less than their full claim were contained in Section 12(d) which provided that a composition should only be confirmed by the Court if, among other things, "it is for the best interests of the creditor". That standard was carried forward into § 366 of Chapter XI (11 U.S.C. § 766). The "best interests" standard was based on the assumption that bank and trade creditors tended to have adequate information about the debtor's business and its owner's character and potential and could cooperate when making concessions. Although there was room for debate as to its precise contours, under the standard, one—if not indeed the principal—limitation on the majority's power to make concessions for the claims of all unsecured creditors was that the composition offer the creditors a distribution of not less than they would realize in a straight bankruptcy liquidation. That was the limit to which the bankrupt's capacity (a) to collude with some creditors at the expense of others, or (b) to force the acquiescence of all the creditors in a detrimental composition by delaying and frustrating the collection and distribution of assets by concealment and diversion. See Fleischmann & Devine Inc. v. Saul Wolfson Dry Goods Co., 299 Fed. 15 (5th Cir.1924); Technical Color & Chemical Works, Inc. v. Two Guys from Massapequa, 327 F.2d 737, 741 (2d Cir.1964).

As the SEC pointed out, "Section 12 was inadequate for corporate reorganization as commonly understood because it never was intended to be employed for such purpose. It was part of a general system of bankruptcy; and, as such, was directed toward the type of business concern ordinarily liquidated through a bankruptcy sale. Both in general conception and in detail it was designed for use by the individual trader or businessman and by the small, close corporation equivalent to the individual businessman. It was designed as a substitute for liquidation in these small cases, setting up a machinery by which the creditors of a bankrupt might obtain a settlement approximating the amount obtainable in liquidation, and by which the honest debtor might continue in business and remain a customer of his creditors. The very paucity of detail in Section 12, the town meeting technique of unlimited creditor control, the failure to provide specifically for secured creditors, the omission to provide especially for stockholders, the neglect of distinction between various classes of creditors, and the failure to recognize the possible existence of holders of corporate securities of the debtor or any likelihood of committees representing their interests—all bore witness to the restricted purview of this section, as applying only to the small, personal enterprise. Moreover, it is significant that the breakdown of the Section 12 composition procedure even in the small cases to which it was intended to apply was due in large measure to the general failure of individual creditors to take an active and continued interest in the proceedings—a condition far more prevalent, and almost inevitable, in the case of large corporations with publicly held securities." SEC, Report on the Study of Protective and Reorganization Committees, Pt. VIII, § III (1940).

The "best interest" standard survived the repeal of Chapter XI and reappeared in the Bankruptcy Act of 1978, 11 U.S.C. § 1129, as the liquidation standard limiting the majority's power to make concessions in all reorganization proceedings.

The "best interests" standard also showed up under § 20b of the Interstate Commerce Act (now 49 U.S.C. § 11,361, § 11,362(a)). There, Congress provided for modification of seniors' obligations (including extension of maturity of debt, lowering of interest rates, and elimination of preferred stock arrearages) upon the consent of 75% in aggregate principal amount of debt or number of shares of each affected class, and a finding by the ICC that the proposed modification is, among other things, "in the best interests of the carrier, of each class of its stockholders and of the holders of each class of its obligations affected by such modification or alterations". In adopting the "best interests" standard, Congress plainly rejected the absolute priority test which measured the surrendered claim by its rights on maturity or liquidation. The limits to be imposed on the rebargain in lieu of the absolute priority guide were, however, uncertain. For discussion of those uncertainties, see Blum, The Interstate Commerce Commission as Lawmaker: The Development of Standards for Modification of Railroad Securities, 27 U.Chi.L.Rev. 603, 654–657 (1960).

(2) The Attack on Absolute Priority and the Bankruptcy Act of 1978

In 1978, Congress repealed Chapter X and enacted a new bankruptcy act which makes substantial changes in the prior law of insolvency reorganization. One significant change is the abandonment of the absolute priority rule for all reorganization bargains which are accepted by at least two-thirds in amount and more than one-half in number of the allowed claims of the creditor class, and two-thirds in amount of any class of equity participants. While the 1978 Act provides that a court may enforce a plan which is not accepted by the requisite numbers and amounts of each class, and that in that circumstance the "fair and equitable" standard measures the limits of a permissible reorganization plan with respect to the non-acquiescing class (§ 1129(b)), it is expected that most plans will be "accepted" by the requisite numbers and amounts of each class. The revised reorganization process contemplates bargaining over a plan by representatives of claimants and the debtor, but under restrictions designed to favor submission of only the debtor's (§ 1121) plan for acceptance. Committees of classes of claimants can consist only of persons appointed by the court and are intended to be the persons with the largest claims in the class—a system which imposes its own limitations on the bargaining process. The SEC's role in the process has been substantially curtailed; and its advisory reports to security holders have been eliminated. The trustee's role has also been materially diminished; a trustee (or examiner to investigate the debtor's affairs and possible prior mismanagement or malefaction) may, but is not required to, be appointed. The trustee or examiner may report to the court the results of its investigation. It is contemplated (§ 1125) that full disclosure (in documents judicially determined to be adequate for the purpose, in light particularly of trustees' or examiners' reports) will be made to the affected voters of each class in soliciting their approval for a plan, and that such disclosure will be sufficient to legitimate the results of the bargaining—i.e., acceptance of a plan by the requisite majorities in numbers and amounts—which will thereupon become enforceable against all members of the class. But even then, the Act sets limits on how much can be conceded by the majority. Liquidation value is the floor set by Section 1129(a)(7) on the permissible concessions.

The 1978 Act resulted from and responded to decades of criticism of the 1938 Act and, in particular, the absolute priority rule.

HOUSE REPORT NO. 95–595.

95 Cong., 1st Sess., 1977, pp. 221–224.

Chapter X was designed for a thorough financial reorganization of a corporation. It contemplates very rigid and formalized procedures, and the imposition of strict financial rules governing a plan * * * [of] reorganization; which, though designed to protect public creditors, have often worked to the detriment of not only the public creditors, but also the public shareholders and private creditors as well. The negative results under chapter X have resulted from the stilted procedures, under which management is always ousted and replaced by an independent trustee, the court and the Securities and Exchange Commission examine the plan of reorganization in great detail, no matter how long that takes, and the court values the business, a time-consuming and inherently uncertain process.*

Chapter X requires application of the absolute priority rule as a standard for confirmation of a plan. Under that rule, senior creditors must be paid in full under the plan before junior creditors or stockholders may receive anything. In 1938, when public securities were usually senior bonds and corporations were more often privately held, the absolute priority rule prevented abuses of the public's rights by insiders of a corporation in reorganization. Today, public classes are more likely to be subordinated debenture holders and stockholders, and the protection of senior classes inures to the benefit of private creditors, often financing consortiums, that have nearly as much influence over the operation of a business as the inside shareholders did in an earlier day. Application of the absolute priority rule under chapter X has more recently led to the exclusion rather than the protection of the public.

Further, the application of that rule requires a full going concern valuation of the business. Though valuation is theoretically a precise method of determining the creditors' and stockholders' rights in a business, more often the uncertainty of predicting the future, required in any valuation, is a method of fudging a result that will support the plan that has been proposed. As Peter Coogan has aptly noted, such a valuation is usually "a guess compounded by an estimate". In a reorganization where time is of the essence, the length and uncertainty of the valuation process is no longer justified in every case.

* * *

* * * Under chapter X, the financial standard for confirmation is the absolute priority rule. Under that rule, creditors are entitled to be paid according to the going-concern value of the business, which is usually higher than the liquidation value of the business, because assets in operation can usually earn more than assets sold for scrap. Under chapter XI, however, creditors are entitled only to the liquidation value of the business. The plan may be confirmed if creditors receive at least what they would receive under a liquidation of the business. The debtor, that is, stockholders, are able to retain for themselves the difference between liquidation value and going-concern value.

The establishment of the two chapters in 1938 was most likely due not only to the desire to differentiate both procedures and standards for small private companies versus large public ones, but also to the

* [Ed. Note] (from p. 225 of Report).

"After the hearing on the plan, the plan, along with the evidence developed at the approval hearing, is sent to the Securities and Exchange Commission. The Commission develops an advisory report on the plan. This process may take anywhere from one to six months or more. The purpose of the advisory report is to inform the creditors and stockholders of the contents of the plan, and of the SEC's evaluation of the plan. Some have argued that creditors and stockholders simply are unable to make an intelligent or informed decision without the SEC's report, all of the valuation evidence developed at the disclosure hearing, and an order of the court finding the plan worthy of consideration and approving the plan. The purpose of the approval hearing, court approval, and an SEC report in chapter X was public investor protection."

inability of Congress or the bankruptcy community, both the bar and academia, to decide what it was that creditors were ultimately entitled to receive: liquidation or going-concern value. They finessed the issue by the adoption of two chapters.

* * *

The consolidated chapter is chapter 11 of proposed title 11. It adopts much of the flexibility of chapter XI of current law, and incorporates the essence of the public protection features of current chapter X. The areas of greatest importance are the financial standard for confirmation; the court hearing on the plan and the report on the plan to creditors and stockholders; the right to propose a plan; and the appointment of a trustee.

II. THE FINANCIAL STANDARD

The premise of the bill's financial standard for confirmation is the same as the premise of the securities law: parties should be given adequate disclosure or relevant information, and they should make their own decision on the acceptability of the proposed plan * * * [of] reorganization. The bill does not impose a rigid financial rule for the plan. The parties are left to their own to negotiate a fair settlement. The question of whether creditors are entitled to the going-concern or liquidation value of the business is impossible to answer. It is unrealistic to assume that the bill could or even should attempt to answer that question. Instead, negotiation among the parties after full disclosure will govern how the value of the reorganizing company will be distributed among creditors and stockholders. The bill only sets the outer limits on the outcome: it must be somewhere between the going-concern value and the liquidation value.

Only when the parties are unable to agree on a proper distribution of the value of the company does the bill establish a financial standard. If the debtor is unable to obtain the consents of all classes of creditors and stockholders, then the court may confirm the plan anyway on request of the plan's proponent, if the plan treats the nonconsenting classes fairly. The bill defines "fairly" in terms of the relative rights among the classes. Simply put, the bill requires that the plan pay any dissenting class in full before any class junior to the dissenter may be paid at all. The rule is a partial application of the absolute priority rule now applied under chapter X and requires a full valuation of the debtor as the absolute priority rule does under current law. The important difference is that the bill permits senior classes to take less than full payment, in order to expedite or insure the success of the reorganization.

* * *

(Excerpt from Memorandum by Homer Kripke

* * *

At a meeting on January 30, 1977, a member of the SEC staff said that Congress had determined in 1938 (the time of enactment of Chapter X as part of the "Chandler Act") that certain protections were needed and that nothing had occurred to change this determination. This kind of thinking is at the root of the present difficulty. The fact is that much has changed and that to some extent the protections of 1938 proved to be a case of overkill. Reconsideration of these protections is in keeping with current desires to discontinue over-regulation which no longer has adequate purpose.

The Chandler Act is now nearly 40 years old, and it is based on the findings in the SEC Protective Committee Study of conditions in the 1920's, fifty years ago. Even before the Chandler Act was passed, there were the beginnings of restriction on the evils of the 1920's in the form of the securities legislation generally, the Glass–Steagall Act, the requirements of audited financial statements, and the generally changed public atmosphere with the SEC as watchdog. After the Chandler Act, there was enacted the Trust Indenture Act of 1939 which puts the indenture trustee in the forefront as protecting the holders of public debt securities. There has also been enacted the Investment Company Act of 1940, which precludes the likelihood of extensive bankruptcies in the investment company field by imposing rigorous capital structure requirements. This had also been accomplished in the public utility field by the Public Utility Holding Company Act of 1935, but that Act had been too recent in 1938 to permit a realization of the extent to which it had precluded repetition of the evils of the 1920's for a substantial segment of the corporate world in which the abuses had been the most extensive.

Moreover, since 1938 there has arisen a large and vigorous plaintiffs' bar, anxious to represent public security holders in any case where they are being unfairly treated. The importance of this group seeking representation of the public cannot be overemphasized. In other contexts, the SEC has earnestly supported the growth and development of this Bar and the private cause of action, on the plea that its own limited staff could not adequately police conditions. In the allocation of its hard-pressed budgetary capabilities, the SEC has depleted its own staff devoted to bankruptcy matters, leaving the aggregate protections still more dependent in the long run on the private plaintiffs' bar.

(3) The New Case for Absolute Priority

As we have seen, the law of corporate reorganization rests on a judgment that claimants against a distressed firm can realize greater value through a recapitalization than through a liquidation or a sale of the going concern to a third party or parties. That judgment having been made, the law then defines the amount and priority of each claim, and provides rules to guide the allocation of participations in the reorganized firm among the claimants. This system, brought to bear in a particular case, turns on a determination of the value of the firm.

First, going concern value must be greater than liquidation value in order for reorganization to be an appropriate alternative. Second, particular allocations of interests in the reorganized firm depend on a prior determination of the total value being allocated.

We also have seen that the Bankruptcy Reform Act of 1978 seeks to leave the final determination of value to negotiation and majoritarian vote instead of to judicial decree and full payment, and in so doing, retreats one step from absolute priority. Commentaries since its enactment question both continuing adherence to the idea that recapitalization preserves value that liquidation destroys, and its mode of solving the problem of valuation and allocation. Ironically, much of this work pursues the program of enhancing the status of absolute priority as the bankruptcy system's governing norm. The historic problem of extraction of value through strategic delay by juniors and corrupt bargains with seniors continues to be treated as a problem that the prevailing system has not solved. Furthermore, the recent commentaries assert that the system's structured bargaining process unduly subordinates what ought to be the system's primary goal—the provision of an optimal capital structure for the reorganized firm. See Bebchuk, A New Approach to Corporate Reorganizations, 101 Harv.L.Rev. 775 (1988).

(a) The "Creditor's Bargain"

The new defense of absolute priority has its roots in an economic model of bankruptcy advanced by Professors Thomas Jackson and Douglas Baird. In this account, bankruptcy is a legal response to the economic problems of debt collection. The creditors are viewed as economic actors with rights in a common pool of assets. Given debtor distress, individual creditor action to pursue rights in the pool under nonbankruptcy law undercuts the broader goal to preserve and maximize the aggregate value of the pool. Bankruptcy law is designed to assure that the value of the common pool is maximized. First, it stays individual creditor actions so as to prevent the disaggregation of the pool; second, it sets out a process assuring that the assets in the pool are deployed so as to maximize their value through sale, either to the creditors or to third parties. See T. Jackson, The Logic and the Limits of Bankruptcy 10–32 (1986).

The assertion that the exclusive focus of the bankruptcy system should be optimal asset deployment leads to the assertion that the system should not focus on, or perhaps even address distributional questions. Instead, the system should defer to substantive nonbankruptcy law, and leave in place the prebankruptcy rights established in the common pool. T. Jackson, supra at 21–27; Baird, Loss Distribution, Forum Shopping and Bankruptcy: A Reply to Warren, 54 U.Chi.L.Rev. 815, 822–824 (1987). Since these prebankruptcy rights are primarily matters of contract, the bankruptcy system's distributional norm should be contractually determined. The law should be shaped by reference to the "creditors' bargain"—the result that the creditors contracted for and, therefore had reason to expect, at the time they extended credit. These "prebankruptcy entitlements" include contracted for priorities. Impairment of these entitlements in bankruptcy should occur only to the extent necessary to maximize net asset distribution to the creditors as a group. See T. Jackson, supra, ch. 9; Jackson and Scott, On the Nature of Bankruptcy: An Essay of Bankruptcy Sharing and the Creditors' Bargain, 75 Va.L.Rev. 155 (1989). Thus does the economic model of bankruptcy return us to the distributional principal that dominated before the enactment of the present Bankruptcy Code—absolute priority.

Economists reiterate this view. Says Weiss, Bankruptcy Resolution: Direct Costs and Violation of Priority of Claims, 27 J. Financial Econs. 285, 286 (1990): "Economists have long argued that bankruptcy courts mistakenly fail to uphold priority of claims." That they should have thus argued for absolute priority comes as no surprise. Absolute priority follows directly from application of a microeconomic model to the problem of debtor distress. Forgiveness of failure does not fit easily into the microeconomic context of evolutionary improvement and survival of the fittest. More particularly, in the economic picture of debt and equity, productivity advantages flow from the uncompromising imposition of downside risk. Firms prosper in part because the equity, as holders of the residual upside claim, press the managers to produce efficiently. On the downside, the equity still presses for efficient production because, as the holder of the residual risk of loss, it will be wiped out in the event of failure. Any relaxation of absolute priority disrupts this system of production incentives.

(b) Alternative Modes of Reorganization

Although the economic model of bankruptcy takes us back to absolute priority, its protagonists rarely suggest that absolute priority be realized by the old means of a judicial valuation and cram down. A number of alternative modes of reorganization have been presented. These share a tendency to question what was once a conventional wisdom—that the market is likely systematically to undervalue the reorganized enterprise and the new securities issued upon the effectiveness of the plan. See Blum, The Law and the Language of Corporate Reorganization, 17 U.Chi.L.Rev. 565, 567–568 (1950).

(1) *Liquidation*

T. Jackson, supra, ch. 9 (1986) and Baird, The Uneasy Case for Corporate Reorganization, 15 J. Legal Studies 127 (1986), suggest that we abandon the recapitalization solution and rely on the market for corporate assets, sold on a going concern basis. The enterprise would be valued in this market, and sold for cash. The cash would be distributed to the claimants in the order of their priority. This system avoids both judicial valuation and the need for dispersed creditor and junior security holders to bargain collectively over value or a revised capital structure. The only significant disputes remaining for resolution within the bankruptcy system would concern the validity, scope and priority of claims.

(2) *All Common Stock Capital Structure/Market Test*

The reform proposition set out in Roe, Bankruptcy and Debt: A New Model for Corporate Reorganization, 83 Colum.L.Rev. 527 (1983), like that of Baird and Jackson, sets value by means of a market transaction. But, unlike Baird and Jackson, Roe would retain recapitalization as a central aspect of bankruptcy reorganization. Roe would simplify the process substantially by (1) requiring a capital structure consisting only of common stock, and (2) offering a segment of the new common stock for sale to, and trading by, the public. The price established in the public sale provides the basis for the valuation of the enterprise as a whole. The value being thus set, the remaining common stock is distributed to the claimants in order of priority. As with the Baird and Jackson, judicial valuation and collective bargaining over value are avoided.

(3) *Options*

Each of the Baird and Jackson and Roe proposals would improve on the present system only to the extent that the auction or market transactions on which they rely provide a more accurate means of valuation. Were the market relied on open to substantial imperfections—such as price volatility based on supply and demand swings not related to fundamental value, or informational problems or manipulation—then the proposal's viability would be open to substantial question. Bebchuk, A New Approach to Corporate Reorganizations, supra, offers another alternative. This, like the Baird and Jackson and Roe alternatives, is designed to avoid valuation by decree or by collective bargaining. Unlike those alternatives, it does not rely on market transactions. Bebchuk's reorganization plan hands the firm and the claimants options instead of unconditioned ownership interests. The parties are then given time to ascertain the value of the options. The firm, in effect, becomes an investment opportunity for the claimants. The burden to establish a value flows to the claimants themselves.

More specifically, Bebchuk would place the securities of the reorganized firm in the hands of the seniors, subject to a call at the option of the firm. The call price would be the amount of the seniors' claim. The junior creditors would receive an option to purchase the firm's securities, the option price being set at the amount of the seniors' claims. Thus, if the juniors determined the value of the firm to be greater than the seniors' claims, they would exercise their option. The proceeds of the exercise would be used by the firm to redeem the firm's securities from the seniors. The juniors would profit to the extent of the difference between the value of the firm and the value of the seniors' claim. Similarly, the equity would have an option to purchase the firm's securities for a price equal to the senior and junior creditors' claims. The model allows for complicating factors such as more than three levels of claim and option exercise by less than all the claimants at a given level.

(4) *Abolition*

Bradley and Rosenzweig, The Untenable Case for Chapter 11, 101 Yale L.J. 1043 (1992), reports the results of a comparative study of bankruptcy filings and security prices of listed companies before and after the effective date of the Bankruptcy Reform Act of 1978. They conclude that chapter 11 is an inefficient device that disserves investors and serves the purpose of "permitting management to extract wealth from the firm's various security holders," id., p. 1077, and recommend its repeal. In its stead they would institute a system in which default results in the automatic cancellation of the firm's equity. The firm's junior debt holders would then inherit the status of residual claimant. In other words, their interests would be transformed into equity. The junior debt holders thereupon would get a chance either to pay the senior creditors or default and have their claims extinguished in turn. Id. pp. 1079–1086. Both their study and their conclusions are challenged in Warren, The Untenable Case for Repeal of Chapter 11, 102 Yale L.J. 437 (1992), and in LoPucki, Strange Visions In a Strange World, 91 Mich.L.Rev. 79 (1992).

Rasmussen, Debtor's Choice: A Menu Approach to Corporate Bankruptcy, 71 Texas L.Rev. 51 (1992), suggests a more moderate alternative to mandatory reorganization. Rasmussen would provide that corporations select in their charters from among a "menu" of different modes of bankruptcy. The menu would include, *inter alia,* chapter 11, chapter 7 liquidation, no bankruptcy (with the possibility of a contingent equity capital structure), and any bankruptcy regime designed by the firm itself.

(c) Counter–Attacks Against Absolute Priority

LoPucki and Whitford, Bargaining Over Equity's Share in the Bankruptcy Reorganization of Large Publicly Held Companies, 139 U.Pa.L.Rev. 125 (1990), use the results of an empirical study of practice under the present Bankruptcy Code to question whether resort should be made to market valuation sources in preference to a structured bargaining approach. They argue that since all valuation—market, judicial, or other—is approximate, "fairness considerations do not compel strict compliance with the absolute priority rule, particularly since, as our data shows, the extent of deviations from the absolute priority rule is modest in large cases." Id. at 189. They contextualize the "creditors' bargain," id. at 180–181:

> "Real creditors live, lend and strike their bargains in a world where they have every reason to believe that defaulting debtors will file bankruptcy petitions, and that in those bankruptcies, the absolute priority rule will not be strictly enforced. Creditors set their terms of credit, including interest rates, accordingly. * * *

> 　　　* * *

> "Even though absolute priority is the doctrinal rule outside of bankruptcy, it is not an accurate description of the actual pattern of distributions in such cases. Bargaining takes place outside

bankruptcy as well, so it is far from clear that any difference exists in the patterns of distribution produced by the bankruptcy and nonbankruptcy systems. Under both systems, absolute priority governs adjudication. Yet under both, the parties are free to, and almost invariably do, enter into settlement agreements that deviate from the absolute priority rule."

But LoPucki and Whitford do recognize that the system permits juniors to delay proceedings in order to capture nuisance value from make-weight legal positions and that reorganization plans tend to be negotiated with this power in mind. They also make an empirical assertion that chapter 11 cram downs are feasible alternatives. They therefore project that hold ups will be less and less of a problem as time passes and practitioners learn that cram downs are feasible. Id. at 186. They make a reform suggestion for dealing with the hold up problem nevertheless—a "preemptive cram down." This relies on the Code's provision in § 105(a) for court power to "issue any order * * * that is necessary or appropriate to carry out the provisions in this title." The bankruptcy judge would make a finding early in the proceeding that the equity interests would not be entitled to any property in a cram down. This frees the collective bargaining process from the threat of an equity hold up.

LoPucki and Whitford's empirical challenge to the assertions of the economic model is complemented by theoretical challenges. Carlson, Philosophy in Bankruptcy, 85 Mich.L.Rev. 1341 (1987), and Carlson, Bankruptcy Theory and the Creditors Bargain, 61 U.Cinn.L.Rev. 453 (1992), sets out an extended critique of the "creditors' bargain" conception. Professor Donald Korobkin offers a "value-based" account that provides a basis for justifying deviations from absolute priority. Korobkin, Rehabilitating Values: A Jurisprudence of Bankruptcy, 91 Colum.L.Rev. 717 (1991). This account is based on the assertion that "bankruptcy law is a response to the many aspects of financial distress—moral, political, personal, social and economic—and, in particular, to the grievances of those who are affected by financial distress." Id. at 721. Under this view, the bankruptcy system provides a process for the ongoing treatment of fundamentally incommensurate values. The bankrupt firm is not merely a pool of assets to be maximized for the creditors' account, but an "evolving and dynamic enterprise" with diverse aims. Id. at 722.

(d) Defenses of Reorganization

Both Bradley and Rosenzweig, supra, and Rasmussen, supra, assert that the bankruptcy reorganization system is inefficient. Is this assertion intuitively correct? For the view that the system's survival implies efficiency, see Easterbrook, Is Corporate Bankruptcy Efficient? 27 J.Fin.Econ. 411 (1990). For reconfirmation of the conventional wisdom that operation under judicial protection better preserves value than does a sale of assets, see LoPucki and Whitford, Corporate Governance in the Bankruptcy of Large Publicly Held Companies, 141 U.Pa. L.Rev. 669, 753–767 (1993). LoPucki and Whitford point out that preparations for an effective quick sale of a large corporation would take around a year, that substantial fees would be incurred, and that the market for assets still may be too undeveloped to produce bids that approximate the firm's going concern value. Shleifer and Vishny, Liquidation Values and Debt Capacity: A Market Equilibrium Approach, 47 J. Finance 1343 (1992), confirm this view. They suggest that most firm assets are specialized and not redeployable. The assets are illiquid in the sense that they have no reasonable use other than "the one they are destined for." The highest valuing users therefore are as likely to be in the same industry. If distress at the bankrupt firm is industry wide, there may be constraints on the purchasing capacity of other firms in the industry. Thus the sale price may not be close to the value in best use, and operation under bankruptcy protection may be the least costly strategy. See also Lang and Stulz, Contagion and Competitive Intra–Industry Effects of Bankruptcy Announcements, 32 J.Fin.Econ. 45 (1992).

(e) Valuation and Risk

The insolvency reorganization puzzle persists in part as a result of the inevitable disparity between the imputed present value of the debtor's assets and the new participations in the debtor as derived in the proceeding, and the price at which the market values these assets and participations upon their later distribution. Imputed present value is affected by the pressures of the bargaining claimants and their experts, and rises to the extent the decisionmaker responds favorably to the juniors' optimism. Market price presumably will be lower due in part to perceived uncertainties generated by the trauma of bankruptcy and in part to institutional factors. See Shleifer and Vishny, supra; LoPucki and Whitford, supra, 141 U.Pa.L.Rev. at 753–767. Whatever this disparity's cause or meaning, should it come at the expense of one set of investors—stockholders, junior creditors, or senior creditors—in preference to another? The commentators who suggest that market pricing provides a feasible basis for deriving bankruptcy valuations would impose the cost principally on the stockholders and junior creditors. The use of imputed reorganization values has historically put the cost on creditors, more heavily on juniors.

A sole lender meaningfully could consent to bear this cost either in a bond contract or later reorganization. But the consent of dispersed investor-creditors never manifests itself clearly and is not easily inferred. Do considerations of efficiency require the cost to be borne by investor-stockholders because they made a bet with limited loss potential on the residual risk interest in the firm? If so do equitable considerations come to bear to counter the balance? If the costs should be shared, what theory supports such sharing and in what proportions? Should dispersed bondholders be exposed to greater costs than is a sole lender by reason of the debtor's nuisance potential?

To the extent that those managing the debtor during reorganization have discretion to vary the risk of the business, should they favor juniors over seniors or seniors over juniors? Or is there some other standard for them to follow? Can the law constrain the managers' investment discretion as a practical matter? See LoPucki and Whitford, supra, 141 U.Pa.L.Rev. at pp. 779–796; Bienenstock, Conflicts Between Management and the Debtor in Possession's Fiduciary Duties, 61 U.Cinn.L.Rev. 543 (1992).

NOTE: EMPIRICAL STUDIES OF REORGANIZATION PROCEEDINGS

How is the 1978 Act working? Empirical studies of bankruptcy proceedings confirm that it operates substantially as planned, at least in the sense that absolute priority does not determine the results of bankruptcy distributions.

LoPucki and Whitford, report the results of a study of the forty-three largest publicly held corporations reorganized between 1979 and 1988. They find, 139 U.Pa.L.Rev. at 194–196, (a) that negotiation determines the results of most proceedings, and that cram downs and judicial adjudication of absolute priority are rare; and (b) that shareholders of insolvent corporations regularly get a share of the distribution, although the share "almost invariably" is a small one when measured as a percentage of the total distribution, rarely exceeding 10 percent. With one exception among the insolvent companies covered in the study, equity participated in the distribution only so long as the general creditors received at least 14 percent on their claims. Id. at 143.

Eberhart, Moore & Roenfeldt, Security Pricing and Deviations from the Absolute Priority Rule in Bankruptcy Proceedings, 45 J. Finance 1457 (1990), report on a similar study of 30 large bankruptcy proceedings commenced between 1979 and 1986. The study finds that the deviations from absolute priority (the amount paid to common divided by total distribution) range from zero to 35 percent, with an average of 7.57 percent. The creditors were paid less than they were owed in 24 of the 30 cases; in these "creditor deficit" distributions, the deviation from absolute priority averaged 9.87 percent. Weiss, Bankruptcy Resolution: Direct Costs and Violation of Priority of Claims, supra, reports the results of a study of 37 bankruptcy proceedings, finding that absolute priority is violated in 29 (or 78 percent) of the cases. In 3 of these cases the equity received a minimal cash settlement; in 15 the equity received 25 percent or less of the equity of the reorganized company; in 12 the equity received more than 25 percent of the new equity. Introducing a geographic distinction, Weiss finds that equity holders are treated better in the New York bankruptcy courts. See also Weiss, Bankruptcy in Corporate America: Direct Costs and Enforcement of Claims, J.Leg.Econ, July 1992, p. 79.

What normative implications arise from these findings? Does a 7 or 10 percent deviation from absolute priority amount to a problem? If so why? Because the cost of debt capital goes up to the extent that the system builds in deviations from absolute priority? Because the deviations violate the expectations of investors in debt securities? Because the returns do not justify the costs of the cumbersome system of collective bargaining? White, Measuring Deviations from Absolute Priority in Chapter 11 Bankruptcy, J.Leg.Econ., July 1992, p. 71, considers whether the data described above imply that the equity receives a comparatively small slice of the pie ("crumbs off the table") or a slice large enough to cause creditors to be less willing to lend. She concludes, id. p. 76, that the equity receive a small share of the payout even when the creditors receive little or nothing "and then receive a sharply increasing share as creditors' payoff rate rises." In cases where the creditors receive less than 90 percent of their claims, the payoff to the equity averages 10 percent of the creditors' claims, while the creditors receive an average of 42 percent of their claims. The creditors, it follows, would have averaged 24 percent more had strict priority been followed, suggesting a "substantial" deviation.

Contrast with these findings an observation made by LoPucki and Whitford. They find that the bargaining dynamic between seniors and juniors in chapter 11 does not turn on projected difficulties with valuation: "In nearly every case, the negotiators knew the company was insolvent and that equity would be entitled to nothing in an adjudication." LoPucki and Whitford, supra, 139 U.Pa.L.Rev. at 195. The key factors behind the practice of awards for equity are aggressive, effective representation for the equity, on the one hand, and the "desire to have a consensual plan," id., on the other. This is partly economic—a trade off in recognition of the juniors' ability to make trouble—and partly cultural—a product of relationships in the bankruptcy community combined with a sharing norm.

(C) REORGANIZATION UNDER THE BANKRUPTCY CODE

---

(1) Overview of the Chapter 11 Proceeding

The Debtor in Possession. Under chapter 11, the firm becomes a "debtor in possession." [m] No trustee is appointed, and the pre-bankruptcy managers remain in place. The automatic stay provided for in section 362 of the Code keeps the creditors in check. [o] The restructuring of the business is facilitated by the power to continue to perform favorable executory contracts and repudiate contracts deemed unfavor-

---

m. A debtor in possession is defined as the debtor, except when a trustee has been qualified. 11 U.S.C. § 1101(1).

o. The stay covers, *inter alia*, all actual and potential judicial or other legal proceedings against the debtor, the enforce-ment of judgments, and the creation and perfection of liens and tax proceedings, 11 U.S.C. § 362(a), but excepts criminal proceedings and actions that enforce the police or other regulatory powers. 11 U.S.C. § 362(b).

able. 11 U.S.C. § 365.[p] New financing is facilitated through the issuance of trustee certificates, which represent a senior claim against the estate. See sections 327(a) and 1107.

Thus protected and financed, management continues to operate the business. In theory, its possession of office can be terminated and a trustee appointed by the bankruptcy court upon motion by a party in interest and a finding of fraud or gross mismanagement, or a finding that the appointment otherwise is in the best interests of creditors and the estate. See 11 U.S.C. § 1104. But the presumption lies with management, and a trustee is unlikely to be appointed as a practical matter.

Management also tends to control the bankruptcy proceeding, as a result of its power to draft and propose a plan of reorganization. Under section 1121(c) of the Code, the debtor has the exclusive right to propose a plan during the first 120 days of the proceeding and any extensions the court permits. LoPucki and Whitford, supra, 139 U.Pa. L.Rev. at 128, found that such extensions are routinely granted for the duration of the proceeding.[q]

Committees and Classes. The diminution of regulatory oversight, both judicial and administrative, by the Bankruptcy Reform Act of 1978 is compensated by an enhanced governance role for creditors' committees. The Code charges the members of such committees with the protection of the interests they represent, specifying that the committee consult with the debtor's managers, investigate its finances and prospects, and participate in the formulation of the plan. 11 U.S.C. § 1103(c). Thus the Code contemplates that the proceeding's core negotiations be conducted by representatives rather than by the interest holders themselves. The Code requires the appointment of a committee of unsecured creditors by the United States Trustee promptly upon adjudication. Active monitors are sought: the Code articulates a preference for larger claimants with representative claims. 11 U.S.C. § 1102(b)(1). But, as a practical matter, this results in committees dominated by bank creditors. LoPucki and Whitford, supra, 139 U.Pa. L.Rev. at 155. Insiders are precluded from membership. Bankruptcy Rule 1007(d). Equity committees are optional. According to LoPucki and Whitford, id. at 159–160, equityholders of insolvent debtors greatly enhance their chance of recovering an award by electing a committee to represent them in the bargaining.

p. Under section 365 contracts are approved or repudiated subject to judicial scrutiny on a business judgment basis. When a contract is repudiated, the nonbreaching party can file a claim for damages in the proceeding. Contracts that may not be assumed or assigned are identified in section 365(c). These include personal services transactions that would not be assignable under contract law, loan commitments and leases already terminated.

q. The debtor that fails to meet the 120 day deadline and does not receive an extension may still file a plan, but no longer has the exclusive right to do so. Any party in interest, which includes the trustee, a creditor's committee, an equity security holders' committee, a creditor, an equity security holder, or any indenture trustee, may also file a plan.

Under chapter 11, creditors have "claims" and equityholders have "interests". The Code contemplates that claims and interests be separated into "classes" for purposes of confirmation, and that each member of a "class" be treated in the same way by the plan. 11 U.S.C. § 1123(a)(4). The Code does not, however, require that all similar claims or interests be placed in the same class. Instead, it sets out a negatively phrased rule: a claim or interest may be placed in a particular class "only if such claim or interest is substantially similar to the other claims or interests of such class". 11 U.S.C. § 1122(a). Thus, holders of debentures and trade debt claimants can be placed in different classes even though both are general creditors. It follows that a plan treating substantially similar claims in a different manner presupposes the placement of the claimants in a different class. Class formation by the intermediaries who conduct the proceeding thus becomes a stage of a wider allocational politics.

Disclosure. The plan's proponent must provide those voting with "adequate information" by means of a disclosure statement before soliciting consents. This regime of mandatory disclosure contrasts sharply with that administered by the SEC under the federal securities laws. In bankruptcy, "adequate information" is a relative proposition. It is defined as "information of a kind, and in sufficient detail, as far as is reasonably practicable in light of the nature and history of the debtor and the condition of the debtor's books and records, that would enable a hypothetical reasonable investor typical of holders of claims or interests of the relevant class to make an informed judgment about the plan." 11 U.S.C. § 1125(a)(1).[r] Compliance with the standard is a matter of bankruptcy court discretion. The system provides this flexibility with a view to the different characteristics of different proceedings—some debtors are larger and more complicated than others, some creditor groups are better informed than others, speed matters more in some proceedings, and costs vary. The capital is already sunk in any event. 5 Collier on Bankruptcy ¶ 1125.03.

The disclosure statement is exempted from registration requirements under the federal and state securities laws, although the SEC still has a privilege to be heard on the issue of whether a disclosure statement contains adequate information. 11 U.S.C. § 1125(d).[s] Sec-

---

r. The "typical" investor is defined in section 1125(a)(2) in terms of a "relationship with the debtor" and an "ability to obtain information" similar to that of other members of the class.

s. Public Service Co. v. Consolidated Utilities and Communications, 846 F.2d 803 (1st Cir.1988), confirms that section 14 of the 1934 Act does not apply to the conduct of solicitations of support for plans of reorganization. See also Century Glove, Inc. v. First American Bank, 860 F.2d 94 (3d Cir.1988).

In 1983, the SEC indicated that it would materially curtail its discretionary involvement in bankruptcy proceedings. It would no longer, on its own motion, undertake an active role in chapter 11 cases, although it would "be receptive to specific requests made by the bankruptcy judge and the U.S. trustee for advice with respect to matters within its area of special expertise, such as, for example, the adequacy of information contained in a disclosure statement." Commissioner Beavis Longstreth, The Securities and Exchange Commission's Role in Bankruptcy Reorganization Proceedings, November 21, 1983, CCH Fed.Sec. L.Rep. ¶ 83,463. Thereafter, it initiated a procedure to reevaluate its bankruptcy role. See SEC Corporate Reorganization

tion 1125(e) adds a safe harbor from the antifraud provisions of the securities laws, conditioned on a solicitation "in good faith and in compliance with the applicable provisions of this title."

Note that the "prepackaged bankruptcy" procedure, discussed supra p. 253, avoids this process.

Approval. Once the court approves the disclosure statement, the statement and proposed plan are disseminated to each class for a vote. Acceptance or rejection of a plan is assessed as to each class. For creditor acceptance, two thirds of amount and more than one half in number is required. 11 U.S.C. § 1126(c). The requirement for equity holders is two thirds in amount. 11 U.S.C. § 1126(d). The percentage requirements are calculated only as among those who actually voted.

If a plan proposes that a certain class is not entitled to any payment or compensation, the class is automatically deemed to have not accepted the plan. Contrariwise, classes "unimpaired" within the meaning of section 1124 of the Code are automatically deemed to have accepted the plan. Solicitation of their votes is not required for approval. 11 U.S.C. § 1126(f). "Unimpaired" claims or interests meet one of three definitions set out in section 1124. Either, (1) the plan "leaves unaltered the legal, equitable and contractual rights to which such claim or interest entitles the holder of such claim or interest;" (2) the plan reinstates the claim or interest by curing any default (other than a default under an ipso facto or bankruptcy clause), reinstating its maturity, and otherwise leaving unaltered the holder's rights under the claim; or (3) the plan pays cash in the allowed amount of a claim or liquidation preference of an interest.

Confirmation. The following are the principal requirements that must be met in order for a plan to be confirmed:

(1) *Good Faith.* The plan must have been proposed in good faith and not in violation of any law. 11 U.S.C. § 1129(a)(3).

(2) *Feasibility.* The court must conclude that confirmation is not likely to be followed by liquidation or further financial reorganization, "unless such liquidation or reorganization is proposed in the plan". 11 U.S.C. § 1129(a)(11).

(3) *Best Interest of Creditors.* Each holder of a claim or interest of each impaired class must have either accepted the plan, or, in the alternative, be provided with the liquidation value of his claim. 11 U.S.C. § 1129(a)(7)(A).[t] In other words, if the plan does not provide for each member of a class to receive at least what would have been obtained had the debtor been liquidated under chapter 7, a single negative vote defeats the plan. Application of this "best interest" test entails two valuations. First, the court must determine how much the dissenter is receiving under the plan. Then the court must construct a

Rel. No. 384 [1989–1990 Transfer Binder] CCH Fed.Sec.L.Rep. ¶ 84,502.

t. In the case of secured creditors who made the § 1111(b)(2) election, see infra p. 316, liquidation value is defined as "property of a value, as of the effective date of the plan, that is not less than the value of such creditor's interest in the estate's interest in the property that secures such claims."

hypothetical liquidation of the debtor, as of the effective date of the plan.

(4) *Class Vote.* Each class must have accepted the plan or be unimpaired by the plan. 11 U.S.C. § 1129(a)(8). This requirement can be avoided, and the plan "crammed down" on a dissenting class, if the plan satisfies the absolute priority rule, as laid down in section 1129(b). But even if the plan satisfies the "cram down" test in section 1129(b), at least one class must have accepted the plan, not including acceptance by any insider group. 11 U.S.C. § 1129(a)(10).

Absolute Priority Under Chapter 11.

HOUSE REPORT NO. 95–595

95th Cong., 1st Sess, 1977, pp. 408–418.

§ 1129. Confirmation of Plan

* * *

Subsection (b) permits the court to confirm a plan notwithstanding failure of compliance with paragraph (8) of subsection (a). The plan must comply with all other paragraphs of subsection (a) * * *. This subsection contains the so-called cramdown. It requires simply that the plan meet certain standards of fairness to dissenting creditors or equity security holders. The general principle of the subsection permits confirmation notwithstanding nonacceptance by an impaired class if that class and all below it in priority are treated according to the absolute priority rule. The dissenting class must be paid in full before any junior class may share under the plan. If it is paid in full, then junior classes may share. Treatment of classes of secured creditors is slightly different because they do not fall in the priority ladder, but the principle is the same.

Specifically, the court may confirm a plan over the objection of a class of secured claims if the members of that class are unimpaired or if they are to receive under the plan property of a value equal to the allowed amount of their secured claims, as determined under proposed 11 U.S.C. 506(a). The property is to be valued as of the effective date of the plan, thus recognizing the time-value of money. As used throughout this subsection, "property" includes both tangible and intangible property, such as a security of the debtor or a successor to the debtor under a reorganization plan.

The court may confirm over the dissent of a class of unsecured claims, including priority claims, only if the members of the class are unimpaired, if they will receive under the plan property of a value equal to the allowed amount of their unsecured claims, or if no class junior will share under the plan. That is, if the class is impaired, then they must be paid in full or, if paid less than in full, then no class junior may receive anything under the plan. This codifies the absolute priority rule from the dissenting class on down.

With respect to classes of equity, the court may confirm over a dissent if the members of the class are unimpaired, if they receive their liquidation preference or redemption rights, if any, or if no class junior shares under the plan. This, too, is a codification of the absolute priority rule with respect to equity. * * *

One requirement applies generally to all classes before the court may confirm under this subsection. No class may be paid more than in full.

The partial codification of the absolute priority rule here is not intended to deprive senior creditor[s] of compensation for being required to take securities in the reorganized debtor that are of an equal priority with the securities offered to a junior class. Under current law, seniors are entitled to compensation for their loss of priority, and the increased risk put upon them by being required to give up their priority will be reflected in a lower value of the securities given to them than the value of comparable securities given to juniors that have not lost a priority position.

Finally, the proponent must request use of this subsection. The court may not confirm notwithstanding nonacceptance unless the proponent requests and the court may then confirm only if subsection (b) is complied with. The court may not rewrite the plan.

A more detailed explanation follows:

* * *

The procedure followed is simple. The court examines each class of claims or interests designated under section 1123(a)(1) to see if the requirements of section 1129(b) are met. If the class is a class of secured claims, then [* * * certain] tests * * * must be complied with in order for confirmation to occur. * * * While section 1129(a) does not contemplate a valuation of the debtor's business, such a valuation will almost always be required under section 1129(b) in order to determine the value of the consideration to be distributed under the plan. Once the valuation is performed, it becomes a simple matter to impose the criterion that no claim will be paid more than in full.

* * *

* * * [W]hen an impaired class [of unsecured claims] that has not accepted the plan is to receive less than full value under the plan * * *, the plan may be confirmed * * * if the class is not unfairly discriminated against with respect to equal classes and if junior classes will receive nothing under the plan. The second criterion is the easier to understand. It is designed to prevent a senior class from giving up consideration to a junior class unless every intermediate class consents, is paid in full, or is unimpaired. This gives intermediate creditors a great deal of leverage in negotiating with senior or secured creditors who wish to have a plan that gives value to equity. One aspect of this test that is not obvious is that whether one class is senior, equal, or junior to another class is relative and not absolute. Thus from the perspective of trade creditors holding unsecured claims, claims of senior and subordinated debentures may be entitled to share on an equal basis

with the trade claims. However, from the perspective of the senior unsecured debt, the subordinated debentures are junior.

This point illustrates the lack of precision in the first criterion which demands that a class not be unfairly discriminated against with respect to equal classes. From the perspective of unsecured trade claims, there is no unfair discrimination as long as the total consideration given all other classes of equal rank does not exceed the amount that would result from an exact aliquot distribution. Thus if trade creditors, senior debt, and subordinate debt are each owed $100 and the plan proposes to pay the trade debt $15, the senior debt $30, and the junior debt $0, the plan would not unfairly discriminate against the trade debt nor would any other allocation of consideration under the plan between the senior and junior debt be unfair as to the trade debt as long as the aggregate consideration is less than $30. The senior debt could take $25 and give up $5 to the junior debt and the trade debt would have no cause to complain because as far as it is concerned the junior debt is an equal class.

However, in this latter case the senior debt would have been unfairly discriminated against because the trade debt was being unfairly over-compensated; of course the plan would also fail unless the senior debt was unimpaired, received full value, or accepted the plan, because from its perspective a junior class received property under the plan. Application of the test from the perspective of senior debt is best illustrated by the plan that proposes to pay trade debt $15, senior debt $25, and junior debt $0. Here the senior debt is being unfairly discriminated against with respect to the equal trade debt even though the trade debt receives less than the senior debt. The discrimination arises from the fact that the senior debt is entitled to the rights of the junior debt which in this example entitle the senior debt to share on a 2:1 basis with the trade debt.

Finally, it is necessary to interpret the first criterion from the perspective of subordinated debt. The junior debt is subrogated to the rights of senior debt once the senior debt is paid in full. Thus, while the plan that pays trade debt $15, senior debt $25, and junior debt $0 is not unfairly discriminatory against the junior debt, a plan that proposes to pay trade debt $55, senior debt $100, and junior debt $1 would be unfairly discriminatory. In order to avoid discriminatory treatment against the junior debt, at least $10 would have to be received by such debt under those facts.

The criterion of unfair discrimination is not derived from the fair and equitable rule or from the best interests of creditors test. Rather it preserves just treatment of a dissenting class from the class's own perspective.

* * *

EXCERPT FROM DEBATES ON BANKRUPTCY
REFORM ACT OF 1978

Cong.Rec. pp. H. 11,104–11,105 (Sept. 28, 1978).

Although many of the factors interpreting "fair and equitable" are specified in paragraph (2), others, which were explicated in the description of section 1129(b) in the House report, were omitted from the House amendment to avoid statutory complexity and because they would undoubtedly be found by a court to be fundamental to "fair and equitable" treatment of a dissenting class. For example, a dissenting class should be assured that no senior class receives more than 100 percent of the amount of its claims. While that requirement was explicitly included in the House bill, the deletion is intended to be one of style and not one of substance.

Paragraph (2) provides guidelines for a court to determine whether a plan is fair and equitable with respect to a dissenting class. It must be emphasized that the fair and equitable requirement applies only with respect to dissenting classes. Therefore, unlike the fair and equitable rule contained in chapter X and section 77 of the Bankruptcy Act under section 1129(b)(2), senior accepting classes are permitted to give up value to junior classes as long as no dissenting intervening class receives less than the amount of its claims in full. If there is no dissenting intervening class and the only dissent is from a class junior to the class to which value * * * [has] been given up, then the plan may still be fair and equitable with respect to the dissenting class, as long as no class senior to the dissenting class has received more than 100 percent of the amount of its claims.

Paragraph (2) contains three subparagraphs, each of which applies to a particular kind of class of claims or interests that is impaired and has not accepted the plan. Subparagraph (A) applies when a class of secured claims is impaired and has not accepted the plan. The provision applies whether or not section 1111(b) applies. The plan may be crammed down notwithstanding the dissent of a secured class only if the plan complies with clause (i), (ii), or (iii).

Clause (i) permits cram down if the dissenting class of secured claims will retain its lien on the property whether the property is retained by the debtor or transferred. It should be noted that the lien secures the allowed secured claim held by such holder. The meaning of "allowed secured claim" will vary depending on whether section 1111(b)(2) applies to such class.

If section 1111(b)(2) applies then the "electing" class is entitled to have the entire allowed amount of the debt related to such property secured by a lien even if the value of the collateral is less than the amount of the debt. In addition, the plan must provide for the holder to receive, on account of the allowed secured claims, payments, either present or deferred, of a principal face amount equal to the amount of the debt and of a present value equal to the value of the collateral.

For example, if a creditor loaned $15,000,000 to a debtor secured by real property worth $18,000,000 and the value of the real property had dropped to $12,000,000 by the date when the debtor commenced a proceeding under chapter 11, the plan could be confirmed notwithstanding the dissent of the creditor as long as the lien remains on the collateral to secure a $15,000,000 debt, the face amount of present or extended payments to be made to the creditor under the plan is at least $15,000,000, and the present value of the present or deferred payments is not less than $12,000,000. The House report accompanying the House bill described what is meant by "present value".

Clause (ii) is self explanatory. Clause (iii) requires the court to confirm the plan notwithstanding the dissent of the electing secured class if the plan provides for the realization by the secured class of the indubitable equivalence of the secured claims. The standard of "indubitable equivalence" is taken from In re Murel Holding Corp., 75 F.2d 941 (2d Cir.1935) (Learned Hand, Jr.).

Abandonment of the collateral to the creditor would clearly satisfy indubitable equivalence, as would a lien on similar collateral. However, present cash payments less than the secured claim would not satisfy the standard because the creditor is deprived of an opportunity to gain from a future increase in value of the collateral. Unsecured notes as to the secured claim or equity securities of the debtor would not be the indubitable equivalent. With respect to an oversecured creditor, the secured claim will never exceed the allowed claim.

* * *

Subparagraph (B) applies to a dissenting class of unsecured claims. The court must confirm the plan notwithstanding the dissent of a class of impaired unsecured claims if the plan provides for such claims to receive property with a present value equal to the allowed amount of the claims. Unsecured claims may receive any kind of "property," which is used in its broadest sense, as long as the present value of the property given to the holders of unsecured claims is equal to the allowed amount of the claims. Some kinds of property, such as securities, may require difficult valuations by the court; in such circumstances the court need only determine that there is a reasonable likelihood that the property given the dissenting class of impaired unsecured claims equals the present value of such allowed claims.

Alternatively, under clause (ii), the court must confirm the plan if the plan provides that holders of any claims or interests junior to the interests of the dissenting class of impaired unsecured claims will not receive any property under the plan on account of such junior claims or interests. As long as senior creditors have not been paid more than in full, and classes of equal claims are being treated so that the dissenting class of impaired unsecured claims is not being discriminated against unfairly, the plan may be confirmed if the impaired class of unsecured claims receives less than 100 cents on the dollar (or nothing at all) as long as no class junior to the dissenting class receives anything at all. Such an impaired dissenting class may not prevent confirmation of a plan by objection merely because a senior class has elected to give up value to a junior class that is higher in priority than the impaired dissenting class of unsecured claims as long as the above safeguards are met.

———

NOTES

1. *Cash Value.*

Does the 1978 Bankruptcy Act require the pay-out to claimants in a reorganization to be close to, if not actually in, immediate cash value? The words of sections 1124, 1129(a), and 1129(b) suggest this. But compare the reference in the debates, supra, to the "reasonable likelihood" that payoff equals present value, and the reference in the House Report, supra, to compensatory treatment.

What is the consequence of departure from cash or its equivalent as the sole mode of payment in insolvency reorganization in a case where the senior creditors insist that their claims can only be satisfied by converting the debtor's business into cash or its equivalent by selling it promptly as a going concern to a third party? The stockholders or junior creditors, will generally oppose the sale because the sale price will squeeze them out or leave them with little. They have little to lose and may gain much from delay and retention of the business. In support of their position, they can make (among others) two contentions. One is that the cash proceeds will be less than the "intrinsic" value of the enterprise—to the claimants against it or to possible other buyers. Hence the juniors will be deprived improperly of a share in "available" values if the assets are thus sold. The other is that the procedural safeguards of chapter 11, which entitle the juniors to notice and a hearing and some opportunity to vote, will in some way enhance the enterprise's value or enable the juniors to prove the first argument. But that proof is difficult to make without allowing delay which is likely to kill the quick sale, and in any event, without a valuation proceeding—the process which it is a crucial purpose of chapter 11 to avoid. Is such a sale of the going concern permissible under chapter 11, or does chapter 11 offer the junior claimants power to prevent it? If the latter, on what theory? See In re The Lionel Corp., 722 F.2d 1063 (2d Cir.1983), where the court, applying section 363(b) of the Code, ruled that a cash sale of assets out of the ordinary course of business had to be supported by a business justification other than the interests of the creditors.

2. *Liquidation Value.*

If a plan is "accepted" under § 1129(a), must the reorganization court, in determining whether a claimant has received not less than he would have received in liquidation determine that value for the enterprise in liquidation and that value for each new security offered in satisfaction of surrendered claims to see whether the latter equals not less than the claimant's share of the former? Such a valuation was required under pre-Code law, and appears also to be necessary under the Code. See 5 Collier on Bankruptcy ¶ 1129.02(7) (15th ed. 1991). But, as the New Haven Inclusion Cases, 399 U.S. 392, 435–482 (1970) and In the Matter of the Valuation Proceedings Under Sections 303(c) and 306 of the RRRA of 1973, 445 F.Supp. 994 (Special Court RRRA 1977) suggest, there is room to argue over whether liquidation value means the value (1) produced by sale of the entire enterprise as scrap (i.e., piece by piece) or (2) produced by sale of the entire enterprise as a going concern or (3) produced by a combination of sale of some divisions as going concerns and others as scrap, or by some intermediate process. And even if scrap value is the goal, the search could be for the higher of the present value of the proceeds of (1) an orderly liquidation over a number of years (which may be a constitutional requirement) or (2) an instantaneous distress sale. Moreover, any valuation process seeking a maximum liquidation value for a corporation with public investors will entail estimates of a range of expectations which is often not likely to be much narrower (see Atlas Pipeline case, p. 8, supra) than that involved in determining going concern values, since it turns on uncertainties as to the period over which sales of various properties can be effected, the prices and terms of those sales, the credit-worthiness of the buyers, the cost of maintaining some piece of the debtor's organization over the period necessary to effect the sales, and the discount rates to be applied to both estimated receipts and estimated expenses in order to produce a "present value." The cases do not suggest that such a process is any more likely to produce an accurate immediate cash value for the debtor's assets than the effort to determine going concern value in previous cases.

(2) The Treatment of Secured Creditors

SECURED CREDITORS UNDER THE BANKRUPTCY CODE
Appendix E

---

(3) The New Value Exception to the Absolute Priority Rule

Norwest Bank Worthington v. Ahlers, 485 U.S. 197 (1988), concerned the reorganization of a family farm. The farmer owed more than $1 million to a bank, secured by the farmland, equipment, crops, livestock and proceeds. The farmer's reorganization plan provided that the farmer retain the equity in the farm in exchange for a promise to contribute labor, experience, and expertise. The farmer relied on an exception to the absolute priority rule, enunciated in Case v. Los Angeles Lumber Products Co., 308 U.S. 106, 121–122 (1939), for new participations by equity holders "based on a contribution in money or money's worth, reasonably equivalent in view of all the circumstances to the participation of the stockholder." A unanimous Supreme Court found that the farmer's undertaking did not meet the requisites of the *Los Angeles Lumber* exception, 485 U.S. at 204–205:

> "Viewed from the time of approval of the plan, respondents' promise of future services is intangible, inalienable, and, in all likelihood, unenforceable. * * * Unlike 'money or money's worth,' a promise of future services cannot be exchanged in any market for something of value to the creditors *today*. In fact, no decision of this Court or any Court of Appeals, other than the decision below, has ever found a promise to contribute future labor, management, or expertise sufficient to qualify for the *Los Angeles Lumber* exception to the absolute priority rule. In short, there is no way to distinguish between the promise respondents proffer here and those of the shareholders in *Los Angeles Lumber;* neither is an adequate consideration to escape the absolute priority rule."

The "new value" exception to the absolute priority rule has come into play twice previously in these materials. First in In re Atlas Pipeline, supra p. 8, and again in Consolidated Rock v. Du Bois, supra p. 279 and the discussion that followed it at pp. 293–296. Its present status has been a heavily litigated issue ever since the *Ahlers* decision.

Should the *Ahlers* court have taken a more aggressive posture, and met the *Los Angeles Lumber* dicta with dicta of its own to the effect that the new value exception was ill-conceived and should not henceforth be held out in reorganizations? On one view, the answer to this question is no. A firm may be worth more as a going concern than in liquidation because an owner-manager of the pre-bankruptcy firm may have technical expertise, relational ties or other capital to contribute to the reorganized firm. Opening room for negotiation for the contribution of this capital makes it possible to enhance the value of the estate and thus advances the purposes of bankruptcy reorganization.

On another view, an open-ended "new value" permission could serve as a loop hole in the absolute priority scheme, making it possible for courts to evade the rule through the approval of the issue of watered securities to the old equity. How should the new value exception be framed so as to minimize this problem? Should the decision on new equity contributions be left up to the senior claimants? That is, as Judge Easterbrook suggests in the case that follows, should new value be treated as a question of creditor consent? If the creditors holding the residuary interest in the firm do *not* consent to the contribution by the equity holders, what justification is there for a judicial decree that overrides their appraisal? To the extent that such a decree is possible, the "absoluteness" of absolute priority becomes a matter of degree.

———

KHAM & NATE'S SHOES NO. 2, INC.
v. FIRST BANK OF WHITING

United States Court of Appeals, Seventh Circuit, 1990.
908 F.2d 1351.

Before WOOD, Jr., and EASTERBROOK, Circuit Judges, and ESCHBACH, Senior Circuit Judge.

EASTERBROOK, Circuit Judge.

[This is a bank creditor's appeal from an order confirming a chapter 11 reorganization plan for Kham & Nate's Shoes No. 2, Inc., the operator of four shoe stores. The bankruptcy judge had allowed Beard and Parker, the stockholders of the debtor, to retain their interests on the theory that their guarantees of new loans to be made as a part of the reorganization were "new value." For a report of another phase of the case, see infra p. 330.]

IV

* * *

Judge Coar approved a "cram-down" plan in this case. Unsecured creditors (including Bank) will not be paid in full. Bank objected to the plan, and the court overrode its objection after finding that the plan would be "fair and equitable". Yet the court did not extinguish the interests of every class junior to the unsecured creditors. Instead it allowed the stockholders to retain their interests, reasoning that by guaranteeing a $435,000 loan to be made as part of the plan, Beard and Parker contributed "new value" justifying the retention of their stock. The size of the new debt made the risk of the guarantees "substantial", the court found. The risk also exceeded the value of the retained stock, because "given the history of Debtor and the various risks associated with its business", the stock would have only "minimal" value. Beard and Parker thus would contribute more than they would receive, so the court allowed them to keep their stock.

There is something unreal about this calculation. If the stock is worth less than the guarantees, why are Beard and Parker doing it? If the value of the stock is "minimal", why does Bank object to letting Beard and Parker keep it? Is *everyone* acting inconsistently with self-interest, as the court's findings imply? And why, if the business is likely to fail, making the value of the stock "minimal", could the court confirm the plan of reorganization? Confirmation depends on a conclusion that the reorganized firm is likely to succeed, and not relapse into "liquidation, or the need for further financial reorganization". 11 U.S.C. § 1129(a)(11). If, as the bankruptcy court found, the plan complies with this requirement, then the equity interest in the firm *must* be worth something—as Beard, Parker, and Bank all appear to believe.

Stock is "property" for purposes of § 1129(b)(2)(B)(ii) even if the firm has a negative net worth, Norwest Bank Worthington v. Ahlers, 485 U.S. 197, 208, 108 S.Ct. 963, 969, 99 L.Ed.2d 169 (1988). An option to purchase stock also is "property". The bankruptcy judge gave Beard and Parker a no-cost option to buy stock, which they could exercise if they concluded that the shares were worth more than the risk created by the guarantees. Whether we characterize the stock or the option to buy it as the "property", the transaction seems to run afoul of § 1129(b)(2)(B)(ii) for it means that although a class of unsecured creditors is not paid in full, a junior class (the stockholders) keeps some "property".

Only the "new value exception" to the absolute priority rule could support this outcome. Dicta in cases predating the 1978 Code said that investors who put up new capital may retain interests equal to or lower in value than that new contribution. These interests are not so much "retained" as purchased for the new value (the "option" characterization of the transaction). Some firms depend for success on the entrepreneurial skills or special knowledge of managers who are also shareholders. If these persons' interests are wiped out, they may leave the firm and reduce its value. If they may contribute new value and retain an interest, this may tie them to the firm and so improve its prospects.

In principle, then, the exchange of stock for new value may make sense. When it does, the creditors should be willing to go along. Creditors effectively own bankrupt firms. They may find it worthwhile, as owners, to sell equity claims to the managers; they may even find it worthwhile to give the equity away in order to induce managers to stay on and work hard. Because the Code allows creditors to consent to a plan that impairs their interests, voluntary transactions of this kind are possible. Only collective action problems could frustrate beneficial arrangements. If there are many creditors, one may hold out, seeking to engross a greater share of the gains. But the Code deals with holdups by allowing half of a class by number (two-thirds by value) to consent to a lower class's retention of an interest. 11 U.S.C. § 1126(c). Creditors not acting in good faith do not count toward the one-third required to block approval, § 1126(e). When there is value to be gained by allowing a lower class to kick in new value and keep its interest, the creditors should be willing to go along. *Ahlers*, 485 U.S. at 207, 108 S.Ct. at 968. A "new value exception" means a power in the *judge* to "sell" stock to the managers even when the creditors believe that this transaction will *not* augment the value of the firm. To understand whether the Code gives the judge this power (and, if it does, the limits of the power), it is necessary to examine the genesis of the doctrine.

The Bankruptcy Act of 1898 required plans of reorganization to be "fair and equitable" but did not define that phrase. It also allowed creditors to consent to plans that impaired their interests, but the consent had to be unanimous. The absolute priority rule came into being as a cross between the interpretation of "fair and equitable" and a rule of contract law. Northern Pacific Ry. v. Boyd, 228 U.S. 482, 33 S.Ct. 554, 57 L.Ed. 931 (1913). Because contracts give creditors priority over shareholders, a plan of reorganization had to do the same. But under the 1898 Act bankruptcy also was a branch of equity, so it is not surprising that equitable modifications of the doctrine developed. One of these was the "new value exception" to the absolute priority doctrine. So far as the Supreme Court is concerned, however, the development has been 100% dicta.

Kansas City Terminal Ry. v. Central Union Trust Co., 271 U.S. 445, 46 S.Ct. 549, 70 L.Ed. 1028 (1926), is the genesis of the exception. The Court conceived the absolute priority rule as barring any retention of interest by a shareholder if any layer of creditors is excluded. It used this rule to veto a decision by the secured creditor to allow the shareholder a stake when junior creditors were cut out and objected. Yet the senior creditor, which as a practical matter owned 100% of the firm, must have had a reason to suffer the continued existence of the shareholder. The plan in *Kansas City Ry.* was identical in principle to selling the firm to the secured creditor at auction, and the secured creditor giving some stock to the manager and former shareholder. Only the fact that both steps were rolled into one plan of reorganization gave the junior creditor an opportunity to say no (as a practical matter to hold out for some portion of the gains). The Court said in dicta that this right to object did not give the junior creditor as potent a power as it might, because the judge could modify the strict priority equitably if the shareholder agreed to contribute new value.

Case v. Los Angeles Lumber Products Co., 308 U.S. 106, 60 S.Ct. 1, 84 L.Ed. 110 (1939), came next. The bankruptcy judge took the hint in *Kansas City Ry.* and allowed shareholders to retain an interest in exchange for their promise to contribute value in the form of continuity of management, plus financial standing and influence in the community that would enable the debtor to raise new money. It allowed the shareholders to retain their interests even though the class of senior creditors objected (because unanimity could not be achieved)—a dramatic step from the suggestion in *Kansas City Ry.* that new value plus the *consent* of the creditor whose claim exceeded the value of the firm would suffice. The Supreme Court reversed, holding that new value must mean "money or money's worth", 308 U.S. at 121–22, 60 S.Ct. at 10–11. It did not remark on the difference between consent and objection from the creditors, and it did not really need to given its conclusion that non-monetary value is insufficient.

Cases in the lower courts proceeded to apply the dicta in *Case* and *Kansas City Ry.* without noticing the difference between consent and objection by the creditors. But see SEC v. Canandaigua Enterprises Corp., 339 F.2d 14, 21 (2d Cir.1964) (Friendly, J.), questioning the doctrine on this basis; Henry J. Friendly, Some Comments on the Corporate Reorganization Act, 48 Harv.L.Rev. 39, 77–78 (1934). Perhaps this distinction was not an essential one in the administration of a common law doctrine, especially not when (a) the unanimity rule made the lack of consent the norm, and (b) bankruptcy was a branch of equity.

Everything changed with the adoption of the Code in 1978. The definition of "fair and equitable" is no longer a matter of common law;

§ 1129(b)(2) defines it expressly. Holdouts that spoiled reorganizations and created much of the motive for having judges "sell" stock to the manager-shareholders no longer are of much concern, now that § 1126(c) allows the majority of each class (two-thirds by value) to give consent. And bankruptcy judges no longer have equitable powers to modify contracts to achieve "fair" distributions. Bankruptcy judges enforce entitlements created under state law. Butner v. United States, 440 U.S. 48 (1979); Levit v. Ingersoll Rand Financial Corp., 874 F.2d 1186, 1197–98 (7th Cir.1989); In re Iowa R.R., 840 F.2d 535 (7th Cir.1988). "[W]hatever equitable powers remain in the bankruptcy courts must and can only be exercised within the confines of the Bankruptcy Code." *Ahlers,* 485 U.S. at 206.

Whether the "new value exception" to the absolute priority rule survived the codification of that rule in 1978 is a question open in this circuit. In re Stegall, 865 F.2d 140, 142 (7th Cir.1989). The language of the Code strongly suggests that it did not, and we are to take this language seriously even when it alters pre-Code practices. Pennsylvania Department of Welfare v. Davenport, ___ U.S. ___, 110 S.Ct. 2126, 2130–31 (1990); United States v. Ron Pair Enterprises, Inc., 489 U.S. 235 (1989); Levit, 874 F.2d at 1196–97. See also Douglas G. Baird & Thomas H. Jackson, Bargaining After the Fall and the Contours of the Absolute Priority Rule, 55 U.Chi.L.Rev. 738, 746–47 & n. 23, 756–60 (1988). The legislative history reinforces the implication of the text. The Bankruptcy Commission proposed a modification of the absolute priority rule, and its proposal was not warmly received. See, e.g., Victor Brudney, Bankruptcy Commission's Proposed "Modifications" of the Absolute Priority Rule, 48 Am.Bankr.L.J. 305 (1974). Congress moved in the other direction, enacting the rule in an uncompromising form: "The general principle of the subsection permits confirmation notwithstanding non-acceptance by an impaired class if that class and all below it in priority are treated according to the absolute priority rule. The dissenting class must be paid in full before any junior class may share under the plan." H.R.Rep. No. 95–595, 95th Cong., 1st Sess. 413 (1977), U.S.Code Cong. & Admin.News 1978, pp. 5787, 6369. Neither the report nor any part of the text of the Code suggests a single exception to this blanket rule.

Bank asks us to hold that the new value exception vanished in 1978. We stop short of the precipice, as the Supreme Court did in *Ahlers,* 485 U.S. at 203–04 n. 3, for two reasons: first, the consideration for the shares is insufficient even if the new value exception retains vitality; second, although Bank vigorously argues the merits of the new value exception in this court, it did not make this argument in the bankruptcy court. Despite Bank's failure to preserve its argument, the history and limits of the rule before 1978 are pertinent to our analysis because, as the Court held in *Ahlers,* 485 U.S. at 205–06, at a minimum the Code forbids any expansion of the exception beyond the limits recognized in *Case.*

Case rejected the argument that continuity of management plus financial standing that would attract new investment is "new value".

According to the Court, only an infusion of capital in "money or money's worth" suffices. *Ahlers* reinforces the message, holding that a promise of future labor, coupled with the managers' experience and expertise, also is not new value. It remarked that the promises of the managers in *Case* "[n]o doubt * * * had 'value' and would have been of some benefit to any reorganized enterprise. But ultimately, as the Court said * * *, '[t]hey reflect merely vague hopes or possibilities.' The same is true of respondents' pledge of future labor and management skills." 485 U.S. at 204, (citations omitted). The Court observed, ibid., again quoting from *Case,* that the promise was "intangible, inalienable, and, in all likelihood, unenforceable. It 'has no place in the asset column of the balance sheet of the new [entity].' "

Guarantees are no different. They are intangible, inalienable, and unenforceable by the firm. Beard and Parker may revoke their guarantees or render them valueless by disposing of their assets; although a lender may be able to protest the revocation, the debtor cannot compel the guarantor to maintain the pledge in force. Guarantees have "no place in the asset column" of a balance sheet. We do not know whether these guarantees have the slightest value, for the record does not reveal whether Parker and Beard have substantial unencumbered assets that the guarantees would put at risk. If Beard and Parker were organizing a new firm in Illinois, they could not issue stock to themselves in exchange for guarantees of loans. Illinois requires the consideration for shares to be money or other property, or "labor or services actually performed for the corporation", Ill.Rev.Stat. ch. 32 ¶ 6.30. So Beard and Parker could subscribe for shares against a promise of labor, but the firm could not issue the shares until the labor had been performed. A guarantee does not fit into any of the statutory categories, and there is no reason why it should. One who pays out on a guarantee becomes the firm's creditor, a priority higher than that of stockholder. A guarantor who has *not* paid has no claim against the firm. Promises inadequate to support the issuance of shares under state law are also inadequate to support the issuance of shares by a bankruptcy judge over the protest of the creditors, the real owners of the firm.

Debtor relies on In re Potter Material Service, Inc., 781 F.2d 99 (7th Cir.1986), but it does not support the bankruptcy judge's decision. The new value in *Potter* was a combination of $34,800 cash plus a guarantee of a $600,000 loan. If Beard and Parker had contributed substantial cash, we would have a case like *Potter.* They didn't, and we don't. To the extent *Potter* implies that a guarantee alone is "new value", it did not survive *Ahlers. Potter* observed that the guarantor took an economic risk, 781 F.2d at 103. *Ahlers* holds that *detriment* to the shareholder does not amount to "value" to the firm; there must be an infusion of new capital. See John D. Ayer, Rethinking Absolute Priority after Ahlers, 87 Mich.L.Rev. 963 (1989). A guarantee may be costly to the guarantor, but it is not a balance-sheet asset, and it therefore may not be treated as new value. The plan of reorganization should not have been confirmed over Bank's objection.

NOTE: THE NEW VALUE EXCEPTION

1. *Caselaw.*

Some courts, more receptive to new value contributions than that in *Kham & Nate's,* treat proposals for cash contributions by equity holders with a two part test. The new capital must (1) represent a substantial contribution, and (2) equal or exceed the value of the new interest in the corporation. The first leg of the test, "substantiality," involves the comparison of the contribution with the amount of pre-petition claims and the amount of debt discharged under the plan. In In re Pullman Construction Industries, 107 B.R. 909, 936–937, 948–950 (Bkrtcy.N.D.Ill.1989), a $450,000 contribution that amounted to less than 2 percent of pre-petition claims and less than 4 percent of debt discharged failed the test. See also Matter of Snyder, 967 F.2d 1126 (7th Cir.1992). How, if at all, does the two part test solve the analytical problems presented by the new value exception? Is a "substantial" contribution required as a means to the end of increasing the equity capitalization of the reorganized firm? Does the requirement follow from a mistrust of the value of the equity's contribution of human capital? Or does the "substantial" contribution represent a payment for a purchase of control?

Other courts have read *Ahlers* more narrowly than did Judge Easterbrook in *Kham & Nate's.* Under this view, the Bankruptcy Act of 1978 effected the elimination of the exception. See In re Bryson Properties XVIII, 961 F.2d 496, 503–505 (4th Cir.1992); In re Outlook/Century, Ltd., 127 B.R. 650 (Bkrtcy.N.D.Cal.1991); In re Lumber Exchange Ltd. Partnership, 125 B.R. 1000 (Bkrtcy.D.Minn.1991). The issue was finessed in In re Greystone III Joint Venture, 948 F.2d 134 (5th Cir.1991). There the court found room for a new value exception in neither "the Code's language, nor in the context of a previous, different reorganization law, nor in legislative history, nor in policy." But, later, on petition for rehearing en banc, the Fifth Circuit withdrew the panel's opinion on the new value exception and limited its decision to a narrower ground. 948 F.2d 142.

Does the 1978 Act's narrowing of the absolute priority rule from (a) a rule that assists dissenting *individual* creditors in challenging plans to which the *requisite majorities of creditors consent,* to (b) a rule that protects dissenting majorities of *classes* of creditors against the cramdown of plans to which *such majorities did not consent,* suggest a structural reason for reading section 1129(b) to preclude any dilution of the absolute priority rule through the new value exception? Is it relevant that the Supreme Court cases under chapter X of the 1938 Act had been eroding the import of the new value exception?

2. *New Value, Close Corporations, and Public Corporations.*

These problems with "new value" contributions follow from chapter 11's awkward amalgamation of old chapters X and XI and their respective absolute priority and best interest of creditors standards. Chapter 11 narrowed the applicability of the absolute priority rule and substituted the composition principle in most reorganizations of public corporations. If two-thirds in amount and a majority in number of a class of bondholders consented to take less than their due, their bargain was not to be subject to review for fairness. Consent by such a number was sufficient to force the other members to give up to juniors distributable values available in the enterprise's assets, presumably on the theory that such consent was sufficiently informed and volitional that those giving it did not need the protection of the absolute priority rule. Only if less than two-thirds consented and a plan was crammed down upon the non-consenting class was the rule's protection to continue. The 1978 Act not only thus limited the applicability of the absolute priority principle to the cram down context, but extended it to the reorganization of close corporations. This extension of absolute priority protection to the creditors of close corporations—formerly deemed able to protect themselves—has given rise to the bulk of the "new value" litigation under the 1978 Act.[u] If, on these fact patterns, we can assume parties who are equipped to bargain with one another and give informed collective consent to participation by equity owners who contribute their personal ability and energy, what need is there for an absolute priority doctrine at all, much less a new value exception to it? One might, accordingly, recommend the development of a new and very loose concept of "new value" that dilutes the pre–1978 doctrine but fits the specific circumstances of the close corporation reorganizing under section 1129(b). The problem with such a rule would lie in its threat further to dilute the rigor of the pre–1978 doctrine in reorganizations of public corporations,[v] or to enable such reorganizations to become management buyouts at the expense of junior creditors and stockholders.

---

u. For a model of the dynamics of bargaining in reorganizations where the debtor has human capital to contribute, see Baird and Picker, A Simple Noncooperative Bargaining Model of Corporate Reorganizations, 20 J. Legal Studies 311 (1991).

v. For an approach to the new value question grounded in the creditor consent norm advanced by Judge Easterbrook in *Kham & Nate's,* see Baird and Jackson, Bargaining After the Fall and the Contours of the Absolute Priority Rule, 55 U.Chi.L.Rev. 738, 760 (1988). This concludes that, given a single class of unsatisfied claimants, they should be given discretion to bargain with an old owner-manager group over the terms of latter's continued participation: "there is little reason to provide an override that will permit old owner-managers to keep a portion of the interest * * * without the consent of the senior class." But they enter a caveat in respect of problems that arise in tripartite situations where a class of senior creditors wishes to combine with an owner-manager

so as to freeze out an intermediate class of creditors. Id. pp. 760–781. For defenses of the new value exception, see Warren, A Theory of Absolute Priority, 1991 Ann. Surv.Amer.L. 9, 33, 45 (creditors get opportunity to present valuation evidence; consent rule creates creditor holdout possibilities); Markell, Owners, Auctions, and Absolute Priority in Bankruptcy Reorganizations, 44 Stan.L.Rev. 69, 112–123 (1991) (supports new value transactions, but only with accompanying changes in the Bankruptcy Code to facilitate an effective auction of the equity in the reorganized firm). Those inclined to argue for judicial sanction of new value transactions over the objection of creditors should refer to Korobkin, Rehabilitating Values: A Jurisprudence of Bankruptcy, 91 Colum.L.Rev. 717 (1991), for assistance in constructing a justification. Korobkin's "value based" account of bankruptcy, see supra p. 306, holds open a door to a revised concept of absolute priority.

5. LENDER LIABILITY

We have seen that borrowers have opportunities to take actions that reduce the value of their lenders' claims. Sometimes, as in *RJR Nabisco,* supra, this opportunism stems from equityholders' attempts to maximize their returns during prosperous times. At other times, as in *Katz v. Oak Industries,* supra, this behavior stems from the maximizing equityholders' response to a distress situation. We also have seen that lenders' defense against such conduct is preeminently a matter for the drafter of the bond contract. In theory, an overlay of fairness concepts supplements the contract, inviting courts to intervene and protect long term lenders who stumble into positions of exposure. In practice, the courts tend to decline this invitation. Aside from cases of misrepresentation or material nondisclosure (and, as discussed in the next section, cases where the opportunistic debtor is in such extreme distress as to cause its conduct to fall within the parameters of fraudulent conveyance doctrine), the law displays no affirmative commitment to affirmative lender protection. It instead opens a field for lender self-protection through contract.

If symmetry in the structure of the law were the paramount consideration in this area, one would expect that the self-protected lender would be free to exercise its contract rights without fear of judicial intervention on good faith or other fairness grounds on behalf of the borrower thereby disadvantaged. But symmetry is not the paramount consideration here. "Lender liability" has been a recent growth area—a financial topic brushed with multimillion dollar judgments and the other trappings of the "litigation explosion." Fischel, The Economics of Lender Liability, 99 Yale L.J. 131, 132 n. 6 (1989), catalogs "major awards" against banks of up to $105 million.

Fischel, supra at 138–139, notes that in most situations, lenders are unlikely to attempt to extract concessions from borrowers after the execution and delivery of the debt contract. Lenders have reputations to worry about, and able borrowers can find substitute loans elsewhere. But Fischel goes on to identify two situations in which these circumstantial guarantees of cooperation fail and lenders may be induced to dishonor a commitment to lend, or, where the loan already has closed, call a technical default. First, external events can alter the economics of the relationship after the time the commitment or loan is made, as where interest rates rise sharply. Second, where the borrower and the lender have a particularly close relationship—as where the lender invests in specialized information about the borrower and time constraints make it difficult for the borrower to find a substitute—the lender may extract concessions by threatening to withhold advances.

So, although the lender's failure to self-protect through contract gives the borrower the opportunity to transfer wealth from the lender for its own account, successful contractual self-protection by the lender turns the tables and gives it the opportunity to extract uncontemplated benefits from the borrower. Should the law deal with this phenomenon by following the pattern of cases of borrower opportunism, and put the burden of self protection on the victim? Or, should good faith constraints be imposed on the lender? If the borrower is to be protected by a good faith constraint, does a consistency problem arise? If so, does bondholder protection in cases of borrower opportunism follow from the legitimate imposition of lender liability? Or, can some material distinction be articulated between the unprotected borrower and the unprotected bondholder or other lender, so as to justify differential treatment? Or should the inconsistency be taken as a signal that lender liability should be rolled back forthwith?

One leading lender liability case, **K.M.C. Co. v. Irving Trust Co.,** 757 F.2d 752 (6th Cir.1985), centered on the refusal of a bank, without any notice, to advance the last $800,000 on a line of credit of $3.5 million to a debtor that was in shaky condition. Whether the debtor was so shaky as to be at the point of collapse was a disputed point. The bank had discretion to refuse the advance, but the loan agreement was silent on whether, and how much advance notice was required before it exercised such discretion. A jury decided that the failure to give notice (and thus give the debtor an opportunity to obtain other financing) by a lender which was fully secured, violated the lender's obligation of good faith, and rendered the lender liable for the debtor's subsequent collapse. The Court of Appeals upheld the jury verdict, reasoning that (1) the implied notice requirement was necessary to give the borrower time to obtain alternate financing, for without it the borrower's continued existence would be entirely at the whim or mercy of the lender, (2) the lender needed a valid business reason to avoid the notice requirement, (3) the good faith constraint also covered the loan's demand provision, and (4) the fact that the lender was fully secured weighed heavily in the good faith determination.ʷ

Another leading lender liability case is **State National Bank of El Paso v. Farah Manufacturing Co.,** 678 S.W.2d 661 (Tex.Ct.App.1984), in which a group of banks invoked a contract provision to block the return of an ousted chief executive officer. One year later the officer returned and restored the borrower to a prosperity that contrasted with its losses under the management of the bank approved c.e.o. The borrower recovered $19 million from the banks on the claim, *inter alia,* that they fraudulently imposed the provision, having never intended to

---

w. Fischel, The Economics of Lender Liability, supra, at 140–143, takes issue with the result in *K.M.C. v. Irving Trust.* He makes three assertions. First, no actionable opportunism occurred, since K.M.C.'s ability to meet its obligations was far from clear. Second, the lender's action was consistent with the debt contract. The provision giving the lender sole discretion respecting continued funding embodied a considered risk allocation; in exchange for conceding the discretion the borrower paid a lower interest rate. Third, the case's notice requirement opens the door to borrower opportunism: between the receipt of notice and the cut off date the borrower can draw down the full line of credit and employ the funds in derogation of the lender's interests.

call a default in the first place. See also United California Bank v.
Prudential Insurance Co., 140 Ariz. 238, 681 P.2d 390 (Ct.App.1983)
(liability for failure to close real estate takeout financing).

Kham & Nate's Shoes No. 2, Inc. v. First Bank of Whiting, 908
F.2d 1351 (7th Cir.1990) (Easterbrook, J.), invites comparison with
K.M.C. v. Irving Trust. In *Kham & Nate's,* a debtor with unsecured
loans outstanding to a bank needed more credit but could not provide
adequate security. The bank agreed to open a $300,000 line of credit if
the debtor filed a petition under chapter 11 and the court approved an
order under section 364(c)(1) of the Bankruptcy Code giving post petition borrowings under the line a super priority. The order was given,
the line of credit was opened, and the debtor drew down about $75,000.
The credit agreement provided that the bank could terminate financing
on five days notice. After a month the bank terminated the line of
credit. Three years later, in connection with the submission of its
fourth plan of reorganization, the debtor requested that the bankruptcy
court treat the $65,000 still owing to the bank as unsecured indebted-
ness. The bankruptcy court ruled that the bank had behaved inequitably in terminating the line of credit and subordinated its claim under
section 510(c) of the Bankruptcy Code. The Seventh Circuit disagreed.
Said Judge Easterbrook, 908 F.2d at 1356–1359:

"Cases subordinating the claims of creditors that dealt at arm's
length with the debtor are few and far between. Benjamin v. Diamond,
563 F.2d 692 (5th Cir.1977) (*Mobile Steel Co.*), suggests that subordination depends on a combination of inequitable conduct, unfair advantage
to the creditor, and injury to other creditors. Debtor submits that
conduct may be 'unfair' and 'inequitable' for this purpose even though
the creditor complies with all contractual requirements, but we are not
willing to embrace a rule that requires participants in commercial
transactions not only to keep their contracts but also do 'more'—just
how much more resting in the discretion of a bankruptcy judge assessing the situation years later. Contracts specify the duties of the parties
to each other, and each may exercise the privileges it obtained. Banks
sometimes bind themselves to make loans (commitment letters and
letters of credit have this effect) and sometimes reserve the right to
terminate further advances. Courts may not convert one form of
contract into the other after the fact, without raising the cost of credit
or jeopardizing its availability. Unless pacts are enforced according to
their terms, the institution of contract, with all the advantages private
negotiation and agreement brings, is jeopardized. * * *

"* * * 'Good faith' is a compact reference to an implied undertaking not to take opportunistic advantage in a way that could not have
been contemplated at the time of drafting, and which therefore was not
resolved explicitly by the parties. * * *

"We do not doubt the force of the proverb that the letter killeth,
while the spirit giveth life. Literal implementation of unadorned

language may destroy the essence of the venture. Few people pass out of childhood without learning fables about genies, whose wickedly literal interpretation of their 'masters' wishes always leads to calamity. Yet knowledge that literal enforcement means some mismatch between the parties' expectation and the outcome does not imply a general duty of 'kindness' in performance, or of judicial oversight into whether a party had 'good cause' to act as it did. * * *

"Bank did not break a promise at a time Debtor was especially vulnerable, then use the costs and delay of obtaining legal enforcement of the contract as levers to a better deal. Debtor and Bank signed a contract expressly allowing the Bank to cease making further advances. The $300,000 was the maximum loan, not a guarantee. The Bank exercised its contractual privilege after loaning Debtor $75,000; it made a clean break and did not demand improved terms. It had the right to do this for any reason satisfactory to itself. * * *

"Although Bank's decision left Debtor scratching for other sources of credit, Bank did not create Debtor's need for funds, and it was not contractually obliged to satisfy its customer's desires. The Bank was entitled to advance its own interests, and it did not need to put the interests of Debtor and Debtor's other creditors first. To the extent K.M.C., Inc. v. Irving Trust Co., 757 F.2d 752, 759–63 (6th Cir.1986), holds that a bank must loan more money or give more advance notice of termination than its contract requires, we respectfully disagree. First Bank of Whiting is not an eleemosynary institution. It need not throw good money after bad, even if other persons would catch the lucre. See Secon Service System, Inc. v. St. Joseph Bank & Trust Co., 855 F.2d 406, 419 (7th Cir.1988); Mid–State Fertilizer Co. v. Exchange National Bank, 877 F.2d 1333 (7th Cir.1989). See also Comment, What's So Good About Good Faith? The Good Faith Performance Obligation in Commercial Lending, 55 U.Chi.L.Rev. 1335 (1988).

"Debtor stresses, and the bankruptcy judge found, that Bank would have been secure in making additional advances. Perhaps so, but the contract did not oblige Bank to make all advances for which it could be assured of payment. *Ex post* assessments of a lender's security are no basis on which to deny it the negotiated place in the queue. Risk must be assessed *ex ante* by lenders, rather than *ex post* by judges. If a loan seems secure at the time, lenders will put up the money; their own interests are served by making loans bound to be repaid. What is more, the bankruptcy judge's finding that Bank would have been secure in making additional advances is highly questionable. The judgment of the market vindicates Bank. If more credit would have enabled Debtor to flourish, then other lenders should have been willing to supply it. Yet no one else, not even the SBA, would advance additional money to Debtor.

* * *

"Although Debtor contends, and the bankruptcy judge found, that Bank's termination of advances frustrated Debtor's efforts to secure credit from other sources, and so propelled it down hill, this is legally irrelevant so long as Bank kept its promises. It is factually questionable too. Why would Bank shoot itself in the foot—spurning what the bankruptcy judge thought to be sure repayment while leaving an outstanding balance of $164,000 that it could not expect to collect if Debtor collapsed? At all events, Debtor could have asked for further orders under § 364 making potential lenders secure and ensuring a flow of credit; it did not. It could have asked Judge Toles to clarify his financing order, so that other creditors would know that Bank's priority was limited to $75,000; it did not. A straightforward inference is that even high priority would not have induced other institutions to put up money—just as high priority did not make Bank feel sufficiently secure."

Professor Dennis Patterson takes issue with Judge Easterbrook's statements of the facts of *Kham & Nate's* and of the applicable law. See Patterson, A Fable from the Seventh Circuit: Frank Easterbrook on Good Faith, 76 Iowa L.Rev. 503 (1991). See also D. Patterson, Good Faith and Lender Liability: Toward A Unified Theory (1990).

PROBLEM

Given *K.M.C. v. Irving Trust*, what result in the following case? Insurance Company buys $30,000,000, fifteen year private placement notes from Manufacturer during a time of low interest rates, pursuant to a note agreement containing a full and tight set of business covenants and financial maintenance tests. The issue constitutes approximately 25 per cent of the capitalization of Manufacturer. A further 25 per cent is provided pursuant to a revolving credit agreement with a group of banks. Three years into the life of the loan, the economy goes into stagflation: interest rates rise sharply while the economy stays flat. Manufacturer had expected further economic expansion and had invested in additional output. The economy upsets Manufacturer's plans. A cash crunch results from a combination of excess inventory and lower than expected sales. Manufacturer fails to meet a ratio test by a small margin as a result. Insurance Company takes the opportunity to declare an event of default, upon due notice. Manufacturer, which cannot cure the default, requests a waiver in exchange for an additional prepayment or a slightly higher rate of interest. Insurance Company, which has been taken over by an entrepreneur and is reducing its participation in the private placement market, refuses and accelerates the loan. Is Insurance Company liable if,

(a) Manufacturer is forced to refinance with a floating rate loan from a factor that is 5 to 7 per cent higher than the rate on the private placement?

(b) The acceleration causes the banks to demand payment on the revolving credit agreement, forcing Manufacturer in chapter 11. It emerges two years later with a more expensive capital structure after incurring substantial costs.

Would it make a difference if, when negotiating the covenants, the Insurance Company had assured Manufacturer that "It required these protections to protect its policyholders but made it a practice to be reasonable when its borrowers encountered ordinary cyclical difficulties?" What provision of the loan agreement would come to bear in respect of this representation?

———

NOTE: LENDER LIABILITY AS A CONTROLLING PARTY

Lenders can be held for losses sustained or liabilities incurred by borrowers if the lender is deemed to be in "control" of the borrower. Unlike stockholders in control, lenders in control do not have limited liability. See Douglas–Hamilton, Creditor Liabilities Resulting from Improper Interference with the Management of a Financially Troubled Debtor, 31 Bus.Law. 343 (1975). Conventional business covenants and other negative regulations of borrower conduct are not deemed to be "control" for this purpose. See Lloyd, Financial Covenants in Commercial Loan Documentation: Uses and Limitations, 58 Tenn.L.Rev. 335, 352–353 (1991).

In recent years, issues have arisen respecting the control concept shaping lender liability for toxic waste cleanup expenses under the Comprehensive Environmental Response Compensation and Liability Act ("CERCLA"), 41 U.S.C. §§ 9601–9657.

CERCLA imposes liability on "any person who at the time of disposal of any hazardous substance owned or operated any * * * facility at which such hazardous substances were disposed of," 42 U.S.C. § 9607(a)(2), but excludes from the definition of "owner or operator" any "person, who, without participating in the management of a * * * facility, holds indicia of ownership primarily to protect his security interest in the * * * facility."

United States v. Fleet Factors Corp., 901 F.2d 1550 (11th Cir. 1990), was the first Court of Appeals opinion to interpret this language. The case concerned the conduct of a lender, Fleet Factors, in the course of the chapter 7 liquidation of its borrower, Swainsboro Print Works ("SPW"). Fleet had a security interest in SPW's facility and equipment—a site that later required a $400,000 EPA cleanup. Fleet took an active role in business decisions during the course of the liquidation. It also foreclosed on its security interests, contracted with a liquidator to conduct an auction of the property, and later hired a second firm to cart off all the unsold equipment. Years later, the government included Fleet among the defendants in its CERCLA action to recover the cleanup costs.

The Court ruled against Fleet's summary judgment motion. Ambiguous statutory terms, it said, should be construed in favor of liability to advance the remedial goal of the statute. Said the court, 901 F.2d at 1557–1559:

"* * * Under the standard we adopt today, a secured creditor may incur section 9607(a)(2) liability, without being an operator, by participating in the financial management of a facility to a degree indicating a capacity to influence the corporation's treatment of hazardous wastes. It is not necessary for the secured creditor actually to involve itself in the day-to-day operations of the facility in order to be liable—although such conduct will certainly lead to the loss of the protection of the statutory exemption. Nor is it necessary for the secured creditor to participate in management decisions relating to hazardous waste. Rather, a secured creditor will be liable if its involvement with the management of the facility is sufficiently broad to support the inference that it could affect hazardous waste disposal decisions if it so chose. * * *

"* * * Nothing in our discussion should preclude a secured creditor from monitoring any aspect of a debtor's business. Likewise, a secured creditor can become involved in occasional and discrete financial decisions relating to the protection of its security interest without incurring liability.

* * *

"Our ruling today should encourage potential creditors to investigate thoroughly the waste treatment systems and policies of potential debtors. If the treatment systems seem inadequate, the risk of CERCLA liability will be weighed into the terms of the loan agreement. Creditors, therefore, will incur no greater risk than they bargained for and debtors, aware that inadequate hazardous waste treatment will have a significant adverse impact on their loan terms, will have powerful incentives to improve their handling of hazardous wastes.

"Similarly, creditors' awareness that they are potentially liable under CERCLA will encourage them to monitor the hazardous waste treatment systems and policies of their debtors and insist upon compliance with acceptable treatment standards as a prerequisite to continued and future financial support. * * * Once a secured creditor's involvement with a facility becomes sufficiently broad that it can anticipate losing its exemption from CERCLA liability, it will have a strong incentive to address hazardous waste problems at the facility rather than studiously avoiding the investigation and amelioration of the hazard."

A panel of the Ninth Circuit added some limiting language to the *Fleet Factors* reading of "participation in management" in **In re Bergsoe Metal Corp.,** 910 F.2d 668, 672–673 (9th Cir.1990):

"* * * It is clear from the statute that whatever the precise parameters of "participation," there must be *some* actual management of the facility before a secured creditor will fall outside the exception. Here there was none, and we therefore need not engage in line drawing.

"* * * Lenders normally extend credit only after gathering a great deal of information about the proposed project, and only when they have some degree of confidence that the project will be successful. A secured creditor will always have some input at the planning stages of any large-scale project and, by the extension of financing, will perforce encourage those projects it feels will be successful. If this were 'management,' no secured creditor would ever be protected.

" * * * That a secured creditor reserves certain rights to protect its investment does not put it in a position of management. What is critical is not what rights the [lender] had, but what it did. The CERCLA security interest exception uses the active 'participating in management.' Regardless of what rights the [lender] may have had, it cannot have participated in management if it never exercised them."

Based on these opinions, what advice would you give a client engaged in lending to industrial corporations on a secured basis? Should the *Fleet Factors* liability standard be extended, as a common law proposition, to cover all cases of tort liability?

SECTION B. PREFERRED STOCKHOLDERS' RIGHTS

1. PREFERRED STOCK FINANCING

(A) INTRODUCTION
HUNT, WILLIAMS AND DONALDSON, BASIC BUSINESS FINANCE

358–61 (5th Ed.1974).

The preferred stock represents a type of corporate financing which is somewhat paradoxical as between its nominal characteristics and its practical application. On the surface, it appears to provide the corporation with a security coupling the limited obligation of the bond with the flexibility of the common stock—a combination that would be unusually attractive to the issuer. Unfortunately, general experience does not bear out such expectations.

From the purely legal point of view the preferred stock is a type of ownership and thus takes a classification similar to that of the common stock. Accounting practice recognizes this by placing preferred stock along with common stock in the net worth section of the balance sheet, and tax laws interpret preferred dividends as a distribution of net profits to the owners rather than a cost of the business, as in the case of bond interest. * * * Unlike the bond, the preferred stock does not contain any promise of repayment of the original investment; and as far as the shareholders are concerned, this must be considered as a permanent investment for the life of the company. Further, there is no legal obligation to pay a fixed rate of return on the investment.

The special character of the preferred stock lies in its relationship to the common stock. When a preferred stock is used as a part of the corporate capital structure, the rights and responsibilities of the owners as the residual claimants to the asset values and earning power of the business no longer apply equally to all shareholders. Two types of owners emerge, representing a voluntary subdivision of the overall ownership privileges. Specifically, the common shareholders agree that the preferred shareholder shall have "preference" or first claim in the event that the directors are able and willing to pay a dividend. In the case of what is termed a nonparticipating or *straight preferred stock*, which is the most frequent type, the extent of this priority is a fixed percentage of the par value of the stock or a fixed number of dollars per share in the case of stock without a nominal or par value.

* * *

In most cases the prior position of preferred stock also extends to the disposition of assets in the event of liquidation of the business. Again, the priority is only with reference to the common stock and does not affect the senior position of creditors in any way. It has meaning and value only if asset values remain after creditors have been fully satisfied—a condition which is by no means certain in the event of liquidation following bankruptcy. * * *

So far, we have considered the preferred stock in terms of the formal rights and responsibilities inherent in this type of security. The impression created is that of a limited commitment on dividends coupled with considerable freedom in the timing of such payments. In reality, experience with preferred stocks indicates that the flexibility in dividend payments is more apparent than real. The management of a business which is experiencing normal profitability and growth desires to pay a regular dividend on both common and preferred stock because of a sense of responsibility to the corporate owners and/or because of the necessity of having to solicit further equity capital in the future. The pressure for a regular common dividend in many cases assures the holder of a preferred stock that his regular dividend will not be interrupted, even in years when profits are insufficient to give common shareholders a comparable return, for it is very damaging to the reputation of a common stock (and therefore its price) if preferred dividend arrearages stand before it. The fact that most preferred issues are substantially smaller in total amount than the related common issue means that the cash drain of a preferred dividend is often less significant than the preservation of the status of the common stock.

The result is that management comes to view the preferred issue much as it would a bond, establishing the policy that the full preferred dividend must be paid as a matter of course. The option of passing the dividend still exists, but it is seen as a step to be taken only in case of unusual financial difficulty.[1] Under such a circumstance, the obvious question presents itself: Why, then, use preferred stock as a means of raising permanent capital? Why not use bonds instead? The primary advantage of the preferred stock becomes identical with that of a bond, namely, the opportunity to raise funds at a fixed return which is less than that realized when the funds are invested. On the other hand, the dividend rate on preferred stock is typically above the interest rate on a comparable bond and may have the additional disadvantage of not developing a tax shield. Of course, the bond is more likely to have a sinking fund, so that the *burden* of bond and preferred stock may not be greatly different.

The differential in cost between a preferred stock and an alternative debt issue may be considered a premium paid for the option of postponing the fixed payments. If management is reluctant to exercise this option, it is likely that the premium will be considered excessive. However, the closer a company gets to its recognized debt limits, the more management is likely to appreciate the option to defer the dividend on a preferred stock issue and be willing to pay a premium for this potential defense against a tight cash position.

———

The deductibility of interest payments gives debt a relative advantage over preferred from the issuer's point of view. This tax differential has contributed to a relative decline in the use of preferred as a financing vehicle in the post-war era. By now, the very survival of preferred as a form of financing has become a subject matter for explanation. Financial economic commentators explain its continued issuance in terms of the issuer's debt capacity. Elsaid, The Function of Preferred Stock in the Corporate Financial Plan, 25 Financial Analysts' J. 112 (1969), concluded that preferred stock tends to be issued in order to improve the borrowing base for debt financing. Heinkel and Zechner, The Role of Debt and Preferred Stock as a Solution to Adverse Investment Incentives, 25 J. Financial & Quantitative Analysis 1 (1990) reconfirm this conclusion from the point of view of agency theory. Their model shows that preferred creates incentives for the firm's common holders to invest, and thus ameliorates the underinvestment problem that follows from the issuance of debt (see the discussion supra p. 188). A new issue of preferred counters the agency costs of debt, and thereby enhances the firm's debt capacity.

These theoretical assertions are at bottom expansions on the simple proposition that additional equity increases the equity cushion and thus creates room for cheaper debt. Unsurprisingly, preferred stock, being equity, has this effect. In fact, preferred usually is issued by firms under duress to bolster their equity cushions. Preferred stock financing most often is employed by firms, such as public utilities, the capital

---

1. The experience of the 1930's is evidence of the fact that such periods do occur; and it must be recognized that in such conditions of severe economic recession, large numbers of preferred issues will stand in arrears.

structures of which are subject to government regulation. They issue preferred in order to satisfy legally mandated debt equity ratios. In addition, banks and bank holding companies, pressed by regulatory agencies to expand equity their capital base, have issued extraordinary quantities of preferred in recent years. These issues often carry an adjustable rate of interest geared to the prevailing rate of interest of various U.S. treasury securities, but within a limiting range. Short term issues of bank preferred also have appeared. Preferred stock also has been widely employed in the recapitalization programs of firms having difficulty meeting the obligations assumed in high leverage restructurings undertaken during the 1980s. As with the banks, the objective is to increase the firm's equity cushion with the minimum possible dilution of the upside potential of the common stock.

A tax advantage figures into preferred stock financing, partially offsetting the disadvantages of the lack an issuer deduction for dividend payments. The intercorporate dividend exclusion, I.R.C. §§ 243, 244, results in preferred stock dividends attracting less federal income tax than bond interest when the preferred is held by a corporation. Hence preferred stock—particularly that issued by high grade public utilities—can offer a more attractive investment opportunity than unsecured bonds to insurance companies and other corporate institutional investors, and thus may cost the issuer less. See Fisher & Wilt, Non–Convertible Stock As a Financing Instrument 1950–1965, 23 J. Finance 611 (1968).

(B) THE PREFERRED STOCK CONTRACT

Like bonds or debentures, preferred stock is essentially a security which combines priority with a ceiling on the claim to income and principal. Unlike bonds or debentures, however, the preferred stock's claim is to priority in payment, but not to an unconditional right to be paid. Indeed, in many states dividends may not be paid unless the enterprise has some form of surplus or earnings available therefor. And no repayments may be made on dissolution or in redemption, unless assets are available therefor after all debts have been satisfied. See infra, pp. 348–355.

(1) *Financial Terms*

The provisions for current dividends may vary greatly in the force of their compulsion to make payments, ranging from the mandatory and fully cumulative dividend to the discretionary and wholly non-cumulative dividend. The preferred stock contract generally provides, in the event of dissolution of the enterprise, for the payment prior to any distribution to the common stockholders, of a specified sum plus an amount equal to all dividends in arrears, and if dissolution is voluntary, often a premium. Usually, the contract also provides for redemption at the option of the corporation at a specific price plus an amount equal to all dividends in arrears and a premium (See pp. 352–355, infra). Apart from providing for payment of dividends and principal, the preferred stock contract may contain protective provisions designed to minimize risk of non-payment, (e.g., sinking fund provisions, requirements for the maintenance of a minimum working capital, prohibitions against creation of prior preferred stock without the consent of the existing preferred, class voting for alterations,[x] etc.) most of which are comparable to the protective provisions developed for bonds and debentures.

Although the preferred stock contract is primarily addressed to protecting the stockholders' prior claims to dividends and principal in the event that the enterprise shrinks, it may also embody an opportunity to share in the growth of the enterprise. Indeed, in an expanding economy, preferred stock is not likely to offer a particularly attractive investment unless it has that opportunity. The usual device for offering such an opportunity, while preserving priority in the event of contraction, is the conversion privilege—the right of the stockholder to convert the preferred stock into common stock by exchanging a share of preferred for a specified number of shares of common, or at a designated value for as many shares of common as may be purchased at specified prices. (See pp. 397–447, infra).

Finally it may be noted that during the past forty years, investment bankers have suggested, and counsel have created, a variety of other hybrid instruments designed to allocate risk and return as the presumed optimal needs of assorted participants and transactions required. See generally, Hu, New Financial Products, the Modern Process of Financial Innovation, and the Puzzle of Shareholder Welfare, 69 Tex.L.Rev. 1273 (1991). Concomitantly corporate law has come to tolerate variations not merely in debt instruments, but in the terms of equity. Thus, as the "official comment" to Section 6.01 of the Revised Model Business Corporation Act (RMBCA) notes (Harcourt Brace Jovonavich, The Model Business Corporation Act Annotated 307):

> It is possible under modern corporation statutes to create classes of "common" shares that have important preferential rights and classes of "preferred" shares that are subordinate in all important economic aspects or that are indistinguishable from common shares in either voting rights or entitlement to participate in the assets of the corporation upon dissolution. The revised Model Act breaks away from the inherited concepts of "common" and "preferred" shares and develops more general language to reflect the actual flexibility in the creation of classes of shares that exists in modern corporate practice. The words "common shares" or "preferred shares" are no longer used in the revised Model Act, though the words appear

---

x. Comparable protective prohibitions may be found in corporation laws which require a class vote of the preferred stock for increases in the par value or number of outstanding shares, or for the issuance of prior preferred stock. See e.g., RMBCA § 10.04; NYBCL §§ 801 and 804; compare Del.Corp.Law §§ 242(a) and 242(b)(2).

The original Model Business Corporation Act, reported in 1950, is referred to as "MBCA"; the Revised Model Business Corporation Act is referred to as "RMBCA".

in a few instances in examples appearing in the Official Comment.

(2) *Voting Power*

Normally, the preferred stock's interest in directing the affairs of the enterprise is not significantly different from that of a bondholder, since like the latter, albeit more marginally, preferred stock has a prior and limited claim on earnings of the going concern and on assets in liquidation, which generally may be terminated by redemption at the option of the common. Both bondholders and preferred stockholders have an entirely different interest in the enterprise than does the common stock, which is the residual claimant of the benefits of operations and the first to sustain the burdens of loss.

To be sure, formally the preferred stockholder is an "owner" with an "equity" interest, like a common stockholder, and, therefore, in some states may be entitled to vote like a holder of common stock. In most states, the preferred stock may be denied the vote if the corporate charter so provides. See, e.g., Del.Corp.Law § 151(a); RMBCA § 6.01(c); NYBCL §§ 501, 613. Since the matter is thus effectively left to the common stock to decide in the first instance, the preferred is not generally given voting power, except as statutes may require with respect to specially prescribed matters.

For example, the preferred stockholders are generally entitled by statute (and often by charter) to vote as a class on charter amendments which adversely affect them. The occasions for which such an apparently irrevocable right to a class vote may be specified in some detail as in RMBCA § 10.04, or set out in a more generalized statement, as in Del.Corp.Law § 242(b)(2), which prescribes class voting on those charter amendments which would increase or decrease the par value or aggregate number of authorized shares, or "alter or change the powers, preferences or special rights of the shares of such class so as to affect them adversely." See also NYBCL § 804. Some statutes indirectly add an express provision for a class vote where stockholder approval is sought for a merger or consolidation. See RMBCA § 11.03; NYBCL § 903(a)(2). Where the statute does not make such provision, as in the case of Delaware's statute, the question arises whether a class vote can be implied from the right to vote as a class on amendments. The Delaware courts have held in the negative, see infra pp. 395–397.

In deference to the substantially increased interest of the preferred in controlling the enterprise, and particularly in the distribution of dividends, the corporate charter may provide that the preferred stock shall vote for the election of directors (and possibly on other matters) upon the occurrence of default in the payment of dividends for a specified period.[y] Generally there is no statutory requirement that it

---

y. In theory, default in the payment of dividends is not the only contingency upon which to predicate the creation of voting rights. Violation of other protective provisions in the preferred stock contract, such as minimum sinking fund requirements, minimum working capital requirements, limitations on dividends payable to junior

so provide. The Securities and Exchange Commission, with respect to corporations subject to Sections 6 and 7 of the Public Utility Holding Company Act of 1935, has required the preferred contract to vest power to elect a majority of the Board if dividends are in arrears "in an amount equal to four full quarter-yearly payments." PUHCA Rel. No. 13,106 (2/16/56) 4 CCH Fed.Sec.L.Rep. ¶¶ 36,691, 36,693. See also § 18(a) of the Investment Company Act of 1940, 15 U.S.C. § 80a–18(a). Comparable provisions were generally recommended by the SEC in Advisory Reports under Chapter X with respect to corporations emerging from reorganization with preferred stocks in their capital structures.

The New York Stock Exchange has moved in the same direction, although not nearly so far, with respect to corporations whose preferred stock is listed on the Exchange. It requires preferreds as a class to be given power to elect "at least two directors [who almost always constitute a small minority] upon default of the equivalent of six quarterly dividends"—(NYSE Listed Company Manual, § 703.05D). And the American Stock Exchange has also inched along toward the same goal; it "will not view favorably applications for the listing of * * * nonvoting Preferred Stocks which do not acquire voting rights upon specified default (maximum two years) in the payment of fixed dividend requirements." (American Stock Exchange Guide, Original Listing Requirements, § 124).

It will be noted that default is defined as the failure to pay an aggregate (rather than a consecutive) number of quarterly dividends. The voting power is bestowed upon the preferred by class, rather than by share, in recognition of the possibility (generally the actuality) that the number of preferred shares will be significantly smaller than the number of common shares, even on those occasions when the investment of the preferreds is considerably larger than the investment of common stockholders.

Should the investment contract explicitly require a limit to the continuance of a shift in control on default in preferred stock dividends? Compare Baron v. Allied Artists Pictures Corp., infra, p. 346.

(3) *Authorization and Amendment*

The terms of the preferred stock contract are contained in the corporate charter, and may also appear on the stock certificate. However, both its initial terms and any alterations in those terms must find authorization in the State's corporation law. The authorization for initial terms is generally embodied in broad and permissive statutory language. Many states permit corporate charters to authorize preferred on an open-ended basis. Under such a "blank check," the terms of an issue are fixed by subsequent resolution of the board of directors.

securities, prohibitions against creating senior securities, etc., may provide the occasion for creating voting rights in the preferred, and in some states, in bonds. (Del.Corp.Law § 221; NYBCL § 518(c)). The creation of voting power for bondholders, with attendant control of the enterprise, may be a more substantial means for enforcing protective covenants, than the right to seek judicial assistance.

Thus the new financing goes forward without the need to submit the terms for shareholder approval.[z]

The statutes commonly contain express and specific provisions governing the process of alteration. These statutory provisions are deemed to be incorporated in the preferred stock contract. Hence, the interpretive questions which arise as to the meaning of the contract will often turn on statutory language and structure as well as on the language of the particular contract. They may pose difficult problems of integrating the former with the latter, by way of resolving contradictions or ambiguities or supplying material to cover omissions.

Relatively few disputes are encountered in the day to day application of the terms of preferred stock contracts. But, as with debt securities, a considerable body of case law has developed in response to efforts to amend or alter the preferred stock contract. Such efforts are made, normally, when the common stockholders desire to shift the initially agreed-upon allocation of risks and returns, to the disadvantage of the preferreds. The risks against which the preferreds have purchased the priorities and protective features of their contract at the cost of accepting a limited return will have materialized—e.g. there is an opportunity to sell all the assets of the enterprise at a price which the common stock regards as relatively favorable, or earnings will have been inadequate for a period of years, so that preferred dividends will have been passed or sinking fund payments skipped—and the future, although apparently improving, will look less roseate than when the original arrangements were made. Hence, the preferreds' arrearage priority will constitute an apparently insurmountable obstacle to the flow of dividends to the common, the preferreds' dividend rate will seem unduly high, and the protective features of the investment contract (sinking fund obligations, working capital restrictions, liquidation price, call premium) unduly burdensome. The common will then seek (a) to acquire a larger share of future returns by eliminating the preferreds' right to arrears and reducing their promised or expected future returns, and (b) to increase the preferreds' risks for the future by modifying or eliminating the protective features of the investment contract. Comparable attempts may be involved in connection with the distribution of the assets of the enterprise on liquidation, or of new participations in a substantially changed enterprise in the case of a bona fide merger. In those events, the commons may seek advantageous alteration of the distribution of shares promised to, or reasonably expected by, the preferreds.

Inevitably the occasions for such attempted reallocations of participations will be said to be, and may actually be, occasions for substantial changes in the economic dimensions of the enterprise. Inevitably also, those changes, such as infusion of new capital or an arm's length

---

z. The Board's issuance of such stock on terms contrived to impede or effectively preclude takeovers (discussed pp. 963–965 infra) is one of the more imaginative uses of preferred stock to allocate power for corporate governance—possibly in the interest of the common stock, but certainly in the interest of preserving existing management.

merger with another enterprise, will be said by management to be necessary or appropriate for the increased prosperity of the enterprise. The question then arises whether the proposed alterations of the investment contract are equally necessary and appropriate, either to facilitate the presumably desirable economic changes in the enterprise or otherwise.

2. CLAIMS TO DIVIDENDS

(a) *Preferred Stock Dividend Provisions*

Since the income priority of preferred stock is a matter of contract, a great variety of delineations of priority may occur—ranging from a requirement that dividends shall be paid if appropriate surplus exists (Arizona Western Ins. Co. v. L.L. Constantin & Co., 247 F.2d 388 (3d Cir.1957); cf. L.L. Constantin & Co. v. R.P. Holding Corp., 56 N.J.Super. 411, 153 A.2d 378 (1959) (interpreting the same charter language to be insufficiently explicit to overcome the directorial discretion that the statute authorizes)) to a non-cumulative priority (i.e., a priority that only blocks dividends to common during the current payment period; past skipped dividends do not accumulate as arrearages even if the enterprise was profitable). Intermediate forms most frequently encountered are the fully cumulative preferred (i.e., the failure to pay dividends in any period, whether or not the enterprise had earnings during that period, does not relieve the enterprise of the obligation to pay those unpaid dividends before common dividends can be paid) and the preferred which is cumulative only if earned (i.e., unpaid dividends only cumulate or accrue if they have not been paid for periods for which there were earnings), a contingency which leaves wide room for dispute. See e.g., Kern v. Chicago & Eastern Ill. R.R. Co., 6 Ill.App.3d 247, 285 N.E.2d 501 (1972); Koppel v. Middle States Petroleum Corp., 197 Misc. 479, 96 N.Y.S.2d 38 (Sup.Ct.N.Y.County 1950).[a]

(b) *Board Discretion to Withhold Payment*

In all cases other than that of mandatory dividend preferred, directors have discretion to withhold payment of dividends. Should courts or legislatures fashion standards limiting the exercise of that discretion, or are the considerations discussed in Hunt, Williams, and Donaldson, supra, p. 335, sufficient to contain such discretion? Should

---

a. In addition to its limited preference—both to dividends and to assets—preferred stock may participate along with common stock in residual earnings and assets. The extent of such participation is a matter of contract, and will vary with the needs of the corporation for capital and the marketability of its stock at the time when capital is needed. See e.g., Zahn v. Transamerica Corp., 162 F.2d 36 (3d Cir. 1947). In the absence of contractual provision for participation, however, the majority view is that a preferred stock is limited by the amount of its priority as to dividends, and as to assets in liquidation, and is not entitled to share in residual earnings or assets. See St. Louis Southwestern Ry. Co. v. Loeb, 318 S.W.2d 246 (Mo.1958); Squires v. Balbach Co., 177 Neb. 465, 129 N.W.2d 462 (1964). On the terms of preferred stock generally; see Buxbaum, Preferred Stock—Law and Draftsmanship, 42 Calif.L.Rev. 243 (1954).

the same standards confine directors' discretion to withhold dividends on non-cumulative preferred as on fully cumulative preferred?

(1) *Noncumulative Preferred*

The discretion question has been litigated extensively in respect of noncumulative preferred. The facts giving rise to these disputes work along the following lines. No dividends are paid on either the noncumulative preferred or the underlying common for many years. During this period the corporation may be profitable—but because the business is capital intensive, management retains all earnings available for dividends. Then, when times improve, management starts the dividend flow again. The noncumulative preferred is paid its limited annual dividend, and the common, the dividend to which is not subject to a limitation once the preferred is paid, is paid a much larger dividend.[b] The preferred argues that, on these facts, "noncumulative" does not have its literal meaning.

The leading cases, Wabash Railway Co. v. Barclay, 280 U.S. 197 (1930) (Holmes, J.) and **Guttman v. Illinois Central R. Co.,** 189 F.2d 927 (2d Cir.1951) (Frank, J.), cert. denied, 342 U.S. 867 (1951), rule against the preferred. Judge Frank, in *Guttman,* opted for literalism even while recognizing that the noncumulative arrangement opens possibilities for opportunistic manipulation for the benefit of the common:

"Here we are interpreting a contract into which uncoerced men entered. Nothing in the wording of that contract would suggest to an ordinary wayfaring person the existence of a contingent or inchoate right to arrears of dividends.[13] The notion that such a right was promised is, rather, the invention of lawyers or other experts, a notion stemming from considerations of fairness, from a policy of protecting investors in those securities. But the preferred stockholders are not—like sailors or idiots or infants—wards of the judiciary. As courts on occasions have quoted or paraphrased ancient poets, it may not be inappropriate to paraphrase a modern poet, and to say that "a contract is a contract is a contract." To be sure, it is an overstatement that the courts never do more than carry out the intentions of the parties: In the interest of fairness and justice, many a judge-made legal rule does impose, on one of the parties to a contract, obligations which neither party actually contemplated and as to which the language of the contract is silent. But there are limits to the extent to which a court

---

b. Eisenberg v. Chicago Milwaukee Corp., 537 A.2d 1051 (Del.Ch.1987), offers a contemporary variation on this fact pattern. There the issuer paid no dividends on either its noncumulative preferred or its common, and then, after the 1987 stock market crash, made a tender offer for the preferred.

13. Berle, a most brilliant legal commentator on corporate finance, who may be credited with the authorship of plaintiff's basic contention, admitted that "popular interpretation," including that of "investors and businessmen," holds "non-cumulative" to mean "that dividends on noncumulative preferred stock, once passed or omitted, are 'dead'; can never be made up." See Berle, Non-cumulative Preferred Stock, 23 Columbia L.Rev. 358, 364, 365 (1923).

may go in so interpolating rights and obligations which were never in the parties' contemplation. In this case we consider those limits clear.

"In sum, we hold that, since the directors did not "abuse" their discretion in withholding dividends on the non-cumulative preferred for any past years, (a) no right survived to have those dividends declared, and (b) the directors had no discretion whatever to declare those dividends subsequently.

"From the point of view of the preferred stockholders, the bargain they made may well be of a most undesirable kind. Perhaps the making of such bargains should be prevented. But, if so, the way to prevent them is by legislation, or by prophylactic administrative action authorized by legislation, as in the case of the S.E.C. in respect of securities, including preferred stocks, whether cumulative or noncumulative, issued by public utility holding companies or their subsidiaries.[15] The courts are not empowered to practice such preventive legal medicine, and must not try to revise, extensively, contracts already outstanding and freely made by adults who are not incompetents."

As Judge Frank indicated, some commentators have interpreted the noncumulative feature to bar accruals only for years in which the corporation has no earnings. The New Jersey courts have adopted this interpretation.

Under this approach, retained earnings serve to create a dividend credit for preferred stockholders which must be satisfied before dividends can be paid on the common. In **Sanders v. Cuba Railroad Co.,** 21 N.J. 78, 120 A.2d 849 (1956), the Supreme Court of New Jersey (Jacobs, J.) rejected an opportunity to realign itself with the *Wabash Railway* and *Guttman* decisions:

"This much is quite apparent—if the common stockholders, who generally control the corporation and will benefit most by the passing of the dividends on the preferred stock, may freely achieve that result without any dividend credit consequences, then the preferred stockholders will be substantially at the mercy of others who will be under temptation to act in their own self-interest. See Note, Dividend Rights of Non–Cumulative Preferred Stock, 61 Yale L.J. 245, 251 (1952); Note, Right of Non–Cumulative Preferred Stockholders to Back Dividends Earned But Unpaid, 74 U.Pa.L.Rev. 605, 608 (1926). While such conclusion may sometimes be compelled by the clear contractual arrangements between the parties there is no just reason why our courts should not avoid it whenever the contract is silent or is so general as to leave adequate room for its construction. In any event, New Jersey's doctrine has received wide approval in legal writings and there does not

---

15. See In the Matter of The North American Company, 4 S.E.C. 434, 462 (1939) (dissenting opinion).

There it is pointed out, inter alia, that the provisions of many cumulative preferred stocks create bargains that are most undesirable, but which the courts nevertheless enforce.

There are those who think that no sort of preferred stock should be permitted because, among other things, of the unavoidable perplexities which they frequently occasion for conscientious directors owing allegiance to classes of stockholders with interests often in conflict.

seem to be any present disposition in this court to reject it or limit its
sweep in favor of the Supreme Court's approach in the Wabash Railway
case. * * * "

Why should anyone buy non-cumulative preferred stock?

(2) *Board Discretion and Voting Control*

Suppose the holders of a class of cumulative preferred stock gain
the right under the charter to elect a majority of the board of directors
if the issuer defaults in the payment of six quarterly dividends. The
defaults occur and the preferred holders elect themselves to the board.
The new board returns the corporation to profitability. But the preferreds' board members never declare the payment of the preferred
dividends in arrears. So doing would cause the vote to revert to the
common stock and possibly cost them their control. Would the common stockholders at some point have a right to have these board
elections declared invalid?

This was the question in **Baron v. Allied Artists Pictures Corp.,**
337 A.2d 653 (Del.Ch.1975). Holders of preferred stock of Allied Artists
Pictures had been electing the board for ten years when a class of
common holders sought avoidance of the election. As of the 1974
election, preferred arrearages exceeded $280,000. A corporation called
Kalvex held 52 percent of the preferred and thereby controlled the
corporation even though the holding amounted only to 7½ percent of
the total equity. Kalvex nominated the board and top officers of Allied;
these nominees drew annual salaries from Allied totalling $402,088,
including $100,000 for the president. But Allied also had returned to
profitability under Kalvex control, recently having produced hits like
Cabaret and *Papillon.*

The board had been disabled from paying dividends for a number of
years under the terms of a tax deficiency settlement with the IRS. One
final payment was left to be made under this at the time of the 1974
board election. As of the fiscal year ended June 30, 1973, Allied's
capital surplus available for dividend payments amounted to only
$118,000.

The court sustained the 1974 election, subject to an ultimate limit
on the preferred stockholders' hegemony:

"Plaintiff stresses that he is not asking the Court to compel the
payment of the dividend arrearages, but only that a new election be
held because of the preferred board's allegedly wrongful refusal to do
so. * * *

"Plaintiff here appears to be asking that an exception be carved
from * * * well established principles [delegating discretion over dividend declarations to the board] where the nonpayment of dividends and
arrearages results in continued control by the very board which determines not to pay them. As I understand his argument, he asks for a
ruling that a board of directors elected by preferred shareholders whose
dividends are in arrears has an absolute duty to pay off all preferred
dividends due and to return control to the common shareholders as

soon as funds become legally available for that purpose, regardless of anything else. Thus, in effect, he would have the court limit the discretion given the board by the certificate of incorporation, and make the decision to pay arrearages mandatory upon the emergence of a lawful financial source even though the corporate charter does not require it (as perhaps it did in *Petroleum Rights*). He has offered no precedent for such a proposition, and I decline to create one.

* * *

"When the yearly hit-and-miss financial history of Allied from 1964 through 1974 is considered along with the Internal Revenue obligation during the same time span, I cannot conclude, as a matter of law, that Allied's board has been guilty of perpetuating itself in office by wrongfully refusing to apply corporate funds to the liqu.dation of the preferred dividend arrearages and the accelerated payment of the Internal Revenue debt. Thus I find no basis on the record before me to set aside the 1974 annual election and to order a new one through a master appointed by the court.

* * *

"It is clear, however, that Allied's present board does have a fiduciary duty to see that the preferred dividends are brought up to date as soon as possible in keeping with prudent business management.

* * *

"This is particularly true now that the Internal Revenue debt has been satisfied in full and business is prospering. It cannot be permitted indefinitely to plough back all profits in future commitments so as to avoid full satisfaction of the rights of the preferred to their dividends and the otherwise normal right of the common stockholders to elect corporate management. While previous limitations on net income and capital surplus may offer a justification for the past, continued limitations in a time of greatly increased cash flow could well create new issues in the area of business discretion for the future."

––––––––––––

Why should Wolf and his associates have been so reluctant to allow control of Allied Artists to pass back again to the common? Executives' compensation—$100,000 for Wolf, $400,000 for the lot—really does not seem excessive by the standards of the time. Accordingly, why such a desperate grip on the corporate windpipe? In any event, since Wolf and the others had succeeded so well with *Cabaret* and *Papillon,* wouldn't the common stockholders have been happy to reelect them to their directorships? Compare Levin v. Mississippi River Fuel Corporation, 386 U.S. 162 (1967); and see Baron v. Allied Artists Pictures Corp., 395 A.2d 375 (Del.Ch.1978).

3. CLAIMS TO PRINCIPAL, INCLUDING ARREARAGES

(A) ALTERATION BY AMENDMENT

(1) Liquidation Provisions

The preferred stock contract typically provides that on the "liquidation, dissolution or winding up" of the corporation, the preferred stockholder is entitled to payment of a specified amount before any assets are distributable to common stockholders or to holders of any other security junior to his. The "principal" amount thus distributable is generally equal to the par value or the amount paid on the original issuance of the preferred stock, but it need not be equal to either. In addition to the "principal" amount of the claim, the preferred stock contract usually entitles the holder to priority of payment of all dividend arrearages on dissolution, and to a premium if the dissolution is voluntary.[c] Payment is usually required to be made in cash.

The protective significance of the liquidation preference is not only affected by the fact that as an economic matter the protection it offers is most likely to be sought when it is least likely to be available—i.e., when the enterprise is insolvent—but it is diminished by the narrow scope attributed by courts to the typical language in which it is embodied. Thus questions have been raised as to what conduct or acts invoke the liquidation preference, and whether it is the voluntary or involuntary liquidation preference that is triggered by such transactions. Does the customary language prescribing a preference in the event of any "liquidation, dissolution or winding up", cover the sale of substantially all the assets, so that on such a sale, the preferreds can assert a right to receive distribution of the proceeds, as against the "corporation's" claim to retain the proceeds and engage in new business

---

c. Occasionally common stockholders have sought to prevent payment of preferred dividend arrearages on dissolution, on the ground that, notwithstanding the terminal character of the payment, it should be viewed only as a return of "principal" or of capital, and the arrearage component should be treated as a dividend, payable only if lawful sources for dividends (e.g., surplus) are available. Hence, although the value of distributable assets may be great enough to permit payment to preferred stockholders of their liquidation or dissolution "principal" and accumulated arrears, the common stockholders contend that an absence of accounting surplus precludes the payment of the arrears component—the value of which is thus left for distribution to the common stock as the residual takers. Whatever may be the statutory restrictions on payment of pre-ferred dividends on a current basis by reason of requirements that dividends be paid only from some type of accounting surplus (see infra, p. 442), does it follow—either in logic or in policy, or as a matter of law or of contract—that such restrictions preclude priority of payment of the preferred's contractually specified amounts on dissolution? Compare Hay v. Hay, 38 Wash.2d 513, 230 P.2d 791 (1951) and Matter of Chandler & Co., Inc., 230 N.Y.S.2d 1012 (Sup.Ct.1962) with Wouk v. Merin, 283 App.Div. 522, 128 N.Y.S.2d 727 (1st Dept. 1954). Since voluntary dissolution generally requires the common stock to consent to liquidation of the enterprise and to relinquish its use of the capital contributed by the preferred, such action is likely to occur only in unusual circumstances. Hence, the premium is of little practical benefit.

activities? See Treves v. Menzies, 37 Del.Ch. 330, 142 A.2d 520 (1958); Maffia v. American Woolen Co., 125 F.Supp. 465 (S.D.N.Y.1954); Rothschild International Corporation v. Liggett Group Inc., infra p. 372. Or is still other action—e.g., dissolution or distribution of assets—required before the clause is triggered? See Craddock–Terry Co. v. Powell, 181 Va. 417, 25 S.E.2d 363 (1943); Geiger v. American Seeding Machine Co., 124 Ohio St. 222, 177 N.E. 594 (1931).

Similar problems of interpretation arise with respect to whether the conventional language of the liquidation preference clause covers a merger of the preferred stockholder's corporation into another corporation, in which the preferred stockholder and common stockholder of the old corporation each received common stock of the surviving corporation. (Compare Petry v. Harwood Electric Co., 280 Pa. 142, 124 A. 302 (1924) with Rothschild Int'l Corp. v. Liggett Group, Inc., infra p. 372 Anderson v. Cleveland–Cliffs Iron Co., 87 N.E.2d 384, 394–396 (Ohio C.P.1948) and Adams v. United States Distributing Corp., 184 Va. 134, 149–151, 34 S.E.2d 244, 251–252 (1945)). Can the charter lawfully provide that, notwithstanding express statutory provisions authorizing and prescribing the consequences of mergers and sales of assets, such transactions trigger the preferred stock liquidation preference? Compare Jones v. St. Louis Structural Steel Co., 267 Ill.App. 576 (1932); Langfelder v. Universal Laboratories, Inc., 163 F.2d 804 (3d Cir.1947).

Compare the constituencies authorized to vote on a merger (RMBCA § 11.03; Del.Corp.Law § 251; NYBCL § 903); sale of assets (RMBCA § 12.02; Del.Corp.Law § 271; NYBCL § 909); dissolution (RMBCA § 14.02; Del.Corp.Law § 275; NYBCL §§ 1001–1002), and amendment (RMBCA §§ 10.03, 10.04; NYBCL §§ 803, 804; Del.Corp.Law § 242(b)(2)).

GOLDMAN v. POSTAL TELEGRAPH, INC.

United States District Court, District of Delaware, 1943.
52 F.Supp. 763.

LEAHY, District Judge. Diversity and the requisite amount establish jurisdiction.

* * *

Postal Telegraph, Inc., incorporated under the laws of Delaware in 1939 (herein called "Postal"), agreed to transfer to Western Union, Telegraph Company (herein called "Western Union"), another Delaware corporation, all its assets. At the time of the agreement plaintiff owned 500 shares of non-cumulative preferred stock of Postal which, by the terms of Postal's certificate of incorporation, entitled all preferred stockholders to a payment of $60 a share on liquidation before any distribution could be made to its common stockholders. On July 5, 1943, defendant Postal proposed to its stockholders three resolutions authorizing (1) the sale of all its assets to Western Union, conditioned upon the approval by Postal's stockholders of an amendment to its certificate of incorporation referred to in (2); (2) the amendment of Postal's certificate of incorporation so as to provide that the holders of defendant's non-cumulative preferred stock would receive in lieu of $60 per share on liquidation one share of Western Union B stock; * and (3) formal dissolution of Postal. At the stockholders' meeting held on August 10, 1943, these resolutions were passed by a requisite vote over plaintiff's express objection. This suit followed.

The Postal–Western Union agreement provides that for the transfer of all the assets of Postal to Western Union, Postal will receive as part consideration 308,124 shares of Class B stock of Western Union. The entire amount of Class B stock to be received from Western Union will have a value substantially less than the aggregate liquidation preference of the preferred stock of Postal. Consequently, under its certificate of incorporation Postal's common stockholders—whose equity is deeply under water—would be entitled to receive nothing if ordinary liquidation occurred. Subject to various adjustments which do not have my immediate attention, Western Union will assume approximately $10,800,000 of Postal's liabilities. Postal's economic position is shown by its steady losses, aggregating over $13,500,000 from February 1, 1940, to May 31, 1943. These losses have been financed, in part, by advances from the Reconstruction Finance Corporation. In facing further corporate existence, two courses were open to Postal: (a) To submit to government ownership or (b) to seek some type of merger with or absorption by Western Union.

In order to complete the proposed transfer of assets to Western Union, the vote of a majority of the outstanding stock of Postal was required under the Delaware law, sec. 65. See Rev.Code of Delaware of 1935, c. 65, Sec. 2097. Postal's outstanding preferred was 256,769.9 and the number of shares of common was 1,027,076.6. Hence, if all the preferred voted in favor of the plan, it would still be necessary to obtain the affirmative vote of approximately 400,000 shares of common. In order to obtain such vote, Postal's directors determined it advisable that the preferred's rights on liquidation be modified, so as to provide that out of the 308,124 shares of Class B stock of Western Union to be received by Postal, 256,770 shares would be distributed share for share for each of Postal's preferred and the balance of the Class B—51,354 shares—would be distributed to Postal's common stockholders, which was to be in the ratio of $\frac{1}{20}$ of a share of Class B Western Union stock for each share of common stock of Postal.

---

* [Ed. Note] The amendment added the following to the provisions of the certificate of incorporation dealing with the rights of preferred stockholders:

"*Provided, however, that notwithstanding the provisions of the next preceding paragraph in this subdivision (e) contained, if substantially all of the assets of the Corporation or of its operating subsidiaries are sold to the Western Union Telegraph Company then upon any liquidation, dissolution or winding up of the affairs of the Corporation the holders of shares of the Non–Cumulative Preferred Stock shall be entitled to receive for each share out of the assets of the Corporation (in lieu of the cash payments in said next preceding paragraph specified) one share of the Class B Stock of the Western Union Telegraph Company before any distribution or payment shall be made to the holders of shares of Common Stock; but they shall be entitled to no further or other participation in any distribution or payment.*"

As part of the plan, Western Union would also change its present 1,045,592 shares of capital stock into an equal number of shares of Class A stock without par value, which stock would be entitled to a non-cumulative dividend of $2 per share in each year before any dividends could be paid upon the Class B stock. After such dividend payment, the Class A and Class B stock are to participate on an equal basis in any dividends.

* * * Plaintiff here seeks, on behalf of himself and all other non-assenting shareholders, to enforce the liquidating rights which he contends are secured to him by the certificate of incorporation of Postal prior to the adoption of the resolution to amend it under Sec. 26. Defendant moved to dismiss on the ground that the complaint failed to state a cause of action.

* * *

[Plaintiff contends] that defendant could not agree to sell its assets conditioned upon the power of the corporation to amend its certificate of incorporation as a part of the transaction. There is no merit to this view. When the statute provides the amendment may be made from time to time, when and as desired, it means the amendment may be effectuated at any time; and there is no limitation with respect to the circumstances or the exigencies of the situation upon the exercise of the power. See Havender v. Federal United Corp., 23 Del.Ch. 104, 2 A.2d 143; 11 A.2d 331; Hartford Accident, etc., Co. v. Dickey Clay Co., Del.Ch., 24 A.2d 315.

Craddock–Terry Co. v. Powell, 181 Va. 417, 25 S.E.2d 363, relied on by plaintiff, is distinguishable. In the Craddock & Co. case the corporation sought, in connection with the contract for the sale of its assets, to force the minority to take shares in the buyer corporation which were of a lesser value than the seller corporation's stockholders were entitled to receive under the liquidation provisions of the latter's certificate of incorporation. In that case, no attempt was made to pursue the statutory provisions for amendment; an attempt was made to accomplish by the contract of sale itself the alteration of the seller corporation's stockholders' preference rights. It is one thing to alter a preference pursuant to valid statutory authority; it is another to ignore a grant of power and attempt to accomplish the same result without the benefit of statutory reclassification.

In the case at bar, I see no reason why a Delaware corporation cannot agree to sell its assets conditioned upon the seller corporation amending its certificate of incorporation as a part of the transaction. In fact, such a condition may well become a part of the urgent necessities of a particular transaction. Here, for example, 256,770 shares of preferred, if entitled to $60 a share on dissolution, would be entitled to receive approximately $15,000,000 on liquidation. The present value of the Class B stock of Western Union to be received by Postal in exchange for its assets, at about $19 a share, admittedly amounts to only $4,888,000. If the preferential right of $60 a share remains unaltered, it would be impossible in this case to obtain the vote of the common stockholders in favor of the sale and dissolution, because there could not possibly be any rational basis, under the circumstances, for the common stock voting in approval. One thing is certain. Nothing can be accomplished, either in law or in life, by calling the recalcitrants names. The reality of the situation confronting Postal's management called for some inducement to be offered the common stockholders to secure their favorable vote for the plan. It seems to me of little moment whether that approval was voiced at one or two meetings. The fact is something had to induce the common stockholders to come along. This court and the Delaware courts have recognized the strategic position of common stock to hamper the desires of the real owners of the equity of a corporation, and the tribute which common stock exacts for its vote under reclassification and reorganization. Cf. MacCrone v. American Capital Corp., D.C.Del., 51 F.Supp. 462, at page 469; and MacFarlane v. North American Cement Corporation, 16 Del.Ch. 172, 180, 157 A. 396. And, as stated, separate meetings of Postal's stockholders could have been called to (a) amend under Sec. 26 and (b) approve a sale of assets under Sec. 65; for purposes of convenience and the saving of expense, both steps were taken at one meeting. Nothing in the Delaware law forbids such a procedure. Secs. 26 and 65 contain no limitations on the time or the necessary circumstances which must exist for the exercise of the grant of majority power given under the statutes, except the procedural ritual contained in those statutes.

Accordingly, I conclude for the reasons hereinabove mentioned that defendant's motion to dismiss has merit. A form of decree for my consideration may be submitted upon notice.*

(2) Redemption Provisions

A corporation's power to redeem its stock, i.e., to compel its return in exchange for cash or property, is a function of the investment contract. The corporation statutes authorize such provisions in investment contracts [d] and the redemption is to be effected by the corporation

---

* [Ed.Note] The Goldman case involved the question whether amendment of the liquidation preference may be effected when expressly and separately proposed. Does it follow from Goldman that such an amendment may be effected if it is not separately proposed but is embodied in the proposal for, or the corporate contract of, sale of assets? Compare Craddock–Terry Co. v. Powell, 181 Va. 417, 25 S.E.2d 363 (1943), involving sale of all assets to a subsidiary created for the purpose of eliminating arrears on the parent's preferred stock and Opelka v. Quincy Memorial Bridge Co., 335 Ill.App. 402, 82 N.E.2d 184 (1948) which emphasizes the distinction between stockholder approval of a sale of assets or a dissolution, and stockholder approval of a modification of the corporate charter to effect a change in the previously agreed upon distribution of the proceeds of the sale upon dissolution.

d. The corporation's power to redeem should not be confused with the stockholder's unilateral option to compel repurchase (either as a direct obligation or, as an upstream conversion, e.g., N.J.Statutes 14A:7–6; Del.Corp.Law § 151(e)) which is occasionally given to stockholders, but is subject to the prevailing constraints on corporate distributions which might impair capital or be made from sources other than an appropriate surplus. Cf. Schneider v. Foster–Thornburg Hardware Co., 33 F.Supp. 271 (S.D.W.Va.1940); Mueller v. Kraeuter & Co., 131 N.J.Eq. 475, 25 A.2d 874 (1942).

in accordance with the provisions of the stock contract. From the point of view of the corporation (and, therefore, the common stock) the fixed claim on earnings represented by preferred stock becomes onerous when interest rates fall below the rates prescribed in the preferred stock. At that point, it may be in the interest of the corporation to replace the outstanding preferred stock with a senior security carrying the lower, current rate of interest or dividends. Whatever may be the questions about corporate power to redeem in the absence of such express contractual authorization, there is no doubt that by contract such power can be created,[e] subject to the statutory limits imposed on corporate distributions.[f]

There is no legal requirement for the redemption price to be any minimum amount, but as a practical matter it is not likely to be less than the issue price of the stock. Indeed, to the extent that the stock represents a desirable investment when issued, and will only be redeemed when it represents an even more desirable investment, the purchaser of the security regards with disfavor the unilateral power of the corporation to redeem it. Accordingly, the redemption price will generally include a premium above the issue price, in order to compensate the investor for the loss of a desirable investment. Redemption is not an inevitable attribute of a senior security, because there may be times when the capacity of the issuer to obtain senior capital is so limited that not only is a high interest or dividend rate required in order to attract investors, but the promise must be perpetual (see e.g., In re Childs Co., infra p. 389) or unrecallable for a fixed period. The power thus given by contract to the corporation to redeem the preferred stock at its option may also be used to favor the common stock by relieving the corporation of other obligations which, however, are not as readily quantified as the dividend rate. Thus, common stock may seek to eliminate restrictions on payment of dividends, minimum working capital requirements, or negative covenants (e.g., against issuance of senior securities) in preferred stock. Or, provisions of the tax law may make a bond preferable to preferred stock. Finally, the redemption power enables the corporation to compel, or to frustrate, the exercise of a conversion privilege.

Apart from the purely financial utility to the common stock of the power to redeem, there is the opportunity which possession of that power gives for other "adjustments" in the enterprise—adjustments which are more likely to occur in the case of closely held than of publicly held corporations. On the one hand, it enables the common stock to force out senior security holders whom it regards as unduly intrusive or too demanding, and, on the other hand, it enables "insiders" to bail out if they hold senior securities.

---

e. Corporation statutes often authorize expressly the inclusion in the articles of incorporation of power to redeem stock (e.g. RMBCA § 6.01, NYBCL § 512; Del. Corp.Law § 151(b)).

f. See, e.g., MBCA §§ 66, 67, NYBCL § 513, Del.Corp.Law § 243.

When the power of redemption is exercised, the corporation is, in effect, distributing assets to security holders. Insofar as bonds are being redeemed, the only restrictions upon such distributions are apt to come from the bankruptcy law's prohibition which protects creditors generally against the debtor giving preferences to selected creditors, or from prohibitions embodied in other securities contracts which forbid prior distributions to the bonds being redeemed. When stock is being redeemed, not only the contractual restrictions on distributions, but all the statutory restrictions on distributions (e.g., the requirements with respect to the existence of adequate surplus or earnings) come into play.[g]

The legal issues with respect to the meaning and operation of redemption provisions, therefore, involve primarily questions of interpretation of particular contracts and statutes.[h] Even though the redemption complies with the requirements of the contract and statute, however, problems comparable to those generated by a repurchase may exist—questions of conformity to statutory policy, or of fairness between shareholders of the same class or of different classes. For example, if the relevant norms, whether statutes, rules of a stock exchange, or articles of incorporation,[i] contain no requirement of pro rata or by-lot selection, what considerations should govern the Board's exercise of power, in redeeming less than all the shares, to select particular shares for redemption? If there are dividend arrearages on the stock to be redeemed, what considerations should affect the Board's exercise of power to redeem less than all the shares? Consider SEC, Public Utility Holding Company Act Release No. 13, 106 (2/16/56) (4 CCH Fed.Sec.L.Rep. ¶¶ 36,691, 36,693) which prohibits (with respect to companies subject to the Public Utility Holding Company Act of 1935)

---

g. Redemption of preferred stock may involve repayment of "capital" plus payment of a call premium plus payment of arrearages. The repayment of capital can presumably be reflected by a charge to capital (Del.Corp.Law §§ 151, 243, 244; MBCA § 67; NYBCL § 513) or by a reduction of capital or a charge to capital surplus; but difficult, if not significant, questions remain as to the permissible sources for payment of the call premium and of any arrearages. Is the premium payable from any kind of surplus—earned surplus, capital surplus (reduction or appreciation)? Are the arrearages payable only from the kind of surplus available for dividends? Or is the transaction viewed as a kind of liquidation, so that premium and arrears are payable from "any" source?

h. E.g., if the Board of Directors adopts a resolution to redeem, and notice of redemption is given to stockholders, but the Board later resolves to cancel the redemption, (A) what considerations are relevant in determining whether the preferred stockholders are permitted to force the re-demption? (Is the analogy to declaration of dividends relevant?) (B) What considerations are relevant in determining whether the common stockholders are permitted to force redemption? Taylor v. Axton–Fisher Tobacco Co., 295 Ky. 226, 173 S.W.2d 377 (1943); Zahn v. Transamerica Corp., 162 F.2d 36 (3d Cir.1947); Borst v. East Coast Shipyards, Inc., 105 N.Y.S.2d 228 (Sup.Ct. 1951).

i. The New York Stock Exchange requires each listed company to agree that it "will not select any of its securities listed on the Exchange for redemption otherwise than by lot or pro rata." New York Stock Exchange Listed Company Manual, Section 901.01(9). Few statutes require redemption to be on a pro rata or by lot basis. Compare General Investment Co. v. American Hide & Leather Co., 98 N.J.Eq. 326, 331, 129 A. 244, 246 (1925) with Martin v. American Potash & Chemical Corp., 33 Del.Ch. 234, 92 A.2d 295 (1952); Cf. Snyder v. Memco Engineering & Manufacturing Co., 23 A.D.2d 671, 257 N.Y.S.2d 213 (1965).

any acquisition of, including redemption of, less than all shares if there are arrearages, unless the Commission approves the transaction.

Finally, it should be noted that, paralleling the structure of debt contracts, preferred stock contracts often contain sinking fund provisions—scheduled mandatory redemptions of stated numbers of shares. These provisions, like redemption provisions, are subject to legal constraints on corporate distributions. Sinking fund preferred has become much more common (along with floating rate preferred) since the late 1970s, when rising and volatile interest rates caused perpetual preferred issues to have a poor market reception. In addition, the National Association of Insurance Commissioners instituted a regulatory change that made sinking fund preferred a more attractive holding than perpetual from an accounting point of view. For discussion of the relative costs of sinking fund preferred and perpetual preferred, see McDaniel, Sinking Fund Preferred Stock, 13 Financial Management, (Spring 1984), pp. 45–52; Gombola and Ogden, Effects of a Sinking Fund on Preferred Stock Marketability: A Probit Analysis, 27 Q.J.Bus. Econ. 41 (1988) (reporting that sinking fund provisions enhance the marketability of preferred). For a look at the predicament of a holder of perpetual preferred issued in the early 1960s—a period of low interest rates—in the late 1970s and early 1980s—a period of high rates, see Dalton v. American Investment Co., 490 A.2d 574 (Del.Ch. 1985).

BOWMAN v. ARMOUR & CO.

Superior Court, Cook County, 1959.
17 Ill.2d 43, 160 N.E.2d 753.   Amendment

Opinion of SBARBARO, J.

On January 11, 1955, plaintiff, Johnston A. Bowman, brought this action against the defendants for a declaratory judgment that an amendment to Armour's articles of incorporation and action taken pursuant thereto was illegal, unfair and unconstitutional. * * * The amendment in question, which was duly presented to Armour's stockholders on December 7, 1954, changed the redemption provisions of Armour's $6 Cumulative Convertible Prior Preferred Stock (herein called "Prior Stock") from $115 per share plus accumulated dividends to the date of redemption to a price of $120 per share payable in 5% debentures of a like principal amount maturing on November 1, 1984, and one warrant for the purchase of one share of common stock of the Company. This amendment also waived the preemptive rights of the common stock as to the shares to be issued upon the exercise of these warrants. The stockholders adopted this amendment by the affirmative vote of the holders of 352,922 shares of Prior Stock, or 70.6% of the 500,000 shares of Prior Stock authorized and outstanding on that date, and 81.7% of the shares of common stock outstanding on that date.

The evidence showed that the amendment was adopted as part of a plan for the retirement of the Prior Stock, and the proxy material furnished to the stockholders stated that if the amendment were adopted, the Company would promptly issue its notice of redemption in order to effectuate the plan. Thus, in accordance with the articles of incorporation as amended by the stockholders, the Board of Directors of the Company, at a meeting held on December 7, 1954, after the stockholders' meeting, authorized the issuance of the debentures and warrants, called the Prior Stock for redemption on December 21, 1954, and authorized the issuance of a notice of such redemption to each Prior Stockholder. * * *

The rights of the Prior Stockholders were determined by a contract, the terms of which are found in the articles of incorporation of the Company and in the provisions of the Illinois Business Corporation Act which was in force at the time when the Prior Stock was issued. Tennant versus Epstein, 356 Ill. 26, 189 N.E. 864 (1934). Thus the issue is drawn: Did the Act authorize the amendment in question? For the same contract creating a right may, by other terms and conditions, make the right defeasible by appropriate action of the stockholders. Plaintiffs are bound by their contract and cannot be heard to question action taken in accordance therewith, whether such action be taken by the stockholders or by the Company. Western Foundry Co. versus Wicker, 403 Ill. 260, 85 N.E.2d 722, 8 A.L.R.2d 878 (1949).

"The rights of the holders of the preferred stock—their so-called preemptive rights, their rights to retain their shares as against a call thereof, and their rights as to dividends—are all purely contractual. If no term of the contract authorizes a change in such rights as originally stated, then they cannot be changed. Statutes in existence when the stock is issued (and perhaps also those in existence when stock is acquired by individual shareholders) are, however, a part of the contract, and if such statutes authorize a change, then any seemingly absolute statement of such rights in other parts of the contract necessarily is to be read as subject to the changes so authorized, and such rights cannot properly be described as 'vested' in any sense which implies that they are not subject to such changes. That principle is plain and elementary." Zobel versus American Locomotive Co., 44 N.Y.S.2d 33, 35–36 (S.Ct.N.Y.1943).

Section 52 of the Business Corporation Act provides, in part:

"Right to Amend Articles of Incorporation: A corporation may amend its articles of incorporation, from time to time, in any and as many respects as may be desired, provided that its articles of incorporation as amended contain only such provisions as might be lawfully contained in original articles of incorporation if made at the time of making such amendment, and, if a change in shares or an exchange or reclassification of shares is to be made, such provisions as may be necessary to effect such change, exchange or reclassification as may be desired and is permitted by this Act.

"In particular, and without limitation upon such general power of amendment, a corporation may amend its articles of incorporation, from time to time, so as: * * * (g) To change the designation of all or any part of its shares, whether issued or unissued, and to change the preferences, qualifications, limitations, restrictions, and the special or relative rights in respect of all or any part of its shares, whether issued or unissued."

Section 14 of the Act provides, in part:

"Authorized Shares. Each corporation shall have power to create and issue the number of shares stated in its articles of incorporation. Such shares may be divided into one or more classes, any or all of which classes may consist of shares with par value or shares without par value, with such designations, preferences, qualifications, limitations, restrictions and such special or relative rights as shall be stated in the articles of incorporation." (This section goes on to set forth, "without limiting the authority herein contained," certain classes of stock which a corporation may issue.)

It is my opinion that Section 52(g), especially when read together with the introductory paragraphs of Sections 14 and 52 quoted above, clearly authorize the adoption of the amendment by Armour's stockholders. In adopting Section 52, the General Assembly used the broadest language at its disposal to allow amendments to the articles of incorporation of Illinois companies. I do not see how I can carve out from this broad grant of authority the action taken by Armour and its stockholders in 1954. A plain mandate from the Legislature may not be treated so lightly by the judiciary. * * *

The rule that a person buying into a corporation does so with the assumed knowledge that his contract may be changed by appropriate action of the stockholders is not a harsh rule. It is one of the fundamental concepts of Illinois corporate law that protection against arbitrary action is found in the requirement that a two-thirds majority of those affected by the amendment must vote in favor of it in order to have it adopted. This may result in a form of paternalism as charged by plaintiffs, but to hold otherwise would be to ask the judiciary to indulge in a judicial paternalism that would be limitless.

* * *

Next presented is plaintiff's contention that even if the plan may be said to have been authorized by the literal expressions of the Business Corporation Act, I should declare it ineffective as to them because it is unfair and contrary to equity and good conscience. They cite the well-known rule of law that the exercise of a statutory grant of power is always subject to the historical process of an equity court to judge whether there has been an oppressive exercise of the power granted. About this rule there can be no question, if it is properly understood and applied. The rule in Illinois, as in most other states, is that a recapitalization effected in accordance with power conferred by a corporation act may not be interfered with unless actual or constructive fraud is proved. Western Foundry Co. versus Wicker, supra; Kreicker versus Naylor Pipe Company, 374 Ill. 364, 29 N.E.2d 502 (1940); see Hofeller versus General Candy Corporation, 275 Ill.App. 89 (1934).

And when fraud such as this is urged as a basis for upsetting a recapitalization, it must be of such a nature as to impel the conclusion that it emanated from acts of bad faith or reckless indifference to the rights of others interested, rather than from an honest error of judgment. Barrett versus Denver Tramway Corporation, 146 F.2d 701, 706–707 (3d Cir.1944), and cases therein cited. This again may be traced to a common sense and democratic concept that barring unusual circumstances not here present, stockholders of a corporation know what is in their best interest. However, since the fairness of this action by the Company has been so strongly assailed and so vigorously defended, I feel I should discuss the evidence on this subject.

From the elaborate testimony and stipulations introduced by the parties, the following facts appear:

(1) Armour has had for many years and undoubtedly will have for many years in the future a heavy long-term debt which requires substantial annual interest and sinking fund payments.*

(2) Armour has had for many years and undoubtedly will have for many years in the future a need to spend substantial amounts of money each year for modernization and maintenance of its plants as well as for desirable diversification.

(3) Inflation required Armour to invest more and more funds into its working capital. This condition has existed for many years and will undoubtedly continue in the future.

(4) The earnings of Armour have been sporadic.**

(5) As a result of these factors, there was a shortage of funds with which to conduct the company's business. This fact is further testified to by the extensive current bank loans which the Company has had outstanding ever since 1946.

(6) Because of this shortage of funds, the dividend payments on the Prior Stock were often omitted, and there were dividends in arrears for seventeen of the twenty years during which the Prior Stock was outstanding. As of November 1, 1954, there were arrearages on the

* [Ed. Note] According to the Illinois Supreme Court opinion (infra, p. 363), in 1954, prior to the proposed plan of recapitalization, Armour's capital structure (in thousands of dollars) contained:

Long Term Debt	$124,699
Prior Stock	50,000
Common Stock	20,329
Capital and Paid in Surplus	33,619
Earned Surplus	134,079
	$362,726

** [Ed. Note] Armour's net income, as disclosed in appellee's brief in the Illinois Supreme Court and Moody's Manual of Industrials was as follows (in thousands of dollars):

Year	Total	Per Share of Common	Year	Total	Per Share of Common
1945	$ 9,172	$1.41	1953	10,339	1.81
1946	30,291	4.27	1954	1,557	.35
1947	30,950	4.91	1955	10,108	2.49
1948	(1,966)	(1.22)	1956	13,867	3.60
1949	588	(.60)	1957	3,370	.56
1950	19,039	3.94	1958	5,560	1.19
1951	16,029	3.20	1959	14,067	2.73
1952	7,140	1.02	1960	16,221	3.10

Prior Stock of $18.50 per share.*** Courts are not unaware of the problems posed by continuing arrearages in preferred stock dividends. For example, in Zogel versus American Locomotive Co. supra, the court said, at page 35:

"The existence of a large amount of unpaid cumulative dividends may well be and in many cases is detrimental to the interests of a company, and no showing is here made which enables the court to say that that is not true in this case."

Again, in Hottenstein versus York Ice Machinery Corporation, 136 F.2d 944, 952–953 (3d Cir.1943), the court said: "As a practical matter we know that it is difficult to refinance corporate indebtedness when there are heavy arrearages of accumulated dividends outstanding. A corporation so situated reasonably may expect litigation and its concomitant miseries."

(7) During the twenty years when the Prior Stock was outstanding, the common stock received a total of $1.60 per share in dividends. The Company was faced with two unhappy groups of stockholders.

These problems had been under consideration by the officers and directors of the Company for at least several years prior to 1954. In early 1954, Wertheim & Co., through Milton Steinbach, was commissioned by the President of the Company to analyze the plans which had been submitted by stockholders and to devise a plan of recapitalization which would alleviate the Company's financial difficulties. They arrived at this plan which was presented to the Board of Directors (in substantially the same form as ultimately adopted) in September of 1954. The Board acted upon it with the results herein set forth.

It appears that the plan of recapitalization had the following effects on the Company:

(1) The plan will result in more funds becoming available to the Company because of a tax saving of up to $1,560,000 annually. This tax saving occurs because of the different tax treatment given to interest on debentures as compared with dividends on preferred stock.

*** [Ed. Note] The history of Armour's dividend payments is as follows (from appellee's brief and Moody's Manual of Industrials):

| | Preferred | | Common |
	Dividends Paid	Arrearages	Cash Div. Paid
1945	$ 6.00	$28.50	—
1946	9.50	25.00	—
1947	31.00	—	—
1948	6.00	—	$.90
1949	3.00	3.00	—
1950	—	9.00	—
1951	6.00	9.00	—
1952	3.00	12.00	—
1953	6.00	12.00	—
1954	—	18.00	—
1955			
1959			None

(2) The plan will result in additional equity capital being invested in the Company upon the exercise of the warrants. Testimony showed that $2,250,000 or more has already been received by the Company from this source and that up to $8,000,000 total may be similarly received.

(3) The elimination of the accrued dividends and conversion possibility (about which more will be said later) benefitted the company and placed the common stock in a better position to enable it to reflect in market value the earnings of the company. This will help the common to become a fit vehicle for equity financing and acquisitions in the future.*

It is my opinion, therefore, that the plan of recapitalization adopted by Armour resulted in an improvement both in the capital structure of the Company and in the operating end of the Company. This was the main reason for its adoption. I turn now to analyze the changes wrought by the plan on the former Prior Stockholder, comparing the one share of Prior Stock he held before the adoption of the plan with the $120 of debentures and one warrant he held after.

(1) His annual return from his investment is unchanged, but there is a much greater assurance of payment now because interest must be

---

* [Ed. Note] Appellee's brief in the Illinois Supreme Court urged the fairness of the recapitalization in large part as a predicate to raising equity capital in the future. The brief said:

"Armour could not have raised additional capital through new long-term debt because the restrictive provisions of the existing debt would prevent * * * Armour from incurring any additional debt with a maturity of more than one year, except subordinated debt, and except certain deferred payment obligations for the purchase price of property.

"Prior to the plan of recapitalization, Armour could not have raised additional capital by common stock financing without engaging in an unorthodox financing of the most flagrant nature due to the low price at which the common stock would have had to be sold. Armour's shareholders would not have permitted Armour to try to raise additional capital by this means.

" * * *

"A major purpose of the plan was to increase the value of the common stock by improvement of Armour's capital structure so that ultimately it could be used as a means of equity financing. Armour believed this objective could be accomplished by the combined elimination of the conversion privilege and existing preferred dividend arrearages, and by the benefit obtained from tax saving.

* * * [T]he conversion privilege of six for one threatened a radical dilution of the common stock from approximately four million to seven million shares and that this possibility operated as depressant on the value of the common stock.

* * *

"In addition to this possible use of the common stock for equity financing in the future, the warrants issued in redemption of the Prior Stock resulted in Armour raising additional equity capital. Each warrant gave the holder thereof an option to purchase one share of common stock at the following prices: $12.50 per share during the years 1954–1956, $15 per share during the years 1957–1959, $17.50 per share during the years 1960–1961, and $20.00 per share during the years 1962–1964. Between the date of issuance of these warrants and the trial below, $2,250,000 in additional equity capital had been raised by the exercise of these warrants and there existed the possibility that a total of $6,000,000 would be raised by this means."

According to Moody's Manual of Industrials, Armour's assets (per books) decreased from some $470,000,000 at the end of 1954 to some $398,000,000 at the end of 1960. During that period, no new long term debt was incurred and no new equity capital was sought, or (except by reason of exercise of employee stock options and the warrants issued in the recapitalization) obtained.

paid on the debentures if earned, but payment of dividends was a discretionary act on the part of the Board of Directors. Also, the coverage is greater on the debentures: Armour had to earn $6,250,000 before taxes to pay dividends on the Par Stock in full, but it has to earn only $3,000,000 before taxes to pay interest on the debentures in full.

(2) The holders of the Prior Stock had no right to return of capital except at Armour's option. On the other hand, the debentures will mature on November 1, 1984, and there are elaborate sinking fund provisions to protect this maturity.

(3) One share of Prior Stock could be converted into six shares of common stock at the option of the holder. This right of conversion was terminated on December 21, 1954, and the debentures are not convertible. The evidence showed that no share of Prior Stock had ever been converted into common; that at no time could such conversion have ever taken place without loss to the holder in terms of market value; and that at all times since the adoption of the plan, the new package received for one share of Prior Stock could have been sold and more than six shares of common bought with the proceeds on the open market.* I am convinced that the conversion privilege was never realistic or attractive.** The directors knew this and the stockholders

---

* [Ed. Note] The market prices of Armour's common and preferred stocks and 5% debentures and warrants were as follows (according to Moody's Manual for Industrials):

	H L 1960	H L 1959	H L 1958	H L 1957
Debentures	90–81³⁄₈	86¹⁄₂–79	80–69¹⁄₂	78¹⁄₂–62¹⁄₂
Common	42³⁄₈–29	37³⁄₈–23	24⁵⁄₈–12¹⁄₈	16⁵⁄₈–10³⁄₈
Warrants	29¹⁄₂–15¹⁄₄	22³⁄₈–11³⁄₈	12⁷⁄₈–4⁵⁄₈	6¹⁄₂–3¹⁄₂

	H L 1956	H L 1955	H L 1954
Debentures	87¹⁄₂–70¹⁄₄	85–78¹⁄₄	80¹⁄₂–77¹⁄₂
Common	24–15³⁄₄	18–13¹⁄₂	14⁷⁄₈–8⁵⁄₈
Warrants	11⁷⁄₈–4¹⁄₄	8¹⁄₄–5¹⁄₂	8–4⁵⁄₈
Preferred	–	–	106³⁄₄–85³⁄₄

During 1951–1953 the preferred stock ranged in price (annually) between approximately 77 and 95 and the common stock between approximately 8¹⁄₂ and 12¹⁄₂.

** [Ed. Note] To test the correctness of this conclusion, consider the following possible dispersion of earnings per share (e/sh) and probabilities (Pr.) for Armour's common and preferred on three contingencies—events A, B and C:

	COMMON			PREFERRED		
	I 1 share	II 6 shares		III 1 sh. w/o conversion right	IV 1 share converted	V best choice
	e/sh Pr.	e/sh Pr.		e/sh Pr.	e/sh	e/sh Pr.
Event A	$4 × .2= .8	$24 × .2=4.8		$6 × .2= 1.2	$24	$24 × .2= 4.8
Event B	$2 × .3= .6	$12 × .3=3.6		$6 × .3= 1.8	$12	$12 × .3= 3.6
Event C	0 × .5= 0	0 × .5=0		$4 × .5= 2.0	0	$ 4 × .5= 2.0
Mean	$1.4	$8.4		$5	$ 8.4	$10.4

The "best choice" for the holder of the convertible preferred who looks to the future (Col. V) offers protection on the down side (by refraining from converting) combined with gain on the upside (by converting whenever in the future the contingencies look most favorable). At any given time, the convertible preferred should sell at a price higher than six shares of com-

apparently did also. The directors were also of the opinion that the conversion privilege operated to depress the value of the common stock and to prevent its use as a vehicle for acquisition and equity financing. I cannot find that the removal of the conversion right was in any respects unfair.

(4) After the plan, the Prior Stockholder had no right to the $18.50 dividends which had accrued on his share of Prior Stock of $100 stated value, but he did have $120 of debentures and the warrant. There was nothing unfair about this change. Armour's earned surplus was not supported by cash or liquid securities which would have been available for the payment of these accrued dividends. The Company's need for cash and its continuing heavy bank loans outstanding have been referred to above. The dividends on the Prior Stock could not be paid out of bricks and mortar, and the cash needs of the Company were such that it was within the discretion of the Board of Directors to withhold the payment of further cash dividends. The retention of this cash for operations, to meet the payments required on the long-term debt and to furnish needed funds for other corporate purposes outlined above is something that is committed to the directors' discretion.

The many other points raised by the plaintiffs concerning the fairness of the plan have been considered, but I do not believe that any extension of these remarks is necessary. Suffice it to say that the burden is on the plaintiffs to show that unfairness which would require me to hold the plan invalid. Dratz versus Occidental Hotel Co., supra. This burden has not been sustained. "True, plaintiffs say that the plan is so unfair to the preferred stockholders in favor of the common stockholders that it amounts to fraud, but as has been indicated above, that is here nothing more than an emphatic way of saying that as a matter of business judgment plaintiffs would rather keep what they now have. No actual bad faith is shown, and neither is there such unfairness, if any, as would justify an inference of fraud." Zobel versus American Locomotive Co. supra, * * *.

The former Prior Stockholders received in exchange for their stock marketable securities of the Company with a much greater assurance of annual return and a somewhat higher market value. The plan as noted above, redounded to the benefit of the Company. I think it was fair to all concerned. 98½% of the Prior Stock has been exchanged in accordance with this plan. The holders of these shares apparently agree with me.

From what has been said, it is also clear that plaintiffs have not been deprived of rights without the due process of law within the

mon. The reason for this is that at any given time, the conversion privilege has value (compare Col. IV with Col. III); and, assuming a known dividend policy, the value of the preferred exceeds the value of six common because its claim on the expected earnings will not go below $4, (to that extent making its owner better off than the owner of six shares of common stock) and its opportunity to share in all earnings above $6 leaves its owner no worse off than the owner of six shares of common stock. The entitlement of the holder to protection against exposure to the worst part of the dispersion and to share in the best part is a value that is not eliminated by comparing the constantly higher price of the preferred with the price of six shares of common.

purview of the fourteenth amendment to the Federal Constitution or the similar provisions of the state constitution. Dratz versus Occidental Hotel Co., supra; Goldman versus Postal Telegraph Inc., supra.

Further, the Western Foundry Co. case, supra, laid to rest any doubt that defeasible rights of preferred stockholders are not "vested." They may constitutionally be altered by appropriate corporate and stockholder action. The reason for this is that it is not unconstitutional to alter a right which the stockholder consented in advance to have alterable. So long as the rights of the stockholder lie within the confining box of stock ownership, he cannot complain of action taken in accordance with statutory power. Only by giving the plaintiffs a status as creditors—which was done in this case—can they escape from these limitations of the stockholder-corporation relationship. See Langfelder versus Universal Laboratories, 163 F.2d 804, 807 (3d Cir.1947); Mayfield versus Alton Ry. Gas & Electric Co., 198 Ill. 528, 65 N.E. 100 (1902).   * * *

————

On appeal, the Supreme Court of Illinois (Hershey, J.) reversed, holding the amendment invalid under the Illinois Business Corporation Act. Bowman v. Armour & Co., 17 Ill.2d 43, 160 N.E.2d 753 (1959). A critical part of the Supreme Court's opinion is the following (17 Ill.2d at 50–55, 160 N.E.2d at 757–60):

"The language of subparagraph (g) of section 52, authorizing amendment of articles of incorporation makes rights and privileges of preferred stock defeasible to the extent that amendments are authorized. The question here is not one of the existence of the power to amend nor is the question here one of the authority to divest certain rights and privileges. Rather, the question is whether this quoted language gives to Armour the right to amend to the extent that holders of the prior shares are required to surrender their ownership in said stock and accept in lieu thereof the earnings bonds as specified.

"The amendment, whether it is viewed as effecting a purchase of the prior stock with bonds or as a compulsory redemption thereof, obviously contemplates that the fundamental relationship of stockholder as between the holders of the prior stock and Armour will be changed and the prior stockholders will become mere creditors of the company.

"A share of stock in a corporation is a unit of interest in the corporation and it entitles the shareholder to an aliquot part of the property or its proceeds to the extent indicated. The interest of a shareholder entitles him to participate in the net profits in proportion to the number of his shares, to have a voice in the selection of the corporate officers and, upon dissolution or liquidation, to receive his portion of the property of the corporation that may remain after payment of its debts. A change in preferences, qualifications or relative rights may increase or decrease the right to participate in profits, the right to participate in distribution of the assets of the corporation on dissolution or liquidation, or other indicia of ownership manifest by the ownership of corporate stock. But the change here contemplated is more than that; it is a compulsory redemption or a purchase of the stock rather than a divestiture of certain rights and privileges.

"The plan of recapitalization here is not a divestiture of rights or privileges or an increase or decrease in relative rights of shares but it is, as we have said, a compulsory redemption or purchase that results in a change of the status of the shareholder from that of a shareholder to that of a creditor. The ownership of some equity in the corporation is not modified or changed leaving some resulting ownership, but it is liquidated and a corporate owner prior to the amendment finds that subsequent to the amendment he is a creditor.

"A corporation has no inherent right to redeem its preferred stock and can do so only if authorized by law. Fletcher Cyclopedia, Corporations, vol. 11, Permanent Ed., sec. 5309. Section 14 of our Business Corporation Act provides for the issuance of preferred shares and further provides that the same may be redeemed 'at not exceeding the price fixed by the articles of incorporation. * * *' The articles of Armour expressly provided that the prior stock could be redeemed at a price of $115 per share plus accrued dividends.

* * *

"It is the position of the plaintiffs that the only way the stock can be redeemed is by compliance with the provisions of the article and the payment in dollars of the sum therein provided. The plaintiffs assert that the word 'price,' as used in the statute, is definable only to mean money and not bonds or other evidences of debt.

* * *

"The word 'price' is used in the redemption language of section 14 and is also found in section 15 of the Business Corporation Act with reference to the issuance of preferred or special shares in a series. It is there provided that there may be variations between series of stock as to price. Further, in section 18 of the Business Corporation Act, the word 'price' is not found, and in that section it is obvious that when the legislature wished to broaden the meaning of the term it did not use the word 'price' but used the word 'consideration' and defined it to include many things—money, property, labor or services actually performed.

"A consideration of these sections can lead us only to the conclusion that when the legislature makes reference to the payment of money it uses the word 'price.' When it is concerned with a broader definition it found adequate words to express its intention.

* * *

"It seems to us to be evident that the effect of the amendment here sought to be sustained was, in fact, a purchase with bonds by the Armour Company of its own outstanding preferred stock without the consent of the owners of said stock. While the Business Corporation

Act does, under certain circumstances, permit a corporation to purchase its own stock, it can do so only when the shareholder is willing to
sell, and no amendment passed with the approval of a two-thirds vote of
the shareholders can force him to sell.

"Further, that section 52(g) should be construed as we have indicated is made more clear by referring to the express safeguards found in
the Business Corporation Act applicable to merger. Section 61 expressly provides that on merger the shares of each merging corporation may
be converted into shares or other securities or obligations of the
corporation. Section 70 provides safeguards for shareholders who may
dissent from the merger by permitting them to obtain the fair market
value of their shares. To construe section 52 as to authorize the
recapitalization plan here under consideration would mean that a
minority shareholder would not have the protection on recapitalization
that the legislature has provided on merger, even though the recapitalization plan could more drastically affect his interest than would a
merger. It is obvious to us that the legislature did not intend to
authorize a recapitalization program by amendment of the nature and
to the extent of the one here involved but, rather, by the language of
section 52(g) contemplated only changes in relative rights, privileges,
restrictions or limitations.

    * * *

"For the reasons stated, the decree of the superior Court of Cook
County is reversed and the cause is remanded to that court for the
entry of a decree in accordance with the views here expressed. * * * "

NOTES

1. In the final disposition of the case in December 1959, the
plaintiff and those stockholders participating in the suit received 7.26
shares of common stock for each surrendered share of preferred. The
number of common shares was computed by adding to the 6 shares
attributable to the conversion right 1.26 shares reflecting stock dividends between 1954 and 1959.

2. Suppose a corporation with an issue of redeemable preferred
outstanding sells all of its assets, with the result that the state business
corporation law extends to all dissenting shareholders, including the
preferred, the right to an appraisal of the "fair value" of their shares.
Will the redemption price of the preferred constitute an upward limit
on its "fair value" in the appraisal proceeding? **Breniman v. Agricultural Consultants, Inc.,** 829 P.2d 493 (Colo.Ct.App.1992), rules (over a
dissenting opinion) that fair value in such an appraisal proceeding may
be greater than the redemption price. According to the court, "fair
value" is "akin to fair market value, which is the value a shareholder
would receive for his stock if he were able to sell it in an arms-length
transaction." How much higher than the redemption price is the
market price of an issue of redeemable preferred likely to rise?

(B) ALTERATION BY MERGER
BOVE v. THE COMMUNITY HOTEL CORPORATION OF NEWPORT, RHODE ISLAND

Supreme Court of Rhode Island, 1969.
105 R.I. 36, 249 A.2d 89.

[The plaintiffs held shares of $100 par value, 6 percent cumulative preferred stock of The Community Hotel Corporation of Newport, Rhode Island. Dividends on the 4,335 outstanding shares of the stock had not been declared for 24 years; dividend arrearages totalled $645,-000, or $148.75 per share.

[The board of Community Hotel organized a shell corporation called Newport Hotel Corp. and caused Community Hotel to agree to merge into it. Under the merger, each of Community Hotel's outstanding 6 percent preferred shares, together with all accrued dividends, would be converted into 5 shares of Newport common; each share of Community Hotel's outstanding 2,106 shares of common stock would be converted into one share of Newport common. Under section 7-5-3 of the Rhode Island statute, the merger required the approval of the holders of two thirds of each class of stock.

[The court, per Justice Joslin, affirmed a judgment denying the issuance of an injunction against the accomplishment of the merger.]

It is true, of course, that to accomplish the proposed recapitalization by amending Community Hotel's articles of association under relevant provisions of the general corporation law would require the unanimous vote of the preferred shareholders, whereas under the merger statute, only a two-third vote of those stockholders will be needed. Concededly, unanimity of the preferred stockholders is unobtainable in this case, and plaintiffs argue, therefore, that to permit the less restrictive provisions of the merger statute to be used to accomplish indirectly what otherwise would be incapable of being accomplished directly by the more stringent amendment procedures of the general corporation law is tantamount to sanctioning a circumvention or perversion of that law.

The question, however, is not whether recapitalization by the merger route is a subterfuge, but whether a merger which is designed for the sole purpose of cancelling the rights of preferred stockholders with the consent of less than all has been authorized by the legislature. The controlling statute is § 7-5-2. Its language is clear, all-embracing and unqualified. It authorizes any two or more business corporations *which were or might have been organized* under the general corporation law to merge into a single corporation; and it provides that the merger agreement shall prescribe " * * * the terms and conditions of consolidation or merger, the mode of carrying the same into effect * * * *as well as the manner of converting the shares of each of the constituent corporations into shares or other securities of the corporation resulting* *from or surviving such consolidation or merger,* with such other details and provisions as are deemed necessary." [3] (italics ours) Nothing in that language even suggests that the legislature intended to make *underlying purpose* a standard for determining permissibility. Indeed, the contrary is apparent since the very breadth of the language selected presupposes a complete lack of concern with whether the merger is designed to further the mutual interests of two existing and nonaffiliated corporations or whether alternatively it is purposed solely upon effecting a substantial change in an existing corporation's capital structure.

Moreover, that a possible effect of corporate action under the merger statute is not possible, or is even forbidden, under another section of the general corporation law is of no import, it being settled that the several sections of that law may have independent legal significance, and that the validity of corporate action taken pursuant to one section is not necessarily dependent upon its being valid under another. * * *

We hold, therefore, that nothing within the purview of our statute forbids a merger between a parent and a subsidiary corporation even under circumstances where the merger device has been resorted to solely for the purpose of obviating the necessity for the unanimous vote which would otherwise be required in order to cancel the priorities of preferred shareholders. * * *

A more basic problem, narrowed so as to bring it within the factual context of this case, is whether the right of a holder of cumulative preferred stock to dividend arrearages and other preferences may be cancelled by a statutory merger. That precise problem has not heretofore been before this court, but elsewhere there is a considerable body of law on the subject. There is no need to discuss all of the authorities. For illustrative purposes it is sufficient that we refer principally to cases involving Delaware corporations. * * *

* * * [The Court contrasted the Delaware Supreme Court's decision in Keller v. Wilson & Co., 21 Del.Ch. 391, 190 A. 115 (1936), which ruled that the statutory power authorizing stockholders to amend charters did not permit an amendment cancelling accrued dividends on preferred stock, with its 1940 decision in Federal United Corp. v. Havender, 24 Del.Ch. 318, 11 A.2d 331 (1940), which ruled that the Delaware merger statute did authorize cancellation of such accruals by merger with a wholly-owned subsidiary, even though the effect of the merger was identical to that of a prohibited charter amendment. The Court then continued:]

The *Havender* approach is the one to which we subscribe as being the sounder, and it has support in the authorities. * * *

3. The quoted provision is substantially identical to the Delaware merger statute (Del.Rev.Code (1935) C. 65, § 2091) con- strued in Federal United Corp. v. Havender, 24 Del.Ch. 318, 11 A.2d 331.

The plaintiffs do not suggest, other than as they may have argued that this particular merger is a subterfuge, that our merger statute will not permit in any circumstances a merger for the sole reason that it affects accrued, but undeclared, preferred stock dividends. Rather do they argue that what should control is the date of the enactment of the enabling legislation, and they point out that in *Havender,* Federal United Corp. was organized and its stock was issued subsequent to the adoption of the statute authorizing mergers, whereas in this case the corporate creation and the stock issue preceded adoption of such a statute. That distinguishing feature brings into question what limitations, if any, exist to a state's authority under the reserved power to permit by subsequent legislation corporate acts which affect the preferential rights of a stockholder. More specifically, it raises the problem of whether subsequent legislation is repugnant to the federal and state constitutional prohibitions against the passage of laws impairing the obligations of contracts, because it permits elimination of accumulated preferred dividends by a lesser vote than was required under the law in existence at the time of the incorporation and when the stock was issued.

The mere mention of the constitutional prohibitions against such laws calls to mind Trustees of Dartmouth College v. Woodward, 17 U.S. 518, 4 Wheaton 518, 4 L.Ed. 629, where the decision was that a private corporation charter granted by the state is a contract protected under the constitution against repeal, amendment or alteration by subsequent legislation. Of equal significance in the field of corporation law is Mr. Justice Story's concurring opinion wherein he suggested that application of the impairment clause upon acts of incorporation might be avoided if a state legislature, coincident with granting a corporate charter, reserved as a part of that contract the right of amendment or repeal. With such a reservation, he said, any subsequent amendment or repeal would be pursuant, rather than repugnant, to the terms of the contract and would not therefore impair its obligation.

Our own legislature was quick to heed Story's advice, * * * and since at least as far back as 1844 the corporation law has read in substance as it does today viz., " * * * The charter or articles of association of every corporation hereafter created may be amended or repealed at the will of the general assembly." Section 7–1–13.

    * * *

The plaintiffs * * * insist that any legislation, if enacted subsequent to the creation of a corporation and the issuance of its preferred stock, may not be a source of authority for corporate action which deprives a holder of his stock or of its preferential rights or of the dividends accrued thereon. An attempt to do so, they say, constitutes an unconstitutional exercise of the reserved power. On this issue, as on most others in this case, the authorities are not in accord.

On the one side, there is a body of law which speaks of the threefold nature of the stockholder's contract and, while agreeable to an exercise of the reserved power affecting only the contractual relationship between the state and the corporation, rejects as unconstitutional any exercise which affects the relationship between the stockholder and the corporation or between the stockholders inter sese. Wheatley v. A.I. Root Co., 147 Ohio St. 127, 69 N.E.2d 187; Schaad v. Hotel Easton Co., 369 Pa. 486, 87 A.2d 227.   Under this view, subsequent legislation purporting to permit a corporate act to cancel accrued preferred dividends would obviously be an improper exercise of the power inasmuch as the essence of a preferred stockholder's contract is its definition of his relationship with the corporation and with the other stockholders vis-à-vis such matters as the distribution of the profits of the enterprise or the division of its capital and surplus account in the event of liquidation.

The other side of the argument considers that the question is primarily one of statutory construction and that so long as the statute authorizes the corporate action, it should make no difference whether its enactment preceded or postdated the birth of the corporation or the issuance of its stock.   The basis for this viewpoint is that the terms of the preferred stockholder's contractual relationship are not restricted to the specifics inscribed on the stock certificate, but include also the stipulations contained in the charter or articles of association as well as the pertinent provisions of the general corporation law.   One of those provisions is, of course, the reserved power; and so long as it is a part of the preferred shareholder's contract, any subsequent legislation enacted pursuant to it, even though it may amend the contract's original terms, will not impair its obligation in the constitutional sense.   It is as if the stock certificate were inscribed with the legend "All of the terms and conditions hereof may be changed by the legislature acting pursuant to the power it has reserved in G.L.1956, § 7–1–13."

* * *

On the basis of our own precedents we conclude that the merger legislation, notwithstanding its effect on the rights of its stockholders, did not necessarily constitute an improper exercise of the right of amendment reserved merely because it was subsequent.

* * * [P]laintiffs also contend that [the merger] is unfair and inequitable to them, and that its consummation should, therefore, be enjoined.   By that assertion they raise the problem of whether equity should heed the request of a dissenting stockholder and intervene to prevent a merger notwithstanding that it has received the vote [8] of the designated proportions of the various classes of stock of the constituent corporations.

* * *

This case involves a merger, not a recapitalization by charter amendment, and in this state the legislature, looking to the possibility

---

8. For purposes of this proceeding we have accepted the implied assumption of all of the parties that the proposed merger will receive the required vote and we have not sua sponte suggested that the suit might more properly have awaited that eventuality.

that there might be those who would not be agreeable to the proposed merger, provided a means whereby a dissatisfied stockholder might demand and the corporation be compelled to pay the fair value of his securities. G.L.1956, §§ 7–5–8 through 7–5–16 inclusive. Our inquiry then is to the effect of that remedy upon plaintiff's right to challenge the proposed merger on the ground that it is unfair and inequitable because it dictates what shall be their proportionate interests in the corporate assets. Once again there is no agreement among the authorities. Vorenberg, "Exclusiveness of the Dissenting Stockholder's Appraisal Right," 77 Harv.L.Rev. 1189. See also Annot. 162 A.L.R. 1237, 1250. Some authorities appear to say that the statutory remedy of appraisal is exclusive. Beloff v. Consolidated Edison Co., 300 N.Y. 11, 87 N.E.2d 561; Hubbard v. Jones & Laughlin Steel Corp., D.C., 42 F.Supp. 432. Others say that it may be disregarded and that equity may intervene if the minority is treated oppressively or unfairly, Barnett v. Philadelphia Market Co., 218 Pa. 649, 67 A. 912; May v. Midwest Refining Co., 1 Cir., 121 F.2d 431, cert. denied 314 U.S. 668, 62 Sup.Ct. 129, 86 L.Ed. 534, or if the merger is tainted with fraud or illegality, Adams v. United States Distributing Corp., 184 Va. 134, 147, 34 S.E.2d 244, 250, 162 A.L.R. 1227; Porges v. Vadsco Sales Corp., 27 Del.Ch. 127, 32 A.2d 148. To these differing views must also be added the divergence of opinion on whether those in control or those dissenting must bear the burden of establishing that the plan meets whatever the required standard may be. Vorenberg, supra; 77 Harv.L.Rev. 1189, 1210–1215.

In this case we do not choose as between the varying views, nor is there any need for us to do so. Even were we to accept that view which is most favorable to plaintiffs we still would not be able to find that they have been either unfairly or inequitably treated. The record insofar as it relates to the unfairness issue is at best sparse. In substance it consists of the corporation's balance sheet as of September 1967, together with supporting schedules. That statement uses book, rather than the appraised, values, and neither it nor any other evidentiary matter in any way indicates, except as the same may be reflected in the surplus account, the corporation's earning history or its prospects for profitable operations in the future.

Going to the figures we find a capital and surplus account of $669,948 of which $453,000 is allocable to the 4,530 issued and outstanding shares of $100 par value preferred stock and the balance of $216,948 to surplus. Obviously, a realization of the book value of the assets in the event of liquidation, forced or otherwise, would not only leave nothing for the common stockholders, but would not even suffice to pay the preferred shareholders the par value of their stock plus the accrued dividends of $645,000.

If we were to follow a rule of absolute priority, any proposal which would give anything to common stockholders without first providing for full payment of stated value plus dividend accruals would be unfair to the preferred shareholders. It could be argued that the proposal in this case violates that rule because an exchange of one share of Community

Hotel's preferred stock for five shares of Newport's common stock would give the preferred shareholders securities worth less than the amount of their liquidation preference rights while at the same time the one to one exchange ratio on the common would enrich Community Hotel's common stockholders by allowing them to participate in its surplus.

An inherent fallacy in applying the rule of absolute priority to the circumstances of this case, however, is its assumption that assets would be liquidated and that nothing more than their book value will be realized. But Community Hotel is not in liquidation. Instead it is a going concern which, because of its present capitalization, cannot obtain the modern debt-financing needed to meet threatened competition. Moreover, management, in the call of the meeting at which it was intended to consider and vote on the plan, said that the proposed recapitalization plan was conceived only " * * * after careful consideration by your Board of Directors and a review of the relative values of the preferred and common stocks by the independent public accountants of the Corporation. The exchange ratio of five new common shares for each share of the existing preferred stock was determined on the basis of the book and market values of the preferred and the inherent value of the unpaid preferred dividends." Those assertions are contained in a document admitted as an exhibit and they have testimonial value.

When the varying considerations—both balance sheet figures and management's assertions—are taken into account, we are unable to conclude, at least at this stage of the proceedings, that the proposed plan is unfair and inequitable, particularly because plaintiffs as dissidents may avail themselves of the opportunity to receive the fair market value of their securities under the appraisal methods prescribed in § 7–5–8 through § 7–5–16 inclusive.

The plaintiffs argue that due consideration will not be given to their dividend accruals under the appraisal. We do not agree. Jeffrey v. American Screw Co., 98 R.I. 286, 201 A.2d 146, requires that the securities of a dissident invoking the statute must be appraised by a person "versed in the intricacies of corporate finance." Such a person will find when he looks to *Jeffrey* for guidance that the evaluation process requires him to consider " * * * all relevant value factors including market value, book value, asset value, and other intrinsic factors probative of value." Certainly, unpaid dividend arrearages fall within that directive and are a relevant factor to be considered in arriving at the full and fair cash value of the plaintiffs' preferred stock. While we make no decision one way or the other on the exclusiveness of appraisal as a remedy for a dissident, we do decide that its availability is an element or a circumstance which equity should weigh before intervening. When that is done in this case, we find no ground for intervention.

For the reasons stated, the judgment appealed from is affirmed.

ROTHSCHILD INTERNATIONAL CORPORATION
v. LIGGETT GROUP INC.

Supreme Court of Delaware, 1984.
474 A.2d 133.

HORSEY, Justice.

This appeal is from a summary judgment Order of the Court of Chancery dismissing a purported class action filed by the owners of 7% cumulative preferred stock in Liggett Group, Inc. ("Liggett"), a Delaware corporation. The suit arises out of a combined tender offer and reverse cash-out merger whereby the interests of the 7% preferred shareholders were eliminated for a price of $70 per share, an amount $30 below the liquidation preference stated in Liggett's certificate of incorporation. Plaintiff-appellant asserts claims for breach of contract and breach of fiduciary duty based on the non-payment of the $30 premium.

I

Plaintiff, Rothschild International Corp., filed a class action in the Court of Chancery on behalf of 7% cumulative preferred stockholders of Liggett against defendants Liggett, Grand Metropolitan Limited ("GM"), a corporation of England, GM Sub Corporation ("GM Sub"), a Delaware corporation formed for the purpose of acquiring Liggett, and GM Sub II, a wholly-owned Delaware subsidiary of GM. The class was to consist of those 7% shareholders who tendered their preferred stock for $70 per share in response to GM's tender offer and those who did not so tender and were cashed out for the same per share price in the subsequent merger of GM Sub II into Liggett.*

On motion by defendants, GM was dismissed as a party to the action for lack of personal jurisdiction; similarly, the case against GM Sub II was dismissed as GM Sub II had ceased to exist by virtue of its merger into Liggett in August, 1980. After such dismissal, but during the pendency of plaintiff's motion for class certification, both sides moved for summary judgment on the merits of plaintiff's claims. Upon consolidation of the motions and presentation of oral argument, the Court granted defendants' motion for summary judgment.

On appeal, plaintiff contends that the takeover of Liggett via the combined tender offer and merger in essence effected a liquidation of

---

* [Ed. Note] According to the trial court (Rothschild International Corporation v. Liggett Group, Inc., 463 A.2d 642, at 644), "Under the terms of Liggett's charter, the 7% Preferred had no right to vote as a class on a merger proposal. As a consequence, even though less than 40% of the 7% Preferred tendered their shares in response to the offer, GM Sub's combined acquisition of an overwhelming majority of both Liggett's common stock and the $5.25 Convertible Preferred gave it sufficient voting power to approve a follow up merger proposal whereby all remaining shareholders of Liggett other than GM Sub were eliminated in return for the payment of cash for their shares."

the company thus warranting payment to the holders of the 7% preferred stock of the $100 liquidation value set forth in Liggett's charter. Plaintiff's breach of contract and breach of fiduciary duty claims are premised on a single assertion—that GM's plan of acquisition was equivalent to a liquidation. However, as we view the record, the transaction did not involve a liquidation of Liggett's business. Hence, we must affirm.

II

A.

There is no dispute of facts. Liggett's certificate of incorporation provided that "[i]n the event of any liquidation of the assets of the Corporation (whether voluntary or involuntary) the holders of the 7% Preferred Stock shall be entitled to be paid the par amount of their 7% Preferred shares and the amount of any dividends accumulated and unpaid thereon. * * * " [1] Under the terms of Liggett's charter, each share of the 7% security carried a $100 par value. Plaintiff makes two interrelated arguments: (1) that the economic effect of the merger was a liquidation of Liggett's assets "just as if [Liggett] were sold piece meal to Grand Met"; and (2) that any corporate reorganization that forcibly liquidates a shareholder's *interests* is tantamount to a liquidation of the *corporation* itself. From this, plaintiff argues that it necessarily follows that defendants' failure to pay the preferred shareholders the full liquidation price constituted a breach of Liggett's charter. We cannot agree with either argument.

Preferential rights are contractual in nature and therefore are governed by the express provisions of a company's certificate of incorporation. Stock preferences must also be clearly expressed and will not be presumed. See Wood v. Coastal States Gas Corp., Del.Supr., 401 A.2d 932 (1979); Ellingwood v. Wolf's Head Oil Refining Co., Del.Supr., 88 A.2d 743 (1944). See also Hibbert v. Hollywood Park, Inc., Del.Supr., 457 A.2d 339 (1983); Shanghai Power Co. v. Delaware Trust Co., Del.Ch., 316 A.2d 589, 594 (1974).

Liggett's charter stated that the $100 liquidation preference would be paid only in the event of "any liquidation of the assets of the Corporation." The term "liquidation", as applied to a corporation, means the "winding up of the affairs of the corporation by getting in its assets, settling with creditors and debtors and apportioning the amount of profit and loss." W. Fletcher, Corporations § 7968 (1979). See Sterling v. Mayflower Hotel Corp., Del.Supr., 93 A.2d 107, 112 (1952).

Our view of the record confirms the correctness of the Chancellor's finding that there was no "liquidation" of Liggett within the well-defined meaning of that term. Clearly the directors and shareholders of Liggett determined that the company should be integrated with GM, not that the corporate assets be liquidated on a "piece meal" basis.

---

1. The certificate also provided that its 7% Cumulative Preferred stock could not be redeemed, called or converted into any other security. The stock also guaranteed a fixed 7% return per annum.

The fact is that Liggett has retained its corporate identity. Having elected this plan of reorganization, the parties had the right to avail themselves of the most effective means for achieving that result, subject only to their duty to deal fairly with the minority interests.

Thus, we must construe Liggett's liquidation provision as written and conclude that the reverse cash-out merger of Liggett did not accomplish a "liquidation" of Liggett's assets. Only upon a liquidation of its assets would Liggett's preferred shareholders' charter rights to payment of par value "spring into being." Rothschild International Corp. v. Liggett Group, Del.Ch., 463 A.2d 642, 647 (1983).

Sterling v. Mayflower Hotel Corp., supra is in point on this issue. There, this Court held that a merger is not equivalent to a sale of assets. In so holding, the Court followed the well-settled principle of Delaware Corporation Law that "action taken under one section of that law is legally independent, and its validity is not dependent upon, nor to be tested by the requirements of other unrelated sections under which the same final result might be attained by different means." Orzeck v. Englehart, Del.Supr., 195 A.2d 375, 378 (1963).

It is equally settled under Delaware law that minority stock interests may be eliminated by merger. And, where a merger of corporations is permitted by law, a shareholder's preferential rights are subject to defeasance. Stockholders are charged with knowledge of this possibility at the time they acquire their shares. Federal United Corp. v. Havender, Del.Supr., 11 A.2d 331, 338 (1940). Accord, Langfelder v. Universal Laboratories, Inc., D.Del., 68 F.Supp. 209 (1946), aff'd 3rd Cir., 163 F.2d 804, 806–807 (1947); Hottenstein v. York Ice Machinery Corp., 3rd Cir., 136 F.2d 944, 950 (1943).

Plaintiff claims that reliance on *Sterling* and *Havender* for a finding that Liggett was not liquidated is misplaced. To support this claim, plaintiff variously argues: (1) that as *Sterling* and *Havender* predated cash mergers, they are not dispositive as to whether a Liggett-like takeover could constitute a liquidation; (2) that the relied-on authorities viewed a merger as contemplating the continuance of a stockholder's investment in the corporate enterprise; and (3) that because of the *Sterling/Havender* view of a merger and the unique features of the 7% preferred stock, the 7% shareholders could reasonably expect to be paid the $100 liquidation preference in any circumstance effecting a total elimination of their investment in Liggett.

The short answer to plaintiff's arguments is that, as a matter of law, stock issued or purchased prior to the Legislature's authorization of cash mergers does not entitle the stockholder to any vested right of immunity from the operation of the cash merger provision. Coyne v. Park & Tilford Distillers Corp., Del.Supr., 154 A.2d 893 (1959). Further, it is settled that the State has the reserved power to enact laws having the effect of amending certificates of incorporation and any rights arising thereunder. Id. at 897. As plaintiff is charged with knowledge of the possible defeasance of its stock interests upon a merger, Singer v. Magnavox Co., Del.Supr., 380 A.2d 969, 978 (1977), plaintiff cannot successfully argue for relief on the basis of the uniqueness of the 7% stock and the stockholders' "reasonable expectations" theory.

B.

Plaintiff also claims that Liggett and GM, acting through its subsidiary GM Sub, breached their fiduciary duties to accord to the 7% shareholders fair and equitable terms of conversion. Simply stated, plaintiff argues that, irrespective of whether a de facto liquidation occurred, "[a]ny payment less than the full liquidation price was not 'entirely fair' to the 7% Preferred stockholders."

We agree with the Chancellor that plaintiff's "fairness" argument presumes a *right* of the 7% shareholders to receive full liquidation value and does not *per se* raise the issue of the intrinsic fairness of the $70 price offered at the time of the tender offer and merger. However, even assuming *arguendo* that plaintiff did present a fairness issue, it is well settled that "the stockholder is entitled to be paid for that which has been taken from him, *viz.*, his proportionate interest in a going concern." Tri–Continental Corp. v. Battye, Del.Supr., 74 A.2d 71, 72 (1950). Moreover, the measure of "fair value" is not "liquidation value." Rather, the 7% shareholders were entitled only to an amount equal to their proportionate interests in Liggett as determined by "all relevant factors." 8 Del.C. § 262; Weinberger v. UOP, Inc., Del.Supr., 457 A.2d 701 (1983); Tri–Continental Corp. v. Battye, supra.

Thus, having reviewed the transaction, we find that the Chancellor did not err as a matter of law in granting defendants' motion for summary judgment.

* * *

Affirmed.

NOTES

1. The reasoning of *Rothschild v. Liggett* is extended so as to defeat the proposition that a merger constitutes a redemption of preferred stock in Rauch v. RCA Corp., 861 F.2d 29 (2d Cir.1988), and Dart v. Kohlberg, Kravis, Roberts & Co., 1985 WL 21145 (1985).

2. In **Kirschner Bros. Oil, Inc. v. Natomas Co.,** 185 Cal.App.3d 784, 229 Cal.Rptr. 899 (1986), preferred holders in pursuit of a class veto of a transaction unsuccessfully advanced a "de facto" argument. The merger agreement in question provided for the acquisition of the issuer by reverse triangular merger of an acquisition subsidiary of the acquirer into the issuer. The merger agreement provided that the preferred receive preferred stock of a new holding company formed in connection with the transaction. Class votes by both the preferred and common of the issuer were provided for. But the merger agreement also provided

that in the event the preferred did not approve the transaction by class vote, the transaction would go forward anyway; the preferred would be left outstanding, holding stock of an issuer the common stock of which was held by the acquirer. Here the control parties took advantage of a provision of the California statute excusing the requirement of a class vote by preferred shares of surviving corporations the rights and preferences of which were left unchanged by the merger. The preferred argued that in the context of a reverse triangular merger they should not be deemed shareholders of the "surviving corporation," but de facto, holders of shares of the transferor. The court held against them, and also held that the transaction structure did not constitute a breach of fiduciary duty.

3. The Delaware Chancery Court was asked to subject to fairness scrutiny the treatment accorded to a class of preferred in connection with a management buyout in **Dart v. Kohlberg, Kravis, Roberts & Co.**, 1985 WL 21145 (Del. Ch. 1985). The claim survived a motion to dismiss.

The preferred stock in question was first issued by Amstar Corp. in 1967. It initially sold for $12.50 per share, and was entitled to a $0.68 per share annual dividend. The Certificate provided for redemption at the issuer's option for $13.125 per share, and entitled the holders to $12.50 upon liquidation. The Certificate also provided that no change could be made of any of the express terms of the preferred stock which would adversely affect the holder of the stock without an affirmative vote of two-thirds of the holders of the stock.

In 1982 and 1983 two other corporations began accumulating significant positions in Amstar common. As a result, Amstar's managers began looking for a friendly acquisition partner. They entered into discussion with KKR Associates. In October 1983 Amstar and KKR Associates entered into an agreement pursuant to which KKR would form an acquisition subsidiary which would merge into Amstar. The common stockholders of Amstar would receive $47 cash for their shares; KKR Associates would be left with the common stock of Amstar; management would receive stock options designed to leave it holding 8 percent of the stock of Amstar post-merger.

Initially, the merger agreement made no provision for the preferred. It later was amended to provide for a cash out of the preferred at $8 per share (a premium over the then market price), subject to an affirmative vote by two-thirds of the holders of the preferred. But only 60 percent of the preferred cast affirmative votes. As a result, the preferred was not cashed out and remained outstanding as a security of a privately held and heavily indebted Amstar.

The court discussed the plaintiff's claim as follows:

"Although the plaintiff has not shown any legal basis for his claim that the preferred stockholders should have been permitted to vote as a separate class on the entire merger, inequitable action does not become permissible simply because it is legally possible. Schnell v. Chris–Craft Industries, Inc., Del.Supr., 285 A.2d 437 (1971). Although everything done by defendants may have been in strict compliance with the letter of Delaware law, it is possible that the totality of actions resulted in an impermissible inequity to the holders of the preferred stock. The difficulty with the challenged transaction is that it was highly leveraged and a majority of the preferred stockholders ended up still owning their shares although they preferred to be bought out. The assets of the corporation were used as sole security for the loans obtained for the purpose of buying out the common stock and the public preferred stockholders were left holding their shares in a corporation which, as a result of the transaction, has a much greater debt and therefore perhaps a lessened ability to pay preferred dividends. Such a leveraged buy-out calls for judicial scrutiny to prevent possible abuse. On the present record, therefore, which does not contain the fruits of full discovery, it can be at least reasonably inferred that plaintiff has a cause of action, however imperfectly stated and however speculative, as to the allegations which attack the leveraged buy-out and its effect on the preferred stockholders."

DALTON v. AMERICAN INVESTMENT CO.
Delaware Court of Chancery, 1985.
490 A.2d 574.

[This case concerned the 1980 acquisition of American Investment Company ("AIC") by a wholly owned subsidiary of Leucadia, Inc. AIC had 5.5 million common shares outstanding and two issues of preferred. The plaintiffs held noncallable 5½% Series B having a stated redemption and liquidation value of $25. Because of increases in interest rates after the issue of the Series B in 1961, the stock, which had no trading market, had a market value of less than $9 during the events in question.

[AIC had been on the market for an acquirer before Leucadia came along. Two years earlier, Household Finance Corporation ("HFC") offered to acquire AIC for a total consideration of $75 million, distributed $12 per share to the common and $25 per share to the preferred. The deal aborted when the Justice Department objected on antitrust grounds. Thereafter, the President of AIC, Brockmann, continued to market the company, alluding to the book value of the common stock, about $13.50, as the basis on which a successful offer should be made.

[Leucadia's initial offer was $13 for the common and nothing for the preferred. Brockmann then suggested that "something should be done" for the preferred, and Leucadia added an offer to increase the dividend rate on the preferred from 5½% to 7% and set up a sinking fund to retire the stock over 20 years.

[The merger negotiations also involved a third party interested in purchasing some of AIC's receivables. The deal included a sale of $130 million of these receivables to the third party for $120 million cash. As a result, AIC came to Leucadia with a pot of cash containing much more than the $72.2 million purchase price. All of the directors of AIC owned common; their holdings collectively amounted to 12% of the outstanding common. One director held preferred. No preferred class vote was held. In the pooled vote for the merger, the Series B holders voted 170,000 of the 280,000 shares outstanding against the merger.]

Plaintiffs suggest that what Brockmann and the other directors did was note that HFC had offered to pay a total of $75.7 million to acquire AIC, broken down into components of $66.5 million for the common ($12 per share × roughly 5.5 million shares) and $9.2 million for the total of the two series of preferred ($25 per share × some 361,000 shares). They say that simple arithmetic shows that AIC's 1980 book value of $13.50 for the common shares multiplied by the 5.5 million common shares outstanding worked out to approximately $75 million. Since it was not necessary for a potential acquirer to cash out the preferred shareholders in order to gain control of the company, and since the AIC board viewed the offer of HFC to purchase the preferred shares at their redemption value of $25 per share as having been a potential "Christmas present" to the preferred shareholders anyway, plaintiffs charge that what Brockmann did, with the board's ultimate approval, was to suggest the book value of the common stock as the starting point for any merger offer so as to assure that the whole of any new offer would go totally to the owners of the common shares.

* * *

Plaintiffs Claims

In sum, plaintiffs contend that the failure of the defendant directors to treat their interests evenhandedly with those of the common shareholders has damaged them financially by leaving them as minority shareholders in a de-listed company and as the owners of an unmarketable preferred stock paying only a meager return when measured by present-day standards. They charge that the defendant directors knowingly took the action which has served to lock them in as preferred shareholders of AIC when, had they properly exercised the fiduciary duty of fair dealing owed to all shareholders, they could have extricated the plaintiffs at a fair price as well. For this alleged wrong, plaintiffs demand monetary damages.

* * *

[D]efendants point out that Leucadia's view of the preferred shares as "cheap debt", and the fact that Leucadia was well aware that it could accomplish its goal of acquiring AIC without the need to purchase the preferred shares, left Brockmann and the other members of AIC's board with absolutely no leverage with which to negotiate a pay-out for the preferred. Moreover, had they attempted to do so once Leucadia made its offer, two consequences were possible—both being fraught with danger insofar as AIC's board was concerned.

First, if AIC's board had attempted to persuade Leucadia to reduce its $13 per share for the common by some portion in order that the difference might be used to cash out the preferred shareholders, such conduct could have been viewed as a breach of the fiduciary duty of fair dealing owed to the common shareholders and subjected the board members to suit for this reason. Alternatively, such an effort by the AIC board might have caused Leucadia to believe that it could acquire the common shares for less than $13 per share, in which event Leucadia might have reduced its offer for the common and still offered nothing for the preferred—again subjecting the board to potential suit by the common shareholders. And, of course, there was always the possibility that if AIC's board rejected the proposal for its failure to include a price for the preferred shares, Leucadia could have backed off and gone the tender offer route for the common shares so as to acquire control in that manner and bring about a merger under its own terms at some later date.

[The court reasoned that the "Hobson's choice defense raised by the defendant directors * * * misses the point" and that case turned on "the factual determination of whether or not Leucadia's offer was made in response to a solicitation by Brockmann and the other director defendants."]

When the trimmings of precedent and fiduciary duty are brushed aside, plaintiffs' argument, reduced to its simplest terms, is (1) that between the HFC proposal in 1978 and the Leucadia merger in 1980 the price per share for the common stock was increased from $12 to $13 per share while the preferred shareholders went from $25 per share to no cash consideration whatever, and (2) that during the interval between the two events Brockmann and the AIC board were soliciting offers at book value, or $13.50, for the common shares while seeking nothing for the preferred. From these two premises plaintiffs proceed to the conclusion that the difference between the HFC and Leucadia proposals was necessarily a direct result of the efforts by the AIC board to increase the cash consideration from the common stock with knowledge that such an increase would be at the expense of the preferred shares. Having thus bridged the gap to arrive at this factual conclusion, plaintiffs then plug it into the legal principle which holds that it is improper for those in a fiduciary position to utilize the merger process solely to promote the interests of one class of shareholders to the detriment, and at the expense, of the members of a minority class of shareholders. Thus plaintiffs reach their final position that they have been injured monetarily by the failure of the defendant directors to adhere to their fiduciary duty to deal fairly with all shareholders in a merger context.

[The court ruled against the plaintiffs on a finding of causation. Reviewing the evidence on the formulation of the Leucadia offer, it found that the offer had been determined by the offeror's business interests and had not been "made in direct response to a veiled solicitation by Brockmann."]

(C) OTHER MODES OF ALTERATION OR ELIMINATION

Apart from recapitalizations and mergers, problems of fairness can be raised by other efforts to modify preferred stockholders' rights, even though the alterations conform, in all formal respects, to the requirements of charter and statute. Not only is the ultimate asset priority embodied in the liquidation preference of preferred stock subject to amendment (RMBCA §§ 10.03, 10.04; Del.Corp.Law § 242; NYBCL §§ 801–804), but the income priority embodied in the preferential claim to dividends may also be amended (see e.g., Johnson v. Bradley Knitting Co., 228 Wis. 566, 280 N.W. 688 (1938); Blumenthal v. Di Giorgio Fruit Corp., 30 Cal.App.2d 11, 85 P.2d 580 (1938); Western Foundry Co. v. Wicker, 403 Ill. 260, 85 N.E.2d 722 (1949)). So too, the amendment process is available to modify the various protective features of the preferred stock contract which are designed to increase the likelihood of the payment of dividends and of the liquidation or redemption priority (such as a sinking fund provision or a special provision restricting the payment of dividends to common stock), and other features which affect its investment value, such as the noncallable feature, the redemption price, or the conversion rights or voting rights. See e.g. Morris v. American Pub. Util. Co., 14 Del.Ch. 136, 122 A. 696 (1923); compare Breslav v. New York & Queens Elec. Light & P. Co., 249 App.Div. 181, 291 N.Y.S. 932 (2nd Dept.1936), aff'd without opinion, 273 N.Y. 593, 7 N.E.2d 708 (1937) with Beloff v. Consolidated Ed. Co., 300 N.Y. 11, 87 N.E.2d 561 (1949) and N.Y. § 801(b)(12). See Note, Limitations on Alteration of Shareholders' Rights by Charter Amendment, 69 Harv.L.Rev. 538 (1954).

Are the same considerations that impelled Judge Leahy to find apparently unconstrained freedom to bind dissenters to amendment of the liquidation preference in the *Goldman* case likely to affect amendment of the protective, redemption, or other features of the preferred stock contract?

Why do the commons seek such amendments?

Why do the preferreds consent to them?

(1) Repurchase

Eisenberg v. Chicago Milwaukee Corp., 537 A.2d 1051 (Del.Ch. 1987), involved a company that had effectively sold off most of its business in 1985 and thereafter held approximately $300 million in cash and real estate appraised at $90 million while it sought a new business or businesses. It had outstanding approximately 2.5 million shares of common stock and 464,000 shares of noncumulative preferred stock with an annual dividend preference of $5 per share (approximately $2.34 million annually) and an aggregate liquidation preference of approximately $46,400,000. The company declined to pay dividends on the preferred during the years in which it sought a new line of business. By reason of the default in preferred dividends, the preferred stockholders elected two of the company's ten directors. The eight common stock directors and their affiliates owned no appreciable amount of the preferred, but did own approximately 41 percent of the common stock.

The preferred stock traded during the period from 1985 to October 16, 1987 at prices ranging between $52.50 and $80.25, gradually declined in price during 1987 and reached its low of $52.50 on October 16. On Black Monday, October 19, 1987, the stock dropped to $42.50. By October 27 the price had declined to $41.50. The directors, deciding to take advantage of the sharp price decline, caused the company to make a tender offer for its preferred stock at $55 per share and announced that the company would move to delist the stock. Holders of the preferred sought to enjoin the tender offer on the grounds that (1) the tender solicitation materials were misleading in failing, among other things, to disclose the conflict of interest of the common stock directors and their purpose to take advantage of the price drop resulting after Black Monday, and (2) the tender offer was improperly coercive.

On the claim that the materials were misleading, the court started with the premise that the corporation and its directors owed the preferred the "exacting duty of disclosure imposed upon corporate fiduciaries" and found, as claimed by the plaintiffs, that duty not to have been met. On the coercion claim, the court also rested on fiduciary theory and reasoned as follows, 537 A.2d p. 1061–1062:

"The plaintiff argues that the Offer is inequitably coercive, because: (i) it was purposefully timed to coincide with the lowest market price for the Preferred since 1983, (ii) the offer occurs against the background of an announced Board policy of not paying dividends, despite CMC's present ability to do so, and (iii) CMC has announced that it intends to seek the delisting of the Preferred shares.

"The defendants respond that the Offer, while perhaps "coercive" in the sense that its economic merits may make it more attractive to tender than not to tender, is not "actionably" coercive, because the defendants have committed no wrongful or inequitable coercive act.

"In these circumstances the coercion issue is not easy to decide. To be sure, the directors have timed the Offer to coincide with the lowest Preferred stock price levels since 1983. They have also made a business judgment (one that at this stage must be presumed valid) not to pay dividends on, or to redeem, the Preferred. Given those circumstances, Preferred stockholders may perceive, not unreasonably, that unless they tender, they may not realize any return on or value for their investment in the foreseeable future. In that sense the offer does have coercive aspects. And the coercion may be attributed, at least to some extent, to acts of the directors (namely, their timing of the Offer and their no-dividend policy) rather than to market forces alone.

"If these were the only relevant circumstances (and if proper disclosure was made of all material facts), the Court would have difficulty concluding, at least on this preliminary record, that the Offer

is inequitably coercive. In what sense do corporate directors behave
inequitably if they cause the corporation to offer to purchase its own
publicly-held shares at a premium above market, even if the market
price is at an historic low? So long as all material facts are candidly
disclosed, the transaction would appear to be voluntary. The only
arguable inequity is that if the offer is successful, it may result in a
decrease in the number and market value of the outstanding shares
and in the number of shareholders. That state of affairs, in turn,
would create the possibility that shares not tendered will be delisted
and/or deregistered. However, that possibility and its disclosure in the
offering materials, without more, has been held to be not wrongfully
coercive. See Klein v. Soundesign Corp., supra at 8; Fisher v. Plessey
Co., 559 F.Supp. 442, 451 (S.D.N.Y.1983).

"In this case, however, the defendants have done more than simply
acknowledge the possibility of delisting and deregistration; they have
told the Preferred stockholders that CMC *intends to request* delisting
of the Shares from the NYSE." (Emphasis added.) It is that disclosure
which tips the balance and impels the Court to find that the Offer, even
if benignly motivated, operates in an inequitably coercive manner.

"CMC's directors are fiduciaries for the Preferred stockholders,
whose interests they have a duty to safeguard, consistent with the
fiduciary duties owed by those directors to CMC's other shareholders
and to CMC itself. Those directors have disclosed that they intend to
seek to eliminate a valuable attribute of the Preferred stock, namely,
its NYSE listing. That listing is the source of that security's market
value, and its elimination will adversely affect the interests of nontendering Preferred shareholders. On what basis are the defendants, as
fiduciaries, entitled to do that? Defendants do not claim that they are
obliged to seek delisting in order to protect a paramount interest of the
corporation or an overriding interest of the common stockholders.
What they seem to argue is that the criticized disclosure is not coercive
because it is not material, because if the criteria for listing are no
longer met, the stock will be delisted automatically, irrespective of and
without regard to any action of the directors.

"That argument has two infirmities. First, it is inconsistent with
the Offer to Purchase, which discloses that if the listing criteria are no
longer met, the NYSE "would consider" delisting the shares. That
disclosure does not say that delisting will be automatic. Second, if the
defendants are correct in their argument that delisting will occur
automatically as a matter of law, then they need not disclose that CMC
"intends to request delisting." Such a disclosure is unnecessary and,
therefore, misleading. The only apparent purpose of such a disclosure
would be to induce shareholders to tender by converting a possibility of
delisting into a likelihood or certainty. On that basis it must be
concluded that the Offer is inequitably coercive."

The source of the directors fiduciary duties to the preferred in the repurchase transaction is not entirely clear. It is plain that there was no fiduciary (or contractual) duty either to redeem the preferred or to liquidate, notwithstanding the long period during which the company's assets consisted principally of cash and it was engaged in no business. Possibly a contractual duty to pay dividends during that period could be spelled out, but neither logic nor case law imposes such a duty. In the absence of either a fiduciary or contractual obligation of the common to the preferred in the above respects, in what sources can any such duty be rooted, whether to disclose motives or to refrain from the kind of coercion involved? To be sure, fiduciary obligations of those kinds can be rooted in the relationship of management or directors to the common stock, or even controlling common stock to minority common stock. But on what theory can (or should) such obligations be found to run to preferred stock? If the case for a duty is to be made, is it better made on a contractual or fiduciary theory?

(2) Dissolution

Suppose a controlling stockholder, holding all the common and an entire issue of first preferred, seeks to dissolve the corporation, and a shareholder holding second preferred seeks to enjoin the dissolution on the ground that continuance of the corporation eventually would result in dividend payments on the second preferred? This was the claim in **Burton v. Exxon Corp.,** 583 F.Supp. 405 (S.D.N.Y.1984). Exxon held all of the first preferred stock and 90 percent of the common stock of Eurgasco, a corporation formed during the 1930s to explore for oil and gas in Eastern Europe. Eurgasco had never paid any dividends on any of its stock. By 1977, dividend arrearages on the first preferred amounted to $6.5 million. Plaintiff owned shares of an issue of second preferred stock on which arrearages totalled $2.3 million in 1977.

Eurgasco's only reason for continued existence was the prosecution of claims for compensation of assets nationalized by the Hungarian government after World War II. Between 1977 and 1980, Eurgasco received $9 million in total payment of these claims and earned $823,000 of interest income on these funds. Between 1977 and 1980, Eurgasco declared a series of large dividends, all of which were paid in compliance with its charter to Exxon as the holder of the first preferred. By the time the stream of claims payments stopped in 1980, Eurgasco had $2.8 million left. Its board, comprised of Exxon nominees, determined to dissolve it. This would result in the entire $2.8 million being paid to Exxon as first preferred holder, since the stock still had $2.8 million of dividend arrearages plus a liquidation preference of $2.3 million. But the votes of two-thirds of the holders of the second preferred were required to approve the dissolution, and most of these holders either voted no or failed to return proxies. As a result, Exxon filed a petition for judicial dissolution in the Delaware courts. Plaintiff brought a federal action to enjoin the dissolution proceeding, claiming breaches of fiduciary duty.

The court, applying *Sinclair v. Levien,* infra p. 575, held that the dividend payments constituted self dealing on the part of Exxon. The test, it said, "is not whether the minority stockholders were entitled to the item transferred but whether the minority stockholders were excluded from, or damaged by, the transfer * * * to the * * * majority stockholder." The fact that the charter did not entitle plaintiffs to dividend payments did not block the self dealing finding, but was "important only in so far as deciding whether the dividend decision was intrinsically fair."

The plaintiff claimed that the dividends were unfair on the theory that, given prevailing interest rates in the late 1970s, the rate of return on reinvested funds exceeded the rate of arrearage accruals, permitting Eurgasco to reinvest the funds so as to cause the eventual payment of arrearages on both issues of preferred. The court rejected the claim and ruled that the dividends were intrinsically fair, and that the plaintiff's case against the dissolution proceeding accordingly was moot. The court gave two reasons. First, high returns on reinvested funds were not certain at the time the decision to make the dividends was made in 1977. At the rate levels prevailing in 1977, it would have taken until 2024 to pay down all the arrearages. That the higher rates prevailing in 1978–1983 would have brought forward the payoff date to 1991 did not change matters. Second, the board owed fiduciary duties to the first preferred as well as the second preferred. Had the board decided to retain the funds, the first preferred might have successfully claimed a breach of fiduciary duty. Citing *Baron v. Allied Artists,* the court stated that "[i]n keeping with prudent business management, the board of directors does have a fiduciary duty to see that preferred dividend arrearages are brought up to date as soon as possible."

Suppose you were the judge presiding over Exxon's Delaware proceeding to dissolve Eurgasco. How would you rule?

(3) Coerced Exchange

In **Barrett v. Denver Tramway Corporation,** 53 F.Supp. 198 (D.Del.1943), affirmed, 146 F.2d 701 (3d Cir.1944), abnormal wartime earnings created a source of large dividends for the common stock of Denver Tramway Corporation which could be distributed if only the arrearages on the preferred could be eliminated. The corporation effectively cancelled the preferred's arrearages by the device of authorizing a new prior preferred stock and offering to exchange two shares of the new stock for each share of the old preferred. Each prior preferred share carried a liquidation price equal to about one half the sum of the liquidation price plus the arrearage on each old share, and dividends on the new stock were comparably scaled to produce approximately the same dividends on two shares of new preferred as were provided on one share of old. Those holders of old preferred who accepted the offer could expect dividends from the bulging earnings. Those who did not accept the offer remained with their old preferred, whose claims were subordinate to those of the new preferred, and were therefore unable to receive dividends if these new preferred were not fully paid.   The common stock gambled on the whip-saw effect to induce the exchange and thus eliminate the arrearage obstacle to the flow of dividends to it—and it won.   When dissident holders of old preferred challenged the scheme as unfair (even if technically conforming to the Delaware statute), the court (Leahy, J.) reluctantly held the scheme not to be unfair under Delaware caselaw.

4. LIMITATIONS ON PERMISSIBLE ALTERATIONS

We have seen that the process by which preferred stock's contractual claims to principal (on liquidation or redemption) or to arrearages are altered and circumvented may vary in form—whether it be by amendment of the charter, by merger, by exchange offer, or otherwise. In addition to problems of contract interpretation and charges of violation of statutory process, each such claim may also generate assertions of entitlement to other kinds of protection against exploitation by the commons—and to judicial consideration.   These claimed entitlements are to (A) fairness of treatment, (B) adequate disclosure, and (C) class voting.

(A) FAIRNESS

At the outset it is necessary to consider why the courts examine, and sometimes even seek to impose limitations of "fairness" on alterations of preferred stockholders' rights at the petition of dissenting preferred stockholders.

If the preferred's investment contract, by its terms, ever expressly provides for the possibility of any such changes, even by a class vote, that feature of the contract is rarely pressed on the attention of the investor in selling him the stock.   Nor, certainly, is there any reason to believe that the possibility of effecting such alterations by contrived merger is called to the attention of the investor.   Hence, for courts to find buried in the contracts drafted by the commons' representatives, or to import from the local corporations code, the preferreds' consent, even to the power of a majority of the class, to amend or merge or "voluntarily" exchange arrears out of existence or otherwise alter particular preferences or protection, is not to suggest that the preferreds actually bargained for those terms.   Nor is it to find that they were communicated to, or understood by, those buying the stock—except possibly by the osmotic process that makes the market an efficient discounter not only of economic information and contingencies, but of legal changes and potential for maneuver.

If the obscurity of the message with respect to the potential for altering their rights conveyed to investors by the investment contract should invite judicial willingness to consider limits on the scope of that potential, the politics of the readjustment process likewise suggest imposition of limits on such "rebargaining". As we saw in the case of debt securities, the need to import such limits is no less, and indeed a good deal more, compelling in the case of a voluntary recapitalization or amendment or merger than in the case of an insolvency readjustment. Apart from their disadvantage of economic position as against the commons (derived from the different impact of delay in payment on the preferreds and commons)[j] the preferreds are also at a disadvantage in the *process* of bargaining in a recapitalization, a disadvantage substantially greater than that of bondholders.[k] To those impediments must be added the fact that preferred stock recapitalization may be described as a bargain only by a loose euphemism. No real bargaining takes place. Inevitably the plan originates with management, in contrast to the diversity of plans and bargainers which is possible, if no longer contemplated, by the insolvency reorganization process. The proxy apparatus is in control of management, which thus has the advantage of primary access to the finances and facilities to solicit consents and the ability to control the information disclosed to those solicited, as well as ability to time the plan on short notice. In the past, management has not been required either to spell out the character of the economic disaster it was proposing for the preferreds or to indicate that there might be less costly alternatives. In contrast, the insolvency reorganization process, even under Chapter 11, envisions bargaining by committees which have some potential for exposing claimants to the

j. Delay favors the juniors and disfavors the seniors, albeit somewhat more in the insolvency situation than in the circumstances inviting recapitalization. Investors in preferred stock look for a continuous cash return; the possibility of increment in the value of their stock from corporate reinvestment of the cash flow is, by definition, limited. Moreover, delay in the flow of dividends will further depress the market price of their stock, while a resumption of that flow may increase it. Hence, the promise of an immediate cash flow—even though much less than is due—is an irresistible temptation to sacrifice larger future increments, which the presumed prosperity would produce for the preferreds before the commons could receive anything. To be sure, common stock also has some interest in avoiding delay. Its price on the market is adversely affected by the lack of dividends and the size of the arrearage obstacle to its receipt of dividends. But the cost of delay is apt to be less to the common stockholder, because he is gambling principally on the preferreds' capital; and the residual character of his invest-ment position in a depressed enterprise which appears to have "turned the corner" implies that he has a larger proportionate interest in any improvement in the enterprise (and the retention of its earnings) than does the preferred stockholder.

k. The preferreds are likely to be widely scattered and disorganized, in contrast to the common stock represented by management functioning as a coherent bargaining unit. And financial intermediaries or institutional investors, around which an opposition bargaining unit can be formed, are often less likely to hold substantial positions in preferred stock than in bonds. Moreover, to the extent that bondholders have a much more substantial stake in the outcome of an insolvency reorganization (which involves a complete reallocation of their full participations) than do preferred stockholders in an arrearage elimination or other particular alteration, the incentive is greater to make the expenditures necessary for organization and to engage in strenuous bargaining and litigation.

possibility of alternatives that are less disadvantageous
proposed by the debtor.

In such circumstances, it may be an overstatement †
the common stockholders can impose their will unila
preferreds when they propose a recapitalization.   Bu·
denied that there is considerably greater freedom of action ior ᴜⁱᴜ
common stockholders and substantially less protection for the preferred
stockholders than is present for seniors in insolvency reorganization.
As an observer of the process has remarked, "through the bargaining
leverage of common stockholdings" preferreds have regularly "been
euchred, cajoled, coerced, elbowed and traded out of their legal rights." [l]
Accordingly, there is much to be said for judicial intervention in, if not
actual supervision of the process.   There is little doubt that courts have
recognized this "political" reason for setting limits on the recapitalization bargain.   The chief difficulty appears to have been their inability
to formulate standards or criteria for determining the appropriate
limits of the bargain.   See Brudney, Standards of Fairness and the
Limits of Preferred Stock Modifications, 26 Rutgers L.Rev. 445 (1973).

(1) Doctrinal Bases

If "tribute" may thus be exacted from the preferred stock by the
commons in recapitalizations or other restructurings or in bona fide
cash-out mergers, on what legal theory are courts empowered to prevent or limit such exaction if the transaction is not found to violate any
statutory strictures?   Is any such theory revealed in the materials so
far studied?

Is the problem appropriately addressed as a matter of contract
interpretation?   That is, does the preferred stock contract permit the
proposed transaction?   For example, is the "consent" of the dispersed
preferred stockholders to an amendment or a proposal that is timed
and made by the common (as in *Barrett, Bove,* or *Armour*) the kind of
approval that the investment contract should be deemed to have
contemplated or permitted?   What theory of contract interpretation
precludes (or permits) either (i) a bona fide merger with a stranger in
which the common stock is cashed out but the preferred stock remains
outstanding in the old corporate form in which the acquirer now owns
all the common stock (*Dalton*), or (ii) a management buyout (*Dart*) or
parent subsidiary merger (*Kirschner*) on similar terms?

If contract interpretation does not adequately address the preferreds' problems in the above transactions, does the relationship of
commons to preferreds permit the fiduciary notion to be invoked to
protect the preferreds against such exaction of tribute by the commons?
If so, how do fiduciary constraints operate?   Is light shed by the
following standard of scrutiny in respect of fiduciary duty to preferred

l. In the Matter of International Paper
& Power Co., 2 S.E.C. 1004, 1023–24 (1937).

stockholders articulated by Chancellor Allen, in **Jedwab v. MGM Grand Hotels, Inc.,** 509 A.2d 584, 594–595 (Del.Ch.1986):

"[W]ith respect to matters relating to preferences or limitations that distinguish preferred stock from common, the duty of the corporation and its directors is essentially contractual and the scope of the duty is appropriately defined by reference to the specific words evidencing that contract; where however the right asserted is not to a preference as against the common stock but rather a right shared equally with the common, the existence of such right and the scope of the correlative duty may be measured by equitable as well as legal standards.

"With this distinction in mind the Delaware cases which frequently analyze rights of and duties towards preferred stock in legal (i.e., contractual) terminology (e.g., *Wood v. Coastal States Gas Corp.,* supra; Judah v. Delaware Trust Company, Del.Supr., 378 A.2d 624 (1977); *Rothschild International Corp. v. Liggett Group, Inc.,* supra) may be made consistent with those cases that apply fiduciary standards to claims of preferred shareholders (e.g., David J. Greene & Co. v. Schenley Industries, Inc., Del.Ch., 281 A.2d 30 (1971); Lewis v. Great Western United Corporation, Del.Ch., C.A. No. 5397, Brown, V.C. (September 15, 1977)).

* * *

"Assuming that plaintiff and the other preferred shareholders have a "right" recognized in equity to a fair apportionment of the merger consideration (and such a right to require directors to exercise appropriate care) it becomes material to know what legal standard is to be used to assess the probability that a violation of that right will ultimately be proven. Plaintiff asserts that the appropriate test is one of entire or intrinsic fairness. That test is the familiar one employed when fiduciaries elect to utilize their power over the corporation to effectuate a transaction in which they have an interest that diverges from that of the corporation or the minority shareholders. See, *Weinberger v. UOP, Inc.,* supra; Gottlieb v. Heyden Chemical Corp., Del.Supr., 91 A.2d 57 (1952).

"Our Supreme Court has made it quite clear that the heightened judicial scrutiny called for by the test of intrinsic or entire fairness is not called forth simply by a demonstration that a controlling shareholder fixes the terms of a transaction and, by exercise of voting power or by domination of the board, compels its effectuation. (The apparent situation presented in this action.) It is in each instance essential to show as well that the fiduciary has an interest with respect to the transaction that conflicts with the interests of minority shareholders. Aronson v. Lewis, Del.Supr., 473 A.2d 805, 812 (1984). Speaking in the context of a parent dealing with a controlled but not wholly-owned subsidiary our Supreme Court has said:

The basic situation for the application of the rule [requiring a fiduciary to assume the burden to show intrinsic fairness] is the one in which the parent has received a benefit to the exclusion and at the expense of the subsidiary.

* * *

"A parent does indeed owe a fiduciary duty to its subsidiary when there are parent-subsidiary dealings. However, this alone will not evoke the intrinsic fairness standard. This standard will be applied only when the fiduciary duty is accompanied by self-dealing—the situation when a parent is on both sides of a transaction with its subsidiary. Self-dealing occurs when the parent, by virtue of its domination of the subsidiary, causes the subsidiary to act in such a way that the parent receives something from the subsidiary to the exclusion of, and detriment to, the minority stockholders of the subsidiary.

Sinclair Oil Corporation v. Levien, Del.Supr., 280 A.2d 717, 720 (1971)."

If fiduciary principles apply to preferred stock, as *Jedwab* suggests, then did the leveraged buyout in *Dart,* supra p. 376, create a case for intrinsic fairness scrutiny? What benefit did the majority receive "to the exclusion and at the expense" of the preferred?

———

(2) Substantive Criteria

Whether the theory that justifies judicial intervention to protect the preferreds is rooted in contract or fiduciary considerations or in some other grounds, it inevitably implicates the question of substantive fairness of the transaction. Is the test of substantive fairness whether the "get" is in some sense the equivalent of the "give up"? How should the courts and parties measure each? Or is some other standard of fairness involved? Answers to, or at least consideration of, some of these issues is offered in the following materials.

(1) *The Matured Claim*

Under Chapter X of the old Bankruptcy Act, it was suggested, in **In re Childs Company,** 69 F.Supp. 856 (S.D.N.Y.1946)), that insolvency reorganization, being a substitute for liquidation, and effectively the economic contingency against which the preferred contracted for liquidation priority over the common, should mature the preferred's claim to its liquidation price and accumulated arrearages. As a consequence, the commons should not participate in the reorganized enterprise until the matured preferred claim was "fully" satisfied. By the same token, the preferred stock should receive no more than such payment in an insolvency reorganization in the course of which the enterprise increased in value so that its assets exceeded its debts and the preferred liquidation claim. Hence, the Court (in approving a plan awarding the old preferred stock only common stock in the reorganized enterprise) ruled that the preferred stock was entitled to receive no more than the amount of its matured claim, even though the stock's going-concern attributes (it was non-callable, had an unusually high rate of dividends and enjoyed the protection of a special sinking fund) gave it an economic value in the market well in excess of the matured liquidation claim.[m]

Apart from the compulsion of bankruptcy, can the decision by the common stockholders to initiate a recapitalization or exchange proposal for the purpose of eliminating preferred stock arrearages or liquidation preferences rationally be viewed as creating, for the preferred stockholders, "matured" rights to be paid the arrearages or liquidation preferences at once, analogous to the matured liquidation rights generated for them by insolvency reorganization? Do the considerations which, in the latter circumstance, impel the assumption that the reorganization matures the preferreds' liquidating rights even though no liquidation is actually taking place, justify a similar assumption that the common's voluntary decision to seek dividends for themselves (and therefore to eliminate the obstacle to the flow of dividends presented by the preferred stock arrearages or liquidation preferences) matures the preferred stock's right to arrearages or liquidation preferences? If so, do the considerations which induced Congress in the Bankruptcy Act of 1978 to adopt the liquidation standard as the limit of the concessions which a senior class may make, justify applying the same standard as the limit of concessions in preferred stock recapitalizations? In any event should the payoff in new common shares be required to have a present cash value equal to the surrendered claim?

Will such a test discourage common stockholders from initiating arrearage elimination proposals? See Bove case, supra p. 366.

If so, what interests will be harmed?

(2) *The Investment Value Doctrine*

The Public Utility Holding Company Act of 1935 called for a breakup of the huge public utility holding companies which had been

---

m. In a summary of its Advisory Report on the plan, which was sent to security holders who were to vote on the Plan, the SEC said (24 SEC 512, 521–522 (1946)):

"Under the charter the present preferred stockholders would be entitled to about $7,650,000 ($3,731,600 of par value plus unpaid accrued dividends of $3,918,-180) if the company were liquidated at December 31, 1946. Some of the holders contended that the preferred stock, which is noncallable and bears a 7 percent dividend, is entitled to more than this liquidation priority. We agree with the Trustee that under the law the liquidation preference set forth in the charter controls in this respect.

"On the basis of our estimate of earnings and our valuation of the equity for the preferred and common stockholders of about $10,300,000, exclusive of possible proceeds from the law suit of Finn v. Empire Trust Co., et al., we concluded that a reasonable participation for the preference stockholders would appear to fall between 70 percent and 75 percent of the equity of the debtor in an all common stock capitalization.

"Such an allocation would appear to compensate the preferred stockholders fully, including compensation for the entire bundle of preferred rights they surrender by accepting a common stock position. To counterbalance the change of position, the preferred stockholders receive voting control, the major interest in any proceeds from the lawsuit of Finn v. Empire Trust Co., et al., and the right to about three fourths of the probably substantial future earnings and dividends of the company.

"We, therefore, concluded that a plan with approximately our suggested allocation would be fair and equitable and would meet the legal requirements that senior security holders must be fully compensated before junior interests can participate in a reorganization."

assembled during the previous two decades; and, generally speaking, it sought to restrict their operations to one or more systems whose operations were integrated and confined to a single State and States contiguous thereto. It also had as one of its major objectives the simplification of the corporate and capital structures of holding company systems and the redistribution of voting power among security holders on a fair and equitable basis.

The volume and complexity of the corporate and capital structures which were required to be simplified (see e.g. p. 506, infra) and the nature and scope of the geographical dispersion of the properties required to be integrated presented extremely difficult and novel problems which it was the task of the Commission to resolve. Opponents of the legislation had asserted that the law would cause dumping and forced liquidation of securities, demoralizing the market therefor, and they characterized the integration and simplification requirements as a "death sentence". The Congress, on the other hand, contemplated that this program should not destroy any legitimate investment values, and the Commission was given a mandate to bring about the required integration and simplification in keeping with that objective.

Compliance with the integration and simplification requirements took various forms. They included liquidations, mergers and consolidations, separation of large systems into smaller, integrated systems, divestment of nonutility properties unrelated to the utility business, sale of nonretainable utility properties to other systems with whose properties they could be integrated, sale of the securities of nonretainable subsidiaries to the public at competitive bidding or pursuant to a rights offering to stockholders of the parent company and distribution of securities pro rata among stockholders.

The Commission was authorized to approve a simplification plan under Section 11(e) of the Act only if, *inter alia,* it found the plan to be "fair and equitable" (15 U.S.C. § 79k), the same formula which Congress had formerly embedded in Section 77 (11 U.S.C. § 205) and Section 77B (48 Stat. 912) of the Bankruptcy Act, and later inserted in Chapter X of the Bankruptcy Act. In ruling upon simplification plans, the Commission developed the so called "investment value" doctrine to implement the "fair and equitable" standard contained in Section 11. That doctrine was designed to meet the problem created by the disparity—often substantial—between the "value" of a security when it is assessed as a continuing claim on a going concern and the value of the corporation's available assets which the same security would, by its terms, be entitled to receive in a liquidation, recapitalization, merger, or other form of corporate readjustment compelled by Section 11 of the Holding Company Act. To honor the contractual provision might be to entitle the security holder in any given case to more (or less) than the going-concern value of the security he is being forced to surrender. But except for the compulsion of Section 11, senior-security holders might not have the right to force, and junior-security holders might not have the desire to make, the proposed readjustment. And the regulatory compulsion of Section 11, unlike the compulsion of bankruptcy, was not a contingency contemplated in allocating risk and return in the senior security contract. The investment-value doctrine rests on the assumption that Congress did not intend enforcement of the overriding public policy of holding-company simplification to have its effect visited on one class with a corresponding windfall to another class of security holders, or to result in shifting investment values from one class of security holders to another. On that premise, both the Commission and the Supreme Court concluded that the act (1) in effect, overrides the security contract—i.e., precludes a corporate readjustment which it compels, from being a "maturing" event under the security contract merely by reason of such compulsion, even though the particular form of readjustment occurring was a contingency apparently explicitly provided for in the contract, and (2) requires surrendering security holders to receive the long-term going-concern values which their securities have when the act compels their surrender—i.e., their claims are to be measured by their going-concern values rather than by the formal requirements of their contracts or by some other norm.

The "investment value" standard (as invoked in In the Matter of Eastern Gas and Fuel Associates, 30 SEC 834 (1950), approved and enforced Civ.Action No. 50–168 (D.Mass.)) is illustrated, and advocated, in Note, A Standard of Fairness for Compensating Preferred Shareholders in Corporate Recapitalizations, 33 U.Chi.L.Rev. 97 (1965), as follows:

"Consider, for example, a strong corporation which expects to have $100,000 in earnings available annually for its shareholders and which has 10,000 shares of common and 10,000 shares of 5%, $100–par preferred each with $20 of arrears. The investment value of the preferred shares would be the sum of the value of the contract without arrears and the value of the arrears, determined as follows:

(1) The value of the contract without arrears is derived from the preferred dividend requirement of $50,000 per year. The value of this right is the present value of $50,000 per year in perpetuity, capitalized at a rate which properly reflects the risk of not earning the dividend. Because the corporation is strong and the risk is small, a proper capitalization rate might be 7%. The value of the contractual right to dividends is thus $714,073.

(2) The second component of the preferred shares' investment value is the value of the arrears. If the company earns $100,000 annually and pays $50,000 in preferred dividends, $50,000 will be available for payments on the arrears. Assuming depreciation charges sufficient to maintain the plant at a level necessary to earn $100,000 and assuming a willing board of directors, if the entire sum is devoted to that purpose the arrears will be paid off in four years ($20 on each of 10,000 shares; $200,000 total arrearage accruals). The present value of $50,000 per year for four years must be determined. Since the risk of not earning this sum is greater than the risk of not earning the first $50,000 of the corporation's expected annual

income, it should be capitalized at, perhaps, 10%. Thus, the present value of the arrears is $158,493, and the total value of the preferred rights is $872,566.

The preferred should be given either cash or securities of this value. If the new capital structure is to consist of one class of securities such as common stock, the preferred should be given a percentage of that stock equal to the ratio of the preferred's investment value to the value of the entire equity. The value of the entire equity is determined by capitalizing the expected annual earnings available for the equity interest, $100,000, in perpetuity at the appropriate rate considering the risk of not achieving those earnings (e.g., 8½%). On this basis, the total equity is worth $1,176,405 and the preferred would be entitled to 74% of the new single class of stock to be issued. If more than one class of securities is to be issued, the preferred should be given the most senior package of shares which will, if present expert expectations are realized, have a market value equal to the preferred's present investment value. The expected market value of the new shares is estimated in the same manner in which the investment value of the old shares was determined. The earnings attributable to the new shares are capitalized at a rate which the market would probably require of a security of similar quality in a similarly-situated company.

"In this way, 'the equitable equivalent of the securities' investment value on a going concern basis' is most accurately determined, and it is on the basis of this determination that the preferred should be made whole in the event of a recapitalization."

(3) *"Funding" Standards*

Professor Latty proposed a test of fairness in a classic article entitled, Fairness—The Focal Point in Preferred Stock Arrearage Elimination, 29 Va.L.Rev. 1 (1942), which he characterized as a "funding theory." His notion is to treat the arrears as being reinvested in additional preferred stock, so that the preferred stock claim to future earnings at the time of recapitalization may be viewed as an amount equal to the rate of dividends prescribed in the investment contract, but applied to a base consisting of the original investment plus the arrears. Thus, a $100 6% stock with $50 of arrears would be treated for purposes of testing fairness, as a $150 investment carrying a right to $9 in annual dividends with no claim to payment of arrears, i.e., the arrearage claim would be commuted into a remote liquidation claim plus a claim to income until liquidation. On that premise, the preferreds' rightful share of the enterprise would be determined by ascertaining the ratio of the preferreds' $9 claim to the total stream of anticipated income. Thus, if income were expected to be $1,000,000 and there were outstanding 100,000 shares of the preferred stock, the preferreds would be entitled to 90% of the recapitalized enterprise if it were recapitalized on a one stock basis.

How would the results of applying Professor Latty's proposal differ from (i) the results of applying the investment value test and (ii) the results of invoking the appraisal remedy?

(4) *Procedural and Related Devices*

If no very meaningful criteria of fairness can be formulated to prescribe the limits of a bargain to eliminate preferred stock arrearages, do any of the following suggestions, either alone or in combination, offer assistance:

Fixing the burden of proof. See, e.g., the provisions in the Nebraska Statutes (Rev.Stat., Art. 20 § 21–2059) (1987):

> "In case of any proposed amendment of the articles of incorporation changing the existing priority rights, or provisions of any class of shares outstanding, a shareholder adversely affected may apply to any court of competent jurisdiction to restrain and enjoin the corporation from adopting any such amendments on the ground of fraud or unfairness. * * * [T]he court shall enjoin the proposed amendment if the proponents fail to show that, to a reasonable probability, it is fair, just, and equitable to all shareholders affected thereby."

Consider also the following suggestion:

> "The primary objection to tightening judicial control is the risk of unwise interference with legitimate business affairs. A distinction can be drawn, however, between the activity of a corporation in managing a business enterprise and its function as a vehicle for collecting and using capital and distributing profits and losses. The former involves corporate functioning in competitive business affairs in which judicial interference may be undesirable. The latter involves only the corporation-shareholder relationship, in which the courts may more justifiably intervene to insist on equitable behavior.

> "It is therefore suggested that when a plan is challenged in the courts, the defendant corporation should be required to show either that the plan is fair or that in its broad outlines the plan fulfills some substantial business purpose. If the corporation proves the latter, the dissenters should have the burden of proving that the recapitalization is unfair. Since it is usually quite difficult to establish either fairness or unfairness, this procedure would favor the corporation when it is demonstrably acting pursuant to legitimate corporate ends and would favor the dissenting shareholders when their rights are being modified solely for the private purposes of management or those in control." Note, Protection For Shareholder Interests in Recapitalizations of Publicly Held Corporations, 58 Col.L.Rev. 1030, 1066–7 (1958).

Administrative supervision of the propriety of the recapitalization bargain. See Orschel, Administrative Protection for Shareholder in California Recapitalizations, 4 Stan.L.Rev. 215 (1952); see also Cal. Corp.Code §§ 25110–25113, 25120, 25142 (West Ed.1985 & Supp.1992).

(B) DISCLOSURE

Some vote of the preferred stockholders, whether by class or in solution with the common, is generally required for alteration of preferred contract entitlements. Will the preferred stockholder's interests be materially aided by conditioning the effectiveness of the vote or approval upon the adequacy of the information given about the proposed alteration?   Arguably, at least, the inequality of bargaining position previously referred to would justify the imposition of a detailed disclosure requirement on the common.   Do the disclosure requirements in the proxy rules promulgated by the Securities and Exchange Commission under Section 14 of the Securities Exchange Act provide the preferred stockholder with information sufficient to induce him to act critically in assessing the fairness of a recapitalization plan?   Does the answer turn on the rigor with which the rules require disclosure of future oriented information such as the magnitude or duration of improvements in earnings anticipated by management or of the magnitude of benefits expected to flow to the common stockholders or management from the recapitalization proposal, or the reasons for the proposed alterations?   See Eisenberg v. Chicago Milwaukee Corp., supra p. 378.

(C) CLASS VOTING

(1) *Class Voting Provisions and Their Limitations*

State business corporation laws now ordinarily require class voting as a condition to certificate amendments that alter preferred stockholders' rights and preferences.   See Del.Corp.L. sec. 242(b)(2);   RMBCA § 10.04.   These provisions somewhat ameliorate fairness problems respecting adjustment of preferred stockholders' rights.   State corporation statutes are less thoroughgoing in their provision for preferred class votes in respect of mergers and acquisitions, however.   Recall that the issuer in the *Bove* case, supra p. 366, evaded a statute requiring a unanimous preferred class vote for a direct certificate amendment by engineering a merger pursuant to which a two-thirds class vote sufficed.

Delaware has permitted a more extreme version of this move. **Warner Communications Inc. v. Chris–Craft Industries, Inc.,** 583 A.2d 962 (Del.Ch.1989), concerned a merger consummated without class voting that adversely affected the rights of a class of preferred.   The holder of the preferred claimed a right to a class vote under two charter provisions.   The first provided that a two-thirds vote of the particular class of preferred was necessary for the issuer to "amend, alter or repeal any of the provisions of the Certificate of Incorporation or By-Laws * * * so as to affect adversely any of the preferences, rights, powers or privileges" of the class of preferred.   The second provided that a two thirds class vote of all outstanding shares of preferred "shall be necessary to alter or change any rights, preferences or limitations of the Preferred stock so as to affect the holders of all such shares adversely * * *."   Chancellor Allen held that neither provision applied to merger votes.   As to the first provision, the impairment of rights stemmed from the conversion of the stock pursuant to a merger under section 251 of the Delaware statute rather than from an "amendment" or "repeal" under section 242. The second provision was not so narrowly phrased. But, because it tracked language in section 242 (read by the court to apply only to direct amendments and not to provide for class voting rights in mergers), it was held inapplicable. The court ascribed to the drafter the "general understanding" that Delaware's merger and certificate amendment provisions operate separately under the "bedrock doctrine of independent legal significance." Given this, said the court, it is "extraordinarily unlikely" that the provision could have been intended to apply to mergers. See also *Rothschild v. Liggett Group,* supra p. 372; Sullivan Money Management, Inc. v. FLS Holdings Inc., CCH Fed.Sec.L.Rep. ¶ 97,292 (Del. Ch. 1992).

The court's reading of the charter language in *Warner* can be questioned. First, reference should be made to statutes of other jurisdictions under which a class vote would have been required in *Warner.* See RMBCA § 11.03(f)(1); N.Y.Bus.Corp.L. secs. 804(a)(2), 903(a)(2). The drafting technique employed in these statutes is noteworthy—the drafter makes a reference back to the provision requiring a class vote for a charter amendment. That is, the merger statute singles out for a class vote merger plans containing provisions that, if included in a certificate amendment, would trigger the statutory class voting requirement for certificate amendments. This statutory drafting practice requires a court to compare the effects of the merger with the specified transactions provided for in the amendment provision in order to determine whether a class vote is required in the merger. The difficulties encountered in such a comparison are illustrated by transactions such as those in the *Kirschner* and *Dart* cases, which leave the preferred stock unchanged. In any event, it is plausible to interpret the phrase "alter or change any rights * * * so as to affect the holders of all such shares adversely" in the *Warner* certificate to include mergers. Cf. Shidler v. All American Life & Financial Corp., 298 N.W.2d 318 (Iowa 1980) (applying a statute requiring a class vote of common stockholders in respect of an amendment that would cancel shares to apply to a cashout merger). Thus, contrary to the Court's analysis, the fact that the second provision in the *Warner* charter tracked the language of section 242 of the Delaware statute arguably supported a class vote in a merger: the language in effect referred back to the basic section that defines situations appropriate for a class vote.

The ruling of the leading case interpreting language similar to that contained in the *Warner* charter also should be noted. In Levin v. Mississippi River Corp., 386 U.S. 162 (1967), which concerned possible preemption of state corporate law on share voting by the Interstate Commerce Act, the Court held that a charter provision requiring a class vote in respect of an alteration or change in "the preferences, qualifications, limitations, restrictions and special or relative rights" of the preferred applied in the case of a consolidation with another railroad pursuant to which the preferred received common stock. Given this ruling, it is plausible to assume that the drafters of the subsequent generation of preferred stock contracts would have seen no reason to include more specific language respecting merger votes.

Quite apart from the legal question whether a class vote is available or required in the merger is the practical question whether the availability of the vote offers the class much protection if its members are dispersed and unorganized. See, e.g., the *Bove, Barrett,* and *Armour* cases supra. Possibly the requirement of a class vote stimulates the common, *ex ante,* to offer a higher price for a cashout or alteration of the preferred's rights than it would offer in the absence of a class vote. And the stimulus may be more powerful if a supermajority vote is required. See Interstate Commerce Act section 20b, 49 U.S.C. § 11,363(a)(1) (75 percent); NYSE Company Manual, A–281 (66⅔ percent) But the question remains whether that stimulus is sufficient to preclude significant overreaching by the common stock.

Does the existence of appraisal rights offer the preferred stock adequate protection? See the *Bove* case, supra p. 366.

2. *Drafting Practice.*

Note, Arrearage Elimination and the Preferred Stock Contract: A Survey and a Proposal for Reform, 9 Cardozo L.Rev. 1335, 1345–53, 1361–70 (1988), presents the results of a survey of the contracts governing 97 preferred stock issues of 52 industrial corporations chartered in Delaware. Only fourteen percent of the issues had provisions for a class vote in respect of a merger.

Fifty-two percent of the issues surveyed were listed on the New York Stock Exchange and thus subject to the Exchange's listing requirement of a two-thirds supermajority class vote for adverse certificate amendments. NYSE Company Manual, A–281 (1984). But only about one half of these listed stocks actually included the supermajority provision, presumably because of a liberal policy of granting exceptions on the part of the Exchange. Of the listed stocks, twenty-two percent provided for merger class votes.

SECTION C. CONVERTIBLE SECURITIES AND WARRANTS

INTRODUCTION

A "warrant" is a long term option on the common stock of a corporation granted for consideration by the corporation itself. A "convertible bond" is a bond that incorporates the privilege of conversion into the common stock of the corporate issuer. "Conversion" is the act of exchanging one class of securities for another. It is, at bottom, a contractual device, and may be attached to preferred stock as well as bonds." The addition of a conversion privilege to a bond's bundle of

---

n. Common stock is not the only available underlying security. Bonds can be made convertible into preferred stock of the issuer or common stock of a subsidiary or sister corporation. Debt which is convertible into stock of an issuer other than

rights in effect grants the holder a long term option on the issuer's common stock. The convertible bond thus includes the economic substance of a warrant. Such a bond-warrant unit can be packaged and sold directly at a comparable cost of capital to the issuer. Under this alternative mode of financing, the issuer sells a straight bond and attaches a warrant.°

Convertibles and bonds with attached warrants are "hybrids"— they combine features of debt and equity in a single security. The option that effects the combination gives rise to distinct problems of valuation. Its attachment and sale also gives the issuer distinct opportunities to hinder and frustrate the holders' expectations. Convertibles and warrants accordingly present special problems of contract drafting, and give rise to a constant flow of litigation in which holders ask judges to intervene to protect them from issuer opportunism.

1. VALUATION

The complexities involved in valuing convertible debt stem from the need to value not merely its straight debt characteristics, but also its claim as an option, and then to combine the variables.

Options come in a number of sizes and shapes. Convertibles and warrants, which embody a call on *the issuer* to sell stock to the holder, should be distinguished from the option which is a "call" on a *third party* to sell (or a "put" to a third party to buy) stock of a named issuer to (or from) the option holder. The latter options, which tend to have short durations, do not represent an overhang on the common stock of an issuer since they do not require issuance of any more stock. Such instruments permit investors to fine-tune their risk-return choices.

the debtor is called "exchangeable" debt. It can take the form either of a convertible obligation in which the bond is tendered for exchange to the second corporation, or it can take the form of a bond with attached warrants that entitle the holder to purchase the stock of the other company.

Conversion need not be optional only with the holder; bonds convertible at the option of the issuer have appeared in the past.

Although the conventional convertible security contemplates the conversion, at the option of the security-holder, of his senior or prior ranking investment position into a junior security, there have been security contracts which contemplate conversion of a junior security into a senior security, known as upstream convertibles. Conversion into a superior ranking stock is prohibited in some states (e.g., RMBCA § 602(a)(5); NYBCL § 519(a)(1)), but is permitted in others. See e.g., N.J.Statutes § 14A:7–9(1); Del.Gen.Corp.Law § 151(e).

New Jersey and Delaware also authorize security contracts in which the right to convert may be vested in the corporation rather than in the security holder. (Id.)

Convertible securities are not the only means by which the purchaser of the limited return of a senior security may, as part of the same investment, acquire an interest in the growth of residual earnings and in the increase in value of the common stock. Most costly to the enterprise and most attractive to the investor is a participating senior security. The investor in such a security is entitled to the priority of income and assets of a senior investment, and in addition, he shares in the residual earnings and assets without foregoing his seniority (as would the holder of a convertible on conversion) or paying an additional sum as would the holder of a warrant.

o. The warrant portions of the unit may or may not be detachable, i.e., the debt and warrant portions separate into two distinct securities.

The trading markets in these options are part of the larger "market" that affects managers who are concerned with the cost of their capital. They nevertheless provide a useful beginning point for a presentation of convertible bond valuation.

The seller of a call option receives money up front in exchange for assuming an obligation to sell the stock at the exercise price if the option holder decides to purchase it. The seller of a put option also receives cash up front, but in exchange for assuming an obligation to buy the stock at the exercise price if the option holder decides to sell it. The seller of a call profits if the stock price stays low; the holder of a call profits only if the stock price rises. The seller of a put profits if the stock price rises; the holder of a put profits if the stock price stays low.

The "theoretical" value of a call option is the current price of the stock on which it is a claim less the exercise price of the option. When the price of the stock is higher than the exercise price of the option, the option has a "theoretical" value equal to the difference between the stock price and the exercise price. When the price of the stock is lower than the exercise price of the option, the option has a zero "theoretical" value. But so long as the option continues to be exercisable after the date on which it is being valued, it is possible for its "market" value to be greater than its "theoretical" value. An option with an exercise price of 6 on stock which has a market price of 5, has a "theoretical" value of zero. But if it continues to represent a call on the stock for some period in the future, either determinate or indeterminate, and the stock may at some point rise above 6, the option has a positive market value even though its "theoretical" value is zero. The option inevitably has some value because of the combination of the possibility that the price of the stock will rise while the option is exercisable and the impossibility of the option ever being worth less than zero.[p]

According to Ross, Westerfield and Jordan, Principles of Corporate Finance 642–645 (1991), five factors determine the value of a call option:

Stock price. The higher the stock price, the higher the value of the call.

Exercise price. The higher the exercise price, the lower the value of the call.

Duration. The longer the time to the expiration date, the higher the value of the call.

Risk free rate of return. The higher the risk free rate of return, the higher the value of the call. What accounts for this factor, given that, as we have seen with both stocks and bonds, the higher the risk free rate of return, the higher the discount rate, and the lower the value of the security? The explanation lies in the fact that another element of

p. Significantly, the holders of such options are not involved (directly) in the conflict of interest that confronts management or common stockholders (vis-a-vis holders of convertible bonds or preferred stock) because of management's or common share's power to increase or decrease the variance of the corporation's returns by shifting its assets.

value, the exercise price, entails a cash outflow in the future with a negative present value. Thus, the higher the risk free rate of return, the higher the discount rate, the lower the negative present value of the outflow, and the higher the value of the option.

Volatility of stock. The more volatile the price of the stock, the higher the value of the call. What accounts for this factor, given that, as we have seen, because investors are risk averse, the greater the variance in the stream of payments, the less their value? Here the explanation lies in the proposition that the market value of the option can never go below zero. Return to the example of a call option with an exercise price of 6 on a stock with a current price of 5. Now make a limiting assumption—the stock will have one of two prices for the duration of the life of the call, $5.50 or $7. If the stock turns out to be worth only $5.50, the option is worthless. But, despite that possibility, the option has a present value because the stock may be worth $7. Now let us change the limiting assumption. The stock will be worth $5.25 or $7.25. On this new fact pattern the stock is more volatile. But the option is worth more. Changing the lower of the two possible stock prices from $5.50 to $5.25 does not make the option any less valuable because the option is worth zero in either event. But the increase in the upper price from $7 to $7.25 makes the option worth more when it is in the money. Thus, assuming the same mean return, the wider the dispersion of possible returns on the company's assets, the greater the value of the option, because it cannot be worth less than zero but can constitute a claim on the upper end of the dispersion.

The five factors identified above were first combined into a formula for valuing options in Black and Scholes, The Pricing of Options and Corporate Liabilities, 81 J.Pol.Econ. 637 (1973). Relying on the insight that an investor can create a riskless hedge by buying shares of stock and simultaneously selling options on the stock, their formula sets the value of an option at any one time as a function of the relation among current value of the underlying security, the exercise price of the option, the short term interest rate, the time until expiration, and the variance of the expected return on the stock.

Black and Scholes contributed a powerful insight about the interrelationship of senior and junior securities along with their valuation formula. Once a corporation sells debt, they asserted, its stock represents a call on the firm's assets. The firm's equity literally has an option: It can repay the debt and buy back the firm, the exercise price of the option being the principal amount of the debt; in the alternative, it can default and leave the firm to the debt holders. This insight, taken together with the option pricing model, implies that the conflict of interest between the debt and the equity is sharper than previously assumed. For further discussion of this point, see infra pp. 529–530.

BRATTON, THE ECONOMICS AND JURISPRUDENCE
OF CONVERTIBLE BONDS

1984 Wis.L.Rev. 667, 672–680.

Convertible bond valuation is a complicated matter involving a large set of stochastically related variables. * * *

1. PRINCIPAL VARIABLES

The issuer incorporating a conversion privilege into its bonds grants a future claim on its equity. For investors, this future claim gives convertible bonds the advantage of combining desirable features of straight bonds, such as fixed income payments and principal repayment, with the upside potential of common stock.[18] In exchange for the future equity claim, bondholders customarily accept a coupon rate lower than that of an equivalent straight bond,[19] less restrictive business covenants, and subordinated status. To issuers, these concessions give convertibles advantages over straight debt, such as cost savings, increased future capacity to incur senior debt, and greater flexibility to advance the interests of the common stockholders.[20] The value of the conversion privilege stems from these mutual perceptions of advantage.

The following Figure illustrates the upside and downside interrelations of the three constituent elements of value—debt value, conversion value, and conversion premium—for a typical convertible bond[22] at various possible values of the issuing corporation.

18. Convertible bonds tend to be used during periods of rising stock prices. * * *

19. For the past few years, 300 basis points has been the rule of thumb on the coupon rate differential. * * *

20. See J. Weston & E. Brigham, Essentials of Managerial Finance 592–93 (5th ed. 1979); Fleischer & Cary, supra note 7, at 474–75; Reiling, Warrants in Bond–Warrant Units: A Survey and Assessment, 70 Mich.L.Rev. 1411, 1419–20, 1424–25 (1972).

Surveys of issuers' motivations for using convertibles are numerous. See C. Pilcher, Raising Capital With Convertible Securities 22 (1955) (survey of 1948–52 industrial issues; 83% of issuers sought delayed equity financing); Brigham, An Analysis of Convertible Debentures: Theory and Some Empirical Evidence, 21 J.Fin. 35, 50 (1966) (survey of 1961–63 issues; 73% of issuers sought delayed equity financing, 27% sought reduced interest costs); Broman,

The Use of Convertible Subordinated Debentures by Industrial Firms 1949–59, Q.Rev.Econ. & Bus., Spring 1963, at 65 (survey of 1949–59 issues; delayed equity financing motivation dominated); Hoffmeister, Use of Convertible Debt in the Early 1970s: A Reevaluation of Corporate Motives, Q.Rev.Econ. & Bus., Summer 1977, at 23, 26 (survey of 1970–72 issues; 34% of issuers primarily sought delayed equity financing, 30% sought reduced interest costs).

22. The bond has a 20 year term. Conversion is optional with the holder at any time over the entire term of the bond. The issuer may redeem the bond for its face value plus a small premium at any time during the term. The coupon rate is 300 basis points below the rate available on a comparable nonconvertible bond.

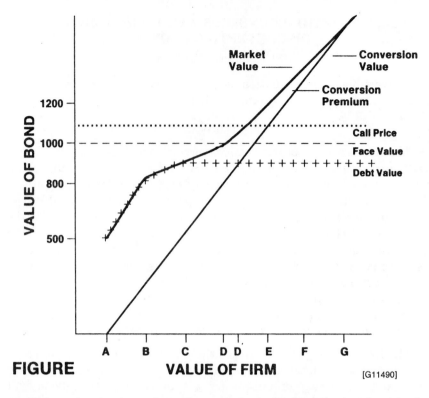

FIGURE   **VALUE OF FIRM**   [G11490]

Debt value is the value of an equivalent straight bond with the same coupon rate. It is sensitive to the variables dominant in straight bond valuation, such as interest rate levels and the issuer's equity cushion. *Conversion value* is the value of the amount of common stock into which the bond can be converted. It depends on the market value of the underlying common stock and the price, the "conversion price," * at which the bonds, taken at their face value, are convertible.[25] If the conversion price is a constant, conversion value is subject to the same determinants as the stock price, and goes up and down in lockstep with it. Although arbitrage possibilities prevent the bond from selling below the higher of debt or conversion value, nothing prevents it from selling above the higher of these two values. *Conversion premium* is the

* [Ed. note] The conversion price may be made subject to change, or "reset," over the life of the issue. Under an issuer-favorable reset provision, the conversion price would increase in set amounts at intervals over the life of the bond. Under a holder-favorable reset, a downside change in the market price of the stock would provide the basis for a calculation of a reduction in the conversion price. A provision of the latter sort results in a dispute in Zimmerman v. Home Shopping Network, Inc., 1990 WL 140890 (Del.Ch. 1990).

25. Commonly set 10 to 20% above the market price of the underlying common

stock at the time of issue, conversion price may remain constant for the life of the conversion privilege * * * or be stepped up at stated intervals.

The "conversion ratio" expresses the number of shares of common stock the bondholder receives upon conversion:

Conversion Ratio = $\dfrac{\text{Face Value}}{\text{Conversion Price}}$

For example, a bond with a face value of $1000 and a conversion price of $50 has a conversion ratio of 20. * * *

amount by which market value exceeds debt or conversion value. If we characterize the conversion privilege as a long term option on the underlying common, the premium represents the option's value.

Assume that the bond illustrated in the Figure is priced, issued and sold for its $1000 face value with a conversion price of $50. Assume further that at the time of the bond's issue the issuer's stock is trading at $40 and the issuer's value is at D. Debt value at issue is $900, reflecting the convertible's lower coupon rate. Conversion value is $800, reflecting that the $50 conversion price exceeds the $40 market price of the underlying common. The premium at issue is $100, the difference between the higher of debt or conversion value and the initial $1000 market price. Valuation at issue reflects the expectation that the issuer's value will increase substantially during the early years of the bond's term.

Looking to the right of D in the Figure, we see the bond's conversion value and market value rising in tandem with higher issuer values, illustrating the convertible bond's upside potential. Debt value, in contrast, is limited by a fixed coupon rate and does not rise significantly.[31] As issuer values increase, the market behavior of the convertible increasingly mirrors the market behavior of the underlying common stock and the premium accordingly becomes progressively smaller. Eventually, at G, the issuer's value and the dividend payout on the underlying common have increased so much that the expected return on the underlying common exceeds the expected return on the bonds. As a result, the premium disappears and the holders convert.

We see the bond's downside market behavior by looking to the left of D. Conversion value declines in tandem with the issuer's value and the premium disappears as the decline in value becomes extreme. Debt value, protected by the bond contract, shows more stability and resilience. At B, the bond's market value has fallen so far as to have become nearly contiguous with debt value; this is the "bond floor." As the issuer's value goes into extreme decline to the left of B, even the bond floor begins seriously to give way. With the issuer's value at A, we reach the end of the line—a hypothetical bankruptcy liquidation pursuant to which the holders of the convertible issue receive $500 per bond and the stockholders receive nothing.

2. ELEMENTS OF THE CONVERSION PREMIUM

We have seen that calculating the conversion value, given a constant conversion price, is a matter of valuing the underlying common, and that calculating the debt value is a matter of straight bond valuation. Valuing the conversion premium, in contrast, is a matter of valuing the conversion privilege. Sorting out the interrelated variables which constitute and affect the premium is the central problem of convertible bond valuation.

---

31. If the Figure were to show the convertible's value as a function of different levels of prevailing interest rates, rather than of different firm values, then movement to the right on the horizontal axis would cause the debt value line to drop.

The premium arises, first and foremost, from investors' perception that advantages lie in having two imperfectly correlated elements of value—debt value and conversion value—combined in the same security. One advantage of the combination comes from the bond's limited downside risk. The downside risk of holding the bond is less than that of holding the amount of common into which it is convertible because debt value provides a floor should issuer values decline.[33] The limited downside risk causes the bond to sell for more than its conversion value even when we are to the right of D in the Figure, where higher issuer values cause conversion value to surpass debt value. But since the relative importance of bond floor protection decreases as issuer values increase, the premium also decreases as issuer values increase.

Another advantage comes from the bondholder's potential upside participation. The bond in the Figure still sells at a premium to the left of D, even though debt value exceeds conversion value at these lower issuer values. This premium results not from bond floor downside protection but from the market's hopes that conversion value has upside potential. Since this upside potential's relative importance decreases as issuer values decrease, the premium diminishes so as to disappear entirely when bankruptcy liquidation is reached at A.

The premium also results from the convertible's income stream. So long as the convertible's coupon rate exceeds the underlying common's dividend payout rate, it is a more advantageous holding than the common. Indeed, so long as the coupon rate exceeds the dividend rate, arbitrage possibilities will prevent the bond from selling as low as conversion value, except immediately prior to declaration of a dividend or an adverse change in conversion terms.[35] Conversely, as is the case in the Figure, if the dividend payout rate eventually exceeds the coupon rate at higher issuer values, the premium will be entirely eliminated.[36]

The premium is also sensitive to the conversion privilege's durability—the longer its life, the greater its value. Conversely, the premium is reduced if the issuer retains the power to shorten the duration of the conversion privilege.[37] Issuers customarily retain this power in the form of a redemption or "call" right—the right to pay off the bond prior to maturity at the "call price," usually fixed at par plus a small premium.

3. Call Rights and Convertible Bond Valuation

Call rights will reduce the size of the conversion premium in varying degrees depending upon the likelihood that the issuer actually

33. This floor also gives the convertible greater price stability than the underlying common possesses. One therefore can expect a positive correlation between the size of the premium and the size of the variance in the price movements of the underlying stock.

35. * * * Given the stated condition, the bond always sells above its conversion value and the investor will not find it optimal to convert at any time prior to maturity, since conversion would result in the premium's destruction.

36. At that point, voluntary conversion should occur, preventing the occurrence of a negative premium. * * *

37. Thus convertible bond contract provisions affect the valuation calculus by their effect on the duration of the conversion privilege.

will exercise them. Issuer call policies in turn depend on a number of factors, including bond contract provisions, market restraints on management actions, and, at bottom, management awareness.

Most issuers reserve the right to call issues of convertible bonds at any time.[38] The idea is to force conversion at such time as issuer growth causes conversion value to exceed the call price. Since conversion value is the higher figure, the bondholder converts.[39] Forced conversion through call advances stockholder interests: if the total value of the issuer is the sum of the value of the debt and equity claims upon it, then permitting convertibles further to appreciate in value as the issuer grows permits the bondholders' claim on the issuer's equity to increase at the stockholders' expense.

In theory, then, a stockholder optimal call policy dictates call as soon as the bond's conversion value exceeds its call price.[40] In the real world, however, such a call policy would have to permit conversion value to rise somewhat higher than that—probably about 20% higher—in order to assure that a drop in the market price of the stock during the period between the call and the redemption date[42] does not discourage voluntary conversion and force the issuer to cash out bondholders on the redemption date.

Actual issuer call practices fall short of this stockholder optimal point by a wide margin. The median issuer delays call until conversion value exceeds call price by 43.9%,[43] a surprising result in view of issuers' assiduous reservation of the contractual right to pursue a stockholder optimal policy.**

The call problem illustrates the riskiness of investment in the conversion premium. According to one analyst, it is an average of six times more risky than investment in the underlying common. The same analyst tells us that the investors exact a high rate of return—49% annually—for bearing this risk. These market statistics indicate that the bargain embodied in convertible securities, although peculiar

---

38. Until recently only a minority of currently publicly traded convertible bond issues contained contract provisions prohibiting call, and even within this minority the protection tended to apply only during the first five years of the issue's life. See 13 Value Line Convertible Surv. 262 (May 3, 1982).

Due to investor pressure, in 1982 new convertible bond issues began to contain call prohibitions applicable for the first two years of the issue's life. See N.Y. Times, Mar. 6, 1983, § F, at 10, col. 1.

39. On the redemption date both bond and conversion privileges disappear and are replaced with the right to claim the call price. Needless to say, the conversion premium disappears also.

40. To the contrary, it is not optimal for the issuing corporation to call the convertible when its call price exceeds its mar-

ket value. The amount paid in excess of market value would amount to a wealth transfer from the stockholders to the convertible bondholders.

42. Trust indentures specify a notice period of 30 to 60 days between the call notice and the redemption date.

43. See Ingersoll, Corporate Call Policies, supra note 35, at 466. Ingersoll based his study on all convertible bond issues called between 1968 and 1975.

** [Ed. note] Asquith and Mullins, Convertible Debt: Corporate Call Policy and Voluntary Conversion, 46 J. Finance 1273 (1991), offers an additional explanation for the delay of issuer calls. The tax deductibility of the interest on the uncalled bond builds a cash flow bias in favor of delayed call until the dividend payments on the stock are higher than the after tax cost of the debt.

in some particulars, at bottom is sound because an efficient market correctly perceives the risk and requires a commensurately big return. This conclusion would not meet with approval in all quarters, however.

KLEIN, THE CONVERTIBLE BOND: A PECULIAR PACKAGE

123 U.Pa.L.Rev. 547, 553–560 (1975).

It should be clear by this point that the bond with warrant attached is itself a peculiar package—a combination of two elements, the bond and the warrant, that are at opposite ends of the spectrum of risk and certainty. Bearing that in mind, we can now turn to convertible bonds, which are basically the same package, but with one more element that seems as unrelated to the other two as they are to each other. This added element consists of a rather bizarre kind of gamble on changes in the market rate of interest. In the case of the convertible, the exercise of the option to convert is tied to a surrender of the fixed payments established in the pure bond element of the security. In the event of conversion, any changes, subsequent to issuance, in the market value of the right to fixed payments become irrelevant. * * * [W]hen the holder contemplates purchase he will properly take account of the coupon rate and terminal value in determining the present value of the bond. He knows that if he were buying a straight bond its value would change as the market rate of interest changed, but the value of the convertible bond will change as the market rate of interest changes if, and only if, the value of the common has not risen to the point where conversion is appropriate. Specification of the complex relations suggested by this observation is beyond the scope of this paper, but the following observations seem in order. First, the practically random relation between the interest rate and the price of this particular common stock injects a variable that increases the already complex, difficult, and uncertain task of valuing a convertible bond (and derivatively, the other outstanding securities of the same company). Second, this particular variable can be eliminated by the use of the bond with warrant attached. Finally, and consequently, it is difficult to imagine any rational investor who would willingly choose to include this variable, this bizarre gamble, in the investment package represented by the other features of the convertible bond, unless he thereby obtained the investment at a markedly lower price than that at which he could obtain separately the other desirable elements of the package.*

* * * In an unregulated market one would expect that the use of a package or tie-in like that reflected in a convertible bond would reduce the potential proceeds to the company, unless there are substantial savings in flotation costs achieved by selling the package as opposed to selling the separate elements (and in an efficient securities market it is

---

*[Ed. Note] It has been suggested ("Equity–Linked Debt" by E. Phillip Jones and Scott P. Mason of the Harvard Business School) that if issue quality and issue date are held reasonably constant, both the coupon rate and the conversion premiums tend to be higher for units of debt with warrants than for units of debt which are convertible.

hard to see why there should be such savings). Selling a package consisting of a bond and an option is like selling a package consisting of a combination of apples and oranges—it deprives the seller of the opportunity to obtain the best possible price by fully exploiting the separate demands for each product. * * *

A priori one would expect the same analysis to apply to a financial package consisting of disparate elements. It will be recalled that in the case of convertible bonds, the package consists of the bond, the option, and the bizarre gamble on the market rate of interest—analogous to a package of apples, oranges, and a lottery ticket * * *. [A] buyer looking for the *precise* package embodied in a particular convertible bond would be rare, and would be a potential customer for each element of the package even if those elements were sold separately.[†] * * *

By this point, if not earlier, one should have begun to question why companies ever issue convertible bonds, at least for the purpose of raising new capital. A number of reasons have been suggested, but only two have even enough superficial purely economic rationality to deserve consideration. One reason is associated with the view that a convertible bond is basically debt financing, with the conversion privilege as a "sweetener." The reason for adding the sweetener by issuing a convertible, rather than a straight bond, is to reduce the interest cost, or to put the same idea in slightly different terms, to permit the sale of a bond at an interest cost such that the company's appearance as a good credit risk will not be impaired. * * * The cost of raising the money is not reduced at all, of course; it is just disguised, unless there is only a negligible chance that the price of the common will, in fact, rise to the point where conversion will be attractive to the bondholders. By selling the conversion privilege the company in effect receives a payment for a gamble on the common stock, and uses that payment to reduce the apparent cost of capital. I offer no insight into who is deceived—management, existing shareholders, or purchasers of the bonds, or all of them.

The other most significant reason for issuing convertibles is associated with the view that they are essentially a form of deferred equity financing. The idea behind this view is that management may want to raise equity capital, but it considers that the current market price of the common is too low. Convertible bonds are issued, therefore, with the idea that they will be converted into common when the value of the common rises to a point where the company can force conversion by

---

† [Ed. Note] Convertible debt may attract at least two distinct groups of investors who might not otherwise be brought into the corporate fold: (1) those who because of legal restrictions must contemplate a debt instrument or a preferred stock, but who are willing to assume a subordinate position in a highly leveraged capital structure because of the possibility of gain through the accompanying conversion, warrant or option; and (2) those sophisticated investors in common stock whose primary interest is the option, which is made more attractive because it is attached to a debt investment with more permissive margin requirements and a steadier cash flow than are available for common stock, and a lower commission rate on the purchase.

calling the bond. But if the common looks like such a good buy, why let the purchasers of the convertible bonds in on the expected rise in value? Is it not true that by selling the option, the company's officers are gambling that the stock will not perform as well as the buyers expect? If the market price of the common rises and the bonds are converted, then, to be sure, the company will receive more for the stock than it would have received if it had sold the stock at the time of issuance of the bond, but it will receive less than it would have received for the stock if the bond, with its conversion privilege, had never been issued.[†] * * *

* * *

NOTE: CONVERTIBLE BOND VALUATION AND INVESTOR PROTECTION

Does the Efficient Markets Hypothesis imply that notwithstanding the difficulties in valuing convertibles, the market operates to price them "correctly"? Is there reason to believe that the market does not price convertibles efficiently? See Wang, supra p. 119 at 377–386. Are the following views expressed by the SEC (in Public Service Co. of Indiana, 26 S.E.C. 338, 350–352 (1947) in connection with the issuance of convertible securities by public utility companies) merely a quaint relic?:

" * * * A convertible debenture combines the investment features of a debenture with the speculative aspects of a long term option warrant to obtain stock at a fixed price. So long as the market value of the stock is close to the conversion price, the price of the debentures will be determined by the investment value of the debentures *qua* debentures plus whatever value is attributed to the option to purchase stock at that price in the future. If, however, the market price of the stock rises above the conversion price, the price of the debenture will fluctuate with the value of the stock. Should the price of the stock become very high and raise the price of the debenture proportionately, the latter will lose all of the stability normally associated with a debenture and because of the low yield the holder will be interested in retaining it only as a convenient means of speculating in the stock into which the debenture is convertible. The fact that the debenture gradually loses its investment quality and takes on the speculative characteristics of common stock may frequently confuse and delude the investor.[21]

---

† [Ed. Note] If, as is frequently the case, a substantial period of time must elapse before the new real capital results in increased earnings, the use of convertibles costs current interest charges but spares the common stock investors the need to divide future expanded earnings at today's cost of current, and as yet unexpanded, earnings. On the other hand, it has been suggested that conversion is most likely to occur at a time when the conversion price is materially below the price at which the corporation could issue common stock and when the corporation has little or no need for the capital it will receive from the issuance of the common stock.

21. See Graham and Dodd, Security Analysis (2d Ed., 1940), p. 293:

"Furthermore, the conversion feature, being essentially an option to obtain common stock, is an interest that has been carved out of the common stockholders' equity. As such, it represents a potential share in both the company's surplus and future earnings, a fact often overlooked or misunderstood by investors in the appraisal of common stock values. The value of the conversion privilege is, therefore, based on the opportunity to share in the profits of the company, without the normal risks of ownership, by obtaining the stock at a lower price than the value of the stock equity at the time of conversion. In the instant case, the conversion price has been fixed at $40, approximately the current market value of the stock. Conversions effected when the market price of the stock has risen above that price not only require the company to issue stock at a lower price than would be obtained through a public offering but result in a dilution of the equity of existing stockholders. Because of the difficulty in predicting future market fluctuations and measuring the amount of that dilution, it is unlikely that stockholders will be adequately compensated for this dilution in the price they can obtain either for the warrants they acquire or for the debentures, if they are sold before the market price of the common stock has risen. In addition, the possibility that additional shares equal to 25 percent of the total shares now outstanding may be issued under the conversion option makes it extremely difficult to appraise the stock on the basis of its present earning power and a statement regarding its earnings per share may frequently mislead an unwary investor."

Comparable views were expressed by the Commission with respect to issuance of warrants in insolvency reorganizations. See In The Matter of Childs Company, 24 S.E.C. 85, 120–122 (1946); See also Consolidated Rock Products Co., supra p. 279.

Would you expect convertible bond prices to be more or less volatile than prices of straight bonds? Prices of common stocks? Beatty, Lee and Chen, On the Nonstationarity of Convertible Bond Betas: Theory and Evidence, 28 Q.Rev.Econs. & Bus. 15 (1988) reports on an empirical study of the price behavior of a sample of 97 convertible bonds traded between 1976 and 1979. The convertible prices and returns were compared to those of the bond and stock markets. Twenty of the 97 issues exhibited the characteristics of equities; 77 of the 97 issues exhibited the characteristics of debt securities.

———

"It must be recognized that there is something insidious about even a good convertible bond; it can easily prove a costly snare to the unwary. To avoid this danger the investor must cling determinedly to a conservative viewpoint. When the price of his bond has passed out of the investment range, he must sell it; most important of all, he must not consider his judgment impugned if the bond subsequently rises to a much higher level. The market behaviour of the issue, once it has entered the speculative range, is no more the investor's affair than the price gyrations of any speculative stock about which he knows nothing."

2. CONFLICTS OF INTEREST

(A) PROTECTIVE CONTRACT PROVISIONS

Imagine a convertible bond (or warrant) issued without any contract provision for the adjustment of the terms of the option in the event of changes in the issuer's capital structure. The bond has a conversion price of $20. The stock price rises to $20 from $15 at the time of original issue. Now the issuer splits its common stock two-for-one. The price of a share of stock drops to $10, destroying much of the value of the conversion privilege. The issuer could achieve the same result through four consecutive quarterly 25% stock dividends (assuming the stock's value stays constant during the period). If the issuer were to mount a successful rights offering to its existing common stockholders, it could cause the common stock price to fall to $10, provided that it priced the shares offered below $10 and sold a sufficient number. In sum, conversion value is destroyed when the issuer increases the number of common shares outstanding without proportionately increasing their value.

Conversion value also is destroyed whenever, as with a dividend, the issuer disgorges assets for less than equivalent consideration. Total destruction of conversion value occurs when the issuer, the underlying common, or both cease to exist altogether. Any number of voluntary issuer actions can accomplish this—a recapitalization, merger, or liquidation and dissolution. As a matter of law, the conversion privilege is diminished or lost in all of these cases if the contract does not provide for its survival. Compare B.S.F. Co. v. Philadelphia Nat'l Bank, 204 A.2d 746 (Del.1964); Parkinson v. West End. St. Ry., 173 Mass. 446, 53 N.E. 891 (1899) (Holmes, J.).

These dilutive or destructive actions are so easy to effect and impair the bond's conversion value so substantially (in the case of a warrant, they can destroy the security's value completely), that provisions protecting against them are universal in convertible bond and warrant contracts. These "anti-dilution" provisions protect against dilutive and partially destructive actions by triggering proportionate reductions in the conversion price. Conversion value remains unaffected by the action as a result. They protect against destructive events such as mergers, recapitalizations, and liquidations by creating a right to convert into the securities or other consideration being distributed to the common stockholders in connection with the particular transaction. They also often provide for advance notice of dilutive and destructive actions. This is a lesser order of protection: like notice in advance of a call, it permits the holder to realize on the bond's conversion value prior to the consummation of the issuer action. It provides only cold comfort where, as in the case that follows, the conversion price exceeds the conversion value.

It is safe to assume that the governing contract in every one of the cases that follows in this section contained "standard" anti-dilution language. How effective were these provisions in preserving the value of the option for which the holders bargained?

American Bar Foundation, Commentaries on Indentures,
Article Thirteen, Conversion—Sample Provision, 1971

Appendix C

GARDNER AND FLORENCE CALL COWLES
FOUNDATION v. EMPIRE INC.

United States District Court, Southern District of New York, 1984.
589 F.Supp. 669 vacated on other grounds, 754 F.2d 478 (2d Cir.1985).

WHITMAN KNAPP, District Judge.

Before us is defendants' motion pursuant to Fed.R.Civ.P. 12(b)(6) to dismiss the complaint for failure to state a claim upon which relief can be granted. For reasons which follow, we grant this motion.

This case involves a merger between defendant Empire Incorporated ("Empire") and Exco Acquisition Corporation ("Exco") in which Empire was the survivor. Plaintiffs, holders of convertible subordinated debentures issued by Empire prior to the merger, claim that the terms of the merger violated certain contractual rights set out in the Indenture under which the debentures were issued, and further that defendants' actions constituted a breach of fiduciary duty owed them as debenture holders.

FACTS

Plaintiffs are the owners of $1.3 million face value of 9% convertible subordinated debentures issued by Empire in January of 1981, which debentures are due and payable on December 31, 2005. Empire sold approximately $25 million of these debentures. The debenture holders had the right to convert to Empire common stock at the ratio of 20.51 shares of stock for every $1,000 face value of debenture; or, put differently, to acquire Empire common at "conversion price" of $48.75 per share.

When the debentures were issued approximately 3 million shares of Empire common stock were outstanding. Both the debentures and the common stock were listed and trading on the New York Stock Exchange. Immediately prior to the issuance of the debentures in January 1981, Empire common was trading at approximately $49 per share (just over the $48.75 conversion price). In August of 1982 the stock traded as low as $9.50 per share. When the merger was announced in October of 1982 the stock was trading at around $20 per share, and at $27 per share immediately prior to the occurrence of the merger (still well below the $48.75 conversion price).

On June 9, 1983 Exco merged into Empire. Exco had issued 3 million shares of common stock, all of which were purchased by defendants Robert W. Plaster, S.A. Spencer, H.N. Forman, Harold M. Witt, Allen & Company and Reliance Insurance Company, for the aggregate amount of $30,000, ($.01 per share). Following approval by 96% of the Empire common shareholders who participated in the merger vote, each share of outstanding Empire common could be exchanged for $22 in cash and one new $9 face amount 9% subordinated debenture with a market value of $5. Empire shareholders thus received $27, in the form of cash plus one new debenture, upon surrender of each share of Empire common.[1] This amounted to a $7 premium over the then $20 market price. Following the repurchase of the outstanding stock, each share of Exco common stock was converted into one share of Empire common.

Prior to the merger each debenture holder was given the opportunity to convert, under the above formula, and receive the same consideration received by the Empire shareholders in the merger. The debenture holders were also informed that following the merger their debentures would continue to be convertible to Empire common. None of the debenture holders took advantage of this opportunity, presumably because the debentures were trading at a higher price than the consideration they would have received had they chosen to convert.

* * *

Count I

Count I of the amended complaint alleges that Empire breached its obligation under the Indenture by maintaining the conversion ratio of 20.51 shares per $1,000 face value of debenture instead of adjusting this ratio pursuant to § 4.05(c) of the Indenture. That section provides in part:

> In case the company shall * * * distribute to all holders of shares of its Common Stock evidences of its indebtedness or securities or assets (excluding cash dividends or cash distributions payable out of consolidated net income or retained earnings of the Company and its consolidated Subsidiaries, or dividends payable in shares of Common Stock) or rights to subscribe therefor * * * the conversion price in effect immediately prior to such distribution shall be adjusted * * *. Such adjustment shall become effective on the date of such distribution retroactively to immediately after the opening of business on the day following the record date for the determination of shareholders entitled to receive such distribution * * *.

Plaintiffs assert that the cash payment made in exchange for the surrender of the old Empire stock constituted a massive distribution of assets that should have triggered the application of this section and an

1. In order to finance this transaction, in addition to the $3 million invested by the defendants for Exco Series A Preferred Stock, defendants arranged for a series of loans worth $1 billion which were secured by liens on the assets of Empire. Defendants also provided their personal guarantees in the aggregate of $5 million to secure the financing.

adjustment of the conversion ratio. Whether or not this transaction constituted a distribution of assets in the abstract, however, a contextual reading of this section together with the remainder of the section of which it is a part (i.e., § 4.05(a)(b)) and other sections of the Indenture, indicates that this is not the type of transaction that was intended to invoke an adjustment of the conversion ratio under the quoted section. In light of the universally expressed need for certainty of terminology in the interpretation of bond contracts,[3] we must reject plaintiffs' tortuous reading of this provision.

* * *

An examination of § 4.05 reveals that the transactions it was intended to govern anticipate a limited cast of characters—the company, shareholders and debenture holders—so that changes in their relative positions can be adjusted through the application of the fairly simple formula the section provides. Subsection (a) calls for the adjustment of the conversion ratio where the company changes the number of outstanding shares through the issuance of stock dividends, stock splits, stock combinations and reclassifications. Subsection (b) requires an adjustment where the company issues warrant to buy stock at below market price levels. The quoted provision (subsection (c)) anticipates distribution to shareholders in the form of dividends. All of the above are transactions to which the § 4.05 formula is readily applicable.

* * *

Additionally, the Indenture contains a separate provision— § 4.06 [4]—which specifically governs mergers, consolidations and reorganizations. This section, in contrast to § 4.05, anticipates a change in the relationship of the shareholders to the corporation. Thus, 4.06 mandates that in certain corporate reorganizations, the debenture holder is entitled to an opportunity to convert into common stock prior

---

3. See, e.g., Broad v. Rockwell (5th Cir. 1981) 642 F.2d 929 (en banc), cert. denied (1981) 454 U.S. 965, 102 S.Ct. 506, 70 L.Ed.2d 380.

4. Section 4.06 provides:

In case of any reclassification or change of outstanding shares of Common Stock deliverable upon conversion of the Debentures (other than a change in par value or from par value to no par value, or from no par value to par value, or as a result of a subdivision or combination), or in case of any consolidation of the Company with one or more other corporations (other than a consolidation in which the Company is the continuing corporation and which does not result in any reclassification or change of outstanding shares of Common Stock issuable upon conversion of the Debentures), or in case of the merger of the Company into another corporation, or in case of

any sale or conveyance to another corporation of the property of the Company as an entirety or substantially as an entirety, the Company, or such successor or purchasing corporation, as the case may be, shall execute with the Trustee a supplemental indenture (which shall conform to the Trust Indenture Act of 1939 as in force at the date of the execution of such supplemental indenture) providing that the holder of each Debenture then outstanding shall have * * * the right to convert such Debenture into the kind and amount of shares of stock or other securities and property, including cash, receivable upon such reclassification, change, consolidation, merger, sale or conveyance by a holder of the number of shares of Common Stock into which such Debenture might have been converted immediately prior to such reclassification, change, consolidation, merger, sale or conveyance.

to the merger, and thus participate in the consideration given to the old shareholders. In such a situation, the use of a mathematical conversion formula like that contained in § 4.05 would be impossible to apply to the new entity formed and the complex interrelationship of the parties involved.[5]

With the introduction of § 4.06 to the task of interpreting the terms of the indenture before us, it thus becomes even clearer that an adjustment of the conversion ratio as requested by the plaintiffs is inapplicable to the Empire–Exco merger. Section 4.06 applies to mergers. Section 4.05 does not. The fact that § 4.06 by its terms does not apply to this merger because Empire was the surviving corporation is of no consequence to the determination of this motion. The sole question before us with respect to Count I is the applicability of § 4.05(c). "That [interpretation of a contract] will be chosen which best accords with the sense of the remainder of the contract, and that interpretation is favored which will make every part of the contract effective." *Broad,* supra, 642 F.2d at 947. Under this sound rule, we find § 4.05(c) to be inapplicable to the Empire–Exco merger, and dismiss Count I.

[The court went on to dismiss plaintiff's allegations of a breach of an implied covenant of fair dealing and breach of a fiduciary duty owed to plaintiffs as debentureholders. These sections of the opinion are set out infra pp. 434–436.]

NOTE: CONVERTIBLE BOND CONTRACTS

1. Anti-dilution provisions give rise to endless interpretive problems. Many cases, like *Cowles Foundation v. Empire,* concern the questions whether a particular issuer action is within a particular contingency provided for in the contract, and thus protected or unprotected. See, e.g., Prescott, Ball & Turben v. LTV Corp., 531 F.Supp. 213 (S.D.N.Y.1981) and Stephenson v. Plastics Corp. of America, 276 Minn. 400, 150 N.W.2d 668 (1967) (whether a spin off of a subsidiary is a "dividend" or "capital reorganization"). Other cases raise the question whether the agreement is to be read to preserve the option holder's proportionate interest in the enterprise by altering the price or rate at which his security is convertible to stock to reflect proposed alterations in the structure of the enterprise (e.g., stock splits, capital distributions, etc.), or should be read to force him to elect either to exercise the option or to suffer the dilution when an alteration in capital structure is proposed. See e.g., Pittsburgh Terminal Corporation v. The Baltimore

---

5. We note that although plaintiffs devote several pages to discussion of the § 4.05 conversion rate, including presentations of four "hypotheticals" dealing with the conversions required where distributions are made of assets worth $\frac{1}{2}$, $\frac{3}{4}$, $\frac{7}{8}$ and $\frac{15}{16}$ of Empire's stock, nowhere do they state precisely what conversion should have been effected in the situation at bar. Defendants have calculated that the formula would in fact yield a negative result—which conclusion plaintiffs dispute without providing a mathematical answer of their own.

and Ohio Railroad Company infra p. 422; Meckel v. Continental Resources Co., 758 F.2d 811 (2d Cir.1985); Merritt–Chapman & Scott Corp. v. New York Trust Co., 184 F.2d 954 (2d Cir.1950). As already noted, the latter alternative is effected by providing, instead of an adjustment of the conversion price or rate, that the bondholder shall receive notice of the proposed alteration and be required to exercise his conversion option or forego the proposed distribution within the noticed period. Generally, the burden to draft against specific contingencies is imposed by courts on the bondholder. Should the burden of specificity instead lie with the issuer?

2. *Good faith provisions.* The limitations on the effectiveness of standard form anti-dilution clauses have not escaped the notice of the corporate bar. Many private placement debt contracts contain a so-called "good faith" anti-dilution provision. This catches all actions not otherwise covered which "materially and adversely affect the conversion rights of the holders." See Kaplan, Piercing the Corporate Boilerplate: Anti–Dilution Clauses in Convertible Securities, 33 U.Chi.L.Rev. 1, 18 n. 27 (1965). In theory this shifts the risk of dilution and destruction back to the issuer.

3. *Call.* The integration of the conversion privilege with redemption provisions is a constant source of problems. At the time of the call, the bondholder is generally forced by the terms of the security to opt either to convert and lose the benefit of seniority or to accept the cash call price and terminate his investment. Problems which may be created by the interplay between the call provisions (particularly their "notice" requirements) and the conversion privileges are illustrated in the Pittsburgh Terminal Corporation case, infra p. 422; Jamie Securities Co. v. The Limited, Inc., 880 F.2d 1572 (2d Cir.1989); Mueller v. Howard Aircraft Corp., 329 Ill.App. 570, 70 N.E.2d 203 (1946); Green v. Hamilton Int'l Corp., 493 F.Supp. 596 (S.D.N.Y.1979) (invoking Rule 10b–5); Van Gemert v. The Boeing Co., 520 F.2d 1373 (2d Cir.1975), certiorari denied 423 U.S. 947 (1975); compare Meckel v. Continental Resources Co., 758 F.2d 811 (2d Cir.1985).

4. *Issue of additional common stock.* How should the convertible bond contract deal with a subsequent issue in an arms length transaction of common stock for a price lower than the conversion price? Fifty years ago standard anti-dilution provisions employed a "conversion price" formula. Under this, the conversion price was adjusted downward whenever stock was sold below the conversion price. The idea was that the conversion privilege was an option on a specified portion of the issuer's earnings. The operative theory of injurious dilution changed during the 1950s and 1960s. The contracts then provided for downward adjustment of the conversion price only in response to below market offerings of new stock and rights to existing common stockholders. The new theory was that the contract should (a) protect not a percentage claim on earnings but the current market level of conversion value and conversion premium, and (b) operate only when stockholders receive a benefit at the bondholders expense (which presumably is impossible if the offering is made at the market price) and that

otherwise there should be parity of treatment. See Kaplan, supra at 18; Bratton, supra at 687 n. 76.

(B) DUTIES IMPLIED IN LAW

Does the inclusion of a conversion privilege in a bond import a status change, so that the convertible bondholder benefits from an issuer fiduciary duty where the holder of a straight bond does not? If so, does the duty extend only to actions impairing the value of the conversion privilege and not to actions impairing the bond's debt value? If no fiduciary duty obtains, does the conversion privilege's susceptibility to easy impairment give rise to a contractual good faith duty that supports judicial intervention to restrain issuer action materially diluting or otherwise impairing the value of the conversion privilege? Finally, does the interest in the corporation's equity carried by the conversion privilege import bondholder standing to enforce management duties to the corporation by means of a derivative action?

The cases that follow deal with these questions.

HARFF v. KERKORIAN

Court of Chancery of Delaware, 1974.
324 A.2d 215.

QUILLEN, Chancellor:

This action is a combined derivative and class action challenging a singular corporate act—the declaration and payment of a $1.75 per share dividend by Metro–Goldwyn–Mayer, Inc., in the late fall of 1973.

Plaintiffs are holders of 5% convertible subordinated debentures due 1993 which were issued by Metro–Goldwyn–Mayer, Inc. (MGM), pursuant to an Indenture Agreement between MGM and The Chase Manhattan Bank (Trustee) dated July 1, 1968. On November 21, 1973, the Board of Directors of MGM declared a cash dividend, the first cash dividend since 1969, in the amount of $1.75 per share of common stock. Plaintiffs contend that the dividends were declared improvidently and for the financial benefit of defendant Kerkorian, a member of the Board of Directors as well as the controlling stockholder of MGM. Plaintiffs allege that the declaration of cash dividends (1) damaged MGM by depleting its capital, thereby endangering its future prospects and (2) damaged the debenture holders in that it impaired the value of the conversion feature and caused a decline in the market value of the debentures themselves.

On this basis, plaintiffs are simultaneously maintaining a derivative action on behalf of the corporation as well as a class action on behalf of all holders of MGM's convertible debentures, excluding the members of the Board of Directors. The defendants are the individual directors of MGM and the corporation itself. In connection with the derivative claim, plaintiffs seek to recover from the individual defendants, on behalf of the corporation, the amount of the cash dividends which was paid pursuant to the November 21 declaration and damages for the loss of the use of the funds which were appropriated to make the dividend payments. In addition, plaintiffs request that all damages which may be recovered on the derivative claim be placed in a constructive trust "for the benefit of the class members." With regard to the class action, plaintiffs seek to recover money damages for class members.

Defendants have moved to dismiss the derivative action on the ground that plaintiffs lack standing to maintain an action on behalf of MGM due to the fact that they are not stockholders. Defendants also seek dismissal of the class action on the following grounds: * * * (2) although plaintiffs' rights and remedies as holders of convertible debentures are governed by the Indenture Agreement pursuant to which the convertible debentures were issued, plaintiffs have failed to allege that the defendants have breached any of the terms of that Agreement and, therefore, plaintiffs have failed to state a cause of action * * *.

I.

STANDING TO MAINTAIN DERIVATIVE ACTIONS

Defendants first contend that plaintiffs do not have standing to sue derivatively as they are not stockholders of MGM. * * * Plaintiffs, on the other hand, argue that the convertibility of their debentures into common stock of MGM provides them with the necessary standing to sue on behalf of MGM. Plaintiffs emphasize the fact that they are not suing on behalf of themselves but rather are seeking to enforce a claim which belongs to the corporation which management refused to assert.

* * *

But it has been generally accepted under Delaware law that only one who was a stockholder at the time of the transaction or one whose shares devolved upon him by operation of law may maintain a derivative action. Folk, The Delaware General Corporation Law, pp. 485–486. For purposes of a derivative action, an equitable owner is considered a stockholder. * * * But Delaware law seems clear that stockholder status at the time of the transaction being attacked and throughout the litigation is essential. * * *

The holder of an option to purchase stock is not an equitable stockholder of the corporation. Gamble v. Penn Valley Crude Oil Corp., 34 Del.Ch. 359, 364, 104 A.2d 257, 260 (Ch.1954). Debenture holders are not stockholders and their rights are determined by their contracts. Wolfensohn v. Madison Fund, Inc., Del.Supr., 253 A.2d 72, 75 (1969). A holder of a convertible bond "does not become a stockholder, by his contract, in equity any more than at law." Parkinson v. West End St. Ry. Co., 173 Mass. 446, 53 N.E. 891, 892 (1899), an opinion by Justice Holmes.

Plaintiffs conceded at oral argument that creditors generally are not entitled to sue derivatively. Nor does this case involve any statutorily recognized rights where debenture holders are deemed to be stockholders. Compare 8 Del.C., § 221. Nevertheless, plaintiffs contend that the convertibility feature of the debentures which they hold sets them apart from other creditors and gives them standing to maintain a derivative suit. Plaintiffs rely on Hoff v. Sprayregan, S.D.N.Y., 52 F.R.D. 243 (1971), wherein it was held that convertible debenture holders had standing to institute a derivative suit. In *Hoff,* the plaintiffs had alleged a violation of the Securities Exchange Act of 1934, which classifies convertible debentures within the definitional meaning of "equity security." 15 U.S.C.A. § 78c(a)(11). On the basis of this definitional section in the Federal Act, the District Court found that the convertible debenture holders were "stockholders" for purposes of bringing the derivative action.

In this case, plaintiffs are not suing under the Federal Act and they do not contend that they are stockholders of MGM. They do, however, argue that the result in *Hoff* should be followed due to their interest in the stock of the corporation. They also assert that inasmuch as the minority stockholders of MGM received their proportionate share of the dividends complained of, such stockholders are not in as favorable a position as are the plaintiffs to challenge the wrong to the corporation. According to the plaintiffs, such stockholders would either be precluded entirely from suing derivatively or would, at best, be faced with a very strict burden of proof.

Notwithstanding these arguments, the conclusion is inescapable that plaintiffs are creditors of MGM and simply do not have standing to maintain a stockholder's derivative action under Delaware law.

* * *

II.

THE CLASS ACTION

* * *

The basis upon which plaintiffs assert the class claim is an alleged breach by defendants of their fiduciary duty to refrain from acting in their own self interest. Plaintiffs contend that the dividends were improvidently declared and that they evidenced self-dealing on the part of the defendants since they were the controlling stockholders of MGM. The harm which plaintiffs claim they suffered as a result of the breach by defendants was the reduction of the market value of their debentures and the impairment of the conversion feature of their securities. Plaintiffs suggested at oral argument that the issue to be decided is whether or not the declaration of the challenged dividend constituted a breach of the defendants' fiduciary duties. A more fundamental question which must be dealt with, however, is whether or not any fiduciary duties existed as between defendants and the convertible debenture holders.

Plaintiffs do not contend that the payment of dividends resulted in the insolvency of MGM nor do they allege that the dividends violated any Delaware statute. And, although counsel for plaintiffs at oral argument categorized the declaration of dividends as amounting to fraud, plaintiffs have failed to allege fraud in their complaint on the class claim. The authorities cited by plaintiffs for the proposition that creditors can maintain an action against management for violation of rights which exist independently of the Indenture Agreement all involved either fraud or insolvency. E.g., Noble v. European Mortgage & Investment Corporation, 19 Del.Ch. 216, 165 A. 157 (Ch.1933); Slater Trust Co. v. Randolph–Macon Coal Co., 166 F. 171 (S.D.N.Y.1908). It is apparent that unless there are special circumstances which affect the rights of the debenture holders as creditors of the corporation, e.g., fraud, insolvency, or a violation of a statute, the rights of the debenture holders are confined to the terms of the Indenture Agreement pursuant to which the debentures were issued. Helvering v. Southwest Consol. Corporation, 315 U.S. 194, 200, 62 S.Ct. 546, 551, 86 L.Ed. 789 (1942); City of Covington v. Sanitation District No. 1, 301 S.W.2d 885, 890 (Ky.1957); see 19 Am.Jur.2d, Corporations, § 1069.

Part of the investment which plaintiffs have made in MGM is undeniably the right to convert their debentures into common stock of MGM. With this investment, however, runs no guarantee that the market value of the common stock will appreciate. The fact that the market value of the common stock is not sufficiently attractive to make conversion profitable at a particular time does not give rise to a cause of action against management. To the contrary, the legal payment of large cash dividends is a valid means by which a corporation can discourage convertible debenture holders from exercising their right to convert their debentures into common stock. 4 Cavitch, Business Organizations, § 92.01[3].

It is my opinion that no fiduciary duties existed as between the parties and that the rights of the convertible debenture holders in this case are confined to the terms of the Indenture Agreement. As plaintiffs have failed to allege any default under that Indenture the class claim must be dismissed. The effect of the "no-action" clause contained in § 8.04 and as well the "no-recourse" clause found in § 15.01 of the Indenture need not be determined. Summary judgment on the class claim is granted in favor of the defendants. It is so ordered.

HARFF v. KERKORIAN

Supreme Court of Delaware, 1975.
347 A.2d 133.

PER CURIAM:

This appeal arises in a combined derivative and class action brought by holders of convertible subordinate debentures against the corporation and its directors, claiming damages for wrongful declaration of dividend. The Court of Chancery dismissed the derivative action and granted summary judgment in favor of the defendants in the class action. See Opinion below at 324 A.2d 215. The plaintiffs appeal both rulings.

I.

The Court of Chancery ruled that debenture holders lack standing under Delaware law to sue derivatively because they are not "stockholders" under 8 Del.C. § 327. We affirm that ruling for the reasons stated in the Opinion below. See 324 A.2d at 218–220.

II.

As to the class action, in response to the plaintiffs' claim of breach of fiduciary duty by the directors, the Court of Chancery held that the complaint failed to state a claim upon which relief may be granted because the right upon which the plaintiffs rely is not within the terms of the Indenture to which the plaintiffs are confined in the absence of "fraud, insolvency, or a violation of a statute". 324 A.2d at 222. And the Court of Chancery found no assertion of fraud in the complaint stating: " * * * although counsel for plaintiffs at oral argument categorized the declaration of dividends as amounting to fraud, plaintiffs have failed to allege fraud in their complaint on the class claim." 324 A.2d at 221.

It was error to so conclude. The class action claim alleged in the complaint (paragraphs 25 and 26) incorporated by reference all of the allegations contained in paragraphs 12 through 24 of the complaint; and paragraph 22 alleged:

> "22. The $10,500,000 dividend was conceived and effectuated by the individual defendants fraudulently and in breach of their fiduciary duties for the personal benefit of Kerkorian."

The claim of fraud is thus clearly sounded in the complaint; and it permeates the plaintiffs' position *vis a vis* the Indenture limitations: the plaintiffs argue that the "dividend was wrongfully declared"; that this "tort claim is wholly unrelated to and unaffected by any contract rights that the plaintiffs may have under the Indenture Agreement"; that the directors "were not merely negligent but were guilty of wrongful acts"; that "here, tortious acts have been committed"; that the "alleged wrongful declaration of a dividend is a tort"; that if " 'special circumstances' are necessary [to enable debenture holders to assert a right not included in the Indenture], * * * the intentional looting of a corporation clearly qualifies as such."

While the plaintiffs' demonstrated reluctance to use the word "fraud" is remarkable, there can be no doubt that the issue of fraud is sufficiently asserted to require trial of that issue.

Accordingly, the summary judgment in favor of the defendants in the class action is reversed and the cause remanded for trial of the issue of fraud.

We abstain from passing at this stage upon the various collateral questions presented by the parties, here and below. Those questions may be best examined and determined in the light of a further development of the facts of the case upon the trial of the fraud issue.

* * *

Reversed and remanded.*

PROBLEM: FAIR AND UNFAIR DIVIDENDS

Suppose W Corp., earning $800,000 annually after taxes with 1,000,000 shares of common stock outstanding selling at $10 per share, issues $200,000 principal amount 8% debentures convertible into common stock at prices ranging from 15 to 25 over a period of 10 years. The proceeds of the debentures are used to open a new line of business which also prospers, so that 5 years later, when the conversion price is 20, W Corp. is earning $1.30 per share and its stock is selling at 18. A subsidiary is formed to conduct the new line of business, its stock is distributed as a dividend to W stockholders, share for share, and the price of W stock returns to 10. Are the holders of the convertibles "unfairly" treated if W has ample earned surplus to cover the distribution, and the conversion terms provide: "In case the Company shall declare a dividend upon the capital stock payable otherwise than out of earnings or surplus (other than paid-in surplus) or otherwise than in capital stock, the purchase price per share in effect immediately prior to the declaration of such dividend shall be reduced by an amount equal, in the case of a dividend in cash, to the amount thereof payable per share of the capital stock or, in the case of any other dividend, to the fair value thereof per share of the capital stock as determined by the Board of Directors of the Company."

Would they be "unfairly" treated if the company had no earned surplus when the convertibles were issued and at the end of each year thereafter it distributed all its annual earnings, and partly as a result thereof, during each year its stock sold at no higher than 12?

Would they be "unfairly" treated if W, having a large accumulated earned surplus, paid a cash dividend of 90 cents each year?

Can a contract be drafted which would provide "fair" treatment for the convertible holders? See Wood v. Coastal States Gas Corp., 401 A.2d 932 (Del.Ct.1979).

-----

* [Ed.Note] The "interest" of holders of convertible securities as "shareholders" has been at issue not merely in suits raising the question of their standing to bring derivative actions to police managerial misbehavior (see Hoff v. Sprayregan, 52 F.R.D. 243 (S.D.N.Y.1971) suggesting a conflict with Harff, discussed in Note 26 Syracuse L.Rev. 730 (1975)) but also in claims that management owes them the same fiduciary obligations owed to shareholders and that they are shareholders for purposes of determining the corporation's entitlement to assert the attorney-client privilege against revealing documents to debenture-holder plaintiffs. See Valente v. Pepsico Inc., 68 F.R.D. 361 (D.Del.1975).

What limits, if any, does "fairness" impose on the commons' right to dilute or frustrate the expectations of the convertible holder whose contract does not forbid *all* dividends?

PITTSBURGH TERMINAL CORPORATION v. THE BALTIMORE AND OHIO RAILROAD COMPANY

United States Court of Appeals, Third Circuit, 1982.
680 F.2d 933, cert. denied, 459 U.S. 1056 (1982).

The Baltimore and Ohio Railroad Company (B & O) operated a railroad and also owned substantial non-rail assets, such as real estate, timber and mineral reserves. It had outstanding, and listed on the New York Stock Exchange (NYSE), both common stock and 4.5% debentures due in 2010 which were convertible into common stock at a ratio of 10 shares for each $1000 face amount of debenture. Prior to 1977 the Chesapeake and Ohio Railway Company (C & O) acquired over 99 percent of the B & O common stock. Since all the B & O stock was owned by C & O and 13 individuals, it was de-listed from the NYSE. The convertible debentures however continued to be listed and traded on the NYSE. Because the B & O did not pay dividends after 1961 and there was no market for its common stock after C & O acquired 99 percent of it, there was no incentive for the holders of the convertible bonds to convert.

Under regulations of the Interstate Commerce Commission (ICC), railroad corporations were prohibited from engaging in non-rail business; therefore, B & O's and C & O's assets not used in rail transportation remained undeveloped. Beginning in 1973, C & O segregated its own non-rail assets and placed them in a separate corporation, Chessie Resources, Inc., so that they could be developed free of constraints imposed by the ICC. With the same objective, C & O's parent (Chessie) created a Restructuring Committee in January 1977, to plan the transfer by B & O of its assets to Mid–Allegheny Corporation (MAC), a wholly-owned B & O subsidiary, and then to distribute the MAC stock as a dividend to B & O's 14 common stockholders.

Ostensibly in order to avoid the possible necessity to file a registration statement under the Securities Act of 1933 with respect to that distribution, the Restructuring Committee sought to distribute the MAC stock as a dividend before the many B & O debenture holders could convert to B & O common stock, and while there was only a total of 14 common stockholders of B & O. Avoidance of such registration would save expenses and eliminate the practical difficulties entailed in placing a value on B & O's non-rail assets; and the distribution to the 14 stockholders would also have the effect of depriving the holders of the convertible debentures of any share of that dividend. In order to preclude conversion by the debenture holders * and the concomitant

* [Ed.Note] The debentures were callable at $102.5 (in 1977), but to eliminate them by call might require disclosures that would induce conversions. See Zahn v. Transamerica Corporation, 162 F.2d 36 (3d Cir.1947); Speed v. Transamerica Corpora-

necessity to register the stock, the Restructuring Committee decided to avoid giving notice of the MAC transaction to the convertible debenture holders prior to the record date of the dividend-in-kind—by declaring the dividend payable to the holders of record on the date of declaration—December 13, 1977. By the terms of the dividend resolution, distribution of the MAC stock to B & O stockholders was to be made to the record holders promptly after the SEC should signify that registration of the MAC stock was unnecessary, or if registration was determined to be necessary, promptly after such registration.

[The Court (Judge Gibbons) said:]

I.

* * *

Conversion rights to the bondholders are protected in the event of merger or sale. Article V, section 12 of the Indenture provides:

> SECTION 12. The Company covenants and agrees that it will not declare and/or pay any dividend on its common stock payable in stock or create any rights to subscribe for stock or securities convertible into stock unless in any such case notice of the taking of a record date for the determination of the stockholders entitled to receive such dividend, distribution or right is given at least ten days prior thereto by at least one publication in an Authorized Newspaper. A copy of each such published notice shall promptly after such publication be filed with the Trustee.

When the convertible debentures were issued in 1956, B & O entered into a listing agreement with the NYSE relating to them, which incorporated by reference B & O's earlier listing agreements. Listing Agreement A–12653 for an earlier bond issue, incorporated by reference in that for the 1956 convertible debenture issue, provides:

> 4. The Corporation will give the Exchange at least ten days' notice in advance of the closing of the transfer books, or of the taking of a record of its stockholders for any purpose.

> 5. The Corporation will publish promptly to the holders of any of its securities listed on the Exchange any action taken by the Corporation with respect to dividends or to the allotment of rights to subscribe or to any rights or benefits pertaining to the ownership of its securities listed on the Exchange; and shall give prompt notice to the Exchange of any such action; and shall afford the holders of its securities listed on the Exchange a proper period within which to record their interests and to exercise their rights; and shall issue all such rights in form approved by the Exchange and will make the same transferable, payable and deliverable in the Borough of Manhattan, in the City of New York. (455a).

tion, 235 F.2d 369 (3d Cir.1956). Compare Van Gemert v. Boeing Co., 520 F.2d 1373 (2d Cir.1975), cert. denied, 423 U.S. 947 (1975) with Meckel v. Continental Resources Co., 758 F.2d 811 (2d Cir.1985).

In addition to the Listing Agreements, the B & O is bound by the Rules of the NYSE. Section A–2 of its Manual, "Timely Disclosure," provides:

A corporation whose securities are listed on the New York Stock Exchange, Inc., is expected to release to the public any news or information which might reasonably be expected to materially affect the market for those securities. This is one of the most important and fundamental purposes of the listing agreement which each corporation enters into with the exchange.

509 F.Supp. at 1008.

In November of 1977, * * * plaintiff Monroe Guttmann wrote to the Secretary of B & O:

As one of the very few public owners of B & O common stock, we are concerned that we may not be made aware of any dividend the directors declare on the common stock in sufficient time to convert any of our convertible debentures.

Although it may not be customary to do so in view of the fact that declaration of a dividend may not be widely publicized, if publicized at all, we ask that you notify us promptly of any such dividend declaration so that we will have an opportunity to convert debentures in time to receive such dividend if we choose to do so.

Will you please let me know what provisions there are in the by-laws of the company that govern the time which must elapse between the declaration of a dividend, the record date and the payable date.

To this pointed inquiry the Secretary, on November 17, 1977, replied:

Thank you for your letter of November 11. We appreciate your concern as a holder of B & O Convertible Debentures as to whether B & O would fail to disclose the declaration of a dividend in its common stock.

You may be assured that if B & O should have any information to announce regarding dividend action on B & O stock, such information will be disseminated promptly to the public at large. Because we cannot prefer you over the public at large advance advice cannot be sent to you, but I will make sure that you get a copy of such press release. We are not in a position to help you with respect to your decision whether or not to convert.

There is no by-law provision relating to the timing of the declaration, record, and payment dates.

By the time of Guttmann's inquiry and the Secretary's reply, the Restructuring Committee's plan to structure the MAC transaction so as to avoid timely notice to the convertible bondholders was well advanced.

* * *

II.

The first of these consolidated actions was commenced by Pittsburgh Terminal Corporation on December 28, 1977, and the others soon followed. On March 7, 1978 the District Court issued a preliminary injunction restraining the defendants from proceeding with the dividend in MAC stock. Defendants appealed from that order, and when they agreed to hold sufficient shares of B & O and MAC stock to satisfy the claims of the convertible debenture holders, should they prevail, this court reversed that injunction.

* * *

[T]he consolidated cases went to trial on amended complaints challenging the December 13, 1977 actions of the B & O Board of Directors. The complaints alleged that these actions violated section 10(b) of the Securities and Exchange Act, 15 U.S.C. § 78j(b), the contractual rights of the convertible debenture holders under the provisions of the Indenture, their rights as third party beneficiaries of the NYSE listing agreements, the obligations of B & O under the rules of the NYSE, and the fiduciary duties of directors and of majority stockholders under Maryland law. The District Court, over defendants' objection, held that the convertible debenture holders had standing to make these claims, but rejected each of them. * * *

III.

A. *Purchase or Sale*

Section 10(b) prohibits the use of manipulative or deceptive devices or contrivances "in connection with the purchase or sale of any security." The District Court held that a contract to obtain common stock in exchange for the surrender of a convertible debenture is a contract for purchase or sale of a security, and thus that the debenture holders could sue.

* * *

[W]e hold that the conversion option in a convertible debenture qualifies as a contract for the purchase or sale of a security * * *.

B. *Duty to Speak*

The Bondholders contend that by fixing the dividend date and the record date of the MAC dividend so as to prevent them from exercising their conversion option in time to participate in that dividend, the defendants violated section 10(b) and SEC Rule 10b–5(a) and (c), 17 C.F.R. 240.10b–5(a) and (c) (1981). It is undisputed that the defendants made a knowing decision to time the December 13, 1977 transactions so as to prevent the Bondholders from obtaining timely notice of them. Defendants contend that the decision was lawful because they made no affirmative misrepresentation and because they were under no affirmative obligation to speak.

In Chiarella v. United States, 445 U.S. 222, 228, 100 S.Ct. 1108, 1114, 63 L.Ed.2d 348 (1980), the Court observed that "one who fails to disclose material information prior to the consummation of a transaction commits fraud only when he is under a duty to do so." It held that a printer, who had no fiduciary obligation to a corporation or its shareholders, and who did not receive information as a result of the breach of any fiduciary relationship, could not be liable for a criminal violation of section 10(b). "He was not [the sellers'] agent, he was not a fiduciary, he was not a person in whom the sellers had placed their trust and confidence." 445 U.S. at 232, 100 S.Ct. at 1116. The defendants contend that *Chiarella* requires an affirmance, because like the printer who happened upon material market information, none of them had a duty to speak.

To put that contention in context, we note that the Bondholders were on December 13, 1977, holders of options to acquire B & O equity securities, while C & O was a majority holder of those securities having voting control of B & O. The convertible debentures were listed on the NYSE, and the listing agreement applicable to them imposed on B & O the affirmative duties (a) to give ten days notice to the Exchange of a record date for a dividend, and (b) to "afford the holders of its securities listed on the Exchange a proper period within which to record their interests and exercise their rights." These requirements of the listing agreement parallel those in SEC Rule 10b–17, which provides:

> (a) It shall constitute a "manipulative or deceptive device or contrivance" as used in section 10(b) of the Act for any issuer of a class of securities * * * to fail to give notice in accordance with paragraph (b) of this section of the following actions relating to such class of securities:

> (1) A dividend or other distribution in cash or in kind, except an ordinary interest payment on a debt security, but including a dividend or distribution of any security of the same or another issuer; * * *

* * * B & O is the issuer of the convertible debentures, the MAC distribution is a dividend of a security, and that dividend related to the convertible debentures since it was material to a decision about exercising the conversion option. The convertible debentures were not simple debt securities, for which the information about dividends ordinarily would not be material.

Whatever may be the fiduciary duty of majority stockholders and corporate directors under Maryland law to general unsecured creditors, we are here dealing with securities having an equity option feature. Maryland follows the settled rule that a control stockholder owes a fiduciary obligation not to exercise that control to the disadvantage of minority equity participants. Cooperative Milk Service v. Hepner, 198 Md. 104, 81 A.2d 219, 224 (1951). Similarly, Maryland directors must act as fiduciaries to all equity participants. Coffman v. Maryland Pub. Co., 167 Md. 275, 173 A. 248, 254 (1934); Lawson v. Baltimore Paint and Chemical Corp., 347 F.Supp. 967, 975 (D.Md.1972). Although no Maryland case has been called to our attention presenting the precise issue of fiduciary obligations to holders of securities containing stock options, we would be very much surprised if Maryland or any other state would today hold that no such obligations were owed by an issuer of such securities and its directors. Moreover the scope of the obligation of the fiduciary depends upon the nature of the interest of the beneficiary. If the beneficiary of a fiduciary duty needs information in order intelligently to protect that interest, the withholding of it, especially when withholding it confers advantage upon others (in this case C & O and Chessie), is an obvious breach of duty.

The 1956 Indenture under which B & O borrowed the sums evidenced by the convertible debentures was made in New York and the loan transaction completed there. B & O's obligation, therefore, is a New York contract. The law of that state is "that in every contract there is an implied covenant that neither party shall do anything which will have the effect of destroying or injuring the right of the other party to receive the fruits of the contract * * *." Kirke La Shelle Co. v. Paul Armstrong Co., 263 N.Y. 79, 87, 188 N.E. 163, 167 (1933). See Van Gemert v. Boeing Co., 553 F.2d 812, 815 (2d Cir.1977); Restatement (Second) of Contracts § 205 (1981). Defendants in this case took steps to prevent the Bondholders from receiving information which they needed in order to receive the fruits of their conversion option should they choose to exercise it. As a matter of New York contract law, B & O had a duty to speak.

In the present context we do not look to the listing agreement. Rule 10b–17, the Maryland law of fiduciary obligations, and the New York law of contracts, as sources of independent causes of action, though they well may be. Rather we look to them as sources of a duty to speak, breach of which under section 10(b) and Rule 10b–5(a) and (c) gives rise to a cause of action for fraud. Those four independent sources of duty to speak in the circumstances of this case amply serve, separately or collectively, to distinguish it from Chiarella v. United States, supra. We need not consider other sources of such duty relied on by the Bondholders.

C. *Scienter*

The defendants urge that even if they were under a duty to speak, their decision not to do so in this instance did not involve the scienter required by the Supreme Court's interpretation of section 10(b).

* * *

On the facts as found * * * the District Court erred in ruling that the defendants lacked the scienter required for a section 10(b) violation.

We hold, therefore, that on the facts found by the District Court, the December 13, 1977 transaction, designed to deprive the Bondholders of timely notice in order to exercise their conversion option if they should so desire was a manipulative or deceptive device or contrivance in violation of section 10(b).

* * *

GARTH, Circuit Judge, concurring in part and concurring in the judgment.

I agree that the judgment of the district court must be reversed. However, in concluding that the defendants violated Rule 10b–5, * * * I would predicate their duty to disclose the Mid–Allegheny Corporation (MAC) dividend solely on the provisions of Rule 10b–17, * * *, rather than on the complex of theories set forth in Part III–B of Judge Gibbons' opinion. I thus would not reach the question whether the defendants had a duty to disclose under the New York Stock Exchange (NYSE) listing agreement, the Maryland law of fiduciary obligations, or the New York law of contracts.

* * *

Rule 10b–17 provides that the failure of an issuer to give ten days' prior notice of the declaration of a dividend *relating to* a publicly traded security constitutes a "manipulative or deceptive device or contrivance" within the prohibitions of section 10(b) of the Securities Exchange Act of 1934, 15 U.S.C. § 78j(b) (1976). Here, it is undisputed that while the common stock of the Baltimore & Ohio Railroad Company was not publicly traded or listed on any national securities exchange (99.63 percent of the common stock was owned by the Chesapeake & Ohio Railway Company), the convertible debentures were publicly traded and were listed on the NYSE. Thus, the B & O convertible debentures are a publicly traded class of securities within the meaning of Rule 10b–17.[2] It is also undisputed that the B & O failed to give ten days' notice of its action in declaring the MAC stock dividend to the National Association of Securities Dealers (NASD), or to the NYSE in accordance with the procedures set forth in the B & O's listing agreement with that Exchange. Thus, the only remaining question to be answered is whether the declaration of the MAC dividend was an action "relating to" the publicly traded convertible debentures within the meaning of Rule 10b–17. If Rule 10b–17 applies, a duty of disclosure arises, the breach of which provides the predicate for a violation of Rule 10b–5. See generally Chiarella v. United States, 445 U.S. 222, 235, 100 S.Ct. 1108, 1118, 63 L.Ed.2d 348 (1980).

* * *

It is obvious that a stock dividend declared on common stock comes within the terms of Rule 10b–17. It would be anomalous if a stock dividend which becomes payable simply by the exercise of converting a debenture were not considered as "relating to such class of [convertible debenture] securities." It seems to me that in the context of Rule 10b–

---

2. Rule 10b–17 is not limited to equity securities. That dividends or other distributions relating to debt securities are covered by the Rule is evident from the Rule's exclusion from its notice requirement of "ordinary interest payment[s] on a debt security." Rule 10b–17(a)(1). This clearly indicates that dividends or other distributions relating to debt securities, other than ordinary interest payments, are governed by the Rule. If Rule 10b–17 covers equity and debt securities, it must cover a mixed debt-equity security such as a convertible debenture.

17, a dividend "relates to" a security if the declaration of that dividend makes the security significantly more or less valuable, whether by directly increasing or decreasing the value of the security or by enabling the holder of the security to take steps which would either augment the security's worth or prevent the diminution of its value.

Here, the convertible debentureholders claim that the value of the non-rail assets of the B & O which are represented by the MAC dividend roughly approximates $250 million. Prior to the declaration of the MAC dividend, the debentures included the right to convert to B & O common stock which represented both rail and non-rail assets; after the dividend declaration, the debentures were convertible into B & O common stock which no longer represented the non-rail assets and *only* represented the rail assets. Tested by the definition set out above, it is evident to me that the declaration of such a dividend in which the convertible debentureholders could share in both categories of assets by exercising their conversion option, is an action which clearly "relates to" this class of securities.

Accordingly, I agree with Judge Gibbons, who has reached a similar conclusion in his opinion where he has indicated that the MAC dividend "related to the convertible debentures since it was material to a decision about exercising the [debentures'] conversion option." Op. of Gibbons, J., at 941. Under the analysis I have suggested, the defendants had a duty under Rule 10b–17 to give advance notice to the NASD or the NYSE (and through them to the convertible debentureholders) of the declaration of the MAC dividend. The conceded failure of the defendants to give such notice rendered them liable in damages under Rule 10b–5. That being the case, there is no need to consider whether any other theory is viable which would impose a duty upon the defendants to give notice to the holders of the convertible debentures.

Accordingly, I join Judge Gibbons' opinion except for Part III–B, and concur in the reversal of the judgment below.

ADAMS, Circuit Judge, dissenting.

* * * Unlike my two colleagues, I conclude that B & O was under no legal obligation—pursuant to Rule 10b–17 or otherwise—to provide plaintiffs with advance notice of the MAC dividend. I therefore respectfully dissent.

* * *

The traditional view is that the convertible debenture holder is a mere creditor until conversion, whose relationship with the issuing corporation is governed by contract and statute.

* * *

Justice Holmes expanded upon this principle, holding for the Supreme Court of Massachusetts that the debenture holder had no right, apart from contract, to object to corporate actions that dilute or destroy the value of the conversion option: * * *

* * *

It is simply an option to take stock as it may turn out to be when the time for choice arrives. The bondholder does not become a stockholder, by his contract, in equity any more than at law. * * *

* * * [T]he contract does not prevent the corporation from consolidating with another in such a way as to make performance impossible, any more than it prevents the issue of new stock in such a way as to make performance valueless.

Parkinson v. West End St. Ry. Co., 173 Mass. 446, 53 N.E. 891, 892 (1899). * * * And in Lisman v. Milwaukee, L.S. & W. Ry. Co., 161 F. 472 (E.D.Wis.1908), aff'd 170 F. 1020 (7th Cir.1909), the court held that convertible debenture holders could not complain when the railroad company in which they had invested merged with another railroad. The fact that the parties "were bound to" have anticipated such a consolidation when they entered into the option contract was dispositive.

The rights and remedies of convertible debenture holders have expanded since the turn of the century. Most notably, the Securities Exchange Act of 1934 accords convertible debenture holders the federal statutory rights of "equity security holders," able, for example, to employ section 10(b) of the Act to protect against fraud or manipulative devices. 15 U.S.C. § 78j. Congress's explicit recognition of convertibles as equity, as well as debt, securities has had significant consequences. In Kusner v. First Pennsylvania Corp., 531 F.2d 1234 (3d Cir.1976), for instance, this Court held that a convertible debenture holder, who alleged that he had purchased the securities in reliance on a false and misleading prospectus, had standing to sue under section 10(b). *Kusner* depicts the precise sort of situation in which a section 10(b) remedy is appropriate for debenture holders in their role as equity investors. As the Court explained, in such a case, the debenture holder's need for accurate information about the corporation was as pressing as any shareholder's: * * *.

* * *

The mere availability of a securities act remedy for fraud, however, does not answer the question whether the common law rule of *Parkinson* remains the applicable standard by which to judge whether or not a corporation has, indeed, acted fraudulently. That question was addressed and analyzed perceptively in a recent en banc Fifth Circuit decision, Broad v. Rockwell International Corp., 642 F.2d 929 (5th Cir.), cert. denied, 454 U.S. 965, 102 S.Ct. 506, 72 L.Ed.2d 380 (1981). There, the plaintiff debenture holders complained that when the company in which they had invested was acquired by another entity in a cash merger, they lost their right to convert into common stock. The Court concluded that the plaintiffs had "received * * * all to which they were contractually entitled under the Indenture" and that, as a result, no violation of section 10(b) could have occurred: * * *.

* * *

Significantly, although the commentators have been careful to consider the situation in which a corporation distributes its assets in forms other than ordinary cash or stock dividends, the indenture at issue here contains no such provision. While the indenture does address a variety of potentially diluting acts—including a change in the par value of the outstanding common stock; a change of outstanding common stock from par to no par; and a possible consolidation, merger, or sale of the company—we have been directed to no provision in the indenture here that addresses the situation in which the company spins off a portion of its assets to a subsidiary and distributes those assets, in the form of a stock dividend, to its common shareholders. * * * Had the B & O indenture contained a more broadly inclusive notice clause, B & O might have been required to inform the debenture holders prior to the declaration of the MAC dividend. The sample provision quoted above [from the Model Indenture], for example, requires notice both for dividends "payable in stock of any class" and for "any other distribution," excluding normal cash dividends. Kaplan, supra note 4, at 13 n. 24.* But the fact remains that the B & O indenture contains no such clause. Accordingly, the plaintiffs cannot rely upon the terms of the indenture as a source of B & O's purported duty to speak.

Apparently mindful of the limited protection afforded to them by the indenture, the plaintiffs maintain that, notwithstanding any lack of an adequate notice provision within the indenture, New York's law of fair dealing required that in any event notice be given prior to the declaration of the MAC dividend. Judge Gibbons credits this argument, concluding that, in failing to give notice, B & O violated the principle "that in every contract there is an implied covenant that neither party shall do anything which will have the effect of destroying or injuring the right of the other party to receive the fruits of the contract. * * *" At 941 (quoting Kirke La Shelle Co. v. Paul Armstrong Co., 263 N.Y. 79, 87, 188 N.E. 163, 167 (1933)).

Such an analysis is clearly inappropriate. By its terms, the principle of fair dealing expressed in *Kirke* and quoted by Judge Gibbons applies only when one party infringes the other's *rights* "to receive the fruits of the contract." Here, under the well-settled *Parkinson* doctrine, Pittsburgh Terminal *had no right,* under the contract, to receive advance notice of the MAC dividend because *no anti-dilution provision to that effect had been included in the indenture.* Thus, the risk of dilution was "inherent in the investment made by the holders of Debentures * * * [B & O] did nothing that could be described as 'destroying or injuring the right of the other party to receive the fruits

* [Ed.Note] Judge Adams pointed out that " * * * at least one commentator has suggested that it is advisable to insert in the indenture a provision giving holders of convertible securities adequate notice in the event that 'the Company shall propose * * * to pay any dividend payable in stock of any class to the holders of its Common Stock *or to make any other distribution to* the holders of its Common Stock (other *than a cash dividend payable out of earnings or earned surplus legally available for the payment of dividends * * *).'* Kaplan, supra * * * Such a notice provision would clearly encompass the kind of arrangement against which Pittsburgh Terminal has complained in the case at bar."

of the contract,' because * * * the benefits that the holders of Debentures received were all the rights to which they were contractually entitled." Broad v. Rockwell International Corp., supra at 958.

* * *

II.

The conclusion that B & O was under no contractual obligation to provide advance notice of the MAC dividend to its convertible debenture holders does not, of course, end the inquiry. For while it is clear that, as a general rule, the debenture holders rights are limited to those specified in the indenture, the Court today has determined that SEC Rule 10b–17 furnishes an independent statutory source from which to derive a duty, on the part of B & O, to provide notice of the MAC dividend. I turn, therefore, to an examination of this issue.

* * *

I do not disagree that the MAC dividend may have been "material" to the debenture holders' decision whether or not to convert their securities into shares of common stock. Nor do I take issue with Judge Garth's determination that the debentures were less valuable after the declaration of the dividend. Nonetheless, in my view, these considerations are not sufficient to establish that the dividend declaration "related to" the class of debenture securities as that term is used in Rule 10b–17. Put simply, Rule 10b–17 never was meant to deal with a situation similar to that before us today.

Nothing in the Commission's "Notice of Proposed Rule Making" or in the language of the rule itself suggests that Rule 10b–17 was intended to override the common law and accord debenture holders significant additional *substantive* rights. When the Rule was proposed by the Securities Exchange Commission in 1971, it was described as a rule "to require companies whose securities are publicly traded to furnish public investors with timely advance notice of the *right to receive dividend[s] and other rights which accrue to holders of record* of a specified class of securities as of a specialized date ('the record date')." 36 Fed.Reg. 3430 (1971). In other words, the Rule was designed to ensure that purchasers of securities receive all the fruits of the transaction *to which they legally are entitled*—namely, distributions made after the sale but before the change in ownership is reflected in the corporation's record books.

* * *

III.

Had the debenture holders foreseen the possibility that B & O would spin off its nonrail assets, arguably they may have bargained for—and paid for—the right to advance notice of the event.[9] Despite

---

9. Concededly, the debenture holders themselves do not, in the average case, bargain individually with the issuing corporation. See Note, Convertible Securities:

the well-settled precedent of *Pratt* and *Parkinson,* however, the B & O indenture did not require such notice to the debenture holders and the price of the debenture presumably reflected this fact. For this Court today—almost thirty years after the drafting of the indenture—to ignore what was set forth as the intent of the parties and fundamentally to alter the terms of the contract is, in my view, not only legally erroneous but improvident.[10]

I therefore respectfully dissent.

NOTE: SUBSEQUENT PROCEEDINGS IN *PITTSBURGH TERMINAL*

Doubt was cast on the precedential status of the discussion of issuer duties in Judge Gibbons' plurality opinion in **Lorenz v. CSX Corp.,** 736 F.Supp. 650, 658–659 (W.D.Pa.1990). The district court made the following comments:

[T]he appellate Opinion rested on that one narrow ground—the effect of Rule 10b–17. In announcing the judgment of the Court, Judge Gibbons identified several other sources of a duty to speak, including the New York Stock Exchange Listing Agreement, New York contract law, and Maryland and New York fiduciary law. Judge Adams on the other hand dissented, disagreeing with Judge Gibbons on all these sources. Judge Garth joined Judge Gibbons to form a majority, but only on the Rule 10b–17 violation. He declined to reach any of the other alleged sources of a duty to speak, leaving those questions open for future consideration. * * *

* * *

* * * [T]he Indenture is designed and intended to be an all-encompassing document.

[I]f there is an independent fiduciary duty owed to debenture holders, it is satisfied if the defendants comply with the terms of the Indenture. Broad v. Rockwell International Corp., 642 F.2d

Holder Who Fails to Convert Before Expiration of the Conversion Period, 54 Cornell L.Rev. 271, 272 (1969). But attorneys or investment bankers normally perform this function on behalf of the debenture holders as a class, see e.g., Hills, supra note 4; Kaplan, supra note 4, and there is no suggestion in this case that those persons who bargained on behalf of the B & O debenture holders did so other than with diligence and vigor.

10. In this regard it is instructive to consider the views expressed by Judge Tyler in Entel v. Guilden, 223 F.Supp. 129, 131–32 (S.D.N.Y.1963):

One of the chief economic functions of a corporation, obviously, is to facilitate aggregations of capital. To further this function, there has developed a broad range of modes of investment within the corporate framework. Each such mode is a bundle of legal rights and duties; the market price for each bundle is no doubt determined at least in part by what the bundle contains. Thus, courts should act with conservatism in changing the content of any of these bundles in ways which would give the holders of some bundles less, and holders of other bundles more, than bargained for in the marketplace.

929, 958–959 (5th Cir.1981). Applying New York law, that Court held that there can be no breach of fiduciary duty without a predicate breach of the Indenture. Plaintiffs have not charged defendant railroads with breach of the Indenture and have not identified any source of notice duty in the contract.

GARDNER & FLORENCE CALL COWLES FOUNDATION v. EMPIRE INC.

United States District Court, Southern District of New York, 1984.
589 F.Supp. 669, vacated on other grounds, 754 F.2d 478 (2d Cir.1985).

WHITMAN KNAPP, District Judge.

[The opinion's fact statement and first section is set out supra pp. 411–414.]

Counts II and III

Both Counts II and III are conditioned upon a finding of breach of contract in Count I, and they must fall along with it. Plaintiffs contend in Count II that even if neither § 4.05 nor § 4.06 applies to the Empire–Exco merger, they are entitled to relief based upon defendants' breach of an implied covenant of good faith and fair dealing. An implied covenant, however, derives its substance directly from the language of the Indenture, and "cannot give the holders of Debentures any rights inconsistent with those set out in the Indenture." *Broad,* supra, 642 F.2d at 957. As we have found that plaintiffs' contractual rights were not violated, there can have been no breach of an implied covenant.

* * *

Count IV

Count IV alleges that defendant Plaster, as an officer, director and controlling shareholder of Empire, and aided by the other defendants, breached a fiduciary duty owed to plaintiffs as debenture holders. Plaintiffs claim that the merger, as "orchestrated" by the defendants, resulted in a financial windfall for the common shareholders, at a corresponding cost to plaintiffs who now bear the risk that Empire may not be able to satisfy its obligation to pay the debentures when due. Further, plaintiffs allege that defendants' actions effectively destroyed the value of their conversion right because the new Empire stock into which they are now entitled to convert is worth considerably less than the old Empire stock.

Fiduciary duties in a debenture contract, however, do not exist in the abstract, but are derived from the Indenture itself. As stated by the *Broad* court: "We may assume without deciding * * * that [defendant] was charged with a fiduciary duty to the holders of Debentures. But since we have determined * * * that [defendant] fully complied with its obligations under the Indenture * * * [defendant] can have no liability for breach of fiduciary duty." 642 F.2d at 958–59. As we, likewise, have found (as discussed above) that defendants have not breached the terms of the Indenture, we cannot find liability for breach of fiduciary duty.

Plaintiffs strongly rely on Green v. Hamilton (S.D.N.Y. July 14, 1981) Docket No. 76 Civ. 5433 (MJL). That case is, however, clearly distinguishable from the one at bar. *Green* concerned a contention that the defendant corporation, in a successful attempt to induce debenture holders to redeem their debentures rather than convert them into common stock, issued an intentionally false and misleading press release concerning the imminence of an impending merger. Had the debenture holders, who relied upon these false statements, chosen instead to convert, they would have participated in the merger consideration, which was greater than the consideration they received upon redemption. No such misrepresentation is—or could be—alleged in the case at bar.

Similarly, in the other case relied upon by plaintiffs, Pittsburgh Terminal Corp. v. Baltimore & O.R. Co., (3d Cir.1982) 680 F.2d 933, cert. denied 459 U.S. 1056, 103 S.Ct. 475, 476, 74 L.Ed.2d 621, it was alleged that defendants had intentionally failed to notify debenture holders of an upcoming dividend, thus depriving them of an opportunity to convert and participate in that dividend. Again, no such failure to advise is—or could be—here alleged.

The facts of this case are, rather, closely aligned with the *Broad* case, where actions taken by the issuer in connection with a merger severely impaired the value of the debenture holders' conversion rights. The *Broad* Court found no liability where the terms of the Indenture, as bargained for, were enforced.

"A purchaser of Debentures * * * takes the risks inherent in the equity feature of the security, risks that are shared with the [common stockholders]. One of those risks is that [the issuer] might merge with another company—which is effectively the risk that any individual investor's assessment of the value of [the common stock] based on [the issuer's] prospects for the future, will be replaced by the collective judgment of the market place and other investor's in [the issuer] who might vote in favor of the merger. This—like the risk that [the issuer's] future operations might be lackluster, with the result that conversion might never be economically attractive—is simply a risk inherent in this type of investment."

Broad, supra, 642 F.2d. We shall follow that well-reasoned decision. Defendants in the case at bar were under a duty to carry out the terms of the contract, but not to make sure that plaintiffs had made a good investment. The former they have done; the latter we have no jurisdiction over.

The fact that defendant Plaster was financially successful in the merger is not, contrary to plaintiff's contentions, itself proof (indeed, does not even necessarily suggest) that he breached a fiduciary duty. The details of the merger proposal were communicated in full both to the shareholders, who voted in its favor, and to the debenture holders, who were given the opportunity to convert. The shareholders presumably approved the merger because the consideration they received was significantly greater in value than the market value of the Empire stock. By the same token, the debenture holders presumably declined to convert because their debentures were trading at an even higher value.

Plaintiffs have presented the court with absolutely no evidence to support their suggestion that as a result of the merger Empire will be unable to satisfy its contractual obligation to the debenture holders. Moreover, the actions of the shareholders and debenture holders at the time of the merger strongly indicate that the conversion right had long been rendered valueless by the operation of the market.[6]

Where, as here, defendants have fully complied with their obligations under the Indenture, there is no liability for breach of fiduciary duty. We therefore dismiss Count IV.

NOTE: JUDICIAL FAIRNESS STANDARDS AND CONVERTIBLE BONDS

1. *The Weight of Authority.*

Cowles Foundation v. Empire follows Broad v. Rockwell Int'l, 642 F.2d 929 (5th Cir.1981) (en banc), cert. denied, 454 U.S. 965 (1981) in declining to intervene against a merger limiting or eliminating the value of a conversion privilege on either a fiduciary or good faith theory. This approach now appears to be authoritative. Chancellor Allen dispelled any doubts about the meaning of the *Harff v. Kerkorian* reversal in **Simons v. Cogan,** 542 A.2d 785, 790–791 (Del.Ch.1987):

"Thus, there exists a body of judicial opinion willing to extend the protection offered by the fiduciary concept to the relationship between an issuer and the holders of its convertible debt securities. These seeds, however, have fallen upon stones. None of the appellate opinions actually represent a holding so extending that concept and, indeed, each of those cases evidence the fact that prevailing judicial opinion remains to the contrary.

"In relying upon the district court opinion in *Green,* plaintiff invites this court to reinterpret the reading of Harff v. Kerkorian that it made in Norte & Co. v. Manor Healthcare Corp., Del.Ch., C.A. No. 6827, Berger, V.C. (November 21, 1985) * * *

"The flaws in the *Green* analysis are two. First, and most simplistically, that case simply misreads, in my opinion, the clear implication of the Supreme Court opinion in Harff. See Norte & Co. v. Manor

---

6. Plaintiffs claim that their right to convert was "illusory" because the merger agreement provided that if more than $4 million in principal amount of debentures were converted, the merger would have been aborted. This provision was also communicated in Empire's Proxy Statement, but is nevertheless irrelevant as none of the debenture holders chose to convert.

Healthcare Corp., Del.Ch., C.A. No. 6827, Berger, V.C. (November 21, 1985) in which this court reviewed that matter and concluded differently than did the *Green* court.[9] Second, and more substantively, the analysis of the *Green* opinion is not persuasive when viewed independently. * * *

"[W]ere I free to pass upon the question presented in *Harff* and *Norte & Co.* for the first time, I could find nothing in *Green* or in the other federal opinions cited above to suggest that an alteration in the traditional structure governing the legal relationship between corporations and holders of their convertible debt is warranted. That traditional approach has not been shown to be inadequate in any important way. Underwriters of convertible securities do have an interest in negotiating protections on points regarded as material by ultimate purchasers of those securities. The development of elaborate anti-destruction and anti-dilution provisions in indentures attests to the relative effectiveness of this mechanism of defining rights and obligations of issuers. See ABF Commentaries at 290–301.

"The tide has no doubt long run away from a world of hard and fast rules with predictable outcomes and towards a world in which it is common for courts to evaluate specific behavior in the light cast by broadly worded principles.[10] Working amid such flows, however, courts must be wary of the danger to useful structures that they entail. To introduce the powerful abstraction of "fiduciary duty" into the highly negotiated and exhaustively documented commercial relationship between an issuer of convertible securities and the holders of such securities would, or so it now appears to me, risk greater insecurity and uncertainty than could be justified by the occasional increment in fairness that might be hoped for."

The Delaware Supreme Court affirmed, restating this position in Simons v. Cogan, 549 A.2d 300 (Del.1988). See also Pittelman v. Pearce, 6 Cal.App.4th 1436, 8 Cal.Rptr.2d 359 (1992) (leveraged buyout).

Glinert v. Wickes Companies, Inc., 1990 WL 34703 (Del. Ch.) takes a similar approach to the claims of a class of warrant holders. The holders advanced fiduciary and good faith claims against a reclassification precedent to a merger that had the effect of limiting the upside potential of equity not held by insiders, thus wiping out the value of their options.

2. *The Facts of the Cases.*

(a) Was the merger in *Cowles Foundation v. Empire* unfair to the convertible bondholders? Did the controlling parties in the case de-

---

9. Subsequently to the issuance of the *Norte & Co.* opinion the Supreme Court, while not discussing the point, has had occasion to cite the Chancery opinion in *Harff v. Kerkorian.* See Revlon, Inc. v. MacAndrews & Forbes Holdings, Inc., Del. Supr., 506 A.2d 173, 182 (1986).

10. Professor P.S. Atiyah has brilliantly captured the zeitgeist in his inaugural lecture at Oxford University, which has been reprinted by the Iowa Law Review. See Atiyah, From Principles to Pragmatism: Changes in the Function of the Judicial Process and the Law, 65 Iowa L.Rev. 1249 (1980).

prive bondholders of any substantial element of value? If so, was it because the merger entailed substantial borrowing by the issuer or because the merger caused the value of the common to decline? Did the merger cause the holders to lose the possibility of any, or limit the probability of sufficient, appreciation due to a rise in the value of the common?

The facts *Simons v. Cogan,* supra, are similar, but bear comparison. The case concerned 8½% subordinated debentures of Knoll International ("Knoll"), convertible into its Class A common stock at a $19.20 conversion price. More than 90% of the issuer's voting stock was held by a parent corporation, Knoll Holding. In 1986–1987, the parent mounted a tender offer and second step merger to cash out the minority shareholders of Knoll. The tender offer and merger price was $12 per share. Knoll survived the merger, but as a wholly-owned subsidiary. In connection with the merger, Knoll issued a supplemental indenture providing that upon conversion of the debentures, the holders would receive $12 cash instead of Knoll common stock.

On the day before the announcement of the cash-out transaction, Knoll's class A common traded for 9¼ and the debentures traded at 86. The plaintiffs alleged that the debentures declined in value upon the announcement of the supplemental indenture, trading at 73¼ immediately thereafter. The Supreme Court opinion reports, 549 A.2d at 301, that an "additional" supplemental indenture was executed that increased the interest rate on the debentures from 8½% to 9⅞%. The opinion does not specify the time at which this "additional" accommodation of the bondholders was announced. Thus its relationship with the asserted drop in the market price of the debentures is unclear.

Assume that no additional supplemental indenture was issued and the merger caused the bonds to drop to 73¼. Why did the bonds' price drop—due to loss of debt value, conversion value or premium? Was the lost value captured by the stockholders or parent corporation? Was the transaction unfair?

Why would did the issuer provide the "additional" supplemental indenture? Would an interest rate increase make the bondholders whole for their loss in respect of the merger? Will the approach taken by the Delaware courts in the case make it more or less likely that future issuers will offer stepped up interest rates to convertible bondholders who lose value due to mergers?

(b) Would application of a judicially formulated fairness requirement in cases like *Cowles Foundation v. Empire* and *Simons v. Cogan* increase the cost and reduce the number of presumably value enhancing mergers—either because acquiring entities would not increase the offering price so as to accommodate the holders of convertibles, or because the stockholders of the issuing corporation would not accept a lesser share price?

What action should the indenture trustee take in cases like these? Does it fail in its duties or obligations when it agrees to a supplemental indenture substituting (or adding) the acquiring entity as obligor under the indenture?

Suppose these cases had gone the other way and the courts had imposed a contractual good faith duty to protect the bondholders from impairment of the value of the conversion privilege in mergers. Suppose further that actors in the financial markets thought the duty was too costly and drafted the next generation of bond contracts to negate it explicitly. Would the duty apply to the subsequent generation of contracts? Would the subsequent explicit allocation of risk amount to a market decision that the court had been wrong in the first place? If the duty were imposed as a fiduciary proposition would market actors have been in a position thus to "contract out"?

Should a court which finds all contracts to have been complied with by the merger nevertheless impose an overriding restriction of fairness? Should the concept of fairness be the same in arms-length mergers as in parent-subsidiary mergers? How should the bondholders be compensated for unfair treatment? By valuing the lost possibility of gain under the conventional option pricing formula? Consider also the extension of the conversion privilege to the stock of the acquirer, diluted to reflect the ratio of cash received in the merger to the market price of the acquirer's stock. See Broad v. Rockwell Int'l. Corp., 642 F.2d 929, 953 (5th Cir.1981).

Is there any difference between cases involving mergers and cases, like *Harff* and *Pittsburgh Terminal,* involving large dividends, so far as concerns the expectations of the parties?

(c) If an acquiring company acquires only 90% or 95% of a corporation's outstanding stock so that there ceases to be a public market for the stock, should the holders of convertible bonds have a cause of action for loss of the value of their conversion rights? See Kessler v. General Cable Corp., 92 Cal.App.3d 531, 155 Cal.Rptr. 94 (2d Dist.1979), for a negative answer. How would one draft a bond contract to protect against such a loss? Does it matter that the acquiring company acquires its 95% stake by means of a tender offer?

3. *The Impact of Efficient Markets*

Under the efficient markets hypothesis, does the price of preferred stock or of a convertible security impound a discount for (1) the power of the common stock to effect alterations in the contractual entitlements of the preferred stock, (2) the discretion vested in the common stock to dilute the value of the convertible security within the limits permitted by the convertible contract, and (3) the malleability of the legal rules governing such matters? If so, is the efficient markets hypothesis an argument for precluding judicial intervention to protect preferred stock and convertibles against such "unfair" treatment?

SECTION D.   CORPORATE LAW
LEGAL CAPITAL RULES

State corporation statutes contain provisions that regulate capital structure for the benefit of creditors and senior security holders. These "legal capital" rules restrict the corporation's discretion to make distributions to equityholders for the purpose of protecting the seniors' equity cushion. These rules have been on the books for a century or more, and have the appearance of a substantial body of corporate law. But they are generally understood to be ineffective as a shield to protect creditors from debtor opportunism. In theory, the legal capital rules serve the function of a dividend covenant in an indenture, note agreement, or preferred stock contract. See supra p. 189. But, although in form they operate notwithstanding the solvency of the enterprise, in fact the rules do little more than block distributions to the shareholders of insolvent corporations. They thus in effect restate the constraint of fraudulent conveyance law. See supra. pp. 254–269.

Today the prevailing view is that creditors' and preferred stockholders' interests are better left to regulation through negotiated contracts than to regulation by positive law. The following introduction to the legal capital rules is included to show why this view prevails. For further reading, see T. Fiflis, Accounting Issuers for Lawyers (4th ed. 1991); B. Manning and J.J. Hanks, A Concise Textbook on Legal Capital (3d ed. 1990); Kummert, State Statutory Restrictions on Financial Distributions by Corporations to Shareholders, 59 Wash.L.Rev. 187 (1984); Hackney, The Financial Provisions of the Model Business Corporation Act, 70 Harv.L.Rev. (1957).

1.   THE STATED CAPITAL REQUIREMENT

[T]he corporation statutes of all states contemplate (1) that *some* consideration will be paid by stockholders for the stock issued to them, (2) that the consideration will be of a *quality* which is acceptable under statutory specifications, and (3) that the *amount* of consideration will be "sufficient" or "adequate" as tested by some standard. One standard of adequacy, of course, could be the corporation's willingness to accept as adequate what the subscriber offers in exchange for its shares. The difficulty with making conclusive the corporation's acceptance, however, is that the corporation may agree to accept less in actual value for its stock than the amount stated on its books. Either because the interests of the promoters are so served, or because the stockholder and the corporation are otherwise not dealing at arm's length, the agreed consideration paid by the stockholder may be given an inflated value by the corporation and be accepted in exchange for stock of par value equal to the inflated value ("watered" stock). Or, the stock may be issued for no measurable consideration (i.e., as a bonus); or it may be issued for cash which is less than its par value (i.e., at a discount). In any of those circumstances, there may have been complete disclosure, or in any event nothing misleading, as between the stockholder paying the consideration and the promoters and executives of the corporation duly authorized to issue the stock. Hence, as a matter of tort or contract law, there is no basis for any action by the corporation against the stockholder.

But the corporate books will record the consideration at a specified amount on the asset side of the balance sheet, and will reflect on the liability side of the balance sheet an amount of capital with respect to the stock issued therefor. Under the traditional learning, the amount of capital is viewed either as a representation to those extending credit, or as legally imposed assurance to third parties—creditors and stockholders alike—of the receipt of something of value equal to that amount, and of the dedication of that economic value to the enterprise's long range effort to earn profits, and to the ultimate payment of its debts.

Hence, notwithstanding the fact that as between the purchasing stockholder and the issuing corporation no one may be misled, the "adequacy" of the consideration paid by a stockholder for his stock is measured by the amount of capital stated to be represented by the issued shares. If the amount of the consideration (in money, or in tangible or intangible property valued by the board of directors) is equal to par or the capital stated, the stockholder has fulfilled not merely his contract, but such obligations as external policy (either legislatively or judicially defined) imposes. If, however, the amount of the consideration is less than par or the stated capital, then, notwithstanding the fact that he may have complied with his contract with the corporation, the stockholder has failed to meet his legal obligations to relying creditors or, possibly, to third party claimants generally. The problems which such failure has generated have not been satisfactorily solved by the courts—or in more recent legislative efforts as interpreted by the courts. Solution of the problems requires:

(1) Identifying the nature of the misrepresentation or misleading appearance created by the inaccurate statement of the transaction on the corporate books. Is it with respect to the value entered as an asset, or to the statement of the amount of capital, or both?

(2) Determining who shall be liable and in what amount. Should liability be imposed upon the directors or upon the recipients of watered stock or both, and if upon either or both, should liability turn on whether they know or have reason to know of the water?

(3) Determining to whom they shall be liable and in what amount. Should liability run only to creditors, on the theory that capital is in some way a symbol of a fund held in trust for them; or on a theory of fraud, should liability run only to those creditors who rely on the misrepresentation; or should it also run to fellow stockholders on the theory of a statutory obligation to all persons interested in the enterprise; or should liability be to the corporation at large, notwithstanding its willingness to accept less consideration than it appears to have

agreed upon? [q] Should stockholders be liable only to make good the
water or for all the corporate indebtedness? And in any event, should
the remedy against them permit cancellation of their stock?

In recent years watered stock problems have rarely produced
litigation, because of the ease with which they may be avoided in
planning. The efforts to eliminate "the outmoded concepts of stated
capital and par value" embodied in the latest version of the RMBCA
(see Appendix F infra) have not yet taken root in many states. Hence
in most jurisdictions, "watered stock" problems still inhere in every
issuance of stock and are present when stock is issued for property as in
corporate acquisitions of, or mergers with, going concerns, or in the
incorporation of going concerns formerly conducted as sole proprietor-
ships or partnerships, or for services.

2. DIVIDENDS AND DISTRIBUTIONS

(A) TRADITIONAL STATUTES

As Hackney, supra, points out, historically "there have been, other
than an insolvency test, two methods of defining the funds available for
dividends: one which 'prohibits distributions except from surplus as
normally computed in a corporate *balance sheet,*' and one which 'prohibits payments except from current or past *net profits* most frequently
determined by a corporate profit and loss statement.' "

Balance Sheet Test. Traditional legal capital schemes employ the
balance sheet as the basis for regulating distributions of corporate
assets to shareholders. The distributions covered by the statutes include dividends, stock repurchases and any other transactions entailing
a net outflow of assets to shareholders.

In general, under the "balance sheet" test, distributions are prohibited if, after giving effect to the transaction, the firm's total assets
would be less than the sum of its liabilities (including preferred stock
liquidation price) and its "stated capital" account. "Stated capital" is a
dollar figure representing the number of outstanding shares multiplied
by their "par value." Par value is set in the certificate of incorporation. The par value amount is left to the drafter's discretion. It can
range from 1 cent upward, but must be equal to or less than the
original issue price of the stock. In the alternative, a firm's charter
can specify that its stock will not have a par value. Where the firm
issues no par stock, stated capital is determined by multiplying the
stock's "stated value"—a dollar figure designated by the board at the

---

q. See Dodd, Stock Watering—The Judicial Valuation of Property for Stock Issue
Purposes (1930); Ballantine, Corporations
(1946) pp. 465–485; 789–820; Lattin, Corporations (1971) pp. 465–492; Henn and

time of the stock's issue—by the number of outstanding shares.[r] The particular stated value figure, like the par value figure, is within the firm's discretion. Where shares are issued for a consideration greater than their par or stated value, the difference between the par or stated value and the consideration received is entered into a separate surplus account. Traditionally, this is termed the "capital surplus" account. On a contemporary balance sheet, this account may be termed "additional paid in capital" or "capital in excess of par."

Restating the basic legal capital test, distributions are permitted out of "surplus" accounts—whether additional paid in capital or retained earnings—but may not be made out of stated capital. The surplus accounts thus equal total assets minus the sum of liabilities and stated capital. This is the simplest of the stated capital tests in the statutes. Del.Corp.L. § 170; N.Y.Bus.Corp.L. § 510.[s]

Earned Surplus Test. Under the "earned surplus" or "net profits" standard, dividends and distributions are limited to amounts carried in the enterprise's balance sheet as "earned surplus" or "retained earnings." MBCA § 45(a). In theory, resort to this standard relieves the firm of the necessity to compute or recompute "capital," and limits its dividends or distributions to some form of profits, current or accumulated. In practice, under both generally accepted accounting principles and the statutes, it is possible to alter the earned surplus account by drawing on capital surplus or including (or excluding) some capital transactions.

Alexander, Laws of Corporations (3rd Ed. 1983) pp. 428–435.

r. This represents an initial floor for stated capital. A company is usually free to increase its stated capital from this floor by board resolution or to reduce it, sometimes by board action alone (Del.Corp.L. § 244; NYBCL § 516) and sometimes by board action and stockholder consent (NYBCL § 802).

s. The following balance sheet serves to illustrate the test:

ABC Corp.

Total assets	$10,000,000
Liabilities	
Accounts payable	$ 2,000,000
Funded debt	2,000,000
Shareholders' Equity	
Common stock, 1,000,000 shares outstanding, par value $1 per share	$ 1,000,000
Additional paid in capital	4,000,000
Retained earnings	1,000,000
Total liabilities and equity	$10,000,000

Based on this balance sheet, the common stock must have been issued originally for $5 per share. Stated capital here is the $1,000,000 "common stock" entry. The $4,000,000 additional paid in capital represents the difference between the stock's $1 par value and the $5 received for each share on original issue. Now we apply the basic test:

The maximum dividend a firm may make is the amount by which total assets are greater than liabilities plus stated capital. Total assets = $4,000,000 liabilities + $1,000,000 stated capital + allowable dividend. ABC may make a maximum dividend of $5,000,000.

Restating the test, dividends may only be made out of surplus accounts: $4,000,000 additional paid in capital + $1,000,000 retained earnings = $5,000,000 total surplus accounts. ABC may make a maximum dividend of $5,000,000.

Nimble Dividends. Many states, Delaware included, provide a significant exception to the rule against distributions where stated capital is impaired. This allows dividends to the extent of the firm's earned profits during the dividend year or the previous year, regardless of the absence of a surplus. Del.Corp.L. § 170(a). Such distributions are called "nimble dividends."

Insolvency. Finally, most corporation laws include an equity insolvency restriction against dividends and other distributions to shareholders. Equity insolvency occurs when a debtor cannot meet its obligations as they become due. The statutes provide, first, that a firm already insolvent in the equity sense may make no distributions to shareholders, and second, that a solvent firm may not make a distribution if, as a result, the firm would be left insolvent in an equity sense.

The statutory restrictions on dividends and distributions are troublesome for many reasons. In large part the rules are infected by the intrinsic ambiguity of the terms used in the statutes, which predicate dividends and distributions to stockholders on determination of a firm's "assets" or "liabilities" or "capital," and the existence of "surplus," "earned surplus," "retained earnings," "net profits," or the like.[t] To the extent that the legal meanings of those terms is determined by reference to generally accepted accounting principles, management (and common stock) can legitimately manufacture sources for, and make payments of, dividends or distributions that result in little protection for seniors. Thus, without the consent, or possibly even the knowledge, of the seniors, it is possible for management (sometimes common stockholder consent is required) simply to reduce stated capital, and thereby create some form of distributable surplus, or to write up the value of assets on the books so as to create a form of distributable surplus. Similarly, the statement of earned surplus on a corporation's balance sheet may be manipulated to make available sources for distributing dividends that are rooted in capital and do not reflect current or historical accumulation of profits. While there is some variation among the states in the application of each of the standards, the net result is to create a flimsy shield for seniors against the

---

t. Note that only "distributions" come with the purview of the legal capital rules. Whether or not a transaction constitutes a "distribution" within the meaning of the statute can be a subject of dispute. C–T of Virginia, Inc. v. Barrett, 958 F.2d 606 (4th Cir.1992), is a prominent recent instance. The question there was whether the payments to tendering stockholders in an LBO constituted a "distribution" within the meaning of the Virginia legal capital rules. The statute defined distribution as a "direct or indirect transfer of money * * * or incurrence of indebtedness by a corporation to or for the benefit of its shareholders in respect of any of its shares." The court, commenting that "[a] corporate acquisition, structured as a merger, is simply a different animal from a distribution," held that the payment was not a distribution. The encumbering of the corporation's assets was not an "incurrence of indebtedness" within the meaning of the statute, even though the closing of the loan transaction occurred simultaneously with the closing of the merger, because the management of the firm promoting the LBO was identical with that of the pre-merger LBO target. Furthermore, said the court, the fact that all phases of the transaction closed simultaneously meant that the debt was not incurred "for the benefit of the shareholders" within the meaning of the statute!

distribution of assets to juniors notwithstanding behavior by management that is consistent with the statutes.

In part also, the concepts involved are inadequate for their purpose because they are tied to valuation notions that—at least for publicly owned enterprises—are dysfunctional. The traditional legal capital and earned surplus rules rely on numbers generated through the application of accounting principles to the many and various actions undertaken by a firm. They, therefore, inherit all the intrinsic shortcomings of accounting numbers as measures of the economic value of the firm. The distribution which seniors seek to restrict is, of necessity, the payment of tangible assets, generally cash. And their fear of not being repaid rests on an assumed ultimate insufficiency of tangible assets to repay them when their principal is due or the enterprise is forced to liquidate. Their effort, therefore, is to secure the availability of tangible or salable assets at all times—as if senior claims were matured on each occasion when distributions are made to juniors. The balance sheet and surplus approach is congruent with that effort. But the focus on preserving realizable liquidation values during the interim period between the making of the senior investment and its maturity is at odds with the valuation assumptions underlying the senior investment at both its beginning and its end. When seniors advance money to the enterprise, their expectation of repayment is rooted in their belief in the likely success of the enterprise as a going concern. And as the reorganization materials, supra, indicate, in insolvency also, the value to which seniors look for reimbursement is more often the going concern value of the enterprise than its liquidation value.

The apparent contradiction in approaches to valuation raises the question whether protection of seniors during the interim period should depend on static values, such as costs recorded on the balance sheet, or even the appraised value of assets, or on going concern values; and to the extent that cost-oriented balance sheet values dominate in delineating the seniors' protection, the further question is raised whether the cost to the juniors of protecting senior capital by this means is higher than any rational allocation of risks would suggest.

Finally, it may be noted that the rules restricting the payment of dividends predicate payments on premises that may well result in the wrong signals to investors. For example, they base dividends on the history of the enterprise, whether reflected in its capital, surplus, or accumulated earnings, and thus offer only modestly relevant (and frequently misleading) information about the future.

(B) NEW MODEL STATUTES

Wide recognition of the shortcomings of the legal capital rules has prompted a law reform movement. California has radically revised its legal capital rules. Furthermore, the Revised Model Business Corporation Act (RMBCA) includes a streamlined set of legal capital rules that abandon most of the traditional concepts.[u]

California removes the legal significance from a stock's par value. Its statute does not bar the use of par value, but it does remove the concepts of par value, capital and surplus from distribution decision-making. The California scheme allows distributions from retained earnings in all cases. In other cases, distributions may be made if certain financial ratios, similar to covenants used in debt contracts, are satisfied. Cal.Gen.Corp.Law § 500. The statute retains an equity insolvency limitation on distributions. Id. § 501. Additionally, corporations making distributions to junior shareholders must maintain assets in excess of liabilities in an amount equal to or greater than the aggregate liquidation preferences of senior stock. Id. § 502. If preferred arrearages have piled up, no distributions may be made to junior stockholders unless retained earnings exceed the proposed dividend plus the arrearages. Id. § 503. Stock purchasers are obligated to pay in only what they agreed to. Id. § 410.

Under the RMBCA a corporation may still issue stock with a par value, but, like the California statute, the Act removes any legal significance for par. See RMBCA § 2.02(b)(2)(iv). The concept of watered stock disappears along with par, and stock purchasers are simply obligated to pay the contractually ordered price for their shares.[v]

The RMBCA extensively revises the rules on shareholder distributions. The Act retains an equity insolvency test. RMBCA § 6.40(c)(1). Concurrent with it, the Act employs a net worth test. RMBCA § 6.40(c)(2). This is, at bottom, a balance sheet insolvency test, providing that a corporation may not make a distribution to shareholders if its total assets do not exceed its total liabilities, plus total liquidation preferences. Id. With the addition of liquidation preferences, the Act adjusts its net worth concept to deviate from balance sheet solvency under generally accepted accounting principles. It specifies that the dollar amounts of the sum of all the outstanding preferred stock's liquidation preferences shall be considered a liability in the net worth calculation.

u. The Model Business Corporation Act was extensively revised in 1980. See Committee on Corporate Laws, Changes in the Model Business Corporation Act—Amendments to Financial Provisions, 34 Bus.Law. 1867 (1979), and again in 1984. In 1987, further refinements were made which, in combination with the two earlier revisions, resulted in a Revised Model Business Corporation Act that substantially altered the legal capital scheme. See Committee on Corporate Laws, Changes in the Model Business Corporation Act—Amendments Pertaining to Distributions, 42 Bus.Law. 259 (1986).

v. Directors have a responsibility under the RMBCA and fiduciary law to ensure that the price they demand is fair relative to other shareholders.

The RMBCA does not incorporate the concepts of par and stated capital and does not differentiate among surpluses. A corporation may still affix a par value to shares or create legal capital, but for the purpose of regulating distributions, such actions are meaningless.[w]

w. Stock dividends are recognized as the meaningless transaction that they are. See RMBCA § 1.40(b) (excluding share dividends from definition of distribution). Without concepts of par and capital, no tinkering is necessary if stock dividends are declared. RMBCA § 6.23(a).

With regard to stock reacquisition, the RMBCA does away with the legal fiction of treasury shares and the hypertechnical distinction between treasury stock and authorized but unissued shares. The Act treats reacquired shares as authorized but unissued, RMBCA § 6.31(a), and payment for them is clearly a distribution. See RMBCA § 1.40(b).

Sensing difficulties with an entanglement of accounting concepts within the statute, the drafters of the RMBCA require only that the accounting system used be reasonable. The Act appears to favor a system that imbues a reviewing court with discretion instead of a system that purports to mandate certain accounting principles as law.

Part III: CAPITAL STRUCTURE AND LEVERAGE
INTRODUCTION

In Part II, the primary concern was with rights of holders of outstanding senior securities and the protection they might reasonably claim against actions by the holders of common stock or their delegees (i.e., management) under the "incomplete" securities contracts embodied in preferred stock or bonds or debentures. The problems may to a large extent be said to be matters of "contract." But the necessities of the relationship vest considerable discretion in management to use collective resources in ways that favor common stock at the expense of seniors. That discretion is not substantially narrowed by the institutional arrangements under which the "contracts" are drafted and entered into, or eliminated by market forces. Hence rules of law restrict the discretion of management, both procedurally by facilitating senior monitoring of managerial behavior and substantively by limiting permissible behavior. Next we turn to questions about why management issues any debt, how much debt is appropriate, and to what extent (and for whose benefit) the law should restrict (or require) the issuance of debt or senior securities.

One of the most widely debated issues in financial theory continues to be whether the value of the corporate enterprise can be enhanced by a judicious use of leverage, i.e. by financing corporate investments with senior securities as well as common shares. The conventional view until thirty-five years ago was that within appropriate limits the inclusion of bonds or other senior securities in the corporation's capital structure increases the total value of the firm and is advantageous to common stockholders. Beyond some point of maximum advantage, however, additional increments of debt or other fixed obligations are said to have the opposite effect and to reduce enterprise value and hence the value of common shares. Under this view, because capital structure is relevant to the value of the firm, a significant task of financial management is to issue debt and equity in roughly optimal proportions.

The belief that there is an advantage in financing with one mix of securities rather than another was challenged by a number of writers—most notably, Modigliani and Miller in a celebrated 1958 article.[a] Briefly stated, the M and M analysis (following an earlier discussion by Durand) argued that the value of the firm is independent of its capital structure and is determined solely by capitalizing the expected stream of operating income at a discount rate appropriate to the company's business risk. The external arrangement of claims against the income

a. F. Modigliani and M.H. Miller, The Cost of Capital, Corporation Finance and the Theory of Investment, 48 Amer.Econ. Rev. 261 (1958).

stream, it is argued, can have no influence on the value placed on that stream by the market. If this view is correct, then unless extraneous factors such as taxes intervene, management should cease searching for an optimal capital structure and concentrate instead on other goals.

Discussions of the M–M thesis led, in turn, to new theories about the benefits of including debt in corporate capital structures. These revived theories of optimal capital structure entail examination of bankruptcy costs, tax benefits incidental to borrowing, and asserted corporate governance or "agency cost" benefits. These theories circulated in tandem with the high leverage restructurings of the 1980s, and were offered as justifications for them. But the collapse of the junk bond market in 1989 and associated events stopped the restructuring movement. See Appendix C, Part 2, infra. We will see in this Part that these events give rise to a new round of questions about the components of an optimal capital structure.

The Durand and M and M positions and the import of bankruptcy and agency costs and other extraneous factors are discussed in section A of this part. It should be noted that the questions raised by M and M in connection with capital structure also have bearing on the dividend decision of the firm, a problem which is taken up in Part IV.

Design of the corporation's capital structure is, of course, largely a matter within the discretion of management. Nevertheless, the law has occasionally played a role in capital structure decisions, particularly with respect to public utilities, which in the aggregate constitute the largest nongovernmental issuers of debt securities. In addition, as suggested, the tax law undoubtedly has an important, if indeterminate, influence on capital structure by reason of the deductibility of interest payments on debt obligations as compared with the non-deductibility of dividends on preferred and common stock.

The materials in section B illustrate some of the legal standards which courts and regulatory agencies apply when authorized or obliged to review management's financing decisions. In contrast to the legal materials considered in Part II, many of the cases that follow focus upon the *anticipated effect* of the firm's capital structure choices rather than upon the *realized consequences* of choices earlier made.

SECTION A.   THE LEVERAGE EFFECT

---

1.   THE COST OF CAPITAL AND
THE VALUE OF THE FIRM

The term "cost of capital" is widely used in the literature of investment decision-making and generally refers to the minimum rate of return which a firm requires as a condition for undertaking an investment. If the rate of return on a proposed investment project exceeds this required minimum, or if the anticipated cash flows from the project discounted at this rate exceed its cost, the investment should be accepted by the firm. Theoretically, the effect of such acceptance (once the news has been communicated to investors) will be to enhance the market value of the owners' equity. See discussion supra, pp. 40 and 65. As a matter of formal definition, therefore, "the cost of capital for a firm is a discount rate with the property that an investment with a rate of profit above (below) this rate will raise (lower) the value of the firm". Gordon, The Investment, Financing And Valuation Of The Corporation 218 (1962). The following excerpt from Farrar and Meyer, Managerial Economics 63–67 (1970), points up some of the attendant analytic problems:

"The calculation of net present value [of a proposed investment], even in simplest form, obviously has one indispensable requirement: someone must stipulate what value or values of the interest rate, r, are to be used for discounting purposes. This, in turn, raises a fundamental question regarding just what the cost of capital incurred by the firm in making such an investment may be, since almost by any definition, the discount rate, r, must bear some relationship to the firm's costs of raising funds, or of diverting funds from other uses to a particular expenditure.

"Everything * * * suggests that this return must be based (at least conceptually) on an opportunity cost, and furthermore, that the opportunity cost in question must be that borne by the firm's owners in foregoing alternative uses for the funds. Beyond this initial presumption, however, it is easy to become mired in a mass of extremely messy details; for shareholders, clearly, have access to a variety of investment vehicles, each of which offers different risk and return combinations. *Which* alternative vehicle, and *which* rate of return should be used to capitalize any particular investment opportunity's expected cash flows often is a source of contention, both among managers and managerial economists.

"Historically, economists have sought an answer to this question by focusing attention on returns available to the firm's owners through the purchase of proportionally larger fractions of all the company's outstanding securities, both debt and equity. By doing so, shareholders may effectively hold—and obtain investment returns on—a proportional share, not simply of the firm's equity, but of *all* its assets. Should the new capital budgeting project be comparable in all important respects to the types of assets already held, the rate of return at which existing cash flows are capitalized also should serve to *value* expected cash flows from the new undertaking.

"There are several virtues to selecting a financial asset, or combination of financial assets, having the firm's risk characteristics as a basis for evaluating the company's cost of capital. First of all, a company can, in fact, usually sell these securities in open capital markets to provide a *source of funds* for direct investment purposes. Alternatively, the firm's own securities also may provide a perfectly satisfactory *use of funds* either for reinvestment by stockholders of dividend payments, or through the firm itself by repurchasing (and retiring) its own outstanding debt and equity securities. Both conceptually and practically, then, a firm's own securities may represent a very real investment opportunity that can either be purchased, if internally generated funds exceed the amounts needed for 'real' investment opportunities, or can be sold to provide additional funds should the reverse be true. Consider, for example, the hypothetical, downward sloping demand curve for physical assets—'real investment' opportunities—in Fig. 4–5. Suppose in addition that returns on the company's securities are capitalized by investors in the securities markets at the $r = 8$ percent rate of return indicated by the figure's horizontal, straight line demand curve for financial assets. Rational investment policy for this (hypothetical) firm in an environment without taxes or transactions costs of any kind, then, would require the expenditure of precisely $200,000 on capital equipment; accepting *all* those projects whose rates of return exceed 8 percent, and *no* projects whose returns are less than that amount. Should internally generated funds fall short of the optimal $200,000 capital budget, additional shares could (and presumably should) be sold to raise the needed funds; should internally generated funds exceed $200,000, the remainder could be paid out as dividends to shareholders who, on their own, can obtain such returns (if they so desire) by purchasing additional securities on the open market.

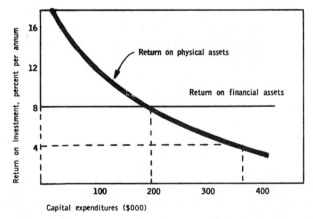

FIG. 4–5   A comparison of returns on physical and financial assets.
[A5611]

"The world in which most of us live, however, is not tax-free and also may contain non-negligible transactions costs for the purchase or sale of securities. Thus, corporate decisions to pay dividends, retain funds for investment in physical assets, raise additional capital through the sale of new securities, or use funds for the repurchase and retirement of outstanding securities may have a very important impact on each shareholder's well being. As a very simple example, consider a shareholder in the hypothetical corporation whose investment opportunities are displayed in Fig. 4–5 and whose marginal personal tax bracket is 50 percent. A dollar's worth of dividend payments to this investor, then, will add only 50 cents to his disposable personal income. Reinvested in additional shares of the firm's stock, this (before tax) dollar adds no more to its owner's welfare than would an investment by the firm itself in assets yielding as little as 4 percent. Thus, a perfectly rational management bent on maximizing its shareholder's welfare might well, in some circumstances, choose to retain earnings for investment in projects whose yields actually are less than the company's cost of capital.[7]

"Internally generated funds, then, often are considered by managements to be low in cost. Saying the same thing differently, the *opportunity cost* of ploughing earnings back into a firm rather than distributing them as dividends to stockholders generally is not thought to be great. While such a view may be defensible from a managerial standpoint, it at least raises a question regarding whether or not stockholders value dividends differently from capital gains—that is, the increase in share price on the securities markets resulting from an increase in the firm's assets (generally from reinvested earnings) and earning power. If stockholders do not value dividends and capital gains differently, the sharp distinctions conventionally made between the costs of internal funds, long-term debt, preferred stock, and new stock issues are rather difficult to reconcile with the maximization of returns to ownership as a basic managerial objective.   * * *

"The question of the cost of capital also can become intermingled with the measurement of risk. Quite obviously, if a firm can borrow unlimited sums of money at, say, 6 percent, it should do so—unless risk is a factor—as long as it has investment opportunities offering higher returns. Borrowing in this fashion is called *leveraging* the stockholders' investment. However, the extent to which various forms of fund raising are used, normally affects the firm's exposure to risk, imposing definite limits on the extent to which leverage or borrowing can be indulged. Conventional wisdom tells us that additional debt financing, other things being equal, will increase a firm's risk. Thus, lenders tend to insist at some point that additional debt be balanced by additional equity, either from the retention and reinvestment of internally generated funds or from the sale of additional shares of stock. Of course, if the proportions of debt to equity in the firm's capital structure were rigidly fixed, the relevant discount rate would simply be a weighted average of returns on the company's debt and equity securities. The difficulty with such an approach, obviously, is that risk appraisal generally is influenced importantly by the mix of debt and equity—and this, in turn, usually influences the *true costs* assigned both to borrowing and to the capitalization of the firm's equity securities.

"Inflation or inflationary expectations also can condition the costs to a firm of borrowing. The rate charged for debt financing tends to

---

7. Theoretically, no corporation whose securities are publicly traded ever should encounter such a situation, for by repurchasing these securities the corporation can at least recover its capital costs—in our illustrative example, the 8 percent return on its own financial assets.

increase as or if inflationary expectations arise. Debt generally represents a fixed obligation on the part of the borrower to pay a certain sum of money to the lender on a specified date. If general price inflation is expected, any fixed payment will be expected to decline in real purchasing power before repayment. In such circumstances, the lender often insists on a higher interest charge to offset his expected loss in real value. The cost of debt to a borrower depends, of course, on the extent to which the additional interest charge eventually offsets, or fails to offset, any subsequent decline in the purchasing power of money.

" * * * Generally speaking, a growth stock is an asset whose holders do not expect or even desire a large current dividend payment, but do expect considerable growth in the value of their holdings; that is, they expect to enjoy most of the return on their investment as capital gains. For firms that enjoy such status, new common stock issue may appear to be a relatively inexpensive means of financing certain kinds of capital acquisitions, especially the acquisition of other firms (through merger) * * *.

"In sum, the *cost of capital* as perceived by a firm's management can depend on a very large number of considerations: the structure of corporate and individual income taxes, the growth characteristics and reputation of the firm, the status of money markets (and, therefore the interest rates charged on different classes of debt), the general state of the stock market and stockholders' expectations, and so forth. Under the circumstances, it is hardly surprising that most firms adopt a more or less arbitrary rule of thumb about the cost they will attach to their use of capital, and employ it as a discount rate in present value calculations. Typically, these rule of thumb estimates run between 8 and 20 percent (after taxes) for United States corporations, with exceptions usually lying above the higher rather than below the lower figure. Exact figures for any firm, or even for any particular capital budgeting decision, usually will be difficult to define with precision and will depend, for the reasons outlined, on the circumstances faced by the firm, its management and its stockholders. In a sense, this rule of thumb figure represents a distillation of managerial experiences regarding the costs of acquiring and using capital. The firm's management, by using such a figure, presumes that it can raise enough capital to meet all demands yielding such a return, and that by accepting all investments having such a yield, it will maximize the value to the firm's owners of the assets under their control."

DURAND, COSTS OF DEBT AND EQUITY FUNDS FOR BUSINESS: TRENDS AND PROBLEMS OF MEASUREMENT

(National Bureau of Economic Research, Inc.)

Haverford College, June 19–21, 1952.

TABLE I
Balance Sheet of the ABC Manufacturing Company

Assets		$30,000,000
Liabilities		
Total Current	$ 6,000,000	
Common stock, 1,000,000 shares at $15 per share	15,000,000	
Surplus	9,000,000	
	$24,000,000	
Total		$30,000,000

Income Statement of the ABC Manufacturing Company

Net operating income	2,500,000
Dividends paid	2,000,000
Transferred to Surplus	500,000
Earnings per share	$2.50
Dividends per share	$2.00

* * *

Could a corporation [whose balance sheet and income statement are summarized in Table I] profitably finance additional plant by issuing $10 million of 4 percent bonds, provided the expansion were expected to earn $800,000 annually, or 8 percent? The estimated income after the proposed expansion is shown below:

Net income, current operations	$2,500,000
[Net income, proposed operations ($800,000 less $400,000 interest)]	400,000
Net income	$2,900,000
Dividends (old rate)	2,000,000
	$ 900,000

But if the bond issue could be arranged, would the stockholders consider the transaction attractive? The expansion has the advantage of increasing the prospective earnings from $2.50 a share to $2.90. It also has the disadvantage of increasing the risk because the proposed bond issue is so large that dividends might be curtailed for several years—even if the expected earnings were realized; and the entire financial position of the company might be jeopardized if earnings fell off sharply.

* * *

* * * Suppose, for example, that 12½ percent, or eight times earnings, is considered a fair capitalization rate as long as the company remains debt free, and that an increase to 15 percent, or six and two-thirds times earnings, is considered an adequate adjustment to compensate for the risk of carrying $10 million in debt. These assumed rates are completely arbitrary * * * [It is sufficient for the present argument merely to assume that the stockholders consider the rates satisfactory.] The necessary stock appraisals can then be made easily, as shown below. These calculations imply that the proposed expansion is inadvisable.

Earnings per share from current operations	$ 2.50
Multiplier	8
Investment value per share	$20.00
Projected earnings after expansion	$ 2.90
Multiplier	6⅔
Investment value	$19.33

Because the stockholders suffer a decline in the investment value of their holdings, the small increase in earnings is not sufficient to compensate for the additional risk.

Required Return

The preceding example showed that the risks incurred in borrowing may discourage investment, even though the rate of return on the new investment exceeds the interest cost of borrowed money. Specifically, the possibility of earning 8 percent in this example did not justify borrowing at only half that rate. But a still higher rate of return would have justified the investment. The following calculations show how to ascertain a rate that is just high enough to offset the risk. It is assumed that the risk will be just offset if the prospective per share earnings capitalized at 15 percent maintain the value of the common stock at $20.00.

Required value of stock per share	$20.00
Capitalization rate	.15
Required earnings, per share	3.00
Required earnings, 1,000,000 shares	3,000,000
Earnings previously available	2,500,000
Additional earnings required	500,000
Interest charges	400,000
Required earnings before interest	900,000
Rate of required earnings	9%

The required rate of earnings—9 percent for this example—is in a sense the cost to this corporation of borrowing the needed money. Of course, it is not an out-of-pocket cost, but a sort of opportunity cost—the minimum rate that the new investment must earn without being actually disadvantageous to the stockholders. But perhaps this is too broad an interpretation of cost, and the reader is, therefore, free to choose for himself. * * * For the remainder of this paper, the required rate of earnings will be referred to as the *required return* and will be abbreviated, RR. * * *

Although the RR discussed above refers to bond financing, there is also a RR when a corporation sells stock, and sometimes even when it finances expansion with cash retained from operations. If the stockholders in the previous example had been deterred from authorizing the proposed expansion because the expected returns were inadequate to justify the inherent risk incurred by bond financing, they might have considered preferred stock, common stock, and perhaps a judicious combination of common stock and bonds. Would the expected return have been sufficient to justify any of these alternatives? And if not, what rate of return would have been sufficient? * * * When capital is raised by a common stock issue, the old stockholders will suffer a dilution of earning power and hence a dilution of investment value unless the new investment is capable of earning enough to maintain per-share earnings at the old level. The RR depends upon the old level of earnings and the price at which the new shares must be sold. If the stockholders of the ABC Company wanted to raise $10 million by selling 500,000 shares on the market at $20.00, the new investment would have to earn $1,250,000 or 12½ percent to avoid dilution of earnings. Hence 12½ percent is the RR.

II. THE PROBLEM OF SECURITY APPRAISAL

It should be clear enough that any practical application of the principles of the RR necessitates a sound, effective, and generally acceptable system of security appraisal. Yet at present, no such system exists. Naturally some differences of opinion concerning details may always be expected. But present differences run much deeper than details. On the single question of capitalizing earnings, involved in most appraisal methods, there appear to be two systems in current use that arise from fundamentally different assumptions, lead to substantially different results in calculating the RR, and have radically different implications for financial policy. An analysis of these two systems will therefore prove illuminating and will further highlight the need of providing a sound conceptual groundwork for research on investment problems and the costs of capital.

The accompanying sample balance sheet and income statement contain enough data to illustrate the fundamental difference between the two methods of capitalizing earnings. This hypothetical company is financed partly with bonds, partly with common stock; and the problem at hand is to estimate the value of the common stock on the assumption that the bonds, which are well protected, sell in the market at par. Since the purpose of the illustration is to focus attention on the problem of capitalizing earnings, questions of assets and book value will be neglected entirely, and the important matter of the corporate income tax will be deferred for later treatment.

Balance Sheet of the PDQ Manufacturing Company [Abridged]

Assets		$30,000,000
Liabilities		
Total Current	$5,000,000	
Bonded debt, 4 percent debentures	5,000,000	
Common stock, 1,500,000 shares at $10 per share	15,000,000	
Earned surplus	5,000,000	
Total		$30,000,000

Income Statement of the PDQ Manufacturing Company

Sales	$30,000,000
Cost of goods sold	28,000,000
Net operating income	2,000,000
Interest	200,000
Net income	$1,800,000

One approach, hereafter called the NOI Method, capitalizes net operating income and subtracts the debt as follows:

Net operating income	$2,000,000
Capitalization rate, 10%	× 10
Total value of company	20,000,000
Total bonded debt	5,000,000
Total value of common stock	15,000,000
Value per share, 1,500,000 shares	$10.00

The essence of this approach is that the total value of all bonds and stock must always be the same—$20 million in this example—regardless of the proportion of bonds and stock. Had there been no bonds at all, for example, the total value of the common stock would have been $20 million, and had there been $2.5 million in bonds, the value would have been $17.5 million. Hereafter, the total of all stocks and bonds will be called the "total investment value" of the company.

The alternative approach, hereafter called the NI Method, capitalizes net income instead of net operating income. The calculations are as follows:

Net operating income	$2,000,000
Interest	200,000
Net income	1,800,000
Capitalization rate, 10%	× 10
Total value of common stock	18,000,000
Value per share, 1,500,000 shares	$12.00

Under this method, the total investment value does not remain constant, but increases with the proportion of bonds in the capital structure. In the table below, three levels of bond financing are assumed: $5 million, $2.5 million, and no bonds at all. At each level, the value of the stock is

Assumed amount of bonds	None	$ 2,500,000	$ 5,000,000
Value of common stock	$20,000,000	19,000,000	18,000,000
Total investment value	$20,000,000	$21,500,000	$23,000,000

obtained, as above, by capitalizing at 10 percent the residual income after bond interest. The implied relation in this table is that an increase of $2.5 million in bonded debt (total capitalization remaining constant) produces a corresponding increase of $1.5 million in total investment value. However, such a relationship cannot continue indefinitely as the proponents of the NI Method clearly point out. As the debt burden becomes substantial, the bonds will slip below par, and the stock will cease to be worth ten times earnings.

* * *

* * * The most obvious difference between the two methods is that the NI Method results in a higher total investment value and a higher value for the common stock except for companies capitalized entirely with stock. For such companies the two methods give identical results provided the same capitalization rate is used. This difference alone marks the NI Method as more liberal than the NOI Method, but the distinction between the optimism of the NI Method and the pessimism of the NOI Method will grow sharper as the discussion progresses. The NI Method, it will appear, takes a very sanguine view of the risks incurred in business borrowing; the NOI Method takes a more sober view.

Proponents of the NOI Method argue that the totality of risk incurred by all security holders of a given company cannot be altered by merely changing the capitalization proportions. Such a change could only alter the proportion of the total risk borne by each class of security holder. Thus if the PDQ Company had been capitalized entirely with stock—say 2,000,000 shares instead of 1,500,000—the stockholders would have borne all the risk. With $5 million in bonds in lieu of the additional 500,000 shares, the bondholders would have incurred a portion of this risk. But because the bonds are so well protected, this portion would be small—say in the order of 5 or ten percent. Hence the stockholders would still be bearing most of the risk, and with 25 percent fewer shares the risk per share would be substantially greater.[8]

The advocates of the NI Method take a position that is somewhat less straightforward. Those who adhere strictly to this method contend: first, that *conservative* increases in bonded debt do not increase the risk borne by the common stockholders; second, that a package of securities containing a *conservative* proportion of bonds will justifiably command a higher market price than a package of common stock alone.

The first contention seems to have little merit; it runs counter to the rigorous analysis offered by the advocates of the NOI Method; and it seems to imply that the security holders of a business can raise

8. This proposition can be stated rigorously in terms of mathematical expectation. In brief, the argument runs along the following lines. The future income of a company has a definite, though perhaps unknown, mathematical expectation. If this income is to be divided up among types of security holder according to some formula, the income of each type will also have a definite mathematical expectation. Finally, the sum of the mathematical expectations for each type will necessarily equal the total for the entire income *no matter how that income is divided up.*

In spite of the logical merits of this proposition, the basic assumption may be objectionable. One of my critics opines that the totality of risk is increased when a business borrows and that even the NOI Method is optimistic.

themselves by their own bootstraps.[9] The second contention appears to be correct, however, and it certainly merits critical analysis.

Since many investors in the modern world are seriously circumscribed in their actions, there is an opportunity to increase the total investment value of an enterprise by effective bond financing. Economic theorists are fond of saying that in a perfectly fluid world one function of the market is to equalize risks on all investments. If the yield differential between two securities should be greater than the apparent risk differential, arbitragers would rush into the breach and promptly restore the yield differential to its proper value. But in our world, arbitragers may have insufficient funds to do their job because so many investors are deterred from buying stocks or low-grade bonds, either by law, by personal circumstance, by income taxes, or even by pure prejudice. These restricted investors, including all banks and insurance companies, have to bid for high-grade investments almost without regard to yield differentials or the attractiveness of the lower grade investments. And these restricted investors have sufficient funds to maintain yield differentials well above risk differentials. The result is a sort of super premium for safety; and a corporation management can take advantage of this super premium by issuing as many bonds as it can maintain at a high rating grade.

---

2. THE MODIGLIANI–MILLER POSITION AND THE REVISED CONCEPT OF OPTIMAL CAPITAL STRUCTURE

The net operating income approach to enterprise valuation stressed by Durand was further elaborated in an article by Modigliani and Miller, "The Cost of Capital, Corporation Finance and the Theory of Investment," 48 Am.Econ.Rev. p. 261 (1958). In contrast to Durand, however, M–M concluded not merely that the firm's cost of capital ought, theoretically, to be independent of its capital structure, but that generally speaking such independence *actually exists* under realistic conditions. The M–M thesis, and the extensive debate that it provoked, are well summarized in the following excerpts.

VAN HORNE, FINANCIAL MANAGEMENT AND POLICY
271–275; 276–281; 284–288; 293–296 (9th Ed.1992).

TRADITIONAL APPROACH

The traditional approach to valuation and leverage assumes that there is an optimal capital structure and that the firm can increase the

---

9. The argument * * * implies that a business can incur any amount of debt without increasing the proprietors' risk. Recognizing that this is a practical absurdity, the advocates of the NI Method say merely that a business can incur a limited amount of debt without increasing the proprietors' risk. * * *

total value of the firm through the judicious use of leverage. The approach suggests that the firm initially can lower its cost of capital and raise its total value through leverage. Although investors raise the equity-capitalization rate, the increase in k_e does not offset entirely the benefit of using "cheaper" debt funds. As more leverage occurs, investors increasingly penalize the firm's equity capitalization rate until eventually this effect more than offsets the use of "cheaper" debt funds.

In one variation of the traditional approach, shown in Fig. 10–2, k_e is assumed to rise at an increasing rate with leverage, whereas k_o is assumed to rise only after significant leverage has occurred. At first, the weighted-average cost of capital declines with leverage because the rise in k_e does not offset entirely the use of cheaper debt funds. As a result, the weighted-average cost of capital, k_o, declines with moderate use of leverage. After a point, however, the increase in k_e more than offsets the use of cheaper debt funds in the capital structure, and k_o begins to rise. The rise in k_o is supported further, once k_j begins to rise. The optimal capital structure is the point at which k_o bottoms out. In the figure, this optimal capital structure is point X. Thus the traditional position implies that the cost of capital is not independent of the capital structure of the firm and that there is an optimal capital structure.

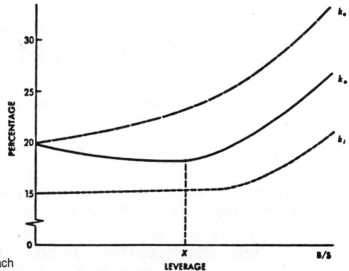

Figure 10-2
Traditional approach

MODIGLIANI–MILLER POSITION

Modigliani and Miller (MM) advocate that the relationship between leverage and the cost of capital is explained by the net operating income approach. They make a formidable attack on the traditional position by offering behavioral justification for having the cost of capital, k_o, remain constant throughout all degrees of leverage. As their assumptions are extremely important, it is necessary to spell them out.

1. Capital markets are perfect. Information is costless and readily available to all investors. There are no transaction costs, and all securities are infinitely divisible. Investors are assumed to be rational and to behave accordingly.

2. The average expected future operating earnings of a firm are represented by subjective random variables. It is assumed that the expected values of the probability distributions of all investors are the same. The MM illustration implies that the expected values of the probability distributions of expected operating earnings for all future periods are the same as present operating earnings.

3. Firms can be categorized into "equivalent return" classes. All firms within a class have the same degree of business risk. As we shall see later, this assumption is not essential for their proof.

4. The absence of corporate income taxes is assumed. MM remove this assumption later.

Simply put, the Modigliani–Miller position is based on the idea that no matter how you divide up the capital structure of a firm among debt, equity, and other claims, there is a conservation of investment value. That is, because the total investment value of a corporation depends upon its underlying profitability and risk, it is invariant with respect to relative changes in the firm's financial capitalization. Thus, the total pie does not change as it is divided into debt, equity, and other securities. The sum of the parts must equal the whole; so regardless of financing mix, the total value of the firm stays the same, according to MM. * * *

The support for this position rests on the idea that investors are able to substitute personal for corporate leverage, thereby replicating any capital structure the firm might undertake. Because the firm is unable to do something for its stockholders (leverage) that they cannot do for themselves, capital structure changes are not a thing of value in the perfect capital market world that MM assume. Therefore, two firms alike in every respect except capital structure must have the same total value. If not, arbitrage will be possible, and its occurrence will cause the two firms to sell in the market at the same total value.

ARBITRAGE SUPPORT ILLUSTRATED

Consider two firms identical in every respect except that Company A is not levered, while Company B has $30,000 of 12 percent bonds outstanding. According to the traditional position, Company B may have a higher total value and lower average cost of capital than Company A. The valuation of the two firms is assumed to be the following:

		Company A	Company B
O	Net operating income	$10,000	$10,000
F	Interest on debt		3,600
E	Earnings available to common stockholders	$10,000	$6,400
k_e	Equity-capitalization rate	0.15	0.16
S	Market value of stock	$66,667	$40,000
B	Market value of debt		30,000
V	Total value of firm	$66,667	$70,000
k_o	Implied overall capitalization rate	15%	14.3%
B/S	Debt-to-equity ratio	0	75.0%

MM maintain that this situation cannot continue, for arbitrage will drive the total values of the two firms together. Company B cannot command a higher total value simply because it has a financing mix different from Company A's. MM argue that by investing in Company A, investors in Company B are able to obtain the same dollar return with no increase in financial risk. Moreover, they are able to do so with a smaller investment outlay.[3] Because investors would be better off with the investment requiring the lesser outlay, they would sell their shares in Company B and buy shares in Company A. These arbitrage transactions would continue until Company B's shares declined in price and Company A's shares increased in price enough to make the total value of the two firms identical.

If you are a rational investor who owns 1 percent of the stock of Company B, the levered firm, worth $400 (market value) you should

1. Sell the stock in Company B for $400.
2. Borrow $300 at 12 percent interest. This personal debt is equal to 1 percent of the debt of Company B, your previous proportional ownership of the company.
3. Buy 1 percent of the shares of Company A, the unlevered firm, for $667.67.

Prior to this series of transactions, your expected return on investment in Company B's stock was 16 percent on a $400 investment, or $64. Your expected return on investment in Company A is 15 percent on a $666.67 investment, or $100. From this return you must deduct the interest charges on your personal borrowings, so your net dollar return is

Return on investment in Company A	$100
Less interest ($300 × 0.12)	36
Net return	$ 64

Your net dollar return, $64, is the same as it was for your investment in Company B; however, your cash outlay of $366.67 ($666.67 less personal borrowings of $300) is less than the $400 investment in

3. This arbitrage proof appears in Franco Modigliani and Merton H. Miller, "Reply to Heins and Sprenkle," American Economic Review, 59 (September 1969), 592–95.

Company B, the levered firm. Because of the I
would prefer to invest in Company A under th(
In essence, you "lever" the stock of the unleve
personal debt.*

The action of a number of investors undert
transactions will tend to drive up the price of C
its k_e, drive down the price of Company B, ai
arbitrage process will continue until there is n(
reducing one's investment outlay and achieving the sam.. _.
At this equilibrium, the total value of the two firms must be the same.
As a result, their average costs of capital, k_o, also must be the same.
The principle involved is simply that investors are able to reconstitute
their former positions by offsetting changes in corporate leverage with
changes in personal leverage.

* * *

TAXES AND CAPITAL STRUCTURE

The irrelevance of capital structure rests on an absence of market
imperfections. No matter how one slices the corporate pie between
debt and equity, there is a conservation of value, so that the sum of the
parts is always the same. In other words, nothing is lost or gained in
the slicing. To the extent that there are capital market imperfections,
however, changes in the capital structure of a firm may affect the total
size of the pie. That is to say, the firm's valuation and cost of capital
may change with changes in its capital structure. One of the most
important imperfections is the presence of taxes. In this regard, we
examine the valuation impact of corporate taxes in the absence of
personal taxes and then the combined effect of corporate and personal
taxes.

CORPORATE TAXES

The advantage of debt in a world of corporate taxes is that interest
payments are deductible as an expense. They elude taxation at the
corporate level, whereas dividends or retained earnings associated with
stock are not deductible by the corporation for tax purposes. Consequently, the total amount of payments available for both debtholders
and stockholders is greater if debt is employed.

To illustrate, suppose that the earnings before interest and taxes
are $2,000 for companies X and Y, and they are alike in every respect
except in leverage. Company Y has $5,000 in debt at 12 percent

---

* [Ed. Note] Suppose, however, that an
investor borrows to buy stock in levered
firm *B*, thus apparently doubling the leverage effect by adding his own to the corporation's borrowing. Will he then have succeeded in outrunning investors in *A* shares
and hence be willing to pay a premium for
that opportunity? The answer (which the
reader is left to illustrate for himself) is
that the investor can accomplish the same
results by simply borrowing more to buy
an equivalent proportionate stock interest
in *A*. Once again, therefore, the inducement to pay a premium for *B* is non-existent, at least theoretically.

whereas Company X has no debt. If the tax rate (federal and
is 40 percent for each company, we have

	Company X	Company Y
Earnings before interest and taxes	$2,000	$2,000
Interest—income to debtholders	0	600
Profit before taxes	2,000	1,400
Taxes	800	560
Income available to stockholders	$1,200	$840
Income to debtholders plus income to stockholders	$1,200	$1,440

Thus, total income to both debtholders and stockholders is larger for
levered Company Y than it is for unlevered Company X. The reason is
that debtholders receive interest payments without the deduction of
taxes at the corporate level, whereas income to stockholders is after
corporate taxes have been paid. In essence, the government pays a
subsidy to the levered company for the use of debt. Total income to all
investors increases by the interest payment times the tax rate. In our
example, this amounts to $600 \times 0.40 = $240. This figure represents a
tax shield that the government provides the levered company * * *.*

* [Ed. Note] This is a shield that homemade leverage cannot duplicate or overcome. As has been seen, a corporation
with bonds outstanding can deduct all interest payments in computing its taxable
income. By contrast, a corporation with
an all-stock capital structure computes its
taxable income without deducting dividends, and without regard to interest payments made at the shareholder level by
shareholders who are borrowing. If a corporate tax rate of 50 percent is assumed,
the comparative results can be illustrated
as follows:

CORP. A

100,000 shares, par value $50

E/s before tax	E/s after tax	Probability of occurrence
$12	$6	$1/3$
$ 8	$4	$1/3$
$ 4	$2	$1/3$

CORP. B

50,000 shares, par value $50
$2.5 million bonds at 5%

E/s before tax	E/s after tax	Probability of occurrence
$21.50 ($24—$2.50)	$10.75	$1/3$
$13.50 ($16—$2.50)	$ 6.75	$1/3$
$ 5.50 ($ 8—$2.50)	$ 2.75	$1/3$

The expected value of A's after-tax earnings is thus $4 per share; that of B, $6.75
per share. Assume a multiplier of 12.5 for
A, so that the market value of a share of A
is $50. Now, however, it can no longer be
asserted that a B share will also sell at
only $50 despite higher expected earnings,
since the investor cannot duplicate the B
income stream by engaging in personal
leverage and buying 2 shares of A. Thus,
if an investor borrows $50 at 5% and pur-
chases a second share of A, he achieves the
following result after allowing for the $2.50
interest charges he will owe on the loan:

* * * [T]he greater the amount of debt, the greater the tax shield and the greater value of the firm, all other things the same. Thus, the original MM proposition as subsequently adjusted for corporate taxes suggests that an optimal strategy is to take on a maximum amount of leverage. Clearly, this is not consistent with the behavior of corporations, and alternative explanations must be sought.

* * * [T]he tax savings associated with the use of debt are not certain. If reported income is consistently low or negative, the tax shield on debt * * * is reduced or even eliminated. As a result, the near full or full cash-flow burden of interest payments would be felt by the firm. If the firm should go bankrupt and liquidate, the potential future tax savings associated with debt would stop altogether. We must recognize also that Congress can change the corporate tax rate. Finally, the greater the possibility of going out of business, the greater the probability the tax shield will not be effectively utilized. All of these things make the tax shield associated with debt financing less than certain.

* * *

* * * [T]he uncertain nature of the interest tax shield, together with the possibility of at least some tax shelter redundancy, may cause firm value to rise less with leverage than the corporate tax advantage alone would suggest. * * * As leverage increases, the uncertainty associated with the interest tax shield comes into play. At first, the diminution in value is slight. As more leverage occurs, tax shield uncertainty causes value to increase at an ever-decreasing rate and perhaps eventually to turn down. Under these conditions, the value of the firm is

$$\begin{matrix} \text{Value of} \\ \text{firm} \end{matrix} = \begin{matrix} \text{Value if} \\ \text{unlevered} \end{matrix} + \begin{matrix} \text{Pure value of} \\ \text{corporate tax} \\ \text{shield} \end{matrix} - \begin{matrix} \text{Value lost through} \\ \text{tax shield} \\ \text{uncertainty} \end{matrix}$$

[?26a]

The last two factors combined give the present value of the corporate tax shield. The greater the uncertainty associated with the shield, the less important it becomes.

CORPORATE PLUS PERSONAL TAXES

* * * [T]he presence of taxes on personal income may reduce or possibly eliminate the corporate tax advantage associated with debt. If

Earnings on 2 A shares	Probability of occurrence
$9.50 [(2 × $6)—$2.50]	$\frac{1}{3}$
$5.50 [(2 × $4)—$2.50]	$\frac{1}{3}$
$1.50 [(2 × $2)—$2.50]	$\frac{1}{3}$

While the spread of probable outcomes is the same on 2 shares of *A* as on 1 share of *B,* the expected return on *A* is $1.25 less than on *B* ($6.75—$5.50) and indeed the investor is clearly worse off by that amount at every possible outcome. It follows that investors will pay more for *B* than for *A* and hence that corporate leverage will attract a premium once taxes are taken into account.

returns on debt and on stock are taxed at the same personal tax rate, however, the corporate tax advantage remains. This can be seen by taking our earlier example and applying a 30 percent personal tax rate to the debt and stock returns:

	Company X	Company Y
Debt income	0	$600
Less personal taxes of .30		− 180
Debt income after personal taxes	0	420
Income available to stockholders	$1200	$840
Less personal taxes of .30	− 360	− 252
Stockholders income after personal taxes	840	588
Income to debt holders and stockholders after personal taxes	$840	$1,008

Although the total after-tax income to debt holders and stockholders is less than before, the tax advantage associated with debt remains.

* * *

* * * Therefore, the corporate tax advantage of debt remains exactly the same if debt income and stock income are taxed at the same personal tax rate.

We know that stock income is comprised both of dividends and capital gains * * *. Dividend income by and large is taxed at the same personal tax rate as interest income. Capital gains are often taxed at a lower rate.* * * *

For now we assume that overall stock income (dividends and capital gains) is taxed at a lower personal tax rate than is debt income (interest). In this situation, the corporate tax advantage associated with corporate debt is reduced. * * *

* * * If the company is concerned with only after-tax income to the investor, it would finance either with debt or with stock, depending upon the relative values of t_{pd} [personal income tax on debt income] and t_c [corporate income tax]. If the personal tax rate on debt income exceeds the corporate tax rate, the company would finance with stock, because the after-tax income to the investor would be higher. If t_{pd} is less than t_c, however, it would finance with debt, because after-tax

---

* [Ed. Note:] [T]he Tax Reform Act of 1986 made important tax-rate and structural changes in the Internal Revenue Code which affect the above analysis. The rate on larger corporations was reduced to 34%, while rates on individuals were cut to a maximum of 28% (raised to 31% in 1990 and proposed to be raised again in 1993). The long-standing distinction between capital gain and ordinary income was eliminated, with the result that dividends and gains from the sale of stock (no matter how long the seller's holding period) were taxed at the same marginal rate. But the rate differential between ordinary income and capital gains was reopened in 1990, to stand at 31% to 28%. Before 1986, in contrast, dividends were taxed at a maximum rate of 50%, while long-term capital gains were taxed at a maximum rate of only 20%.

income to the investor would be greater here.   If t_{pd} equals t_c, it would be a matter of indifference whether debt or stock were employed.**

* * *

EFFECT OF BANKRUPTCY COSTS

Another important imperfection affecting capital structure decisions is the presence of bankruptcy costs. * * * [B]ankruptcy costs are more than legal and administrative expenses of bankruptcy; they involve inefficiencies in operating a company when it is about to go bankrupt [or during insolvency proceedings *] as well as liquidation of assets at distress prices below their economic values. * * *

If there is a possibility of bankruptcy, and if administrative and other costs associated with bankruptcy are significant, the levered firm may be less attractive to investors than the unlevered one.   With perfect capital markets, zero bankruptcy costs are assumed.   If the firm goes bankrupt, assets presumably can be sold at their economic values with no liquidating or legal costs involved.   Proceeds from the sale are distributed according to the claim on assets * * *.   If capital markets are less than perfect, however, there may be administrative costs, and assets may have to be liquidated at less than their economic values. These costs and the shortfall in liquidating value from economic value represent a drain in the system from the standpoint of debt holders and equity holders.

** [Ed. Note:] Plainly income taxes on the investor can affect the value to the investor of the tax shield which the interest deduction offers to the corporation. There is considerable argument over whether, as suggested by Miller [Debt and Taxes, 32 J. of Fin. 261 (1977)], the interplay of the tax on investors and the tax consequences of the corporate interest deduction combined with shifting investor clienteles will make capital structure irrelevant for individual firms.   As described by Bradley, Jarrell and Kim, On the Existence of an Optimal Capital Structure: Theory and Evidence, 39 J. of Fin. 857 (1984):

"The general academic view by the mid–1970s, although not a consensus, was that the optimal capital structure involves balancing the tax advantage of debt against the present value of bankruptcy costs.   No sooner did this general view become prevalent in the profession than Miller presented a new challenge by showing that under certain conditions the tax advantage of debt financing at the firm level is exactly offset by the tax disadvantage of debt at the personal level.   Since then there has developed a burgeoning theoretical literature attempting to reconcile Miller's model with the balancing theory of optimal

capital structure * * *.   The general result of this work is that if there are significant 'leverage-related' costs, such as bankruptcy costs, agency costs of debt, and loss of non-debt tax shields, if the income from equity is untaxed, then the marginal bondholder's tax rate will be less than the corporate rate and there will be a positive net tax advantage to corporate debt financing.   The firm's optimal capital structure will involve the trade off between the tax advantage of debt and various leverage-related costs. The upshot of these extensions of Miller's model is the recognition that the existence of an optimal capital structure is essentially an empirical issue as to whether or not the various leverage-related costs are economically significant enough to influence the costs of corporate borrowing."

* [Ed. Note:] E.g., costs attributable to reluctance of creditors to permit sale of some assets in order to obtain cash with which better to exploit other assets; difficulty of raising additional capital for profitable projects, reluctance of suppliers (including skilled labor) and customers to continue dealing except on costlier terms to the debtor.   See Gordon and Malkiel, Corporation Finance, in Aaron, H.J. and Pechman, J.A. (Editors) How Taxes Affect Economic Behavior (1981) pp. 131–163 et seq.

In the event of bankruptcy, security holders as a whole receive less than they would in the absence of bankruptcy costs. To the extent that the levered firm has a greater possibility of bankruptcy than the unlevered one has, the levered firm would be a less attractive investment, all other things the same. The possibility of bankruptcy usually is not a linear function of the debt-to-equity ratio, but it increases at an increasing rate beyond some threshold. As a result, the expected cost of bankruptcy increases in this manner and would be expected to have a corresponding negative effect upon the value of the firm and upon its cost of capital. Creditors bear the ex-post cost of bankruptcy, but they will probably pass on the ex-ante cost to stockholders in the form of higher interest rates. Hence the stockholders would bear the burden of ex-ante bankruptcy costs and the subsequent lower valuation of the firm. Because bankruptcy costs represent a "dead weight" loss, investors are unable to diversify away these costs even though the market equilibration process is assumed to be efficient.

Now it may be argued that if creditors and stockholders could get together informally, they could work out an agreement outside of the court. By so doing, bankruptcy costs could be avoided, with both parties sharing in the gain. Even if such a workout were "costless," Ronald M. Giammarino shows that creditors often prefer costly arbitration.[18] The crux of his argument is that there is asymmetric information between the two parties, and enforcement of contracts is costly.

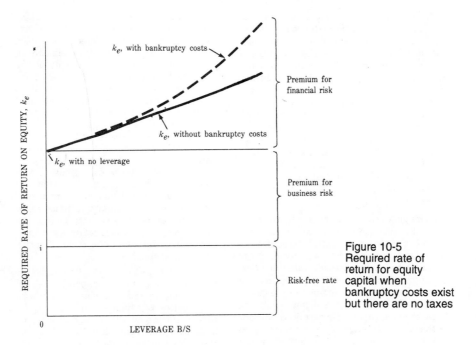

Figure 10-5
Required rate of return for equity capital when bankruptcy costs exist but there are no taxes

18. Ronald M. Giammarino, "The Resolution of Financial Distress," *Review of Financial Studies*, 2, No. 1 (1989), 25–49. A similar conclusion is reached by David T. Brown, "Changing Incentive Conflicts in Reorganization: The Role of Bankruptcy Law," *Review of Financial Studies*, 2, No. 1 (1989), 109–23.

As a result, investors are likely to penalize the price of the stock as leverage increases. The nature of the penalty is illustrated for a no-tax world in Fig. 10–5. Here the required rate of return for investors, k_e, is broken into its component parts. There is the risk-free rate, i, plus a premium for business risk. This premium is depicted on the vertical axis by the difference between the required rate of return for an all-equity capital structure and the risk-free rate. As debt is added, the required rate of return rises and this increment represents a financial risk premium. In the absence of bankruptcy costs, the required return would rise in a linear manner according to our earlier discussion of taxes, and this relationship is shown. However, with bankruptcy costs and an increasing probability of bankruptcy with leverage, the required rate of return would be expected to rise at an increasing rate beyond some point. At first there might be a negligible probability of bankruptcy, so there would be little or no penalty. As leverage increases, so does the penalty; for extreme leverage, the penalty becomes very substantial indeed.[*]

TAXES AND BANKRUPTCY COSTS

Our earlier discussion of taxes and capital structure concluded that leverage is likely to result in a net tax advantage * * *. As the company increases its degree of leverage, the present value of the tax shield will increase. In this restricted context, the total value of the firm is

$$\text{Value of firm} = \begin{array}{c} \text{Value as} \\ \text{unlevered} \\ \text{firm} \end{array} + \begin{array}{c} \text{Present} \\ \text{value} \\ \text{of net tax} \\ \text{shield on} \\ \text{debt} \end{array} \qquad (10\text{--}11)$$

As leverage is increased, the second term on the right increases in a linear manner, so that the value of the firm also increases. With more and more leverage, the tax shield uncertainty lessens the increment in value that occurs. Despite this occurrence, if we look at only the net tax effect, then a high proportion of debt would be optimal.

If we allow for bankruptcy costs and if the probability of bankruptcy increases at an increasing rate with leverage, extreme leverage is likely to be penalized by investors. (As discussed earlier, bankruptcy

---

[*] [Ed. Note:] The existence of creditors creates the possibility that stockholders will alter the firm's investments so as to shift risks (i.e., increase the variance) as asset values approach the amount of creditors' claims, or decline to invest in order to accept "safe" investments at times when the creditor would get too large a benefit from the foregone opportunity in view of the risk involved. (See p. 188, supra). While creditors seek *ex ante* to guard against such behavior by protective cove- nants, they cannot deny to stockholders (except at prohibitive cost) sufficient discretion to expose them (creditors) to such risks. The cost of guarding against such behavior, either by contract in anticipation of, or by monitoring during, periods of temptation, particularly when confronting financial distress short of bankruptcy, is an added cost of leverage. See C.W. Haley and L.W. Schall, The Theory of Financial Decisions (2nd Ed.1979), Ch. 14. It is presumably worth the benefit. See, p. 475, infra.

costs represent a drain in the system to securityholders.) In a world of both taxes and bankruptcy costs, it is likely that there would be an optimal capital structure. Whereas the net tax effect would have a positive influence on value, bankruptcy costs would exert a negative influence. The value of the firm would increase as leverage was first employed because of the tax advantage of debt. Gradually, however, the prospect of bankruptcy would become increasingly important. This, together with the tax shield uncertainty, would cause the value of the firm to increase at a decreasing rate. As more and more leverage was undertaken, the bankruptcy effect eventually would offset the tax effect, and the value of the firm would decline. * * *

The joint effect of taxes and bankruptcy costs is illustrated in Fig. 10–6. * * * The optimal capital structure by definition is the point at which the value of the firm is maximized. Thus, we have a tradeoff between the positive linear tax effects associated with leverage and the nonlinear expected bankruptcy costs that come when leverage is pushed beyond a point. While taxes and bankruptcy costs are probably the most important imperfections when it comes to capital structure decisions, there are others which bear on the problem.

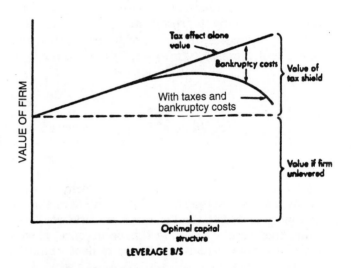

Figure 10-6
Value of firm
with taxes and
bankruptcy costs

OTHER IMPERFECTIONS

Other capital market imperfections impede the equilibration of security prices according to their expected returns and risks. As a result, these imperfections may result in leverage having an effect on the value of the firm apart from taxes and bankruptcy costs. The imperfections must be not only material, they must be one-directional. We know that transaction costs restrict the arbitrage process described earlier, but the net effect of this imperfection is not predictable as to direction if, in fact, there is a net effect at all. In what follows, we examine certain additional imperfections that may have a predictable effect on the capital structure question.

CORPORATE AND HOMEMADE LEVERAGE NOT BEING PERFECT SUBSTITUTES

The perceived risks of personal leverage and corporate leverage may differ. Despite the implication in the MM analysis that personal and corporate leverage are perfect substitutes, there are various reasons for suspecting that this may not be the case. For one thing, if investors borrow personally and pledge their stock as collateral, they are subject to possible margin calls. Many investors view this possibility with alarm. Moreover, personal leverage involves a certain amount of inconvenience for investors, which they do not experience with corporate leverage. In addition, stockholders have limited liability with a stock investment, whereas their liability with personal loans is unlimited. Moreover, the cost of borrowing may be higher for the individual than for the corporation. For these reasons, personal leverage may not be a perfect substitute for corporate leverage in the minds of many investors.

Arbitrage need not occur in terms of the individual actually borrowing in the market, however. The same thing may be accomplished by changing one's holdings of bonds. Moreover, the arbitrage process is not confined to individuals. If opportunities for profit exist, financial intermediaries may enter the scene and replicate the financial claims of either the levered or the unlevered company and buy the stock of the other. The free entry of financial intermediaries without cost will assure the efficient functioning of the arbitrage process, which in turn will result in the irrelevance of corporate leverage.* Therefore we are inclined to discount the importance of this argument.

INSTITUTIONAL RESTRICTIONS

Restrictions on investment behavior may retard the arbitrage process. Many institutional investors, such as pension funds and life insurance companies, are not allowed to engage in the "homemade" leverage that was described. Regulatory bodies often restrict stock and bond investments to a list of companies meeting certain quality standards, such as only a "safe" amount of leverage. If a company breaches that amount, it may be removed from the acceptable list, thereby precluding certain institutions from investing in it. This reduction in investor demand can have an adverse effect on the market value of the company's financial instruments.

* * *

If other imperfections and behavioral factors dilute the arbitrage argument of MM, the point at which the firm value line turns down with leverage in Fig. 10–6 would be sooner or later than that depicted. The greater the importance of the other imperfections we have discussed, the less effective the arbitrage process becomes, and the greater the case that can be made for an optimal capital structure.

---

* [Ed. Note:] But note discussion of the   arbitrage process, supra pp. 137–142.

* * *

AGENCY COSTS MORE BROADLY DEFINED

The [possibility of] expropriation of wealth * * * illustrate[s] the need for debt holders to monitor the actions of equity holders. Monitoring requires the expenditure of resources, and the costs involved are one form of *agency costs*. * * * Michael C. Jensen and William Meckling have expounded a sophisticated theory of agency costs.[27] Among other things, they show that regardless of who makes the monitoring expenditures, cost is borne by stockholders. Debt holders, anticipating monitoring costs, charge higher interest. The higher the probable monitoring costs, the higher the interest rate, and the lower the value of the firm to its shareholders, all other things the same.

Complete protection would require the specification of extremely detailed protective covenants and extraordinary enforcement costs. Virtually every decision of the firm would need to be monitored. Not only would there be substantial legal and enforcement costs, but the firm would operate inefficiently. All of these agency costs go to reduce the overall value of the firm. As residual owners of the firm, stockholders have an incentive to see that such monitoring costs are minimized—up to a point. There is a tradeoff. In the absence of any protective covenants, debt holders may charge very high interest rates, and these rates may cost stockholders more than the agency costs associated with reasonable protective covenants.

It is not that monitoring costs per se are bad for the owners of a company; it is that monitoring needs to be efficient. As more and more safeguards and enforcement procedures are imposed, debt holders' protection rises, but at a decreasing rate. Beyond a point, the reduction in interest rate is more than offset by escalating agency costs, which ultimately are borne by the stockholders. An optimal balance needs to be struck between monitoring costs and the interest rate charged on a debt instrument at the time it is sold. Some activities of the firm are relatively inexpensive to monitor; others are expensive. Dividend and financing decisions can be monitored with only moderate cost, whereas the production and investment decisions of the firm are much more costly to monitor. The relative costs of monitoring need to be taken into account in determining the protective covenants that should be used.

In addition, the firm should endeavor to see that efficient monitoring occurs. To the extent that management together with an outside auditor or appraiser can produce information at a lower cost than the lender can, it should undertake the production of such information. (This assumes that the "quality" of the information is the same.) The important thing to realize is that ultimately the costs of monitoring are borne by the stockholders. It is always in their interest to see that

27. * * * Theory of the Firm: Managerial Behavior, Agency Costs and Ownership Structure, 3 Journal of Financial Economics (October 1976), 305–60. For a somewhat different approach, see Stewart C. Myers, "Determinants of Corporate Borrowing," 5 Journal of Financial Economics (November 1977) 147–75.

monitoring is efficiently administered. * * * In order to control agency costs, equity holders may need to limit the amount of debt financing.

The presence of monitoring costs acts as a disincentive to the issuance of debt. If capital markets were perfect with the exception of these costs and we lived in a no-tax world, the firm would not want to issue any debt. In the real world of corporate income tax, the issuance of debt is attractive. Like bankruptcy costs, though, monitoring costs may limit the amount of debt that it is optimal for a firm to issue. It is likely that the amount of monitoring required by debt holders increases with the amount of debt outstanding. When there is little or no debt, lenders may engage in only limited monitoring, whereas with a great deal of debt outstanding they may insist upon extensive monitoring. In turn, this monitoring may involve considerable costs. As a result, Fig. 10–6, showing the relationship between taxes, bankruptcy costs and firm value would need to be modified. Monitoring costs would act as a further factor decreasing firm value for extreme leverage. The situation is illustrated in Fig. 10–8. The optimal capital structure occurs at point x, somewhat before that which occurs with taxes and bankruptcy costs alone, point y.

DEBT AND THE INCENTIVE TO MANAGE EFFICIENTLY

Working in the other direction is the notion that high debt levels create incentives for management to be more efficient.[28] By taking on the cash-flow obligation to service debt, it is claimed that management's "feet are held close to the fire." As a result, there is said to be an incentive not to squander funds in wasteful activities, whether it be an investment, a perquisite, a company plane, or whatever. The idea is that levered companies may be leaner because management cuts the fat. Contrarily, the company with little debt and significant free cash flow, after investing in all worthwhile projects, may have a tendency to squander funds. In the absence of other incentives, "running scared" to make debt payments may have a salutary effect on efficiency.

FINANCIAL SIGNALING

Closely related to monitoring costs and agency relationships is the notion of signaling. Because strict managerial contracts are difficult to enforce, managers may use capital structure changes to convey information about the profitability and risk of the firm. The implication is that insiders know something about the firm that outsiders do not. As a manager, your pay and benefits may depend upon the firm's market

---

28. A number of people have made this argument, but it is articulated perhaps best in Michael C. Jensen's "The Takeover Controversy: Analysis and Evidence," Midland Corporate Finance Journal, 4 (Summer 1986), 12–21.

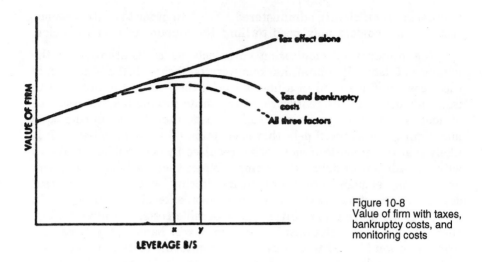

Figure 10-8
Value of firm with taxes,
bankruptcy costs, and
monitoring costs

value. That gives you an incentive to let investors know when the firm is undervalued. You could make an announcement, "Our firm is undervalued," but you are more sophisticated than that; and you know that investors would probably be as convinced as if you were boasting about your child. So you alter your firm's capital structure by issuing more debt. Increased leverage implies a higher probability of bankruptcy; and since you would be penalized contractually if bankruptcy occurred, investors conclude that you have good reason to believe that things really are better than the stock price reflects. Your actions speak louder than words. Increased leverage is a positive sign.

ASYMMETRIC INFORMATION

More formally, a signaling effect assumes there is information asymmetry between management and stockholders. When financing an investment project management will want to issue the overvalued security, if it is acting in the interests of current stockholders. As Myers and Majluf suggest, it will issue stock if it believes the existing stock is overvalued and debt if it believes the stock is undervalued.[30] However, investors are not unmindful of this phenomenon, so debt issues are regarded as "good news" and stock issues as "bad news."

The greater the asymmetry in information between insiders (management) and outsiders (security holders), the greater the likely stock price reaction to a financing announcement. In general, empirical evidence is consistent with the asymmetry of information idea. Around the time of the announcement, leverage-increasing transactions tend to result in positive excess returns to stockholders, whereas leverage-decreasing transactions result in the opposite. The evidence overall is

30. Stewart C. Myers and Nicholas S. Majluf, "Corporate Financing and Investment Decisions When Firms Have Information That Investors Do Not Have," Journal of Financial Economics, 13 (June 1984), 187–222. For refinement along the lines of adverse selection, see Michael Brennan and Alan Kraus, "Efficient Financing under Asymmetric Information," Journal of Finance, 42 (December 1987), 1225–43.

consistent with a financial signaling effect accompanying the choice of security employed in the capital structure.

FROM WHERE DOES VALUE COMETH?

This is not to say that capital structure changes cause changes in valuation. Rather, it is the signal conveyed by the change that is significant. This signal pertains to the underlying profitability and risk of the firm, as that is what is important when it comes to valuation. Financial signaling is a topic of considerable interest in the writing on finance, but the various models are difficult to evaluate. Unless the managerial contract is very precise, the manager is tempted to give false signals. Moreover, there simply may be more effective and less costly ways to convey information than by altering the firm's capital structure. * * *

NOTES

1. *Agency Theory.*

As Van Horne [b] explains, agency theory breaks with the irrelevance model of capital structure. It relaxes Modigliani and Miller's assumptions of perfect information and an absence of costly contracts, and thereby makes possible a microeconomic account of the capital structures that we observe in practice. The agency costs of debt rise as leverage increases and at some point outweigh the benefits of debt. One of these costs is the cost of bankruptcy identified by Van Horne, supra. As Van Horne notes, bankruptcy carries out of pocket and other significant costs. Agency theory identifies two additional costs of debt [c]:

Asset substitution. Equity holders can increase the value of their interest in the firm at the expense of the debt if the firm disposes of the

---

b. The foregoing passage from Van Horne summarizes the main points of an extensive body of economics. Those interested in a more detailed overview should consult Harris & Raviv, The Theory of Capital Structure, 46 J. Finance 297 (1991). This breaks the literature on determination of relative amounts of debt and equity into four "categories of determinants," id. pp. 299, 306, 320:

(a) The agency cost explanation. Mixing debt and equity ameliorates conflicts of interest among various groups with claims to the firm's resources.

(b) The asymmetric information approach. Mixes of debt and equity mitigate information asymmetries between management and the capital markets by conveying information and mitigating inefficiencies in the firm's investment decisions.

(3) Product markets. Mixes of debt and equity influence the nature of the products the firm produces and the nature of product market competition.

(4) Corporate control contests. Mixes of debt and equity influence the outcome of control contests by affecting the distribution of votes and distribution of cash flows. Harris and Raviv conclude that the four determinants are "for the most part, complementary," id. at 342. An accompanying survey of empirical studies of capital structure choices lead them to conclude that and these are "broadly consistent with the theory." Id. at 350. See also Mello and Parsons, Measuring the Agency Cost of Debt, 47 J.Finance 1887 (1992) (proposing a model to measure the agency cost of debt).

c. See Bratton, Corporate Debt Relationships: Legal Theory in a Time of Restructuring, 1989 Duke L.J. 92, 127.

assets it holds at the time the money is borrowed and substitutes riskier assets. This opportunistic predilection follows from application of the Black–Scholes option pricing model to the firm as a whole. See Black and Scholes, The Pricing of Options and Corporate Liabilities, 81 J.Pol.Econ. 637 (1973) and the discussion infra, pp. 529–530. Under Black–Scholes, equities are viewed as combinations of options to buy and sell a firm's assets. Stockholders, in effect, hold an option to buy back the firm from the holders of the firm's debt. The stock, accordingly, is valued as an option. The value of an option increases with the volatility of the firm's stream of net cash flows. Given borrowing, stockholders will want the firm to switch to investments in high-variance projects. These could be projects less valuable to the firm, considered as a whole, than substitute projects with lower variance. Contract provisions in the firm's capital structure that prevent this asset substitution therefore cause the firm to be more valuable than it otherwise would be, given the presence of debt.[d]

Underinvestment. Where the firm's ability to repay its debt depends on positive returns from new investments, the firm's equity holders have an incentive to cause the firm to turn down certain kinds of profitable investment opportunities. Assume that the firm's projected cash flows from existing assets are insufficient to pay down existing debt. A new investment opportunity comes along with a positive net present value. The firm's equity holders have an incentive to cause the firm to make the investment only if its net present value exceeds the face value of the debt. Otherwise, the project operates to benefit only the creditors. Given limited liability, the equity holders might as well walk away. See Myers, Determinants of Corporate Borrowing, 5 J.Fin. Econ. 147 (1977). This underinvestment incentive causes the firm, taken as a whole, to forego profitable investments. Provisions to prevent underinvestment in the firm's capital structure therefore cause the firm to be more valuable than it otherwise would be.

Each of asset substitution, underinvestment, and bankruptcy become more problematic and generate larger and larger agency costs, as the firm's leverage increases. Similarly, the risks of these costs in respect of a particular loan become greater as the loan's term becomes longer.

d. Rose–Ackerman, Risk Taking and Ruin: Bankruptcy and Investment Choice, 20 J.Legal Studies 277 (1991), offers a model integrating the point that managers prefer suboptimal levels of debt with the point that highly levered debtors tend to engage in asset substitution. She takes the position that the conventional picture of investment in terms of a utility function defined over the mean and variance of returns does not capture the situation of the corporate manager. The manager equates the downside possibility of firm liquidation with financial ruin, due to interests in career, reputation and self esteem. The manager thus seeks to avoid bankruptcy for its own sake, rather than simply treating it as a low level of return in a continuous distribution. The upshot is that given a continuous risk of liquidation, the manager's investment policy will reflect creditor rather than equity holder interests. But, in a situation of distress, if all choices are losing propositions, the same manager will select high variance projects that impose high costs on creditors.

Agency theory, although built on an acknowledgment of market failure, goes on to assert that market trading and other simple purchase and sale arrangements can go some distance in reducing the agency costs of debt. Two possible market correctives for the agency costs are emphasized. One is portfolio diversification by the creditors. But, of course, the risk of opportunism by the equity cannot be diversified out of a portfolio containing only debt. There results the second corrective—"unification." This is the ownership of a fraction of each of the outstanding ownership interests in the firm's capital structure, whether debt or equity, in a proportion corresponding to the interest's fractional share of the whole. But, since these devices do not completely solve the conflict of interest problem, complex financial contracting results. These cost-reductive capital structures turn out to create new conflict of interest problems. These problems encourage further diversification, unification and complex contracting. See A. Barnea, R. Haugen and L. Senbet, Agency Problems and Financial Contracting 2–12, 63–66 (1985); Carney, The Theory of the Firm: Investor Coordination Costs, Control Premiums and Capital Structure, 65 Wash.U.L.Q. 1, 11–19 (1987).

2. *Law and Capital Structure.*

If institutional arrangements and tax considerations suggest that there can be an optimal capital structure, does a management which fails substantially—by some criteria and measure of substantiality yet to be developed—to create such capital structure violate its duty to its stockholders? If not, why not? If so, may management's obligation be policed by imposing (1) liability for failure to borrow "enough," or an order directing management to borrow more; or (2) liability for borrowing "too much", or an order directing management to reduce debt?

3. *Monitoring.*

Berlin, Bank Loans and Marketable Securities: How Do Financial Contracts Control Borrowing Firms? Fed. Res. Bank of Philadelphia Bus. Rev., July–Aug. 1987 at 16–17, comments as follows on monitoring costs and the structure of lending relationships:

" * * * When a firm requires outside finance, lenders either must monitor the firm's affairs or provide incentives for firm insiders to run the firm efficiently. Marketed securities do provide such incentives, but security holders will seldom be willing to bear the costs of monitoring the firm. By depositing their funds in a bank, savers hire an agent to make loans and monitor the investments on their behalf.

"The goal of the theory of financial intermediation is to provide insights into the role of intermediaries and other contractual alternatives in credit markets. But these theoretical inquiries may also interest crystal ball gazers who want to know whether marketable securities will increasingly replace bank loans as a source of funds for business.

"Many observers have claimed that technological improvements have lowered costs to individual security holders of obtaining and processing information about firms. In particular, the largest firms are watched closely by many market specialists, and individual investors may have found that the cost of purchasing and interpreting this information in a timely fashion is decreasing. In fact, the larger firms have reduced their reliance on bank loans, and money center banks that have traditionally specialized in providing services to larger firms have shifted away from commercial lending. Should information costs continue to fall, the theory predicts that more firms will rely primarily on marketed securities.

"At the same time, the theory provides a counterweight to predictions that banks' commercial lending will soon become a thing of the past. Since diversification reduces the agency costs of intermediated lending, greater opportunities to diversify loan portfolios should increase the efficiency of bank lending. Thus, the theory suggests that relaxed interstate banking restrictions should enhance banks' ability to compete in credit markets. Also, firms in unsettled markets and firms entering new markets should continue to rely primarily on bank loans, because bond contracts are too inflexible. Finally, since bank monitoring benefits all security holders, even firms that sell securities will continue to borrow through a mixture of bank loans and direct securities."

----

3. LEVERAGE AND MANAGEMENT DISCIPLINE

The passage from Van Horne in the preceding subsection suggests that "high debt levels create incentives for management to be more efficient." This proposition played a leading part in the justification of the leveraged restructurings of the 1980s. It is developed more fully in the materials that follow.

(A) MANAGEMENT'S VIEW OF OPTIMAL
CAPITAL STRUCTURE
DONALDSON, MANAGING CORPORATE WEALTH
(1984) pp. 42–62.

* * *

Top management's commitment to continuous growth means that it must have a matching strategy for providing the requisite funds. Nowhere is this necessity more apparent than in the funding of existing product markets.

* * *

As management considers the flow of funds for strategic investments in established product markets * * * corporate managers prefer sources that most nearly satisfy certain conditions. These include:

availability on an open-ended and continuous basis; compatibility with the level of management's perceived needs; a high degree of certainty as to amount and timing; reasonable cost to the organization; and the absence of terms which would contravene management's normal prerogatives over its funds. Not all sources of funds satisfy these conditions.

The Limitations of the Public Capital Market

Top managers of major industrial corporations have had decades of individual experience with the capital market. Such experience tends to persuade many (probably most) that the public capital market is an untrustworthy ally when it comes to their corporation's vital interests. They recognize that the U.S. economy provides a well-organized and relatively efficient system for distributing private and institutional savings among various investing enterprises and that, by and large, the market is more than adequate to meet the needs of any individual business. But they also know that their enterprise does not survive by and large. It survives from moment to never-ending moment, or it does not survive at all.

Watching the public equity and debt markets' sharp cyclical fluctuations, therefore, many corporate managers come to believe in the reality of a market window for financing. This window opens and shuts at times not of their choosing, and its timing may or may not coincide with the vital needs of a particular competitive venture. Consequently, they are loathe to entrust the success of those ventures to the public markets, no matter how large and well-established the companies they direct.

* * *

The objective evidence of the external capital markets' limited role in funding established product markets lies in the collective experience of the mature industrial companies studied. In this combined record of financing, covering more than 120 company-years, there were only two issues of common or preferred stock for cash. These accounted for about one percent of the $8.5 billion of new long-term capital added to the companies during this period. (By coincidence an equal amount of equity was repurchased so that the net addition was zero.)

The managements which made use of the public equity market as a contingency reserve did so under extraordinary circumstances and outside their normal funding frameworks. These companies did not *plan* to use public equity for cash.

* * *

Students of corporate finance have often wondered why industrial managements do not use new external equity more extensively to fund the normal growth of established businesses. No single answer suffices because the issues are complex and involve subjective as well as objective factors. However, this study calls attention to two considerations that influence management's decisions. The first is corporate leaders' inevitable disposition to regard their equity as undervalued—good times or bad. This disposition results from their plans and commitment to better performance in the future and from their conviction that outsiders are always ill-informed. Expectations for next year's sales and earnings always look better to the insiders who have responsibility—and the self-confidence—for delivering them than last year's results do to a skeptical and detached investor. Thus, *next year* always promises a better price.

A second deterrent to the use of equity in funding ongoing investment is management's preference for continuous, reliable, and predictable sources of funds. In a mature organization the necessity to turn to the public equity market for supplemental funds is often seen as a public admission of misjudgment or mismanagement. Had management accurately foreseen its capital requirements (for the established product markets), it would have priced its products more aggressively, controlled expenses more carefully, or retained more earnings (i.e., it would have conserved cash in such a way as to fund the growth on its own). Thus, these managers attached a negative connotation to the market signal associated with a new equity issue. Management abhors surprises, especially those that are considered bad news.

Use of the public debt market is another matter. In this regard management was prepared to fund some of its ongoing strategic needs from a source which can be unreliable at times. Of the $8.5 billion of new funds invested by these companies between 1969 and 1978, long-term debt funded some 26 percent. The strategy for dealing with the attendant uncertainty can be summed up in one word: conservatism. In essence, the managers of these mature industrial companies sought to conduct their own affairs so that *they* could *always* borrow if necessary, even in bad times. They did so by keeping their borrowing within tight limits and by providing wide margins of safety over and above the lender's minimum lending rules. They made it a practice to live within the standards of an A credit rating at the least and within moderate debt/equity ratios. As a result, they were in a position to regard debt as an automatic extension of internally generated funds and to treat it, for planning purposes at least, as though it were an assured, off-balance sheet, liquid asset reserve. Each increment of retained earnings could be assumed to bring an additional unit of debt capacity along with it.

These practices and attitudes indicate that top management views the capital market as essentially *private* insofar as its firm's vital requirements are concerned. These corporate managers expect that the equity required to sustain their established businesses will be generated from within, and that any necessary debt will be readily forthcoming from a captive public debt equity market. The evidence of their thinking is apparent in the companies' investment statistics. During the period under review, 74 percent of the new funds were generated internally, with the balance provided by long-term debt with an overall debt/equity ratio of 1 to 3.

* * *

[But the resort to debt as a source of permanent capital is not a joyous ploy. As Donaldson later points out (pp. 54–56):]

* * * For all but one of the companies, debt was an acceptable, if not desirable, source of long-term funds and a regular part of the corporate supply. In the case of the exception the zero debt target was a corporate objective which could be traced back to the founders' experience in the 1930s, when bankruptcies precipitated by default on debt contracts were common. To quote one of the founders, "What do you do with borrowed dollars? I think most of us believe something unwise."

Although most of the corporate managers were less extreme than this in their views, they shared a preference for debt policies they characterized as conservative. They pointed out that debt was easy to increase and hard to cut back. They recognized that debt limits were arbitrary, but they took comfort in a line which looked conservatively drawn. Debt was desirable in that it allowed them to grow at a faster rate, perhaps faster than the average; but too much debt deprived the company of its ability to meet unexpected needs and survive. Some managers expressed their thinking about a debt reserve in terms of avoiding circumstances in which "the next financing had to be equity."

* * *

Corporate managers considered a variety of factors as they set these debt limits. Among them were: the needs of the business; the need for a substantial reserve for both offensive and defensive use; the use of debt by close competitors in the funding of competitive strategy; the opinions of the capital-market power centers—bankers, analysts, and credit rating agencies; and the managers' own subjective sense of the riskiness of any given amount of debt. The ultimate risk with which the managers were concerned was the loss of independence and control consequent upon falling into the hands of "those damn banks." As the executive who described the banks in these terms went on to say:

> They will cut you off and they will be cold-blooded as hell. I don't want to be in the position where our money market center can control me.

Listening to these comments, it is hard to remember that the speaker is a top executive in a large, mature, and profitable corporation—not a sidewalk entrepreneur. Yet many of his peers in other companies expressed the same concerns although they phrased them more elegantly.

* * *

Short of the extreme event of losing control, the value of a conservative debt limit was seen to lie in its ability to guarantee continued funding flexibility (through debt and equity) in the face of competitive uncertainty. Access to the capital markets *regardless of conditions* was the key consideration. Of course, the level of debt deemed conservative was to some degree a function of need and experience. New levels of debt brought on by urgent competitive spending priorities could and did become the new conservatism, if found to be tolerable over an extended period of time. However, beneath these judgments was management's abiding concern for organizational survival. As one executive remarked:

> The debt policy [of our company] reflects a primary emphasis on freedom—that if we maintain the debt limits we have set, we will be free from bank restrictions and the banks will not inhibit our activities. This, along with our earnings goals are *parts of the whole concept of a desirable quality of life* for management. (Emphasis added.)

* * *

A Strategy of Self–Sufficiency

The financial strategy that emerges from a study of these industrial firms can best be characterized as one of self-sufficiency. It springs from management's desire for self-preservation in an environment generally regarded as hostile and unpredictable. In addition, it accords with a business climate in which intense competition is the norm and which lacks a public or private safety net for those who fall. Thus, financial self-sufficiency complements the organizational goals of survival and independence which are basic to management's corporate mission.

In practice, this strategy means that managements rely heavily on retained earnings to meet the demand for funds from their existing businesses. Retained earnings are particularly appropriate for this purpose because they are the source about which management has the best information and over which it has the greatest control. Accordingly, they lend themselves to the close coordination in the flow of funds which strategic investments require. As has been seen, corporate managers work with most of their strategic investment budget tightly set; they cannot separate the demand for funds from their supply. As one senior financial executive observed, "One can't pull back from long-term goals simply because of short-term changes."

* * *

In the following chapter we shall look more closely at the ways in which the concept of financial self-sufficiency influences the character of management's financial goal setting. For now, we must turn to the price management pays for its independence and control over strategic investment. That price is *the need to live within limits*. The sources of funds that are continuous, predictable, reliable, and free of discretionary restrictions are also limited in magnitude and in timing. Management must order its strategic investments to fit the available capital at the available time; it must plan carefully and live within its plans. Further, each business unit or division must learn to accomplish its objectives with its share of plannable resources—or find some way to renegotiate allocations with its internal competitors.

As should be readily apparent, this price tag significantly diminishes the possibility of spontaneous or opportunistic investment. The internal capital market as it has been defined is a finite capital market. Unless management is willing to expose its strategies to the uncertainties of the external capital market and to the judgments of independent investors, it cannot escape this limitation. Most managements are reluctant to do so.

* * *

The key to the interdependence among a company's financial goals lies in the scarcity of corporate purchasing power (actual or perceived) by which management implements its decisions. As has been seen, every financial goal can be classified in terms of its immediate impact on the flow of funds within the firm. Some goals, chiefly those related to the competitive drives of the product market and to organizational well-being, define the demand for funds. Others, chiefly those related to the capital markets, define their supply. Given an infinite supply of funds these relationships do not impinge on management's plans. If the supply of funds is finite, however, as most of these top managers believed, then the demand for funds does become a financial planning problem.

Readers versed in classical financial theory and traditional interpretations of American capitalism may be surprised by the notion that management's investment funds are limited. From traditional perspectives the deep pockets of the American debt and equity markets are always available to fund any appropriate investment by any company at any time. The basic limitation on corporate growth is not the scarcity of funds, therefore, but rather the scarcity of opportunities for profitable investment (i.e., investment that promises a return equal to or in excess of the market's cost of capital). In other words, the firm could get all the capital it needed for the right opportunity and *at the right price.*

This last principle is the implicit assumption in all discounted cash flow analyses. However, it was significantly qualified by the large majority of the managements studied during the period under review. Their behavior conformed with an environment of capital scarcity rather than capital abundance. Why such behavior would appear rational has already been indicated in the preceding chapters. As has been seen, most managers give paramount importance to a reliable, predictable stream of funds to support vital competitive strategies and long-term organizational survival. External debt and equity markets are perceived as ill informed and untrustworthy, particularly in periods of heightened uncertainty. Self-sufficiency is given priority as the prerequisite of true independence, and line managers are disciplined by the insistence that they earn their own pocket money. Thus even the largest and most creditworthy industrial corporations function under the tight discipline of capital scarcity in funding existing product markets.

Once this discipline has been recognized, however, it also becomes apparent that the company's key financial goals are part of a comprehensive goals system which must be reconciled and balanced. An adjustment in one goal will inevitably require a compensatory adjustment elsewhere. A fundamental and persistent balance must be struck between demand-related and supply-related goals, just as actual funds flows must be balanced. Priorities among conflicting goals must be established so that critical tradeoffs can be made.

* * *

(B) DEBT AS DISCIPLINE

The conservative debt financing practices discussed by Donaldson came to be identified with suboptimal management performance. The association of the two began when MM articulated the tax-adjusted version of their position. Merton Miller, The Modigliani–Miller Propositions After Thirty Years, 2 J. Econ. Perspectives 99, 112 (1988), recalls the appearance of the management critique:

"In many ways this tax-adjusted MM proposition provoked even more controversy than the original invariance one, which could be, and often was, shrugged off as merely another inconsequential paradox from some economists' frictionless dreamworld. But this one carried direct and not very flattering implications for the top managements of companies with low levels of debt. It suggested that the high bond ratings of such companies, in which the management took so much pride, may actually have been a sign of their incompetence; that the managers were leaving too much of their stockholders' money on the table in the form of unnecessary corporate income tax payments, payments which in the aggregate over the sector of large, publicly held corporations clearly came to many billions of dollars.

"We must admit that we too were somewhat taken aback when we first saw this conclusion emerging from our analysis. The earlier modeling of the tax effect in our 1958 paper, which the 1963 paper corrected, had also suggested tax advantages in debt financing, but of a smaller and more credible size. By 1963, however, with corporate debt ratios in the late 1950s not much higher than in the low tax 1920s (see Miller, 1963) we seemed to face an unhappy dilemma: either corporate managers did not know (or perhaps care) that they were paying too much in taxes; or something major was being left out of the model. Either they were wrong or we were."

Stating Miller's point more broadly, management's desire to be self sufficient and secure comes at the cost of maximum return on capital invested. As Donaldson points out, outside debt financing gives rise to management insecurity. The inference arises that debt financing can cause management to perform more productively. From an agency cost point of view, then, debt does more than perform a financial signalling function. Grossman and Hart, Corporate Financial Structure and Managerial Incentives, in McCall (Ed.), The Economics of Information and Uncertainty, at pp. 108–110, (1982), pursues this point. The authors suggest that if management causes the firm to issue debt, "shareholders know that it is personally costly to management not to profit maximize [because managers lose the perquisites of their position when the firm becomes bankrupt]. Hence * * * the market will recognize that profits will be higher and so the firm will have a high market value." Since management gains when the firm has a high market value, issuance of debt serves to give management an incentive to maximize the firm's value. Debt, on this view is a bonding rather than a signaling device; "the former involves agents communicating their endogenous intentions; the latter involves agents communicating their exogenous characteristics."

Grossman and Hart's suggestion of a governance role for debt has been more fully developed by Jensen in what he calls "the control hypothesis" in Agency Costs of Free Cash Flow, Corporate Finance and Takeovers, 76 Amer.Econ.Rev. (Papers and Proceedings) 323–325 (1986):

"Managers have incentives to cause their firms to grow beyond the optimal size. Growth increases managers' power by increasing the resources under their control. It is also associated with increases in managers' compensation, because changes in compensation are positively related to the growth in sales. * * * The tendency of firms to reward middle managers through promotion rather than year-to-year bonuses also creates a strong organizational bias toward growth to supply the new positions that such promotion-based reward systems require.

         * * *

"Free cash flow is cash flow in excess of that required to fund all projects that have positive net present values when discounted at the relevant cost of capital. Conflicts of interest between shareholders and managers over payout policies are especially severe when the organization generates substantial free cash flow. The problem is how to motivate managers to disgorge the cash rather than investing it at below the cost of capital or wasting it on organization inefficiencies.

"The agency costs of debt have been widely discussed, but the benefits of debt in motivating managers and their organizations to be efficient have been ignored. I call these effects the 'control hypothesis' for debt creation.

         * * *

"Debt creation, without retention of the proceeds of the issue, enables managers to effectively bond their promise to pay out future cash flows. Thus, debt can be an effective substitute for dividends, something not generally recognized in the corporate finance literature. By issuing debt in exchange for stock, managers are bonding their promise to pay out future cash flows in a way that cannot be accomplished by simple dividend increases. In doing so, they give shareholder recipients of the debt the right to take the firm into bankruptcy court if they do not maintain their promise to make the interest and principal payments. Thus debt reduces the agency costs of free cash flow by reducing the cash flow available for spending at the discretion of managers. These control effects of debt are a potential determinant of capital structure.

"Issuing large amounts of debt to buy back stock also sets up the required organizational incentives to motivate managers and to help them overcome normal organizational resistance to retrenchment which the payout of free cash flow often requires. The threat caused by failure to make debt service payments serves as an effective motivating force to make such organizations more efficient. Stock repurchase for debt or cash also has tax advantages. * * *

"Increased leverage also has costs. As leverage increases, the usual agency costs of debt rise, including bankruptcy costs. The optimal debt-equity ratio is the point at which firm value is maximized, the point where the marginal costs of debt just offset the marginal benefits.

"The control hypothesis does not imply that debt issues will always have positive control effects. For example, these effects will not be as important for rapidly growing organizations with large and highly profitable investment projects but no free cash flow.

       * * *

"The control function of debt is more important in organizations that generate large cash flows but have low growth prospects, and even more important in organizations that must shrink. In these organizations the pressures to waste cash flows by investing them in uneconomic projects is most serious." [e]

---

e. Harris and Raviv, Capital Structure and the Informational Role of Debt, 45 J. Finance 321 (1990) offers a model of management discipline and debt financing that complements Jensen's. In this model, self serving managers need to be disciplined, and the capital markets cannot get full information on investment and performance. Debt disciplines management by giving creditors the option to force the firm into liquidation. Debt also generates information: (1) the firm's ability to perform the debt contract is informationally significant, and (2) proceedings in the event of default generate information and changes in operating policy. An optimal capital structure trades th~ values created by these advantages against the costs of default.

SECTION B. CAPITAL STRUCTURE, PUBLIC POLICY, AND LEGAL STANDARDS

1. HIGH LEVERAGE

The 1980s saw a sudden increase in aggregate American indebtedness. The standard measure of all obligations, public and private, other than those of financial intermediaries, increased by an average of 11.8 percent per year during 1985, 1986, and 1987. This aggregate, expressed as a percentage of gross national product, yields an aggregate national debt equity ratio. From 1945 to 1983 this figure stayed around 140 percent. In fact, except during the Depression era, this figure had been stable for as far back into the Nineteenth century as data are available. The figure began increasing in 1983. By 1988 it had risen to 181 percent, a level previously experienced only in the early 1930s. The increase occurred because businesses increased their leverage in relation to net worth, breaking longstanding financing patterns in so doing.

Much of this increase stemmed from the joint appearance of the leveraged restructuring and the junk bond. Their dual rise and impact are described in Appendix C, Part 2. We turn to them at this point to consider their policy implications. Specifically, were the leveraged restructurings beneficial or detrimental to the wider economy? If they were detrimental, was there any effective way to regulate them, or would the costs of any such regulation outweigh the benefits?

In considering these questions bear in mind that an economic downturn prompted an abrupt turnabout in corporate financing patterns in late 1990 and early 1991. According to Anders, Merchants of Debt: KKR and the Mortgaging of American Business 273 (1992), the "Age of Leverage" ended suddenly: In 1990 and 1991 companies moved to issue more stock and pay off debt, credit upgrades became common once more, and the "harsh 'discipline of debt' abated as companies' balance sheets returned to more normal levels." Is the change of financial norms prevailing in the business world a sign that the leverage movement of the 1980s was a failure? Or is the change a species of efficient contractual adjustment to a change of economic conditions that gives rise to the inference that the leverage movement was a success?

(a) The Governance Defense

JENSEN, ECLIPSE OF THE PUBLIC CORPORATION
Harv.Bus.Rev., September–October 1989, p. 61
pp. 65–66, 67, 68, 69, 72.

Active investors are creating a new model of general management. These investors include LBO partnerships such as Kohlberg Kravis Roberts and Clayton & Dubilier; entrepreneurs such as Carl Icahn, Ronald Perelman, Laurence Tisch, Robert Bass, William Simon, Irwin Jacobs, and Warren Buffett; the merchant banking arms of Wall Street houses such as Morgan Stanley, Lazard Freres, and Merrill Lynch; and family funds such as those controlled by the Pritzkers and the Bronfmans. Their model is built around highly leveraged financial structures, pay-for-performance compensation systems, substantial equity ownership by managers and directors, and contracts with owners and creditors that limit both cross-subsidization among business units and the waste of free cash flow. Consistent with modern finance theory, these organizations are not managed to maximize earnings per share but rather to maximize value, with a strong emphasis on cash flow.

* * *

A central weakness and source of waste in the public corporation is the conflict between shareholders and managers over the payout of free cash flow—that is, cash flow in excess of that required to fund all investment projects with positive net present values when discounted at the relevant cost of capital. For a company to operate efficiently and maximize value, free cash flow must be distributed to shareholders rather than retained. But this happens infrequently; senior management has few incentives to distribute the funds, and there exist few mechanisms to compel distribution.

* * *

[The] perceived "leveraging of corporate America" is perhaps the central source of anxiety among defenders of the public corporation and critics of the new organizational forms. But most critics miss three important points. First, the trebling of the market value of public-company equity over the last decade means that corporate borrowing had to increase to avoid a major deleveraging.

Second, debt creation without retention of the proceeds of the issue helps limit the waste of free cash flow by compelling managers to pay out funds they would otherwise retain. Debt is in effect a substitute for dividends—a mechanism to force managers to disgorge cash rather than spend it on empire-building projects with low or negative returns, bloated staffs, indulgent perquisites, and organizational inefficiencies.

By issuing debt in exchange for stock, companies bond their managers' promise to pay out future cash flows in a way that simple dividend increases do not. "Permanent" dividend increases or multiyear share repurchase programs (two ways public companies can distribute excess cash to shareholders) involve no contractual commitments by managers to owners. It's easy for managers to cut dividends or scale back share repurchases.

* * *

Third, debt is a powerful agent for change. For all the deeply felt anxiety about excessive borrowing, "overleveraging" can be desirable and effective when it makes economic sense to break up a company, sell off parts of the business, and refocus its energies on a few core operations. Companies that assume so much debt they cannot meet the debt service payments out of operating cash flow force themselves to rethink their entire strategy and structure. Overleveraging creates the crisis atmosphere managers require to slash unsound investment programs, shrink overhead, and dispose of assets that are more valuable

outside the company. The proceeds generated by these overdue restructurings can then be used to reduce debt to more sustainable levels,
creating a leaner, more efficient and competitive organization.

* * *

Active investors are creating new models of general management,
the most widespread of which I call the LBO Association. A typical
LBO Association consists of three main constituencies: an LBO partnership that sponsors going-private transactions and counsels and monitors management in an ongoing cooperative relationship; company
managers who hold substantial equity stakes in an LBO division and
stay on after the buyout; and institutional investors (insurance companies, pension funds, and money management firms) that fund the
limited partnerships that purchase equity and lend money (along with
banks) to finance the transactions.

* * *

Management incentives are built around a strong relationship
between pay and performance. Compensation systems in LBO Associations usually have higher upper bounds than do public companies (or no
upper bounds at all), tie bonuses much more closely to cash flow and
debt retirement than to accounting earnings, and otherwise closely link
management pay to divisional performance. * * *

Thus the salary of the typical LBO business-unit manager is almost
20 times more sensitive to performance than that of the typical public-
company manager. * * *

* * *

Intensive use of debt dramatically shrinks the amount of equity in
a company. This allows the LBO general partners and divisional
managers to control a large fraction of the total ownership without
requiring huge investments they would be unable to make or large
grants of free equity. For example, in a company with $1 billion in
assets and a debt ratio of 20%, management would have to raise $80
million to buy 10% of the equity. If that same company had a debt
ratio of 90%, management would have to raise only $10 million to
control a 10% stake. By concentrating equity holdings among managers and LBO partners, debt intensifies the ownership incentives that
are so important to efficiency.

High debt also allows LBO Associations and other private organizations to tap the benefits of risk diversification once provided only by the
public equity market. Intensive use of debt means much of it must be
in the form of public, high-yield, noninvestment-grade securities, better
known as junk bonds. This debt, which was pioneered by Drexel
Burnham Lambert, reflects more of the risk borne by shareholders in
the typical public company. Placing this public debt in the well-
diversified portfolios of large financial institutions spreads equity like
risk among millions of investors, who are the ultimate beneficiaries of
mutual funds and pension funds—without requiring those risks to be

held as equity. Indeed, high-yield debt is probably the most important and productive capital market innovation in the last 40 years.

* * *

The relationship between debt and insolvency is perhaps the least understood aspect of this entire organizational evolution. New hedging techniques mean the risk associated with a given level of corporate debt is lower today than it was five years ago. Much of the bank debt associated with LBOs (which typically represents about half of the total debt) is done through floating-rate instruments. But few LBOs accept unlimited exposure to interest rate fluctuations. They purchase caps to set a ceiling on interest charges or use swaps to convert floating-rate debt into fixed-rate debt. In fact, most banks require such risk management techniques as a condition of lending.

Critics of leverage also fail to appreciate that insolvency in and of itself is not always something to avoid—and that the costs of becoming insolvent are likely to be much smaller in the new world of high leverage than in the old world of equity-dominated balance sheets. The proliferation of takeovers, LBOs, and other going-private transactions has inspired innovations in the reorganization and workout process. I refer to these innovations as "the privatization of bankruptcy." LBOs do get in financial trouble more frequently than public companies do. But few LBOs ever enter formal bankruptcy. They are reorganized quickly (a few months is common), often under new management, and at much lower costs than under a court-supervised process.

* * *

NOTE: DEBT AND CORPORATE GOVERNANCE

A number of empirical studies support Jensen's assertions. See Kaplan, The Effects of Management Buyouts on Operating Performance and Value, 24 J.Financial Econ. 217 (1989) (increases in operating income and net cash flow resulting from a sample of buyouts consummated between 1980 and 1986); Smith, Corporate Ownership Structure and Performance, 27 J.Financial Econ. 143 (1990) (shows an increase in return on operating assets for a sample of buyouts consummated between 1977 and 1986); Lichtenberg and Siegel, The Effect of Leveraged Buyouts on Productivity and Related Aspects of Firm Behavior, 27 J.Financial Econ. 165 (1990) (increases in plant productivity). See also Kaplan and Stein, How Risky is the Debt in Highly Leveraged Transactions? 27 J.Financial Econ. 215 (1990); Muscarella and Vetsuypens, Efficiency and Organizational Structure: A Study of Reverse LBOs, 45 J.Finance 1389 (1990); Baker and Wruck, Organizational Changes and Value Creation in Leveraged Buyouts, 25 J.Financial Econ. 163 (1989); Kaplan, Campeau's Acquisition of Federated: Value Destroyed or Value Added, 25 J.Financial Econ. 191 (1989).

On the other hand, a pair of studies contrasts the performance of leveraged buyouts that closed during the early 1980s with the results of buyouts that closed during the late 1980s. The later transactions performed less well. The later transactions may have involved companies less suited to leveraged restructuring or higher prices. Long and Ravenscraft, The Aftermath of LBOs (Brookings Institution Conference on Takeovers, LBOs, and Changing Corporate Forms, April 1991) (late transactions result in slight decrease in ratio of cash flow to sales); Kaplan and Stein, The Evolution of Buyout Pricing and Financial Structure in the 1980s (CRSP Working Paper No. 327, University of Chicago Graduate School of Business, April 1991) (late transactions involved increase of price paid relative to cash flows).

What material differences distinguish the high leverage capital structures described by Jensen from the public utility holding company pyramids described infra pp. 506–513? How much staying-power is possessed by the new corporate governance structure described by Jensen?

The classic LBO's final phase comes when the restructured firm's owners cash in on their work by selling their equity stake to the public. According to Kaplan, The Staying Power of Leveraged Buyouts, 29 J.Financial Econ. 287 (1991), the median time an LBO remains private is 6.82 years. Financial exigencies can shorten the time period: in "rapid-fire succession" in 1990 and 1991, KKR took public its best performing portfolio companies and used the proceeds of these offerings to pay down debt. Anders, Merchants of Debt: KKR and the Mortgaging of American Business 273 (1992). And, as demonstrated by the equity recapitalization of RJR Nabisco, supra p. 219, public equity sales can occur even before a majority of the equity goes into public hands.

The virtual cessation of restructurings and takeovers after 1990 caused academic discussions of corporate governance to move in a new direction. At least temporarily, commentators stopped looking to high leverage as a source of intensified management discipline, and began to encourage institutional investors actively and collectively to assert themselves in corporate governance. See, e.g., Gilson and Kraakman, Reinventing the Outside Director: An Agenda for Institutional Investors, 43 Stan.L.Rev. 463 (1991); Black, Shareholder Passivity Reexamined, 89 Mich.L.Rev. 520 (1990); Coffee, Liquidity versus Control: The Institutional Investor as Corporate Monitor, 91 Colum.L.Rev. 1277 (1991).

NOTE: BANKRUPTCY COSTS

How should the increased probability of bankruptcy be balanced against the claimed benefits of high leverage as a matter of public policy? Consider the following studies of bankruptcy costs:

"Direct" bankruptcy costs are the legal and other professional fees associated with the bankruptcy filing. "Indirect" bankruptcy costs are opportunity costs, including lost sales and decline in value of inventory, increased operating costs and a reduction in competitiveness. See Weiss, Bankruptcy Resolution: Direct Costs and Violation of Priority of Claims, 27 J.Fin.Econ. 285 (1990). Studies of bankruptcy costs tend to focus on direct costs, which are more easily and reliably measured. Warner, Bankruptcy Costs: Some Evidence, 32 J.Finance 337 (1977), studied a sample of railroad bankruptcies between 1930 and 1955, and found that the direct costs of the larger bankruptcies was 5.3 percent of the market value of the railroads' securities at the time of filing. Ang, Chua and McConnell, The Administrative Costs of Corporate Bankrupt- cy, 37 J.Finance 219 (1982), a study of small firm bankruptcies, found direct costs of 7.5 percent of the liquidating value of the estate. Weiss, supra, studies the bankruptcy proceedings of 37 publicly traded compa- nies and finds direct costs of 3.1 percent of the book value of the debt and 2.8 percent of the book value of total assets.

The leading study of indirect costs is Altman, A Further Empirical Investigation of the Bankruptcy Cost Question, 39 J.Finance 1067 (1984). Altman constructs a figure of lost profits for the three years prior to filing and relates it to the firm's market value. He finds lost profits to be 12.2 percent of the value of retailing firms and 23.7 percent of the value of manufacturing firms. He concludes that total bankruptcy costs are "not trivial," amounting to 20 percent of the value of the firm if measured immediately prior to filing, and on average, 11 to 17 percent of the value of the firm three years prior to filing.

(b) Objections to Leveraged Restructurings

(1) The restructuring movement provoked a national debate. Brat- ton, Corporate Debt Relationships: Legal Theory in a Time of Restruc- turing, 1989 Duke L.J. 92, 162–163, describes the two opposition posi- tions articulated against restructuring as "high" and "guarded" pessi- mism:

"The high pessimists assert that high debt itself creates a risk of financial crisis. They foresee this scenario: as the quantity of debt continues to grow, creditors will at some point lose confidence and abruptly withdraw their funds from the credit markets, causing a drastic curtailment of economic activity. Significantly, those who fear this result also express the traditional judgment that there is 'some- thing wrong' with borrowing. Borrowing stems from weakness and creates risk. Equity, in contrast, stems from strength and creates security. Thus, according to Henry Kaufman, the present heavy debt load undermines the 'integrity' of our financial system; it signifies that those in authority evade their 'responsibilities.' * * * John Kenneth Galbraith compares contemporary events to the most notorious debt disaster of the this century, the utility pyramiding of the 1920s and 1930s. And Felix Rohatyn worries that the increased borrowing occurs during a period of global competitive difficulty for American businesses. He expresses dismay: 'Maybe I'm getting old * * * but, boy, I think that's crazy.'

"Guarded pessimists worry about the incremental effect that higher debt load will have during a cyclical downturn in the economy's nonfinancial performance. Under this view, debtors' distress will contribute to, but will not itself cause, a decline in nonfinancial economic activity. A downturn will cause cash flow problems for debtors. When they fail to pay, they will cause their creditors to have cash flow problems. Further curtailment of economic activity will result. In addition, forced asset sales by strapped debtors will depress asset prices. A wave of bankruptcies will follow. In [Professor Benjamin] Friedman's view, the magnitude of today's debt load makes the prospect of widespread debtor distress intolerable as a matter of financial policy. Under this view, the new indebtedness in the end encourages expansionary monetary policy and inflation."

The macroeconomic arguments against high leverage are laid out in Friedman, Increasing Indebtedness and Financial Stability in the United States 19–24 (National Bureau of Economic Research Working Paper No. 2072, Nov. 1986), and Bernake and Campbell, Is There a Corporate Debt Crisis? 1988 Brookings Papers on Economic Activity 83, 93–96.

(2) Some observers also questioned whether demand for immediate high returns occasioned by restructuring transactions would outstrip the supply of firms with the stable, noncyclical cash flows best suited for restructuring. See Congressional Research Service, Report on Merger Activity and Leveraged Buyouts: Sound Corporate Restructuring or Wall Street Alchemy? 17 (Nov. 1984).

(3) In late 1986, the $120 to $125 billion of junk bonds outstanding were held as follows: $40 billion, insurance companies; $10 to $15 billion, pension funds; $40 billion, mutual funds; $10 billion, savings and loans; $15 billion, individuals. Taggart, The Growth of the "Junk" Bond Market and Its Role in Financing Takeovers, Mergers and Acquisitions 5, 17–18 (Auerbach, ed. 1988). Questions were raised as to whether many of these holders could be relied on to monitor managers at all. Coffee, Shareholders Versus Managers: The Strain in the Corporate Web, in Coffee, Lowenstein and Rose–Ackerman, eds., Knights, Raiders, and Targets: The Impact of the Hostile Takeover 77, 94–95 (1987) states the problem:

"Examining the debtor's financial condition also looks at only one half the equation. If there is a problem with leverage, why is it that creditors would not protect themselves adequately? Here, there are potentially disturbing answers. To the extent that the "junk bond" market is a new institution, it is possible that the necessary monitoring mechanisms may not yet have developed adequately. One aspect of this problem involves the distinct possibility that the creditors purchasing these bonds have little incentive to monitor their debtors. When "junk bond" purchasers are either savings and loan associations or pension funds, these classes of institutions receive their capital from individuals who are largely protected by government insurance (either the Federal Savings and Loan Insurance Corporation (FSLIC) or the Pension Benefit Guaranty Corporation (PBGC)). As a result, these investors have little reason to monitor the level of risk accepted by these financial institutions, and a classic moral hazard problem therefore arises, because the high returns paid on junk bonds are not counterbalanced by high risks to these depositors so long as they can look to government insurance. This is a traditional problem in banking, and the traditional answer has been the use of regulatory monitoring by a variety of agencies. However, in the new era of deregulation, some of these constraints have been relaxed, and financial institutions, such as Continental Illinois, may themselves be under shareholder pressure to accept greater risk. Whatever the reason, the apparent result has been a wave of bank failures unprecedented since the Great Depression.

"Another, even more significant reason for skepticism about whether the credit risks associated with junk bonds have been properly evaluated by their purchasers has been suggested by Peter Drucker. As he points out, pension funds, who are major purchasers of junk bonds, are typically "defined benefit" plans under which the corporate employer's contribution is reduced to the extent that the pension fund's assets earn above-market returns. Because the corporation's financial managers typically also supervise the pension fund, there is a built-in conflict of interest, with the corporation having an incentive to seek above average returns for the fund (and accept above average risks in so doing) in order to minimize its own required contribution.

"Similar observations may be made about mutual funds, and other more general problems may also compromise the efficiency of the debt market * * *."

Some also questioned whether the institutions buying the junk bonds sufficiently understood the accompanying risks so as to be positioned to pay the right price. See Congressional Research Service, Report on the Role of High Yield Bonds [Junk Bonds] in Capital Markets and Corporate Takeovers: Public Policy Implications 4–7 (Dec. 1985).

(c) Regulatory Responses

The 1980s restructuring movement prompted a number of significant changes to corporate law, state antitakeover and constituency statutes being most prominent among them. See infra pp. 1142–1163. The topic of high leverage, narrowly defined, was repeatedly investigated and discussed by lawmakers. But, in the end, very little lawmaking occurred. The principal legislative responses were as follows:

(1) *Legal Investment Laws and Other Regulation of Lending Institutions*

Portfolios of junk bonds held by federally insured savings and loan institutions played a role in the savings and loan crisis of the late 1980s and early 1990s. Congress responded with Section 222 of the Financial Institutions Reform, Recovery and Enforcement Act of 1989, 103 Stat.

183. This added section 28(d) to the Federal Deposit Insurance Act, 12
U.S.C. § 1831e(d) (1989), providing that thrift institutions may not
"acquire or retain any corporate debt security not of investment grade,"
and provides further that the FDIC shall require divestment of such
securities as were held at the time of the statute's enactment "as
quickly as may prudently be done, and in any event not later than July
1, 1994."

Mandated divestment of thrift portfolios was accompanied by stricter scrutiny of bank portfolios. In 1989, the federal banking agencies—
the Office of the Comptroller of the Currency, the Treasury, the FDIC
and the Board of Governors of the Federal Reserve System—coordinat-
ed their definition of "highly leveraged transactions" in order to facilitate the work of bank examiners and comparative analysis of bank
performance. The definition went through different versions until
1992, when the agencies discontinued its use, while continuing to
monitor the banks' risk exposure.

The states also tightened credit standards. Connecticut, for example, revised its legal investment laws for insurance companies, defining
"high yield obligations" as below investment grade and restricting such
obligations as are registered under the 1933 Act to 10 percent of an
insurance company's assets and limiting investment in the high yield
obligations of a particular issuer to 1 percent of assets. Conn.Public
Act No. 91–262 §§ 3(c), 4(c) (1991). Connecticut's Banking Law limits
savings bank investments to top rated securities and securities deemed
"prudent" by board resolution. Conn.Gen.Stats. § 36–96(14) (1990).

Professor Merton Miller objected to the stepped up federal regulation of banks in his 1990 Nobel Memorial Prize Lecture:

"To point out that the market has powerful endogenous controls
against overleveraging does not mean that who holds the highly leveraged securities is never a matter of concern. Certainly the U.S.
Savings and Loan institutions should not have been using government-
guaranteed savings deposits to buy high-risk junk bonds. But to focus
so much attention on the junk bond losses of a handful of these S & L's
is to miss the main point of that whole sorry episode. The current hue
and cry over S & L junk bonds serves merely to divert attention from
those who expanded the government deposit guarantees and encouraged the S & L's to make investments with higher expected returns, but
alas, also with higher risk than their traditional long-term home
mortgages.

* * *

"More is at stake, however, than merely assigning proper blame for
these failed attempts to overrule the market's judgment that this
politically powerful industry was not economically viable. Drawing the
wrong moral from the S & L affair can have consequences that extend
far beyond the boundaries of this ill-fated industry. The American
humorist, Mark Twain, once remarked that a cat, having jumped on a
hot stove, will never jump on a stove again, even a cold one. Our

commercial bank examiners seem to be following precisely this pattern. Commercial banking may not quite be a cold stove at the moment, but it is, at least, a viable industry. Unlike the S & L's, moreover, it plays a critical role in financing businesses, particularly, but not only, those too small or too little known to support direct access to the public security markets. Heavy-handed restrictions on bank loans by examiners misreading the S & L experience will thus raise the cost of capital to, and hence decrease the use of capital by, this important business sector.

"Whether regulatory restrictions of these and related kinds have already gone so far as to produce a 'credit crunch' of the kind associated in the past with monetary contraction is a subject much being argued at the moment, but one I prefer to leave to the specialists in money and banking. My concerns as a finance specialist are with the longer-run and less directly visible consequences of the current anti-leverage hysteria. This hysteria has already destroyed the liquidity of the market for high-yield bonds. The financial future markets, currently under heavy attack for their supposed overleveraging are the next possible candidates for extinction, at least in their U.S. habitats."

Miller, Leverage, 46 J. Finance 479, 487–488 (1991).

What effect would you expect the federal savings bank junk bond divestiture legislation to have had on the junk bond market?

(2) Tax Laws

Federal income tax law responsive to merger and acquisition activity dates back to the conglomerate merger movement of the 1960s.

Congress in 1969 added section 279 to the Internal Revenue Code, which limits the deductibility of interest on "corporate acquisition indebtedness" where such interest exceeds 5 million dollars a year. "Corporate acquisition indebtedness" includes obligations used to provide consideration for the acquisition of the stock or operating assets of another corporation if (1) the indebtedness is subordinated to the claims of general creditors or of other unsecured creditors, (2) the indebtedness is convertible into stock of the issuing corporation, and (3) the debt-equity ratio of the issuing corporation is in excess of 2:1, or interest on total indebtedness is not covered at least three times by projected earnings. In the view taken by Congress, for tax purposes at least, the standards last named were apparently thought to draw the line between true debt and disguised equity. That line has apparently not been effective to prevent significant increase in the issuance of "junk bonds." [f]

f. Comparable difficulties are encountered in distinguishing between debt and equity in the "thin incorporation" cases, generally in the context of closely held enterprises. In the simplest case, the stockholders capitalize their venture with 90% or more debt and 10% or less equity, and parcel out the debt among themselves pro rata with their holdings of stock. The question arises whether the debt is "true" debt (and therefore whether the ostensible interest payments are tax-deductible interest rather than nondeductible dividends, and whether the repayment of principal is truly a non-taxable return of capital or a taxable dividend) or disguised equity. The

In 1987, Congress, concerned over the restructuring movement, considered bills that would have added more bite to section 279. Proposed section 279A would have limited the deductibility of interest on debt incurred in connection with the acquisition of 50 percent of the stock by the issuing corporation or a group of persons acting in concert with the issuing corporation. Proposed section 279H would have denied any interest deduction on debt incurred to acquire stock or assets of a corporation once 20 percent of its stock had been acquired by means of a hostile offer. Both of these bills passed the House but were rejected in the final 1987 Revenue Act legislation.

Congress returned to high leveraged transactions in 1989 and enacted legislation designed to deal with some perceived but narrowly defined tax abuses in leveraged transactions. The Revenue Reconciliation Act of 1989, among other things, limited the current deductibility of high yield original issue discount debt interest, I.R.C. §§ 163(e)(5) and 163(i), and limited the deductibility of interest paid to certain tax exempt payees, I.R.C. § 163(j). See Eustice, Bittker and Eustice's Federal Income Taxation of Corporations and Shareholders para. 4.26 (1991 Cumulative Supp.).

National tax policy is often designed to induce alterations in business practices. The willingness of Congress in 1969 and again in 1989 to limit the deductibility of debt interest in certain restricted circumstances suggests that the corporate interest deduction may not be wholly invulnerable to legislative modification or even to outright repeal. Would repeal make sense as a matter either of economic or of tax policy? Since interest and dividends both represent divisions of the net earnings on invested capital, it can be argued with some force that no distinction should be made between them, and that interest charges should be included as part of the company's taxable net income. The effect would, of course, be to increase the cost of capital for many corporate enterprises, and presumably to reduce private investment, but the tax system would at least then be neutral as between debt and equity financing.

What about a legislative move in the opposite direction, i.e., by allowing a deduction for all forms of distribution to security owners? It has been urged that the corporate tax itself—rather than the distinction between interest and dividends—is the true source of "unneutrality":

"The discriminatory effects of the present Federal tax structure transcend the internal inconsistencies of the corporation tax law. To eliminate these internal 'unneutralities' by the inclusion of bond inter-

case law is voluminous, and only the number of cases exceeds the variety of criteria for determining when the ostensible debt will be treated as equity. Many of the cases are collected and discussed in Mertens, Law of Federal Income Taxation, § 26.10c. See also Caplin, The Caloric Count of a Thin Corporation, 17 N.Y.U.Tax Inst. 771 (1959); 43 Marq.L.Rev. 31 (1959).

In the 1969 Tax Reform Act, Congress enacted legislation (Section 385 of the Internal Revenue Code) containing criteria for determining when ostensible debt is to be treated as equity, and authorized the Commissioner of Internal Revenue to promulgate implementing regulations. To date, the Commissioner has never managed to complete this rulemaking assignment.

est in the tax base would only intensify and perpetuate the inequities of the existing system. To follow the alternative course, allowance for preferred dividends would neutralize the choice of bonds and preferred stock and provide some relief to common stock. But this step would still discriminate against equity financing and would open new avenues of avoidance. To pursue this course to its logical conclusion would allow deduction of common stock dividends, as well, and tax only undistributed profits in the hands of the corporation. Removal of the present 'double taxation' of common stock dividends, in one way or another, appears to offer the best solution. * * * " Lent, Bond Interest Deduction And The Federal Corporation Income Tax, 2 Nat'l Tax.J. 131, 141 (1949).

(3) *Margin Rules*

Also inspired by concern with leverage and the increase in "junk bonds" are the regulations of the Federal Reserve Board which affect the amount of debt permitted in financing, or arranging the financing of tender offers. These resulted from an FRB interpretation of the margin rules so as to make them apply to the issuance of debt securities to finance takeovers by shell corporations without substantial assets. See 12 C.F.R. § 207.112 (1992) (51 Fed.Reg. 1781). For commentary, see Barker, The Federal Reserve and Junk Bond Financing: Anomaly or Inconvenience? 19 Pac.L.J. 769 (1988).

(4) *Debt as Equity*

Reforms of the Internal Revenue Code to limit the deductibility of interest payments tend to be based on the view that the debt issued in highly leveraged transactions is "disguised equity." Economists offer indirect support for this approach, noting that the financial innovations of recent years have caused traditional distinctions between debt and equity securities to collapse. See, e.g., Kopcke and Rosengren, Are the Distinctions between Debt and Equity Disappearing? An Overview, N.E.Econ.Rev., March–April 1990, p. 2.

Are Courts free in insolvency situations or other situations of intra-class conflict to borrow from the Congressional judgment and to treat such debt as equity? Mendales, The New Junkyard of Corporate Finance: The Treatment of Junk Bonds in Bankruptcy, 69 Wash.U.L.Q. 1137 (1991), argues that bankruptcy law in some cases should treat junk bond holders as equity investors rather than creditors. According to Mendales, bankruptcy courts have the authority to recharacterize a junk bond issue as equity, either under the equitable subordination provision of the Code, 11 U.S.C. § 510(c), or under the general power to classify claims and interests asserted against the debtor and the general equity power. Id. at 1152–1157.

Upon which investor constituencies would the subordination effect of according equity treatment to "improper" debt cause the most severe injuries?

2. LEGAL STANDARDS THAT AFFECT
CAPITAL STRUCTURE

(A) STANDARDS OF FEASIBILITY UNDER
THE BANKRUPTCY CODE

(1) *Regulatory Alternatives*

Should the Bankruptcy Code require "safe" capital structures for reorganized companies? Consider the following comments from Rostow and Cutler, Competing Systems of Corporate Reorganization, Chapters X and XI of The Bankruptcy Act, 48 Yale L.J. 1334, 1373–1376 (1939):

"According to the calculus of the economists, it pays socially for business enterprises to be continued as long as their revenues cover out-of-pocket costs, or their out-of-pocket losses are less than the losses which would be incurred by shutting down. So far as the economics of solvency are concerned, inability to pay interest on capitalized debt is not a useful criterion for determining when the enterprise should be subjected to the expense of insolvency proceedings. In the case at least of larger enterprises, which have no market value in any realistic sense, the capital represented by the debt is irrevocably invested in the enterprise, and will generally continue to be used in it for production, whatever is done by way of insolvency proceeding, as long as revenues equal or exceed the costs which must be incurred in order to continue production. Default in payment of charges on capital might well be the occasion for a visitorial inquiry into management, and perhaps for a change in voting rights, in effect eliminating common stock by intra-corporate action rather than by judicial proceeding; but it seems wasteful to make such an event alone the occasion for reorganization proceedings on their present scale.

"Historically, of course, we are committed to the practice of regarding some part of capital as debt, and correlatively, the holders of that debt have the status of current-account creditors for purposes of creditors' remedies. It is probably impossible to change the deep-seated habit of treating bondholders as creditors for such purposes. And so long as default on capitalized debt is regarded as the occasion of reorganization proceedings, it is desirable that the resulting reorganizations be drastic. If we must have a judicial proceeding after default on capitalized debt, that proceeding should thoroughly purge the finances of the business. And the administration of Chapter X, at least, promises that reorganization will have adequate purgative features.

"An acceptable reorganization system should, however, do more than is done by Chapters X and XI to control the future financial structure of reorganized enterprises, in the interest of preventing the recurrence of uneconomic insolvency proceedings. Ideally, such a policy would be expressed by a prohibition in the charter of the new company against any form of capitalization resulting in fixed charges or fixed maturities. All capital returns would be contingent on there being earnings above operating expenses, priority of risk being expressed by priority of claim to income. If habits of finance and of thinking about finance among those who constitute the capital market will keep reorganizers from writing such utopian terms into articles of incorporation, they should at least be required to restrict the quantity or proportion of an enterprise's capital which may be obtained through borrowing. The control of capital structures through reorganization should go further. It is generally regarded as dangerous to have much of the capitalization of a business represented by securities on which a fixed maximum return is payable. Such a financial structure promises a new default with every considerable fluctuation of income, and tempts the directors to speculative managerial policies. If the capitalization of a company carries large fixed or maximum charges, its management, usually holding equities, stands to gain disproportionately from a course of action, however risky, which increases the existing over-all rate of return on capital. And so far no device short of charter restriction has developed for protecting the corporation against its management in this particular financial policy. * * *

"Any substantial revision of the system of corporate reorganization through bankruptcy should start with a reconsideration of the economic function of such proceedings, and should serve the definite policy of making them an occasion to rebuild the financial structure of the debtor enterprise. The plan of reorganization should give management all the discretion it needs to meet the future financing requirements of the business; but that discretion should be restricted so as to forestall the danger of over-speculative business policy, and the waste of premature reorganization."

(2) *Broadway–Exchange*

In **In re Broadway–Exchange Corp.**, 15 S.E.C. 256, 377 (1944), the Securities and Exchange Commission rendered an Advisory Report under Chapter X of the Bankruptcy Act on the reorganization of a corporation whose principal asset was an office building. The plan of reorganization provided in substance:

1. That the existing first mortgage be modified by reducing the principal amount by one-half, to $3,961,000, with interest thereon to be payable only if earned up to 6% per annum, that 25% of net earnings be applied to a sinking fund for the reduction of the mortgage, and that for each $1000 principal amount of presently outstanding first mortgage certificates there be issued to the holder in exchange

(a) a new income first mortgage certificate in the principal amount of $500;

(b) a new voting trust certificate for ten shares of the stock of the new company (totalling 79,220 shares); and

(c) a proportionate share of the balance of cash in the hands of the trustee.

2. That the general or second mortgage income bonds in the principal amount of $2,125,000 be cancelled and discharged of record and that the holder of each $1000 principal amount of presently outstanding general or second mortgage bonds receive a voting trust certificate for one share of stock in the new company (totalling 2,125 shares), or, in lieu thereof, $12.50 in cash, representing the measurement of the value of the claim of such holder in the unmortgaged assets of the debtor.

3. That the new company have authorized 81,345 shares of common stock, and that all of such stock be issued to voting trustees under a voting trust agreement for a period of five years, with a provision for renewal for a further period of five years upon the approval of the holders of 51% of the stock represented by voting trust certificates or as otherwise provided by law.

4. That the new first mortgage certificates and appurtenant voting trust certificates, which are initially to be attached physically in the same instrument, may later be detached and separated, but only upon either (1) the unanimous affirmative vote of the entire board of directors or (2) the affirmative vote of a majority of the entire board and the consent of holders of a majority in principal amount of the certificates outstanding.

The Commission stated in its Advisory Report that the enterprise, viewed in the optimistic glow of wartime occupancy of the building, had estimated earnings of between $255,000 and $265,000 before depreciation, income tax and interest on the proposed new bonds. On any valuation of their claim, the first mortgage bondholders could not be satisfied, even if they received all the mortgaged assets.[g] Thus they and the second mortgage bondholders were to divide the remaining unpledged assets (approximately $66,400), and the stockholders were to be wiped out. In view of the uncertainty as to any value existing for the stock of the reorganized enterprise over the long run, the Commission suggested that the "fairness" standard would be met if the second mortgage bondholders received, in lieu of stock, cash in the amount of $12.50 per $1000, face amount of claim, or a total of $26,562. With respect to feasibility, the Commission said (15 S.E.C. at 267–271):

"Before approving a plan of reorganization, the court is required by the provisions of Chapter X of the Bankruptcy Act to find that it is 'feasible.' This means that the proposed capital structure should be sound. If bonds are issued, there should be reasonable assurance that the earnings will be sufficient in amount and stability to provide regular payments of interest and in reduction of principal so that at maturity the remaining principal can be paid or be readily refunded.

---

g. The record of the plan hearings contains "valuation" estimates for the debtor's fixed property, ranging from $4,500,000 to $6,500,000. The appraiser employed by the disinterested trustee, appraised "the fair worth of the property" at $5,200,000 including $700,000 for the land.

On this subject the United States Supreme Court, in a reorganization case, Consolidated Rock Products Co. v. DuBois, 312 U.S. 510, stated:

'Whether or not the earnings may reasonably be expected to meet the interest and dividend requirements of the new securities is a *sine qua non* to a determination of the integrity and practicability of the new capital structure.'

"The same standards of sound finance are applicable to real estate companies as to other business enterprises. Failure to restrict debt to proper limits with reference to earning power has been a principal cause of widespread defaults on real estate mortgages. As early as 1931, it was estimated that about 60 percent of the outstanding real estate bond issues in the country were in default. Since then additional defaults have occurred, and many publicly financed skyscrapers in the downtown financial district have undergone one or more reorganizations. At the present time proceedings for reorganization of at least four large office buildings in the downtown financial district are pending in this court. Such a record of default does not justify relaxation of the standards of feasibility in the case of real estate enterprises.

"The financial soundness of the proposed bond issue of nearly $4,000,000 is to be judged by the company's reasonably prospective earnings. If such earnings will provide adequate coverage of interest payments and for necessary reduction of principal, the issue should be approved as to feasibility. But, if on review of the evidence, it appears that earnings will not be sufficient to meet debt requirements, the issue cannot be said to be sound. The plan is clearly unfeasible if the express undertakings and promises of the reorganized company are found to be beyond its financial ability to perform.

"Our conclusions as to prospective earnings have been stated. For the next few years—under the continuing stimulus of war conditions resulting in the highest occupancy rate enjoyed in the past 10 years—earnings available for payments of principal and interest may be taken as approximately $260,000 per annum before any provision for depreciation. It is highly uncertain, however, that such earnings will continue after the war and gradually diminishing income is to be expected as the building grows older. Further, the building, now 30 years old, has a limited economic life beyond which it will cease to produce earnings. Mr. Stevens, the appraiser retained by the trustee, has estimated its economic life in good judgment to be not more than 20 years.

"The limited economic life of the building is a factor which serves to emphasize the necessity for retiring debt even more than in the case of many industrial enterprises. Usually an industrial company makes provision by way of depreciation reserves for replacing capital assets which become worn out or obsolete. Earnings set aside annually can be used to buy plant and equipment, enabling the enterprise to keep abreast of developments in the industrial arts, to meet competition and, if successful, to prolong its life indefinitely. Few similar opportunities may be availed of by the owners of office buildings. Worn out equipment may of course be replaced, but there is little that can be done to overcome obsolescence. If a building no longer attracts tenants because it is old or outdated, or because there has been a shift of tenants to other neighborhoods, purchases of new equipment and major alterations are of only limited assistance in staving off eventual loss of income. It is therefore imperative that sufficient earnings be set aside regularly so that the debt of the reorganized company can be very substantially reduced, if not entirely paid off, as the end of the economic life of the building approaches.

"In our view, the evidence indicates that the proposed bond issue should be entirely paid off in 20 years * * *, but even if it be assumed for purposes of argument that the remaining life of the building would justify a bond issue as large as $1,000,000 at the end of 20 years, it would still be necessary to reduce the proposed mortgage by $3,000,000 within that period.

"To pay 6% on the outstanding bonds and to retire $3,000,000 of the $4,000,000 issue at par in 20 years would require 40 regular semiannual payments of about $160,000 each, or total payments in each year exceeding $320,000. Even if interest were paid at only 5% and bonds of $3,000,000 were to be retired at par in 20 years, such a reduction would still require 40 regular semiannual payments totaling about $290,000 in each year. Since even the sums required to retire $3,000,000 of bonds exceed foreseeable earnings, it is obviously not reasonable to expect that a bond issue of $4,000,000 on this property would be retired at par with regular payments of interest at 6%, or even 5%. An issue requiring any such payments would lead with almost predictable certainty to the third default and reorganization in the history of the company.

"An endeavor has been made, however, to minimize the possibility of default by several provisions of the plan. Interest is not to be paid unless earned, which not only deprives the bondholders of a regular return but prevents them from exercising remedies usually conferred upon nonpayment of fixed interest. Furthermore, the funds available for interest payments are to be restricted to 75 percent of the net earnings and the remaining earnings—regardless of what amount of interest is paid—are to be used to purchase bonds in the open market or on tenders. This will mean that although the bonds provide for interest payments 'up to 6%,' the initial rate is likely to be less than 5% * * * and bondholders may, and probably will, receive substantially less than 6% interest in the following years. Meanwhile, one-quarter of the net earnings, it is presumed by the trustee, may be used to buy in bonds at cheap prices in the open market or on tenders * * *.

"In view of the nature of these provisions, the feasibility of the plan would depend in the final analysis on the ability of the reorganized company to buy bonds in cheaply, rather than on its financial ability to honor the bonds at face value. In our opinion, it is highly objectionable to issue bonds containing an express promise to pay a stated principal sum, when it is to be expected that the bonds can be retired only at a very substantial discount. Moreover, it is deceptive to issue bonds containing a promise to pay interest out of earnings up to 6% when there is little prospect that earnings during the life of the building will, in fact, permit a payment approaching that percentage. Even with these proposed interest and sinking-fund provisions, the prospective earning power of the property offers no reasonable assurance that a third reorganization will be avoided upon the maturity of the principal of an issue as large as that proposed. In our opinion, therefore, the proposed plan fails to meet the tests of feasibility and should be disapproved.

"It is argued in support of a large bond issue that there will be tax savings, as compared with a plan providing for a smaller funded debt, although the record does not show the extent of any such savings. Speculation on the tax aspects of the proposed capital structure is likely to be fruitless because of the uncertainty as to the company's income for tax purposes and as to the nature and extent of the tax statutes which may be enacted not only in the immediate future but over the life of the enterprise. Even if it were true that some savings in taxes could be foreseen because of a larger issue of bonds, that factor would not outweigh the necessity that reorganization produce a sound capital structure meeting the statutory requirements of feasibility.

"We recognize that many plans might be devised which would be well adapted to the particular requirements of this case and which would meet the standards of feasibility. In the suggestions which follow we have endeavored to outline certain specific proposals, including some offered by the parties, which appear to us to be sound and appropriate.

"In our opinion, in order to effect a sound reorganization which will meet the requirements of feasibility, the debt of the reorganized company should not exceed approximately $2,500,000. We believe there is merit to the proposal that some interest should be fixed, and suggest that the new bonds provide for 5% interest per annum of which 2½% would be fixed and 2½% cumulative, contingent interest payable if earned. We believe the record clearly indicates that the bonds should mature not later than 20 years, rather than in 30 years as proposed by the plan * * *. All earnings after payment of interest should be paid into the sinking fund for the purpose of retiring bonds by tender or by redemption until the bond issue has been reduced to $1,500,000. Thereafter, 50 percent of earnings after interest might be paid into the sinking-fund and the remainder could be used either for additional sinking-fund payments or for dividend payments as decided by the board of directors. The indenture trustee, and not the company, should handle all sinking-fund operations. We agree that the plan should provide that the sinking-fund should acquire bonds only and not the appurtenant stock."

The District Court (CCH, Fed.Bkrtcy.Law Serv. ¶ 54,803 (1944)) rejected the Commission's recommendation and ruled:

* * *

"It is obvious that the debtor is insolvent and that it has not sufficient assets to meet its liabilities. From the evidence I find that the property at 61 Broadway has a fair value of $5,500,000. On this basis it is clear that a bond issue of more than $4,000,000 is out of the question. I am of the opinion, however, that an issue of $3,961,000 of income bonds is amply justified. It necessarily follows that the general or second mortgage bondholders are entitled only to share in the unmortgaged assets of the debtor as provided in the plan, and further that the present stockholders of the debtor are not entitled to participate in the reorganization. * * *

"The plan as now submitted has been approved by substantially all of the parties appearing in the proceeding with the exception of the Securities and Exchange Commission. I find that the plan in its present form is fair, equitable and feasible."

———

According to Moody's Investors Service (Banks and Finance), the 6% income certificates (with voting trust certificates attached) of the Broadway–Exchange Corporation (name changed to 61 Broadway Corp.) sold at prices ranging from 80 to 120 in 1945.[h] The corporation retired its 6% income certificates on April 1, 1946, paying (with the proceeds of a 10 year first mortgage loan at 4% from Metropolitan Life Insurance Co.) principal, a premium of $50 per $1000 principal, and all interest due. The corporation's voting trust certificates sold at prices ranging from 17 to 33 during 1946, after retirement of the income certificates. Its record of earnings and dividends per share (following a small loss in 1945) was as follows:

	Earnings	Dividends
1946	.17	—
1947	2.24	1.25
1948	2.69	—
1949	1.98	2.00

On May 1, 1950 its property was sold for $9,000,000 subject to the then mortgage indebtedness of $4,365,000.

———

(3) *Questions*

The present Bankruptcy Code carries on the feasibility requirement of Chapter X of the 1938 Act, 11 U.S.C. § 1129(a)(11), and cases under the present Code bring to bear the same considerations that pre–Code cases brought to bear on the feasibility determination. 5 Collier on Bankruptcy ¶ 1129.02[11][a] (15th ed. 1991).

If there can be an optimal capital structure in which debt and equity are so mixed as to produce a maximum aggregate market price

h.   No prices were quoted in 1944.

for the securities of the enterprise, how does the "feasibility" standard relate to that optimum? Feasibility points toward minimizing the risk of ruin so that a capital structure becomes more "feasible" as the fixed charges against the earning power of the enterprise are decreased—i.e., as there is less funded debt and more equity. If that is true, does the search for feasibility exert a pressure against an optimal capital structure and a corresponding strain on the process of arriving at a fair bargain? In the case of Atlas Pipeline Corporation, supra p. 8, if the only security in the new corporation's capital structure were to be common stock, and that common stock were to have a lower aggregate market value than the bonds and stock proposed to be issued in the reorganization, would the first mortgage bondholders be entitled to more—and the second mortgage bondholders to less—than they received under the plan? Why did the seniors in that case, and in Broadway–Exchange Corporation, consent to such heavy leverage?

By what criteria should the courts determine the outer limits of feasibility?

Did Congress impose feasibility limitations on the capital structures of enterprises emerging from insolvency reorganization because the amount of senior securities which may be issued in insolvency reorganization is not determined by their salability in a free market, as it would be, presumably, in the case of a new venture or an established going concern? Compare testimony cited in the Atlas Pipeline Case, supra p. 8. Is the doctrine of "thin" incorporation (see Costello v. Fazio, 256 F.2d 903 (9th Cir.1958)) or the *Deep Rock* doctrine (see Taylor v. Standard Gas & Electric Co., 306 U.S. 307 (1939)) a response to similar considerations, made *after* rather than *before* the issuance of debt which was issued in circumstances reflecting inadequate operation of a free market? Ought the same criteria determine both how much debt may be "recognized" in the thin incorporation cases and how much may be permitted in a feasible capital structure in bankruptcy reorganization?

(B) REGULATION OF EXCESSIVE RISK UNDER THE PUBLIC UTILITY HOLDING COMPANY ACT OF 1935

The pyramidal and highly leveraged capital structures which prevailed in some sections of the public utility industry during, and even after the boom period of the 1920s, is described in the following excerpt from Blair–Smith and Helfenstein, A Death Sentence or a New Lease on Life? A Survey of Corporate Adjustments under the Public Utility Holding Company Act, 94 U.Pa.L.Rev. 148, 150–51, 162–69 (1946):

"We have no statistics on how many holding-company magnates began as brokers' messenger boys, but not a few were primarily financiers, paper-minded rather than operational in their approach to utility system problems. Some of these, possessing or commanding prime financial and legal talent, bent their efforts to the accumulation of voting control over existing utilities and other enterprises, deprived them of all semblance of independence, and smothered them under elaborate paper superstructures.   The operating utilities and other businesses at the base of these pyramids furnished all the revenues derived from outside sources, and a large percentage of revenues were drained off, in numerous instances, by exorbitant service and construction fees charged against them by 'service companies' belonging to the parent holding company or to the individual interests who controlled the system.[7]   What was left of the earnings after expenses, fixed charges, and preferred stock dividend requirements of the operating companies, had to percolate upward through tier upon tier of holding companies to pay the interest and dividends on their outstanding securities.   In such systems the companies in the super-structure were used for the purpose of retaining the insiders' control while the financial investment and risk were passed on to public investors by the flotation of a myriad of holding-company securities carrying no effective power to control the management.   The securities issued to the public were frequently based on inflated 'book value' bearing little or no relation to the amounts actually invested in the revenue-producing properties at the base of the pyramid, and were issued on the most optimistic assumptions as to the earning power of such properties.   " * * *

"[United Light and Power] had its origin in 1910 as a small Maine corporation controlling electric, gas, and transportation companies in Iowa, Illinois, Indiana, Tennessee, and Michigan.   The system had grown slowly up to 1923, when Power was reorganized as a Maryland corporation.   At this time annual consolidated gross revenues were about $12,000,000.   In 1924, Power, through a subholding company, United Light and Railways Company ('Railways'), acquired about 75% of the common stock of a much larger concern, Continental Gas & Electric Corporation ('Continental').   This company, also a holding company, had electric utility subsidiaries operating in Nebraska, Iowa, and Missouri, with consolidated gross revenues of about $21,000,000 annually.   The properties thus acquired were mostly far removed from and were never interconnected with those previously controlled by Power.

"Late in 1924, Power further acquired a substantial common stock interest in American Light & Traction Company ('Traction'), a holding

---

7. The functions of system-owned and affiliated "service companies" varied widely.   Some furnished engineering advice and construction work, some furnished bookkeeping or auditing services, some performed outright every managerial function that an operating company's officers and board of directors could have performed. Whatever they did, the purpose of many of them was to obtain fees (including profits often running to 100% or more) which would be treated as operating expenses or capital costs in the accounts of the paying utilities, but would be received as income by the controlling persons.   Since the com-panies paying the fees were under the control of the very persons who profited from the fees, the system-owned or affiliated service company was in a position to render "services" (whether they were needed or not) at prices which were not limited by competitive conditions or even by the independent business judgment of the paying company's officers.   * * *   These fees, which were passed on to the consumer in the electric and gas rates charged by the utilities, were not subject to ready analysis by state or local regulatory bodies, which usually did not have jurisdiction over the service companies or their records.

company controlling mainly gas companies which operated in Michigan, Wisconsin, and Minnesota, and at more remote points such as San Antonio, Texas, and Binghamton, New York, with consolidated gross revenues of about $33,000,000 annually. The properties of Traction bore no physical or operating relationship either to Power's original group or to the Continental group. Power continued to acquire Traction's stock on the open market, for a time in active competition with the Mellon–Koppers interests, until rapidly rising prices compelled the rival forces to negotiate. Finally, in 1928, Power obtained a majority control of Traction by a deal in which it took over United American Company ('United American') from Koppers. United American had been the holding company through which Koppers had held Traction stock. In the meantime the Mellon–Koppers interests had acquired a substantial block of Power's own voting stock.

"Beginning in 1924, Power also purchased stock of the Detroit Edison Company in aggressive competition with North American Company. It never succeeded in gaining control of Detroit Edison, but the contest had resulted in excessive prices being paid by both purchasers.

"The last important addition to the system occurred in 1930, when Railways subscribed for 35% of the common stock of Northern Natural Gas Company, which was formed primarily to own and operate a gas pipeline from Texas to Wisconsin and neighboring states.

"The growth of the system, primarily through these methods, resulted in an increase in annual gross revenues from about $12,000,000 in 1924 to more than $84,000,000 in 1930, excluding Detroit Edison and Northern Natural.

"Power's system in 1930 consisted of several subholding-company systems comprising some seventy-five companies of various kinds. During the 1930s and the early part of 1940 at least twenty-three corporate entities were eliminated by consolidation or dissolution, and some were sold. * * * In general, however, the complexities that resulted from the system's mode of growth were still present at the beginning of 1940, when the system comprised seven registered holding companies and forty-three other companies (including twenty-two electric and gas utilities, seven transportation, water or ice companies, one system service company, and thirteen companies which were engaged in other businesses). A simplified corporate chart is shown * * * [below] depicting the structure as of December 31, 1939. The solid connecting lines indicate solid control, and the dotted lines indicate holdings of less than majority voting power.

"It will be seen at once from the chart that there were either three or four tiers of holding companies above the utility operating companies in the Traction, Continental, and Northern Natural Gas systems. This structure was in clear conflict with the mandate of Section 11(b)(2),

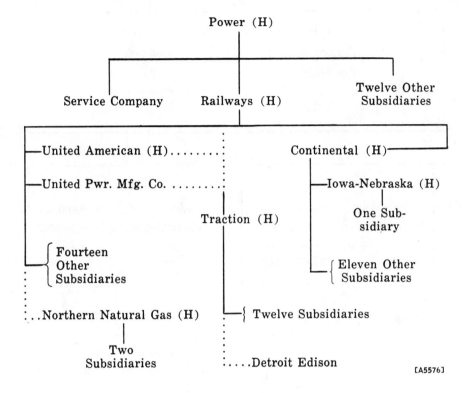

[A5576]

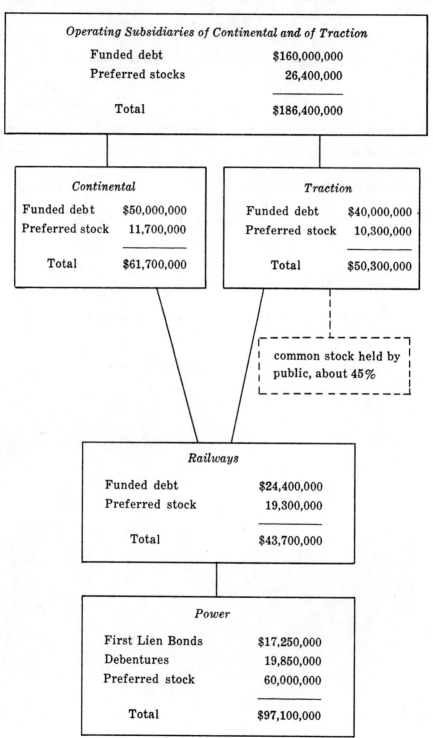

[A5575]

particularly the 'great-grandfather' clause which made it necessary for the Commission to order prompt reduction of the tiers of holding companies to not more than two. This statutory requirement works automatically, but the reasoning behind it is not hard to find. The capitalization and earnings history of the system companies provide the clue.

"The capitalization of the system was highly stratified at each of the principal corporate levels by the existence of outstanding debt and preferred stocks. This stratification is shown on the accompanying chart of publicly held senior securities which are presented as a pyramid that has been inverted, starting with the operating companies at the base and progressing downward toward the point in order to illustrate the principle that the quality of the securities tends to diminish as their degree of removal from the operating base increases. The chart gives the approximate amounts of senior securities outstanding as of the end of 1939, excluding intrasystem holdings and the securities of Detroit Edison and Northern Natural Gas.

"Except for the minority interest in Traction's common stock held by the public (as shown in the chart), Power directly or indirectly held virtually all the junior equity interests in the operating and subholding companies. The junior equity interest in Power itself was represented by Class A and Class B common stocks, which were coequal except that all the voting power was vested in the Class B. It will be noted that these common stocks were subject to no less than $430,000,000 of outstanding senior securities. The junior equity represented by Power's common stocks was about $9,700,000 for the Class A and $4,200,000 for the Class B, on the basis of the consolidated balance sheet. Power had no earned or capital surplus.

"In summary, from base to apex there were at least nine strata of publicly held senior securities with their several fixed interest rates (ranging from 2.75% to 6.5%) and fixed dividend requirements (ranging from 6% to 8%) which had to be paid before any earnings could be attributed to Power's common stock—not to mention the three to four tiers of corporations each with its own expenses, taxes and fixed charges other than interest. Small variations in the amount of revenues taken in by the operating subsidiaries at the base were naturally magnified with each layer of corporate expenses, fixed charges and fixed dividends, with the result that slight fluctuations in system revenues produced violent swings in the consolidated net income figures, and there existed numerous potential blocks in the intrasystem flow of cash earnings.

"In the lush years when the system was put together, this leverage factor was an apparent advantage to Power's common stockholders because so much of the system's capital had been contributed by the public holders of limited-income securities, while any gains in net earnings were to be available for dividends on the common stock.[61]

---

61. About 3% of total consolidated capitalization was represented by Power's common stock, and the voting or Class B stock represented less than 1%.

Actually, however, as far as Power was concerned the leverage worked the other way and the flow of earnings—complex at best—became blocked before they reached even Power's preferred stock which was about $28,000,000 in arrears on its dividends by the end of 1939.

"The earnings flow is, of course, an important factor in any holding-company structure, and the holding company's corporate net income may differ greatly from consolidated net earnings. The latter is merely a statistical figure indicating in general the amount of system net income applicable to the equity securities of the top holding company. It may be very different from what can actually be drawn up in cash by the top company because there often exist many reasons why a subsidiary cannot or should not pay cash dividends equal to the amount of its net income. For example, the subsidiary may need its cash for construction of new facilities, or for debt retirements, or for other purposes; or the payment of dividends may be restricted by indenture covenants, by charter provisions, or by law or regulatory order, for the protection of the investment of senior security holders or to insure adequate utility service to consumers. It is entirely natural that the more corporate complexities there are in the system, the more hazards there are in the flow of earnings. This is well illustrated by a comparison of the consolidated net income with Power's corporate net income in the period 1935–1939:

	Net Income Before Power's Preferred Dividend Requirements	
Year	Consolidated	Corporate
1935	$ 2,411,652	$ 311,268
1936	4,508,261	121,851
1937	5,182,602	402,139
1938	3,091,508	627,594
1939	4,598,654	2,342,432
	$19,792,677	$3,805,284

"Disregarding this factor, however, and taking consolidated figures alone, the magnification of slight changes in operating company revenues is an impressive feature of the stratified security structure. To give an extreme example of this kind of leverage in Power's system, in 1935 an increase of 5% in gross operating revenues produced an increase of 144% in the amount applicable to Power's preferred stock. The fluctuations in consolidated revenues and earnings reported for the calendar years 1931 to 1939 were as follows:

		% of Change Over Preceding Year	
Year Ended December 31	Gross Operating Revenues	Income Applicable to Power's Fixed Charges	Net Income Applicable to Power's Preferred Stock
1931	−6	−19	−25
1932	−8	−35	−47

% of Change Over Preceding Year

Year Ended December 31	Gross Operating Revenues	Income Applicable to Power's Fixed Charges		Net Income Applicable to Power's Preferred Stock
1933	−7	−43	−64	
1934	+4	−13	−35	
1935	+5	+40	+144	
1936	+9	+41	+87	
1937	+5	+ 9	+15	
1938	−3	−28	−40	
1939	+5	+27	+49	

"Faced with the foregoing problems and recognizing the necessity of complying with Section 11, the management of Power co-operated at the hearings and in conferences with the Commission's staff in the difficult process of deciding what steps should be taken, and in what order. After considering the major holding companies and the possibilities of eliminating each, the management concluded that Power lent itself best to dissolution as a major step toward compliance. * * * "

IN THE MATTER OF CONSUMERS POWER CO.
6 S.E.C. 444 (1939).

Consumers Power Company, a subsidiary of The Commonwealth and Southern Corporation, a registered holding company, has, pursuant to the provisions of Section 7 of the Public Utility Holding Company Act of 1935, filed a declaration regarding the issue and sale of $28,594,-000 principal amount of first mortgage bonds, 3¼% Series of 1939 due 1969; and 125,000 shares of no par value common stock.

The Commonwealth and Southern Corporation has filed an application pursuant to Section 10 of the Act for approval of the acquisition by it of the 125,000 shares of common stock which Consumers Power Company proposes to issue, at a price of $28.25 per share. * * *

Consumers Power Company, incorporated under the laws of Maine, does business entirely within the State of Michigan. It engages in the generation and purchase of electricity and in its distribution and sale in 1,133 communities and townships as well as in certain rural areas; in the production of manufactured gas and its distribution and sale in 126 communities and townships; and in the purchase of natural gas and its distribution and sale in 105 communities and townships. The population of the territory served is estimated to exceed 2,000,000. * * *

Consumers Power Company proposes to apply the proceeds from the sale of $10,000,000 principal amount of bonds to reimburse its treasury, in part, for certain expenditures for net property additions. The proceeds from the remaining $18,594,000 principal amount of bonds will be used together with other treasury funds to retire on or before May 1, 1940, $18,594,000 principal amount of the company's First Mortgage Bonds, 3¼% Series of 1935 due 1965, at 104½ plus accrued interest to May 1, 1940. It is proposed to use the net proceeds, amounting to $3,524,187.50[3] from the sale of the 125,000 shares of

3. * * * sometimes stated hereinafter in round numbers, viz., $3,500,000.

common stock to The Commonwealth and Southern Corporation, also to reimburse its treasury for expenditures.

The bonds are to be sold to a group of 33 underwriters * * * at a price of 103½ and accrued interest, which represents a cost of money to the company of 3.07%. It is stated that the bonds will be offered to the public at a price of 105½, resulting in a spread of 2 points. This is equivalent to a yield of 2.97% per year to maturity * * * The estimated net proceeds to be received by the company for the sale of the bonds, after estimated expenses in addition to the underwriting discounts or commissions of $113,448, amount to $29,481,342.

On the basis of a proposed offering of $18,594,000 with the same price and spread indicated above, the sale to the public will aggregate $19,616,670, and the underwriting discounts or commissions will amount to $371,880. Accordingly, without deducting estimated expenses over and above the underwriting discounts or commissions, the company will receive $19,244,790.

CAPITALIZATION

The capitalization (including surplus) of declarant as of September 30, 1939, per books, and pro forma after giving effect to the proposed financing, is as follows: *

	Per Books		Pro Forma	
	Amount	%	Amount	%
Funded Debt	$123,685,000.	51.11	$133,685,000.	52.32
Preferred Stock (cumulative, no par)	$ 70,631,024.50	29.19	$ 70,631,024.50	27.65
Common Stock (no par; 1,686,716 shares per books and 1,811,716 shares pro forma)	$ 35,484,725.	14.67	$ 39,015,975.	15.27
Surplus				
Acquired	$ 312,907.97	0.13	$ 312,907.97	0.12
Earned	11,862,968.99	4.90	11,862,968.99	4.64
Total Common Stock and Surplus	$ 47,660,601.96	19.70	$ 51,191,851.96	20.03
Total Capitalization and Surplus	$241,976,626.46	100.00	$255,507,876.46	100.00

* Table abridged.

EARNINGS

The earning power of the declarant per books for the 12 months ended September 30, 1939, and pro forma to give effect to the sale of bonds and stocks and the retirement of $18,594,000 Bonds 3¾% series of 1935 is indicated by the following table: *

	Per Books	Pro Forma
Gross Income	$14,107,864	$14,107,864
Interest on Funded Debt	4,434,564	4,666,594
Interest on Funded Debt and other Deductions	4,730,731	5,000,007
Net Income	9,377,134	9,107,857
Dividends on Preferred Stock	3,424,822	3,424,822
Balance for Common Stock	5,168,973	4,899,696
Times Earned:		
Interest on Funded Debt	3.2	3.0
Interest on Funded Debt, Other Deductions, and Preferred Dividends	1.7	1.7
Earnings per share of Common Stock	$3.06	$2.70

* Table abridged.

By Chairman Frank:

* * *

The duties imposed by Congress upon this Commission as to the issuance and sale of securities of registered utility holding companies and their utility subsidiaries are substantially greater than its duties under the Securities Act of 1933. Under the Securities Act our statutory duty is solely to see to it that the truth about a security is told in registration statements and prospectuses. But, under the Public Utility Holding Company Act of 1935, our duties are more comprehensive: Congress provided, in Section 6, that, as to utility companies within our jurisdiction, it should be unlawful to issue securities (other than those exempted by statute or by rules thereunder) except in accordance with a declaration filed with us and an order by us permitting the declaration to become effective. And Congress further provided, in Section 7(d), that we permit such a declaration to become effective unless, after considering the evidence, we find that—

"(1) the security is not reasonably adapted to the security structure of the declarant and other companies in the same holding-company system;

"(2) the security is not reasonably adapted to the earning power of the declarant;

"(3) financing by the issue and sale of the particular security is not necessary or appropriate to the economical and efficient operation of a business in which the applicant lawfully is engaged or has an interest;

* * *

"(6) the terms and conditions of the issue or sale of the security are detrimental to the public interest or the interest of investors or consumers."

All of the provisions of Section 7(d), it is clear, impose standards to which financing by public utility companies must conform. Such standards were deliberately set up by Congress after intensive study had revealed the evils which accompanied public utility holding company management of operating companies when such management was not adequately restrained. Congress, by expressly requiring that an application be filed with and approved by the Commission and that the Commission make adverse findings and correlative orders, if utility securities did not conform to the prescribed standards, made it clear that the judgment of company management was not to be conclusive, and that the exercise of managerial discretion was to be restrained by the Commission, if management proposed to issue securities not conforming to the standards of fair and sound financing prescribed by Section 7.   * * *

* * *

We turn, then, to Section 7(d)(3). Here, again, managerial judgment, although it is to be given weight, cannot be conclusive. Moreover, that a security meets the requirements of Section 7(d)(1)—in that it is reasonably adapted to the security structure—or of Section 7(d)(2)—in that it is reasonably adapted to the earnings—clearly does not relieve us of our obligation not to permit its issue and sale if, under Section 7(d)(3), we find that "financing by the issue and sale of the particular security" is not "necessary or appropriate to the economical and efficient operation of [the] business" of the applicant.

With respect to $18,594,000 of such bonds, we make no adverse finding under Section 7(d)(3). That part of the issue would merely replace bonds presently outstanding in the same principal amount and with a higher rate of interest, at a net saving to the company after the cost of the refinancing has been recovered. We have heretofore approved the issuance of refunding bonds prior to maturity under various circumstances where it was clear that the results would be beneficial. In the absence of both (a) a showing that the retirement of debt presently outstanding could be accomplished on favorable terms by the issuance of junior securities and (b) a further showing that the issuance and sale of those bonds is not appropriate at the present time, we make no adverse finding with respect to the refunding issue of bonds in the amount of $18,594,000 under Section 7(d)(3).

The $10,000,000 of Bonds and Section 7(d)(3)

A different question arises as to whether the declaration with respect to $10,000,000 of such bonds (not to be used for refunding) satisfies the standards of Section 7(d)(3). That section, to repeat, provides that we shall permit a declaration to be effective unless we find that "financing by the issue and sale of the particular security is not necessary or appropriate to the economical and efficient operation" of the business in which Consumers Power Co. is engaged. In inquiring whether there has been compliance with that section, we shall assume (without the necessity, for reasons presently appearing, of so finding) that those bonds meet all of the other standards of Section 7(d), i.e., we shall assume that they are reasonably adapted to the declarant's security structure and to its earning power, that the terms and conditions of their issuance and sale are not detrimental to the public interest or to the interest of investors or consumers, and that the underwriting fees in connection with the issue and sale thereof are reasonable.

Giving due regard to the record evidence of the managerial judgment on that subject, the Commission [13] has concluded that the record facts require adverse findings, as to those $10,000,000 of bonds, under Section 7(d)(3), for the following reasons:

(a) The record shows that financing through the sale of bonds, in excess of $18,594,000 for refunding, is not thus *"necessary"* for the economical and efficient operation of Consumers' business, because Consumers could satisfy its capital needs, over and above the need for refunding, by the sale, at reasonable terms, of common stock [in addition to the sale to Commonwealth and Southern of $3,500,000 of such stock] in the amount of $10,000,000, instead of bonds as proposed in its declaration. Consumers Power Co. has enjoyed good earnings. It has, for many years, paid substantial dividends upon its common stock. This alone indicates that its common stock might readily be marketed.

Moreover, Otis & Company has offered to purchase, at a price at least equal to book value, enough common stock to assure Consumers a minimum of $10,000,000 in addition to the $3,531,250 which Commonwealth & Southern proposes to buy.

Our reference to that offer is not in any way intended to indicate that Consumers is under duty to market any of its securities through Otis & Company. We refer to the offer merely because it shows that common stock financing, in the amount of at least $10,000,000 more than is now proposed, is available. It raises a powerful presumption that, if the management of Consumers Power Co. sought to do so, it could easily find a market on reasonable terms, through Otis & Company or other responsible underwriters, for an additional $10,000,000 of its common stock. In the absence of any adequate countervailing evidence, a finding is unavoidable that, to that extent, financing by bonds is not *"necessary* to the economical and efficient operation" of the business of Consumers Power Co.

That leaves open the question of whether or not such bond financing in excess of $18,594,000 is "appropriate" to such operation of Consumers' business. For under Section 7(d)(3), if we find that financing is "not necessary," we must not permit the declaration in regard thereto to become effective if we also find that proposed financing is "not appropriate" to the economical and efficient operation of the business involved. However, if we find that the security is "necessary," the security would satisfy the standard of Section 7(d)(3) that it be "necessary *or* appropriate", and we would not reach the question of whether it is "appropriate." The clear language of the statute requires

---

13. By Commissioners Eicher, Henderson and Frank.

this result and leaves no room for the contention that this interpretation is incongruous in that a relatively weak company, because it is "necessary" for it to sell the senior security, can more easily satisfy the statutory standard than a strong company, which is able to finance with alternative types of securities. This contention, moreover, misconceives both the statute as a whole and the statutory policy which it expresses. The word "appropriate" in Section 7(d)(3) clearly imposes a standard in addition to the standards of Section 7(d)(1), (2) and (6); otherwise, its inclusion would be redundant. That additional standard requires that proposed financing be rejected if there are other available alternatives which are clearly better suited to the needs of the corporation. In other words, a security which satisfies the other tests of Section 7 must still be rejected where (1) it is not "necessary"—i.e., something else is easily available; and (2) it is not "appropriate"—i.e., something unquestionably *better,* something distinctly more appropriate to efficient and economical operation, is easily available.

The facts show that it is not "appropriate" for the economical and efficient operation of Consumers Power Co. to finance by increasing substantially the present amount of its outstanding debt.

The following table * shows that Consumers Power Co.'s ratio of common stock and surplus to its total capitalization is (prior to increasing its debts by $10,000,000 and its common stock by $3,500,000) much less than ratios of other utility companies operating in the middle west area:

Capitalization Ratios (as of December 31, 1938) [a]	Consumers Power Co.	Detroit Edison Co.	Cleveland Elec. Illuminating Co.	The Ohio Power Co.	Duquesne Light Co.
Funded debt and notes	51.3%	47.7%	33.8%	59.6%	38.3%
Preferred Stock	29.2%	None	21.5%	17.3%	15.0%
Common stock and surplus	19.5%	52.3%	44.7%	23.1%	46.7%

* Table abridged.

a. These figures have been treated uniformly throughout in this comparison, the common stock and surplus accounts being used as *per* books without considering the effect which the elimination of possible inflationary items in the property accounts and which the addition to the depreciation reserve (where deficiencies may exist) would have on the capital structure of each of the above companies. * * * There is, however, nothing to indicate that the changes described above, which may be effected by individual companies, will have any material effect on the comparative capitalization ratios.

Moreover, the ratio of the common stock and surplus of Consumers Power Co. to its total capitalization is much smaller than the average of such ratios in 177 public utility subsidiaries of registered holding companies.

Comparisons may also be made on the basis of the ratios of debt, preferred stock and common stock (and surplus), to the depreciated value of the properties; figures prepared on that basis are as follows:

	Property Coverage (as of December 31, 1938) [c]				
	(000 omitted from dollar amounts)				
	Consumers Power Co.	Detroit Edison Co.	Cleveland Elec. Illuminating Co.	The Ohio Power Co.	Duquesne Light Co.
Depreciated property	$217,908	$277,577	$112,411	$104,771	$168,702
Debt related to depreciated property	52%	51%	35%	65%	42%
Debt and preferred stock related to depreciated property	89%	None	58%	84%	58%
Balance of depreciated property remaining for common stock and surplus	11% [b]	49%	42%	16%	42%

b. See footnote a on page 518.

c. * * * Assuming that all of the new money, viz. $3,500,000 from the sale of stock and $10,000,000 from the sale of bonds, would be used for additions to the property account * * * approximately 14% of depreciated property would remain for common stock and surplus. Furthermore, it should be observed that these figures do not reflect the possible existence of inflationary items in Consumers' property account or the property accounts of the companies compared. * * *

The presently outstanding long-term debt of Consumers is 55.23% of its depreciated property. If the $28,594,000 of bonds were issued, and $18,594,000 were used to refund existing debt, and $3,500,000 of its common stock were sold, that debt ratio would become 59.7%. That debt ratio we may assume (but do not decide) is not so excessive as to call for findings that the proposed bond issue in the entire amount of $28,594,000 would not be reasonably adapted to Consumers' security structure, under Section 7(d)(1), or to its earnings, under Section 7(d)(2).

But that the *debt* ratio may meet the standards of Sections 7(d)(1) and (2) is not enough; for Congress imposed not only those standards but also the requirements of Section 7(d)(3). Accordingly, we cannot permit the bonds, in the total amount of $28,594,000, to be issued and sold unless bonds in that amount are "necessary" or "appropriate" to the economical and efficient operation of Consumers' business. And it is impossible to avoid finding that the increase of $10,000,000 in debt is not "appropriate to the economical and efficient operation" of Consumers' business where—

(a) the combined amount of its debt and preferred stock would, after such financing, be (approximately) 80% of its total capitalization, with its common stock, and surplus (approximately) but 20% thereof;

(b) the ratio of its debt and preferred stock to depreciated property, as of December 31, 1938, is (approximately) 89%, leaving (approximately) 11% of depreciated property for common stock and surplus;

(c) the ratio of common stock and surplus to total capitalization and the balance of depreciated property remaining for common stock and surplus, expressed in percentage terms, are, respectively, less than the corresponding ratios and balances, also expressed in percentage terms, in the case of other comparable operating utility companies; and

(d) increased common stock financing, in substitution for increased debt financing, is easily available.

There are cases in which we have permitted debt to be increased without inquiring searchingly into the ratio of common stock and surplus to total capitalization, or into the balance of depreciated property remaining for the common stock after allocation to debt and preferred stock; but in those cases the increase of debt was "necessary" within the meaning of Section 7(d)(3); and, therefore, we were not faced with the question of whether the increased debt was "appropriate," which confronts us in this case.

In making our finding that financing, which will increase debt by $10,000,000, is, in the circumstances, not "appropriate" within the meaning of Section 7(d)(3), we have also considered the following:

In view of past business history, any program of financing must take into account the possibility of future changes in earning power. The corporation may, at a time of financial stress, be confronted with the necessity of obtaining capital for replacement or expansion of plant facilities or to meet maturities. At that time, financing may be possible only if the corporation has not previously exhausted its credit by the issuance of bonds. It is, therefore, not "appropriate" financial policy for a company such as Consumers' not to take advantage of a favorable opportunity to sell common stock, thereby conserving the company's credit.[37]

In this connection, it should be observed that in considering the standard of Section 7(d)(3) we must also consider whether present financing through additional debt, (now not "necessary") will not tend to create such a security structure that the Commission, when dealing with future applications under Section 7 for the issuance of securities by Consumers (which may, at that time, be "necessary"), may be impelled to make an adverse finding under Section 7(d)(1). For the stoppage of the flow of capital to Consumers which would result from such a future adverse finding would be detrimental to the economical and efficient operation of Consumers' business.

That is to say, we are enjoined by Congress to pay reasonable regard to the future as well as the present. The example of the results of railroad financing in past prosperous periods may well have prompted Congress so to provide. We must not ignore the statutory admonition. We must, therefore, not permit, where we can lawfully prevent, present utility financing which is likely to yield a future for the utility industry similar to the present plight of the railroads and their investors.

* * *

37. In view of the other basis of our findings, there is no need to consider, and we do not here consider, the question of the "leverage" value to the present holder of the common stock, of increased debt financing, to the possible disadvantage to the bondholders.

It is urged that, although conservation of credit is desirable, it may well be equally desirable to take advantage of low money rates, and that it is difficult to hazard a guess on how long the opportunity to borrow money at low rates will last. But since Consumers can meet its present needs by common stock financing in a favorable market, at a favorable price, the question of low rates for borrowed money will be irrelevant as far as its present needs are concerned. If the reference is to the future, such a suggestion is no more illuminating: If the company will be able to meet its future needs by common stock financing, (i.e., if future bond financing will not be necessary) the then existing rates for borrowed money will not be significant. If, however, future bond financing becomes necessary, surely the company will be able to sell bonds more cheaply and more easily, if it has not previously issued $10,000,000 of bonds but has instead issued that amount of stock.

It is suggested that Consumers Power Co. stood up under the impact of the depression and earned common dividends throughout that period. But the pleasant past is not an adequate protection against what may be a less pleasant future. The rigidities created by past needless bond financing by then prosperous railroads, account, in no small measure, for their present difficulties. Many railroads which successfully weathered earlier depressions did not fare well in recent times.

We do not at all intimate that Consumers' funded debt "has reached the danger point" or would reach that point if $10,000,000 of additional debt were created. The question as to whether a "danger point" is already at hand properly arises under Section 7(d)(2), and in applying that section we must inquire whether a new issue of securities is reasonably adapted to the corporate earning power. But Congress added Section 7(d)(3), which compels us to go further and to inquire also whether the new security issue is "appropriate to the economical and efficient operation of [the] business." This standard, long before the danger point has been reached, calls for an adverse finding, as to an issue which will substantially add to debt; it commands us to prevent conditions which may, in the future, bring the company into the danger zone.

And so we must not be taken as saying that disaster would follow the increase of Consumers' debt by $10,000,000. But since the more flexible method of financing through the sale of a substantial block of common stock is easily available, it is clear, on the facts of this case, that the sale of bonds in excess of the principal amount of $18,594,000 is not necessary. And, in view of the fact that the ratio of the Company's common stock and surplus to total capitalization is strikingly less than the ratios of comparable utility companies; that the balance of depreciated property, expressed in percentage terms, remaining for common stock is less than the average of corresponding balances of comparable utility companies; and that common stock financing in the amount of $10,000,000 is readily available on favorable terms, we are, for the reasons previously indicated, compelled to find that bond financing, which would increase debt by that amount, is not appropriate to the economical and efficient operation of the company's business.

* * *

It is intimated by Commissioners Healy and Mathews that, if there were no adverse findings and order under Section 7(d)(3) as to the issue and sale of the $10,000,000 of bonds by Consumers, there would be avoided any possible difficulty that might hereafter arise in fixing the price per share on a possible future sale of additional shares of Consumers' common stock to the public. But nothing in our adverse findings and order in this case will necessarily lead to such a sale. Moreover, any such difficulty in fixing the price of Consumers common stock is not insurmountable. And Commissioners Healy and Mathews concede that a similar difficulty will have to be faced by holding companies and this Commission as integration programs develop under Section 11. In view of the foregoing, no such possible difficulty can invalidate our adverse findings and order as to the issue and sale of the $10,000,000 of bonds.

It should also be observed that the adverse findings and order under Section 7(d)(3) in no way affect the preemptive rights of Commonwealth & Southern, as sole common stockholder of Consumers, to purchase additional common shares which may hereafter be sold by Consumers. The significance and effect of those rights are not involved in this case, and it would be inappropriate to discuss these matters here.

* * *

Separate Opinion of Commissioners Healy and Mathews:

* * *

The next question is whether the issue and sale of the first mortgage bonds may be approved under the Holding Company Act. There is no disagreement that the proposed bonds conform to the standards prescribed in Section 7(c) of the Act in that they are first lien bonds and, with respect to over $18,000,000 principal amount of the issue, for the additional reason that they are to be used for the purpose of refunding outstanding bonds of Consumers. It is with respect to the $10,000,000 of new money which is being raised through the issue and sale of the proposed bonds that a majority of the Commission is unable to make the requisite findings under Section 7(d).

* * *

The first question for decision is then, shall we find that the proposed bonds are *not* reasonably adapted to the security structure of the declarant and other companies in the same holding company system? The Consumers' capitalization after the proposed financing will consist of 52.32% funded debt, 27.65% preferred stock and 20.03% common stock and surplus. Though the preferred stock interest is larger and the common stock interest smaller than might be desirable, the disproportion is not such as to affect the bonds. And it is to be remembered that of the $13,500,000 new money which is being raised by Consumers, over 25% is by the sale of common stock, or by contribution, thereby increasing the existing common stock and surplus ratio of 19.7%. The ratio of common stock to total capitalization may or may not be significant. Much depends on what the common stock represents. For example, the common stock and surplus of Public Service Company of Colorado was 27.59% of the total capitalization, but all of the common stock was based on write-ups or intercompany profits and had not cost the holding company anything.

On a pro forma basis the long-term debt will be 53.78% of gross property and 59.70% of depreciated property per books. Upon the application of the proceeds of the proposed financing these ratios would most likely be improved. Such ratios cannot be said to be disproportionate. Indeed, we have often approved the issuance of funded debt where the ratios have been far less favorable. It is unnecessary to detail the long list of instances.   * * *

We think the bonds are reasonably adapted to the security structure of declarant.

The next question is: Shall we find that the proposed bonds are *not* reasonably adapted to the earning power of the declarant? As respects this finding, suffice it to say, that on a pro forma basis the interest on the bonds will be earned three times. This coverage is more favorable than that in other cases which this Commission has approved.   * * * We cannot find that the bonds proposed to be issued are not reasonably adapted to the earning power of the declarant.

Shall we find that the financing by the proposed first mortgage bonds is not necessary or appropriate to the economical and efficient operation of a business in which applicant lawfully is engaged or has an interest? That is our next problem. A majority of the Commission is of the opinion that because there is some indication that Consumers may be able to raise such funds as are necessary through the issue and sale of common stock it follows that financing by first mortgage bonds is not necessary or appropriate to the economical and efficient operation of Consumers. Whatever may be said as to the effect of the "offer" of Otis & Company to negotiate for the purchase of the common for resale to the public, we believe that Consumers, unlike Commonwealth & Southern which has large preferred dividend arrears, can obtain its necessary capital through the sale of common stock to the public. This we believe has already been sufficiently demonstrated by certain other utilities during the past year. And so while financing by first mortgage bonds is not necessary, it does not follow that it is not appropriate to the economical and efficient operation of Consumers. The financing by the proposed bonds should prove most economical to Consumers for the bonds bear a 3¼% coupon and the cost to the company is 3.07%. This is, we believe, the lowest cost of money in the history of Consumers and almost the lowest in the history of the entire public utility industry. In view of this fact, we do not feel justified in overriding the judgment of the management that such a favorable opportunity for borrowing a moderate amount of new money on these terms should be taken advantage of. We are fully aware that a large debt is not conservative financing. We are further aware of the plight of those railroad companies which indulged in excessive funded debt financing. We believe that the history of some of these presents a most solemn warning to the electric and gas utilities. But because of the ratios here, we think that the proposed increase in funded debt has not reached the danger point. We also know that borrowing money at 3.07% through the issuance of bonds creates additional leverage for the common stock. But we consider this an incident of common stock ownership which is permissible until the amount contributed by the senior security holders is so large as to place upon them the risks ordinarily accepted by the common stock, or as to be objectionable for other reasons. Furthermore, while borrowing money at 3.07% is advantageous to the common stock interest it should increase the earnings coverage for the preferred stockholders, since the difference between the rate of return earned by the borrowed capital and the interest paid on that capital is available for preferred dividends. * * *

Chairman Frank in his opinion points out that Consumers' ratio of common stock and surplus to its total capitalization is much less than the ratios of four utility companies operating in the middle west area. There are indications however that the property accounts of one of the four may be inflated, namely, Duquesne Light Company, which has about $8,000,000 of intercompany profits. So too, we think that the comparison to the average ratios of 177 public utility subsidiaries of registered holding companies is not completely meaningful for in many cases there were present write-ups and intercompany profits.

It is stated by Chairman Frank, in speaking of the $10,000,000 of new money, that since this company can raise this money through equity financing it should do so and conserve its credit. This overlooks the fact that Consumers has stood up under the "impact of the depression"; indeed, it continued to earn common dividends throughout the depression. Conservation of credit is admittedly desirable but it may well be equally desirable to take advantage of low money rates. Who can hazard a guess on how long the opportunity to borrow money at low rates will last?

* * *

If, however, it should be established that financing by first mortgage bonds to the extent proposed is inappropriate and that Consumers must finance through the issue and sale of common stock, then it would become necessary to consider whether such common stock must first be offered to Commonwealth & Southern before being offered to the public. The charter of Consumers contains a provision reading as follows:

"In case the stockholders vote to increase the capital stock of the corporation, so much of such increased capital stock as shall be common stock shall be offered exclusively to the common stockholders pro rata, and so much of such increased capital stock as shall be preferred stock shall be offered pro rata to both the preferred and common stockholders; provided, however, that if the corporation shall issue any of its stock, either preferred or common, in payment for property purchased or services rendered the stockholders shall have no right to subscribe for any stock issued for that purpose."

* * *

The order of the Michigan Public Service Commission dated November 10, 1939, finds Consumers entitled to issue and sell 125,000 shares of common stock, saying specifically, "such stock when issued is to be sold to the Commonwealth & Southern Corporation (Delaware) the holder of all its outstanding common stock." The same order later states that it is "ordered that Consumers is hereby authorized and empowered to issue and sell presently, or from time to time, 125,000 shares of its common stock at the price of $28.25 per share to The Commonwealth & Southern Corporation (Delaware) the holder of all of its outstanding common stock," etc.

It is fairly inferable that this order either recognizes Commonwealth & Southern's preemptive right to subscribe for Consumers' new common or is based upon a recognition of the same general principles which underlie the preemptive rule. The preemptive right is given not only for the protection of a shareholder's voting right but principally to protect him against a dilution of the values fairly belonging to him. Surely the Michigan Commission could not justify the sale of these shares to anyone other than Commonwealth and Southern at a price of $28.25 a share. This price is the present book value of the common stock per share. Commonwealth & Southern owns (and this cannot be pointed out too often) all the outstanding common shares. Consequently the issuance to it of additional shares at the book values avoided all problems of either dilution or fattening of the book value of either old or new shares. To emphasize the point let us assume that a corporation has outstanding 1,000 shares of common stock with a book value of $28,000 or $28 per share. Let us assume that the corporation sells to the general public 1,000 new shares for $60 per share or $60,000. The assets of the corporation applicable to common stock then become $88,000 belonging in equity to 2,000 shares. The 2,000 shares are then worth at book values $44 per share. The old 1,000 shares are worth at book $44,000, the new 1,000 shares are worth at book $44,000. In other words, the old shares have been fattened in book value to the extent of $16 per share or a total of $16,000 for all the old shares, while the $60,000 put up by new common stock has been diluted to the extent of $16 per share or $16,000. This sum the public would have contributed to fattening the book value of the old common. [It will be remembered that Otis & Co. intended to resell the stock to the public if it obtained it.] If immediately following such a subscription the corporation were dissolved and liquidated for precisely the book value of its assets, the old common stockholders would receive $44,000 of which $16,000 would have been contributed by the new stockholders. To still further demonstrate the principle involved let us assume that the corporation with 1,000 shares of a book value of $28 per share, or a total of $28,000, issues and sells to the general public 1,000 new shares at $20 a share, or a total of $20,000. The total assets of the corporation applicable to the common stock will then become $48,000, belonging in equity to 2,000 shares. The 2,000 shares are then worth at book $24 per share. The old 1,000 common shares are worth at book $24,000. In other words, the old shares will have been diluted in book value to the extent of $4 a share or a total of $4,000, while the 1,000 shares of new stock costing $20,000 would be fattened to the extent of $4 a share or a total of $4,000. This sum the old stockholders would have contributed to increasing the book value of the new common. If immediately following such a subscription the corporation were dissolved or liquidated for precisely the book value of its assets, the new stockholders would receive $24,000 for stock which had cost them $20,000 the difference of $4,000 having been contributed by the old stockholders. So much for book figures.

It is apparent, of course, that if a public distribution of Consumers' common were to be undertaken or compelled, fairness to both the old and the prospective common stockholders would demand that the price of the stock be fixed at its true and fair value, so far as ascertainable and not merely at book value. If it were fixed too high it would be unfair to the new public buyers; if at a price too low it would be unfair to Commonwealth & Southern and the public holders of its securities. The palpable difficulty of such a task is among the considerations which has led to the insistence of the courts upon the preemptive right. It is a task which in the absence of a public distribution of Consumers' common neither the Michigan Commission nor this Commission, nor either of the companies involved, needed to undertake.

* * *

We would approve the issue of [all] the bonds. We would approve the capital contribution proposed by Commonwealth & Southern. We would permit Consumers in return for this contribution to issue 125,000 shares of common stock, 50,000 shares, one share or no shares.

(C) REGULATION OF RISK SHIFTING

(1) Investment Companies and Variance

Section 18(a) of the Investment Company Act of 1940 (15 USC § 80a–18(a)) provides in part as follows:

"SEC. 18. (a) It shall be unlawful for any registered closed-end company to issue any class of senior security, or to sell any such security of which it is the issuer, unless—

(1) if such class of senior security represents an indebtedness—

(A) immediately after such issuance or sale, it will have an asset coverage of at least 300 per centum;

* * *

(2) if such class of senior security is a stock—

(A) immediately after such issuance or sale it will have an asset coverage of at least 200 per centum; * * *."

To what extent, if at all, do the categorical limitations on leverage for closed end investment companies which are embodied in Section 18(a) mitigate or avert the risks of leverage? In considering this question, note that Section 12 of the Investment Company Act (15 USC § 80a–12) substantially restrains registered investment companies from (1) purchasing securities on margin, (2) effecting short sales, and (3) acquiring more than limited percentages of the securities of other investment companies.

If the object of Section 18(a) and Section 12 is to limit the risks to which managers may subject investors in stocks of investment companies, can management avoid that restraint by increasing the riskiness of portfolio securities? If so, does the restriction of leverage impose a cost upon investors in investment company stocks (loss of the opportunity to adjust to a desired risk-return relationship by investing in a "conservative" portfolio with a high return while levering the portfolio) with no offsetting benefit? See Note, 82 Yale L.J. 1305 (1973). Or are there institutional factors affecting management of investment companies which cause unrestrained leverage, in the case of investment companies, to create risks for the company's senior security holders and public stockholders that are not encountered by investors in industrial or public utility enterprises? Consider the following excerpts from Part Three of the SEC Report on Investment Trusts and Investment Companies (1939), a Report upon which many of the provisions of the Investment Company Act of 1940 are based:

"Another type of consideration connected with the establishment of a multiple-security structure is that a situation is created analogous to, but lacking the protections which exist in, the ordinary margin account. A person purchasing senior securities in an investment company is in effect lending money [82] to the investment company for the use of the common stockholders to invest or to speculate in securities, similar in many ways to a broker's loan to a customer for use in a margin account.[83]

"Yet the customary protection in this situation demanded by a broker is in strong contrast to the protection usually afforded senior security holders by investment companies, even by those investment companies sponsored by brokers. The broker ordinarily keeps daily supervision over the status of a customer's margin account and can

---

82. In the broad sense preferred stockholders may be characterized as lenders to the investment company, even though they do not have a creditor relationship. * * *

83. Both the senior security holder and the broker turn over a definite amount of money to the return of which they have an immediate or ultimate claim and are entitled to a specified and limited compensation for the use of that money, either in interest or dividends. In both cases the funds loaned are used to purchase securities, particularly common stocks.

long before the account reaches the point of being 'under water' compel the customer to supply additional collateral. If additional collateral is not supplied, the broker can sell out the customer's securities in a few hours and fully protect his loan. When the asset value of the investment company has dropped to a dangerously low point, e.g., the preferred stock may actually be 'under water', the senior security holder, particularly the preferred stockholder, ordinarily cannot demand more collateral or that the underlying securities be sold and his claim paid off.[85] If he holds a bond he is almost entirely helpless until its due date, while if he holds a preferred stock, he must await the dissolution of the company, which dissolution is largely determined by the holders of the common stock. Regardless of the extent to which the senior securities are 'under water,' the common stockholder usually continues to manage the funds on which the senior securities have a prior claim. In such a situation the multiple security structure tends to encourage a speculative policy on the part of the common stock management, since speculative transactions at such a point may, with the aid of leverage, reestablish positive values for the common stock and cannot do any substantial damage to the already existing negative values.

" * * *

" * * * The theory of senior securities in the capital structure presumed the existence of a large investment by the common stockholders as a buffer or cushion to insure the safety of the investment of the senior security holders and the regular payment of interest and dividends to them. However, in the financing of investment companies, senior securities apparently have been used for the purpose of obtaining from the public the major part of the capital contribution, while the control of the enterprise has been retained by the sponsors with small proportionate investments through ownership of common stock. Thus, the complex capital structure usually gives rise to another crucial element of conflict within the investment company field; the general public holding the major part of the senior securities has the greatest stake in the enterprise, while the sponsors or insiders, having a much smaller stake, control the enterprise. (at 1593–1595)

" * * *

"The difference in rights and claims awarded the senior and equity securities, respectively, in the multiple-security company subjects the company to pressure in favor of a speculative investment policy. The impetus toward abnormal capital accretion arises from two attributes of the senior-equity structure: (a) The need of such investment companies to maintain a level of earnings and profit greater than the average yield on a diversified list of high-grade investments in order to meet the fixed interest and dividend requirements of the senior securities; and

---

85. Theoretically this does not apply to investment company bonds with a "touch-off" clause. However, "touch-off" clauses are far less effective or timely for the investor than are rights in the usual margin agreement for the broker. In fact, means are often found to avoid the operation of "touch-off" clauses. * * *

(b) The fact that the bulk of the large profits possibly accruing from a policy of speculation with the total funds of the company will inure to the sponsors while the possibility of loss to the sponsor is limited to its comparatively small investment in the company." (at 1668)

The phenomenon adverted to in the SEC Report on Investment Companies is an instance which is generalized in the Black–Scholes option pricing model framework, and is discussed in those terms in Corporate Finance textbooks, as the following excerpt shows.

VAN HORNE, FINANCIAL MANAGEMENT AND POLICY
9th ed. 1992, pgs. 289–292

* * * [T]he equity of a firm can be viewed as a call option on the firm's total value, the value being the associated or underlying asset of the option.   The writers of the option are the debt holders.   For simplicity, assume that debt is represented by discount bonds that pay only at maturity.   We can then view stockholders as having sold the firm to the debt holders with an option to buy it back at a specified price.   The option has an exercise price equal to the face value of debt, and its expiration date is the maturity of the debt. * * * Note that the value of * * * [the stockholders'] option at expiration cannot be negative, because they have limited liability.

* * *

We know * * * that the greater the variance or volatility in value of the underlying asset, the greater the value of the option, all other things the same.   Therefore it is in the interest of the optionholders, in this case the stockholders, to increase the variance of the firm. With a given exercise price * * *, an increase in the dispersion of the probability distribution of possible firm values increases the value of their option.   Thus, by increasing the riskiness of the assets of the firm, stockholders can increase the value of their option.   This works to the disadvantage of the debt holders because there will be a corresponding decrease in the market value of their investment.*

---

* [Ed. Note:] The point may be illustrated by assuming that a corporation with assets initially valued at $90 million issued $40 million face amount of 10% debt, but that the present value of its assets is only $45 million and they earn just enough to pay interest on the debt. Expected earnings (dispersion and probability) are as follows:

Earnings/ (Loss)	Probability	Expected Value
$5 million	25%	$1.25 million
$4 million	50%	$2.00 million
$3 million	25%	$ .75 million
		$4.00 million

The owners of the equity are given the opportunity to sell the assets and reinvest in much riskier assets having expected earnings of:

Earnings/ (Loss)	Probability	Expected Value
$10 million	50%	$5 million
−$2 million	50%	−$1 million
		$4 million

Although the expected return is $4 million in each case, the equity owners have little to lose and a great deal to gain in returns from switching from the old assets to the new investment.   Correspondingly, the debt holders are disadvantaged.   The market value of the stock will rise, and of the debt will fall.   The price impact of such behavior by the common stock may be derived from the Black–Scholes formula.

* * *

[Another mechanism for invoking a comparable alteration of the value of existing debt is to change the debt-equity ratio.] In the context of the option pricing model, issuing debt and retiring stock—thereby increasing the proportion of debt in the capital structure—will result in a decline in the price of the existing debt (per dollar of face value) and an increase in share price. * * *

* * *

* * * In essence, the stockholders have expropriated some of the wealth of the existing debt holders. The new debt holders are not hurt, because they lend money on the basis of the default risk associated with the new capital structure. * * * Only the old debt holders suffer. Similar to a change in the overall risk of the firm in our previous discussion, wealth transfers from the old debt holders to the stockholders.

* * *

Debt holders can protect themselves against expropriation by imposing constraints on the company at the time the loan is made. Known as protective covenants, these covenants may be used to restrict the stockholders' ability to increase the asset riskiness and/or its leverage. * * *

The Modigliani–Miller argument for the irrelevance of capital structure requires that securityholders protect themselves against capital structure changes that work to erode their position. "Me first" rules ensure that one party cannot gain at the expense of the other. Although stockholders usually gain and old debt holders usually lose, it is possible for the reverse to occur. With certain protective covenants, debt holders might obtain a claim on future retained earnings at the expense of stockholders. Therefore stockholders also must assure themselves that their position will not be eroded without compensation. To the extent that "me first" rules are not effective, capital structure decisions may be relevant even in the absence of taxes and bankruptcy costs.

(2) Bank Capital Structures

What relevance do the learning on capital structure and the efforts to regulate capital structure have for the conduct and regulation of bank capital structures and operations? Failing banks and thrifts have been an important problem in recent years. The thin margin furnished by bank capital underlies those troubles to some considerable, albeit indeterminate extent. The banks' debt-equity ratios are notoriously low—often below 10 percent and rarely much higher. Does the role of capital in bank operations differ so significantly from its role in commercial or manufacturing or utility operations as to explain the lower proportion of bank equity capital?

Does the option model of the firm tell us something about bank capital structures? Are depositors the sort of creditor the option model contemplates? If not, do deposit insurers play this role? If not, how should bank capital be regulated? Who benefits when a bank invests in risky assets—that is, makes risky loans? Its depositors? Its stockholders? Its bondholders? Presumably, risky loans serve an economic function and the present system is premised on an assumed price equilibrium for loans reached by negotiations between banks and their risk-taking stockholders and their borrowers, with bank depositors seeking, and presumably occupying, a low risk or riskless position. If the quantity of bank capital does not sufficiently lower the depositors' risk because neither the depositors nor the regulators can define or police capital adequacy, and government insurance is necessary to protect the depositors, then why insist on (or even permit) bank capital in the first place? What function does it serve?

Is bank capital supposed to serve a disciplinary function? If so, how feasible is the discipline or displacement of bank managers by bank stockholders? If displacement is difficult to accomplish, why should bank managers be thought to have any special competence or incentive to perform "correctly" the resource allocating and risk-taking function involved in lending money? Would higher capital requirements mitigate the difficulties? Or is the regulation of bank investments (that is, loans) a better remedy? Finally, if bank management is responsive to stockholder discipline, then, given the option pricing model, are the stockholders, left unregulated, likely to opt for less capital and for investment decisions implying a higher return to themselves and a lower return to depositors than a well functioning free market would permit?

(3) Margin Requirements

Section 7 of the Securities Exchange Act (15 U.S.C. § 78g) empowers the Federal Reserve Board (FRB) to regulate the supply of credit available for buying securities (or selling them short) by limiting the loan value of securities. The difference between the loan value specified by the FRB and the market price of the securities represents the margin which the investor must furnish out of his own resources when he invests. Thus, if the margin requirement were 70% (the maximum loan value being 30%), an individual who purchased 100 shares of a stock selling at $50 a share, "on margin," would be permitted to borrow no more than $1,500 from his broker.

The FRB does not require that the margin level be maintained at the level it specifies—currently 50%—once the initial purchase has been made, but the rules of the stock exchanges do prescribe margin maintenance levels for customers' accounts. The New York Stock Exchange for example, requires that margin never fall below 25%—i.e., that a customer's indebtedness to this broker never exceed 75% of the value of the cash and securities held in his account. If stock values decline below the permitted minimum, the customer will receive a margin call from his broker and be asked to post additional collateral.[l]

l. To implement Section 7 of the Exchange Act, the FRB has promulgated regulations prescribing permissible margin on loans or extensions of credit by brokers

Impetus for margin requirements came from the stock market crash of 1929 and the feeling that excessive use of security credit had in some part been responsible for pushing stock prices to unrealistically high levels. As stock prices began to slide, lenders who had made security loans on as little as 10% margin grew apprehensive and issued calls for more collateral, which their customers were frequently unable to provide. This led to the quick liquidation of customers' portfolios as lenders attempted to retrieve some portion of their loans, and thereby induced a swifter and more severe decline in prices than might otherwise have occurred.[m] The evidence is mixed (see Moore, Stock Market Margin Requirements, 74 J.P.E. 158 (1966)) on whether margin requirements do contribute to a healthier securities market by suppressing speculative zeal during boom periods and avoiding forced sales in periods of contraction.

Do the margin regulations, which (with the exception noted in footnote *l*, supra) do *not* impose restrictions on borrowing in order to purchase straight (i.e., nonconvertible) debt securities, distort the supply schedules of loan and equity funds in the market, and tend to channel more investments into senior securities than would otherwise be made? If so, do the margin regulations thereby interfere with efficient allocation of capital, albeit in the interest of a kind of distributive equity?

Why are there no governmentally imposed margin requirements on other kinds of investment, e.g., real estate? What attitude on the part

and dealers (Regulation T, 12 C.F.R. Part 220), banks (Regulation U, 12 C.F.R. Part 221), and others (Regulation G, 12 C.F.R. Part 207), and extended those regulations to cover transactions in convertible securities and selected over-the-counter securities (12 C.F.R. Part 220), and equity funding plans (12 C.F.R. Parts 207 and 221). To implement the Foreign Bank Secrecy Act which amended Section 7, the FRB promulgated Regulation X (12 C.F.R. Part 224) making it unlawful for any U.S. citizen to borrow from any lender anywhere if the borrowing would have violated margin requirements had it been made in the United States.

m. While reducing the range and intensity of price fluctuation of securities is one of the purposes of the margin restrictions authorized by Section 7, "[T]he main purpose is to give a Government credit agency an effective method of reducing the aggregate amount of the nation's credit resources which can be directed by speculation into the stock market and out of other, more desirable uses of commerce and industry. * * *'" And "a by-product of the main purpose" was to protect the individual investor against himself. (HR Rep. No. 1383, 73rd Cong. 2d Sess. (1934) p. 8). It

has also been suggested that the margin requirements protect broker solvency by setting limits on the extent to which competition may drive brokers to make unsafe loans.

Report of Special Study of the Securities Markets of the Securities and Exchange Commission, H.R.Doc. No. 95, 88th Cong., 1st Sess. (1963) Part 5 at 158; Part 4 at 20.

With respect to each of these objectives, the FRB at one point recommended to Congress that there no longer remains sufficient justification for maintaining securities margins at levels substantially higher than needed to protect brokers and lenders against loss from customer default. The FRB recommended that the task of setting margin requirements to protect brokers and lenders be delegated to the various stock exchanges and over-the-counter regulatory bodies with coordination responsibilities vested with the SEC and CFTC. See Federal Reserve Board, A Review and Evaluation of Federal Margin Regulations, CCH Fed.Sec.L.Rep., ¶ 83,728. Was that recommendation consistent with the FRB's later interpretation of the margin rules in connection with takeovers supra p. 498?

of investors in highly leveraged assets do the margin requirements appear to assume?

Is the unrestrained authority to issue warrants incompatible with restrictions on the purchase of securities on margin? Does the answer turn on whether the margin restrictions are designed more to preserve the stability of stock market prices against speculative "excesses" than to preserve or protect the security holder from bankruptcy?

Is it possible for an investor to be exposed to more risk with a portfolio financed without borrowing than with a portfolio financed by borrowing 80% of the amount needed to purchase the securities? If so, are the margin regulations justifiable on risk minimization grounds? Is such justification sufficient to offset the discriminatory impact which these regulations have on the ability of persons with limited resources to invest in securities? See Rizzi, Portfolio Theory, Capital Requirements and the Marginal Effect of Federal Margin Requirements, 8 Loyola Univ.L.J. 499 (1977).

Efforts at enforcement of these legislative mandates have raised legal problems for which satisfactory solutions remain to be found. In particular, in enforcing the margin regulations, limitations of manpower hobble the SEC. The Exchanges and NASD may be no more able to meet the resulting need.[n] Whether recommendations of the FRB for policing by self-regulatory organizations will alter that balance remains to be seen.

(D) HYPOTHETICAL CAPITAL STRUCTURE IN RATE–MAKING PROCEEDINGS

NEW ENGLAND TEL. & TEL. CO. v. DEPARTMENT OF PUBLIC UTILITIES

Supreme Judicial Court of Massachusetts, 1951.
327 Mass. 81, 97 N.E.2d 509.

QUA, Chief Justice. This is a suit in equity brought by the plaintiff, hereinafter called the company, under G.L. (Ter.Ed.) c. 25, § 5, praying for the annulment of, or other relief from, an order of the department dated March 18, 1949, in a proceeding known as D.P.U. 8181, which disallowed a schedule of rates and charges filed by the company on April 21, 1948. * * *

When this present suit came on for hearing before the single justice of this court, the company and the department presented a stipulation wherein the company waived all issues except those relating to the adequacy of the return and the rate of return allowed by the department, including as still open the subsidiary issues (a) of adequate

---

n. A Report in 1986 by the General Accounting Office on the activities of self-regulatory organizations suggests that they are less than perfect policemen. It was noted by Congressman Wirth in discussing the Report that there is an "inherent problem in self-regulation: the difficulty of an employee disciplining someone upon whom he depends for a livelihood."

return upon stock capital, (b) of a safe ratio of debt capital to total capital, and (c) of the right of the company to earnings upon reinvested surplus.   This stipulation included an agreement as to certain facts, among them being that the average 1949 Massachusetts intrastate rate base upon which the company was entitled to a fair return was $238,264,400, if the company was not entitled to earnings upon surplus reinvested in its plant, or $244,185,500, if the company was entitled to such earnings; that the company's total capitalization, not including surplus, was $410,570,100, consisting of long term debt of $135,000,000, advances from the American Telephone and Telegraph Company of $120,000,000, and common stock amounting to $155,570,100, making a ratio of debt capital to total capital of 62.1%; that the surplus was $9,585,000; that the composite cost of existing long term debt was 3.613% as found by the department, which (according to the stipulation and the findings) could be reduced to 3.45% [2] upon the acquisition of new debt capital at slightly lower cost; and that the composite return on the rate base resulting from the department's order would be 4.887% if the company was not entitled to earnings on reinvested surplus and 4.768% if the company was so entitled.   Reference will be made to other facts agreed in so far as becomes necessary.   It was further agreed that the case should be presented to the single justice upon the pleadings, the facts agreed, and the evidence presented to the department bearing upon rate of return for the determination of the issues "by the court upon its own independent judgment as to both law and fact."

* * *

It is elementary that the fixing of rates is not a proper judicial function.   On the other hand, where a rate established by a public regulatory body is attacked as confiscatory the Constitution of this Commonwealth and seemingly still that of the United States require that there be a full opportunity for judicial review as to both fact and law.   * * * It is the contention of the company here that the rates set up by the order of the department of March 18, 1949 (the 5% rates), do not permit a fair return upon the property of the company devoted to the public service and are confiscatory.   That issue is before us in all its aspects.   It was said, however, in St. Joseph Stock Yards Co. v. United States, 298 U.S. 38, 53, 56 S.Ct. 720, 726, 80 L.Ed. 1033, that "the court will not interfere with the exercise of the rate-making power unless confiscation is clearly established."

Certain undisputed facts form the background of the case and will in large measure determine the outcome.   They are established by a plenitude of figures, charts, and testimony, but their substance may be stated in simple language.   The company is one of the associated companies of the Bell system.   Of its stock 68.9% is held by the American Telephone and Telegraph Company.   During and since World War II there has been an immense increase in the demand for

---

2. This percentage assumes a debt ratio   ment found to be safe, as hereinafter ap-
of approximately 45%, which the depart-   pears.

the company's telephone service. The company has greatly increased its facilities but nevertheless by the summer of 1948 shortly before the hearings began before the department it had not yet been able to catch up with the accumulated applications for service. To enable the company to expand its plant to meet the vast public demand, and in accordance with a custom in the Bell system, the American Telephone and Telegraph Company has advanced to the company on unsecured demand notes at 2.75% the sum of $120,000,000, which amounts to between a quarter and a third of the total capitalization of the company. This money was advanced in the expectation that it would be repaid in accordance with the custom in the system out of new issues of securities by the company. The company is under an absolute obligation to repay these advances but can do so only by means of acquiring new permanent capital either in the form of additional debt capital through bond issues or in the form of additional stock capital through stock issues. But the experts who testified were in agreement, and we suppose it is a matter of common knowledge, that the proportion of debt capital cannot be extended indefinitely without adversely affecting the credit of the company, injuring the market for its stock, and to some degree that for its bonds also. It would seem that the company, with a ratio of 62.1% of debt capital to total capital, is already top-heavy with debt, and that a substantial part of the new capital required must be raised by the sale of stock, how much will be a subject of discussion later in this opinion. And at this time, when it has become necessary to raise a substantial amount of new capital through an issue of stock, we are confronted with the further undoubted facts that high costs of operation since the war have greatly impaired the company's earning capacity relative to the capital invested,[4] so that the dividends upon the stock have decreased from 6% to 4.25%, and as the hearing before the department approached its end the stock, of which the par value is $100, had fallen in the market so that it was hovering around $80 to $85. Moreover, the company is a New York corporation and under New York law cannot issue new stock at less than par. * * * Such in rough outline was the situation with which the company and the department had to deal. The expert witness called by the Attorney General in behalf of the public conceded that the company was faced with a very serious financial problem to which he could see no answer except in some way to increase earnings.

The department approached the problem by way of its so called theory of "prudent investment" upon which it and its predecessor commissions have for many years relied in ascertaining the property "actually used or useful for the convenience of the public". See G.L. (Ter.Ed.) c. 159, § 26. As applied to this case the department describes its method in these words, "our method is to ascertain, through appropriate steps, the value of the company's investment in gross intrastate plant in Massachusetts, to deduct therefrom the amount of the compa-

---

4. The department finds that, although gross revenues in 1948 exceeded those in 1940 by nearly $51,000,000, the net earn-ings in 1948 exceeded those in 1940 by only $126,000.

ny's corresponding depreciation reserve, and to add thereto the amount of working capital, if any, required by the company in its intrastate operations." Application of this method led to the finding of the rate base of $238,264,400, and as hereinbefore stated the parties have now agreed upon this figure, subject to an increase to $244,185,500, if the company is entitled to earnings upon its reinvested surplus.

In determining the fair rate of return upon the rate base the department adopted the "cost of capital" method. As to debt capital this means that the company is entitled to earnings which will pay its actual interest obligations as they accrue on existing debt capital and upon new debt capital required in the immediate future, and as to stock capital, according to a statement of the department in the early part of its decision, it means "the amount which the company would have to pay in order to 'hire' its equity capital under current conditions," subject to the important consequence, which the department apparently recognizes, that commonly a company cannot issue new stock which will have a preferred position over stock already outstanding, and that the rate must therefore be sufficient to pay the same dividends upon all the stock that are required to enable the company to sell new stock.

* * *

In following the department's theories, no particular difficulty is encountered in ascertaining the probable total cost of debt capital after the acquisition of $120,000,000 of required new capital. We understand the stipulation of the parties and the pleadings to mean that the total cost of debt capital would then be 3.45% * * *.

* * *

Cost of stock capital. Debt ratio.

It is in determining the cost of stock capital that serious difficulty arises. In this connection debt ratio becomes a matter of more importance and has greater effect upon the cost of obtaining new capital. The company contended that in order to restore a sound capital structure it was necessary that enough of the required new capital should be in the form of stock capital to reduce the debt ratio to not more than 35%. The department, while recognizing the necessity of reducing the present debt ratio, was of opinion that a reduction to 45% would be safe. The company further contends that debt ratio is a matter for the exclusive determination of the management of the company. As to this last contention, we agree of course that a public regulatory board cannot assume the management of the company and cannot under the guise of rate making interfere in matters of business detail with the judgment of its officers reached in good faith and within the limits of a reasonable discretion. * * * But we think that in this instance, in the circumstances now existing and especially in proceeding upon the "cost of capital" theory, the debt ratio is not a matter of that kind. This company is in effect seeking additional capital and higher rates in order to obtain and support such additional capital. Debt ratio substantially affects the manner and cost of obtaining new capital. It seems to us that to say the department could not even consider debt ratio would be to blind its eyes to one of the elements in the problem before it. From the standpoint of the company it might be better to have no debt capital at all. An honest board of directors might think so and at least from the standpoint of loyalty to the company's interests it would be difficult to say that they had abused their discretion. Yet the evidence shows that such a decision under present conditions might well double or even triple the cost of new capital and increase correspondingly the burden laid upon the public for obtaining it. Surely the department could give consideration to this matter. There was a great deal of evidence on the point which we cannot undertake to summarize here. It included opinion evidence and comparisons with the debt ratios in other companies, not all of which, it is true, were wholly comparable. It appeared, however, beyond question that under conditions existing at the time of the hearing before the department, owing partly to the tax laws and to the increasing aggregations of capital in the hands of insurance companies and savings institutions, which are restricted in their stock investments, debt capital was very plentiful and cheap, while stock capital was difficult to obtain and comparatively expensive. The department also took into consideration the increased Federal income taxes and the State franchise tax incident to new stock capital. These might well amount to millions of dollars annually and might seriously increase the cost to the public of stock capital compared to that of debt capital. We think that the department could properly consider these additional taxes as elements in the problem before it. City of Detroit v. Michigan Public Service Commission, 308 Mich. 706, 715–718, 14 N.W.2d 784. Upon all the evidence, and remembering that the burden of proof is upon the company (G.L. [Ter.Ed.] c. 25, § 5), we were not prepared to say that the refusal of the department to adjust its rates to a reduction in the debt ratio all at once under particularly adverse conditions from the high point of 62.1% to an ideal ratio of 35% or lower and the department's adoption of the figure of 45% were in themselves unlawful or confiscatory.*

In reaching this conclusion we have not overlooked the persuasive effect of G.L. (Ter.Ed.) c. 166, § 2, which in substance limits Massachu-

---

* [Ed.Note] In the recurring appearances of New England Telephone Company before the Supreme Judicial Court of Massachusetts on review of DPU rate orders, the Court approved the action of the Commission insofar as it based rates upon the 45/55 hypothetical ratio at a time when in fact the company's debt-equity ratio was closer to 36/64 (331 Mass. 604, 607, 617–619, 121 N.E.2d 896, 898, 904 (1954)), and it held unconstitutional rates based upon a 50/50 hypothetical ratio when the ratio in fact was close to 45/55 or 46/54 (360 Mass. 443, 275 N.E.2d 493 (1971)). The most that can be gleaned by way of rationale for the latter conclusion is that the DPU must defer to management's conception of appropriate capital structure "within a very substantial range," and a difference of less than 5 percentage points between management's choice and DPU standards is apparently within that range. Existing capital structures can apparently only be rejected by the DPU "if they so unreasonably and substantially vary from usual practice as to impose an unfair burden on the consumer." "In mere differences of opinion between the Department and the Company on the matter of capital structure, the opinions of the Department are not solely by reason thereof entitled to prevail." But see the Diamond State Telephone Co. v. Public Service Comm., 367 A.2d 644 (Del. Sup.Ct.1976).

setts telephone and telegraph companies to a 33⅓% debt ratio. But this statute does not apply to a New York corporation, and its weight as indicating sound policy is greatly weakened by the facts that it was enacted approximately a century ago when the disparity in availability and in cost between debt capital and stock capital could not have been anticipated, and that Massachusetts companies have generally been so few in number and small in size that there has been little occasion to amend the statute to meet changed conditions.

We are unable, however, to follow the finding of the department that a 6% return on stock capital is adequate. We find no evidence to support the proposition that under the prevailing conditions new stock capital could be had at all unless the rate of return thereon was substantially increased above this figure. Several expert witnesses of undoubted competency testified upon the point most elaborately and after careful study and research. They differed somewhat as to the rate of return on stock capital necessary to sell new stock. The lowest estimate was that of the witness called by the Attorney General in the interest of the public, who testified that 8% would be required at a 45% debt ratio. Estimates of experienced witnesses called by the company, some of them, so far as appears, wholly disinterested, were somewhat higher and were based upon a debt ratio of only 35%. All witnesses agreed that the price of the stock must go substantially above par in the market before an issue of new stock could be sold. At the time this testimony was given the stock was selling substantially below par. Even the witness called in behalf of the public testified in substance that in order to float an issue of new stock the intrinsic worth of the stock ought to approach $120 a share, and that increased earnings were necessary. Indeed, the department itself did not attempt to find in the face of this evidence that new stock capital could be obtained at a 6% return. Its finding was that such return was "fair, reasonable, adequate for the company's needs, and likely under normal and representative conditions to maintain the price of the common stock at or above its par of 100." This may or may not be true, but it does not reach to the real point. The question was not what return might maintain the stock at par in some hoped for representative period. The question was a much more immediate and practical one. Here is one of our greatest and most necessary public utilities. It cannot be permitted to fail in its service to the public. It was legally and morally bound to increase its service to meet an insistent public demand. It did so by borrowing $120,000,000 on demand notes from a source which fortunately was available to it. It must repay this money in the near future. It cannot expect to retain this borrowed money indefinitely as part of its capital structure. Its only means of repayment is by obtaining new capital. Concededly it must not increase its debt ratio. It must therefore sell a substantial amount of stock. On the evidence it can do this only if it is allowed a return on stock capital substantially larger than the 6% allowed by the department. On this part of the case we agree with the following two paragraphs taken from the opinion of the dissenting member of the department.

"The fact is, that the investors of New England have apparently lost confidence in these securities. This is indeed unfortunate, but it is true. The stock, which is listed in Boston and New York, is currently selling at about 82, and has not been above 90 in a year or more. The majority has adopted a so-called 'historical basis' of arriving at the cost of equity capital, losing sight of the fact that this company is going to be compelled to float new issues, not in the period of from 1938 to 1946, and certainly not in 1925, but now and on the present market. No witness anywhere in the record, including the Commonwealth's own witness Whiteside, testified that the company could acquire new equity capital at less than 8 per cent. * * *

"The company has been receiving revenues under an emergency rate increase since July, 1947, of about $5,000,000 in excess of its prior '1946' rates. We are now informed that this emergency increase is to be cancelled but that, on the other hand, an increase of almost exactly the same amount over the prior '1946' rates will restore the company's earnings to the point where its stock will go up some twenty points on the market. I feel this is a peculiar logic and one which is lacking in realism. Neither my own observations nor the testimony before us cause me to believe that any such result will follow."

It is repeatedly stated or implied in the decided cases, so far as we know without contradiction, that one of the constitutional rights of a regulated utility is the right to earn a sufficient return to maintain its credit and to obtain additional capital when needed to enable it to serve its public. Bluefield Water Works & Improvement Co. v. Public Service Commission of State of West Virginia, 262 U.S. 679, 693, 43 S.Ct. 675, 67 L.Ed. 1176; * * * Federal Power Commission v. Hope Natural Gas Co., 320 U.S. 591, 603, 64 S.Ct. 281, 88 L.Ed. 333; * * * It is sometimes added that earnings should be sufficient to enable something to be passed to surplus, * * * The department made no provision for surplus. If the "cost of capital" theory on which the department purported to proceed requires the cost of stock capital to be ascertained by reference to some supposedly normal period and in disregard of the stubborn facts existing in the period when the capital must be raised, instead of by reference to "the amount which the company would have to pay in order to 'hire' its equity capital under current conditions" as stated in the department's own definition of that theory, the theory must give way to the extent necessary to afford the utility its constitutional rights. Stated in a different way, if rates are to be fixed on a "cost of capital" theory so that a return of only 3.45% is allowed on debt capital, the theory must be consistently applied, and a sufficient return must be allowed on stock capital so that in fact necessary stock capital can be acquired. We do not see that the situation is materially altered by the hope or even expectation that the American company will take the full 68.9% to which it is entitled out of any new stock issue. It is not bound to take any and might not do so. Moreover, if it took its full share, the necessity for selling a large block to the general public would still exist. For the reasons above set forth, we are forced to conclude that the allowance of only a 6% return on stock capital, where less than 3½% has been allowed on debt capital, and the resulting overall return on both kinds of capital is only 4.887%, if surplus is not entitled to earnings, and 4.768% if surplus is entitled to earnings, was confiscatory and unlawful. It seems proper to add that if we turn away from the method and consider only the result reached, an examination of the decisions of regulatory boards and of courts convinces us that an overall return of approximately 4.8% on the rate base is considerably below that which is reasonably expected and is generally being allowed on the capital of public utilities used and useful in the public service.

Although it is beyond our power to fix rates and we certainly have no desire to attempt that task, yet it is our duty to draw to the best of our ability the line where confiscation begins, and in the circumstances of this case, in order to make our decision as useful as possible and not merely the starting point of a series of attempts to ascertain by the method of trial and error just what figure this court would allow to stand, it seems that we should state where in our judgment on the evidence before us that line must be drawn. The Supreme Court of the United States did this in United Railways & Electric Co. of Baltimore v. West, 280 U.S. 234, 252, 50 S.Ct. 123, 74 L.Ed. 390. As previously stated, there is no dispute as to the cost of debt capital. But on all the evidence, and we have nothing else to go by, it is our opinion that a return of nothing less than 8.5% will suffice to attract new stock capital at a debt ratio of 45% and to enable the company to restore its credit and properly to capitalize its new construction. This is somewhat less than the company asserted and introduced evidence to prove that it must have and is only one half of one per cent more than the expert witness called by the Attorney General testified to be necessary. It should produce an overall composite net return on all capital devoted to the public service (disregarding for the moment surplus reinvested in the business) of 6.23%, as appears below:

45% debt capital × 3.45% net return	=	1.55%	net return on whole capital
55% stock capital × 8.5% net return	=	<u>4.68%</u>	net return on whole capital
Composite net return on total of both kinds of capital		6.23%	

In our opinion therefore a net return of less than 8.5% on stock capital or less than 6.23% on the sum of both kinds of capital is below the level where confiscation begins. It does not follow that a considerably higher return might not fall within the range of reason and might not have been allowed by the department, but our duty is performed by marking the line of confiscation.

Return on reinvested surplus.

But we are of opinion that the company is entitled to a fair return on its surplus which it has reinvested in its business and thus devoted to the public service. This money belongs to the company and not to its customers. The money could have been paid out in dividends to the stockholders. Instead, it has been put into the plant for the benefit of the public, thus obviating the necessity of acquiring capital in some

other manner upon which the company would have been entitled to a fair return. We are not impressed by the argument that this surplus must have been wrongfully exacted from past customers through excessively high rates and so should now be devoted to the public service without compensation. Apart from the obvious impossibility of restoring the money to a past generation of customers, there is not a scintilla of evidence that the money was wrongfully exacted in the first place. As hereinbefore stated good authority supports the proposition that a public utility has a constitutional right to a sufficient return to enable it to accumulate a reasonable surplus. There is no reason to doubt that the rates of the company in past years have been fair and in accordance with the filed schedules which it was obliged to observe and which could have been reduced by the department or its predecessor commission if they were excessive. The allowance of a fair return on reinvested surplus is not the same as a stock dividend, which is forbidden to Massachusetts telephone companies by G.L. (Ter.Ed.) c. 166, §§ 9, 10.
* * *

This brings us at once to the question as to what rate of return the company is entitled to receive on reinvested surplus, which is neither debt capital nor stock capital, but has been derived from both kinds of capital. In a case tried, as this case has been, on the theory of "cost of capital" it seems to us that the line of confiscation in the return on reinvested surplus is the same as that established for the composite return on debt and stock capital, to wit, 6.23%, and that a lower rate of return would be confiscatory, and we so hold.

* * *

NOTE: COST OF CAPITAL AND UTILITY RATE–MAKING

As generally conceived, public utility rate control is designed to prevent utility investors from reaping a return based on full exploitation of the utility's monopoly power, and to restrict those investors to a fair return; the fair return is measured by the rate the utility must pay to attract its investors rather than the juicy percentage it could, if unregulated, obtain for them. Hence, "cost of capital" is regarded as appropriately marking "fair return".

Such a concept of "cost of capital" is not, of course, that of the capital budgeter. The latter, as to a company which comes under his eye, asks "What is this company's actual cost of capital?" The foundation of his answer is the company's *actual* earnings stream, whether that stream is derived from a market characterized by competition, monopoly or pillage. The regulator, on the other hand, sets out prepared to change the enterprise earnings. His "cost of capital" question is: "What would it cost this enterprise to raise money if competition kept it from gouging the public?" The amount thus determined is added to the utility's regular costs to set its permissible level of earnings. More simply, the capital-budgeter's cost of capital is earnings-determined; the regulator's is an earnings determinant.

The regulator accordingly is seeking a normative "cost of capital" *rate* which, once determined, he will apply against the investment in the enterprise to determine permissible dollars of return.[o] In seeking that rate of return, the regulator, under the conventions and law of the subject, has two data sources, each unsatisfactory. The terminology of the subject, not to mention the concepts, is confused and confusing, but the two rate-of-return theories may be reasonably identified as the "comparable risk" theory and the "cost of capital" theory. Each depends on "cost of capital"; the first on that of companies comparable to the regulated utility; the second on that of the company itself.

Under the "comparable risk" theory the regulator derives his normative rate of return from the existing "cost of capital" rates of comparable companies (cf. Universal City Studios case, p. 698 infra). "There is general agreement that a 'fair return' should approximate the going rate for non-regulated securities exposed to comparable risks. But since there are few if any such securities, regulatory commissions must either pass the buck (e.g., by one state allowing its utilities the average rate prevailing in all other states) or make arbitrary choice (e.g., by picking any rate greater than that on long-term government bonds and less than that for risky manufacturing stocks)". Ross, Comments on the Earnings—Price Note, 21 Stanford Law Review 644 (1969).

The other theory, that of internal "cost of capital", proceeds somewhat as follows: Suppose a utility whose $1 million of capital, raised by a common stock issue, is employed under pricing policies that generate a full and steady monopoly net earnings level of $200,000. The market value on its common having risen to $2 million, a discount rate of 10% seems to be what the market is applying. It is then thought proper, in reviewing the charges the utility may lawfully make to consumers, once it comes under regulation, to use 10% as a cost-of-capital rate, but to apply that rate to the investment of $1,000,000 (rather than the market value of $2 million) so as to give the utility a "fair" rather than monopoly return.

There are serious difficulties with using a cost of capital thus derived in order to achieve the ends of utility regulation (putting aside the difficulty of deriving the rate in the first place—see p. 71 supra):

(a) The risk attributed by the market to the monopoly earnings is apt to be higher (and, therefore, the price-earnings ratio lower) than that which the market would apply to the lower regulated level.

(b) The 10% figure would have to be adjusted to the extent that the pre-proceeding share values were influenced by a perception of the likelihood and consequence of regulation.

(c) The utility proceeding does not concern itself with the actual company whose shares are traded on the market but rather with a

o. Obviously the "investment" involved in such a formula is not the "value" of the investors' stake in the enterprise, since "value" is earnings-determined; "invest-ment," as here employed, refers to some way or another of measuring the investors' input.

fictitious entity consisting of that part of the utility's capital which is employed in operations within the territorial and subject matter jurisdiction of the regulator (e.g., Western Electric capital and earnings might be regarded as irrelevant to an AT & T rate case). The 10% rate would have to be varied to the extent that the excluded and included portions of the enterprise were not homogeneous as to risk.

These special aspects of an internal "cost of capital" relevant to utility regulation are easier to state than to solve. For a proposal to handle the circularity problem ((b) above), see Note, An Earnings–Price Approach to Fair Rate of Return in Regulated Industries, 20 Stanford L.Rev. 287 (1968); Robicheck, Regulation and Modern Finance Theory, 33 J.Finance 693 (1978). Even if the figure can be appropriately derived, it may still be rejected as inconsistent with the regulatory goals. It is, for example, common in utility regulation to give considerable weight to historical costs, and to ignore (or stress) particular sorts of appreciation or depreciation which are irrelevant (or central) to the capital budgeter's "cost of capital". It is important to note that the problems indicated above apply not only to the initial regulatory proceeding for the utility, but also to those rate re-setting proceedings in which it is sought to determine whether a previously approved rate level has become inappropriate because of changes in the utility's buying and selling markets.

Finally, in the New England Tel. & Tel. Co. case, a variant of the internal "cost of capital" theory is employed by the Massachusetts court when it indicates that an appropriate objective of rate control is to maintain the utility's common (if properly leveraged) at or above par. Putting aside problems of inflation, regulation to keep a utility's stock down to par seems consistent with the basic goals of utility control. But keeping the stock up to par is perhaps dubious considering that even a monopoly can overbuild or experience a drastic market shrinkage. Ought the monopoly be guaranteed a return, or merely held to a fair one?

Part IV: DIVIDENDS AND RETAINED EARNINGS
INTRODUCTION

How much should a corporation pay out to its shareholders in annual cash dividends, and how much should it retain for reinvestment? Are there "maximizing rules" that ought to be observed by company management in setting the corporation's dividend rate? Does the market respond favorably to, and will it pay a premium for, relatively high dividend payment rates and a record of dividend stability, or are low dividends and a higher rate of reinvestment preferred by investors? In addition, what form should corporate distributions take? Straight cash dividends are the most usual event, but stock dividends and stock repurchases are also common. What are the relative merits of these distribution procedures, and which, if any, is to be preferred?

Like the capital structure question, the relationship of dividend policy to share valuation has been warmly debated by financial theorists and remains a "puzzle" to some extent.[a] Essentially, the issue is whether dividend policy is an active variable which affirmatively affects share prices, or simply a means of distributing funds for which management can find no competitive employment. If the former, identification of an optimal payout rate should be a matter of urgent concern to financial managers. If the latter, dividends may be treated as a "mere detail" to be determined by the availability of competitive investment projects which otherwise preempt the use of corporate funds.

Like the capital structure question, the dividend policy question includes an agency cost problem. Management has incentives to reinvest corporate cash flows suboptimally, thereby setting dividends too low from the shareholders' point of view. If optimal dividend policy is subject to debate even in the case of the firm that makes only competitive investments, the problem of policing the managers inclined to reinvest profits in uncompetitive projects becomes much more difficult.

Before proceeding to the range of views on dividend policy, some background points need to be established. Specifically, we return to the role of dividends in stock valuation.

---

a. See Black, The Dividend Puzzle, 2 J. of Portfolio Management 5 (1976); "The nearly universal policy of paying substantial dividends is the primary puzzle in the economics of corporate finance," Feldstein and Green, Why Do Companies Pay Dividends?, 73 Amer.Econ.Rev. 17 (1983).

SECTION A.   DIVIDENDS AND DIVIDEND POLICY

1.   A THEORY OF STOCK VALUATION

(a) Dividend Capitalization Model

What do investors "really" capitalize when they buy shares—dividends or earnings?   Most financial theorists find it convenient to view the matter, as in Lewellen, Cost of Capital (1969) 88–93, in the following terms:

"The answer here is that investors buy the firm's dividends, not its earnings.   The intuitive rationale is quite straightforward: dividends constitute the only cash flows produced by the firm for its shareholders and therefore represent the one observable return they receive on their investment.   They put up a sum of money to purchase a share of stock—i.e., they forego present consumption—in order to lay claim to a series of subsequent payments that will permit future consumption at a higher level.   This trade-off, as perceived by the multitude of individuals who populate the capital markets, is in fact the essence of the community's collective investment decision.   Such individuals cannot spend a firm's retained earnings on goods and services; they can spend only the dividends—the *cash* payments—they receive.   Retained earnings are not necessarily irrelevant, but they are relevant only insofar as they generate higher *future* dividends.   Unless some incremental cash flow eventually occurs, a corporation's retentions have absolutely no value to its stockholders.

"As an illustration of this argument, take the case of a firm which has been experiencing annual earnings over a period of years ranging from, say, $4 to $8 per share depending on the general level of economic activity.   When the economy is booming, the firm reports earnings near the upper end of that spectrum; in recessions, the lower extreme usually occurs.   Despite these fluctuations, however, the firm has paid exactly $3 a share in dividends for the last decade or more and shows no signs of increasing either its dividends or its reported earnings in the foreseeable future.   As an investor, am I likely to consider myself purchasing an expected annual income stream of $6—which we shall assume is the figure that earnings average out to over the years—or one of $3?   The latter seems the clear choice.   Apparently, the only benefit I obtain from the retained earnings is the reliability of my dividend.   The firm is on a treadmill, reinvesting at just about the rate which keeps its real earning power constant.   It uses what are called "earnings" on its income statement to maintain its plant and equipment, pay its bills to suppliers, and meet its labor costs in such a way that it can afford to part with $3 annually to its stockholders without losing ground.   As far as they are concerned, the $3 is all they can ever expect to receive—despite the fact that the firm's balance sheet indicates it is growing.

"Statements of this sort must, of course, be made a little more carefully when we recognize that investors do not always acquire stock with the intention of holding it indefinitely.   Can the same conclusion be drawn for a securities market in which the participants anticipate capital gains as well as dividends? It can if we attribute the capital gains themselves to the expectation of higher subsequent dividends on the part of the individuals to whom today's shareholders hope eventually to sell their shares. Fortunately, that interpretation does appear legitimate.

"Consider the cash income prospects of an individual who purchases a share of stock with the intention of holding it for n years and then reselling it. In return for his immediate outlay of funds, he anticipates a series of annual dividend payments terminating in the resale of the share involved at (hopefully) an increased price. We may therefore tabulate his cash flow projections as follows:

Year	Expected Receipt
1	d_1
2	d_2
.	.
.	.
.	.
n	$d_n + P_n$

where d_1 denotes the per-share dividend payment predicted for year i and P_n the stock's expected per-share market price at the end of year n. Our investor's decision to acquire this security implies that, in his eyes, the present value of the indicated sequence of cash inflows is equal to or greater than its current market price, P_0. * * *

"The question, then, is: On what grounds can our man reasonably hope for this—or any other—set of receipts? Certainly, he will use the firm's past dividend record to predict the relevant d_1 figures, but what about P_n? How will he attempt to arrive at an estimate of the stock's potential resale value? The suggestion here is that, if he is a rational man interested in profit opportunities, he will impute the same sort of attitude to other investors. He will assume that anyone who may be interested in buying his stock when he wants to sell it will use a valuation model similar to his own in deciding what the share is worth. Thus, the price P_n he foresees can be interpreted as his estimate of the present value he expects the *next* purchaser to place on the stock. * * *

" * * * He must—if only implicitly—predict the dividends and the capital gain his successor can expect if he is to come to a meaningful conclusion about the possible size of his own capital gain.

"But what of P_{n+m}? We cannot really say much about P_n unless we consider the price the second investor in the chain is likely to predict for *his* resale transaction. What will the third man be apt to pay? Well, if we assume that man number 2 performs something akin to a present value analysis, the same should be true of man number 3. * * *

"It should not be necessary to carry the game further to make the intended point. If we keep repeating this process—which in principle we should do in order to predict the successive P_i's—we eventually reach a situation in which the formula for *PV* is an infinite stream of (presumably growing) discounted dividend payments and the last relevant resale price is indefinitely far in the future.   Indeed, once we get past 25 or 30 years of inflows in such an analysis, the subsequent dividends as well as that ultimate price can be ignored because, for any meaningful discount rate *K*, they add virtually nothing to our estimate of *PV*.   As a result, we end up with an expression for the worth of a share of stock in a world where investors actively seek capital gains, which is paradoxically nothing more than the present value of the firm's per-share dividend payments during the foreseeable future.   It is incontrovertible that the only thing investors receive in return for purchasing securities is a series of dividend payments plus a terminal capital gain.   All we need accept is this almost tautological view of the securities market and the conclusion above follows automatically.   Investors in fact 'buy' dividends.   Their capital gains are merely the product of anticipated higher future dividends."

———

For the reasons just expressed, financial theorists generally employ a *dividend capitalization model* of share valuation.   The model assumes that the present value of a share of stock is equal to the value of all future dividend payments, capitalized at a rate reflecting the market's view of the risks associated with the firm's expected income stream.   If we take a highly simplified situation in which the firm's earnings remain constant over time and are fully distributed each year as dividends (i.e., there is no reinvestment), the market value of the shares can be determined by the usual formula for perpetual annuities:

$$Vo = \frac{Do}{1+k} + \frac{Do}{(1+k)^2} + \frac{Do}{(1+k)^3} + \ldots = \frac{D}{k}$$

where Vo is the market value of a share, Do is the expected constant dividend, and k is the market capitalization rate.   If the expected dividend is $2 a year in perpetuity and the market capitalization rate is 8%, the value of each share is $25 $\left(\frac{\$2}{.08} \right)$.

Suppose, however, that the firm decides to retain a portion of its earnings each year.   As the amounts retained are invested in additional income-producing assets, stockholders can expect a growing, rather than a constant, stream of future dividends.   While the dividend capitalization formula remains applicable in concept, the annual growth factor must also be taken into account.   If we represent the ratio of retained earnings to total earnings by the symbol b and the rate of return on such reinvested earnings by the symbol r, the firm's dividends (as well as its earnings and retentions) will grow continuously at a rate of $g = br$.   Under these circumstances the annuity formula must be altered to reflect the fact that the stream of dividend payments is expanding at the annual rate of g:

$$Vo = \frac{Do}{1+k} + \frac{Do\,(1+g)}{(1+k)^2} + \frac{Do\,(1+g)^2}{(1+k)^3} + \cdots$$

As the dividend payments are not constant, the above formula must take each dividend into account separately, and the resulting statement is long and awkward. In consequence, financial writers customarily use the following substitute formula, which is equivalent in mathematical terms but considerably more manageable:

$$Vo = \frac{Do}{k-g} = \frac{Do}{k-br}$$

This formula simply says that market value is equal to the firm's current dividend capitalized at a rate k - g. To illustrate, assume the firm's current earnings are $5 per share; that it plans to retain 60% of its earnings this year and every year; that the expected return on its investments is 16.67%; and that the market capitalization rate is 12%. The current dividend is thus $2 (i.e., .40 × $5), and the expected growth rate is 10% (i.e., .60 × .1667). The value of the firm's shares is:

$$\frac{\$2}{.12 - .10} = \frac{\$2}{.02} = \$100$$

Incidentally, the theoretical literature on this subject always assumes that the growth rate g is smaller than the discount rate k. Why is this assumption necessary, and why is it evidently valid?

(b) The Retention Ratio

A more substantial question can now be considered. How much of its annual earnings *should* the firm retain for reinvestment? Most firms do retain and reinvest some portion of their annual earnings, in many instances the greater portion. The result, as stated, is that dividends can be expected to grow instead of staying constant. While this sounds all to the good, it must be remembered that when funds are retained for reinvestment the *current* dividend is necessarily reduced by the amount held back. Stockholders must give up some dividend income today for the sake of larger dividends in the future; they cannot have it both ways. The question is how to determine the *retention rate* that maximizes shareholder wealth. Which of all the possible dividend streams that might be generated—smaller today but larger later, *much* smaller today but *much* larger later, etc.—has the greatest present value to the company's shareholders?

For the moment we will defer discussion of the possibility of raising money by issuing new securities and assume that retained earnings represent the company's only source of additional funds. The choice between internal and external financing is discussed infra, p. 553.

A solution to the retention rate problem can be found in the relationship between the internal rate of return obtainable from the firm's investment projects and the rate at which the firm's dividends are capitalized by investors in the market. Briefly stated, retention of earnings is justified if the proposed investment offers a yield in excess of the dividend capitalization rate—if, in the customary notation, r (internal rate of return) exceeds k (dividend capitalization rate). Under these circumstances, the value of the company's shares is maximized by retaining 100% of earnings and reducing the current dividend to zero since all funds retained can be reinvested at better than the market rate of return. This relationship between r and k *($r > k$)* presumably prevails in the case of "true" growth companies—IBM in the 1960s, a biotechnology firm today. As a result, shares of such companies often sell at very high multiples of current earnings, reflecting the expectation of super-normal profits. See supra, p. 74.

In contrast, if $r < k$, share price is maximized when the retention rate is zero and all earnings are distributed as dividends. A positive rate of retention under these conditions would merely reduce the value of the company's stock; if the company cannot invest funds at a rate of k or better, it should not be investing internally.

The same logic governs the answer to the retention question if $r = k$. If the firm's investment opportunities promise a rate of return exactly equal to the market capitalization rate, market price per share should be insensitive to the retention ratio. The argument is that funds distributed as dividends can be invested by the stockholders at a rate (k) equal to the firm's internal rate of return, either by purchasing additional shares of the firm itself or by acquiring shares of comparable firms. In this third situation, reinvestment brings about an expansion in assets, earnings and dividends, but the firm has no investment opportunities which promise yields above the normal rate of return. Accordingly, the stockholders gain (or lose) nothing through changes in the firm's retention policy; the market price of their stock remains the same at any retention rate, at least in theory.

All this is nothing more than a restatement of the general rule which governs (or ought to govern) management's capital budgeting decisions. As indicated at pp. 40–42, supra, the standard prescription is that all investment opportunities should be accepted which have a positive net present value, i.e., which promise a rate of return in excess of the company's cost of capital. Thus, the basic comparison is again between r and k.

With these principles in mind, we can turn our attention to the current debate over dividend policy. Let us drop the assumption that the company is restricted to retained earnings as a source of funds and assume that it is free to finance investment projects from external as well as internal sources. Which course is best from the standpoint of the shareholders' wealth position? Should the company dedicate itself to maintaining its current dividend rate and finance its investments by issuing new securities? Or should it simply cut back on current dividends and finance investments out of retained earnings? In terms of the formulas above, which procedure has the effect of minimizing k?

2. THE ROLE OF DIVIDEND POLICY

Economists have been debating dividend policy for more than three decades. Under the traditional point of view, investors prefer a stable pattern of dividends, and dividend increases in some circumstances can cause firm value to increase. Just as the Modigliani–Miller irrelevance proposition challenged traditional views on capital structure, so it challenged this traditional view of dividend policy. Under the irrelevance proposition, dividend policy makes no difference to firm value. The parallel to the capital structure debate continued, and the irrelevance proposition itself came to be questioned in the process of being applied in a real world with taxes and market imperfections. This process gave rise to third point of view. Under this view, low dividends maximize firm value. Since taxes are crucial in this discussion, the Tax Reform Act of 1986 caused the relative strengths of the three positions to change. See Brealey and Myers, Principles of Corporate Finance 376–377 (4th ed. 1991).

(A) THE TRADITIONAL VIEW
GRAHAM, DODD AND COTTLE, SECURITY ANALYSIS
(4th Ed.1962), 515–518.

Dividends and the Multiplier. The fact that the influence of dividends on the price of some common stocks may have been changing in recent years was pointed out * * *. We doubt that anyone at present has sufficient insight into these changes to determine with finality whether they will result in the establishment of a new, long-term pattern of capitalization rates. However, in this interim period of uncertainty—and probably of transition—the analyst cannot suspend his activities. He must cope with this problem as best he can. [W]e suggested one possible approach, which is to classify common stocks into three broad groups for valuation purposes. The next step at this point is to review these groups in more detail and set forth our further views as to the possible treatment of dividends in the capitalization rate for the shares of each group.

It will be recalled that the three general categories were termed the "growth-stock," "below-average," and "middle" groups. Since the nature of the middle group is less distinct than the others, it may be best indicated by defining the two groups which set its limits. Therefore we shall first describe as clearly as possible the determinants of the growth-stock and below-average groups. In this manner the broad nature of the middle group will be automatically designated.

* * * [T]he * * *, the growth-stock group would consist of those issues whose per-share earnings have increased at an average annual rate of at least 7.2 percent; i.e., earnings double in ten years. In addition, these stocks should have a demonstrated ability to earn an attractive return on their book value and to maintain this return on a rapidly expanding capital base. It is to be expected that ordinarily the rate of return on capital will be well above that for, say, Standard & Poor's 425 industrial stocks.[2]

The below-average group consists of those stocks which have (*a*) sold for some recent period of time, such as the average of the last five years, at less than approximately 1½ times their book value and (*b*) earned a return on book value for the same period below that for, say, Standard & Poor's 425 industrial stocks.

We hold no strong brief for the employment of a five-year test period in measuring the market-to-book ratio and the rate of return on the common-stock equity. If the analyst considers a longer or a shorter period desirable he is privileged to use it, but we think it should not be less than three years.

As determined by the foregoing definitions, the "middle" group will thus consist of those shares with the following characteristics: First, the growth rate in per-share earnings will have been less than 7.2 percent per annum—in the last decade quite probably closer to 4 percent. Second, the average return on the common-stock equity for, say, the last three years will have been above that for Standard & Poor's 425 industrial shares.[3] Third, the market-price-to-book-value ratio will have been above 1½ times but probably below 2½ times.

Having divided industrial common stocks into three broad groups, we must next arrive at some general conclusions as to the role of dividends in the valuation process of each group. The reader must allow for the difficulty of the problem here presented and be prepared to exercise caution and judgment in applying the following suggested techniques:

First, in valuing *growth shares* the dividends can be for all practical purposes ignored and sole reliance placed on expected earnings.

Second, in valuing below-average shares, dividends are of paramount importance and should have the traditional weighting along the lines suggested in our 1951 edition and repeated later in this chapter.

---

2. Out of 300 industrial issues reviewed by us, those shares which—judged in terms of increase in average per-share earnings 1955–1959 over 1950–1954—had a growth rate of 7.2 percent or more in the decade of the 1950's earned a 1955–1959 average return on their common-stock equity of 15.6 percent. This compares with 12.8 percent for Standard & Poor's 425 industrials. The market-value-to-book-value ratio over the 1955–1959 period for these "growth" shares averaged 244 percent.

3. The rate of return earned on the common-stock equity may or may not be below that for the growth shares. It is possible that the principal distinguishing feature of a growth share is that its book value is increasing much more rapidly than that of the middle-group share and not necessarily that the return is substantially higher.

Third, in valuing shares in the middle group, the role of dividends is still dominant, but the weighting will be less than in the case of the below-average shares. Since the shares in this group cover the broad gamut between the *below-average and the growth-stock* groups, we doubt that there is some formula or neatly arranged schedule that can be developed for treating the payout rate. Thus the analyst will need to take a compromise position in this regard, such as adopting something less than the suggested 4–to–1 weighting ratio for below-average stocks but something more than the proposed 1–to–1 weighting for growth stocks. It may also involve giving somewhat less consideration to changes in the payout rate as it fluctuates moderately about the typical norm of approximately two-thirds. Thus a change in the payout rate between, say, roughly one-half and three-fourths might modify only slightly the price-earnings ratio. We believe that the more important consideration in valuing these shares lies in determining (*a*) whether a significant change in dividend policy is taking place and (*b*) if so, whether it may have a substantial impact on *expectable* dividends. For example, does an increase in the payout rate herald a slowing down in the growth rate for the company? Contrariwise, does a decrease in the payout rate indicate an attempt to accelerate the growth of the company by husbanding funds for a diversification or acquisition program?

Below-average Shares. As proposed in Chapter 35, we suggest for industrial common stocks in the below-average category and for railroad shares that dividends be given a specific weighting in relation to earnings in the valuation process. As it happens, this can be done in a very simple manner, and in one which will enable us to use the same sort of *earnings multiplier* that is customarily employed. Our suggested formula—excluding possible adjustment for asset values—is as follows:

Value = earnings multiplier $\times$

$\qquad$ (expected dividend + one-third expected earnings)

or

$$V = M(D + \tfrac{1}{3}E)$$

In this formula the multiplier taken is that which would be applied to the earnings alone if the expected dividend is at a "normal" payout rate of two-thirds of earnings. In that case the formula reduces to the conventional one

$$V = M(\tfrac{2}{3}E + \tfrac{1}{3}E) = M \times E$$

On the other hand, if the payout is more than two-thirds, the value will exceed $M \times E$; and conversely if the payout is below two-thirds.

If all the earnings are distributed, the value becomes

$$V = \tfrac{4}{3}M \times E$$

If nothing is paid out, it becomes

$$V = \tfrac{1}{3}M \times E$$

Examples: Assume Companies *A, B, C, D,* and *E* all have expected average earnings of $6 per share and a "normal" multiplier of 12. The expected average dividends, however, are respectively $4, $5, $2, $6, and zero—the latter a highly improbable assumption. Substituting 12 for *M,* 6 for *E,* and the various dividends for *D,* the formula will produce the following valuations for the five companies:

$$\text{Company } A\text{:} \quad V = 12 \times 4 + 12 \times 2 = 72$$
$$\text{Company } B\text{:} \quad V = 12 \times 5 + 12 \times 2 = 84$$
$$\text{Company } C\text{:} \quad V = 12 \times 2 + 12 \times 2 = 48$$
$$\text{Company } D\text{:} \quad V = 12 \times 6 + 12 \times 2 = 96$$
$$\text{Company } E\text{:} \quad V = 12 \times 0 + 12 \times 2 = 24$$

Our formula involves the assumption that a dollar paid out in dividends has four times the weight in the valuation process as the same dollar retained in the business. (This is demonstrated by the ratio of the values derived in the two extreme cases of 100 percent and zero payouts, as in Companies *D* and *E* above.) While this may appear to exaggerate the importance attaching to the payout policy, the various tests that we and others have made of market-price behavior *in this context* give considerable support to that conclusion when applied to below-average companies.

(B) DIVIDENDS AS A FINANCING DECISION

The last selection articulates the traditional view of security analysts that share values react favorably to a generous and stable dividend policy and unfavorably to the converse, except possibly when a particular company's growth prospects are outstanding. The assumption (which is purportedly based on market experience) is that investors prefer a certain pattern of dividend payments (generous, stable, etc.), and that a departure from the preferred pattern will result in a nonoptimal market price for the company's shares.

This view of the effect of dividend policy is by no means universal. Some financial theorists—Modigliani and Miller (M–M) among them [b]— assert that, *once the investment decision of the firm is made known to investors,* the dividend-payout ratio is irrelevant in the valuation process. The value of the firm, they argue, depends solely upon the earning power of its assets. This value is unaffected by how the firm finances its activities, whether by retaining earnings (i.e., withholding dividends) or by selling new securities (i.e., paying dividends, but issuing stock or bonds to obtain funds needed for investment). The net wealth of the company's shareholders, who are (or ought to be) indifferent between a dollar of dividend income and a dollar of capital gain, is said to be the same under either financing procedure. Far from being

b. Miller and Modigliani, Dividend Pol-   34 J. of Bus. 411 (1961).
icy, Growth and the Valuation of Shares,

the subject of an independent policy decision, therefore, dividends (in this view) should simply be a means of disposing of the firm's "residual" cash assets—funds left over after all of the firm's financing needs have been met.

To illustrate the "irrelevance-of-dividends" thesis, assume X Corporation has outstanding 100,000 shares of common stock and no long-term debt; that it earns $1,000,000 annually, or $10 per share, all of which it normally pays out in dividends; and that its stock normally sells at $100, reflecting a 10% capitalization rate. Assume further that management identifies a new investment opportunity (involving the same degree of risk as present operations) which will require an immediate outlay of $1,000,000 and is expected to generate earnings of $200,000 annually in perpetuity. If the investment is made, X's earnings are expected to increase to $1,200,000. As the company has no further investment plans, all earnings from the expanded operation will be distributed as dividends. What financing procedure should X adopt consistent with the goal of maximizing shareholder wealth? Three possibilities exist:

(a) *Retained earnings.* X could distribute no dividends to its shareholders this year and use its current earnings of $1,000,000 to finance the new investment. In that event, the expected dividends for all future years will be $1,200,000 or $12 per share. Capitalizing these future dividends at a 10% rate, the present value of a share of X will be $120.

(b) *New stock issue.* X could pay a dividend of $1,000,000 to its shareholders and finance the new investment by selling $1,000,000 of additional common stock. Present shareholders of X would receive a current cash dividend of $10 per share. Their wealth would consist of the $10 dividend plus the value of the X stock *after* the proposed stock issue and the new investment. The value of X stock, in turn, will depend on the number of additional shares that must be sold in order to raise $1,000,000. If n = the number of shares to be sold and P = the price per share, then

$$n \times P = \$1,000,000.$$

We know that the issue price of the new X shares will be 10 times the expected dividend per share (given a capitalization rate of 10%). Hence:

$$P = 10 \times \$1,200,000/100,000 + n.$$

The expected dividends still rise to $1,200,000 to reflect the new investment, but the number of shares outstanding is increased by n to reflect the new stock issue.

When these equations are solved for n and for P (by substituting the right-hand side of the second equation into the first), it turns out that n = 9090.9 and P = $110. Thus, X can finance the new investment by selling 9090.9 shares for $110 per share. Future dividends will be $1,200,000/109,090.9, or $11 per share. At the 10% capitalization rate, the value of X stock will be $110 per share. Accordingly, for each

X share that they now own, present shareholders will have a $10 cash dividend plus $110 in share value, or total wealth of $120 per share, just as above.

(c) *Bond issue.* *X* could pay a dividend of $1,000,000 to its shareholders and finance the new investment by issuing $1,000,000 of bonds. At 5% interest, after the interest charge of $50,000 *X*'s earnings (and dividends) would be $1,150,000, or $11.50 per share. If the market continues to capitalize *X*'s dividends at a rate of 10%, then the wealth of present shareholders would include the $10 current dividend and *X* stock with a value of $115 per share, for a total of $125, making this financing procedure better than either of the others. On the other hand, M–M (see supra p. 460) argue that the dividend capitalization rate must rise (owing to the greater risk resulting from the issuance of bonds) to offset exactly the increase in expected dividends, so that share value would be the same as with an all-equity capital structure, i.e., $110 per share. In the latter event, the present shareholders of *X* would have total wealth per share of $120, just as in the first two alternatives.

If the total wealth figure is the same with all three financing procedures, shareholders will be indifferent to the company's dividend policy and will be just as happy whether the company finances the new investment out of retained earnings or by issuing new securities. Thus, suppose *X* decides to obtain the needed funds by withholding current dividends. A shareholder who wants cash income to meet consumption needs can either sell some stock or borrow from his broker using his securities as collateral. Shareholders who prefer to reinvest their dividends will have had that done for them by the corporation. On the other hand, suppose *X* elects to pay the current dividend, and then recoups those funds by issuing new securities. Again, a shareholder who prefers consumption will have received a cash payment and can use it for that purpose, while shareholders who prefer to save can reinvest their dividends by buying more *X* securities or securities of a comparable company. Ignoring brokerage costs, and assuming (in accordance with M–M's earlier argument) that corporate leverage has no advantage, it appears that the manner in which *X*'s earnings stream is split between dividends and retentions does not affect the value of the firm even when investor preferences for saving or consumption are taken into account.

What happens to this analysis when federal income taxes are introduced? As has been seen, pp. 463–467, supra, the tax law differentiates between interest payments and dividends. Interest is deductible, dividends are not. Quite obviously, this means that a corporation that finances its investments by issuing bonds will have less tax to pay and will have a larger after-tax income than a corporation that raises capital by issuing stock. Since its after-tax income will be larger, a levered (interest-paying) corporation is certain to be worth more than an unlevered (dividend-paying) corporation, everything else being equal, even if one accepts in full the M–M position that leverage of itself makes no difference to the value of the firm.

But this does not quite end the tax story. If debt is better than stock because of the interest deduction, why don't all firms maintain as high a debt/equity ratio as possible? Why don't they all add debt to their capital structure up to the point where there is a positive probability of bankruptcy? The fact, of course, is that they do not. Indeed, it is a common observation that most firms prefer to draw on *retained earnings* to finance the replacement or expansion of their assets and that the issuance of long-term debt is only the second choice. Thus, external financing, even through debt, is usually resorted to only when internally generated cash-flows are insufficient to cover investment requirements. Why should this be so?

Once again, the tax law—at least as it stood prior to the 1986 Act and other recent changes—provides a clue. As the reader knows, the Internal Revenue Code imposes a shareholder-level tax on corporate dividends at the regular progressive personal rates. Accordingly, if the firm's individual stockholders paid tax on dividends at a higher rate than the corporate rate, then the saving that resulted from the corporate interest deduction would be outweighed by the dividend tax. In that event, as the following illustration shows, retained earnings rather than debt would represent the preferred source of financing.

Assume a firm earned $15 a share this year and now wants to invest in a new project that will cost precisely $15. To finance the project entirely through debt the firm would first distribute the $15 of earnings as a dividend and then "recapture" the amount distributed by issuing a $15 bond. While interest on the bond will be deductible, the saving in corporate tax—which will accrue annually and (we may assume) in perpetuity—has to be compared with the tax payable by the shareholders on the current dividend. Suppose the dividend tax would be at a 60% rate, or $9. If the bond coupon is 8%, or $1.20, the corporate tax (assume it is 50%) saving is 60¢ a year in perpetuity. When this saving is capitalized at the same 8% rate at which the bond interest is capitalized, its present value is $7.50 (60¢ × 12.5), which is $1.50 less than the tax paid on the dividend. It follows that where the shareholders of a corporation are taxable at a higher rate than the corporation itself, they are likely to be better off if the corporation holds back dividends and finances out of retained earnings than if it distributes the dividend and finances by issuing debt. While the retained earnings will ultimately be taxed when the shares are sold (prior to 1987 at the much lower rate applicable to capital gains and after 1990 at a slightly lower capital gains rate), this factor in many cases will not be great enough to outweigh the immediate tax cost of the dividend even when the corporate interest deduction is taken into account.

Suppose, however, that the new project which the above firm has in view will require an investment that *exceeds* the year's earnings—let's say the required investment is $25 a share rather than $15. In respect of the additional $10, the tax law plainly offers an inducement to finance by issuing debt. Here, the corporate-level interest deduction can be had without any offsetting cost in the form of a current dividend. Since *future* interest payments on the "new" capital are deductible, while future dividends on such new capital are not, the firm will normally prefer to issue a $10 bond rather than an additional $10 of new common stock and will presumably do so if the new debt does not create a serious risk of bankruptcy.

As suggested, the observable financing pattern followed by most corporations—resorting first to retained earnings, second to external debt, and last to new equity—has largely conformed to the pattern of incentives and penalties contained in the tax law.

The low payout theorists took this pattern as the basis for a generalization. If dividends are taxed more heavily than capital gains, then the firm should pay the lowest possible cash dividend. The firm thereby transforms the dividends into capital gains taxed at a lower rate. Given two equivalent firms, one of which offers returns in the form of capital gains with the other paying cash dividends, the dividend-paying firm would have the higher cost of equity capital. Moreover, suboptimal reinvestment of cash flows is not necessarily implied by a low payout policy. To the extent that the firm does not have a competitive investment available, it should still avoid paying a dividend and instead repurchase outstanding shares. See infra pp. 600–609. For discussion of the low payout perspective, see Brealey and Myers, Principles of Corporate Finance 383–386 (4th ed. 1991).

The rate and other structural changes made by the Tax Reform Act of 1986 (as modified in 1990) diminish the force of the low payout argument and may in some cases alter the financing pattern described above. Individual tax rates—now, generally, 31 percent for ordinary income and 28 percent for capital gains—are actually *lower* than the maximum corporate rate—now 34 percent. Under this new and more complicated tax picture, it will in many cases be beneficial for the corporation to distribute its earnings as dividends and then recapture the amounts distributed by issuing interest-bearing debt, thus in effect substituting the lower individual for the higher corporate marginal tax rate. The tax argument in favor of higher dividends also gains force from the fact that significant segments of the shareholding community have tax reasons to prefer dividends. Some shareholders, such as pension funds and not-for-profit institutions, are tax exempt. In addition, corporations that hold shares can take advantage of the intercorporate dividend exclusion and pay corporate income tax only 30 percent of any dividends received.

But the tax picture has not changed completely. Tax paying shareholders with long term investment perspectives still can be expected to favor earnings retention. Even though the capital gains rate advantage has been reduced to 3 percent, the time advantage remains. Earnings retention implies a tax deferral until the individual shareholder sells and realizes the gain. Management, which has institutional reasons to want to retain earnings, see infra pp. 561–567, can be expected to continue to cater to this segment of the shareholding population.

––––––

(C) CLIENTELES AND MARKET IMPERFECTIONS

Does the lack of an easy answer to the problem of the taxation of dividends indirectly support the irrelevance position? Or can we expect a revival of the traditional approach in response to the 1986 tax reforms? Consider that, despite the apparent tax advantage of financing out of retained earnings, the market in practice has historically reacted unfavorably when corporations *reduced* their dividend payments to acquire new assets. Does this mean that the tax advantages of corporate leverage outweigh those associated with retained earnings, or possibly, that the latter are in reality less significant than the above illustration implies? Or does the market, because it dislikes uncertainty, pay a premium for dividends and dividend stability? Or do dividends have an informational component to which investors react, perhaps irrationally? These and related issues are examined in the materials that follow.

VAN HORNE, FINANCIAL MANAGEMENT AND POLICY
(9th ed. 1992) pp. 331–335.

INVESTOR CLIENTELE NEUTRALITY

With different tax situations, clienteles of investors may develop with distinct preferences for dividend- or nondividend-paying stocks. Many corporate investors will prefer dividend-paying stocks, whereas wealthy individual investors may prefer stocks that pay no dividends. Tax-exempt investors will be indifferent, all other things the same. * * *

If various clienteles of investors have dividend preferences, corporations should adjust their dividend payout to take advantage of the situation. * * * Suppose that three-fifths of all investors prefer a zero dividend payout, one-fifth prefer a 25 percent payout, and the remaining one-fifth prefer a 50 percent payout. If most companies pay out 25 percent of their earnings in dividends, there will be excess demand for the shares of companies paying zero dividends and for the shares of companies whose dividend payout ratio is 50 percent. Presumably, a number of companies will recognize this excess demand and adjust their payout ratios in order to increase share price. The action of these companies eventually will eliminate the excess demand.

In equilibrium, the dividend payouts of corporations will match the desires of investor groups. At this point, no company is able to affect its share price by altering its dividend. As a result, even with taxes dividend payout will be irrelevant.

Black and Scholes are the principal proponents of [this] neutral position, based on corporations adjusting the supply of dividends to take advantage of any mispricing of stocks in the marketplace.[4]

* * *

INFLUENCE OF OTHER FACTORS ON DIVIDENDS

FLOTATION COSTS

The irrelevance of dividend payout is based upon the idea that in accordance with the investment policy of the firm, funds paid out by the firm must be replaced by funds acquired through external financing. The introduction of flotation costs favors the retention of earnings in the firm. For each dollar paid out in dividends, the firm nets less than a dollar after flotation costs per dollar of external financing. Moreover, the smaller the size of the issue, the greater in general the flotation costs as a percentage of the total amount of funds raised. In addition, stock financing is "lumpy" in the sense that small issues are difficult to sell even with high flotation costs.

TRANSACTION COSTS AND DIVISIBILITY OF SECURITIES

Transaction costs involved in the sale of securities tend to restrict the arbitrage process in the same manner as that described for debt. Stockholders who desire current income must pay brokerage fees on the sale of portions of their stock if the dividend paid is not sufficient to satisfy their current desire for income. This fee varies inversely, per dollar of stock sold, with the size of the sale. For a small sale, the brokerage fee can be a rather significant percentage. Because of this fee, stockholders with consumption desires in excess of current dividends will prefer that the company pay additional dividends. Perfect capital markets also assume that securities are infinitely divisible. The fact that the smallest integer is one share may result in "lumpiness" with respect to selling shares for current income. This, too, acts as a deterrent to the sale of stock in lieu of dividends. On the other hand, stockholders not desiring dividends for current consumption purposes will need to reinvest their dividends. Here again, transaction costs and divisibility problems work to the disadvantage of the stockholder, although in the opposite direction.* * * *

INSTITUTIONAL RESTRICTIONS

Certain institutional investors are restricted in the types of common stock they can buy or in the portfolio percentages they can hold in

---

4. Fischer Black and Myron Scholes, "The Effects of Dividend Yield and Dividend Policy on Common Stock Prices and Returns," Journal of Financial Economics, 1 (May 1974), 1–5. Rosita P. Chang and S. Ghan Rhee, "The Impact of Personal Taxes on Corporate Dividend Policy and Capital Structure Decisions," Financial Management 19 (Summer 1990) 21–31 * * *. [Ed. Note: In their original article, M–M suggested the clientele effect not only with respect to varying tax preferences, but also with respect to the impact of other market imperfections on investor preferences, 34 J. of Bus. 431–432.]

* [Ed. Note] Both disadvantages may be reduced, if not wholly overcome, by dividend reinvestment plans (under which companies offer stockholders a continuing costless opportunity to apply dividends to purchase stock) and comparable stock repurchase plans (under which corporations offer to repurchase or facilitate the sale of corporate stock at minimum cost). See p. 599, infra.

these types. The prescribed list of eligible securities is determined in part by the duration over which dividends have been paid. If a company does not pay a dividend or has not paid dividends over a sufficiently long period of time, certain institutional investors are not permitted to invest in the stock.

Universities, on the other hand, sometimes have restrictions on the expenditure of capital gains from their endowment. Also, a number of trusts have a prohibition against the liquidation of principal. In the case of common stocks, the beneficiary is entitled to the dividend income, but not to the proceeds from the sale of stock. As a result of this stipulation, the trustee who manages the investments may feel constrained to pay particular attention to dividend yield and seek stocks paying reasonable dividends. Though the two influences described are small in aggregate, they work in the direction of a preference for dividends as opposed to retention and capital gains.

PREFERENCE FOR DIVIDENDS

Finally, we must allow for the possibility of a preference for dividends on the part of a sizable number of investors. The payment of dividends may resolve uncertainty in the minds of some. Also, such payments may be useful in diversification of investments in an uncertain world. If in fact investors can manufacture "homemade" dividends, such a preference is irrational. Nonetheless, sufficient statements from investors make it difficult to dismiss the argument. Perhaps, for either psychological or inconvenience reasons, investors are unwilling to manufacture "homemade" dividends.

NOTE: THE SIGNALING EFFECT OF DIVIDENDS

Entirely apart from their more or less direct economic role in relation to retained earnings, dividends are said to have a signaling effect on investors—increase in dividends is said to signal management's favorable expectations about the future profitability of the firm; decrease to signal unfavorable expectations.

Asquith and Mullins, Signalling with Dividends, Repurchases and Equity Issues, pp. 15–16 (1984) (Research Paper 75th Anniversary Colloquium Series Harvard Business School), concludes that dividend changes have significant informational content:

"There are reasons for the efficacy of dividends as signals. Dividend announcements are backed by hard, cold cash. The firm must generate this cash internally or convince the capital markets to supply it. Alternative communications may lack the credibility that comes from saying it with cash. Investors may suspect that statements from management are backed by the ghostwriting of well paid public relations specialists. They may feel that financial statements have been skillfully massaged by the financial staff. In addition, dividend decisions tend to be future oriented as opposed to accounting statements which document past performance.

"Besides credibility, dividends also have the advantage of simplicity and visibility. Many other announcements are, at the same time, complex and detailed in focus. They require time and expertise to decipher. In contrast, few investors fail to notice and understand a check in the mail. An empty mailbox is also easily interpreted. As simple numerical signals, dividends facilitate comparative analysis unlike statements by management which may be difficult to calibrate. Simplicity is especially advantageous for investors holding many firms' shares to achieve the benefits of diversification. Further, dividend signals convey information without releasing sensitive details which may be useful to competitors."

———

There is, however, a puzzling aspect to the signalling effect thus attributed to dividends, or at least to changes in dividends. If management increases dividends, it either foregoes a better use for the funds or distributes the funds because it has no better use for them. The dividend recipient cannot tell from the mere act of paying dividends which circumstances underpin the distribution—whether management sees the future optimistically or has no better use for the funds. If management has no better use for the funds, the dividend signals the opposite information from that which is thought by the "signalling" theorists and the market to be conveyed. And if the dividend is paid notwithstanding management's foregoing a profitable opportunity in order to do so, the signal is no more accurate.

Similar obscurities, if not inaccuracies, attend the decision to reduce or withhold dividends—a decision which except for unusual growth situations is read by the market unfavorably rather than to reflect management's expectation for favorable new investment.

If, as appears to be the case, there is little doubt about how the market reads either dividend decision, can management be said to be culpably misleading if it foresees the opposite, or at any rate a different, consequence from that perceived by the market, but does not so state?

(D) MANAGEMENT DIVIDEND POLICIES AND AGENCY THEORY

LINTNER, DISTRIBUTIONS OF INCOMES OF CORPORATIONS AMONG DIVIDENDS, RETAINED EARNINGS AND TAXES

46 American Economic Review, 97, 99–106 (1956).

* * *

What then can be said in any general way regarding the dividend policies of this diverse group of 28 companies? Several features of central importance stand out clearly. With the possible exception of 2 companies which sought a relatively fixed percentage pay-out, consideration of what dividends should be paid at any given time turned, first and foremost in every case, on the question whether the existing rate of payment should be changed. In studying 196 company-years of dividend action (28 companies, seven years, 1947–1953), we found no instance in which the question of how much should be paid in a given quarter or year was considered without regard to the existing rate as an optimum problem in terms of the interests of the company and/or its stockholders at the given time, after the manner suggested by the usual theoretical formulations of such problems in static terms, even when expectations are considered. Rather, there would be serious consideration of the second question of just how large the change in dividend payments should be only after management had satisfied itself that a change in the existing rate would be positively desirable. Even then, the companies' existing dividend rate continued to be a central bench mark for the problem in managements' eyes. On the basis of our field observations, the dependent variable in the decision-making process is the change in the existing rate, not the amount of the newly established rate as such.

It was equally clear that these elements of inertia and conservatism—and the belief on the part of many managements that most stockholders prefer a reasonably stable rate and that the market puts a premium on stability or gradual growth in rate—were strong enough that most managements sought to avoid making changes in their dividend rates that might have to be reversed within a year or so. This conservatism and effort to avoid erratic changes in rates very generally resulted in the development of reasonably consistent patterns of behavior in dividend decisions. The principal device used to achieve this consistent pattern was a practice or policy of changing dividends in any given year by only part of the amounts which were indicated by changes in current financial figures. Further partial adjustments in dividend rates were then made in subsequent years if still warranted. This policy of progressive, continuing "partial adaptation" tends to stabilize dividend distributions and provides a consistency in the pattern of dividend action which helps to minimize adverse stockholder reactions. At the same time it enables management to live more comfortably with its unavoidable uncertainties regarding future developments—and this is generally true even during at least a considerable part of most cyclical declines, since the failure of dividends to reflect increasing earnings fully and promptly during the preceding upswing leaves more cushion in the cash flow position as earnings start to decline.

Within this context of the decision-making process, it became clear that any reason which would lead management to decide to change an existing rate—and any reason which would be an important consideration in determining the amount of the change—had to seem prudent and convincing to officers and directors themselves and had to be of a character which provided strong motivations to management. Consequently, such reasons had to involve considerations that stockholders and the financial community generally would know about and which management would expect these outside groups to understand and find reasonably persuasive, if not compelling. Current net earnings meet these conditions better than any other factor. Earnings are reported frequently and receive wide publicity in the financial press. Most officers and directors regarded their stockholders as having a proprietary interest in earnings, and many urged the stockholders' special interest in getting earnings in dividends, subject to their interest in regularity of payment. The managements we interviewed very generally believed that, unless there were other compelling reasons to the contrary, their fiduciary responsibilities and standards of fairness required them to distribute part of any substantial increase in earnings to the stockholders in dividends. Even the executives in the minority who were most inclined to view the interests of the company as distinct from those of the stockholders, and who seemed least concerned with their responsibility to frame dividend policy in the best interests of the stockholders as such, were generally concerned with the decline in favorable proxies and in the weakening of their personal positions which they believed would follow any failure to reflect a "fair share" of such added earnings in dividends. Similarly, managements felt that it was both fair and prudent for dividends to the shareholders to reflect some part of any substantial or continued decline in earnings, and that under these circumstances stockholders would understand and accept the cut.

In contrast with earnings, other considerations and aspects of the companies' positions were thought to be less generally known, less widely understood, and less generally and sympathetically recognized by stockholders as factors which should have an important bearing upon dividend distributions. Moreover, no other consideration was nearly as consistently important year by year and company by company. Such things, for instance, as indenture provisions restricting dividends, debts to be discharged at specific dates, or tight liquidity positions were important in particular instances, but dividend decisions were dominated by such considerations rather than by earnings in line with an established policy in less than five percent of the company-years studied, and these exceptions were not clustered in any particular years. In part this finding reflects the general prosperity of the postwar period, but a large part of the explanation almost certainly lies deeper. A prudent foresighted management will always do its best to plan ahead in all aspects of financial policy to avoid getting into such uncomfortable situations where dividends *have* to be cut substantially below those which the company's previous practice would lead stockholders to expect on the basis of current earnings. Stockholder reactions in such situations have been sufficiently vigorous and effective in enough companies that the fear of such a reaction is an effective "burr under the saddle" to all managements, including those which have never been in such difficulty themselves. We might add that a policy geared to considerations other than earnings would have to be explained and justified first on one thing and then on another. Even if there were a perfectly consistent underlying rationale to such a policy, it would be difficult to explain in simple, understandable and persuasive terms, and would probably seem erratic, *ad hoc* or "academic." Moreover, as shown below, companies have generally framed policies (or systematic patterns of behavior) geared to earnings which do quite generally take care of these other considerations in what they regard as a reasonably satisfactory manner.

* * *

Special comment is required, however, regarding the bearing of the magnitude and profitability of current investment opportunities and the ease or stringency of current liquidity positions on each year's dividend decisions within the framework of these two standards. As already indicated, each company's target pay-out ratio and speed-of-adjustment factor reflected the cyclical movements of investment opportunities, working capital requirements, and fund flows in its previous experience along with the other considerations mentioned. Moreover, the standards ran in terms of net earnings as reported to stockholders and many used LIFO accounting for much of their inventories. Generally speaking, after these standards had been established or embodied in informal understandings, the company lived with them and undertook all of its financial planning and capital budgeting in the light of these standards of dividend behavior. Managements deliberately planned ahead so that carrying through their established dividend policy would not involve them in unduly short liquidity positions. Management was generally in a position and was willing to draw down on working capital to help meet such requirements. In general, management's standards with respect to its current liquidity position appeared to be very much more flexible than its standards with respect to dividend policy, and this flexibility frequently provided the buffer between reasonably definite dividend requirements in line with established policy and especially rich current investment opportunities. If investment opportunities were particularly abundant and could not be financed with the funds currently available after dividends had been increased in line with established policies, the remaining investment projects which could be undertaken only through outside financing were re-examined to make sure that they were sufficiently desirable as to justify the company in having recourse to outside capital. If so, the necessary capital was raised and the projects were undertaken; if not, the projects were abandoned. In the companies which as a matter of policy would not go to the outside market except in most extreme circumstances, the capital budget year by year was simply cut to fit the available funds.

In this connection it must be recognized that net earnings generally increase much more than in proportion to increased volume (and similarly on declines). Even though dividend rates are increased somewhat in line with policy described, the current pay-out ratio will decline with increased profits and under this pattern of behavior retained earnings fluctuate still more than in proportion. Marked fluctuations in working capital requirements and investment outlays are consequently "automatically" provided for under this form of conservative dividend behavior to a very considerable extent at least. This fact, together with the marked dependence of capital budgets upon the availability of internal funds (even when outside funds are used) shown in all the studies of this subject, go far to explain the finding that investment requirements as such very generally had relatively little direct effect in modifying the pattern of dividend behavior, except in a limited number of special situations well scattered over the years studied.

———

The import of Lintner's study is generally supported by later research. See Fama and Babiak, Dividend Policies: An Empirical Analysis, 63 J.Amer. Statistical A'ssn. 1132 (1968); DeAngelo, DeAngelo, and Skinner, Dividends and Losses, 47 J. Finance 1837 (1992).

———

Donaldson, Managing Corporate Wealth (1984) makes some additional observations (pp. 51–54):

" * * * Top management teams recognized the importance of dividends as a signal of financial well-being and as a measure of cash-flow volatility. They knew that unexpected discontinuities conveyed a disconcerting prospect of a management surprised by events and not in full control. Consequently they stressed the importance of dividend continuity and emphasized strongly the need for growth to keep pace with earnings and general inflation. However, as these managers thought about dividend policy they were concerned less directly with their shareholders than with the flow of funds within the firm. Thus they concentrated on dividend payout targets instead of dividends per share.

"As is readily apparent, dividend payouts are the obverse of retained earnings: those earnings or cash flows which are not distributed will be available for corporate reinvestment. A dividend policy expressed in terms of a payout rate could be expressed equally well as an earnings retention policy. The implications of this orientation are apparent in the financial planning documents of a company whose profit margins were below the *Fortune* 500 average. From the shareholders' perspective, it would be reasonable to assume that the company's payout would be inversely proportional to its profitability, on the theory that the better the earnings performance, the more justification and opportunity for reinvestment. In reality, the president argued just the reverse in a document circulated to his four top executives:

* * *

[His line of reasoning was that] our performance is below average; it must and can be improved; we are confident of our ability to accomplish our goals; therefore, we are justified in asking our shareholders to make an above-average reinvestment of earnings to fund it. Such self-confident managers assume that the shareholders will agree with their optimistic views and, in time of need, they lean toward the highest acceptable target earnings-retention ratio consistent with the continuity of dividends per share. Indeed, these top managers generally preferred to keep their payouts as low as possible in the belief that "we can make better use of the money than our shareholders can," given reinvestment opportunities and the personal tax advantages of undistributed earnings. None sought to increase payouts as a deliberate policy. All spoke often about the need for a reasonable or fair dividend policy—thereby suggesting that in the absence of such concerns, internal pressures would result in lower payouts.

"Individual definitions of a reasonable payout varied considerably * * *. The companies' current targets ranged from 25 percent to 55 percent of earnings with an average of 38 percent. The study provided no evidence of an objective reasoning process by which these numbers were derived. Rather, the numbers appeared to originate in the level of corporate need, conditioned by past payout practices, the observation of payout levels among comparable companies, current market expectations (particularly in recent years as dividends have appeared to figure more prominently in stock selection), and—occasionally—the direct or indirect prodding of takeover initiatives which focused attention on shareholder reward.

"Running throughout these considerations was the need to conform to the range of general practice; yet the range also offered considerable room for choice, without appearing to violate group norms. In general, the managers were responding to pressure to adjust dividends per share to keep pace with inflation while simultaneously endeavoring to retain more of their earnings than they had in the past. Most companies' current targets called for reduced payouts, and only two exceeded their historical averages.

"Before turning from dividends to debt, it is important to note that on this issue, as on other matters of financial policy, individual managers tended to reflect the viewpoint of the constituency with which they were most closely associated by reason of their organizational responsibilities. Differing viewpoints were often apparent within the same company, as the following comments demonstrate. Not surprisingly, the strongest concern for dividend payments was expressed by the company's chief financial officer * * * [who was 'determined' never to cut the [absolute] dividend payment and to seek to increase it when trends justify. Our 'dividend record * * * is part of the corporate culture.']

"In contrast, a retired chief executive and current board member of the same company commented:

> We have a commitment to good earnings—not to dividends.
> We used to think that a 50% payout was right but now the
> fashion is to pay less. I don't believe in paying out all the
> earnings to the shareholders, and 50% is a reasonable division.
> In bad years, I would favor reducing the dividend if necessary.

Clearly, his organizational identity and viewpoint persisted, despite the
fact that he was now first and foremost a shareholder himself."

————

Is a dividend policy shaped by the considerations described by
Donaldson likely to be optimal from the point of view of a shareholder?
Recall that the leveraged restructurings of the 1980s were justified as
drastic remedies to the problem of management's self-serving financing
and investment decisions. Management's preference for a low but safe
level of debt was but one practice held out as in need of correction. Its
tendency to pay a low dividend and retain an excessive amount of
earnings was another. As might be expected, Professor Michael Jensen
made the leading theoretical statement of this point. Jensen, Agency
Costs of Free Cash Flow, Corporate Finance and Takeover, 76 Amer.
Econ.Rev. 323 (1986), asserts that a firm with substantial available
internally generated funds, or free cash flows, will tend to overinvest
them, accepting marginal investment projects. That is, management
tends to reinvest earnings in investments where r is less than k.
Jensen connects this point to the dividend policy debate. All other
things being equal, an increase in the dividend will reduce the extent of
suboptimal investment and increase the value of the firm. See also
Lang and Litzenberger, Dividend Announcements: Cash Flow Signalling vs. Free Cash Flow Hypothesis? 24 J. Financial Econs. 181 (1989)
(empirical study supporting both free cash flow and signalling explanations).

According to Jensen, then, dividends matter, and high dividends
may be preferable to low dividends depending on the set of investments
available to the firm. Reconsider the "traditional" approach of Graham, Dodd and Cottle, supra, in light of Jensen's approach. Do the
economic assumptions underlying their "traditional" advice to stock
analysts differ materially from Jensen's?

Finally, it should be noted that the recognition of the presence of
agency costs does not, taken alone, require the conclusion that the
management behavior pattern in question is suboptimal. Easterbrook,
Two Agency–Cost Explanations of Dividends, 74 Amer.Econ.Rev. 650
(1984), offers an ingenious agency cost explanation of the dividend
payout pattern described by Lintner and Donaldson. Easterbrook
assumes first, that managers are not perfect agents and that monitoring is costly, and second, that managers' risk aversion causes them to
prefer levels of debt that are suboptimal from a shareholder point of
view. If managers were forced to go to the capital markets to borrow,
effective monitoring would occur and the level of debt would rise.

Easterbrook posits that dividends play a role in causing this to occur, id. at 655, 657:

"The role of dividends in starting up the monitoring provided by the capital market is easy to see. An example of the role of dividends in making risk adjustments may help. Suppose a firm has an initial capitilization of 100, of which 50 is debt and 50 equity. It invests the 100 in a project. The firm prospers, and earnings raise its holdings to 200. The creditors now have substantially more security than they started with, and correspondingly the residual claimants are paying the creditors a rate of interest unwarranted by current circumstances. They can correct this situation by paying a dividend of 50 while issuing new debt worth 50. The firm's capital continues to be 200, but the debt-equity ratio has been restored, and the interest rate on the original debt is again appropriate to the creditors' risk.

"Expected, continuing dividends compel firms to raise new money in order to carry out their activities. They therefore precipitate the monitoring and debt-equity adjustments that benefit stockholders. Moreover, even when dividends are not accompanied by the raising of new capital, they at least increase the debt-equity ratio so that shareholders are not giving (as much) wealth away to bondholders. In other words, dividends set in motion mechanisms that reduce the agency costs of management and that prevent one group of investors from gaining, relative to another, by changes in the firm's fortunes after financial instruments have been issued. The future is always anticipated imperfectly in these contracts, so there will always be some need for *ex post* adjustments and supervision, and dividends play a role in these adjustments."

"The agency-cost explanations have implications for the stability of dividends over time * * *. Because the first function of dividends is to keep firms in the capital markets, we would not expect to see a very strong correlation between short-term profits and dividends. This implication cries out for testing, but it is certainly consistent with the fact that most firms have consistent policies (for example, 20 cents per share per quarter) that are not changed very often. A consistent policy uncouples dividends from profits while maintaining a link to the capital market. One indirect way to examine whether consistent dividends are valued for their effect on agency costs is to examine whether prices appreciate more on an increase in the 'regular' dividend than on an increase of the same present value in 'extraordinary' dividends. Shareholders concerned only about payouts in hand value the two equally; if dividends contain agency costs, regular payouts are more valuable. Evidence indicates that the regular dividend is associated with greater increases in price * * *.

"Profits would have some effect on the risk-adjustment function, but past profits (which inure to debtholders' benefit unless dividends are increased) would be more important explanatory variables than current or anticipated profits. Anticipated profits can be handled by an adjustment of the terms on which money is raised; unanticipated past profits must be paid out to avoid windfalls to debtholders. The agency-cost treatment predicts that increases in dividends lag increases in profit and are uncorrelated with future profits. The lag may be substantial, because small increases (small changes of all sorts) in profits will be anticipated by debtholders, and there will be no need to make adjustments for these changes. Only the unanticipated (relatively large) changes call for adjustments in dividend policy."

————

NOTE: DIVIDENDS AND NEW ISSUES OF COMMON STOCK

In examining the considerations affecting the dividend decision, certain previously discussed problems which management faces in resorting to new equity as a means of financing new investment are relevant (see Consumers' Power case, supra p. 513). Is issuance of new stock affected by the possibility that, notwithstanding the efficient markets hypothesis, if the outstanding stock is in some sense "underpriced," issuance of additional shares at the market price or below it will dilute the equity of the outstanding shares, and if it is "overpriced," the new investors will in some sense be overcharged? Is the latter effect cured by the signalling impact of a new issue—with consequences that should be avoided unless the new issue is necessary? See Asquith and Mullins, Equity Issues and Offering Dilution, 15 J. Financial Econ. 61, 61–62, 65–66 (1986):

* * * An enduring anomaly in financial economics is the reliance of firms on internally generated funds as their chief source of equity financing and their corresponding reluctance to issue common stock * * *. This behavior is less anomalous to financial practitioners. Financial executives, investment bankers and many regulators argue that selling equity causes a firm's stock price to fall. Their view, labelled the price-pressure hypothesis by Scholes * * *, contends that an increase in the supply of shares causes a decline in a firm's stock price because the demand curve for shares is downward sloping. The implication is that each firm's shares are unique, and close substitutes do not exist. In addition, some proponents of this hypothesis argue that the price reduction is short-lived and that a post-offering increase in stock prices or "sweetener" is necessary to market additional shares.

In contrast, the theoretical literature in finance assumes that the demand curve for a firm's shares is essentially horizontal. The prices of securities are determined solely by the risk and expected return associated with a security's future cash flows. Close substitutes for a firm's shares, e.g., securities with similar risk and return characteristics, are either directly available in the capital markets or they can be constructed through combinations of existing securities. Moreover, efficient capital markets rule out new issue price effects not based on changes in a security's expected cash flows. Thus with close substitutes, efficient capital markets and fixed investment policies, the price of any firm's shares should be independent of the number of shares the firm, or any shareholder, chooses to sell. This view of equity financing is also not without challenge. There are also theoretical arguments, other than a downward sloping demand curve, for predicting a stock price decrease with equity issues. Chief among these are the effect of new equity issues on corporate capital structures and the role of stock issues as informative signals.

* * *

Others have theorized that equity issues serve as signals which communicate managers' superior information independent of capital structure considerations. In a world of asymmetric information managers and insiders have superior information compared to investors, and management's decision to issue equity conveys information about a firm's "intrinsic" value. A stock price reduction is produced by rational investors hedging against the risk that, in selling stock, managers are using their superior information to benefit existing shareholders at the expense of new shareholders. A more benign interpretation is that the information available to managers is not favorable enough to preclude selling stock, and thus the decision to issue equity is a negative signal.

The results presented in this paper confirm [the] finding that primary stock issues are more likely to occur after a rise in stock prices. However, the decision to issue equity appears to be related more to the performance of a firm's stock price relative to the market than to the performance of the market as a whole. Regression results for industrial issues indicate that the announcement day price reduction is inversely related to stock price performance in the year prior to the announcement. This finding provides an explanation for why firms tend to issue equity after a rise in stock prices. * * *

* * * [T]he roughly similar price effects observed for primary issues by corporations and registered secondary distributions suggest that the price reduction is not related solely to tax effects or leverage-related information associated with a change in capital structure. The results are generally consistent with the hypothesis that equity sales by firms and knowledgeable investors are viewed by the market as unfavorable signals about a firm's current performance and future prospects. The results are also consistent with the price-pressure hypothesis that there is a downward sloping demand for a firm's shares.

Pilotte, Growth Opportunities and the Stock Price Response to New Financing, 65 J.Bus. 371 (1992), adds a further observation. Pilotte studies a sample of growth firms and mature firms and finds that stock price response to a security offering is a function of the growth opportunities of the issuer and the riskiness of the security offered. The better the growth outlook and the less risky the offering (debt as opposed to equity), the more positive the price response.

3. APPLICABLE LEGAL STANDARDS

The Modigliani–Miller hypothesis on the irrelevance of dividends as against retention assumes a firm in which the interests of the stockholders are perfectly aligned with those of the managers making the dividend decision. If management's interests diverge from those of the stockholders, then a basic assumption of the hypothesis is negated. The different assumptions implicate different legal norms. If the interests are mutual, then a dispute over investment or dividend policy presumably reflects differences only of business judgment, and management should enjoy the wide discretion allowed under the business judgment rule. If the interests diverge, then the breadth of managerial discretion allowed by the business judgment rule suggests that the choice of an optimal dividend policy should be restrained, or stimulated. Such a restraint or stimulus could arise either in the form of irate shareholders exercising their voting rights, or of "penalties" for inefficiency imposed by the capital markets, presumably through lower prices for the company's shares and takeovers. But if, as the debate over takeovers suggests, neither of these forces is likely to be fully effective, then within some indeterminate range, that contemporary managers have discretion to define their own goals and to behave accordingly. See Berle and Means, The Modern Corporation and Private Property (1932); Williamson, The Economics of Discretionary Behavior: Managerial Objectives in a Theory of the Firm (1967). In view of this uncertainty, how confidently can we assume that management's investment decisions are guided by "scientific" capital budgeting principles (or their practical equivalent) and that new investment projects are accepted or rejected only in response to considerations most likely to enhance the value of the company's outstanding shares?

From a legal standpoint, selection of a dividend policy is almost entirely within the discretion of management. Statutory surplus requirements (supra, p. 442) must be met when dividends are paid, but this is rarely a problem for large, publicly held corporations whose balance sheets almost always contain sizable quantities of retained earnings. Nevertheless, as the cases that follow suggest, the law is not without some further impact on corporate distribution policy, especially when that policy is suspected of having manipulative or other illicit goals in view.

DODGE v. FORD MOTOR CO.*

Supreme Court of Michigan, 1919.
204 Mich. 459, 170 N.W. 668.

[Henry Ford owned 58% of the outstanding stock of the Ford Motor Company, which had been incorporated in 1903 with authorized capital stock of $150,000. By 1908, the authorized and issued capital had been increased (by stock dividends) to $2,000,000. In that and subsequent years, the company declared and paid a regular annual cash dividend of 60% on the increased capital of $2,000,000, and between 1911 and 1915 it declared and paid special cash dividends amounting to over $40,000,-000. Mr. Ford, who controlled the board of directors, then made it known that no more special dividends would be paid to shareholders, that profits "would be put back into the business for the purpose of extending its operations and increasing the number of its employees, and that, inasmuch as the profits were to be represented by investment in plants and capital investment the stockholders would have no right to complain." As of July, 1916, the surplus of the corporation was $112,000,000 and it held cash and government securities of almost $54,000,000. Two minority shareholders, the Dodge brothers, owning 10% of the company's shares, brought suit to compel the declaration of a dividend of not less than three-quarters of the corporation's accumulated cash surplus. The lower court decreed that a dividend of $19,275,-000 be paid and the company appealed.]

OSTRANDER, J. * * * When plaintiffs made their complaint and demand for further dividends the Ford Motor Company had concluded its most prosperous year of business. The demand for its cars at the price of the preceding year continued. It could make and could market in the year beginning August 1, 1916 more than 500,000 cars. Sales of parts and repairs would necessarily increase. The cost of materials was likely to advance, and perhaps the price of labor, but it reasonably might have expected a profit for the year of upwards of $60,000,000. * * *

[T]he defendants have offered testimony tending to prove, and which does prove, the following facts. It had been the policy of the corporation for a considerable time to annually reduce the selling price of cars, while keeping up, or improving, their quality. As early as in June, 1915, a general plan for the expansion of the productive capacity of the concern by a practical duplication of its plant had been talked over by the executive officers and directors and agreed upon, not all of the details having been settled and no formal action of directors having been taken. The erection of a smelter was considered, and engineering and other data in connection therewith secured. * * *

The plan, as affecting the profits of the business for the year beginning August 1, 1916, and thereafter, calls for a reduction in the

* Substantially as abridged in Cary, Cases and Materials on Corporations (1969) 1580–3.

selling price of the cars. * * * In short, the plan does not call for and is not intended to produce immediately a more profitable business but a less profitable one; not only less profitable than formerly but less profitable than it is admitted it might be made. The apparent immediate effect will be to diminish the value of shares and the returns to shareholders.

It is the contention of plaintiffs that the apparent effect of the plan is intended * * * to continue the corporation henceforth as a semi-eleemosynary institution and not as a business institution. In support of this contention they point to the attitude and to the expressions of Mr. Henry Ford.

* * *

"My ambition," said Mr. Ford, "is to employ still more men to spread the benefits of this industrial system to the greatest possible number, to help them build up their lives and their homes. To do this we are putting the greatest share of our profits back in the business."

"With regard to dividends, the company paid sixty per cent. on its capitalization of two million dollars, or $1,200,000, leaving $58,000,000 to reinvest for the growth of the company. This is Mr. Ford's policy at present, and it is understood that the other stockholders cheerfully accede to this plan."

He had made up his mind in the summer of 1916 that no dividends other than the regular dividends should be paid, "for the present."

* * *

The record, and especially the testimony of Mr. Ford, convinces that he has to some extent the attitude towards shareholders of one who has dispensed and distributed to them large gains and that they should be content to take what he chooses to give. His testimony creates the impression, also, that he thinks the Ford Motor Company has made too much money, has had too large profits, and that although large profits might be still earned, a sharing of them with the public, by reducing the price of the output of the company, ought to be undertaken. We have no doubt that certain sentiments, philanthropic and altruistic, creditable to Mr. Ford, had large influence in determining the policy to be pursued by the Ford Motor Company—the policy which has been herein referred to.

It is said by his counsel that—

"Although a manufacturing corporation cannot engage in humanitarian works as its principal business, the fact that it is organized for profit does not prevent the existence of implied powers to carry on with humanitarian motives such charitable works as are incidental to the main business of the corporation."

* * *

In discussing this proposition, counsel have referred to decisions [citations omitted]. These cases, after all, like all others in which the subject is treated, turn finally upon the point, the question, whether it appears that the directors were not acting for the best interests of the corporation. * * * There should be no confusion (of which there is evidence) of the duties which Mr. Ford conceives that he and the stockholders owe to the general public and the duties which in law he and his codirectors owe to protesting, minority stockholders. A business corporation is organized and carried on primarily for the profit of the stockholders. The powers of the directors are to be employed for that end. The discretion of directors is to be exercised in the choice of means to attain that end and does not extend to a change in the end itself, to the reduction of profits or to the nondistribution of profits among stockholders in order to devote them to other purposes.

* * * As we have pointed out, and the proposition does not require argument to sustain it, it is not within the lawful powers of a board of directors to shape and conduct the affairs of a corporation for the merely incidental benefit of shareholders and for the primary purpose of benefiting others, and no one will contend that if the avowed purpose of the defendant directors was to sacrifice the interests of shareholders it would not be the duty of the courts to interfere.

We are not, however, persuaded that we should interfere with the proposed expansion of the business of the Ford Motor Company. In view of the fact that the selling price of products may be increased at any time, the ultimate results of the larger business cannot be certainly estimated. The judges are not business experts. * * * We are not satisfied that the alleged motives of the directors, in so far as they are reflected in the conduct of the business, menace the interests of shareholders. It is enough to say, perhaps, that the court of equity is at all times open to complaining shareholders having a just grievance.

[If the expansion plan is for the best interests of the company,] what does it amount to in justification of a refusal to declare and pay a special dividend or dividends? The Ford Motor Company was able to estimate with nicety its income and profits * * *. If the total cost of proposed expenditures [for expansion] had been immediately withdrawn in cash from the cash surplus * * * on hand August 1, 1916, there would have remained nearly $30,000,000 * * *. The large sum appropriated for the smelter plant was payable over a considerable period of time. So that, without going further, it would appear that, accepting and approving the plan of the directors, it was their duty to distribute on or near the first of August, 1916, a very large sum of money to stockholders.

* * * It is obvious that an annual dividend of sixty percent upon $2,000,000 or $1,200,000, is the equivalent of a very small dividend upon $100,000,000, or more.

The decree of the court below fixing and determining the specific amount to be distributed to stockholders is affirmed.

[Concurring opinion of MOORE, J., omitted.]

NOTE: DIVIDENDS AND "CORPORATE OPPORTUNITY"

1. In **Sinclair Oil Corp. v. Levien,** a minority stockholder of Sinclair's 97%–owned Venezuelan subsidiary (Sinven) brought an action for damages and an accounting on the ground that Sinclair had injured Sinven by causing it to distribute "excessive" dividends for the purpose of financing Sinclair's worldwide exploration activities. The plaintiff stressed that between 1960 and 1966 Sinven had paid out $108 million in dividends, which was $38 million more than its earnings during that period. While the plaintiff and other public stockholders received their proportionate share of such dividends, the plaintiff argued that Sinven was thereby effectively disabled from undertaking new investments of its own, and was, in effect, thrown into partial liquidation to serve its parent's need for cash.

The plaintiff was successful in obtaining an accounting order in the Court of Chancery, 261 A.2d 911 (Del.Ch.1969). Finding that Sinclair owed a fiduciary duty to its subsidiary by reason of its control over the latter's board of directors, the Chancellor said (261 A.2d at 921):

"It seems to me that these two facets of the case, extraordinary dividends and the absence of any serious efforts to expand or develop industrially when considered together, are significant in showing how Sinclair managed Venezuelan's business. As to the first of these, the overwhelming inferences from the record are, and I so find as facts, that (a) the dividend payments coincided with Sinclair's substantial needs for large amounts of cash (Sinclair received 97% of the distributions), and (b) Sinclair's need for cash was the dominant factor in the decision to pay the dividends, particularly in 1963. There is indeed little to show that Venezuelan's corporate needs were weighed in the process. Dividends were first paid only when Sinclair could receive them tax-free, and thereafter the amounts were irregular because they were almost a function of Sinclair's need for cash. For example: in 1963 Venezuelan paid $28,000,000 against earnings of about $10,590,-000, and in that year Sinclair borrowed $150,000,000. And the irregular payment schedule was substantially inconsistent with Sinclair's own announced and conservative approach (up to 50% of earnings) to dividends.

"As to the absence of serious expansion or development efforts, the withdrawal of such enormous amounts of cash obviously had an impact on what the Company could do. I recognize that Venezuelan was in something of a bind (as were all oil companies in Venezuela) with limited acreage and no opportunity to acquire more. But Sinclair's response to that challenge was to drain off corporate cash (which it needed) and to limit corporate development. I do not mean to say that Sinclair was under a duty to offer any specific opportunity to Venezuelan (although during the period in question Sinclair made acquisitions and expanded generally through ventures which were prima facie suitable for Venezuelan). I say only that it was obliged to follow a course of fair dealing toward the minority stockholders in the way it managed the corporation's business. (Citation omitted)

"I find that Venezuelan was not treated fairly because of the extraordinary and large cash withdrawals combined with the absence of any serious effort to add to revenue or to use corporate resources available for that purpose. The result was a drying up of the subsidiary and the only reasonable conclusion is that this was done because it was in the interest of Sinclair to do so. It was not in Venezuelan's.

"When these two critical facts are laid side by side they make out a case for an accounting. I am aware that it takes an unusual case to override director judgment on dividends. But when such distributions are prompted by the needs of the fiduciary stockholder and when they dilute equity as they did here, and when they are combined with the absence of any serious effort to develop the company, then the conclusion is inevitable that the fiduciary has failed to apply the corporation's assets for the benefit of *all* stockholders. * * *"

On appeal, the Supreme Court of Delaware reversed (280 A.2d 717 (1971)), stating (at 719–722):

"The Chancellor held that because of Sinclair's fiduciary duty and its control over Sinven, its relationship with Sinven must meet the test of intrinsic fairness. The standard of intrinsic fairness involves both a high degree of fairness and a shift in the burden of proof. Under this standard the burden is on Sinclair to prove, subject to careful judicial scrutiny, that its transactions with Sinven were objectively fair. Guth v. Loft, Inc., 23 Del.Ch. 255, 5 A.2d 503 (Del.Sup.1952); Getty Oil Co. v. Skelly Oil Co., supra.

"Sinclair argues that the transactions between it and Sinven should be tested, not by the test of intrinsic fairness with the accompanying shift of the burden of proof, but by the business judgment rule under which a court will not interfere with the judgment of a board of directors unless there is a showing of gross and palpable overreaching. * * *

"A parent does indeed owe a fiduciary duty to its subsidiary when there are parent-subsidiary dealings. However, this alone will not evoke the intrinsic fairness standard. This standard will be applied only when the fiduciary duty is accompanied by self-dealing—the situation when a parent is on both sides of a transaction with its subsidiary. Self-dealing occurs when the parent, by virtue of its domination of the subsidiary, causes the subsidiary to act in such a way that the parent receives something from the subsidiary to the exclusion of, and detriment to, the minority stockholders of the subsidiary. * * *

"Consequently, it must be determined whether the dividend payments by Sinven were, in essence, a self-dealing by Sinclair. The dividends resulted in great sums of money being transferred from Sinven to Sinclair. However, a proportionate share of this money was received by the minority shareholders of Sinven. Sinclair received nothing from Sinven to the exclusion of its minority stockholders. As such, these dividends were not self-dealing. We hold therefore that the Chancellor erred in applying the intrinsic fairness test as to these dividend payments. The business judgment standard should have been applied.

"We conclude that the facts demonstrate that the dividend payments complied with the business judgment standard. * * * The motives for causing the declaration of dividends are immaterial unless the plaintiff can show that the dividend payments resulted from improper motives and amounted to waste. The plaintiff contends only that the dividend payments drained Sinven of cash to such an extent that it was prevented from expanding.

"The plaintiff proved no business opportunities which came to Sinven independently and which Sinclair either took to itself or denied to Sinven. As a matter of fact, with two minor exceptions which resulted in losses, all of Sinven's operations have been conducted in Venezuela, and Sinclair had a policy of exploiting its oil properties located in different countries by subsidiaries located in the particular countries.

"From 1960 to 1966 Sinclair purchased or developed oil fields in Alaska, Canada, Paraguay, and other places around the world. The plaintiff contends that these were all opportunities which could have been taken by Sinven. The Chancellor concluded that Sinclair had not proved that its denial of expansion opportunities to Sinven was intrinsically fair. He based this conclusion on the following findings of fact. Sinclair made no real effort to expand Sinven. The excessive dividends paid by Sinven resulted in so great a cash drain as to effectively deny to Sinven any ability to expand. During this same period Sinclair actively pursued a company-wide policy of developing through its subsidiaries new sources of revenue, but Sinven was not permitted to participate and was confined in its activities to Venezuela.

"However, the plaintiff could point to no opportunities which came to Sinven. Therefore, Sinclair usurped no business opportunity belonging to Sinven. Since Sinclair received nothing from Sinven to the exclusion of and detriment to Sinven's minority stockholders, there was no self-dealing. Therefore, business judgment is the proper standard by which to evaluate Sinclair's expansion policies.

" * * * Accordingly, Sinclair's decision, absent fraud or gross overreaching, * * * must be upheld."

On the remand, Sinclair was found liable to Sinven on another count for breach of a contract involving inter-company transactions, in the amount of approximately $5,250,000. 314 A.2d 216 (Del.Ch.1973).

2. Should the "intrinsic fairness" standard be invoked if, in an announced two-step takeover, in which the same price is paid to the cashed-out stockholders in each step, the usual quarterly dividend is skipped in anticipation of the closing of the second step merger? Compare Gabelli & Co., Inc. v. Liggett Group Inc., 479 A.2d 276 (Del.1984), holding in the negative, with Smith v. SPNV Holdings, Inc.,

1987 WL 14676 (Del.Ch.1987), which holds open the possibility of intrinsic fairness scrutiny. But cf. Smith v. SPNV Holdings, Inc., 1989 WL 44049 (Del.Ch.1989).

BERWALD v. MISSION DEVELOPMENT COMPANY

Supreme Court of Delaware, 1962.
40 Del.Ch. 509, 185 A.2d 480.

SOUTHERLAND, Chief Justice. Plaintiffs, owners of 248 shares of the stock of Mission Development Corporation, brought suit to compel the liquidation of Mission and the distribution of its assets to its stockholders. Mission answered and filed a motion for summary judgment, based on affidavits and depositions. Plaintiffs tendered no contradictory proof. The Vice Chancellor granted the motion and the plaintiffs appeal.

The facts are as follows:

Defendant, Mission Development, is a holding company. Its sole significant asset is a block of nearly seven million shares of Tidewater Oil Company. Tidewater is a large integrated oil company, qualified to do business in all the States of the Union. It is controlled, through Mission Development and Getty Oil Company, by J. Paul Getty.

Mission Development was formed in 1948 for the purpose of acquiring a block of 1,416,693 shares of Tidewater common stock then owned by Mission Corporation, a Nevada corporation. Its avowed purpose was to invest only in Tidewater stock, and in furtherance of this purpose to acquire additional stock to fortify its position in Tidewater. Accordingly, Mission of Delaware issued to Mission of Nevada 2,833,386 shares of its common stock and received the block of Tidewater stock held by Mission. Appropriate orders under the Investment Company Act were obtained from the Securities and Exchange Commission. The shares of both Mission Development and Tidewater are listed on the New York Stock Exchange.

Mission of Delaware will be hereinafter referred to as "Mission".

From 1948 to 1951 Mission acquired an additional 1,050,420 shares of Tidewater. Thereafter, and by 1960, Mission's holdings of Tidewater, through a 100% stock dividend and annual stock dividends of five per cent, increased to 6,943,957 shares.

In 1954 Tidewater discontinued the payment of cash dividends, thus effecting a discontinuance of Mission's income. Mission, as above noted, received thereafter until 1960 an annual 5% stock dividend, but Mission's proportionate ownership of Tidewater was not thereby increased, and its management accordingly deemed it unwise to distribute the shares as a dividend, since to do so would have decreased its proportionate ownership of Tidewater.

As hereafter shown, Tidewater's discontinuance of cash dividends was prompted by the adoption in 1954 of a policy of corporate expansion and modernization. The use of its available cash for this purpose left it without funds for dividends.

Later in the same year, Tidewater proposed to its stockholders to exchange shares of its cumulative $1.20 preferred stock for shares of its common stock held by the stockholders. Getty Oil Company and Mission were excluded from this offer.

All of the foregoing facts were reported to Mission stockholders by letter of J. Paul Getty, President of the corporation, dated April 11, 1955.

We pause to note that some of the plaintiff's stock in Mission Development was bought in 1956 and 1959.

In 1960 Tidewater discontinued the practice of distributing stock dividends. In the same year it submitted to its stockholders an exchange offer similar to the one made in 1955, again excluding Getty Oil and Mission.

From September 1960 to and including August 1961 Getty Oil Company acquired 510,200 shares of Mission. Some of these were purchased off the market.

In November 1960 this suit was filed.

As above indicated, plaintiffs seek to compel a complete or partial liquidation of the defendant and the distribution of its assets, either through the medium of a winding-up receivership, or by means of a court order compelling the management to distribute, or to offer to distribute, at least part of the Tidewater shares in exchange for Mission shares.

The extreme relief of receivership to wind up a solvent going business is rarely granted. To obtain it there must be a showing of imminent danger of great loss resulting from fraud or mismanagement. Hall v. John S. Isaacs, etc., Inc., Del.Ch., 163 A.2d 288, 293. Like caution is dictated in considering an application to compel a corporation to make a partial distribution.

Since no showing is made of fraud or mismanagement inflicting injury upon the corporation, what is the basis of plaintiff's case?

Plaintiff's argument proceeds as follows:

There is an inherent conflict of interest between the controlling stockholder of Mission, Mr. J. Paul Getty, and the minority stockholders. This arises out of the dividend policy of Tidewater. Because of high income taxes, Mr. Getty, it is said, is not interested in receiving dividends; he is interested in acquiring more shares of Tidewater. To achieve this end, it is charged, he has caused Tidewater to discontinue all dividends and to announce, in 1960, that no dividends could be expected for five years. The necessary effect of this policy, plaintiffs say, was to depress the market value of Mission shares, and enable Mr. Getty to buy more Mission shares at an artificially low price, at the expense of Mission's minority stockholders. This, plaintiffs charge, is just what he has done, as is proved by Getty Oil's purchases of stock in

1960 and 1961. Thus he and Mission have inflicted a serious wrong upon the minority stockholders.

It is quite true that in some cases the interests of a controlling stockholder and of the minority stockholders in respect of the receipt of dividends may conflict, because of the existence of very high income taxes. See Cases and Materials, Baker and Cary, p. 1375. And in some cases this may work hardship on the minority. But we find no such situation here.

It is plain that the whole argument based on a charge of conflict of interest rests upon the claim that Tidewater's dividend policy, and its public announcement of it, were designed to serve the selfish interest of Mr. Getty and not to further its own corporate interests. If the opposite is true—if Tidewater's policy was adopted in furtherance of its own corporate interest—then Mission's stockholders have not been subjected to an actionable wrong and have no complaint. The fact of Mr. Getty's purchase of Mission Development stock then becomes irrelevant.

What does the record show with respect to Tidewater's dividend policy?

In the ten years prior to 1953 Tidewater's expenditure for capital improvements did not exceed $41,100,000 in any one year. Shortly prior to 1954 Tidewater began to expand and modernize its facilities. In February 1955 it closed and subsequently sold its obsolete refinery at Bayonne, New Jersey, and built a new and modern refinery in New Castle County, Delaware at a cost in excess of $200,000,000. Also, it commenced and still continues the expansion and modernization of its refinery facilities at Avon, California, and the increase of its crude oil and natural gas resources. As of November 3, 1960, the budget for new capital projects to be begun in 1961 was $111,000,000.

It is unnecessary to elaborate the point. It is entirely clear from the facts set forth in the affidavits that Tidewater's cash has since 1960 been largely devoted to capital improvements and that, in the opinion of management, funds were not available for dividends. These facts are uncontradicted, and they constitute a refutation of the basic argument of plaintiffs that dividends were discontinued to enable J. Paul Getty to buy Mission stock at a depressed price.

Some point is sought to be made of the unusual action of the Tidewater management in announcing that dividends could not be expected for five years. As defendant's counsel says, this was done out of common fairness to its stockholders and to prospective purchasers of its stock.

It is earnestly argued that plaintiffs should be allowed to go to trial and adduce testimony on the issue of the selfish motives of the controlling stockholder. Plaintiffs say that they could show by expert testimony that the market price of Mission common was artificially depressed.

It is first to be noted that the record of market prices put in by the plaintiffs themselves fails to show any drop in prices coincident with or closely following the announcement of the cessation of dividends. Plaintiffs reply that this fact is meaningless because at that time the market was steadily going up, and say that expert testimony will establish this. The answer to this argument is that if plaintiffs had such proof, they should have come forward with it. "In such a situation, a duty is cast upon the plaintiff to disclose evidence which will demonstrate the existence of a genuine issue of fact * * * if summary judgment * * * is to be denied." Frank C. Sparks Co. v. Huber Baking Co., 9 Terry 9, 48 Del. 9, 96 A.2d 456, 459.

There are other facts in this case that support the conclusion above indicated. The sole corporate purpose of Mission is and has been to hold Tidewater stock. Any investor in its shares could readily ascertain this fact. Because of this he knows, or should know, that he is buying for growth and not for income.

Some point is made of the exclusion of Mission from the exchange offers made by Tidewater to its stockholders in 1954 and 1960. Obviously, for Mission Development to have been included in the exchange would have defeated the very purpose of its corporate existence.

However the various arguments are put they come to this: Plaintiffs are in effect seeking to wind up the corporation, either wholly or partially, because it is doing exactly what it was lawfully organized to do.

We think the plaintiffs have failed to make a case. *No case*

The judgment below is affirmed.

Why would anyone buy shares of Mission Development Co. in the first place? If you fancy Tidewater Oil, why not own its shares and receive its dividends directly? Broad hint: Under I.R.C. § 243 a corporation (Mission) which receives a dividend from another corporation (Tidewater) was at that time allowed to deduct 85% of such dividend from its gross income. Since the corporate tax was then 52%, intercorporate dividends were taxed at the effective rate of only 7.8%, i.e., 52% of 15%. Individuals owning stock in the recipient corporation were taxed at capital gain rates when they sold those shares. The capital gain tax is half the tax on ordinary dividend income, however, and prior to 1969 it could not exceed 25%.

COCHRAN v. CHANNING CORP.

United States District Court, Southern District of New York, 1962.
211 F.Supp. 239.

DAWSON, District Judge. This is a motion by defendant Channing Corporation (Channing) and three of its directors named as individual defendants to dismiss the complaint for failure to state a claim upon which relief can be granted. * * *

The facts alleged by plaintiff and accepted as true for the purposes of this motion are as follows:

The complaint is purportedly brought under Section 10(b) of the Securities Exchange Act of 1934 (par. 1), by plaintiff, a stockholder of Agricultural Insurance Company since November of 1958, allegedly suing in behalf of himself and others similarly situated (pars. 2, 3). Defendant Channing Corporation is a company which is claimed to have dominated the policies of Agricultural since January 1961 (pars. 4, 7). The individual defendants are alleged to be directors of both Channing and Agricultural, two of the three having been such throughout the time covered by the complaint (pars. 5, 7).

In substance, it is claimed that since 1960 Channing and the individual defendants have engaged in a scheme aimed at acquiring for Channing ownership of Agricultural's shares at the lowest possible price, and at utilizing its control for the purpose of (1) realizing on an equity in excess of prevailing market prices for Agricultural's shares, and (2) causing Agricultural's insurance agents to engage, in behalf of a Channing wholly-owned sales subsidiary, in the retail sale of shares of mutual funds managed by Channing (par. 8).

It is further alleged that to effectuate this scheme Channing carried out a program of purchase of Agricultural's shares, withholding from the public any disclosure of its identity or of its program * * *.

The complaint further alleges that Agricultural's directors, dominated by defendants, reduced the quarterly dividend of Agricultural on March 9, 1961, the defendants desiring that reduction in order to facilitate Channing's purchasing program and their alleged plan (pars. 11–12); and that as a result Channing acquired further shares at depressed prices (pars. 13–14).

It is then alleged that because of the dividend reduction and lack of information as to Channing's program of purchases, plaintiff in or about the first week of April, 1961, sold some 500 shares of Agricultural's stock which he would not otherwise have sold, at a price reflecting the depressing effect of the dividend reduction, and a price below what he (and other stockholders) could have obtained later after disclosure of Channing's purchasing program. * * *

The second count of the complaint (pars. 25, 26) substantially repeats the allegations of the first count, except that it omits those relating to violation of Section 10(b) and Rule 10b–5 and instead alleges that the various acts set forth were violations of the fiduciary duties owed by Channing as dominant stockholder and the individual defendants as directors.

Defendant attacks the first cause of action on two grounds: (1) that Section 10(b) and Rule 10b–5 require privity of contract and the plaintiff has not alleged that the shares he sold were purchased by the defendants, and (2) that even if privity had been alleged, the acts of defendants do not constitute a violation of the Securities Exchange Act because there were no verbal misrepresentations made by defendants to plaintiff.

Assuming, arguendo, that privity is not necessary, does the conduct of defendants amount to a violation of Rule 10b–5? The rule is addressed to any person and not merely to insiders. However, since its construction has imposed special burdens upon insiders, it is necessary to determine the status of these defendants. There can be no question that the three directors of Agricultural were insiders as to the affairs of the corporation. Moreover it must be taken as true, as asserted in the complaint, that defendant Channing was in a position to, and in fact did, dominate the policies of Agricultural and must therefore be deemed an insider.

* * *

The fact that the defendants did not make any statements at all does not, in and of itself, deprive plaintiff of relief. The three subsections of Rule 10b–5 are in the disjunctive,* and while subsection (2) seems to require a statement of some sort, subsections (1) and (3) do not. One who causes a reduction of dividend in order more cheaply to purchase the shares of a corporation is most certainly employing a device to defraud and is engaging in a course of business which operates as a fraud upon the seller of those securities.

* * *

The Securities Exchange Act was enacted in part to afford protection to the ordinary purchaser or seller of securities. Fraud may be accomplished by false statements, a failure to correct a misleading impression left by statements already made or, as in the instant case, by not stating anything at all when there is a duty to come forward and speak. It is the use of the inside information that gives rise to a violation of Rule 10b–5. See Matter of Cady, Roberts & Co., Securities Exchange Act Release No. 6668 at p. 4 (November 8, 1961). Lack of communication between defendant and plaintiff does not eliminate the possibility that Rule 10b–5 has been violated.

* * * In the instant case, if the dividend was reduced only to depress the price of the stock, then plaintiff, as a stockholder, was in

---

* [Ed. Note] Section 10(b), together with Rule 10b–5, prohibits the use of manipulative and deceptive devices in connection with the purchase or sale of any security by use of the mails or instrumentalities of interstate commerce. Rule 10b–5 declares:

"It shall be unlawful for any person, directly or indirectly, by the use of any means or instrumentality of interstate commerce, or of the mails, or of any facility of any national securities exchange,

(1) to employ any device, scheme, or artifice to defraud,

(2) to make any untrue statement of a material fact or to omit to state a material fact necessary in order to make the statements made, in the light of the circumstances under which they were made, not misleading, or

(3) to engage in any act, practice, or course of business which operates or would operate as a fraud or deceit upon any person,

in connection with the purchase or sale of any security."

the class of persons expected to rely on the reduction as evidence of decreased valuation.

The Court of Appeals, Second Circuit, has interpreted New York law as stating that there is no difference between active concealment and active fraud by a director. Lesnik v. Public Industrial Corporation, supra. Ultramares, supra, holds that when fraud is alleged direct privity need not be shown. Putting the two cases together this Court is constrained to hold that the plaintiff has asserted a good cause of action under New York State law. The facts alleged in the complaint charge defendants with an active concealment that is legally the exact equivalent of active fraud in its traditional posture; it is alleged that the fraud by defendants was intended to, and in fact did, deceive plaintiff into parting with his stock when disclosure of the truth would have dictated a different course of action.

Concealment = Fraud

The motion of the defendants as to each cause of action must be and hereby is denied.

So ordered.

POLICY STATEMENT ON THE PAYMENT OF CASH DIVIDENDS BY STATE MEMBER BANKS AND BANK HOLDING COMPANIES

(Board of Governors of the Federal Reserve System) November 14, 1985.
1 CCH Federal Banking Law Reporter ¶ 5521.

The Board of Governors of the Federal Reserve System considers adequate capital to be critical to the health of individual banking organizations and to the safety and stability of the banking system: A major determinant of a bank's or bank holding company's capital adequacy is the strength of its earnings and the extent to which its earnings are retained and added to capital or paid out to shareholders in the form of cash dividends.

Normally, during profitable periods, dividends represent an appropriate return of a portion of a banking organization's net earnings to its shareholders. However, the payment of cash dividends that are not fully covered by earnings, in effect, represents the return of a portion of an organization's capital at a time when circumstances may indicate instead the need to strengthen capital and concentrate financial resources on resolving the organization's problems.

As a matter of prudent banking, therefore, the Board believes that a bank or bank holding company generally should not maintain its existing rate of cash dividends on common stock unless 1) the organization's net income available to common shareholders over the past year has been sufficient to fully fund the dividends *and* 2) the prospective rate of earnings retention appears consistent with the organization's capital needs, asset quality, and overall financial condition. Any banking organization whose cash dividends are inconsistent with either of these criteria should give serious consideration to cutting or eliminating its dividends. Such an action will help to conserve the organization's capital base and assist it in weathering a period of adversity. Once earnings have begun to improve, capital can be strengthened by keeping dividends at a level that allows for an increase in the rate of earnings retention until an adequate position has been restored.

The Board also believes it is inappropriate for a banking organization that is experiencing serious financial problems or that has inadequate capital to borrow in order to pay dividends since this can result in increased leverage at the very time the organization needs to reduce its debt or increase its capital. Similarly, the payment of dividends based solely or largely upon gains resulting from unusual or nonrecurring events, such as the sale of the organization's building or the disposition of other assets, may not be prudent or warranted, especially if the funds derived from such transactions could be better employed to strengthen the organization's financial resources.

A fundamental principle underlying the Federal Reserve's supervision and regulation of bank holding companies is that bank holding companies should serve as a source of managerial and financial strength to their subsidiary banks. The Board believes, therefore, that a bank holding company should not maintain a level of cash dividends to its shareholders that places undue pressure on the capital of bank subsidiaries, or that can be funded only through additional borrowings or other arrangements that may undermine the bank holding company's ability to serve as a source of strength. Thus, for example, if a major subsidiary bank is unable to pay dividends to its parent company—as a consequence of statutory limitations, intervention by the primary supervisor, or noncompliance with regulatory capital requirements—the bank holding company should give serious consideration to reducing or eliminating its dividends in order to conserve its capital base and provide capital assistance to the subsidiary bank.

The Board's guidelines on capital adequacy define primary capital to include perpetual preferred stock, and the Board is aware that such instruments have become an increasingly significant element in the capital base of some banking organizations. As part of a balanced capital structure, this instrument can serve as a useful vehicle for supplementing common stockholders' equity, the most critical component of an organization's capital base, and for augmenting primary capital. However, in formulating capital plans and meeting regulatory capital requirements, banking organizations should avoid excessive reliance on preferred stock since this could limit an organization's financial flexibility in the event it encounters serious and protracted earnings weaknesses.

* * *

NOTE: DIVIDENDS AND CONFLICTS OF INTEREST

If contrary to public stockholders' interest in maximizing share values, and within the limits that the markets set, management can exercise a systematic preference for retention of earnings over payment of dividends—a view which as we saw, supra pp. 553–557, has come to be widely accepted,—a dispute over investment policy or dividend policy may reflect conflicts of interest, as well as differing business judgments. In that event, whether dividends are only a residual of investment policy or independently affect share values, the legal norm for assessing the propriety of a particular investment/dividend policy may involve conventional fiduciary considerations as well as business judgment. If such considerations are relevant, the question arises whether they should induce a rule requiring management to justify its retention decisions on a case by case basis or whether they imply a categorical rule which would compel the payment annually or periodically of, e.g., all earnings as dividends.

These questions are presented in their most acute form when dividend policy is determined by controlling stockholders, who are likely to be less concerned than "outside" stockholders with the impact of dividend policy on near-term share prices, and less dependent upon cash dividends from the enterprise. As suggested in the *Mission Development* case, controlling shareholders, having power to modify dividend policy as they choose, may actually prefer a dividend policy which reduces, or does not increase, near-term share prices, but saves them from a tax at ordinary income rates or enables them to purchase minority-held shares more cheaply. See Whittemore v. Continental Mills, 98 F.Supp. 387 (D.C.Me.1951).

These questions also come up with respect to non-owner managed firms. Management's preference for the quiet life and lower levels of risk (and return) in conducting the firm's business may lead to dividend and reinvestment decisions that are suboptimal from a shareholder point of view. More particularly, it has been suggested that (i) management's widespread ownership of stock options leaves it with diminished incentive to pay-out dividends and increased incentive to seek to enhance stock values by reinvesting earnings, and (ii) retained earnings tend to be invested in projects that produce lower returns and lower risk than those financed by new capital.

Do these patterns of conflicting interests give force to Easterbrook's suggestion, supra pp. 567–569, that stockholder preference for dividends reflects the notion that such a policy reduces agency costs? To the extent that payment of dividends requires management to look to the market for capital it substitutes capital market actors for dispersed stockholders as monitors of management's behavior.

A more draconian proposal also has been made for dealing with this problem. It has been suggested that management should be forced to pay out all or some substantial and designated portion of earnings as dividends. A. Rubner, The Ensnared Shareholder 133–36 (1965); Brewster, The Corporation and Economic Federalism, in The Corporation in

Modern Society 72, 81 (E. Mason, ed. 1960).[c] This is a simple suggestion, but it leads quickly to the complicated problem of developing the legal and economic norms by which to determine and measure the mandated payout. If the payout of all earnings were required, management would have to go to the capital market for all the cash needed to expand or meet competition—with explanations that are costly in either case. If payout of only some portion of earnings were required, there would remain the problem of defining appropriate and enforceable criteria for selecting the proper amount. As we saw above, economic theory does not yet offer a determinate answer to the question of the proper amount. An arbitrarily selected percentage could be decreed as a fall back, but would present problems of its own.

Must we conclude that, just as traditional corporate law fails to put adequate restraints on management's powers respecting dividend policy, there is good reason to conclude that the law cannot be reformed so as to impose any effective additional restrictions? Brudney, Dividends, Discretion, and Disclosure, 66 Va.L.Rev. 85, 85–86 (1980), suggests that the situation calls for stepped up disclosure rules: "The inability to impose feasible limits on management's discretion in making the dividend decision underscores the significance of defining the extent of management's obligation to convey the information content of the dividend decision. Questions about the adequacy of management's disclosure arise from the essential ambiguity of signals given by the mere act of declaring or altering a dividend and from the potential, if not intrinsic, conflicts of interest between management and stockholders over dividend policy. That combination of intrinsic ambiguity and divergence of interest invites the examination of compelling management to communicate more clearly the meaning of its dividend action." How might such dividend disclosure rules be drafted? See id. pp. 114–129. For the view that market controls are adequate to deal with management's dividend discretion, see Fischel, The Law and Economics of Dividend Policy, 67 Va.L.Rev. 699 (1981).

SECTION B. STOCK DIVIDENDS
LEWELLEN, THE COST OF CAPITAL
Chapter 8 (1969).

Stock Dividends and Splits

Is it possible for a firm to increase its total market value simply by changing the number of shares it has outstanding? Logic—and the

---

c. While modern corporation statutes no longer compel distribution of earnings in excess of specified reserves (compare New Jersey statutes discussed in Murray v. Beattie Mfg. Co., 79 N.J.Eq. 322, 82 A. 1038 (Err. & App. 1911) with Del.Corp.Law §§ 170, 171; NYBCL § 517(b); there have been efforts to protect minority stockholders of close corporations (where divergence of interest is most often demonstrable) by enacting legislation which would compel payment of a minimum portion of annual profits on the request of a specified percentage of stockholders. See N.C.Bus. Corp. Act § 55–6–40(j). The problems are discussed in Note, 64 Harv.L.Rev. 299 (1950); Note, 56 Nw.U.L.Rev. 503 (1961); Note, 10 Rutgers L.Rev. 723 (1956).

weight of current scholarly opinion—would suggest a negative reply. Given the firm's investments, the level of its borrowing, and therefore its aggregate after-interest-and-tax profit prospects, it should make no difference how many pieces of paper it happens to hand out to its owners. The product

$$V_s = \text{(price per share)} \times \text{(number of shares)}$$

should be a constant. Two shares of stock promising $5 a year should not sell for more in total than one share promising $10. The same argument—in reverse—is the basis for the stock repurchase discussion * * * [below]. If a corporation uses its redundant cash to remove some of its shares from the market and retire them, the price of those remaining should rise correspondingly to reflect higher per-share future income prospects.

Why, then, do firms occasionally split their stock and pay stock dividends—and why does it often seem that the share prices involved do not fall quite in proportion? Thus, it is not unusual to see a $60 stock which is split two-for-one end up selling for more than $30 afterward. One answer commonly given is that, by lowering the shares' price range, the market for them is broadened to include more small investors. People who will not consider a $60 stock because it is "high-priced" will buy it if it trades near $30 instead. They will be attracted to the opportunity to buy what in market terminology is called a "round lot"—100 shares—for $3,000, whereas they would not think of buying 50 shares at $60. If this sounds a little bizarre, there does seem to be some truth in it. A possible reason is that the brokerage commissions on a round lot are smaller per share so that there *is* a slight saving on such purchases as compared with "odd lots" of less than 100 shares. Since this saving is fairly small, however, the main factor seems to be purely psychological. Enough people appear to like lower-priced shares that the firm does get some benefit out of keeping the trading range of its stock at an appropriate level through periodic splits.[9]

A more rational sort of explanation for the same phenomenon involves the effect of stock splits on investors' expectations. The market may interpret the act of splitting in itself as an indication that the firm's subsequent earnings and dividends are likely to be higher than were previously anticipated. The firm in a sense is telling the world that the time has come to bring its share price down to a more manageable level because it looks as though even further increases will soon be forthcoming. This alerts investors to the company's bright future and—if the brightness is in fact there and has just not been fully appreciated before—a price increase is a logical result. In that respect,

---

9. On the other hand, there seems to be a feeling that it is possible to err on the low side as well. Several years ago, the Studebaker Corporation *combined* its stock in the ratio 1:5 in order to raise the relevant price from approximately $7 per share to $35. The concern was that a $7 figure made the company look too "cheap"—i.e., speculative and probably a little disreputable—and thereby discouraged respectable investors from being interested in its shares.

a stock split may be said to contain implicitly some useful information about management's confidence in the firm's prospects.

An even more concrete way of expressing that confidence, of course, is to raise the company's cash dividend simultaneously. This seems the most likely justification for any hopes that a corporation's total market value will increase, particularly in the case of a stock dividend. If a firm "pays" a 5 percent stock dividend—giving its shareholders one additional piece of paper for every 20 they now own—but does not adjust its per-share cash dividend payment downward by the same fraction, the effect is to augment its owners' aggregate annual cash income by 5 percent. It would therefore come as no surprise if it turned out that the per-share price of the company's stock held steady. The basis for such a result, however, is the behavior of the relevant cash payments rather than the presence of extra stock certificates. The firm could achieve the same objective by skipping the latter entirely and simply raising its per-share cash payout.

As an illustration, consider the situation of a company which has been paying $5 per share cash dividend every year for many years. Its earnings have fluctuated, but have exhibited no tendency to grow over time and there is no expectation of higher dividends to come. Its current stock price is $50. Suddenly, one of its products catches on with consumers and it becomes clear that earnings will jump to a new level that will permit dividends to be raised to—and maintained at—$5.25 a share. If the firm increases its payout in that manner, a new stock price of $52.50 can be anticipated. If instead it issues a 5 percent stock dividend and keeps the cash payment at $5.00, the price should continue to be $50. Either way, every original shareholder will own stock worth a total of $52.50, will be receiving $5.25 annually in cash dividends, and will eventually have to pay tax on a $2.50 capital gain. But the cause of these happy circumstances is the improvement in the firm's profit position and thereby in its ability to generate income for its owners—not an increase in the number of pieces of paper those individuals have in their safety deposit boxes.

By way of comic relief, the following news item from the December 20, 1965, *Wall Street Journal* suggests the confusion which often attends discussions of the efficacy of stock dividends. As a charitable gesture, the company and the executive involved will be allowed to remain anonymous:

> The XXX Corporation today declared a 2.5 percent stock dividend payable February 1 to stock of record January 3. It is the first dividend declared by the company since it was formed in 1945. John Doe, Senior Vice–President for Finance, said: "This has been a very good financial year and we felt we should recognize this by a stock dividend to our shareholders. Because of our equipment program, we felt we shouldn't pay it in cash."

Wouldn't a 5 percent dividend have been twice as good?

NOTE: EXPLAINING STOCK SPLITS AND STOCK DIVIDENDS

1. *Stock Splits.*

The two standard explanations of stock splits—management signalling and the return of the stock price to a "normal" trading range—have been the subject of debate.

The downward price adjustment explanation has been contested on the ground that transaction costs (measured as a percentage of transaction value) tend to be an inverse function of stock price, and, at least in the days of fixed commissions, liquidity tended to decrease following a split. Thus there should be no investor affinity for small round lot trading. Copeland, Liquidity Changes Following Stock Splits, 34 J. Finance 115 (1979). Subsequent studies support the price adjustment theory, however. Lamoureux and Poon, The Market Reaction to Stock Splits, 42 J. Finance 1347 (1987), finds that the number of shareholders tends to increase after a split. Lakonishok and Lev, Stock Splits and Stock Dividends: Why, Who and When, 42 J. Finance 913 (1987), confirms the price adjustment explanation with the results of a study of stock split and stock dividend activity by the firms on the University of Chicago's CRSP tape during the period 1963 to 1982. The study shows that during the five years preceding the split, a 70 percent gap tends to open up between the stock prices of splitting firms and control firms. After the split, the price gap narrows and then vanishes.

The signalling explanation is the subject of an analytical objection. If the split is a signal that the company is undervalued, then the market must extract some cost in the case of a false signal. Otherwise it would be impossible to distinguish an undervalued splitting stock from an overvalued splitting stock. But no such cost appears, and the signal could be a negative one in any event—the split could reflect management's judgment that the price has peaked. See Lamoureux and Poon, supra, p. 1348. The Lakonishok and Lev study provides a partial rebuttal to this objection. It looks at pre and post split earnings and dividend records, and concludes that "some signalling" may be occurring. Splitting firms have higher dividend growth than nonsplitting firms during both the pre and post split periods. In the post split period, the most dramatic increase in dividends occurs during the first quarter after the split. The splitting firms' growth advantage diminishes thereafter. This leads to the conclusion that a split signals "mildly good news:" the firm's presplit earnings will stabilize at the newly reached plateau. Lakonishok and Lev, supra, p. 922.

Two further findings respecting splits should be noted. Grinblatt, Masulis and Titman, The Valuation Effects of Stock Splits and Stock Dividends, 13 J. Financial Econs. 461 (1984), reports that even where no other firm-specific event coincides with the split announcement, splits generate a positive abnormal return of 3 percent on announcement and an additional 1 percent abnormal return on the ex-day. Ohlson and Penman, Variance Increases Subsequent to Stock Splits: An Empirical Aberration, 14 J. Financial Econs. 251 (1985), documents the surprising point that stock splits cause stock volatility to rise: volatility increases by an average of 35 percent subsequent to the ex-day. Does this increase in the standard deviation of the stock require the conclusion that the split injures investors? Lamoureux and Poon, supra, contend that the volatility increase is consistent with investor welfare. In their model, the split causes an increase in trading volume. The volume increase causes noise, and thus accounts for the increase of nonsystematic risk. This increased risk increases the firm's value because, to the extent the risk is diversifiable, is creates tax opportunities for high bracket taxpayers in the equity ownership group. They can opt either for short term losses or long term capital gains. For a contrasting explanation centered on trading costs, consult Brennan and Copeland, Stock Splits, Stock Prices, and Transaction Costs, 22 J. Financial Econs. 83 (1988).

2. Stock Dividends.

Lakonishok and Lev, supra, find that firms issuing stock dividends enjoy only slightly higher preannouncement earnings growth than do control firms. They also find that stock dividend firms have slightly lower preannouncement dividend yields than do control firms. Stock price appreciation tends to occur around the announcement date. Lakonishok and Lev explain this by reference to an additional empirical finding: the stock dividend announcement tends to be followed by a relatively large cash dividend increase. Id. pp. 923–925. Notwithstanding this point, management apparently believes that the market does not reduce stock prices even if cash dividends are not effectively increased upon distribution of a stock dividend. See Eiseman and Moses, Stock Dividends: Management's View, 34 Fin.Anal.J. 77 (July–August 1978); Woolridge, Ex Date Stock Price Adjustment to Stock Dividends: A Note, 38 J. Finance 247 (1983).

Lakonishok and Lev, supra, conclude that stock dividends are not just small stock splits. The traditional explanation that managers consider them to be a temporary substitute for cash dividends, although unpersuasive as an economic justification for stock dividends, may be accurate.

3. Frequency.

Lakonishok and Lev, supra, report that stock splits are frequent and persistent—between 5 and 10 percent of the firms they studied split their stock each year. In contrast, the number of firms issuing stock dividends declined steadily, from 13.45 percent in 1968 to 4.48 percent in 1982.

4. Management Explanations.

Compare with the foregoing views the explanation offered for a 2 for 1 stock split by William J. Agee, the Chairman and Chief Executive

Officer of Morrison Knudsen Corp., in a letter to stockholders dated May 26, 1992:

> "The Board of Directors believes that the stock split will stimulate investor interest in the Company and add liquidity to the Company's common stock by increasing the number of shares (and eventually, the number of shareholders)."

NOTE: STOCK DIVIDENDS AS INFORMATION AND THE REGULATION OF DISCLOSURE

The preceding discussion suggests that stock dividends are often intended to express the distributing corporation's optimistic outlook: "business is good and getting better, but we want to retain our cash assets to use for expansion." Additional shares give a kind of recognition to the fact that the company is profitable and has attractive investment opportunities on hand. Suppose, however, that just the opposite is true—business is bad and getting worse and there is simply no cash to spare for stockholders. Might the distribution of a stock dividend then actually serve to obscure the real state of affairs? Securities Exchange Act Release No. 8268, set out below, is based on Accounting Research Bulletin No. 43, ch. 7B (1953), which is also reflected in the listing standards of both the New York Stock Exchange (NYSE Listed Company Manual § 703.02) and the American Stock Exchange (Amer. Stock Exchange Guide § 506, CCH ¶ 10,136). How well, and how directly, does the remedy proposed by the SEC deal with the assumed vice?

SECURITIES EXCHANGE ACT RELEASE NO. 8268
March 7, 1968.

Notice is hereby given that the Securities and Exchange Commission has under consideration a proposal to adopt Rule 10b–12 under the Securities Exchange Act of 1934 (the Act) to preclude an issuer whose stock is publicly offered or traded from misrepresenting the results of its operations by distributing stock dividends or their equivalent to shareholders unless the issuer has earned surplus sufficient to cover the fair value of the shares distributed. The rule would not affect traditional stock splits involving the distribution of at least an additional share for each share outstanding.

Pro rata stock distributions to stockholders in amounts which are relatively small in relation to the number of shares outstanding are a means of conveying the impression that a distribution is being made out of the earned surplus of the company without the drain on current assets that would result from the distribution of a cash dividend. Instances have recently come to the attention of the Commission in which such distributions were utilized by companies having little or no earned surplus, thus creating a misleading impression concerning the results of operations of the company.

The listing standards of the New York Stock Exchange have for a number of years provided that a pro rata distribution to stockholders, without consideration, of less than 25% of the number of shares outstanding prior to the distribution cannot be made in the absence of the transfer of the fair value of the securities so distributed from earned surplus to the capital stock or capital surplus accounts. In the same connection, it has been pointed out that the use of the term "dividend" with reference to such pro rata stock distributions tends to be misleading in the absence of such a transfer from earned surplus to the capital stock or capital surplus accounts of an amount equal to the fair value of the shares so distributed. Moreover, existing standards indicate that such pro rata distributions in the range between 25% and 100% of the shares outstanding prior to the distribution could create the deceptive impression that such distributions are "dividends" if they are of a recurring nature and if transfers of their fair value are not made from earned surplus to the capital stock or capital surplus accounts. Further in this connection, the New York Stock Exchange has observed that a so-called "split up" (stock split) of less than 100% often will not be reflected in appropriate adjustments of price and distribution, and that such attempted adjustments, if they follow each other too closely, may have effects upon the market not consistent with the best interests of the company or its stockholders, or those of the general investing public.

* * *

The text of proposed Rule 10b–12 is as follows:

Rule 10b–12   Employment of Manipulative or Deceptive Devices or Contrivances With Respect to Certain Stock Distributions

(a) It shall constitute a manipulative or deceptive device or contrivance in connection with the purchase or sale of a security within the meaning of Section 10(b) of the Act for an issuer which publicly offers any class of stock, or which has outstanding any class of stock traded, by use of the mails or any means or instrumentality of interstate commerce, or of any facility of any national securities exchange, to issue to the holders thereof shares of any class of stock on a pro rata basis and without consideration,

(1) if directly or indirectly the issuer designates the shares so issued as a stock dividend, or if the number of shares so issued (regardless of how designated) is less than 25% of the number of shares of the same class outstanding immediately prior to such issuance, unless (A) at the time of such issuance, the issuer has earned surplus in an amount at least equal to the fair value of the shares so issued, and (B) the issuer has transferred such amount of earned surplus to the permanent capitalization of the issuer represented by its capital stock and capital surplus accounts, or

(2) if the number of shares so issued is 25% or more, but less than 100%, of the number of shares of the same class outstanding immediately prior to such issuance, unless (A) at the time of such issuance the

issuer has earned surplus in an amount at least equal to the fair value of the shares so issued, and has transferred such amount of earned surplus to the permanent capitalization of the issuer represented by its capital stock and capital surplus account, or (B) the issuance of such shares is not part of a program of recurring pro rata distribution without consideration. The issuer shall have the burden of proving that any given distribution of shares of the kind covered by this subsection is not part of such a program of recurring pro rata distribution without consideration.

(b) The term "fair value" as used in this rule means an amount, determined in accordance with good accounting practice, which closely approximates the current per share market price adjusted to reflect issuance of the additional shares.

(c) This rule shall not prohibit activity by an issuer otherwise proscribed by this rule, if the Commission, upon written request or upon its own motion, exempts such activity, either unconditionally or on specified terms and conditions, as not constituting a manipulative or deceptive device or contrivance comprehended within the purpose of this rule.

———

Even though proposed Rule 10b–12 was never adopted, would a financial statement which accounted for a series of four stock distributions (two of 10% and two of 25%, characterized as "stock split * * * dividends") over a period of years by transfers to capital from capital surplus (in the absence of earned surplus) be misleading (in violation of either Sections 11, 12 or 17 of the Securities Act of 1933 or Rule 10b–5) if it purported to follow generally accepted accounting principles? Compare Monmouth Capital Corporation, Sec.Act.Rel. No. 5169 (July 14, 1971) and S.A.Rel. No. 5255 (June 1, 1972), CCH Fed.Sec.L.Rep. ¶ 72,146, suggesting that where companies do not have retained or current earnings "declaration of a dividend not warranted by the business condition of a company is characteristic of a manipulative scheme."

With the above requirements contrast the statutory provisions authorizing stock dividends to be underpinned by a transfer to capital from surplus (MBCA §§ 18, 45(d); NYBCL § 511). Do these statutes permit a transfer from capital surplus even if the corporation has earned surplus? Do these statutes prescribe the amount of the charge to either type of surplus? If a corporation has sufficient authorized, but unissued, shares, a stock dividend may in most states be declared simply by action of the board of directors, without need for a stockholders' vote (RMBCA § 6.23; NYBCL § 511; Del.Corp.Law §§ 170, 173). On the other hand, a stock split will generally require stockholders' action as well as board action. In the case of par value shares, amendment of the charter will normally be required. In the case of no-par shares, a stock split may be effected by charter amendment (RMBCA §§ 10.03, 10.04; NYBCL § 801), but the same result may often be achieved by action of the board alone. See Hackney, The Financial Provisions of the Model Business Corporation Act, 70 Harv.L.Rev. 1357, 1386 n. 136 (1957) discussing MBCA Section 45(d) (formerly 40(d)).

NOTE: STOCK DIVIDENDS AND CAPITAL GAINS; SAGA OF G.P.U.

On February 23, 1968, the president of General Public Utilities Corporation addressed the following letter to the company's stockholders:

DEAR STOCKHOLDER:

The Board of Directors has under consideration a possible change in the GPU dividend policy. The purpose of this letter is to acquaint you with that fact and the considerations that have caused the Board to embark on such a study. *No decision has yet been made by the Board and we shall advise you promptly when such a decision is made.*

For the last two decades, GPU has followed the policy of distributing quarterly cash dividends to its stockholders equal to approximately 70% to 75% of current earnings. The cash distributions have been increased almost every year in conformity with that policy. In essence, the change in policy under consideration would involve the payment of one cash dividend each year and the distribution of stock dividends during the balance of the year. If this policy change is adopted, it is expected that arrangements will be made to enable any stockholder to sell readily and at minimum cost the shares periodically distributed as stock dividends.

If a program of this character had been in effect in prior years, the aggregate of the cash dividends paid and the value of the shares distributed as stock dividends would have been approximately equal to the cash dividends which were distributed in those years. For example, if this program had been in effect in 1967, each stockholder would have received in 1967, per share of GPU stock, a cash dividend of about 40¢ and stock dividends aggregating about 4% (or about $1.12 in realizable market value) and thus corresponding to the approximately $1.52 which was paid in cash.

This possible change in policy is being considered because the rate of growth of the capital requirements of GPU's subsidiaries is now such that the subsidiaries require very substantial amounts of additional equity capital from GPU every year, and GPU must obtain a part of such capital by the periodic issuance of additional shares. GPU's offering of shares has traditionally taken the form of the issuance of subscription rights to its stockholders. GPU has had a total of eight offerings through subscription rights. On the average, more than half the shares so offered were purchased by stockholders through the exercise of subscription rights. The holders of a substantial portion of the GPU shares have thus evidenced an interest in increasing their investment in GPU whenever additional shares have been made available by the Corporation. This periodic sale of additional shares is an expensive way to raise funds needed for the conduct of the Corporation's affairs. It is clear that retention of cash otherwise payable as dividends and the issuance of stock dividends instead would be a more economical way to provide the needed capital.

At our present rate of growth, the funds made available to GPU by such a stock dividend policy would not fully meet GPU's requirements for additional equity capital and it would be necessary to supplement it periodically with additional offerings of stock (and, indeed, we expect to make such an offering this year, whether or not the policy change is adopted), but the size and frequency of such offerings would be substantially reduced.

It is believed that such a stock dividend program would be in the interest of virtually all GPU stockholders. There is a considerable income tax disadvantage to a stockholder who receives cash dividends and then buys additional shares upon the exercise of subscription rights, i.e. he pays ordinary income tax on the cash dividends he receives and he purchases the additional shares with after-tax dollars. By contrast, we are advised that if he were to receive shares as a dividend under the program under consideration the receipt of such shares would not result in any current income tax liability to him; moreover, if he should sell his dividend shares (whether immediately when issued or at some subsequent date), we are advised that, under present tax laws, the proceeds of such sale would be taxable on a capital gain basis, rather than as ordinary income, and if he had acquired the shares on which the stock dividend was distributed more than six months before the sale, any capital gain realized would be long-term and taxable at the lesser of one-half of the rate applicable to ordinary income or 25% of the gain.*

We are in the process of working out the mechanical means to implement such a policy if it should be adopted. An important ingredient will be the provision of means whereby a stockholder who wishes to do so can sell his dividend shares readily. We contemplate that the stockholder will be furnished with a card enabling him, in advance, to direct a bank to dispose of the dividend shares distributable to him. On this basis, the bank would sell the shares for his account and would remit the net proceeds thereof to the stockholder. Assuming no substantial fluctuation in the market between the time the stock dividends are declared and the sales are made, the level of the net proceeds so realized by the bank for the account of the stockholder during the year should approximate the amount that he would have received as cash dividends if this policy had not been adopted. Consequently, based on

---

*[Ed. Note] The Tax Reform Act of 1986 eliminated the long-standing distinction between ordinary income and capital gain, so that the same tax-rates now applied to dividends and gains from the sale of shares. A rate advantage in favor of capital gains reappeared in 1990, when the top individual rate rose to 31 percent and the capital gains rate stayed at 28 percent. It also continues to be true that cash dividends are taxable when received, while stock dividends are generally received tax-free. The recipient of a stock dividend thus incurs a tax only when (and if) the dividend shares are finally sold.

the advice we have received, the stockholder electing to sell his dividend shares would receive during the year cash for such dividend shares in approximately the same total amount that he would otherwise have received as cash dividends, but if he had acquired more than six months earlier the shares on which the stock dividend was distributed, the income tax payable by him with respect to such net proceeds would be no more than one-half of that which he would otherwise pay.

In the case of stock held by trustees where the life beneficiary of the trust is not the same as the residuary beneficiary, a program of this sort might have disadvantages, if under the terms of the trust or applicable law, stock dividends are treated as a part of capital while cash dividends are treated as income. Our preliminary study indicates that this affects only a relatively few shares.

If the Board concludes that it is feasible and desirable to proceed with this change in policy, we shall apply for a ruling by the Internal Revenue Service confirming the tax advice we have received. If the Board adopts the program, the Board will continue to have authority either to modify the program or to suspend or terminate it if experience should demonstrate that this is desirable or if the need of GPU's subsidiaries for additional equity funds should decline to a level which would make such action appropriate.

As I stated at the beginning of this letter, no decision has yet been made by the Board and we shall advise you promptly when such a decision is made. There is no need or occasion for stockholders to take any action at this time. Our sole purpose in writing you at this stage is simply to inform you of a study which the Board is making on a matter of importance to you, so that you would learn of that fact directly from GPU.

Sincerely,

W.G. KUHNS, *President*

————

A further communication was addressed to the stockholders on April 19, 1968:

To the Stockholders of

GENERAL PUBLIC UTILITIES CORPORATION:

The following is a statement which I intend to make today at the Annual Meeting of Stockholders of the Corporation and which the Board thought you would wish to receive promptly if you were unable to attend the meeting.

I want to advise you that the board has concluded that it will not adopt the possible change in dividend policy which we outlined in our letter to stockholders, dated February 23, 1968. Instead, the Board intends to adhere to the present policy of declaring cash dividends on a quarterly basis.

We have reached this conclusion after extensive study. We believe that the possible change in dividend policy has many virtues and could well serve the interests of the stockholders and the Corporation. However, it has become apparent that a significant number of GPU stockholders were so strongly opposed to the change in policy that its adoption could have a disruptive effect on our over-all financing program and, accordingly, might interfere with the orderly raising of the additional capital required by our rapidly growing business and cause genuine hardship to some of our stockholders.

We know that this decision will please some of our stockholders and that it will disappoint others. We are confident that all stockholders realize that, both in developing the plan and in announcing to all of our stockholders that it was under study, we were attempting to serve the interests of the entire stockholder group.

We should like to thank the stockholders who studied the proposed program and who gave us the benefit of their views. Many stockholders took the time and made the effort to write us about it, some in considerable detail. Each of these communications was considered by us and we wrote an individual reply to each such letter discussing the particular matters raised by each stockholder and, where appropriate, discussing the possible application of the plan to his individual situation. We also discussed the plan in detail with a number of financial analysts, investment bankers, officers of banks and trust companies, executives of mutual funds and representatives of other organizations. I want to highlight a few of the major items raised:

1. As our February 23rd letter indicated, we recognized at the outset that the plan might create problems in the cases of trusts where, under applicable law or the particular trust instrument, cash dividends are treated as income but stock dividends are treated as principal, since it would occasion a shift of receipts from the life tenant to the remainderman of the trust. Subsequent to our February 23rd letter, we met with a number of trust officers to explore the matter in more detail. They have advised us that the proposed change in dividend policy would require forced liquidation by many trusts which, in our opinion, would have a disturbing effect upon the market level of the GPU stock and upon our ability to raise the funds required in the future.

2. All the banks, securities firms and others that hold shares as custodians or investment managers for beneficial owners, advised us the plan would impose a tremendous administrative burden upon them and upon their beneficiaries. They stated that because our plan would involve a departure from the policies of other corporations where the receipt and disbursements of dividends can be programmed on computers, it would be necessary for every account which included GPU shares to be handled on an individual basis which would interfere with the orderly flow of their work.

3. Another factor mentioned by virtually all of the banks and securities firms and many of the individual stockholders was the

complexity of the record keeping that a stock dividend program would involve. We recognized that under the applicable requirements of the Internal Revenue Code the payment of quarterly stock dividends would require quarterly allocations of tax basis in accordance with the formulae prescribed by the Internal Revenue Service. We thought, however, that this would be a relatively minor nuisance to the stockholders. The banks, the securities firms and a great many individual stockholders informed us that our assumption was not correct.

In enumerating these objections, I do not want to suggest that it is our opinion that all of them present necessarily insuperable problems. They do clearly represent, however, the genuinely and firmly held convictions of many of our stockholders.

There is one other aspect of this matter on which I should like to comment. Several stockholders have asked us why we announced publicly that the plan was under consideration before we sought the views of representative stockholders. This obligation is imposed by various statutes and regulations, the standard form of agreement with the New York Stock Exchange and by other legal requirements. In addition, we have always tried to let all stockholders have contemporaneously the pertinent information about material factors affecting their investment. We also wanted the benefit of the comments of large and small stockholders who would not necessarily be reached through the banks and financial analysts. We wanted to be sure that in seeking the views of the banks and financial analysts we put them in a position where they were free to discuss the matter not only within their own organizations, but also with their beneficiaries and clients.

To sum it all up, our stockholders have responded in a most helpful fashion in giving us a better picture of their own objectives and attitudes and this will help us in the years ahead.

Sincerely,

W.G. KUHNS, *President*

While stockholders may have rejected proposals to pay them stock dividends in lieu of cash, they have become members of dividend reinvestment plans (DRPs). DRPs which were first offered by banks in 1968 grew rapidly in the '70s. Notwithstanding the fact that federal income tax is payable on the cash dividends received and reinvested (so that the investor is able to reinvest only the amount received net of tax) these plans attract investors even though comparable investors appear to have rejected stock dividend plans which would have given them the same reinvestment without tax. If dividend reinvestment plans are more attractive to stockholders, notwithstanding their greater cost, than stock dividend plans, is there some rational explanation?

SECTION C. REPURCHASE OF
OUTSTANDING SHARES

---

1. THE ECONOMICS OF SHARE REPURCHASES

BRIGHAM, THE PROFITABILITY OF A FIRM'S PURCHASE OF ITS OWN COMMON STOCK

7 California Management Review 69 (Winter 1964).

On September 4, 1963, American Radiator and Standard Sanitary Corporation announced a stock tender offer to buy about 10 per cent of its outstanding common shares. Thompson Ramo Wooldridge and Interlake Iron Corporation carried out similar operations some months later, and in recent years many other well-known firms have purchased significant amounts of their own stock through the open market.

Although it is not generally possible to be sure of the motives behind these purchases, there seem to be two principal reasons for them. First, many acquisition-minded firms find that companies can frequently be bought more easily on an exchange-of-stock basis than for cash. The acquiring firm could issue new shares to effect the merger, but sometimes it is apparently expedient to buy outstanding stock and use it for this purpose. The second reason for a firm's purchase of its own shares is simply as an investment. Thompson Ramo Wooldridge, for instance, stated that

> the company now has funds in excess of its operating require-
> ments for the foreseeable future. After considering various
> alternatives for the use of these funds, we have concluded that
> the purchase of additional shares of common stock would be
> more beneficial to shareholders from the standpoint of earn-
> ings improvement per share.

This paper examines the rationale behind this second type of purchase—the permanent investment in one's own shares. The under-lying economics are examined briefly, but for the most part the exposi-tion is by example. The paper describes a hypothetical firm operating under what seem to be rather reasonable conditions, and discusses a technique for examining the impact of an investment in its own shares on the firm's profits. * * *

The economic environment. The U.S. economy as a whole has grown rapidly in the postwar era, but not all sectors have shared in this expansion. This has caused serious investment problems for some of the firms operating in the more or less stagnant industries—where demand is increasing too slowly to permit all available internal funds to be invested profitably.

Funds are generated internally as depreciation and profits after taxes, and externally by the sale of debt and equity securities. The "true growth company," by definition, has attractive internal investment opportunities; it can invest its available funds in projects that promise a relatively high internal rate of return, while just the reverse is true for the nongrowth firm. Each company must decide how to best use its internally generated funds and whether, given its investment opportunities, these funds are insufficient, just right, or excessive. Typically the true growth company (Firm G in the example below) finds internal funds to be insufficient for its needs so it periodically issues debt or equity securities; the nongrowth company (Firm N) finds its internal funds to be greater than it can profitably employ in the business.

Figure 1 shows this situation graphically. Here the X-axis gives the total dollars invested during a certain time period, say a year; the Y-axis gives the rate of return on investment; the curves labeled ARR ^{g} and MRR ^{g}, and ARR ^{n} and MRR ^{n}, represent the average and marginal rates of return on investment opportunities for Firms G and N respectively; ACC is the average (and marginal) cost of capital for each of the firms; and the point Q is the total amount of internally generated funds for each company. In the case described in the graph, Firm N should invest I^1 internally and dispose of Q–I^1, and Firm G should invest I^2, obtaining I^2–Q from external sources.

The case of "Firm N." No real-world company has the information necessary to make the precise marginal decisions specified above, but firms do have, or at least can arrive at, "reasonably" good approximations to their internal investment opportunities and their cost of capital. Hypothetical Firm N, a company assumed to be operating in a stagnant industry, is a case in point. Demand for its product is stable, but any effort to increase sales would involve heavy promotional expenditures and would meet with severe price competition from other firms in the industry. Management is reasonably efficient, and the company is doing relatively well under the circumstances. Internal operations generate $2 million per year, $1 million of after-tax profits and $1 million of depreciation. One million shares of stock are outstanding and sell for 13.3 times the $1.00 earnings, or $13.30. This provides investors with an earnings yield (earnings per share divided by price per share) of 7½ per cent. * * *

FIGURE 1. *Hypothetical schedules relating rate of return on invest-*
ment to the dollar amount of investment during the year.

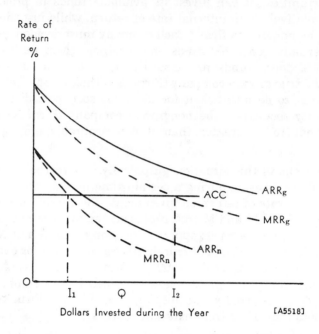

We will assume that this earnings multiplier remains constant, hence the market price of the shares bears a constant relationship to earnings per share.

Suppose that the company, which is debt-free and plans to remain so, can invest all of its depreciation allowances to replace existing equipment as it wears out, and this investment will maintain the present earnings after taxes. If this replacement is not made, however, earnings after taxes will have a permanent decline equal to 10 per cent of the depreciation allowances of the first year. This means, in effect, that the replacement program has an after-tax rate of return of 10 per cent. Suppose, further, that the next most profitable investment opportunity can be taken on in unlimited amounts and will yield 10 per cent before or 5 per cent after taxes in perpetuity. Figure 2 shows Firm N's investment opportunity schedule under this particular set of assumptions.

FIGURE 2. *Hypothetical investment opportunities for nongrowth firm N.*

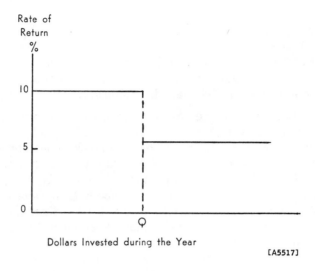

Dollars Invested during the Year

[A5517]

Now assume that Firm N's management's primary goal is to maximize the market value of the common stock; with a constant earnings multiplier, this amounts to maximizing earnings per share. What financial policy does the firm follow with respect to the $2 million of available funds to make earnings per share as high as possible? In practice, four alternatives are open. First, the company can simply build up cash balances, purchase marketable securities, and strengthen its financial position generally. Sometimes, if the business is in a weak position, this may be feasible, but it would not generally be the best choice. A second option is to use surplus funds to buy up other companies and diversify into areas with greater opportunities for growth. This policy has been followed successfully by a number of companies in stagnant industries, coal and textiles for example, but it requires special management skills and will not be considered further here. If these first two alternatives are not followed, then the company must either invest the funds internally or return them to stockholders. The decision to return funds to stockholders usually means increasing dividends, but, as will be shown, it may be better for the company to buy up its own shares.

Now Firm N, by assumption, does not plan to become involved in an acquisition program, wishes to maximize the wealth of its stockholders, and has $2 million available for investment or distribution. If it invests the $1 million of depreciation-generated funds internally at an average rate of 10 per cent after taxes and the retained earnings at 5 per cent, then earnings per share will rise to $1.05 and, with the 13.3 earnings multiplier, the effect is to push the price of the stock up to $14.00. Since there are one million shares outstanding, the value of the firm's equity—the wealth of its shareholders—is $14 million.

Alternatively, it could pay the $1 million out in dividends. If its stockholders are all tax-exempt, they will receive the full $1 million and will have an aggregate wealth position of $14.3 million, the dividend plus the value of the shares. If the stockholders pay, on the average, 30 per cent of the dividends in taxes, then they will end up with but $14.0 million. This is still better than taking on the internal investment, since in that case stockholders are still subject to a capital gains tax liability when they sell their shares.

As an alternative to the cash dividend, the firm could use the $1 million to buy its own shares. After the million dollars have been earned, but before they are paid out, the stock should be selling for about $14.00 (the "normal" value of $13.30 plus the after-tax value of the dividend, or $.70). Assuming that shares can be bought for this price, the $1 million can be used to retire about 71,400 shares; this will cause future earnings to increase to about $1.075. Since the multiplier is assumed to be 13.3, the new price must be about $14.30 as compared to the normal-price-plus-dividend of $14.00 in the event of a cash dividend payment. Continuing stockholders will be subject to (possible) capital gains taxes on the increase in the price of the stock, but these are presumably low because of the difference in capital gains and normal income taxes and the fact that the capital gains taxes * are deferred to the future. In summary, under the assumed conditions, the firm can raise the wealth of its continuing stockholders, without detriment to stockholders who sell out, by taking advantage of the fact that dividends are taxed as normal income.

In actual practice, the firm will probably not be able to purchase a substantial block of its shares at the going market price but may be required to pay a premium. Any price up to $20 per share would leave the remaining stockholders as well off as they would be under either the internal investment alternative or the dividend payment alternative, assuming a 30 per cent average tax rate. Just where the price would actually be set could be decided arbitrarily by the board of directors, or it could be established by the market place. Some interesting questions of equity can be raised at this point (such as, with which group of stockholders should the directors be concerned?), but we shall not attempt to resolve them now. One point remains: The best financial policy open to this hypothetical firm, which is typical of many, is to purchase its own shares.

* * *

It is our contention * * * that diverting funds from dividends to the purchase of shares would not, under the circumstances described, adversely affect the earnings multiplier. We would not recommend a sudden cut in an established dividend; this might well have an adverse impact on the corporation's shares. Financial prudence would indicate that a policy such as the one advocated here should be approached

---

* [Ed. Note] Under the Tax Reform Act of 1986, as modified in 1990, the rate differential between capital gains and ordinary income has been reduced to 3 percent.

cautiously, and that investors should be given time to see and appreciate what the firm is doing and how it is affecting growth in earnings per share.

* * *

FIGURE 3.   *Hypothetical relationships between the capital structure and: (1) The earnings yield on common stock, (2) The after-tax cost of debt, and (3) The average cost of capital.*

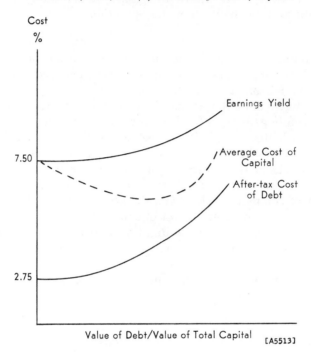

[A5513]

Restructuring the capital structure.   Most financial authorities would agree that the cost of capital for a nongrowth firm should be computed as the weighted average of the cost of debt and equity funds. The cost of equity capital (for a nongrowth firm) is the earnings/price ratio, in our example 7½ per cent, while the cost of debt is the current after-tax interest rate which the firm would be required to pay on new bond issues.   Since, generally speaking the earnings yield on nongrowth common stock is considerably higher than the after-tax cost of debt so long as a "moderate" amount of debt is used, the capital structure that provides firms with a minimum cost of capital must ordinarily include some debt.   These relationships are graphed in Figure 3.

Suppose a firm has achieved its cost-minimizing capital structure. If it is growing and expanding rapidly, it will be able to maintain this optimal structure; if it is not expanding, there may be a tendency for the earnings retention to reduce the proportion of debt in the capital structure.   If this is the case, the firm can benefit by actually taking on debt and using the proceeds to buy and retire its own shares. The impact on the wealth positions of the shareholders can be examined exactly as in the preceding section, and the results are similar; under conditions that appear to be quite realistic debt can be used to provide funds for the purchase of the firm's own shares and all the stockholders will benefit. No one can, on a generalized basis, tell firms exactly how far they should go with this restructuring process, or if they should engage in it at all, but there are undoubtedly many firms whose stockholders would benefit from the operation.

* * *

Conclusions. A substantial number of corporations have been buying and retiring shares of their own common stock, and we have discussed two reasons that might explain this action. First, there are firms that have limited internal investment opportunities available, and if internally generated funds cannot be invested profitably, then it is sometimes better to distribute the excess funds by buying up outstanding shares rather than by paying dividends. This advantage for the stock purchase arises because of tax considerations, but it is very real, nonetheless. The second reason given for the purchase and retirement of common stock is more controversial, as it assumes that firms can reduce their over-all cost of capital through the use of debt in the capital structure. If this assumption is true, then companies that have used retained earnings to retire debt and thus caused their capital structures to be relatively heavily weighted with equity can lower their cost of capital by selling debt and using the proceeds to retire common stock.

NOTE: REPURCHASES—VOLUME AND STATED PURPOSE

1. Contrast with Brigham's suggestions the action of the Board of Governors of the Federal Reserve System on April 8, 1976 in amending its Regulation Y to require prior notification by bank holding companies planning to purchase their own stock. According to the Board:

"The purpose of the amendment is to assist the Board in supervising bank holding companies by providing advance notice of redemptions of bank holding company stock that could have a significant impact on the company's capital structure.

"In particular, the amendment is intended to deter the practice known as 'bootstrapping'—whereby a holding company incurs substantial debt in order to purchase or redeem its own outstanding stock, generally to help a shareholder or shareholder group gain control of the company.

"Effective May 15, the regulatory amendment will require 45 days advance notice to the Board by a bank holding company planning to redeem its own stock.

"Although the Board is aware that there are legitimate reasons for a bank holding company to buy its own stock, it is requiring prior notification of transactions that may result in the following conditions:

"—The 'bootstrapped' bank holding company is left with heavy debts and much reduced, perhaps very little or no equity.

"—Repayment and servicing of the debt depends mainly upon dividends the holding company receives from its subsidiary bank or banks, resulting in substantial pressure on them to pay excessive dividends to the parent company, possibly creating an unsafe or unsound bank condition.

"—The need of the holding company to meet heavy debt service obligations may encourage undue risk-taking aimed at increasing the earnings of its subsidiary bank or banks.

"The Board also wished to forestall bootstrapping due to the difficulties that may be encountered in unwinding such a transaction once it has taken place.

"Where the required prenotification indicates that consummation of a proposed purchase of its own stock by a bank holding company would violate applicable law, or would create an unsafe or unsound condition in a holding company, the Board would, if necessary, use its cease and desist powers to prevent the transaction." *

2. Once the firm has decided what proportion of its annual operating income shall be used to replace existing assets and finance new investments, it will ordinarily distribute any residue (less interest payments) to shareholders as dividends. However, management has the alternative of repurchasing stock, thereby leaving a smaller number of shares outstanding among which future dividends will have to be divided. This alternative distribution procedure has become increasingly popular. In the 1970s, the total value of repurchases grew to 20 percent of the value of dividend payments. The practice grew further in the 1980s, with the result that in many years United States corporations repurchased more stock than they sold. Ross, Westerfield and Jordan, Fundamentals of Corporate Finance 527 (1991).

F.A. Lees, "Repurchasing Common Stock" (Research Bulletin No. 147 of the Conference Board (1983), p. 4), reported the following data on direct stock repurchases: **

	1973	1980	1981	1982 [3]
Companies reporting purchases	522	305	312	297
Companies purchasing 100,000 shares or more..........................	219	134	113	107
Number of firms purchasing 1 million shares or more.....................	32	20	32	25
Shares acquired (millions)	143.8	101.3	148.4	218.9
Largest purchaser (millions)	13.1	12.5	26.4	14.1
	(Gulf Oil)	(Standard Oil Indiana)	(Exxon)	(Brunswick)

[3] Data cover only first 10 months of 1982.

* [Ed. Note] The present version of this regulation requires notice to be given to the Board only in cases where the consideration paid for stock repurchases during the preceding 12 months equals 10 percent of the holding company's consolidated net worth, 12 C.F.R. § 225.4(b) (1992).

** [Ed. Note] Indirect repurchases by or for employee benefit funds, which varied

Source: Fact Sheets, New York Stock Exchange, January, 1980; October 1982. Also Francis J. Walsh, Jr., Repurchasing Common Stock. The Conference Board, Report No. 659, 1975.

This study reported the principal objectives of such repurchases as follows (p. 6):

Principal Objectives of Direct Common Stock Repurchasing Programs, Ranked by 72 Companies

	Rank								Total Mentions [1]
	1	2	3	4	5	6	7	8	
	Number of Times Listed								
Obtaining shares for employee compensation programs	38	9	8	4	3	2			64
Exploiting the investment opportunity	17	10	5	4	3	1			40
Improving earnings per share	2	7	10	2	3	1	1		26
Obtaining shares for acquisitions	2	6	8	6	1			2	25
General corporate purposes (unspecified)	3	9	6	1	3	1			23
Obtaining shares for conversion		12	1	1	1			1	16
Preventing dilution	3	4	5	2		1	1		16
Supporting market price	2	4	3		1	1			11
Increasing book value		1	3	5	2				11
Changing ratio of debt to equity	1	2	1	1	2		1		8
Temporary investment of cash		1	1	4	1	1			8
Preventing unwanted takeover	3	1	2	1					7
Reducing cost of servicing small stockholder	1		3	1					5

[1] Multiple responses.

The circumstances that influenced such repurchase activity by the 69 companies that supplied information (p. 5) were summarized as follows:

	Percent of Responses
Purchase stock aggressively when stock market prices depressed	28%
Purchase stock on an ad hoc basis, depending on current needs	23
Purchase stock on regular, year-to-year basis, irrespective of stock market conditions	22
Purchase stock aggressively when cash flows are large, and there is no higher priority use of funds	16
Purchase stock aggressively when business conditions are weak and investment projects can be deferred	2
Other [1]	10
	100% [a]

[1] Includes: purchase of stock based on favorable long-term trends; purchases timed to minimize average cost per share; exchange of shares on exercise of options; repurchase of stock from resigning employees; special situations only; and when large blocks become available.

[a] Details do not add to 100 percent because of rounding.

During the 1980s large, blue chip firms repurchased enormous quantities of stock. The oil companies, which ran short of opportunities for competitive earnings reinvestment present a prime example.

between 3,640,000 and 5,800,000 shares annually during 1978 through 1982, were said by Lees to have been made principally for "Personnel Relations Objectives." But a more than trivial number of responses (22 responses out of 87) indicated financial or control preservation reasons comparable to the reasons listed for direct repurchases.

Exxon repurchased more than $15 billion of its shares through the end of 1989. But it was joined by many famous corporations in other industries. In 1989, for example, General Electric announced a $10 billion repurchase program and IBM announced a $5 billion program. Ross, Westerfield and Jordan, supra, p. 527. At least prior to 1989, a substantial part of this activity could be attributed to defensive moves against attempted takeovers—efforts to distribute cash in order to make the distributing entity a less attractive target or to fend off a third party bid. In 1985, the year hostile takeover activity first threatened the managers of the largest corporations, there was a marked increase in the percentage of stock repurchased by particular corporations (e.g., Phillips Petroleum: 45.7%; Unocal: 34%; Union Carbide: 55%; CBS: 21.5%; Litton Industries: 35.8%).

Stock repurchases also made the news in the aftermath of the 1987 market crash. See supra pp. 143–146. During the two day period following the crash, a number of large corporations announced plans to buy back a total of $6.2 billion stock. Brealey and Myers, Principles of Corporate Finance 373 (4th ed. 1991). According to Brealey and Myers, these managers were "concerned about the market crash" and their buying programs "helped to stem the slide in prices." Id. pp. 373–374. Did the managers also sense a bargain? Cf. Eisenberg v. Chicago Milwaukee Corp., 537 A.2d 1051 (Del.Ch.1987) (issuer tender offer for an issue of noncumulative preferred commenced Oct. 28, 1987); Cottle v. Standard Brands Paint Co., 1990 WL 34824 (Del.Ch.1990) (issuer tender offer announced Nov. 10, 1987).

---

2. REGULATION OF REPURCHASES—FIDUCIARY AND DISCLOSURE OBLIGATIONS

Publicly held corporations repurchase their outstanding stock for a wide variety of stated reasons. But unless the repurchase is related to a refinancing, the effect of the repurchase is to contract the size of the enterprise and to distribute assets to the selling stockholders. It is a form of partial liquidation. The essential question to be considered in deciding on a repurchase program, therefore, is whether the corporation has a better internal use for the funds. If it does, management should presumably not repurchase. If it does not, the question is whether repurchase is an appropriate mode of distributing excess assets.

Although a repurchase is a distribution of assets, the decision to expend funds in this manner is not necessarily a response to the same considerations that impel payment of dividends. Repurchase is not a device for putting income pro-rata into the hands of stockholders on a continuing basis. Nor is it as explicit a device as dividends to convey signals with respect to future earnings.[d] Precisely because of its potential for unequal treatment of stockholders and for concealment of information, a corporate repurchase may create a variety of "fairness" problems, and is therefore subject to a variety of judicial and statutory restrictions.

Although at one time there was a question whether the corporation had power (in the sense of intra vires) to repurchase its stock (a power which until recently it lacked in England; see Gower, The Principles of Modern Company Law (4th Ed.1979)), statutes in the United States fairly uniformly vest such power in the corporation. However, because repurchase is economically a distribution of assets to stockholders, restrictions comparable to those that apply to payment of dividends apply to repurchase—both contractual (in the corporate charter or debt instruments) and statutory. See NYBCL §§ 513–516, 719; Del.Corp. Law §§ 160, 172, 174, 243. The questions raised by those restrictions[e] are of some significance for close corporations, but do not often arise in the case of large publicly-held enterprises.

(A) SELECTIVE REPURCHASES AT HIGH PRICES— GREENMAIL AND BAILOUTS

Substantial legal problems arise when the repurchases are not made pro-rata.[f]

d. Asquith and Mullins, supra, p. 560, suggest that "dividends and repurchases, although similar, play somewhat different signalling roles. Dividends appear to be perceived by the stock market as regularly scheduled news releases conveying management's ongoing assessment of a firm's prospect. A repurchase is viewed as an 'extra'—a news bulletin justified when management is convinced its stock is substantially undervalued. The market's reaction demonstrates that in both cases, the news is credible, and apparently investors are persuaded. Moreover, both types of distributions create an incentive for management to fulfill the promise implicit in the signal and the integrity of both types of signals is policed by substantial costs associated with false signalling. Both dividends and repurchases are useful tools which managers can employ to create value for shareholders." The information signal given by repurchase or special dividends is commonly viewed as a signal of favorable earnings prospects. See Howe, He, and Kao, One–Time Cash Flow Announcements and Free Cash–Flow Theory: Share Repurchases and Special Dividends, 47 J. Finance 1963 (1992).

e. For example, must, and does, the corporation have sources in distributable surplus, either earned or capital, from which to make payments for the repurchased

stock? See e.g., Bishop v. Prosser—Grandview Broadcasters Inc., 3 Wash.App. 43, 472 P.2d 560 (1970). See complaint in Carter, Hawley, Hale Stores, Inc., by bidder against target expending funds to buy up its stock on the market, on ground, inter alia, that target lacked sufficient retained earnings to permit massive market repurchase of its common stock. Sec.Reg. and L.Rep., Vol. 16, p. 865 (5/18/84). Are directors and officers or recipient stockholders liable (and if so, to whom and in what amounts) for payments in violation of the statutes without regard to their knowledge of, or negligence in ascertaining, the impropriety of the repurchase? Is their liability affected by whether the repurchase makes the corporation insolvent or merely impairs capital? See generally Herwitz; Business Planning: Materials on The Planning of Corporate Transactions (Temp.2nd Ed.1984) 332 et seq.; Kummert State Statutory Restrictions on Financial Distributions By Corporations To Shareholders, 59 Wash.L.Rev. 185 (1984). See also the discussion supra p. 442.

f. Section 6 of the old Model Business Corporations Act and Rules 10b–6 to 10b–8 under the Securities Exchange Act suggest the kinds of repurchases which are unlikely to give rise to such problems—sufficiently so to be exempted from the prohibitions

(1) Fiduciary Duties

(a) Occasionally overpayments are made to selected sellers, as when insiders are "bailed out." Less often it can be shown that corporate assets are paid for the sole benefit of management or a controlling stockholder—as when outsiders are deliberately overpaid (or paid a premium above market) for their stock solely in order to preserve management's control and access to perquisites. In such cases traditional fiduciary strictures seem sufficient to underpin relief against the decisionmakers, and sometimes the recipients, either *ex ante* or *ex post.*

(b) The problem arises more often when it is not, or cannot be, shown that the outsider is bought off *solely* to perpetuate management's control. Such repurchases may put at issue the scope of management's traditional fiduciary obligations to the remaining stockholders under local law, both because "too much" is being paid and because other uses of corporate cash would have been more profitable even if market price or less were paid.

(c) Moreover, quite apart from overpaying or underpaying in some calculable economic sense, management's expenditure of corporate funds to purchase corporate stock in order to preserve its control—by defeating a tender offer or by buying off a "raider" or "greenmailer"— raises other problems of conflict of interest. See Note, 98 Harv.L.Rev. 1045 (1985).

If corporate funds are spent to fend off the "raider" or "greenmailer,"—whether by market purchases, a self-tender or purchase from the "raider" [g]—the stockholders are denied the benefit of at least one potential tender offer or new controller, and possibly others. If the repurchase price equals or exceeds the market price (however computed), the question arises whether the loss to non-selling stockholders is worth the gain to them of the prevention of the "raider's" success.[h]

---

of those provisions. Among the kinds of repurchases thus designated are those likely to affect only close corporations (such as buying out departing "partners" or collecting or compromising debt) as well as those affecting public corporations, such as eliminating fractional shares or small lots, or stabilizing market prices in aid of a public distribution or paying off dissenters seeking appraisal or purchasing stock from employees on termination of their employment pursuant to the contract on the original sale or employment.

g. Analyses of economic models suggesting that self-tenders are preferable to market repurchases (see Bradley and Rosenzweig, Defensive Stock Repurchases, 99 Harv.L.Rev. 1377 (1986); Note, 35 Stan. L.Rev. 701 (1985)) and that greenmail is

defensible (Macey and McChesney, A Theoretical Analysis of Corporate Greenmail, 95 Yale L.J. 13 (1985)) are penetratingly examined in Gordon and Kornhauser, Takeover Defense Tactics: A Comment on Two Models, 96 Yale L.J. 295 (1986).

h. The "loss" derives not merely from the expenditure of corporate cash for a premium, but from the impact of elimination of the threat of the "raider" on the price of the stock. See e.g., Dann and DeAngelo, Standstill Agreements, Privately Negotiated Stock Repurchases and the Market for Corporate Control, 11 J.Fin. Econ. 275 (1983); Bradley and Wakeman, The Wealth Effects of Targeted Share Repurchases, 11 J.Fin.Econ. 301 (1983). If the "raider" contemplated purchase of 100% of the stock in a tender offer, the

The harm thought to attend the "raider's" success is either (1) the possibility of too low a future bid price by the "raider" for the remainder of the company's stock, or (2) the disadvantages (by overreaching or incompetence) to be imposed on the company by the "raider's" expected conduct, as compared to that expected of incumbent management. In either case, the answer turns upon an estimate of the future behavior of the "raider." Even if the issue is phrased so that the propriety of the repurchase at a premium is said to turn on whether it was made at an economically "fair" price (i.e., in some sense, was "worth" it), courts appear willing to make the answer turn on whether management could reasonably have believed that the "raider" would have caused more damage to the corporation than the cost of buying him off. See e.g., Herald Co. v. Seawell, 472 F.2d 1081 (10th Cir.1972); Bennett v. Propp, 41 Del.Ch. 14, 187 A.2d 405 (Sup.Ct.1962); Cheff v. Mathes, 41 Del.Ch. 494, 199 A.2d 548 (Sup.Ct.1964); Kaplan v. Goldsamt, 380 A.2d 556, 559 (Del.Ch.1977). See also Brudney, Fiduciary Ideology in Transactions Affecting Corporate Control, 65 Mich.L.Rev. 259 (1966); Note, Buying Out Insurgent Shareholders With Corporate Funds, 70 Yale L.J. 308 (1960); Note, Targeted Stock Repurchases and the Management Entrenchment Hypothesis, 98 Harv.L.Rev. 1045 (1985). In one of the leading tender offer cases of the 1980s, the question was whether directors could lawfully cause the corporation to offer to buy stock from all its stockholders other than the "raider"; the discrimination against the "raider" was upheld as an appropriate exercise of business judgment (to avoid, among other things, the payment of greenmail!) by a board of which a majority were independent directors. Unocal Corp. v. Mesa Petroleum Co., 493 A.2d 946 (Del.Ct.1985).[i]

The inquiry is heavily tilted in management's favor by the trial procedure—i.e., the bought-out "raider" is either not available to testify (about allegedly pernicious purposes) (cf. Cheff v. Mathes, supra) or may

questions arise not only (1) whether the repurchase price per share for less than 100% of the stock is higher than the tender offer would have been, but (2) whether the surviving stockholders are, as a result of the repurchase, worse off than they would have been if they could have sold to the bidder.

In assessing the loss, questions also arise as to how greenmail payments and other expenses of defending against take-over should be accounted for. If those expenditures (including the greenmail or other repurchase premium) must be expensed, (see FASB proposal in Technical Bulletin No. 85–6, 161 J. of Acct. 25 (March 1986)) may the impact on the company's reported earnings significantly affect the price of its stock?

Some early economic studies defended greenmail on the statistical ground the investment made by a potential hostile offeror leads to positive returns for the target shareholders, and that these positive re-

turns exceed the negative returns that result from the announcement of a greenmail repurchase. See generally, Macey and McChesney, A Theoretical Analysis of Corporate Greenmail, 95 Yale L.J. 13 (1985). Since the possibility of greenmail encourages the hostile offeror's initial investment, it was argued that greenmail should not be prohibited. Subsequent studies affirm a different conclusion. If, after the greenmail transaction, no subsequent offeror shows up, the target shareholders' initial gains are lost. See Ang and Tucker, The Shareholder Wealth Effects of Corporate Greenmail, 11 J. Financial Res. 265 (1988).

i. If as the Court held in Unocal Corp. v. Pickens, 608 F.Supp. 1081 (N.D.Cal. 1985), the Williams Act does not prohibit a selective tender offer, may the SEC by regulation require all tender offers to include all shareholders of a given class? See p. 1022 infra. Should (can) it distinguish between issuer tender offers and third party tender offers?

act to support the integrity of the buy-out, or modify the arrangements to dilute its impropriety (cf. Polk v. Good, 507 A.2d 531 (Del.1986)). Even if the so-called burden of proof is said to be on the directors to "justify" the purchase, it is easily carried so long as the courts defer to the directors' business judgment. When a majority of the board consists of outsiders (i.e., persons not visibly affiliated in interest with management), the assumption appears to be that they are sufficiently disinterested to justify judicial review of their behavior under the very permissive version of the business judgment rule, or a somewhat tighter version of that rule (Cheff v. Mathes, supra; Kaplan v. Goldsamt, supra; Bennett v. Propp, supra; cf. Unocal Corp. v. Mesa Petroleum Co., supra, 493 A.2d at 955; Polk v. Good, 507 A.2d 531 (Del.1986); Turner Broadcasting System v. CBS, Inc., 627 F.Supp. 901 (N.D.Ga. 1985); but see Edelman v. Freuhauf Corp. infra, p. 754)—which is satisfied by a showing of "good faith and reasonable investigation" by the board and "reasonable grounds for believing that a danger to corporate policy" arose by reason of the raider's stock ownership. When a majority of the board is not thus "independent" (either because it is directly involved in receipt of perquisites or is in some sense closely enough related to recipients of perquisites) or the predominantly self-serving character of the repurchase is transparent, (see e.g., Petty v. Penntech Papers, Inc., 347 A.2d 140 (Del.Ch.1975)) the courts seem to assess the behavior by reference to some standard of fairness. Even if the court upholds a challenge to repurchases in the context of preserving control,[j] problems arise as to appropriate forms of relief, at least if the "raider" is not a party to the litigation.

Heckmann v. Ahmanson (214 Cal.Rptr. 177, 168 Cal.App.3d 119 (1985)) bears mention as one of those few occasions when a court imposed a stricture on a stock repurchase in a greenmail context. No less important is its suggestion that a remedy may lie against the greenmailer.

In the Heckman case, stockholders of Walt Disney Productions sued "to recover the pay-off in the greenmailing of Disney"; defendants were both the Disney directors who authorized the pay-off and the Steinberg Group to whom approximately $325 million was paid. Apparently in seeking to fend off the Steinberg Group, the Disney directors placed a heavy debt burden on the Disney enterprise by making an allegedly unfavorable purchase of another company, (Arvida), and

j. The case law has generally allowed such virtually unconstrained managerial discretion in repurchases—often even in the context of tender-offers—that the SEC Advisory Committee on Tender Offers expressed concern "with a target company's repurchase of its stock at a premium to market from a dissident shareholder. Under current law, the ability of a company to repurchase shares from dissident shareholders at a premium has created incentives for investors to accumulate blocks with the intention to sell them back to the issuer at a profit. Not only does such a transaction generally serve little business purpose outside the takeover context but also it constitutes a practice whereby a control premium may be distributed selectively and not shared equally by all shareholders. Moreover, the Committee is concerned about the doubt that such a transaction casts on the integrity of the takeover process. The Committee recommends prohibiting the repurchase at a premium of a block of stock held for less than two years without shareholder approval." SEC Advisory Committee on Tender Offers, Report of Recommendations (1983) 46.

then further levered the enterprise to buy off the Steinberg Group. The Steinberg Group sought to prevent the purchase of Arvida by initiating a derivative suit against Disney, but abandoned that suit as part of its sale of Disney stock to Disney.

In the course of its opinion affirming a preliminary injunction imposing a trust on the approximately $60 million profit the Steinberg Group is alleged to have made, the Court said:

"While there may be many valid reasons why corporate directors would purchase another company or repurchase the corporation's shares, the naked desire to retain their positions of power and control over the corporation is not one of them.

"If the Disney directors breached their fiduciary duty to the stockholders, the Steinberg Group could be held jointly liable as an aider and abettor. The Steinberg Group knew it was reselling its stock at a price considerably above market value to enable the Disney directors to retain control of the corporation. It knew or should have known Disney was borrowing the $325 million purchase price. From its previous dealings with Disney, including the Arvida transaction, it knew the increased debt load would adversely affect Disney's credit rating and the price of its stock. If it were an active participant in the breach of duty and reaped the benefit, it cannot disclaim the burden.

"Where there is a common plan or design to commit a tort, all who participate are jointly liable whether or not they do the wrongful acts.

"The Steinberg Group contends there was no evidence presented to the trial court that the repurchase agreement was motivated by the Disney directors' desire to perpetuate their own control instead of a good faith belief the corporate interest would be served thereby.

"At this point in the litigation, it is not necessary the court be presented with a 'smoking gun.' We believe the evidence presented to the court was sufficient to demonstrate a probability of success on the merits. The acts of the Disney directors—and particularly their timing—are difficult to understand except as defensive strategies against a hostile takeover.

* * *

"Once it is shown a director received a personal benefit from the transaction, which appears to be the case here, the burden shifts to the director to demonstrate not only the transaction was entered in good faith, but also to show its inherent fairness from the viewpoint of the corporation and those interested therein.

* * *

"When the Steinberg Group filed suit against Disney to block Disney's purchase of Arvida it assumed a fiduciary duty to the other shareholders with respect to the derivative claims.

* * *

"One who assumes such a fiduciary role cannot abandon it for personal aggrandizement. (Young v. Higbee (1945) 324 U.S. 204, 213; Lemer v. Boise Cascade, Inc. (1980) 107 Cal.App.3d 1, 7.) In the case before us plaintiffs have demonstrated a reasonable probability the Steinberg Group breached its fiduciary duty to the other shareholders by abandoning the Arvida litigation.

* * *

"The array of law and facts advanced by plaintiffs evaluated against defendants' counter-contentions demonstrates a reasonable probability that plaintiffs will be successful although, we stress, the final decision must await trial and a trial might well produce a different result. As to hardship, we believe the trial court reasonably concluded detriment to the plaintiffs if the proceeds and profits are dissipated or untraceable exceeds any hardship to the Steinberg Group in complying with the investment and accounting provisions of the preliminary injunction.

"The order granting a preliminary injunction is affirmed."

A class action against Steinberg for failure to disclose the green-mail negotiations with Disney in a Schedule 13D filing under section 13(d) of the 1934 Act was settled for $4.25 million. Brown v. Steinberg, CCH Fed.Sec.L.Rep. ¶ 95,680, 1990 WL 161023 (S.D.N.Y.1990).

Greenmail cases in which management has been held to have violated either its fiduciary obligations or its disclosure obligations to stockholders (under 10b–5 or other reporting obligations) are rare. But charges against the recipient of the greenmail for aiding and abetting management to violate its obligations by paying greenmail or for itself being remiss in its disclosure obligations, have repeatedly withstood attack on the pleadings. See Heckman v. Ahmanson, CCH Fed.Sec. L.Rep., ¶ 94,447, 1989 WL 260226 (Cal.Super.Ct.1989); Samuel M. Fein-berg Testamentary Trust v. Carter, 652 F.Supp. 1066, 1082–1084 (S.D.N.Y.1987); Fry v. Trump, 681 F.Supp. 252 (D.N.J.1988).

Should all raiders be liable automatically if the "fiduciaries" caus-ing the repurchase are found to be at fault? If so, what will be the effect upon the incentive for partial takeovers? If not, on what princi-ples can the raider's liability be differentiated from that of the errant fiduciary?

Finally, irrespective of the motives of the greenmailer and the defending managers, consider the question of damages. In **Viacom International, Inc. v. Icahn,** 946 F.2d 998 (2d Cir.1991), the Second Circuit rejected a civil RICO claim asserted by a target against Carl Icahn, the payee of a prior greenmail transaction, on the ground that the target had suffered no damage. The transaction involved the repurchase of 17 percent of the target's stock at a $17 premium over the market price of $62. The market price, said the court, is not the only factor to be considered in determining the value of the stock repurchased. The board had refused Icahn's $75 per share tender offer on the ground that the price was inadequate. In addition, only ten months later the target was acquired by a third party for $111 per share. Were the target's stockholders damaged by the greenmail payment even if the target was not?

(2) Federal Antifraud Provisions

Comparable obligations to the remaining stockholders to refrain from using corporate assets either to preserve control or to overpay sellers were developing in attacks on repurchases brought in derivative suits under Rule 10b–5 (See Schwartz, The Effect of the 1934 Act on Sales of Control, 15 N.Y.L.F. 674 (1969); Israels, Corporate Purchase of its Own Shares—Are There New Overtones?, 50 Cornell L.J. 620 (1965); Kennedy, Transactions by a Corporation in Its Own Shares, 19 Bus.Law 319 (1964); Malley, Corporate Repurchases of Stock and the SEC Rules: An Overview, 29 Bus.Law 117 (1973)) before the decisions of the Supreme Court in Santa Fe Industries, Inc. v. Green, 430 U.S. 462 (1977), Ernst & Ernst v. Hochfelder, 425 U.S. 185 (1976), and Blue Chip Stamps v. Manor Drug Stores, 421 U.S. 723 (1975). Notwithstanding those decisions, there may still be scope for Rule 10b–5 to affect such repurchases.

However, to invoke Rule 10b–5 on the assumption that it applies only to some form of nondisclosure and deceit rather than to unilateral diversion of assets, as required by *Santa Fe Industries, Inc.,* and more pointedly by Pin v. Texaco, Inc., 793 F.2d 1448 (5th Cir.1986) (which held that paying greenmail was not a "manipulation") poses questions as to *who* must be deceived in order for a cause of action to be assertable, and *what* must be disclosed to those who would otherwise be deceived. Thus in **O'Neill v. Maytag,** 339 F.2d 764 (2d Cir.1964), stockholders of National Airlines sued derivatively Pan American World Airways, Inc. (Pan American) and the controlling insiders and directors of National Airlines (National) on account of a transaction in which National and Pan American exchanged blocks of stock which each held in the other (and was required by the Civil Aeronautics Board to dispose of). The Pan American stock had a market price considerably higher than the National stock, but the management of National was alleged to be fearful that if Pan American offered to dispose of its National stock publicly, a single buyer might acquire it and become a threat to the incumbent control. Hence instead of selling its Pan American stock, National exchanged it with Pan American for its own stock, at an alleged loss of approximately $1,800,000—or a use of that amount of corporate cash to preserve management's control.

The Court of Appeals found that since all the directors knew all the facts there could be no deceit or misleading or failure to disclose, and therefore no violations of Rule 10b–5.

Can it be said validly that there was a culpable failure to disclose to the stockholders of National (a) if the repurchase did not require a stockholder vote, or (b) if it did and (i) the public owned more than 50 percent of National's stock or (ii) management owned more than 50 percent of National's stock, and the repurchase did (or did not) trigger appraisal rights under local law? See Note, 66 Col.L.Rev. 1292 (1966). Compare Goldberg v. Meridor, 567 F.2d 209 (2d Cir.1977), cert. denied 434 U.S. 1069; Wright v. Heizer Corp., 560 F.2d 236 (7th Cir.1977); Schoenbaum v. Firstbrook, 405 F.2d 215 (2d Cir.1968), cert. denied 395 U.S. 906 (1969). If disclosure is required, *what* should be disclosed to protect non-selling stockholders of the purchasing corporation?[k]

(3) Tax Legislation

Greenmail became a political issue during the white-hot phase of the 1980s' corporate control market. Direct prohibitions were introduced in Congress, but not enacted. See H.R. 2172, 100th Cong., 1st Sess.; S. 1324, 100th Cong., 1st Sess. But a tax disincentive was enacted in 1987 as section 5881 of the Internal Revenue Code. This imposes a 50 percent excise tax on profit realized in a greenmail transaction. The tax is imposed in addition to corporate tax, resulting in an effective rate of 84 percent. Greenmail is defined as consideration transferred by a corporation to repurchase its stock from a shareholder for less than two years who made or threatened a tender offer, unless the acquisition is pursuant to an offer made on the same terms to all shareholders. For criticism, see Gilson, Drafting an Effective Greenmail Prohibition, 88 Colum.L.Rev. 329 (1988); Zelinsky, Greenmail, Golden Parachutes and the Internal Revenue Code: A Tax Policy Critique of Sections 280G, 4999 and 5881, 35 Villanova L.Rev. 131 (1990).

––––––––––

(B) THE PROBLEM OF THE LOW PRICED REPURCHASE

If non-sellers are disadvantaged when the repurchase is thus made at a price which is "too high" or to preserve control, sellers may be wronged if the repurchase is made at a price which is "too low", in the sense that if the seller had all the information which the buyer had he would not have sold at so low a price.

If such a repurchase is knowingly and intentionally engineered solely in order to favor the management or controlling stockholders, the

---

k. Section 13(a) of the Exchange Act is another source of disclosure obligations in the case of greenmail payments, as BF Goodrich Company discovered when its Form 10–K was alleged by the Commission to be materially deficient in failing to disclose that shares were repurchased in a greenmail transaction from a single seller at a 25 percent premium. In the same proceeding the Commission suggested that the proxy rules were violated because the proxy materials seeking charter amendments ostensibly to make greenmail payments more difficult omitted to disclose the prior payments. SEA Rel. No. 22,792, Jan. 15, 1986, CCH Fed.Sec.L.Rep., ¶ 83,958.

repurchase may then be challenged successfully as a violation of fiduciary duties or as a form of fraud under local law, or possibly for failure of the corporation to comply with its disclosure obligation under Rule 10b–5 or Sections 13(e) and 14(e) or the periodic filing requirements of the Exchange Act of 1934.

Often, however, such a repurchase cannot be shown to serve exclusively the benefit of management or the controller. Legitimate, even if dubiously sufficient, corporate purposes may be asserted, such as the absence of any better investment opportunities (see p. 586 supra) or the need for "extra" stock for future acquisitions or for option plans. In such cases, unequal treatment (i.e., disadvantaging the seller) is a theoretical possibility; and in practice strong temptation to effect such unequal treatment is not lacking. The question is whether the benefits from permitting such repurchases offset the costs. In the past, it might have been argued that the tax benefit to the seller (receipt of capital gain rather than ordinary dividend) justified the repurchase. Since the Tax Reform Act of 1986, that argument is considerably less persuasive. Can a rule be fashioned which disentangles repurchases that are wholly self-serving from those which have legitimate benefits to offer to the corporation and the selling stockholders? If not, should the question of propriety turn on a case by case examination of the center of gravity of the effects of the transaction, or should a categorical prohibition be imposed in deference to fiduciary concerns which impose such prohibitions traditionally when it is impossible to disentangle the receipt of benefits by the fiduciary and by the beneficiaries?[l] In any event, can a rule requiring disclosure solve the problem? Should the criteria for adequate disclosure be the same on a repurchase as in a registration statement on original issuance of stock for cash, or in a third party tender offer?

(1) Fiduciary Duties
KAHN v. UNITED STATES SUGAR CORPORATION
No. 7313, Delaware Court of Chancery, 1985.
1985 WL 4449.

HARTNETT, Vice Chancellor.

This suit was brought as a class action challenging a leveraged cash tender offer made by United States Sugar Corporation ("U.S. Sugar") and a trust existing under its Employee Stock Ownership Plan (the

---

l. Repurchase of stock by closed-end investment companies presented the above problems in pervasive and sufficiently acute forms to impel Congress in Section 23(c) of the Investment Company Act of 1940 to prohibit such repurchases except by public tender solicitations or on the exchanges or similarly "open" markets (with an uncertain, but advance, disclosure requirement) or under other circumstances permitted by the Commission. A fair catalogue of the repurchase practices apparently found to exist and considered improper by the Commission may be inferred from its Regulation § 270.23c–1, and from its admonition in Inv.Co.Act.Rel. No. 3548 (Oct. 3, 1962) against repurchase, notwithstanding full disclosure, "if the issuer has failed to declare dividends on its stock even though substantial earnings are available for this purpose".

"ESOP") to the corporation's stockholders. It was commenced in September of 1983 and on October 18, 1983, an application for a preliminary injunction enjoining the consummation of the offer was denied.

* * *

I find from all the properly admissible evidence that there was a breach of fiduciary duty by the defendants because the disclosures made in the tender offer solicitation materials did not disclose with complete candor all the material facts a stockholder needed to make a fully informed decision as to whether to accept the tender offer. I also conclude that the tender offer was coercive. I further find that it would be impossible to rescind the transaction and that, therefore, an award of damages is the only possible remedy. I find that the amount of damages is $4 per share.

I

Most of the underlying facts are not disputed. Where they are disputed I find the facts to be as stated. The named plaintiffs represent the class of minority, public shareholders of U.S. Sugar who tendered their shares in response to the tender offer by U.S. Sugar and the ESOP. Defendants are U.S. Sugar, the ESOP, and the members of the Board of Directors of U.S. Sugar.

At the time of the tender offer U.S. Sugar was a public company with almost 5 million shares outstanding and its shares were held of record by more than 2,000 shareholders. The shares traded on the over-the-counter market, but only 28% of the outstanding shares were held by the public. The other 72% were owned either by charitable organizations established by Charles Stewart Mott, the founder of U.S. Sugar, or by members of the Mott family (collectively, the "Mott Interests"). The Board of Directors consisted of 14 persons of whom eight were either members of the Mott family or trustees of Mott charities or family trusts. Three were part of management.

* * *

The tender offer came about because the Mott Interests wished to reduce their holdings in U.S. Sugar but did not wish to relinquish their aggregated ability to exercise majority control over the company. The market price for U.S. Sugar stock was already considered to be depressed due to the world sugar glut and the sale of a substantial block of stock would have likely depressed it still further: It was therefore decided that a leveraged tender offer for 75% of the outstanding shares (over 3.5 million shares) was the best means of facilitating the wishes of the Mott Interests, while not depressing the market. Additionally, this tender offer would allow public shareholders to share in the tender offer and thus take advantage of a premium above market price.

Because the Mott Interests planned to tender a substantial number of shares while still retaining majority control, they had competing desires to both receive the highest possible tender offer price and still leave U.S. Sugar as a viable company not unduly burdened with debt. It is asserted by the defendants that these competing interests would tend to assure that those public shareholders who tendered their shares in response to the tender offer would receive as high a price as feasible for their shares, while also assuring that shareholders who did not choose to tender would not be locked into an overburdened corporation. Be that as it may, although more than 93% of the publicly held shares were tendered, more than 42% of the 2,000 shareholders chose not to be completely cashed out but elected to retain some portion of their holdings.

The ESOP was formed as a part of the tender offer plan. It purchased over one million shares at $68 per share with funds borrowed from U.S. Sugar. It was planned that the ESOP would repay U.S. Sugar from the annual tax deductible contributions made to the ESOP by the company.

There being no independent directors on U.S. Sugar's Board, no independent committee of directors could be appointed to review the tender offer and to negotiate on behalf of the public shareholders. However, the existence of the conflicts of interest was disclosed in the tender offer statement.

The tender offer was not intended to be merely the first step of a two-step elimination of public shareholders because those shareholders who did not tender their shares were not to be cashed out in a merger following the tender offer. A substantial number of shares are presently outstanding and held by public shareholders, and there continues to be a market for the trading of U.S. Sugar shares, although it has been trading at a lesser price than it did before the tender offer.

Prior to the challenged transaction, U.S. Sugar was virtually debt free. Chemical Bank, the corporation's traditional bank, was approached and was requested to advance $300 million, $250 million of which was to be used to finance the tender offer while the remaining $50 million would be used for working capital. Chemical Bank determined that U.S. Sugar would generate sufficient cash flow to service such a loan and that its assets would be sufficient to repay the loan in the event a foreclosure became necessary. Using conservative projections as to sugar yields, number of acres planted, etc., it also decided that sufficient cash would be generated to service the debt. The bank further determined that on a "worse case" basis, assuming a foreclosure sale, the assets would be worth at least $369 million (approximately $75 per share.) Chemical Bank, for its loan purposes, concluded that the current market value of U.S. Sugar's assets indicated a real net worth of more than $400 million (more than $80 per share). The replacement cost of U.S. Sugar's assets was estimated by the corporation in 1983 to be over $631 million ($130 per share).

Plaintiffs assert that U.S. Sugar's management disregarded information it had as to the value of its assets and instead arrived at the proposed tender offer price by considering only the price range which could be paid off by a projected cash flow over ten years. This range was $60 to $70 per share.

While consideration of the tender offer price range was still taking place, U.S. Sugar retained First Boston Corporation ("First Boston") to render a fairness opinion on the offering price. It was paid $650,000 for its three weeks of work. Initially First Boston was only informed of the range being considered for the tender offer by the corporation and was not informed of the actual tender offer price of $68 until the Friday before it delivered its opinion on Tuesday, September 13, 1983. In the fairness opinion issued by First Boston it opined that the $68 per share was fair to the public shareholders from a financial point of view.

First Boston was originally engaged to represent the public shareholders, as well as to give an opinion as to fairness. Its representative role was never carried out; it was not asked to recommend an independently arrived at fair price; it did not engage in any negotiations over the offering price with U.S. Sugar; it did not consult with any representatives of the minority shareholders; nor did it solicit outside offers to purchase.

Bear, Stearns & Co. ("Bear, Stearns") was retained to represent the ESOP and U.S. Sugar. It was asked to opine that the price to be offered in the tender offer was reasonable to the ESOP. It was also asked to determine whether after the proposed transaction the fair market value of U.S. Sugar's assets would exceed its liabilities by at least $50 million.

The determination that the corporation's assets had a fair market value which would exceed liabilities by at least $50 million after the tender offer was completed was necessary to allow the Board to make a finding that U.S. Sugar's capital would not be impaired, a finding required by Delaware law. This determination was called for because the distribution to be made under the tender offer would be greater than the net book value of the corporation's assets.

Bear, Stearns did negotiate on behalf of the ESOP. It was responsible for the setting of the offering price at $68 rather than $70 which the officers of U.S. Sugar had originally determined should be the offering price. The $68 price followed Bear, Stearns' decision that the fair price range was between $62 and $68 per share and that any higher price would be unfair to the ESOP.

The Offer to Purchase ("Tender Offering Statement") was sent to the stockholders by U.S. Sugar and the ESOP about September 20, 1983. In response, 1,288,210 shares were tendered by public stockholders. Of the then outstanding publicly held shares only 89,108 were not tendered.

While a different plan might have achieved the objectives of the Mott Interests without involving the public stockholders, I find that the tender offer, as made, required substantial acceptance by the public stockholders if the objectives of the majority stockholders were to be achieved.

II

Plaintiffs contend that the Tender Offering Statement was misleading or coercive and concealed or buried facts [including internal studies of the company's asset value and valuations by First Boston and Bear, Stearns] which, if disclosed, might have led stockholders to conclude that the $68 price was inadequate * * *.

Plaintiffs also assert that the Tender Offering Statement contained disclosures which created the impression that U.S. Sugar's management had arrived at the $68 price based mainly upon the independent valuation opinion of First Boston, that First Boston had been allowed to do a thorough valuation study with no restraints placed upon it, and that the interests of the public shareholders had been adequately represented by First Boston in the process of determining the terms of the offer. These disclosures are claimed to be false and misleading because certain alleged facts were omitted: (1) that U.S. Sugar's management, and not First Boston's, had arrived at the $68 price and that First Boston had never suggested a price which it felt was fair but merely opined as to the fairness of the price suggested by management; (2) that the $68 price was derived from a consideration of the amount which could comfortably be borrowed and repaid rather than from any evaluation of U.S. Sugar's true worth; (3) that management would have paid up to $70 per share if Bear, Stearns had not represented that no price above $68 would be reasonable for the ESOP to pay; (4) that First Boston had accepted a representation that the sale of U.S. Sugar to a third party would not be considered and therefore had made no attempt to solicit outside offers; and (5) that after the meeting of the Board of Directors at which it was unanimously determined that $68 per share was a fair price, Stewart Mott, a director and son of the founder of U.S. Sugar, decided not to tender any of the shares registered in his name.

The tender offer and the disclosures in the Tender Offering Statement are further asserted by the plaintiffs to have been coercive because the shareholders were told that they had a choice between tendering at $68 per share or retaining their stock, which after the transaction would no longer be listed on any exchange, would yield no dividends for a minimum of three years, and would represent ownership in a company burdened by substantial debt.

Plaintiffs claim that the fair value of U.S. Sugar at the time of the tender offer was $122 per share which they claim was the liquidation value of the assets. They request that the Court find that the defendants breached their fiduciary duties by not disclosing all germane facts with complete candor and by structuring a coercive tender offer. They claim that the appropriate remedy is an award of money damages measured by the difference between the $68 tender offering price and $122 which they claim was the true value of the shares at the time of the tender offer, plus prejudgment interest.

On the other hand, defendants contend that the tender offer was not coercive, that all germane facts were fully disclosed and that, in light of this, U.S. Sugar was under no duty to offer any particular price since the shareholders had all the information necessary to make an informed decision whether to accept or to reject the offer. The defendants further assert that the $68 price was fair to the public shareholders and that it was properly arrived at by the financial consultants retained by U.S. Sugar.

III

I find, from the facts adduced at trial, that the disclosures in the Tender Offer Statement did not fully comply with the requirements for disclosure with complete candor which are mandated by Delaware law. Singer v. Magnavox Co., 380 A.2d 969 (Del.Supr.1977); Smith v. Van Gorkom, 488 A.2d 858 (Del.Supr.1985); and Rosenblatt v. Getty Oil Company, 493 A.2d 929 (Del.Supr.1985).

There was a failure to clearly indicate in the proxy materials that the book value of the land, which was the principal asset of U.S. Sugar, was based primarily on the 1931 acquisition costs of the land and that in 1982 the internal real estate department of the corporation had rendered an informal opinion to management that the fee simple holdings of land was in excess of $408 million ($83 per share). The tender offer proxy materials also failed to adequately disclose that a Cash Flow Terminal Value Study prepared by First Boston had shown estimated values as high as $100.50 per share; that Bear, Stearns had made some estimates of value of up to $78 per share; and that First Boston did not actually prepare a thorough valuation study without restraints.

I also find that there was a failure to adequately disclose the methods used to arrive at the $68 tender offer price, especially because it was, for all practical purposes, chosen because that is what the ESOP and the corporation could afford to pay to service the loan obtained to finance the tender offer.

I also find that the method used to select the tender offer price was not likely to assure that the public minority stockholders would receive the true value of their shares and, as will be seen, they did not. The tender offer price, unfortunately, was, in essence, arrived at by determining how much debt the corporation could safely and prudently assume. The public stockholders had to either accept this price and tender their shares or to hold on to their shares only to find, because of the large loan which was to be used to pay for the shares tendered, that their shares would dramatically decline in value with no prospects for any dividends for at least three years.

In some circumstances a corporation is under no obligation to offer a particular tender offer price. Joseph v. Shell Oil Co., 482 A.2d 335 (Del.Ch.1984). Here, however, because of the highly leveraged nature of the transaction it was coercive and therefore defendants had an obligation to offer a fair price.

I acknowledge that the directors of U.S. Sugar were faced with a most difficult scenario because the majority shareholders desired to sell a substantial portion of their shares and yet insisted on retaining control of the corporation. The only feasible way to accomplish this was for the corporation to buy its own shares by the means of a leveraged tender offer. If the price offered had been fair there would not be any problem. The price offered, however, was not fair and it should have been selected with a greater emphasis on the true value of the corporation.

I do not, however, find the statements in the proxy statement setting forth the results which would likely occur if a stockholder did not tender to have been inadequate, improper or coercive. The proxy materials merely set forth that which was obvious: the minority stockholders who did not tender their shares would end up owning shares with a greatly diminished value because of the large debt being created to finance the tender offer.

* * *

Having found that there was a breach of fiduciary duty, I must now find a remedy.

IV

Plaintiffs seek, as damages, the difference between the fair value of the shares and the $68 offering price, plus pre-judgment interest. They correctly point out that it would be impossible now to rescind the transaction.

Most of the testimony adduced at trial relating to value was produced by experts retained by the litigants who expressed their opinion of the fair and intrinsic value of U.S. Sugar's stock at the time of the tender offer. Analyses of U.S. Sugar were performed on behalf of the plaintiffs by Professor James E. Walter and on behalf of the defendants by Mr. Francis C. Schaffer, Mr. W. Stanley Hanson, Jr., First Boston and Bear, Stearns.

A review of this testimony clearly shows the reason that testimony as to value by experts is of such limited use to a trier of fact.

* * *

VIII

The * * * testimony of the expert witnesses * * * is in hopeless disagreement. Each expert presented impressive credentials. Each expressed an opinion as to value based on dozens of value judgment assumptions. While each assumption was based on some data, almost all of the assumptions were fairly debatable and reasonable men using the same data could conclude that a different percentage multiple, or per acreage figure, etc., should be used.

Quite frankly, there is no rational way that I as the trier of fact could conclude that one expression of value was best. All had flaws, all were based on personal assumptions and opinions and all were expressed by obviously knowledgeable and experienced experts who were retained by one side or the other.

* * *

After considering and weighing all the conflicting testimony, the many value judgments and assumptions (some of which were invalid), and the credentials and demeanor of the witnesses, I conclude that the fair value of the assets of U.S. Sugar at the time of the tender offer was $72 per share. The damages, therefore, are equal to $4 per share ($72 less the $68 tender offer price).*

* * *

NOTE: COERCIVE REPURCHASES

Any tender offer at a premium over market price entails an application of pressure on the offerees. Given that fact, what differentiates a "coercive" issuer tender offer, such as that in *Kahn*, from a permissibly "uncoercive" offer?

Cottle v. Standard Brands Paint Co., CCH Fed.Sec.L.Rep. ¶ 95,-306 (Del.Ch.1990), expands on the concept of impermissible coercion:

"A claim for coercion must state that the plaintiffs, the tendering stockholders, 'were wrongfully induced by some act of the defendants to sell their shares for reasons unrelated to the economic merits of the sale.' Ivanhoe Partners v. Newmont Mining Corp., Del.Ch., 533 A.2d 585, 605, aff'd Del.Supr., 535 A.2d 946, 1334 (1987). Thus, a two-tier tender offer in which the buyer plans to freeze out non-tendering stockholders, giving them subordinated securities in the back end, is coercive. Unocal Corp. v. Mesa Petroleum Co., Del.Supr., 493 A.2d 946, 956 (1985). Similarly, a 'tender offered structured and timed so as to effectively deprive stockholders of the ability to choose a competing offer—also at a fair price—that the shareholders might have found preferable' is coercive. Ivanhoe, 533 A.2d at 605 * * *.

"Actionable coercion does not exist, however, simply because a tender offer price is too good to pass up. Id. Further, a self-tender at a premium above the shares' market price does not appear to be actionably coercive, even if paying that premium may adversely affect the market value of the remaining outstanding shares, provided that the offering materials make full disclosure of such an adverse effect. Eisenberg v. Chicago Milwaukee Corp., Del.Ch., 537 A.2d 1051, 1061–62 (1987)".

Is the courts last statement, based on a reading of *Eisenberg v. Chicago Milwaukee,* supra p. 378, consistent with the coercion finding in *Kahn* ?

---

* [Ed. Note] The litigation was later settled. $4,719,708 (calculated as $3.50 per share to holders of 1,348,488 shares) plus interest from February 11, 1986 was to be paid; and from that sum, lawyers' fees and expenses were to be paid in the amount of $1,179,927.

The *Cottle* case concerned an issuer tender offer conducted in the immediate aftermath of the 1987 crash. Early in 1987, the issuer had rejected an outside $28 per share offer for the stock. After the crash, the stock traded for around $16. The offer was structured as a dutch auction at a price of $25 to $28 per share. According to the court: "A dutch auction is a form of tender offer in which the selling stockholders, rather than the buyer, determine the price to be paid for the shares bought. When tendering their shares, stockholders designate the price (here within the $25.00–$28.00 range) at which they are willing to sell. The company then determines the lowest price at which it will be able to purchase the * * * shares and buys, on a pro rata basis if necessary, all shares tendered at or below that lowest price." The offering materials stated that (1) the shares' post offering price was expected to be less than the tender offer price, and (2) the only way the holders could be assured of maximizing the value of their holdings was by tendering all shares at the minimum $25 price.

The court found no infirmities in the dutch auction structure. It did not, said the court, "function much differently from an ordinary tender offer at $25.00." The timing of the offer did not provide a basis for a coercion case either, because plaintiff, unlike the plaintiff in *Kahn,* failed to make an adequate allegation that the offering price was unfair.

---

(2) Federal Securities Laws

(a) Antifraud Rules

COYNE v. MSL INDUSTRIES, INC.

United States District Court, Northern District of Illinois, 1976.
CCH Fed.Sec.L.Rep. ¶ 95,451 [1975–1976 Transfer Binder].

MARSHALL, District Judge.

Plaintiff is a former shareholder in defendant, MSL Industries, Inc. ("MSL"). MSL is a conglomerate in the metal fabrication field and owns seven operating subsidiaries. On January 14, 1974, MSL promulgated a cash tender offer to its shareholders to purchase 200,000 or approximately 15% of its outstanding shares of common stock at $25 per share. Plaintiff tendered all his 1000 shares of MSL stock and received $25,000 for them. Approximately one year later, plaintiff filed this action, claiming that the offering circular (which is pleaded as Exhibit A to the complaint) was false and misleading in that

(a) MSL knew or should have known but failed to disclose that MSL's earnings for fiscal 1974 would be substantially greater than 1973.

(b) it misrepresented that the offer was in the best interests of the company and,

(c) it failed to disclose that the acquisition by MSL of 200,000 of its shares would result in an increase in the value of the shares held by its officers and directors.

Plaintiff alleges that the circular employed in MSL's tender offer violated Section 10(b) of the Securities Exchange Act of 1934, 15 U.S.C. § 78j(b) and Rule 10b–5 promulgated thereunder by the Securities and Exchange Commission. 17 C.F.R. § 240.10b–5. Jurisdiction is present under 15 U.S.C. § 77aa. * * *

* * *

MSL's offering circular is a five-page document containing information about the procedure for tendering shares, the purpose of the offer, and the financial condition of the company. The offer was publicly announced on January 8, 1974, and remained open until January 31, 1974. * * *

The purpose of the tender offer was expressed as follows:

> The Board of Directors, in the exercise of its business judgment, is of the view that the purchase of shares of Common Stock at this time * * * is prudent and in the best interests of the Company. * * *

The offer then stated that MSL intended to retire purchased shares or hold them in the treasury, with the option of using them for stock options, acquisitions, stock dividends or conversions of outstanding convertible debentures. MSL declined to advise its shareholders how to respond to the offer:

> Neither the Company nor the Board of Directors makes any recommendation, that stockholders tender or refrain from tendering any or all of their Shares, and no one has been authorized by either of them to make any such recommendation. Each stockholder must make his own decision as to whether to tender Shares and, if so, how many Shares to tender. * * *

Then the circular stated that the directors, officers, and their spouses would not tender any shares pursuant to the offer.

The circular contained some information about the financial conditions of MSL. On the first page, it stated that the closing price of MSL on the New York Stock Exchange was $21¼ per share immediately before the offer was announced, suggesting that the offered price of $25 was a desirable one for the shareholders. The remaining financial information consisted mostly of market price, sales, and earnings data comparing MSL's performance in 1972 and 1973. With the exception of a drop in market prices during the first few days of 1974, all indicia were increasing. For example, total net sales were $75,308,000 for the nine months ended September 30, 1972, and $87,645,000 during the same period in 1973. Similarly, net earnings increased from $3,479,000 during the first nine months of 1972 to $5,547,000 for the same period in 1973. MSL estimated that net earnings for the entire fiscal year ended December 31, 1973 would be about $3,800,000 more than net earnings in 1972. Finally, the circular noted that book value per share was $31.28 on November 30, 1973.

In the circular, MSL estimated that the purchase of 200,000 shares under the cash tender offer would result in an increase in book value per share and a material increase in earnings per share based upon the level of profits in 1973. However, specific dollar amounts for these increases were not given.

As previously noted, plaintiff tendered his 1,000 shares of common stock in response to the offer and received $25,000 for them and in total, approximately 188,000 shares were tendered to MSL.

It appears from the statements which have been submitted that the first quarter of 1974 witnessed a sharp increase in MSL's earnings which persisted throughout 1974. On March 13, 1974, approximately one and one half months after the January tender offer expired, MSL revised its internal budget projection for 1974, which had been made in November of 1973. The revised budget indicated that the estimated operating profit for MSL's Heads and Threads division, which imports commercial fasteners, had increased about 24%. The March 13 revision also showed that the 1974 net sales projection for Heads and Threads had increased from $34,000,000 to $50,000,000. Subsequent budget revisions during 1974 showed that four other MSL subsidiaries were expected to experience substantial increases in operating profits and net sales. According to MSL, the anticipated increases in sales and profits in 1974 were 80% attributable to increased prices in their products.

In the summer of 1974, Alleghany Corporation negotiated with MSL to purchase MSL securities. Alleghany examined MSL's internal financial reports and projections and developed a take-over proposal. On November 6, 1974, Alleghany promulgated a tender offer to purchase any and all shares of MSL common stock at $50 per share.

* * *

Alleghany planned to hire the President of MSL and two other MSL employees after it obtained control. As presented to the MSL shareholders, the success of Alleghany's take-over bid seemed assured. All MSL directors suggested that it would take all permissible steps to buy the remaining shares. For example, Alleghany noted that the Exchange would likely delist MSL's shares if Alleghany purchased about half the outstanding shares of MSL. Once delisted, the remaining shareholders might not be able to obtain a good price for their MSL securities.

The November Alleghany tender offer also contained more financial information than MSL's earlier tender offer, and this information attests to the upsurge in MSL's earnings. For example, the reported high and low sales prices of MSL on the Exchange had been $26½ and $17¾ for the last quarter of 1973. They were $50 and $40⅛ respectively in the fourth quarter of 1974. The November 1974 offer estimated that earnings for 1974 would be approximately $12.40 per share, as opposed to MSL's estimate of approximately $5.30 per share for 1973 in its January 1974 offer. Estimated book value as of December 31, 1974 would be $45 per share, as opposed to $31.66 per share in 1973.

The November Alleghany offer also contained predictions for the following year, a type of information missing in MSL's January offer. It noted that MSL had estimated that its earnings for 1975 would be between $7.00 and $16 per share, and that after-tax earnings would be about the same as in 1974. MSL and Alleghany cautioned that these projections were based upon experience and assumptions as to future economic conditions. They warned that the estimates could prove to be inaccurate due to uncertain or changing economic forces.

* * *

Plaintiff has not argued his second and third contentions vigorously, and they are without merit. The second contention, that the offer is misleading because it was in the best interests of the nontendering shareholders and not of the company, erroneously distinguishes between the two interests. As defendant urges, a corporation is managed for the benefit of its owners. The nontendering shareholders were the sole owners of MSL after MSL purchased the tendered shares. Thus, the interests of MSL and of the nontendering shareholders were identical.

The third contention, that the offer failed to disclose that the officers' and directors' shares would increase in value, is also without merit. The offer stated that the officers and directors would not tender their shares. It also stated that acceptance of the tender offer would result in an increase in the book value and earnings of nontendered shares. Thus, the offer itself suggested that all nontendered shares, including those of MSL's insiders, would increase in value.

Plaintiff's remaining contention is that MSL knew or should have known when it made its January tender offer that its earnings would rise substantially in 1974, and that MSL failed to disclose this information in its offering circular. Plaintiff interchanges the terms "information," "predictions," and "projections," but he clearly refers to nondisclosure of MSL's expected performance during 1974. This issue is more complex. It requires a statement of general principles, their application to the facts, and a consideration of plaintiff's specific arguments.

One of the purposes of Rule 10b–5 is to require accurate disclosure of material facts relating to the purchase or sale of securities in order to equalize the bargaining position of corporate insiders and uninformed minority shareholders. Speed v. Transamerica Corp., 99 F.Supp. 808, 829 (D.C.Del.1951). Congress intended to substitute a policy of full disclosure for that of caveat emptor. Affiliated Ute Citizens v. United States, 406 U.S. 128, 151 (1972). Purchasers such as MSL are liable for nondisclosure if they conceal existing material facts which would have influenced a reasonable seller's actions. Liability may be imposed for nondisclosure of improving business conditions. Janigan v. Taylor, 344 F.2d 781 (1st Cir.1965), cert. denied, 382 U.S. 879

(1965), or the existence of a new asset or business opportunity, SEC v. Texas Gulf Sulphur Corp., 401 F.2d 833 (2d Cir.1968). See also, Feit v. Leasco Data Processing Corp., 332 F.Supp. 544 (E.D.N.Y.1972). It appears, however, that mere predictions need not be disclosed to satisfy Rule 10b–5. SEC v. Texas Gulf Sulphur Corp., supra, at 848.

The distinction between an existing plan or intent to act in the future and an economic forecast was determinative in Arber v. Essex Wire Corp., 490 F.2d 414 (6th Cir.1974). There, plaintiff owned shares in a closely held corporation which she sold despite advice that they would greatly appreciate if Essex went public. Essex did go public, the value of its shares increased greatly, and plaintiff sued for misrepresentation under Rule 10b–5. After a trial the district court held for the defendant, and the court of appeals affirmed, noting that while plaintiff had alleged that at the time of the sale management had definite plans reasonably certain to increase the value of the stock, she did not prove that management had any material existing plans. The court said that a present plan of future corporate activity may be a material existing fact, but mere speculation is not. Corporate insiders need not give investors the benefit of expert financial analysis or educated guesses and predictions. Insiders need not volunteer economic forecasts.* See also, Kohn v. American Metal Climax, Inc., 458 F.2d 255, 265 (2d Cir.1972); Union Pacific Railroad Co. v. Chicago and North Western Railway Co., 226 F.Supp. 400 (N.D.Ill.1964).

This limitation on the policy of full disclosure is also recognized in SEC guidelines, which do not require issuers to publicly disclose their projections. See Statement on Disclosure of Projections, Securities Act Release No. 5362, CCH Fed.Sec.L.Rep. ¶ 79,211 (1973). If a corporation voluntarily chooses to disclose its economic predictions, however, they will be closely examined for accuracy. See, Beecher v. Able, 374 F.Supp. 341, 348 (S.D.N.Y.1974); cf. Green v. Jonhop, Inc., 358 F.Supp. 413 (D.C.Or.1973).

But with the record in its present state, the facts are unknown. We cannot determine if we are dealing with known facts and plans or mere predictions. All we have are the MSL statements which, understandably, have given rise to the controversy and Mr. Scott's belated affidavit that, as of the time of MSL's January tender offer, "the company was not aware of any information and had not made any analyses from which it concluded that the November [1973] budget projections were materially either understated or overstated." Plaintiff is entitled to challenge the disclaimer of knowledge on cross examination. As for the latter—that the company had not made "any analyses"—its obfuscatory character entitles it to little weight at this stage of these proceedings.

In short, while plaintiff is not entitled to summary judgment on the showing he has made on this issue, neither should he suffer summary

* [Ed. Note] Compare Harkavy v. Apparel Industries, Inc., 571 F.2d 737 (2d Cir. 1978).

defeat in advance of a reasonable discovery opportunity to probe the facts known to MSL at the time it made its offer.

* * *

———

The uncertainties which often color management's projections of sales or earnings, and therefore affect their reliability, are illustrated in **Walker v. Action Industries, Inc.,** 802 F.2d 703 (4th Cir.1986), cert. denied 479 U.S. 1065 (1987) involving an issuer tender offer for which the court declined to require disclosure of the issuer's internal sales and earnings projections which, if "hard", would plainly have been material. The decision relies heavily on the fact that neither the SEC self-tender regulation, Rule 13e–4, nor the regulations authorizing projections in registration statements and proxy materials require disclosure of projections—notwithstanding that the plaintiff's claim appears to have been based on Rule 10b–5. The opinion collects the case law on disclosure of projections in all contexts indiscriminately and essays to summarize the learning. See p. 841 et seq. infra. Further reference should be made to the Supreme Court's recent discussion of disclosure of opinions in *Virginia Bankshares v. Sandberg,* infra p. 847.

(b) Rules 13e–4 and 13e–1

Many of the objectives of issuer stock repurchases may be achieved by discrete market purchases or by self tender offers. Such issuer tender offers, whether made defensively against third party tender offers or otherwise, generate for the issuer's security holders needs for disclosure (particularly as to the issuer's purposes, plans, and proposals), and relief from sales pressure that are comparable to (although far from identical with) those generated by third party tender offers. To meet those needs, the Commission promulgated Rule 13e–4 which, it will be noted, contains both disclosure requirements and substantive restrictions on the manner of making the tender offer. The Commission's authority under either Section 13 or Section 14 to impose such substantive requirements has been the subject of debate. See pp. 1023 et seq. infra. An excerpt from the rule, together with excerpts from the release accompanying the rule, follow:

Rule 13e–4. Tender Offers by Issuers

* * *

(b)(1) It shall be a fraudulent, deceptive or manipulative act or practice, in connection with an issuer tender offer, for an issuer or an affiliate of such issuer, in connection with an issuer tender offer:

(i) to employ any device, scheme or artifice to defraud any person;

(ii) to make any untrue statement of a material fact or to omit to state a material fact necessary in order to make the statements made, in the light of the circumstances under which they were made, not misleading; or

(iii) to engage in any act, practice or course of business which operates or would operate as a fraud or deceit upon any person.

(2) As a means reasonably designed to prevent fraudulent, deceptive or manipulative acts or practices in connection with any issuer tender offer, it shall be unlawful for an issuer or an affiliate of such issuer to make an issuer tender offer unless:

(i) such issuer or affiliate complies with the requirements of paragraphs (c), (d), (e) and (f) of this section,* and

(iii) the issuer tender offer is not in violation of paragraph (b)(1) of this section.

SECURITIES EXCHANGE ACT RELEASE No. 16,112

Securities and Exchange Commission.
August 16, 1979.

TENDER OFFERS BY ISSUERS

Introduction

* * *

II. *Statutory Background*

Some commentators raised questions regarding the Commission's authority to adopt a rule which would regulate the manner in which tender offers by issuers must be made. Those commentators suggested that, based upon the legislative history of the sections of the Act under which the Rule has been adopted, particularly Section 13(e), the Commission's authority is limited to promulgating disclosure requirements in connection with such offers. The Commission does not agree.

* * *

---

* [Ed. Note] Paragraphs (c), (d), (e) and (f) prescribe requirements for filing, disclosure, and dissemination of information, and restrictions on the manner of making the tender offer.

The information required to be disclosed under Rule 13e–4 and Schedule 13E–4 consists, among other things, of the usual financial statements, including income statements, balance sheets and ratios of earnings to fixed charges for the two most recent fiscal years and the latest interim period and for the corresponding interim period for the prior year; earnings and book value per share; and a pro forma presentation disclosing the effect of the tender offer on the figures for the most recent fiscal year and for the latest year-to-date interim period, where material. In addition, information is required about the source of funds for the buy-back, the purposes of the tender offer and any plans or proposals which relate to or would result in an extraordinary corporate transaction such as a merger, a sale or transfer of a material amount of assets, a material change in dividend rates or policies or indebtedness or capitalization, any change in the board, or any acquisition or disposition by the issuer of additional securities of the issuer, any other material change in the issuer's corporate structure of business, and any defensive changes in the issuer's charter or securities structure making it less vulnerable to take-over.

In response to the suggestion of one person who testified during the hearings on the Williams Act that issuers should be subject to Section 14(d), the Commission emphasized that the concerns raised by issuer tender offers may vary from those raised by tender offers made by third parties in an attempt to gain control of the issuer. The Commission informed Congress that:

> (i)f the Commission is given rulemaking power with respect to issuers' purchases as provided in the bill, it could, and presumably would, provide separately for tender offers by issuers following the provisions of [Section 14(d)] to the extent appropriate.

The Commission has determined that regulation of issuer tender offers under Rule 13e–4 is appropriate to ensure that issuer tender offers are conducted in a manner free of the deceptive, manipulative and fraudulent acts and practices set forth in paragraph (b) of the Rule. By providing a regulatory framework governing issuer tender offers, Rule 13e–4 responds to a major Congressional concern underlying the Williams Act to ensure that tender offers are conducted on appropriate terms and conditions in light of the special market and investment decision problems which attend such offers.[18]

* * *

IV. *Summary of Rule 13e–4*

* * *

D. *Disclosure and Dissemination Requirements*

Rule 13e–4(d) sets forth specifically those terms of the tender offer which the issuer or affiliate is required to disclose to security holders in its offering materials. The offering materials must be disseminated to security holders pursuant to the requirements contained in paragraph (e) of the Rule. The issuer or affiliate will be deemed to have published, sent or given the tender offer to security holders upon compliance with the provisions relating to long-form publication, use of shareholder and other lists or summary publication. If any material change occurs in the information published, sent or given to security holders, the offeror is required by Rule 13e–4(e)(2) to disseminate promptly disclosure of such change in a manner reasonably calculated to inform security holders.

E. *Manner of Making the Tender Offer*

* * *

[In response largely to the effects of issuer tender offers as defenses against third party bids, the Commission in SA Rel. No. 6618 (Jan. 14,

---

18. As discussed in the release proposing and adopting Rule 13e–3 under the Act, the Commission believes that it would be appropriate to imply a private right of action under Section 13(e). See Securities Exchange Act Release Nos. 34–14185 (November 23, 1977), 41 FR 60099–60100; 34–16075 (August 2, 1979), 44 FR 46736. The Commission adheres to this view in the context of Rule 13e–4.

1986) and SA Rel. No. 6653 (July 11, 1986) amended Rules 13e–4 and 14e–1 to bring the requirements for issuer tender offers into line with those for third party tender offers with respect to (1) the period for which the offer must be open (at least 20 business days) (2) the period of withdrawal rights (the period of the offer) and (3) the period which must elapse before the required pro rata purchase may be made (the period of the offer).]

5. *Increase in Consideration and Payment for Securities*

Paragraph (f)(4) of the Rule requires that, if the issuer or affiliate subject to the Rule increases the consideration offered after the tender offer is commenced, the issuer or affiliate must pay the increased consideration to all security holders whose tendered securities are accepted for payment. This requirement is patterned after an analogous provision contained in Section 14(d)(7) of the Act. The so-called "best price" provision was designed "to assure fair treatment of those persons who tender their shares at the beginning of the tender period, and to assure equality of treatment among all shareholders who tender their shares." The Commission believes that the principle embodied in Section 14(d)(7) should be equally applicable in the context of an issuer tender offer. In addition, as a means reasonably designed to prevent fraudulent or deceptive conduct, Rule 13e–4(f)(4) is intended to prevent an issuer from misleading security holders with respect to the price it is willing to pay for the securities which are the subject of the tender offer.

Paragraph (f)(5) of the Rule requires that the person making the issuer tender offer must either pay the consideration offered, or return tendered securities, promptly after termination of the tender offer.

6. *Post–Tender Offer Restrictions*

As proposed, the Rule would have prohibited, for the ten business days after termination of the offer, any purchases by the issuer of the securities which are the subject of the tender offer. This provision is essentially an antimanipulation restriction. A tender offer tends to peg the market price of the security which is the subject of the tender offer at or near the offering price, and the purpose of the prohibition on post-offer purchasing activity is to prevent the issuer from supporting the market at that artificial price after termination of the tender offer.

* * * [T]his short "cooling-off" period constitutes a reasonable means to ensure that the market impact of the tender offer on the issuer's securities is dissipated by market activity unaffected by additional purchases by the issuer.

* * * Similarly, in the context of exchange offers, the Rule prohibits purchases by the issuer of any security in a control relationship with the issuer of any security being offered pursuant to the exchange offer, or any security of the same class and series as, or any right to purchase, any such security. Market activity in these securities may affect the market price for the security which is the subject of the tender offer, or the security offered pursuant to an exchange offer. Accordingly, issuer

purchases of those classes of securities may tend to peg the price of the security which is the subject of the tender offer at or near the tender offer price or distort the market for the offered security in an exchange offer.

Although Rule 13e–4 specifically excepts any tender offer subject to Section 14(d) of the Act, which includes tender offers by affiliates of most issuers covered by the Rule, the Commission believes that purchases of the securities covered by paragraph (f)(6) of the Rule by persons in a control relationship with the issuer during the ten day period following termination of the offer may have the same adverse market effects as purchases by the issuer. Accordingly, for purposes of paragraph (f)(6), post-offer purchases by control persons of the issuer shall be deemed to be purchases by the issuer.

* * *

Special problems arise if the issuer repurchases stock during the period of a third party tender offer. The issuer's repurchases are therefore required to comply with the disclosure provisions of Rule 13e–1. Whether, during that period, the issuer should be denied the freedom of market repurchases and be confined to the restrictions entailed in making a competing self tender offer (and thus its management would be restricted to more equal competitive terms with the third party bidder (see SA Rel. No. 6618, Jan. 14, 1986)) is the subject of discussion in Bradley and Rosenzweig, Defensive Stock Repurchases, 99 Harv.L.Rev. 1377 (1986); Note, 38 Stan.L.Rev. 701 (1986); see also Gordon and Kornhauser, Takeover Defense Tactics: A Comment on Two Models 96 Yale L.J. 295 (1986); Bradley and Rosenzweig, Defensive Stock Repurchases and The Appraisal Remedy 96 Yale L.J. 322 (1986).

Rule 13e–1. Purchase of Securities by Issuer Thereof

When a person other than the issuer makes a tender offer for, or request or invitation for tenders of, any class of equity securities of an issuer subject to section 13(e) of the Act, and such person has filed a statement with the Commission pursuant to Rule 14d–1 and the issuer has received notice thereof, such issuer shall not thereafter, during the period such tender offer, request or invitation continues, purchase any equity securities of which it is the issuer unless it has complied with both of the following conditions:

(a) The issuer has filed with the Commission eight copies of a statement containing the information specified below with respect to the proposed purchases:

(1) The title and amount of securities to be purchased, the names of the persons or classes of persons from whom, and the market in which, the securities are to be purchased, including the name of any exchange on which the purchase is to be made;

(2) The purpose for which the purchase is to be made and whether the securities are to be retired, held in the treasury of the issuer or otherwise disposed of, indicating such disposition; and

(3) The source and amount of funds or other consideration used or to be used in making the purchases, and if any part of the purchase price or proposed purchase price is represented by funds or other consideration borrowed or otherwise obtained for the purpose of acquiring, holding, or trading the securities, a description of the transaction and the names of the parties thereto; and

(b) The issuer has at any time within the past 6 months sent or given to its equity security holders the substance of the information contained in the statement required by paragraph (a).

Provided, however, That any issuer making such purchases which commenced prior to July 30, 1968, shall, if such purchases continue after such date, comply with the provisions of this rule on or before August 12, 1968.

3. REGULATION OF STOCK REPURCHASES TO "CORRECT" THE MARKET PRICE

(A) THE PROBLEM OF REPURCHASES TO BRING MARKET PRICE UP TO MANAGEMENT'S JUDGMENT OF CORRECT VALUE

Deliberate "overpayment" in repurchases on the market may be made in order to raise the price of the stock so that it may more profitably be used as currency to purchase new assets or to induce conversion of convertible debt, or merely to reflect a price which management believes to be more consonant with the value of the firm. Whatever may be the uses for which the repurchased corporate stock is intended, if the repurchases are made either (1) to increase the market price of the stock or (2) merely to "peg" it at current levels, substantial questions exist with respect to the propriety of such expenditures of corporate funds:

(a) At best, management seeks to affect the market price because it believes the stock is "undervalued". Do such purchases by the corporation, even if disclosed in advance to the public, inject into the market an artificiality which detracts from the role of the market as the register of equilibrium between a willing seller and a willing buyer? Is management's judgment—whether as a faithful fiduciary or as an errant fiduciary—a "legitimate" pricing factor comparable to the judgments of buyers and sellers seeking to advance their economic interests as investors? Is management's self-interest apt to inject a bias in the repurchase program which should be irrelevant to the market's pricing mechanism—e.g., to keep the price higher than the stock's value justifies in order to win the approval of stockholders?

(b) If the disparity between management's judgment as to the value of the stock and the market's evaluation of the stock is to be cured, is it more appropriate to use corporate cash to affect the price than to disclose the information which will bring the price into line? Should the answer to that question be different if management is a substantial or controlling stockholder than if it owns little or no stock? On the other hand, are there limits to the disclosure which is permissible in order to bring the price of the stock up to management's judgment of an appropriate price? [m] Should those limits be different for assessing the culpability of a controlling stockholder than of management holding little or no stock?

(c) If, notwithstanding the fullest permissible disclosure, the market still evaluates the stock at less than management does, can management ever (even assuming no interest in diversion of values for its own benefit) properly use corporate assets to favor one set of stockholders (the non-sellers) over another (the sellers) by causing the corporation to make a "bargain" purchase on the market? [n]

Consider the following from Brudney, A Note on "Going Private," 61 Va.L.Rev. 1019, 1047–48 (1975):

"* * * Apart from tax advantages, there is reason to question the propriety of market repurchases made only because they are the company's 'best' investment. In theory, management is precluded from distributing assets to some members of the class and not to others. Yet a market repurchase is just such a skewed distribution—to the probable disadvantage rather than to the advantage of the distributees * * *.

"It has been argued that such treatment in a repurchase is a permissible inequality because it is not forced upon the distributee but is voluntarily chosen. However, the voluntary character of the seller's choice is questionable when he does not have knowledge of the relevant facts, including why management thinks the price is

---

m. Consider the communications problems created by a repurchase if management's reason for repurchasing is its belief that the stock is undervalued but it is unable to offer adequate information to persuade the market to raise the price. According to Asquith and Mullins, supra p. 560 at p. 10, such "repurchases should convey valuable information to investors. A repurchase is a signal that managers who possess an insider's knowledge of the firm, are convinced that their stock is worth more than its current price. In addition their conviction is strong enough to lead them to pay a premium for the stock despite the risk of dilution if they are wrong."

n. According to Loomis, Beating the Market by Buying Back Stock, Fortune, April 29, 1985, pp. 29 et seq., it is estimated that $26 billion was spent on repurchases in 1984. The Fortune "study shows that buybacks have made a mint for shareholders who stuck with the companies carrying them out." Those companies showed "a median total return, expressed as an annual average, compounded, of 22.6%" compared to "the equivalent returns for the S & P 500 * * * [of] only 14.1%." All these goodies for the surviving shareholders are achieved "because each $1 spent will buy [from another shareholder] more than $1 of value."

right. If management's belief that the market price is too low actuates the repurchase decision, management is obliged to communicate the reasons and bases for its belief to those from whom it buys.* If it cannot adequately communicate those considerations— either for business reasons or because they are not intelligibly communicable—there is good reason to forbid it from causing purchase of the stock. If it does adequately communicate the reasons, and the market fails to respond by an increased price, a no less difficult question is raised—is it a legally permissible function of management to favor some members of a class of stockholders over others on the basis of its judgment about the inadequacy of market price? It is one thing to force stockholders to choose between remaining stockholders and selling out on the market, on the basis of management's proposal to invest in a new project or to abandon an old one. It is another, to force such a choice [or gamble, which one or the other group of stockholders will presumably lose] on the basis of management's proposal to repurchase the company's stock [when it has the option to distribute the cash pro-rata]. Offer of the former choice, unlike offer of the latter, is unavoidable in the pursuit of the corporation's profit maximizing goal and is not loaded with the temptation to favor management or its supporters over outside stockholders. Those temptations are not fanciful when management owns, or is responsive to those who own, substantial stock so that self-dealing becomes unavoidable. "In any case, is management remiss if it avoids advising the stockholders that it believes the repurchase to be advantageous to the corporation and disadvantageous to the seller, and instead makes the following disclosure?

> 'Neither the Company nor the Board of Directors makes any recommendation that stockholders tender or refrain from tendering any or all of their shares. Each stockholder must make his own decision whether to become a holder of Debentures or to remain a holder of Common Stock.'

" * * * Any repurchase, in order to be valid, presumably would have to be preceded by effective disclosure, including disclosure of management's judgment * * *.

"The possibility that disclosure [must systematically] * * * be inadequate to illuminate management's 'intuition' about a good price, and the likelihood that disadvantageous treatment of selling stockholders could only be avoided by absolute prohibition rather than by case-to-case findings of actual misbehavior, raise questions which require * * * [further] exploration * * *. [O]bjections to corporate repurchases on the market may not adequately be met simply by disclosure. See Fleischer, Mundheim & Murphy, [An Initial Inquiry into the Responsibility to Disclose Market Information, 121 U.Pa.L.Rev. 798, 840–845 (1973).]"

---

* [Ed. Note] Compare Lynch v. Vickers   with TSC Industries, Inc. v. Northway,
Energy Corp., 383 A.2d 278 (Del.Ct.1977)   Inc., 426 U.S. 438 (1976).

It has been urged as the economic justification for repurchase of stock that management, by reason of its "inside" position, can "beat" the efficient market, and systematically perceive price-value disparities, and thus enable the corporation to make bargain purchases. (See Stewart, Should a Corporation Repurchase Its Own Stock? 31 J.Fin. 911 (1976)). If repurchase thus results in favoring one group of stockholders over another, is market efficiency thus enhanced at the cost of behavior that is not consonant with corporate norms? Does the fact that management often purchases corporate stock for itself at bargain prices prior to announcing a corporate repurchase further complicate the problem? See Lee, Mikkelson and Partch, Managers' Trading Around Stock Repurchases, 47 J. Finance 1947 (1992).

NOTE: STOCK REPURCHASES AND DISCLOSURE OF DIVIDEND POLICY

Entirely apart from the impact of the reduction in the number of outstanding shares on the market price of the stock, a program of corporate repurchases is related to the disclosure of relevant information to the extent that the repurchase is a substitute for dividends. Management's reluctance to contract the total amount of dividends paid from year to year may impel it to seek to avoid raising regular dividends in a given year if it is uncertain about being able to pay similar amounts in succeeding years. The same tendency, although to a lesser degree, may affect payment of "extra" dividends. The repurchase, made without fanfare, is in effect an extra dividend, but it avoids the exposure of management to unfavorable inferences if not repeated. Repurchase may well conceal the uncertainty of the pay out. And, of course, in larger terms it may conceal the fact that management has no better investment use for the corporation's funds.[o]

Compare the suggestions that (a) "there is a distinct group of companies using the repurchase technique. If the companies can be viewed as a composite of their ratios, then companies that repurchase have below normal expectations for profits caused either by industry circumstances or poor management or both. It appears that managements use repurchases for cosmetic adjustments to financial ratios so they can avoid the market test of their worth." Norgaard and Norgaard, A Critical Examination of Share Repurchase, 3 Fin.Mgt. 44 (1974) with (b) " * * * though the repurchasing companies did experience significantly poorer operating performance just prior to the time

---

o. Repurchase is not always accompanied by adequate publicity of the fact of repurchase. But even if it is, consider the import of the suggestion that repurchase (whether by tender offer or by open market purchase) is an appropriate mode of signalling that management believes the enterprise is undervalued in the market. (See note d, p. 610 supra.) One trouble with the suggestion is the uncertainty of the signal. A rational management acting in the stockholders' best interests would also distribute, rather than retain or reinvest, corporate funds if it had no better use for them. A repurchase could conceivably signal such a managerial conclusion. Management would not be anxious to articulate that conclusion; it would prefer that such a message be embodied in the act of repurchasing stock. How does the stockholder know which of the two signals is given by the mute act of repurchasing stock?

of the repurchase [than comparable non-repurchasing companies], no significant difference could be found between them after the repurchase. Thus, these operating troubles generally seem to have been overcome. Also, to the extent that operating difficulties are reflected in declining stock prices, management may be choosing to repurchase at a time when it feels the shares are relatively cheap." Ellis and Young, Repurchase of Common Stock (Ronald Press 1971) pp. 104–105.

(B) CORPORATE REPURCHASES AND THE REGULATION OF MARKET MANIPULATION

---

(1) Manipulation

Management repurchases resemble certain classic forms of stock price manipulation. In both cases, after all, purchases are being made for the purpose of increasing the stock price. The resemblance has given rise to questions respecting the applicability of the sections of the 1934 Act that prohibit stock price manipulation. Consider Section 9(a)(2), which provides:

"It shall be unlawful for any person, directly or indirectly, by the use of the mails or any means or instrumentality of interstate commerce, or of any facility of any national securities exchange, or for any member of any national securities exchange—* * * to effect, alone or with one or more other persons, a series of transactions in any security registered on a national securities exchange creating actual or apparent active trading in such security or raising or depressing the price of such security, for the purpose of inducing the purchase or sale of such security by others."

Would Section 9(a)(2) apply to a conventional issuer repurchase program which was not disclosed to the public? Would the federal securities' laws' antifraud provisions apply to such a program? Would either case depend on the subjective purpose of the managers of the issuer?

Note that Section 9(a)(2) by its terms applies only to transactions on national securities exchanges. Would a transaction in an unlisted security which would violate the section if it involved a listed security violate the antifraud provisions of the 1934 Act? If so, would the violation occur because those other provisions incorporate the strictures of Section 9(a)(2), or because some behavior which violates Section 9(a)(2) also violates the antifraud provisions because of the failure to disclose the manipulation? Consider the following discussion of the question by the Securities and Exchange Commission in **Halsey Stuart & Co., Inc.,** 30 S.E.C. 106, 110–112 (1949):

"The contention is correct insofar as the jurisdictional coverage of Section 9(a)(2) is concerned. It is wrong insofar as it intends us to hold that the broad anti-fraud provisions of Section 17(a) of the Securities

Act, and Sections 15(c) and 10(b) of the Exchange Act (and the rules thereunder) relating to over-the-counter securities do not cover activity which would be prohibited by Section 9(a)(2) as to listed securities merely because Section 9(a)(2) is, by its terms, limited to listed securities.

"The basic legal question posed by respondents is whether it is fraud to engage in transactions in an over-the-counter security creating actual and apparent activity and raising its price for the purpose of inducing purchase by others, assuming that such activity can be found. We think it obvious that this is so, and have clearly so held. In Barrett & Company, 9 S.E.C. 319, 328 (1941) we said:

" 'We conclude that the respondents, in continually raising the bids and buying at the higher bid prices, manipulated the price of American Wringer common stock with the intent of raising the price in order to induce the purchase of the stock by others at a price level at which the options they held could be profitably exercised and the stock resold. Transactions of this character, when effected with respect to listed securities, are expressly declared illegal by Section 9(a)(2) of the Securities Exchange Act because they are manipulative and fraudulent. See Sen.Rep. No. 792, 73rd Cong., 2d Sess., pp. 7–9. We think that there is no reasonable distinction in this respect between manipulation of over-the-counter prices and manipulation of prices on a national securities exchange, and that both are condemned as fraudulent by the Securities Exchange Act and, in fact, were fraudulent at common law. * * * We believe that the Securities Exchange Act contemplates that Section 15(c)(1) affords to the over-the-counter market at least as great a degree of protection against manipulation or attempted control as is afforded to the exchange market by Section 9(a). We find, therefore, that respondents' activities constitute an 'act, practice, or course of business' which operated 'as a fraud or deceit' and that respondents thereby violated Section 15(c)(1) of the Securities Exchange Act and paragraph (a) of Rule X–15C1–2 thereunder.'

"A manipulation may be accomplished without wash sales, matched orders, or other fictitious devices. Actual buying with the design to create activity, prevent price falls, or raise prices for the purpose of inducing others to buy is to distort the character of the market as a reflection of the combined judgments of buyers and sellers, and to make of it a stage-managed performance. Whether or not his belief is, in good faith, that the free market has undervalued the securities, the manipulator's design in raising prices is to create the appearance that a free market is supplying demand whereas the demand in fact comes from his planned purpose to stimulate buyers' interest. It is of utmost materiality to a buyer under such circumstances to know that he may not assume that the prices he pays were reached in a free market; and the manipulator cannot make sales not accompanied by disclosure of his activities without committing fraud.

"There is, of course, no subjective evidence of purpose to manipulate in this case and such purpose has been denied. But the facts of the case raise a compelling inference of motive to support or raise the market. Concededly, large insurance companies had 'struck' against buying at the public offering price. Emerging from a syndicate whose members had unsold inventories of over $12,500,000 of bonds (nearly 38% of which was in Halsey's hands), Halsey faced the prospect of a dire loss if market movements were to carry prices down too far for too long. Active trading in this situation subjected Halsey to the reasonable interpretation that its transactions in fact supporting the market, or raising prices, were undertaken in order to minimize or eliminate that risk—were undertaken, in other words, for a manipulative purpose."

———

Most, and possibly all, instances of manipulation may well implicate deception or non-disclosure in violation of the securities acts' general anti-fraud provisions. But even so, can there be manipulative behavior which, although disclosed, artificially affects market prices (e.g., behavior which violates Sections 14(d)(4)–14(d)(7) and Rules thereunder)? Is a requirement of disclosure inadequate to prevent the effects of manipulative behavior at which Congress quite explicitly aimed? In Rel. No. 34–17222 (Oct. 10, 1980), in discussing one of the many proposed (but not adopted) versions of Rule 13e–2 the Commission explained why, notwithstanding specific disclosure requirements contemplated by the Rule for certain issuer repurchase programs and the general anti-fraud provisions, the Commission deemed it necessary in the Rule to prohibit certain kinds of behavior. In the course of the Release, the Commission explained:

> While the Commission believes that the required disclosures are necessary or appropriate to prevent fraud, deception and manipulation, it does not believe that disclosure alone can take the place of the substantive regulation embodied elsewhere in the rule. Disclosure is unlikely to prevent manipulative conduct from having improper effects on the market since market manipulation is not solely a matter of deception and cannot be cured solely by preventing deception. For example, an issuer that every day participated in the opening and closing transactions in its securities could significantly and improperly affect the price of those securities despite the fact that its conduct was fully disclosed. Similarly, disclosure of an issuer repurchase program that involved purchases that dominated the market would not eliminate the effects of that domination. Disclosure of an issuer's efforts to drive the price of its securities up or to maintain it at artificial levels, by engaging several brokers to bid against one another or through other measures, would not cure the ill effects of such a manipulation. Moreover, given the often considerable fluctuations in market conditions and the rapid pace at which market transactions occur, it is questionable whether full and timely disclo-

sure of certain practices could ever be made in a fashion that would protect the markets and investors as fully or efficiently as can more direct prohibitions on manipulative practices. For these reasons, the proposed rule would prohibit the practices proscribed by the purchasing limitations, instead of merely requiring their disclosure.

* * *

Consider whether the anti-manipulation provisions of Section 9(a)(2) are substantive prohibitions, without regard to whether the behavior which violates them also can constitute violation of the anti-fraud and disclosure requirements of Section 10(b) and Rule 10b–5. Consider the same relationships among Sections 14(d)(4)–14(d)(7) and 14(e). Can Congress in enacting such anti-manipulative provisions have empowered the Commission to promulgate substantive rules which restrict behavior or forbid transactions rather than only rules which define and enforce disclosure requirements? Cf. Commission's prophylactic powers under Sections 13(e)(i)(B) and 14(e). If so, is the scope of the permissible substantive rules limited to proscribing behavior which causes injury to investors only by reason of its misleading or deceptive import? Cf. Schreiber v. Burlington North., Inc., infra p. 1015. See Fiflis, Of Lollipops and Law—A Proposal for a National Policy Concerning Tender Offer Defenses 19 U.C.Davis L.Rev. 303, 322–329 (1986).

(2) Stabilization

Section 9 of the Securities Exchange Act of 1934 provides in part:

(a) It shall be unlawful for any person, directly or indirectly, by the use of the mails or any means or instrumentality of interstate commerce, or of any facility of any national securities exchange, or for any member of a national securities exchange—

* * *

(6) To effect either alone or with one or more other persons any series of transactions for the purchase and/or sale of any security registered on a national securities exchange for the purpose of pegging, fixing, or stabilizing the price of such security in contravention of such rules and regulations as the Commission may prescribe as necessary or appropriate in the public interest or for the protection of investors.

* * *

(e) Any person who willfully participates in any act or transaction in violation of subsections (a), (b), or (c) of this section, shall be liable to any person who shall purchase or sell any security at a price which was affected by such act or transaction, and the person so injured may sue in law or in equity in any court of competent jurisdiction to recover the damages sustained as a result of any such act or transaction. In any such suit the court may, in its discretion, require an undertaking for the payment of the costs of such suit, and assess reasonable costs, including reasonable attorneys' fees, against either party litigant. * * *

In Release No. 6127 (Nov. 30, 1959) under the Securities Exchange Act of 1934, the Securities and Exchange Commission proposed to amend its rules on stabilization to make it unlawful to effect any stabilizing transaction except for the purpose of facilitating a particular distribution of securities. In the Release, the Commission said:

"The term 'stabilizing' has generally been accepted to mean the placing of any bid or the effecting of any purchase for the purpose of pegging or fixing the price of a security, or for the purpose of preventing or retarding a decline in the open market price of a security. While the Act specifically prohibits certain types of manipulation, and the Congress recognized stabilization as a form of manipulation, stabilization was not specifically prohibited. The mandate to the Commission under the Act was that the Commission should guard investors and the public from the vicious and unsocial aspects of the practice by such regulation as might be necessary.

"As is generally known, the Commission has been continually studying the problem of whether and to what extent stabilizing should be prohibited, and in what areas it should be regulated and how. In 1955, after obtaining the written views and comments of interested persons, and after a public hearing on the subject, the Commission adopted its Rules 10b–6, 7 and 8 prohibiting certain manipulative activities and regulating others in connection with the distribution of securities. Rule 10b–7 regulates stabilizing for the purpose of facilitating a distribution, and prohibits any person from making any stabilizing bid or purchase in connection with a distribution except in compliance with that rule. In general, the rule requires that such purchases be limited to those necessary to prevent or retard a decline in the open market price of the security, that they be made at price levels restricted as provided in the rule, that purchasers be given notice that the market is being stabilized, and that the Commission receive appropriate notice and reports.

"The Commission has become aware that certain persons have been effecting open market purchases which are intended to create trading activity, or to affect the price of a particular security, under circumstances which do not relate to or are not intended to facilitate a distribution. For example, there have been situations in which * * * issuers or other persons not contemplating any distribution, but interested in 'improving' or 'stimulating' or 'stabilizing' the existing market for a particular security, undertake to make open market purchases of the security. Persons bidding for or purchasing a security for the purpose of affecting the price, otherwise than to facilitate a distribution, may contend that their activities constitute stabilization which is not prohibited in the absence of a Commission rule, rather than illegal manipulation.

"It has been suggested that bids and open market purchases which are intended to affect the price of a security should be prohibited when they are not necessary to facilitate a particular distribution of securities. It is contended that while stabilizing may be in the public interest when it is done in connection with a distribution, because it facilitates an expeditious and orderly distribution and avoids disruption of the existing market for the security, conditions which are necessary under the American system of public financing, no such reason to justify the activity exists in other cases. The Commission's proposal would prohibit all bids or purchases of a security which are intended to peg, fix or stabilize the price of a security unless such transactions are for the purpose of facilitating a particular distribution of securities."

[The proposed amendments were never adopted.]

---

(3) Safe Harbor for Potentially Manipulative Repurchases

Suppose the management of X Corp. wishes to embark on an acquisition program and to use X Corp. stock as currency for acquisitions. It reasonably considers that the company's stock is undervalued on the market where it is priced at 32; and it believes that once the market focuses on the stock, its price will rise to 60. Is it not in the interest of the company's shareholders for the company to bid the price up to its true value? And, as with the discovery of any undervalued situation, would not the company defeat its purpose if it made a prior announcement of its intentions? On the other hand, if the true value of X Corp. is only 32, how can the company hope to benefit by overpaying for the shares? Unless it plans to issue false statements about its prospects and accomplishments, will not the market price fairly quickly settle back to the earlier level? Hence, if management honestly believes that the market undervalues X Corp. stock and that acquisitions can be carried out more easily, or more cheaply, if a better "price-structure" is established, presumably on a permanent basis (and there is no showing of an intention to create a mere temporary run-up) should the law make it impossible for a company to "invest" in its own shares without prior notice? If so, what policy reason would justify such a prohibition? If not, what serious objection can be made to management's proposals? See Davis v. Pennzoil Company, 438 Pa. 194, 264 A.2d 597 (1970).

Until the adoption in 1968 of Section 13(e) of the Securities Exchange Act, the SEC addressed issuer repurchases generally under the anti-fraud provisions of the securities acts, but specifically only by Rule 10b–6 [p] which applied only to repurchases of securities which were the

---

p. Rule 10b–6 provides that it shall constitute "a manipulative or deceptive device or contrivance," as used in § 10(b) of the Act for any issuer, underwriter, or certain

subject of a "distribution." While that term covered more than the conventional issuance of securities to the public through underwriters, its coverage was the subject of considerable tension—e.g., did it extend to the purchase by an issuer or affiliate of a target's stock or the issuer's stock when the issuer has an exchange offer outstanding for the target's stock, or to purchase by an issuer or affiliate of stock when there is outstanding either another class of the issuer's securities immediately convertible to the stock or a shelf registration? The limitations of Rule 10b–6 were increasingly apparent with the growth of market purchases by corporations for the purpose of affecting the prices of their stocks—e.g., in connection with expected or pending mergers, or sales by insiders or maintaining the value of securities pledged by insiders for loans. Those transactions raised sometimes difficult questions under the general anti-manipulative and anti-fraud provisions of Sections 9(a) and 10(b) of the Exchange Act as well as under Rule 10b–6.

For further discussion of Rule 10b–6, see Whitney, Rule 10b–6: The Special Study's Rediscovered Rule, 62 Mich.L.Rev. 567 (1964); Note, The SEC's Rule 10b–6: Preserving a Competitive Market During Distributions, 1967 Duke L.J. 809; Weiss and Liebowitz, Rule 10b–6 Revisited, 39 Geo.Wash.L.Rev. 474 (1971); Wolfson, Rule 10b–6: The Illusory Search For Certainty, 25 Stan.L.Rev. 809 (1973); Securities Underwriting (Bialkin and Grant Eds. P.L.I. 1985) pp. 293–324.

In 1968, Congress added section 13(e) to the Exchange Act[q] in order to give the SEC authority to make comprehensive rules with respect to share repurchases in view of the recent growth in volume of

others participating in a distribution, "directly or indirectly * * * to bid for or purchase for any account in which he has beneficial interest, any security which is the subject of such distribution * * * until after he has completed his participation in such distribution." [The rule exempts nonconvertible investment grade debt and preferred stocks, presumably because price manipulation for such securities is "very difficult."] The Rule then lists several transactions which do not violate that prohibition, including purchases sanctioned by Rules 10b–7 and 10b–8, which are intended primarily to "stabilize" the market during the public offering of a new issue of securities. See Foshay, Market Activities of Participants in Securities Distributions, 45 Va. L.Rev. 907 (1959).

q. Sec. 13(e) provides:

(1) It shall be unlawful for an issuer which has a class of equity securities registered pursuant to section 12 of this title, * * * to purchase any equity security issued by it if such purchase is in contravention of such rules and regulations as the Commission, in the public interest or for the protection of investors, may adopt (A) to define acts and practices which are fraudulent, deceptive, or manipulative, and (B) to prescribe means reasonably designed to prevent such acts and practices. Such rules and regulations may require such issuer to provide holders of equity securities of such class with such information relating to the reasons for such purchase, the source of funds, the number of shares to be purchased, the price to be paid for such securities, the method of purchase, and such additional information, as the Commission deems necessary or appropriate in the public interest or for the protection of investors, or which the Commission deems to be material to a determination whether such security should be sold.

(2) For the purpose of this subsection, a purchase by or for the issuer, or any person controlling, controlled by, or under the common control with the issuer, or a purchase subject to control of the issuer or any such person, shall be deemed to be a purchase by the issuer. * * *

such transactions. The Commission's efforts to promulgate antimanipulative rules under Sec. 13(e) entailed several unadopted proposals over a period of more than fifteen years (for part of that history see SEA Rel. No. 17,222 (Oct. 17, 1980)), and culminated in the adoption in 1984 of Rule 10b–18.

PURCHASES OF CERTAIN EQUITY SECURITIES BY THE ISSUER AND OTHERS; ADOPTION OF SAFE HARBOR

(Securities Exchange Act Release No. 19244, November 17, 1982.)

I. INTRODUCTION

The Commission has considered on several occasions since 1967 the issue of whether to regulate an issuer's repurchases of its own securities. The predicates for this effort have been twofold: first, investors and particularly the issuer's shareholders should be able to rely on a market that is set by independent market forces and not influenced in any manipulative manner by the issuer or persons closely related to the issuer. Second, since the general language of the anti-manipulative provisions of the federal securities laws offers little guidance with respect to the scope of permissible issuer market behavior, certainty with respect to the potential liabilities for issuers engaged in repurchase programs has seemed desirable.

The most recent phase of this proceeding is proposed Rule 13e–2 which was published for public comment on October 17, 1980. This rule would have imposed disclosure requirements and substantive purchasing limitations on an issuer's repurchases of its common and preferred stock. These restrictions, which generally would have limited the time, price, and volume of purchases, also would have been imposed on certain persons whose purchases could be deemed to be attributable to the issuer. In addition, the issuer, its affiliates, and certain other persons would have been subject to a general antifraud provision in connection with their purchases of the issuer's common and preferred stock.

The Commission has recognized that issuer repurchase programs are seldom undertaken with improper intent, may frequently be of substantial economic benefit to investors, and, that, in any event, undue restriction of these programs is not in the interest of investors, issuers, or the marketplace. Issuers generally engage in repurchase programs for legitimate business reasons and any rule in this area must not be overly intrusive. Accordingly, the Commission has endeavored to achieve an appropriate balance between the goals described above and the need to avoid complex and costly restrictions that impinge on the operation of issuer repurchase programs.

In light of these considerations, and based on the extensive public files developed in this proceeding, the Commission has determined that it is not necessary to adopt a mandatory rule to regulate issuer repurchases. Accordingly, the Commission has today withdrawn proposed Rule 13e–2, and, as discussed in this release, is amending Rule 10b–6 to eliminate most issuer repurchase regulation under that rule.* In lieu of direct regulation under Rule 10b–6 and proposed Rule 13e–2, the Commission has determined that a safe harbor is the appropriate regulatory approach to offer guidance concerning the applicability of the anti-manipulative provisions of Rule 10b–5 and Section 9(a)(2) to issuer repurchase programs, New Rule 10b–18 reflects this determination.

The Commission wishes to stress, however, that the safe harbor is not mandatory nor the exclusive means of effecting issuer purchases without manipulating the market. As a safe harbor, new Rule 10b–18 will provide clarity and certainty for issuers and broker-dealers who assist issuers in their repurchase programs. If an issuer effects its repurchases in compliance with the conditions of the rule, it will avoid what might otherwise be substantial and unpredictable risks of liability under the general anti-manipulative provisions of the federal securities laws.[5] * * *

* * * In order to make it clear that Rule 10b–18 is not the exclusive means to effect issuer repurchases, paragraph (c) of the rule provides that no presumption shall arise that an issuer or affiliated purchaser has violated Section 9(a)(2) or Rule 10b–5 if the purchases do not meet the conditions of paragraph (b).

* * *

II. SAFE HARBOR RULE 10b–18

A. *Coverage of Rule 10b–18*

The safe harbor of paragraph (b) is available for any bid or purchase that constitutes a "Rule 10b–18 bid" or a "Rule 10b–18 purchase," as defined in the rule. Paragraph (a)(3) defines a Rule 10b–18 purchase as a purchase of common stock of an issuer by or for the

---

* [Ed. Note] The effect of the amendment to Rule 10b–6 is to eliminate the need to seek specific exemptive or interpretative relief from Rule 10b–6 in order to permit purchases of any class of issuer stock solely because the issuer is engaged in a "technical" distribution. A "technical" distribution refers to the continuous offer of securities that is implicitly being made by reason of securities being outstanding with the public which are convertible into or exchangeable for other securities. The latter are the subject of the "technical" distribution. Rule 10b–6 continues to apply, however, to purchases of any security that is the subject of any other kind of distribution, including shelf registered stock with a plan of distribution at least when a genuine distribution, as distinguished from "ordinary trading," is involved (Rule 10b–6(c)(5)). See generally Manning and Miller, The SEC's Recent Revisions to Rule 10b–6, 11 Sec.Reg.L.J. 195 (1983).

5. Paragraph (b) of the rule provides that any issuer and its affiliated purchasers could not be held liable under the anti-manipulative provisions of Section 9(a)(2) of the Act or Rule 10b–5 under the Act solely by reason of the number of brokers or dealers used, and the time, price, and amount of bids for or purchases of common stock of the issuer, if such bids or purchases are effected in compliance with all of the conditions of paragraph (b) of the rule. Of course, Rule 10b–18 is not a safe harbor from violations of Rule 10b–5 which may occur in the course of an issuer repurchase program but which do not entail manipulation. For example, Rule 10b–18 confers no immunity from possible Rule 10b–5 liability where the issuer engages in repurchases while in possession of favorable, material non-public information concerning its securities.

issuer or any affiliated purchaser of the issuer. Paragraph (a)(4) defines a Rule 10b–18 bid as a bid for securities that, if accepted, or a limit order to purchase securities that, if executed, would result in a Rule 10b–18 purchase.

B. *General antifraud provision*

Under paragraph (b) of proposed Rule 13e–2, a class of issuers defined as "Section 13(e) issuers," their affiliates, affiliated purchasers, and any broker, dealer, or other person acting on behalf of these issuers, affiliates, or affiliated purchasers would have been subject to a broad general antifraud and anti-manipulative prohibition in connection with any bids or purchases of any equity security of the issuer. The commentators that addressed this provision opposed its adoption for essentially two reasons. First, they argued that it was unnecessary in view of existing provisions of the Act such as Section 9(a)(2) and Section 10(b) and Rule 10b–5 thereunder. Second, they argued that the general nature of paragraph (b) would detract from the certainty otherwise provided by the rule.

The Commission has reconsidered the question of whether a general antifraud provision is necessary in this context and has concluded that it is not. The sole purpose of the rule as adopted is to provide a safe harbor from liability under the anti-manipulative provisions of the Act. For that reason, the Commission has determined not to include a general antifraud provision in Rule 10b–18.

C. *Disclosure*

Proposed Rule 13e–2 would have required issuers and affiliated purchasers that sought to repurchase more than two percent of the issuer's stock during any twelve-month period publicly to disclose certain specified information prior to effecting any purchases of the issuer's stock. In addition, those persons would have been required to disclose the specified information to any exchange on which the stock was listed for trading or to the NASD if the stock was authorized for quotation in NASDAQ.

* * *

The proposed disclosure requirements were not intended to be coextensive with other disclosure obligations. Nevertheless, the Commission is persuaded that the obligation to disclose information concerning repurchases of an issuer's stock should depend on whether the information is material under the circumstances, regardless of whether such purchases are made as part of a program authorized by a company's board of directors or otherwise. The Commission has therefore determined not to adopt the specific disclosure requirements contained in paragraph (d) of proposed Rule 13e–2, even as a safe harbor. Other relevant provisions of the federal securities laws and existing policies and procedures of the various self-regulatory organizations impose disclosure responsibilities that appear to be sufficient to ensure that investors and the marketplace in general receive adequate information concerning issuer repurchases. The Commission emphasizes its belief that timely disclosure of all material information in the context of issuer repurchases may significantly facilitate the maintenance of an orderly market for the issuer's stock.

* * *

E. *Purchasing Conditions*

In order to take advantage of the safe harbor provided by Rule 10b–18, an issuer or affiliated purchaser would have to comply with all the conditions of paragraph (b) of the Rule. [The conditions, which are designed to prevent the issuer from dominating the trading market in its shares, impose limits on the timing of its purchases (after the opening and before the closing on any given day), the prices at which it may purchase (forbidding up-ticks), the volume of its purchases and the number of brokers it may use in making its open market purchases.]

Part V: MERGERS AND ACQUISITIONS
INTRODUCTION

A firm which acquires another company—one, perhaps, that is equal to or even larger in size than the acquiring concern—does so ideally for exactly the same reason that it purchases a new piece of machinery, even though the factors that enter into the former undertaking may be much more numerous and complex than those that inspire the latter. Essentially, the decision to invest capital funds rests upon the expectation that the future returns to existing shareholders, discounted to present value at a rate which reflects the risks of the enterprise, will exceed the amount currently to be committed. If this expectation is communicated to and believed by a sufficient number of investors, the shares of the acquiring company will rise to reflect the anticipation of greater returns. Calculation of both expected returns and the appropriate discount rate is not without its difficulties—theoretical as well as practical—but the elements of the calculations are presumably unaffected by the size of the investment project being considered.

Nevertheless, the decision to acquire another enterprise entails financial, tax and legal factors which are rarely significant in small scale capital budgeting decisions. Determining the bond/stock mix with which to finance a merger involves resolution of cost of capital problems of considerably greater complexity than those involved in financing normal asset acquisitions (see supra, pp. 459 et seq.). Accounting procedures for acquisitions or mergers provide new options for affecting the earnings, or at least reported earnings, and ultimately the share value of the combined enterprise. And, the income tax laws affect the decision to merge in a manner not encountered in the simpler setting.

As a legal matter, the economic importance of a merger decision gives special urgency to questions of management's skill, judgment and loyalty to shareholder interests. From the point of view of the acquiring corporation, the initial inquiry is whether "too much" is being paid, whether the consideration flowing from the buyer exceeds the sum of (1) the acquired corporation's "worth" apart from the merger and (2) any value added to the resulting corporation by the combination. In ascertaining the latter, the question must be asked whether there are any rational norms for dividing "synergistic" gains—i.e., if A contributes earnings of 3 and B contributes equally risky earnings of 1 to the A–B merger, and the combined enterprise is expected to earn 6 as a result (for example) of eliminating duplicated expenses, how should the additional 2 be apportioned between the stockholders of A and B? If the combination of two equally risky ventures diversifies the total risk borne by the investors, how should the gain be divided? In addition, entirely apart from whether management has fulfilled its duty of care in the merger bargain, there is the question whether the acquiring corporation is paying for increased size (and the resultant presumed perquisites to management) and increased assurance of management's continuity rather than for share values. Inquiries into whether stockholders of acquired companies are fully paid or stockholders of acquiring companies gain or lose notwithstanding payment of premiums to sellers, or whether acquiring companies have proved more efficient or more profitable than non-acquiring companies of comparable size and risk, are, in fair part, addressed to affirming or denying a systematic bias of management on such counts. But, although the literature is voluminous, and the debate tendentious, the findings (except for gains to stockholders of acquired companies) are inconclusive.

From the point of view of the acquired corporation, similarly, the initial inquiries are whether enough is being received for the value given up, apart from any increased efficiency or profitability flowing from the merger, and whether synergistic or other gains are being appropriately divided. There is also the question of loyalty—whether management (or those in control) received a side payment or other premium for consenting to the acquisition. If circumstances or legal rules place power over the merger decision in a given individual or group, one is entitled to suspect that its exercise does not always go uncompensated, and that the sales price is sometimes less than it would otherwise be, by an amount which exceeds the side payment to management or other controlling persons.

With respect to mergers and acquisitions, corporate law is concerned primarily with prescribing the procedure by which they may be effected, and the organs of the corporation which must consider and approve the transactions. Because of frictions and imperfections in the linkage between management and stockholders in the decision making process, there are occasional legal constraints on the freedom of management in making the merger bargain, including obligations to disclose essential information to security holders. The injection of legal norms to measure the propriety of the merger bargain or to force disclosure occurs largely for the benefit of stockholders on the sellers' side of the transaction, presumably because problems of fair division more often arise when business ownership is terminated for cash or securities than when it is extended to embrace additional operating assets.

SECTION A. THE MOVE TO MERGE

A series of merger movements has shaped and reshaped the corporate landscape during this century. The first occurred at the turn of the century; a second followed during the 1920s; and a third came during the period 1941–1947. The fourth period began after 1950. In a sense the fourth period has continued ever since, albeit with varying degrees of intensity. This extended post war merger movement has had two peaks of activity. The first, which was connected with the rising stock markets of the 1960s, was characterized by the conglomerate merger. The second, which accompanied the rising stock markets of the 1980s, was characterized by the bust-up takeover and its defensive counterpart, the leveraged buyout.

Explaining this activity is an ongoing enterprise. The problem of articulating an answer to the question as to why corporations merge, which is not easily solved even in static conditions, is repeatedly complicated by the stream of developments in merger and acquisition practice. Consider first the situation of a quarter century ago. The conglomerate merger was a new development that challenged traditional explanations of mergers. Traditionally, gains resulting from corporate combinations had been accounted for in terms of changes in the operation of the surviving firm. These changes either (1) restrained competition, that is, the combined firm possessed enhanced power in the product market, or (2) entailed operating efficiencies, that is, the combined firm gained from cross-breeding technologies or other synergies, or gained from the introduction of superior internal control systems or other management improvements. The "pure" conglomerate merger entailed neither of these. The commentators, accordingly, identified several additional possible sources of gain. Many of these arose from institutional imperfections rather than productive opportunities. The tax system provided favorable treatments for the surviving firm in certain mergers. The accounting system created extraordinary opportunities for the managers of the surviving firm to select favorable, arguably manipulative, accounting treatments. Other sources of gain identified were financial in nature. Discussion focused on the fact that an all equity combination could automatically increase the earnings per share of the surviving corporation even though the combined dollar amount of earnings did not increase, so long as the price earnings ratio of the acquiring corporation was higher than that of the acquired firm. Some also noted that conglomerate combinations created a portfolio effect (although others, referring to the capital asset pricing model, pointed out that actors in marketplace already would have captured this gain through diversification). Still others noted that the larger, more secure combined firm gained by virtue of lower borrowing costs. See Lintner, Expectations, Mergers and Equilibrium in Purely Competitive Securities Markets, 61 Amer.Econ.Rev. 101 (1971). Compare Scott, On the Theory of Conglomerate Mergers, 32 J.Finance 1235 (1977).

During the middle 1980s corporate actors in pursuit of gain through combination changed the landscape again. But this time they "busted up" many of the conglomerates constructed in the pursuit of gain through combination during the 1960s. Where the markets had once rewarded unrelated diversification, now they punished it. See Morck, Shleifer, and Vishny, Do Managerial Objectives Drive Bad Acquisitions? 45 J.Finance 31, 47 (1990); Bhagat, Shleifer, and Vishny, Hostile Takeovers in the 1980s: The Return to Corporate Specialization, Brookings Papers on Economic Activity 1 (1990). Once again commentators on mergers and acquisitions began their analysis with the traditional notion that gain through combination is best explained in terms of operating results. But, once again, reference to the usual sources of operating gain—market power, synergy and management improvement—could not account for all developments in the marketplace. At the core of the problem was the proliferation of hostile acquisition activity and everyday realization by target shareholders of 50 percent premiums over the market value of target equity.[a]

KRAAKMAN, TAKING DISCOUNTS SERIOUSLY: THE IMPLICATIONS OF "DISCOUNTED" SHARE PRICES AS AN ACQUISITION MOTIVE

88 Colum.L.Rev. 891 (1988).
pp. 893–905, 907–911, 913, 925–930.

I. AN OVERVIEW OF ACQUISITION GAINS

Three possibilities might occur to an observer who first learned that acquirers routinely pay large premia over share price for the assets of target firms: (1) acquirers may be discovering more valuable uses for target assets; (2) share prices may "underprice" these assets; or, finally, (3) acquirers may simply be paying too much. These same possibilities point to a useful typology of current explanations of acquisition gains. A broad class of "traditional" gains hypotheses assumes that acquirers can create or claim new value to pay for acquisition premia. These explanations accord with the assumption that informed share prices fully reflect asset values. They include all ways in which acquirers might expect to increase the net cash flows of targets, for example, by improving management or redeploying assets. A second class of "discount" hypotheses asserts that while acquirers' bid prices reflect real private gains, these gains result because share prices discount the underlying value of target assets. Finally, a third and more troubling class of "overbidding" hypotheses questions whether bid prices and takeover premia reflect real opportunities for acquisition gains at all. Under these theories, managers of acquiring firms may misperceive or misvalue targets out of "hubris,"[6] or they may pursue

----

a. Nathan and O'Keefe, The Rise in Takeover Premiums: An Exploratory Study, 23 J.Financial Econs. 101 (1989), charts the rise in merger and takeover premiums during the period 1963–1985. They find that between 1963–1973 and 1974–1985 the mean cash tender offer premium rose from 29 percent to 70 percent, and the mean stock merger premium rose from 32 percent to 67 percent. Also, takeover premiums rose steadily throughout the period. They also find that the structural shift took place in 1973–1974, the time of the oil crisis and the final collapse of the bull market of the 1960s. They conclude that as a general proposition takeover premiums are negatively related to the business cycle, as measured by the Standard and Poor's Stock index. They conjecture that the economic disruptions of 1973–1974 caused an increase in the heterogeneity of investors' beliefs about firm value. Id. pp. 118–119.

6. Roll, The Hubris Hypothesis of Corporate Takeovers, 59 J.Bus. 197 (1986).

distinctly managerial interests such as corporate growth at great cost to shareholder interests.

The extent to which this third class of acquisition hypotheses might explain takeover premia remains a difficult issue. Nevertheless, a prosperous acquisitions market and a large empirical literature both suggest that most acquisitions do generate private gains, at least as measured by their impact on share prices. Target shareholders earn large returns in the form of premia, while shareholders of acquiring firms do not seem to suffer losses and may also register gains.[8] Since a primary role for private gains in motivating takeovers seems likely, inquiry must turn to the traditional and discount hypotheses. The question thus becomes: What mix of opportunities can explain these gains and the size of acquisition premia?

A. *Traditional Gains Hypotheses*

Most traditional accounts of motives and gains in the acquisitions literature favor active and resourceful acquirers who seek to increase cash flows from target assets through the redeployment or better management of these assets. The reorganization of assets can lead to synergy benefits, while new management may slash operating costs and increase returns in a variety of ways.[9] In either case, acquisitions create both private gains for the participating parties and net social gains. In addition, there are less prominent, if no less traditional, accounts of how acquisitions might create private gains by imposing costs on third parties. Acquirers might exploit monopoly power,[10] or breach "implicit contracts" between target shareholders and creditors,

8. See Jarrell, Brickley & Netter, The Market for Corporate Control: The Empirical Evidence Since 1980, 2 J.Econ.Perspectives 49, 53 (1988); Jensen & Ruback, The Market for Corporate Control: The Scientific Evidence, 11 J.Fin.Econ. 5, 9–22 (1983). Recent studies provide additional evidence of aggregate gains from mergers and takeovers. See, e.g., Dennis & McConnell, Corporate Mergers and Securities Returns, 16 J.Fin.Econ. 143, 152–79 (1986); Malesta & Thompson, Partially Anticipated Events, 14 J.Fin.Econ. 237 (1985). Basic ambiguities in the interpretation of these market studies, however, leave the issue of aggregate gains far from closed. See, e.g., Magenheim & Mueller, Are Acquiring–Firm Shareholders Better Off After an Acquisition than They Were Before?, *in* Knights, Raiders, and Targets: The Impact of the Hostile Takeover 172 (J. Coffee, L. Lowenstein & S. Rose–Ackerman eds. 1988) [hereinafter Knights, Raiders, and Targets]; Roll, Empirical Evidence on Takeover Activity and Shareholder Wealth, *in* Knights, Raiders, and Targets, supra, at 241.

9. For overviews of acquisition hypotheses, see Jarrell, Brickley & Netter, supra

note 8, at 54–58; Jensen & Ruback, supra note 8, at 22–33; Roll, supra note 8. The specialized literature on acquisition gains is large. The synergy hypothesis, including gains from vertical integration and economies of scale, is the most strongly supported traditional account. See, e.g., Bradley, Desai & Kim, The Rationale Behind Interfirm Tender Offers: Information or Synergy?, 11 J.Fin.Econ. 183, 185–87 (1983); McConnell & Nantell, Corporate Combinations and Common Stock Returns: The Case of Joint Ventures, 40 J.Fin. 519, 520–21 (1985) (extrapolating from joint ventures to merger gains); Roll, supra note 8, at 245–46. However, the case for pure "financial synergies," including diversification and co-insurance gains in conglomerate mergers, is not persuasive. See Amihud & Lev, Risk Reduction as a Managerial Motive for Conglomerate Mergers, 12 Bell J.Econ. 605, 610–15 (1981); Roll, supra note 8, at 15–16.

10. Indirect evidence strongly suggests that market power is not an important acquisition motive. See Eckbo, Horizontal Mergers, Collusion, and Stockholder Wealth, 11 J.Fin.Econ. 241, 251–68 (1983).

employees, or incumbent managers.[11]

Two further accounts of acquisition gains straddle the line between traditional and discount hypotheses. One of these is a "private information" theory, which assumes that the market may be uninformed about the real value of target assets. In this case, acquirers who privately learn key information can exploit true discrepancies between share prices and asset values. The possibility of such information is a traditional caveat to the identification of share prices and asset values. Yet its practical significance seems largely limited to friendly transactions. Short of hiring informers, hostile acquirers lack access to inside information about targets. In addition, evidence that unsuccessful bids fail to increase the share prices of target firms over the long run also suggests that hostile bids do not release key inside information.[12]

The second of these accounts concerns the import of tax savings for acquisition premia. The tax hypothesis may be either a traditional or a discount hypothesis depending on the nature of the asserted tax gain. In most instances, it is a traditional hypothesis that turns on corporate-level tax savings. Acquirers are said to garner significant tax gains by stepping up the basis on target assets, transferring valuable operating loss carryovers ("NOLs"), or increasing their interest deductions by borrowing against target assets.[13] These forms of the tax hypothesis are variations on the better management theory, although here management is tax management and the potential savings at issue are

---

11. Among the most provocative revisionist accounts of private gains in takeovers are implicit contract theories that locate private gains in the redistribution of surplus from nonshareholder factors of target firms to acquiring firms. Thus, several commentators portray takeovers as a species of shareholder opportunism vis-a-vis incumbent managers. E.g., Coffee, Shareholders Versus Managers: Strains in the Corporate Web, 85 Mich.L.Rev. 1, 24 (1986); Knoeber, Golden Parachutes, Shark Repellents and Hostile Tender Offers, 76 Am.Econ.Rev. 155, 159–61 (1986). This view suggests that acquirers profit in part by breaching implicit agreements to pay incumbent managers deferred compensation or to provide other perquisites. Professors Shleifer and Summers generalize the implicit contract perspective to other major corporate factors including employees and creditors. A. Shleifer & L. Summers, Breach of Trust in Hostile Takeovers 13–15 (National Bureau of Economic Research Working Paper No. 2342, 1987). The implicit contract perspective obscures the consequences of seemingly straightforward changes in management policy. Lower labor or management costs are no longer obvious efficiencies on this view; they may also result from breaches of implicit agreements. Thus, implicit contract theories inject an element of normative

uncertainty into the analysis of operational gains that parallels the uncertain interpretation of share discounts.

12. See Bradley, Desai & Kim, supra note 9 (share prices of targets gradually fall to pre-offer levels within five years after unsuccessful bids). Share prices would presumably remain at post-bid levels if the market believed that hostile bids were based on inside information. Many other studies have replicated Bradley, Desai and Kim's result although doubt remains as to whether targets of unsuccessful bids typically lose all offer-related gains in share prices. See, e.g., Jarrell, The Wealth Effects of Litigation by Targets: Do Interests Diverge in a Merge?, 28 J.L. & Econ. 151 (1985); Ruback, Do Target Shareholders Lose in Unsuccessful Control Contests, in The Economic Effects of Mergers and Acquisitions (A. Auerbach ed. forthcoming 1988).

13. See A. Auerbach & D. Reishus, The Effects of Taxation on the Merger Decision (National Bureau of Economic Research, Inc. Working Paper No. 2192, Mar. 1987); R. Gilson, M. Scholes & M. Wolfson, Taxation and the Dynamics of Corporate Control: The Uncertain Case for Tax Motivated Acquisitions *in* Knights, Raiders and Targets, supra note 8, at 271.

purely distributional gains.[14]   Recent studies suggest that each of these corporate-level tax gains has played some role in acquisitions and, more importantly, in management buyouts.[15]   Yet, apart from leveraged buyouts, their role seems to have been modest in the recent past; tax effects seldom appear to have been primary motives for acquisitions.[16]

* * *

B. *Discount Hypotheses*

True discount hypotheses rely on neither private information nor a traditional inquiry into how acquirers might extract larger net cash flows from target assets.   The discount claim assumes that acquisition premia reflect the existing value of target assets, a value that may be much higher than the pre-bid market value of target shares.   A discount hypothesis must explain why these values differ.   Apart from specialized tax claims, two broad explanations of discounts are possible: the misinvestment hypothesis and the market hypothesis.

The misinvestment hypothesis comes closest to traditional accounts of takeover gains.   This account locates discrepancies between share prices and asset values in a rational mistrust of managers' future investment decisions.   As such, it belongs to the broader family of agency cost theories.   Unlike accounts of manager-shareholder conflict over operating slack and perquisites, however, the misinvestment hypothesis follows more recent analyses of manager-shareholder conflict over the distribution of corporate returns.[20]   In this view, managers exercise discretionary control over what Professor Jensen terms "free cash flows"—those cash flows exceeding the investment requirements of the firm's existing projects.   If managers are reluctant to distribute

14. This point is made most forcefully by considering that alternative transactions would permit target managers to realize most tax gains for shareholders that are ordinarily attributed to acquisitions. See R. Gilson, M. Scholes & M. Wolfson, supra note 13 (arguing that acquisitions ordinarily do not dominate alternative means of realizing corporate-level tax gains unless acquisitions have a marginal advantage in reducing transactions costs).

15. See A. Auerbach & D. Reishus, Taxes and the Merger Decision, *in* Knights, Raiders and Targets, supra note 8, at 310 (tax losses and credits potentially important in 20% of mergers but fewer apparent tax benefits from stepping up asset basis or leverage); A. Auerbach & D. Reishaus, supra note 13, at 27–29 (use of tax losses and credits by acquiring companies appears to have "some impact" on merger activity, while interest deductions "could not have been an important factor" during 1968–83). The evidence that tax gains are critical in many management buyouts is more persuasive.   See Lowenstein, Management

Buyouts, 85 Colum.L.Rev. 730, 759–67 (1985); K. Lehn & A. Poulsen, Sources of Value in Leveraged Buyouts 18–22 (working paper) (Feb. 1987) (on file at the Columbia Law Review).

16. See Roll, supra note 8, at 246–48; supra note 15 (citing sources).

20. See, e.g., Coffee, supra note 11, at 16–24; Easterbrook, Two Agency–Cost Explanations of Dividends, 74 Am.Econ.Rev. 650 (1984); E. Jacobs, The Agency Cost of Corporate Control: The Petroleum Industry 35 (Massachusetts Institute of Technology Center for Energy Policy Working Paper Studies No. 86–021, 1986); Jensen, Agency Costs of Free Cash Flow, Corporate Finance, and Takeovers, 76 Am.Econ.Rev. 323 (1986).   Tax-based discount theories, see supra notes 13–19 and accompanying text, are variations on the misinvestment hypothesis, since they implicitly assume that target managers "misinvest" by failing to channel free cash flows into low-tax distributions, such as share repurchases or corporate liquidations.   See M. King, supra note 17, at 8–9.

these cash flows and are unable—or unwilling—to discover profitable new investments, shareholders must inevitably price firms at below informed appraisals of their asset values.[21]

Although the misinvestment hypothesis is conceptually related to traditional accounts of acquisition gains arising from improvements in the operational management of target firms, there is an important difference. Ongoing mismanagement of targets' assets reduces their cash flows. Thus, low share prices may accurately mirror the value of mismanaged target assets; there may be no discounts. By contrast, under the misinvestment hypothesis, discounts can arise even though targets' assets are put to their best uses. These discounts, which acquirers can exploit, result from the ongoing or expected misinvestment of surplus cash flows that exceed targets' operating requirements. Acquiring firms can profit, then, merely by purchasing discounted shares at any price up to the full value of targets' assets.

The alternative discount hypothesis—the market hypothesis—fits less easily with standard accounts of the securities market. In this view, share prices may discount asset values for reasons endogenous to the formation of market prices. Financial economics conventionally assumes that share prices are best estimates, given available information, of the present value of expected corporate cash flows available for distribution to shareholders. Thus, share prices should fully capitalize the value of corporate assets in the hands of existing managers. In real markets, this assumption is an approximation; it is unlikely to be either precisely correct or, given the sensitivity of share prices to new information, wholly misguided. It is a very good approximation in the standard view. By contrast, the market hypothesis asserts that discounts arise because share prices are sometimes very poor estimates of the expected value of corporate assets.

Modern objections to identifying share prices with asset values typically fall into two classes. The first class includes "valuation" challenges that question whether a single valuation model can apply across the markets for shares and firms or within the share market itself. Even if traders in both the asset and share markets value corporate assets similarly, share prices might nonetheless discount asset values simply because assets and shares differ in ways that

---

21. Agency-cost analyses focusing on distribution policy build upon evidence that managers often seek to maximize total corporate resources, including debt capacity. G. Donaldson, Managing Corporate Wealth: The Operation of a Comprehensive Financial Goals System 54–56 (1984). Maximizing resources may lead in turn to investments with a negative net present value. Managerial incentives to misinvest in this fashion are variously attributed to organizational inertia; a desire to increase size (or sales) per se; and the close correlation among firm size, managerial career opportunities, and managerial compensation. Jensen, supra note 20, at 323. In addition, misinvestment may follow from managers' relative risk aversion in comparison to that of shareholders. Coffee, supra note 11, at 16–24. Whatever the mix of managerial motives, however, it must be strong enough to force real prospective losses in order to generate share discounts. Neither risk aversion nor empire building alone can explain discounts unless the firm faces restricted investment opportunities.

matter to traders.[23] For example, the share prices of firms holding liquid assets might discount asset values if traders placed an intrinsic value on the right to liquidate firms in the asset market—a right that minority shareholders in these firms would necessarily lack. Alternatively, overlapping clienteles of traders within the securities market might have heterogeneous demands for timing, magnitude, or tax attributes of shareholder distributions.[25] In this case, shares might sell at either a discount or a premium relative to asset values.

The second and more prominent class of objections to equating share prices with asset values challenges the price setting role of informed traders. Thus, there is a growing theoretical literature on "mispricing" behavior, which argues that uninformed traders may introduce persistent biases or cumulative noise into share prices or that speculative trading might lead to positive or negative price "bubbles." [26] Large-scale noise trading—arising from misconceived strategies, erroneous valuation assumptions, fashion and fads, or simple pleasure in trading [27]—might distort share prices and generate discounts or premia through the sheer pressure of trading. In addition, some commentators suggest that noise trading further distorts share prices by encouraging informed traders to speculate on noise and by imposing "noise trader risk" on all traders in a noisy market. Finally, noise theorists find evidence of mispricing in the long-term price behavior of both individual firms and the entire market.

* * * What remains uncertain is how effectively share prices estimate the full present value of corporate cash flows, as distinct from

---

23. Professors Louis Lowenstein and Martin Shubik vigorously urge this point as part of their broader advocacy of the market hypothesis. See, e.g., Lowenstein, Pruning Deadwood in Hostile Takeovers: A Proposal for Legislation, 83 Colum.L.Rev. 294 (1983); Shubik, Corporate Control, Efficient Markets, The Public Good, and Economic Theory and Advice, *in* Knights, Raiders and Targets, supra note 8, at 31, 41–45. A separate argument is that traders in the asset and share markets systematically differ in their valuations of underlying assets or cash flows. This occurs, for example, when corporate acquirers have different risk preferences or valuation models than traders in shares. See, e.g., Gordon & Kornhauser, supra note 22, at 825. This argument, unlike the claim that shares and assets differ, leads back to the problematic overbidding hypothesis. See supra notes 6–8 and accompanying text.

25. See, e.g., Thompson, The Information Context of Discounts and Premiums on Closed–End Fund shares, 6 J.Fin.Econ. 151, 180–82 (1978) (suggesting heterogeneous demands as possible source of discounts on closed-end funds). Heterogeneous demand implies downward sloping demand curves for equity rather than the horizontal demand curves predicted by common forms of the efficient capital markets hypothesis. Compare Gilson & Kraakman, supra note 22, at 570 & n. 67 (evidence suggesting horizontal demand) with Shleifer, Do Demand Curves for Stocks Slope Down?, 41 J.Fin. 579 (1986) (inferring downward sloping demand from price increases after inclusion in index funds).

26. E.g., Black, Noise, 41 J.Fin. 529 (1986) (cumulative noise in price following uninformed trading).

27. A variety of sources for noise trading have been proposed. See, e.g., Black, supra note 26, at 531 (noise trading by mistake or because trading yields direct utility); Schiller, Fashions, Fads and Bubbles in Financial Markets, *in* Knights, Raiders and Targets, supra note 8, at 56, 60–65 (fashions and fads); Trueman, A Theory of Noise Trading in Securities Markets, 43 J.Fin. 83 (1988) (rational noise trading by uninformed fund managers to fool investors); J. Delong, A. Shleifer, L. Summers & R. Waldmann, The Economic Consequences of Noise Trading, 4–5 (CRSP Working Paper No. 218, Sept., 1987) (irrational belief or cognitive bias).

predicting near-term share prices, and how large residual mispricing effects are likely to be. The market hypothesis simply asserts that recurrent discrepancies between share prices and asset values can explain major portions of at least some acquisition premia.

Stepping back from the market hypothesis, then, it is apparent that neither this account nor the misinvestment theory of acquisition gains is easily evaluated. * * * Fortunately, however, one task does not require such an evaluation: namely, examining the discount claim in its own right as a motive for acquisitions. Evidence of discounts can support either hypothesis. * * *

II. The Case for Discounts

Market discounts must satisfy three conditions to be meaningful. First, potential acquirers and market professionals must be able to form reliable asset or break up values for the firm "as is;" that is, as its component assets are already managed and deployed. Asset values in this sense are particularly credible when assets can be separated from the functions of top management. Thus, natural resources or established corporate divisions may lend themselves to reliable valuation, while start-up projects or undeveloped investment opportunities might be impossible to value with confidence. Second, share prices must fall significantly below asset values. And third, potential acquirers must accept appraisals within the consensus range as useful—perhaps as minimal—estimates of what target assets will be worth to themselves and competing bidders.

Although these conditions are difficult to test, the case for discounts is nonetheless persuasive. Certain specialized firms that hold easily priced assets provide direct evidence of discounting. In addition, pervasive discounting can explain much recent acquisition behavior, including breakup acquisitions,[32] management buyouts, and the sheer size of takeover premia. Finally, support for discounts can be found in many forms of corporate restructuring, including the wave of share repurchases and recapitalizations that swept American corporations during the mid–1980s.

A. *Discounts on Specialized Firms*

Specialized firms whose shares clearly trade below the value of their assets provide direct evidence of discounting. * * * The closed-end investment fund is the best example of such a firm, and discounts on closed-end funds have long been viewed as important anomalies by financial economists. Yet discounts appear to be common among holding companies and natural resource companies, which are also firms that possess easily accessible and seemingly reliable asset values. Thus, even though reliable appraisals are not readily available for most firms, the suggestion is clear: If discounts appear wherever we are able

---

32. Breakup acquisitions of multidivisional firms rely on the preplanned resale of target divisions in order to finance premia and generate gains. The asset values of such firms are the aggregate appraisal values of their constituent divisions, net of the costs of centralized management.

to detect them, we have good reason to suspect that they may occur elsewhere.   * * *

Although there have been numerous investigations of discounts on closed-end funds, none has satisfactorily accounted for their origins.   * * * Not surprisingly, competing explanations divide along the familiar lines of the market-or-manager dichotomy.   * * * In particular, the market-based accounts seem to challenge basic hypotheses in financial economics, while agency cost theories have difficulty explaining why the past performance of funds is only a modest predictor of discounts. If there is a significant risk of agency losses, it has not yet materialized—or at least not since the Great Depression.

   * * *

Other than closed-end funds, holding companies, and natural resource companies, there is no direct evidence of discounts due to the absence of reliable appraisals.   * * *

Nevertheless, difficulty in observing discounts across all categories of firms does not diminish the significance of their presence on closed-end funds and natural resource firms.   These examples create a presumption in favor of the discount claim.   They cannot be ignored unless they can be explained or distinguished as anomalous by some still undiscovered characteristic of the securities market. * * *

B.   *Acquisition Behavior*

Given a basic presumption in favor of discounts, the discount claim becomes an intuitively attractive explanation over a broad spectrum of corporate activity.   In particular, it accords well with at least two aspects of acquisition behavior where traditional hypotheses falter. One is the sheer size of premia in hostile acquisitions and management buyouts.   The other is the recent prominence of break up acquisitions that exploit perceived differences between the share prices and asset values of conglomerate firms.

Consider first the size of acquisition premia.   In recent years, premia have averaged about 50% of share value in management buyouts and 50% or more in hostile acquisitions.   Most studies suggest that acquisitions of all kinds are either zero or positive net present value transactions on average.   Thus, assuming that most acquirers reasonably expect to recover their premia costs, the obvious question is: How can they be so sure?   Apart from possible tax gains, which few commentators believe to dominate premia, we are left to choose among market discounts and the usual suspects including the displacement of inefficient management, synergy gains, or the exploitation of private information. * * *

An evaluation of these assumptions shows the superiority of the discount claim.   Large premia are easily explained if reliable appraisals of large firms can reveal the existence of market discounts.   Under these circumstances, acquirers can calculate discounts with standard appraisal techniques and thereby learn, within the limits of appraisal error, whether the bulk of their premia costs are a simple purchase of assets at their existing values. That is, acquirers learn that their premia costs largely pay for assets that are worth the price if they merely continue to perform as they have in the past. By contrast, the synergy and better management hypotheses require acquirers to value novel and still hypothetical changes in targets' operating assets, while the information hypothesis demands that acquirers routinely discover dramatic good news relative to market expectation about targets.

* * *

Many commentators implicitly recognize the difficulty of valuing hypothetical changes by surmising that the cost of searching for opportunities to extract operating gains is a principal determinant of takeover activity.[70] But this assumption encounters institutional difficulties. Casual evidence of several kinds suggests that acquirers rely heavily upon routine appraisals of the existing value of target assets rather than farsighted assessments of their potential value. Investment bankers deploy standard valuation programs in advising their clients; second bidders enter bidding contests on short notice; and outside analysts offer roughly similar and often accurate predictions of acquisition values as soon as firms are rumored to be "in play." Moreover, the rapid convergence of offer prices in auctions suggests common criteria for estimating value that seem unlikely to result from operating gains. Of course, consensus in the acquisitions market might also follow if first bidders fully revealed common opportunities for exploiting operating gains through their offers. But precisely because operating gains are complex and potentially unique to particular firms, this prospect seems unlikely. In contrast, the discount claim organizes many of the basic features of today's takeover market—large premia, acquirers' "wish lists," rapid decisions, and routine bidding contests— into a comprehensible game. It is a sporty game.

Finally, the discount claim can help to explain breakup acquisitions. Breakup acquisitions, whether hostile or friendly, present a clear analogy to the liquidation of closed-end investment funds. Where discounted funds hold portfolios of stocks, breakup targets are typically conglomerates holding several divisions that acquirers can resell piecemeal with their managements and markets intact. Although the prima facie likelihood of immediate operating gains from conglomerate breakups is greater than the likelihood of similar gains from management buyouts or acquisitions of natural resource firms, conglomerates still would have to impose enormous costs on their operating divisions for acquirers to generate 50% premia merely by eliminating the conglomerate structure. Operating gains in breakup acquisitions more plausibly occur—as in management buyouts—at the time when corporate assets are resold. Acquirers expect profits from the breakup and resale of target divisions, and these profits, in turn, may reflect the

70. See, e.g., Easterbrook & Fischel, The Proper Role of a Target's Management in Responding to a Tender Offer, 94 Harv. L.Rev. 1161 (1981); Schwartz, Search Theory and the Tender Offer Auction, 2 J.Law, Econ. & Organization 229 (1986).

synergy or management gains that are available to the third-party
purchasers of target assets.   Standing alone, however, these resale
profits seem unlikely to explain large initial premia paid to target
shareholders.   Acquirers and their financial backers cannot predict *ex
ante* the synergy and management gains of end purchasers.   Once
again, operating gains would have to be improbably large to support
prepayments of 50% premia, particularly since these gains must be
divided between acquirers and end purchasers in negotiated transactions.   While breakups may ultimately generate large operating or
synergy gains, then, the discount claim presents a more compelling
account of initial premia.

             * * *

IV.   DISCOUNTS AS AN ACQUISITION MOTIVE

A.   *Joint Gains*

The most important way in which discounts can prompt takeovers
is in combination with other sources of acquisition gains such as
operating gains or private information.   Only large discounts can
trigger takeovers in isolation if, as I have argued, target shareholders
ordinarily capture most of the value of discounts.   Nevertheless, small
gains from other sources might transform firms with modest discounts
into attractive targets, provided that these ancillary gains are—unlike
discounts—uniquely available to particular acquirers.   This possibility
assumes that acquirers are able to capture most unique gains for their
own accounts.   Like pre-bid purchases on the open market, such gains
give first bidders a strategic edge.   They are unavailable to rival
bidders, and they are likely to be invisible or at least difficult to value
for defending managers or the market at large.

A simple example can clarify how such appropriate gains might
affect acquisition decisions on the margin.   Suppose that a target trades
at a 30% discount below its asset value of $500,000,000, and that an
acquirer can purchase 10% of the target's stock at the discounted price.
In addition, assume that a tender offer for the remaining 90% must be
priced at the target's pro rata asset value in order to discourage
management resistance, including the solicitation of rival bids.   In this
case, a potential bidder would anticipate a gross return of $15,000,000
($0.10 \times 0.30 \times \$500,000,000$) from the target's discount.   Thus, if the
expected costs of a successful bid—including professional fees, financing
and solicitation costs, contingent liabilities, defensive tactics, and transition expenses—totaled, say, $20,000,000, no acquirer would bid on the
basis of the target's discount alone.   If, however, an acquirer expected
even minor synergy gains (on the order of $10,000,000) in addition to
discount gains, a hostile bid would become an attractive proposition.

[I]f large discounts can offset premia and subsidize first-stage
transaction costs, even uncertain synergies or management gains might
suffice to motivate buyout syndicates or breakup acquirers.   Thus, the
joint-gains hypothesis can accommodate conflicting evidence about the
"real" motive behind these transactions and explain one of their most

puzzling features: why buyers pay "second premia" when breakup assets are resold, buyout targets go public, or residual shares in recapitalized firms appreciate in the market. Second premia on this account are merely the rewards of forecasting previously uncertain operating gains.

The joint-gains hypothesis also bears on efforts to test the discount claim. First, it suggests that discount levels alone cannot reliably predict takeovers. Given a distribution of acquirers' opportunities to exploit unique gains, takeovers might occur at all discount levels. The discount claim is probabilistic; larger discounts only increase the likelihood of acquisitions. But second, and more promising, the joint-gains model predicts that average takeover premia may vary *inversely* with synergies or other acquirer-specific gains. The reason is that without acquirer-specific gains, only large discounts—which, by hypothesis, yield large premia—are likely to trigger takeovers. Put differently, acquirers who locate opportunities for large, unique gains do not need to bid for heavily discounted targets that command large premia.

B. *Changing Acquisition Risks*

The second occasion for takeovers in a world of discounts stems from management failure to respond to changing acquisition risks. [T]akeovers may occur before targets learn to adapt to exogenous events that modify the economics of takeovers by inflating discounts or lowering takeover costs.

The prime example of such a window of opportunity for acquirers is the most recent wave of takeovers (extending from 1981 to the present) and the even larger wave of corporate restructurings that these takeovers seem to have triggered. Commentators agree on at least two underlying causes of this dramatic increase in takeovers. One is the rapid expansion of institutional support for takeovers, including a specialized capital market. The second is the joint impact of severe inflation during the 1970's and sustained economic expansion in the 1980's. Both factors profoundly altered acquisition risks. A maturing acquisitions market dramatically lowered takeover costs, while rising nominal and real asset values raised discount levels by upsetting existing relationships among corporate cash flows, debt obligations, and distribution policies.[131] The predictable consequence was a burst of takeover activity that persists today as managers continue to adapt financial policies to the new acquisitions climate.

A subsidiary question is precisely how rising asset values act to increase discount levels under both the market and the misinvestment

---

131. Shleifer & R. Vishny, supra note 76 at 5. Professors Shleifer and Vishny, who focus on management buyouts, stress the tax savings and the discount opportunities which rise from the larger net asset values that result when inflation reduces debt obligations and increases firms' free cash flows. For a market hypothesis of how inflation might introduce bias directly into share prices, see Modigliani & Cohn, Inflation, Rational Valuation, and the Market, 35 Fin. Analysts J., Mar./Apr. 1979, at 24. By contrast, Professor Jensen excludes past inflation but adds deregulation, relaxed antitrust enforcement, and industry-specific factors to the causes of recent takeover and restructuring activity. Jensen, supra note 55, at 316–17.

hypotheses. First, consider Professor Jensen's application of the misinvestment hypothesis to the energy industry. In his view, a sharp increase in oil prices coincided with a sharp decrease in the marginal productivity of new investment in the energy industry during the late 1970's.[132] Rather than reflect the declining profitability of new investment, however, investment spending rose to match the rising cash flows generated by higher prices. The result could only have been a dramatic increase in discount levels for oil firms.

Although Professor Jensen describes this conjuncture as unusual in its dimensions,[133] the misinvestment hypothesis suggests that the same result must occur whenever exogenous events increase the asset values of discounted firms. Without offsetting changes in the investment and distribution policies of such firms, larger discretionary cash flows can only mean more misinvestment and lower returns on total equity. Share prices, then, must always lag behind the revaluation of assets until managers can credibly limit their investment discretion by, *inter alia,* converting equity into debt.

The market hypothesis dictates much the same result. On this view, shares trade at depressed prices due to uninformed trading or speculative biases. Informed traders must look partly to existing prices and disbursement policies to anticipate price changes. Disbursement policies, in turn, influence prices by "focusing" investors on either the asset values of discounted firms or the easily valued terms of debt securities. Thus, share prices cannot fully—or even proportionately—reflect increases in asset values without offsetting changes in disbursement expectations. Exogenous events may increase the free cash flows of discounted firms, but share prices fail to reflect the asset values of these firms even *before* their reappraisals. Unless the market revises its expectations about the distribution policies of these firms—after, for example, announcements of share repurchases or higher dividends—savvy traders must expect even larger discounts when discounted assets are revalued.

In sum, almost any theory that builds financial policy into the formation of share prices implies that these prices must be "sticky" with respect to changes in asset values. * * *

NOTE: MOTIVATIONS FOR MERGERS

1. *Downward–Sloping Demand.*

Booth, Discounts and Other Mysteries of Corporate Finance, 79 Calif.L.Rev. 1055 (1991), stresses that the misinvestment and market explanations of discounts are not mutually exclusive. According to

---

132. Jensen, supra note 55, at 329–32; see also E. Jacobs, supra note 20, at 30 (elaborating on Jensen's analysis).

133. Jensen, supra note 55, at 331.

Booth, id. pp. 1058–1059, "both explanations are nothing more than alternative formulations of the same basic truth: stocks, like other commodities have downward-sloping demand curves. In other words, the price of a share for purposes of the trading market is established by the lowest-valuing current shareholder or, stated another way, the highest-valuing potential shareholder while the price of a share for the purposes of a tender offer or other acquisition is set by the highest-valuing current shareholder or highest-valuing bidder." Stout, Are Takeover Premiums Really Premiums? Market Price, Fair Value, and Corporate Law, 99 Yale L.J. 1235 (1990), also suggests that takeover premiums stem from heterogeneous investor beliefs and downward sloping demand.

2. *Overpayment.*

Kraakman, supra, makes reference to traditional investment practices in accounting for the behavior of bidders in the mergers and acquisitions market. He describes the bidder as an investor of capital who conducts a valuation of a potential investment. This valuation approach to mergers brings recognition of the uncertainty that inheres in management decisions respecting investments. See Trautwein, Merger Motives and Merger Prescriptions, 11 Strategic Mgt.J. 283, 287 (1990). Unfortunately, uncertainty also inheres in the explanatory discussion. Kraakman has to make a critical assumption before going on to assert that the discounts exist and to propose his management and misinvestment explanations. The assumption is that the valuing managers reach cognizably accurate conclusions most of the time—that value in fact is present, despite inevitable uncertainty. As Kraakman acknowledges, supra p. 654, there is a view to the contrary. Under this, the bidding firms have a tendency to overvalue acquired firms—value in fact may not be present much of the time. Roll, Empirical Evidence on Takeover Activity and Shareholder Wealth, in Coffee, Lowenstein and Rose–Ackerman, eds., Knights, Raiders, and Targets: The Impact of the Hostile Takeover, 241, 249–250 (1988), ascribes overbidding to the hubris of the bidders' managers:

"A recent paper of mine [Roll, The Hubris Hypothesis of Corporate Takeovers, 59 J.Bus. 197 (1986)] advances a behavioral explanation for the takeover phenomenon. My argument is that bidding firm managers intend to profit by taking over other firms, possibly because they *believe* that synergy is present, that the target has inefficient management, etc. Their intentions are not fulfilled, however, because the market price already reflects the full value of the firm, (i.e., there is actually no synergy nor inefficient management involved). Why, then, do bidding firms persist in their pursuit of the target? Because the *individual* decision makers in the bidding firm are infected by overweaning pride and arrogance (hubris) and thus persist in a belief that their own valuation of the target is correct, despite objective information that the target's true economic value is lower.

"The hubris explanation is heavily dependent on improper recognition of the "winner's curse," a concept familiar to scholars of bidding theory. The idea of the winner's curse is simple: Whoever makes the winning bid for a valuable object is likely to be a bidder with a positive valuation error. In auctions with only a few bidders, the winner is likely to have made the biggest (positive) error. Optimal-bidding theory recognizes this problem and prescribes a lower bid than the valuation in general. The extent of downward bias in the bid depends on the variability in the bidder's distribution of values, perhaps subjectively determined, and the number of competitors.

* * *

"Hubris cannot be the sole explanation of the takeover phenomenon because it implies that every bid announcement should elicit a price decline in the bidding firm's shares. Some papers have even found an average increase. Furthermore, if all bids were inspired by hubris, stockholders could easily stop them by the simple expedient of a prohibition in the corporate charter. On the other hand, a strict prohibition would be irrelevant to a fully diversified shareholder since a hubris-driven takeover is a wealth transfer, from one of his or her issues to another (ignoring the deadweight takeover costs). We do not observe such stringent antibid charter provisions, which must imply that stockholders at least believe that an occasional bid by a firm might have positive individual and aggregate benefits."

Others offer contrasting descriptions of the motivations of overpaying managers. Morck, Shleifer and Vishny, supra, combine management self-interest and management concern for the market value of the firm. In their view, the particular mix of motivations varies with the transactional circumstances. Managers, they say, are more likely to overbid where they detect personal benefits. This is a situation where the acquisition contributes to long term firm growth, enhances job security, or enables the manager to diversify the risk on human capital. Id. pp. 31–32. Morck, Shleifer and Vishny accompany their description with an empirical study of 326 acquisitions consummated between 1975 and 1987, and report on several situations where acquiring firms systematically overpay. Specifically, returns to the shareholders of bidding firms are lower where managers pursue unrelated diversification and buy growth. Also, firms with bad managers do much worse with their acquisitions than do firms with good managers. Id. pp. 33–34, 45–47. See also Lang, Stulz, and Walkling, Managerial Performance, Tobin's Q and the Gains from Successful Takeovers, 24 J. Financial Econ. 137 (1989) (uses the ratio of firm market value to replacement cost of assets as a measure of management quality, and shows that well managed companies earn significant positive returns when they acquire poorly managed companies and that poorly managed companies earn significant negative returns when they acquire well managed companies).

Can the proposition that acquirers overbid be squared with evidence of the stock price effects of takeovers? Roll reports, supra pp. 241–242, (1) that studies of target stock prices show price increases of 20 percent for mergers and 30 percent for tender offers in the period around the takeover event; (2) that studies of bidding firm prices have mixed results: some show positive price movements, some show negative price movements; and (3) that whether the bidding firm price movements are positive or negative, they tend to be small in percentage terms and less statistically significant than those of target firms. If bidding firms tend to overpay, should not their stock prices show statistically significant declines in response to tender offers? Black, Bidder Overpayment in Tender Offers, 41 Stan.L.Rev. 597, 614–615 (1989), argues that we should not necessarily expect the stock price to decline in response to an overly high bid.

Assume, with Black, id. pp. 623–634, that some bidders are likely to overpay, that capital, product and labor market constraints do not prevent overpayment, that investors can anticipate overpayment at least some of the time, but that, despite this, many takeovers may lead to efficiency gains. Does the phenomenon of overpayment have implications for the law regulating mergers and acquisitions? If overpayment should be regulated, who should do the regulating, courts or shareholders? See Dent, Unprofitable Mergers: Toward a Market–Based Legal Response, 80 Nw.U.L.Rev. 777 (1986) (proposing that courts enjoin bids causing significant declines in bidder stock prices), and Coffee, Regulating the Market for Corporate Control: A Critical Assessment of the Tender Offer's Role in Corporate Governance, 84 Colum.L.Rev. 1145, 1269–72 (1984) (suggesting approval by bidder shareholders).

For a decidedly contrary empirical study, see Bradley, Desai, and Kim, Synergistic Gains From Corporate Acquisitions and their Division Between the Stockholders of Target and Acquiring Firms, 21 J. Financial Econs. 3 (1988) (average synergistic gain in tender offers studied is a 7.4 percent increase in combined wealth of bidder and target shareholders). For a study of market constraints on overbidding, see Mitchell and Lehn, Do Bad Bidders Become Good Targets? 98 J.Pol.Econ. 372 (1990).

3. *Further Reading.*

For summaries of the recent explanatory literature, see Romano, A Guide to Takeovers: Theory, Evidence, and Regulation, 9 Yale J.Reg. 119 (1992); Trautwein, Merger Motives and Merger Prescriptions, 11 Strategic Mgt.J. 283 (1990); Roll, Empirical Evidence on Takeover Activity and Shareholder Wealth, in Coffee, Lowenstein, and Rose–Ackerman, eds., Knights, Raiders, and Targets: The Impact of the Hostile Takeover 241 (1988). For more on financial motivations, see Bruner, The Use of Excess Cash and Debt Capacity as a Motive for Merger, 23 J. Financial & Quan. Anal. 199 (1988); Billingsley, Johnson and Marquette, Bankruptcy Avoidance as a Merger Incentive, 14 Managerial Finance 25 (1988); for more on management displacement, see Martin and McConnell, Corporate Performance, Corporate Takeovers, and Managerial Turnover, 46 J. Finance 671 (1991) (compares performance of takeover targets where senior executive is displaced with those where senior executive is retained; displacement targets showed significant negative abnormal returns compared to the rest of their industries during pre-takeover period, other targets showed slight positive returns); for more on tax gains, see Hayn, Tax Attributes of Shareholder Gains in Corporate Acquisitions, 23 J. Financial Econs. 121 (1989); for a study of gains from labor concessions, see Rosett, Do Union Wealth Concessions Explain Takeover Premiums? 27 J. Financial Econs. 263 (1990).

4. *Partial Combinations.*

The complete combination of two or more businesses in one corporate solution presents one set of questions and problems. The partial combination which occurs when one party acquires control, but less than 100 percent of the equity, of another party presents another. Such a combination potentially embodies many of the operating aspects of a total combination, but leaves a visible conflict of interest between stockholders in the two enterprises. The benefits sought from such acquisitions are said to include the exploitation of the subsidiary by the parent in collateral transactions, as much as appropriately shared gain from the relationship. A puzzling question presented by the potential for such exploitation is why, or under what circumstances, the controller should determine that it can gain more by owning 100 percent of the subsidiary than by such collateral exploitation. Perhaps at some point the controller senses an increased awareness of fiduciary obligations and the potential for violating them, and being liable for such violation.

SECTION B.   ACCOUNTING AND TAXES

---

1.   ACCOUNTING FOR MERGERS— PURCHASE OR POOLING

Appendix A, Section 2

2.   TAX TREATMENT OF MERGERS

(a) Reorganization Transactions *

The purchase of one corporation's assets by another for cash, or a mixture of cash and debt, is obviously a "taxable" transaction under the Internal Revenue Code. With limited exceptions, the selling corporation (S) recognizes gain or loss with respect to the assets sold, while the buying corporation (B) takes a basis for those assets (for purposes of

---

* Discussion of reorganizations is adapted from Surrey, Warren, McDaniel and Ault, Federal Income Taxation (1978), with further reference to Bittker and Eustice, Federal Income Taxation of Corporations and Shareholders (5th ed. 1987).

computing depreciation as well as gain or loss on subsequent resale) equal to their cost. If S liquidates following the sale (as it might do if all of its assets were disposed of in the transaction) and distributes the proceeds of sale to its shareholders, the latter recognize individual gains or losses measured by the difference between the amount received in the liquidation and the particular shareholder's basis for the stock which he surrenders.

The "purchase" just referred to may take the form of a so-called cash merger—S merges into B under a State statute, with the shareholders of S receiving cash pursuant to the merger plan—or it may take the form of a sale of assets by S to B followed by the liquidation of S. Yet another common procedure—different in form but with similar economic consequences—would entail a purchase by B (again, for cash or cash and debt) of all of the stock of S from S's individual shareholders, with S then being liquidated into B (or perhaps kept alive as a wholly-owned subsidiary). Under Code § 338, B may elect to treat a stock purchase *as if* it were an asset purchase, so that the tax results associated with the latter—taxable gain or loss to S and its shareholders, and a cost-basis to B for S's assets—occur here as well even though S's assets are acquired and held only indirectly, i.e., through B's ownership of S stock.

As an alternative to a taxable purchase, the Code also permits one corporation to acquire another through the medium of a tax-free reorganization. The Code provisions governing corporate reorganizations are detailed and elaborate. In general, however, they provide for non-recognition of any gain or loss realized by a corporation or its shareholders as a result of certain readjustments of the corporate capital structure.

The corporate reorganization [b] sections cover a great variety of corporate transformations. The congressional policy is that while such readjustments may produce changes in the conduct of a business enterprise, they do not involve a change in the nature of the relation of the owners of the enterprise to that enterprise sufficient to warrant taxation of gain or allowance of loss. Because the sections permit nonrecognition and, hence, postponement of gain, and, as a corollary, require nonrecognition and postponement of loss, special provisions are needed to reflect such nonrecognition in the cost or other basis of the corporate assets and stock involved.

The corporate readjustments covered range from the absorption of one corporation into another engaged in a completely different business to a mere change in the place of incorporation. They relate to small corporations and large corporations, to successful growing corporations and to corporations in bankruptcy and receivership, to closely held family corporations and to publicly owned corporations, to business corporations and to personal investment companies. Because the reorganization sections mirror most of the corporate transformations that

---

b. The term "reorganization" does not here refer primarily to bankruptcy reorganizations, though it does include insolvency proceedings.

occur in the business world, they are one of the most complex parts of the Code.

Code sections 354(a) and 361(a) are the central provisions establishing nonrecognition of gain or loss in corporate reorganizations. They depend for their operation on the existence of a "reorganization," a term defined in section 368(a). Of the situations there described, the three following largely cover the merger area:

TYPE (A)—STATUTORY MERGERS AND CONSOLIDATIONS. Under section 368(a)(1)(A), a "merger" or "consolidation" effected pursuant to a state statute permitting such transactions qualifies as a reorganization. A merger occurs when one or more corporations transfer their assets to another existing corporation—as where corporation X merges into existing corporation Y. A consolidation occurs when two or more corporations transfer their assets to a newly created corporation—as where corporation X and corporation Y consolidate into new corporation Z. Corporations X and Y may be parent and subsidiary or may be corporations not previously related.

TYPE (B)—ACQUISITION OF STOCK IN EXCHANGE FOR VOTING STOCK. Under section 368(a)(1)(B), a qualified reorganization exists when one corporation acquires the stock of another corporation solely in exchange for all or a part of the voting stock of the acquiring corporation, as where corporation Y acquires the stock of corporation X, so that thereafter corporation Y, in effect, owns corporation X. Corporation X may either be operated as a subsidiary or liquidated and merged into corporation Y. If corporation X is liquidated (which may be accomplished under section 332 without recognition of gain or loss to corporation Y), the end result does not differ from a statutory merger as described above. In either event, the shareholders of corporation X become shareholders in corporation Y. They may be minority or majority shareholders, depending on the amount of stock issued by corporation Y, which, in turn, depends on the relative sizes of corporations X and Y.

The acquisition of X stock, if it is to constitute a reorganization, must be solely in exchange for the voting stock of corporation Y. This "solely for voting stock" requirement has been strictly applied, and it can create troublesome practical problems. Thus, if the acquiring corporation agrees to pay certain expenses of the transferor-shareholders, such as legal fees, disqualification presumably results. Likewise, a problem may arise where the acquiring corporation enters into employment contracts with those shareholders. If these contracts are deemed partly in payment for the stock, disqualification results. If some of the shareholders of corporation X are unwilling to exchange their stock for stock of corporation Y, apparently corporation X can redeem their stock without disqualifying the entire transaction; but if funds for redemption were furnished by corporation Y, the requirement of the statute is not satisfied.

To qualify the acquisition as a type (B) reorganization, the acquiring corporation must have or obtain control of the acquired corporation. "Control" is defined in section 368(c) as 80% ownership of the total combined voting power of all classes of stock entitled to vote and 80% of the total number of shares of all other classes of stock. The entire 80% (or more) of the stock need not be acquired in one transaction. Any particular acquisition is a reorganization if after that acquisition corporation *Y* is in "control" of corporation *X*. Hence, a previous acquisition of some shares of corporation *X* for cash or nonvoting stock, or for voting stock but without "control," would not constitute a reorganization. However, the earlier acquisition would not necessarily prevent a later acquisition for voting stock from being interpreted as a reorganization if, after the later acquisition, the requisite 80% of the shares of corporation *X* were held by corporation *Y* as a result of the several acquisitions. Likewise, if corporation *Y* had previously acquired "control" of corporation *X*, whether in a taxable transaction or in a reorganization, a subsequent acquisition of shares in corporation *X* would presumably be a reorganization. Acquisition of control over a period of time, sometimes called "creeping control," was permitted for the first time in 1954. Under prior law, a corporation which had previously purchased more than 20% of another corporation's stock apparently could not acquire the balance in a type (B) reorganization.

Application of the "creeping control" rule is somewhat uncertain. An acquisition for cash, related in time or by plan to an acquisition for stock, would be treated as one transaction and would prevent a "reorganization" since the "acquisition" would not be solely for voting stock. Thus, if corporation *Y* acquired 50% of the stock of corporation *X* on January 1 for cash and acquired the remaining 50% on July 1 in exchange for voting stock, presumably the later exchange would not be a reorganization. The later exchange would qualify, however, if the two transactions were widely separated in time, or if it could be proved that they were independently conceived.

TYPE (C)—ACQUISITION OF ASSETS IN EXCHANGE FOR VOTING STOCKS. The acquisition by one corporation of another corporation through the acquisition of substantially all of its assets—as where corporation *Y* acquires the assets rather than the stock of corporation *X*—qualifies as a reorganization under section 368(a)(1)(C). The acquisition, in general, must be "solely" in exchange for the voting stock of corporation *Y*.[c] Corporation *X* need not receive any specific percentage of the shares of corporation *Y;* it is enough that in return for its assets it become a shareholder of corporation *Y*. The important point is that corporation *Y* has obtained all or "substantially all" of corporation *X*'s assets, thus generally, paralleling, with regard to quantity, the type (B) acquisition described above. Having transferred substantially all of its assets to corporation *Y*, corporation *X* must liquidate, transferring the consideration it received on the transfer, plus any retained assets, to its shareholders, who thus become shareholders of corporation *Y* just as did the shareholders in the type (A) and type (B) situations.

c. There are two exceptions: (i) Assumption by *Y* of *X*'s liabilities is permitted, and (ii) up to 20% of the value of *X*'s assets may be acquired for a consideration other than voting stock (e.g., cash), though in such event any liabilities assumed by *Y* are treated as money paid for *X*'s property.

As to the meaning of "substantially all," transfers of 90% and even 85% of the assets have qualified. Lower percentages may also qualify if the retained assets are used to pay creditors. The IRS has said that the particular percentage of assets transferred is not determinative, but that instead "the nature of the properties retained by the transferor, the purpose of retention, and the amount thereof" must be considered.

Triangular Reorganizations. For various reasons—accounting convenience, employee relations, liability limitations, relations with creditors—corporation *Y* may wish to acquire the assets or stock of corporation *X* by using a wholly-owned subsidiary as the vehicle for the acquisition. Thus, typically, corporation *Y* would form a new subsidiary, *Y*-sub, and transfer to it an appropriate number of corporation *Y* voting common shares. *Y*-sub would then acquire the assets of corporation *X* in (for example) a type (A) statutory merger, or would acquire at least 80% of the voting stock of corporation *X* in a type (B) stock-for-stock exchange, exchanging not its own but its parent's (*Y*'s) stock for the assets or stock of corporation *X*. In yet another variation, *Y*-sub, holding nothing but its parent's stock, would merge into corporation *X* (the latter being the survivor), with corporation *Y* receiving newly issued stock of corporation *X* in place of its stock in *Y*-sub and the shareholders of corporation *X* exchanging all of their *X* stock for the *Y* shares previously held by *Y*-sub. Both types of acquisition—the "forward" merger of corporation *X* into *Y*-sub and the "reverse" merger of *Y*-sub into corporation *X*—are now authorized by most state corporation statutes and qualify as reorganizations for tax purposes under sections 368(a)(2)(D) and (E). The aim of the latter provisions, generally speaking, is to extend the reorganization definition to transactions in which a controlled subsidiary acquires property (the assets or stock of corporation *X*) in exchange for the stock of its parent, and which would otherwise qualify if the property were acquired by the parent directly.

COMPARISON OF TYPE (A), TYPE (B), AND TYPE (C) REORGANIZATIONS.

Subparagraphs (A), (B), and (C) of section 368(a)(1) thus cover various methods by which several corporations may be combined into one ownership. A chain store absorbing a corner grocery store (obtaining its assets directly under (C), or obtaining its stock under (B) and then liquidating it or keeping it alive as a subsidiary, or pursuing a statutory merger under (A), so that the owners of the grocery are really "selling" their business for stock) could be within any of the three subsections. So could be the amalgamation of two industrial giants.

The type (B) and type (C) reorganizations both relate to the tax-free acquisition of a corporate business, the first by the acquisition of stock from the shareholders of the corporate business, and the second by the acquisition of the corporate assets. They are intended to supplement the type (A) acquisition through a statutory merger or consolidation under state law, and thus to permit tax-free acquisition in situations where the relevant corporate law does not permit a statutory merger or consolidation, as where there is no state law permitting mergers or where the state merger law does not cover corporations of another state.   These alternatives may also be used where state merger laws exist, but the parties wish to avoid some of their requirements.

While the three subparagraphs thus, essentially, provide rules for the different nontax methods by which a corporate acquisition can occur, differing economic and legal (non-tax) consequences may still attend each form, so that the existence of a choice is not without utility. For example, in a statutory merger the acquiring corporation automatically assumes all the liabilities of the seller, whereas in an asset acquisition such complete assumption of liabilities is not obligatory; on the other hand, in a statutory merger the acquiring corporation may issue non-voting preferred stock bonds or even cash, but it may not do so in a tax-free stock or asset [d] acquisition; in a statutory merger, stockholders of one or both corporations generally have voting and appraisal rights which may not be available at all, or to the same extent, in an asset acquisition; in an exchange of shares, the acquiring corporation may remain with a minority partner (i.e., 20% stockholder of the acquired corporation) whereas in an asset acquisition, the stockholders become participants in a single homogenized unit.   For a general discussion of the variations in form and their consequences, see Bittker and Eustice, Federal Income Taxation of Corporations and Shareholders (5th Ed.1987).

For nonrecognition to occur, it is necessary not only that the exchange of assets or of stock be pursuant to a reorganization as defined in section 368(a), but also that one or more of the exchange provisions be applicable.   These exchange provisions are chiefly found in sections 354 and 361.

Section 361(a) provides for nonrecognition of gain or loss to the corporation transferring its assets (corporation X in the examples above) pursuant to a qualified reorganization, provided that the transfer is solely in exchange for stock or securities of the transferee corporation.   Thus, corporation X would have a tax-free exchange as respects the assets transferred by it in exchange for stock or securities of the transferee in type (A) or type (C) reorganization.

Where section 361 is applicable, the basis of the transferor-corporation for stock or securities of the transferee is the same as the transferor's basis for the assets given up in the exchange.   The transferee corporation's basis for the assets it received is the same as the basis of those assets in the hands of the transferor.   This is a matter of some significance because it determines the amount of the deduction for depreciation which the transferee may enjoy.

Section 354 relates to the shareholder in the reorganization exchange.   In general, under section 354(a)(1), no gain or loss is recognized to a shareholder upon an exchange, pursuant to a plan of reorganization solely for stock or securities in the same corporation, or in another corporation which is also a party to reorganization.   Thus, in a type (B) reorganization the shareholders of corporation X (in the

---

d.   But see note c supra, p. 672.

examples above) are exchanging the stock in corporation X, a party to the reorganization, for stock of corporation Y, also a party to the reorganization. In a type (C) reorganization, if the plan of reorganization provides for the liquidation of corporation X, its shareholders will receive, upon liquidation, stock or securities of corporation Y, a party to the reorganization, for stock of corporation X, also a party to the reorganization.

Section 358(a) prescribes the basis rules for the shareholders in section 354(a) exchanges. While gain or loss is thus not recognized by the shareholder at the time of the reorganization exchange, the basis of stock or securities received tax-free by a shareholder is the same as the basis of the stock or securities given up in the exchange; hence the shareholder's gain or loss is deferred until the new property is finally sold for cash.

The tax benefits flowing from these provisions are often said to be a determinant of corporate combinations. Whether or not anticipation of tax benefits is a significant impetus for corporate combination, there is no doubt that tax considerations materially affect the forms which the combinations will take. Generally, the crucial consideration is that after the merger a stockholder of a merging company will have changed the form of his wealth into an entirely different and often more freely marketable security than he held before, without having incurred the tax that would have been payable had the original security been sold and the proceeds reinvested in stock of the merged enterprise. In addition to the benefit to the seller from thus being able to defer the tax on his gain, merger encourages the buyer to pay for assets with its stock, rather than cash. To the extent that a buoyant stock market gives a large block of stock a higher exchange value than cash value, the buyer derives an advantage. This is partially offset by the disadvantage of foregoing the higher tax basis (and correspondingly higher depreciation deduction) for the seller's depreciable assets that would attach to a taxable acquisition, e.g., a purchase for cash.

(b) Nonreorganization Transactions

The reader of the preceding discussion of tax free reorganizations who recalls this book's previous references to the mergers and acquisitions market of the 1980s will ask how, if at all, the elaborate structure of tax relief just described figured into that course of events. In the conglomerate merger boom of the 1960s and early 1970s the consideration paid to the shareholders of the acquired firm tended to be stock of the acquiring corporation, making reorganization tax treatment feasible. Transactions in the 1980s market, in contrast, tended to have a significant portion of cash consideration procured as the proceeds of borrowing. These therefore tended to be nonreorganization transactions, with the shareholders of the target paying capital gains tax on their transactional gains.

Any tax benefits in nonreorganization transactions lie on the side of the acquiring corporation. Before the Tax Reform Act of 1986, these came in three varieties:

(1) Where the acquiring corporation booked the assets of the acquired corporation at fair value, the step-up in the dollar amount of the basis of the assets resulted in increased depreciation deductions (to the extent that the acquisition included assets depreciable for tax purposes).

(2) Where the target company had generated losses, its net operating loss carryovers could (subject to various restrictions) be transferred to the acquirer and used to shield its income from tax.

(3) Where the acquiring corporation borrowed all or part of the acquisition price, it increased its tax deductions from interest.

For discussion of the impact of these tax incentives on the economics of acquisition activity before the effective date of the Tax Reform Act of 1986, see Gilson, Scholes and Wolfson, Taxation and the Dynamics of Corporate Control: The Uncertain Case for Tax–Motivated Acquisitions, in Coffee, Lowenstein and Rose–Ackerman, eds., Knights, Raiders, and Targets: The Impact of the Hostile Takeover 271 (1988).

The Tax Reform Act of 1986 diminished both the availability and magnitude of these tax advantages. First of all, the Act made nonreorganization transactions significantly more expensive from the point of view of the target's shareholders by eliminating preferential treatment of capital gains. Second, the Act repealed the *General Utilities* doctrine, formerly embodied in sections 337 and 338 of the Code, so as to place a substantial tax cost in the way of the step-up in the basis of the target assets. The *General Utilities* doctrine assured that the target corporation did not realize a taxable gain in respect of the increase in value of its assets resulting from the acquisition. Its 1986 repeal resulted in the assets of the target being deemed to be sold to the acquirer. As a result, capital gains tax resulted at both the corporate and shareholder level. According to Ginsburg and Levin, Mergers Acquisitions, and Leveraged Buyouts, ¶ 1203.01 (1991), the "GU Repeal makes it unlikely that it will be advantageous to structure acquisitions * * * to achieve a step-up in the basis of [the transferor's] assets." Third, the 1986 Act tightened restrictions, contained in section 382 of the Code, on the availability of target net operating loss carryovers to acquiring firms. See Ginsburg and Levin, supra, chapter 12; H.R. Conference Report No. 99–841, 99th Cong., 2d Sess. (1986). Amendments to the Internal Revenue Code enacted in 1989 and 1990 to restrict the deductibility of acquisition-related interest costs are discussed supra p. 496. For an exposition of "positive interactions" between these tax provisions and corporate law, see Levmore, The Positive Role of Tax Law in Corporate and Capital Markets, 12 J.Corp.L. 483 (1987).

SECTION C.   FORMAL ASPECTS OF MERGER

1. THE MECHANICS OF THE PROCESS

SCHULMAN AND SCHENK, SHAREHOLDERS' VOTING AND APPRAISAL RIGHTS IN CORPORATE ACQUISITION TRANSACTIONS

38 Bus.Law. 1529–1536 (1983).

* * *

STATUTORY PATTERNS

Essentially, acquisitions fall into three general categories—merger, purchase of assets, and purchase of shares. There are variations on these three basic techniques and, at times, the transactions become quite complex. This section describes a variety of acquisition transactions and tracks the statutory treatment of shareholder rights in each. The purpose is to highlight those situations in which the structure of the acquisition—its form—plays a critical role in the availability of shareholder rights.

The effect of form on shareholder rights is illustrated by provisions in the Model Business Corporation Act (Model Act). (Although the American Bar Association's Committee on Corporate Laws has tentatively adopted a revised Model Act, none of the proposed changes in the relevant acquisition provisions affect the shareholder rights problems we consider.) [3] In a merger, a statutory procedure by which the merged corporation disappears and all of its assets and liabilities pass by operation of law to the surviving party, the general rule is simple. Shareholders of both merger constituents obtain voting and dissenters' rights.[4] However, if the survivor's shareholders' proportionate investment interest is not substantially diluted in the merger—i.e., the survivor does not issue in the merger more than twenty percent of its previously outstanding shares—these shareholders may be denied voting and dissenters' rights.* In these small-scale mergers, the drafters

---

3. In this article, we cite to the Model Act and to the comparable provisions in the tentatively adopted revision of the Act.

4. Model Business Corp. Act §§ 73(a), (b), 80(a)(1) (1982); id. §§ 11.03(a)–(f), 13.-02(a)(1) (Exposure Draft 1983). A pattern of generally affording voting and appraisal rights to the shareholders of merger constituents is found in nearly all of the corporate acts. However, a few jurisdictions generally deny appraisal rights to the shareholders of a merger survivor. See, e.g., * * *; Md.Corps. & Ass'ns Code Ann. § 3–202(c)(2) (Supp.[1992]); N.Y.Bus.Corp. Law § 910(a)(1)(A)(ii) ([Consol.Supp.1992]).

See also Connecticut and Georgia's unusual limitations on voting rights. Conn.Gen. Stat.Ann. § 33–366(b) (West Supp.[1987]); Ga.Code Ann. § 22–1003(a) (Supp.[1982]). * * *

* [Ed. Note] In this connection, it may be noted that stockholder approval is required by the New York Stock exchange as a "prerequisite" to listing securities to be issued in mergers or acquisitions if the newly issued common stock "could result in an increase in outstanding common shares of 18½% or more * * *" NYSE Listed Company Manual § 703.08(A) (rev. ed. 1985).

of the Model Act concluded that the acquiring corporation should be able to conduct the transaction without approval by its shareholders and certainly without giving them the right to opt out of the venture by exercising the right to dissent.[7]

At this point, one might infer that the policy of the Model Act is to afford rights to the shareholders of parties constituent to an acquisition, except when the shareholders do not face a significant alteration of investment. However, the logical pattern in the merger provisions frequently appears to yield to pure formalism. To simplify the discussion, we will separate the rights of an acquiror's shareholders from those of an acquired's shareholders, considering the former first.

Merger is not the only form of acquisition that may have a significant effect upon an acquiror's shareholders. For example, Corporation *A* may acquire the net assets of Corporation *T* in exchange for thirty percent of its previously outstanding shares. *A* may also acquire *T*, through a voluntary share exchange, by offering to purchase all the *T* shares from *T*'s shareholders in exchange for the same thirty percent of *A* shares. In both cases, the acquisition produces a significant dilution in the proportionate equity interest of the shareholders holding shares of *A* before the acquisition. Had *A* paid this same consideration as a merger survivor, the Model Act would provide rights for its shareholders. Yet in either of the purchase transactions described above, *A*'s shareholders apparently are denied rights. The Model Act is stonily silent regarding voting or appraisal rights for the shareholders of a corporation conducting an asset purchase or voluntary share exchange. Thus, as far as acquiror shareholders' rights are concerned, the statute appears to invite management to avoid rights by adopting a nonmerger form of acquisition.

Even if Corporation *A* prefers to conduct the acquisition as a merger and issues thirty percent of its shares as the merger consideration, *A*'s management may be able to circumscribe rights for its shareholders. This rights-limiting technique is the triangular or three-party merger. In this type of acquisition, a corporation intending to acquire another by merger does so not directly by merging the target into itself (a two-party merger), but indirectly through a subsidiary.

Until 1969 the Model Act may not have authorized the triangular merger as an acquisition technique. Prior to that time, like most corporate statutes, the Act apparently authorized as merger consideration only shares, securities, or obligations of the surviving party, thereby sanctioning only two-party mergers in which the survivor

---

7. Conard, Amendments of Model Business Corporation Act Affecting Dissenters' Rights (Sections 73, 74, 80 and 81), 33 Bus. Law. 2587, 2595 (1978).

A second exception to the grant of shareholder rights in mergers occurs in a short-form merger, that is, one between a parent and a 90% or more owned subsidiary. Model Business Corp. Act §§ 75, 80(a)(1), (c) (1982); id. §§ 11.04, 13.02(a)(1)(ii) (Exposure Draft 1983). Because the parent's shareholders are not significantly affected by the merger, they are denied both voting and dissenters' rights. The minority shareholders, if any, of the subsidiary have dissenters' rights, but are denied voting rights since they obviously could not block the merger.

supplied such consideration. In 1969, the Model Act adopted broadened merger consideration provisions. Beginning at about that time, similar changes in the merger consideration provisions were enacted in the great majority of jurisdictions. These amended provisions not only authorize the use of cash or other property as merger consideration, but also explicitly sanction the use of shares or securities of *any* corporation, thus permitting three-party mergers in which a subsidiary uses its parent's shares as the merger consideration. In these transactions, the subsidiary is funded with its parent's shares (P shares) and merges with the target in either a forward or reverse triangular merger. In a forward triangle the target merges into the subsidiary and the target shares are converted into the P shares held by the subsidiary. When the transaction is consummated, the subsidiary, which remains wholly owned by the parent, now possesses the assets and is responsible for the liabilities of the target. A reverse triangle is used when business or tax considerations demand that the target remain in existence. The transaction is more complex than the forward triangle. Basically, the subsidiary merges into the target and the plan of merger requires that the target's shareholders convert their shares into the P shares held by the subsidiary. The parent's share ownership in the subsidiary is converted into newly issued shares of the target. After completion of the transaction, the target is the nominal survivor to the merger with its assets and liabilities intact, but realistically it has been acquired by the parent, which holds all of the target's outstanding shares.

In either type of triangle, the parent has conducted an acquisition by merger, but has done so through a surrogate corporation without becoming a party to the merger. In form, the parent is a shareholder of a merger constituent—its subsidiary corporation. As such, the parent seems entitled to whatever shareholder rights are available in the merger, and its board will exercise such rights. Nothing in the Model Act specifically extends rights to the parent's shareholders.

The Model Act also does not provide rights for acquiror shareholders in the newest form of acquisition, the compulsory share exchange. This procedure, adopted in the Model Act in 1976, but not yet in widespread use, is intended as a simplified substitute for the reverse triangular merger. Under this form of acquisition, all shareholders (or shareholders of a particular class of shares) of the acquired company must transfer their shares to the acquiring corporation for the consideration set forth in the plan of exchange. Thus, assuming that the exchange involves all classes of target shares, the target remains alive as a wholly owned subsidiary of the acquiror—precisely the result obtained by a reverse triangular merger. Although the Act requires approval of the plan by the boards of both corporations and grants voting and dissenters' rights to the shareholders of the target, it provides no rights for the acquiror's shareholders. This omission caps off the pattern in the Act whereby the rights granted to shareholders of merger survivors apparently may be avoided by selecting any form of acquisition other than a two-party merger. There is nothing extraordinary in this aspect of the Model Act. Most of the corporate acts display this pattern of explicitly granting rights to shareholders of an acquiror only when they are shareholders of a merger survivor.

The Model Act is generally less form-oriented in its treatment of shareholders of an acquired corporation. If the target is a merger constituent, its shareholders obtain voting and dissenters' rights. When a corporation transfers all or substantially all of its assets outside the regular course of business, its shareholders are granted voting rights and, with some exceptions, dissenters' rights. If a corporation is acquired by the purchase of its shares in either a compulsory or voluntary share exchange, its shareholders still receive a fair measure of protection. In a compulsory share exchange, target shareholders receive both the right to vote and to dissent. In a voluntary share exchange the acquired corporation is not itself a party to the transaction. The acquiror offers to purchase the target's shares from its shareholders, each of whom decides whether he wishes to sell. There are no voting or dissenters' rights since no corporate action by the acquired corporation occurs and its shareholders are not compelled to exchange their shares. Shareholder protection rests on the individual right to sell or retain shares.

Although the above summary suggests that the Model Act's treatment of shareholders of an acquired corporation follows a sensible, nonformalistic pattern, at times the Act apparently places a premium on form in awarding rights to such shareholders. For example, the seller's shareholders do not obtain dissenters' rights when their corporation sells its assets for cash on terms requiring the distribution of the sale proceeds within one year. Thus, shareholders cashed out as part of an asset sale cannot dissent and obtain payment for shares, although shareholders of a target acquired in a merger or compulsory share exchange retain dissenters' rights even if cash is the acquisition consideration. A comparable pattern is found in many jurisdictions. Even more dramatically, in Delaware and a few other states, while shareholders of a corporation acquired in a merger generally can exercise appraisal rights, the statute never grants appraisal to the shareholders of an asset seller.

Before concluding this discussion of the rights of shareholders of an acquired corporation, we will note two cases where the Model Act, consistent with the vast majority of corporate statutes, seemingly denies any rights to those who in practical effect are shareholders of an acquired corporation. The first involves a venture structured in a parent-subsidiary configuration, with all or substantially all of the operating assets held by the subsidiary. If the subsidiary is acquired by merger or purchase of its assets, the transaction would not appear to generate rights for the parent's shareholders. As in the case of a triangular merger, the parent is not formally a party to the transaction but only the shareholder of a party. Thus, the parent's shareholders apparently receive no say in the acquisition despite the fact that all or substantially all of the venture's operating assets have been transferred.

The second case occurs when a smaller corporation acquires a larger and, in the process, effectively becomes the acquired corporation. To illustrate this upside-down acquisition, a corporation may purchase the assets of a larger venture and issue as payment a large block of stock constituting a majority of its outstanding shares. While the nominal acquiror effectively has been acquired, its formal role is that of an asset purchaser and under the literal language of the Model Act and other typical statutory formulations, the shareholders of the nominal acquiror are deprived of rights.

As written, the corporate statutes frequently seem to make form determinative in the award of shareholder rights. But did the drafters intend to base the award of significant rights on formalistic distinctions? *

PROBLEM

X Corporation has outstanding 5,000 shares of preferred stock and 100,000 shares of common stock. It has authorized, but unissued, another 100,000 shares of common stock. Y Corporation has outstanding 100,000 shares of common stock and, authorized but unissued, another 100,000 shares of common and 5,000 shares of blank check preferred stock. X and Y are roughly comparable in amounts of assets, returns and risks; and X's common stock sells at a slightly higher price than Y's common stock.

X and Y wish to combine on a basis that enables either company to exchange one share of its common stock for one share of the other's, and X's preferred stockholders to remain preferred stockholders.

The formal options for combining include:

I. Statutory merger Y (or X) into X (or Y) (triangular merger of X into Y' (Y subsidiary) or the reverse; or of Y into X' (X subsidiary) or the reverse).

II. X (or Y) acquires the other's shares by plan of exchange.

III. X (or Y) acquires Y's (or X's) assets by purchase for stock and assumes the others' debts. The other may or may not dissolve.

IV. X (or Y) acquires majority of Y (or X) shares (for cash) (for stock).

    A. Acquirer merges with acquired.

    B. Acquirer dissolves acquired.

    C. Acquirer sells acquired's assets to itself for its stock and assumes acquired's debt and dissolves acquired.

---

* [Ed. Note] The history of state merger legislation is discussed in (1) Balotti, The Elimination of the Minority Interests By Merger Pursuant to Section 251 of the General Corporation Law of Delaware, 1 Del.J.Corp.L. 63 (1976); Carney, Fundamental Corporate Changes, Minority Shareholders and Business Purposes, 1980 Am.Bar.Found.Research J. 69; Weiss, The Law of Take Out Mergers: A Historical Perspective, 56 N.Y.U.L.Rev. 624 (1981); Weiss, The Law of Take–Out Mergers: Weinberger v. UOP, Inc. Ushers in Phase Six, 4 Cardozo L.Rev. 245 (1983).

Questions for transaction implementing each option (consult Revised Model Business Corporation Act (Appendix F); New York Business Corporation Law; Del.Gen'l Corp.Law (Appendix G)):

1. What action, if any, must the Board of X or Y take?

2. Are the stockholders of X or Y required to take some action for the transactions to be consummated?

3. Which stockholders?

   — Who votes?

   — Who can or cannot be deprived (by charter or otherwise) of power to vote, or to vote as a class?

   — What percent of what base vote is required?

4. Which stockholders, if any, of which corporation have appraisal rights?

5. Which stockholders inherit liabilities? Which liabilities?

6. Which stockholders have liquidation rights?

7. Apart from impact on stockholders, what business or other considerations might make one form of amalgamation preferable to another?

FARRIS v. GLEN ALDEN CORP.

Supreme Court of Pennsylvania, 1958.
393 Pa. 427, 143 A.2d 25.

COHEN, Justice. We are required to determine on this appeal whether, as a result of a "Reorganization Agreement" executed by the officers of Glen Alden Corporation and List Industries Corporation, and approved by the shareholders of the former company, the rights and remedies of a dissenting shareholder accrue to the plaintiff.

Glen Alden is a Pennsylvania corporation engaged principally in the mining of anthracite coal and lately in the manufacture of air conditioning units and fire-fighting equipment. In recent years the company's operating revenue has declined substantially, and in fact, its coal operations have resulted in tax loss carryovers of approximately $14,000,000. In October 1957, List, a Delaware holding company owning interests in motion picture theaters, textile companies and real estate, and to a lesser extent, in oil and gas operations, warehouses and aluminum piston manufacturing, purchased through a wholly owned subsidiary 38.5% of Glen Alden's outstanding stock.[1] This acquisition enabled List to place three of its directors on the Glen Alden board.

On March 20, 1958, the two corporations entered into a "reorganization agreement," subject to stockholder approval, which contemplated the following actions:

1. Glen Alden is to acquire all of the assets of List, excepting a small amount of cash reserved for the payment of List's expenses in

---

1. Of the purchase price of $8,719,109, $5,000,000 was borrowed.

connection with the transaction. These assets include over $8,000,000 in cash held chiefly in the treasuries of List's wholly owned subsidiaries.

2.   In consideration of the transfer, Glen Alden is to issue 3,621,-703 shares of stock to List. List in turn is to distribute the stock to its shareholders at a ratio of five shares of Glen Alden stock for each six shares of List stock. In order to accomplish the necessary distribution, Glen Alden is to increase the authorized number of its shares of capital stock from 2,500,000 shares to 7,500,000 shares without according preemptive rights to the present shareholders upon the issuance of any such shares.

3.   Further, Glen Alden is to assume all of List's liabilities including a $5,000,000 note incurred by List in order to purchase Glen Alden stock in 1957, outstanding stock options, incentive stock options plans, and pension obligations.

4.   Glen Alden is to change its corporate name from Glen Alden Corporation to List Alden Corporation.

5.   The present directors of both corporations are to become directors of List Alden.

6.   List is to be dissolved and List Alden is to then carry on the operations of both former corporations.

Two days after the agreement was executed notice of the annual meeting of Glen Alden to be held on April 11, 1958, was mailed to the shareholders together with a proxy statement analyzing the reorganization agreement and recommending its approval as well as approval of certain amendments to Glen Alden's articles of incorporation and bylaws necessary to implement the agreement. At this meeting the holders of a majority of the outstanding shares, (not including those owned by List), voted in favor of a resolution approving the reorganization agreement.

On the day of the shareholders' meeting, plaintiff, a shareholder of Glen Alden, filed a complaint in equity against the corporation and its officers seeking to enjoin them temporarily until final hearing, and perpetually thereafter, from executing and carrying out the agreement.[2]

The gravamen of the complaint was that the notice of the annual shareholders' meeting did not conform to the requirements of the Business Corporation Law, 15 P.S. § 2852–1 et seq., in three respects: (1) It did not give notice to the shareholders that the true intent and purpose of the meeting was to effect a merger or consolidation of Glen Alden and List; (2) It failed to give notice to the shareholders of their right to dissent to the plan of merger or consolidation and claim fair

2.   The plaintiff also sought to enjoin the shareholders of Glen Alden from approving the reorganization agreement and from adopting amendments to Glen Alden's articles of incorporation, certificate of incorporation and bylaws in implementation of the agreement. However, apparently because of the shortness of time, this prayer was refused by the court.

value for their shares, and (3) It did not contain copies of the text of certain sections of the Business Corporation Law as required.[3]

By reason of these omissions, plaintiff contended that the approval of the reorganization agreement by the shareholders at the annual meeting was invalid and unless the carrying out of the plan were enjoined, he would suffer irreparable loss by being deprived of substantial property rights.[4]

The defendants answered admitting the material allegations of fact in the complaint but denying that they gave rise to a cause of action because the transaction complained of was a purchase of corporate assets as to which shareholders had no rights of dissent or appraisal. For these reasons the defendants then moved for judgment on the pleadings.[5]

The court below concluded that the reorganization agreement entered into between the two corporations was a plan for a *de facto* merger, and that therefore the failure of the notice of the annual meeting to conform to the pertinent requirements of the merger provisions of the Business Corporation Law rendered the notice defective and all proceedings in furtherance of the agreement void. Wherefore, the court entered a final decree denying defendants' motion for judgment on the pleadings, entering judgment upon plaintiff's complaint and granting the injunctive relief therein sought. This appeal followed.

When use of the corporate form of business organization first became widespread, it was relatively easy for courts to define a "merger" or a "sale of assets" and to label a particular transaction as one or the other. See, e.g., 15 Fletcher, Corporations §§ 7040–7045 (rev. vol. 1938); In re Buist's Estate, 1929, 297 Pa. 537, 541, 147 A. 606; Koehler v. St. Mary's Brewing Co., 1910, 228 Pa. 648, 653–654, 77 A. 1016. But prompted by the desire to avoid the impact of adverse, and to obtain the benefits of favorable, government regulations, particularly federal tax laws, new accounting and legal techniques were developed by lawyers and accountants which interwove the elements characteristic of each, thereby creating hybrid forms of corporate amalgamation. Thus, it is no longer helpful to consider an individual transaction in the abstract and solely by reference to the various elements therein determine

---

3. The proxy statement included the following declaration: "Appraisal Rights.

"In the opinion of counsel, the shareholders of neither Glen Alden nor List Industries will have any rights of appraisal or similar rights of dissenters with respect to any matter to be acted upon at their respective meetings."

4. The complaint also set forth that the exchange of shares of Glen Alden's stock for those of List would constitute a violation of the pre-emptive rights of Glen Alden shareholders as established by the law of Pennsylvania at the time of Glen Alden's incorporation in 1917. The defendants answered that under both statute and prior common law no pre-emptive rights existed with respect to stock issued in exchange for property.

5. Counsel for the defendants concedes that if the corporation is required to pay the dissenting shareholders the appraised fair value of their shares, the resultant drain of cash would prevent Glen Alden from carrying out the agreement. On the other hand, plaintiff contends that if the shareholders had been told of their rights as dissenters, rather than specifically advised that they had no such rights, the resolution approving the reorganization agreement would have been defeated.

whether it is a "merger" or a "sale". Instead, to determine properly the nature of a corporate transaction, we must refer not only to all the provisions of the agreement, but also to the consequences of the transaction and to the purposes of the provisions of the corporation law said to be applicable. We shall apply this principle to the instant case.

Section 908, subd. A of the Pennsylvania Business Corporation Law provides: "If any shareholder of a domestic corporation which becomes a party to a plan of merger or consolidation shall object to such plan of merger or consolidation * * * such shareholder shall be entitled to * * *, [the fair value of his shares upon surrender of the share certificate or certificates representing his shares]." Act of May 5, 1933, P.L. 364, as amended, 15 P.S. § 2852–908, subd. A.[6]

This provision had its origin in the early decision of this Court in Lauman v. Lebanon Valley R.R. Co., 1858, 30 Pa. 42. There a shareholder who objected to the consolidation of his company with another was held to have a right in the absence of statute to treat the consolidation as a dissolution of his company and to receive the value of his shares upon their surrender.

The rationale of the Lauman case, and of the present section of the Business Corporation Law based thereon, is that when a corporation combines with another so as to lose its essential nature and alter the original fundamental relationships of the shareholders among themselves and to the corporation, a shareholder who does not wish to continue his membership therein may treat his membership in the original corporation as terminated and have the value of his shares paid to him. See Lauman v. Lebanon Valley R.R. Co., supra, 30 Pa. at pages 46–47. See also Bloch v. Baldwin Locomotive Works, C.P.Del. 1950, 75 Pa.Dist. & Co.R. 24, 36–38.

Does the combination outlined in the present "reorganization" agreement so fundamentally change the corporate character of Glen Alden and the interest of the plaintiff as a shareholder therein, that to refuse him the rights and remedies of a dissenting shareholder would in reality force him to give up his stock in one corporation and against his will accept shares in another? If so, the combination is a merger within the meaning of section 908, subd. A of the corporation law. See Bloch v. Baldwin Locomotive Works, supra. Cf. Marks v. Autocar Co., D.C.E.D.Pa.1954, 153 F.Supp. 768. See also Troupiansky v. Henry Disston & Sons, D.C.E.D.Pa.1957, 151 F.Supp. 609.

If the reorganization agreement were consummated plaintiff would find that the "List Alden" resulting from the amalgamation would be quite a different corporation than the "Glen Alden" in which he is now a shareholder. Instead of continuing primarily as a coal mining

---

6. Furthermore, section 902, subd. B provides that notice of the proposed merger and of the right to dissent thereto must be given the shareholders. "There shall be included in, or enclosed with * * * notice [of meeting of shareholders to vote on plan of merger] a copy or a summary of the plan of merger or plan of consolidation, as the case may be, and * * * a copy of subsection A of section 908 and of subsections B, C and D of section 515 of this act." Act of May 5, 1933, P.L. 364, § 902, subd. B, as amended, 15 P.S. § 2852–902, subd. B.

company, Glen Alden would be transformed, after amendment of its articles of incorporation, into a diversified holding company whose interests would range from motion picture theaters to textile companies, Plaintiff would find himself a member of a company with assets of $169,000,000 and a long-term debt of $38,000,000 in lieu of a company one-half that size and with but one-seventh the long-term debt.

While the administration of the operations and properties of Glen Alden as well as List would be in the hands of management common to both companies, since all executives of List would be retained in List Alden, the control of Glen Alden would pass to the directors of List; for List would hold eleven of the seventeen directorships on the new board of directors.

As an aftermath of the transaction plaintiff's proportionate interest in Glen Alden would have been reduced to only two-fifths of what it presently is because of the issuance of an additional 3,621,703 shares to List which would not be subject to pre-emptive rights. In fact, ownership of Glen Alden would pass to the stockholders of List who would hold 76.5% of the outstanding shares as compared with but 23.5% retained by the present Glen Alden shareholders.

Perhaps the most important consequence to the plaintiff, if he were denied the right to have his shares redeemed at their fair value, would be the serious financial loss suffered upon consummation of the agreement. While the present book value of his stock is $38 a share, after combination it would be worth only $21 a share. In contrast, the shareholders of List who presently hold stock with a total book value of $33,000,000 or $7.50 a share, would receive stock with a book value of $76,000,000 or $21 a share.

Under these circumstances it may well be said that if the proposed combination is allowed to take place without right of dissent, plaintiff would have his stock in Glen Alden taken away from him and the stock of a new company thrust upon him in its place. He would be projected against his will into a new enterprise under terms not of his own choosing. It was to protect dissident shareholders against just such a result that this Court one hundred years ago in the Lauman case, and the legislature thereafter in section 908, subd. A, granted the right of dissent. And it is to accord that protection to the plaintiff that we conclude that the combination proposed in the case at hand is a merger within the intendment of section 908, subd. A.

Nevertheless, defendants contend that the 1957 amendments to sections 311 and 908 of the corporation law preclude us from reaching this result and require the entry of judgment in their favor. Subsection F of section 311 dealing with the voluntary transfer of corporate assets provides: "The shareholders of a business corporation which acquires by sale, lease or exchange all or substantially all of the property of another corporation by the issuance of stock, securities or otherwise shall not be entitled to the rights and remedies of dissenting shareholders * * *." Act of July 11, 1957, P.L. 711, § 1, 15 P.S. § 2852–311, subd. F.

And the amendment to section 908 reads as follows: "The right of dissenting shareholders * * * shall not apply to the purchase by a corporation of assets whether or not the consideration therefor be money or property, real or personal, including shares or bonds or other evidences of indebtedness of such corporation. The shareholders of such corporation shall have no right to dissent from any such purchase." Act of July 11, 1957, P.L. 711, § 1, 15 P.S. § 2852–908, subd. C.

Defendants view these amendments as abridging the right of shareholders to dissent to a transaction between two corporations which involves a transfer of assets for a consideration even though the transfer has all the legal incidents of a merger. They claim that only if the merger is accomplished in accordance with the prescribed statutory procedure does the right of dissent accrue. In support of this position they cite to us the comment on the amendments by the Committee on Corporation Law of the Pennsylvania Bar Association, the committee which originally drafted these provisions. The comment states that the provisions were intended to overrule cases which granted shareholders the right to dissent to a sale of assets when accompanied by the legal incidents of a merger. See 61 Ann.Rep.Pa.Bar Ass'n 277, 284 (1957).[7] Whatever may have been the intent of the *committee,* there is no evidence to indicate that the *legislature* intended the 1957 amendments to have the effect contended for. But furthermore, the language of these two provisions does not support the opinion of the committee and is inapt to achieve any such purpose. The amendments of 1957 do not provide that a transaction between two corporations which has the effect of a merger but which includes a transfer of assets for consideration is to be exempt from the protective provisions of sections 908, subd. A and 515. They provide only that the shareholders of a corporation which acquires the property or purchases the assets of another corporation, *without more,* are not entitled to the right to dissent from the transaction. So, as in the present case, when as part of a transaction between two corporations, one corporation dissolves, its liabilities are assumed by the survivor, its executives and directors take over the management and control of the survivor, and, as consideration for the transfer, its stockholders acquire a majority of the shares of stock of the survivor, then the transaction is no longer simply a

---

7. "The amendment to Section 311 expressly provides that a sale, lease or exchange of substantially all corporate assets in connection with its liquidation or dissolution is subject to the provisions of Article XI of the Act, and that no consent or authorization of shareholders other than what is required by Article XI is necessary. The recent decision in Marks v. Autocar Co., D.C.E.D.Pa., Civil Action No. 16075 [153 F.Supp. 768] is to the contrary. This amendment, together with the proposed amendment to Section 1104 expressly permitting the directors in liquidating the corporation to sell only such assets as may be required to pay its debts and distribute any assets remaining among shareholders (Sec-

tion 1108, [subd.] B now so provides in the case of receivers) have the effect of overruling Marks v. Autocar Co., * * * which permits a shareholder dissenting from such a sale to obtain the fair value of his shares. The Marks case relies substantially on Bloch v. Baldwin Locomotive Works, 75 [Pa.] Dist. & Co.R. 24, also believed to be an undesirable decision. That case permitted a holder of stock in a corporation which *purchased* for stock all the assets of another corporation to obtain the fair value of his shares. That case is also in effect overruled by the new Sections 311 [subd.] F and 908 [subd.] C." 61 Ann.Rep.Pa.Bar Ass'n, 277, 284 (1957).

purchase of assets or acquisition of property to which sections 311, subd. F and 908, subd. C apply, but a merger governed by section 908, subd. A of the corporation law. To divest shareholders of their right of dissent under such circumstances would require express language which is absent from the 1957 amendments.

Even were we to assume that the combination provided for in the reorganization agreement is a "sale of assets" to which section 908, subd. A does not apply, it would avail the defendants nothing; we will not blind our eyes to the realities of the transaction. Despite the designation of the parties and the form employed, Glen Alden does not in fact acquire List, rather, List acquires Glen Alden, cf. Metropolitan Edison Co. v. Commissioner, 3 Cir., 1938, 98 F.2d 807, affirmed sub nom., Helvering v. Metropolitan Edison Co., 1939, 306 U.S. 522, 59 S.Ct. 634, 83 L.Ed. 957, and under section 311, subd. D [8] the right of dissent would remain with the shareholders of Glen Alden.

We hold that the combination contemplated by the reorganization agreement, although consummated by contract rather than in accordance with the statutory procedure, is a merger within the protective purview of sections 908, subd. A and 515 of the corporation law. The shareholders of Glen Alden should have been notified accordingly and advised of their statutory rights of dissent and appraisal. The failure of the corporate officers to take these steps renders the stockholder approval of the agreement at the 1958 shareholders' meeting invalid. The lower court did not err in enjoining the officers and directors of Glen Alden from carrying out this agreement.*

Decree affirmed at appellants' cost.

NOTE

In **Terry v. Penn Central Corporation,** 668 F.2d 188, 192–194 (3d Cir.1981), the court was concerned with whether a triangular merger involving PCC Holdings, Inc., a wholly owned subsidiary of Penn Central Corporation, and Colt Industries, Inc., in which Colt was to be merged into PCC in exchange for Penn Central stock, constituted a "merger" to which Penn Central was a party so as to trigger the voting and dissenters' appraisal rights of Penn Central stockholders. The

8. "If any shareholder of a business corporation which sells, leases or exchanges all or substantially all of its property and assets otherwise than (1) in the usual and regular course of its business, (2) for the purpose of relocating its business, or (3) in connection with its dissolution and liquidation, shall object to such sale, lease or exchange and comply with the provisions of section 515 of this act, such shareholder shall be entitled to the rights and remedies of dissenting shareholders as therein provided." Act of July 11, 1975, P.L. 711, 15 P.S. § 2852–311, subd. D.

* [Ed. Note] According to Moody's Industrial Manual (1960), on April 21, 1959 Glen Alden merged List by exchange of one Glen Alden share for one List share and by issuance of an additional Glen Alden share to holders of each 4 Glen Alden shares; at the end of 1958, Glen Alden had outstanding approximately 1,750,000 shares and List approximately 4,210,000 shares.

court concluded that Penn Central was not a party to the merger between its subsidiary and Colt, and it rejected the de facto merger doctrine as a mechanism for construing the transaction and the statute so as to make Penn Central a party to the merger. The court relied upon the emphatic action of the Pennsylvania legislature immediately after the Glen Alden case in explicitly repealing the de facto merger doctrine in Pennsylvania. But its opinion alluded to circumstances in which that doctrine (which had been held applicable to a triangular merger in Penn Central Securities Litigation, 367 F.Supp. 1158 (E.D.Pa. 1973)) might not be ignored by a court. For similar rejection of the de facto merger doctrine with respect to voting power of the parent's stockholders in triangular mergers, see Equity Group Holdings v. D.M.G., Inc., 576 F.Supp. 1197 (S.D.Fla.1983).

HARITON v. ARCO ELECTRONICS, INC.

Court of Chancery of Delaware, 1962.
40 Del.Ch. 326, 182 A.2d 22.
Aff'd, 41 Del.Ch. 74, 188 A.2d 123 (1963).

SHORT, Vice Chancellor. Plaintiff is a stockholder of defendant Arco Electronics, Inc., a Delaware corporation. The complaint challenges the validity of the purchase by Loral Electronics Corporation, a New York corporation, of all the assets of Arco. Two causes of action are asserted, namely (1) that the transaction is unfair to Arco stockholders, and (2) that the transaction constituted a de facto merger and is unlawful since the merger provisions of the Delaware law were not complied with.

Defendant has moved to dismiss the complaint and for summary judgment on the ground that the transaction was fair to Arco stockholders and was, in fact, one of purchase and sale and not a merger.

Plaintiff now concedes that he is unable to sustain the charge of unfairness. The only issue before the court, therefore, is whether the transaction was by its nature a de facto merger with a consequent right of appraisal in plaintiff.

Prior to the transaction of which plaintiff complains Arco was principally engaged in the business of the wholesale distribution of components or parts for electronics and electrical equipment. It had outstanding 486,500 shares of Class A common stock and 362,500 shares of Class B common stock. The rights of the holders of the Class A and Class B common stock differed only as to preferences in dividends. Arco's balance sheet as of September 30, 1961 shows total assets of $3,013,642. Its net income for the preceding year was $273,466.

Loral was engaged, primarily, in the research, development and production of electronic equipment. Its balance sheet shows total assets of $16,453,479. Its net income for the year ending March 31, 1961 was $1,301,618.

In the summer of 1961 Arco commenced negotiations with Loral with a view to the purchase by Loral of all of the assets of Arco in exchange for shares of Loral common stock. I think it fair to say that the record establishes that the negotiations which ultimately led to the transaction involved were conducted by the representatives of the two corporations at arms length. There is no suggestion that any representative of Arco had any interest whatever in Loral, or vice versa. In any event, Arco rejected two offers made by Loral of a purchase price based upon certain ratios of Loral shares for Arco shares. Finally, on October 11, 1961, Loral offered a purchase price based on the ratio of one share of Loral common stock for three shares of Arco common stock. This offer was accepted by the representatives of Arco on October 24, 1961 and an agreement for the purchase was entered into between Loral and Arco on October 27, 1961. This agreement provides, among other things, as follows:

1. Arco will convey and transfer to Loral all of its assets and property of every kind, tangible and intangible; and will grant to Loral the use of its name and slogans.

2. Loral will assume and pay all of Arco's debts and liabilities.

3. Loral will issue to Arco 283,000 shares of its common stock.

4. Upon the closing of the transaction Arco will dissolve and distribute to its shareholders, pro rata, the shares of the common stock of Loral.

5. Arco will call a meeting of its stockholders to be held December 21, 1961 to authorize and approve the conveyance and delivery of all the assets of Arco to Loral.

6. After the closing date Arco will not engage in any business or activity except as may be required to complete the liquidation and dissolution of Arco.

Pursuant to its undertaking in the agreement for purchase and sale Arco caused a special meeting of its stockholders to be called for December 27, 1961. The notice of such meeting set forth three specific purposes therefor: (1) to vote upon a proposal to ratify the agreement of purchase and sale, a copy of which was attached to the notice; (2) to vote upon a proposal to change the name of the corporation; and (3) if Proposals (1) and (2) should be adopted, to vote upon a proposal to liquidate and dissolve the corporation and to distribute the Loral shares to Arco shareholders. Proxies for this special meeting were not solicited. At the meeting 652,050 shares were voted in favor of the sale and none against. The proposals to change the name of the corporation and to dissolve it and distribute the Loral stock were also approved. The transaction was thereafter consummated.

Plaintiff contends that the transaction, though in form a sale of assets of Arco, is in substance and effect a merger, and that it is unlawful because the merger statute has not been complied with, thereby depriving plaintiff of his right of appraisal.

Defendant contends that since all the formalities of a sale of assets pursuant to 8 Del.C. § 271 * have been complied with the transaction is in fact a sale of assets and not a merger. In this connection it is to be noted that plaintiffs nowhere allege or claim that defendant has not complied to the letter with the provisions of said section.

The question here presented is one which has not been heretofore passed upon by any court in this state. In Heilbrunn v. Sun Chemical Corporation, Del., 150 A.2d 755, the Supreme Court was called upon to determine whether or not a stockholder of the *purchasing* corporation could, in circumstances like those here presented, obtain relief on the theory of a de facto merger. The court held that relief was not available to such a stockholder. It expressly observed that the question here presented was not before the court for determination. It pointed out also that while Delaware does not grant appraisal rights to a stockholder dissenting from a sale, citing Argenbright v. Phoenix Finance Co., 21 Del.Ch. 288, 187 A. 124, and Finch v. Warrior Cement Corp., 16 Del.Ch. 44, 141 A. 54, those cases are distinguishable from the facts here presented, "because dissolution of the seller and distribution of the stock of the purchaser were not required as a part of the sale in either case." In speaking of the form of the transaction the Supreme Court observes:

"The argument that the result of this transaction is substantially the same as the result that would have followed a merger may be readily accepted. As plaintiffs correctly say, the Ansbacher enterprise [seller] is continued in altered form as a part of Sun [purchaser]. This is ordinarily a typical characteristic of a merger. Sterling v. Mayflower Hotel Corp., 33 Del. 293, 303, 93 A.2d 107, 38 A.L.R.2d 425. Moreover the plan of reorganization *requires* the dissolution of Ansbacher and the distribution to its stockholders of the Sun stock received by it for the assets. As a part of the plan, the Ansbacher stockholders are compelled to receive Sun stock. From the viewpoint of Ansbacher, the result is the same as if Ansbacher had formally merged into Sun.

"This result is made possible, of course, by the overlapping scope of the merger statute and the statute authorizing the sale of all the corporate assets. This possibility of overlapping was noticed in our opinion in the Mayflower case.

"There is nothing new about such a result. For many years drafters of plans of corporate reorganization have increasingly resorted to the use of the sale-of-assets method in preference to the method by merger. Historically at least, there were reasons for this quite apart from the avoidance of the appraisal right given to stockholders dissenting from a merger."

Though it is said in the Heilbrunn case that the doctrine of de facto merger has been recognized in Delaware, it is to be noted that in each of the cases cited as recognizing the doctrine, namely, Drug, Inc. v. Hunt, 35 Del. 339, 168 A. 87 and Finch v. Warrior Cement Corp., supra,

* [Ed. note] See text of Delaware statute,   Appendix G.

there was a failure to comply with the statute governing sale of assets. In both cases the sales agreement required delivery of the shares of the purchasing corporation to be made directly to the shareholders of the selling corporation. It was, of course, held in each case that no consideration passed to the selling corporation and that therefore the transaction did not constitute a sale of the assets of the selling corporation to the purchasing corporation. No such failure to comply with the provisions of the sale of assets statute is present in this case. On the contrary, as heretofore observed there was a literal compliance with the terms of the statute by this defendant.

The doctrine of de facto merger in comparable circumstances has been recognized and applied by the Pennsylvania courts, both state and federal. Lauman v. Lebanon Valley Railroad Co., 30 Pa. 42; Marks v. Autocar Co., D.C., 153 F.Supp. 768; Farris v. Glen Alden Corporation, 393 Pa. 427, 143 A.2d 25. The two cases last cited are founded upon the holding in the case first cited which was decided on common law principles. The basis for the holding in the Lauman case is not at all clear. The transaction involved was a merger of two railroads and the special Pennsylvania statute authorizing the merger made no provision for a dissenting shareholder to be allowed the fair value of his shares. The theory of the court's holding was to the effect that a shareholder could not be compelled to exchange his shares for stock in a new corporation since to do so would be to deprive him of his property without due process of law. The later Pennsylvania cases adopt the de facto merger approach and stress the requirement of dissolution and distribution of the purchaser's stock among the seller's shareholders. The Farris case demonstrates the length to which the Pennsylvania courts have gone in applying this principle. It was there applied in favor of a stockholder of the purchasing corporation, an application which our Supreme Court expressly rejected in Heilbrunn.

The right of appraisal accorded to a dissenting stockholder by the merger statutes is in compensation for the right which he had at common law to prevent a merger. Chicago Corporation v. Munds, 20 Del.Ch. 142, 172 A. 452. At common law a single dissenting stockholder could also prevent a sale of all of the assets of a corporation. 18 C.J.S. Corporations § 515, p. 1194. The Legislatures of many states have seen fit to grant the appraisal right to a dissenting stockholder not only under the merger statutes but as well under the sale of assets statutes. Our Legislature has seen fit to expressly grant the appraisal right only under the merger statutes. This difference in treatment of the rights of dissenting stockholders may well have been deliberate, in order "to allow even greater freedom of action to corporate majorities in arranging combinations than is possible under the merger statutes." 72 Harv.L.Rev. 1132, "The Right of Shareholders Dissenting From Corporate Combinations To Demand Cash Payment For Their Shares."

While plaintiff's contention that the doctrine of de facto merger should be applied in the present circumstances is not without appeal, the subject is one which, in my opinion, is within the legislative domain. Moreover it is difficult to differentiate between a case such as the present and one where the reorganization plan contemplates the ultimate dissolution of the selling corporation but does not formally require such procedure in express terms. The Supreme Court of Iowa in Graeser v. Phoenix Finance Co., 218 Iowa 1112, 254 N.W. 859, wherein the court considered the identical state of facts which were presented to this court in Argenbright v. Phoenix Finance Co., supra, had this to say: "We think the evidence fairly shows that, while the plan pursued contemplated the ultimate dissolution of the old Phoenix Corporations, this was not inconsistent with the sale of their corporate assets to the Phoenix Finance Corporation, in accordance with the provisions of the Delaware statute. * * * Under the agreements thus made, the cash, stock, and securities of Phoenix Finance Corporation, which were given in exchange for the assets of the St. Louis and Des Moines companies, became the property of these respective companies, and these corporations did not cease to exist, as would be the necessary result of a consolidation, but still continued in existence as corporate entities." By the same token, Arco continued in existence as a corporate entity following the exchange of securities for its assets. The fact that it continued corporate existence only for the purpose of winding up its affairs by the distribution of Loral stock is, in my mind, of little consequence. The argument underlying the applicability of the doctrine of de facto merger, namely, that the stockholder is forced against his will to accept a new investment in an enterprise foreign to that of which he was a part has little pertinency. The right of the corporation to sell all of its assets for stock in another corporation was expressly accorded to Arco by § 271 of Title 8, Del.C. The stockholder was, in contemplation of law, aware of this right when he acquired his stock. He was also aware of the fact that the situation might develop whereby he would be ultimately forced to accept a new investment, as would have been the case here had the resolution authorizing dissolution followed consummation of the sale. Argenbright v. Phoenix Finance Co., supra; Finch v. Warrior Cement Corp., supra. Inclusion of the condition in the sale agreement does not in any way add to his position to complain.

There is authority in decisions of courts of this state for the proposition that the various sections of the Delaware Corporation Law conferring authority for corporate action are independent of each other and that a given result may be accomplished by proceeding under one section which is not possible, or is even forbidden under another. For example, dividends which have accrued to preferred stockholders may not be eliminated by an amendment to the corporate charter under § 242, Title 8. Keller v. Wilson & Co., 21 Del.Ch. 391, 190 A. 115. On the other hand, such accrued dividends may be eliminated by a merger between the corporation and a wholly owned subsidiary. Federal United Corporation v. Havender, 24 Del.Ch. 318, 11 A.2d 331; Hottenstein v. York Ice Machinery Corp., D.C.Del., 45 F.Supp. 436, Id., 3 Cir., 136 F.2d 944. In Langfelder v. Universal Laboratories, D.C., 68 F.Supp. 209, Judge Leahy commented upon these holdings as follows:

" * * * Havender v. Federal United Corporation, Del.Sup., 11 A.2d 331 and Hottenstein v. York Ice Machinery Corp., D.C.Del., 45 F.Supp. 436; Id., 3 Cir., 136 F.2d 944 hold that in Delaware a parent may merge with a wholly owned subsidiary and thereby cancel old preferred stock and the rights of the holders thereof to the unpaid, accumulated dividends, by substituting in lieu thereof stocks of the surviving corporation. Under Delaware law, accrued dividends after the passage of time mature into a debt and can not be eliminated by an amendment to the corporate charter under Sec. 26 of the Delaware Corporation Law, Rev.Code 1935, § 2058. But the right to be paid in full for such dividends, notwithstanding provisions in the charter contract, may be eliminated by means of a merger which meets the standard of fairness. The rationale is that a merger is an act of independent legal significance, and when it meets the requirements of fairness and all other statutory requirements, the merger is valid and not subordinate or dependent upon any other section of the Delaware Corporation Law."

In a footnote to Judge Leahy's opinion the following comment appears:

"The text is but a particularization of the general theory of the Delaware Corporation Law that action taken pursuant to the authority of the various sections of that law constitute acts of independent legal significance and their validity is not dependent on other sections of the Act. Havender v. Federal United Corporation proves the correctness of this interpretation. Under Keller v. Wilson & Co. accrued dividends are regarded as matured rights and must be paid. But, this does not prevent a merger, good under the provisions of Sec. 59, from having the incidental effect of wiping out such dividend rights, i.e., Sec. 59 is complete in itself and is not dependent upon any other section, absent fraud. The same thing is true with most other sections of the Corporation Law."

The situation posed by the present case is even stronger than that presented in the Havender and York Ice cases. In those cases the court permitted the circumvention of matured rights by proceeding under the merger statute. Here, the stockholder has no rights unless another and independent statute is invoked to create a right. A holding in the stockholder's favor would be directly contrary to the theory of the cited cases.

I conclude that the transaction complained of was not a de facto merger, either in the sense that there was a failure to comply with one or more of the requirements of § 271 of the Delaware Corporation Law, or that the result accomplished was in effect a merger entitling plaintiff to a right of appraisal.

Defendant's motion for summary judgment is granted. Order on notice.

NOTE: OTHER CONSEQUENCES OF DE FACTO MERGER

In **Rath v. Rath Packing Co.,** 257 Iowa 1277, 136 N.W.2d 410
(1965) challenge was made to a "Plan and Agreement of Reorganization" entered into between Rath Packing Co. (an Iowa corporation) and
Needham Packing Co. (a Delaware corporation) under which Rath was
to issue newly created common and preferred stock to Needham,
assume all of Needham's debts and liabilities, elect two Needham
officers to its Board, and change its name to Rath–Needham Corporation. Needham was to transfer all of its assets to Rath, distribute the
new Rath–Needham shares to its stockholders in liquidation and then
dissolve. Notwithstanding the fact that Rath was a much larger
corporation than Needham, the plan contemplated that Rath would
issue 5.5 shares of its common and two shares of its convertible
preferred in exchange for each 5 shares of Needham common. If the
new preferred were converted, the old Needham stockholders would
own a majority of the outstanding shares of Rath–Needham.

On a book basis the value of Rath common as of January 2, 1965
was reduced by the amalgamation from $27.99 to $15.93 per share.
Each share of Needham's common was increased in book value from
$6.61 to $23.90 (if all the preferred were converted). If the preferred
were not converted, Needham shareholders would enjoy a priority in
liquidation slightly in excess of the book value of all Needham shares
and a prior claim of approximately 80 cents a share on dividends over
Rath stockholders. Shortly prior to the time the terms of the Plan
were made public, Rath and Needham shares sold on the American
Stock Exchange for about the same price, but almost immediately
thereafter the price of Needham shares increased and Rath's decreased,
so that the former sold for 50% more than the latter. Needham's and
Rath's earnings per share records compared as follows:

	Rath	Needham
1961	(1.91)	.18
1962	(.83)	.80
1963	.81	.39
1964	.41	.61
1965	(3.12)	2.15

A vote of Rath stockholders was necessary in order to increase the
number of authorized shares, to change the corporation's name and to
elect the Needham directors. Approximately 60% of the outstanding
Rath shares voted in favor of the transaction. Minority shareholders of
Rath sought to enjoin the transaction on the ground that it constituted
a merger, and that it had not been approved by the holders of two-
thirds of the outstanding shares of Rath, as required by the Iowa Code.
The Code authorized amendments of the charter, such as were called
for by the Plan, by a majority vote.

The trial court accepted the Hariton approach, and interpreted the
Iowa Code to give corporate management the option to choose between
the consequences of amalgamating the two enterprises by the process

taken and amalgamating them by a formal statutory merger. Hence it dismissed the complaint. The Iowa Supreme Court reversed and directed the issuance of an injunction against effectuation of the Plan, on the ground that the effect of the Plan was identical with that of a merger, and that the statutory voting requirements for merger had not been met. The Court rejected the Hariton approach, denied that the Code gave management a choice of methods in effecting a combination which produces the same continuing single enterprise as would a merger, and ruled that the merger provisions of the Code imposed constraints on the amendment provisions. The Court said (136 N.W.2d at 416–417):

"It is apparent that if the sections pertaining to amending articles and issuing stock are construed to authorize a merger by a majority vote of shareholders they conflict with the sections specifically dealing with the one matter of mergers which require a two-thirds vote of shareholders. The two sets of sections may be harmonized by holding, as we do, that the merger sections govern the matter of merger and must be regarded as an exception to the sections dealing with amending articles and issuing stock, which may or may not be involved in a merger.

"The construction we give these sections is in accord with the cardinal rule that, if reasonably possible, effect will be given to every part of a statute. * * *

"The merger sections make it clear the legislature intended to require a two-thirds vote of shareholders and accord so-called appraisal rights to dissenters in case of a merger. It is unreasonable to ascribe to the same legislature an intent to provide in the same act a method of evading the required two-thirds vote and the grant of such appraisal rights. The practical effect of the decision appealed from is to render the requirements of a two-thirds vote and appraisal rights meaningless in virtually all mergers. It is scarcely an exaggeration to say the decision amounts to judicial repeal of the merger sections in most instances of merger.

"It is obvious, as defendants' counsel frankly stated in oral argument, that corporate management would naturally choose a method which requires only majority approval of shareholders and does not grant dissenters the right to be paid the fair value of their stock. The legislature could hardly have intended to vest in corporate management the option to comply with the requirements just referred to or to proceed without such compliance, a choice that would invariably be exercised in favor of the easier method."

The question whether a transaction constitutes a *de facto* merger to be treated as if it were *de jure* may arise in contexts other than claims of minority or dissenting stockholders to exercise voting or appraisal rights. For example, an arrangement such as in the *Rath* or *Hariton* cases may be asserted to be a *de facto* merger by creditors of the acquired corporation if not all of the obligations of that corporation were assumed by the acquiring corporation and the stock of the acquiring corporation has been distributed to the stockholders of the acquired corporation together with its few remaining assets. See, e.g., Kloberdanz v. Joy Manufacturing Co., 288 F.Supp. 817 (D.Colo.1968); McKee v. Harris–Seybold Co., Division of Harris Intertype Corp., 109 N.J.Super. 555, 264 A.2d 98 (1970), affirmed, 118 N.J.Super. 480, 288 A.2d 585 (1972); Turner v. Bituminous Cas. Co., 397 Mich. 406, 244 N.W.2d 873 (1976); but cf. Ray v. Alad Corp., 19 Cal.3d 22, 560 P.2d 3 (1977). In addition, asset purchasers' exposure to products liability and environmental claims has expanded dramatically during the past two decades. See generally Symposium, 67 Wash.U.L.Q. 325 (1989); Shecter, Acquiring Corporate Assets Without Successor Liability: Is It a Myth? 1986 Colum.Bus.L.Rev. 137; Roe, Mergers, Acquisitions and Tort: A Comment on the Problem of Successor Corporation Liability, 70 Va.L.Rev. 1559 (1984).

A particular process of combining firms (e.g., statutory merger or sale of assets) may offer public stockholders more protection (such as voting rights, appraisal rights, liquidation rights or immunity from the old corporation's obligations) than other processes of combining. By the same token, however, that process may impose its costs on the controlling or majority stockholders or on "the enterprise." In that event, should management or the majority or controlling stockholder be allowed, without restriction, to avoid those costs by effecting the combination by some other technique—e.g., instead of merger, by sale of assets, or by contract with a newly created partial subsidiary, or by partnership or leasing arrangement with another corporation owned by the controllers? Pratt v. Ballman—Cummings Furniture Co., 254 Ark. 570, 495 S.W.2d 509 (1973); Good v. Lackawanna Leather Co., 96 N.J.Super. 439, 233 A.2d 201 (1967).

To what extent should "business" considerations, like limiting the buyer's assumption of the seller's obligations, avoiding local bulk sales taxes, or avoiding the need to try to assign non-assignable contracts be permitted to validate the form in which the transaction is cast, if use of that particular form imposes costs on stockholders or consumers or employees that would be avoided if the transaction were cast in another form?

In determining whether one form of combination is the functional equivalent of another, and is (or is not) permissible in lieu of the other, should the criteria that courts use vary depending upon whether (1) the claim being pursued is that of a stockholder of the acquired corporation (i.e. the enterprise whose management relinquishes control) rather than of a stockholder of the acquirer (see e.g. claim of appraisal rights in an "upside-down" merger, Morley Brothers v. Clark, 361 N.W.2d 763 (Mich.1984)); (2) the complainant is a stockholder claiming (a) loss of voting or appraisal rights, (b) loss of protection against liability for the obligations of the old company, or (c) liquidation rights; (3) the complainant is a creditor of the old corporation (compare Philadelphia Elec. Co. v. Hercules, Inc., 762 F.2d 303 (3d Cir.1985) with Terry v. Penn

Central, supra p. 688 or a consumer injured by the old corporation's product; or (4) the complainants are employees injured in the old corporation's service or seeking carry-over of collective bargaining entitlements or pension rights?

2. APPRAISAL

See Appendix G for the statutory provisions for appraisal in Delaware and New York, Delaware General Corporation Law, section 262 and New York Business Corporation Law, sections 623 and 910.

FRANCIS I. duPONT & CO. v. UNIVERSAL CITY STUDIOS, INC.
Court of Chancery of Delaware, 1973.
312 A.2d 344.

DUFFY, Justice.

This is the decision upon exceptions to an Appraiser's final report determining the value of minority shares in a corporation absorbed in a short form merger.

A.

On March 25, 1966 Universal Pictures Co. (Universal) was merged into Universal City Studios, Inc. (defendant) under 8 Del.C. § 253. [The merger was] effected by MCA, Inc., the common parent. MCA owned 92% of Universal and 100% of defendant. The minority stockholders of Universal were offered $75 per share which plaintiffs rejected and then perfected their appraisal rights.

On March 29, 1973 the Appraiser filed a final report, in which he found the value of the Universal stock to be $91.47 per share. Both parties filed exceptions and this is the decision thereon after briefing and oral argument.

B.

The parties' ultimate disagreement is, of course, over the value of the stock. Plaintiffs submit that the true value is $131.89 per share, defendant says it is $52.36. The computations are as follows:

Plaintiffs

Value Factor	Value	Weight	Result
Earnings	$129.12	70%	$ 90.38
Market	144.36	20%	28.87
Assets	126.46	10%	12.64
	Value per share		$131.89

Defendant

Value Factor	Value	Weight	Result
Earnings	$ 51.93	70%	$ 36.35
Dividends	41.66	20%	8.33
Assets	76.77	10%	7.68
	Value per share		$52.36

Appraiser

Value Factor	Value	Weight	Result
Earnings	$ 92.89	80%	$ 74.31
Assets	85.82	20%	17.16
		Value per share	$91.47

The parties differ as to details of the report to which each assigns error, but their exceptions spring from fundamentally different views of several basic elements of the appraisal.[3] These are, principally: (1) Universal's earnings and selection of the proper multiplier for capitalization of those earnings; (2) the correct asset value per share; (3) whether an independent dividend value should have been used; (4) whether a market value for Universal's stock should have been reconstructed; and (5) the correct weight to be given each of the value factors found to be relevant by the Appraiser.

C.

At the heart of the dispute is the different picture each side draws of the nature of Universal's business, its place in the broader industry of which that business was a part, and the prospects of the industry generally and of Universal in particular. The parties apparently agree that at the date of merger Universal was engaged in the production and distribution of feature motion pictures. But agreement ends there.

Defendant takes exception to the Appraiser's failure to find that in the years prior to merger the industry was declining and that Universal was ranked near its bottom. And it argues that Universal was in the business of producing and distributing feature motion pictures for theatrical exhibition. It contends that such business, generally, was in a severe decline at the time of merger and that Universal, in particular, was in a vulnerable position because it had failed to diversify, its feature films were of low commercial quality and, unlike other motion picture companies, substantially all of its film library had already been committed to distributors for television exhibition. In short, defendant pictures Universal as a weak ("wasting asset") corporation in a sick industry with poor prospects for revival.

The stockholders see a different company. They say that Universal's business was indeed the production and distribution of feature films, but not merely for theatrical exhibition. They argue that there was a dramatic increase in the television market for such feature films at the time of the merger. This new market, they contend, gave great new value to a fully amortized film library and significantly enhanced the value of Universal's current and future productions. They equate

---

3. In Tri–Continental Corporation v. Battye, Del.Supr., 31 Del.Ch. 523, 74 A.2d 71 (1950), the Supreme Court formulated the concept of value to be determined in an appraisal: it is a "proportionate interest in a going concern * * * the true or intrinsic value of * * * stock which has been taken by the merger." It directed that "all factors and elements which reasonably might enter into the fixing of value" must be considered in an appraisal, including "market value, asset value, dividends, earning prospects, the nature of the enterprise and any other facts which were known or which could be ascertained as of the date of the merger and which throw any light on future prospects of the merged corporation * * *."

the television market to the "acquisition of a new and highly profitable business whose earnings potential was just beginning to be realized at the time of the merger." Finally, say plaintiffs, the theatrical market itself was recovering in 1966. Thus, they paint the portrait of a well situated corporation in a rejuvenated industry.

The Appraiser agreed with the stockholders that the theatrical market was recovering and that the new television market had favorable effects and would continue to provide a ready market for future films to be released by Universal. However, he declined to give the stockholders the benefit of all inferences as to specific value factors which they maintained those conclusions required.

D.

I first consider earnings. Both parties disagree, for different reasons, with the result of the Appraiser's analysis of Universal's earnings as a value factor. He concluded that Universal's earnings value should be derived by calculating the mean average of earnings per share for the years 1961 through 1965, the five years preceding the merger.[4] So doing, he arrived at average earnings of $5.77 per share. He then adopted a multiplier of 16.1, which is the average price earnings ratio of nine motion picture companies,[5] to capitalize Universal's earnings.

The stockholders accept the multiplier selected by the Appraiser but argue that he should have used the 1965 earnings of $8.02 per share rather than the mean average of the five years preceding the merger. * * *

* * *

It is established Delaware law that for appraisal purposes earnings are to be determined by averaging the corporation's earnings over a reasonable period of time. In re Olivetti Underwood Corp., Del.Ch., 246 A.2d 800 (1968); Sproborg v. City Specialty Stores, 35 Del.Ch., 560, 123 A.2d 121 (1956). The determination must be based upon historical earnings rather than on the basis of prospective earnings. Application of Delaware Racing Association, Del.Supr., 213 A.2d 203 (1965). The five-year period immediately preceding the merger is ordinarily considered to be the most representative and reasonable period of time over which to compute the average. Application of Delaware Racing Association, supra; In re Olivetti Underwood Corporation, supra.

Our cases have recognized that an appraiser, in certain circumstances, may justify adjusting average earnings by eliminating "unusual and isolated" items from reported earnings or, in a "most unusual situation" by limiting or expanding the number of years over which the average is taken. Adams v. R.C. Williams & Company, 39 Del.Ch. 61,

---

4. Those earnings per share were:

1961	$3.32
1962	4.96
1963	6.22
1964	6.32
1965	8.02

5. Those companies were Columbia, MGM, Paramount, Republic, 20th Century Fox, United Artists, M.C.A., Walt Disney and Warner Brothers.

158 A.2d 797 (1960). But I agree with the Appraiser's finding that no such situation has been shown here.

The stockholders argue that averaging past earnings is proper only when the earnings history has been erratic. In support of that proposition, Mr. Stanley Nabi, managing partner of a NYSE brokerage house and an investment and financial analyst, testified that the accepted practice among security analysts is to capitalize present earnings, and to give the trend of earnings important consideration in the selection of the multiplier. The stockholders argue that Universal's earnings history was not erratic but, in fact, had a steady and rapid growth. They contend that the Appraiser 'therefore should have used the current (1965) earnings as the figure to be capitalized.

This argument is not persuasive even if Mr. Nabi's testimony as to the accepted practice among security analysts for capitalizing earnings is conceded to be correct. Whatever that practice may currently be, the policy of Delaware law is that averaging earnings over the five years immediately preceding the merger should be the rule and not the exception. In short, a choice among alternative techniques for capitalizing earnings has been made and no persuasive conceptual reason has been shown to change that choice now.

The stockholders also argue that Universal's earlier earnings, particularly those of 1961, were not representative of Universal's earning power at the time of merger because television was a relatively minor factor in such earnings. They offered a number of alternatives to the Appraiser and, on the exceptions, press their contention that he should have used 1965 earnings of $8.02 per share.

I do not agree with the shareholders that the "pre–1986 earnings had become an anachronism" at the time of merger. I view Universal's situation at that time as one of change in the nature of its market, not in the fundamental nature of its business. It was undoubtedly clear at the time of merger that the new television market had contributed substantially to Universal's earnings and would continue to do so for at least the short term. It was also evident that television presented a relatively permanent new market. But I do not think it realistic to say that that market was of such a revolutionary character as to assure for time without end either a trend of increasing earnings or a comparatively high level of earnings. Compare Adams v. R.C. Williams & Company, supra. The fact is that, with or without the television market, Universal's earning experience over the long term remains subject to the variables in its managerial and artistic talent, the ability and ingenuity of competitors and the uncertainties of public tastes in entertainment.

Certainly the figures show, as plaintiffs argue, that the trend in earnings was on the rise from 1961 through 1965 but that is not a reason in law for abandoning the averaging approach required under *Delaware Racing* and other Supreme Court decisions, nor does it provide a basis for eliminating any one year as unusual or isolated under *Adams.* The trend has significance in the choice of the multiplier.

* * *

I conclude, therefore, that the Appraiser correctly used the mean average of earnings for the five years immediately preceding the merger.

Defendant agrees that the earnings to be capitalized is the five-year average of $5.77 per share, but says that the Appraiser erred in adopting as a multiplier the industry price earnings ratio (16:1). It argues that even if such ratio were appropriate, the correct figure is not more than 12.7 and it contends that the maximum multiplier permitted under our case law is 10, except under special circumstances not present here. Plaintiffs do not except to the Appraiser's multiplier. Specifically, defendant says a multiplier of 9 is fair both in terms of Universal's prior history and its position in that industry.

Admittedly many of the cases and treatises approve a multiplier of 10 or thereabouts. But that is based largely on the economics and pricing structure of an earlier day and, under the circumstances here present, the use of any such number would be artificial.

* * *

The earnings value (16.1 $\times$ $5.77 = $92.89) determined by the Appraiser will be approved.

E.

I turn now to asset value. Plaintiffs say that at the time of merger the net figure was $126.46, defendant says it was $76.77, the Appraiser determined it to be $85.82.

The parties have argued at some length their respective views of the adjustments which should be made to Universal's book value, but I do not propose to discuss each of these in detail. * * *

I conclude that for appraisal purposes a share of Universal stock should be assigned an asset value of $91.72.

F.

The Appraiser declined to include market value of Universal stock as a value factor because there was not a reliable market for it and none could be constructed. Defendant agrees with that conclusion. Plaintiffs urged the Appraiser to find a reconstructed value of $144 a share.

The Delaware law is that in the absence of a reliable market for stock, a reconstructed market value "must be given consideration", if one can be made. Application of Delaware Racing Association, supra.

I agree with plaintiffs that, on a comparative basis, Universal's financial performance was more impressive than that of MCA, but I am not persuaded that a reliable basis for valuation can be established by applying MCA price earnings ratio to Universal's 1965 earnings. Certainly there was a market for MCA shares and Universal's earnings and experience contributed to whatever value that buyers and sellers in that market placed upon MCA at any given time. But to reach through the MCA curtain and find Universal, is to grasp at shadows, and to attempt to divine (in this case where we deal with hard dollars) what buyers would have paid for Universal had they the chance, is to substitute fantasy for fact. This simply involves too much speculation about too many intangibles. Accordingly, market value will not be included as an appraisal index.

G.

Defendant urged the Appraiser to capitalize the historical dividends of Universal and assign to them an independent value of $41.66 for appraisal purposes. He declined to do so. Plaintiffs agree.

I agree with the Appraiser's conclusion, based upon Felder v. Anderson, Clayton & Co., supra, that dividends largely reflect the same value as earnings and so should not be separately considered. *Delaware Racing,* with its policy and history of "no dividends", was obviously a unique case entirely unlike that presented here.

H.

Finally, I consider the weighting factor, an issue as to which the parties are in least disagreement. The views of the Appraiser and the parties are as follows:

Value Factor	*Plaintiffs*	*Defendant*	*Appraiser*
Earnings	70%	70%	80%
Assets	10%	10%	20%
Market value	20%	—	—
Dividend Distribution	—	20%	—

As this table shows, the parties agree on the weight which should be assigned to earnings and assets, respectively. They differ on allocation of the remaining 20% which each argues should be assigned to separate factors, both of which the Appraiser and the Court have rejected. The Appraiser, in effect, divided the 20% equally between the two components he used.

In my own view, a more precise division of that 20% should be made by applying to it a factor derived from the allocations about which the parties agree. I think this is particularly desirable because both sides agree that earnings are entitled to seven times as much weight as assets. Applying such factors ($7/8$ for earnings, $1/8$ for assets) to the remaining 20%, I conclude that the earnings percentage should be increased by 17.5%, while the asset percentage should be increased by 2.5%.

* * *

I conclude that the value of a share of Universal stock on the date of merger should be determined to be as follows:

Value Factor	Value	Weight	Result
Earnings	$92.89	87.5%	$81.28
Assets	91.72	12.5%	11.47
		Value per share	$92.75

———

[On appeal the decision of Justice Duffy was affirmed (334 A.2d 216 (1975)). In connection with the proper determination of "earnings value" the Supreme Court said at 218:]

It is well settled that in an appraisal proceeding under 8 Del.C. § 262, the shares must be valued on a going concern basis. Sporborg v. City Speciality Stores, 35 Del.Ch. 160, 123 A.2d 121, 123 (1956). This approach necessitates not only the Court's examination of historical earnings but also a perusal of the corporation's stability and future prospects as of the date of merger. The prospective financial condition of the subject corporation and the risk factor inherent in the corporation and the industry within which it operates are vital factors to be considered in arriving at a realistic present earnings value. These considerations are manifested in the valuation process through the choice of a capitalization factor, or multiplier. The multiplier will be low if the financial outlook for a corporation is poor, or high if prospects are encouraging. When the multiplier is computed with the past earnings record (in this case $5.77 per share), the resultant figure is deemed to best approximate the present earnings value of a share of stock. The multiplier adopted by the Appraiser and the Court below was 16.1 and that figure, as well as the means used to arrive at such number, are the primary issues upon which appellant bases its appeal.

The choice of a multiplier is a most difficult task and one which is often the subject of parties' exceptions, since its use leads to an approximation of value for which creditable arguments can always be made for increase or decrease. Professor Dewing states in his work, "The Financial Policy of Corporation" (5th Ed., 1953):

"[T]he determination of this rate is at best a matter of guess-work, but guesswork supported by the evidence of prices at which business of various kinds are being actually valued at any one time. * * * "

* * *

The appellees assert that the 16.1 figure should be affirmed. The appellant contends that improper criteria were used by the Appraiser and the Court in determining the multiplier and that the figure is impermissibly high. For this latter proposition, appellants cite Professor Dewing, whose works in the past have been accorded deferential treatment in Delaware. At page 388 of his work, "The Financial Policy of Corporations," (5th Ed.1953) Professor Dewing states that a multiplier of 10 is the highest value that can be assigned to a business. We, however, do not find such a view to be persuasive, but instead concur with the findings of Swanton, supra, (where a multiplier of 14 was fixed), which recognized that Professor Dewing's capitalization chart was not the "be-all and end-all," and it did not "freeze the subject matter for all time," especially since "contemporary financial history" reveals a "need for flexibility." (at 246).

Appellants contend that the Appraiser and the Chancellor looked solely to the price-earnings ratios of nine other motion picture companies on March 25, 1966, and averaged them together to arrive at a 16.1 multiplier. We agree with the appellant insofar as the 16.1 figure is arrived at through precise mathematical calculations involving the price-earnings ratios of these nine other companies. We disagree however that this was the sole consideration * * *

* * * The Chancellor included a table in the opinion which showed that in 1961, earnings per share were $3.32, and that the earnings steadily increased until in 1965, they were at $8.02 per share. The record shows that during these years, none of the companies except Disney could show a steady growth trend. Within the industry, there was pronounced volatility of earnings, with years of deficit and decline. Universal, on the other hand, was able to show a steady growth, even during the period of 1962 and 1963, when the industry was suffering greatly. As for the "predictability" of certain of its television income, the Chancellor was taking cognizance of the Appraiser's report, which specified that Universal was to receive "substantial future income" in the sum of over $48,000,000 as a result of the leasing of major portions of its film library to television networks. Such commitments were labeled "guaranteed" by the Appraiser, and he noted that they would result in net earnings from television of at least $16.63 per share over the following four years. Further income could be expected from renewal of television contracts as well as from release of future films and subsequent leases to television. The evidence presented was sufficient to warrant a departure from Dewing's capitalization chart. The steady upward trend in Universal's earnings and the vast amount of money guaranteed to inure to Universal are persuasive factors indicating future economic success and stability. This situation is analogous to Swanton, supra, because increased revenue from television contracts is guaranteed in future years and is not represented in present earnings. It is true that a corporation in the motion picture industry, such as Universal, is subject to the whims of public taste and the artistic talents of its employees. Fluctuation in earnings is indeed a trademark of the motion picture industry and Universal was as vulnerable to non-acceptance of its theatrical productions as any other company. However, as of the date of the merger, Universal had exhibited a better earnings picture than any other motion picture company and had, through its television contracts, provided a buffer which would tend to offset for several years any theatrical losses. Therefore a relatively high multiplier was warranted.

There are other factors not alluded to in the opinion which support a high multiplier in this case. The years of 1964 and 1965 showed a marked resurgence for the motion picture industry after a long period of slumping profits due to competition from television. The stock market reflected the turnaround of the industry by rising from the stock price index of 49 in 1963 (the mean price of Columbia, MGM, 20th Century Fox, United Artists, Paramount, Warner Brothers) to a mean of about $64 per share figure in 1966. Further, on March 25, 1966, the Dow Jones and Standard and Poors Indices showed an average price to earnings ratio of approximately 17.3, 17.4. Universal's growth rate during the years 1961 through 1965 amounted to 142 per cent or a compound rate of 25 per cent a year. This record, showing no yearly volatility, was far superior to those other companies within the industry and was also superior to the rate of growth of the stocks listed in the Dow Jones and Standard and Poors Indices.

Appellant contends that the use of the average price earnings ratio of the nine other companies in the industry was improper in that those companies were not comparable and did not reflect the corporate managerial policies which were unique to Universal. Alternatively, it is contended that if companies within the industry were to be used in arriving at a multiplier, only those companies which were financially and otherwise comparable should have been used. In addition, appellant contends it was error as a matter of law for the average industry price earnings ratio to have been computed on the basis of one day's market price. We disagree.

Universal was a subsidiary of MCA and its stock was predominantly owned by the parent corporation. There was such a low percentage of Universal stock available to the public that no reliable data existed upon which to project a market value. Since Universal had no market value, it had no price-earnings ratio and a multiplier was therefore needed which would reflect the amount of public confidence in Universal's future and would, when multiplied with earnings, give a dollar figure closely approximately the earnings value of a share of Universal stock. "Without a market price for reference the selection of an appropriate multiplier takes on added import as a key factor in determining value." David J. Greene & Co. v. Dunhill International, Inc., Del.Ch., 249 A.2d 427, 434 (1968).

There being no valid market price for Universal's stock, and therefore no valid price-earnings ratio, the Appraiser was without a fixed mathematical method whereby factors relating solely to Universal's own stability and growth potential could be given effect in the form of a multiplier. Therefore, the Appraiser referred to the industry price-earnings ratio on the date of the merger as a starting point in the fixing of a multiplier. The use of price-earnings ratios of comparable businesses on the date of merger as a factor in evaluating another company, and here as a vital first step in arriving at a multiplier, is reasonable and has support in Delaware case law. In Felder v. Anderson, Clayton & Co., 39 Del.Ch. 76, 159 A.2d 278 (1960), a five-year industry average price-earnings ratio served as a starting point for arriving at a multiplier for a corporation involved in a merger. The five-year average was adopted because the market was in a boom phase. Though the motion picture industry was in a period of rejuvenation at the time of Universal's merger, a look at the price-earnings ratios over the five-year period preceding the merger as compared with the 16.1 average on the date of merger, reveals figures not disproportionate. The 16.1 figure being representative of the industry's past record, we see no reason to depart from the holdings of Levin v. Midland–Ross Corporation, 41 Del.Ch. 276, 194 A.2d 50 (1963) and David J. Greene & Co. v. Dunhill International, Inc., Del.Ch., 249 A.2d 427 (1968), where the price-earnings ratios of comparable companies and of Standard & Poors' national stock averages were calculated as of the date of merger and were used as comparative measures to aid in the determination of a multiplier for the subject corporations. The determination of value as of the day of merger being the Court's endeavor, it is appropriate that the price-earnings ratios of comparable companies, serving as barometers of risk within the industry, be referred to solely on the day of merger in the absence of extraordinary deviation from the past price-earnings record.

As for the appellant's contention that error was committed below by the use of certain non-comparable companies in arriving at the 16.1 figure, we are not persuaded to reverse. The "imponderables of the valuation process" and the concomitant broad discretion traditionally granted to evaluators of corporate shares of stock, compel an acceptance of the method of determining a multiplier unless there is a clear abuse of discretion amounting to an error at law, i.e., such as the use of only one value factor at the expense of other factors. *Tri Continental,* supra.

* * *

We accept the findings below that the companies used to initially provide a basis for a multiplier for Universal were in fact "comparable" to Universal. True, some of the companies were more diversified than Universal, and some produced more award winning movies than Universal. Nevertheless, all nine companies were heavily engaged in the production and distribution of motion pictures and were therefore subject to the same public moods and reactions that affected Universal. We note that, based on its past record and managerial plans for the future, Universal was in a position to suffer less than other companies from woes generally affecting the industry. We are not prepared to delineate one or more companies within the same industry as Universal, as being non-comparable, when influxes applicable to one are applicable to all, but register in varying degrees as measured by financial growth or depletion. See David J. Greene & Co. v. Dunhill International, Inc., Del.Ch., 249 A.2d 427, 433 (1968). In that case, the Court admonished the Appraiser below for including in a group of companies, for purposes of ascertaining a multiplier based on comparability, five companies that were productive in a related field, but not within the industry. Nevertheless, the use of the price-earnings ratios of three companies which competed with the company under evaluation, "to a limited degree," was not found to have unwarranted effects in the choice of a multiplier.

From the foregoing, and after applying the standard of review applicable to the selection of earnings multipliers, we conclude that the 16.1 figure reached below is within the range of reason.

* * *

Affirmed.

NOTE: VALUATION OF DISSENTERS' STOCK UNDER THE "DELAWARE BLOCK"

1. A Note in 79 Harvard Law Review 1453, 1468–1469 (1966) observes that:

"Consideration of at least the three factors discussed [namely, assets, market value and earnings] helps to minimize the effect of defects in any one and to assure that no single computation will be determinative. Even if perfectly accurate values could be derived for assets, market, and earnings, the three figures will seldom be identical. Although each is a suitable measure of stock for certain purposes, each requires the appraiser to make different assumptions as to stockholder objectives.

"Once the various elements have been computed, they must be balanced in order to arrive at a figure that will represent fair consideration for the dissenter's stock. The relative weights will necessarily vary according to the type of business involved and the special circumstances surrounding the particular company. Less weight should be given a particular element when the estimate of its value is unreliable; in at least one instance a value factor was given lower weight because it was substantially out of line with the others, causing the court to lose confidence in its accuracy.

"The Delaware courts require the appraiser to state the percentage weight he has assigned to each value factor. The percentages are understood to be only crude estimates and are commonly expressed in round numbers. Nevertheless, such a procedure forces the appraiser to analyze the relative importance of each element and to justify his conclusions, and it affords a more concrete basis for review by the courts. It guards to some extent against the possibility that the figures will be merely a compromise between the contentions of the parties or an intuitive judgment."

2. Supplementing the Harvard Law Review Note, a Note in 30 Okl.L.Rev. 629, 641–642 (1977) summarizes the weighting process as follows:

The following chart indicates the weights as determined by several leading cases, the majority of which are Delaware decisions.

Percentage Weight (Dollar Values)

	Asset	Market	Earnings	Dividend	(Result)
1–	50 ($ 129.00)	25 ($ 90.00)	25 ($ 83.00) —		($ 108.00)
2–(a)	40 (139.60)	30 (113.00)	30 (149.00) —		(131.74)
(b)	20 (32.54)	45 (12.13)	35 (16.90) —		(17.88)
3–	20 (46.57)	30 (14.00)	25 (11.97)	25 ($14.28)	(20.08)
4–	40 (42.35) —		60 (13.00) —		(24.74)
5–	20 (700.05) —		80 (365.23) —		(432.09)
6–	50 (35.67)	25 (18.69)	25 (8.82) —		(24.71)
7–	25 (5996.00)	40 (1305.00)	25 (1201.90)	10 (00.00)	(2321.30)
8–	60 (128.08)	10 (66.00)	30 (43.26) —		(96.42)
9–	50 (11.20)	25 (3.67)	25 (1.05) —		(6.79)
10–	25 (10.62)	50 (14.25)	25 (00.00) —		(9.78)
11–	50 (242.81)	25 (69.00)	25 (00.00) —		(138.65)
12–	12.5 (91.72) —		87.5 (92.89) —		(92.75)
13–	—	55 (29.00)	45 (39.79) —		(33.86)
[14–	20 (15.41)	40 (4.88)	40 (2.52) —		(6.04)*]
[15–	50 (103.16)	10 (26.50)	40 (52.60) —		(75.27)*]
[16–	90 (85.51)	5 (15.00)	5 (23.90) —		(78.74)*]
[17–	25 (1,712,000)		75 (1,885,000) —		(1,842,000)*]

*[Ed. note] 14: In re Valuation of Common Stock of Libby, McNeill & Libby, 406 A.2d 54 (Me.1979). 15: Piemonte v. New Boston Garden Corp., 377 Mass. 719, 387 N.E.2d 1145 (1979). 16: Sarrouf v. New England Patriots Football Club, Inc., 397 Mass. 542, 492 N.E.2d 1122 (1986). 17: In re Valuation of McCloon Oil Co., 565 A.2d 997 (Me.1989). Figures for the *McCloon* case are absolute dollar values rather than per share values.

Basis for Determination

1. In re General Realty & Utilities Corp., 29 Del.Ch. 480, 52 A.2d 6 (Ch. 1947). The assets, mostly securities and real estate, were weighted more because the corporation depended more upon the assets than upon good management.

2. Jacques Coe & Co. v. Minneapolis–Moline Co., 31 Del.Ch. 368, 75 A.2d 244 (Ch.1950). (a) Preferred Stock: Asset value weighted more because it formed such a large part of the present worth.

(b) Common Stock: Market value was more accurate because of active trading in the stock. Earnings value was of less importance because no dividends had been recently paid.

3. Heller v. Munsingwear, Inc., 33 Del.Ch. 593, 98 A.2d 774 (Ch.1953). Assets were downgraded because they were so out of line with other values.

4. Sporborg v. City Specialty Stores, Inc., 35 Del.Ch. 560, 123 A.2d 121 (Ch.1956). Market value was disregarded because it was found to be artificially sustained. Asset value was weighted more than normal because the corporation had recently expanded and improved assets, and such was not yet reflected in the earnings value.

5. Felder v. Anderson, Clayton & Co., 39 Del.Ch. 76, 159 A.2d 278 (Ch.1960). There was no market value for the stock in this case. The asset value was discounted because the court found that the method utilized by the appraiser (depreciated replacement cost) was more than the actual asset value if not so discounted.

6. Levin v. Midland–Ross Corp., 41 Del.Ch. 276, 194 A.2d 50 (1963). Asset value was stressed because approximately 50 per cent of corporate assets were liquid at the time of the appraisal, and the court determined that these were the intrinsic value of the corporation.

7. Application of Delaware Racing Ass'n, 42 Del.Ch. 406, 213 A.2d 203 (Sup.Ct.1965), affirming 42 Del.Ch. 175, 206 A.2d 664 (Ch.1965). Assets were discounted and market value stressed because the court determined that the market was the only place where the value of the corporation, a raceway with obsolete facilities and depressed earnings, could be adequately measured. Lack of dividends considered to balance the weighting of market value.

8. Swanton v. State Guaranty Corp., 42 Del.Ch. 477, 215 A.2d 242 (Ch. 1965). Assets stressed to reflect the fact that the corporation had engaged in a policy of investment in capital appreciation. Such a weighting would allow consideration of future prospects of such a policy.

9. Poole v. N.V. Deli Maatschappij, 243 A.2d 67 (Del.1968). Assets stressed because of nature of corporation as a holder of tobacco-producing lands.

10. In re Olivetti Underwood Corp., 246 A.2d 800 (Del.Ch.1968). Earnings are considered such an important factor in the value of a corporation that they are weighted even though nonexistent. Market value stressed because the market for such stocks had been in existence for some time and was a strong indicator of value.

11. Brown v. Hedahl's–Q B & R, Inc., 185 N.W.2d 249 (N.D.1971). Asset value stressed because of the nature of the corporation as an auto parts retailer.

12. Universal City Studios, Inc. v. Francis I. duPont & Co., 334 A.2d 216 (Del.1975), modifying, 312 A.2d 344 (Del.Ch.1973). Earnings value stressed because at the time of merger corporation had a better than average earnings picture. There was no market for the stock.

13. Gibbons v. Schenley Indus., Inc., 339 A.2d 460 (Del.Ch.1975). Assets ignored because majority were in idle and obsolete manufacturing plants. Court determined that assets are to be valued as to ability to generate earnings. Here the vast amount of corporate earnings came from distribution agreements for imported whisky. Market value was determined to be reliable, and court found a growing trend to favor market value when possible.

---

3. Although, as Weinberger v. U.O.P., infra, p. 766 and Rosenblatt v. Getty Oil Co., infra p. 802, indicate, Delaware no longer requires the block-weighting method of valuing in appraisal proceedings, other states continue to regard that method as appropriate. See Piemonte v. New Boston Garden Corp., 377 Mass. 719, 387 N.E.2d 1145 (1979); Sarrouf v. New England Patriots Football Club, Inc., 397 Mass. 542, 492 N.E.2d 1122 (1986); BNE Massachusetts Corp. v. Sims, 588 N.E.2d 14 (Mass.Ct.App.1992); In re Valuation of Common Stock of Libby, McNeill and Libby, 406 A.2d 54 (Me.1979); Dibble v. Sumter Ice and Fuel Co., 283 S.C. 278, 322 S.E.2d 674 (1984); Ford v. Courier–Journal Job Printing Co., 639 S.W.2d 553 (Ky.App.1982). So too has the comptroller of the currency with respect to dissenters from mergers involving national banks. See Austin, Commercial Bank Dissenters' Appraisals, 101 Banking Law Journal 302, 318–319 (1984). See also Schaefer, The Fallacy of Weighting Asset Value and Earnings Value in the Appraisal of Corporate Stock, 55 S.Cal.L.Rev. 1031 (1982). What is the rationale for the use in appraisal proceedings of the block-weighting

method of valuing—a method which either necessarily does (Schaefer, supra), or empirically may often, undervalue the dissenters' shares?

4. On what theory and evidence should weights be assigned to the various "values"?

(a) Is the "asset value" computed from book figures? Or does it represent the net liquidation value determined by expert testimony as to the price at which the enterprise's assets could be sold piecemeal? Or is there some other "current value" or "going concern" value to be discovered? See Sarrouf v. New England Patriots Football Club, Inc., 397 Mass. 542, 492 N.E.2d 1122 (1986). See Hackney, Accounting Principles in Corporation Law, 30 L. & Contemp. Probs. 791, 819–821 (1965); Comment, supra, 34 Emory L.J. 117, 135–138 (1985). If "going concern" value is the target, is it relevant to note or seek a price or prices that would be paid by hypothetical (or real) third party purchasers for the entire enterprise or for separate operating divisions? Cf. Kahn v. Household Acquisition Corp., 591 A.2d 166, 175 (Del.1991).

(b) If the enterprise's securities are traded in reasonable depth in a liquid market why is there any need to consider "intrinsic value" or "asset value"? On the other hand, if for any special reason or configuration of reasons the market for the enterprise's securities is not "efficient," why allow "market value" to enter into the computation at all?

(c) Which, if any, of the "values" seems to attract the highest weight? What considerations may influence that result?

(d) Schaefer, supra, suggests that the dissenter is entitled to be paid on the basis of the "best use" or highest value of the enterprise (e.g., as between "asset" and "earnings" values) because that is the value management should pursue and choose. Is this a correct suggestion? If not, does the theory of appraisal suggest some basis other than maximizing dissenters' wealth as the determinant of their entitlement? What basis? What is the relevance of the prohibition contained in most statutes against taking the effects of the merger into account? Must the court keep its focus on pre-merger going concern value? What considerations justify such a focus? Given that, in the end, present value always comes from *future* payments, might pre-merger going concern value be expanded into a capacious basis for appraisal valuation on the assumption that all conceivable future cash generating scenarios figure into present value? Consider these questions in connection with Rapid–American v. Harris, which follows.

5. Does the theory on which appraisal rights rest require or permit the dissenter's shares to be discounted because of a lack of "control"? Or is the dissenter entitled to an aliquot share of the value of the firm? Compare Cavalier Oil Corp. v. Harnett, 564 A.2d 1137 (Del.1989), Rapid–American v. Harris, infra, MT Properties Inc. v. CMC Real Estate Corp., 481 N.W.2d 383 (Minn.Ct.App.1992), Perlman v. Permonite Manufacturing Co., 568 F.Supp. 222 (N.D.Ind.1983), aff'd, 734 F.2d 1283 (7th Cir.1984), and Hernando Bank v. Huff, 609 F.Supp. 1124 (N.D.Miss.1985), with Ford v. Courier–Journal Job Printing Co.,

supra. Is it inconsistent with the dissenter's entitlement to be free from a discount for holding minority shares to allow a dissenter from a parent's merger with subsidiaries to share in the value of the parent's control of the subsidiaries? See Rapid–American v. Harris, which follows.

RAPID–AMERICAN CORP. v. HARRIS

Supreme Court of Delaware, 1992.
603 A.2d 796.

MOORE, Justice.

[Rapid–American Corp. ("Rapid") was a publicly held conglomerate that received 99 percent of its revenues and most of its income from three wholly-owned subsidiaries: (1) McCrory Corp., a retailer, contributing more than half of Rapid's net sales and profits, (2) Schenley Industries, a distiller, contributing 25 percent of Rapid's net sales and profits, and (3) McGregor–Duniger, Inc., a clothing manufacturer, contributing less than 1 percent of Rapid's net sales and profits. Rapid was heavily leveraged, capitalized with close to 75 percent long and short term debt.

[In 1974, Rapid's CEO and Chairman, Meshulam Riklis, began purchasing its shares in the open market. Two corporate vehicles conducted the purchases: Kenton Corp. ("Kenton"), controlled by Riklis, and American Financial Corp. ("AFC"), controlled by Carl Lindener. Rapid also contemporaneously repurchased large blocks of its own shares, causing Riklis' control of Rapid's outstanding shares to increase. By 1980, Kenton and AFC controlled 46.5 percent of Rapid's outstanding stock. That year, Rapid agreed to merge with Kenton into a newly reformed, privately-held Rapid, owned 60 percent by Riklis and 40 percent by Lindener. Rapid's other shareholders received a package worth $28, including a $45 face amount 10 percent subordinated debenture, and $3.25 cash.

[Harris, who owned 58,400 shares, brought an appraisal proceeding and sought $73 per share. The Chancery court awarded $51 per share plus simple interest. Both sides appealed.]

I.

* * *

Rapid employed an independent Transaction Review Committee ("TRC") to evaluate the merger price. The TRC retained Bear Stearns & Co. to provide financial advice. The TRC also employed Standard Research Consultants ("SRC") to determine, among other things, the fairness of the proposed transaction to Rapid's shareholders. Arthur H. Rosenbloom, SRC's head consultant and expert witness at trial, led the investigation. The examination continued for approximately six months. SRC ultimately concluded that the $28.00 compensation package was fair to Rapid's shareholders.

SRC's valuation technique considered Rapid on a consolidated basis. It evaluated Rapid based on an analysis of earnings and dividends. *Harris,* slip op. at 7. SRC calculated price/earnings ratios for each subsidiary and adjusted its figures to include certain dividend ratios. It figured each subsidiaries' contribution to the parent's operating income for a set period of time to calculate Rapid's ultimate value. SRC then tested its figures against various established financial ratios of similarly situated corporations. Id.

Harris retained Willamette Management Associates, Inc. ("WMA") to evaluate the merger consideration. In contrast to SRC's technique, WMA separately evaluated each of Rapid's subsidiaries. WMA reasoned that its "segmented" approach to valuation was particularly appropriate because of the difficulty of finding a conglomerate comparable to Rapid.

* * *

The Court of Chancery adopted WMA's comparative analysis. Id. at 19. It examined each of Rapid's subsidiaries as a separate entity. Id. It then compared the subsidiaries to a group of comparable publicly-traded companies. Id.

WMA examined the financial statements of the subsidiaries and the comparables to develop certain pricing multiples. Id. at 20. These multiples were based on revenues, pre-interest and tax earnings, earnings "before depreciation, amortization, interest and taxes [and] tangible book value of invested capital * * *." Id. WMA specifically treated each subsidiary and comparable on a debt-free basis in an effort to factor out the vagaries of "managerial discretion" and to treat the companies on a "level playing field." Id. The analysis yielded a market value of invested capital for each segment. Id. The trial court also considered an average of the subsidiaries' financials for the five years preceding the merger, but placed special emphasis on the twelve months before the merger. Id. at 20–21. After calculating the market value of invested capital for each segment, the court subtracted out the market value of all senior debt and preferred equity to calculate the value of each segment's common equity. Id. at 13, 21. The trial court also considered "various parent-level" factors. Id.

The Vice Chancellor rejected WMA's inclusion of a "control premium" in its final evaluation of each Rapid subsidiary. Id. at 21–22. It found that the addition of a "control premium" violated Delaware law. Id. at 29, 35, 38. The court reasoned that the "control premium" contravened the proscription against weighing factors affecting valuation "at the shareholder level." Id. at 29.

II.

* * *

We now turn to the specific merits of Rapid's appeal to determine whether the trial court abused its discretion. We first consider Rapid's claim that the court's "segmented" valuation technique violated Delaware law because it supposedly assessed Rapid's value on a liquidation basis instead of considering it as a going concern. Rapid argues that the court's valuation approach was identical to the liquidation technique rejected in Bell v. Kirby Lumber Corp., Del.Ch., 395 A.2d 730 (1978), modified, Del.Supr., 413 A.2d 137 (1980).

* * *

Bell best illustrates the law. Kirby Lumber Corporation ("Kirby"), the company subject to the appraisal in *Bell,* was a manufacturing concern primarily engaged in the production of lumber and plywood. *Bell,* 395 A.2d at 732. Kirby also held a vast acreage of timberland. Id. at 733. Kirby harvested the timber on a "sustained yield" basis to maintain a steady and constant supply of natural resources for its wood production operations. Id.

The dissenting shareholders argued that the court should have evaluated Kirby on its acquisition value. Id. at 735–36. They claimed that Kirby's natural resources were much more valuable than its worth as an on-going concern. Id. The dissenters thus maintained that the court should have set Kirby's "fair value" at the price a third party would have paid for the company instead of relying on an evaluation of earnings or market price. Id.

The trial court rejected the dissenters' argument. Id. at 736. It reasoned that the liquidation value incorrectly assumed that Kirby would not have continued in its pre-merger form as an on-going concern. Id. This Court affirmed. *Bell,* 413 A.2d at 142. We agreed that the dissenters' liquidation approach violated the statute and improperly failed to consider Kirby's value apart from its acquisition value. Id.

* * *

We find nothing in the record to convincingly support the claim that the court's "segmented" valuation technique was either identical or even similar to the liquidation approach rejected in *Bell.* The modified WMA valuation explicitly considered Rapid's subsidiaries as going concerns. See *Harris,* slip op. at 34–35. It placed special emphasis on financial data cumulated from operating results and not liquidation values. Id. at 19–22.

The "segmented" technique itself also did not manifest a liquidation analysis. Instead, the "segmented" approach best mirrored economic reality. Indeed, even Riklis admitted that "Rapid's value is best found in the sum of its parts." Id. at 10.

* * *

III.

We now consider the merits of Harris' cross-appeal. The trial court determined the publicly traded equity ("PTE") value of Rapid's shares after adopting WMA's "segmented" comparative valuation technique. See *Harris,* slip op. at 22–38. The court, however, refused to add a "control premium" to the PTE for each of Rapid's operating subsidiaries. The court, citing [Cavalier Oil Corp. v. Harnett, 564 A.2d 1137 (Del.1989)], reasoned that adding a "control premium" violated 8 Del.C. § 262 because it contravened the general proscription against weighing any additional factors affecting valuation "at the shareholder level." Id. at 29, 35, 38.

* * * Harris maintains that WMA's valuation technique only compared its subsidiaries' PTE's with the individual shares of similar corporations trading in the market. He notes that the market price of these comparable corporations are discounted and do not reflect a control premium. Harris concludes that the trial court effectively treated Rapid as a minority shareholder in its wholly-owned subsidiaries. Harris contends that the trial court gave the new, privately-held Rapid, a windfall at his expense.

* * *

We disagree with the trial court's characterization of the "control premium" in this case as an impermissible shareholder level adjustment. Its reliance on *Cavalier* and *Bell* is misplaced. The "control premium" Harris urged the trial court to adopt represented a valid adjustment to its valuation model which "applied a [bonus] at the company level against all assets * * *." *Cavalier,* 564 A.2d at 1144.

* * *

Tri–Continental recognized that a court had the authority to discount the value of the enterprise at the corporate level. 74 A.2d at 76. The company appraised in *Tri–Continental* was a leveraged closed-end mutual fund. Id. at 73. The court understood that the shares of a leveraged closed-end mutual fund ordinarily trade at a discount of its underlying assets. Id. at 76. The court concluded:

> [T]he full value of the corporate assets to the corporation is not the same as the value of those assets to the common stockholder because of the factor of discount. To fail to recognize this conclusion * * * is to fail to face the *economic facts* and to commit error.

Id. (Emphasis added).

Cavalier also recognized the importance of assigning a realistic market value to the appraised corporation. 564 A.2d at 1144. * * * The court, however, rejected shareholder level discounting. It found that an appraisal explicitly considering the minority discount at the shareholder level both injects speculative elements into the calculation, and more importantly:

> [F]ail[s] to accord to a minority shareholder the full proportionate value of his shares [which] imposes a penalty for lack of control, and unfairly enriches the majority shareholders who may reap a

windfall from the appraisal process by cashing out a dissenting shareholder, a clearly undesirable result.

Id. at 1145.

Rapid misses the fundamental point that Harris was not claiming a "control premium" at the shareholder level. Harris urged the trial court to add a premium at the parent level to compensate all of Rapid's shareholders for its 100% ownership position in the three subsidiaries. WMA's valuation technique arrived at comparable values using the market price of similar shares. These shares presumptively traded at a price that discounted the "control premium."

The trial court's decision to reject the addition of a control premium within the WMA valuation model placed too much emphasis on market value. * * * Recent price changes in the stock market dramatically illustrate the defects of an *overstated* reliance on market price to determine a corporation's intrinsic value in an appraisal proceeding. * * *

Rapid was a parent company with a 100% ownership interest in three valuable subsidiaries. The trial court's decision to exclude the control premium at the *corporate level* practically discounted Rapid's entire inherent value. The exclusion of a "control premium" artificially and unrealistically treated Rapid as a minority shareholder. Contrary to Rapid's arguments, Delaware law *compels* the inclusion of a control premium under the unique facts of this case.[2] Rapid's 100% ownership interest in its subsidiaries was clearly a "relevant" valuation factor and the trial court's rejection of the "control premium" implicitly placed a disproportionate emphasis on pure market value. See *Weinberger*, 457 A.2d at 712–13; *Munds*, 172 A. at 456.

We also reject Rapid's implicit claim that the inclusion of a "control premium" violates our decision in *Bell*. Rapid seems to contend that a "control premium" is only payable when the corporation is liquidated. It concludes that the addition of a "control premium" incorrectly inflates Rapid's worth to an acquisition value instead of pricing its inherent value as a going concern.

We reject Rapid's arguments because *Bell* is easily distinguishable on its facts. Unlike *Bell*, the WMA valuation technique did not assume that an acquiror would liquidate Rapid. WMA's valuation technique added the "control premium" to reflect market realities. Rapid may have had a different value as a going concern if the court had considered that it enjoyed a 100% interest in its three major subsidiaries.

We recognize that the term "control premium" may be misleading here. The past decade has proven that an acquiror is often willing to

---

2. We are fully aware of the Court of Chancery's decision in Cede & Co. v. Technicolor, Inc., Del. Ch., Civ.A. No. 7129, Allen, C. 1990 WL 161084 (Oct. 19, 1990), which explicitly rejected the inclusion of a "control premium" in a calculation of the intrinsic value of dissenting shares. Id. at 50–52 & n. 41. We note that *Cede* is factually distinguishable and did not consider a corporate level "control premium." We now express no view on the particular merits of the trial court's holding in *Cede*, a case in which an appeal is now pending before this Court.

pay a "control premium" in return for a majority interest in a corporation. Nonetheless, the WMA valuation technique utilized the control premium as a means of making its valuation more realistic. Under the circumstances presented here, the trial court was under a duty to assess the value of Rapid's full ownership in its subsidiaries.

* * *

Accordingly, we reverse the Court of Chancery and remand. The court must consider the "control premium," together with all other traditional valuation elements, and determine what, if any, additional value is to be ascribed to Harris' stock above the $51.00 per share initial finding.

———

On remand, the Chancery Court awarded the plaintiffs the "control premium" they requested—$23 per share for a total value per share of $73. Harris v. Rapid–American Corp., 1992 WL 69614 (Del.Ch.).

NOTE: VALUATION OF DISSENTERS' STOCK AFTER THE "DELAWARE BLOCK"

1. *Constituents of Premiums.*

What value factors comprise the control premiums awarded by the court? Reconsider Kraakman's discussion of the constituents of takeover premiums, supra pp. 654–665. If the control premiums awarded in *Rapid–American* are made up of the same elements as the takeover premiums in Kraakman's discussion, are they not impermissible elements of value "arising from the accomplishment or expectation of the merger" within section 262? Does the determination of whether a premium arises from the merger depend on its particular components? If the premium stems from perceptions of management misinvestment or expectations of other synergistic gains, is it impermissible in an appraisal proceeding, while a premium due to market pricing imperfections may be awarded? In that case, given Kraakman's discussion, how workable is the distinction between value elements arising from the merger and value elements independent of the merger?

2. *Problem.*

At what point does a permissible "segmented" analysis become an impermissible liquidation approach? At what point does the valuation depart from permissible "corporate level" considerations into impermissible "shareholder level" territory"? Consider the following problem.

Conglom Corp. operates three wholly owned subsidiaries, Manufacturing Corp. (M), Retail Corp. (R), and Timber Corp. (T). M and R each contribute approximately 40 percent of Conglom's sales and profits. T contributes 20 percent. Conglom has no significant parent level business. Conglom's stock trades at 30; the total market value of the stock is $100 million. Then, Nasticorp mounts a hostile tender offer for $45 cash per share, a total of $150 million. Conglom's managers encourage the shareholders not to tender because $45 is "too low." Nasticorp acquires 85 percent of Conglom's stock. In a subsequent second step merger, the consideration is set at $45. Before execution of the merger agreement, Nasticorp retains investment bankers who, after exhaustive study, determine the value of Conglom to be $150 million, after subtracting its debt at market value. They value M at $60 million, R at $60 million, and T at $30 million on a "going concern" basis. Shareholder (S) brings an appraisal proceeding under section 262.

A disgruntled former employee of Nasticorp leaks a document to S. This internal memorandum is a study of Conglom conducted prior to the takeover. This describes a "reorganization plan" pursuant to which Nasticorp will sell R and T in the corporate asset market after the acquisition. According to the memo, (1) Nasticorp expects to realize between $60 and $70 million for T and $55 to $65 million for R, and (2) Nasticorp will retain M because it is a good "fit" with its other manufacturing businesses; given the fit, M is worth $70 million to Nasticorp.

S introduces the memorandum as evidence of Conglom's value. Should the court admit the memorandum? If the memorandum is relevant evidence, what role should it play in the valuation? Is projected sale price of T of $60 to $70 million a part of the *ex ante* going concern value of T or a "liquidation" figure? Does one have to know what the potential acquirers would do with the assets? Can S assert the $70 million figure for T on a "control premium" theory?

Suppose S introduces evidence that Conglom's managers were considering an arm's length sale of T for $60 to $70 million with a subsequent dividend of the proceeds to its shareholders? Is this evidence of "going concern" value?

Suppose Nasticorp introduces evidence that Conglom's value is $150 million based on a comparison with three "comparable" conglomerates, each of which operates a retail, manufacturing and timber subsidiary. Does this submission block consideration of a higher "segmented" valuation submitted by S's expert?

What result in this case if the Delaware block approach is taken? How would the asset value of Conglom be calculated, and what weight should it take in the block?

Suppose the firm being appraised has a single operating division wholly-owned by a parent doing no other business. May the court include a control premium in its appraisal?

3. *Valuation Techniques.*

The abandonment of the block valuation approach has been followed by increasingly sophisticated valuation techniques in Delaware appraisal proceedings. The court's choice of technique plays a determinative role. Compare the analysis of comparable companies in Francis I. duPont & Co. v. Universal City Studios, supra, with the analysis adopted by the Chancery court in **Cede & Co. v. Technicolor,** 1990 WL 161084 (Del.Ch.) (finding the merger price to exceed appraised value).

As to the role of expert presentations of discounted cash flow ("DCF") models, Chancellor Allen commented as follows: 1990 WL 161084 at pp. 23–24 & n. 17:

"An appraisal action is a judicial, not an inquisitorial, proceeding. The parties, not the court, establish the record and the court is limited by the record created. The statutory command to determine fair value is a command to do so in a judicial proceeding, with the powers and constraints such a proceeding entails. Accepting that the expert testimony has been so structured as to largely foreclose the court from accepting parts of one DCF model and sections of the other, it follows that the court must decide which of the two principal experts has the greater claim overall to have correctly estimated the intrinsic value of Technicolor stock at the time of the merger. Having decided that question, it will be open to me to critically review the details of that expert's opinion in order to determine if the record will permit, and judicial judgment require, modification of any inputs in that model. What the record will not permit is either a completely independent judicially created DCF model or a pastiche composed of bits of one model and pieces of the other.

"For good reasons aside from technical competence, one might be disinclined to do so. Simply to accept one expert's view or the other would have a significant institutional or precedential advantage. The DCF model typically can generate a wide range of estimates. In the world of real transactions (capital budgeting decisions for example) the hypothetical, future-oriented, nature of the model is not thought fatal to the DCF technique because those employing it typically have an intense personal interest in having the best estimates and assumptions used as inputs. In the litigation context use of the model does not have that built-in protection. On the contrary, particularly if the court will ultimately reject both parties DCF analysis and do its own, the incentive of the contending parties is to arrive at estimates of value that are at the outer margins of plausibility—that essentially define a bargaining range. If it is understood that the court will or is likely to accept the whole of one witness's testimony or the other, incentives will be modified. While the incentives of the real world applications of the DCF model will not be replicated, at least the parties will have incentives to make their estimate of value appear most reasonable. This would tend to narrow the range of estimates, which would unquestionably be a benefit to the process." *

Chancellor Allen dealt with the two contrasting DCF models presented by the parties' experts as follows, pp. 66–77:

"The most basic conceptual difference in the two DCF models used is this: Professor Rappaport assumes (and Mr. Torkelsen does not) that for every company its particular set of comparative advantages estab-

---

* [Ed. Note] This paragraph appears as the court's footnote.

lish, as of any moment, a future period of some greater or lesser length during which it will be able to earn rates of return that exceed its cost of capital. Beyond that point, the company (as of the present moment of valuation) can expect to earn no returns in excess of its cost of capital and therefore, beyond that point, no additional shareholder value will be created. Professor Rappaport calls this period during which a company's net returns can be predicted to exceed its costs of capital, the company's 'value growth duration,' which is a coined term. * * * [This] is an application of elementary notions of neo-classical economics: profits above the cost of capital in an industry will attract competitors, who will over some time period drive returns down to the point at which returns equal the cost of capital. At that equilibrium point no new competition will be attracted into the field. The leading finance text includes a reference to this concept of a future period beyond which there is no further value created. See R. Brealey & S. Myers, Principles of Corporate Finance (3d ed. 1988) at 65–66. The existence of such a point in time does not mean that there is no value attributed to the period beyond that point, but rather that there is no further value growth.

"I accept as sound (as a 'technique * * * generally considered acceptable in the financial community' Weinberger at 713) the methodology of Professor Rappaport. See, e.g., In Re Pullman Constr. Indus., 107 Bankr. 909 (Bankr.N.D.Ill.1989). [But its] distinctive feature— forecasting net cash flows for a 'value growth duration' ('VGD') rather than a defined period (often 5 years)—is, however, difficult to apply here. There were no firms closely comparable to Technicolor in order to estimate VGD with confidence (in my opinion). * * *

"In the final analysis, however, Professor Rappaport used a period to project Technicolor's most important net cash flows similar to that employed by Mr. Torkelsen (5 years). Therefore, the practical significance of this conceptual difference between the DCF model used by Rappaport and that used by Torkelsen is in connection with what each does with cash flows at the end of the projection period, that is how each creates the terminal or residual value component of his DCF analysis. To estimate residual value Rappaport capitalizes a constant (last forecasted year) cash flow; he assumes no new value creation beyond the forecast period (but nevertheless much of his total value is attributed to the residual value). In creating his estimation of residual value Torkelsen, on the other hand, increases the last forecasted year's net cash flows by 5% each year (for inflation) into infinity, before capitalizing those flows. * * *

"This 5% growth assumption adds very substantial additional value to the discounted present value of a share of Technicolor stock. That assumption alone contributes $16.56 in per share value (making all other assumptions PVR makes). * * *

* * *

"Neither approach can be said to be wrong as a matter of logic nor * * * is either methodology inconsistent with the record. Thus, methodology cannot be decisive on choice of the most dependable of the two opinions. The impacts of methodological differences are only expressed through specific application, which of course involves substantive assumptions about the business and its future. Thus, the financial impact of the most important methodological difference—the 5% growing cash flow—is itself derivative from the cash flows generated in the last year. That difference at $16.56 a share of present value is huge in this context, but it would be larger still, or smaller, if the net cash flows projected were different. That significant $16.56 per share difference is also affected by the discount rate.

"Therefore, while I believe it is incumbent upon the court to examine the experts' methods, where as here those methods each present a reasonable approach recognized in the world of financial analysis, other factors, such as the projection of future cash flows, the cost of capital and sources of corroboration are necessary in order to make the overall assessment concerning which opinion is more likely to estimate fair value as defined in Section 262.

* * *

"The cost of capital supplies the discount rate to reduce projected future cash flows to present value. The cost of capital is a freestanding, interchangeable component of a DCF model. It also allows room for judicial judgment to a greater extent than the record in this case permits in other areas of the DCF models.

* * *

"Professor Rappaport used the Capital Asset Pricing Model (CAPM) to estimate Technicolor's costs of capital as of January 24, 1983. That model estimates the cost of company debt (on an after tax basis for a company expected to be able to utilize the tax deductibility of interest payments) by estimating the expected future cost of borrowing; it estimates the future cost of equity through a multi-factor equation and then proportionately weighs and combines the cost of equity and the cost of debt to determine a cost of capital.

"The CAPM is used widely (and by all experts in this case) to estimate a firm's cost of equity capital. It does this by attempting to identify a risk-free rate for money and to identify a risk premium that would be demanded for investment in the particular enterprise in issue. In the CAPM model the riskless rate is typically derived from government treasury obligations. For a traded security the market risk premium is derived in two steps. First a market risk premium is calculated. It is the excess of the expected rate of return for a representative stock index (such as the Standard & Poor 500 or all NYSE companies) over the riskless rate. Next the individual company's 'systematic risk'—that is the nondiversified risk associated with the economy as a whole as it affects this firm—is estimated. This second element of the risk premium is, in the CAPM, represented by a coefficient (beta) that measures the relative volatility of the subject firm's stock price relative to the movement of the market generally.

The higher that coefficient (i.e., the higher the beta) the more volatile or risky the stock of the subject company is said to be. Of course, the riskier the investment the higher its costs of capital will be.

"The CAPM * * * cannot, of course, determine a uniquely correct cost of equity. Many judgments go into it. The beta coefficient can be measured in a variety of ways; the index rate of return can be determined pursuant to differing definitions, and adjustments can be made, such as the small capitalization premium, discussed below. But the CAPM methodology is certainly one of the principal 'techniques or methods * * * generally considered acceptable [for estimating the cost of equity capital component of a discounted cash flow modeling] in the financial community * * *.' Weinberger v. UOP, Inc. at 713. See, e.g., Northern Trust Co. v. C.I.R., 87 T.C. 349, 368 (1986).

"In accepting Professor Rappaport's method for estimating Technicolor's costs of capital, I do so mindful of the extent to which it reflects judgments. That the results of the CAPM are in all instances contestable does not mean that as a technique for estimation it is unreliable. It simply means that it may not fairly be regarded as having claims to validity independent of the judgments made in applying it.

"With respect to the cost of capital aspect of the discounted cash flow methodology (in distinction to the projection of net cash flows and, in most respects, the terminal value) the record does permit the court to evaluate some of the variables, used in that model chosen as the most reasonable of the two (i.e., Professor Rappaport's) and to adjust the cost of capital accordingly. I do so with respect to two elements of Professor Rappaport's determination of costs of equity for the various Technicolor divisions. These businesses were all (excepting One Hour Photo, Consumer Photo Processing and Standard Manufacturing) assigned a cost of equity of 22.7% and a weighted average cost of capital of 20.4%. The remaining businesses were assigned a cost of equity of 20.4% and a weighted average cost of capital of 17.3%.

"In fixing the 22.7% cost of equity for film processing and other businesses Professor Rappaport employed a 1.7 beta which was an estimate published by Merrill Lynch, a reputable source for December 1982. That figure seems intuitively high for a company with relatively stable cash flows. Intuition aside, however, it plainly was affected to some extent by the striking volatility in Technicolor's stock during the period surrounding the announcement of [a] proposal to acquire Technicolor for $23 per share. Technicolor stock rapidly shot up to the $23 level from a range of $9 to $12 in which it traded for all of September and the first week of October. Technicolor stock was thus a great deal more volatile than the market during this period. Applying the same measure of risk—the Merrill Lynch published beta—for September yields a significantly different beta measurement: 1.27. Looking at other evidence with respect to Technicolor betas I conclude that 1.27 is a more reasonable estimate of Technicolor's stock beta for purposes of calculating its cost of capital on January 24, 1983, than 1.7, even though that latter figure represents a December 1982 estimation.

"The second particular in which the record permits and my judgment with respect to weight of evidence requires a modification of Mr. Rappaport's cost of capital calculation relates to the so-called small capitalization effect or premium. This refers to an unexplained inability of the capital asset pricing model to replicate with complete accuracy the historic returns of stocks with the same historic betas. The empirical data show that there is a recurring premium paid by small capitalization companies. This phenomena was first noted in 1981 and has been confirmed. The greatest part of the additional return for small cap companies appears to occur in January stock prices. No theory satisfactorily explaining the phenomena has been generally accepted.

"Professor Rappaport classifies Technicolor as a small capitalization company and expressed the view that its cost of equity would include a 4% premium over that generated by the CAPM.

"The question whether the premium can be justified in this instance is difficult because of the inability of academic financial economists to generate an accepted theory of the phenomena. While Technicolor may qualify as a small cap company, the particulars of its situation are different from many small cap companies. It was an old, not a new company. It existed in a relatively stable industry—motion picture film processing. That industry was an oligopoly and Technicolor was a leader. It had 'brand name' identification. Do these distinctive characteristics that Technicolor had in common with many giant capitalization companies, matter at all in terms of the 'small cap' anomaly? One cannot say. Yet the impact of a 4% increase in the cost of equity (yielding a 3.44% increase in the cost of capital of the Film Processing & Videocassette divisions) would be material to the value of the company and the appraisal value of a share. In these circumstances, I cannot conclude that it has been persuasively shown that the statutory fair value of Technicolor stock would more likely result from the inclusion of a small capitalization premium than from its exclusion. In this circumstance, I conclude it should not be considered.

"Thus, in summary, I find Professor Rappaport's calculation of a cost of capital follows an accepted technique for evaluating the cost of capital; it employs that technique in a reasonable way and, except for the two particulars noted above, in a way that is deserving of adoption by the court. Applying these adjustments they lead to a cost capital of 15.28% for the main part of Technicolor's cash flow and 14.13% for the One Hour Photo related cash flows."

See also In re Shell Oil Co., 607 A.2d 1213 (Del.1992); Harris v. Rapid–American Corp., 1990 WL 146488 (Del.Ch.1990); In re Radiology Assoc., Inc., 611 A.2d 485 (Del.Ch.1991).

NOTE: THE DEBATE OVER APPRAISAL RIGHTS

1. *The Purpose of the Appraisal Remedy.*

Compare the following statements on the wisdom of continuing or extending appraisal rights to shareholders in publicly held corporations:

(a) "Permissions and protections have a way of getting scrambled in corporation law. We are schooled today to view the special statutory provisions of sales of all assets as protections to shareholders, designed to temper management's centralized control of so important a transaction. Historically, however, these sections were put into the corporation acts in order to soften the rigor of the judicial rule which protected the shareholder by requiring unanimous shareholder approval for such a sale. Before the statutory provisions on sales of assets, the single dissenter could enjoin the transaction; after the statute, the management could nearly always muster the required majority vote * * *.

"The early supporters of the appraisal remedy may not have forseen that its availability would help to free corporate managements (the 'majority') from some of the risk of injunction. Those who have proposed the remedy or its extension have always argued their concern for the lot of the dissident minority. But this may have been just good politics, and some may have been playing for the backlash effect. * * *

"How might we go about developing a sensible body of law providing for the appraisal remedy?

"We should begin by scrapping (to the extent that one ever can) all of our past thinking about the topic. It is infected with its conceptual and irrelevant ancestry. Evolution in this case will not work. We should start over.

"The second step is to reset the problem into functional economic terms. The appraisal remedy is of virtually no economic advantage to the usual shareholder except in highly specialized situations. The remedy is, or can be, a substantial nuisance to the remaining shareholders and to the enterprise as a whole. Enterprises should not be required to stay liquid to stave off appraisal claims. Similarly, the need of the enterprise to make rapid decisions should be kept firmly in mind. These considerations counsel against any extension of the appraisal device except in cases of extreme and extraordinary need.

"It may well be that we do not need the appraisal remedy for shareholders at all. It is clear beyond question that shareholders as a lot have little or no real concern with the kinds of transactions—the 'fundamental' transactions—to which the appraisal remedy has been linked in the past. It is commonplace to observe that the modern shareholder is a kind of investor and does not think of himself as or act like an 'owner.' He hires his capital out to the managers and they run it for him; how they do it is their business, not his, and he always votes 'yes' on the proxy * * *. Shareholders have been cheerfully carrying all kinds of real economic risks without the benefit of an appraisal remedy. When the appraisal remedy has been available to them, it has been much like finding an Irish Sweepstakes ticket—not earned, unrelated to their work, usually worth nothing, and once in a great while, a windfall. * * *

"If we are to have the remedy at all, the key point on which it should turn is the presence or absence of a market. If the remedy has any function, it is to provide a way for an unhappy investor to get out when he has no other feasible way to get out. The remedy should not be thought of as a punishment for management, and triggering transactions should not be selected on the theory that they are 'fundamental' or that they are immoral. Neither should sheer economic risk of loss be sufficient justification for the remedy. Appraisal should be considered an economic substitute for the stock exchange and its use should be limited to situations in which the exchange, or some kind of a reasonable market, is not available * * *." Manning, The Shareholder's Appraisal Remedy: An Essay for Frank Coker, 72 Yale L.J. 223, 228–229, 260–261 (1962).

(b) "The thrust of Dean Manning's critique of the appraisal right is twofold: that it ill-serves the shareholder who uses it, and ill-serves the corporation against which it is asserted.[236] On the shareholder side Manning notes that the procedure the shareholder must follow is highly technical, long, and expensive; that if the corporation's stock is publicly traded, the courts will not go beyond an inquiry into market price (a proposition which the cases do not fully support), while if it is not publicly traded the amount of the award is unpredictable; and that when the award is finally made it will be taxable, whereas the transaction dissented from may very well have produced tax-free benefits to the shareholder. Generally speaking, these criticisms are accurate, although many of them are equally applicable to many other legal rights which must be asserted through litigation. However they are hardly dispositive, because in themselves they indicate not that the remedy is unsound, but merely that its usefulness, like the usefulness of all legal rights, may be limited by the boundaries of reality and legislative drafting.

"But when he turns to the effect of the appraisal right on the corporation, Manning does conjure up problems intended to bring the very soundness of the right into question. First, he argues that the assertion of appraisal rights may wipe out the enterprise.

'Even a relatively modest number of shareholders claiming the appraisal remedy may constitute a severe economic threat to the corporate enterprise. * * * If some shareholders go the appraisal road, a sudden and largely unpredictable drain is imposed upon the corporation's cash position. This demand for a cash pay-out to

---

236. Manning actually begins his critique with another point—that the presence of the appraisal remedy has often influenced the courts to cut down the availability, or even preclude the granting, of other types of relief, particularly injunctive relief based on unfairness. The true extent of this tendency is very difficult to determine, see Vorenberg, Exclusiveness of the Dissenting Stockholder's Appraisal Right, 77 Harv.L.Rev. 1189 (1964), but in any event the problem is not intrinsic to the appraisal remedy and is therefore legislatively remediable. Cf. Lattin, A Reappraisal of Appraisal Statutes, 38 Mich. L.Rev. 1165 (1940).

shareholders often comes at a time when the enterprise is in need of every liquid dollar it can put its hands on.

'Some kind of corporate surgery is going on; the enterprise is much more apt to be in need of a blood transfusion than a leeching. * * * [T]he period following the closing will likely be a period of intense activity as a general reshuffling takes place in the administrative, productive, and distributional arrangements of the combined enterprise. The management hopes that in time these steps will prove economic; but in the short run many of them will require a cash in-put.'

The gravity of the 'threat to the corporate enterprise' seems highly exaggerated. No evidence is adduced that corporations involved in mergers are 'in need of a blood transfusion,' and my own observation has been that most mergers involve two perfectly healthy enterprises. Even then, of course, there may be a short-run cash output, but it is unlikely to be material in terms of cash resources. Furthermore, in considering the appraisal right from the shareholder's point of view, Manning stresses that the procedure by which the right must be asserted is a long and weary one. If that is so, then by the time a dissenter is actually paid off the short-run period of adjustment will be far behind.

"Second, Manning argues that the payments made to dissenters may lead creditors to start a run on the corporation's treasury.

" * * * Again, no evidence is adduced, and again my own observation has been that while the 'trade creditors, suppliers, [and] banks' are indeed at the door following a merger, they are kneeling, not pounding. Their object is not to get out, but to get in—at best, to garner all the business of the reconstituted enterprise, at worst, to retain the business they had. Furthermore, the time when payment must actually be made to dissenting shareholders will, as Manning's earlier point emphasizes, lie in the dim, distant future.

* * *

" * * * [E]ven assuming that the market fairly reflects the value of the stock in question in its normal operations, remitting a dissenting shareholder to the market will fail to adequately protect him where (1) his block is so large that the mere act of selling the block will depress the market—and it has already been seen that large blocks are common even in stock listed on the New York Stock Exchange—or (2) the very effect of the structural change, when it is announced, is to depress the market price, because the change is an ill-considered one. In other words, even in a well-functioning market, remitting the dissenting shareholder to the market place will be unsatisfactory in just those cases where the shareholder would seem most entitled to appraisal— where his shareholding is a large one, so that his expectations are likely to be oriented around the enterprise rather than the market, or where the structural change is ill-considered, so that the market price after the change is announced is lower than that prevailing before the announcement.

"A final problem with eliminating appraisal rights in publicly held corporations is that in such corporations the appraisal right not only serves the function of permitting shareholders to withdraw under certain circumstances at a fair price, but also serves as a check on management. Granted that a certain proportion of shareholders in publicly held corporations will vote in favor of any management proposal, no matter how ill-conceived, and granted that management is not necessarily either highly skilled or disinterested in the making of structural changes, it may be appropriate to structure the decision-making process in publicly held corporations so that more than a bare majority or even a two-thirds majority is needed to carry management's decision. As Professor Folk has pointed out:

> '[I]t is important to maintain some internal or external control to offset the power of the directors, unless one assumes that directors, especially when backed by a shareholder majority, should have unrestrained discretion. Appraisal rights * * * have, in the past, served as a countervailing power to force the insiders to tailor their plans to minimize the number of dissenters by getting the best deal possible. A high vote requirement (including a class vote) plays the same sort of role. When either weapon is removed, the insiders lack the real self-interest to fashion a plan acceptable to a sufficient number of shareholders. [Folk, De Facto Merger In Delaware, 49 Va.L.Rev. 1261, 1293 (1963)]'

"It has already been seen that the appraisal right presents many difficulties from the shareholder's perspective: It is always technical; it may be expensive; it is uncertain in result, and, in the case of a publicly held corporation, is unlikely to produce a better result than could have been obtained on the market; and the ultimate award is taxable. It is, in short, a remedy of desperation—generally speaking, no shareholder in a publicly held corporation who is in his right mind will invoke the appraisal right unless he feels that the change from which he dissents is shockingly improvident and that the fair value of his shares before the change will far exceed the value of his shares after the change. But may not the existence of just such a right—a switch which will be pulled only in case of emergency—be desirable in connection with transactions of the utmost gravity, in which self-interest and lack of investment skills may seriously obscure management's vision?

"In short, while it would not be irrational to eliminate appraisal rights as to shares which are traded under conditions which are likely to insure the existence of a continuous and relatively deep market, it seems more advisable to retain the appraisal right even in such cases, partly to protect the fair expectations of those shareholders whose legitimate expectations center on the enterprise rather than on the market, and partly to serve as a well-designed emergency switch to check management improvidence." Eisenberg, The Legal Roles of Shareholders and Management in Modern Corporate Decision Making, 57 Calif.L.Rev. 1, 72–74, 84–86 (1969).

(c) Developing themes touched upon by Professor Eisenberg, Professor Fischel, in The Appraisal Remedy in Corporate Law, 1983 American Bar Foundation Research Journal 875, suggests that the appraisal right is best understood as a component of the contract for which a rational investor in stock would bargain, ex ante. So viewed, that right benefits all stockholders, not merely dissenters, because it solves the prisoners' dilemma created for dispersed stockholders when they are confronted with the opportunity to vote on a merger proposal, and pro tanto it acts as a restraint on management or majorities in trading off individual investors' entitlements in the course of negotiating the merger.

On a similar tack, Professors Kanda and Levmore, in The Appraisal Remedy and Goals of Corporate Law, 32 U.C.L.A.L.Rev. 429 (1985), explore a variety of goals that the appraisal remedy might serve. For the most part, they examine appraisal as a mechanism to help stockholders obtain accountability from, and monitor the behavior of, management and insiders beset with temptations to exploit outside stockholders—both on the occasion of merger and at earlier and, perhaps, later times. Kanda and Levmore also suggest that the appraisal remedy may protect the shareholders' inframarginal valuations of the stock. That is, it reflects an understanding that shareholders do not all value their share identically, and that the marginal, or market price understates their average valuation of the shares. This approach leads to an intractable valuation problem, as Kanda and Levmore point out. Individual shareholders' subjective valuations cannot be objectively determined. Therefore, an appraisal statute can protect inframarginality goals only in an inexact way, with rules of thumb that block transactions that undersell shares at the market price. For further discussion of inframarginality and appraisal rights, see Stout, Are Takeover Premiums Really Premiums? Market Price, Fair Value, and Corporate Law, 99 Yale L.J. 1235, 1284–1295 (1990).

2. *Statutory Reform.*

If the principal role of the appraisal remedy is to restrict or discourage management's slack or acceptance of side payments in negotiating mergers, is it an effective mechanism for the performance of that function? The dissenter in an appraisal proceeding is appropriately paid his fair value from the assets of the corporation, not from those of its management or its merger partner. What is the likely impact on managerial efforts (in negotiating a merger) to maximize stockholder returns or to refrain from taking side payments of (a) the fact that the corporation is the only source of payment of fair value in an appraisal proceeding, (b) the substantive provisions of most appraisal statutes [e] that exclude from the "fair value" to which the dissenter is entitled any of the gains from the merger, and (c) the procedural provisions of most appraisal statutes that create impediments to the

---

e. But see RMBCA § 13.01(3) (and Official Comment thereon suggesting "equitable" adjustment in the case of "squeeze- outs" of dissenters); Delaware after UOP v. Weinberger, infra p. 766; New York BCL § 623(h)(4), infra Appendix G.

dissenter's successful exercise of appraisal rights by way of pitfalls on an intricate and easily lost path to judicial relief? (See Kaplan, Problems in the Acquisition of Shares of Dissenting Minorities, 34 B.U.L.Rev. 291 (1954).) *

What is the likely effect on the protective value of the appraisal remedy of the provisions of Sections 80 and 81 of the old Model Act (substantially embodied in Chapter 13 of the Revised Model Act) which have been explained as follows in A Report of the Committee on Corporate Laws of the ABA Section of Corporation, Banking and Business Law, to alter §§ 73, 74, 80 and 81 of the Model Act (33 Business Lawyer 2592–2593 (1978))?

* * * [Section 80] and section 81 deal with one of the classic tensions in corporation law—the tension between the desire of the company leadership to enter new fields, acquire new enterprises, and rearrange investor rights, and the desire of investors to adhere to the rights and the risks on the basis of which they invested. Most contemporary corporation codes in the United States attempt to resolve this tension through a combination of two devices. On the one hand, the majority is given an almost unlimited power to change the nature and shape of the enterprise and the rights of its members. On the other hand, the members who dissent from changes are given a right to withdraw their investment at a fair valuation.

This pattern of accommodation has been sharply criticized from two directions. From the viewpoint of dissident investors, it is criticized for providing little help to the ordinary investor because its technicalities make its use difficult, expensive and risky. From the viewpoint of the corporate leadership, it is criticized because it fails to protect the corporation from suits on grounds of unfairness or fraud toward dissenting shareholders, and from demands that are motivated by the hope of a nuisance settlement, or by fanciful conceptions of value.

The Committee acknowledges that dissenters' rights as defined in present statutes sometimes work unfairly and inefficiently, but believes that in the majority of cases they lead to a satisfactory solution of conflicting interests. The provisions of sections 80 and 81 are designed to increase the frequency with which dissenters' rights lead to economical and satisfying solutions, and to decrease the frequency with which they lead to delay, expense and dissatisfaction. They seek this aim primarily by motivating the parties to settle their differences in private negotiations, without resort to judicial appraisal proceedings.

---

* E.g., the requirements of (a) being a record owner rather than a beneficial owner, (b) voting against the merger or simply not voting for it, (c) giving notice prior to the meeting or within a stated period after the meeting or after the effective date of the merger or after the filing date of the merger papers, or after the corporation gives notice (see e.g., Schneyer v. Shenan-doah Oil Corp., 316 A.2d 570 (Del.Ch.1974)), and (d) satisfying other prevalent procedural conditions to get into court. In addition, the dissenters must generally encounter considerable delay in receipt of payment (but cf. RMBCA, § 13.25) and uncertainty about the payment of attorneys' fees (compare Delaware Corporation Law, § 262(h) with RMBCA § 13.31).

This approach involves a substantial change in the prevailing concept of the dissenter's right. The right has sometimes been characterized as the "appraisal right," implying that its object is to provide each dissenter with a judicial appraisal. In the Committee's view, the objective should be that each dissenter would receive a fair payment without the formality of judicial appraisal, which involves delays and uncertainties, and legal expenses which are prohibitive to small investors. Appraisal is the ultimate sanction to be invoked only when the parties fail to reach reasonable terms of settlement. In line with this conception, the accompanying comments studiously avoid the term, "appraisal right," and refer rather to "dissenters' rights to obtain payment for their shares," or more colloquially to the "cashout right."

These sections contain several devices designed to increase the incentive to settle. The corporation is required to pay promptly on effectuation of the proposed corporate action, without waiting for a final agreement on value. If the dissenter is not satisfied with the preliminary payment, he must designate the amount which he will accept in full settlement. Either party who holds to an arbitrary or vexatious position may be required to pay part or all of the other's attorneys' fees. A minor exception to the rule of immediate payment is made for shares purchased after the proposed corporate action was announced.

Assertion of dissenters' rights has been procedurally eased. The corporation must notify dissenters of their rights at each stage of the procedure, and must supply financial statements for the dissenters' enlightenment.

While the difficulty of asserting dissenters' rights is diminished, provisions have been inserted to reduce the opportunities for assertion of dissenters' rights for speculative or obstructionist purposes. The right to receive immediate payment is limited to dissenters who purchased before the corporation announced the proposed corporate action. A dissenter who acts vexatiously, arbitrarily, or not in good faith may be assessed with part or all of the corporation's counsel fees and other expenses.

In one important respect, the accompanying proposals would reduce the area of application of dissenters' rights. Under present law, mergers give rise to dissenters' rights without regard to the size of the companies involved. If a billion-dollar automobile company were to absorb by merger a million-dollar mock-up shop (increasing the automobile company's assets by $1/10$ of one percent), dissenting shareholders of the auto company would suddenly have a right to demand payment of the appraised value of their shares. The accompanying proposal would deny this right to the dissenters of the larger company when the increase in its shares amounts to no more than 20 percent. The shareholders of the smaller company would have dissenters' rights in every case, since the change in their status is always substantial.

In some other respects, the accompanying amendments broaden the area of corporate events to which dissenters' rights attach. Amendments which adversely affect shareholders' rights by diminished voting, preemptive or preferred dividend rights are added to the triggers of dissenters' rights.

The accompanying proposals as a whole are designed to benefit both minority shareholders and controlling shareholders. Minority shareholders benefit because the assertion of their rights is made easier, and penalties are introduced for vexatious obstruction by corporate management. Controlling shareholders benefit directly and indirectly. They benefit directly by the added incentives for dissenters to settle without a judicial appraisal. They benefit indirectly because the provision of an adequate appraisal right diminishes the justification for courts to enjoin or set aside corporate changes because of the absence of an "adequate remedy at law," or because the corporate action "would operate as a fraud."

SECTION D. FAIRNESS AND DISCLOSURE
INTRODUCTION

Ideally, the management or controllers of each of the corporate parties to a merger bargain for a maximum enhancement of share values. It is, of course, possible that such maximization will not materialize because of errors in the bargaining process, incompetence of the bargainers or bargaining disadvantages of the one against the other. Arguably, failures to maximize resulting from such circumstances must be accepted, at least if the statutorily specified majority of the stockholders knowingly vote to support the managerial decision to merge.

Apart from the danger of a bad bargain, there may also, and perhaps often, be a lack of identity of interest between those doing the "bargaining" and the public stockholders. This can be seen most easily in a case like Farris v. Glen Alden, supra. There, List, the "acquiring company," was in control of Glen Alden at the time the merger between the two took place; the List directors effectively sat on both sides of the bargaining table. As a result, the exchange rate for the publicly owned shares of Glen Alden was unilaterally determined by List's management rather than through arm's length negotiation. To be sure, unilateral decision was unavoidable once List had obtained control and could not of itself constitute a violation of fiduciary duty. But given the evident, and indeed quite natural, tendency of the List directors to view their obligation to List and its stockholders as primary, and to regard Glen Alden's public stockholders as "outsiders," the value placed on the latter's interest might be expected to be as low as reasonable pessimism would allow.

In this context the possibility that the public stockholders may be treated unfairly is evident, and it should not be surprising to find that a merger between one corporation and another that it controls is very often challenged by public stockholders of the latter. The question that confronts the courts in these cases is—what constitutes "fair treatment" of the public or outside investors of the subsidiary? This issue continues to be important because of the persistence of partial takeovers (through cash tender offer or other means) of public companies by other firms. Typically, the takeover process begins with a corporation's acquiring a controlling, but not a 100% interest, in what is then the target company. In some instances partial ownership is merely a transitory step towards full ownership and is followed fairly promptly by merger of the new subsidiary into the acquiring company. In others the status of parent and subsidiary is preserved for an extended period: the parent operates the subsidiary as such through a board of directors composed of its own nominees, but then ultimately elects to merge the subsidiary into itself, thereby obtaining direct ownership of all the subsidiary's assets.

Under either circumstance, the public stockholders of the merging subsidiary receive stock or other securities of the parent, or cash, for their minority shares. Once again, given the parent's practical power to impose terms on the subsidiary, the question that arises is whether the treatment of the minority stockholders is "fair."

This fairness question is almost exclusively a feature of mergers between controlling and controlled corporations, and the cases that follow are almost all of that sort. By contrast, where merger takes place between companies that are unrelated—neither having representation on the board of the other (Hariton v. Arco Electronics, supra, is an example)—the expectation is that each side will bargain exclusively in its own interest, that the outcome will truly be an arm's length deal, and that fiduciary problems of the kind that afflict related-party dealings will not arise. Even here, however, the facts may well be otherwise in many cases. The target company's managers possess an economic "power," after all, since they alone have access to the proxy machinery and their approval is required before the acquiring company's merger proposal can be placed before the target company's stockholders. It would not be altogether surprising to learn that at least some managers will insist upon a personal consideration—long-term employment contracts, stock options or the like—before consenting to approve the merger, in which event the purchase price that is finally communicated to the stockholders may well be less than all they are entitled to. More than a hint of this appears in the court's opinion in Singer v. Magnavox, 380 A.2d 969 (Del.1977) (in which a target's management that was "shocked at the inadequacy of" an $8 per share bid was able soon thereafter to agree upon a $9 per share price and employment contracts) and it is of course the heart of the dispute in Rosenfeld v. Black, infra. Nevertheless, decided cases on the subject of "side-payments" are few. The reason may reside in the difficulty of detection; in effect, quantitative proof of wrongdoing on the part of individual managers—which is what is needed if fiduciary rules are to be enforced directly in these circumstances—is virtually unattainable.

One form of legal restraint which might be imposed to prevent inequality between outside or public stockholders on the one hand, and inside or controlling stockholders, on the other, would be to require equal treatment in *form.* All stockholders in the absorbed firm would be entitled to receive the same form of participation in the continuing enterprise; none would be required to accept a different form of pay-out (e.g., cash or non-participating senior securities) than the others. That form of restraint has been rejected by most state legislatures, deliberately in the short form merger legislation and apparently no less explicitly in long form merger statutes. This, in turn, has posed for the courts the question how to resolve any incompatibility between what some would see as the stockholders' right to remain stockholders and the legislation which apparently permits insiders to *force* the outsiders out of the firm by giving them a cash (or non-participating senior security) pay-out. Can—or should—such legislation be interpreted narrowly to permit freeze-outs only when some economically tolerable function is served by the transaction, or is the legislation a carte blanche? If the former, how should courts define an economically tolerable function and determine whether it is being served, and on whom should the burden of proof be placed to demonstrate that such a function exists and could not be as well performed by procedures which do not freeze out the outside stockholders?

In any event, even if the disparate formal treatment of insiders and outsiders is to be tolerated, should restraints of "fairness" with respect to the substance of the exchange be imposed upon the essentially self-dealing transaction? And if a test of "fairness" is the appropriate restriction to impose upon mergers, either because of a systematic divergence of interest between management and stockholders with respect to the merger decision or because of self-dealing where one of the parties to the merger controls the other, what criteria should determine fairness, and what ought to be the procedural requirements for testing compliance with those criteria?

1. FREEZE–OUTS: "BUSINESS PURPOSE" AND THE APPRAISAL REMEDY

INTRODUCTORY NOTE

Managers and controlling stockholders may on occasion use corporate cash to repurchase stock in order to "take the corporation private," or freeze-out the public stockholders. Somewhat different considerations affect the transaction and assessment of its propriety when managers who own little stock are the beneficiaries, as in management buy-out cases, than when controlling shareholders are the beneficiaries. In the former case, traditional fiduciary-agency notions are involved— collective assets are being diverted by agents to themselves, effectively unilaterally, with no offsetting benefit to stockholders other than a "fair" price—i.e., a price that presumably gives stockholders the fairly derived present value of their stock, and produces no present gain for the management-agent, or possibly a "fair" sharing of any gain. In the latter case, the relevant fiduciary constraints import horizontal equity—i.e., equality of treatment for all members of the class of stockholders—more than restrictions on an agent dealing with his principal's property.

Possibly differing likelihoods of social gain impel different protective rules for public stockholders in the one case than in the other. In the former case, the social gain is said to result from the added incentive to management by reason of its acquisition of substantial ownership interest and the more effective monitoring of management by a smaller group of sophisticated creditor-investors who may also be equity participants.[f] The latter case, at least where the controller is a parent corporation, is likely to involve termination of a structure which tempts the parent to overreach its subsidiary in intercompany transactions. In that circumstance the freeze-out is said to be justified by both efficiency reasons (for the parent to avoid the cost of the protective veneer to prevent successful challenges to intercompany transactions) and equitable considerations (to avoid the danger to minority stockholders of continuous over-reaching in such transactions).

There is vast literature on the "freeze-out" in publicly held corporations and the variation of it known as "going private." Some of the literature (such as Lipton and Steinberger, Take–Overs and Freeze–Outs (1986 rev.) is intensely "practical." Other writing is more speculative. See e.g., Borden, Going Private—Old Tort, New Tort or No Tort?, 49 N.Y.U.L.Rev. 987 (1974); Greene, Corporate Freeze-out Mergers: A Proposed Analysis, 28 Stan.L.Rev. 487 (1976); Brudney & Chirelstein, A Restatement of Corporate Freezeouts, 87 Yale L.J. 1354 (1978); Note, 84 Yale L.J. 903 (1975); Carney, Fundamental Corporate Changes, Minority Shareholders and Business Purposes, 1980 ABF Research Journal 69; Jensen, Agency Costs of Free Cash Flow, Corporate Finance and Takeovers, 76 Amer.Econ.Rev. (Papers and Proceedings) 323 (1986); Thompson, Squeeze-out Mergers and the "New" Appraisal Remedy, 62 Wash. U.L.Q. 415 (1984); Weiss, The Law of Take Out Mergers: A Historical Perspective, 56 N.Y.U.L.Rev. 624 (1981); Oesterle and Norberg, Management Buyouts: Creating or Appropriating Shareholder Wealth? 41 Vand.L.Rev. 207 (1988); Hazen, Management Buyouts and Governance Paradigms, 25 Wake Forest L.Rev. 1 (1990); De Mott, Puzzles and Parables: Defining Good Faith in the MBO Context, 25 Wake Forest L.Rev. 15 (1990); Sommer, "Going Private" Seventeen Years Later, 70 Wash.U.L.Q. 571 (1992).

f. See p. 744 infra. If "efficiency" is enhanced by such a "private" capital structure, the question arises—how to tell when it is "efficient" for a corporation so capitalized to "go public" once more, and whether any mechanism other than the market is necessary or appropriate to constrain a company from shuttling back and forth from public to private to public, etc.

(A) GOING PRIVATE

COGGINS v. NEW ENGLAND PATRIOTS FOOTBALL CLUB, INC.

Massachusetts Supreme Judicial Court, 1986.
397 Mass. 525, 492 N.E.2d 1112.

LIACOS, J.   On November 18, 1959, William H. Sullivan, Jr. (Sullivan), purchased an American Football League (AFL) franchise for a professional football team.   The team was to be the last of the eight original teams set up to form the AFL (now the American Football Conference of the National Football League).   For the franchise, Sullivan paid $25,000.   Four months later, Sullivan organized a corporation, the American League Professional Football Team of Boston, Inc.   Sullivan contributed his AFL franchise; nine other persons each contributed $25,000.   In return, each of the ten investors received 10,000 shares of voting common stock in the corporation.   Another four months later, in July, 1960, the corporation sold 120,000 shares of nonvoting common stock to the public at $5 a share.

Sullivan had effective control of the corporation from its inception until 1974.   By April, 1974, Sullivan had increased his ownership of shares from 10,000 shares of voting stock to 23,718 shares, and also had acquired 5,499 shares of nonvoting stock.   Nevertheless, in 1974 the other voting stockholders ousted him from the presidency and from operating control of the corporation.   He then began the effort to regain control of the corporation—an effort which culminated in this and other law suits.

In November, 1975, Sullivan succeeded in obtaining ownership or control of all 100,000 of the voting shares, at a price of approximately $102 a share (adjusted cash value), of the corporation, by that time renamed the New England Patriots Football Club, Inc. (Old Patriots).[3] "Upon completion of the purchase, he immediately used his 100% control to vote out the hostile directors, elect a friendly board and arrange his resumption of the presidency and the complete control of the Patriots.   In order to finance this coup, Sullivan borrowed approximately $5,348,000 from the Rhode Island Hospital National Bank and the Lasalle National Bank of Chicago.   As a condition of these loans, Sullivan was to use his best efforts to reorganize the Patriots so that the income of the corporation could be devoted to the payment of these personal loans and the assets of the corporation pledged to secure them.   At this point they were secured by all of the voting shares held by Sullivan.   In order to accomplish in effect the assumption by the corporation of Sullivan's personal obligations, it was necessary, as a matter of corporate law, to eliminate the interest of the nonvoting shares."[4]

3. Sullivan owned 87,320 shares outright, and had entered a contract with his cousin, the defendant Mary H. Sullivan, providing for future purchase of her 12,680 shares and an irrevocable proxy to vote her shares.

4. These findings of fact were made by a Federal District Court judge in the unre-

ported decision of Pavlidis v. New England Patriots Football Club, Inc., No. 76–4240–S (D.Mass. July 22, 1983), aff'd in part and rev'd in part, 737 F.2d 1227 (1st Cir.1984). The trial judge in the case at bar adopted these findings as his own.

On October 20, 1976, Sullivan organized a new corporation called the New Patriots Football Club, Inc. (New Patriots). The board of directors of the Old Patriots and the board of directors of the New Patriots executed an agreement of merger of the two corporations providing that, after the merger, the voting stock of the Old Patriots would be extinguished, the nonvoting stock would be exchanged for cash at the rate of $15 a share, and the name of the New Patriots would be changed to the name formerly used by the Old Patriots.[6] As part of this plan, Sullivan gave the New Patriots his 100,000 voting shares of the Old Patriots in return for 100% of the New Patriots stock.

General Laws c. 156B, § 78(c)(1)(iii), as amended through St.1976, c. 327, required approval of the merger agreement by a majority vote of each class of affected stock. Approval by the voting class, entirely controlled by Sullivan, was assured. The merger was approved by the class of nonvoting stockholders at a special meeting on December 8, 1976.[7] On January 31, 1977, the merger of the New Patriots and the Old Patriots was consummated.

David A. Coggins (Coggins) was the owner of ten shares of nonvoting stock in the Old Patriots. Coggins, a fan of the Patriots from the time of their formation, was serving in Vietnam in 1967 when he purchased the shares through his brother. Over the years, he followed the fortunes of the team, taking special pride in his status as an owner.[8] When he heard of the proposed merger, Coggins was upset that he could be forced to sell. Coggins voted against the merger and commenced this suit on behalf of those stockholders, who, like himself, believed the transaction to be unfair and illegal. A judge of the Superior Court certified the class as "stockholders of New England Patriots Football Club, Inc. who have voted against the merger * * *

---

6. Additional findings as to the purpose of this merger made by the Federal judge, as adopted by the trial judge, are: "Purported reasons for the merger [were] stated in the [proxy materials]. Three reasons are given: (1) the policy of the [National Football League] to discourage public ownership of member football teams, (2) the difficulty in reconciling management's obligations to the NFL with its obligations to public stockholders, and (3) the cost and possible revelation of confidential information resulting from the obligations of publicly owned corporations to file reports with various public bodies. * * * I find, however, that while some of the stated reasons may have been useful by-products of the merger, the true reason for the merger was to enable Sullivan to satisfy his $5,348,000 personal obligation to the banks. The merger would not have occurred for the considerations stated as reasons in the Proxy Statement. * * * The Proxy Statement is an artful attempt to minimize the future profitability of the Pa-

triots and to put a wash of corporate respectability over Sullivan's diversion of the corporation's income for his own purposes."

7. On the date of the meeting, 139,800 shares of nonvoting stock were outstanding, held by approximately 2,400 stockholders. The Sullivan family owned 10,826 shares. Of the remaining 128,974, a total of 71,644 voted in favor of the merger, 22,795 did not vote, and 34,535 voted against. The plaintiffs in this case are stockholders of 2,291 of the 34,535 voting against the merger.

Prior to the 1976 amendment of G.L. c. 156B, § 78(c)(1)(iii), that section required a two-thirds vote of approval for a merger from each class of stock. The two-thirds requirement was reinstated in 1981 by St. 1981, c. 298, § 4.

8. It was, in part, the goal of the Old Patriots, in offering stock to the public, to generate loyal fans.

but who have neither turned in their shares nor perfected their appraisal rights * * * [and who] desire only to void the merger."

The trial judge found in favor of the Coggins class but determined that the merger should not be undone. Instead, he ruled that the plaintiffs are entitled to rescissory damages, and he ordered that further hearings be held to determine the amount of damages. After the judge rendered his decision, motions were made to permit intervention by plaintiffs in two related cases, Pavlidis v. New England Patriots Football Club, Inc., 737 F.2d 1227 (1st Cir.1984), and Sarrouf v. New England Patriots Football Club, Inc., post 542 (1986).[9] The trial judge allowed the motion of the *Pavlidis* plaintiffs, and allowed the motion of the *Sarrouf* plaintiffs, but only as to those plaintiffs in the *Sarrouf* action who were not granted relief in that case.

* * *

We conclude that the trial judge was correct in ruling that the merger was illegal and that the plaintiffs have been wronged. Ordinarily, rescission of the merger would be the appropriate remedy. This merger, however, is now nearly ten years old, and, because an effective and orderly rescission of the merger now is not feasible, we remand the case for proceedings to determine the appropriate monetary damages to compensate the plaintiffs. * * *

Scope of judicial review. In deciding this case, we address an important corporate law question: What approach will a Massachusetts court reviewing a cash freeze-out merger employ? This question has been considered by courts in a number of other States. See A.M. Borden, Going Private § 4.09, and cases cited (rev. 1986); 1 M. Lipton and E.H. Steinberger, Takeovers and Freezeouts § 9.05, and cases cited (rev. 1986).

The parties have urged us to consider the views of a court with great experience in such matters, the Supreme Court of Delaware. We note that the Delaware court announced one test in 1977, but recently has changed to another. In Singer v. Magnavox Co., 380 A.2d 969, 980 (Del.1977), the Delaware court established the so-called "business-purpose" test, holding that controlling stockholders violate their fiduciary duties when they "cause a merger to be made for the sole purpose of eliminating a minority on a cash-out basis." Id. at 978. In 1983, Delaware jettisoned the business-purpose test, satisfied that the "fairness" test "long * * * applicable to parent-subsidiary mergers, Sterling v. Mayflower Hotel Corp., Del.Supr., 93 A.2d 107, 109–110 (1952), the expanded appraisal remedy now available to stockholders, and the broad discretion of the Chancellor to fashion such relief as the facts of a

---

9. The plaintiffs in *Pavlidis* "voted to accept the New Patriots' offer of $15.00 per share for their common stock in the [Old] Patriots corporation. They now claim that they were induced to accept this offer by a misleading proxy statement * * * contain[ing] various misrepresentations * * *. They seek to rescind the merger or to receive a higher price per share for the stock they sold." 737 F.2d at 1229–1230. The plaintiffs in *Sarrouf* objected to the merger but sought the statutory remedy of appraisal. See *Sarrouf,* supra at 543; G.L. c. 156B, § 85 (1984 ed.). * * *

given case may dictate" provided sufficient protection to the frozen-out minority.   Weinberger v. UOP, Inc., 457 A.2d 701, 715 (Del.1983).

* * * We note that the "fairness" test to which the Delaware court now has adhered is, as we later show, closely related to the views expressed in our decisions.   Unlike the Delaware court, however, we believe that the "business-purpose" test is an additional useful means under our statutes and case law for examining a transaction in which a controlling stockholder eliminates the minority interest in a corporation.[†] * * * This concept of fair dealing is not limited to close corporations but applies to judicial review of cash freeze-out mergers.   * * *

The defendants argue that judicial review of a merger cannot be invoked by disgruntled stockholders, absent illegal or fraudulent conduct.   They rely on G.L. c. 156B, § 98 (1984 ed.).[12]   In the defendants' view, "the Superior Court's finding of liability was premised solely on the claimed inadequacy of the offering price."   Any dispute over offering price, they urge, must be resolved solely through the statutory remedy of appraisal.

We have held in regard to so called "close corporations" that the statute does not divest the courts of their equitable jurisdiction to assure that the conduct of controlling stockholders does not violate the fiduciary principles governing the relationship between majority and minority stockholders.   * * *

The dangers of self-dealing and abuse of fiduciary duty are greatest in freeze-out situations like the Patriots merger, where a controlling stockholder and corporate director chooses to eliminate public ownership.[14]   It is in these cases that a judge should examine with closest scrutiny the motives and the behavior of the controlling stockholder.   A showing of compliance with statutory procedures is an insufficient substitute for the inquiry of the courts when a minority stockholder claims that the corporate action "will be or is illegal or fraudulent as to him."   G.L. c. 156B, § 98.   Leader v. Hycor, Inc., 395 Mass. 215, 221 (1985) (judicial review may be had of claims of breach of fiduciary duty and unfairness).

---

† [Ed. Note] The "business purpose" requirement is alluded to in Berkowitz v. Power/Mate, infra p. 744 and asserted in Alpert v. 28 Williams Street Corp., 63 N.Y.2d 557, 473 N.E.2d 19 (1984); Perl v. IU International Corp., 607 P.2d 1036 (Hawaii 1980); Dower v. Mosser Industries, Inc., 648 F.2d 183 (3d Cir.1981); Shivers v. Amerco, 670 F.2d 826 (9th Cir.1982); Bryan v. Brock & Blevins Co., Inc., 490 F.2d 563 (5th Cir.1974), cert. denied, 419 U.S. 844 (1974); and Laird v. Interstate Commerce Commission, 691 F.2d 147 (3d Cir.1982) (elimination of household costs of communicating with and otherwise servic-ing public stockholders can constitute valid business purpose).

12. "The enforcement by a stockholder of his right to receive payment for his shares in the manner provided in this chapter shall be an exclusive remedy except that this chapter shall not exclude the right of such stockholder to bring or maintain an appropriate proceeding to obtain relief on the ground that such corporate action will be or is illegal or fraudulent as to him." G.L. c. 156B, § 98.

14. All freeze-out mergers are not alike. See Brudney and Chirelstein, A Restatement of Corporate Freezeouts, 87 Yale L.J. 1354, 1356, and sources cited (1978).

A controlling stockholder who is also a director standing on both sides of the transaction bears the burden of showing that the transaction does not violate fiduciary obligations.

* * *

Factors in judicial review.   The defendants concentrate their arguments on the finding of the Superior Court judge that the offered price for nonvoting shares was inadequate.   They claim that his conclusion that rescissory damages are due these plaintiffs is based wholly on a finding of price inadequacy.   The trial judge, however, considered the totality of circumstances, including the purpose of the merger, the accuracy and adequacy of disclosure in connection with the merger, and the fairness of the price.   The trial judge correctly considered the totality of circumstances, even though he failed to attach adequate significance to each of these factors and to structure them correctly in his analysis.

Judicial scrutiny should begin with recognition of the basic principle that the duty of a corporate director must be to further the legitimate goals of the corporation.   The result of a freeze-out merger is the elimination of public ownership in the corporation.   The controlling faction increases its equity from a majority to 100%, using corporate processes and corporate assets.   The corporate directors who benefit from this transfer of ownership must demonstrate how the legitimate goals of the corporation are furthered.   * * *   Because the danger of abuse of fiduciary duty is especially great in a freeze-out merger, the court must be satisfied that the freeze-out was for the advancement of a legitimate corporate purpose.   If satisfied that elimination of public ownership is in furtherance of a business purpose, the court should then proceed to determine if the transaction was fair by examining the totality of the circumstances.

The plaintiffs here adequately alleged that the merger of the Old Patriots and New Patriots was a freeze-out merger undertaken for no legitimate business purpose, but merely for the personal benefit of Sullivan.   * * *   Consequently, the defendants bear the burden of proving, first, that the merger was for a legitimate business purpose, and, second, that, considering totality of circumstances, it was fair to the minority.

The decision of the Superior Court judge includes a finding that "the defendants have failed to demonstrate that the merger served any valid corporate objective unrelated to the personal interests of the majority shareholders.   It thus appears that the sole reason for the merger was to effectuate a restructuring of the Patriots that would enable the repayment of the [personal] indebtedness incurred by Sullivan * * *." *   The trial judge considered the defendants' claims that

---

* [Ed. Note] In Tanzer v. International General Industries, Inc., 379 A.2d 1121 (Del.1977), the Delaware Supreme Court concluded that the parent's or controlling stockholders' business needs could constitute a sufficient business purpose to permit a cash-out merger.   Other jurisdictions have been even more flexible in finding

the policy of the National Football League (NFL) requiring majority ownership by a single individual or family made it necessary to eliminate public ownership. He found that "the stock ownership of the Patriots as it existed just prior to the merger fully satisfied the rationale underlying the policy as expressed by NFL Commissioner Pete Rozelle. Having acquired 100% control of the voting common stock of the Patriots, Sullivan possessed unquestionable authority to act on behalf of the franchise at League meetings and effectively foreclosed the possible recurrence of the internal management disputes that had existed in 1974. Moreover, as the proxy statement itself notes, the Old Patriots were under no legal compulsion to eliminate public ownership." Likewise, the defendants did not succeed in showing a conflict between the interests of the league owners and the Old Patriots' stockholders. We perceive no error in these findings. They are fully supported by the evidence. Under the approach we set forth above, there is no need to consider further the elements of fairness of a transaction that is not related to a valid corporate purpose.

Remedy. The plaintiffs are entitled to relief. They argue that the appropriate relief is rescission of the merger and restoration of the parties to their positions of 1976. We agree that the normally appropriate remedy for an impermissible freeze-out merger is rescission. Because Massachusetts statutes do not bar a cash freeze-out, however, numerous third parties relied in good faith on the outcome of the merger. The trial judge concluded that the expectations of those parties should not be upset, and so chose to award damages rather than rescission.

* * * Ordinarily, we would remand with instructions for the trial judge to determine whether rescission would be in the corporation's best interests, but such a remedy does not appear to be equitable at this time. This litigation has gone on for many years. There is yet at least another related case pending (in the Federal District Court). Furthermore, other factors weigh against rescission. The passage of time has made the 1976 position of the parties difficult, if not impossible, to restore. A substantial number of former stockholders have chosen other courses and should not be forced back into the Patriots corporation. In these circumstances the interests of the corporation and of the plaintiffs will be furthered best by limiting the plaintiffs' remedy to an assessment of damages.

We do not think it appropriate, however, to award damages based on a 1976 appraisal value. To do so would make this suit a nullity, leaving the plaintiffs with no effective remedy except appraisal, a position we have already rejected. Rescissory damages must be determined based on the present value of the Patriots, that is, what the stockholders would have if the merger were rescinded. Determination of the value of a unique property like the Patriots requires specialized

---

valid business purposes, including elimination of the household costs of servicing public stockholders and complying with federal regulations. See e.g., Cross v. Communications Channels, Inc., 456 N.Y.S.2d 971 (Sup.Ct.1982); Laird v. I.C.C., 691 F.2d 147 (3d Cir.1982).

expertise, cf. Correia v. New Bedford Redevelopment Auth., 375 Mass. 360, 367 (1978) (valuation of unusual property may require unusual approach), and, while the trial judge is entitled to reach his own conclusion as to value, Piemonte v. New Boston Garden Corp., 377 Mass. 719, 731 (1979), the credibility of testimony on value will depend in part on the familiarity of the witness with property of this kind. On remand, the judge is to take further evidence on the present value of the Old Patriots on the theory that the merger had not taken place.

Each share of the Coggins class is to receive, as rescissory damages, its aliquot share of the present assets.[15]

The trial judge dismissed the plaintiffs' claims against the individual defendants based on waste of corporate assets. The remedy we order is intended to give the plaintiffs what they would have if the merger were undone and the corporation were put back together again. The trial judge's finding that the sole purpose of the merger was the personal financial benefit of William H. Sullivan, Jr., and the use of corporate assets to accomplish this impermissible purpose, lead inescapably to the conclusion that part of what the plaintiffs otherwise would have benefitted by, was removed from the corporation by the individual defendants. We reverse the dismissal of the claim for waste of corporate assets and remand this question to the trial court. The present value of the Patriots, as determined on remand, should include the amount wrongfully removed or diverted from the corporate coffers by the individual defendants.

* * *

The case is remanded to the Superior Court for further proceedings consistent with this opinion.

So ordered.

NOTE: BUSINESS PURPOSE AND FAIRNESS

1. **Berkowitz v. Power/Mate Corp.**, 139 N.J.Super. 36, 342 A.2d 566 (1975), presents, in the language of the opinion, "a classic example of the now popular concept of 'going private' which, in the vernacular of the financial community, has become the 'newest game in town'. Numerous privately held companies which were taken 'public' by their insiders during the boom market for new issues that prevailed during the late 1960s are now, as a result of the current stock market depression, seeking—through the same insiders—to buy back the public's interest at a fraction of the price paid by the public for its stock." Power/Mate was engaged in manufacturing and marketing electronic

---

15. Our discussion in Sarrouf v. New England Patriots Football Club, Inc., post 547–551 (1986), of appropriate methods of valuation may be of some help to the remand judge.

modular and laboratory power supply equipment. It went public with about 29 percent of its stock in December 1968 at a price of $5 per share. Its stock fluctuated in price during 1969 and the first half of 1970 between a low bid of $2¼ and a high bid asked of $18 per share. During 1971 through 1974 the stock's price declined, and in early 1975 it was quoted at $1.25 offered, $2 asked. The two insiders (owning 69 percent of the stock) decided to take the company private by merging out the public stockholders into a dummy corporation formed for the purpose at $2 per share. The company complied with all statutory requirements of New Jersey law and of the federal securities laws. But, as the court pointed out, "neither the parameters of the Business Corporation Act nor the regulations of the SEC dispose of the matter at issue here. Those who control the affairs and conduct of a corporation, whether public or private, have a fiduciary duty to all the stockholders and the powers they by virtue of their majority status are powers held by trust." It went on to suggest "that a merger which serves no business purpose other than the termination of the minority stockholder's interest is *ipso facto* a breach of the controlling stockholder's fiduciary duties to the minority." But it declined to rely on the requirement that would invalidate the freeze-out unless there was a business purpose other than eliminating the minority stockholders. Instead it said:

"Enough has been shown by the pleadings, the undisputed facts and the testimony to raise serious questions as to the fairness of this 'freeze-out' of the minority stockholders. By their own admission the controlling stockholders of Power/Mate intend to acquire the public's stock at a price advantageous to them. Some measure of their gain may be found in the fact that after payment of the purchase price to the minority stockholders, the insiders will have achieved a gain of $.66 a share in the book value of the stock they will hold in the new Power/Mate. This represents an absolute gain to them of $148,648 in the book value of their stock, after deducting merger expenses estimated at approximately $40,000.

"Then, again, the timing of the merger suggests that the insiders have chosen a most opportune time—in relation to Power/Mate's earnings record since it went public—to buy out the minority at an unreasonably low price. Coupled with this is the fact that the two principal officers of Power/Mate gave themselves bonuses of $100,000 each so as to significantly reduce the company's earnings only three months prior to the proposed merger. While we can only speculate at this juncture, it may be doubted whether the market price of Power/Mate stock would have remained at $1.25 bid and $2 asked had the company announced earnings for the six-month period ending December 31, 1974 in excess of $1 a share. Since the justification for the $2 a share being offered to the minority is closely tied to the market price of the stock, the conduct of the insiders obviously may have adversely affected the market price. Closer scrutiny of this aspect of the transaction is clearly warranted.

"As noted in *Outwater,* supra, and in countless other decisions of the courts of this state and elsewhere, corporate officers and directors who engage in self-dealing transactions have a heavy burden of showing that they have not violated their fiduciary obligations to the minority stockholders. At a minimum their conduct is subject to a searching inquiry to determine whether it conforms to accepted concepts of fairness and equity. It may well be that the public stockholders of Power/Mate would benefit from the purchase of their stock. If so, the question at issue is whether the price they are being offered for their interest in Power/Mate is a fair and reasonable one.

"Defendants urge in effect that any price offered the minority in excess of the market price is *per se* fair and reasonable. This surely is an anomalous position inasmuch as the principal justification for the transaction is that there really is no market for the public stock, and hence the 'market price' may only be an arbitrary if not an altogether fictitious concept in this setting. Nor does the report of the independent consultant add much weight to defendants' position. His conclusions as to the fairness of the price being offered to the Power/Mate stockholders is based largely upon a comparison with a series of cash offers in other 'freeze-out' or 'going private' transactions which presumably may suffer from the same basic infirmity as that involved here, i.e., the prices offered were determined not as the result of arms-length bargaining but by the corporate insiders. Such transactions are surely not a barometer by which one can or should measure the fairness of the price offered here.

"Finally, defendants urge that injunctive relief is not an appropriate remedy. It is suggested that the minority stockholders can be adequately compensated by an award of money damages if it is ultimately determined that the terms of this merger are unfair. This argument, of course, presumes that a 'freeze-out' of the minority stockholders via the merger route is permissible under our law so long as the price paid is a fair one, and further presumes this court has the power to fix the price to be paid to the minority stockholders for their stock. Neither presumption is free from doubt, and until such doubts are resolved the consummation of the merger should be enjoined. See Brundage v. New Jersey Zinc Co., supra, 48 N.J. at 461–463, 226 A.2d 585."

2. In view of the possibilities for discord and for agreement among the stockholders of close corporations, should the concepts, "business purpose" and "fairness" serve the same function and have the same meaning in assessing the propriety of freeze-outs (1) by controllers of close corporations, (2) by parent corporations, as in the *Weinberger* and *Rabkin* cases, infra, and (3) by individual controllers of publicly held corporations, as in the *Berkowitz* and *Coggins* cases?

(B) MANAGEMENT BUYOUTS

INTRODUCTORY NOTE

The management buyout usually involves (a) the purchase by a newly formed company of all the stock or assets of a functioning company for cash, (b) obtained largely from institutional lenders or banks and intermediate or junior lenders, (c) with old management, their outside equity partners, and/or the junior lenders receiving the bulk of the equity in the new company. The institutional lenders sometimes also participate in the equity. The essence of the technique is the substantial use of debt capital—creating a debt equity ratio which is considerably higher than would normally be tolerable [g]— coupled with the commitment of the management team to remain with the company after the buy-out. Management's percentage ownership of equity is said to increase (by bargain purchase) from a median of 3.8% to 10.4%.

The buyout is typically powered by a combination of tax incentives [h] and the belief that the company, usually a mature enterprise with substantial future earning power, is undervalued by the market. By taking the corporation private at an advantageous price, management can acquire for itself a potentially substantial equity in a "new" firm with earnings expected to pay off the debt incurred to buy out the old firm within a few years. If management is also a controlling stockholder, it can (along with its participation in the new firm) collect the cash proceeds of the sale, or it can keep the cash in the old corporate shell and exploit the public stockholders of the old firm by converting it into a closed end investment company.[i] The attractiveness of such buyouts is enhanced for management by their utility as a defense mechanism to a threatened takeover.

Whether the management buyout involves taking a public company private or a management buyout of a subsidiary or division of a conglomerate, the central legal issues are embedded in the question whether the public investors (of the bought-out company or of the parent) are being treated fairly. The problem arises in large part because management inevitably has a significant information advantage over public investors about the value of the assets and earning

---

g. For discussion of the fraudulent conveyance or subordination problems of leveraged buyouts, see supra p. 254. Can the management leveraged buyout be said to constitute a non-market transaction, such as is at the root of the Deep Rock doctrine, in which incumbent creditors of, and investors in, the target are no more able to protect themselves against those who lend for the buyout than against the lenders in the Deep Rock type of case? If so, is the subordination of the lenders who enable the leveraged buy-out a feasible remedy in an insolvency proceeding?

h. In addition to the interest and depreciation deductions to which leveraged buyout promoters look primarily as mechanisms permitting fullest possible use of ESOPS and of earnings to repay debt, there may be additional tax benefits, such as possible uses of the dividend received deduction. The Tax Reform Act of 1986 has reduced the deductions available to fuel such transactions. See supra p. 466.

i. See SEA Rel. No. 15,572 (2/15/79); In the Matter of Wood Corporation, SEA Rel. No. 15,337 (11/16/78); In the Matter of Spartek Corporation, SEA Rel. No. 15,-567 (2/14/79).

prospects of the enterprise.[j] In buyouts of subsidiaries or divisions, the subsidiary's management possibly has such an advantage over the selling parent and its public stockholders.

In either case, management is subject to the temptation to take advantage of its information by overreaching public investors on price in what is often effectively a unilateral transaction. The principal restraint on that temptation is the possibility of bids from third parties. Those bids are said to increase the average premium of 50% paid to stockholders to 70%. Since the company's own assets are the substantial underpinning for the financing to purchase the company, once the company is priced by management any other company can compete with a higher bid if it is interested in purchasing the assets. The management buyout is thus, in form at least, considerably less coercive of the public stockholders than is "going private" by controlling stockholders. But an investor group with inside information and no need for dividends can leverage the company's assets a great deal more than can a third party, particularly a public company. The greater the magnitude of the proposed leverage, the fewer are the number of public companies able to finance a competitive bid by borrowing as much as the informed private investors group can against the assets of the target company. Notwithstanding the information disadvantages affecting outside bidders, if management and its associates bid more than the third party, the transaction would seem to be less plainly a case of taking advantage in a self-dealing transaction than if there is no other bidder—unless management places significant blocks in the path of the third party bidder. See MacAndrews and Forbes Holdings v. Revlon, Inc., 501 A.2d 1239, 1248–1251 (Del.Ch.1985), aff'd, 505 A.2d 454 (Del. 1985).

In the case of management buyout of a public company when no third party bidder enters the picture, the conflicts of interest are etched in the question whether management fulfills its duty to the public investors if it takes for itself any or all the upside opportunities facilitated by the loan on the sole security of the firm's assets which it obtains in order to buy out the public for its personal benefits. See Coggins v. New England Patriots Football Club, Inc., supra p. 735. Also present, as has been pointed out,[k] are questions generated by management's ability to paint the record so as to depress the price of the stock it seeks to buy out or to preempt the bidding, as by granting options for blocks of stock to itself or crown jewels to its lenders. Moreover, tax and investment advantages over public investors may permit the insiders to yield on the price at which the assets are sold, to the detriment of public investors—e.g., if the insiders are controlling stockholders, and the buy-out takes the form of an asset sale to a buyer in whom the insiders have a substantial interest, the insiders may retain control of

j. Those advantages are occasionally discovered in litigation and required, on fiduciary theory, to be shared. See e.g., Joseph v. Shell Oil Co., 482 A.2d 335, 341 (Del.Ch.1984).

k. Lowenstein, Management Buyouts, 85 Colum.L.Rev. 730, 739–742 (1985).

the old corporation and turn it into a closed end investment company or mutual bond fund. And in the case of mergers, the special interests in the new corporation given to management or insiders encourage them similarly to yield on price.

In the case of leveraged buyouts by managements of subsidiaries and divisions, the bargaining power and information disparities between the parties are not as great as in the buyout of public investors. But added conflicts arise because, for example, the seller is expected to indemnify the buyer (essentially the old management) against liability for falsehood in the representations which are in effect made by that buyer.

Significant efficiency gains are said to result from management buyouts by reason of the combined effect of (a) reduction in management discretion to waste mature companies' excess cash flow because the need to pay interest on the debt incurred for the buyout restricts managerial discretion to make suboptimal use of the excess, (b) the parallel ownership of debt and equity on monitoring costs, and (c) the added incentive to management from increased equity ownership. See Jensen, The Eclipse of the Public Corporation, supra p. 487, Jensen, Agency Costs of Free Cash Flow, Corporate Finance and Takeovers, 76 Amer.Econ.Rev. (Papers and Proceedings) 323 (1986). See also, Kaplan, The Effect of Leveraged Buyouts on Operations and Value, 24 J. Financial Econ. 217 (1989); Palepu, Consequences of Leveraged Buyouts, 27 J. Financial Econ. 247 (1990). It is suggested that such efficiency gains occur principally in the case of "mature" companies, which are said to be the prime generators of "excess" cash flows and correspondingly "wasteful" management. It is not entirely clear how large is the proportion of buyouts involving such companies. But in any event, questions arise as to the extent of gains in operating efficiency that result from such buyouts, the extent to which post-buyout increases in enterprise value reflect pre-buyout inside information advantages, and whether the benefits of the process exceed the costs resulting from investor suspicions about unfair sharing between public investors and management of any such gains. The last question is not made easier to answer in any particular case by the difficulties encountered in attempting to identify a "mature" company or "excess" cash flows or "wasteful" corporate management—let alone the difficulties in defining and determining "fair" share.

For an illuminating analysis of management buyouts, the gains and costs they offer, and innovative suggestions for controlling the process productively see Lowenstein, Management Buyouts, 85 Colum.L.Rev. 730 (1985). For additional discussion taking a range of positions, see Hazen, Management Buyouts and Corporate Governance Paradigms, 25 Wake Forest L.Rev. 1 (1990); DeMott, Puzzles and Parables: Defining Good Faith in the MBO Context, 25 Wake Forest L.Rev. 15 (1990); Macey, Auction Theory, MBOs and Property Rights in Corporate Assets, 25 Wake Forest L.Rev. 85 (1990); Vagts, The Leveraged Buyout and Management's Share, 25 Wake Forest L.Rev. 129 (1990); Brown, In Defense of Management Buyouts, 65 Tul.L.Rev. 57

(1990); Repetti, Management Buyouts, Efficient Markets, Fair Value and Soft Information, 67 N.C.L.Rev. 121 (1988); Oesterle and Norberg, Management Buyouts: Creating or Appropriating Shareholder Wealth, 41 Vand.L.Rev. 207 (1988); Booth, Management Buyouts, Shareholder Welfare and the Limits of Fiduciary Duty, 60 N.Y.U.L.Rev. 630 (1985).

FIELD v. ALLYN
Court of Chancery of Delaware, 1983.
457 A.2d 1089.

BROWN, Chancellor.

This is a decision after trial in a class action brought on behalf of the former minority shareholders of the Pittsburgh and Lake Erie Railroad Company, a Delaware corporation. The suit attacks both a tender offer and a subsequent cash-out merger whereby a newly-formed company, after purchasing a 92.6 per cent interest in the corporation from the previous owner of that interest, acquired, and thus eliminated, the remaining 7.4 per cent public minority interest. While the facts of the matter are predictably complex and involved, the end result which has given rise to the plaintiffs' complaint is relatively simple to understand.

* * *

What the plaintiffs complain about is the fact that the four individual defendants, two of whom were key officers of the Pittsburgh and Lake Erie Railroad Company at the time, were able to put together a highly-leveraged plan whereby, with the financial assistance of the defendant Beloit Corporation and with virtually no cash outlay of their own, they, along with Beloit Corporation, were able to acquire complete ownership of the Pittsburgh and Lake Erie Railroad Company by means of using the assets of the corporation to finance the cost of its acquisition. To understand the situation the following facts will suffice.

The Pittsburgh and Lake Erie Railroad Company (hereafter referred to as "the P & LE") is a Class I railroad operating a system of more than 377 miles of main line track serving the industrial complexes of the greater Pittsburgh, Pennsylvania and Youngstown, Ohio areas. The company was formed in 1875. As of March 1979, shortly before the tender offer and merger complained of, the assets of the P & LE included 10,744 freight cars and 56 locomotives. These particular assets, referred to hereafter as the rolling stock, had an unencumbered, appraised value of between $118 million and $124 million at the time. Since its rolling stock far exceeded its own needs, it was the practice of the P & LE over the years to lease these cars to other railroads on a per diem basis for use around the country. The leasing of its cars on this basis produced substantial revenue.

In 1979 the total book value of all of the P & LE's assets was some $168 million. In an era in which railroads had declined generally, the

P & LE had been able to survive. It had a history of good management and profitability and was basically well maintained. It had a good record of earnings and stability from a financial standpoint. In recent years this was necessarily attributable in part to the efforts of the defendant, Henry G. Allyn, Jr., its President and Chief Executive Officer, and the defendant, Gordon E. Neuenschwander, its Vice President and General Counsel. Both Allyn and Neuenschwander were also directors.

* * *

[Penn Central Transportation Corp. (Penn Central) owned 92.6% of P & LE stock.]

In 1973 the defendant Bernard B. Smyth, a Pittsburgh lawyer and business consultant, was approached by others with regard to putting together a group of investors for the purpose of attempting to purchase the P & LE from the Penn Central Trustees. At that time the Trustees indicated that Penn Central's P & LE stock interest was not for sale.

* * *

[Smyth persisted, and with the help of one, Garland, planned a leveraged buy-out of P & LE by obtaining a loan on its rolling stock and using the borrowed funds to pay the Penn Central Trustees for the P & LE common stock.]

Both Garland and Smyth also recognized that it was absolutely necessary to include Allyn and Neuenschwander as part of any such acquisition plan. Since such a leveraged purchase as Garland had in mind would be dependent upon the cash flow and income derived from the operation of the railroad, it was vital to keep the successful incumbent management in place if their acquisition plan was to have any chance of success.

Accordingly, Garland, Smyth, Allyn and Neuenschwander thereafter merged their respective interests in a common desire to acquire, if possible, the P & LE, the majority interest which, by then, was openly being touted for sale by the Penn Central Trustees. These four defendants are referred to collectively hereafter as the "Pittsburgh Group." In due course, they also formed a corporation, The Pittsburgh and Lake Erie Company (hereafter referred to as "PLECO"), for the purpose of carrying out this enterprise. For the initial price of $1 per share, 255 shares each in PLECO were issued to Garland and Allyn and 160 shares each were issued to Smyth and Neuenschwander.

* * *

[Smyth and Garland encountered difficulties in getting the needed loan and failed at first.]

Garland continued to pursue the matter, however, and in November 1978, through certain business brokers, he was introduced to The First National Bank of Boston (hereafter "FNBB"). As a result of this meeting, the machinery by which the Pittsburgh Group, through PLE-CO, acquired the P & LE was put in place.

* * *

[FNBB agreed to make the loan to PLECO but insisted that the Pittsburgh Group provide at least $11,250,000 in equity.]

Garland and Smyth then set about to produce the additional equity demanded by FNBB. After negotiations, the defendant Beloit Corporation, a former client of Smyth, agreed to participate in the proposed transaction in return for a 51 per cent interest in PLECO (but with the understanding that the Pittsburgh Group would retain control of the board of directors of PLECO). For this interest, Beloit loaned PLECO $800,000 and agreed to purchase $11,200,000 in PLECO preferred stock upon the closing of a deal with Penn Central for the acquisition of Penn Central's P & LE stock. Beloit also agreed to advance up to $4,000,000 in additional loans to PLECO if such were needed to achieve 100 per cent ownership of the P & LE.

* * *

[After acquiring 92.6% of P & LE stock from Penn Central for $90.25 per share, PLECO made a tender offer for the remainder of the P & LE stock. Of the 52,366 outstanding minority shares 34,804 were voluntarily tendered and paid for at $115 per share. The remaining shares were merged out in a short form merger for the same price.]

With PLECO now owning 100 per cent of the P & LE, the final pegs of the acquisition plan were put in place. Specifically, the P & LE, as now fully controlled by PLECO, entered into a sale of its rolling stock to FNBB for the sum of $60 million. FNBB, in turn, leased this rolling stock back to the P & LE over a period of ten years, at an annual rental of $6 million per year, with interest. Under the terms of the leaseback, the rolling stock is to again become the property of the P & LE at the end of the ten-year lease period, assuming of course that all obligations of the P & LE under the lease are fulfilled.

Upon receipt of the $60 million sale price from FNBB, the P & LE declared a dividend to PLECO in the sum of $60 million. PLECO then paid the $60 million to FNBB so as to pay off the bridge loan. This, in turn, freed the 92.6 per cent stock interest acquired by PLECO from Penn Central from its pledge to FNBB as security for the bridge loan. As a result, PLECO ended up with an unencumbered 100 per cent ownership of the P & LE. The four individual defendants, along with the defendant Beloit, own all of the outstanding stock in PLECO. The respective interests of these defendants in the authorized voting stock structure of PLECO is as follows:

Beloit Corporation	1,020 shares	— 51 %
Allyn	255 shares	— 13.4%
Neuenschwander	160 shares	— 8.4%
Garland	255 shares	— 13.4%
Smyth	160 shares	— 8.4%

(The remaining 5 per cent, or 100 shares, was issued originally to two business brokers as a finder's fee for putting Garland in touch with FNBB. These shares were subsequently repurchased by PLECO for the sum of $1,150,000 and retained as treasury shares.)

As can be seen from the foregoing, the effect of the financial machinations successfully employed by the Pittsburgh Group was to use the credit of the P & LE's rolling stock as the means to obtain the funds needed to acquire a 100 per cent ownership interest in the P & LE, the only sacrifice along the way being their surrender of a 51 per cent interest in their enterprise to Beloit so as to provide the equity participation required in order to obtain the bridge loan. The bridge loan, obviously, was the key to the success of the entire plan. But at the same time the ability to use the credit of the assets of the corporation to finance their acquisition of the stock of the corporation was the foundation on which the plan of the Pittsburgh Group was structured. And two of the four members of the Pittsburgh Group—Allyn and Neuenschwander—were officers and directors of the P & LE both at the time that the plan was conceived as well as during the time that it was carried out.

Plaintiffs find great fault in this. As former minority shareholders of the P & LE they feel that they have been wronged by the involvement of Allyn and Neuenschwander as a part of the acquisition group. For example, they point out that originally Allyn, as President and Chief Executive Officer of the P & LE, owned but 69 shares of the P & LE. These shares were sold to PLECO during the tender offer for the sum of $7,935. For a mere $255 Allyn had previously acquired what turned out to be his 13.4 per cent interest in PLECO. Since PLECO now owns 100 per cent of the P & LE, Allyn in effect now has a 13.4 per cent interest in the P & LE. Thus, as plaintiffs compute it, he went from a minimal shareholder position in the P & LE to a 13.4 per cent equity position in the P & LE, and helped eliminate the minority shareholders in the process, all because he was able to use the assets of the company he was running to finance the cost of the acquisition. They make a similar case with regard to Neuenschwander who originally owned 32 shares of the P & LE.

As noted at the outset, this is a class action. Plaintiffs represent two separate classes. The plaintiff Field represents the class of minority shareholders who were eliminated by the merger. Plaintiff Fanucchi represents the class of minority shareholders who tendered their shares in response to the tender offer of PLECO. On behalf of his class Fanucchi contends that the tender offer solicitation materials of PLECO omitted certain material matters. Underlying the position of both Field and Fanucchi, however, is the contention that the entire acquisition was illegal—from the purchase of the Penn Central interest through the tender offer and on through the merger—and that as a consequence both the tender offer and the merger should be declared void and the minority shareholders returned to an equity position with regard to the P & LE.

In the final analysis plaintiffs have settled on two main theories. First, they say that in reality the overall transaction amounted to a sale of substantially all of the assets of the P & LE, and that as such it is void since it was not approved by the board of directors of the P & LE nor was it submitted to the vote of its shareholders as required by 8 Del.C. § 271. Second, they contend that Allyn and Neuenschwander breached the fiduciary duty owed by them to the corporation and its minority shareholders, thus fatally tainting the acquisition of the Pittsburgh Group and PLECO. As presented, I find no substance to either argument.

The suggestion that the situation here really involved a sale of assets, and thus was governed by the section of the Delaware General Corporation Law applicable to such transactions, requires little comment.

* * *

The short answer here is that there was no effort made on behalf of the P & LE to sell its rolling stock to PLECO and the Pittsburgh Group pursuant to 8 Del.C. § 271, and the plaintiffs can establish no legal wrong simply by branding it as such.

The fiduciary duty argument of the plaintiffs is, I think, similarly strained. This suit was initiated by an application for a temporary restraining order to prevent the short form merger from taking place. At that time it was contended that the case was a simple one involving the taking of a corporate opportunity by Allyn and Neuenschwander in violation of Guth v. Loft, Inc., Del.Supr., 23 Del.Ch. 255, 5 A.2d 503 (1939). The restraining order application was denied on the basis that a likelihood of success on the merits of that legal theory had not been demonstrated. This was attributable primarily to the underlying premise of such a corporate opportunity theory, namely, that Allyn and Neuenschwander were obligated in some way to cause the P & LE itself to purchase the 92.6 per cent stock interest of its majority shareholder, Penn Central, so as to convert the 7.4 per cent minority shareholders into the 100 per cent owners of the company. Subsequently, the complaint was amended and the corporate opportunity theory was abandoned.

Despite this plaintiffs still rely on certain principles taken from the Guth v. Loft decision as well as those set forth in Brophy v. Cities Service Co., Del.Ch., 31 Del.Ch. 241, 70 A.2d 5 (1949), a leading case which prohibits corporate fiduciaries from trading in the stock of their corporation based upon inside information. As best that I can discern plaintiffs are attempting to patch together the Guth v. Loft and Brophy decisions, together with certain general statements taken from the recent decision of Lynch v. Vickers Energy Corp., Del.Ch., 383 A.2d 278 (1978), to come up with the proposition that the fiduciary duty of loyalty owed by a corporate officer and director to his shareholders, when coupled with the prohibition against using his corporate position for personal profit, absolutely prohibits such an officer and director from participating with others in any plan to acquire the corporation, regardless of the fairness of the plan to the minority shareholders of the corporation, if it is the ultimate intention of the acquisition plan to use the assets and revenue generating capability of the corporation to finance the cost of the acquisition. I cannot conclude that those cases stand for such a broad-based principle.

While the general statements of fiduciary duty taken by the plaintiffs from those decisions are unassailable, I have trouble in making them fit the factual context of the present matter. Conceding, of course, that Allyn and Neuenschwander owed a fiduciary duty to the P & LE and its shareholders—both the minority shareholders as well as Penn Central—in what manner did they utilize their fiduciary positions for their own personal gain? What advantage was gained by PLECO and the Pittsburgh Group by virtue of their corporate offices?

On the facts of the matter there is no evidence that Allyn or Neuenschwander did anything to give the Pittsburgh Group or PLECO any advantage over any other party wishing to bid for the Penn Central's interest in the P & LE. On the record they were scrupulous throughout to avoid any appearance of impropriety. This was confirmed by the testimony of a representative of the Penn Central Trustees. They did nothing to slant things in favor of their group. They were candid with all interested purchasers as to the business and financial status of the P & LE. They knew that their position was a delicate one. They advised both Penn Central and the board of directors of the P & LE of their participation in the Pittsburgh Group from the outset.

In addition, Allyn and Neuenschwander did not participate personally in the negotiations leading up to the financing of the acquisition by PLECO. This was done exclusively by Garland and Smyth. The most that can be said is that the ownership interests of Allyn and Neuenschwander in PLECO perhaps lent strength to the ability of PLECO to obtain the precarious financing required for such a highly leveraged purchase of the P & LE. It provided perhaps an added assurance to prospective lenders that Allyn and Neuenschwander would be staying on to run the railroad and thus continue its successful operation so as to generate the funds to pay off the acquisition financing. But this same assurance could have been provided by any other acquisition group through the use of long-term employment contacts for Allyn and Neuenschwander even in the absence of a shareholder interest.

This, of course, leads to the main contention of the defendants. The ability to utilize the rolling stock or other assets of the P & LE to finance the acquisition of all of its outstanding stock did not accrue to PLECO because of the fact that Allyn and Neuenschwander held fiduciary positions with the P & LE. It was a potential means of financing available to any person, corporation or investment group that was interested in acquiring the P & LE, and it was made possible to all such interested parties because of the unusual fact that a 92.6 per cent shareholder was desirous of selling its entire holdings.

One in a fiduciary position to a corporation and its shareholders is not absolutely prohibited from dealing in all transactions in which his corporation may have an interest. It is only a misuse of the fiduciary position that is prohibited. For instance, it is implicit in Brophy v. Cities Service Co., supra, that so long as a fiduciary is not profiting by inside information he is free to trade in the market place in his company's stock. He is also free to take a business opportunity for himself once his corporation has properly rejected the opportunity or if it is established that it is not in a position to take it, Guth v. Loft, supra; and this is true even if he learns of the opportunity through his fiduciary position. Compare, Fliegler v. Lawrence, Del.Supr., 361 A.2d 218 (1976). He is even free to deal directly with outside shareholders so long as he does not take advantage of superior knowledge derived from his insider status. Lank v. Steiner, Del.Supr., 43 Del.Ch. 262, 224 A.2d 242 (1966).

As a consequence I agree with the defendants that it cannot be a breach of a fiduciary duty for a director or corporate officer to benefit personally from a wholly non-corporate transaction, unless he has derived some specialized or unique advantage from his fiduciary position. If he is merely doing that which any non-fiduciary could do, even if it can be said in a sense to constitute a "use" of the corporate assets, and if he is doing so without using his fiduciary position to gain a particular advantage over others, I find it difficult to conclude that he is breaching his fiduciary duty to his corporation and its shareholders. I find such to be the case here on the facts of the matter.

I think that this conclusion also disposes of the plaintiffs' argument that in order for Allyn and Neuenschwander to be permitted to participate in such an acquisition plan the minority shareholders of the P & LE, or such of them who might be interested, must be afforded an opportunity to participate in it also. For one thing I see no particular logic to such an argument. It is an argument that any time that an acquisition group desires to include a corporate officer or director within its number, it must also take in so many of the minority shareholders as may desire to come along.

More importantly, such an argument is again based on the fiduciary duty premise. But if the corporate officer or director has no fiduciary duty not to participate in such a leveraged acquisition plan in the absence of particular facts that would show an improper use of his corporate office on his part, then I can see no fiduciary duty owed to minority shareholders to somehow permit them to retain their equity position in the corporation.

I note again that plaintiffs have offered no authority from any jurisdiction which either deals with directly or supports directly the proposition on which they are relying with regard to the alleged breach of fiduciary duties on the part of Allyn and Neuenschwander. As a consequence I find on the facts of the matter that no such breach has been established.

As to the separate claims of the plaintiff Fanucchi on behalf of his class that the tender offer disclosures were inadequate, I find it to be unfounded. As I view it, the offering circular contained a full disclosure of all germane facts concerning the acquisition of the P & LE and thus it met the standard of candor set forth in Lynch v. Vickers Energy Corporation, supra. Specifically, the roles of Allyn and Neuenschwander in PLECO were fully disclosed. The purchase of the Penn Central interest in the P & LE and the bridge loan by which it was accomplished was set forth. The offering circular also explained the future transactions which PLECO intended to undertake, including the merger, the sale and leaseback of the P & LE rolling stock, and the proposed dividend to PLECO of sufficient funds to repay the bridge loan. In short, an outline of the entire acquisition plan of PLECO and the Pittsburgh Group was fully disclosed to the minority shareholders.

Without going into the various matters which the plaintiff Fanucchi feels were improperly omitted, I find no substantial likelihood that their disclosure would have been viewed by a reasonable investor as significantly altering the total mix of the information made available. TSC Industries, Inc. v. Northway, Inc., 426 U.S. 438, 96 S.Ct. 2126, 48 L.Ed.2d 757 (1976); Lynch v. Vickers Energy Corporation, supra. They are simply representative of the usual handful of nondisclosure allegations that are typically thrown into a shareholder action such as this just in case one of them might accidently hit the mark. Here, they do not.

On the evidence I find that the minority shareholders of the P & LE who tendered their shares to PLECO in response to the tender offer did so after full disclosure by PLECO and consequently there is no basis to this aspect of the claim made on their behalf by the plaintiff Fanucchi.

* * *

Should the presence of a third party bidder for the assets of a corporation affect or alter the obligations of (1) management to refrain from using corporate assets to effect a management buyout, and (2) independent directors in assessing the propriety of the management buyout offer?

EDELMAN v. FRUEHAUF CORPORATION

United States Court of Appeals, Sixth Circuit, 1986.
798 F.2d 882.

[This case involved a proposed cash tender offer by the so-called Edelman group for all the Fruehauf Corp. stock (which had sold in the low $20 per share range a few months earlier) for $44.]

MERRITT, Circuit Judge.

* * *

In response to the Edelman group's offer, members of Fruehauf's management negotiated with Merrill Lynch to arrange a two-tier leveraged buyout by management and Merrill Lynch. Under this deal, a corporation formed for purposes of the buyout would purchase approximately 77% of Fruehauf's stock in a cash tender offer for $48.50 per share. This tender offer would be funded using $375 million borrowed from Merrill Lynch, $375 million borrowed from Manufacturers Hanover, and $100 million contributed by Fruehauf Corporation. Next, Fruehauf would be merged with the acquiring corporation, and the remaining Fruehauf shareholders would receive securities in the new corporation valued at $48.50. Total equity contribution to the new company would be only 25 million dollars—10 to 15 million dollars from management and the rest from Merrill Lynch. In return for their equity contribution, management would receive between 40 and 60 percent control of the new company (depending on the amount of their equity contribution). Under this arrangement, Fruehauf would also pay approximately $30 million to Merrill Lynch for loan commitment fees, advisory fees, and a "breakup fee" that Merrill Lynch would keep even if the deal did not go through. Additionally, the deal would contain a "no-shop" clause restricting Fruehauf's ability to attempt to negotiate a better deal with another bidder. A special committee composed of Fruehauf's outside directors approved the proposed management leveraged buyout, and Fruehauf's board authorized the buyout. * * *

Like the District Court, we conclude on the basis of strong evidence that Fruehauf's Board of Directors unreasonably preferred incumbent management in the bidding process—acting without objectivity and requisite loyalty to the corporation. Their actions were not taken in a good faith effort to negotiate the best deal for the shareholders. They acted as interested parties and did not treat the Fruehauf managers and the Edelman group in an even handed way but rather gave their colleagues on the Board, the inside managers, the inside track and accepted their proposal without fostering a real bidding process.

The evidence for this conclusion is clear. Several directors admitted their bias in their depositions. In disclosing the management transaction, to the stockholders, the Board made it appear that the management proposal was the best bid obtainable after giving Edelman a reasonable opportunity to top the bid. In fact the Board accepted the leverage buyout proposal of the management and Merrill Lynch without giving Edelman an opportunity to bid further and then rejected out of hand Edelman's offer a couple of days later to acquire the company on the same terms as management but at a higher price. While refusing to talk to Edelman or promote an open bidding process, the Board agreed to pay well over $30 million in corporate funds to Merrill Lynch as financing and advisory fees so that the management buyout could be consummated. (Over half of this amount would be paid even if another bidder prevailed.) The Board also made available $100 million of corporate funds for management's use in the purchase of shares and entered into an agreement severely limiting the Board's ability to negotiate another offer.

There are other indicia of the Board's intention to preempt the bidding in favor of management. For example, the committee of outside directors employed as its advisor the investment banker that was in the process of negotiating management's buyout proposal and clearly favored that course. Then no effort was made to get a counter offer. Additionally, the Board amended Fruehauf's stock option plan, incentive compensation plan, and pension plan to provide that if anyone obtained a 40% interest in Fruehauf without the Board's approval, all company-issued options in Fruehauf stock would be immediately exercisable, all incentive compensation payments normally due Fruehauf's salaried employees in due course would become immediately due, and the $70 to $100 million of overfunding in the pension plan, which had been available for corporate use, would be irrevocably committed to the pension fund. These measures had the effect of making Fruehauf a less attractive takeover target, and thereby, of dampening the bidding process. Later, in response to the threat of litigation, the Board again amended these plans to provide for acceleration of stock options and incentive compensation payments in the event anyone became a 40% shareholder, even with Board approval. Counsel admits that it is from these plans that members of management would obtain the money for their equity contributions to the management buyout. The Board also further amended the pension plan to give advance board approval to any 40% acquiror who pays at least $48.50 per share. In short, it appears that the Board simply decided to make a deal with management no matter what other bidders might offer. The entire factual pattern is consistent with that purpose.

Under Michigan law, a "transaction between a corporation and 1 or more of its directors or officers" is invalid unless the transaction is "fair and reasonable" or is properly authorized or ratified by disinterested directors or shareholders after complete disclosure. Mich.Comp. Laws § 450.1545. "When the validity of [such] a contract * * * is questioned, the burden of establishing its validity" is on the Board. Id. at § 450.1546. Michigan law is similar to the general law on this subject. See Radol v. Thomas, 772 F.2d 244, 257 (6th Cir.1985).

In this case, the Board has failed to carry its burden of establishing that the management buyout was fair and reasonable in light of the circumstances. * * * The evidence here compels the conclusion that the directors simply "rubber stamped" the management buy-out proposal.

* * *

Given the Board's unreasonable conduct in violation of Michigan law, as found by the District Court, we agree with the District Court that the remedy should be injunctive relief. All sides agree that Fruehauf is on the auction block. Once it becomes apparent that a takeover target will be acquired by new owners, whether by an alleged "raider" or by a team consisting of management and a "white knight," it becomes the duty of the target's directors to see that the shareholders obtain the best price possible for their stock. "The directors' role change[s] from defenders of the corporate bastion to auctioneers charged with getting the best price for the stockholders at a sale of the company." Revlon, Inc. v. McAndrews & Forbes Holdings, Inc., 506 A.2d 173, 182 (Del.Sup.1986). When, in violation of this duty, directors take measures that are intended to put an end to the bidding, those measures may be enjoined. See Revlon, 506 A.2d at 184 (enjoining directors from agreeing to a "no-shop" clause, which prevented them from negotiating with other bidders). In light of the clear failure of the Board to provide for a fair auction, the District Court was correct to devise injunctive relief setting a framework for an open bidding process.

* * *

As Judge Guy pointed out in dissent at the hearing, the most controversial provisions of the District Court's injunction are its provisions restraining the defendants from using corporate funds to effectuate the buyout, including financing, commitment, legal and other similar fees. Our treatment of those provisions should not suggest that under the business judgment rule we would never allow corporate funds to be used to encourage bidders or even to encourage management buyouts. Obviously some marginal costs to finance the flow of information are necessary, and advisory fees for lawyers and investment bankers to structure and conduct the bidding process will have to be paid. It may be that in some instances—where the neutrality and objectivity of the Board is clearly present—commitment fees of various bankers should be paid.

But in this case, as the District Court found, the degree of the Board's largess in favor of the managers, their bankers and Merrill Lynch is out of proportion. The Board was willing to make over $130 million available to its managers to insure their success. The evidence clearly suggests that the Board's purpose was not to create a fair bidding process but to make sure that the managers and Merrill Lynch bought the company and that other bidders would be turned away. In light of this conduct, the District Court was correct to restrain the Board from making Fruehauf money available to fund the management buyout. Where evidence of bias is clearly present, an injunction insuring neutrality is necessary and each bidder must stand on its own bottom in respect to funding.

We believe this position is consistent with the development of the law. The original common law rule prohibiting transactions with interested directors was found to be too inflexible and was gradually modified. See Model Business Corp. Act § 41 and accompanying notes (2nd ed. 1971) (stating that such transactions should not be void per se and tracing history of development); W. Cary & M. Eisenberg, Cases and Materials on Corporations 563–74, 613–37 (5th ed. 1980). Vague principles granting deference to managers and directors whose interests clearly conflict with the corporation have not worked well in buyout situations and firm rules insuring open bidding are considered necessary by most scholars who have investigated the problem. See generally, Lowenstein, Management Buyouts, 85 Col.L.Rev. 730 (1985).

Accordingly, the judgment of the District Court, as modified herein, is affirmed.

   * * *

NOTES

1. *Further Proceedings in Edelman v. Fruehauf.*

The court ordered bidding contest proceeded after the court's decision. Both the Edelman and Merrill groups submitted bids, but the Special Committee's outside financial advisers were unable to recommend one bid over the other. Edelman refused to go higher. Merrill stated a willingness to increase its offer, but only if a settlement could be worked out with the Edelman group. A two part Merrill proposal emerged: (1) Merrill would purchase Edelman's 2 million shares for $49 per share and pay $21 million of "expenses" in exchange for a release; (2) Merrill would offer $49.50 cash for 14.575 million shares and a package of securities for the remaining shares in a second-step merger. The Committee valued this offer at between $47.50 and $49.25 as against a value of $45 to $48.50 for the Edelman offer. The Board accepted the Merrill offer. The arrangement was sustained in **Priddy v. Edelman,** 883 F.2d 438 (6th Cir.1989).

2. *Management Buyouts and Hostile Tender Offers.*

Edelman v. Fruehauf shows that board action respecting proposed management buyouts often occurs in the context a multisided contest for corporate control involving inside and outside bidders. In these cases the courts apply fiduciary standards for management responses to hostile tender offers and management conduct of bidding competitions. Several of the leading cases articulating these standards turn on rulings that board action in favor of a management proposal violate fiduciary norms. See *Mills Acquisition v. MacMillan,* infra p. 1101, *Revlon, Inc. v. MacAndrews & Forbes Holdings, Inc.,* infra p. 1095, *Hanson Trust PLC v. ML SCM Acquisition, Inc.,* infra p. 1133.

NOTE: THE "MARKET CHECK" AND "FAIRNESS" OPINIONS

Does the practice of delegating decisionmaking authority to a committee of outside directors that, in turn, retains its own investment bankers and counsel provide an adequate guarantee against overreaching by management due to its structural and informational advantages? Does the prevention of overreaching require, as a practical matter, a *per se* rule that the outside committee sell control of the corporation to the highest bidder? If so, what procedures assure that the highest possible price is obtained for the shareholders? Compare the transactions that precipitated *Metropolitan Life v. RJR Nabisco*, supra p. 207, described in **In re RJR Nabisco**, CCH Fed.Sec.L.Rep. ¶ 94,194 (Del.Ch.1989), with those at issue in **In re Fort Howard Corp. Shareholders Litigation**, 1988 WL 83147 (Del.Ch.1988). In *Nabisco*, a management buyout proposal led to an extended and elaborate auction won by an outside bidding group whose bid had a lower face value than that of the management group. In *Fort Howard*, a special committee accepted the proposal of a management buyout group after opening a thirty day window in which the management offer was public information and the committee was willing to share proprietary information with interested outside bidders. No bids were solicited, however. The Delaware court raised an eyebrow at the facts that the corporation's C.E.O., a member of the buyout group, selected both the chair and outside counsel of the special committee, that the C.E.O. discussed the proposal with the committee chair, and that he joined the chair in selecting the other two members of the committee. But the court sustained the procedure nevertheless. Compare also, In re Formica Corp. Shareholders Litigation, CCH Fed.Sec.L.Rep. ¶ 94,362 (Del.Ch. 1989), in which the special committee conducted an active solicitation of competing bids during the "market check" period and negotiated actively with several interested parties. These cases are analyzed in De Mott, supra.

In a case like *Fort Howard*, where no outside bids are solicited, is it sufficient that the committee's outside investment bankers opine that the consideration is "fair" ? Outside fairness opinions became a necessary component of merger and acquisition transactions during the 1980s. Liability considerations, particularly in respect of the duty of care, made it almost inconceivable that a board of directors would approve a sale of the firm without an outside opinion on the fairness of the price. A practical necessity such as this does not necessarily guaranty substantive adequacy, however. Practice respecting the preparation of these opinions has been criticized repeatedly. See Bebchuk and Kahan, Fairness Opinions: How Fair are They and What Can be Done About It? 1989 Duke L.J. 27.[1]

Should the courts go a step farther and hold investment bankers liable for negligently prepared opinions by analogy to cases respecting accountants or attorneys? Do outside investment bankers owe a fiduciary duty of care and loyalty as agents in connection with the transaction? If so, to whom? To the special committee? The target board?

---

[1]. Bebchuk and Kahan make several recommendations, 1989 Duke L.J. at 53. First, the courts should develop a definition of fair price and investment banks should disclose their own definitions of fair price in their opinions. Second, the weight attached to a fairness opinion should depend on whether the opinion contains information about the range of fair prices and on the sensitivity of the price estimate. Third, courts should be sensitive to conflicts of interest on the part of the investment bankers. If the banker is paid by a contingent fee, is involved in other aspects of the transaction, or has prior dealings with the corporation, the court should discount the opinion.

The target? The shareholders of the target? A pair of New York cases suggest that a duty to the shareholders obtains. **Wells v. Shearson Lehman/American Express, Inc.,** 127 A.D.2d 200, 514 N.Y.S.2d 1 (1987), rev'd on other grounds, 72 N.Y.2d 11, 530 N.Y.S.2d 517, 526 N.E.2d 8 (1988), concerned an opinion rendered in connection with a $1.1 billion management buyout of Metromedia in 1984. Metromedia paid Shearson $750,000 for the opinion, $685,000 in brokers fees, and promised an additional $3.2 million if the merger went through. The opinion was included in proxy material sent to the shareholders. Within a year of the buyout, Metromedia sold its television assets for $2 billion. Thereafter, it sold most of its remaining assets for $2.5 billion—a total of $4.5 billion. The court denied Shearson's motion to dismiss the plaintiff's negligence complaint on an agency theory. Liability, said the court, did not depend on privity of contract between the bankers and the shareholders. This approach is reasserted in **Schneider v. Lazard Freres & Co.,** 159 A.D.2d 291, 552 N.Y.S.2d 571 (1990), an action against the firms that advised the RJR Nabisco board. The firms, which had addressed their opinions to the committee only, argued against liability as subagents of the board by making reference to the traditional idea that the board represents not the shareholders but the corporate entity. The court, rejecting the argument, said that "the sale of control of a corporation is not corporate business of the type governed by traditional principles of corporate governance * * *." Fiflis, Responsibility of Investment Bankers to Shareholders, 70 Wash. U.L.Q. 497 (1992), approves of liability to shareholders. Oesterle, Fairness Opinions as Magic Pieces of Paper, 70 Wash.U.L.Q. 541 (1992), takes the position that the firm, not the shareholder, is the client and any shareholder action for breach of the relationship should be a derivative action. Carney, Fairness Opinions: How Fair Are They and Why We Should Do Nothing About It, 70 Wash.U.L.Q. 523 (1992), argues that courts are ill suited to articulate the necessary standards of care, and that as a result, the costs of investment banker liability would outweigh the benefits. At least one Delaware court has taken the position that the special committee's investment banker is not an agent of the shareholders. In re Shoe–Town, Inc. Stockholders Litigation, 1990 WL 13475 (Del.Ch.1990).

(C) FREEZE–OUTS, FIDUCIARY STANDARDS AND APPRAISAL RIGHTS

INTRODUCTORY NOTE

Freeze-outs often occur in close corporations. They also arise more than occasionally in mergers of publicly held corporations, as where the depressed stock market of 1974 and 1975 stimulated the "going private" form of freeze-out in *Berkowitz*. But, more often, they occur after a corporation has acquired a controlling interest in a publicly-held corporation either by market purchases or by purchases from controlling stockholders. When the acquirer owns a large enough proportion of the subsidiary's stock to make it feasible to do so, it absorbs the subsidiary—either by merger or by liquidation—in a transaction which results in the parent acquiring all the productive assets of the subsidiary and the minority public stockholders receiving only cash.

Do the cases determine whether the public stockholder can be *required* to accept cash or non-participating senior securities rather than a continuing participation in the merged enterprise; and if so does the requirement govern *all* cases or are there circumstances in which they cannot thus be "frozen out"? Can those circumstances be determined on any coherent principle or principles? In any event, the further question remains whether in any particular case the amount of cash or securities involved can be challenged as inadequate by an appraisal proceeding or an action for damages or by an effort to enjoin the transaction as unfair or to unscramble it.

In addressing those questions consider whether there are valid bases for distinguishing among (a) mergers that are purely internal rearrangements which effect no change in the enterprise other than elimination of "outside" stockholders, such as the "going private" transactions illustrated by the *Berkowitz* and *Coggins* cases,[m] (b) mergers in which 3rd parties are taking over and something new is added, such as a transfer of all the assets to a stranger in a transaction in which the controlling insiders are given stock or other participations in the combined enterprise and the outsiders are given only cash or senior securities, (c) absorption by the successful take-over bidder of the previously untendered stock within a short period after the successful take-over, as in the *Rabkin* case, infra p. 781, or Radol v. Thomas, infra p. 1000, and (d) absorption by a parent of a subsidiary which it has controlled for many years.

(1) In **L.D. Kellogg v. Georgia Pacific Paper Corp.**, 227 F.Supp. 719 (W.D.Ark.1964), Georgia Pacific, having acquired 99.6% of the stock of The Crossett Company from the latter's controlling stockholders and on the market, apparently at $55 per share, sought to liquidate Crossett, distributing to itself the going concern and to the minority public stockholders $54.85 per share (apparently the book value), in cash. The minority public stockholders had been offered the opportunity to sell out to Georgia Pacific at $55. In a suit by the minority public stockholders to enjoin the liquidation, both because the Arkansas statutes did not permit distributions of such different types of assets to the same class of stockholders and because the amounts distributed to the public were inadequate, the District Court (Henley, J.) said (at pp. 722–25):

"From its consideration of the facts of record in the light of what appear to be governing provisions and principles of law the Court is persuaded that while some of the contentions of the defendants may

---

m. Stockholders may be forced out of an enterprise formally by techniques other than merger (such as sale of assets followed by dissolution, or bankruptcy, or reverse stock split) or informally by inducing sale of their stock after withholding dividends or by issuing additional stock to insiders.

have some relevancy on the question of what relief is to be granted plaintiffs, none of them can be sustained as far as the legality of the plan of liquidation is concerned, and that plaintiffs are entitled at this time to a binding adjudication that the plan adopted was illegal.

"The Arkansas statutes prescribe the method by which the affairs and assets of dissolved domestic corporations are to be liquidated. Ark.Stats. §§ 64–806, 64–807, and 64–811. Without stopping to abstract those statutory provisions in detail, they contemplate that the trustees in liquidation shall collect the corporate assets, pay or provide for the payment of corporate debts and liabilities, and distribute remaining assets in cash or in kind to the former stockholders in proportion to their stock ownership. Those statutes do not contemplate that the trustees in the absence of an agreement among the stockholders shall turn the corporate business and physical assets over to one stockholder or group of stockholders while requiring some other stockholder or stockholders to accept cash as his or their distributive share in liquidation.

"As to the legality of the plan of liquidation, the case of Mason v. Pewabic Mining Co., 133 U.S. 50, 10 S.Ct. 224, 33 L.Ed. 524, decided in 1890, appears to be in point here. In that case the Pewabic Mining Company was in distressed financial condition; the majority stockholders of Pewabic were apparently not willing to put any more money into that corporation. Instead, they organized a new corporation which they controlled. It was decided that Pewabic would be dissolved; that Pewabic's assets would be turned over to the new corporation in satisfaction of the stock interest of the majority stockholders, and that the owners of the minority stock would be paid in cash for their stock on the basis of a valuation fixed by the majority. It was held that this method of winding up the affairs of Pewabic was illegal and was subject to injunction.

* * *

"The correctness of the Pewabic decision is manifest. To say that majority stockholders may dissolve a corporation and proceed to take over the business and principal assets for themselves while at the same time forcing the minority to take mere cash for their interests, the payments to be based on a valuation made by the majority, would be to confer upon the majority the power to confiscate the minority interest, thus depriving the minority shareholders of their interest in an existing business with its attendant possibilities of growth and appreciation in value, an interest which may be worth much more than the present cash value of the minority shares. Such should not be permitted.

"In coming to the conclusion that the plan for the liquidation of Crossett which was adopted was illegal the Court does not mean to suggest that Georgia–Pacific or the Trustees have been guilty of any fraud or conscious oppression or conscious violation of any fiduciary duty. On the contrary, the Court assumes, and for summary judgment purposes must assume, that the defendants acted with subjective conscientiousness and fairness, and that the price offered for the minority stock was a fair price. But, those are not the questions before the Court at the moment.

"While the interests of plaintiffs in Crossett were very small proportionately, those interests constituted property rights which plaintiffs are entitled to have declared and protected. When Georgia–Pacific decided to bring about the dissolution of Crossett rather than to continue its corporate existence and operations, it assumed the obligation to liquidate Crossett in accordance with law. It had a right to distribute the assets in kind or to put them on the block for sale and divide the proceeds, in either case treating all stockholders alike. It had no right to take over The Crossett Company as a going business and eliminate plaintiffs' interests in that company by cash payments.

"To the argument that the method of liquidation selected was the only feasible one and was the alternative most beneficial to plaintiffs there is a conclusive answer. Georgia–Pacific was not required to dissolve and liquidate Crossett. Having chosen to dissolve and liquidate, it was required to do so lawfully. That a lawful liquidation might have produced less money or value to plaintiffs than the method selected is beside the point. Plaintiffs had the right to insist on a lawful liquidation, and they have done so.

"The Court is going no further at this time than to declare and adjudicate that Georgia–Pacific's method of liquidating Crossett was not in accordance with law, and that plaintiffs are entitled to some relief. What specific relief should be awarded plaintiffs presents a serious problem which the Court is not now in a position to solve. Although plaintiffs are entitled to a protection of their rights, they have come into a court of equity, and the framing of an appropriate remedy rests to some extent in the discretion of the Court to be exercised within the framework of general principles of equity. The determination of the relief to be awarded plaintiffs may involve a balancing of the comparatively small interests of the plaintiffs, on the one hand, against the very large and significant interests involved on the other hand. Rights of innocent third parties may have intervened, which rights may have to be protected.

"Without at all prejudging the matter, it may not be feasible to undo what has been done already. Or it may be that to divest Georgia–Pacific of its ownership of the Crossett properties might inflict undue hardship on Georgia–Pacific without any corresponding benefit to plaintiffs. It is possible that the plaintiffs may have to take money, and they may come out with less than Georgia–Pacific has offered. But, at the very least, they are entitled to the fair value of their stock, determined impartially, and are not required to accept a value fixed by the majority stockholders. * * *

" * * * The Court understands from counsel on both sides that in the past some settlement negotiations have been conducted. Those negotiations should be renewed in light of the Court's views herein set forth. If the negotiations are not fruitful, within about thirty days the Court will on short notice call a conference of counsel at which counsel should be prepared to discuss with the Court questions of further proceedings looking toward termination of the litigation by settlement or otherwise."

Can the result enjoined by the court in the *Kellogg* case[n] be achieved without raising any questions of statutory power through the device of a sale of all of the assets of the subsidiary to the parent in exchange for (1) cash or (2) the stock of the subsidiary held by the parent plus enough cash to pay off the minority stockholders? Compare Cal.Corp.Code § 1001(d)[o] with Alcott v. Hyman, 208 A.2d 501 (Del.Sup.Ct.1965) and Abelow v. Midstates Oil Corp., 41 Del.Ch. 145, 189 A.2d 675 (1963); Lebold v. Inland Steel Co., 82 F.2d 351 (7th Cir.1936); same case 125 F.2d 369 (7th Cir.1941); same case 136 F.2d 876 (7th Cir.1943); certiorari denied 320 U.S. 787.

(2) Are different ends intended to be served by permitting freeze-out in the short form merger (See RMBCA § 11.04, Del.Gen.Corp.Law § 253) than in long form mergers? Should these differences affect the exclusivity of the appraisal remedy in the two cases?

(3) Do the statutes authorizing long form merger and liquidation (Compare Cal.Corp.Code § 1101[p] with RMBCA Sections 11.01–11.06

n. See also In re San Joaquin Light & Power Corp., 52 Cal.App.2d 814, 127 P.2d 29 (4th Dist.1942); Zimmermann v. Tidewater Associated Oil Co., 61 Cal.App.2d 585, 143 P.2d 409 (4th Dist.1943).

o. Cal.Corp.Code § 1001 provides:

(d) If the buyer in a sale of assets pursuant to subdivision (a) of this section or subdivision (g) of Section 2001 is in control of or under common control with the seller, the principal terms of the sale must be approved by at least 90 percent of the voting power unless the sale is to a domestic or foreign corporation in consideration of the nonredeemable common shares of the purchasing corporation or its parent.

(e) Subdivision (d) does not apply to any transaction if the Commissioner of Corporations, the Superintendent of Banks, the Insurance Commissioner or the Public Utilities Commission has approved the terms and conditions of the transaction and the fairness of such terms and conditions pursuant to Section 25142, Section 696.5 of the Financial Code, Section 838.5 of the Insurance Code or Section 822 of the Public Utilities Code.

p. Sections 1101(e) and 1101.1 of the Corporations Code provide that in a statutory merger

1101(e) " * * * Each share of the same class or series of any constituent corporation (other than the cancellation of shares held by a constituent corporation or its parent or a wholly-owned subsidiary of either in another constituent corporation) shall, unless all shareholders of the class or series consent and except as provided in Section 407 [treatment of fractional shares], be treated equally with respect to any distribution of cash, property, rights, or securities. Notwithstanding subdivision (d) [which permits payment of cash for shares], except in a short-form merger * * * the nonredeemable common shares of a constituent corporation may be converted only into nonredeemable common shares of the surviving corporation or a parent party if a constituent corporation or its parent owns, directly or indirectly, shares of another constituent corporation representing more than 50 percent of the voting power of the other constituent corporation prior to the merger, unless all of the shareholders of the class consent and except as provided in Section 407.

1101.1 The last two sentences of Section 1101 do not apply to any transaction if the Commissioner of Corporations, the Superintendent of Banks, the Commissioner of Insurance or the Public Utilities Commission has approved the terms and conditions of the transaction and the fairness of such terms and conditions pursuant to Sec-

and 14.02–14.07; NYBCL Sections 902(a)(3) and 1005; Del.Corp.Law Sections 251(b)(4) and 281) permit distribution of different kinds of property to members of the same class of shareholders (e.g., a portion of the assets to some, and the remainder of the assets to others)? If equality of treatment of holders of a class of securities is required when distributions are made to the class (e.g., NYBCL § 501(c); cf. Cawley v. SCM Corp., 530 N.E.2d 1264 (N.Y.1988)) may (should) that requirement be read into the statutory provisions governing merger and liquidation so as to require distributions that are equal in form, equal in substance, or neither? See Beaumont v. American Can Co., 160 A.D.2d 174, 553 N.Y.S.2d 145 (1990). Apart from whether the statutes may be construed to permit disparate treatment of any kind, of members of the same class of stockholders (see Krafcisin v. LaSalle Madison Hotel Co., CCH Fed.Sec.L.Rep. ¶ 93,586 (N.D.Ill.1973)), there is also the question whether merger or liquidation which gives "outside" or minority shareholders cash or redeemable securities while inside or controlling shareholders receive the residual equity participation in the continuing enterprise, may, by reason of that fact alone, be unfair or enjoinable. Outwater v. Public Service Corp., 103 N.J.Eq. 461, 143 A. 729 (1928), affirmed, 104 N.J.Eq. 490, 146 A. 916 (1928), the *Berkowitz* case, supra p. 741 and the *Kellogg* case, supra, p. 761 suggest an affirmative answer, in contrast to many other decisions.

Do requirements of "business purpose" and "fairness" suggest a tolerable middle ground? Does a categorical prohibition of freeze-outs rest on a premise comparable to that underlying the denial of a premium to sellers of control? Is the analogy apposite for the phenomenon of "going private"? Compare Jutkowitz v. Bourns, No. CAOOD268 Cal.Superior Court, (11/19/75) with Jones v. H.F. Ahmanson & Co., infra p. 928. Can it be argued that the occasions on which insiders determine to freeze-out outsiders, at least in public corporations, are likely to be only those in which the former will have reason to believe that earnings will improve, so that valuation on the basis of past earnings will be inaccurate and valuation on the basis of future earnings cannot adequately be made by persons lacking the predictive capacity of insiders? If so, does it follow that a rule of fairness on a case by case basis will be inadequate, or at least will have serious defects—i.e., it will be difficult to apply with any accuracy and will be likely to result in a determination of equivalence between the cash payout and the continuing participation which is systematically biased in favor of insiders or controllers? Does it follow that a categorical denial of disparate treatment is preferable to a rule of fairness? Or will a categorical denial give the minority a nuisance value that is more costly to the majority than is the cost to the minority of a "fairness" rule? Compare Gabhart v. Gabhart, 267 Ind. 370, 370 N.E.2d 345 (1977).

tion 25142 or Section 696.5, 5750, or 5802   the Insurance Code.
of the Financial Code or Section 838.5 of

WEINBERGER v. UOP, INC.

Supreme Court of Delaware, 1983.
457 A.2d 701.

MOORE, Justice:

This post-trial appeal was reheard en banc from a decision of the Court of Chancery.[1] It was brought by the class action plaintiff below, a former shareholder of UOP, Inc., who challenged the elimination of UOP's minority shareholders by a cash-out merger between UOP and its majority owner, The Signal Companies, Inc.[2] Originally, the defendants in this action were Signal, UOP, certain officers and directors of those companies, and UOP's investment banker, Lehman Brothers Kuhn Loeb, Inc.[3] The present Chancellor held that the terms of the merger were fair to the plaintiff and the other minority shareholders of UOP. Accordingly, he entered judgment in favor of the defendants.

Numerous points were raised by the parties, but we address only the following questions presented by the trial court's opinion:

1) The plaintiff's duty to plead sufficient facts demonstrating the unfairness of the challenged merger;

2) The burden of proof upon the parties where the merger has been approved by the purportedly informed vote of a majority of the minority shareholders;

3) The fairness of the merger in terms of adequacy of the defendants' disclosures to the minority shareholders;

4) The fairness of the merger in terms of adequacy of the price paid for the minority shares and the remedy appropriate to that issue; and

5) The continued force and effect of Singer v. Magnavox Co., Del.Supr., 380 A.2d 969, 980 (1977), and its progeny.

In ruling for the defendants, the Chancellor re-stated his earlier conclusion that the plaintiff in a suit challenging a cash-out merger must allege specific acts of fraud, misrepresentation, or other items of misconduct to demonstrate the unfairness of the merger terms to the minority. We approve this rule and affirm it.

The Chancellor also held that even though the ultimate burden of proof is on the majority shareholder to show by a preponderance of the evidence that the transaction is fair, it is first the burden of the plaintiff attacking the merger to demonstrate some basis for invoking the fairness obligation. We agree with that principle. However, where corporate action has been approved by an informed vote of a majority of

1. Accordingly, this Court's February 9, 1982 opinion is withdrawn.

2. For the opinion of the trial court see Weinberger v. UOP, Inc., Del.Ch., 426 A.2d 1333 (1981).

3. Shortly before the last oral argument, the plaintiff dismissed Lehman Brothers from the action. Thus, we do not deal with the issues raised by the plaintiff's claims against this defendant.

the minority shareholders, we conclude that the burden entirely shifts to the plaintiff to show that the transaction was unfair to the minority. See, e.g., Michelson v. Duncan, Del.Supr., 407 A.2d 211, 224 (1979). But in all this, the burden clearly remains on those relying on the vote to show that they completely disclosed all material facts relevant to the transaction.

Here, the record does not support a conclusion that the minority stockholder vote was an informed one. Material information, necessary to acquaint those shareholders with the bargaining positions of Signal and UOP, was withheld under circumstances amounting to a breach of fiduciary duty. We therefore conclude that this merger does not meet the test of fairness, at least as we address that concept, and no burden thus shifted to the plaintiff by reason of the minority shareholder vote. Accordingly, we reverse and remand for further proceedings consistent herewith.

In considering the nature of the remedy available under our law to minority shareholders in a cash-out merger, we believe that it is, and hereafter should be, an appraisal under 8 Del.C. § 262 as hereinafter construed. We therefore overrule Lynch v. Vickers Energy Corp., Del.Supr., 429 A.2d 497 (1981) (Lynch II) to the extent that it purports to limit a stockholder's monetary relief to a specific damage formula. See Lynch II, 429 A.2d at 507–08 (McNeilly & Quillen, JJ., dissenting). But to give full effect to section 262 within the framework of the General Corporation Law we adopt a more liberal, less rigid and stylized, approach to the valuation process than has heretofore been permitted by our courts. While the present state of these proceedings does not admit the plaintiff to the appraisal remedy per se, the practical effect of the remedy we do grant him will be co-extensive with the liberalized valuation and appraisal methods we herein approve for cases coming after this decision.

Our treatment of these matters has necessarily led us to a reconsideration of the business purpose rule announced in the trilogy of Singer v. Magnavox Co., supra; Tanzer v. International General Industries, Inc., Del.Supr., 879 A.2d 1121 (1977); and Roland International Corp. v. Najjar, Del.Supr., 407 A.2d 1032 (1979). For the reasons hereafter set forth we consider that the business purpose requirement of these cases is no longer the law of Delaware.

I.

The facts found by the trial court, pertinent to the issues before us, are supported by the record, and we draw from them as set out in the Chancellor's opinion.

Signal is a diversified, technically based company operating through various subsidiaries. Its stock is publicly traded on the New York, Philadelphia and Pacific Stock Exchanges. UOP, formerly known as Universal Oil Products Company, was a diversified industrial company engaged in various lines of business, including petroleum and petro-chemical services and related products, construction, fabricated metal products, transportation equipment products, chemicals and plastics, and other products and services including land development, lumber products and waste disposal. Its stock was publicly held and listed on the New York Stock Exchange.

In 1974 Signal sold one of its wholly-owned subsidiaries for $420,-000,000 in cash. See Gimbel v. Signal Companies, Inc., Del.Ch., 816 A.2d 599, aff'd, Del.Supr., 816 A.2d 619 (1974). While looking to invest this cash surplus, Signal became interested in UOP as a possible acquisition. Friendly negotiations ensued, and Signal proposed to acquire a controlling interest in UOP at a price of $19 per share. UOP's representatives sought $25 per share. In the arm's length bargaining that followed, an understanding was reached whereby Signal agreed to purchase from UOP 1,500,000 shares of UOP's authorized but unissued stock at $21 per share.

This purchase was contingent upon Signal making a successful cash tender offer for 4,300,000 publicly held shares of UOP, also at a price of $21 per share. This combined method of acquisition permitted Signal to acquire 5,800,000 shares of stock, representing 50.5% of UOP's outstanding shares. The UOP board of directors advised the company's shareholders that it had no objection to Signal's tender offer at that price. Immediately before the announcement of the tender offer, UOP's common stock had been trading on the New York Stock Exchange at a fraction under $14 per share.

The negotiations between Signal and UOP occurred during April 1975, and the resulting tender offer was greatly oversubscribed. However, Signal limited its total purchase of the tendered shares so that, when coupled with the stock brought from UOP, it had achieved its goal of becoming a 50.5% shareholder of UOP.

Although UOP's board consisted of thirteen directors, Signal nominated and elected only six. Of these, five were either directors or employees of Signal. The sixth, a partner in the banking firm of Lazard Freres & Co., had been one of Signal's representatives in the negotiations and bargaining with UOP concerning the tender offer and purchase price of the UOP shares.

However, the president and chief executive officer of UOP retired during 1975, and Signal caused him to be replaced by James V. Crawford, a long-time employee and senior executive vice president of one of Signal's wholly-owned subsidiaries. Crawford succeeded his predecessor on UOP's board of directors and also was made a director of Signal.

By the end of 1977 Signal basically was unsuccessful in finding other suitable investment candidates for its excess cash, and by February 1978 considered that it had no other realistic acquisitions available to it on a friendly basis. Once again its attention turned to UOP.

The trial court found that at the investigation of certain Signal management personnel, including William W. Walkup, its board chairman, and Forrest N. Shumway, its president, a feasibility study was made concerning the possible acquisition of the balance of UOP's outstanding shares. This study was performed by two Signal officers, Charles S. Arledge, vice president (director of planning) and Andrew J. Chitiea, senior vice president (chief financial officer). Messrs. Walkup, Shumway, Arledge and Chitiea were all directors of UOP in addition to their membership on the Signal board.

Arledge and Chitiea concluded that it would be a good investment for Signal to acquire the remaining 49.5% of UOP shares at any price up to $24 each. Their report was discussed between Walkup and Shumway who, along with Arledge, Chitiea and Brewster L. Arms, internal counsel for Signal, constituted Signal's senior management. In particular, they talked about the proper price to be paid if the acquisition was pursued, purportedly keeping in mind that as UOP's majority shareholder, Signal owed a fiduciary responsibility to both its own stockholders as well as to UOP's minority. It was ultimately agreed that a meeting of Signal's Executive Committee would be called to propose that Signal acquire the remaining outstanding stock of UOP through a cash-out merger in the range of $20 to $21 per share.

The Executive Committee meeting was set for February 28, 1978. As a courtesy, UOP's president, Crawford, was invited to attend, although he was not a member of Signal's executive committee. On his arrival, and prior to the meeting, Crawford was asked to meet privately with Walkup and Shumway. He was then told of Signal's plan to acquire full ownership of UOP and was asked for his reaction to the proposed price range of $20 to $21 per share. Crawford said he thought such a price would be "generous", and that it was certainly one which should be submitted to UOP's minority shareholders for their ultimate consideration. He stated, however, that Signal's 100% ownership could cause internal problems at UOP. He believed that employees would have to be given some assurance of their future place in a fully-owned Signal subsidiary. Otherwise, he feared the departure of essential personnel. Also, many of UOP's key employees had stock option incentive programs which would be wiped out by a merger. Crawford therefore urged that some adjustment would have to be made, such as providing a comparable incentive in Signal's shares, if after the merger he was to maintain his quality of personnel and efficiency at UOP.

Thus, Crawford voiced no objection to the $20 to $21 price range, nor did he suggest that Signal should consider paying more than $21 per share for the minority interests. Later, at the Executive Committee meeting the same factors were discussed, with Crawford repeating the position he earlier took with Walkup and Shumway. Also considered was the 1975 tender offer and the fact that it had been greatly oversubscribed at $21 per share. For many reasons, Signal's management concluded that the acquisition of UOP's minority shares provided the solution to a number of its business problems.

Thus, it was the consensus that a price of $20 to $21 per share would be fair to both Signal and the minority shareholders of UOP. Signal's executive committee authorized its management "to negotiate" with UOP "for a cash acquisition of the minority ownership in UOP, Inc., with the intention of presenting a proposal to [Signal's] board of directors * * * on March 6, 1978". Immediately after this February 28, 1978 meeting, Signal issued a press release stating:

> The Signal Companies, Inc. and UOP, Inc. are conducting negotiations for the acquisition for cash by Signal of the 49.5 per cent of UOP which it does not presently own, announced Forrest N. Shumway, president and chief executive officer of Signal, and James V. Crawford, UOP president.
>
> Price and other term. of the proposed transaction have not yet been finalized and would be subject to approval of the boards of directors of Signal and UOP, scheduled to meet early next week, the stockholders of UOP and certain federal agencies.

The announcement also referred to the fact that the closing price of UOP's common stock on that day was $14.50 per share.

Two days later, on March 2, 1978, Signal issued a second press release stating that its management would recommend a price in the range of $20 to $21 per share for UOP's 49.5% minority interest. This announcement referred to Signal's earlier statement that "negotiations" were being conducted for the acquisition of the minority shares.

Between Tuesday, February 28, 1978 and Monday, March 6, 1978, a total of four business days, Crawford spoke by telephone with all of UOP's non-Signal, i.e., outside, directors. Also during that period, Crawford retained Lehman Brothers to render a fairness opinion as to the price offered the minority for its stock. He gave two reasons for this choice. First, the time schedule between the announcement and the board meetings was short (by then only three business days) and since Lehman Brothers had been acting as UOP's investment banker for many years, Crawford felt that it would be in the best position to respond on such brief notice. Second, James W. Glanville, a long-time director of UOP and a partner in Lehman Brothers, had acted as a financial advisor to UOP for many years. Crawford believed that Glanville's familiarity with UOP, as a member of its board, would also be of assistance in enabling Lehman Brothers to render a fairness opinion within the existing time constraints.

Crawford telephoned Glanville, who gave his assurance that Lehman Brothers had no conflicts that would prevent it from accepting the task. Glanville's immediate personal reaction was that a price of $20 to $21 would certainly be fair, since it represented almost a 50% premium over UOP's market price. Glanville sought a $250,000 fee for Lehman Brothers' services, but Crawford thought this too much. After further discussions Glanville finally agreed that Lehman Brothers would render its fairness opinion for $150,000.

     * * *

     * * * [T]he Lehman Brothers team concluded that "the price of either $20 or $21 would be a fair price for the remaining shares of

UOP". They telephoned this impression to Glanville, who was spending the weekend in Vermont.

On Monday morning, March 6, 1978, Glanville and the senior member of the Lehman Brothers team flew to Des Plaines to attend the scheduled UOP directors meeting. Glanville looked over the assembled information during the flight. The two had with them the draft of a "fairness opinion letter" in which the price had been left blank. Either during or immediately prior to the directors' meeting, the two-page "fairness opinion letter" was typed in final form and the price of $21 per share was inserted.

On March 6, 1978, both the Signal and UOP boards were convened to consider the proposed merger. Telephone communications were maintained between the two meetings. Walkup, Signal's board chairman, and also a UOP director, attended UOP's meeting with Crawford in order to present Signal's position and answer any questions that UOP's non-Signal directors might have. Arledge and Chitiea, along with Signal's other designees on UOP's board participated by conference telephone. All of UOP's outside directors attended the meeting either in person or by conference telephone.

First, Signal's board unanimously adopted a resolution authorizing Signal to propose to UOP a cash merger of $21 per share as outlined in a certain merger agreement and other supporting documents. This proposal required that the merger be approved by a majority of UOP's outstanding minority shares voting at the stockholders meeting at which the merger would be considered, and that the minority shares voting in favor of the merger, when coupled with Signal's 50.5% interest would have to comprise at least two-thirds of all UOP shares. Otherwise the proposed merger would be deemed disapproved.

UOP's board then considered the proposal. Copies of the agreement were delivered to the directors in attendance, and other copies had been forwarded earlier to the directors participating by telephone. They also had before them UOP financial data for 1974–1977, UOP's most recent financial statements, market price information, and budget projections for 1978. In addition they had Lehman Brothers' hurriedly prepared fairness opinion letter finding the price of $21 to be fair. Glanville, the Lehman Brothers partner, and UOP director, commented on the information that had gone into preparation of the letter.

Signal also suggests that the Arledge–Chitiea feasibility study, indicating that a price of up to $24 per share would be a "good investment" for Signal, was discussed at the UOP directors' meeting. The Chancellor made no such finding, and our independent review of the record, detailed infra, satisfies us by a preponderance of the evidence that there was no discussion of this document at UOP's board meeting. Furthermore, it is clear beyond peradventure that nothing in that report was ever disclosed to UOP's minority shareholders prior to their approval of the merger.

After consideration of Signal's proposal, Walkup and Crawford left the meeting to permit a free and uninhibited exchange between UOP's non-Signal directors. Upon their return a resolution to accept Signal's offer was then proposed and adopted. While Signal's men on UOP's board participated in various aspects of the meeting, they abstained from voting. However, the minutes show that each of them "if voting would have voted yes".

On March 7, 1978, UOP sent a letter to its shareholders advising them of the action taken by UOP's board with respect to Signal's offer. This document pointed out, among other things, that on February 28, 1978 "both companies had announced negotiations were being conducted".

Despite the swift board action of the two companies, the merger was not submitted to UOP's shareholders until their annual meeting on May 26, 1978. In the notice of that meeting and proxy statement sent to shareholders in May, UOP's management and board urged that the merger be approved. The proxy statement also advised:

> The price was determined after *discussions* between James V. Crawford, a director of Signal and Chief Executive Officer of UOP, and officers of Signal which took place during meetings on February 28, 1978, and in the course of several subsequent telephone conversations. (Emphasis added.)

In the original draft of the proxy statement the word "negotiations" had been used rather than "discussions". However, when the Securities and Exchange Commission sought details of the "negotiations" as part of its review of these materials, the term was deleted and the word "discussions" was substituted. The proxy statement indicated that the vote of UOP's board in approving the merger had been unanimous. It also advised the shareholders that Lehman Brothers had given its opinion that the merger price of $21 per share was fair to UOP's minority. However, it did not disclose the hurried method by which this conclusion was reached.

As of the record date of UOP's annual meeting, there were 11,488,-302 shares of UOP common stock outstanding, 5,688,302 of which were owned by the minority. At the meeting only 56%, or 3,208,652, of the minority shares were voted. Of these, 2,953,812, or 51.9% of the total minority, voted for the merger, and 254,840 voted against it. When Signal's stock was added to the minority shares voting in favor, a total of 76.2% of UOP's outstanding shares approved the merger while only 2.2% opposed it.

By its terms the merger became effective on May 26, 1978, and each share of UOP's stock held by the minority was automatically converted into a right to receive $21 cash.

II.

A.

A primary issue mandating reversal is the preparation by two UOP directors, Arledge and Chitiea, of their feasibility study for the exclusive use and benefit of Signal. This document was of obvious significance to both Signal and UOP. Using UOP data, it described the advantages to Signal of ousting the minority at a price range of $21–$24 per share.

* * *

The Arledge–Chitiea report speaks for itself in supporting the Chancellor's finding that a price of up to $24 was a "good investment" for Signal. It shows that a return on the investment at $21 would be 15.7% versus 15.5% at $24 per share. This was a difference of only two-tenths of one percent, while it meant over $17,000,000 to the minority. Under such circumstances, paying UOP's minority share-holders $24 would have had relatively little long-term effect on Signal, and the Chancellor's findings concerning the benefit to Signal, even at a price of $24, were obviously correct. Levitt v. Bouvier, Del.Supr., 287 A.2d 671, 673 (1972).

Certainly, this was a matter of material significance to UOP and its shareholders. Since the study was prepared by two UOP directors, using UOP information for the exclusive benefit of Signal, and nothing whatever was done to disclose it to the outside UOP directors or the minority shareholders, a question of breach of fiduciary duty arises. This problem occurs because there were common Signal–UOP directors participating, at least to some extent, in the UOP board's decision-making processes without full disclosure of the conflicts they faced.[7]

B.

In assessing this situation, the Court of Chancery was required to:

examine what information defendants had and to measure it against what they gave to the minority stockholders, in a context in which 'complete candor' is required. In other words, the limited function of the Court was to determine whether defendants had disclosed all information in their possession germane to the trans-action in issue. And by 'germane' we mean, for present purposes, information such as a reasonable shareholder would consider im-portant in deciding whether to sell or retain stock.

* * *

* * * Completeness, not adequacy, is both the norm and the man-date under present circumstances.

---

7. Although perfection is not possible, or expected, the result here could have been entirely different if UOP had appoint-ed an independent negotiating committee of its outside directors to deal with Signal at arm's length. See, e.g., Harriman v. E.I. duPont de Nemours & Co., 411 F.Supp. 133 (D.Del.1975). Since fairness in this context can be equated to conduct by a theoretical, wholly independent, board of directors act-ing upon the matter before them, it is unfortunate that this course apparently was neither considered nor pursued. Johnston v. Greene, Del.Supr., 121 A.2d 919, 925 (1956). Particularly in a parent-subsidiary context, a showing that the ac-tion taken was as though each of the con-tending parties had in fact exerted its bar-gaining power against the other at arm's length is strong evidence that the transac-tion meets the test of fairness. Getty Oil Co. v. Skelly Oil Co., Del.Supr., 267 A.2d 883, 886 (1970); Puma v. Marriott, Del.Ch., 283 A.2d 693, 696 (1971).

Lynch v. Vickers Energy Corp., Del.Supr., 383 A.2d 278, 281 (1977)
(Lynch I). This is merely stating in another way the long-existing
principle of Delaware law that these Signal designated directors on
UOP's board still owed UOP and its shareholders an uncompromising
duty of loyalty.

* * *

Given the absence of any attempt to structure this transaction on
an arm's length basis, Signal cannot escape the effects of the conflicts it
faced, particularly when its designees on UOP's board did not totally
abstain from participation in the matter. There is no "safe harbor" for
such divided loyalties in Delaware. When directors of a Delaware
corporation are on both sides of a transaction, they are required to
demonstrate their utmost good faith and the most scrupulous inherent
fairness of the bargain. Gottlieb v. Heyden Chemical Corp., Del.Supr.,
91 A.2d 57, 57–58 (1952). The requirement of fairness is unflinching in
its demand that where one stands on both sides of a transaction, he has
the burden of establishing its entire fairness, sufficient to pass the test
of careful scrutiny by the courts. Sterling v. Mayflower Hotel Corp.,
Del.Supr., 93 A.2d 107, 110 (1952); Bastian v. Bourns, Inc., Del.Ch., 256
A.2d 680, 681 (1969), aff'd, Del.Supr., 278 A.2d 467 (1970); David J.
Greene & Co. v. Dunhill International Inc., Del.Ch., 249 A.2d 427, 431
(1968).

There is no dilution of this obligation where one holds dual or
multiple directorships, as in a parent-subsidiary context. Levien v.
Sinclair Oil Corp., Del.Ch., 261 A.2d 911, 915 (1969). Thus, individuals
who act in a dual capacity as directors of two corporations, one of whom
is parent and the other subsidiary, owe the same duty of good management to both corporations, and in the absence of an independent
negotiating structure (see note 7, supra), or the directors' total abstention from any participation in the matter, this duty is to be exercised in
light of what is best for both companies. Warshaw v. Calhoun, Del.
Supr., 221 A.2d 487, 492 (1966). The record demonstrates that Signal
has not met this obligation.

C.

The concept of fairness has two basic aspects: fair dealing and fair
price. The former embraces questions of when the transaction was
timed, how it was initiated, structured, negotiated, disclosed to the
directors, and how the approvals of the directors and the stockholders
were obtained. The latter aspect of fairness relates to the economic
and financial considerations of the proposed merger, including all
relevant factors: assets, market value, earnings, future prospects, and
any other elements that affect the intrinsic or inherent value of a
company's stock. Moore, The "Interested" Director or Officer Transaction, 4 Del.J.Corp.L. 674, 676 (1979); Nathan & Shapiro, Legal Standard
of Fairness of Merger Terms Under Delaware Law, 2 Del.J.Corp.L. 44,
46–47 (1977). See Tri–Continental Corp. v. Battye, Del.Supr., 74 A.2d
71, 72 (1950); 8 Del.C. § 262(h). However, the test for fairness is not a

bifurcated one as between fair dealing and price. All aspects of the issue must be examined as a whole since the question is one of entire fairness. However, in a non-fraudulent transaction we recognize that price may be the preponderant consideration outweighing other features of the merger. Here, we address the two basic aspects of fairness separately because we find reversible error as to both.

D.

Part of fair dealing is the obvious duty of candor required by Lynch I, supra. Moreover, one possessing superior knowledge may not mislead any stockholder by use of corporate information to which the latter is not privy. Lank v. Steiner, Del.Supr., 224 A.2d 242, 244 (1966). Delaware has long imposed this duty even upon persons who are not corporate officers or directors, but who nonetheless are privy to matters of interest or significance to their company. Brophy v. Cities Service Co., Del.Ch., 70 A.2d 5, 7 (1949). With the well-established Delaware law on the subject, and the Court of Chancery's findings of fact here, it is inevitable that the obvious conflicts posed by Arledge and Chitiea's preparation of their "feasibility study", derived from UOP information, for the sole use and benefit of Signal, cannot pass muster.

The Arledge–Chitiea report is but one aspect of the element of fair dealing. How did this merger evolve? It is clear that it was entirely initiated by Signal. The serious time constraints under which the principals acted were all set by Signal. It had not found a suitable outlet for its excess cash and considered UOP a desirable investment, particularly since it was now in a position to acquire the whole company for itself. For whatever reasons, and they were only Signal's, the entire transaction was presented to and approved by UOP's board within four business days. Standing alone, this is not necessarily indicative of any lack of fairness by a majority shareholder. It was what occurred, or more properly, what did not occur, during this brief period that makes the time constraints imposed by Signal relevant to the issue of fairness.

The structure of the transaction, again, was Signal's doing. So far as negotiations were concerned, it is clear that they were modest at best. Crawford, Signal's man at UOP, never really talked price with Signal, except to accede to its management's statements on the subject, and to convey to Signal the UOP outside directors' view that as between the $20–$21 range under consideration, it would have to be $21. The latter is not a surprising outcome, but hardly arm's length negotiations. Only the protection of benefits for UOP's key employees and the issue of Lehman Brothers' fee approached any concept of bargaining.

As we have noted, the matter of disclosure to the UOP directors was wholly flawed by the conflicts of interest raised by the Arledge–Chitiea report. All of those conflicts were resolved by Signal in its own favor without divulging any aspect of them to UOP.

This cannot but undermine a conclusion that this merger meets any reasonable test of fairness. The outside UOP directors lacked one material piece of information generated by two of their colleagues, but shared only with Signal. True, the UOP board had the Lehman Brothers' fairness opinion, but that firm has been blamed by the plaintiff for the hurried task it performed, when more properly the responsibility for this lies with Signal. There was no disclosure of the circumstances surrounding the rather cursory preparation of the Lehman Brothers' fairness opinion. Instead, the impression was given UOP's minority that a careful study had been made, when in fact speed was the hallmark, and Mr. Glanville, Lehman's partner in charge of the matter, and also a UOP director, having spent the weekend in Vermont, brought a draft of the "fairness opinion letter" to the UOP directors' meeting on March 6, 1978 with the price left blank. We can only conclude from the record that the rush imposed on Lehman Brothers by Signal's timetable contributed to the difficulties under which this investment banking firm attempted to perform its responsibilities. Yet, none of this was disclosed to UOP's minority.

Finally, the minority stockholders were denied the critical information that Signal considered a price of $24 to be a good investment. Since this would have meant over $17,000,000 more to the minority, we cannot conclude that the shareholder vote was an informed one. Under the circumstances, an approval by a majority of the minority was meaningless. Lynch I, 383 A.2d at 279, 281; Cahall v. Lofland, Del.Ch., 114 A. 224 (1921).

Given these particulars and the Delaware law on the subject, the record does not establish that this transaction satisfies any reasonable concept of fair dealing, and the Chancellor's findings in that regard must be reversed.

E.

Turning to the matter of price, plaintiff also challenges its fairness. His evidence was that on the date the merger was approved the stock was worth at least $26 per share. In support, he offered the testimony of a chartered investment analyst who used two basic approaches to valuation: a comparative analysis of the premium paid over market in ten other tender offer-merger combinations, and a discounted cash flow analysis.

In this breach of fiduciary duty case, the Chancellor perceived that the approach to valuation was the same as that in an appraisal proceeding. Consistent with precedent, he rejected plaintiff's method of proof and accepted defendants' evidence of value as being in accord with practice under prior case law. This means that the so-called "Delaware block" or weighted average method was employed wherein the elements of value, i.e., assets, market price, earnings, etc., were assigned a particular weight and the resulting amounts added to determine the value per share. This procedure has been in use for decades. See In re General Realty & Utilities Corp., Del.Ch., 52 A.2d 6, 14–15 (1947). However, to the extent it excludes other generally accepted techniques used in the financial community and the courts, it is now clearly outmoded. It is time we recognize this in appraisal and other stock valuation proceedings and bring our law current on the subject.

While the Chancellor rejected plaintiff's discounted cash flow method of valuing UOP's stock, as not corresponding with "either logic or the existing law" (426 A.2d at 1360), it is significant that this was essentially the focus, i.e., earnings potential of UOP, of Messrs. Arledge and Chitiea in their evaluation of the merger. Accordingly, the standard "Delaware block" or weighted average method of valuation, formerly employed in appraisal and other stock *valuation cases shall no longer exclusively control such proceedings.* We believe that a more liberal approach must include proof of value by any techniques or methods which are generally considered acceptable in the financial community and otherwise admissible in court, subject only to our interpretation of 8 Del.C. § 262(b), infra. See also D.R.E. 702–05. This will obviate the very structured and mechanistic procedure that has heretofore governed such matters. See Jacques Coe & Co. v. Minneapolis–Moline Co., Del.Ch., 75 A.2d 244, 247 (1950); Tri–Continental Corp. v. Battye, Del.Ch., 86 A.2d 910, 917–18 (1949); In re General Realty and Utilities Corp., supra.

Fair price obviously requires consideration of all relevant factors involving the value of a company. This has long been the law of Delaware as stated in Tri–Continental Corp., 74 A.2d at 72:

> The basic concept of value under the appraisal statute is that the stockholder is entitled to be paid for that which has been taken from him, viz., his proportionate interest in a going concern. By value of the stockholder's proportionate interest in the corporate enterprise is meant the true or intrinsic value of his stock which has been taken by the merger. In determining what figure represents this true or intrinsic value, the appraiser and the courts must take into consideration all factors and elements which reasonably might enter into the fixing of value. Thus, market value, asset value, dividends, earning prospects, the nature of the enterprise and any other facts which were known or which could be ascertained as of the date of merger and which throw any light on *future prospects* of the merged corporation are not only pertinent to an inquiry as to the value of the dissenting stockholders' interest, but *must be considered* by the agency fixing the value. (Emphasis added.)

This is not only in accord with the realities of present day affairs, but it is thoroughly consonant with the purpose and intent of our statutory law. Under 8 Del.C. § 262(h), the Court of Chancery:

> shall appraise the shares, determining their *fair* value exclusive of any element of value arising from the accomplishment or expectation of the merger, together with a fair rate of interest, if any, to be paid upon the amount determined to be the *fair* value. In deter-

mining such *fair* value, the Court shall take into account *all relevant factors* * * * (Emphasis added)

See also Bell v. Kirby Lumber Corp., Del.Supr., 413 A.2d 137, 150–51 (1980) (Quillen, J., concurring).

It is significant that section 262 now mandates the determination of "fair" value based upon "all relevant factors". Only the speculative elements of value that may arise from the "accomplishment or expectation" of the merger are excluded. We take this to be a very narrow exception to the appraisal process, designed to eliminate use of *pro forma* data and projections of a speculative variety relating to the completion of a merger. But elements of future value, including the nature of the enterprise, which are known or susceptible of proof as of the date of the merger and not the product of speculation, may be considered. When the trial court deems it appropriate, fair value also includes any damages, resulting from the taking, which the stockholders sustain as a class. If that was not the case, then the obligation to consider "all relevant factors" in the valuation process would be eroded. We are supported in this view not only by *Tri–Continental Corp.*, 74 A.2d at 72, but also by the evolutionary amendments to section 262.

Prior to an amendment in 1976, the earlier relevant provision of section 262 stated:

(f) The appraiser shall determine the value of the stock of the stockholders * * * The Court shall by its decree determine the value of the stock of the stockholders entitled to payment therefor * * *

The first references to "fair" value occurred in a 1976 amendment to section 262(f), which provided:

(f) * * * the Court shall appraise the shares, determining their fair value exclusively of any element of value arising from the accomplishment or expectation of the merger * * *.

It was not until the 1981 amendment to section 262 that the reference to "fair value" was repeatedly emphasized and the statutory mandate that the Court "take into account all relevant factors" appeared [section 262(h)]. Clearly, there is a legislative intent to fully compensate shareholders for whatever their loss may be, subject only to the narrow limitation that one can not take speculative effects of the merger into account.

Although the Chancellor received the plaintiff's evidence, his opinion indicates that the use of it was precluded because of past Delaware practice. While we do not suggest a monetary result one way or the other, we do think the plaintiff's evidence should be part of the factual mix and weighed as such. Until the $21 price is measured on remand by the valuation standards mandated by Delaware law, there can be no finding at the present stage of these proceedings that the price is fair. Given the lack of any candid disclosure of the material facts surrounding establishment of the $21 price, the majority of the minority vote, approving the merger, is meaningless.

The plaintiff has not sought an appraisal, but rescissory damages of the type contemplated by Lynch v. Vickers Energy Corp., Del.Supr., 429 A.2d 497, 505–06 (1981) (Lynch II). In view of the approach to valuation that we announce today, we see no basis in our law for *Lynch II's* exclusive monetary formula for relief.* On remand the plaintiff will be permitted to test the fairness of the $21 price by the standards we herein establish, in conformity with the principle applicable to an appraisal—that fair value be determined by taking "into account all relevant factors" [see 8 Del.C. § 262(h), supra]. In our view this includes the elements of rescissory damages if the Chancellor considers them susceptible of proof and a remedy appropriate to all the issues of fairness before him. To the extent that *Lynch II,* 429 A.2d at 505–06, purports to limit the Chancellor's discretion to a single remedial formula for monetary damages in a cash-out merger, it is overruled.

While a plaintiff's monetary remedy ordinarily should be confined to the more liberalized appraisal proceeding herein established, we do not intend any limitation on the historic powers of the Chancellor to grant such other relief as the facts of a particular case may dictate. The appraisal remedy we approve may not be adequate in certain cases, particularly where fraud, misrepresentation, self-dealing, deliberate waste of corporate assets, or gross and palpable overreaching are involved. Cole v. National Cash Credit Association, Del.Ch., 156 A. 183, 187 (1931). Under such circumstances, the Chancellor's powers are complete to fashion any form of equitable and monetary relief as may be appropriate, including rescissory damages. Since it is apparent that this long completed transaction is too involved to undo, and in view of the Chancellor's discretion, the award, if any, should be in the form of monetary damages based upon entire fairness standards, i.e., fair dealing and fair price.

Obviously, there are other litigants, like the plaintiff, who abjured an appraisal and whose rights to challenge the element of fair value must be preserved. Accordingly, the quasi-appraisal remedy we grant the plaintiff here will apply only to: (1) this case; (2) any case now pending on appeal to this Court; (3) any case now pending in the Court of Chancery which has not yet been appealed but which may be eligible for direct appeal to this Court; (4) any case challenging a cash-out merger, the effective date of which is on or before February 1, 1983; and (5) any proposed merger to be presented at a shareholders' meeting,

---

* [Ed. Note] On the first remand, in Lynch v. Vickers Energy Corp. (Lynch I), the trial court valued the Vickers stock as though in an appraisal proceeding, and concluded that plaintiffs had not been damaged because they had received more than fair value for their shares. (402 A.2d 5 (Del.Ch.1980)). On appeal, the Delaware Supreme Court affirmed in part, reversed in part, and remanded (429 A.2d 497 (1981)). (Lynch II) It ruled that in a cause of action for damages for having been induced fraudulently to sell stock, the actual value of the stock is relevant in determin-

ing whether plaintiff may recover the damages he seeks. But where the claim is for a failure to make adequate disclosure in breach of fiduciary duty, plaintiff is entitled to an accounting or rescission. This can be accomplished without interfering with the completed transaction, "by ordering damages which are the monetary equivalent of rescission and which will, in effect, equal the increment in value that Vickers [the bidder] enjoyed as a result of acquiring and holding the TransOcean [the target] stock in issue" (429 A.2d at 501).

the notification of which is mailed to the stockholders on or before February 23, 1983. Thereafter, the provisions of 8 Del.C. § 262, as herein construed, respecting the scope of an appraisal and the means for perfecting the same, shall govern the financial remedy available to minority shareholders in a cash-out merger. Thus, we return to the well established principles of Stauffer v. Standard Brands, Inc., Del. Supr., 187 A.2d 78 (1962) and David J. Greene & Co. v. Schenley Industries, Inc., Del.Ch., 281 A.2d 30 (1971), mandating a stockholder's recourse to the basic remedy of an appraisal.

III.

Finally, we address the matter of business purpose. The defendants contend that the purpose of this merger was not a proper subject of inquiry by the trial court. The plaintiff says that no valid purpose existed—the entire transaction was a mere subterfuge designed to eliminate the minority. The Chancellor ruled otherwise, but in so doing he clearly circumscribed the thrust and effect of *Singer*. Weinberger v. UOP, 426 A.2d at 1342–43, 1348–50. This has led to the thoroughly sound observation that the business purpose test "may be * * * virtually interpreted out of existence, as it was in *Weinberger*".[9]

The requirement of a business purpose is new to our law of mergers and was a departure from prior case law. See Stauffer v. Standard Brands, Inc., supra; David J. Greene & Co. v. Schenley Industries, Inc., supra.

In view of the fairness test which has long been applicable to parent-subsidiary mergers, Sterling v. Mayflower Hotel Corp., Del. Supr., 93 A.2d 107, 109–10 (1952), the expanded appraisal remedy now available to shareholders, and the broad discretion of the Chancellor to fashion such relief as the facts of a given case may dictate, we do not believe that any additional meaningful protection is afforded minority shareholders by the business purpose requirement of the trilogy of *Singer, Tanzer, Najjar,* and their progeny. Accordingly, such requirement shall no longer be of any force or effect.

The judgment of the Court of Chancery, finding both the circumstances of the merger and the price paid the minority shareholders to be fair, is reversed. The matter is remanded for further proceedings consistent herewith. Upon remand the plaintiff's post-trial motion to enlarge the class should be granted.

* * *

Reversed and Remanded.[*]

---

9. Weiss, The Law of Take Out Mergers: A Historical Perspective, 56 N.Y.U.L.Rev. 624, 671, n. 300 (1981).

[*] [Ed. Note] After UOP, does it become relevant in an appraisal proceeding that the target was the subject of a two-tier pricing bid—i.e., what impact should the higher price in the first tier bid have on the determination of the fair value sought in a merger (a) in Delaware? (b) in a block weighting valuation jurisdiction?

On the remand, the Court of Chancery awarded members of the plaintiffs' class damages of $1 per share and interest from February 1, 1983, the date of the Delaware Supreme Court's en banc decision to remand. The Supreme Court upheld that award and in its order said:

"Plaintiffs contend, inter alia, that the Court of Chancery erred (a) in placing the burden of proof on them, (b) in deciding not to award rescissory damages, (c) in awarding an inadequate amount of damages, and (d) in not awarding interest on the damages from the date of the wrong. We conclude that these contentions are without merit."

The decision not to award rescissory damages was based on the Chancellor's proclaimed inability "to formulate a post merger value for a share of UOP stock [frozen out in "a long completed merger"] with a sufficient degree of certainty to put the theory to work." That inability was a function of the length of time between the merger and the decision on remand, and the resulting incalculability of the relevant variables which are essential to be taken into account in "constructing" rescissory damages for a freeze-out merger. How likely is it that rescissory damages will be calculable "with a sufficient degree of certainty to put the theory to work" in any freeze-out merger involving a parent and subsidiary each of which has substantial operating assets?[q]

NOTE: RABKIN v. HUNT CHEMICAL

In **Rabkin v. Philip A. Hunt Chemical Corp.,** 498 A.2d 1099 (Del.1985) the court elaborated on its teaching in Weinberger about the exclusivity of the appraisal remedy and the significance of procedural fairness in a cash-out merger. The case involved a challenge to the merger of Hunt Corp. into Olin Corp. in July 1984. On March 1, 1983 Olin Corp. had bought 63.4% of the Hunt common stock for $25 per share from a holding company. At the latter's insistence, Olin undertook, at the time of its purchase on March 1, 1983, to pay at least the equivalent of $25 per share to the holders of the remaining Hunt stock if within one year thereafter it absorbed Hunt by merger, consolidation, tender offer or the like. Although, according to the evidence obtained in discovery in the case, Olin quite plainly always had contemplated acquiring 100% of Hunt, it waited until after the year had run, then obtained a banker's opinion that $20 per share was fair for Hunt stock, and merged out the remaining Hunt common stock at $20 on July 5, 1984.

The merger procedure entailed a statement by Olin's CEO to Hunt's President of the terms of the merger on the evening of March 27, 1984, and the issuance on March 28 of a joint press release

q. The breadth of the valuation methods open to the Chancellor under *Wein-* *berger* is explained in Kahn v. Household Acquisition Corp., 591 A.2d 166 (Del.1991).

announcing the merger on those terms. According to the Supreme Court, Moore, J. (498 A.2d at 1103–1108):

Later that day the Hunt Board appointed a Special Committee, consisting of the four Hunt outside directors, to review and determine the fairness of Olin's merger proposal. These directors met on April 4, 1984, and retained Merrill Lynch as their financial advisor and the law firm of Shea and Gould as legal counsel. This committee met again on three other occasions. At the May 10, 1984 meeting the Special Committee heard a presentation by the lawyers for several plaintiffs who had filed class actions on behalf of the minority shareholders to enjoin the proposed merger. A representative of Merrill Lynch advised the meeting that $20 per share was fair to the minority from a financial standpoint, but that the range of values for the common stock was probably $19 to $25 per share.

The outside directors subsequently notified the Hunt board that they had unanimously found $20 per share to be fair but not generous. They therefore recommended that Olin consider increasing the price above $20. The next day, May 11, 1984, Olin informed the Hunt Special Committee that it had considered its recommendation but declined to raise the price. The Hunt outside directors then met again on May 14, 1984, by teleconference call, and at a meeting of the Hunt board on May 15, also held by teleconference, the Special Committee announced that it had unanimously found the $20 per share price fair and recommended approval of the merger.

On June 7, 1984, Hunt issued its proxy statement favoring the merger. That document also made clear Olin's intention to vote its 64% of the Hunt shares in favor of the proposal, thereby guaranteeing its passage. There was no requirement of approval by a majority of the minority stockholders.

     * * *

II.

Taken together, the plaintiffs' complaints challenge the proposed Olin–Hunt merger on the grounds that the price offered was grossly inadequate because Olin unfairly manipulated the timing of the merger to avoid the one year commitment, and that specific language in Olin's Schedule 13D, filed when it purchased the Hunt stock, constituted a price commitment by which Olin failed to abide, contrary to its fiduciary obligations.

A.

The issue we address is whether the trial court erred, as a matter of law, in dismissing these claims on the ground that absent deception the plaintiffs' sole remedy under *Weinberger* is an appraisal. The plaintiffs' position is that in cases of procedural unfairness the standard of entire fairness entitles them to relief that is broader than an appraisal. Indeed, the thrust of plaintiffs' contentions is that they eschew an appraisal, since they consider Olin's manipulative conduct a breach of its fiduciary duty to pay the $25 per share guaranteed by the one year commitment. Furthermore, plaintiffs contend that an appraisal is inadequate here because: (1) the alleged wrongdoers are not parties to an appraisal proceeding, and thus are not personally accountable for their actions; (2) if such misconduct is proven, then the corporation should not have to bear the financial burden which only falls upon it in an appraisal award; and (3) overreaching and unfair dealing are not addressed by an appraisal.

The defendants answer that the plaintiffs' claims were primarily directed to the issue of fair value, and that under *Weinberger,* appraisal is the only available remedy.

* * *

In ordering the complaints dismissed the Vice Chancellor reasoned that:

> Where, * * * there are no allegations of non-disclosures or misrepresentations, *Weinberger* mandates that plaintiffs' entire fairness claims be determined in an appraisal proceeding.
>
> *Rabkin,* 480 A.2d at 660.

Id. We consider that an erroneous interpretation of *Weinberger,* because it fails to take account of the entire context of the holding.

* * *

Thus, the trial court's narrow interpretation of *Weinberger* would render meaningless our extensive discussion of fair dealing found in that opinion. In *Weinberger* we defined fair dealing as embracing "questions of when the transaction was timed, how it was initiated, structured, negotiated, disclosed to the directors, and how the approvals of the directors and the stockholders were obtained." 457 A.2d at 711. While this duty of fairness certainly incorporates the principle that a cash-out merger must be free of fraud or misrepresentation, *Weinberger's* mandate of fair dealing does not turn solely on issues of deception. We particularly noted broader concerns respecting the matter of procedural fairness.

* * *

Although the Vice Chancellor correctly understood *Weinberger* as limiting collateral attacks on cash-out mergers, her analysis narrowed the procedural protections which we still intended *Weinberger* to guarantee. Here, plaintiffs are not arguing questions of valuation which are the traditional subjects of an appraisal. Rather, they seek to enforce a contractual right to receive $25 per share, which they claim was unfairly destroyed by Olin's manipulative conduct.

While a plaintiff's mere allegation of "unfair dealing", without more, cannot survive a motion to dismiss, averments containing "specific acts of fraud, misrepresentation, or other items of misconduct" must be carefully examined in accord with our views expressed both here and in *Weinberger.* See 457 A.2d at 703, 711, 714.

III.

A.

* * *

The Court of Chancery stated that "[t]he gravamen of all the complaints appears to be that the cash-out price is unfair." *Rabkin,* 480 A.2d at 658. However, this conclusion, which seems to be more directed to issues of valuation, is neither supported by the pleadings themselves nor the extensive discussion of unfair dealing found in the trial court's opinion. There is no challenge to any method of valuation or to the components of value upon which Olin's $20 price was based. The plaintiffs want the $25 per share guaranteed by the one year commitment, which they claim was unfairly denied them by Olin's manipulations.

* * *

B.

In *Weinberger* we observed that the timing, structure, negotiation and disclosure of a cash-out merger all had a bearing on the issue of procedural fairness. 457 A.2d at 711. The plaintiffs contend *inter alia* that Olin breached its fiduciary duty of fair dealing by purposely timing the merger, and thereby unfairly manipulating it, to avoid the one year commitment * * *

> It is apparent that, from the outset, Olin anticipated that it would eventually acquire the minority interest in Hunt. Olin's chief executive officer expected as much when the Agreement was executed and, in evaluating the Agreement, Olin prepared computations based upon the assumption that it would acquire 100% of Hunt.

Rabkin, 480 A.2d at 657–58.

> * * * Olin's alleged attitude toward the minority, at least as it appears on the face of the complaints and their proposed amendments, coupled with the apparent absence of any meaningful negotiations as to price, all have an air reminiscent of the dealings between Signal and UOP in *Weinberger.* See 457 A.2d at 711.[7] * * * As we said in *Weinberger:*

---

7. As we noted in *Weinberger,* the use of an independent negotiating committee of outside directors may have significant advantages to the majority stockholder in defending suits of this type. See 457 A.2d at 709–711; 709 n. 7. The efficacy of that procedure was recently indicated by our opinion in Rosenblatt v. Getty Oil Company, Del.Supr., 493 A.2d 929, 937–939 (1985). However, we recognize that there can be serious practical problems in the use of such a committee as even *Rosenblatt* demonstrated. See 493 A.2d at 933–936; Her-

zel & Colling, Establishing Procedural Fairness in Squeeze–Out Mergers After Weinberger v. UOP, 39 Business Law. 1525, 1534–37 (1984); Weiss, Balancing Interests in Cash–Out Mergers: The Promise of Weinberger v. UOP, Inc., 8 Del.J.Corp. Law 1, 50–53 (1983). Thus, we do not announce any rule, even in the context of a motion to dismiss, that the absence of such a bargaining structure will preclude dismissal in cases bottomed on claims of unfair dealing.

There is no "safe harbor" for such divided loyalties in Delaware.
* * *

> The requirement of fairness is unflinching in its demand that where one stands on both sides of a transaction, he has the burden of establishing its entire fairness, sufficient to pass the test of careful scrutiny by the courts.
>
> There is no dilution of this obligation where one holds dual or multiple directorships, as in a parent-subsidiary context. Levien v. Sinclair Oil Corp., Del.Ch., 261 A.2d 911, 915 (1969). Thus, individuals who act in a dual capacity as directors of two corporations, one of whom is parent and the other subsidiary, owe the same duty of good management to both corporations, * * *

Id. 457 A.2d at 710. These are issues which an appraisal cannot address, and at this juncture are matters that cannot be resolved by a motion to dismiss.

In our opinion the facts alleged by the plaintiffs regarding Olin's avoidance of the one year commitment support a claim of unfair dealing sufficient to defeat dismissal at this stage of the proceedings. The defendants answer that they had no legal obligation to effect the cash-out merger during the one year period. While that may be so, the principle announced in Schnell v. Chris–Craft Industries [8] establishes that inequitable conduct will not be protected merely because it is legal. At the very least the facts alleged import a form of overreaching, and in the context of entire fairness they deserve more considered analysis than can be accorded them on a motion to dismiss.

Similarly, the plaintiffs' pleas arising from the language in Olin's Schedule 13D (referred to by the trial court as the claim for promissory estoppel) should not have been dismissed on the ground that appraisal was the only remedy available to the plaintiffs challenging the entire fairness of the merger.

IV.

In conclusion we find that the trial court erred in dismissing the plaintiffs' actions for failure to state a claim upon which relief could be granted. As we read the complaints and the proposed amendments, they assert a conscious intent by Olin, as the majority shareholder of Hunt, to deprive the Hunt minority of the same bargain that Olin made with Hunt's former majority shareholder, Turner and Newall. But for Olin's allegedly unfair manipulation, the plaintiffs contend, this bargain also was due them. In short, the defendants are charged with bad faith which goes beyond issues of "mere inadequacy of price." Cole v. National Cash Credit Association, Del.Ch., 156 A. 183, 187–88 (1931). In *Weinberger* we specifically relied upon this aspect of *Cole* in acknowledging the imperfections of an appraisal where circumstances of this sort are present. See 457 A.2d at 714.

---

8. The trial court's narrow interpretation of this principle misconceives the thrust of *Schnell.* See *Rabkin,* 480 A.2d at 661.

Necessarily, this will require the Court of Chancery to closely focus upon *Weinberger's* mandate of entire fairness based on a careful analysis of both the fair price and fair dealing aspects of a transaction. See 457 A.2d at 711, 714. We recognize that this can present certain practical problems, since stockholders may invariably claim that the price being offered is the result of unfair dealings. However, we think that plaintiffs will be tempered in this approach by the prospect that an ultimate judgment in defendants' favor may have cost plaintiffs their unperfected appraisal rights. Moreover, our courts are not without a degree of sophistication in such matters. A balance must be struck between sustaining complaints averring faithless acts, which taken as true would constitute breaches of fiduciary duties that are reasonably related to and have a substantial impact upon the price offered, and properly dismissing those allegations questioning judgmental factors of valuation. Cole v. National Cash Credit Association, 156 A. at 187–88. Otherwise, we face the anomalous result that stockholders who are eliminated without appraisal rights can bring class actions, while in other cases a squeezed-out minority is limited to an appraisal, provided there was no deception, regardless of the degree of procedural unfairness employed to take their shares. Without that balance, *Weinberger's* concern for entire fairness loses all force.

Accordingly, the decision of the Court of Chancery dismissing these consolidated class actions is REVERSED. The matter is REMANDED with directions that the plaintiffs be permitted to file their proposed amendments to the pleadings.

On the remand of the *Rabkin* case, Chandler, V.C., demonstrated the "degree of sophistication in such matters" that the Delaware courts are not without. He ruled that the plaintiffs failed to prove that Olin Corp. deliberately timed the cash-out merger so as to violate "its duty of fair dealing in connection with the one year price commitment." Nor had Olin otherwise violated the terms of its section 13D promise to pay a fair price to the minority if it cashed them out after a year. **Rabkin v. Olin Corp.**, CCH Fed.Sec.L.Rep. ¶ 95,255 (Del.Ch., 1990).

NOTE

In assessing the "fairness" of a second step merger, should different criteria determine "fairness" in a case like Rabkin than in a case in which the bidder merges out the untendered stock soon after acquiring control, but (a) did not previously state the price at which it intended to absorb the untendered shares by merger or (b) did not indicate whether (or that) it had any intention to effect such absorption?

In **Joseph v. Shell Oil Co.**, 498 A.2d 1117 (Del.Sup.Ct.1985) the Vice Chancellor rejected a defense that appraisal was necessarily the exclusive remedy for a claim challenging a tender offer and proposed merger between a subsidiary (Shell Oil Co.) and its parent. In the course of the opinion the court said (498 A.2d at 1121–1122):

"Defendant SPNV has moved for a dismissal of the *van der Woude* action for failure to state a claim upon which relief may be granted. SPNV argues that the only remedy in response to van der Woude's complaint would be an appraisal proceeding pursuant to 8 Del.C. § 262. Weinberger v. UOP, Inc., 457 A.2d 701 (Del.1983); Rabkin v. Hunt Chemical Corp., 480 A.2d 655 (Del.Ch.1984). In *Weinberger,* however, the Delaware Supreme Court stated that although a plaintiff's remedy in response to a successful challenge to a merger transaction should ordinarily be confined to an appraisal, the historic power of Chancery to grant other relief was not diminished. And in situations where an appraisal would be inadequate, it could not be the sole remedy. The Delaware Supreme Court suggested that in cases where fraud, misrepresentation, self-dealing, deliberate waste of corporate assets, or gross and palpable overreaching existed, appraisal might well be inadequate.

"It is most difficult at a preliminary stage to ascertain if an appraisal proceeding will ultimately provide an adequate remedy if the allegations of the plaintiff are proven to be correct. Unfortunately, the opinion in *Weinberger* does not give much guidance as how a trial court is to determine before all the facts are ascertained whether the appraisal remedy would be adequate.

* * *

"Because all inferences in the allegations in a complaint must be construed in favor of the plaintiffs, and because each suit is unique, complaints asserting a claim of unfair dealing as to a tender offer or freezeout merger must be read carefully to determine if an appraisal will provide an adequate remedy if the claims prove to be true. Great care must be taken not to unjustifiably relegate objecting stockholders to an appraisal proceeding because to do so might have the result of precluding the imposition of an adequate remedy for serious breaches of fiduciary duty.

"The allegations of overreaching by the defendants * * * are sufficient to raise a reasonable doubt that an appraisal proceeding under 8 Del.C. § 262 will give the shareholders of Shell an adequate remedy to address what seems to have been unfair dealing. This is especially so in view of the fact that the burden of persuasion to show the entire fairness of the transaction is on the defendants, no negotiations as to price occurred, no vote of the shareholders or directors of Shell will ever occur, there is no guarantee that the short-form merger will ever take place, and even if it does, only less than 10% of the Shell shareholders will be entitled to an appraisal. I, therefore, cannot find from the present record that it appears with a reasonable certainty that an appraisal pursuant to 8 Del.C. § 262 will grant plaintiffs an adequate remedy.

"Quite candidly, this result presents procedural problems. Obviously some of the issues in the trial now set for March, especially as to value, will be the same as the issues which would ordinarily arise in an appraisal proceeding and it might be better to address questions of value in an appraisal context. I cannot, however, on the present record, with its unusual factual circumstances, deny the plaintiffs their right to seek what might be their only adequate remedy to redress what may be grievous breaches of fiduciary duty by some of the defendants. The motion to dismiss for failure to state a claim upon which relief can be granted, therefore, must be denied."

CEDE & CO. v. TECHNICOLOR, INC.

Supreme Court of Delaware, 1988.
542 A.2d 1182.

Before HORSEY, MOORE and HOLLAND, JJ.

HORSEY, Justice:

We accepted this interlocutory appeal from the Court of Chancery to address a question of first impression in this Court: the standing and right of a minority shareholder who has dissented from a cash-out merger and commenced an appraisal proceeding under 8 Del.C. § 262 to assert and pursue a later-discovered individual claim of fraud in the merger through an action for rescissory damages against the participants for breach of fiduciary duty to the shareholder. This issue arises from a cash-out merger of the minority shareholders of Technicolor Incorporated ("Technicolor"), a Delaware corporation, accomplished by MacAndrews & Forbes Group Incorporated ("MAF") through the merger of its wholly-owned subsidiary, Macanfor Corporation ("Macanfor"), into Technicolor, following approval by a majority of Technicolor's shareholders.

* * * The plaintiffs are Cinerama, Incorporated, a beneficial owner of 201,200 shares of Technicolor common stock, approximately 4.5% of the total issued and outstanding common stock, and Cede & Company, the record owner of the shares of Technicolor owned beneficially by Cinerama.[1] * * *

The sole defendant in the appraisal action is Technicolor, the surviving corporation of the merger. The several individual and corporate defendants in the fraud action include Technicolor, all but two of the members of Technicolor's Board of Directors at the time of the merger, and the chief architects of the merger, MAF, Macanfor, and Ronald O. Perelman, controlling shareholder and Chairman of MAF.[3]

---

1. Hereinafter, Cinerama, Incorporated and Cede & Company shall be collectively referred to as "Cinerama."

3. Perelman was Chairman of the Board and Chief Executive Officer of MAF. In addition to his position in MAF, he personally owned 38.4% of the common stock of MAF and, together with the other officers and directors of MAF, collectively owned more than 50% of the common stock of MAF.

* * *

I

* * * The litigation results from a cash-out merger of MAF's subsidiary, Macanfor, into Technicolor, which purportedly became effective on January 24, 1983, following a special meeting of the shareholders of Technicolor and their approval of the proposed merger. Prior to the shareholder vote on the merger, the Technicolor directors, purportedly by unanimous vote, waived Technicolor's charter requirement mandating a supermajority shareholder vote of 95% to effect a merger. The waiver by the directors of the supermajority requirements of the Technicolor charter, along with the merger itself, needed the approval of the Technicolor shareholders before becoming effective. The amendment to Technicolor's charter and the merger both received more than the required vote for approval, two-thirds of Technicolor's outstanding stock, with approximately 82% of Technicolor's shares being held by MAF/Macanfor at this time.[4]

Cinerama previously rejected Macanfor's tender offer of $23 per share for its shares and voted against the merger. Several days before the merger's effective date, Cinerama made demand upon Technicolor for appraisal of their shares pursuant to 8 Del.C. § 262(d)(1), and later within the required 120 days Cinerama commenced its appraisal action under 8 Del.C. § 262(e), requesting the Court of Chancery to determine the fair value of their Technicolor holdings. Cinerama alleges that it did not then seek to enjoin or otherwise attack the merger because it relied on Technicolor's representations made in connection with the tender offer and accompanying merger and, thus, had no basis for believing that any claim lay against defendants for fraud or unfair dealing in connection with the merger.

* * *

Document discovery was essentially completed by Cinerama in mid–1985; thereafter, Cinerama began deposing the various Technicolor officers and directors. * * * Cinerama, in December 1985, discovered in deposing Charles S. Simone, a former director of Technicolor, that Simone had not voted with the other directors in purportedly waiving the 95% supermajority shareholder vote requirement of Technicolor's charter and had opposed and voted against the merger with Macanfor. As a consequence, Cinerama alleges in its fraud action that Technicolor's shareholder vote was legally insufficient for approval of the merger, causing the merger to be "void" *ab initio.*[5]

---

4. Macanfor purchased 3,534,181 shares of Technicolor pursuant to a tender offer for all of Technicolor's outstanding common stock at a price of $23 per share, which, when combined with the 220,000 shares previously acquired, gave MAF/Macanfor control of approximately 82% of Technicolor's stock.

5. In absence of a waiver by the unanimous vote of the Board of Directors, since 95% of the issued and outstanding shares were not recorded as voting in favor of the merger at the January 24, 1983, shareholder meeting and MAF/Macanfor held less than 95% of the issued and outstanding shares, Cinerama alleges that the merger was not permitted under the terms of Technicolor's certificate of incorporation.

* * * Cinerama filed a second suit in the Court of Chancery in January 1986, alleging fraud in the merger and unfair dealing on the part of defendants. As noted, Cinerama's fraud action charges Technicolor and the other defendants with multiple acts of wrongdoing and breaches of fiduciary duty in the merger, including: waste of assets, self-dealing, intentional and negligent misrepresentation, unfair dealing, accepting a grossly unfair price for Technicolor stock, and carrying out an unlawful merger in violation of Technicolor's certificate of incorporation. Through its fraud action, Cinerama seeks a judgment rescinding the merger or, alternatively, an award of rescissory damages and damages for all losses resulting from defendants' wrongdoing. Prior to answering, all of the defendants, in March 1986, moved to dismiss Cinerama's fraud action on grounds previously outlined—that Cinerama, having elected to file an appraisal petition, could not simultaneously pursue a fraud action arising out of the same merger.

In April 1986, Cinerama filed * * * motions, to amend and enlarge its appraisal petition to include the same allegations of fraud and unfair dealing contained in its fraud action or to consolidate the two actions. Following the Court of Chancery's rulings denying the respective parties' motions and cross-motions, the parties secured leave to file this interlocutory appeal.

* * *

II

For the first time, this Court addresses the standing and right of a shareholder dissenting from a cash-out merger to pursue under Delaware law both an appraisal remedy under 8 Del.C. § 262 and a subsequent individual action for rescissory damages based on a later-discovered claim of fraud in the merger. The disparate nature of the two causes of action has been previously addressed by this Court in Weinberger v. UOP, Inc., Del.Supr., 457 A.2d 701 (1983), and in Rabkin v. Philip A. Hunt Chem. Corp., Del.Supr., 498 A.2d 1099 (1985). In each case, we stated that a statutory appraisal proceeding under section 262 and a rescissory suit for fraud, misrepresentation, self-dealing and other actionable wrongs violative of "entire fairness" to minority shareholders serve different purposes and are designed to provide different, and not interchangeable, remedies.

* * *

Weinberger directs that [its] "liberalized approach" to appraisal shall be used to determine the value of a cashed-out minority's share interest on the day of the merger, reflecting all relevant information regarding the company and its shares. Id. at 713. This includes information concerning future events not arising solely "from the accomplishment or expectation of the merger," 8 Del.C. § 262(h), which, if made public, can affect the current value of the shares and "which

are known or susceptible of proof as of the date of the merger * * *."
457 A.2d at 713; 8 Del.C. § 262(h).[8]

* * * [I]n a section 262 appraisal action the only litigable issue is
the determination of the value of the appraisal petitioners' shares on
the date of the merger, the only party defendant is the surviving
corporation and the only relief available is a judgment against the
surviving corporation for the fair value of the dissenters' shares. In
contrast, a fraud action asserting fair dealing and fair price claims
affords an expansive remedy and is brought against the alleged wrongdoers to provide whatever relief the facts of a particular case may
require. In evaluating claims involving violations of entire fairness,
the trial court may include in its relief any damages sustained by the
shareholders. See *Rabkin,* 498 A.2d at 1107; *Weinberger,* 457 A.2d at
713. In a fraud claim, the approach to determining relief *may* be the
same as that employed in determining fair value under 8 Del.C. § 262.[9]
However, an appraisal action may not provide a complete remedy for
unfair dealing or fraud because a damage award in a fraud action may
include "rescissory damages if the [trier of fact] considers them susceptible of proof and a remedy appropriate to all issues of fairness before
him." *Weinberger,* 457 A.2d at 714. *Weinberger* and *Rabkin* make this
clear distinction in terms of the relief available in a section 262 action
as opposed to a fraud in the merger suit.

III

A.

Whether Cinerama's Subsequent Fraud Action Is Foreclosed
by Its Original Election of an Appraisal Remedy

Applying these principles to the record before us, we find the
Chancellor was clearly correct in refusing to dismiss Cinerama's fraud
action. Given the distinctive nature of the remedies available to a
cashed-out shareholder, the Chancellor properly declined to find Ciner-

---

8. Information and insight not communicated to the market may not be reflected
in stock prices; thus, minority shareholders being cashed out may be deprived of
part of the true investment value of their
shares. See generally R. Clark, Corporate
Law 507 (1986); Fama, Efficient Capital
Markets: A Review of Theory and Empirical Work, 25 J.Fin. 383 (1970). The issue
we are addressing is not the manipulation
of the transaction, see *Rabkin,* 498 A.2d at
1104–05, nor the suppression or misstatement of material information by insiders
defrauding the market, see Basic Inc. v.
Levinson, ___ U.S. ___, 108 S.Ct. 978, 99
L.Ed.2d 194 (1988). Instead, we recognize
that the majority may have insight into
their company's future based primarily on
bits and pieces of *nonmaterial* information
that have value as a totality. See Clark,
supra at 508. It is this information that, if
available in a statutory appraisal proceeding, the Court of Chancery must evaluate

to determine if future earnings will affect
the fair value of shares on the day of the
merger. See 8 Del.C. § 262(h). To obtain
this information the appraisal petitioner
must be permitted to conduct a "detailed
investigation into the facts that is warranted by the acute conflict of interest and the
potential for investor harm that is inherent in freeze-out transactions." Clark, supra at 508.

9. This Court in *Weinberger* recognized
that "[i]n this breach of fiduciary duty
case, the Chancellor perceived that the approach to valuation was the same as that
in an appraisal proceeding." 457 A.2d at
712. Although this Court overruled the
exclusivity of the method used by the
Chancellor, we did not reverse the Chancellor's decision to use the appraisal valuation approach for cases involving breaches
of fiduciary duties.

ama to lack standing to pursue its fraud claim. To rule that Cinerama, having elected to pursue an appraisal remedy under section 262, without apparent knowledge of a claim of fraud in the merger, was foreclosed from asserting a later-discovered claim of fraud in the merger, would have been clearly contrary to the teachings of *Weinberger* and *Rabkin.*

* * *

The Chancellor correctly equated the right of a shareholder who loses share membership through misrepresentation, conspiracy, fraud, or breach of fiduciary duty to seek redress with the right of a shareholder who dissents from a merger and seeks appraisal of his shares to seek redress after discovery of allegedly wrongful conduct. Fairness and consistency require equal recourse for a former shareholder who accepts a cash-out offer in ignorance of a later-discovered claim against management for breach of fiduciary duty and a shareholder who discovers such a claim after electing appraisal rights.

Moreover, policy considerations militate against foreclosing a shareholder electing appraisal rights from later bringing a fraud action based on after-discovered wrongdoing in the merger. Experience has shown that the great majority of minority shareholders in a freeze-out merger accept the cash-out consideration, notwithstanding the possible existence of a claim of unfair dealing, due to the risks of litigation. See Joseph v. Shell Oil Co., Del.Ch., 498 A.2d 1117, 1122 (1985). With the majority of the minority shareholders tendering their shares, only shareholders pursuing discovery during an appraisal proceeding are likely to acquire the relevant information needed to pursue a fraud action if such information exists. Such shareholders, however, would not have any financial incentive to communicate their discovered claim of wrongdoing in the merger to the shareholders who tendered their shares for the consideration offered by the majority and, by tendering, have standing to file suit. Thus, to bar those seeking appraisal from asserting a later-discovered fraud claim may effectively immunize a controlling shareholder from answering to a fraud claim.

Defendants assert that it is inconsistent (or unfair) to permit both the fraud action and the appraisal action to proceed simultaneously. This argument is misguided. Cinerama is not seeking (nor would our courts permit) inconsistent remedial relief, but rather is simply pleading alternative causes of action. In the instant case, the merger occurred. If the merger was properly consummated, then 8 Del.C. § 262 affords Cinerama a claim for the fair value of its Technicolor shares. See Felder v. Anderson, Clayton & Co., Del.Ch., 159 A.2d 278 (1960). If the merger was not lawfully effected, Cinerama should be entitled to recover rescissory damages, rendering the appraisal action moot.

Based upon the appraisal/fraud distinctions found in *Weinberger* and *Rabkin,* policy concerns, and considerations of equity, as a matter of law we affirm the Court of Chancery's ruling denying defendant's motion to dismiss Cinerama's fraud action. Under the record before us, the Chancellor properly allowed Cinerama to pursue both a statutory appraisal remedy and its fraud action; therefore, the defendants' cross-appeal, asserting that Cinerama lacked standing to pursue its fraud action, fails.

B.

Whether Cinerama May Assert in its Appraisal Proceeding Its Claim of Fraud in the Merger

The Court of Chancery correctly denied Cinerama's motion to amend and enlarge its appraisal action to include its claim for rescissory relief for conspiracy, illegality, fraud, and breach of fiduciary duty. As previously noted, statutory appraisal is limited to "the payment of fair value of the shares * * * by the surviving or resulting corporation." 8 Del.C. § 262(i). A determination of fair value does not involve an inquiry into claims of wrongdoing in the merger. See Felder v. Anderson, Clayton & Co., Del.Ch., 159 A.2d 278 (1960); see also Weiss, Balancing Interest in Cash–Out Mergers: The Promise of Weinberger v. UOP, Inc., 8 Del.J.Corp.L. 1, 8–9 (1983). In contrast, in a fraud action seeking monetary relief for unfair dealing, the focus of the suit is whether wrongdoing can be established, see *Weinberger,* 457 A.2d at 714. Hence, the necessary party defendants in a "fraud in the merger" action are the alleged wrongdoers because it is they who arguably caused the injury and should pay any damage award. To permit Cinerama to amend its statutory appraisal action to include its fraud claims would impermissibly broaden the legislative remedy. It would also fail to bring before the Court the necessary parties for the fashioning of any appropriate relief for a fraud.

Finally, to judicially expand an appraisal proceeding to include unfair dealing claims would likely create unforeseeable administrative and procedural problems for litigants and the courts. In most cases only a small proportion of shareholders will have perfected appraisal rights and thus have access to the expanded appraisal remedy. See Joseph v. Shell Oil Co., 498 A.2d at 1122; see also *Rabkin,* 498 A.2d at 1107; 8 Del.C. § 262(d). If shareholders are permitted to litigate fraud claims in appraisal proceedings, shareholders not seeking appraisal would be required to litigate "entire fairness" claims identical to the claims litigated by shareholders with perfected appraisal rights but through separate actions. This would create a substantial risk of inconsistent judgments and raise issues of collateral estoppel. * * *

C.

Whether Cinerama Should Be Put to an Election of Remedies Before Trial or Both Claims Should Be Consolidated for Trial

On this issue we find the Court of Chancery to have erred. Cinerama's motion to consolidate, for purposes of trial as well as discovery, its fraud and appraisal actions should have been granted. No rule of law required the Court to put Cinerama to an election of remedies before judgment.

* * *

An appraisal proceeding and an equitable action for rescissory damages (for illegality or other wrongdoing in extinguishing minority shareholder interests) do not involve the assertion of inconsistent rights. The appraisal action seeks the enforcement of a statutory right that is different and distinct from the alleged wrong sought to be redressed by Cinerama's fraud action. The remedies, though very different, are not inconsistent or repugnant because one remedy is premised on a state of facts that is the alternative to, rather than the converse of, the state of facts that forms the basis for recovery under the other remedy.

* * *

Cinerama should not have been barred from proceeding to trial on its alternate claims for relief. During the consolidated proceeding, if it is determined that the merger should not have occurred due to fraud, breach of fiduciary duty, or other wrongdoing on the part of the defendants, then Cinerama's appraisal action will be rendered moot and Cinerama will be entitled to receive rescissory damages. If such wrongdoing on the part of the defendants is not found, and the merger was properly authorized, then Cinerama will be entitled to collect the fair value of its Technicolor shares pursuant to statutory appraisal and its fraud action will be dismissed. Under either scenario, Cinerama will be limited to a single recovery judgment.

Cinerama, therefore, is entitled to proceed simultaneously with its statutory and equitable claims for relief. What Cinerama may not do, however, is recover duplicative judgments or obtain double recovery.

* * *

Consolidation of the actions is also necessary to put Cinerama in a position equivalent to the position it would arguably be in had defendants exercised "complete candor" in disclosing all material information associated with the merger to the minority shareholders. Had Cinerama known at the time of the merger what it arguably learned through discovery, it is reasonable to assume that Cinerama would have first brought suit to enjoin the merger,[13] and if unsuccessful, Cinerama could still have perfected its appraisal rights.

To require Cinerama to make a binding election of remedies no later than the time that it announced itself to be ready for trial would deprive Cinerama of a cause of action it would have possessed had management made a full disclosure of all material information prior to the merger, as mandated by *Weinberger*. See 457 A.2d at 710. Assuming the defendants failed to exercise "complete candor" with the minority shareholders, the minority should not be placed in a worse position than if management had acted with "complete candor." See Bershad v. Curtiss–Wright Corp., Del.Supr., 535 A.2d 840 (1987). Thus, we hold

---

13. At this late date, there is a strong reluctance to "unwind" a merger. See, e.g., Weinberger, 457 A.2d at 714; Updyke Assocs. v. Wellington Management Co., Del.Ch., C.A. No. 6298, Brown, V.C. (Feb. 3, 1982).

that Cinerama should be permitted to exercise its appraisal rights while seeking rescissory damages in a consolidated action, subject to the limitation of a single recovery judgment.

* * *

Affirmed in part; Reversed in part; and Remanded.*

NOTE

1. The admonition in the Cinerama case that a party may not assert in an appraisal proceeding "claims of wrongdoing in the merger" has received a gloss in two later cases. In **Cavalier Oil Corp. v. Harnett,** 564 A.2d 1137 (Del.1989) (involving a group of closed corporations), possibly because the parties' settlement of prior litigation between them implied agreement on the assertion of the claim in the appraisal proceedings, a claim for an earlier misappropriation by the parent group of a corporate opportunity that should have been shared with the subsidiary was held triable in the appraisal proceeding. The court suggested a distinction between asserting in an appraisal proceeding misbehavior by an absorbing parent corporation in the course of its prior dealings with the subsidiary (thus affecting the fair value of the latter by reason of its potential recovery from the former for such misbehavior) and claiming wrongdoing in the merger "itself," which Cinerama appears to forbid. In **Alabama By–Products Corp. v. Phil H. Neal, Jr.,** 588 A.2d 255 (Del.1991), the Delaware Supreme Court affirmed a ruling by the Vice–Chancellor (in raising the price to which the dissenting stockholders of the subsidiary were entitled from the $75.60 per share offered by the parent to $180.67 per share), which refused to entertain a claim for unfair dealings in the merger itself, but admitted evidence offered in support of that claim as relevant and proper in assessing the correctness of the valuation. In the course of its opinion, the court said:

"In the case *sub judice* there is no dispute that the Court of Chancery properly dismissed the petitioners' claim for unfair dealing, noting that 'to authorize the joinder of appraisal and unfair dealing actions as proposed here would result in a hybrid appraisal action, effectively broadening the legislative remedy afforded * * *.' However, the Court of Chancery then stated, 'if corporate fiduciaries engage in self-dealing and fix the merger price by procedures not calculated to yield a fair price, these facts should, and will, be considered in assessing the credibility of the respondent corporations' valuation contentions * * *.'

"* * * The petitioners argue that after their unfair dealing claim was properly dismissed from the appraisal proceeding, the Court of Chancery was nevertheless entitled to consider the evidence of unfair dealing for the alternative purpose for which it was introduced, i.e., to impeach the respondents' credibility. We agree.

* [Ed. Note] The Chancellor allowed no recovery on the remand of the action against the directors (C.A. No. 8358, June 21, 1991) or in the related appraisal proceeding (C.A. No. 7129, Oct. 19, 1990).

"The respondents' argument fails to recognize the distinction between the propriety of 'considering an act of unfair dealing, which may relate to a party's credibility, and the impropriety of considering an action for unfair dealing in an appraisal proceeding. Although the justiciable issue in an appraisal action is a limited one, the statute specifically provides that "all relevant factors" are to be considered by the Court of Chancery in 'determining the fair value' of shares which are subject to appraisal (* * * Cavalier Oil Corp. v. Hartnett, 564 A.2d at 1142–43; Weinberger v. UOP, Inc., 457 A.2d at 713.) There is nothing in the appraisal statute or this Court's prior holdings, including Cede, which suggests that the Court of Chancery may not consider the respondents' conduct at the time of the merger in assessing the credibility of the respondents' testimony in support of their valuation contentions in an appraisal proceeding.

"This court has recognized that the weight to be ascribed to expert valuation necessarily depends on the validity of the assumptions underlying them * * *. Where those assumptions are values supplied by others, the conduct of such other persons is probative of their credibility and of the information being supplied to the expert. The credibility of the respondents was squarely an issue in this appraisal proceeding because the experts retained by the respondents relied upon the information supplied to them by the respondents * * *."

2. In any particular state, the appraisal proceeding may be determined to be rigorously limited to a valuation process without inquiry into other "wrongs" entailed in the merger, and that process itself may be narrowly confined to ascertaining only the market price of the dissenter's stock. (See Armstrong v. Marathon Oil Co., 32 Ohio St.3d 397, 513 N.E.2d 776 (1987), cert. denied, ___ U.S. ___ (1991). As the appraisal proceeding thus confines inquiry more and more narrowly, does (or should) appraisal become less the exclusive remedy for a shareholder who objects to the terms of the merger, particularly in a parent-subsidiary merger or freeze-out? Cf. Stepak v. Schey, 51 Ohio St.3d 8, 553 N.E.2d 1072 (1990). Can (or must) the value of outstanding claims for breach of fiduciary duty held at the time of the merger by the acquired corporation against its officers and directors be taken into account in the appraisal price? See Porter v. Texas Commerce Bancshares, 1989 WL 120358 (Del. Ch.).

NOTE: THE EXCLUSIVITY OF THE APPRAISAL REMEDY

1. *The Ambiguity of the Appraisal Remedy.*

There is considerable uncertainty over the implications of the existence of the appraisal remedy. There is the question raised in *Technicolor* as to whether if that remedy is sought, the merger can be challenged for unfairness, overreaching, fraud or the like either in the appraisal proceeding or collaterally. See also Graham v. Exxon Corp., 480 F.Supp. 12 (S.D.N.Y.1978); In re Jones & Laughlin Steel Corp., 488

Pa. 524, 412 A.2d 1099 (1980); Breed v. Barton, 54 N.Y.2d 82, 444 N.Y.S.2d 609, 429 N.E.2d 128 (1981); Dofflemyer v. W.F. Hall Printing Co., 432 A.2d 1198 (Del.1981); Dofflemyer v. W.F. Hall Printing Co., 558 F.Supp. 372, 381 (D.Del.1983); Baugh v. Citizens and Southern National Bank, 248 Ga. 180, 281 S.E.2d 531 (1981); Coggins v. New England Patriots Football Club, Inc., supra p. 735. There is also the question whether if a challenge for fraud is brought, the plaintiff can also seek appraisal. Compare In re Jones & Laughlin Steel Corp., 328 Pa.Super. 442, 477 A.2d 527 (1984) (holding appraisal available for stockholders who had settled a collateral claim for violation of proxy rules and Rule 10b–5) with Coggins v. New England Patriots Football Club, Inc., supra p. 735.

Of larger import, is the question whether the mere existence of the appraisal remedy precludes a challenge to enjoin consummation of a long-form merger between parent and subsidiary (as well as between strangers) on grounds of illegality, unlawfulness, overreaching or fraud (i.e., deception or failure to make adequate disclosure) or otherwise. *Weinberger* and *Rabkin* disclose some of the ambiguities in Delaware. In New York, the uncertainty is reflected in the legislative history of Section 623(k) of the merger law, see note *, Appendix G, p. G–29 infra. In many states the judicial allusion to the exclusivity of the appraisal remedy as the mechanism for vindicating a dissenter's rights in a merger often suggests an exception for cases of outright fraud or deception,[r] as well as for cases of "unlawfulness" or "illegality." See e.g., Coggins v. New England Patriots Football Club, Inc., supra p. 735.[s] Connecticut seems to be explicit and to leave no room for such exception.[t] California takes a somewhat different approach.[u]

---

r. For difficulties encountered in identifying "deception," as distinguished from overreaching, compare Singer v. Magnavox Co., 380 A.2d 969 (Del.1977) with Singer v. Magnavox Co., CCH Fed.Sec.L.Rep., ¶ 95,-830 (D.Del.1977). See also Goldberg v. Meridor, infra, p. 836.

s. See also Stepak v. Schey, 51 Ohio St.3d 8, 553 N.E.2d 1072 (1990) (fraud exception confirmed, but allegation that lock-up action prevented auction "is essentially a complaint regarding the price" making appraisal exclusive remedy); Stringer v. Car Data Systems, Inc., 841 P.2d 1183 (Or. Sup.Ct.1992); Schloss v. Chesapeake & Ohio Ry., 73 Md.App. 727, 536 A.2d 147 (1988); Pritchard v. Mead, 155 Wis.2d 431, 455 N.W.2d 263 (Wis.Ct.App.1990); Dowling v. Narragansett Capital Corp., 735 F.Supp. 1105 (D.R.I.1990); Columbus Mills, Inc. v. Kahn, 259 Ga. 80, 377 S.E.2d 437 (1989); Oppenheimer v. Brenner Companies Inc., 107 N.C.App. 16, 419 S.E.2d 354 (1992); Yeager v. Paul Semonin Co., 691 S.W.2d 227 (Ky.App.1985); Mullen v. Academy Life Insurance Co., 705 F.2d 971 (8th Cir.1983) (dealing with New Jersey law); Perl v. IU International Corp., 607 P.2d 1036 (Hawaii 1980).

t. See Yanow v. Teal Industries, Inc., 422 A.2d 311 (Conn.1979) (case involves short form merger, but statutory language covers all mergers); cf. Stauffer v. Standard Brands, Inc., 187 A.2d 78 (Del.1962).

u. See Small, Corporate Combinations Under the New California General Corporation Law, 23 U.C.L.A.L.Rev. 1190, 1217 et seq. (1976); Buxbaum, The Dissenters' Appraisal Remedy, 23 U.C.L.A.L.Rev. 1229, 1244–1247 (1976). Section 1312 of the California General Corporation Law provides:

"(a) No shareholder of a corporation who has a right under this chapter to demand payment of cash for the shares held by the shareholder shall have any right at law or in equity to attack the validity of the reorganization or short-form merger, or to have the reorganization or short-form merger set aside or rescinded, except in an action to test whether the number of shares required to authorize or approve the reorganization have been legally voted in favor thereof; but any holder of shares of a class whose terms and provisions specifically set forth the amount to be paid in respect to them in the event of a reorganization or

The ambiguity about the exclusivity of the appraisal remedy is not dispelled by the draftsmen of the Model Act, at least in the explanation of the Committee on Corporate Laws of the ABA Section on Corporation Banking and Business Law for making the remedy exclusive in § 80(d) which is embodied in § 13.02 of RMBCA as modified in the following Comment to § 13.02(b):

"* * * Section 13.02(b) basically adopts the New York formula as to exclusivity of the dissenters' remedy of this chapter. The remedy is the exclusive remedy unless the transaction is 'unlawful' or 'fraudulent.' The theory underlying this section is as follows: when a majority of shareholders has approved a corporate change, the corporation should be permitted to proceed even if a minority considers the change unwise or disadvantageous, and persuades a court that this is correct. Since dissenting shareholders can obtain the fair value of their shares, they are protected from pecuniary loss. Thus in general terms an exclusivity principle is justified. But the prospect that shareholders may be 'paid off' does not justify the corporation in proceeding unlawfully or fraudulently. If the corporation attempts an action in violation of the corporation law on voting, in violation of clauses in articles of incorporation prohibiting it, by deception of shareholders, or in violation of a fiduciary duty—to take some common examples—the court's freedom to intervene should be unaffected by the presence or absence of dissenters'

short-form merger is entitled to payment in accordance with those terms and provisions * * *.

"(b) If one of the parties to a reorganization or short-form merger is directly or indirectly controlled by, or under common control with, another party to the reorganization or short-form merger, subdivision (a) shall not apply to any shareholder of such party who has not demanded payment of cash for such shareholder's shares pursuant to this chapter; but if the shareholder institutes any action to attack the validity of the reorganization or short-form merger or to have the reorganization or short-form merger set aside or rescinded, the shareholder shall not thereafter have any right to demand payment of cash for the shareholder's shares pursuant to this chapter. The court in any action attacking the validity of the reorganization or short-form merger or to have the reorganization or short-form merger set aside or rescinded shall not restrain or enjoin the consummation of the transaction except upon 10–days prior notice to the corporation and upon a determination by the court that clearly no other remedy will adequately protect the complaining shareholder or the class of shareholders of which such shareholder is a member.

"(c) If one of the parties to a reorganization or short-form merger is directly or indirectly controlled by, or under common control with, another party to the reorganization or short-form merger, in any action to attack the validity of the reorganization or short-form merger or to have the reorganization or short-form merger set aside or rescinded, (1) a party to a reorganization or short-form merger which controls another party to the reorganization or short-form merger shall have the burden of proving that the transaction is just and reasonable as to the shareholders of the controlled party, and (2) a person who controls two or more parties to a reorganization shall have the burden of proving that the transaction is just and reasonable as to the shareholders of any party so controlled."

The California Supreme Court reads the exclusivity provision broadly to preclude collateral challenges to the validity of arm's-length mergers, including post-merger suits seeking only damages because those controlling the absorbed company violated fiduciary duties (e.g. by accepting side payments) and because of fraud in the merger. The court suggests that the damages claim and the controllers' misconduct may (must?) be considered in the appraisal proceeding in determining the fair value to which the claimant is entitled. Steinberg v. Amplica, Inc., 42 Cal.3d 1198, 233 Cal. Rptr. 249 (1986).

See also Sturgeon Petroleums Ltd. v. Merchants Petroleum Co., 147 Cal.App.2d 134, 195 Cal.Rptr. 29 (1983).

rights under this chapter. Because of the variety of situations in which unlawfulness and fraud may appear, this section makes no attempt to specify particular illustrations. Rather, it is designed to recognize and preserve the principles that have developed in the case law of Delaware, New York and other states with regard to the effect of dissenters' rights on other remedies of dissident shareholders. See Weinberger v. UOP, Inc. * * *. See also Vorenberg, 'Exclusiveness of the Dissenting Stockholders' Appraisal Right,' 77 Harv.L.Rev. 1189 (1964)."

2. *Contrasting Results in Appraisal and Unfairness Cases.*

If remedy is available with respect to the same merger both by way of an appraisal proceeding and an unfairness challenge, is there a rationale for valuations in the appraisal that exceed those in the unfairness challenge? Compare Greene & Co. v. Schenley Industries, Inc., 281 A.2d 30 (Del.Ch.1971), in which the Vice–Chancellor denied the objecting stockholders' request (based on grounds of unfair self dealing) for a preliminary injunction against consummation of a merger in which dissenters received a package valued at $29 per share for their common stock, with Gibbons v. Schenley Industries, Inc., 339 A.2d 460 (Del.Ch.1975), in which the appraised fair value of the same common stock was $33.86 per share. Similarly, the absorption of Shell Oil Company by its parent, Royal Dutch Petroleum Company, resulted in an award of $60 or $62 per share to the subsidiary's stockholders who brought a fairness challenge and much later $71.20 per share to dissenters who sought appraisal. Compare also Sarrouf v. New England Patriots Football Club, Inc., 397 Mass. 542, 492 N.E.2d 1122 (1986) with the Coggins case, supra p. 735.

The contrast between the results in the appraisal proceedings and the values found in the fairness challenges to identical mergers is puzzling. The difference could be a function of different valuation techniques. It might also reflect differences in the evidence introduced by the different parties in two separate proceedings. Apart from such explanations, the differences in the theories of recovery in the two proceedings suggest that the results are incongruous. Thus, if the standard of fairness is supposed to take account of the gains resulting from the merger, but the appraisal value is precluded from doing so, how can the latter produce a higher payment per share to complaining stockholders than the former—at least in the absence of a finding that the merger reduced aggregate value?

If the exclusivity of the appraisal remedy is limited to transactions for which appraisal rights are given, is there room for fairness challenges in those cases for which appraisal rights do not exist such as sales of assets under Del.Corp.Law, Section 271 or, occasionally, mergers not involving marketable securities?

3. *Policy Considerations.*

In any event, even where appraisal is said not to be the exclusive remedy, there remains the question whether its availability does, or should, affect the nature of the judicial assessment of the fairness of the merger.[v] Does the change in the concept of, and in the modes of determining, fair value in appraisal proceedings expressed in the *Weinberger* case, in the RMBCA (Appendix F), and in the New York Business Corporation Law (Appendix G) suggest that appraisal is an adequate substitute for other remedies and should remain exclusive? Or are there, and should there be, restrictions by way of "fairness" requirements on the terms which insiders can impose on the outside or public stockholders in a merger and remedies, *in addition to appraisal,* available to public stockholders to enforce those restrictions.

"In answering * * * [those questions], it is important to remember that the object of appraisal is to give dissident stockholders an opportunity to avoid the consequences of merger, not to undo the merger or to press directly for better terms. Appraisal statutes generally make explicit that the claim for which the dissenter is to be compensated in cash is the value of his shares 'exclusive of any element of value arising from the expectation or accomplishment of the merger or consolidation' * * *. [T]he appraisal process is thus designed to generate a claim on behalf of dissenting stockholders equal to the value of their shares in the old firm, just as if it had continued on its customary course without the intervention of a merger bid. Hence, where the merger is perceived as producing gains for the combined enterprise, the appraisal price by itself is inadequate to permit the subsidiary's stockholders to receive any part of those gains. By the same token, it is not the object of the appraisal proceeding to require an overreaching parent to redistribute any portion of the merger gains among the subsidiary's public stockholders.[*] [Nor can the cashed-out objecting shareholder fairly be said to choose appraisal and its risks rather than continue with the enterprise, and therefore properly to be exposed to the limitations of the appraisal remedy.]

* * *

"* * * [T]he individual right of appraisal is not directly responsive to the problem of fiduciary abuse in mergers between parents and subsidiaries. Appraisal is predicated more on the conception of managerial incompetence in valuing the old enterprise and negotiating a

---

v. For a discussion of the impact of the availability of appraisal rights on the right to challenge a merger on grounds of unfairness, see Vorenberg, Exclusiveness of the Dissenting Stockholder's Appraisal Right, 77 Harv.L.Rev. 1189 (1964). See also Bove v. Community Hotel Corp., supra p. 366.

*[Ed. Note] Overreaching by a parent may be the most frequently encountered form of impropriety to the public stockholders of an acquired company in a merger, but it is not the only form. Side payments by the acquirer to the controllers of a public corporation and underpayment of the public investors in an arm's-length merger are not unknown. The appraisal proceeding does not address those forms of impropriety directly, if at all. See Steinberg v. Amplica, Inc., 42 Cal.3d 1198, 233 Cal.Rptr. 249 (1986), suggesting that, but not explaining how, claims of improper side payments and underpayment may be vindicated in an appraisal proceeding, and therefore cannot underpin a collateral challenge to the merger and the insiders. Even if a briber must, in effect, account to the shareholders of the absorbed corporation for the amount of the bribe (and may thus be doubly liable) in an appraisal proceeding valuing the absorbed corporation's stock, the question remains whether that accounting adequately vindicates the victims' claims or imposes effective sanctions on the bribees.

price for it than on the notion of a conflict of interest which results in a diversion of a portion of the merger proceeds to a controlling parent. Moreover, it neither imposes its cost solely on the stockholders of the acquiring company nor seeks to reimburse all the victims of the inadequate merger price, that is, *all* the public stockholders of the acquired company. Finally, appraisal is merely an option-out alternative, and as such it focuses on the premerger value of the acquired company's shares. In short, it neither serves nor is designed to serve as a remedy for the fiduciary misbehavior at which the fairness challenge is directed." Brudney and Chirelstein, Fair Shares in Mergers and Take–Overs, 88 Harv.L.Rev. 297, 304–307 (1974).

Finally, (1) in evaluating the effect of authorizing the appraisal remedy to preclude a challenge for unfairness as a mechanism for protecting public stockholders against underpayment in parent-subsidiary mergers, and (2) in seeking to explain higher awards per share in appraisals sought by dissenters from mergers than in fairness challenges, consider the following summary of the remarks of an experienced Delaware practitioner in commenting on the impact of the Weinberger decision (BNA Secr.Reg. & L.Rep., Vol. 15, p. 2000 (10/28/83)):

"The practical impact of the *Weinberger* holding that disaffected shareholders must resort to the appraisal remedy instead of resorting to class actions to block cash-out mergers is the most significant aspect of the decision, * * *. While a class action proceeds on behalf of all class members, unless any affirmatively opt out, the appraisal remedy requires a shareholder to opt in to participate in the action. It is rare, he said, for more than 5 percent of all shareholders to opt in to an appraisal proceeding, whereas only about 5 percent usually opt out of a class action. As a result, he said, 'the risk in a cash-out merger transaction can be reduced by about 20 times.' "

2.   FAIRNESS

Even if the availability of appraisal should have little or no effect on the availability of judicial remedies or access to courts for challenging self dealing or "corrupt" mergers, should it make a difference if the question before the court is whether to enjoin the as yet unconsummated merger rather than whether to adjust the merger price after consummation? In answering that question, consider (a) the difficulties confronting a plaintiff in finding the evidence to prove entitlement to, and sustaining the unusually heavy burden he carries in seeking, a preliminary injunction (see Greene & Co. v. Schenley Industries, Inc., 281 A.2d 30 (Del.Ch.1971)), and (b) the problems he faces even if the court is prepared to grant a preliminary injunction. See Gimbel v. Signal Companies, Inc., 316 A.2d 599 (Del.Ch.1974) and 316 A.2d 619 (Del.1974) (requiring plaintiff to post a bond for $25 million notwithstanding court's finding that plaintiff was entitled to a preliminary injunction).

Should the nature of the limits on the terms of a merger and the remedies available to public stockholders vary depending upon whether the merger is (a) a bona fide arm's-length transaction between strangers, (b) a transaction between strangers in which, however, one of them makes side payments to the management or controlling stockholders of the other, (c) a transaction imposed by a parent upon a subsidiary in which it owns less than 85 percent or 90 percent of the outstanding stock or (d) a short form merger?

ROSENBLATT v. GETTY OIL CO.

Supreme Court of Delaware, 1985.
493 A.2d 929.

MOORE, Justice:

In this class action brought on behalf of the minority stockholders of Skelly Oil Company (Skelly) we review a Court of Chancery decision holding that the 1977 stock-for-stock merger of Skelly and Mission Corporation (Mission) into Getty Oil Company (Getty) was entirely fair to the plaintiffs.

For the first time since Weinberger v. UOP, Inc., Del.Supr., 457 A.2d 701 (1983), we address certain principles upon which the parties' basic disputes are centered. These include the allocation of the burden of proof on the fairness issue, the continued viability of the Delaware Block method of valuation, and the circumstances necessitating disclosure by a majority stockholder of the price it ultimately is prepared to pay the minority for its elimination. Applying the fairness analysis in *Weinberger*, we conclude that Getty, as the majority shareholder of Skelly, dealt fairly with the Skelly minority throughout the transaction. We also conclude that the stock exchange ratio in this merger was the product of sound valuation methods and arm's length bargaining. Accordingly, we affirm the trial court's decision on the merits.

I.

A somewhat detailed factual discussion is helpful to an understanding of the issues before us.

A.

Background and Operations of the Companies

Immediately before this merger Getty directly owned 7.42% of Skelly's outstanding shares and 89.73% of Mission, which in turn held 72.6% of Skelly's stock.

Getty was a large petroleum company concerned primarily with the exploration for and development of crude oil and natural gas throughout the world. Its operations and activities were integrated vertically to include the exploration and development of petroleum, natural gas, and minerals both on land and offshore; the production and refining of petroleum and natural gas, both domestically and in other countries; the transportation of these products by its own fleet of five domestic and twelve international flag vessels, as well as by rail car, tank truck, and pipeline; the manufacturing of petroleum products and chemicals; and the wholesale and retail distribution of these products in the United States and Philippines.

Apart from Getty's operations and significant assets, qualifying it as an integrated oil company, Getty had important subsurface properties of oil and natural gas reserves in the United States, Canada, Spain, the Middle East, and the North Sea.

* * *

Getty owned uranium, coal, gold, copper and oil shale reserves in the United States, and maintained an interest in uranium—gold ore reserves in Australia's Northern Territory.

Like Getty, Skelly was an integrated oil company with far flung, diversified operations and activities at the time of the merger. Skelly had significant domestic off-shore petroleum reserves in the production stage, as well as large leaseholdings on-shore in North America [and internationally]. * * * Skelly's operations included oil and gas exploration and development, the production, transportation, refining and sale of crude oil and natural gas, and wholesale and retail marketing.

Mission was a Nevada corporation controlled by Getty, and was primarily an investment company with minimal assets other than its Skelly stock.

B.

Merger Discussions and Negotiations

Until his death on June 6, 1976, J. Paul Getty, the majority shareholder of Getty, had continually opposed the merger of Getty and Skelly. His reasons were varied, but they apparently centered on his notion that a healthy competition existed between the two companies which enhanced their profitability to a greater extent than the synergy to be anticipated from a merger.

However there were others with differing views.[5] At the May 1976 annual meeting of Mission an attorney representing Joseph Gruss, a Skelly minority shareholder, argued for a merger of Mission into Getty, and threatened suit on his client's behalf.

* * *

[As a result, on July 15, at the instigation of Getty's then executive Vice President (Berg) a meeting of the principal officers of both Getty and Skelly was held to discuss a merger.]

All acknowledged the desirability of a merger. The consensus was that the fairest way to achieve this result would be an exchange of common stock, continuing shareholder participation in a larger post-

---

5. One advantage of a merger was the reduction in exploration, development, and production costs, given the increased reserves of the surviving corporation. Another advantage was the elimination of duplicative managerial positions.

merger company. Thereafter, a memorandum was distributed summarizing the pertinent legal considerations affecting the proposal.

Generally, it was agreed at the July 15 meeting that DeGolyer and MacNaughton (D & M), a Dallas, Texas, petroleum engineering firm with an outstanding reputation, would assist the parties in evaluating their respective oil, gas and mineral reserves. D & M had worked periodically with both Skelly and Getty since 1939, and had prepared annual estimates of oil and gas reserves for both companies for many years. In addition, D & M had begun preparing annual reports on Getty's mineral properties for the last several years prior to the merger. Accordingly, D & M was contacted on July 15, 1976 by Getty and Skelly and asked to estimate the reserves of both companies, to make an economic valuation based on those estimates, and then to deliver this analysis to the companies for their use in negotiating the merger exchange ratio.

After the July 15 Dallas meeting, Getty and Skelly promptly began evaluating their respective surface and subsurface assets. It is clear that both parties devoted substantial internal resources in preparing to negotiate the exchange ratio of Getty and Skelly stock. In addition, both companies hired reputable investment banking firms to assist in the valuation task, and to render opinions on the fairness of the merger's ultimate terms. Getty retained Blyth, Eastman, Dillon & Co. ("Blyth Eastman"), and Skelly chose Smith Barney, Harris Upham & Co. ("Smith Barney").

Significantly, Skelly and Getty approached the merger with entirely different objectives which remained constant throughout the negotiations. Already, Getty had been threatened with suit by Gruss, a Skelly minority shareholder, and had every expectation that the transaction would lead to litigation. Thus, it carefully sought to comply with applicable Delaware law in meeting the test of complete fairness. It was for this reason that in negotiating the exchange ratio Getty recommended use of the Delaware Block method to value the companies' stock.[6] Skelly's object on behalf of its minority shareholders was one of direct economic interest—to obtain the best possible price for its stock by a highly favorable exchange ratio of Skelly to Getty shares.

In utilizing the Delaware Block method, Skelly attempted to maximize the weight given to surface assets, while minimizing the importance of subsurface properties, i.e., oil, gas, and mineral reserves. This tactic was born of Getty's far more significant estimated reserves. Skelly also emphasized current earnings, because of its 1976 record profits. Finally, because the market price of Getty's stock was much higher, Skelly tried to reduce the weight given this element of value.

---

6. At that time, this was the exclusive technique used in appraisal and other stock valuation proceedings. Elements of value, including assets, earnings, and market price are given a dollar figure, assigned percentage weights, and then summed to yield a weighted average value per share. See, e.g., Sporborg v. City Speciality Stores, Inc., Del.Ch., 123 A.2d 121, 124 (1956); Heller v. Munsingwear, Inc., Del.Ch., 98 A.2d 774, 777 (1953); In re General Realty & Utilities Corp., Del.Ch., 52 A.2d 6, 14–15 (1947).

* * *

[The court recited that in the course of the negotiations between representatives of the two companies during the period July 15, 1976– November 13, 1976, when both boards approved a merger, there was considerable disagreement over proper components of value and much hard bargaining (possibly even anger by the Getty representatives at the inconsistencies they attributed to Skelly). Getty anticipated an exchange ratio of .45–.55 shares of Getty for each share of Skelly, but Skelly proposed .7 shares on the morning of November 1. By the afternoon Getty was offering a ratio of .57 shares and Skelly was proposing .61. At a trade association meeting on November 7, Getty offered a ratio of .5875 and Skelly accepted. Their boards approved on November 13, 1976, their stockholders assented on January 25, 1977 (including 89.4% of the Skelly minority shares that voted) and the companies were merged on January 31, 1977.]

II.

* * *

As to the fairness of the merger price, plaintiffs claim that exclusive use of the Delaware Block method yielded a value of $110 per share, considerably less than Skelly's appraised asset value of $195 per share. Plaintiffs argue that they suffered a dilution of their earnings and dividends per share. Finally, they claim that the merger price was flawed by certain fundamental misconceptions of Getty's negotiators regarding the future prospects of both companies.

As to fair dealing, plaintiffs contend that Getty failed to disclose a projected $52 million reduction in earnings. Plaintiffs also allege that Getty used its controlling position to force Skelly's acceptance of the merger, that Getty coerced Skelly into using the Delaware Block method, and generally, that Getty dominated Skelly's negotiators.

In response, Getty asserts first, as to fairness of price, the Delaware Block method was the sole valuation technique approved by Delaware courts in 1976, and that the resulting Getty–Skelly exchange ratio was entirely fair to the Skelly minority. Moreover, no dilution of dividends was in fact suffered by the minority. Second, as to its conduct, Getty contends that it acted fairly throughout the course of the transaction.

* * *

III.

* * *

A.

In Weinberger v. UOP., Del.Supr., 457 A.2d 701, 710 (1983), we stated that "[t]he requirement of fairness is unflinching in its demand that where one stands on both sides of a transaction, he has the burden of establishing its entire fairness, sufficient to pass the test of careful scrutiny by the courts." Id. [citing Sterling v. Mayflower Hotel Corp.,

Del.Supr., 93 A.2d 107, 110 (1952); Bastian v. Bourns, Inc., Del.Ch., 256 A.2d 680, 681 (1969), aff'd, Del.Supr., 278 A.2d 467 (1970); David J. Greene & Co. v. Dunhill International, Inc., Del.Ch., 249 A.2d 427, 431 (1968)]. We further stated that the concept of fairness has two aspects, fair dealing and fair price, both of which must be examined together in resolving the ultimate question of entire fairness. *Weinberger,* 457 A.2d at 711.

As to fair dealing, we noted in *Weinberger* that the concept included issues of when the transaction was timed, how it was initiated, structured, negotiated, and disclosed to the board, and how director and shareholder approval was obtained. Id. We consider all the foregoing principles applicable here. * * *

B.

Beginning with the burden of proof, we agree with the trial court that the plaintiffs' allegations were sufficient to challenge the fairness of the merger ratio. *Weinberger,* 457 A.2d at 703. Clearly, Getty, as majority shareholder of Skelly, stood on both sides of this transaction and bore the initial burden of establishing its entire fairness. Id. However, approval of a merger, as here, by an informed vote of a majority of the minority shareholders, while not a legal prerequisite, shifts the burden of proving the unfairness of the merger entirely to the plaintiffs. See id. Getty, nonetheless, retained the burden of showing complete disclosure of all material facts relevant to that vote. See id.

C.

On the basis of this record we are satisfied that Getty dealt fairly with Skelly throughout the transaction. Indeed, the adversarial nature of the negotiations completely supports a conclusion that they were conducted at arm's length. There is no credible evidence indicating that Getty, as the majority shareholder, dictated the terms of this merger. If anything, the facts are to the contrary. Thus, what we have here is more than the theoretical concept of what an independent board might do under like circumstances. Johnston v. Greene, Del. Supr., 121 A.2d 919, 925 (1956). Instead, it is clear that these contending parties to the merger in fact exerted their bargaining power against one another at arm's length. This is of considerable importance when addressing ultimate questions of fairness, since it may give rise to the proposition that the directors' actions are more appropriately measured by business judgment standards. Compare Sinclair Oil Corporation v. Levien, Del.Supr., 280 A.2d 717, 720 (1971); Getty Oil Company v. Skelly Oil Company, Del.Supr., 267 A.2d 883, 886–887 (1970); Beard v. Elster, Del.Supr., 160 A.2d 731, 738 (1960); Puma v. Marriott, Del.Ch., 283 A.2d 693, 695 (1971). The facts show that prior to the initiation of merger negotiations Getty knew that it would be sued. Thus, it sought to structure the transaction to meet the standards imposed by Delaware law. At the initial meeting held on July 15, 1976, Getty and Skelly management were given a legal research memorandum on valuation methods approved by Delaware courts. Moreover, Getty was cognizant of the potential conflicts among the interlocking managements of both companies. Accordingly, at the July 15, 1976 meeting, when Getty designated Kenneth Hill of Blyth Eastman as its chief negotiator, Hill immediately resigned from Skelly's board on which he had served for ten years. Similarly, a partner in the law firm Hays, Landsman & Head, resigned from the Skelly board because the law firm was representing Getty.

As to the structure of the actual negotiations, Getty and Skelly agreed on July 15, 1976 to have D & M [a well reputed petroleum engineering firm] estimate their respective reserves and analyze their future prospects. Getty and Skelly also agreed to evaluate separately their respective surface assets and then, negotiate those values. The Chancellor properly found that both corporations devoted substantial economic resources and manpower to the latter effort. The trial court also properly found that the objectives of Getty and Skelly were vastly different. Getty sought a safe harbor for the merger; Skelly sought the highest price possible. See *Weinberger,* 457 A.2d at 710.

As to the negotiations themselves, it is obvious that the divergence in objectives insured the arm's length quality of the bargaining between the Getty and Skelly teams on asset value.[7] In fact, Skelly's attempt to obtain the highest possible value, irrespective of the inconsistencies in its approach, nearly caused the collapse of negotiations on at least two occasions: on September 29, when the surface asset books were exchanged, and on November 1 when Skelly opened with a bid of .7. Moreover, Skelly's persistent efforts to obtain a high price forced the parties to turn to D & M to render, alone, the final subsurface asset value. The evidence indicates that this course of action favored Skelly, given Getty's far greater reserves and D & M's practice of making ultra-conservative reserve estimates.

Plaintiffs seek to compare this action to *Weinberger* by claiming that a memorandum, dated October 14, 1976, prepared by Robert J. Menzie, a Getty financial officer, was never disclosed to Skelly. In particular, plaintiffs liken this document, projecting a $52,165,000 after-tax decrease in Getty's 1976 earnings, in comparison to its 1975 earnings, to the Arledge and Chitiea report in *Weinberger,* which indicated that the majority shareholder, Signal, still considered the elimination of the minority an "outstanding investment opportunity" even at a price higher than that actually being offered. See *Weinberger,* 457 A.2d at 705, 708, 712. However, the two reports are factually and legally different. First, it is not clear that Skelly and its negotiators were unaware of Getty's projected earnings decrease.

---

7. On July 15, or 16, 1976, Hara, Skelly's president, formed a team to negotiate the merger for Skelly, consisting of Hara, Harold C. Stuart, an outside director with 18 years on the Skelly board, and Robert Miller, then executive vice-president of Skelly. Similarly, Getty selected Kenneth Hill of Blyth Eastman to be its chief nego-tiator; Hill resigned his Skelly director-ship on July 15, 1976. This independent bargaining structure, while not conclusive, is strong evidence of the fairness of the merger ratio. See *Weinberger,* 457 A.2d at 709–11; 709 n. 7. However, the use of such a committee is not essential to a finding of fairness.

Second, the Arledge–Chitiea report, used secretly by and exclusively for Signal, was prepared by two Signal directors, who were also UOP directors, using UOP information obtained solely in their capacities as UOP directors. *Weinberger,* 457 A.2d at 705. Here, the decreased earnings projection was prepared by a member of Getty's management for Getty's use as part of its annual reporting function. Moreover, there is not the slightest indication that its disclosure could have materially affected the exchange ratio negotiations. See id. at 709, 712. Third, the merger in *Weinberger* was expressly conditioned on approval of a majority of UOP's minority shareholders; here, there was no such condition. See id. at 707.

While it has been suggested that *Weinberger* stands for the proposition that a majority shareholder must under all circumstances disclose its top bid to the minority, that clearly is a misconception of what we said there.[8] The sole basis for our conclusions in *Weinberger* regarding the non-disclosure of the Arledge–Chitiea report was because Signal appointed directors on UOP's board, who thus stood on both sides of the transaction, violated their undiminished duty of loyalty to UOP. It had nothing to do with Signal's duty, as the majority stockholder, to the other shareholders of UOP.[9]

As to the approval of the merger proposal by the Getty and Skelly boards, the record shows that their action was taken on an informed basis. See Smith v. Van Gorkom, Del.Supr., 488 A.2d 858, 872 (1985); Aronson v. Lewis, Del.Supr., 473 A.2d 805, 812 (1984); Kaplan v. Centex Corp., Del.Ch., 284 A.2d 119, 124 (1971). At Skelly's board meeting, the directors were fully briefed by Smith Barney and by Blyth Eastman, on the basis of copies of valuation books prepared and distributed by the two investment banks. Skelly's directors had been given copies of the proxy statement prior to the meeting. Skelly's board received a legal opinion on the merger, as well as copies of D & M's final estimate. The directors also heard from the attorney representing Gruss, the Skelly shareholder who had been threatening suit since May 1976. The record also shows that certain Skelly directors, including outside director Stuart, who controlled more stock than the plaintiff class, questioned Getty representatives Garber and Thompson, as well as Skelly management, on the fairness of the exchange ratio. Following this discussion, Copley, Jones, and Williams, who were Getty and Mission officers, as well as Skelly directors, were excused from the Skelly board meeting. Outside director Stuart moved to approve the proposed merger ratio. The resolution was unanimously adopted. Copley, Jones, and Williams returned and concurred with the resolution. At the Getty board meeting, Getty's directors were given a similar, in-depth briefing on the proposed merger, and voted to approve it.

---

8. See Herzel and Colling, Establishing Procedural Fairness in Squeeze–Out Mergers After Weinberger v. UOP, 39 Bus.Law. 1525, 1532 (1984); Herzel and Colling, Squeeze–Out Mergers in Delaware—The Delaware Supreme Court Decision in Weinberger v. UOP, 7 Corp.L.Rev. 195, 207 (1984).

9. See Payson and Inskip, Weinberger v. UOP, Inc.: Its Practical Significance In The Planning and Defense of Cash–Out Mergers, 8 Del.J.Corp.L. 83, 89 (1983).

D.

Regarding the second aspect of fairness, fair price, we note initially that "in a non-fraudulent transaction * * * price may be the preponderant consideration outweighing other features of the merger". *Weinberger*, 457 A.2d at 711. Fair price involves all relevant economic factors of the proposed merger, such as asset value, market value, earnings, future prospects, and any other elements that affect the inherent or intrinsic value of a company's stock. Id. Thus, in *Weinberger* we authorized proof of value in appraisal and other stock valuation cases by any techniques or methods generally considered acceptable in the financial community and otherwise admissible in court. Id. at 713. In addition, we ruled that the Delaware Block formula was no longer the *exclusive* mechanism of value precluding other generally accepted techniques. Id. at 712–13. We stated further that only speculative elements of value due to the accomplishment of the merger are excluded from 8 Del.C. § 262(h). However, elements of future value known or susceptible of proof at the date of the merger do not fall within this narrow exclusion and may be considered, along with damages, including rescissory damages. Id.* While the plaintiffs challenge the defendant's use of the Delaware Block method, that was the only valuation technique permitted at that time. In any event, *Weinberger* did not abolish the block formula, only its exclusivity as a tool of valuation. We find no legal error or abuse of discretion by the Chancellor's action in accepting its use here.

In terms of the concept of fair price, *Weinberger* is consistent with Sterling v. Mayflower Hotel Corp., Del.Supr., 93 A.2d 107 (1952), where this Court stated that the correct test of fairness is "that upon a merger

---

* [Ed. Note] In Tanzer v. International General Industries, Inc., 402 A.2d 382 (Del. Ch.1979) the Vice Chancellor noted that "Unfortunately, Delaware law gives only limited guidance as to how to scrutinize 'entire fairness' other than in determining the burden of proof." And even that last point is no longer so clear. In his opinion upholding a parent-subsidiary cash-out merger, the Vice Chancellor recited, and sought to apply, the entire catechism of procedural and substantive factors enunciated by the Delaware Supreme Court. In the course of the opinion the court rejected the notion that in a proceeding challenging "fairness" sharing synergistic gains from merger was an appropriate measure. It went on to say, 402 A.2d at 394–395:

The only practical time to consider the synergistic effect, if any, would be during an appraisal pursuant to 8 Del.C. § 262. Unfortunately, for the Tanzers, the Delaware appraisal statute presently precludes its consideration. It is not for this Court, however, to substitute its judgment for that of the General Assembly. If the synergistic effect is to be considered by this Court in an appraisal proceeding, it should be legislatively mandated. The failure of a dominant stockholder to recognize the possible synergistic effect of a merger in arriving at a price to be offered for the shares of the stockholders being frozen out, is not therefore valid grounds to challenge the merger.

Even if a possible synergistic effect should have been recognized and given value in this case, the Tanzers have introduced no evidence that the 29% premium offered by I.G.I. for Kliklok stock owned by the minority stockholders does not adequately compensate the minority stockholders for such possible synergistic effect.

Does the Supreme Court's reference to "elements of future value" that do not fall within "this narrow exclusion [speculative elements due to accomplishment of the merger]" leave room for a requirement of sharing?

the minority stockholder shall receive the substantial equivalent in value of what he had before". *Sterling,* 93 A.2d at 114.

In *Sterling,* the plaintiffs challenged the fairness of the terms of a stock-for-stock merger of Mayflower Hotel Corporation into its parent/majority shareholder, Hilton Hotel Corporation. Id. at 108. Inquiring into whether the facts supported the fairness of the stock conversion ratio, the Court in *Sterling* carefully scrutinized a pre-merger, outside study comparing the book values, market values, and earnings, but not the asset values of the two companies. Id. at 109, 115. Disposing of plaintiffs' objection to the report's failure to appraise physical assets and to determine net asset value, this Court stated that while all relevant factors must be considered, no one factor is in every case given greatest weight.

The Court stated further that the relative importance of the several tests of value depends upon the circumstances of each case. Id. The Court in *Sterling* then reasoned that net asset value was of less importance than earning power given the nature of the assets of the two companies. Id. 115–16.

After careful scrutiny of the methods employed by the parties, the process of information gathering, the negotiations, and all relevant economic and financial factors, we conclude that the Chancellor's findings regarding fairness of the price paid the Skelly minority shareholders were entirely correct.

As noted earlier, Getty and Skelly were given a legal opinion on mergers under Delaware law at the July 15, 1976 meeting. Thus, from the outset, both sides were aware of the exclusive valuation method then approved by the courts of this State, the so-called Delaware Block formula. Both parties sought to follow this method in reaching the ultimate stock exchange ratio. They were entirely correct in doing so. See, e.g., Universal City Studios, Inc. v. Francis I. duPont & Co., Del.Supr., 334 A.2d 216, 218 (1975); Application of Delaware Racing Ass'n, Del.Supr., 213 A.2d 203, 209–13 (1965); Tri–Continental Corp. v. Battye, Del.Supr., 74 A.2d 71, 72 (1950). At the time there had not been any judicial relaxation of the exclusivity of this method as ultimately occurred in *Weinberger,* 457 A.2d at 712–13.

* * *

Based on the components of the .5875 exchange ratio, Skelly succeeded in obtaining an equal weighting of earnings and assets, despite Getty's recognition that assets were of prime importance, and that under Delaware law assets are often given greatest weight. *Bell,* 413 A.2d at 142; *Abelow,* 173 A.2d at 171. As to the three-year weighted earnings average used, it must be observed that the 1976 annualized income was Skelly's highest in history. Moreover, the 1976 earnings were given a triple weight. See Universal City Studios, Inc. v. Francis I. duPont & Co., Del.Supr., 334 A.2d 216, 218 (1975); Adams v. R.C. Williams & Co., Del.Ch., 158 A.2d 797, 800 (1960). Second, we note that Skelly's earning power, relative to Getty, was at its zenith.

* * *

Third, Skelly succeeded in belittling the market price of the companies' stocks, notwithstanding that Getty shares were selling at a much higher price. See In re Olivetti Underwood Corp., Del.Ch., 246 A.2d 800, 809 (1968). Finally, the record is replete with evidence of Skelly's recognition that the relative positions of the two companies would not be as favorable to Skelly within the foreseeable future, and that the merger would result in a more competitive, efficient company, thereby benefiting the Skelly stockholders who would maintain a continued ownership interest in the surviving company. The inference is that the recognition impelled Skelly to set a year-end deadline for the merger and to try again on November 7.

To rebut the claim of fair price, plaintiffs presented the conclusions of a corporate finance expert who charged both parties with errors in arriving at the exchange ratio.

* * *

Plaintiffs' expert presented an analysis of ten comparable arm's length oil mergers producing a consideration equal to or greater than asset value per share.

As for the plaintiffs' expert testimony, we agree with the trial court's conclusion that it was unpersuasive, based on the noncomparability of the ten mergers selected, and on the unverified asset values employed. See David J. Greene & Co. v. Dunhill International, Inc., Del.Ch., 249 A.2d 427, 433 (1968). In addition, this testimony concludes that Skelly's minority shareholders should have received Getty stock equivalent to the liquidation value of Skelly. This contention was laid to rest in *Sterling,* 93 A.2d at 116. In Delaware a company is valued as a going concern, not on what can be obtained by its liquidation. * * * With respect to the claimed dilution of earnings and dividends, these issues were raised in the negotiations, and the Getty team agreed to raise Getty's 1977 dividend to prevent dilution. The evidence of dilution presented by defendant and Delaware case law indicate that the alleged 26% earnings dilution did not taint the fairness of the merger ratio. See Bastian v. Bourns, Inc., Del.Ch., 256 A.2d 680, 683–84 (1969), aff'd, Del.Supr., 278 A.2d 467 (1970) (in exchange merger, future prospects of survivor corporation and ready investor market outweighed earnings dilution); David J. Greene & Co. v. Dunhill International, Inc., Del.Ch., 249 A.2d 427, 436 (1968) (earnings dilution plus uncertainty of earnings multiplier and possible taking of a corporate opportunity warranted preliminary injunction of exchange merger).

After an exhaustive review of the facts and evidence relating to the issue of fairness, we conclude that Getty dealt fairly with Skelly's minority shareholders from the genesis of the merger through approval by the respective boards of the two companies. We also conclude that the price received by the Skelly shareholders was fair.

* * *

V.

Having examined the fairness of the merger, including the propriety of the delegation to D & M, we consider the plaintiffs' claim that the Skelly proxy statement does not satisfy the standards of Lynch v. Vickers Energy Corp., Del.Supr., 383 A.2d 278, 281 (1977). In *Lynch,* this Court held that to ascertain whether certain individual directors and the majority shareholder, Vickers Energy Corporation, had met their duty of complete candor, "the limited function of the Court was to determine whether defendants had disclosed [to the minority shareholders] all information in their possession germane to the transaction in issue". Id. at 281. The *Lynch* court defined as germane, in a tender offer context, any information which a reasonable shareholder would consider important in deciding whether to sell or retain stock. Id. (ceiling price and ceiling asset value in tender offer held germane). See *Weinberger,* 457 A.2d at 709 (insiders' report that cash-out merger price up to $24 was good investment held germane); Michelson v. Duncan, Del.Supr., 407 A.2d 211, 222 (1979) (alleged terms and intent of stock option plan held not germane); Schreiber v. Pennzoil Co., Del.Ch., 419 A.2d 952, 958–59 (1980) (management fee of $650,000 held germane). Cf. Kaplan v. Goldsamt, Del.Ch., 380 A.2d 556, 561 (1977). The court in *Lynch* also stated that disclosure of all germane facts was required. *Lynch,* 383 A.2d at 281.

Recently, in Smith v. Van Gorkom, Del.Supr., 488 A.2d 858, 890 (1985), we noted that "germane" means "material" facts. The term "germane" has no well accepted meaning in the disclosure context, while "material" does. Moreover, it is clear from the Delaware cases that the materiality standard of TSC Industries, Inc. v. Northway, Inc., 426 U.S. 438, 449, 96 S.Ct. 2126, 2132, 48 L.Ed.2d 757 (1976), applies.

* * *

* * * Even the seminal case of Lynch v. Vickers Energy Corp., Del.Supr., 383 A.2d 278 (1977), employing the term "germane" for the first time, relied upon this concept of materiality by citing TSC Industries, Inc. v. Northway, Inc. in support of its reasoning. See *Lynch,* 383 A.2d at 281.

* * *

Plaintiffs claim that the Skelly proxy statement failed to disclose the D & M delegation and the parties' understanding that D & M's methods were to remain secret. * * * [The court held that disclosure in the proxy statement had been adequate, both because the information was not material and because it was sufficiently disclosed.]

VI.

After careful scrutiny of the entire transaction, we conclude that Getty dealt fairly with the Skelly minority shareholders in the merger. In our opinion the exchange ratio ultimately agreed upon was entirely fair as the product of a careful evaluation of all relevant factors and arm's length bargaining.

* * *

Affirmed.

———

NOTE: THE STANDARD OF REVIEW

1. The Delaware Court of Chancery had occasion to apply the standard of review articulated in *Rosenblatt* in **Citron v. E.I. DuPont de Nemours & Co.,** 584 A.2d 490 (Del.Ch.1990). According to Vice Chancellor Jacobs, *Sinclair Oil Corp. v. Levien,* supra p. 575, holds that the entire fairness standard is triggered when the plaintiff demonstrates "that the parent corporation stood on both sides of the transaction *and* * * * dictated its terms" (emphasis in original), while *Rosenblatt* requires only a showing that the parent corporation stood on both sides of the transaction. Thus, in a case where the merger is negotiated and approved by disinterested directors and ratified by a fully informed majority of the minority stockholders, business judgment scrutiny does not apply because the parent stands on both sides. Under *Rosenblatt,* minority stockholder ratification after disinterested director intervention operates to shift the burden of persuasion on the issue of entire fairness to the plaintiff.

2. Do the opinions of the Delaware courts in parent-subsidiary mergers suggest that procedural fairness, effected by adherence to forms that imitate arm's-length bargaining, is the crucial test of fairness in such mergers? Whatever may be the substantive standard of fairness that can be deciphered from the opinions, does its application implicate such unconstrained judicial discretion that the court's ultimate decision is the result of its perception of procedural fairness? See Burgman and Cox, Reappraising the Role of the Shareholder in the Modern Public Corporation, *Weinberger's* Procedural Approach to Fairness in Freeze–Outs, 1984 Wis.L.Rev. 593; Note, 93 Yale L.J. 1113 (1984).

In any event, what is the teaching of these cases for corporate counsel in staging the merger?

———

MILLS v. ELECTRIC AUTO–LITE CO.

United States Court of Appeals, Seventh Circuit, 1977.

552 F.2d 1239.

Certiorari denied, 434 U.S. 922, 98 S.Ct. 398, 54 L.Ed.2d 279, rehearing denied 434 U.S. 1002, 98 S.Ct. 649, 54 L.Ed.2d 499 (1977).

[In Mills v. Electric Auto–Lite Co., 396 U.S. 375 (1970), the Supreme Court accepted the conclusion of the District Court and Court of Appeals (which was not challenged by petitioners) that proxy solicitations sent to the stockholders of Electric Auto–Lite Co. (Auto–Lite) to solicit approval of a merger with Mergenthaler Linotype Company

(Mergenthaler), which owned some 54% of Auto–Lite's common stock, into a newly formed corporation called Eltra were materially misleading. The proxy statement did disclose that Mergenthaler owned 54% of the stock of Auto–Lite, but in stating that Auto–Lite's Board of Directors recommended approval of the merger it failed to state that Auto–Lite's directors were nominees of Mergenthaler and were under the control and domination of Mergenthaler. The Supreme Court ruled that if the latter omission was material, it was unnecessary to prove reliance by each or any particular stockholder who voted for the merger without further proof of causality or reliance being necessary. The Court rejected the rationale of the Court of Appeals that "causality" or "reliance" was to be determined by proof of the fairness of the terms of the merger. In rejecting that argument, the Court said:

" * * * The decision below, by permitting all liability to be foreclosed on the basis of a finding that the merger was fair, would allow the stockholders to be bypassed, at least where the only legal challenge to the merger is a suit for retrospective relief after the meeting has been held. A judicial appraisal of the merger's merits could be substituted for the actual and informed vote of the stockholders.

"The result would be to insulate from private redress an entire category of proxy violations—those relating to matters other than the terms of the merger. Even outrageous misrepresentations in a proxy solicitation, if they did not relate to the terms of the transaction, would give rise to no cause of action under § 14(a). Particularly if carried over to enforcement actions by the Securities and Exchange Commission itself, such a result would subvert the congressional purpose of ensuring full and fair disclosure to shareholders.

"Further, recognition of the fairness of the merger as a complete defense would confront small shareholders with an additional obstacle to making a successful challenge to a proposal recommended through a defective proxy statement. The risk that they would be unable to rebut the corporation's evidence of the fairness of the proposal, and thus to establish their cause of action, would be bound to discourage such shareholders from the private enforcement of the proxy rules that 'provides a necessary supplement to Commission action.' J.I. Case Co. v. Borak, 377 U.S., at 432.⁵"

---

5. The Court of Appeals' ruling that "causation" may be negated by proof of the fairness of the merger also rests on a dubious behavioral assumption. There is no justification for presuming that the shareholders of every corporation are willing to accept any and every fair merger offer put before them; yet such a presumption is implicit in the opinion of the Court of Appeals. That court gave no indication of what evidence petitioners might adduce once respondents had established that the merger proposal was equitable, in order to show that the shareholders would nevertheless have rejected it if the solicitation had not been misleading. Proof of actual reliance by thousands of individuals would, as the court acknowledged, not be feasible, see R. Jennings & H. Marsh, Securities Regulation, Cases and Materials 1001 (2d ed. 1968); and reliance on the *nondisclosure* of a fact is a particularly difficult matter to define or prove, see 3 L. Loss, Securities Regulation 1766 (2d ed. 1961). In practice, therefore, the objective fairness of the proposal would seemingly be determinative of liability. But, in view of the many other factors that might lead shareholders to prefer their current position to that of owners of a larger, combined enterprise, it is pure conjecture to assume

In remanding the case for appropriate relief, the Court said:

"Monetary relief will, of course, also be a possibility. Where the defect in the proxy solicitation relates to the specific terms of the merger, the district court might appropriately order an accounting to ensure that the shareholders receive the value that was represented as coming to them. On the other hand, where, as here, the misleading aspect of the solicitation did not relate to terms of the merger, monetary relief might be afforded to the shareholders only if the merger resulted in a reduction of the earnings or earnings potential of their holdings. In short, damages should be recoverable only to the extent that they can be shown. If commingling of the assets and operations of the merged companies makes it impossible to establish direct injury from the merger, relief might be predicated on a determination of the fairness of the terms of the merger at the time it was approved. These questions, of course, are for decision in the first instance by the District Court on remand, and our singling out of some of the possibilities is not intended to exclude others."

On remand, the District Court concluded that the merger should not be rescinded, but that the terms of the merger had been unfair, and awarded damages to plaintiffs in the amount of $1,233,918. On appeal, the Court of Appeals reversed. The court agreed with the district court's rejection of the theory of damages based on reduction of Auto–Lite's earnings or potential earnings by reason of the merger. The court indicated that the commingling of Auto–Lite's assets and management with Mergenthaler's, made it unfeasible to determine how much of the post-merger performance of the Auto–Lite division was attributable to what Auto–Lite brought to the merged enterprise (and should have been paid for) and how much was attributable to what Mergenthaler added. Hence, "the post-merger earnings of Auto–Lite and Mergenthaler cannot supply a reliable guide to whether the merger terms were fair to Auto–Lite minority shareholders." The Court (Swygert, J.) went on to say]:

IV

A

The district court based its award of damages on an assessment of the fairness of the merger terms at the time the merger took place. It evaluated five criteria in making this assessment: (1) the market value of each corporation's stock; (2) each corporation's earnings; (3) the book value of each corporation's assets; (4) the dividends that each corporation paid on its stock; and (5) other "qualitative factors" indicating the strength of each corporation. The court found market value to be an unreliable criterion and discounted the importance of dividends. It found that the comparative earnings and book values of each corporation were significant and demonstrated that the merger terms were

---

that the fairness of the proposal will always be determinative of their vote. Cf. *Wirtz v. Hotel, Motel & Club Employees Union*, 391 U.S. 492, 508 (1968).

unfair to the Auto–Lite minority. The court did not indicate what significance it was attributing to "qualitative factors."

Based on these findings the court held that the merger would have been fair if the Auto–Lite minority shareholders had received the equivalent of 2.35 shares of Eltra common for each share of Auto–Lite that they held and Mergenthaler shareholders had received one share of Eltra common for each share of Mergenthaler that they held. It also found that the effective exchange ratio for the actual merger, where the Auto–Lite minority shareholders received 1.88 shares of Eltra preferred for each share of Auto–Lite common that they held, was 2.25 to 1 in terms of Eltra common. It then awarded damages of $1,233,918.35 to plaintiffs based on the differential of .10 between the effective exchange ratio of 2.25 to 1 and the fair exchange ratio of 2.35 to 1.[6]

B

The district court discounted the significance of the comparative market values of Auto–Lite and Mergenthaler stock during the five year period preceding the merger because it found that purchases of Auto–Lite stock by Auto–Lite itself and by Mergenthaler, and of Mergenthaler stock by the American Manufacturing Company, made market value an unreliable indicator during that period of the true worth of the two parties to the merger. Defendants challenge the district

---

6. The district court used the following method of reaching the figure of $1,233,918.35:

(1) Since each share of Auto–Lite was exchanged for the equivalent of 2.25 shares of Eltra common while each share of Mergenthaler was exchanged for one share of Eltra common, the holder of one share of Auto–Lite received 67.38 percent of the interest in Eltra distributed for one share of Auto–Lite and one share of Mergenthaler, because $2.25/(2.35 + 1) = .6738$.

(2) If a fair exchange ratio of 2.35 had been employed, the holder of one share of Auto–Lite would have received 70.15 percent of the interest in Eltra distributed for one share of Auto–Lite and one share of Mergenthaler, because $2.35/(2.35 + 1) = .7015$.

(3) Since $70.15 - 67.38 = 2.77$, the Auto–Lite minority shareholders were unfairly deprived of 2.77 percent of the combined value of an Auto–Lite share and a Mergenthaler share for each share of Auto–Lite that they held.

(4) In July 1963, the month following the merger, the average market value of the Eltra stock that was distributed for one share of Mergenthaler was $25.25 and the average market value of the Eltra stock that was distributed for one share of Auto–Lite was $58.39. Accord-

ingly, the combined value of one share of Mergenthaler and one share of Auto–Lite was $25.25 + $58.39 = 83.64.

(5) 2.77 percent of $83.64 is $2.317. Since there were 532,500 minority shares of Auto–Lite, the total damages were $532,500 \times \$2.317 = \$1,233,918.35$.

The district court's method of calculation was mathematically unsound. First, there was an arithmetic error in step one because $2.25/(2.35 + 1)$ is .6923 rather than .6738. The more fundamental error, however, lies in the court's premise in steps 3, 4, and 5 that the 2.77 percent figure could be multiplied by the combined market value of one share of Auto–Lite and one share of Mergenthaler to calculate the per share dollar loss which the Auto–Lite shareholders had suffered. It is circular reasoning to use the market value generated by the actual merger. If a different exchange ratio had been employed, the market value of Eltra stock undoubtedly would have been different. Moreover, the mathematical significance of the 2.77 percent figure is questionable.

What the court should have done, if its differential of .10 were correct, was simply multiply the differential by the number of minority Auto–Lite shares to calculate the number of additional Eltra common shares that should have been distributed to plaintiffs to make the merger terms fair.

court's assessment while plaintiffs contend that it was correct, at least for the period after 1960. We agree with defendants.

* * *

We must * * * decide what period of time should be used in calculating a price ratio between each corporation's stock. Since prices from the period immediately preceding the merger are the most likely to reflect the actual value of each corporation at the time the merger was consummated, we begin with a presumption that a short period is appropriate. Accordingly, we hold that the average market value for approximately the six month period preceding the merger should be used unless there are special factors indicating that this period is unreliable. Six months is long enough so that very short term price fluctuations will not play an unfairly important role and short enough so that the calculated ratio does not reflect business conditions that have substantially changed as of the time of the merger.

In this case the ratio between the average price of Auto–Lite and the average price of Mergenthaler during 1963 prior to the formulation of the merger terms in late May was 2.1. Our confidence that this figure accurately reflects the relative worth of the two corporations bolstered by the fact that the ratio for 1962 was also 2.1 and was 2.0 for 1961. The similarity of these numbers is evidence that the ratio immediately preceding the merger was not the result of a short term anomaly caused either by the merger itself or by other factors.

* * *

C

After finding that market value provided an inaccurate measure of the true worth of Auto–Lite and Mergenthaler, the district court determined whether the merger terms were fair on the basis of comparative earnings and book value. Given our conclusion that market prices were an accurate gauge of actual value, we must decide whether the other criteria on which the district court relied should properly be considered in evaluating whether the merger was fair.

We hold that when market value is available and reliable, other factors should not be utilized in determining whether the terms of a merger were fair. Although criteria such as earnings and book value are an indication of actual worth, they are only secondary indicia. In a market economy, market value will always be the primary gauge of an enterprise's worth. In this case thousands of shares of Auto–Lite and Mergenthaler were traded on the New York Stock Exchange during the first part of 1963 by outside investors who had access to the full gamut of financial information about corporations, including earnings and book value. If we were to independently assess criteria other than market value in our effort to determine whether the merger terms were fair, we would be substituting our abstract judgment for that of the market. Aside from the problems that would arise in deciding how much weight to give each criterion, such a method would be economically unsound.

D

We turn now to a determination of whether the merger terms were fair, based on the comparative market price of each corporation's stock during the first part of 1963. The simplest method of resolving this issue would be to compare the price ratio, in this case 2.1, to the effective exchange ratio, which we have previously established as 2.31. Under this framework the merger would be fair since the effective exchange ratio gave the Auto–Lite minority shareholders more Eltra stock than they were entitled to in the judgment of the market.

This method of calculation, however, assumes that the new corporation that results from a merger is worth exactly as much as the sum of what its two component parts were worth before the merger. As Professors Brudney and Chirelstein have cogently pointed out, this assumption is usually false because a merger produces a synergistic effect resulting in the merged corporation being worth more than the sum of the two old corporations. Brudney & Chirelstein, Fair Shares in Corporate Mergers and Takeovers, 88 Harv.L.Rev. 297, 308–09 (1974). They demonstrate that fairness requires that minority shareholders be compensated not only for the market value of their shares in the old corporation but also for the share of the synergism generated by the merger that is proportionate to the interest that those shares represented in the combined premerger value of the two old corporations. Id. at 313–25.

We adopt the approach formulated by Professors Brudney and Chirelstein and will attempt to apply it to this case. At the time of the merger * * * [t]he combined premerger value of the two corporations was $27,825,737 + $67,133,197 = $94,958,934.[16]

In the month following the merger, Eltra common stock had an average market value of $25.25 per share. Eltra preferred stock had an average market value of $58.39 per 1.88 shares, the amount of stock which Auto–Lite shareholders had received for each share of Auto–Lite that they had held. The postmerger value of Eltra was therefore * * * $99,240,849. The difference between the combined premerger value of Auto–Lite and Mergenthaler and the postmerger value of Eltra, which was $99,240,849 − $94,958,934 = $4,281,915, can be attributed to the synergism generated by the merger.

According to the fairness formula * * * the minority shareholders of Auto–Lite should have received Eltra stock worth at least as much as the premerger market value of their holdings in Auto–Lite and a share of the synergism produced by the merger proportionate to the percentage of the combined premerger value of Auto–Lite and Mergenthaler which their holdings represented. The premerger value of the Auto–

---

16. Although Mergenthaler owned more than half of the Auto–Lite stock, this holding should not be independently count-ed as part of the combined value of the two corporations because it was already reflected in the value of Mergenthaler stock.

Lite minority shares was $27,825,737, which represented 29.3 percent of $94,958,934, the combined premerger value of Auto–Lite and Mergenthaler. Thus, to satisfy the constraints of fairness, the Auto–Lite minority shareholders should have received stock worth at least $27,-825,737 + (.293 × $4,281,915) = $29,080,338. This would be equivalent to 1,151,696.5 shares of Eltra common at $25.25 per share. Had this many shares been distributed to the Auto–Lite minority shareholders, the exchange ratio would have been 1,151,696.5/532,550 = 2.16 to 1.

The Auto–Lite minority shareholders actually received preferred stock worth $58.39 on the market for each share of Auto–Lite that they had held. As a group, their Eltra holdings were worth 532,550 × $58.39 = $31,095,594. This was $31,095,594 − $29,080,338 = $2,015,-256 more than fairness required. This result can be expressed in terms of Eltra common shares. Since the effective exchange ratio of the merger was 2.31 to 1, the property given the Auto–Lite minority was worth 2.31 − 2.16 = .15 shares of Eltra common per share of Auto–Lite more than what a fair amount would have been.

We therefore hold that the terms of the merger were fair and that plaintiffs should recover no damages. A numerical example may help to show the justice of this result. In early 1963, an Auto–Lite shareholder with one hundred shares and a Mergenthaler shareholder with 210 shares each owned stock worth approximately $5225. After the merger, the former Auto–Lite shareholder had 188 shares of Eltra preferred worth approximately $5839 while the former Mergenthaler shareholder had 210 shares of Eltra common worth approximately $5302. Both individuals benefitted from the merger, but the former Auto–Lite minority shareholder benefitted more.*

In seeking criteria to define fairness in a parent-subsidiary merger, is it appropriate to consider, as benefits to be shared, the taxes avoided by the parent's stockholders (but not by the parent) by the transaction, and to attribute some sort of worth to the nuisance value which the subsidiary and its public stockholders give up? E.g., if the subsidiary's consent is necessary for the merger with the parent whose only asset is 70 percent of the subsidiary's stock, and resort to merger rather than liquidation of the parent will reduce the federal income tax burden on its stockholders, but cost the subsidiary and its public stockholders nothing, does fairness require the subsidiary or its public stockholders to receive any compensation for giving consent to the merger? If so, how do we determine the proper amount? [w] Should the result be

* [Ed. Note] The Seventh Circuit's decision in *Mills,* as well as the Brudney and Chirelstein analysis, are criticized in Lorne, A Reappraisal of Fair Shares in Controlled Mergers, 126 U.Pa.L.Rev. 956 (1978), and in Deutsch, The Mysteries of Corporate Law: A Response, 88 Yale L.J. 235 (1978); see also Toms, Compensating Shareholders Frozen Out in Two–Step Mergers, 78 Col.L.Rev. 548 (1978); Booth, The New Law of Freeze–Out Mergers, 49 Missouri L.Rev. 517 (1984).

w. Cf. E.I. du Pont de Nemours & Co. v. Collins, 432 U.S. 46 (1977) in which the Court upheld SEC action under § 17(b) of

different if the combination is required by law rather than desired by the parent for its own benefit? In any event, is such information "material" so as to be required to be disclosed in a proxy statement? See Sulzer v. Associated Madison Companies, Inc., Fed.Sec.L.Rep. (CCH) ¶ 92,053 (M.D.Fla.1985).

NOTE: MARKET PRICE AS A MEASURE OF FAIR SHARE

Is it correct to measure fairness, as the *Mills* court did, by reference to market prices, on the assumption that "In a market economy, market value will always be the primary gauge of an enterprise's worth"? Reconsider the discussion of takeover premiums, supra, pp. 654–669, along with the following materials.

1. It has been suggested that there are different, if not separate, markets for the entire firm or for a control block of its stock and for small units of its stock (see Kornhauser and Gordon, 60 N.Y.U.L.Rev. 761 (1986); Shubik, Corporate Control, Efficient Markets, and The Public Good, in Coffee, Lowenstein and Rose–Ackerman, supra, at p. 31). Whether or not those markets function separately or are so related that the efficiency of the latter market extends to the former, there is good reason to believe that the latter market is likely to be systematically distorted, and therefore wholly inappropriate, as a measure of the values of parent and subsidiary at the time of their merger.

Thus, securities analysts recognize that the publicly traded stock of the subsidiary often, particularly as the parent owns increasingly larger proportions of the total stock, sells at a discount from the price at which the same stock would have sold if there were no parent, or at less than its pro-rata share of the going concern value of the enterprise. A variety of reasons is offered for the distortion—such as the thinness of the market and the uncertainty among investors generated by the fear that in the continuing relations between the two enterprises the parent will inevitably exercise discretion (lawfully as well as unlawfully, but substantially undetectably) to divert assets to itself instead of sharing them with the subsidiary and its public stockholders. In addition to the fear of such exploitation on a continuing basis, there is the no less plausible fear that the parent will force a merger of the two companies on terms disadvantageous to the subsidiary—but which it will be difficult to challenge effectively or at tolerable cost because their propriety turns on information (e.g., predictions about the future) of a kind that has not been made public and that cannot be extracted from the parent.

the Investment Company Act, permitting a merger which denied such compensation. Section 17(b) authorizes the SEC to permit transactions between affiliates if their terms are, inter alia, "reasonable and fair and do not involve overreaching on the part of any person concerned," a standard under which the SEC has approved—and required—some kinds of sharing in mergers.

See also Smith v. Telecommunications, Inc., 134 Cal.App.3d 338, 184 Cal.Rptr. 571 (1982) (holding subsidiary's minority shareholders entitled to share in use of parent's tax loss to offset subsidiary's gain on sale of assets and liquidation).

There is also reason to believe that the market price of the stocks of both parent and subsidiary will be inaccurate at about the time of a merger because of systematic impediments to the flow of information which not only clouds public perception but reinforces public fears. The parent can, and if it contemplates absorbing the subsidiary by merger it is likely to, control both the use of accounting conventions and the release of operating or financial information so as to cause the market price of the subsidiary's stock to drop below its "intrinsic value", and the market price of its own stock to rise above its "intrinsic value", in anticipation of the merger which if assessed by the comparative stock prices will thus inaccurately measure the comparative contributions to the merger.[x]

Finally, it may be noted that if the "give-up" by the subsidiary stockholders is to be measured by a standard of fairness which entitles them to some compensation for their contribution to the gains produced by the merger, the market will be unable adequately to measure that contribution because the relevant information is, by definition, solely within the parent's possession and therefore not reflected in the price of the subsidiary's stock. Nor can the market register, as of the time of the merger, the value of the combined enterprise, if that value depends upon (a) information not reflected in the price of the subsidiary's stock and (b) gains to be produced by aspects of the combination's operation then known only to the parent. Moreover, the market for the combined enterprise's securities may be affected by variables irrelevant to the merger—e.g., a depression in the market generally at the time of the merger.[y] To be sure, those variables may be more relevant if the "get" takes the form of stock of the combined enterprise than if it takes the form of senior securities. But there is little reason to permit changes in money rates or other irrelevancies during the progress of, or soon after, a merger to affect the rights of the subsidiary's public stockholders, particularly since the form of the merger (allowing the parent the option to cancel) inevitably constitutes a one way street directing movement only in the parent's favor.

2. A Report of the Committee on Corporate Laws of the American Bar Association Section of Corporation, Banking and Business Law

---

x. Not only may reported earnings be understated for the subsidiary and overstated for the parent by "legitimate" application of a variety of accounting conventions, but dividend policies and substantive decisions (maintenance) may be taken with a view to advantaging the parent in the rate of exchange in the ultimate merger. Apart from thus misstating the past, the parent may fail to state what it, but not the public, knows about the future—and time the merger when a new development in the subsidiary is about to reach fruition. The shorter the period between the decision to absorb and the initiation of the merger transaction, the easier it is to prevent discovery of the distortions in the information flow and therefore of the im-

proper price-value relationship. It is also possible in any relatively short period for the parent to manipulate the prices of the stocks—both the subsidiary's and its own— so as to support the distortion caused by corruption of the information flow.

y. Thus, for example, if the whole market drops after the merger, the price of the surviving company's stock may be less than the sum of the prices of the stocks of the two subsidiaries, a configuration that would hardly justify the conclusion that no gain resulted from the merger or that the parent and subsidiary each participated in the new enterprise in the correct proportions.

(supra p. 729) resulted in elimination of the "stock market exception" to appraisal rights from the Model Business Corporation Act. The recommendation for this major change of policy was made "in the light of facts which have become more visible since the stock market exception was added to the Model Act in 1969. The 1970s have demonstrated again the possibility of a demoralized market in which fair prices are not available, and in which many companies publicly offer to buy their own shares because the market grossly undervalues them. Under these circumstances, access to market value is not a reasonable alternative for a dissenting shareholder. Moreover, a shareholder may be disqualified by state or federal securities laws from using the market because his shares are 'restricted,' because he is an 'insider' who has acquired shares within six months, or because he possesses 'inside information.' Even if the dissenter is free to use the market, he may find it impractical to do so because his holdings are large and the market is thin. In any event, the market cannot reflect the value of the shares 'excluding any appreciation or depreciation in anticipation' of the corporate change which gives rise to the dissenters' rights.

"The argument for the stock market exception was probably strongest in those cases where a large listed corporation absorbs by merger a much smaller corporation, and would thereby (in the absence of the stock market exception) confer cashout rights on the large corporation's shareholders even though the change in their rights would be minimal. In such cases dissenters' rights are now eliminated by the accompanying amendment to section 73(d).

(33 Bus.Law. 2595–2596 (1978)).

The Reporters' Study No. 1 (Transactions In Control) of the ALI project on corporate governance also supports elimination of the stock market exception albeit on somewhat different reasoning: "Since the market price of the shares will be affected both by the public announcement of the proposed transaction and (in many cases) by the leakage of information * * * before public announcement, availability of a trading market to dispose of one's shares is not the practical equivalent of an appraisal proceeding that expressly disregards the effect of the transaction." (pp. 9–10)

3. Whether market price is determinative, merely relevant or irrelevant to evaluating fairness in either appraisal or collateral challenge, is it appropriate to discount the public stockholder's entitlement by reason of his lack of "control"? Or is the stockholder entitled to equal treatment in such proceedings even if he is not entitled to share the premium on sale of control? See Rapid–American Corp. v. Harris, supra p. 712 and the cases cited in note (4) supra p. 711.

EASTERBROOK AND FISCHEL, CORPORATE
CONTROL TRANSACTIONS

93 Yale L.J. 698, 703–715 (1982).

* * *

II. Equal Treatment, Fiduciary Duty, and Shareholders' Welfare

Many scholars, and a few courts, conclude that one aspect of fiduciary duty is the equal treatment of investors. Their argument takes the following form: fiduciary principles require fair conduct; equal treatment is fair conduct; hence, fiduciary principles require equal treatment. The conclusion does not follow. The argument depends upon an equivalence between equality and fair treatment, which we have questioned elsewhere. To say that fiduciary principles require equal (or even fair) treatment is to beg the central question— whether investors would contract for equal or even roughly equal treatment.[17]

Our analysis of this question requires that a distinction be drawn between rules that maximize value *ex ante* and actions that maximize the returns of certain investors *ex post*. A simple example illustrates the point. A corporation may choose to invest its capital in one of two ventures. Venture 1 will pay $100, and the returns can be divided equally among the firm's investors. Thus, if there are 10 investors in the firm, the expected value to each investor is $10. Venture 2 will pay $150, in contrast, but only if the extra returns are given wholly to five of the ten investors. Thus, five "lucky" investors will receive $20 apiece, and the unlucky ones $10. Because each investor has a 50 percent chance of being lucky, each would think Venture 2 to be worth $15. The directors of the firm should choose Venture 2 over Venture 1 because it has the higher value and because none of the investors is worse off under Venture 2.

Now consider Venture 3, in which $200 in gains are to be divided among only five of the ten investors with nothing for the rest. If investors are risk neutral, fiduciaries should choose Venture 3 over Venture 2 (despite the fact that some investors end up worse off under Venture 3), because the expected value to each investor is $20 under Venture 3 and only $15 under Venture 2.

In sum, if the terms under which the directors obtain control of the firm call for them to maximize the wealth of the investors, their duty is to select the highest-paying venture and, following that, to abide by the rules of distribution. If unequal distribution is necessary to make the

---

17. Lawyers beg this question with regrettable frequency. As George Stigler observed: "Since the fairness of an arrangement is a large factor in the public's attitude toward it, the lawyers as representatives of the public seek to give their schemes the sheen of justice. They employ to this end two approaches. One is to invoke any widely-held belief—on the tacit

but convincing ground that any position is invulnerable against nonexistent attack." Fairness is an invulnerable position; who is for unfairness? But for lawyers fairness is "a suitcase full of bottled ethics from which one freely chooses to blend his own type of justice." Stigler, The Law and Economics of Public Policy: A Plea to the Scholars, 1 J.Legal Stud. 1, 2, 4 (1972).

stakes higher, then duty requires inequality. The *ex post* inequality
under Ventures 2 and 3 is no more "unfair" than the *ex post* inequality
of a lottery, in which all players invest a certain amount but only a few
collect. The equal treatment of the investors going into Ventures 2 and
3, and the gains they receive from taking chances, make the *ex post*
inequality both fair and desirable.[19]

We hope that our analysis of Ventures 2 and 3 above are uncontroversial. If corporate control transactions sufficiently resemble Ventures 2 and 3, this analysis supplies a guide for analyzing the fiduciary
duties of corporate managers. A class of control transactions resembles
Ventures 2 and 3 if: (1) control changes and financial restructurings
produce gains for investors to enjoy; (2) the existence or amount of the
gain depends upon unequal distribution; and (3) shareholders would
prefer the unequal distribution to a more equal distribution of smaller
gains from an alternative transaction (or no transaction). We address
these issues in the remainder of Part II and conclude by advancing a
fiduciary principle under which managers always are free to engage in
transactions resembling Venture 2. For practical reasons, however,
our principle prohibits transactions resembling Venture 3.

A. *The Potential Gains From Control Transactions*

It should be clear that managers do not always maximize the
wealth of investors. We have already discussed the costs of principal-
agent relationships. Because managers have only a small stake in the
fortunes of the firm, these costs may be quite high. Managers may not
work as hard as they would if they could claim a higher share of the
proceeds—they may consume excessive perquisites, and they may select
inferior projects for the firm without bearing the consequences of their
action. Corporate control transactions can reduce agency costs if better
managers obtain control of the firm's assets or if they alter the
incentive structure facing existing managers. Corporate takeovers, and
subsequent changes in management, increase the wealth of investors.[20]

The sale of a control bloc of stock, for example, allows the buyer to
install his own management team, producing the same gains available
from a tender offer for a majority of shares but at lower cost to the
buyer. Because such a buyer believes he can manage the assets of a

---

19. The firm's managers could not easily justify a choice of Venture 2 or 3, followed by a "surprise" equal distribution of
the proceeds among the 10 investors. In
the example we posed, the firm obtained
the higher returns only by agreeing to
unequal distribution. It might get away
with a breach of these conditions once, but
Ventures 2 and 3 or their equivalent soon
would become unavailable. Besides, if the
firm promises to pay some investors unequally when it undertakes the venture,
the managers could not be "fair" to the
unlucky investors without being unfair to
the lucky ones. *See* Broad v. Rockwell
Int'l Corp., 642 F.2d 929, 955–60 (5th Cir.
1981) (en banc) (fiduciary duties require
managers to abide by bargains and disregard considerations of fairness), cert. denied, 102 S.Ct. 506 (1981).

20. Responses of a Target's Management to Tender Offers, supra note 6, at
1168–88. For related arguments about the
sources of gains in corporate control
changes, see Borden, Going Private—Old
Tort, New Tort, or No Tort?   49
N.Y.U.L.Rev. 987, 1006–13 (1974); Corporate Fair Shares, supra note 4, at 308;
Carney, Fundamental Corporate Changes,
Minority Shareholders, and Business Purposes, 1980 Am.Bar Found.Res.J. 69.

firm more profitably, he is willing to pay a premium over the market price to acquire control. The premium will be some percentage of the anticipated increase in value once the transfer of control is effectuated. If there were no anticipated increase in value, it would be irrational for the buyer to pay the premium. There is a strong presumption, therefore, that free transferability of corporate control, like any other type of voluntary exchange, moves assets to higher valued uses.

Other transactions present similar opportunities for gain. The freezeout of minority shareholders may create gains when it facilitates a takeover. Transfers of control are expensive, and apart from the obvious cost of the premium over the market price necessary to induce the sale of control, the purchaser must invest considerable sums in research to determine which firms can be operated profitably after a shift in control. Transfers of control will occur only if the purchaser believes it can recoup these costs. Recoupment is difficult. Although the purchaser benefits if the share prices of the target firm appreciate after the transfer in control, this gain accrues equally to shareholders who did not sell to the purchaser. By eliminating free-riding shareholders in a freezeout, the purchaser may recoup the costs of the acquisition by appropriating the gains from the transfer of control. Such a freezeout clearly increases expected aggregate shareholders' wealth if it increases the likelihood of a profitable transfer of control.

In addition, a freezeout of minority shareholders in a longstanding subsidiary will produce gains if the value of the combined entity is greater than the sum of the separate values of the parent and the subsidiary. Such an increase in value may be attributable to economies of scale, centralized management and corporate planning, or economies of information. Moreover, a freezeout of the minority shareholders of a subsidiary is beneficial if it reduces the cost of policing conflicts of interest and enables the firm to make additional cost-justified investments. A parent may not send new projects to a subsidiary, for example, if the parent's investors must guarantee loans to finance the projects. Under these circumstances, the parent's investors bear a proportionally greater risk of loss than the minority shareholders in the subsidiary, but they do not receive a proportionally greater share of any gains. Thus, the elimination [of] the minority shareholders can increase the likelihood that profitable new ventures will be undertaken.

Other control transactions attack agency costs directly. Although public ownership of a firm may be value-maximizing at one time, changes in the firm's line of business or financial structure may make it worthwhile for the firm to "go private" later. When firms go private they eliminate—or substantially reduce—the separation of ownership and control that creates the clash of interest between principal and agent. Other things being equal, the lower agency costs mean higher returns to investors. In addition, going-private transactions may eliminate costs attributable to public ownership, which include substantial (and increasing) expenditures for legal and auditing fees, stockholder relations and compliance with myriad disclosure obligations mandated by the SEC and organized stock exchanges. By going private, the firm can avoid these costs of compliance and reduce the risk of liability resulting from failure to comply with uncertain disclosure obligations. Moreover, the avoidance of disclosure obligations can benefit the firm if it might have to sacrifice prospective business opportunities if disclosure were required.

* * *

Some corporate control transactions that do not produce gains, however, are not always self-deterring. Looting may explain certain transfers of control. Some going-private transactions may be motivated by a desire to exploit inside information rather than to reduce agency costs. And sometimes a manager may appropriate control of a corporate opportunity even though the firm would have been able to exploit the opportunity more profitably.

At least for publicly-traded firms, the market offers information that distinguishes value-increasing control transactions from others in which looting or mismanagement may be in store. The information is contained in the price of a firm's shares. If the control change is associated with an increase in price, the investors apparently do not fear looting or other harm to the firm. If a syndicate acquires a control bloc of shares, and the price of the remaining shares *rises,* relative to the market as a whole, then the shareholders are betting on the basis of available information that the new controller will be better for their interests than the old. Precisely the same reasoning can be used when analyzing whether a manager has appropriated a corporate opportunity that could have been used more profitably by the firm. If the firm's share prices do not fall after the taking of the corporate opportunity, investors do not believe that they have been injured. Many studies of these price changes have been made; they show gains in the overwhelming majority of control transactions.

Fewer price signals are available in going-private transactions, because such a transaction frequently eliminates public trading of the firm's shares. Even these transactions, however, leave some traces. If the price paid to frozen-out shareholders is higher than the price that the shares commanded before the transaction, the buyer anticipates that the transaction will produce gains. There is little percentage in paying $15 for shares selling at $10. If the only purpose of the transaction is to eliminate minority shareholders, it is irrational for the controlling shareholder to pay a premium over the market price. By using corporate assets to pay minority shareholders more than their shares are worth, the controlling shareholder will have decreased the value of his own holdings and therefore be worse off as a result.

* * *

B. *The Gains May Depend on Unequal Division*

In many cases the apportionment of the gain makes little difference to the success of the transaction. If the gain from taking over a corporation exceeds the cost incurred by the acquiror, he would be indifferent to who receives the premium that is necessary to obtain control. But the fact that apportionment is irrelevant to the acquiror in many cases does not mean that apportionment of gains is always immaterial—in some marginal cases apportionment is the decisive factor. Suppose that a prospective acquiror of control concludes that, by expending $10, he can create a 50 per cent chance of producing $30 in gains. If the prospective acquiror is risk-neutral, the transaction will go forward because the expected gains of $15 exceed the $10 cost of the transaction. If the fiduciary principle is interpreted to require the prospective acquiror to share the $20 gain in the event it is realized, however, and absorb the entire loss if the gain is not realized, the deal may become unprofitable because the costs exceed the expected gains.

In theory, the law could require sharing of the $5 expected gain, but courts could not calculate this amount because they could not observe the *ex ante* risk of failure. Moreover, a large part of the cost to the acquiror is an opportunity cost—the money the acquiror could have made by devoting his talents to other projects. Another cost is the premium required to compensate risk-averse acquirors for risk-bearing. Because it would be difficult or impossible to compute opportunity costs and risk premia in the context of litigation, it would be difficult or impossible to implement a sensible sharing rule. Even if opportunity costs could be approximated, judicial errors would arise, and beneficial control changes would be stifled.

A sharing requirement also may make an otherwise profitable transaction unattractive to the prospective seller of control. To illustrate, suppose that the owner of a control bloc of shares finds that his perquisites or the other amenities of his position are worth $10. A prospective acquiror of control concludes that, by eliminating these perquisites and other amenities, he could produce a gain of $15. The shareholders in the company benefit if the acquiror pays a premium of $11 to the owner of the controlling bloc, ousts the current managers, and makes the contemplated improvements. The net gains of $4 inure to each investor according to his holdings, and although the acquiror obtains the largest portion because he holds the largest bloc, no one is left out. If the owner of the control bloc must share the $11 premium with all of the existing shareholders, however, the deal collapses. The owner will not part with his bloc for less than a $10 premium. A sharing requirement would make the deal unprofitable to him, and the other investors would lose the prospective gain from the installation of better managers.[30]

---

30. The common law recognizes that unequal distribution of gains facilitates the transfer of assets to higher-valued uses. Someone who discovers a lode of ore need not share the knowledge (and the profits) with the farmer under whose land the ore lies but may, instead, send an agent to buy the farm for the going price of farmland. A sharing requirement would lead to less searching for ore and lower wealth for society. See Leitch Gold Mines v. Texas Gulf Sulfur, 1 Ont.2d 469 (1969). See also Laidlaw v. Organ, 15 U.S. (2 Wheat.) 178 (1817). Cf. Northeastern Tel. Co. v. AT & T, 651 F.2d 76, 88–91 (2d Cir.1981) (a multi-product firm need not share joint costs of production among many products, because pricing all products at fully distributed cost would reduce allocative efficiency); Fischel, supra note 6, at 9–26 (analysis of how disclosure obligations of Williams Act

Other value-increasing transactions would also be deterred by a sharing requirement. First, as we have noted above, sometimes a purchase of control is profitable to the purchaser only if he can prevent minority shareholders from sharing in the gains. Freezeouts of minority shareholders after a transfer of control perform precisely this function. Second, if the controlling shareholder in a going-private transaction or merger of a subsidiary into a parent corporation must underwrite the costs of future value-increasing transactions and thereby incur a proportionally greater risk of loss than the minority shareholders in the event expectations are not realized, the deal may become unprofitable to the controlling shareholder if he must share the gains with minority shareholders if all goes well. Thus, a sharing principle in these transactions leads to a reduction in total wealth as people desist from entering into otherwise profitable transactions.

There are other ways in which the gains from corporate control transactions may depend on unequal distribution. Because investors in the firm must cooperate to transfer control, sharing creates incentives to "free ride." In a tender offer, for example, shareholders must tender rather than hold their shares if the bid is to succeed; in a merger (other than a short-form merger), they must vote favorably rather than abstain. If gains must be shared equally, however, each shareholder may find it worthwhile not to cooperate in the transaction. To illustrate, suppose that all of the gains from a tender offer must be shared equally among the investors in the target corporation and that, if there is a follow-up merger, non-tendering shareholders cannot be eliminated for less than the tender offer price. When a prospective acquiror makes a bid, the investors recognize that the acquiror can profit only to the extent it causes the value of shares to rise. If the bidder is offering $50 per share, the reasoning runs, it cannot profit unless value eventually rises above $50. Under the legal rules assumed above, it may be rational for every shareholder to spurn the $50 offer and hope that enough other shareholders tender to make the offer succeed: If there is a follow-up merger, the "fair" price cannot be less than $50 for the untendered shares. If there is no follow-up merger, the shareholder expects the price to exceed $50. Each shareholder, in other words, may attempt to take a free ride on the efforts of the bidder and other shareholders. To the extent free riding prevails, it reduces the chance that the beneficial transaction will go forward.

A final reason why the gains from beneficial transactions may depend on unequal division is that sharing rules may lead to costly attempts to appropriate greater parts of the gains. The appropriation problem arises because most gain-sharing rules do not produce completely predictable results—it is difficult to determine the "fair" price. If all investors are entitled to a "fair" share of the bounty, each will find it advantageous to claim as much as possible and fight for his

decrease incentive of bidders to produce valuable information); Jovanovic, Truthful Disclosure of Information, 13 Bell J.Econ. 36 (1982); Kronman, Mistake, Disclosure, Information, and the Law of Contracts, 7 J.Legal Stud. 1 (1978); Kronman, Contract Law and Distributive Justice, 89 Yale L.J. 472 (1980).

claim. He would spend as much as a dollar, on the margin, to claim another dollar of the benefits. It is possible for a substantial part of the gain to be frittered away, therefore, as claimants attempt to make the argument that they are entitled to more.[32] Fear for this eventuality may cause otherwise beneficial control transactions to fall through; in any event resources will be wasted in litigation or other skirmishings.

C. *Investors Prefer the Fiduciary Principle That Maximizes Aggregate Gains*

Do investors prefer a larger pie even if not everyone may have a larger slice in every case? We argue here that they do, for two reasons. First, their expected wealth is greatest under this interpretation of the fiduciary principle, and second, they may deal with any risk by holding diversified portfolios of investments.

Clearly, if control transactions produce gains, and if the gains depend on unequal allocation, then the expected wealth of the shareholders in the aggregate is maximized by a rule allowing unequal allocation. *All* share prices *ex ante* will be highest when the probability of a value-increasing transaction in the future is the greatest. Shareholders can realize this value at any time by selling their shares, or they can hold the shares and take the chance of gaining still more as a result of the unequal allocation of gains *ex post*.

This argument may seem to disregard the fact that many investors are risk averse—they prefer a sure $10, say, to a one in ten chance of receiving $100. On the surface, therefore, it seems that investors might benefit from equal or fair division of gains notwithstanding the loss of some gains as a result. This argument, however, ignores the lessons of modern portfolio theory. By investing in many firms simultaneously, risk averse investors can reduce the risk of losses without extinguishing profitable-but-risky transactions.[33]

* * *

The risks involved in corporate control transactions are diversifiable. Corporate control transactions are pervasive. There are mergers, takeovers, freezeouts, tender offers, going-private transactions and related events in abundance. Indeed, there is a strongly negative correla-

---

32. The same problem arises whenever there are profits to which several parties can stake—or create—plausible claims. See, e.g., Hirshleifer & Riley, The Analytics of Uncertainty and Information: An Expository Survey, 17 J.Econ.Lit. 1375, 1389–91 (1979); Posner, The Social Costs of Monopoly and Regulation, 83 J.Pol.Econ. 807 (1975); Spence, Job Market Signalling, 97 Q.J.Econ. 355 (1973). Markets usually devise antidotes for such rent-seeking expenditures. See Barzel, Some Fallacies in the Interpretation of Information Costs, 20 J.Law & Econ. 291 (1977). A rule of corporation law allowing unequal division of gains in control transactions is one such response.

33. There is a burgeoning literature on the theory of portfolio management. For a succinct and lucid description, see Langbein & Posner, supra note 14, at 77–83. More complete discussion of diversification may be found in J. Lorie & M. Hamilton, The Stock Market: Theories and Evidence 171–256 (1973); Langbein & Posner, Market Funds and Trust–Investment Law, 1976 Am.Bar Found.Research J. 1.

tion among the risks. An investor with a reasonably diversified portfolio would be on the winning side of some transactions and the losing side of others. For example, if shareholders of one corporation obtain little of the gain from a given merger, the shareholders of the other corporation obtain more. An investor holding a diversified portfolio with stock in both corporations is concerned with the total gain from the transaction, not with how the gain is allocated. Indeed, the investor with shares of both would see any expense in allocating the gain as pure loss. To the extent an unequal allocation raises the number and amount of gain transactions, therefore, investors with diversified portfolios would prefer to allow the unequal allocation to continue.

* * *

We have shown that the *ex post* inequality under Ventures 2 and 3, like the *ex post* inequality in a lottery, is not "unfair" if, *ex ante,* all investors have an equal chance to win and can eliminate risk through diversification. We now consider a potential objection to this reasoning. One might argue that this *ex ante* equality is absent in corporate control transactions because insiders systematically benefit at the expense of outsiders. Small shareholders, the argument runs, consistently will be frozen out, deprived of control premiums, and otherwise disadvantaged by insiders.

The argument loses its plausibility on close examination. One need not be wealthy to be on the "winning side" of a control transaction, and neither wealth nor status as an insider ensures being a winner. If corporation A purchases from corporation B a control block of shares in corporation C, a small (or outside) shareholder might participate in the gains by holding shares in any of the three firms. Similarly, if corporation D merges with corporation E (its long-held subsidiary) and freezes out the minority shareholders of corporation E, these shareholders may participate in the gains by holding shares of corporation D. Small shareholders also may participate in the gains resulting from tender offers, going private transactions, allocation of a corporate opportunity to a parent rather than a subsidiary, and other types of corporate control transactions, simply by holding shares in the firm that produces the gains. There is no need for the small shareholder to identify these situations in advance. By holding a diversified portfolio containing the securities of many firms, the small shareholder can ensure that he will participate in the gains produced. All shareholders therefore have a chance of receiving the gains produced by corporate control transactions—if not an equal chance, at least enough of a chance to allow diversification of the risk. There remain cases in which it is impossible for an investor to share in gains or diversify away the risk by holding stock in both firms. This would be true, for example, where one of the firms is privately held. The shareholder can minimize this non-diversifiable risk, however, by not investing in firms that are controlled by an individual or a privately-held firm.

D. *Market Value as a Benchmark Under the Fiduciary Principle*

In the circumstances we have discussed, shareholders unanimously prefer legal rules under which the amount of gains is maximized, regardless of how the gains are distributed. The ideal transaction is one like Venture 2 above, in which the gains are unequally distributed but all shareholders are at least as well off as they were before the transaction. Shareholders may also benefit from transactions in which the distribution of gains leaves some shareholders worse off than before the transaction—as in Venture 3—but there are probably few such transactions. We cannot imagine why gains would depend on making some investors worse off, and we have not encountered any example of such a transaction. In a world of costly information, investors will view Venture 2 transactions very differently from Venture 3 transactions, which would raise all-but-insuperable difficulties in determining whether the transaction produced gain. One can imagine instances, of which looting is a good example, in which the person acquiring control pays a premium to some investor(s) in order to obtain control and obliterate the remaining claims, recouping the premium without putting resources to a more productive use. A requirement that all investors receive at least the market value of their positions prior to the transactions would be a useful rule-of-thumb for separating beneficial deals from potentially harmful ones. If every investor receives at least what he had before, and some receive a premium, the transaction *must* produce gains.

The requirement that everyone receive at least the value of his investment under existing conditions serves much the same function as the rule against theft. A thief *might* be able to put stolen resources to a better use than his victim, but if so then he can pay for those resources. Thus, a requirement of payment increases the likelihood that transactions are value-increasing. Moreover, the proscription of theft also reduces the incentive of property owners to take elaborate precautions against theft. For example, investors might resort to costly monitoring devices to reduce the chance of confiscation of their shares. When all transactions are consensual, these precautions become unnecessary. By prohibiting confiscation, therefore, the fiduciary principle reduces wasteful expenditures while simultaneously reducing the number of socially inefficient corporate control transactions.[35]

---

35. A rule against confiscation would be created by contract even if it were not part of existing law. Whoever controlled a corporation would find it advantageous to insert an anti-confiscation provision in the articles of incorporation. If he did not, the firm could not expect to receive much for its shares. New shareholders would fear confiscation and would take (expensive) steps to protect their interest. Because no firm has monopoly power over investment opportunities, the expected costs of these precautions would reduce by an equal amount the price that purchasers would be willing to pay. Thus the sums that the controlling party receives would reflect the costs created by the risk of confiscation. Cf. Grossman & Hart, Disclosure Law and Takeover Bids, 35 J.Fin. 323 (1980) (analyzing consequences and incentive effects of disclosure regulations).

For a different analysis of the import of the notion of equality of treatment see Brudney, Equal Treatment of Shareholders in Corporate Distributions and Reorganizations, 71 Calif.L.Rev. 1072 (1983).

3. FEDERAL DISCLOSURE RULES

Appendix B, Section 2 provides background materials on the federal mandatory disclosure system.

(A) DISCLOSURE OF FACTS IMPLICATING STATE REMEDIES

INTRODUCTORY NOTE

If "fairness" is a criterion for which it is difficult to find substantive content or meaningful applications in local law, can it be invoked any more meaningfully under the federal securities legislation? In particular, do Rules 10b–5 [z] and 14a–9 [a] come to bear so as to regulate

z. Section 10 of the Securities Exchange Act of 1934 provides:

It shall be unlawful for any person, directly or indirectly, by the use of any means or instrumentality of interstate commerce or of the mails, or of any facility of any national securities exchange—

* * *

(b) To use or employ, in connection with the purchase or sale of any security registered on a national securities exchange or any security not so registered, any manipulative or deceptive device or contrivance in contravention of such rules and regulations as the Commission may prescribe as necessary or appropriate in the public interest or for the protection of investors.

Rule 10b–5 provides:

It shall be unlawful for any person, directly or indirectly, by the use of any means or instrumentality of interstate commerce, or of the mails, or of any facility of any national securities exchange,

(1) to employ any device, scheme, or artifice to defraud,

(2) to make any untrue statement of a material fact or to omit to state a material fact necessary in order to make the statements made, in the light of the circumstances under which they were made, not misleading, or

(3) to engage in any act, practice, or course of business which operates or would operate as a fraud or deceit upon any person,

in connection with the purchase or sale of any security.

a. Section 14(a) of the Securities Exchange Act of 1934 provides:

(a) It shall be unlawful for any person, by the use of the mails or by any means or instrumentality of interstate commerce or of any facility of a national securities exchange or otherwise, in contravention of such rules and regulations as the Commission may prescribe as necessary or appropriate in the public interest or for the protection of investors, to solicit or to permit the use of his name to solicit any proxy or consent or authorization in respect of any security (other than an exempted security) registered pursuant to section 78l of this title.

Rule 14a–9 provides:

(a) No solicitation subject to this regulation shall be made by means of any proxy statement, form of proxy, notice of meeting or other communication, written or oral, containing any statement which, at the time and in the light of the circumstances under which it is made, is false or misleading with respect to any material fact, or which omits to state any material fact nec-

the substance of merger transactions? [b]

Sections 10(b) and 14(e) of the Exchange Act, if not the other provisions of Section 10 and Section 14, carry suggestions of being limited to requiring disclosure and to prohibiting only deceptive or manipulative or fraudulent conduct. Do their prohibitions therefore fail to reach behavior which is merely unilaterally overreaching, and apply only to behavior which is in some sense deceptive? Do they reach behavior which denies or coerces investor's choices in mergers? To the former question, the Supreme Court in **Santa Fe Industries, Inc. v. Green,** 430 U.S. 462 (1977) gave an unequivocally affirmative answer with respect to Section 10(b); and to the latter question it gave a somewhat less unequivocal negative answer with respect to Section 14(e) in Schreiber v. Burlington Northern Co., see p. 1015 infra.

The Santa Fe Industries case dealt with a short form Delaware merger under which public stockholders of the subsidiary (Kirby Lumber Corporation) claimed that the long time parent (Santa Fe Industries, Inc.) took too large a share of the subsidiary for itself (or paid the public investors less than the true value of their participation) and that such unilateral overreaching, without deception or manipulation,[c] violated Rule 10b–5 under the Securities Exchange Act. The Supreme Court (White, J.) said:

"The language of § 10(b) gives no indication that Congress meant to prohibit any conduct not involving manipulation or

essary in order to make the statements therein not false or misleading or necessary to correct any statement in any earlier communication with respect to the solicitation of a proxy for the same meeting or subject matter which has become false or misleading.

* * *

b. We will see the SEC's efforts to implement Section 13 of the Exchange Act by prescribing disclosure requirements in connection with issuer tender offers and going private transactions. Discussion of "fairness" is required in the filings under Rule 13e–3.

Merger transactions are likely also to be subject to the requirements of the Securities Act of 1933, (including Section 11 (and 12 and 17(a)), because Rule 145 promulgated by the Commission under that Act interprets mergers to constitute an "offer" or "sale" of, or an "offer to sell" (the securities of the surviving company) within § 2(3) of that Act. While the registration requirements under the '33 Act can be met by the distribution to stockholders of a single document that combines the disclosures required in a prospectus and those required in a proxy statement" the '33 Act may impose obligations under §§ 11 and 12 which demand more diligence in searching for information, lower thresholds of culpa-

bility, and fuller disclosure than are required under Rules 10b–5 and 14a–9.

c. [From the court's opinion] The * * * complaint asserted that, based on the fair market value of Kirby's physical assets as revealed by the appraisal included in the information statement sent to minority shareholders, Kirby's stock was worth at least $772 per share. The complaint alleged further that the merger took place without prior notice to minority stockholders; that the purpose of the merger was to appropriate the difference between the "conceded pro rata of value of the physical assets" and the offer of $150 per share—to "freez[e] out the minority stockholders at a wholly inadequate price,"; and that Santa Fe, knowing the appraised value of the physical assets, obtained a "fraudulent appraisal" of the stock from Morgan Stanley and offered $25 above that appraisal "in order to lull the minority stockholders into erroneously believing that [Santa Fe was] generous." This course of conduct was alleged to be "a violation of Rule 10b–5 because defendants employed a 'device, scheme or artifice to defraud' and engaged in an 'act, practice or course of business which operates or would operate as a fraud or deceit upon any person, in connection with the purchase or sale of any security.'"

deception. * * * Thus the claim of fraud and fiduciary breach in this complaint states a cause of action under any part of Rule 10b–5 only if the conduct alleged can be fairly viewed as 'manipulative or deceptive' within the meaning of the statute.

III

"It is our judgment that the transaction, if carried out as alleged in the complaint, was neither deceptive nor manipulative and therefore did not violate either § 10(b) of the Act or Rule 10b–5.

"As we have indicated, the case comes to us on the premise that the complaint failed to allege a material misrepresentation or material failure to disclose. * * * On the basis of the information provided, minority shareholders could either accept the price offered or reject it and seek an appraisal in the Delaware Court of Chancery. Their choice was fairly presented, and they were furnished with all relevant information on which to base their decision.[14]

"We therefore find inapposite the cases relied upon by respondents and the court below, in which the breaches of fiduciary duty held violative of Rule 10b–5 included some element of deception.

" * * * [T]he cases do not support the proposition, adopted by the Court of Appeals below and urged by respondents here, that a breach of fiduciary duty by majority stockholders, without any deception, misrepresentation, or nondisclosure, violates the statute and the Rule.

"It is also readily apparent that the conduct alleged in the complaint was not 'manipulative' within the meaning of the statute. Manipulation is 'virtually a term of art when used in connection with securities markets.' *Ernst & Ernst*, 425 U.S., at 199. The term refers generally to practices, such as wash sales, matched orders, or rigged prices, that are intended to mislead investors by artificially affecting market activity. * * * No doubt Congress meant to prohibit the full range of ingenious devices that might be used to manipulate securities prices. But we do not think it would have chosen this 'term of art' if it had meant to bring within the scope of § 10(b) instances of corporate mismanagement such as

14. In addition to their principal argument that the complaint alleges a fraud under clauses (a) and (c) of Rule 10b–5, respondents also argue that the complaint alleges nondisclosure and misrepresentation in violation of clause (b) of the Rule. Their major contention in this respect is that the majority stockholder's failure to give the minority advance notice of the merger was a material nondisclosure, even though the Delaware short-form merger statute does not require such notice. Brief for Respondents, at 27. But respondents do not indicate how they might have acted differently had they had prior notice of the merger. Indeed, they accept the conclusion of both courts below that under Delaware law they could not have enjoined the merger because an appraisal proceeding is their sole remedy in the Delaware courts for any alleged unfairness in the terms of the merger. Thus the failure to give advance notice was not a material nondisclosure within the meaning of the statute or the Rule. Cf. TSC Industries, Inc. v. Northway, Inc., 426 U.S. 438 (1976).

this, in which the essence of the complaint is that shareholders were treated unfairly by a fiduciary.

IV

"The language of the statute is, we think, 'sufficiently clear in its context' to be dispositive here, *Ernst & Ernst,* 425 U.S., at 201; but even if it were not, there are additional considerations that weigh heavily against permitting a cause of action under Rule 10b–5 for the breach of corporate fiduciary duty alleged in this complaint. Congress did not expressly provide a private cause of action for violations of § 10(b). Although we have recognized an implied cause of action under that section in some circumstances, Superintendent of Insurance v. Bankers Life & Cas. Co., supra, at 13 n. 9, * * * we are reluctant to recognize a cause of action here to serve what is 'at best a subsidiary purpose' of the federal legislation.

"A second factor in determining whether Congress intended to create a federal cause of action in these circumstances is 'whether "the cause of action [is] one traditionally relegated to state law. * * * " ' Piper v. Chris–Craft Industries, Inc., 45 U.S.L.W., at 4192, quoting Cort v. Ash, 422 U.S., at 78. The Delaware Legislature has supplied minority shareholders with a cause of action in the Delaware Court of Chancery to recover the fair value of shares allegedly undervalued in a short-form merger. See p. 2, supra. Of course, the existence of a particular state law remedy is not dispositive of the question whether Congress meant to provide a similar federal remedy, but as in *Piper* and *Cort,* we conclude that 'it is entirely appropriate in this instance to relegate respondent and others in his situation to whatever remedy is created by state law.' 422 U.S., at 84; 45 U.S.L.W., at 4193.

"The reasoning behind a holding that the complaint in this case alleged fraud under Rule 10b–5 could not be easily contained. It is difficult to imagine how a court could distinguish, for purposes of Rule 10b–5 fraud, between a majority stockholder's use of a short-form merger to eliminate the minority at an unfair price and the use of some other device, such as a long-form merger, tender offer, or liquidation, to achieve the same result; or indeed how a court could distinguish the alleged abuses in these going private transactions from other types of fiduciary self-dealing involving transactions in securities. The result would be to bring within the Rule a wide variety of corporate conduct traditionally left to state regulation. * * * Federal courts applying a 'federal fiduciary principle' under Rule 10b–5 could be expected to depart from state fiduciary standards at least to the extent necessary to ensure uniformity within the federal system. Absent a clear indication of congressional intent, we are reluctant to federalize the substantial portion of the law of corporations that deals with transactions in securities, particularly where established state policies of corporate regulation would be overridden. As the Court stated in Cort v. Ash, supra, 'Corporations are creatures of state law, and investors commit their funds to corporate directors on the understanding that, except where federal law *expressly* requires certain responsibilities of directors with respect to stockholders, state law will govern the internal affairs of the corporation.' 422 U.S., at 84 (emphasis added)."

GOLDBERG v. MERIDOR

United States Court of Appeals, Second Circuit, 1977.
567 F.2d 209.

FRIENDLY, Circuit Judge.

In this derivative action, * * * David Goldberg, a stockholder of Universal Gas & Oil Co., Inc. (UGO) * * * sought to recover damages and to obtain other relief against UGO's controlling parent, Maritimecor, S.A., * * *; Maritimecor's controlling parent, Maritime Fruit Carriers Co. Ltd., * * *; a number of * * * directors of one or more of these companies * * * [and others] with respect to transactions which culminated in an agreement providing for UGO's issuance to Maritimecor of up to 4,200,000 shares of UGO stock and its assumption of all of Maritimecor's liabilities (including a debt of $7,000,000 owed to UGO) in consideration of the transfer of all of Maritimecor's assets (except 2,800,000 UGO shares already held by Maritimecor). It suffices at this point to say that the complaint, filed February 3, 1976, alleged that the contract was grossly unfair to UGO and violated both § 10(b) of the Securities Exchange Act and the SEC's Rule 10b–5 and common law fiduciary duties.

* * *

* * * The amended complaint, * * * [alleged that] the "agreement and transfer was fraudulent and unfair in that the assets of Maritimecor were overpriced and of insufficient value, the liabilities of Maritimecor either exceeded the value of its assets or were so great that the net assets value was insufficient consideration, * * * [and that] the foregoing transactions constituted the employment of a device, scheme or artifice to defraud, the making of untrue statements of material fact and the omission to state material facts necessary in order to make the statements made, in the light of the circumstances under which they were made, not misleading, and the engaging in acts, practices, and courses of conduct which operated as a fraud or deceit upon UGO as the seller of up to 4,200,000 shares of UGO's common stock for Maritimecor's liabilities and assets, and upon UGO's minority stockholders.["]

Defendants filed motions to dismiss the amended complaint for failure to state a claim under § 10(b) of the Securities Exchange Act and Rule 10b–5. In answer to defendants' argument "that deception and non-disclosure is a requirement for a 10b–5 case" which was disputed as a matter of law, plaintiff's counsel submitted an affidavit asserting that "insofar as plaintiff Goldberg, a minority shareholder is concerned, there has been no disclosure to him of the fraudulent nature of the transfer of Maritimecor assets and liabilities for stock of UGO". Counsel annexed two press releases dated August 1 * and December 19, 1975, which described the agreement for and the consummation of the UGO–Maritimecor transaction.   * * * Counsel requested that he be given leave to replead should the court find any defect in the manner of pleading.   * * * [The district court's refusal to permit amendment of the complaint to include reference to the two press releases or otherwise to claim deception was held to be an abuse of discretion, and the Court of Appeals treated the case as if an amendment, at least in the two respects noted, had been allowed. It went on to say that "If the complaint were thus amended, we would deem it clear that, so far as this court's decisions are concerned, the case would be governed by * * * " Schoenbaum v. Firstbrook, 405 F.2d 215 (2d Cir.1968), certiorari denied 395 U.S. 906 (1969) rather than by Popkin v. Bishop, 464 F.2d 714 (2d Cir.1972)].

* * *

III

The ruling that this case is attracted by *Schoenbaum* rather than by *Popkin* by no means ends our inquiry. Rather it brings us to the serious question whether *Schoenbaum* can be here applied consistently with the Supreme Court's decision in Santa Fe Industries, Inc. v. Green * * *. We think it can be and should.

The problem with the application of § 10(b) and Rule 10b–5 to derivative actions has lain in the degree to which the knowledge of officers and directors must be attributed to the corporation, thereby negating the element of deception. Our first important encounter with this problem was in Ruckle v. Roto American Corp., 339 F.2d 24 (2 Cir.1964). We rejected the attribution, saying 339 F.2d at 29:

> We come then to the question whether it is possible within the meaning of Section 10(b) and Rule 10b–5 for a corporation to be defrauded by a majority of its directors. We note at the outset that in other contexts, such as embezzlement and conflict of interest, a majority or even the entire board of directors may be held to have defrauded their corporation. When it is practical as well as just to do so, courts have experienced no difficulty in rejecting such cliches as the directors constitute the corporation and a corporation, like any other person, cannot defraud itself.

---

* [Ed. Note] According to the Court the August 1 press release held out an inviting picture that as a result of the transaction, UGO will replace Maritimecor as the principal operating subsidiary of MFC and, as such, will engage in a diversified line of shipping and shipping related activities including the sale of ships and ship-building contracts, the operation of reefers and tankers, and upon their delivery, product carriers and oil drilling rigs, and underwriting marine insurance, when allegedly the truth was that UGO had entered into a transaction that would ensure its doom.

If, in this case, the board defrauded the corporation into issuing shares either to its members or others, we can think of no reason to say that redress under Rule 10b–5 is precluded, though it would have been available had anyone else committed the fraud. There can be no more effective way to emasculate the policies of the federal securities laws than to deny relief solely because a fraud was committed by a director rather than by an outsider. Denial of relief on this basis would surely undercut the congressional determination to prevent the public distribution of worthless securities.

Although it was there claimed that certain directors withheld information from others, the above quoted passage indicated in dictum that not only the majority but even the entire board, fully informed, could be held to have defrauded the corporation if they all had an interest in a transaction adverse to it. Less than a month later, however, another panel declined to follow the *Ruckle* dictum. O'Neill v. Maytag, 339 F.2d 764, 767 (2 Cir.1964).

The future, both in this circuit and in others, lay with the *Ruckle* dictum rather than with *O'Neill.* * * *

        * * *

Schoenbaum, then, can rest solidly on the now widely recognized ground that there is deception of the corporation (in effect, of its minority shareholders) when the corporation is influenced by its controlling shareholder to engage in a transaction adverse to the corporation's interests (in effect, the minority shareholders' interests) and there is nondisclosure or misleading disclosures as to the material facts of the transaction. * * *

* * * [We] do not read *Green* as ruling that no action lies under Rule 10b–5 when a controlling corporation causes a partly owned subsidiary to sell its securities to the parent in a fraudulent transaction and fails to make a disclosure or, as can be alleged here, makes a misleading disclosure. The Supreme Court noted in *Green* that the court of appeals "did not disturb the District Court's conclusion that the complaint did not allege a material misrepresentation or nondisclosure with respect to the value of the stock" of Kirby; the Court's quarrel was with this court's holding that "neither misrepresentation nor nondisclosure was a necessary element of a Rule 10b–5 action", 430 U.S. at 470, 97 S.Ct. at 1299, and that a breach of fiduciary duty would alone suffice, see fn. 8. It was because "the complaint failed to allege a material misrepresentation or material failure to disclose" that the Court found "inapposite the cases [including *Schoenbaum*] relied upon by respondents and the court below, in which the breaches of fiduciary duty held violative of Rule 10b–5 included some element of deception", 430 U.S. at 475, 97 S.Ct. at 1301, see fn. 15. * * *

Here the complaint alleged "deceit * * * upon UGO's minority shareholders" and, * * * misrepresentation as to the UGO–Maritimecor transaction at least in the sense of failure to state material facts "necessary in order to make the statements made, in the light of the circumstances under which they were made, not misleading," Rule 10b–5(b).[3] The nub of the matter is that the conduct attacked in *Green* did not violate the " 'fundamental purpose' of the Act as implementing a 'philosophy of full disclosure' ", 430 U.S. at 478, 97 S.Ct. at 1303; the conduct here attacked does.

Defendants contend that even if all this is true, the failure to make a public disclosure or even the making of a misleading disclosure would have no effect, since no action by stockholders to approve the UGO–Maritimecor transaction was required. Along the same lines our brother Meskill invoking the opinion in *Green,* 430 U.S. at 474 n. 14, 97 S.Ct. at 1301 n. 14, contends that the defendants' acts were not material since plaintiff has failed adequately to allege what would have been done had he known the truth.

In TSC Industries, Inc. v. Northway, Inc., 426 U.S. 438, 449, 96 S.Ct. 2126, 2133, 48 L.Ed.2d 757 (1976), a case arising under Rule 14a–9, the Court laid down the standard of materiality as "a showing of a substantial likelihood that, under all the circumstances, the omitted fact would have assumed actual significance in the deliberations of the reasonable shareholder" or, putting the matter in another way, "a substantial likelihood that the disclosure of the omitted fact would have been viewed by the reasonable investor as having significantly altered the 'total mix' of information made available." When, as in a derivative action, the deception is alleged to have been practiced on the corporation, even though all the directors were parties to it, the test must be whether the facts that were not disclosed or were misleadingly disclosed to the shareholders "would have assumed actual significance in the deliberations" of reasonable and disinterested directors or created "a substantial likelihood" that such directors would have considered the "total mix" of information available to have been "significantly altered." * * * Here there is surely a significant likelihood that if a reasonable director of UGO had known the facts alleged by plaintiff rather than the barebones of the press releases, he would not have voted for the transaction with Maritimecor.

Beyond this Goldberg and other minority shareholders would not have been without remedy if the alleged facts had been disclosed. * * * Blumenthal v. Roosevelt Hotel, Inc., 202 Misc. 988, 115 N.Y.S.2d 52 (Sup.Ct.N.Y.Co.1952), and Williams v. Bartell, 34 Misc.2d 552, 226 N.Y.S.2d 187 (Sup.Ct.N.Y.Co.), modified, 16 A.D.2d 21, 225 N.Y.S.2d 351 (1st Dept.1962), were suits by stockholders acting in their own behalf to enjoin the sale of all corporate assets or a merger transaction as to which New York afforded dissenters the remedy of an appraisal. While the appraisal remedy was not exclusive, the existence of that remedy was held to require a plaintiff seeking an injunction to demonstrate a

---

3. We do not mean to suggest that § 10(b) or Rule 10b–5 requires insiders to characterize conflict of interest transactions with pejorative nouns or adjectives. However, if Maritimecor was in the par- lous financial condition alleged in the opposing affidavit of plaintiff's counsel, a disclosure of the acquisition of Maritimecor that omitted these *facts* would be seriously misleading.

strong balance of equities in his favor. The UGO–Maritimecor transaction was not of the sort that would afford UGO's stockholders any right of appraisal. Where an appraisal remedy is not available, the courts of New York have displayed no hesitancy in granting injunctive relief, * * *.

The availability of injunctive relief if the defendants had not lulled the minority stockholders of UGO into security by a deceptive disclosure, as they allegedly did, is in sharp contrast to *Green,* where the disclosure following the merger transaction was full and fair, and, as to the pre-merger period, respondents accepted "the conclusion of both courts below that under Delaware law they could not have enjoined the merger because an appraisal proceeding is their sole remedy in the Delaware courts for any alleged unfairness in the terms of the merger," fn. 14. Indeed, we have quite recently recognized that the availability of an injunctive action under New York law constituted a sufficient basis for distinguishing the conclusion in the *Green* footnote with respect to materiality, SEC v. Parklane Hosiery Co., Inc., 558 F.2d 1083, 1088 (2 Cir.1977). * * *

Defendants also rely on statements in Part IV of the *Green* opinion which lend them some support if taken in isolation and out of context. Thus the Court, quoting from Piper v. Chris–Craft Industries, Inc., 430 U.S. 1, 40, 97 S.Ct. 926, 51 L.Ed.2d 124 (1977), said that one factor in determining whether a case was covered by § 10(b) and Rule 10b–5, was "whether 'the cause of action [is] one traditionally relegated to state law * * *.'" But the Court quickly added, after referring to the Delaware appraisal statute, that "Of course, the existence of a particular state law remedy is not dispositive of the question whether Congress meant to provide a similar federal remedy," and it would be hard to think of a cause of action more "traditionally relegated to state law" than the one asserted in the *Superintendent of Insurance* case, which, as has been said, made "just plain stealing" a fraud under Rule 10b–5, on the basis that Begole failed to tell the directors "in advance that he was going to steal", Jennings & Marsh, Securities Regulation 997–98 (1977). Defendants rely also on the Court's fears of the difficulty of future line-drawing among various kinds of breach of fiduciary duty involving securities transactions. But this was said in support of drawing the line so as to require plaintiffs to make claims of nondisclosure or misleading disclosure, not as directing the lower courts to dismiss cases where it was claimed that fiduciaries had failed to disclose their self-dealing or had made a misleading disclosure, even though no disclosure was required by state law. Similarly we fail to see how defendants gain from the Court's quotation of its statement in the *Superintendent of Insurance* case, 404 U.S. at 12, 92 S.Ct. at 169, that "Congress by § 10(b) did not seek to regulate transactions which constitute no more than internal corporate mismanagement"—a statement that originally seemed intended only to remove *negligent* corporate misconduct from the reach of the statute. We readily agree that if all that was here alleged was that UGO had been injured by "internal corporate mismanagement", no federal claim would have been stated.

But a parent's looting of a subsidiary with securities outstanding in the hands of the public in a securities transaction is a different matter; in such cases disclosure or at least the absence of misleading disclosure is required. It would be incongruous if Rule 10b–5 created liability for a casual "tip" in the bar of a country club, as we held in SEC v. Geon Industries, Inc., 531 F.2d 39 (2 Cir.1976), but would not cover a parent's undisclosed or misleadingly disclosed sale of its overvalued assets for stock of a controlled subsidiary with securities in the hands of the public.

The order dismissing the complaint is reversed and the case is remanded to the district court for further proceedings, including amendment of the complaint, consistent with this opinion.

[The opinion of MESKILL, Circuit Judge, concurring in part and dissenting in part, is omitted.]

NOTE: FIELD v. TRUMP

The scope of *Goldberg* was narrowed in **Field v. Trump,** 850 F.2d 938 (2d Cir.1988). That case was an action by public stockholders of Pay'n Save Corporation (Pay'n Save) for damages for violation of the 1934 Act by reason of arrangements among (1) the controlling stockholders of the corporation, (2) a group of dissidents and (3) friendly third party bidders seeking control. The claim rested upon a series of transactions designed to relieve the controlling stockholders and management of the corporation from the disturbing presence of the dissident group that owned approximately 18.4% of the corporation's stock. By agreement with the controlling stockholders, the bidders made a tender offer to buy ⅔ of the target stock for $22.50 per share in cash and to cash out the balance of the shares at the same price by merger. Within four days after making the tender offer the bidders withdrew it, and having negotiated to buy the dissident group's stock for $23.50 per share and pay them an additional $1.50 per share to meet their "fees and expenses" in resisting the contemplated transaction, the bidders made what they called a new tender offer at $23.50 per share to all the public stockholders and the insiders. In addition to the claim that the "new" offer violated § 14(d)(7), the plaintiff public stockholders claimed violations of Rule 10(b)(5) and §§ 14(a) and 14(e) of the 34 Act because of the inadequacy of the disclosures made in various documents related to the tender offer and merger, and in an earlier proxy statement by Pay'n Save. Most of those claimed violations essentially alleged that the target's officers and directors breached their fiduciary duties of loyalty and care under local law and failed to disclose those breaches to the public stockholders. In rejecting those claims, the court (Winter, J.) said that the policy against using Rule 10(b)(5) to federalize state corporation law was equally applicable to §§ 14(a) and 14(e). It went on to say (850 F.2d at 947–949):

"In * * * Data Probe Acquisition Corp. v. Datatab, Inc., 722 F.2d 1 (2d Cir.1983), cert. denied, 465 U.S. 1052, 104 S.Ct. 1326, 79 L.Ed.2d 722

(1984), we refused to 'embark * * * on a course leading to a federal
common law of fiduciary obligations.' Id. at 4; see also Lewis v.
McGraw, 619 F.2d 192, 195 (2d Cir.) (per curiam), cert. denied, 449 U.S.
951, 101 S.Ct. 354, 66 L.Ed.2d 214 (1980). Similarly, we have implicitly
expressed our disapproval of the use of Section 14(a) and Rule 14a–9 'as
an avenue for access to the federal courts in order to redress alleged
mismanagement or breach of fiduciary duty.' Maldonado v. Flynn, 597
F.2d 789, 796 (2d Cir.1979). We noted further in *Maldonado* that

> [e]fforts to dress up [state-law claims] in a § 14(a) suit of clothes
> have consistently been rejected, including allegations of failure to
> disclose a disputed legal theory regarding the legality of transac-
> tions approved by the board, failure to disclose an alleged ulterior
> motive for a fully described corporation action, or failure to disclose
> lack of skill or judgment in approving a transaction intended for
> the corporation's benefit.

Id. (citations omitted). Other courts have taken similar positions with
respect to Section 10(b) and Rule 10b–5.

> * * *

"Language in Judge Friendly's opinion in Goldberg v. Meridor, 567
F.2d 209 (2d Cir.1977), cert. denied, 434 U.S. 1069, 98 S.Ct. 1249, 55
L.Ed.2d 771 (1978), a case not cited by the plaintiff, qualifies the broad
proposition that there is no cause of action under Section 10(b) for nondisclosure of facts material only to support an action for breach of a
fiduciary duty under state law. * * *

> [But Judge Friendly conceded] * * * that if all that was here
> alleged was that UGO had been injured by *'internal corporate
> mismanagement,' no federal claim would have been stated. But a
> parent's looting of a subsidiary with securities outstanding in the
> hands of the public in a securities transaction is a different matter;
> in such cases disclosure or at least the absence of misleading
> disclosure is required.*

Id. at 220–21 (emphasis added).

"We believe the following line to be drawn by our cases. Allegations that a defendant failed to disclose facts material only to support
an action for breach of state-law fiduciary duties ordinarily do not state
a claim under the federal securities laws. Certainly this is true of
allegations of garden-variety mismanagement, such as managers failing
to 'maximiz[e] value for * * * shareholders,' Amended Complaint ¶ 54,
of directors failing 'to adequately inform themselves,' id., or of managers acting in a generally self-entrenching fashion. But where the
remedy of an injunction is needed (and is available under state law) to
prevent irreparable injury to the company from willful misconduct of a

self-serving nature, disclosure of facts necessary to make other statements not misleading is required where the misleading statements will lull shareholders into forgoing the injunctive remedy.

"In *Goldberg,* a parent corporation had transferred its assets and liabilities to a controlled subsidiary with public shareholders in exchange for more stock of the subsidiary. Contemporaneous press releases by the parent painted 'an inviting picture * * * of the transaction,' 567 F.2d at 214. However, the parent's liabilities exceeded the shareholders' net equity by some $10 million, and the transaction transformed the subsidiary from a financially healthy corporation to a firm impaired by a $3.6 million deficit in current liabilities unable to meet its obligations and finding its assets seized by creditors. Id. at 212. Although the parent's control of the subsidiary obviated the legal need for shareholder approval and the disclosure attendant to proxy solicitation, the parent's optimistic press release tended to dispel any suspicion of the transaction. Lack of information about the parent's true financial condition in turn caused the public shareholders of the subsidiary to forgo the opportunity to seek an injunction under state law to prevent irreparable injury to the company.

"*Goldberg* also involved out-and-out 'looting' and 'stealing.' Those facts did not require us to distinguish between conduct that is 'reasonable' and 'unreasonable,' or 'informed' and 'uninformed,' distinctions that are the hallmark of state fiduciary law. Compare *Maldonado,* 597 F.2d at 796 (criticizing use of Section 14(a) to redress mismanagement and breaches of fiduciary duty), with Weisberg v. Coastal States Gas Corp., 609 F.2d 650, 655 (2d Cir.1979) (distinguishing *Maldonado* in light of 'allegations of a cover-up of massive bribes and of kickbacks to directors'), cert. denied, 445 U.S. 951, 100 S.Ct. 1600, 63 L.Ed.2d 786 (1980). There is no allegation in the present case of willful misconduct of a self-serving nature that called for injunctive relief lest Pay'n Save's shareholders be irreparably harmed. At best, plaintiff alleges that the directors failed to maximize the return to shareholders, and thus his claims are not actionable under Sections 10(b), 14(a) or 14(e).

"This conclusion does not dispose completely of the federal claims in Count II, however, because some of the nondisclosure allegations go beyond descriptions of ordinary breaches of fiduciary duties."

The court went on to consider, as presumably sufficient to invoke the Meridor theory, the claimed failure to disclose the possible motives of the dissident group in demanding (and receiving) an amount equal to $25.00 per share, and the social and professional relationships among the officers and directors of Pay'n Save which presumably might have produced their willingness to accept the bidders' offer that gave the dissidents more per share than the other stockholders received. It rejected those claimed violations of the disclosure obligations as being insufficiently material "as a matter of law".

NOTE: THE PROBLEMATIC INTEGRATION OF STATE LAW AND FEDERAL ANTIFRAUD RULES

1. The notion that a sufficient test of the materiality of the information required to be disclosed under the Federal securities laws anti-fraud provisions should be the likelihood that the behavior it discloses would subject its perpetrator to liability under local law (for violation of fiduciary obligations, tort, breach of contract or otherwise) has generated intractable problems for the courts. Plainly, too generous a view of the disclosure obligation will involve the federal courts in decision of ambiguous local law questions as well as in enforcing local law. Too narrow a view will falsify the promise of *Meridor.*

The resulting tensions are reflected in the difficulties, both in theory and in practice, that have attended the judicial effort to draw the line between a non-culpable failure to disclose improper motives or to set out facts which sufficiently readily suggest inferences of self-preferment by controllers and the culpable failure to disclose "material" information about the differential effects of the transactions on controllers and on public investors (e.g., tax benefits, new compensation, sales of stock options). The courts frequently purport to rely on the elusive difference between "motive" or "purpose" and "effect." But their denigratory references to the irrelevance of "impure motive" or "unclean heart" are not accompanied by articulation of criteria to distinguish factual circumstances which will impel a court to treat the claim as one of inadequate disclosure appropriately made under the Federal securities laws from those which will impel it to hold that the claim is one merely for breach of fiduciary duty or other local law misbehavior simply cloaked in the guise of inadequate disclosure.

This problem frequently arises when the complaint is that the controlling insiders' or parents' purpose in engaging in the transaction was to prefer or favor themselves over the public investors, and that they failed to disclose that purpose, e.g., Biesenbach v. Guenther, 588 F.2d 400 (3d Cir.1978); Kademian v. Ladish Co., 792 F.2d 614 (7th Cir.1986); Lewis v. Chrysler Corp., 949 F.2d 644 (3d Cir.1991). If local law makes the purpose relevant to breach of fiduciary duty (as when it is held to be such a breach if the purpose is the "sole" or "a primary" or "a principal" purpose of the alleged misbehavior or self-preference (e.g., Cheff v. Mathes, 41 Del.Ch. 494, 199 A.2d 548 (Del.1964); Panter v. Marshall Field & Co., 646 F.2d 271 (7th Cir.1981), cert. denied, 454 U.S. 1092 (1981); Unocal Corp. v. Mesa Petroleum Co., 493 A.2d 946 (Del.Ct. 1985)) is failure to disclose such a purpose any less material than failure to disclose the time spent and facts examined by the directors in evaluating a merger bid? (See e.g., Smith v. Van Gorkom, infra p.

1131,) or a receipt of kickbacks? See e.g., SEC v. Kalvex Inc., 425 F.Supp. 310, 315 (S.D.N.Y.1975). Virginia Bankshares v. Sandberg, infra p. 847 further complicates this inquiry, as is evident from comparing the opinion in Mendell v. Greenberg, 927 F.2d 667 (2d Cir.1990), with the opinion in the same case after *Virginia Bankshares,* 938 F.2d 1528 (2d Cir.1990). For discussion of the problems encountered in application of the federal disclosure requirements to information bearing on managerial integrity or competence, see Steinberg, Corporate Internal Affairs: A Securities and Corporate Law Perspective (1983), Ch. 2; Longstreth, SEC Disclosure Policies Regarding Management Integrity, 38 Bus.Law. 1413 (1983); Loss, Fundamentals of Securities Regulation 801–809 (1988); Ferrara, Starr and Steinberg, Disclosure of Information Bearing on Management Integrity and Competence, 76 Nw.U.L.Rev. 555 (1981).

In any event, does the explicit requirement under Rules 13e–3 and 13e–4 and perhaps under the proxy rules with respect to mergers and similar transactions and schedule 14D–9 with respect to disclosure of transactions' purposes, alternatives, and reasons shed light on how Rules 10b–5 and 14a–9 should be interpreted in this respect? See Howing v. Nationwide Corp., infra p. 863.

2. The question arises whether the information about the possibility of local law litigation which disclosure should reveal can be said to be "in connection with the purchase or sale of a security" under Rule 10b–5—so that the legal action in response to the information to be taken by the objecting stockholders who lack the votes to block the transaction can be found to be sufficiently "causally" related to the securities transaction. In a jurisdiction or in circumstances which remit merger objectors solely to appraisal so that the corporation's purchase or sale of securities cannot be blocked or undone by a fairness-based injunctive proceeding, can the "materiality" criterion be met? See infra p. 868. Is the materiality requirement under *Meridor* (involving Rule 10b–5) replicated by the causality requirement under *Virginia Bankshares*, infra (involving Rule 14a–9)? Consider the materiality to the sale of a security of the offense of misappropriating the proceeds of the sale, or of deceptively offering unsuitable capital goods to a start-up company that sells its securities on the belief that the capital goods are adequate for its purposes. Compare Superintendent of Insurance v. Bankers Life and Casualty Co., 404 U.S. 6 (1971) with Pross v. Katz, 784 F.2d 455 (2d Cir.1986).

3. Brandeis' notion, said later by Frankfurter to tincture the federal securities legislation, that to require disclosure will inhibit misbehavior by corporate insiders and others, lends considerable support to the theme of Meridor that links the disclosure requirement to behavior which does (or might) constitute violation of local law. Does the concept of "materiality" require disclosure of enough information to cause (1) a plaintiff predictably to prevail in the litigation against alleged misbehavers under local law? (2) A reasonable person reasonably to expect to prevail in the litigation? (3) A reasonable person plausibly, or at least not irresponsibly, to commence the litigation? See Note, 91 Harv.L.Rev. 1874 (1978); Alabama Farm Bureau Mutual

Casualty Co. v. American Fidelity Life Ins. Co., 606 F.2d 602 (5th Cir.1979), reh'g denied, 610 F.2d 818 (5th Cir.1980), cert. denied, 446 U.S. 933 (1980); Healey v. Catalyst Recovery of Pennsylvania Inc., 616 F.2d 641 (3d Cir.1980); Kidwell ex rel. Penfold v. Meikle, 597 F.2d 1273 (9th Cir.1979).

What information should be required to be disclosed about the doctrines (or operation) of local law which might be violated by the behavior involved? Compare e.g., In the Matter of Franchard Corporation, 42 SEC 163 (1964) with Imperial Financial Services, Inc., 42 SEC 717 (1965); see Condec Corp. v. Farley, 573 F.Supp. 1382 (S.D.N.Y.1983) (disclosure in Section 13(d) filing).

Consider the ruling of the court in **Pavlidis v. New England Patriots Football Club, Inc.**, 737 F.2d 1227, 1234–1235 (1st Cir.1984) on a matter on which the Massachusetts courts relied heavily in finding an appraisal value of $80 per share:

"Appellants argue that the proxy statement should have disclosed not only the Patriots' share of the income from the Tampa Bay and Seattle expansion franchises, but also the sale prices of the franchises themselves. They point out that in order to decide whether to vote in favor of the merger or against it, they had to judge whether the offered price of $15.00 per share represented the 'fair value' of their stock. If they judged that the 'fair value' of their stock was considerably higher than $15.00, they would vote against the merger. If a majority of shareholders voted against the merger, New Patriots would be forced to raise its offering price or abandon the merger plans; if those who opposed the merger were in the minority, they could still exercise their statutory appraisal rights in order to obtain a judicial determination of the 'fair value' of their shares. Appellants argue that the value of the NFL expansion franchises was some indication of the value of the Patriots franchise, that the value of the Patriots franchise was a material component of the corporation's 'net asset value', and that the 'net asset value' was a significant part of the 'fair value' of Patriots shares. By this circuitous route appellants arrive at the conclusion that the sale prices of the Tampa Bay and Seattle franchises were material and should have been disclosed to Patriots stockholders.

"The district court did not focus on the relevance of the franchise value in a statutory appraisal proceeding. Instead, it found that franchise value would only be relevant in a liquidation of Patriots' assets, and that this information was 'not material because there was a negligible chance that nonvoting stockholders would participate in a liquidation in the near future'.

"Although it is possible that franchise value *would* be material in the context of an appraisal proceeding, we think it unlikely that § 14(a) requires a corporation to disclose every piece of information that might be relevant in a state appraisal proceeding. In fact, several courts have suggested that for a corporation to include asset appraisals in a proxy statement might constitute a violation of § 14(a) because such appraisals are inherently speculative and may mislead shareholders. See, e.g.,

South Coast Services Corp. v. Santa Ana Valley Irrigation Co., 669 F.2d 1265, 1271 (9th Cir.1982) ('Both the courts and the S.E.C. have consistently discouraged the inclusion of appraised asset valuations in proxy materials'); Gerstle v. Gamble–Skogmo, Inc., 478 F.2d 1281, 1292 (2d Cir.1973) ('[I]t is clear that the policy embodied in the note to Rule 14a–9 [which gives examples of misleading disclosures] has consistently been enforced to bar disclosure of asset appraisals as well as future market values, earnings, or dividends'). Given these cases, we find that Patriots had no duty to appraise its assets and disclose their value, particularly when the relevance of doing so would simply be to help a shareholder decide whether to assert a statutory 'appraisal right'. Nor do we see any duty to disclose the similarly speculative piece of information here at issue, the relevance of which is related only to this asset value.

* * *

"Even if we were to assume that Patriots had a duty to disclose any information that would have been relevant in a Massachusetts appraisal proceeding, it was by no means obvious in 1976, when the proxy statement was drafted, that the value of NFL expansion franchises would play a significant role in such a proceeding. Appellants rely heavily on a case decided several years later, in which a Massachusetts court considered 'net asset value' an important component of the fair value of the stock in a professional hockey team and used the sale price of a new franchise as the starting place for determining the 'asset value' of the established team's franchise. Piemonte v. New Boston Garden Corp., 377 Mass. 719, 387 N.E.2d 1145 (1979). We note, however, that the SEC has not imposed a clairvoyance requirement on the drafters of proxy statements: the drafters are charged with disclosing information that is material 'at the time and in the light of the circumstances' under which the proxy statement is drafted. See Rule 14a–9(a). At the time the Patriots' proxy statement was drafted, the role of new franchise prices in determining the value of an existing franchise was not established, and the significance of 'net asset value' itself varied from one appraisal proceeding to the next. See, e.g., Endicott Johnson Corp. v. Bade, 37 N.Y.2d 585, 587, 376 N.Y.S.2d 103, 106, 338 N.E.2d 614, 616 (1975) ('[T]he weight to be accorded to [net asset value, investment value, and market value] varies with the facts and circumstances in a particular case'). At the time the Patriots' proxy statement was written, the sales prices of expansion franchises were not material to the shareholders' decision whether or not to vote in favor of the merger."

VIRGINIA BANKSHARES, INC. v. SANDBERG
Supreme Court of the United States, 1991.
___ U.S. ___, 111 S.Ct. 2749, 115 L.Ed.2d 929.

Justice SOUTER delivered the opinion of the Court.

* * *

I

In December 1986, First American Bankshares, Inc., (FABI), a bank holding company, began a "freeze-out" merger, in which the First American Bank of Virginia (Bank) eventually merged into Virginia Bankshares, Inc., (VBI), a wholly owned subsidiary of FABI. VBI owned 85% of the Bank's shares, the remaining 15% being in the hands of some 2,000 minority shareholders. FABI hired the investment banking firm of Keefe, Bruyette & Woods (KBW) to give an opinion on the appropriate price for shares of the minority holders, who would lose their interests in the Bank as a result of the merger. Based on market quotations and unverified information from FABI, KBW gave the Bank's executive committee an opinion that $42 a share would be a fair price for the minority stock. The executive committee approved the merger proposal at that price, and the full board followed suit.

Although Virginia law required only that such a merger proposal be submitted to a vote at a shareholders' meeting, and that the meeting be preceded by circulation of a statement of information to the shareholders, the directors nevertheless solicited proxies for voting on the proposal at the annual meeting set for April 21, 1987. In their solicitation, the directors urged the proposal's adoption and stated they had approved the plan because of its opportunity for the minority shareholders to achieve a "high" value, which they elsewhere described as a "fair" price, for their stock.

Although most minority shareholders gave the proxies requested, respondent Sandberg did not, and after approval of the merger she sought damages in the United States District Court for the Eastern District of Virginia from VBI, FABI, and the directors of the Bank. She pleaded two counts, one for soliciting proxies in violation of § 14(a) and Rule 14a–9, and the other for breaching fiduciary duties owed to the minority shareholders under state law. Under the first count, Sandberg alleged, among other things, that the directors had not believed that the price offered was high or that the terms of the merger were fair, but had recommended the merger only because they believed they had no alternative if they wished to remain on the board. At trial, Sandberg invoked language from this Court's opinion in Mills v. Electric Auto–Lite Co., 396 U.S. 375, 385 (1970), to obtain an instruction that the jury could find for her without a showing of her own reliance on the alleged misstatements, so long as they were material and the proxy solicitation was an "essential link" in the merger process.

The jury's verdicts were for Sandberg on both counts, after finding violations of Rule 14a–9 by all defendants and a breach of fiduciary duties by the Bank's directors. The jury awarded Sandberg $18 a share, having found that she would have received $60 if her stock had been valued adequately.

* * *

On appeal, the United States Court of Appeals for the Fourth Circuit affirmed the judgments, holding that certain statements in the proxy solicitation were materially misleading for purposes of the Rule, and that respondents could maintain their action even though their votes had not been needed to effectuate the merger. 891 F.2d 1112 (1989). * * *

II

[The Court ruled that the Board's statement that it approved the merger to provide the public shareholders an opportunity to "achieve a high value" for their shares was material within the rule of TSC Industries, Inc. v. Northway, Inc., 426 U.S. 438 (1976), even though it amounted to a statement of opinion. Said the court, the shareholders would consider knowledge of the directors' beliefs "important to know." The court next considered the petitioner's contention that a statement of opinion was not a statement "with respect to * * * material fact[s]" within the meaning of Rule 14a–9. The court, contrary to standard common law fraud doctrine, ruled that a misstatement of the speaker's belief would not be actionable if the misstatement was only with respect to "the psychological fact of the speaker's belief." But a misstatement such as the one at issue in the case, which misstated the speaker's reasons "and also mislead about the stated subject matter," was actionable.]

III

The second issue before us, left open in Mills v. Electric Auto–Lite Co., 396 U.S., at 385, n. 7, is whether causation of damages compensable through the implied private right of action under § 14(a) can be demonstrated by a member of a class of minority shareholders whose votes are not required by law or corporate bylaw to authorize the transaction giving rise to the claim. * * *

Although a majority stockholder in *Mills* controlled just over half the corporation's shares, a two-thirds vote was needed to approve the merger proposal. After proxies had been obtained, and the merger had carried, minority shareholders brought a *Borak* action. 396 U.S., at 379. The question arose whether the plaintiffs' burden to demonstrate causation of their damages traceable to the § 14(a) violation required proof that the defect in the proxy solicitation had had "a decisive effect on the voting." Id., at 385. The *Mills* Court avoided the evidentiary morass that would have followed from requiring individualized proof that enough minority shareholders had relied upon the misstatements to swing the vote. Instead, it held that causation of damages by a material proxy misstatement could be established by showing that minority proxies necessary and sufficient to authorize the corporate acts had been given in accordance with the tenor of the solicitation, and the Court described such a causal relationship by calling the proxy solicitation an "essential link in the accomplishment of the transaction." Ibid. In the case before it, the Court found the solicitation essential, as contrasted with one addressed to a class of minority shareholders without votes required by law or by-law to authorize the action proposed, and left it for another day to decide whether such a minority shareholder could demonstrate causation. Id., 396 U.S., at 385, n. 7.

In this case, respondents address *Mills'* open question by proffering two theories that the proxy solicitation addressed to them was an "essential link" under the *Mills* causation test. They argue, first, that a link existed and was essential simply because VBI and FABI would have been unwilling to proceed with the merger without the approval manifested by the minority shareholders' proxies, which would not have been obtained without the solicitation's express misstatements and misleading omissions. On this reasoning, the causal connection would depend on a desire to avoid bad shareholder or public relations, and the essential character of the causal link would stem not from the enforceable terms of the parties' corporate relationship, but from one party's apprehension of the ill will of the other.

In the alternative, respondents argue that the proxy statement was an essential link between the directors' proposal and the merger because it was the means to satisfy a state statutory requirement of minority shareholder approval, as a condition for saving the merger from voidability resulting from a conflict of interest on the part of one of the Bank's directors, Jack Beddow, who voted in favor of the merger while also serving as a director of FABI. * * * Under the terms of Va.Code § 13.1–691(A) (1989), minority approval after disclosure of the material facts about the transaction and the director's interest was one of three avenues to insulate the merger from later attack for conflict, the two others being ratification by the Bank's directors after like disclosure, and proof that the merger was fair to the corporation. On this theory, causation would depend on the use of the proxy statement for the purpose of obtaining votes sufficient to bar a minority shareholder from commencing proceedings to declare the merger void.

* * * [N]either theory presents the proxy solicitation as essential in the sense of *Mills'* causal sequence, in which the solicitation links a directors' proposal with the votes legally required to authorize the action proposed. As a consequence, each theory would, if adopted, extend the scope of *Borak* actions beyond the ambit of *Mills,* and expand the class of plaintiffs entitled to bring *Borak* actions to include shareholders whose initial authorization of the transaction prompting the proxy solicitation is unnecessary.

Assessing the legitimacy of any such extension or expansion calls for the application of some fundamental principles governing recognition of a right of action implied by a federal statute * * *.

* * *

* * * This is not the first effort in recent years to expand the scope of an action originally inferred from the Act without "conclusive guidance" from Congress, see Blue Chip Stamps v. Manor Drug Stores, 421 U.S., at 737, and we may look to that earlier case for the proper response to such a plea for expansion. There, we accepted the proposition that where a legal structure of private statutory rights has devel-

oped without clear indications of congressional intent, the contours of that structure need not be frozen absolutely when the result would be demonstrably inequitable to a class of would-be plaintiffs with claims comparable to those previously recognized. Faced in that case with such a claim for equality in rounding out the scope of an implied private statutory right of action, we looked to policy reasons for deciding where the outer limits of the right should lie. We may do no less here, in the face of respondents' pleas for a private remedy to place them on the same footing as shareholders with votes necessary for initial corporate action.

* * *

* * * It will be recalled that in *Blue Chip Stamps* we raised concerns about the practical consequences of allowing recovery, under § 10(b) of the Act and Rule 10b–5, on evidence of what a merely hypothetical buyer or seller might have done on a set of facts that never occurred, and foresaw that any such expanded liability would turn on "hazy" issues inviting self-serving testimony, strike suits, and protracted discovery, with little chance of reasonable resolution by pretrial process. Id., at 742–743. These were good reasons to deny recognition to such claims in the absence of any apparent contrary congressional intent.

The same threats of speculative claims and procedural intractability are inherent in respondents' theory of causation linked through the directors' desire for a cosmetic vote. Causation would turn on inferences about what the corporate directors would have thought and done without the minority shareholder approval unneeded to authorize action. * * * The issues would be hazy, their litigation protracted, and their resolution unreliable. Given a choice, we would reject any theory of causation that raised such prospects, and we reject this one.[12]

* * *

The theory of causal necessity derived from the requirements of Virginia law dealing with postmerger ratification seeks to identify the essential character of the proxy solicitation from its function in obtaining the minority approval that would preclude a minority suit attacking the merger. Since the link is said to be a step in the process of barring a class of shareholders from resort to a state remedy otherwise available, this theory of causation rests upon the proposition of policy

---

12. In parting company from us on this point, Justice KENNEDY emphasizes that respondents in this particular case substantiated a plausible claim that petitioners would not have proceeded without minority approval. FABI's attempted freeze-out merger of a Maryland subsidiary had failed a year before the events in question when the subsidiary's directors rejected the proposal because of inadequate share price, and there was evidence of FABI's desire to avoid any renewal of adverse comment. The issue before us, however, is whether to recognize a theory of causation generally, and our decision against doing so rests on our apprehension that the ensuing litigation would be exemplified by cases far less tractable than this. Respondents' burden to justify recognition of causation beyond the scope of *Mills* must be addressed not by emphasizing the instant case but by confronting the risk inherent in the cases that could be expected to be characteristic if the causal theory were adopted.

that § 14(a) should provide a federal remedy whenever a false or misleading proxy statement results in the loss under state law of a shareholder plaintiff's state remedy for the enforcement of a state right. Respondents agree with the suggestions of counsel for the SEC and FDIC that causation be recognized, for example, when a minority shareholder has been induced by a misleading proxy statement to forfeit a state-law right to an appraisal remedy by voting to approve a transaction, cf. Swanson v. American Consumers Industries, Inc., 475 F.2d 516, 520–521 (CA7 1973), or when such a shareholder has been deterred from obtaining an order enjoining a damaging transaction by a proxy solicitation that misrepresents the facts on which an injunction could properly have been issued. Cf. Healey v. Catalyst Recovery of Pennsylvania, Inc., 616 F.2d 641, 647–648 (CA3 1980); Alabama Farm Bureau Mutual Casualty Co. v. American Fidelity Life Ins. Co., 606 F.2d 602, 614 (CA5 1979), cert. denied, 449 U.S. 820 (1980). Respondents claim that in this case a predicate for recognizing just such a causal link exists in Va.Code § 13.1–691(A)(2) (1989), which sets the conditions under which the merger may be insulated from suit by a minority shareholder seeking to void it on account of Beddow's conflict.

This case does not, however, require us to decide whether § 14(a) provides a cause of action for lost state remedies, since there is no indication in the law or facts before us that the proxy solicitation resulted in any such loss. The contrary appears to be the case. Assuming the soundness of respondents' characterization of the proxy statement as materially misleading, the very terms of the Virginia statute indicate that a favorable minority vote induced by the solicitation would not suffice to render the merger invulnerable to later attack on the ground of the conflict. The statute bars a shareholder from seeking to avoid a transaction tainted by a director's conflict if, *inter alia*, the minority shareholders ratified the transaction following disclosure of the material facts of the transaction and the conflict. Va.Code § 13.1–691(A)(2) (1989). Assuming that the material facts about the merger and Beddow's interests were not accurately disclosed, the minority votes were inadequate to ratify the merger under state law, and there was no loss of state remedy to connect the proxy solicitation with harm to minority shareholders irredressable under state law.[13] Nor is there a claim here that the statement misled respondents into entertaining a false belief that they had no chance to upset the merger, until the time for bringing suit had run out.[14]

13. In his opinion dissenting on this point, Justice KENNEDY suggests that materiality under Virginia law might be defined differently from the materiality standard of our own cases, resulting in a denial of state remedy even when a solicitation was materially misleading under federal law. Respondents, however, present nothing to suggest that this might be so.

14. Respondents do not claim that any other application of a theory of lost state remedies would avail them here. It is clear, for example, that no state appraisal remedy was lost through a § 14(a) violation in this case. Respondent Weinstein and others did seek appraisal under Virginia law in the Virginia courts; their claims were rejected on the explicit grounds that although "[s]tatutory appraisal is now considered the exclusive remedy for stockholders opposing a merger," App. to Pet. for Cert. 32a; see Adams v. United States Distributing Corp., 184 Va. 134, 34

* * *

The judgment of the Court of Appeals is reversed.

It is so ordered.

[Opinion of Scalia, J. concurring in part and in the judgment omitted.]

Justice STEVENS, with whom Justice MARSHALL joins, concurring in part and dissenting in part.

While I agree in substance with Parts I and II of the Court's opinion, I do not agree with the reasoning in Part III.

In Mills v. Electric Auto–Lite Co., 396 U.S. 375 (1970), the Court held that a finding that the terms of a merger were fair could not constitute a defense by the corporation to a shareholder action alleging that the merger had been accomplished by using a misleading proxy statement. The fairness of the transaction was, according to *Mills*, a matter to be considered at the remedy stage of the litigation.

* * *

The case before us today involves a merger that has been found by a jury to be unfair, not fair. The interest in providing a remedy to the injured minority shareholders therefore is stronger, not weaker, than in *Mills*. The interest in avoiding speculative controversy about the actual importance of the proxy solicitation is the same as in *Mills*. Moreover, as in *Mills*, these matters can be taken into account at the remedy stage in appropriate cases. Accordingly, I do not believe that it constitutes an unwarranted extension of the rationale of *Mills* to conclude that because management found it necessary—whether for "legal or practical reasons"—to solicit proxies from minority shareholders to obtain their approval of the merger, that solicitation "was an essential link in the accomplishment of the transaction." *Id.*, at 385, and n. 7. In my opinion, shareholders may bring an action for damages under § 14(a) of the Securities Exchange Act of 1934, 48 Stat. 895, 15 U.S.C. § 78n(a), whenever materially false or misleading statements are made in proxy statements. That the solicitation of proxies is not required by law or by the bylaws of a corporation does not authorize corporate officers, once they have decided for whatever reason to solicit proxies, to avoid the constraints of the statute. I would therefore affirm the judgment of the Court of Appeals.

Justice KENNEDY, with whom Justice MARSHALL, Justice BLACKMUN, and Justice STEVENS join, concurring in part and dissenting in part.

* * * With respect, I dissent from Part III of the Court's opinion.

S.E.2d 244 (1945), cert. denied, 327 U.S. 788, 66 S.Ct. 807, 90 L.Ed. 1014 (1946), "dissenting stockholders in bank mergers do not even have this solitary remedy available to them," because "Va.Code § 6.1–43 specifically excludes bank mergers from application of § 13.1–730 [the Vir-ginia appraisal statute]." App. to Pet. for Cert. 31a, 32a. Weinstein does not claim that the Virginia court was wrong and does not rely on this claim in any way. Thus, the § 14(a) violation could have had no effect on the availability of an appraisal remedy, for there never was one.

* * *

The Court seems to assume, based upon the footnote in *Mills* reserving the question, that Sandberg bears a special burden to demonstrate causation because the public shareholders held only 15 percent of the Bank's stock. Justice STEVENS is right to reject this theory. Here, First American Bankshares, Inc. (FABI) and Virginia Bankshares, Inc. (VBI) retained the option to back out of the transaction if dissatisfied with the reaction of the minority shareholders, or if concerned that the merger would result in liability for violation of duties to the minority shareholders. The merger agreement was conditioned upon approval by two-thirds of the shareholders, App. 463, and VBI could have voted its shares against the merger if it so decided. To this extent, the Court's distinction between cases where the "minority" shareholders could have voted down the transaction and those where causation must be proved by nonvoting theories is suspect. Minority shareholders are identified only by a *post hoc* inquiry. The real question ought to be whether an injury was shown by the effect the nondisclosure had on the entire merger process, including the period before votes are cast.

The Court's distinction presumes that a majority shareholder will vote in favor of management's proposal even if proxy disclosure suggests that the transaction is unfair to minority shareholders or that the board of directors or majority shareholder are in breach of fiduciary duties to the minority. If the majority shareholder votes against the transaction in order to comply with its state law duties, or out of fear of liability, or upon concluding that the transaction will injure the reputation of the business, this ought not to be characterized as nonvoting causation. Of course, when the majority shareholder dominates the voting process, as was the case here, it may prefer to avoid the embarrassment of voting against its own proposal and so may cancel the meeting of shareholders at which the vote was to have been taken. For practical purposes, the result is the same: because of full disclosure the transaction does not go forward and the resulting injury to minority shareholders is avoided. The Court's distinction between voting and nonvoting causation does not create clear legal categories.

There is no authority whatsoever for limiting § 14(a) to protecting those minority shareholders whose numerical strength could permit them to vote down a proposal. One of Section 14(a)'s "chief purposes is 'the protection of investors.' " J.I. Case Co. v. Borak, 377 U.S., at 432. Those who lack the strength to vote down a proposal have all the more need of disclosure. The voting process involves not only casting ballots but also the formulation and withdrawal of proposals, the minority's right to block a vote through court action or the threat of adverse consequences, or the negotiation of an increase in price. The proxy rules support this deliberative process. These practicalities can result in causation sufficient to support recovery.

The facts in the case before us prove this point. Sandberg argues that had all the material facts been disclosed, FABI or the Bank likely would have withdrawn or revised the merger proposal. The evidence in the record, and more that might be available upon remand, see infra, at 2758–2759, meets any reasonable requirement of specific and nonspeculative proof.

FABI wanted a "friendly transaction" with a price viewed as "so high that any reasonable shareholder will accept it." App. 99. Management expressed concern that the transaction result in "no loss of support for the bank out in the community, which was important." Id., at 109. Although FABI had the votes to push through any proposal, it wanted a favorable response from the minority shareholders. Id., at 192. Because of the "human element involved in a transaction of this nature," FABI attempted to "show those minority shareholders that [it was] being fair." Id., at 347.

The theory that FABI would not have pursued the transaction if full disclosure had been provided and the shareholders had realized the inadequacy of the price is supported not only by the trial testimony but also by notes of the meeting of the Bank's board which approved the merger. The inquiry into causation can proceed not by "opposing claims of hypothetical diffidence and hypothetical boldness," ante, at 2765, but through an examination of evidence of the same type the Court finds acceptable in its determination that directors' statements of reasons can lead to liability. Discussion at the board meeting focused upon matters such as "how to keep PR afloat" and "how to prevent adverse reac[tion]/perception," App. 454, demonstrating the directors' concern that an unpopular merger proposal could injure the Bank.

* * *

Though I would not require a shareholder to present such evidence of causation, this case itself demonstrates that nonvoting causation theories are quite plausible where the misstatement or omission is material and the damage sustained by minority shareholders is serious.
* * *

I conclude that causation is more than plausible; it is likely, even where the public shareholders cannot vote down management's proposal. Causation is established where the proxy statement is an essential link in completing the transaction, even if the minority lacks sufficient votes to defeat a proposal of management.

* * *

The majority avoids the question whether a plaintiff may prove causation by demonstrating that the misrepresentation or omission deprived her of a state law remedy. I do not think the question difficult, as the whole point of federal proxy rules is to support state law principles of corporate governance. Nor do I think that the Court can avoid this issue if it orders judgment for petitioners. The majority asserts that respondents show no loss of a state law remedy, because if "the material facts of the transaction and Beddow's interest were not accurately disclosed, then the minority votes were inadequate to ratify the merger under Virginia law." Ante, at 2766. This theory requires us to conclude that the Virginia statute governing director conflicts of interest, Va.Code § 13.1–691(A)(2) (1989), incorporates the same definition of materiality as the federal proxy rules. I find no support for that proposition. If the definitions are not the same, then Sandberg may have lost her state law remedy. For all we know, disclosure to the minority shareholders that the price is $42 per share may satisfy Virginia's requirement. If that is the case, then approval by the minority without full disclosure may have deprived Sandberg of the ability to void the merger.

In all events, the theory that the merger would have been voidable absent minority shareholder approval is far more speculative than the theory that FABI and the Bank would have called off the transaction. Even so, this possibility would support a remand, as the lower courts have yet to consider the question. We are not well positioned as an institution to provide a definitive resolution to state law questions of this kind. Here again, the difficulty of knowing what would have happened in the hypothetical universe of full disclosure suggests that we should "resolv[e] doubts in favor of those the statute is designed to protect" in order to "effectuate the congressional policy of ensuring that the shareholders are able to make an informed choice when they are consulted on corporate transactions." *Mills,* 396 U.S., at 385.

I would affirm the judgment of the Court of Appeals.

NOTE

Would the 14a–9 action have survived in *Sandberg* if the merger had occurred under *Delaware* law? The facts would have been different in two respects. First, appraisal rights would have been available to minority shareholders of the transferor corporation, and second, a well-worn, if not well-defined path to an injunction against the consummation of the merger due to material misstatements would have been available under *Weinberger v. UOP.* Presumably, the plaintiff would argue, by reference to *Goldberg v. Meridor* and its progeny, that the failure to make full disclosure of material facts caused it either (1) to forego perfecting appraisal rights, or (2) to forego seeking an injunction against consummation of the merger in the Delaware courts. The second possibility arguably affords transaction and damage causation, and the first possibility affords damage causation. The opinion of the court in *Sandberg* refers to this state remedies argument without passing on its validity, and the opinion of Justice Kennedy refers to it with approval.

Does *Sandberg* give rise to a negative inference respecting *Goldberg,* despite the court's reservation of the state remedies question? *Sandberg* appears to be motivated by two principles: first, the scope of federal intervention in corporate transactions governed by state law should be kept to the minimum necessary to effectuate the purposes of the securities laws; second, those purposes should, in turn, be read narrowly. Do these principles require the avoidance of federal regulation of internal corporate affairs as an indirect consequence of enforcement of a federal disclosure requirement? Or, is there still a point at which the federal purpose to require disclosure of material information in connection with a corporate transaction dominates over the competing aversion to interfere in internal affairs? Cases in the lower federal courts since *Sandberg* reconfirm the possibility of liability on a *Goldberg* theory. Howing Co. v. Nationwide Corp., 972 F.2d 700 (6th Cir.1992) (13e–3 case), noted infra p. 868; Urbach v. Sayles, CCH Fed.Sec.L.Rep. ¶ 96,247 (D.N.J.1991) (10b–5 case); Wilson v. Great American Industries, Inc., 770 F.Supp. 85 (N.D.N.Y.1991), aff'd, 979 F.2d 924 (2d Cir.1992) (14a–9 case). See also Scattergood v. Perelman, 945 F.2d 618 (3d Cir.1991) (recognizing the possibility that a foregone state injunction proceeding might secure the basis for a 14a–9 proceeding, even as it extends the *Sandberg* voting causation analysis to a 10b–5 action). But cf. Roosevelt v. E.I. Du Pont de Nemours & Co., 958 F.2d 416 (D.C.Cir.1992) (broader reading of *Sandberg*). Is the materiality requirement met by the possibility that disclosure of the information would enable the objecting stockholder to obtain relief from the SEC? See, e.g., United States v. Margala, 662 F.2d 622 (9th Cir.1981); Madison Consultants v. FDIC, 710 F.2d 57 (2d Cir.1983); Susman v. Lincoln American Corp., 517 F.Supp. 931 (N.D.Ill.1981), on remand, 550 F.Supp. 442 (N.D.Ill.1982).

(B) FEDERAL DISCLOSURE REQUIREMENTS IN CONNECTION WITH FREEZE–OUTS

SECURITIES EXCHANGE ACT RELEASE No. 16,075

Securities and Exchange Commission.
August 2, 1979.

Going Private Transactions by Public Companies or Their Affiliates

* * *

(a) Overview of Application of Rule 13e–3

Rule 13e–3 and Schedule 13E–3 operate in essentially the manner proposed. Thus, the application of the rule will depend on three factors: (1) whether the transaction involved is a Rule 13e–3 transaction; (2) if so, whether an exception from the application of Rule 13e–3 is available; and (3) if no exception is available, whether the equity securities which are the subject of the Rule 13e–3 transaction are of a class which is registered pursuant to Section 12 of the Exchange Act or of a class of an issuer which is required to file periodic reports pursuant to Section 15(d) of the Exchange Act.

A Rule 13e–3 transaction is defined to mean any transaction or series of transactions involving one or more of the *transactions specified in paragraph* (a)(4)(i) [e.g., purchase by issuer or affiliate of, or tender offer by either for, issuer's securities; solicitation by either for consent to merger, recapitalization or sale of assets by issuer] which has either a reasonable likelihood or purpose of producing, directly or indirectly, any of the effects specified in paragraph (a)(4)(ii).

* * *

Rule 13e–3 is triggered by a specified transaction which has either the reasonable likelihood or purpose of causing either (i) the termination of reporting obligations under the Exchange Act, by virtue of the class of securities being held of record by less than 300 persons, or (ii) the securities to be neither listed on any exchange nor authorized to be quoted on an inter-dealer quotation system of any registered national securities association. Accordingly, in the above illustration, delisting of a class of equity securities from an exchange would not trigger the application of Rule 13e–3 if the securities were nevertheless authorized to be quoted on an inter-dealer quotation system of a registered national securities association * * *. In order to be effective, the disclosure required by Rule 13e–3 must be received by security holders before consummation of the transaction or the earliest transaction in a series of transactions having a specified effect. These tests ensure that this objective will be accomplished.

* * *

Questions have been raised as to whether multi-step sale of assets transactions * * * fall within the definition of a Rule 13e–3 transaction. Typically, transactions of this type involve a cash sale of substantially all of the assets of a public company ("seller") to another company ("purchaser"), often a private company not otherwise engaged in a trade or business, with the management of the business continuing to be conducted by the managers of the seller. In some cases, the sale of assets, if approved, may be followed closely by a tender offer by the seller to repurchase its shares for cash out of the proceeds received from the sale. Another variation of such transaction involves a second sale of the seller's assets (which, after the sale, consists solely of cash) to a tax exempt bond fund. The seller is then dissolved and its shareholders receive shares of the tax exempt fund.

A multi-step sale of asset transactions of the type described above which involves an issuer tender offer or purchases by the issuer would normally constitute a Rule 13e–3 transaction.

* * *

If the requirements of a Rule 13e–3 transaction are present, the application of the rule would be triggered unless an exception is available. Accordingly, the second factor to be considered is the availability of the exceptions set forth in paragraph (g). The exceptions * * * [include 2 significant provisions].

First, Rule 13e–3(g)(1) excepts second-step, clean-up transactions which occur within one year of a tender offer by or on behalf of a bidder who, as a result of such tender offer, became an affiliate, provided that the equal consideration, disclosure and other requirements of the rule are met. The Commission believes that if a transaction is structured to meet the conditions of that rule it may safely be viewed as a unitary transaction which is not within the purview of the purposes of Rule 13e–3.

Second, Rule 13e–3(g)(2) provides an exception for transactions, including recapitalizations, in which, *inter alia,* security holders are offered only an equity security which is either common stock or has essentially the same attributes as the equity security which is the subject of the Rule 13e–3 transaction. The Commission believes that such transactions are also outside the purpose of Rule 13e–3 since all holders of that class of security are on an equal footing and are permitted to maintain an equivalent or enhanced equity interest.

The third factor to be considered in the application of Rule 13e–3 is the status under the Exchange Act of the issuer or the class of equity securities of the issuer. If the class of equity securities, which is subject to the Rule 13e–3 transaction, is registered pursuant to Section 12 of the Exchange Act (a "Section 12 issuer"), Rule 13e–3(b) [17 CFR 240.13e–3(b)] would apply. * * *

Since the provisions of Rule 13e–3 are not exclusive, the transaction would also be subject to other applicable provisions of the Federal securities laws.

* * *

(c) Disclosure Requirements

Rule 13e–3(e) establishes the information required to be included in the disclosure document furnished to holders of the class of equity securities which is the subject of the transaction. This disclosure provision consists of two elements: (1) the information required by items 1 through 6 and 10 through 16 of Schedule 13E–3 [17 CFR 240.13e–100], or a fair and adequate summary thereof, and items 7, 8 and 9 of the Schedule and (2) any other information required to be disclosed pursuant to any other applicable rule or regulation under the Federal securities laws.

* * *

(e) Schedule 13E–3

Schedule 13E–3 establishes specific disclosure requirements for Rule 13e–3 transactions. As noted in General Instruction E to the Schedule, these requirements are in addition to those of other applicable provisions of the Federal securities laws and supersede such requirements where there is a conflict. The Commission believes that the Schedule will provide more meaningful disclosures to investors in the context of a Rule 13e–3 transaction.

* * *

Item 8 requires the issuer or affiliate to state whether it reasonably believes the Rule 13e–3 transaction is fair or unfair to unaffiliated security holders. The issuer or affiliate is also required to provide a detailed discussion of the material factors upon which that belief is based. This discussion is required to address the extent to which the following factors were taken into account: (1) whether the transaction is structured so that approval of at least a majority of unaffiliated security holders is required; (2) whether the consideration offered to unaffiliated security holders constitutes fair value; (3) whether the majority of non-employee directors has retained an unaffiliated representative to act solely on behalf of unaffiliated security holders for the purposes of negotiating the terms of the transaction and/or preparing a report concerning the fairness of the transaction; (4) whether the Rule 13e–3 transaction was approved by a majority of the directors of the issuer who are not employees of the issuer; and (5) whether a report, opinion or appraisal of the type described in item 9 of the Schedule was obtained. In order to minimize meaningless, boilerplate responses an instruction specifies that conclusory statements are not considered sufficient disclosure in responding to this requirement.*

* * *

* * * [T]he Commission believes that increased discussion of factors bearing upon fairness to unaffiliated security holders is necessary in view of the potential for abuse which exists in a Rule 13e–3 transaction. The absence of arms-length negotiations which is characteristic of going private transactions requires that unaffiliated security holders be furnished with detailed information so that they can determine whether their rights have been adequately protected.[11]

* * *

———

Securities Exchange Act Release No. 34–16,076 which bears the same date (August 2, 1979) as the release adopting Rule 13e–3 states "Rule 13e–3 and Schedule 13E–3 presently require disclosure of projections where it is necessary to make the required statements, in the light of the circumstances under which they are made, not materially misleading. Voluntary disclosure of projections is also encouraged by the Commission if made in accordance with Guides 62 and 5." The Commission proposed, in Release No. 34–16,076, that Rule 13e–3 be amended to require projections. It proposed that Item 10 be added to Schedule 13E–3 to require the filing person to "State whether or not the issuer or affiliate has furnished, directly or indirectly, a projection

---

* [Ed. Note] Item 7 requires a statement of purposes and reasons for the transaction, alternatives considered and reasons for rejecting them, and effects of the transaction on the issuer, its affiliates and non-affiliated security holders.

Item 9 requires a statement of reports, opinions or appraisals received from an outside party which are material to the transaction, a summary of the reports, opinions or appraisals and an offer to make them available for inspection and copying.

11. The materiality of information which would be useful to security holders in challenging the transaction under state law is well established. See e.g., Wright v. Heizer Corp., 560 F.2d 236, 250 (7th Cir. 1977), cert. denied, 434 U.S. 1066 (1978) and SEC v. Parklane Hosiery Co., 558 F.2d 1083, 1088–9 (2d Cir.1977).

of revenues, income (loss), or earnings (loss) per share prepared by or on behalf of the issuer during the preceding eighteen months to a person who has made a loan * * * [to the issuer] or a person who has furnished a report, opinion, or appraisal described in Item 9 of this schedule"; to "Briefly describe the reason for furnishing the projection to the [above] * * * person and the use which was to be made of it * * *"; and to "Furnish a fair and adequate summary of such projection. * * *"

The proposal has not been adopted.

———

NOTE: PROXY STATEMENTS INVOLVING FREEZE–OUTS

Early in the development of the "going private" and management buy-out movement, in February 1979, the Commission issued Securities Exchange Act Rel. No. 15,572, Fed.Sec.L.Rep., (CCH) ¶ 24,115 in which it published the views of its Division of Corporation Finance about the need for issuers engaged in such transactions to make full and adequate disclosure in soliciting proxies. The release discussed items of information requested in the proxy statements and the level of disclosure to be reached in answering those items in order, presumably, not to violate Rule 14a–9.

The Division expressed concern that principal shareholders or management may have failed, in the proxy material in the past, adequately to highlight actual or potential conflicts of interest in the transactions for which proxies were sought. It urged disclosure of those conflicts of interest, including differential tax effects of the transaction on affiliates and non-affiliates, employment contracts by affiliates, and disparities between sale price and tangible book value per share.

In addition, the Division urged, as Schedule 14A requires, express statements of "the reasons for and the effect of the transaction." Issuers were urged to describe the legal effects, tax consequences, and effects on market liquidity of the transaction. In setting out the "reasons for" the transaction issuers were urged to focus on the reasons why (including personal goals and financial circumstances such as tax benefits and diversification gains) management was proposing the transaction. "Such reasons are relevant because under state law the Board of Directors generally must authorize submission of the plan to shareholders for their approval." In order to clarify the "reasons", the proxy statement should contain "a brief description of any prior offers or alternatives * * * that were considered within a reasonable period prior to the date" of the proposed transaction and the reasons for rejecting them.

In connection with disclosure of the employment arrangements, the Division urged a comparison of average old compensation with new compensation. The Division also urged, again as Schedule 14A requires, that the management discuss the aspects of the transaction bearing upon "the fairness of the price offered"—including where appropriate, a comparison with alternatives considered or prior offers or negotiations with respect to any extraordinary corporate transaction, and information about redundant assets which could aid the Buyer in financing the purchase.

Finally, the suggestion was made that in describing the material features of the plan and its general effect on the rights of existing shareholders, the proxy statement should indicate if appraisal rights are not available, "what rights may be available under state law to shareholders who object to the transaction."

Several of the admonitions thus set forth with respect to disclosure in proxy statements appear as affirmative mandates in the filings required under Rule 13e–3.

The rigor, or lack thereof, that courts have read into the disclosure requirements both of Rule 13e–3 and Schedule 14D–9 and of the admonitions with respect to the proxy rules contained in Release No. 34–15,572 may be observed in cases like Starkman v. Marathon, infra p. 872; Lewis v. Oppenheimer & Co., 481 F.Supp. 1199 (S.D.N.Y.1979); and In re Dataproducts Corp. Shareholder Litigation, CCH Fed.Sec. L.Rep. ¶ 96,227 (Del.Ch.1991). The SEC has been more aggressive in prescribing disclosure in Schedule 14D–9, at least with respect to some aspects of merger negotiations. See, e.g., In re Lionel Corp., SEA Rel. No. 30,121 (Dec. 1990), CCH Fed.Sec.L.Rep. ¶ 84,908.

NOTE: RULE 13E–3 IN OPERATION

Rule 13e–3 applies to management buyouts by virtue of the managers' status as "affiliates" if the issuer. But where a leveraged buyout occurs and management is not included in the buyout group, the transaction does not fall within Rule 13e–3, even if the pre-buyout managers are offered employment contracts or after the fact opportunities to make equity investments. The RJR Nabisco leveraged buyout is a prominent example of such a transaction. Since such transactions arguably present the same problems of unequal information as transactions within the scope of the rule, the SEC considered expanding the scope of the rule in 1989. Kofele–Kale, The SEC's Going Private Rules—Analysis and Developments, 19 Sec.Reg.L.J. 139 (1991).

Does Rule 13e–3 cause managers to offer higher premiums in going private transactions? Davis and Lehn, Information Asymmetries, Rule 13e–3, and Premiums in Going–Private Transactions, 70 Wash.U.L.Q. 587 (1992), says "No." Davis and Lehn present the results of an empirical study of going-private transactions during 1980 to 1988. They compare (1) management-initiated transactions to third-party transactions, and find that premiums in third party transactions are slightly lower than in management transactions, and (2) transactions in which management is an equity participant to transactions in which it is not, and find that the average premium is slightly smaller but the median premium slightly larger where management holds equity. Id.

pp. 595–96. To test the suggestion that these results are due to the salubrious effects of the enactment of the Rule in 1979, Davis and Lehn go on to compare premiums in management buyouts from 1976 to 1978 with those from 1980 to 1982. They find that the average premium is *higher* for the *pre*–Rule period. Id. p. 596.

Is it clear that third party bids are the appropriate measure of the propriety of the conduct of management buyouts? Or can it be argued that holders of common should be entitled to a significantly greater payment where fiduciaries purchase the firm's assets?

HOWING CO. v. NATIONWIDE CORP.

United States Court of Appeals, Sixth Circuit, 1991.
927 F.2d 263.

Before MERRITT, Chief Judge; GUY, Circuit Judge; BROWN, Senior Circuit Judge.

MERRITT, Chief Judge.

In this securities action by minority public shareholders arising from a freeze-out merger of a subsidiary, Nationwide Corporation, with its parent, Nationwide Mutual, which at the time of the merger owned approximately 85% of the shares of the subsidiary, we previously reversed the District Court's dismissal of plaintiffs' claims under SEC Rule 13e–3, governing going-private transactions or freeze-out mergers; and we then remanded the case to the District Court for further proceedings. We refer the reader to our earlier opinion for a detailed statement of the facts and the law applicable to such mergers under Rule 13e–3. See Howing Co. v. Nationwide Corp., 826 F.2d 1470 (6th Cir.1987), cert. denied, 486 U.S. 1059 (1988).

I. Materiality Under Rule 13e–3

In our earlier opinion, we found that the defendant corporations in their going-private offer to the minority public shareholders had violated Item 8 required under Rule 13e–3 by making no effort to state, discuss or explain in reasonable detail the net book value, the going concern value or the liquidation value of the company whose minority interests were purchased. On remand, the District Court concluded that such a discussion would not have provided a shareholder with information of "material" value under the legal standard of "materiality" in securities transactions set out in TSC Indus. v. Northway, Inc., 426 U.S. 438, 96 S.Ct. 2126, 48 L.Ed.2d 757 (1976). The District Court therefore granted summary judgment for the defendant corporations which were responsible for the proxy statement we had previously found defective under Item 8 of Rule 13e–3.

The District Court based its grant of summary judgment on the ground that it is so clear and beyond dispute that the information on these values would not be of significance to a shareholder that no reasonable trier of fact—in this case a jury—could reach a contrary conclusion. We do not agree that the insignificance of the information is so clear, and we therefore remand the case for trial. The instructions for Item 8 of Rule 13e–3, as we have previously observed, are clear and specific in their requirement for a discussion of book, going concern and liquidation value in the fairness section of the proxy statement. They say that the issuer "should discuss in reasonable detail," among other things, the net book value, going concern value and liquidation value and "to the extent practicable, the weight assigned each factor." This and other information is specifically required by the SEC because these freeze-out transactions, unlike tender offers and other market transactions, are conducted outside the discipline of the competitive market place in which freedom of contract is the norm. As the SEC has noted, such "going private transactions present an opportunity for overreaching" and are "coercive" because of "the lack of arms-length bargaining and the inability of [minority shareholders] to influence corporate decisions to enter into such transactions." Exchange Act Release No. 34–17,719, reprinted in 8 Fed.Sec.L.Rep. (CCH) ¶ 28,709, at 17,245–42 (April 18, 1981).

Although we agree with the District Court that the general *TSC* standard of materiality is applicable to transactions governed by Rule 13e–3, the clear and specific language of the instructions to Item 8 creates in effect a presumption that a discussion of book, going concern and liquidation value in the proxy statement would be material to a reasonable shareholder. The presumed fact—that the investor would likely find disclosure of such information significant—follows from Item 8's insistence that the information be stated.

The failure to state the information triggers the presumption which the defendants may then rebut in the normal way under Rule 301 of the Federal Rules of Evidence. If the party adverse to the presumption offers no evidence contradicting the presumption of materiality, the court will instruct the jury that it may presume the omissions are material. If the adverse party presents evidence suggesting the insignificance of the omitted information, the right of the plaintiffs to have the jury consider the significance of the information persists, and the jury may infer that the information would be significant, unless and until evidence has been received which would require a directed verdict for the defendants on the significance of the information. The persuasiveness of the evidence so far presented by the defendants does not rise to that level, and hence the District Court should not have granted summary judgment.

The Supreme Court has made use of rebuttable presumptions in analogous factual circumstances in securities law cases. In a 10b–5 action, the Court upheld the use of a rebuttable presumption of reliance where a company misled sellers of its stock by not disclosing that it was engaged in merger negotiations. Basic Inc. v. Levinson, 485 U.S. 224, 108 S.Ct. 978, 99 L.Ed.2d 194 (1988). The Court justified adopting this rebuttable presumption because of the "unnecessarily unrealistic evidentiary burden" that plaintiffs otherwise would have had in showing how they would have acted if the omitted information had been stated. Id., 108 S.Ct. at 990. See also Affiliated Ute Citizens of Utah v. United States, 406 U.S. 128, 153–54, 92 S.Ct. 1456, 1472, 31 L.Ed.2d 741 (1972) (upholding rebuttable presumption of reliance where material omission made in proxy statement). Similarly, in the instant case, in which the question is what "would be" the reaction of reasonable shareholders to the information, the omission should raise a rebuttable presumption. The likelihood that the factors the SEC has enumerated in Item 8(b) will be material is sufficiently strong that omission of such factors without explanation of the reason for the omission will result in a rebuttable presumption of their materiality.

Establishing a presumption of materiality as to factors listed in Item 8(b) is in accord with other courts that have recognized the appropriateness of a "heightened" *TSC* materiality standard in coercive securities transactions such as this one. For example, in Pavlidis v. New England Patriots Football Club, Inc., 737 F.2d 1227, 1231 (1st Cir.1984), the First Circuit concluded that a heightened *TSC* standard should govern in a freeze-out merger where an allegedly misleading proxy statement was drafted at the direction of a shareholder who owned the controlling interest in a corporation at the time of a merger. Discussing materiality in the context of § 14(a) of the Securities Act and Rule 14a–9 promulgated thereunder, the Court found that certain facts may be material in the context of a "one-sided transaction" which otherwise would not be material in the context of an adversarial transaction. Id. Specifically, the First Circuit stated that, even though § 14(a) requires any party soliciting proxies to disclose all material information regardless of status or interest, a self-dealing insider may have a "heavier burden of disclosure" in meeting the § 14(a) disclosure requirements. Id.; accord Plaza Securities Co. v. Fruehauf Corp., 643 F.Supp. 1535, 1544 (E.D.Mich.1986) ("disclosures and nondisclosures [pursuant to Rule 13e–3] must be especially rigorous" where management involved in leveraged buyout designed to take company private) * * *.

In this action, defendants have not rebutted this presumption so as to avoid trial because they have not established the lack of significance of the information with sufficient clarity. The facts do not justify the grant of summary judgment on the ground that a reasonable investor would not find an explanation of book, going concern and liquidation value of any significance.

For example, plaintiffs' expert stated, and defendants' evaluator, First Boston Corp., appears to agree, that a relevant factor in a book value analysis is the multiplier, which is a number multiplied by book value to yield total selling price. According to plaintiffs' expert testimony, which is not effectively contradicted by defendants, insurance companies typically sell in a range from one to four times book value, with unhealthy companies selling in the lower range and more profitable companies selling at higher ratios. The cash out price of $42.50 paid by defendants is only slightly greater than book value, with a resulting multiplier of 1.025. Thus, it may well be that a reasonable shareholder would have found a discussion of this low multiplier (and of the multiplier range typical in purchases of insurance companies) important in deciding how to vote his shares.

We note that determining the value of a company from its book value multiplied by some "appropriate" industry multiplier is often an inexact method of valuation because book value measures nothing more than the value of a company's assets (minus liabilities) at the time the assets are added to a company's books. Obviously, in some cases, book value multiplied by some industry multiplier will not be a useful method to calculate a company's value. Accordingly, the corporation would state in its proxy materials that book value is not relevant to the "fairness" opinion, setting forth the factors leading it to this determination of irrelevancy. Where a defendant does base its "fairness" opinion in part on a comparison of book value to the cash out price, it should discuss in reasonable detail the multiplier used and why that multiplier is appropriate. In the instant case, the record strongly suggests that defendants used book value as an important factor in determining the "fairness" of the transaction and that they sought to use a multiplier of one. Some discussion of book value and the appropriateness of this multiplier for a company like Nationwide Corp. was warranted in the proxy materials.

Likewise, defendants did not discuss in the proxy materials the going concern and liquidation values or explain why they were not discussed. Like book value, defendants merely stated in conclusory language that they had considered these factors without stating what they were, how they were derived or their significance. In the proceeding below, defendants claimed that liquidation and going concern values were considerably lower than the cash out price offered minority shareholders. They presented evidence that Nationwide Corp. had no significant assets which could be sold for more than their book value, that New York insurance law would have frozen more than half of the value of total shareholders' equity ($260 million out of $462.2 million) that could be distributed in a liquidation and that Nationwide Corp. lacked an independent sales force which would have greatly decreased its value if sold as a going concern. See Howing Co. v. Nationwide Corp., No. 1–83–1693, at 7–9, 1989 WL 200973 (S.D.Ohio, Nov. 16, 1989). In response, plaintiffs introduced plausible expert testimony which contradicted defendants' contentions and which suggested that liquidation and going concern values were higher than the cash out price offered to minority shareholders. Because reasonable minds could have differed on whether the omitted discussion of liquidation and going concern values would be significant to a reasonable shareholder, the District Court erred in not letting the jury make this determination.

* * *

II. *State Law Fiduciary Claim*

* * *

Ohio law, while recognizing that a majority shareholder must pay minority shareholders a "fair price" for their shares, nonetheless limits recovery in almost every situation to recovery under the state's appraisal statute, Ohio Rev.Code Ann. § 1701.85 (Supp.1989). See *Armstrong,* 513 N.E.2d 776, 798; see also Stepak v. Schey, 51 Ohio St.3d 8, 553 N.E.2d 1072 (1990). * * * Because Ohio law as set forth in *Armstrong* dictates otherwise, plaintiffs' argument on appeal, that the district court applying Ohio law should have inquired into the "entire fairness" of the transaction, must fail.

Plaintiffs also contend that Nationwide Mutual did not disclose material facts concerning the merger price in its proxy statement. As to this issue, we find that summary judgment should not have been granted. Following the general statement of a majority shareholder's fiduciary duty, Ohio courts seem to acknowledge that a majority shareholder owes minority shareholders a fiduciary duty to disclose "pertinent facts concerning the merger." *Stepak,* 553 N.E.2d at 1078 (Holmes, J., concurring); see also *Armstrong,* 513 N.E.2d at 798 (acknowledging that other causes of action may be available under breach of fiduciary duty claim so long as not seeking additional compensation under theory of inadequate price).

As we determined in Section I of this opinion, plaintiffs have presented evidence that defendants omitted material information in their proxy statement that is required by Rule 13e–3. On appeal, plaintiffs contend that the omission of this same information (required by Rule 13e–3) constitutes a violation of Nationwide Mutual's majority shareholder fiduciary duty. Because Ohio law seemingly permits limited recovery on the narrow ground that full disclosure was not made in the majority shareholder's proxy statement, the district court on remand should try this state law claim.

In effect, plaintiffs have only one claim (although stated alternatively as a legal claim for a violation of Rule 13e–3 and as an equitable claim for a violation of the majority shareholders fiduciary duty): that non-fraudulent, material omissions concerning the "fairness" of the cash out price were made in the proxy statement. Because plaintiffs do not claim in the briefs on appeal that Nationwide Mutual, the majority shareholder, failed to disclose specific information other than that required by Rule 13e–3, we do not reach the question whether, under Ohio law, a majority shareholder has additional disclosure burdens beyond those required by federal law. * * *

We have reviewed all of plaintiffs' claims on appeal and conclude that the District Court erred in granting summary judgment on plaintiffs' Rule 13e–3 claim, as described above, and on plaintiffs' claim under Ohio law that Nationwide Mutual breached its fiduciary duty as majority shareholder to disclose the information specified under Item 8 of Rule 13e–3. Accordingly, to this extent, the judgment of the District Court is reversed and the case remanded for trial on the two remaining issues.

RALPH B. GUY, Jr., Circuit Judge, dissenting.

I believe that the district court judge properly analyzed the issues in this case and found them appropriate for disposition by summary judgment. I would affirm on the basis of the district court's opinion.

NOTE: FURTHER PROCEEDINGS IN *HOWING*

Does *Virginia Bankshares v. Sandberg,* supra p. 847 imply that a plaintiff class of minority shareholders lacking power to block a merger cannot establish damage causation in a 13e–3 action? The Supreme Court, presumably seeking an answer to this question, remanded *Howing* for reconsideration in light of *Sandberg.* In **Howing Co. v. Nationwide Corp.,** 972 F.2d 700 (6th Cir.1992), the Sixth Circuit answered in the negative and confirmed its earlier ruling. The Supreme Court thereupon denied certiorari, ___ U.S. ___, 113 S.Ct. 1645 (1993). The Sixth Circuit opinion questioned whether the *Sandberg* analysis of causation carries over to the 13e–3 context, but went on to articulate a nonvoting theory of causation based on the loss of a state remedy. Had the defendant made a full and fair disclosure, said the court, the plaintiffs would have voted no or not voted, qualified for the appraisal remedy, and exercised their appraisal rights. The court added that "we would be hesitant to hold that Congress intended to provide the protection of an implied right of action, but that causation could never be established in those cases where the minority shareholders, lacking sufficient votes to block the transaction, had their greatest need for such protection."

One judge dissented on the ground that, on the facts of the case, no forfeiture of appraisal resulted from the 13e–3 violation. The named plaintiffs, dissatisfied with the price, simply chose to bypass appraisal in favor of a class action. The majority dealt with this point by making reference to *Mills v. Electric Auto–Lite.* Given a finding of materiality, it said, the shareholder establishes a causal relation between the 13e–3 violation and the loss of state remedy by proving "that the proxy solicitation was an essential link in the chain of events that deprived him of his state-law remedy."

Does a foregone appraisal proceeding establish damage causation but not transaction causation? If the merger occurs in a jurisdiction that makes appraisal the exclusive remedy in cash out merger cases, does it matter in the 13(e) context that the plaintiff therefore had no possibility of a state law injunction against the transaction, and thus cannot show transaction causation?

(C) DISCLOSURE IN AID OF INFORMED CHOICE: USES OF "MATERIALITY"

(1) Prevailing Definitions of "Materiality"

(a) **TSC Industries Inc. v. Northway, Inc.,** 426 U.S. 438 (1976) involved a suit for injunctive relief, and ultimately money damages, for injuries caused by alleged falsehoods and omissions of material facts in proxy statements, in violation of Rule 14a–9. The District Court denied plaintiff's motion for summary judgment, but the Court of Appeals (512 F.2d 324 (7th Cir.1975)) reversed and held that the proxy material was defective as a matter of law. In reversing the Court of Appeals, the Supreme Court defined the standard of materiality for proxy statements under § 14 and Rule 14a–9 as follows (426 U.S. at 449):

"The general standard of materiality that we think best comports with the policies of Rule 14a–9 is as follows: an omitted fact is material if there is a substantial likelihood that a reasonable shareholder would consider it important in deciding how to vote. This standard is fully consistent with *Mills* general description of materiality as a requirement that 'the defect have a significant *propensity* to affect the voting process.' It does not require proof of a substantial likelihood that disclosure of the omitted fact would have caused the reasonable investor to change his vote. What the standard does contemplate is a showing of a substantial likelihood that, under all the circumstances, the omitted fact would have assumed actual significance in the deliberations of the reasonable shareholder. Put another way, there must be a substantial likelihood that the disclosure of the omitted fact would have been viewed by the reasonable investor as having significantly altered the 'total mix' of information made available."

It then went on to rule that a parent (which had acquired approximately 34 percent of a subsidiary's stock by a negotiated purchase from a controlling stockholder in February 1969 and proposed a liquidation—sale of assets (which was the equivalent of a merger) in October 1969, in which the public stockholders of the subsidiary would be paid some 50 percent less than the controlling stockholder had been paid eight months earlier) may not be obliged to disclose, inter alia, the following facts, because they could not be deemed "as a matter of law" to be "material".

(i) Investment bankers hired by the parent were said, in the proxy materials submitted to stockholders, to have reached their conclusion that the merger exchange was "fair" in reliance, in part, on "the substantial premium over current market values" being offered to the public stockholders of the subsidiary—i.e., the excess of the market price of the package of parent's securities which the subsidiary's stockholders would receive over the price of the surrendered securities of the subsidiary. But the proxy materials did not disclose that, in a subsequent explanation to the parent (made before the proxy material was issued, however) of their conclusion that the premium was "substantial", the bankers set forth their calculations, which showed that they believed the prices of the packages of the parent's securities (on which the premium rested) would decline subsequent to the merger by $1.75 per share for the subsidiary's preferred and $2.63 per share for its common. Such a price reduction would reduce the true value of the premium reflected in prices at the time of the proxy statement from $3.23 to $2.10 per share for the subsidiary's preferred stock and from

$2.94 to $1.62 per share for the subsidiary's common stock. The bankers' belief in the later decline in the price of the offered package was held not to be necessarily material, because as of the time of their opinion the predicted decline would not have rendered the premium less than "substantial", since the premium would at that time nevertheless have been about 19 percent for the package offered to the subsidiary's preferred and 14 percent for the package offered to its common; and

(ii) Purchases of the parent's securities by the parent, and by a fund of which one of its directors was president, amounted to 8.5 percent of all reported transactions in the parent's securities during the period between its acquiring control of the subsidiary and the announcement of the "merger". Because there was insufficient proof that those purchases constituted a manipulation—i.e., were planned in concert for the purpose of manipulating the price—by the parent and the director, the failure to state that such purchases had been made was held not to be necessarily a material omission.

(b) **Lynch v. Vickers Energy Corp.,** 383 A.2d 278 (Del.1977) was an action for damages by a tendering stockholder against Esmark, Inc. (Esmark), its wholly owned subsidiary Vickers Energy Corporation (Vickers) and the directors of TransOcean Oil, Inc. (TransOcean) 53.5% of whose common stock was owned by Vickers, on a complaint charging that in the tender offer which Vickers made for the balance of TransOcean's common stock, defendants (1) made less than a full and frank disclosure in the tender offer of the value of TransOcean's net assets; and (2) coerced the minority shareholders, through use of their superior bargaining position and control over the corporate assets and processes, to sell their respective shares for a grossly inadequate price.

After trial on the merits, the Vice–Chancellor entered judgment for defendants, ruling that plaintiff had failed to prove either actionable coercion or fraudulent misrepresentation 351 A.2d 570 (1976).

The Delaware Supreme Court, in reversing that judgment stated (383 A.2d 278 at 281):

> "The Court's duty was to examine what information defendants had and to measure it against what they gave to the minority stockholders, in a context in which 'complete candor' is required. In other words, the limited function of the Court was to determine whether defendants had disclosed all information in their possession germane to the transaction in issue. And by 'germane' we mean, for present purposes, such as a reasonable shareholder would consider important in deciding whether to sell or retain stock. Compare TSC Industries Inc. v. Northway Inc., 426 U.S. 438 (1976). The objective, of course, is to prevent insiders from using special knowledge which they may have to their own advantage and to the detriment of the stockholders. Compare Speed v. Transamerica Corp., D.Del., 99 F.Supp. 808, 829 (1951); Talbot v.

James, 259 S.C. 73, 190 S.E.2d 759, 764 (1972); 3 Loss Securities Regulation 1433–1434." *

Tested by that standard, the Supreme Court concluded, as a matter of law, that Vickers' tender offer circular was defective in that:

(i) in announcing that the value of TransOcean's net assets was "not less than $200,000,000 (approximately $15.00 per share) and could be substantially greater," it failed to disclose that defendants were in possession of estimates by the Vice President of TransOcean, a petroleum engineer, that the net asset value was between $250.8 million (approximately $20 per share) and $300 million,[d] and

(ii) in soliciting tenders at $12 per share, the tender offer circular stated that Vickers had, pursuant to a program of open market purchases, acquired 265,000 shares of TransOcean at an average price of $11.49 per share, but failed to disclose that in connection with that purchase program Vickers had authorized open market purchases of TransOcean's shares at a price of $15 per share. The trial court had concluded that the $15 authorization price "was nothing more than a procedural convenience and not an accurate reflection of Vickers' opinion as to the true value of TransOcean's shares." Accordingly, it ruled that nondisclosure thereof was not fatal. In reversing, the Supreme Court said:

> "But, again, the Court incorrectly weighed the quality of the information before it ruled on the claim of nondisclosure. Whether the authorization price accurately stated Vickers' opinion as to true value of TransOcean's shares, or whether it was a tool of convenience established to facilitate the acquisition of TransOcean's shares in a fluctuating market, is not relevant in a context involving the fiduciary obligation of full disclosure. What is important is the fact that the authorization price was germane to the terms of the tender offer, and as such it should have been disclosed to the minority shareholders.

> "Reversed and remanded for proceedings consistent herewith."

(2) The Materiality of "Soft" Information

The particular items of information that must be disclosed in the schedules under the registration requirements of the 1933 Act or under

* [Ed. Note] In its initial opinion the Delaware Supreme Court's last two sentences read: "And by 'germane' we mean information which has a significant connection, or close relationship, to the transaction at hand. The objective, of course, is to prevent insiders from using special knowledge which they may have to their own advantage and to the detriment of the stockholders."

Do the changes in the opinion, made in the course of denying a motion for reargument addressed to other points, import a change in the initially announced standard

of materiality? See Symposium, 3 Del.J. of Corp.Law 244 (1978).

d. The Supreme Court ruled that the probative value of that estimate, which the lower court had discounted, was for the stockholders, not the court to assess, so that "it was a breach of the fiduciary duty of candor for defendants to fail to disclose the * * * estimate to those persons to whom they owed the duty and whose stock Vickers was attempting to acquire." Did the court further narrow the disclosure required in Delaware in Rosenblatt v. Getty Oil Co., supra?

Sections 12, 13 and 14 of the 1934 Act are presumably automatically deemed to be "material." In addition, the statute implicitly, and regulations explicitly, request disclosure in filed statements of any other material information or additional information that is necessary to make the filed information not misleading. Also, the disclosure requirements derived from the general antifraud provisions of the 1934 Act either expressly or implicitly require disclosure of material information.

Nothing on the face of the statutes expressly requires or forbids disclosure of soft or future-oriented information. During the period of SEC hostility toward disclosure of such information, requiring disclosure of these items as "other material information" was not an option. But, once the SEC withdrew the disclosure bar in 1979, the mandatory disclosure question came up repeatedly. See Appendix B, Section 2 for discussion of the change in the SEC's position.

Analytically, there is little reason to deny that such information sometimes is material. At the same time, there is little reason to assert that it always is material. Sometimes it may be material, and at other times it may not. The question is how *relevant* and how *reliable* the information must be so as to justify its use by a reasonable investor in estimating the future price of the corporation's securities. At some level, any information, soft or hard, is of such little relevance, or so unreliable, or both, that an investor would not use it. At all points above that level, the rational investor finds the information useful. But the fact that a particular piece of information is in some way useful does not necessarily mean that it should be disclosed. Particularly where soft information is involved, there is a large range of uncertainty about the analytic inferences that may properly be made from the underlying information to the estimate of future prices and the intensity with which those estimates are held by their makers. Thus "materiality" depends not merely on the location of some minimum level of analytic utility. The question is where, beyond that point, relevance and reliability combine to require disclosure.

Future oriented information entails not only traditional soft information, such as projections and appraisals, but also information about contemplated transactions that are contingent, and have varying degrees of imminence. As with traditional soft information, such contingent information poses problems if it is required to be disclosed, either in filings with the Commission or in public communications to investors.

STARKMAN v. MARATHON OIL CO.

United States Court of Appeals, Sixth Circuit, 1985.
772 F.2d 231.

MERRITT, Circuit Judge.

Like Radol v. Thomas, 772 F.2d 244 (6th Cir.1985), this action arises out of U.S. Steel's November, 1981 acquisition and eventual

merger with Marathon Oil Company. The plaintiff here, Irving Starkman, was a Marathon shareholder until selling his shares on the open
market for $78 per share on November 18, 1981, the day before U.S.
Steel's tender offer for 51% of Marathon's outstanding shares at $125
per share was announced. On October 31, 1981, Mobil Oil had initiated
its takeover bid for Marathon, a bid which Marathon actively resisted
by urging its rejection by Marathon shareholders and by seeking and
eventually finding a "white knight" or alternative, friendly merger
partner-tender offeror, U.S. Steel. Starkman claims that Marathon's
board violated Rule 10b–5 and its fiduciary duty to him as a Marathon
shareholder by failing to disclose various items of "soft" information—
information of less certainty than hard facts—in its public statements
to shareholders during the period after Mobil's hostile tender offer and
prior to Steel's friendly tender offer. In particular, he says that
Marathon should have told shareholders that negotiations were underway with U.S. Steel prior to the consummation of those negotiations in
an agreement, and that internal and externally-prepared asset appraisals and five-year earnings and cash flow projections should have been
disclosed to shareholders so that they could make a fully informed
choice whether to sell their shares or gamble on receiving a higher
price in a possible Steel–Marathon merger.

The District Court granted summary judgment for Marathon, finding that these items of soft information had either been sufficiently
disclosed or were not required to be disclosed because their nondisclosure did not render materially misleading Marathon's other affirmative
public statements. For the reasons stated below, we affirm the judgment of the district Court.

I. BACKGROUND

We have discussed the background and structure of U.S. Steel's
acquisition of Marathon Oil at some length in Radol v. Thomas, 772
F.2d 244 (6th Cir.1985), and our attention here will therefore be focused
on the facts which are especially relevant to Starkman's Rule 10b–5
claims.

In the summer of 1981, Marathon was among a number of oil
companies considered to be prime takeover targets. In this atmosphere, Marathon's top level management began preparations against a
hostile takeover bid. Harold Hoopman, Marathon's president and chief
executive officer, instructed the company's vice presidents to compile a
catalog of assets. This document, referred to as the "Strong Report" or
"internal asset evaluation," estimated the value of Marathon's transportation, refining and marketing assets, its other equipment and
structures, and the value of proven, probable, and potential oil reserves
as well as exploratory acreage. Hoopman and John Strong, who was
responsible for combining materials received from various divisions into
the final report, both testified that the Strong report was viewed as a
"selling document" which placed optimistic values on Marathon's oil
and gas reserves so as to attract the interest of prospective buyers and

ensure that Marathon could either ward off an attempt to capture Marathon at a bargain price or obtain the best offer available.

In estimating proven, probable, and potential reserves and exploratory acreage, the Strong Report was based on information that was not available to the general public, for example in annual reports, because only the value of proven reserves was normally included in such public documents. The Strong Report defined proven reserves as those actually producing, probable reserves as reserves for properties where some production had been established and additional production was likely, and potential reserves as reserves for properties where production had not yet been established but where geologic evidence supported wildcat drilling. These reserves were valued using a discounted cash flow methodology, under which the present value of oil reserves is calculated by summing risk discounted expected net revenues from the particular field over the life of the field, and then discounted into present value by dividing by an estimated interest rate. This valuation method, a standard procedure for determining the cash value of oil and gas properties, required projections of price and cost conditions prevailing as far as 20 years into the future. For example, the Strong Report assumed that the rate of increase in oil prices would average over 9% per year from 1980–1990.

Using this methodology, the Strong Report valued Marathon's net assets at between $19 billion and $16 billion (depending on which set of interest rates was used to discount back to present value), a per share value of between $323 and $276. The value of oil and gas reserves made up $14 billion of the $19 billion estimate and $11.5 billion of the $16 billion estimate. A similar report using identical methodology was prepared in mid-July 1981 by the investment banking firm of First Boston, which had been hired by Marathon to assist in preparing for potential takeover bids. The First Boston Report was based only upon proven and probable oil reserves and was also intended to be used as a "presentation piece" to avoid a takeover or maximize the price obtained in a takeover. It placed Marathon's value at between $188 and $225 per share.

Some perspective on the values arrived at in the Strong and First Boston reports can be gained from other, publicly available appraisals of Marathon's assets prepared during 1981. The Herold Oil Industry Comparative Appraisal placed Marathon's appraised value at $199 per share, and two other reports by securities analysts said Marathon had an appraised value of between $200 and $210 per share.

Marathon's market value, however, was well below these appraised values. On October 29, 1981, Marathon closed at $63.75 per share. The next day, Mobil Oil announced its tender offer to purchase up to approximately 68% of outstanding Marathon common stock for $85 per share in cash. Mobile proposed to follow the tender offer with a going private or freezeout merger in which the remaining shareholders of Marathon would receive sinking fund debentures worth approximately $85 per share.

On October 31, 1981, Marathon's board of directors met in emergency session and unanimously decided that the Mobil offer was "grossly inadequate" and approved a vigorous campaign to persuade Marathon shareholders not to tender to Mobil, and to simultaneously seek a "white knight." On November 11 and 12, Marathon's Board made public statements to the shareholders recommending rejection of Mobil's bid as "grossly inadequate" and against the best interests of the company. We explore these statements in more detail below, as they are a primary focus of Starkman's claims of inadequate disclosure. However, at the time these statements to shareholders were made, Marathon representatives had already contacted all of the 30 to 35 companies who could possibly undertake an acquisition topping Mobil's bid, and, in particular, had begun negotiations with U.S. Steel on November 10. The Strong and First Boston reports were given to Steel on that same day, on the condition that they be kept confidential, and on November 12, Marathon's vice president for finance delivered five-year earnings forecasts and cash flow projections to Steel in Pittsburgh.

On November 17, Hoopman and David Roderick, Steel's president, reached agreement on the terms of Steel's purchase of Marathon, and, after Board approval, an agreement was signed on November 18, 1981. Under the terms of the agreement, Steel would make a tender offer for up to 31 million shares (about 51%) of Marathon stock for $125 per share in cash, to be followed by a merger proposal in which each remaining Marathon shareholder would receive one $100 face value, 12 year, 12½ per cent guaranteed note per share of common stock. On November 19, Steel mailed its tender offer to Marathon shareholders, and Hoopman sent a letter to Marathon shareholders describing the two-stage deal and stating the opinion of Marathon's Board that the agreement was fair to Marathon shareholders. Steel's offer was successful, with over 91% of the outstanding shares tendered, and the second stage freezeout merger was approved by a two-thirds majority of the remaining shareholders in February, 1982.

II. MARATHON'S PUBLIC STATEMENTS
AND DISPOSITION BELOW

There are three public statements by Marathon management at issue here. First, Marathon's November 11, 1981, press release, which states, in pertinent part, that:

> Our Board of Directors has determined that Mobil Corporation's unsolicited tender offer is grossly inadequate. The offer is not in the best interests of Marathon Oil or its shareholders. It doesn't reflect current asset values and it doesn't permit the long-term investor the opportunity to participate in the potential values that have been developed.
>
> * * *
>
> We plan to do everything we possibly can to defeat this offer. We are determined to stay independent.

The next day, as required by Rule 14e–2, Marathon mailed a letter to its shareholders stating its position regarding Mobil's tender offer. The letter urged rejection of the offer, stating that Marathon's Board was "convinced that the Mobil offer is grossly inadequate and does not represent the real values of the assets underlying your investment in Marathon." The letter described a number of alternative courses of action that were being considered by the Board, including "repurchase of Marathon shares, acquisition of all or part of another company, a business combination with another company, (and) the declaration of an extra ordinary dividend and a complete or partial liquidation of the Company," and concluded by again urging rejection of Mobil's attempt to "seize control of Marathon's assets at a fraction of their value," and stating that "[w]e are convinced that you and our other shareholders would be well served if Marathon remains independent."

Attached to this letter was a copy of Marathon's Schedule 14D–9, filed pursuant to Rule 14d–9, 17 C.F.R. § 240.14d–9, in which the board informed the SEC that it had recommended rejection of the Mobil offer as "grossly inadequate." Item 4(b)(iv) of Marathon's Schedule 14D–9 listed as a factor supporting this recommendation the board's belief that based on current economic and market factors, "this is an extremely inopportune time to sell the Company and, in any event, that its shareholders would be better served if the Company were to remain independent."

Item 7 of this same schedule described "Certain Negotiations and Transactions" by Marathon:

> At a meeting of the Board of Directors held on October 31, 1981, the Board considered and reviewed the feasibility and desirability of exploring and investigating certain types of possible transactions, including, without limitation, repurchases of Company Common Shares, the public or private sale of equity or other securities of the Company, a business combination between the Company and another company, the acquisition of a significant interest in or the entire Company or of one or more of its significant business segments by another company, a joint venture between the Company and one or more other companies, the acquisition by the Company of all or part of the business of another Company, a complete or partial liquidation of the Company or the declaration of an extraordinary dividend. After considerable discussion, the Board resolved that it was desirable and in the best interest of the Company and its shareholders to explore and investigate, with the assistance and advice of First Boston, such transactions, although the Board noted that the initiation or continuation of such activities may be dependent upon Mobil's future actions with respect to the Mobil Offer. There can be no assurance that these activities will result in any transaction being recommended to the Board of Directors or that any transaction which is recommended will be authorized or consummated.

Starkman argues that the failure of any of these communications to disclose the Strong and First Boston reports and the five-year earnings and cash flow projections constituted an omission of material facts which rendered these communications materially misleading, and that Marathon not only failed to adequately disclose its search for a white knight and its negotiations with Steel but actually gave the false impression that the Board was endeavoring to preserve Marathon as an independent entity. He argues that the Strong and First Boston reports, the five-year cash and earnings projections, and the fact of ongoing negotiations with U.S. Steel were all material facts because knowledge of them would have affected a reasonable shareholder's evaluation of the likelihood that Marathon would succeed in negotiating a higher price takeover, and thereby affect such a shareholder's decision to sell his shares. He contends that shareholders were not adequately informed of Marathon management's search for a "white knight" and of the negotiations with Steel, and that failure to disclose more information regarding these negotiations rendered statements suggesting that Marathon might remain independent materially misleading. Similarly, Starkman contends that if he had been told of the Strong and First Boston reports and the five-year earnings and cash flow projections, and also that Marathon management was using these figures in seeking an alternative bidder, then he would have anticipated a much higher bid than he did, and that failure to release this information rendered materially misleading the affirmative statements Marathon did make.

* * *

The District Court summarily disposed of the claim that the five-year earnings and cash flow projections should have been disclosed, concluding that disclosure of such information is simply not required under Marsh v. Armada Corp., 533 F.2d 978, 986–87 (6th Cir.1976), cert. denied, 430 U.S. 954, 97 S.Ct. 1598, 51 L.Ed.2d 803 (1977), and Arber v. Essex Wire Corp., 490 F.2d 414, 421 (6th Cir.1974), cert. denied, 419 U.S. 830, 95 S.Ct. 53, 42 L.Ed.2d 56 (1974).

As to disclosure of the negotiations with Steel, the District Court cited Reiss v. Pan American World Airways, Inc., 711 F.2d 11, 14 (2d Cir.1983), and Staffin v. Greenberg, 672 F.2d 1196, 1206 (3d Cir.1982), in ruling that Marathon's 14D–9 disclosure that the acquisition of all or part of another company, or merger with another company, was being considered as an alternative to the Mobil offer sufficed to meet whatever disclosure obligation may have existed.

III.　DISCUSSION

A.　Introduction

* * *

Aptly described as a "judicial oak which has grown from little more than a legislative acorn," Blue Chip Stamps v. Manor Drug Stores, 421 U.S. 723, 737, 95 S.Ct. 1917, 1926, 44 L.Ed.2d 539 (1975), Rule 10b–5 has been the source of a wide-ranging federal common law of securities fraud, clearly applicable to the tender offer context, provided that, as here, there has been a purchase or sale of a security. See 3 L. Loss, Securities Regulation 1445 (2d ed. 1961).

Despite occasional suggestions by commentators, see, e.g., Bauman, Rule 10b–5 and the Corporation's Affirmative Duty to Disclose, 67 Geo.L.J. 935 (1979), and the courts, Zweig v. Hearst Corp., 594 F.2d 1261, 1266 (9th Cir.1979), that Rule 10b–5 imposes an affirmative obligation on the corporation to disclose all material information regardless of whether the corporation has made any other statements, the established view is that a "duty to speak" must exist before the disclosure of material facts is required under Rule 10b–5. See Flynn v. Bass Brothers Enterprises, Inc., 744 F.2d 978, 984 (3d Cir.1984) (citing Chiarella v. United States, 445 U.S. 222, 235, 100 S.Ct. 1108, 1118, 63 L.Ed.2d 348 (1980); Staffin v. Greenberg, 672 F.2d 1196, 1202 (3d Cir.1982)). Provided that such a duty to speak exists, a further limitation on the duty to disclose is imposed by the requirement that only misstatements of material facts and omissions of material facts necessary to make other required statements not misleading are prohibited by Rule 10b–5. The Supreme Court's definition of "material" in the context of an alleged violation of Rule 14a–9, governing disclosure requirements in proxy statements, has been adopted for cases involving Rule 10b–5 in the tender offer context.

* * *

In structuring the disclosure duties of a tender offer target, we begin therefore with the basic proposition that only material facts— those substantially likely to affect the deliberations of the reasonable shareholder—must be disclosed, and then *only* if the nondisclosure of the particular material facts would make misleading the affirmative statements otherwise required by the federal securities laws and SEC regulations.

Our adherence to this basic proposition ensures that target management's disclosure obligations will strike the correct balance between the competing costs and benefits of disclosure. The benefits of disclosure in ensuring that shareholders who are suddenly faced with a tender offer will not be forced to respond without adequate information are clearly recognized in Section 14(e) of the Williams Act, 15 U.S.C. § 78n(e), which somewhat broadens the reach of Rule 10b–5 to statements made "in connection with any tender offer" and which provides the statutory authority for SEC rules imposing affirmative disclosure obligations on tender offer targets. On the other hand, tender offers remain essentially contests in which participants on both sides act under the "stresses of the marketplace," and "[p]robably there will no more be a perfect tender offer than a perfect trial." Electronic Specialty Co. v. International Controls Corp., 409 F.2d 937, 948 (2d Cir.1969) (Friendly, J.). Under these conditions, imposing an "unrealistic requirement of laboratory conditions," id., would place target management under the highly unpredictable threat of huge liability for the failure to disclose, perhaps inducing the disclosure of mountains of documents and hourly reports on negotiations with potential tender offerors, a deluge of information which would be more likely to confuse than guide the reasonable lay shareholder and which could interfere with the negotiation of a higher tender offer and actually reduce the likelihood that a shareholder will benefit from a successful tender offer at a premium over the market. It is with these competing considerations in mind that we turn to the particular disclosure claims made here.

B.   Assets Appraisals and Earnings Projections

We first address Starkman's contention that Marathon should have disclosed the Strong and First Boston reports and the five-year earnings projections and forecasts given to Steel. Under the authority of Section 14(e) of the Williams Act, the SEC requires a tender offer target to make two affirmative statements regarding an offer. First, Rule 14e–2 requires that the target company mail or publish a statement to its shareholders within 10 days of the tender offer stating its position (or stating it cannot take a position) and giving reasons for the position. Under Rule 14d–9, a Schedule 14D–9 must be filed with the SEC "as soon as practicable" after the recommendation letter is sent to shareholders. The information to be included in the Schedule 14D–9 is described in 17 C.F.R. § 14d–101. Significantly, although Item 4 of the Schedule 14D–9 is to contain a statement of the reasons for the target's position with respect to the offer, and Item 8 requires disclosure of any additional information as "may be necessary to make the required statements, in light of the circumstances under which they are made, not misleading" neither the shareholder recommendation letter nor the Schedule 14D–9 must contain internal asset appraisals, appraisals done by outside consultants such as First Boston, or earnings and cash flow projections.

Since there is no SEC rule specifically requiring the disclosure of this information, we must determine whether Rule 10b–5 requires its disclosure as material information, the nondisclosure of which would render misleading other statements made by Marathon. The starting point in this analysis is the underlying regulatory policy toward disclosure of such information, since regulatory rules reflect careful study of general conditions prevailing in the securities marketplace and provide guidelines upon which corporate officers and directors are entitled to rely.

The SEC's policy toward the inclusion of appraised asset valuations, projections and other "soft" information in proxy materials, tender offers and other disclosure documents has undergone a gradual evolution toward *allowing* the inclusion of such information in some special contexts, provided that the assumptions and hypotheses underlying predicted values are also disclosed.

In 1976, future earnings projections were deleted from a list of examples of potentially misleading disclosures in proxy statements in the note which followed Rule 14a–9. See Securities Act Release No.

5699, reprinted in [1975–76 Transfer Binder] Fed.Sec.L.Rep. (CCH) ¶ 80, 461 (1976). And, effective July 30, 1979, the SEC adopted a "safe harbor" rule for projections, under which a statement containing a projection of revenues and earnings would not be considered to be a materially misleading misstatement or omission for purposes of liability under the federal securities laws provided the statement was prepared with a reasonable basis and was disclosed in good faith. See Securities Act Release No. 6084 reprinted in [1979 Transfer Binder] Fed.Sec. L.Rep. (CCH) ¶ 82,117, at 81,939 (June 25, 1979).

With respect to asset appraisals, Rule 13e–3, 17 C.F.R. § 240.13e–3, requires disclosure of the information called for by Items 7, 8, and 9 of Schedule 13E–3, 17 C.F.R. § 240.13e–100, in the context of freezeout mergers. Item 8 of Schedule 13E–3 requires disclosure of factors important in determining the fairness of such a transaction to unaffiliated shareholders, and these factors include liquidation value; Item 9 of that same schedule says that a summary of any outside appraisal must be furnished, with the summary including a discussion of the procedures and methods of arriving at the findings and recommendations of the appraisal. However, a 1979 SEC-proposed amendment under which an issuer would have to disclose any projection given to an appraisal furnisher was never adopted, see 2 Fed.Sec.L.Rep. (CCH) ¶ 23–706, at 17,245–21 through 21A, and, even more importantly, in Radol v. Thomas, 772 F.2d 244 No. 83–3598, (6th Cir.1985), we have rejected the position that SEC rules regarding freezeout mergers and proxies should determine the disclosure obligations of target management in the first stage of a two-tier tender offer.[6]

Finally, we note that until March, 1982, Regulation S–K, the source for disclosure obligations in annual reports, registration documents and other documents that must be filed with the SEC, provided in Instruction 2 to Item 2(b) that estimates of probable or possible oil and gas reserves should not be disclosed in any document publicly filed with the SEC. See Securities Act Release No. 6008, reprinted in [1978 Transfer Binder] Fed.Sec.L.Rep. (CCH) para. 81,768, at 81,104 (Dec. 19, 1978). The underlying reason was that "estimates of probable or possible reserves and any value thereof are not sufficiently reliable to be included * * * and may be misleading to investors." Id. In March, 1982, well after Steel's tender offer, Item 102 of Regulation S–K was amended to *allow* disclosure of "estimated" as well as proved reserves where such estimates have previously been provided to a person who is offering to acquire or merge with the subject company, see Securities

---

6. In addition, while the note to Rule 14a–9 lists "predictions as to specific future market values" as a potentially misleading proxy statement disclosure, the SEC in 1980 authorized disclosure of good faith appraisals made on a reasonable basis in proxy contests in which a principal issue is the disposition of the issuer's assets, provided that the valuations are accompanied by "disclosure which facilitates shareholders' understanding of the basis for and limitations on the projected realizable values." Exchange Act Release No. 34–16833, reprinted in 3 Fed.Sec.L.Rep. (CCH) ¶ 24,-117 (May 23, 1980). This same release cautioned, however, that where "valuations are so qualified and subject to material limitations and contingencies, inclusion in proxy soliciting material of specific realizable values may be unreasonable." 3 Fed.Sec.L.Rep. (CCH) at 17, 621–13.

Act Release No. 6383, reprinted in [1937–1982 Accounting Series Release Transfer Binder] Fed.Sec.L.Rep. (CCH) ¶ 72,328, at 63,003 (March 3, 1982). The Strong and First Boston reports contain estimates of probable and possible reserves, and the disclosure of this information was actually prohibited at the time of Steel's tender offer, and only *permitted* since that time.

Thus, at the time of Steel's tender offer, the SEC did not require disclosure of earnings projections in any context, and required disclosure of asset appraisals, in summary form, only in the special context of freezeout mergers, which differs markedly from the setting of a first-stage tender offer. Although the SEC allowed disclosure of projections, provided they were prepared on a "reasonable basis" and in "good faith," and also allowed disclosure of similarly supported asset appraisals in some proxy contests, it forbade the disclosure of estimates of probable and potential oil and gas reserves, a major component of the Strong and First Boston appraisals. Absent compelling authority to the contrary, we are reluctant to impose liability on Marathon for failing to disclose asset appraisals based on hypothetical valuations which the SEC did not then permit to be disclosed in most contexts, particularly since Section 23(a) of the Securities and Exchange Act, 15 U.S.C. § 78w(a)(1) provides that no liability under the federal securities laws shall be imposed for "any act done or omitted in good faith, conformity with a rule, regulation, or order of the Commission."

* * *

Rather than suggesting a duty to disclose the Strong and First Boston reports, however, our cases firmly establish the rule that soft information such as asset appraisals and projections must be disclosed only if the reported values are virtually as certain as hard facts.

This Court has recently held that a target's failure to disclose an appraisal based on five-year cash flow and earnings projections and intended to be used as a selling document in ongoing merger discussions did not violate Rule 10b–5. Biechele v. Cedar Point, Inc., 747 F.2d 209 (6th Cir.1984). Chief Judge Lively's opinion for the court reasoned that the report was a "selling document" which "contained projections and speculative assumptions which were little more than predictions of future business success," and valuations based on the replacement cost of assets which could be misleading to shareholders, since they varied from balance sheet information prepared according to accepted accounting principles. Id. at 216. Similarly, in James v. Gerber Products Co., 587 F.2d 324, 327 (6th Cir.1978), we held that the failure to disclose interim earnings reports in connection with a shareholder's sale of stock back to the issuing company did not violate Rule 10b–5, because "such sales figures, projections, forecasts and the like only rise to the level of materiality when they can be calculated with substantial certainty." And in Arber v. Essex Wire Corp., 490 F.2d 414, 421 (6th Cir.), cert. denied, 419 U.S. 830, 95 S.Ct. 53, 42 L.Ed.2d 56 (1974), another case involving a corporate stock repurchase, then Judge McCree said that while a fixed plan of future corporate activity might, under some circumstances, be viewed as a material fact, Section 10(b) and Rule 10b–5 did not require a corporate insider to disclose his educated guesses or predictions, and "[i]n short, the law mandates disclosure only of existing material facts. It does not require an insider to volunteer any economic forecast." See also Marsh v. Armada Corp., 533 F.2d 978, 987 (6th Cir.1976), cert. denied, 430 U.S. 954, 97 S.Ct. 1598, 51 L.Ed.2d 803 (1977) (failure to make a projection of future earnings in freezeout merger proxy statement not actionable under Rule 10b–5).

Our cases fully support a rule under which a tender offer target must disclose projections and asset appraisals based upon predictions regarding future economic and corporate events only if the predictions underlying the appraisal or projection are substantially certain to hold. An example is when the predictions in fact state a fixed plan of corporate activity. If a target chooses to disclose projections and appraisals which do not rise to this level of certainty, then it must also inform the shareholders as to the basis for and limitations on the projected realizable values.[7]

The Third Circuit has enunciated a different test, under which "courts should ascertain the duty to disclose asset valuations and other soft information on a case by case basis, by weighing the potential aid such information will give the shareholder against the potential harm, such as undue reliance, if the information is released with a proper cautionary note." Flynn v. Bass Brothers Enterprises, 744 F.2d at 988. The court listed several factors the courts have considered in determining the reliability of soft information, including the qualifications of those who prepared the appraisal, the degree of certainty of the data on which it was based, and the purpose for which it was prepared. 744 F.2d at 986, 988 (compiling cases); see also Panter v. Marshall Field, 646 F.2d at 292–93.

By its very nature, however, this sort of judicial cost-benefit analysis is uncertain and unpredictable, and it moreover neglects the role of the market in providing shareholders with information regarding the target's value through competing tender offers. Our approach, which focuses on the certainty of the data underlying the appraisal or projection, ensures that the target company's shareholders will receive all essentially factual information, while preserving the target's discretion to disclose more uncertain information without the threat of liability, provided appropriate qualifications and explanations are made.

Under this standard, Marathon plainly had no duty to disclose the Strong and First Boston reports, because these reports contained esti-

---

7. We note that this rule is fully consistent with the recent statement by the SEC Advisory Committee on Tender Offers that "current disclosures of projections and valuations given to a bidder by a target company are essentially meaningless and can be misleading without disclosure of the underlying assumptions," and with that Committee's recommendation that "[w]here the bidder discloses projections or asset valuations to target company shareholders, it must include disclosure of the principal supporting assumptions provided to the bidder by the target." See SEC Advisory Committee on Tender Offers, Report of Recommendations, at 29 (July 8, 1983).

mates of the value of probable, potential and unexplored oil and gas reserves which were based on highly speculative assumptions regarding the path of oil and gas prices, recovery rates and the like over a period of thirty to fifty years. Disclosure of such estimated values could well have been misleading without an accompanying mountain of data and explanations. There is no reported case actually holding that disclosure of appraised values of oil and gas reserves is required, and several which agree with our decision that such disclosure is not required.[8]

Similarly, Marathon had no duty to disclose the five-year earnings and cash flow projections given to Steel and First Boston. This information does not rise to the level of substantial certainty triggering a duty to disclose. Biechele v. Cedar Point; James v. Gerber Products Corp., both supra.

Further, disclosure of the asset appraisals and earnings and cash flow projections was not required in order to ensure that other statements in Marathon's 14D-9 and in its letter recommending rejection of Mobil's bid were not misleading. Marathon stated that Mobil's $85 offer was "grossly inadequate" and disclosure of highly uncertain information indicating that Marathon had a net asset value of over $200 per share would only have supported this statement, and could have actually misled shareholders into thinking that the market would actually support a price of $200 per share.

C.

Starkman's contention that Marathon should have disclosed more information regarding its search for a white knight and its negotiations with Steel are equally without merit. The SEC and the courts have enunciated a firm rule regarding a tender offer target's duty to disclose ongoing negotiations: so long as merger or acquisition discussions are preliminary, general disclosure of the fact that such alternatives are being considered will suffice to adequately inform shareholders; a duty to disclose the possible terms of any transaction and the parties thereto arises only after an agreement in principle, regarding such fundamental terms as price and structure, has been reached. See Item 7 of Schedule 14D-9, 17 C.F.R. § 240.14d-101 (1984); Greenfield v. Heublein, Inc., 742 F.2d 751, 756-57 (3d Cir.1984), cert. denied, 469 U.S. 1215, 105 S.Ct. 1189, 84 L.Ed.2d 336 (1985) (rejecting an "intent to merge" trigger standard); Staffin v. Greenberg, 672 F.2d 1196, 1207 (3d Cir.1982); Reiss v. Pan American World Airways, Inc., 711 F.2d 11, 14 (2d Cir.1983).[9]

---

8. See, e.g., Sunray v. DX Oil Co. v. Helmerich & Payne, Inc., 398 F.2d 447, 450-51 (10th Cir.1968) ("any statement concerning oil reserves other than in the category of 'proved' could certainly be misleading to any investor other than one who is an expert in the industry"); Caspary v. Louisiana Land and Exploration Co., 579 F.Supp. 1105 (S.D.N.Y.1983), aff'd, 725 F.2d 189 (2d Cir.1984) (no duty to disclose internal projections regarding oil recovery rates

and exploration costs); Bradshaw v. Jenkins, [1983-84 Transfer Binder] Fed.Sec. L.Rep. (CCH) ¶ 99,719 (W.D.Wash. March 9, 1984) (no duty to disclose consultant's estimated value of energy loan portfolio).

9. Greenfield v. Heublein also held that Hublein's voluntary statement in response to a New York Stock Exchange inquiry that it knew of no reason for an unusual increase in trading activity in its stock

The rationale emerging from these cases is that when dealing with complex bargaining which may fail as well as succeed and which may succeed on terms which vary greatly from those originally anticipated, the disclosure of preliminary discussions could very easily mislead shareholders as to the prospects of success, and by making public an impending offer, push the price of the target's stock toward the expected tender price, thereby depriving shareholders of the primary inducement to tender—a premium above market price—and forcing the offeror to abandon its plans or greatly increasing the cost of the offer. See Staffin v. Greenberg, 672 F.2d at 1207.

In the instant case, Marathon's shareholder recommendation letter and its Schedule 14D–9 stated that the company was considering a number of alternatives, including a merger with another firm. These statements adequately informed the shareholders of Marathon's plans. Additional statements in these documents to the effect that Marathon's board believed the best result would be for Marathon to remain independent were not misleading when read in their full context, and at most expressed a sincere hope which the board found unrealistic under the pressure of Mobil's offer.

Finally, Starkman's claims for fraud and breach of fiduciary duty are completely unsupported by authority in his brief, and were similarly neglected in his arguments below. We therefore affirm and adopt the reasoning of the District Court finding that no claim for fraud has been made out because Marathon did not fail to disclose any information necessary to make its other public statements not misleading, and that the directors' statements, made at a time of extraordinary pressure on the board, comported in all respects with federal law and did not breach a fiduciary duty to Marathon's shareholders.

Accordingly, the judgment of the District Court is affirmed.

May a failure to file "soft" information which is not required to be filed in Schedule 14D–9 or under Rule 10b–5 be found to violate local fiduciary disclosure obligations, and if so is the violation sanctionable? See Weinberger v. Rio Grande Industries, Inc., 519 A.2d 116 (Del.Ch. 1986).

------

when in fact it knew of ongoing merger negotiations was not false or misleading because the merger negotiations had not been formally disclosed and there was no indication that the information had been leaked or that insider trading had occurred. 742 F.2d at 759. This holding is directly contrary to the position taken by the SEC in that case as amicus that while a company may respond with "no comment" to stock exchange inquiries regarding unusual market activity, it may not state that no corporate development accounts for the stock activity when in fact it knows that merger negotiations are under way. This related position has not altered the Commission's longstanding policy that negotiations need not otherwise be disclosed unless an agreement in principle has been reached.

BASIC INCORPORATED v. LEVINSON

Supreme Court of the United States, 1988.
485 U.S. 224, 108 S.Ct. 978, 99 L.Ed.2d 194.

BLACKMUN, J., delivered the opinion of the Court, in which BRENNAN, MARSHALL, and STEVENS, JJ., joined, and in Parts I, II, and III of which WHITE and O'CONNOR, JJ., joined. WHITE, J., filed an opinion concurring in part and dissenting in part, in which O'CONNOR, J., joined. REHNQUIST, C.J., and SCALIA and KENNEDY, JJ., took no part in the consideration or decision of the case.

Justice BLACKMUN delivered the opinion of the Court.

This case requires us to apply the materiality requirement of § 10(b) of the Securities Exchange Act of 1934, 48 Stat. 881, as amended, 15 U.S.C. § 78a et seq. (1934 Act), and the Securities and Exchange Commission's Rule 10b–5, promulgated thereunder, see 17 CFR § 240.-10b–5 (1987), in the context of preliminary corporate merger discussions. We must also determine whether a person who traded a corporation's shares on a securities exchange after the issuance of a materially misleading statement by the corporation may invoke a rebuttable presumption that, in trading, he relied on the integrity of the price set by the market.

I

Prior to December 20, 1978, Basic Incorporated was a publicly traded company primarily engaged in the business of manufacturing chemical refractories for the steel industry. As early as 1965 or 1966, Combustion Engineering, Inc., a company producing mostly alumina-based refractories, expressed some interest in acquiring Basic, but was deterred from pursuing this inclination seriously because of antitrust concerns it then entertained. * * * In 1976, however, regulatory action opened the way to a renewal of Combustion's interest. The "Strategic Plan," dated October 25, 1976, for Combustion's Industrial Products Group included the objective: "Acquire Basic Inc. $30 million." * * *

Beginning in September 1976, Combustion representatives had meetings and telephone conversations with Basic officers and directors, including petitioners here, concerning the possibility of a merger. During 1977 and 1978, Basic made three public statements denying that it was engaged in merger negotiations.[4] On December 18, 1978,

---

4. On October 21, 1977, after heavy trading and a new high in Basic stock, the following news item appeared in the Cleveland Plain Dealer:

"[Basic] President Max Muller said the company knew no reason for the stock's activity and that no negotiations were under way with any company for a merger. He said Flintkote recently denied Wall Street rumors that it would make a tender offer of $25 a share for control of the Cleveland-based maker of refractories for the steel industry." * * *

On September 25, 1978, in reply to an inquiry from the New York Stock Exchange, Basic issued a release concerning increased activity in its stock and stated that

"management is unaware of any present or pending company development that would result in the abnormally heavy trading activity and price fluctuation in company shares that have been experienced in the past few days." * * *

Basic asked the New York Stock Exchange to suspend trading in its shares and issued a release stating that it had been "approached" by another company concerning a merger. * * * On December 19, Basic's board endorsed Combustion's offer of $46 per share for its common stock, * * * and on the following day publicly announced its approval of Combustion's tender offer for all outstanding shares.

Respondents are former Basic shareholders who sold their stock after Basic's first public statement of October 21, 1977, and before the suspension of trading in December 1978. Respondents brought a class action against Basic and its directors, asserting that the defendants issued three false or misleading public statements and thereby were in violation of § 10(b) of the 1934 Act and of Rule 10b–5. Respondents alleged that they were injured by selling Basic shares at artificially depressed prices in a market affected by petitioners' misleading statements and in reliance thereon. The District Court adopted a presumption of reliance by members of the plaintiff class upon petitioners' public statements that enabled the court to conclude that common questions of fact or law predominated over particular questions pertaining to individual plaintiffs. See Fed.Rule Civ.Proc. 23(b)(3). The District Court therefore certified respondents' class. On the merits, however, the District Court granted summary judgment for the defendants. It held that, as a matter of law, any misstatements were immaterial: there were no negotiations ongoing at the time of the first statement, and although negotiations were taking place when the second and third statements were issued, those negotiations were not "destined, with reasonable certainty, to become a merger agreement in principle." * * *

The United States Court of Appeals for the Sixth Circuit affirmed the class certification, but reversed the District Court's summary judgment, and remanded the case. 786 F.2d 741 (1986). The court reasoned that while petitioners were under no general duty to disclose their discussions with Combustion, any statement the company voluntarily released could not be " 'so incomplete as to mislead.' " Id., at 746, quoting SEC v. Texas Gulf Sulphur Co., 401 F.2d 833, 862 (CA2 1968) (en banc), cert. denied, sub nom. Coates v. SEC, 394 U.S. 976 (1969). In the Court of Appeals' view, Basic's statements that no negotiations were taking place, and that it knew of no corporate developments to account for the heavy trading activity, were misleading. With respect to materiality, the court rejected the argument that preliminary merger discussions are immaterial as a matter of law, and held that "once a statement is made denying the existence of any discussions, even discussions that might not have been material in absence of the denial are material because they make the statement made untrue." 786 F.2d, at 749.

On November 6, 1978, Basic issued to its shareholders a "Nine Months Report 1978." This Report stated:

"With regard to the stock market activity in the Company's shares we remain unaware of any present or pending developments which would account for the high volume of trading and price fluctuations in recent months." * * *

The Court of Appeals joined a number of other circuits in accepting the "fraud-on-the-market theory" to create a rebuttable presumption that respondents relied on petitioners' material misrepresentations, noting that without the presumption it would be impractical to certify a class under Fed.Rule Civ.Proc. 23(b)(3).   See 786 F.2d, at 750–751.

We granted certiorari, 484 U.S. ___ (1987), to resolve the split * * * among the Courts of Appeals as to the standard of materiality applicable to preliminary merger discussions, and to determine whether the courts below properly applied a presumption of reliance in certifying the class, rather than requiring each class member to show direct reliance on Basic's statements.

II

* * *

Pursuant to its authority under § 10(b) of the 1934 Act, 15 U.S.C. § 78j, the Securities and Exchange Commission promulgated Rule 10b–5.[6]

* * *

The Court previously has addressed various positive and common-law requirements for a violation of § 10(b) or of Rule 10b–5.   * * * The Court also explicitly has defined a standard of materiality under the securities laws, see TSC Industries, Inc. v. Northway, Inc., 426 U.S. 438 (1976), concluding in the proxy-solicitation context that "[a]n omitted fact is material if there is a substantial likelihood that a reasonable shareholder would consider it important in deciding how to vote."   Id., at 449.   Acknowledging that certain information concerning corporate developments could well be of "dubious significance," id., at 448, the Court was careful not to set too low a standard of materiality; it was concerned that a minimal standard might bring an overabundance of information within its reach, and lead management "simply to bury the shareholders in an avalanche of trivial information—a result that is hardly conducive to informed decisionmaking."   Id., at 448–449.   It further explained that to fulfill the materiality requirement "there must be a substantial likelihood that the disclosure of the omitted fact would have been viewed by the reasonable investor as having significantly altered the 'total mix' of information made available."   Id., at 449.   We now expressly adopt the TSC Industries standard of materiality for the § 10(b) and Rule 10b–5 context.

---

6. In relevant part, Rule 10b–5 provides:

"It shall be unlawful for any person, directly or indirectly, by the use of any means or instrumentality of interstate commerce, or of the mails or of any facility of any national securities exchange,

* * *

"(b) To make any untrue statement of a material fact or to omit to state a material fact necessary in order to make the statements made, in the light of the circumstances under which they were made, not misleading * * * in connection with the purchase or sale of any security."

III

The application of this materiality standard to preliminary merger discussions is not self-evident. Where the impact of the corporate development on the target's fortune is certain and clear, the TSC Industries materiality definition admits straightforward application. Where, on the other hand, the event is contingent or speculative in nature, it is difficult to ascertain whether the "reasonable investor" would have considered the omitted information significant at the time. Merger negotiations, because of the ever-present possibility that the contemplated transaction will not be effectuated, fall into the latter category.[9]

A

Petitioners urge upon us a Third Circuit test for resolving this difficulty.[10] * * * Under this approach, preliminary merger discussions do not become material until "agreement-in-principle" as to the price and structure of the transaction has been reached between the would-be merger partners. See Greenfield v. Heublein, Inc., 742 F.2d 751, 757 (CA3 1984), cert. denied, 469 U.S. 1215 (1985). By definition, then, information concerning any negotiations not yet at the agreement-in-principle stage could be withheld or even misrepresented without a violation of Rule 10b–5.

Three rationales have been offered in support of the "agreement-in-principle" test. The first derives from the concern expressed in TSC Industries that an investor not be overwhelmed by excessively detailed and trivial information, and focuses on the substantial risk that preliminary merger discussions may collapse: because such discussions are inherently tentative, disclosure of their existence itself could mislead investors and foster false optimism. See Greenfield v. Heublein, Inc., 742 F.2d, at 756; Reiss v. Pan American World Airways, Inc., 711 F.2d 11, 14 (CA2 1983). The other two justifications for the agreement-in-principle standard are based on management concerns: because the requirement of "agreement-in-principle" limits the scope of disclosure obligations, it helps preserve the confidentiality of merger discussions

---

9. We do not address here any other kinds of contingent or speculative information, such as earnings forecasts or projections. See generally Hiler, The SEC and the Courts' Approach to Disclosure of Earnings Projections, Asset Appraisals, and Other Soft Information: Old Problems, Changing Views, 46 Md.L.Rev. 1114 (1987).

10. See Staffin v. Greenberg, 672 F.2d 1196, 1207 (CA3 1982) (defining duty to disclose existence of ongoing merger negotiations as triggered when agreement-in-principle is reached); Greenfield v. Heublein, Inc., 742 F.2d 751 (CA3 1984) (applying agreement-in-principle test to materiality inquiry), cert. denied, 469 U.S. 1215 (1985). Citing Staffin, the United States Court of Appeals for the Second Circuit has

rejected a claim that defendant was under an obligation to disclose various events related to merger negotiations. Reiss v. Pan American World Airways, Inc., 711 F.2d 11, 13–14 (CA2 1983). The Seventh Circuit recently endorsed the agreement-in-principle test of materiality. See Flamm v. Eberstadt, 814 F.2d 1169, 1174–1179 (CA7) (describing agreement-in-principle as an agreement on price and structure), cert. denied, ___ U.S. ___ (1987). In some of these cases it is unclear whether the court based its decision on a finding that no duty arose to reveal the existence of negotiations, or whether it concluded that the negotiations were immaterial under an interpretation of the opinion in TSC Industries, Inc. v. Northway, Inc., supra.

where earlier disclosure might prejudice the negotiations; and the test also provides a usable, bright-line rule for determining when disclosure must be made. See Greenfield v. Heublein, Inc., 742 F.2d, at 757; Flamm v. Eberstadt, 814 F.2d 1169, 1176–1178 (CA7), cert. denied, ___ U.S. ___ (1987).

None of these policy-based rationales, however, purports to explain why drawing the line at agreement-in-principle reflects the significance of the information upon the investor's decision. The first rationale, and the only one connected to the concerns expressed in TSC Industries, stands soundly rejected, even by a Court of Appeals that otherwise has accepted the wisdom of the agreement-in-principle test. "It assumes that investors are nitwits, unable to appreciate—even when told—that mergers are risky propositions up until the closing." Flamm v. Eberstadt, 814 F.2d, at 1175. Disclosure, and not paternalistic withholding of accurate information, is the policy chosen and expressed by Congress. We have recognized time and again, a "fundamental purpose" of the various securities acts, "was to substitute a philosophy of full disclosure for the philosophy of *caveat emptor* and thus to achieve a high standard of business ethics in the securities industry." SEC v. Capital Gains Research Bureau, Inc., 375 U.S. 180, 186 (1963). * * * The role of the materiality requirement is not to "attribute to investors a child-like simplicity, an inability to grasp the probabilistic significance of negotiations," Flamm v. Eberstadt, 814 F.2d, at 1175, but to filter out essentially useless information that a reasonable investor would not consider significant, even as part of a larger "mix" of factors to consider in making his investment decision. TSC Industries, Inc. v. Northway, Inc., 426 U.S., at 448–449.

The second rationale, the importance of secrecy during the early stages of merger discussions, also seems irrelevant to an assessment whether their existence is significant to the trading decision of a reasonable investor. To avoid a "bidding war" over its target, an acquiring firm often will insist that negotiations remain confidential, see, e.g., In re Carnation Co., Exchange Act Release No. 22214, 33 SEC Docket 1025 (1985), and at least one Court of Appeals has stated that "silence pending settlement of the price and structure of a deal is beneficial to most investors, most of the time." Flamm v. Eberstadt, 814 F.2d, at 1177.

We need not ascertain, however, whether secrecy necessarily maximizes shareholder wealth—although we note that the proposition is at least disputed as a matter of theory and empirical research [12]—for this

---

12. See, e.g., Brown, Corporate Secrecy, the Federal Securities Laws, and the Disclosure of Ongoing Negotiations, 36 Cath. U.L.Rev. 93, 145–155 (1986); Bebchuk, The Case for Facilitating Competing Tender Offers, 95 Harv.L.Rev. 1028 (1982); Flamm v. Eberstadt, 814 F.2d, at 1177, n. 2 (citing scholarly debate). See also In re Carnation Co., Exchange Act Release No. 22214, 33 SEC Docket 1025, 1030 (1985) ("The impor- tance of accurate and complete issuer disclosure to the integrity of the securities markets cannot be overemphasized. To the extent that investors cannot rely upon the accuracy and completeness of issuer statements, they will be less likely to invest, thereby reducing the liquidity of the securities markets to the detriment of investors and issuers alike").

case does not concern the timing of a disclosure; it concerns only its accuracy and completeness. We face here the narrow question whether information concerning the existence and status of preliminary merger discussions is significant to the reasonable investor's trading decision. Arguments based on the premise that some disclosure would be "premature" in a sense are more properly considered under the rubric of an issuer's duty to disclose. The "secrecy" rationale is simply inapposite to the definition of materiality.

The final justification offered in support of the agreement-in-principle test seems to be directed solely at the comfort of corporate managers. A bright-line rule indeed is easier to follow than a standard that requires the exercise of judgment in the light of all the circumstances. But ease of application alone is not an excuse for ignoring the purposes of the securities acts and Congress' policy decisions. Any approach that designates a single fact or occurrence as always determinative of an inherently fact-specific finding such as materiality, must necessarily be over- or underinclusive. In *TSC Industries* this Court explained: "The determination [of materiality] requires delicate assessments of the inferences a 'reasonable shareholder' would draw from a given set of facts and the significance of those inferences to him. * * *" 426 U.S., at 450. After much study, the Advisory Committee on Corporate Disclosure cautioned the SEC against administratively confining materiality to a rigid formula.[14] Courts also would do well to heed this advice.

We therefore find no valid justification for artificially excluding from the definition of materiality information concerning merger discussions, which would otherwise be considered significant to the trading decision of a reasonable investor, merely because agreement-in-principle as to price and structure has not yet been reached by the parties or their representatives.

The Sixth Circuit explicitly rejected the agreement-in-principle test, as we do today, but in its place adopted a rule that, if taken literally, would be equally insensitive, in our view, to the distinction between materiality and the other elements of an action under Rule 10b–5:

> "When a company whose stock is publicly traded makes a statement, as Basic did, that 'no negotiations' are underway, and that the corporation knows of 'no reason for the stock's activity,' and that 'management is unaware of any present or pending corporate development that would result in the abnormally heavy trading activity,' information concerning ongoing

14. "Although the Committee believes that ideally it would be desirable to have absolute certainty in the application of the materiality concept, it is its view that such a goal is illusory and unrealistic. The materiality concept is judgmental in nature and it is not possible to translate this into a numerical formula. The Committee's advice to the [SEC] is to avoid this quest for certainty and to continue consideration of materiality on a case-by-case basis as problems are identified."

Report of the Advisory Committee on Corporate Disclosure to the Securities and Exchange Commission 327 (House Committee on Interstate and Foreign Commerce, 95th Cong., 1st Sess.) (Comm.Print) (1977).

acquisition discussions becomes material *by virtue of the statement denying their existence.*

* * *

In analyzing whether information regarding merger discussions is material such that it must be affirmatively disclosed to avoid a violation of Rule 10b–5, the discussions and their progress are the primary considerations. However, once a statement is made denying the existence of any discussions, even discussions that might not have been material in absence of the denial are material because they make the statement made untrue." 786 F.2d, at 748–749 (emphasis in original).

This approach, however, fails to recognize that, in order to prevail on a Rule 10b–5 claim, a plaintiff must show that the statements were *misleading* as to a *material* fact. It is not enough that a statement is false or incomplete, if the misrepresented fact is otherwise insignificant.

C

Even before this Court's decision in TSC Industries, the Second Circuit had explained the role of the materiality requirement of Rule 10b–5, with respect to contingent or speculative information or events, in a manner that gave that term meaning that is independent of the other provisions of the Rule. Under such circumstances, materiality "will depend at any given time upon a balancing of both the indicated probability that the event will occur and the anticipated magnitude of the event in light of the totality of the company activity." SEC v. Texas Gulf Sulphur Co., 401 F.2d, at 849. Interestingly, neither the Third Circuit decision adopting the agreement-in-principle test nor petitioners here take issue with this general standard. Rather, they suggest that with respect to preliminary merger discussions, there are good reasons to draw a line at agreement on price and structure. In a subsequent decision, the late Judge Friendly, writing for a Second Circuit panel, applied the Texas Gulf Sulphur probability/magnitude approach in the specific context of preliminary merger negotiations. After acknowledging that materiality is something to be determined on the basis of the particular facts of each case, he stated:

"Since a merger in which it is bought out is the most important event that can occur in a small corporation's life, to wit, its death, we think that inside information, as regards a merger of this sort, can become material at an earlier stage than would be the case as regards lesser transactions—and this even though the mortality rate of mergers in such formative stages is doubtless high."

SEC v. Geon Industries, Inc., 531 F.2d 39, 47–48 (CA2 1976). We agree with that analysis.

Whether merger discussions in any particular case are material therefore depends on the facts. Generally, in order to assess the probability that the event will occur, a factfinder will need to look to indicia of interest in the transaction at the highest corporate levels.

Without attempting to catalog all such possible factors, we note by way of example that board resolutions, instructions to investment bankers, and actual negotiations between principals or their intermediaries may serve as indicia of interest. To assess the magnitude of the transaction to the issuer of the securities allegedly manipulated, a factfinder will need to consider such facts as the size of the two corporate entities and of the potential premiums over market value. No particular event or factor short of closing the transaction need be either necessary or sufficient by itself to render merger discussions material.[17]

As we clarify today, materiality depends on the significance the reasonable investor would place on the withheld or misrepresented information.[18] The fact-specific inquiry we endorse here is consistent with the approach a number of courts have taken in assessing the materiality of merger negotiations. Because the standard of materiality we have adopted differs from that used by both courts below, we remand the case for reconsideration of the question whether a grant of summary judgment is appropriate on this record.

---

17. To be actionable, of course, a statement must also be misleading. Silence, absent a duty to disclose, is not misleading under Rule 10b–5. "No comment" statements are generally the functional equivalent of silence. See In re Carnation Co., supra. See also New York Stock Exchange Listed Company Manual § 202.01, reprinted in 3 CCH Fed.Sec.L.Rep. ¶ 23,515 (premature public announcement may properly be delayed for valid business purpose and where adequate security can be maintained); American Stock Exchange Company Guide §§ 401–405, reprinted in 3 CCH Fed.Sec.L.Rep. ¶¶ 23, 124A–23, 124E (similar provisions).

It has been suggested that given current market practices, a "no comment" statement is tantamount to an admission that merger discussions are underway. See Flamm v. Eberstadt, 814 F.2d, at 1178. That may well hold true to the extent that issuers adopt a policy of truthfully denying merger rumors when no discussions are underway, and of issuing "no comment" statements when they are in the midst of negotiations. There are, of course, other statement policies firms could adopt; we need not now advise issuers as to what kind of practice to follow, within the range permitted by law. Perhaps more importantly, we think that creating an exception to a regulatory scheme founded on a pro-disclosure legislative philosophy, because complying with the regulation might be "bad for business," is a role for Congress, not this Court. See also id., at 1182 (opinion concurring in the judgment and concurring in part).

18. We find no authority in the statute, the legislative history, or our previous decisions, for varying the standard of materiality depending on who brings the action or whether insiders are alleged to have profited. See, e.g., Pavlidis v. New England Patriots Football Club, Inc., 737 F.2d 1227, 1231 (CA1 1984) ("A fact does not become more material to the shareholder's decision because it is withheld by an insider, or because the insider might profit by withholding it"); cf. Aaron v. SEC, 446 U.S. 680, 691 (1980) ("scienter is an element of a violation of § 10(b) and Rule 10b–5, regardless of the identity of the plaintiff or the nature of the relief sought").

We recognize that trading (and profit making) by insiders can serve as an indication of materiality, see SEC v. Texas Gulf Sulphur Co., 401 F.2d, at 851; General Portland, Inc. v. LaFarge Coppee S.A., CCH Fed.Sec.L.Rep. (1982–1983 Transfer Binder) ¶ 99,148, p. 95,544 (ND Tex.1981). We are not prepared to agree, however, that "[i]n cases of the disclosure of inside information to a favored few, determination of materiality has a different aspect than when the issue is, for example, an inaccuracy in a publicly disseminated press release." SEC v. Geon Industries, Inc., 531 F.2d 39, 48 (CA2 1976). Devising two different standards of materiality, one for situations where insiders have traded in abrogation of their duty to disclose or abstain (or for that matter when any disclosure duty has been breached), and another covering affirmative misrepresentations by those under no duty to disclose (but under the ever-present duty not to mislead), would effectively collapse the materiality requirement into the analysis of defendant's disclosure duties.

IV

A

We turn to the question of reliance and the fraud-on-the-market theory. Succinctly put:

"The fraud on the market theory is based on the hypothesis that, in an open and developed securities market, the price of a company's stock is determined by the available material information regarding the company and its business. * * * Misleading statements will therefore defraud purchasers of stock even if the purchasers do not directly rely on the misstatements. * * * The causal connection between the defendants' fraud and the plaintiffs' purchase of stock in such a case is no less significant than in a case of direct reliance on misrepresentations." Peil v. Speiser, 806 F.2d 1154, 1160–1161 (CA3 1986).

Our task, of course, is not to assess the general validity of the theory, but to consider whether it was proper for the courts below to apply a rebuttable presumption of reliance, supported in part by the fraud-on-the-market theory. * * *

This case required resolution of several common questions of law and fact concerning the falsity or misleading nature of the three public statements made by Basic, the presence or absence of scienter, and the materiality of the misrepresentations, if any. In their amended complaint, the named plaintiffs alleged that in reliance on Basic's statements they sold their shares of Basic stock in the depressed market created by petitioners. * * * Requiring proof of individualized reliance from each member of the proposed plaintiff class effectively would have prevented respondents from proceeding with a class action, since individual issues then would have overwhelmed the common ones. The District Court found that the presumption of reliance created by the fraud-on-the-market theory provided "a practical resolution to the problem of balancing the substantive requirement of proof of reliance in securities cases against the procedural requisites of [Fed.Rule Civ. Proc.] 23." The District Court thus concluded that with reference to each public statement and its impact upon the open market for Basic shares, common questions predominated over individual questions, as required by Fed.Rule Civ.Proc. 23(a)(2) and (b)(3).

Petitioners and their *amici* complain that the fraud-on-the-market theory effectively eliminates the requirement that a plaintiff asserting a claim under Rule 10b–5 prove reliance. They note that reliance is and long has been an element of common-law fraud, see e.g., Restatement (Second) of Torts § 525 (1977); Prosser and Keeton on The Law of Torts § 108 (5th ed. 1984), and argue that because the analogous express right of action includes a reliance requirement, see, e.g., § 18(a) of the 1934 Act, as amended, 15 U.S.C. § 78r(a), so too must an action implied under § 10(b).

We agree that reliance is an element of a Rule 10b–5 cause of action. See Ernst & Ernst v. Hochfelder, 425 U.S., at 206 (quoting

Senate Report). Reliance provides the requisite causal connection between a defendant's misrepresentation and a plaintiff's injury. * * * There is, however, more than one way to demonstrate the causal connection. Indeed, we previously have dispensed with a requirement of positive proof of reliance, where a duty to disclose material information had been breached, concluding that the necessary nexus between the plaintiffs' injury and the defendant's wrongful conduct had been established. See Affiliated Ute Citizens v. United States, 406 U.S., at 153–154. Similarly, we did not require proof that material omissions or misstatements in a proxy statement decisively affected voting, because the proxy solicitation itself, rather than the defect in the solicitation materials, served as an essential link in the transaction. See Mills v. Electric Auto–Lite Co., 396 U.S. 375, 384–385 (1970).

The modern securities markets, literally involving millions of shares changing hands daily, differ from the face-to-face transactions contemplated by early fraud cases, and our understanding of Rule 10b–5's reliance requirement must encompass these differences.

> "In face-to-face transactions, the inquiry into an investor's reliance upon information is into the subjective pricing of that information by that investor. With the presence of a market, the market is interposed between seller and buyer and, ideally, transmits information to the investor in the processed form of a market price. Thus the market is performing a substantial part of the valuation process performed by the investor in a face-to-face transaction. The market is acting as the unpaid agent of the investor, informing him that given all the information available to it, the value of the stock is worth the market price." In re LTV Securities Litigation, 88 F.R.D. 134, 143 (ND Tex.1980).

> * * *

B

Presumptions typically serve to assist courts in managing circumstances in which direct proof, for one reason or another, is rendered difficult. See, e.g., D. Louisell & C. Mueller, Federal Evidence 541–542 (1977). The courts below accepted a presumption, created by the fraud-on-the-market theory and subject to rebuttal by petitioners, that persons who had traded Basic shares had done so in reliance on the integrity of the price set by the market, but because of petitioners' material misrepresentations that price had been fraudulently depressed. Requiring a plaintiff to show a speculative state of facts, i.e., how he would have acted if omitted material information had been disclosed, see Affiliated Ute Citizens v. United States, 406 U.S., at 153–154, or if the misrepresentation had not been made, see Sharp v. Coopers & Lybrand, 649 F.2d 175, 188 (CA3 1981), cert. denied, 455 U.S. 938 (1982), would place an unnecessarily unrealistic evidentiary burden on the Rule 10b–5 plaintiff who has traded on an impersonal market. Cf. Mills v. Electric Auto–Lite Co., 396 U.S., at 385.

Arising out of considerations of fairness, public policy, and probability, as well as judicial economy, presumptions are also useful devices for allocating the burdens of proof between parties. See E. Cleary, McCormick on Evidence 968–969 (3rd ed. 1984); see also Fed.Rule Evid. 301 and notes. The presumption of reliance employed in this case is consistent with, and, by facilitating Rule 10b–5 litigation, supports, the congressional policy embodied in the 1934 Act. In drafting that Act, Congress expressly relied on the premise that securities markets are affected by information, and enacted legislation to facilitate an investor's reliance on the integrity of those markets:

> "No investor, no speculator, can safely buy and sell securities upon the exchanges without having an intelligent basis for forming his judgment as to the value of the securities he buys or sells. The idea of a free and open public market is built upon the theory that competing judgments of buyers and sellers as to the fair price of a security brings [*sic*] about a situation where the market price reflects as nearly as possible a just price. Just as artificial manipulation tends to upset the true function of an open market, so the hiding and secreting of important information obstructs the operation of the markets as indices of real value." H.R.Rep. No. 1383, supra, at 11.

See Lipton v. Documation, Inc., 734 F.2d 740, 748 (CA11 1984), cert. denied, 469 U.S. 1132 (1985).

The presumption is also supported by common sense and probability. Recent empirical studies have tended to confirm Congress' premise that the market price of shares traded on well-developed markets reflects all publicly available information, and, hence, any material misrepresentations.[24] It has been noted that "it is hard to imagine that there ever is a buyer or seller who does not rely on market integrity. Who would knowingly roll the dice in a crooked crap game?" Schlanger v. Four–Phase Systems Inc., 555 F.Supp. 535, 538 (SDNY 1982). Indeed, nearly every court that has considered the proposition has concluded that where materially misleading statements have been disseminated into an impersonal, well-developed market for securities, the reliance of individual plaintiffs on the integrity of the market price may be presumed. Commentators generally have applauded the adoption of one variation or another of the fraud-on-the-market theory. An investor who buys or sells stock at the price set by the market does so in reliance on the integrity of that price. Because most publicly

---

24. See In re LTV Securities Litigation, 88 F.R.D. 134, 144 (ND Tex.1980) (citing studies); Fischel, Use of Modern Finance Theory in Securities Fraud Cases Involving Actively Traded Securities, 38 Bus.Law. 1, 4, n. 9 (1982) (citing literature on efficient-capital-market theory); Dennis, Materiality and the Efficient Capital Market Model: A Recipe for the Total Mix, 25 Wm. & Mary L.Rev. 373, 374–381, and n. 1 (1984). We need not determine by adjudication what economists and social scientists have debated through the use of sophisticated statistical analysis and the application of economic theory. For purposes of accepting the presumption of reliance in this case, we need only believe that market professionals generally consider most publicly announced material statements about companies, thereby affecting stock market prices.

available information is reflected in market price, an investor's reliance on any public material misrepresentations, therefore, may be presumed for purposes of a Rule 10b–5 action.

C

The Court of Appeals found that petitioners "made public, material misrepresentations and [respondents] sold Basic stock in an impersonal, efficient market. Thus the class, as defined by the district court, has established the threshold facts for proving their loss." 786 F.2d, at 751. The court acknowledged that petitioners may rebut proof of the elements giving rise to the presumption, or show that the misrepresentation in fact did not lead to a distortion of price or that an individual plaintiff traded or would have traded despite his knowing the statement was false. Id., at 750, n. 6.

Any showing that severs the link between the alleged misrepresentation and either the price received (or paid) by the plaintiff, or his decision to trade at a fair market price, will be sufficient to rebut the presumption of reliance. For example, if petitioners could show that the "market makers" were privy to the truth about the merger discussions here with Combustion, and thus that the market price would not have been affected by their misrepresentations, the causal connection could be broken: the basis for finding that the fraud had been transmitted through market price would be gone. Similarly, if, despite petitioners' allegedly fraudulent attempt to manipulate market price, news of the merger discussions credibly entered the market and dissipated the effects of the misstatements, those who traded Basic shares after the corrective statements would have no direct or indirect connection with the fraud.[29] Petitioners also could rebut the presumption of reliance as to plaintiffs who would have divested themselves of their Basic shares without relying on the integrity of the market. For example, a plaintiff who believed that Basic's statements were false and that Basic was indeed engaged in merger discussions, and who consequently believed that Basic stock was artificially underpriced, but sold his shares nevertheless because of other unrelated concerns, e.g., potential antitrust problems, or political pressures to divest from shares of certain businesses, could not be said to have relied on the integrity of a price he knew had been manipulated.

V

* * *

---

29. We note there may be a certain incongruity between the assumption that Basic shares are traded on a well-developed, efficient, and information-hungry market, and the allegation that such a market could remain misinformed, and its valuation of Basic shares depressed, for 14 months, on the basis of the three public statements. Proof of that sort is a matter for trial, throughout which the District Court retains the authority to amend the certification order as may be appropriate. See Fed.Rule Civ.Proc. 23(c)(1) and (c)(4). See 7B C. Wright, A. Miller & M. Kane, Federal Practice and Procedure 128–132 (1986). Thus, we see no need to engage in the kind of factual analysis the dissent suggests that manifests the "oddities" of applying a rebuttable presumption of reliance in this case. * * *

The judgment of the Court of Appeals is vacated and the case is remanded to that court for further proceedings consistent with this opinion. It is so ordered.

———

Justice WHITE, with whom Justice O'CONNOR joins, concurring in part and dissenting in part.

I join Parts I–III of the Court's opinion, as I agree that the standard of materiality we set forth in TSC Industries, Inc. v. Northway, Inc., 426 U.S. 438, 449 (1976), should be applied to actions under § 10(b) and Rule 10b–5. But I dissent from the remainder of the Court's holding because I do not agree that the "fraud-on-the-market" theory should be applied in this case.

I

Even when compared to the relatively youthful private cause-of-action under § 10(b), see Kardon v. National Gypsum Co., 69 F.Supp. 512 (ED Pa.1946), the fraud-on-the-market theory is a mere babe. Yet today, the Court embraces this theory with the sweeping confidence usually reserved for more mature legal doctrines. In so doing, I fear that the Court's decision may have many adverse, unintended effects as it is applied and interpreted in the years to come.

A

At the outset, I note that there are portions of the Court's fraud-on-the-market holding with which I am in agreement. Most importantly, the Court rejects the version of that theory, heretofore adopted by some courts, which equates "causation" with "reliance," and permits recovery by a plaintiff who claims merely to have been harmed by a material misrepresentation which altered a market price, notwithstanding proof that the plaintiff did not in any way rely on that price. * * * I agree with the Court that if Rule 10b–5's reliance requirement is to be left with any content at all, the fraud-on-the-market presumption must be capable of being rebutted by a showing that a plaintiff did not "rely" on the market price. For example, a plaintiff who decides, months in advance of an alleged misrepresentation, to purchase a stock; one who buys or sells a stock for reasons unrelated to its price; one who actually sells a stock "short" days before the misrepresentation is made—surely none of these people can state a valid claim under Rule 10b–5. Yet, some federal courts have allowed such claims to stand under one variety or another of the fraud-on-the-market theory.

Happily, the majority puts to rest the prospect of recovery under such circumstances. A nonrebuttable presumption of reliance—or even worse, allowing recovery in the face of "affirmative evidence of nonreliance," Zweig v. Hearst Corp., 594 F.2d 1261, 1272 (CA9 1979) (Ely, J., dissenting)—would effectively convert Rule 10b–5 into "a scheme of investor's insurance." Shores v. Sklar, 647 F.2d 462, 469, n. 5 (CA5

1981) (en banc), cert. denied, 459 U.S. 1102 (1983). There is no support in the Securities Act, the Rule, or our cases for such a result.

B

But even as the Court attempts to limit the fraud-on-the-market theory it endorses today, the pitfalls in its approach are revealed by previous uses by the lower courts of the broader versions of the theory. Confusion and contradiction in court rulings are inevitable when traditional legal analysis is replaced with economic theorization by the federal courts.

In general, the case law developed in this Court with respect to § 10(b) and Rule 10b–5 has been based on doctrines with which we, as judges, are familiar: common-law doctrines of fraud and deceit. See, e.g., Santa Fe Industries, Inc. v. Green, 430 U.S. 462, 471–477 (1977). Even when we have extended civil liability under Rule 10b–5 to a broader reach than the common law had previously permitted, * * * we have retained familiar legal principles as or guideposts. See, e.g., Herman & MacLean v. Huddleston, 459 U.S. 375, 389–390 (1983). The federal courts have proved adept at developing an evolving jurisprudence of Rule 10b–5 in such a manner. But with no staff economists, no experts schooled in the "efficient-capital-market hypothesis," no ability to test the validity of empirical market studies, we are not well equipped to embrace novel constructions of a statute based on contemporary microeconomic theory.[4]

The "wrong turns" in those Court of Appeals and district court fraud-on-the-market decisions which the Court implicitly rejects as going too far should be ample illustration of the dangers when economic theories replace legal rules as the basis for recovery. Yet the Court today ventures into this area beyond its expertise, beyond—by its own admission—the confines of our previous fraud cases. * * * Even if I agreed with the Court that "modern securities markets * * * involving millions of shares changing hands daily" require that the "understanding of Rule 10b–5's reliance requirement" be changed, * * * I prefer that such changes come from Congress in amending § 10(b). The Congress, with its superior resources and expertise, is far better equipped than the federal courts for the task of determining how modern economic theory and global financial markets require that established legal notions of fraud be modified. In choosing to make these decisions itself, the Court, I fear, embarks on a course that it does not genuinely understand, giving rise to consequences it cannot foresee.

---

4. This view was put well by two commentators who wrote a few years ago:

"Of all recent developments in financial economics, the efficient capital market hypothesis ("ECMH") has achieved the widest acceptance by the legal culture. * * *

"Yet the legal culture's remarkably rapid and broad acceptance of an economic concept that did not exist twenty years ago is not matched by an equivalent degree of *understanding*." Gilson & Kraakman, The Mechanisms of Market Efficiency, 70 Va.L.Rev. 549, 549–550 (1984) (footnotes omitted; emphasis added).

While the fraud-on-the-market theory has gained even broader acceptance since 1984, I doubt that it has achieved any greater understanding.

For while the economists' theories which underpin the fraud-on-the-market presumption may have the appeal of mathematical exactitude and scientific certainty, they are—in the end—nothing more than theories which may or may not prove accurate upon further consideration. Even the most earnest advocates of economic analysis of the law recognize this. See, e.g., Easterbrook, Afterword: Knowledge and Answers, 85 Colum.L.Rev. 1117, 1118 (1985). Thus, while the majority states that, for purposes of reaching its result it need only make modest assumptions about the way in which "market professionals generally" do their jobs, and how the conduct of market professionals affects stock prices, * * * I doubt that we are in much of a position to assess which theories aptly describe the functioning of the securities industry.

Consequently, I cannot join the Court in its effort to reconfigure the securities laws, based on recent economic theories, to better fit what it perceives to be the new realities of financial markets. I would leave this task to others more equipped for the job than we.

C

At the bottom of the Court's conclusion that the fraud-on-the-market theory sustains a presumption of reliance is the assumption that individuals rely "on the integrity of the market price" when buying or selling stock in "impersonal, well-developed market[s] for securities." * * * Even if I was prepared to accept (as a matter of common sense or general understanding) the assumption that most persons buying or selling stock do so in response to the market price, the fraud-on-the-market theory goes further. For in adopting a "presumption of reliance," the Court also assumes that buyers and sellers rely—not just on the market price—but on the "integrity" of that price. It is this aspect of the fraud-on-the-market hypothesis which most mystifies me.

To define the term "integrity of the market price," the majority quotes approvingly from cases which suggest that investors are entitled to " 'rely on the price of a stock as a reflection of its value.' " * * * But the meaning of this phrase eludes me, for it implicitly suggests that stocks have some "true value" that is measurable by a standard other than their market price. While the Scholastics of Medieval times professed a means to make such a valuation of a commodity's "worth," I doubt that the federal courts of our day are similarly equipped.

Even if securities had some "value"—knowable and distinct from the market price of a stock—investors do not always share the Court's presumption that a stock's price is a "reflection of [this] value." Indeed, "many investors purchase or sell stock because they believe the price inaccurately reflects the corporation's worth." See Black, Fraud on the Market: A Criticism of Dispensing with Reliance Requirements in Certain Open Market Transactions, 62 N.C.L.Rev. 435, 455 (1984) (emphasis added). If investors really believed that stock prices reflected a stock's "value," many sellers would never sell, and many buyers never buy (given the time and cost associated with executing a stock transaction). As we recognized just a few years ago: "[I]nvestors act on inevitably incomplete or inaccurate information, [consequently] there are always winners and losers; but those who have 'lost' have not necessarily been defrauded." Dirks v. SEC, 463 U.S. 646, 667, n. 27 (1983). Yet today, the Court allows investors to recover who can show little more than that they sold stock at a lower price than what might have been.[7]

I do not propose that the law retreat from the many protections that § 10(b) and Rule 10b–5, as interpreted in our prior cases, provide to investors. But any extension of these laws, to approach something closer to an investor insurance scheme, should come from Congress, and not from the courts.

II

Congress has not passed on the fraud-on-the-market theory the Court embraces today. That is reason enough for us to abstain from doing so. But it is even more troubling that, to the extent that any view of Congress on this question can be inferred indirectly, it is contrary to the result the majority reaches.

* * *

III

Finally, the particular facts of this case make it an exceedingly poor candidate for the Court's fraud-on-the-market theory, and illustrate the illogic achieved by that theory's application in many cases. Respondents here are a class of sellers who sold Basic stock between October, 1977 and December 1978, a fourteen-month period. At the time the class period began, Basic's stock was trading at $20 a share (at the time, an all-time high); the last members of the class to sell their Basic stock got a price of just over $30 a share. * * * It is indisputable that virtually every member of the class made money from his or her sale of Basic stock. The oddities of applying the fraud-on-the-market theory in this case are manifest. First, there are the facts that the plaintiffs are sellers and the class period is so lengthy—both are virtually without precedent in prior fraud-on-the-market cases.

Second, there is the fact that in this case, there is no evidence that petitioner's officials made the troublesome misstatements for the purpose of manipulating stock prices, or with any intent to engage in underhanded trading of Basic stock. Indeed, during the class period, petitioners do not appear to have purchased or sold any Basic stock whatsoever. * * * I agree with amicus who argues that "[i]mposition

---

7. This is what the Court's rule boils down to in practical terms. For while, in theory, the Court allows for rebuttal of its "presumption of reliance"—a proviso with which I agree, * * * in practice the Court must realize, as other courts applying the fraud-on-the-market theory have, that such rebuttal is virtually impossible in all but the most extraordinary case. * * *

Consequently, while the Court considers it significant that the fraud-on-the-market presumption it endorses is a rebuttable one, * * * the majority's implicit rejection of the "pure causation" fraud-on-the-market theory rings hollow. In most cases, the Court's theory will operate just as the causation theory would, creating a non-rebuttable presumption of "reliance" in future 10b–5 actions.

of damages liability under Rule 10b–5 makes little sense * * * where a defendant is neither a purchaser nor a seller of securities." See Brief for American Corporate Counsel Association as Amicus Curiae 13.

* * *

Third, there are the peculiarities of what kinds of investors will be able to recover in this case. As I read the District Court's class certification order, * * * there are potentially many persons who did not purchase Basic stock until after the first false statement (October 1977), but who nonetheless will be able to recover under the Court's fraud-on-the-market theory. Thus, it is possible that a person who heard the first corporate misstatement and disbelieved it—i.e., someone who purchased Basic stock thinking that petitioners' statement was false—may still be included in the plaintiff-class on remand. How a person who undertook such a speculative stock-investing strategy—and made $10 a share doing so (if he bought on October 22, 1977, and sold on December 15, 1978)—can say that he was "defrauded" by virtue of his reliance on the "integrity" of the market price is beyond me. And such speculators may not be uncommon, at least in this case. * * *

Indeed, the facts of this case lead a casual observer to the almost inescapable conclusion that many of those who bought or sold Basic stock during the period in question flatly disbelieved the statements which are alleged to have been "materially misleading." Despite three statements denying that merger negotiations were underway, Basic stock hit record-high after record-high during the 14–month class period. * * *

And who will pay the judgments won in such actions? I suspect that all too often the majority's rule will "lead to large judgments, payable in the last analysis by innocent investors, for the benefit of speculators and their lawyers." Cf. SEC v. Texas Gulf Sulphur Co., 401 F.2d 833, 867 (CA2 1968) (en banc) (Friendly, J., concurring), cert. denied, 394 U.S. 976 (1969). * * *

NOTE: MISREPRESENTATIONS, SILENCE, MERGERS AND OTHER SOFT INFORMATION

1. *Misrepresentations.*

Macey and Miller, Good Finance, Bad Economics: An Analysis of the Fraud-on-the-Market Theory, 42 Stan.L.Rev. 1059, 1072, 1075–76 (1990), takes issue with the result in the case. Putting the matter into a hypothetical contract framework, Macey and Miller argue that most investors would agree in advance to permit management fraud in some cases, so long as management's actions cause the stock value to be maximized in the long run. They assert that legal intervention against management fraud is necessary only where as a result of the fraud the stock price goes up, thus externalizing the social cost of the lie. Where, as in *Basic*, the misrepresentation causes the stock price to go down, the firm's cost of capital goes up, and the cost is internalized, there should be no liability. For a response to this, see Ayres, Back to *Basics: Regulating How Corporations Speak to the Market*, 77 Va.L.Rev. 945 (1991).

2. *Merger Negotiations and Silence.*

Suppose Basic had made a "no comment" response to all inquiries about merger negotiations. Would it thereby have breached a duty to disclose to a stockholder in plaintiff's position? If not, would the price-and-structure rule come to bear, despite the *Basic* opinion?

Justice Blackmun refers to financial economics to support the "fraud on the market" theory of reliance. But what approach is counselled by the precepts of financial economics on the matter of disclosure of merger negotiations?

Consider, in connection with these questions, the opinion of Judge Easterbrook in **Flamm v. Eberstadt,** 814 F.2d 1169 (7th Cir.1987), cert. denied, 484 U.S. 853 (1987). The 10b–5 plaintiff there sold stock of a tender offer target corporation after the tender offer but before the announcement of a competing friendly tender offer at a higher price. Plaintiff contended that the target's search for a White Knight should have been disclosed. Unlike the corporation in *Basic*, no false denials had been issued.

Judge Easterbrook, approved the price-and-structure rule as follows, pp. 1176–1177:

"[Plaintiff contends] that silence is not beneficial to all investors, that there is a conflict of interest between investors who sell before the disclosure and investors who hold, thereby receiving the benefits later on. See Ronald J. Gilson, The Law and Finance of Corporate Acquisitions 977 (1986). Perhaps so, although the corporation is not required by the securities law to favor hair-trigger sellers over other investors. From a longer perspective, however, even this conflict disappears. Investors who wanted to prescribe their managers' behavior during merger discussions would favor a rule of silence until the discussions had reached agreement on price and structure. Such discussions may occur anytime during the life of the firm. Ex ante, each investor's chance of selling during that window is small. The chance of selling for "too little" is offset by an identical chance of buying at a bargain; every sale has a buyer and a seller. Over the long run, then, the prospect of selling for too little and buying a bargain are a wash, leaving only the prospect of receiving (or scaring away) beneficial opportunities to merge. All investors would prefer whichever approach maximized their anticipated wealth. The legal rule governing disclosure is like this hypothetical bargain among investors. It applies to all firms, to all investors be they buyers or sellers, at all times. In selecting a legal rule, a court must consider the effects on all investors in all firms, not just the effects on the plaintiff.

"Even the unlucky investors, such as Flamm, who sell their stock in a particular firm too soon can take comfort in knowing that they do not lose the whole gain. To the extent the appearance of White Knights is predictable, the probability of a White Knight appearing in this contest will be reflected in the price of the stock. Most buyers during tender offer contests are arbitrageurs, professional investors who are exceptionally knowledgeable. These professionals make money by taking risk—they take the risk that all bids will vanish (and the price fall here to $11.75) in exchange for the prospect of gain from the offer (here at $17) and the chance of a higher bid. When Flamm sold his stock, he passed to the arbitrageurs the risk that the price would fall to $11.75, or even to $17 (he received $17⅜); the arbitrageurs did not take the risk off Flamm's shoulders for free but were compensated by the possibility (remote as of December 29!) of a higher price. Undoubtedly many arbitrageurs had learned that Goldman, Sachs was shopping for a deal. Their bids reflected the value of a potential deal, and Flamm received this value without knowing about the prospects himself. It is not right to reply that the arbitrageurs—"speculators", transient investors—are swiping gains that "belong" to the longer-term investors such as Flamm. Arbitrageurs must compete among themselves to buy stock. The more likely the gain from a later White Knight bid, the more any given arbitrageur is willing to pay for stock. To make a profit the arbitrageur must put his hands on the stock; to acquire the stock he must outbid other arbitrageurs, who have the same end in view; the competition ultimately passes back to Flamm and the other original investors the gains from the probability of a White Knight bid, as of December 29 (or any other date), less the premium for taking risk off Flamm's hands. Premature disclosure could have reduced the chances of an acquisition by a White Knight, and therefore reduced the bids made in the market for Flamm's stock.

"So silence pending settlement of the price and structure of a deal is beneficial to most investors, most of the time. We do not think that the securities laws war against the best interests of investors. Rule 10b–5 is about *fraud* after all, and it is not fraudulent to conduct business in a way that makes investors better off—that all investors prefer ex ante and that most prefer ex post. Cf. Dirks v. SEC, 463 U.S. 646, 653–59 (1983) (liability depends on a "duty" to disclose, duty defined in part to ensure the welfare of investors as a group).

"We agree, too, with the conclusion of the other circuits that the benefits of certainty supply additional support for the price-and-structure rule. If disclosure must occur at an earlier date, how much earlier? That would be a fertile ground for disputation. No matter how soon the firm announced the negotiations, investors could say that it should have done so a little sooner. * * * "

Consider also the solution proposed by Professor Ayres. He places the question in a hypothetical contract model and reasons that a default rule in which corporations warrant the honesty of their statements would best suit market actors. He suggests that corporations contract out of the default rule in their certificates of incorporation by committing in advance to silence in merger negotiation situations. See Ayres, supra at 954–956.

Since the *Basic* decision, courts have taken a range of positions on questions concerning disclosure of proposed transactions or proposed actions respecting publicly disclosed transactions. Compare Taylor v. First Union Corp., 857 F.2d 240 (4th Cir.1988) (banks' agreement in principle to merge if interstate banking becomes legal not material), with Kronfeld v. Trans World Airlines, Inc., 832 F.2d 726 (2d Cir.1987), cert. denied, 485 U.S. 1007 (1988) (securities issuer should have disclosed that corporate restructuring alternatives were under study by investment bankers).

3. *Projections and Silence.*

Reconsider *Starkman v. Marathon* in light of *Basic.* First, would a different result have followed in the case had the court adopted the circumstantial test enunciated by the Third Circuit in *Flynn v. Bass Brothers,* infra p. 989? Does either the *Flynn* test or the bright line exclusion for preliminary negotiations applied in *Starkman* survive *Basic*? Would *Basic* require a different result in *Starkman* on the issue respecting the disclosure of internal appraisal reports? Should the *Starkman* court have required disclosure of the negotiations with U.S. Steel? If the case came up today, would *Basic* require disclosure of those negotiations?

NOTE: MATERIALITY AND CONTEXT

Is the materiality determination respecting a given transaction the same no matter what the disclosure context? Footnote 18 of Justice Blackmun's opinion indicates this—otherwise, it says, the materiality and duty to disclose inquiries begin to collapse into one another. At the same time, the opinion suggests that materiality is a factual determination focusing on probability and magnitude. The question, in effect, is whether an abstract reasonable investor would want the information without regard to context.

Can this neat analytical separation be maintained in practice? Or, given the indeterminacy of the materiality inquiry, will normative considerations going beyond the welfare of a hypothesized rational investor inevitably come into the determination? Consider the following problems:

a. Take internal asset appraisals or earnings projections such as those at issue in the *Starkman* case. Assume that management would be comfortable in releasing this information to analysts or including the information in a selling document put together by an investment banker. But management has grounds to question the ultimate reliability of the projection. Should the projection be considered material and its disclosure be mandatory in any of the following transactions:

1. a registration statement covering a public issue of addition-
    al shares of stock?

2. proxy materials issued in connection with a friendly merg-
    er?

3. proxy materials issued in connection with the merger of a
    51% owned subsidiary with a parent corporation?

4. a cash tender offer by the corporation to repurchase 15% of
    its outstanding shares?

5. market purchases of stock by the corporation's top manag-
    ers?

6. filings by the corporation with the SEC under section 13(a)
    of the 1934 Act (e.g., on form 10K or 10Q)?

b. Would your analysis differ if the same projection was an
external analysis employed by a hostile offeror as the basis for a hostile
tender offer?

c. Now take merger negotiations comparable to those in *Basic*,
and assume that the issuer has made no statement about them. Try
questions 1, 3, 4, 5 and 6.

d. Assume that a particular set of merger negotiations about
which the corporation has made no disclosures has been found to be
immaterial for purposes of a periodic filing under the '34 Act because
the transaction was very uncertain of accomplishment and disclosure
could have caused the transaction to abort. Does it follow that insider
should be allowed to trade without disclosing the negotiations because
they are not material?

———

**BRUDNEY, A NOTE ON MATERIALITY AND
SOFT INFORMATION UNDER THE
FEDERAL SECURITIES LAWS**
75 Va.L.Rev. 723 (1989).
732, 735–745.

* * *

II. MATERIALITY—NORMATIVE PROBLEMS

* * *

The federal securities laws impose a duty to disclose upon a variety
of persons in a variety of circumstances. Two justifications dominated
the initial decision to impose a duty to disclose items of information
that are relevant to investors' efforts to assess the prices of corporate
securities. One rested on the notion that it is desirable to deny to
persons having exclusive possession of certain kinds of information an
advantage over others with whom they effectively transact, but who

cannot lawfully get such information. Whether based on conceptions of fiduciary duty or on a broader rationale, such an advantage over the investing public is to be denied to corporations issuing their securities to the public or buying them back and to corporate insiders (and an assortment of market insiders). The other justification for requiring disclosure is to increase the quantity and improve the quality of corporate information available to investors (without regard to whether the person obliged to disclose is contemplating transacting) so as to facilitate intelligent investment decisions and the efficiency of securities markets in pricing securities and in allocating financial capital to real capital. The two justifications are not mutually exclusive, even though each is supported by different calculations of net benefits (apart from their utility to investors in making a buy, sell, hold, or vote decision) under the particular rules of disclosure it powers. Still another justification for requiring disclosure—that underpinning the Williams Act—has a somewhat different premise than the other two. While it too seeks to make relevant information available to public investors, its basic thrust is to compel disclosure by persons who are outsiders to the corporation involved.

The normative considerations that underlie the above justifications are best seen by examining them in context * * *.

* * *

A. The Transactional Context—Insiders

The bulk of the litigation over the meaning of the materiality of future-oriented information has occurred in the context of transactional disclosure by insiders. The requirement of disclosure in that context—e.g., distribution of securities to the public, insider trading, or corporate repurchase of its own stock in freezeouts, self-tenders, or otherwise—is designed more to deny a trading advantage over the investing public to those possessors of exclusive information than it is to enhance the public investor's ability to make informed investment decisions. The purpose of the requirement helps to define the limits of what must be disclosed. Undisclosed items of information that favor the interests of the knowledgeable transactor are likely to be more reliable, if not also more relevant, to the trading public investor than undisclosed information that does not suggest that the insider will gain from the transaction. Thus, when an insider is buying, projections, asset appraisals, or pending merger negotiations that suggest an increase in the price of a corporation's stock are likely to be of more interest to the rational public transactor than unfavorable projections or asset appraisals. And when the insider is selling, the undisclosed unfavorable information about future prices is likely to be of more interest to the rational public transactor than undisclosed favorable information.

The stronger the interest of the trading public investor in learning of particular undisclosed projections, asset appraisals, or merger discussions that are available to inside transactors, the less relevant the underlying data need be to future prices and the less certain need be the likelihood that the predicted or expected events will materialize in order for the insider's information to be material. Favorable projections or asset appraisals that are problematic, or negotiations for a favorable merger that are still very uncertain, may thus reasonably be required to be disclosed by a buying insider but not by a selling insider. In short, notwithstanding the public investor may in theory desire all relevant information in the interest both of reliability and of protecting himself from being overloaded with information, the materiality of the undisclosed information may rationally vary with the context.

Quite apart from the interest of the trading public investor, the interests of others, and of society in encouraging or discouraging the particular transactions to which the information relates, must be considered in determining the materiality of a projection, asset appraisal, or merger negotiation. Thus, insiders, such as managers or advisers, who contemplate buying or selling their corporation's securities must either gain less by disclosing advantageous inside information, or lose all gain by forgoing the proposed transaction altogether. The prevailing view under the federal securities laws is that the costs thus imposed upon transacting insiders and society of requiring disclosure are less than the benefits to transacting public investors and to society. The premises underlying that view suggest that the benefits are increased by requiring more disclosure—i.e., a wider spectrum of relevance and reliability for items of disclosable information—as a condition for permitting the insider to transact.

The net social benefit from discouraging trading by corporate officials may be greater than the net benefit from discouraging most corporate efforts to repurchase the corporation's securities on the market. When a controlling block or a substantial portion of the corporation's stock is owned by one person or a coherent group, corporate dealing in its own securities, particularly repurchase of its own securities, is not significantly different from insider trading. When corporate stock is not so owned—e.g., management does not own a substantial portion of the stock—corporate transacting is less like trading by insiders. But it still entails a significant, generally insurmountable, asymmetry of information between the corporation and those with whom it deals and probably net social costs. Only if there is good reason to encourage or little reason to discourage such asymmetry in a corporation's transactions with its public investors is there a basis for distinguishing the content of the trading corporation's disclosure obligation from that of trading insiders. Such a reason might be found in corporate repurchases for housekeeping purposes, in contrast to most other kinds of corporate repurchases.

In each case, the transacting public investor has the same interest in learning of projections, asset appraisals, or merger negotiations. But if the cost of abstention that is imposed by the disclosure requirement on some kinds of "inside" transactors, like the repurchasing corporation, is more (or the social gain from such abstention is less) than on other kinds of transactors, like the corporate insider, there is reason to argue for a lower threshold of materiality in the information that must be disclosed than in the latter kinds of cases. Indeed, for many types of such transactions, discouraging them, to the extent of broadly delineating the range of information that must be disclosed, may be an independent goal. In short, analysis of the values to be vindicated by the obligation to disclose in particular contexts is necessary in order to determine the appropriate level of the threshold of materiality. The same earnings projections or merger negotiations may be material, and therefore should be disclosed, if an insider is trading or a corporation is going private, but not for isolated corporate stock repurchases in the market.

B. The Nontransactional Context

Disclosure is also required by the federal securities laws in circumstances that do not entail transacting by specially knowledgeable persons, but in which public investors may be buying or selling. * * *

Arguably in such cases, the best interests of rational investors are to receive all relevant information, subject only to the constraint of overload. * * * In the absence of any incentive for the discloser of the information to gain from trading on the basis of it, the reliability of the information is not likely to be adversely affected by the self-serving considerations that characterize insider transactions or corporate trading. Hence, one reason for encouraging more complete disclosure by specially knowledgeable persons is lacking in cases of disclosure by nontraders.

More importantly, as we have seen, to require disclosure imposes costs upon the corporation and society if the disclosure is "premature" or otherwise advantages competitors. Disclosure of a projection, asset appraisal, or other information whose import may be unassailable as a matter of logic, may properly not be required to be disclosed because of its costs to the corporation and its nontransacting stockholders. Each of these costs is likely to increase as the disclosed information's relevance decreases or uncertainty increases.

If the reason for requiring disclosure by a trading corporation or insider is to deny the transactor the informational advantage that it has over the opposite party rather than to educate the public investor, then, as we have seen, the denial equally may be effected by making the disclosure duty contingent upon transacting—i.e., by a rule that requires disclosure or abstention. * * * On the other hand, if the duty to disclose is imposed not for the purpose of denying a transactional advantage, but rather to facilitate informed investment decisions, the duty is not contingent but is absolute. The transacting investors' needs presumably require disclosure of all available information, and the concept of materiality serves as the measure of what should, and what need not be disclosed. In that context, a relatively low threshold of materiality implicates higher costs to the corporation and to society generally than does a high threshold.

* * *

In this connection, it is relevant to consider the criteria for determining when disclosure of information about pending arm's-length merger negotiations is required of the parties in the absence of an express mandate. Early disclosure of negotiations—at a time when many questions are open and results are uncertain and can be influenced by further events—may imperil the consummation or affect the terms of the potential merger. The interests of the acquirer, the acquired company's shareholders, and society generally, as well as the possibly conflicting interests of the acquired company's management, are all affected by the discouraging or encouraging effect that early disclosure would have on the outcome of the negotiations.

To determine whether or when an affirmative obligation arises to make some disclosure about pending negotiations implicates the question of when past information about the corporation's affairs, for which the corporation can (or should be) held responsible, is rendered so inaccurate by the merger or other negotiations as to impugn the continued accuracy of the import of the past information. Resolution of that question is affected in part by a definition of the corporation's responsibility for prevailing public information about its affairs and in part by the definition to be given to the "materiality" of the effect of the negotiations on that import. Such a definition must take account of the incentives of the parties to distort and of the relative costs and benefits of lower and higher thresholds of materiality on the initiation, continuation, and conclusion of merger negotiations. That account does not lend itself to easy calculation or to simple policy solutions— even if one reasonably concludes that it is preferable to impose an affirmative obligation to disclose on nontrading parties only when an agreement in principle is reached.

NOTE: SOURCES OF LEGAL OBLIGATIONS TO DISCLOSE ON THE PART OF NON–TRANSACTORS

1. *Basic v. Levinson* makes it clear that although Rule 10b–5 is aimed primarily at transactional advantages by persons who are buying or selling, it is violated when a corporation makes false statements about material facts concerning its affairs, even though the corporation is not, and does not contemplate, buying and selling or otherwise dealing in its own securities. But suppose the corporation in *Basic* had made no affirmative misstatements and instead had kept silent about the merger? Does Rule 10b–5 impose an affirmative duty to disclose material information, even though the corporation is not in the market, and therefore does not have the option of refraining from dealing in lieu of disclosure? Courts have said that it does, but have not been clear as to which language of Rule 10b–5 imposes this obligation. See Financial Industrial Fund, Inc. v. McDonnell Douglas Co., 474 F.2d 514 (10th Cir.1973), cert. denied, 414 U.S. 874 (1973); SEC v. Texas Gulf

Sulphur Co., Inc., 401 F.2d 833, 850 n. 12 (2d Cir.1968), cert. denied, 394 U.S. 976 (1969); Marx v. Computer Sciences Corp., 507 F.2d 485 (9th Cir.1974). Some courts have imposed a duty to disclose on the premise that materiality alone is enough, at least in the circumstances of merger negotiations. See, e.g., Flamm v. Eberstadt, supra; Staffin v. Greenberg, 672 F.2d 1196 (3d Cir.1982); Reiss v. Pan American World Airways, Inc., 711 F.2d 11 (2d Cir.1983). But cf. footnote 17 in Basic v. Levinson, supra. Other courts have indicated that the materiality of information possessed by non-transactors does not alone implicate any duty to disclose it; some externally imposed duty to disclose must be found before materiality vel non is relevant. See Glazer v. Formica Corp., 964 F.2d 149 (2d Cir.1992) (merger); Taylor v. First Union Corp., 857 F.2d 240 (4th Cir.1988), cert. den., 489 U.S. 1080 (1989); Roeder v. Alpha Industries, Inc., 814 F.2d 22 (1st Cir.1987); State Teachers Retirement Board v. Fluor Corp., 654 F.2d 843 (2d Cir.1981). Commentators also make this assertion. See Brown, Corporate Communications and the Federal Securities Laws, 53 Geo.Wash.L.Rev. 741 (1985); Goelzer, Disclosure of Preliminary Merger Negotiations, 46 Md.L.Rev. 974 (1987).

If the non-transacting corporation does have a duty to disclose material information, what gives rise to the duty? Plainly any announcement (whether in an annual report, a press release, at a securities analysts' meeting, in a magazine or newspaper article or in an executive's speech) must be complete—in the sense that it must not omit information which would materially contradict or qualify the information that is disclosed. See e.g., Kreindler v. Sambo's Restaurant Inc. [1982–1983 Transfer Binder] Fed.Sec.L.Rep. (CCH) ¶ 99,121 (S.D.N.Y.1983). The problem arises when information previously disclosed becomes misleading by reason of subsequent events. On one view, the corporation is under an obligation to disclose the correct information—by application of Rule 10b–5(2). It is not hard to see the relevance of 10b–5 if the change in condition—even though unforeseen—occurs within a few days after the release. But see Greenfield v. Heublein, Inc., 742 F.2d 751, 759–760 (3d Cir.1984), cert. denied, 469 U.S. 1215 (1985); Backman v. Polaroid Corp., 910 F.2d 10 (1st Cir.1990) (en banc). The question then becomes whether the obligation can be extended in time indefinitely[c] on the theory that in the continuous flow of corporate information there is a basis for finding a continuous obligation to disclose in order to correct the continuing impact of prior information which has become inadequate (e.g., Texas Gulf Sulphur's discovery) or incorrect. Compare Securities Act Release No. 5092 (October 15, 1970) (asserting that 1934 Act reporting companies have continuing obligation to make "full and prompt announcements of material facts," noting no source of the obligation other than stock exchange rules and corporation's interest in preserving opportunities

---

c. Cf. S.E.C. v. Manor Nursing Centers, 458 F.2d 1082, 1096 (2d Cir.1972). This duty is to be distinguished from the duty to correct a statement which was false or misleading when made and discovery of its misleading character occurs after it has been disseminated. See Fischer v. Kletz, 266 F.Supp. 180 (S.D.N.Y.1967); United States v. Natelli, 527 F.2d 311, 314 (2d Cir.1975).

for repurchasing its own stock) with SEC v. Shattuck Denn Mining Corp., 297 F.Supp. 470, 475–477 (S.D.N.Y.1968); see Bromberg, Disclosure Programs for Publicly Held Companies, 1970 Duke L.J. 1139, 1159–1162. A narrower view of the role of past information flow as a predicate for a current duty to disclose was announced in Starkman v. Marathon Oil Co., 772 F.2d 231 (6th Cir.1985), supra p. 872. See Block, Barton and Garfield, Affirmative Duty to Disclose Material Information * * * 40 Bus.Law. 1243 (1985). The difficulties with and uncertain limits on the requirement to update are illustrated in Backman v. Polaroid Corp., 910 F.2d 10 (1st Cir.1990). See generally Loss & Seligman, Securities Regulation, pp. 3510–3529 (3d ed. 1991).

A different ground for implying such a disclosure obligation (which does not require disclosure as extensive as is implied by some of the above cases) is the notion that communication of erroneous information by strangers or externally generated erroneous rumors about corporate affairs require correction by the corporation. See Jacobs, Litigation and Practice under Rule 10b–5, p. 1077 (rev. ed. 1985). The case law indicates that erroneous information spread by persons with close connection to the corporation in the context of corporate business such as, for example, underwriters during a distribution, may require correction (Green v. Jonhop, Inc., 358 F.Supp. 413 (D.Or.1973)) whereas rumors initiated by newspaper correspondents without any apparent or acknowledged access to sources inside the company may not require correction (cf. Electronic Specialty case, infra p. 985). How closely "entangled" with the corporation the appearance and activity of the informant must be in order to require correction by the corporation (e.g., if a newspaper reporter or securities analyst has received information from a corporate executive and does (or does not) make the attribution to his source) poses questions which the case law has not yet resolved. See e.g., State Teachers Retirement Board v. Fluor Corp., 654 F.2d 843 (2d Cir.1981); Elkind v. Liggett & Myers, Inc., 635 F.2d 156, 162–164 (2d Cir.1980); and Zuckerman v. Harnischfeger Corp., 591 F.Supp. 112 (S.D.N.Y.1984). See Sheffey, Securities Law Responsibility of Issuers to Respond to Rumors and Other Publicity: Reexamination of a Continuing Problem, 57 Notre Dame L.Rev. 755 (1982).

Another, even narrower, theory on which the corporate duty to disclose, even though it is not in the market, may be rested is the notion that the corporation's failure to disclose promptly facilitates insider trading—and in an appropriate case can make it liable for aiding and abetting insider trading (Brennan v. Midwestern United Life Ins. Co., 417 F.2d 147 (7th Cir.1969), certiorari denied 397 U.S. 989 (1970)); Sharon Steel Corp., SEA Rel. No. 18,271 (Nov. 19, 1981), Fed.Sec.L.Rep. (CCH) ¶ 83,049. Cf. New York Stock Exchange Policy on Disclosure, infra, p. 913. Unusual market activity in a company's stock may be a sign that inside information (generally about significant transactions or internal reports) has leaked, and its effects can only be curtailed if the company issues an announcement. There is considerable difficulty, however, in determining under what circumstances the company should be required to make the disclosure or to examine undisclosed developments in order to ascertain the cause of the market activity, or to ask the exchange to suspend trading until the examination as to whether a disclosure should be made takes place. There may be occasions on which there is no "leak," or the company cannot reasonably be expected to know of it or find it. And if ongoing transactions are the subject of the leak, any announcement about them may jeopardize their consummation. In enforcing any standard against the company there is the further question of liability, which, at least in an action for damages under Rule 10b–5, is complicated by the need to establish scienter by the company. See State Teachers Retirement Board v. Fluor Corp., 654 F.2d 843 (2d Cir.1981); Weintraub v. Texasgulf, Inc., 564 F.Supp. 1466 (S.D.N.Y.1983); Sharon Steel Corp., supra.

Finally, more broadly, the fraud on the market concept provides conceptual support for the disclosure obligation as well as for the presumption of reliance established in *Basic*. See, e.g., HSL, Inc. v. Daniels, CCH Fed.Sec.L.Rep. ¶ 99,557 (N.D.Ill.1983). At one level, the presumption of reliance serves the end of assuring market price accuracy. The duty to disclose serves the same end by assuring the efficient market informational raw material.

If such a duty to disclose does exist, whatever its source, it creates a risk of a conflict between the market's need for the information and the corporation's need to protect the corporation against loss of an opportunity by disclosing the information prematurely. This corporate interest, to which reference was made in the *Texas Gulf Sulphur* case,[f] was widely thought to be a compelling interest before Justice Blackmun's *Basic* opinion. Should *Basic* be read to negate this assumption about when there is a duty to disclose and establish a rule of disclosure of all material information no matter what the interest of the issuer? Such a reading seems unlikely to wear well in the context of litigated cases. Can a court take the corporation's interest into account *sub silentio* by holding that the information is not, taken in all the circumstances, material? Or should the courts discuss the problem directly? The SEC, interpreting some specific disclosure rules of its own, stresses the

---

f. Texas Gulf Sulphur Co. was not held to be at fault for failing to disclose its unusual ore strike to the public, at least until it had an opportunity to purchase—or acquire an option to purchase—adjacent lands which might also be rich in ore. The Court said (401 F.2d 833, 850, n. 12 (2d Cir.1968)):

"We do not suggest that material facts must be disclosed immediately; the timing of disclosure is a matter for the business judgment of the corporate officers entrusted with the management of the corporation within the affirmative disclosure requirements promulgated by the exchanges and by the SEC. Here, a valuable corporate purpose was served by delaying the publication of the K–55–1 discovery. We do intend to convey, however, that where a corporate purpose

is thus served by withholding the news of a material fact, those persons who are thus quite properly true to their corporate trust must not during the period of non-disclosure deal personally in the corporation's securities or give to outsiders confidential information not generally available to all the corporations' stockholders and to the public at large."

See also Segal v. Coburn Corp. of America, Fed.Sec.L.Rep. (CCH) ¶ 94,002 [1973 Tr.Binder] (E.D.N.Y.1973); Matarese v. Aero–Chatillon Corporation, Fed.Sec. L.Rep. (CCH) ¶ 93,322 [Tr.Binder 1971–1972] (S.D.N.Y.1971).

Why, if Texas Gulf Sulphur Co. is obliged to disclose its discovery to its stockholders before dealing with them, is it not also obliged to disclose to adjacent landowners prior to dealing with them?

need to balance "the informational need of investors against the risk that premature disclosure of negotiations may jeopardize completion of the transaction." SEC Rel. Nos. 33–6835, 34–26831 (May 18, 1989).[g] What principles should inform the striking of such a balance in the context of litigated cases? Is it an attribute of ownership of stock that each stockholder is entitled to prompt disclosure of information about the corporation lest its value be unevenly divided—between those stockholders who sell and those who fail to sell? Or must each stockholder risk the consequences of such individual ignorance in order to favor a common good? Is it appropriate to permit particular stockholders to fail to share in that common good so long as the information is not systematically exploited by insiders? If the corporate benefit from concealing the opportunity justifies withholding the information until the benefit is realized, questions remain, of course, as to the determination of when the corporate benefit is quite satisfied, and the timing of the communication which is ultimately required.

Is the practical solution to be found in requiring a firm which is not itself transacting in securities to disclose material information unless there is a good business reason to refrain from disclosing? Or should the firm be permitted to withhold information unless something external occurs to require its disclosure (e.g., increased trading on rumors that affect market price)? See, e.g., Sharon Steel Corp., SEA Rel. No. 18,271 supra p. 911.

2. The New York Stock Exchange Listed Company Manual admonishes (Rule 202.05) that a "listed company is expected to release quickly to the public any news or information which might reasonably be expected to materially affect the market for its securities * * *. A listed company should also act promptly to dispel unfounded rumors which result in unusual market activity or price variations." In addition, the Manual describes in some detail (3 Fed.Sec.L.Rep. (CCH) ¶ 23,513 et seq.) the procedures and practices with respect to timely disclosure by which listed companies are expected to be guided. Not only are companies urged to confine the dissemination of material developments to a limited group within the company, but when the developments implicate so many people, particularly outsiders, that "maintaining security * * * is virtually impossible", an immediate announcement should be made. Elaborate instruction is also provided for (a) dissemination of information to securities analysts, to institutional managers, etc. particularly by keeping an "open door" policy, (b) avoiding disclosure to member firms of non-public information, (c) dealing with rumors of unusual market activity, and (d) procedures for public release of information.

Comparable disclosure policies are contained in the American Stock Exchange Company Guide (see 3 Fed.Sec.L.Rep. (CCH) ¶¶ 23,-124A, 23,124B), and in considerably less detail in the By Law Sched. D

---

g. See also Securities Act Release No. 5092 (October 15, 1970), discussing the obligation of issuers to insure prompt disclosure of all material corporate developments, both favorable and unfavorable.

§ 2(e) of the N.A.S.D. Manual (see Brown, Corporate Communications and the Federal Securities Laws, 53 Geo.Wash.L.Rev. 741 at 758–775 (1985)).

———

NOTE: FRAUD ON THE MARKET DOCTRINE

1. When is a trading context sufficiently efficient to give rise to the presumption of reliance? The *Basic* opinion refers to "open and developed" markets. Suppose plaintiff buys a piece of an initial public offering of a small local firm, relying on a local stockbroker's sales pitch, having thrown the prospectus into the trash unread? Here the trading market is undeveloped. Yet a number of decisions erect a presumption of reliance in this situation—reliance on the integrity of the new offerings process. See Ross v. Bank South, N.A., 837 F.2d 980 (11th Cir.1988), vacated, 848 F.2d 1132 (1988); T.J. Raney & Sons v. Fort Cobb, Okla. Irrigation Fuel Auth., 717 F.2d 1330 (10th Cir.1983), cert. denied, 465 U.S. 1026 (1984); Shores v. Sklar, 647 F.2d 462 (5th Cir.1981) (en banc), cert. denied, 459 U.S. 1102 (1983); In re Taxable Bonds Litigation, CCH Fed.Sec.L.Rep. ¶ 96,836 (E.D.La.1992). For the contrary approach, see Vervaecke v. Chiles, Heider & Co., 578 F.2d 713 (8th Cir.1978); Stinson v. Van Valley Development Corp., 714 F.Supp. 132 (E.D.Pa.1989) (fact that new issue was nationally marketed does not by itself prove open and developed trading market); Rose v. Arkansas Valley Envtl. Auth., 562 F.Supp. 1180, 1201–03 (W.D.Mo.1983).

On the other hand, in some courts the fact that a stock is traded on the NASDQ over-the-counter network does not automatically support the presumption of reliance. Cammer v. Bloom, 711 F.Supp. 1264 (D.N.J.1989), suggests that the plaintiff seeking application of the presumption should allege some or all of the following specific facts in addition to a NASDQ listing: (1) average weekly trading volume, (2) the number of analysts following the stock; (3) the number of market makers, (4) status as a seasoned issuer eligible to file an S–3 registration statement; and (5) facts showing a cause and effect relationship between material information and movement in the stock price.

For the view that reasonable investors should self-protect when purchasing new issues, see Carney, The Limits of the Fraud on the Market Doctrine, 44 Bus. Lawyer 1259 (1989). See also Black, Fraud on the Market: A Criticism of Dispensing With Reliance Requirements in Certain Open Market Transactions, 62 N.C.L.Rev. 435, 452–53 (1984).

2. Suppose a short seller loses money when forced to cover by a rising stock price, and then sues claiming that misstatements by the corporation caused damage through the rise in market price? The Third Circuit held the fraud on the market presumption to be unavailable—the fraud was on the market, not the plaintiff, who complained of injury due to the reliance of other investors. Zlotnick v. TIE Communications, 836 F.2d 818 (3d Cir.1988).

3.   Does either of the extensive literature on noise trading or the disturbing fact of the October 19, 1987 stock market crash, see supra p. 143, have any bearing on the appropriateness of utilizing the ECMH in formulating the 10b–5 cause of action?   For a "no" answer to this question see Fischel, Efficient Capital Markets, the Crash, and "Fraud on the Market Theory," 74 Cornell L.Rev. 907 (1989).

Professor Ayres answers more equivocally.   He notes that Justice Blackmun employs only semi-strong EMH and seems to have only speculative efficiency in mind.   This, says Ayres, is enough to support the assertion of market reliance.   Ayres, supra at 983–984.   Justice White's response addresses allocative efficiency.   And, says Ayres, market prices can be influenced by deceptions without being efficient in the fundamental sense.   The fundamental value problem would pertain to the amount of damages.   Id. at 984–85.

SECTION E.   TRANSFER OF CONTROL

1.   SALE OF STOCK

PERLMAN v. FELDMANN

United States Court of Appeals, Second Circuit, 1955.
219 F.2d 173.
Certiorari denied, 349 U.S. 952, 75 S.Ct. 880, 99 L.Ed. 1277 (1955).

CLARK, Chief Judge.   This is a derivative action brought by minority stockholders of Newport Steel Corporation to compel accounting for, and restitution of, allegedly illegal gains which accrued to defendants as a result of the sale in August, 1950, of their controlling interest in the corporation.   The principal defendant, C. Russell Feldmann, who represented and acted for the others, members of his family,[1] was at that time not only the dominant stockholder, but also the chairman of the board of directors and the president of the corporation.   Newport, an Indiana corporation, operated mills for the production of steel sheets for sale to manufacturers of steel products, first at Newport, Kentucky, and later also at other places in Kentucky and Ohio.   The buyers, a syndicate organized as Wilport Company, a Delaware corporation, consisted of end-users of steel who were interested in securing a source of supply in a market becoming ever tighter in the Korean War.   Plaintiffs contend that the consideration paid for the

---

[1] The stock was not held personally by Feldmann in his own name, but was held by the members of his family and by personal corporations.   The aggregate of stock thus had amounted to 33% of the outstanding Newport stock and gave working control to the holder.   The actual sale included 55,552 additional shares held by friends and associates of Feldmann, so that a total of 37% of the Newport stock was transferred.

stock included compensation for the sale of a corporate asset, a power held in trust for the corporation by Feldmann as its fiduciary. This power was the ability to control the allocation of the corporate product in a time of short supply, through control of the board of directors; and it was effectively transferred in this sale by having Feldmann procure the resignation of his own board and the election of Wilport's nominees immediately upon consummation of the sale.

The present action represents the consolidation of three pending stockholders' actions in which yet another stockholder has been permitted to intervene. Jurisdiction below was based upon the diverse citizenship of the parties. Plaintiffs argue here, as they did in the court below, that in the situation here disclosed the vendors must account to the nonparticipating minority stockholders for that share of their profit which is attributable to the sale of the corporate power. Judge Hincks denied the validity of the premise, holding that the rights involved in the sale were only those normally incident to the possession of a controlling block of shares, with which a dominant stockholder, in the absence of fraud or foreseeable looting, was entitled to deal according to his own best interests. Furthermore, he held that plaintiffs had failed to satisfy their burden of proving that the sales price was not a fair price for the stock per se. Plaintiffs appeal from these rulings of law which resulted in the dismissal of their complaint.

The essential facts found by the trial judge are not in dispute. Newport was a relative newcomer in the steel industry with predominantly old installations which were in the process of being supplemented by more modern facilities. Except in times of extreme shortage Newport was not in a position to compete profitably with other steel mills for customers not in its immediate geographical area. Wilport, the purchasing syndicate, consisted of geographically remote end-users of steel who were interested in buying more steel from Newport than they had been able to obtain during recent periods of tight supply. The price of $20 per share was found by Judge Hincks to be a fair one for a control block of stock, although the over-the-counter market price had not exceeded $12 and the book value per share was $17.03. But this finding was limited by Judge Hincks' statement that "[w]hat value the block would have had if shorn of its appurtenant power to control distribution of the corporate product, the evidence does not show." It was also conditioned by his earlier ruling that the burden was on plaintiffs to prove a lesser value for the stock.

Both as director and as dominant stockholder, Feldmann stood in a fiduciary relationship to the corporation and to the minority stockholders as beneficiaries thereof. Pepper v. Litton, 308 U.S. 295, 60 S.Ct. 238, 84 L.Ed. 281; Southern Pac. Co. v. Bogert, 250 U.S. 483, 39 S.Ct. 533, 63 L.Ed. 1099. His fiduciary obligation must in the first instance be measured by the law of Indiana, the state of incorporation of Newport. Rogers v. Guaranty Trust Co. of New York, 288 U.S. 123, 136, 53 S.Ct. 295, 77 L.Ed. 652; Mayflower Hotel Stockholders Protective Committee v. Mayflower Hotel Corp., 89 U.S.App.D.C. 171, 193 F.2d 666, 668. Although there is no Indiana case directly in point, the most closely analogous one emphasizes the close scrutiny to which Indiana subjects the conduct of fiduciaries when personal benefit may stand in the way of fulfillment of trust obligations. In Schemmel v. Hill, 91 Ind.App. 373, 169 N.E. 678, 682, 683, McMahan, J., said: "Directors of a business corporation act in a strictly fiduciary capacity. Their office is a trust. Stratis v. Andreson, 1926, 254 Mass. 536, 150 N.E. 832, 44 A.L.R. 567; Hill v. Nisbet, 1885, 100 Ind. 341, 353. When a director deals with his corporation, his acts will be closely scrutinized. Bossert v. Geis, 1914, 57 Ind.App. 384, 107 N.E. 95. Directors of a corporation are its agents, and they are governed by the rules of law applicable to other agents, and, as between themselves and their principal, the rules relating to honesty and fair dealing in the management of the affairs of their principal are applicable. They must not, in any degree, allow their official conduct to be swayed by their private interest, which must yield to official duty. Leader Publishing Co. v. Grant Trust Co., 1915, 182 Ind. 651, 108 N.E. 121. In a transaction between a director and his corporation, where he acts for himself and his principal at the same time in a matter connected with the relation between them, it is presumed, where he is thus potential on both sides of the contract, that self-interest will overcome his fidelity to his principal, to his own benefit and to his principal's hurt." And the judge added: "Absolute and most scrupulous good faith is the very essence of a director's obligation to his corporation. The first principal duty arising from his official relation is to act in all things of trust wholly for the benefit of his corporation."

In Indiana, then, as elsewhere, the responsibility of the fiduciary is not limited to a proper regard for the tangible balance sheet assets of the corporation, but includes the dedication of his uncorrupted business judgment for the sole benefit of the corporation, in any dealings which may adversely affect it. Young v. Higbee Co., 324 U.S. 204, 65 S.Ct. 594, 89 L.Ed. 890; Irving Trust Co. v. Deutsch, 2 Cir., 73 F.2d 121, certiorari denied 294 U.S. 708, 55 S.Ct. 405, 79 L.Ed. 1243; Seagrave Corp. v. Mount, 6 Cir., 212 F.2d 389; Meinhard v. Salmon, 249 N.Y. 458, 164 N.E. 545, 62 A.L.R. 1; Commonwealth Title Ins. & Trust Co. v. Seltzer, 227 Pa. 410, 76 A. 77. Although the Indiana case is particularly relevant to Feldmann as a director, the same rule should apply to his fiduciary duties as majority stockholder, for in that capacity he chooses and controls the directors, and thus is held to have assumed their liability. Pepper v. Litton, supra, 308 U.S. 295, 60 S.Ct. 238. This, therefore, is the standard to which Feldmann was by law required to conform in his activities here under scrutiny.

It is true, as defendants have been at pains to point out, that this is not the ordinary case of breach of fiduciary duty. We have here no fraud, no misuse of confidential information, no outright looting of a helpless corporation. But on the other hand, we do not find compliance with that high standard which we have just stated and which we and other courts have come to expect and demand of corporate fiduciaries. In the often-quoted words of Judge Cardozo: "Many forms of conduct permissible in a workaday world for those acting at arm's length, are forbidden to those bound by fiduciary ties. A trustee is held to something stricter than the morals of the market place. Not honesty alone, but the punctilio of an honor the most sensitive, is then the standard of behavior. As to this there has developed a tradition that is unbending and inveterate. Uncompromising rigidity has been the attitude of courts of equity when petitioned to undermine the rule of undivided loyalty by the 'disintegrating erosion' of particular exceptions." Meinhard v. Salmon, supra, 249 N.Y. 458, 464, 164 N.E. 545, 546, 62 A.L.R. 1. The actions of defendants in siphoning off for personal gain corporate advantages to be derived from a favorable market situation do not betoken the necessary undivided loyalty owed by the fiduciary to his principal.

The corporate opportunities of whose misappropriation the minority stockholders complain need not have been an absolute certainty in order to support this action against Feldmann. If there was possibility of corporate gain, they are entitled to recover. In Young v. Higbee Co., supra, 324 U.S. 204, 65 S.Ct. 594, two stockholders appealing the confirmation of a plan of bankruptcy reorganization were held liable for profits received for the sale of their stock pending determination of the validity of the appeal. They were held accountable for the excess of the price of their stock over its normal price, even though there was no indication that the appeal could have succeeded on substantive grounds. And in Irving Trust Co. v. Deutsch, supra, 2 Cir., 73 F.2d 121, 124, an accounting was required of corporate directors who bought stock for themselves for corporate use, even though there was an affirmative showing that the corporation did not have the finances itself to acquire the stock. Judge Swan speaking for the court pointed out that "The defendants' argument, contrary to Wing v. Dillingham [5 Cir., 239 F. 54], that the equitable rule that fiduciaries should not be permitted to assume a position in which their individual interests might be in conflict with those of the corporation can have no application where the corporation is unable to undertake the venture, is not convincing. If directors are permitted to justify their conduct on such a theory, there will be a temptation to refrain from exerting their strongest efforts on behalf of the corporation since, if it does not meet the obligations, an opportunity of profit will be open to them personally."

This rationale is equally appropriate to a consideration of the benefits which Newport might have derived from the steel shortage. In the past Newport had used and profited by its market leverage by operation of what the industry had come to call the "Feldmann Plan." This consisted of securing interest-free advances from prospective purchasers of steel in return for firm commitments to them from future production. The funds thus acquired were used to finance improvements in existing plants and to acquire new installations. In the summer of 1950 Newport had been negotiating for cold-rolling facilities which it needed for a more fully integrated operation and a more marketable product, and Feldmann plan funds might well have been used toward this end.

Further, as plaintiffs alternatively suggest, Newport might have used the period of short supply to build up patronage in the geographical area in which it could compete profitably even when steel was more abundant. Either of these opportunities was Newport's, to be used to its advantage only. Only if defendants had been able to negate completely any possibility of gain by Newport could they have prevailed. It is true that a trial court finding states: "Whether or not, in August, 1950, Newport's position was such that it could have entered into 'Feldmann Plan' type transactions to procure funds and financing for the further expansion and integration of its steel facilities and whether such expansion would have been desirable for Newport, the evidence does not show." This, however, cannot avail the defendants, who—contrary to the ruling below—had the burden of proof on this issue, since fiduciaries always have the burden of proof in establishing the fairness of their dealings with trust property. Pepper v. Litton, supra, 308 U.S. 295, 60 S.Ct. 238; Geddes v. Anaconda Copper Mining Co., 254 U.S. 590, 41 S.Ct. 209, 65 L.Ed. 425; Mayflower Hotel Stockholders Protective Committee v. Mayflower Hotel Corp., 84 U.S.App.D.C. 275, 173 F.2d 416.

Defendants seek to categorize the corporate opportunities which might have accrued to Newport as too unethical to warrant further consideration. It is true that reputable steel producers were not participating in the gray market brought about by the Korean War and were refraining from advancing their prices, although to do so would not have been illegal. But Feldmann plan transactions were not considered within this self-imposed interdiction; the trial court found that around the time of the Feldmann sale Jones & Laughlin Steel Corporation, Republic Steel Company, and Pittsburgh Steel Corporation were all participating in such arrangements. In any event, it ill becomes the defendants to disparage as unethical the market advantages from which they themselves reaped rich benefits.

We do not mean to suggest that a majority stockholder cannot dispose of his controlling block of stock to outsiders without having to account to his corporation for profits or even never do this with impunity when the buyer is an interested customer, actual or potential, for the corporation's product. But when the sale necessarily results in a sacrifice of this element of corporate good will and consequent unusual profit to the fiduciary who has caused the sacrifice, he should account for his gains. So in a time of market shortage, where a call on a corporation's product commands an unusually large premium, in one form or another, we think it sound law that a fiduciary may not appropriate to himself the value of this premium. Such personal gain at the expense of his coventurers seems particularly reprehensible when made by the trusted president and director of his company. In this case the violation of duty seems to be all the clearer because of this triple role in which Feldmann appears, though we are unwilling to say, and are not to be understood as saying, that we should accept a lesser obligation for any one of his roles alone.

Hence to the extent that the price received by Feldmann and his codefendants included such a bonus, he is accountable to the minority stockholders who sue here. Restatement, Restitution §§ 190, 197 (1937); Seagrave Corp. v. Mount, supra, 6 Cir., 212 F.2d 389. And plaintiffs, as they contend, are entitled to a recovery in their own right, instead of in right of the corporation (as in the usual derivative actions), since neither Wilport nor their successors in interest should share in any judgment which may be rendered. See Southern Pacific Co. v. Bogert, 250 U.S. 483, 39 S.Ct. 533, 63 L.Ed. 1099. Defendants cannot well object to this form of recovery, since the only alternative, recovery for the corporation as a whole, would subject them to a greater total liability.

The case will therefore be remanded to the district court for a determination of the question expressly left open below, namely, the value of defendants' stock without the appurtenant control over the corporation's output of steel. We reiterate that on this issue, as on all others relating to a breach of fiduciary duty, the burden of proof must rest on the defendants. Bigelow v. RKO Radio Pictures, 327 U.S. 251, 265–266, 66 S.Ct. 574, 90 L.Ed. 652; Package Closure Corp. v. Sealright Co., 2 Cir., 141 F.2d 972, 979. Judgment should go to these plaintiffs and those whom they represent for any premium value so shown to the extent of their respective stock interests.

The judgment is therefore reversed and the action remanded for further proceedings pursuant to this opinion.

SWAN, Circuit Judge. With the general principles enunciated in the majority opinion as to the duties of fiduciaries I am, of course, in thorough accord. But, as Mr. Justice Frankfurter stated in Securities and Exchange Comm. v. Chenery Corp., 318 U.S. 80, 85, 63 S.Ct. 454, 458, 87 L.Ed. 626, "to say that a man is a fiduciary only begins analysis; it gives direction to further inquiry. To whom is he a fiduciary? What obligations does he owe as a fiduciary? In what respect has he failed to discharge these obligations?" My brothers' opinion does not specify precisely what fiduciary duty Feldmann is held to have violated or whether it was a duty imposed upon him as the dominant stockholder or as a director of Newport. Without such specification I think that both the legal profession and the business world will find the decision confusing and will be unable to foretell the extent of its impact upon customary practices in the sale of stock.

The power to control the management of a corporation, that is, to elect directors to manage its affairs, is an inseparable incident to the ownership of a majority of its stock, or sometimes, as in the present instance, to the ownership of enough shares, less than a majority, to control an election. Concededly a majority or dominant shareholder is ordinarily privileged to sell his stock at the best price obtainable from the purchaser. In so doing he acts on his own behalf, not as an agent of the corporation. If he knows or has reason to believe that the purchaser intends to exercise to the detriment of the corporation the power of management acquired by the purchase, such knowledge or reasonable suspicion will terminate the dominant shareholder's privilege to sell and will create a duty not to transfer the power of management to such purchaser. The duty seems to me to resemble the obligation which everyone is under not to assist another to commit a tort rather than the obligation of a fiduciary. But whatever the nature of the duty, a violation of it will subject the violator to liability for damages sustained by the corporation. Judge Hincks found that Feldmann had no reason to think that Wilport would use the power of management it would acquire by the purchase to injure Newport, and that there was no proof that it ever was so used. Feldmann did know, it is true, that the reason Wilport wanted the stock was to put in a board of directors who would be likely to permit Wilport's members to purchase more of Newport's steel than they might otherwise be able to get. But there is nothing illegal in a dominant shareholder purchasing from his own corporation at the same prices it offers to other customers. That is what the members of Wilport did, and there is no proof that Newport suffered any detriment therefrom.

My brothers say that "the consideration paid for the stock included compensation for the sale of a corporate asset", which they describe as "the ability to control the allocation of the corporate product in a time of short supply, through control of the board of directors; and it was effectively transferred in this sale by having Feldmann procure the resignation of his own board and the election of Wilport's nominees immediately upon consummation of the sale." The implications of this are not clear to me. If it means that when market conditions are such as to induce users of a corporation's product to wish to buy a controlling block of stock in order to be able to purchase part of the corporation's output at the same mill list prices as are offered to other customers, the dominant stockholder is under a fiduciary duty not to sell his stock, I cannot agree. For reasons already stated, in my opinion Feldmann was not proved to be under any fiduciary duty as a stockholder not to sell the stock he controlled.

Feldmann was also a director of Newport. Perhaps the quoted statement means that as a director he violated his fiduciary duty in voting to elect Wilport's nominees to fill the vacancies created by the resignations of the former directors of Newport. As a director Feldmann was under a fiduciary duty to use an honest judgment in acting on the corporation's behalf. A director is privileged to resign, but so long as he remains a director he must be faithful to his fiduciary duties and must not make a personal gain from performing them. Consequently, if the price paid for Feldmann's stock included a payment for voting to elect the new directors, he must account to the corporation for such payment, even though he honestly believed that the men he voted to elect were well qualified to serve as directors. He can not take pay for performing his fiduciary duty. There is no suggestion that he did so, unless the price paid for his stock was more than its value. So it seems to me that decision must turn on whether finding 120 and conclusion 5 of the district judge are supportable on the evidence. They are set out in the margin.[1]

Judge Hincks went into the matter of valuation of the stock with his customary care and thoroughness. He made no error of law in applying the principles relating to valuation of stock. Concededly a controlling block of stock has greater sale value than a small lot. While the spread between $10 per share for small lots and $20 per share for the controlling block seems rather extraordinarily wide, the $20 valuation was supported by the expert testimony of Dr. Badger, whom the district judge said he could not find to be wrong. I see no justification for upsetting the valuation as clearly erroneous. Nor can I agree with my brothers that the $20 valuation "was limited" by the last sentence in finding 120. The controlling block could not by any possibility be shorn of its appurtenant power to elect directors and through them to control distribution of the corporate product. It is this "appurtenant power" which gives a controlling block its value as such block. What evidence could be adduced to show the value of the block "if shorn" of such appurtenant power, I cannot conceive, for it cannot be shorn of it.

The opinion also asserts that the burden of proving a lesser value than $20 per share was not upon the plaintiffs but the burden was upon the defendants to prove that the stock was worth that value. Assuming that this might be true as to the defendants who were directors of Newport, they did show it, unless finding 120 be set aside. Furthermore, not all the defendants were directors; upon what theory the plaintiffs should be relieved from the burden of proof as to defendants who were not directors, the opinion does not explain.

The final conclusion of my brothers is that the plaintiffs are entitled to recover in their own right instead of in the right of the corporation. This appears to be completely inconsistent with the theory advanced at the outset of the opinion, namely, that the price of the stock "included compensation for the sale of a corporate asset." If a corporate asset was sold, surely the corporation should recover the compensation received for it by the defendants. Moreover, if the plaintiffs were suing in their own right, Newport was not a proper party. The case of Southern Pacific Co. v. Bogert, 250 U.S. 483, 39 S.Ct. 533, 63 L.Ed. 1099, relied upon as authority for the conclusion that the plaintiffs are entitled to recover in their own right, relates to a situation so different that the decision appears to me to be inapposite.

I would affirm the judgment on appeal.

---

1. "120. The 398,927 shares of Newport stock sold to Wilport as of August 31, 1950, had a fair value as a control block of $20 per share. What value the block would have had if shorn of its appurtenant power to control distribution of the corporate product, the evidence does not show."

"5. Even if Feldmann's conduct in cooperating to accomplish a transfer of control to Wilport immediately upon the sale constituted a breach of a fiduciary duty to Newport, no part of the moneys received by the defendants in connection with the sale constituted profits for which they were accountable to Newport."

NOTE: THE PROPOSED RULE OF EQUAL OPPORTUNITY

1. Perlman v. Feldmann has been interpreted narrowly by some commentators, broadly by others. Most frequently, perhaps, the decision is explained by grouping it with "looting" cases such as Gerdes v. Reynolds, 28 N.Y.S.2d 622 (Sup.Ct.1941), in which the control shares of an investment company were sold at a premium to purchasers who used their position of dominance to loot the corporation, selling portfolio securities and appropriating the proceeds. Finding that the seller knew or should have known of the danger of looting, which did in fact occur, the court held the seller liable for the premium received on the sale of the control shares and for the amount of the corporation's losses. See also Harris v. Carter, 582 A.2d 222 (Del.Ch.1990) (imposing a duty of care on the selling stockholder as a matter of Delaware law). *Feldmann* is said to be based on similar considerations, with the harm to the corporation being loss of opportunities for Feldmann-plan financing and other benefits. See Hill, The Sale of Controlling Shares, 70 Harv.L.Rev. 986, 989 (1957).

A different, though related, explanation for the outcome in Feldmann stems from the fact that the premium paid for Feldmann's stock was in reality payment of a premium price for Newport's steel output. As the company could not ethically take advantage of the market situation by charging higher prices for its product, the question is whether the controlling shareholder, as a fiduciary, was at liberty to take for himself the whole value of the premium price which a steel purchaser would otherwise have been willing to pay. It is said the decision can best be understood as holding that stockholders must be allowed to share equally in profits resulting from strong market demand whether such profits are realized through sale of the product or sale of stock. See Manning, The Shareholder's Appraisal Remedy, 72 Yale L.J. 223, 225 (1962). Under a third view, the court's opinion reflects a belief that control is a corporate asset, or is held in trust for the corporation, and cannot be sold for private gain. As a result, the decision should be read as requiring the controller-fiduciary to disgorge the amount received in excess of the investment value of his shares shorn of control. Berle, "Control" in Corporate Law, 58 Col.L.Rev. 1212 (1958); Jennings, Trading in Corporate Control, 44 Calif.L.Rev. 1 (1956); but see, Honigman v. Green Giant Co., 208 F.Supp. 754 (D.Minn.1961), aff'd, 309 F.2d 667 (8th Cir.1962), cert. denied 372 U.S. 941 (1963).

Another interpretation of the *Feldmann* decision is suggested in Andrews, The Stockholder's Right to Equal Opportunity in the Sale of Shares, 78 Harv.L.Rev. 505, 515–18 (1965):

"The rule to be considered can be stated thus: whenever a controlling stockholder sells his shares, every other holder of shares (of the same class) is entitled to have an equal opportunity to sell his shares, or a pro rata part of them, on substantially the same terms. Or in terms of the correlative duty: before a controlling stockholder may sell his shares to an outsider he must assure his fellow stockholders an equal opportunity to sell their shares, or as high a proportion of theirs as he ultimately sells of his own * * *.

"Now let us look briefly at what the rule means. First, it neither compels nor prohibits a sale of stock at any particular price; it leaves a controlling stockholder wholly free to decide for himself the price above which he will sell and below which he will hold his shares. The rule only says that in executing his decision to sell, a controlling stockholder cannot sell pursuant to a purchase offer more favorable than any available to other stockholders. Second, the rule does not compel a prospective purchaser to make an open offer for all shares on the same terms. He can offer to purchase shares on the condition that he gets a certain proportion of the total. Or he can even make an offer to purchase 51 per cent of the shares, no more and no less. The only requirement is that his offer, whatever it may be, be made equally or proportionately available to all stockholders.

"Obviously if a purchaser offers to buy only 51 per cent of the shares, and the offer must be made equally available to all stockholders, no stockholder accepting the offer can count on selling all his shares. There are established mechanics for dealing with this situation. The purchaser makes a so-called tender offer, indicating the price at which he wants to buy and how many shares, and inviting all stockholders to tender their stock if they wish to sell at that price. If more shares are tendered than the purchaser is willing to take, then he purchases pro rata from each tendering stockholder. The device of a tender offer has been widely used when a purchaser wants to buy from the public; indeed the New York Stock Exchange Company Manual contains provisions dealing with tender offers, designed to ensure that such offers are made equally accessible to all stockholders.

"The asserted right would prevent just what happened in Feldmann: a private sale by a controlling stockholder at a price not available to other stockholders. But there are two modes of compliance with the rule: either the purchaser can extend his offer to all stockholders, or the seller can offer participation in the sale to his fellow stockholders. A sale is prevented from taking place only when the purchaser is unwilling to buy more than a specified percentage of the shares, and the seller will sell only if he can sell out completely. Indeed, even under these circumstances it is an overstatement to say the rule would prevent a sale taking place, since the minority stockholders may consent to the sale. They may even sell to the purchaser at a lower price than what he pays the controlling stockholder, provided they are adequately informed of what is going on. Thus the rule only operates to prevent a sale when (1) the purchaser is unwilling to purchase more shares, (2) the seller insists on disposing of all his shares, and (3) the minority stockholders are unwilling to stay in the enterprise under the purchaser's control.

* * *

" * * * There is a substantial danger that following a transfer of controlling shares corporate affairs may be conducted in a manner detrimental of the interests of the stockholders who have not had an opportunity to sell their shares. The corporation may be looted; it may just be badly run. Or the sale of controlling shares may operate to destroy a favorable opportunity for corporate action. Recent events confirm that gross mismanagement may follow a sale of controlling shares.

"The equal opportunity rule does not deal directly with the problem of mismanagement, which may occur even after a transfer of control complying with the rule; but enforcement of the rule will remove much of the incentive a purchaser can offer a controlling stockholder to sell on profitable terms. Indeed, in the case of a purchasing looter there is nothing in it for the purchaser unless he can buy less than all the shares; there is no profit in stealing from a solvent corporation if the thief owns all the stock. But the controlling stockholder will be loath to sell only part of his shares (except at a price that compensates him for all of his shares) if he expects the purchaser to destroy the value of what he keeps. The rule forces the controlling stockholder to share equally with his fellow stockholders both the benefits of the price he receives for the shares he sells and the business risks incident to the shares he retains. This will tend strongly to discourage a sale of controlling shares when the risk of looting, or other harm to the corporation, is apparent; and it will provide the seller with a direct incentive to investigate and evaluate with care when the risks are not apparent, since his own financial interest continues to be at stake."

Andrews elsewhere affirms that a sale of control shares may have advantageous effects to the corporation and its shareholders—as when inefficient managers are replaced by a purchaser who can, or believes he can, do better. Andrews concedes that the prevention of sales in such circumstances "would be a high price to pay for the prevention of harm in other cases," but denies that the rule would have that effect. Would it? Compare Javaras, Equal Opportunity in the Sale of Controlling Shares: A Reply to Professor Andrews, 32 U.Chi.L.Rev. 420 (1965); Katz, The Sale of Corporate Control, 38 Chi.Bar Rec. 376 (1957); Manne, Mergers and the Market for Corporate Control, 73 J.P.E. 110 (1965).

The incentive to pay a premium derives from either (or both) the expectation of diverting assets to the new controller or the expectation of exercising control so as to enhance the value of all shareholders' (including the new controller's) pro-rata interest in the enterprise. To the extent that diversion of assets is the principal incentive (see Meeker and Joy, Price Premiums for Controlling Shares of Closely Held Bank Stock, 53 J. of Bus. 297 (1980)), the premium represents the capitalized value of the power of controllers thus to appropriate corporate property for themselves, by reason presumably of the porous restraints otherwise imposed upon them by law. See Brudney, Equal Treatment of Shareholders in Corporate Distributions and Reorganizations, 71 Calif.L.Rev.

1072, 1122–1126 (1983). Cf. Barclay and Holderness, Private Benefits from Control of Public Corporations, 25 J.Financial Econs. 371 (1989) (empirical study of 63 block trades between 1978 and 1982 involving at least 5 percent of the common stock of NYSE or Amex firms, concluding that the premium represents the value of corporate benefits accruing to the blockholder alone). To the extent that the principal incentive is pro-rata gain, as Andrews has pointed out, the buyer of control should not be willing to pay more per share for the minimum number of shares needed for control than for the balance of the shares.

Assuming both incentives, the propriety of allowing the payment of a premium to a selling controller implicates a determination whether the amount by which the new controller is likely to augment the value of the enterprise (by innovation and reduction of agency costs) exceeds the amount of the enterprise's assets which he is likely to divert to himself. See Hamilton, Private Sale of Control Transactions: Where We Stand Today, 36 Case Western Reserve L.Rev. 248 (1985). See also Levmore, A Primer on the Sale of Corporate Control, 65 Tex.L.Rev. 1061 (1987). But in addition to that determination is it also relevant to consider the possibility, if not the probability, that the new controller will divert to himself more than his predecessor did? In any event is he entitled to more than "fair" compensation for his services in reducing agency costs? While the amount of that compensation is hard to determine, the question is whether in theory he is entitled to any more (i.e., requires any more as an incentive), and in practice he is likely to take any more. The ultimate question is whether the net benefits of a sharing rule (that overdeters some beneficial transactions) are equal to, greater or less than the net benefits of a free sale rule (that underdeters harmful transactions). In the absence of empirical proof, should the answer to that question turn on the assumptions one makes about acquisitive behavior when corporate control changes hands? Or is a middle ground possible? See Elhauge, The Triggering Function of Sale of Control Doctrine, 59 U.Chi. L.Rev. 1465 (1992).

Do (should) different considerations affect accountability by the seller of control to the other stockholders for a premium received from a buyer who expressly indicates to the seller an interest in acquiring 100% of the stock (or all the assets) of the affected corporation and a willingness to pay the seller a premium? Compare Brown v. Halbert, 271 Cal.App.2d 252, 76 Cal.Rptr. 781 (1969) with Tryon v. Smith, 191 Or. 172, 229 P.2d 251 (1951).

Should the buyer be accountable? See Doleman v. Meiji Mutual Life Ins. Co., 727 F.2d 1480 (9th Cir.1984) for a suggestion that the buyer is not accountable (or obliged to offer the minority the same price it paid for the control block) unless it can be shown that the buyer conspired with the seller of control to induce the latter to violate its fiduciary obligations to the minority. But if the seller owes no duty to account for the control premium, under what circumstances can it violate fiduciary duties?

To what extent does the following empirical study provide a basis for answers to foregoing questions? Holderness & Sheehan, The Role of Majority Shareholders in Publicly Held Corporations: An Exploratory Analysis, 20 J.Fin.Econ. 317 (1988), measures the returns to minority shares of 21 listed companies that announced sales of majority blocks from 1978 to 1982 where the announcement was not accompanied by an announcement of a tender offer for the minority shares. Such stock had statistically significant abnormal returns of 9.4 per cent during the 30 days surrounding the announcement and 5.5 per cent for the two days surrounding the announcement. Exactly what does the fact that the market expects increased returns tell us about the benefits and costs of the sale of control? An increase in the stock price indicates the market's assessment of a probable increase in the payment stream, but not the mode of increase in the payment stream—whether increased dividend payout, future tender offer for the minority shares, or cash out merger at a premium over the market price.

In any event, with the exception of Brown v. Halbert, supra, most cases since Perlman v. Feldmann have rejected a requirement that the seller of control account to other stockholders for the premium received, at least in the absence of good reason to believe, or to investigate whether, the buyer is a looter or the buyer has a structural conflict of interest with the seller's business. The leading case is **Zetlin v. Hanson Holdings, Inc.,** 48 N.Y.2d 684, 421 N.Y.S.2d 877, 397 N.E.2d 387 (1979), in which the plaintiff challenged the sale of a 44.4 percent control block at a 100 percent premium over market. The New York Court of Appeals rejected the plaintiff's suggestion of an equal opportunity rule with the following comment: "This rule would profoundly affect the manner in which controlling stock interests are now transferred. It would require, essentially, that a controlling interest be transferred only by means of an offer to all stockholders, i.e., a tender offer. This would be contrary to existing law and if so radical a change is to be effected it would best be done by the Legislature."[h]

State legislatures have, in fact, effected radical changes in legal control of the conduct of purchasers of control blocks in recent years. But the equal opportunity rule has not figured in this legislation. Under the "control share" antitakeover statutes enacted in a number of jurisdictions during the 1980s, a majority of the disinterested shareholders must, in some cases, approve the purchase prior to consummation of a subsequent merger giving the purchaser 100 per cent of the target's stock. In other states they must approve the attachment of voting rights to the stock after the purchase. One state, Pennsylvania, has added a "profit disgorgement" provision under which a party that acquires 20 per cent of a firm's stock and disposes of the stock within 18

---

h. Moreover, notwithstanding such cases as Essex Universal Corp. v. Yates, 305 F.2d 572 (2d Cir.1962), which hold that the quantum of ownership that signifies control is an empirical question, such obligation as may be imposed on a seller of control has been held in Delaware to be triggered only if the seller owns a majority of the stock or has exercised actual domination and control in directing operation of corporate affairs. In re Sea–Land Corp. Shareholders Litigation, CCH Fed.Sec. L.Rep. ¶ 93,923 (Del.Ch.1988).

months must turn any profit realized on the disposition to the firm. See infra pp. 1144–1162 for discussion of these statutes and their impact on shareholder value.

2. Are different considerations and different standards of propriety involved when the transaction in control consists of a purchase by existing stockholders rather than by a stranger, or of the relinquishment of control allocated by corporate charter to one class of stock to other classes?

(a) **Jones v. H.F. Ahmanson & Co.,** 1 Cal.3d 93, 81 Cal.Rptr. 592, 460 P.2d 464 (1969), involved the creation of United Financial Corporation of California (United Financial) by the owners (including H.F. Ahmanson & Company) of approximately 85% of the stock of the relatively closely held United Savings and Loan Association of California (Association). The controlling group, in effect, contributed their stock in Association to United Financial in exchange for United's stock at an exchange rate equivalent to 1 for 250. Minority stockholders of Association were not offered the same opportunity. There had been no public market for Association stock. A market for United Financial's stock was created, both by original issue of its stock and by secondary distributions of a portion of the control group's holdings of that stock, and the United Financial stock was listed on the New York Stock Exchange. Association stock was the principal asset of United Financial. By the device of creating the holding company and marketing its stock those in control were able to enjoy the high prices which Association's earning power entitled the shares of the enterprise to receive in a public market. The Supreme Court of California in reversing dismissal of a claim by a minority shareholder that the control group had violated their fiduciary duty to the minority by refusing to allow them to participate in the exchange of Association stock for United Financial stock, said (460 P.2d at 476–78):

"After United Financial shares became available to the public it became a virtual certainty that no equivalent market could or would be created for Association stock. United Financial had become the controlling stockholder and neither it nor the other defendants would benefit from public trading in Association stock in competition with United Financial shares. Investors afforded an opportunity to acquire United Financial shares would not be likely to choose the less marketable and expensive Association stock in preference. Thus defendants chose a course of action in which they used their control of the Association to obtain an advantage not made available to all stockholders. They did so without regard to the resulting detriment to the minority stockholders and in the absence of any compelling business purpose. Such conduct is not consistent with their duty of good faith and inherent fairness to the minority stockholders. Had defendants afforded the minority an opportunity to exchange their stock on the same basis or offered to purchase them at a price arrived at by independent appraisal, their burden of establishing good faith and inherent fairness would have been much less. At the trial they may present evidence tending to show such good faith or compelling business purpose that would render their action fair under the circumstances. On appeal from the judgment of dismissal after the defendants' demurrer was sustained we decide only that the complaint states a cause of action entitling plaintiff to relief.

" * * *

"In so holding we do not suggest that the duties of corporate fiduciaries include in all cases an obligation to make a market for and to facilitate public trading in the stock of the corporation. But when, as here, no market exists, the controlling shareholders may not use their power to control the corporation for the purpose of promoting a marketing scheme that benefits themselves alone to the detriment of the minority. Nor do we suggest that a control block of shares may not be sold or transferred to a holding company. We decide only that the circumstances of any transfer of controlling shares will be subject to judicial scrutiny when it appears that the controlling shareholders may have breached their fiduciary obligation to the corporation or the remaining shareholders.

" * * *

"From the perspective of the minority stockholders of the Association, the transfer of control under these circumstances to another corporation and the resulting impact on their position as minority stockholders accomplished a fundamental corporate change as to them. Control of a closely held savings and loan association, the major portion of whose earnings had been retained over a long period while its stockholders remained stable, became an asset of a publicly held holding company. The position of the minority shareholder was drastically changed thereby. His practical ability to influence corporate decision-making was diminished substantially when control was transferred to a publicly held corporation that was in turn controlled by the owners of more than 750,000 shares. The future business goals of the Association could reasonably be expected to reflect the needs and interest of the holding company rather than the aims of the Association stockholders thereafter. In short, the enterprise into which the minority stockholders were now locked was not that in which they had invested.

* * *

"Judicial protection has also been afforded the shareholder who is the victim of a 'de-facto merger' to which he objects.

* * *

"Appraisal rights protect the dissenting minority shareholder against being forced to either remain an investor in an enterprise fundamentally different than that in which he invested or sacrifice his investment by sale of his shares at less than a fair value. (O'Neal and Derwin, Expulsion or Oppression of Business Associates (1961), supra, 62.) Plaintiff here was entitled to no less. But she was entitled to more. In the circumstances of this case she should have been accorded the same opportunity to exchange her Association stock for that of United Financial accorded the majority."

(b) **Honigman v. Green Giant Co.,** 208 F.Supp. 754 (D.C.Minn. 1961) aff'd, 309 F.2d 667 (8th Cir.1962), cert. denied, 372 U.S. 941 (1963) involved a challenge to the recapitalization of the Green Giant Company whose outstanding stock consisted of 21,233 preferred shares, 44 shares of Class A common and 428,988 shares of Class B common. The Class A and Class B common were identical in all respects except that sole voting power was vested in the Class A stock. 26 shares of the Class A stock were owned by one, Cosgrove, a dominant figure in the company's growth. The company had a net worth of approximately $23,500,000 at the end of its 1960 fiscal year and gross sales in excess of $64,000,000 during that year. Under the proposed plan of recapitalization, Class A and Class B would each be converted into a single class of new common. Class B would be converted at once, at the rate of one share of new common for each share of Class B. Class A would be converted in steps over a ten-year period, at the end of which each share of Class A would have become 1000 shares of new common. Thus the Class A stock would shift from ownership of .01% of the equity and 100% of the voting power to 9.3% of the equity and 9.3% of the voting power. The Class B would shift from ownership of 99.99% of the equity and no voting power to 90.7% of the equity and equivalent voting power. The plan was overwhelmingly approved by the Class B stockholders. After completion of the plan, the market value of the old Class B shares, as converted into new common, rose by more than 33%.

A dissenting Class B shareholder brought an action on behalf of the corporation and other Class B stockholders to set aside the plan on the ground, *inter alia,* that the Class A stockholders were not entitled to any premium.

The District Court held that a premium of some sort could lawfully be exacted by the Class A stock as the price of sharing voting power, and viewed the case as turning on the fairness of the amount of the premium. It concluded "that the premium shares issued to the Class A stockholders is commensurate with the benefit received by the corporation and that the plan is fair and reasonable to the Class B stockholders."

What standards should properly apply to determine whether the premium "is commensurate with the benefit received"? See Manacher v. Reynolds, 39 Del.Ch. 401, 165 A.2d 741 (1960).

(c) Is "control" a value for which the Government should pay when it takes, by condemnation at the current market price, all the outstanding, widely traded stock of an enterprise in which no person or group owns a controlling interest? See Short v. Treasury Commissioners [1948] 1 K.B. 116. Would a private purchaser be obliged to pay a premium for 100 percent ownership?

NOTE: FEDERAL DISCLOSURE REQUIREMENTS AND SALES OF CONTROL

1.   Transfers of control which are accompanied by resignation of directors and election of the transferees' nominees are subject to Subsection (f), added in 1968 to Section 14 of the Securities Exchange Act of 1934, which provides:

> (f) If, pursuant to any arrangement or understanding with the person or persons acquiring securities in a transaction subject to subsection (d) of this section or subsection (d) of section 13 of this title, any persons are to be elected or designated as directors of the issuer, otherwise than at a meeting of security holders, and the persons so elected or designated will constitute a majority of the directors of the issuer, then, prior to the time any such person takes office as a director, and in accordance with rules and regulations pre- scribed by the Commission, the issuer shall file with the Commission, and transmit to all holders of record of securities of the issuer who would be entitled to vote at a meeting for election of directors, information substantially equivalent to the information which would be required by subsection (a) or (c) of this section to be transmitted if such person or persons were nominees for election as directors at a meeting of such security holders.

2.   Efforts to obtain a share of the premium or its equivalent by invoking Rule 10b–5 have been made by stockholders who were not included among the sellers of control, but for the most part they have been unsuccessful. The only success was in **Ferraioli v. Cantor,** 281 F.Supp. 354 (S.D.N.Y.1967) in which the court denied defendants' mo- tion for summary judgment on a complaint under Rule 10b–5 by persons who had sold their stock on the market before they knew that control was being sold. The plaintiff had sold shares of General Baking Corporation at the market price of 8⅞ while the defendant, Dennison Corp., which was the controlling person, and other shareholders who were invited by it to share the opportunity, sold their General Baking shares to Goldfield Corp. at 12½, and elected Goldfield's representatives to the board. The plaintiff, suing only on behalf of selling stockholders, complained that he was denied an equal opportunity to sell, although certain shareholders "associated with Dennison" were given the favor- able opportunity. The court's opinion is less than clear, but seems to rest principally on the notion that denial of an equal opportunity to some shareholders to share in the offer to others to participate in the sale of control may have constituted "an act, practice or course of business which operated or would operate as a fraud or deceit upon any person". That assertion may have rested on the possibility that the other offerees (i.e., tippees) purchased on the market after getting the offer. The litigation was finally settled (January 1969) in favor of those shareholders who sold at about the time that the controlling persons

made their sale, by payment of $2 per share to the holders of 38,500 shares. (CCH Fed.Sec.L.Rep. ¶ 92,336).

The *Ferraioli* opinion was disputed in Christophides v. Porco, 289 F.Supp. 403, 405 (S.D.N.Y.1968) and repudiated in Haberman v. Murchison, 468 F.2d 1305 (2d Cir.1972). In the light of later Supreme Court decisions there is no scope for Rule 10b–5 to operate on the suit of stockholders who neither purchase nor sell stock (at least if control of the corporation has not been transferred by means of acquisition or sale of corporate securities by the corporation). But there remains ample scope for Rule 10b–5 when control has been sold and plaintiffs or the controlled corporation are buyers or sellers of stock. For example, any stockholder who sells before or contemporaneously with, but not knowing of, the sale of control is formally entitled to invoke Rule 10b–5 if he has been deceived or if a material fact has not been disclosed. This is true certainly with respect to sales he has made to the seller of control and possibly to the buyer of control or on the market. So also is it true of an investor who buys stock of the corporation not knowing that control is about to be, or is being, transferred, if a material fact which should have been disclosed has been omitted. Stockholders who sell *after* the purchase of control, but before it has been announced, whether they sell to the person buying control or to the person selling control or on the market, may have a cause of action under Rule 10b–5—as may an investor who buys on the market after, but before any announcement of, the transfer of control.

In all such cases where no affirmative misrepresentations have been made, the questions are first, whether and when either seller or buyer of control has an obligation to make any disclosure about the transfer of control, and second, what must be disclosed by either of them in order for the plaintiff to be able successfully to claim an omission to state a material fact. Answers to those questions are complicated by the fact that a rule requiring announcement of a contemplated transfer of control before the transfer is consummated will place obstacles in the way of consummating the deal even if no premium is involved. Moreover, the premises on which the sale of control by a stockholder constitutes inside material "corporate" information are not self-evident. In any event is it the potential transfer or the contemplated price (or both) that is material to an "outside" stockholder *prior* to the transaction? *After* the transfer of control, the question whether the failure to disclose the transfer or the price can underpin a cause of action under Rule 10b–5 seems more easily answered. Presumably, the facts about the shift in control and the price paid constitute items of information which a buyer, proceeding on the assumption that the old controllers still control the enterprise, would want to know. These and related questions turning on the distinction between deception of, and unfairness to, non-included stockholders are discussed in Schiff, Sale of Control: The Equal Opportunity and Foreseeable Harm Theories Under Rule 10b–5, 32 Bus.Law 507–522 (1977); Lipton, Sale of Corporate Control: Going Private, 31 Bus.Law 1689 (1976); Schwartz, The Sale of Control and the 1934 Act: New Directions for Federal Corporate Law, 15 NYLF 674 (1969); Hazen, Transfers of Corporate Control, 125 U.Pa.L.Rev. 1023 (1977).

2.　SALE OF OFFICE

If control through stock ownership commands a premium from the purchaser, does control through occupancy of office also command such premium?　Consider the following statement from the testimony of Professor Samuel L. Hayes in the Hearings before Subcommittee on Securities of the Committee on Banking and Currency, United States Senate (90th Cong. 1st Sess.) on S. 510.　Appendix No. 2, p. 230:

"Overtures to incumbents

"In virtually every cash tender we examined where those in control supported the bid, there was evidence that the bidder had negotiated with management prior to the announcement of his offer.　On the other hand, where opposition arose, it appeared that the bidder had sprung his tender as a complete surprise to the incumbents.

"This observation emphasizes the fact that the viewpoint of management and that of the shareholders of a company subject to takeover bid do not always coincide.　An offer may strike fear in the managers, even though it looks like a good deal for the company's shareholders. This is not surprising, for while the tender offer is virtually interwoven with considerations of power, job security, and other perquisites of office, for the average shareholder it is confined to the choice between holding or selling one stock.

"No astute bidder has failed to note this distinction, and many have moved to exploit it.　Our study indicates that typically a bidder will accompany his surprise tender offer announcement with a telephone call to the principals of the subject company.　The bidder will give assurances about his intention to retain the current management team and to give it the latitude to run its own operation.　Even if the acquiring company later decides that the old top managers must be replaced, their contracts can usually be bought for cash settlement."

———

Do the "astute bidder" for, and the "current management" of, the target encounter legal obstacles if such arrangements can fairly be said to be payments for sale of office or "governing power" belonging to the target rather than to its managers?　Consider **Rosenfeld v. Black,** 445 F.2d 1337 (2d Cir.1971), cert. denied, 409 U.S. 802 (1972), dealing with a transaction between Lazard Freres (Lazard) and an indirect subsidiary of Dun and Bradstreet, Inc. (D & B) with respect to a mutual fund of which Lazard was the founder and contractual investment advisor. Under the arrangements, Lazard was to terminate its advisory relationship with the Lazard Fund, and through the Fund's proxy apparatus to recommend to its stockholders that it merge into Moody's Capital Fund, a newly created mutual fund subsidiary of D & B which would retain another D & B subsidiary (Moody's A & D) as its investment advisor; for a substantial consideration Lazard also agreed not to become associated, either as investment advisor or manager, with any other registered investment company for five years, or to permit its name to be used in connection with such enterprises; and for a similar period to offer the consulting service of some of its personnel and to be available to perform some other services for the new fund and its advisor. The Fund's stockholders sought, derivatively, an accounting by Lazard for the consideration paid to it. In the course of its opinion, reversing a summary judgment for defendants, the Court (Friendly, J.) said:

We start from one of the "well-established principles of equity," recognized in Insurance Securities "that a personal trustee, corporate officer or director, or other person standing in a fiduciary relationship with another, may not sell or transfer such office for personal gain." There are ample authorities to support this proposition * * *. The reason for the rule is plain. A fiduciary endeavoring to influence the selection of a successor must do so with an eye single to the best interests of the beneficiaries. Experience has taught that, no matter how high-minded a particular fiduciary may be, the only certain way to insure full compliance with that duty is to eliminate any possibility of personal gain.

* * * [We] see no reason to doubt that, on the facts of this case, Lazard in its position as investment adviser came within the scope of this principle. * * * Lazard's influence with the Fund's stockholders can scarcely be questioned. Lazard had organized the Fund, and people had bought shares in it because of their trust and confidence in Lazard. All the Fund's personnel were furnished by Lazard. Unless the pattern differed from that of the industry, Lazard effectively managed the Fund's investments, despite the ultimate authority of the directors, quite as a trustee would do. If Lazard did not wish to continue as adviser and chose to recommend a successor and assist in the latter's installation, it was obliged to forego personal gain from the change of office, no matter how deeply or rightly it was convinced it had made the best possible choice.[9] It is wholly immaterial that the prospect of receiving future management fees if it had continued as an adviser would have been an asset of Lazard rather than of the Fund; the same would be true of a trustee's right to receive future commissions or a

---

9. While the moving affidavit seeks to make the Moody transaction appear as a once in a lifetime opportunity, it is plain that the Fund had many other choices. It could have merged with a fund already being operated and engaging in continuous sales, possibly one whose advisory contract provided for a lower management fee. It could also have hired another adviser, perhaps on better terms, or performed its own management, very likely at less cost, see Investment Company Report Table III-5, p. 103. It might have become closed-end to avoid further shrinkage. The $4 billion of assets already being managed by Moody's Investors Service could be regarded as a detriment rather than an advantage. See Investment Company Report 261–62. There might also be concern lest D & B's issuance to Lazard of stock having a market value of some $3,000,000 might have a negative influence on any future negotiations to reduce the management fee. Even if an independent examination would reject all such possibilities in favor of the Moody merger, the prophylactic rationale behind the prohibition of fiduciary profit in this situation would remain.

corporate president's right to receive future salary and other benefits. Even ratification by the beneficiaries would not save a fiduciary from accountability for any amounts realized in dictating or influencing the choice of a successor unless this was secured with notice that the beneficiaries were entitled to the profit if they wished, cf. United Hotels Co. of America v. Mealey, 147 F.2d 816, 819 (2d Cir.1945), and it is questionable whether even such ratification by a majority of the beneficiaries could bind others or the Fund itself. Quite apart from the question hereafter discussed whether the proxy statement was misleading as to the terms of the Lazard–D & B agreement, it is clear in any event that the Fund's stockholders were never asked to—and did not—ratify it.

* * *

It is argued that, however all this might otherwise be, a different result is demanded because Lazard's advisory contract necessarily terminated under § 15(a)(4) of the Investment Company Act and that, pursuant to § 15(a), the stockholders of the Fund authorized a new contract with Moody's A & D, allegedly on full disclosure, an issue we will discuss below.

Insofar as the argument hinges merely on the statutory nonassignability of the contract with the consequent inference that there was no advisory office that Lazard could sell or transfer, it proves too much. The same could be said of an alleged sale of corporate office or directorship or, in the absence of appropriate provisions in the dispositive instrument, of an executor's or trustee's position. The role of Lazard, as organizer of the Fund and its practical control of the proxy machinery used to recommend the approval of Moody's A & D as new adviser, made it quite as active and influential as a corporate president who recommends a successor to his board of directors, or a trustee who puts the name of a successor before a judge. Indeed, the very fact of nonassignability demonstrates that any payment made to the outgoing adviser by his successor in these circumstances over and above the value of any continuing services represents consideration not for lawful assignment of the contract—which is prohibited—but primarily for the use of influence in securing stockholder approval of the successor who expects to profit from the post. While it is true that the advisory contract is not conceptually an asset of the Fund, it is equally true that the expectation of profits under that contract is not an asset which, under the Act, the adviser can assign outright. Hence, if plaintiffs are correct in asserting that Lazard's few covenants were only a minor part of the consideration for D & B's payment to Lazard, Lazard and D & B must have assumed that the outgoing adviser was in a position to help effect the transfer of his office and that his efforts in so doing were worth valuable consideration.

* * *

In 1975 Congress amended the Investment Company Act to permit investment advisers of investment companies and their affiliates to receive "any amount or benefit in connection with a sale of securities of or any other interest in such investment adviser * * * which results in an assignment of an investment advisory contract * * *, if * * * there is not imposed an unfair burden on such [investment] company * * *", and for three years thereafter the adviser substantially disassociates from the investment company (i.e. 75% of the latter's directors must not be "interested persons" of the former) (15 U.S.C. § 80–15(f)).

SECTION F.   THE TENDER OFFER

---

1.   BACKGROUND

(A) WHY TENDER OFFERS?

---

(1) Introduction

A tender offer is an invitation addressed to all shareholders of the target corporation to tender their shares for sale at a specified price, either in cash or in securities of the tender offeror. The offer is sometimes for 100 percent of the target company's shares, sometimes merely for a controlling block. But on the assumption that almost all tender offers seek at least control of the target company, the question may be asked why that phenomenon has developed in contrast to the conventional form of merger, particularly since tax and accounting considerations (pooling and tax free exchanges) often argue in favor of merger, at least over a cash purchase. In addition, tender offerors may lack the opportunity for detailed investigation of the target and the protective warranties and covenants which the acquirer conventionally obtains in a negotiated merger.

The tender offer technique is most often used instead of the merger when management of the target company either opposes the combination or is unwilling actively to sponsor the merger even though it does not feel obliged to resist the takeover.

The acquiring company may seek the takeover or the control position for the same reason or range of reasons that impels mergers. Thus it may envision gains from economies of scale or other synergy, or, possibly, product market dominance. Or it may see a bargain purchase because it believes there are values implicit in the target company (in its assets or divisions as salable commodities) which are not reflected in its market price.

Whatever may be the acquirer's reasons, inevitably it acts only in cases in which the target's stock, or assets, are thought to be undervalued in the market or the acquirer expects to enhance the target's value—as is evident from the necessity to pay a substantial premium above market price—averaging around 50% in the late 1980s—if the tender offer is to be successful. The target company's management may oppose the takeover effort because it thinks the price inadequate (or the offeror's plans detrimental to non-tendering stockholders) and/or because it is reluctant to lose its perquisites. The prevalence, as well as the significance, of the latter is suggested by the fact that larger premiums are paid in hostile takeovers than in negotiated mergers. A fair part of the difference can presumably be saved for the bidder by making appropriate overtures to the target's management.

Whether the takeover movement offers economic benefits to society remains a much debated subject. Some commentators view takeover bidders as primarily financial manipulators who bootstrap acquisitions, or looters and raiders who intend to pay too little for 100 percent control and, if they get less than 100 percent, to milk the acquired company. In any event, takeovers are said to waste capital and management energy which is better spent on internal improvements, and result in undue concentrations of power.[i] Others see the takeover as the best method available to displace an inefficient management and put the firm's assets to a "better" social use, and at least by its threat to goad such management into better performance.[j] These factors are said to benefit the stockholders of the target company and society at large, because the acquirer will either pay the old stockholders more than market price or bring them into a more prosperous enterprise and will make the entire enterprise more profitable and therefore more productive for society.

It is generally agreed that stockholders of target companies gain significantly from successful tender offers if measured by the premiums they receive, or the increased prices of their stocks; but there is dispute over whether the stockholders of acquiring companies gain much, if anything, whether measured by stock market prices or otherwise, and some doubt whether gains accrue in aggregate and on average to all

---

i. See e.g., Stein, Takeover Threats and Managerial Myopia, 96 J.Pol.Econ. 61 (1988); Coffee, Regulating the Market for Corporate Control: A Critical Assessment of the Tender Offer's Role In Corporate Governance, 84 Colum.L.Rev. 1145 (1984); Lowenstein, Pruning Deadwood in Hostile Takeovers: A Proposal for Legislation, 83 Colum.L.Rev. 249 (1983).

j. E.g., Manne, Mergers and the Market for Corporate Control, 73 J.Pol.Econ. 110 (1965); Easterbrook and Fischel, The Proper Role of a Target's Management in Re-

sponding to a Tender Offer, 94 Harv.L.Rev. 1161 (1981); Gilson, A Structural Approach to Corporations: The Case Against Defensive Tactics in Tender Offers, 33 Stan.L.Rev. 819 (1981); Bebchuk, The Case for Facilitating Competing Tender Offers, 95 Harv.L.Rev. 1028 (1982); Bebchuk, Toward Undistorted Choice and Equal Treatment in Corporate Takeovers, 98 Harv. L.Rev. 1693 (1985); Schwantz, The Fairness of Tender Offer Prices in Utilitarian Theory, 17 J.Leg.Studies 165 (1988).

stockholders.[k]   There is also dispute over whether social gain results from the process, even apart from the costs of the process itself in the form of the fees and expenses of bankers, lawyers, accountants, etc. Some suggest that the social cost of hostile take-overs (i.e. displacement of employees, managers, supply arrangements, etc.) can in theory and does, at least occasionally in fact, exceed the private gains to shareholders of both companies.   Others argue that target companies are relatively less prosperous than others in their field, have a highly liquid position, large cash flow and small debt, and in general have inadequate management.   The debt generated in the corporate structure (of targets and bidders) by takeover efforts is said to result in less managerial discretion to misinvest and to produce more efficient monitoring of management.   Others have suggested that such descriptions do not fit all, or indeed most, target companies.[l]   In any event, the expenditures by such managements on defensive maneuvers and the correlative diversion of their energies from seeking enhanced productivity for the enterprise are alleged to be wasteful costs of the takeover movement. And the claim that benefits flow from the increased leverage produced by defensive maneuvers raises other questions.

Enough has been shown in the area to suggest that the takeover process can serve a useful purpose in displacing (and possibly in threatening to displace) inefficient or corrupt incumbent management and benefiting both sets of stockholders.   But the process may be beneficial in some cases and unduly costly in others.   In the absence of a principled basis for differentiating ex ante the beneficial and the costly, general rules for *all* takeovers offer uncertain comfort.   This uncertainty must affect the effort in any calculus of appropriate regulation, to weigh the cost of protecting public investors (and possibly other participants or constituents) against the benefits accruing from such protection, if such protection increases the cost of (or otherwise impedes) the takeover process.

Debate over these questions continued throughout the heated market for corporate control of the 1980s.   Some of the debate's flavor is indicated in the following excerpts.

k. See the discussion supra pp. 666–669; Mitchell and Lehn, Do Bad Bidders Become Good Targets? 98 J.Pol.Econ. 372 (1990); Scherer, Takeovers: Present and Future Dangers, The Brookings Review, Winter/Spring 1986, pp. 15–20 (suggesting that takeover targets in the 1960s and 1970s did not underperform relative to their manufacturing sector peers, and that post-acquisition manufacturing lines acquired by tender offer takeovers or by white knight alternatives were not managed either clearly better or clearly worse than the average of the industries to which the acquired lines belonged).

l. See note k, supra; see also Mueller, The Case Against Conglomerate Mergers in R.D. Blair and R.F. Lanzilloti (eds.) The Determinants and Effects of Mergers: An International Comparison (1980); FTC Economic Report on Mergers (1969) 70–81.

(2) Social Gain

SECURITIES AND EXCHANGE COMMISSION REPORT OF RECOMMENDATIONS OF ADVISORY COMMITTEE ON TENDER OFFERS (ADVISORY COMMITTEE REPORT)

July 8, 1983.
(pp. 7–9, xix–xxv).

ECONOMICS OF TAKEOVERS AND THEIR REGULATION

A. *Economic Consequences*

There is a broad range of opinion among Committee members as to the economic consequences of takeovers. Some members believe that takeovers create real value for both bidders' and target companies' shareholders and should be encouraged. The economic benefit identified is measured in terms of increases in the market value of the shares of tender offer participants at the time of such transactions. In addition to encouraging takeover transactions through deregulation, these members would reduce the costs of such transactions by limiting the defensive measures of target companies.[7] Such members are concerned that as the costs of acquisition increase, all corporations that are potential targets trade for less in the market because their values as future acquisitions are less.

At the opposite end of the spectrum of views on the economic consequences of takeovers are those that believe that hostile takeovers, particularly partial acquisitions, are socially and economically detrimental. Certain Committee members are concerned that the mere threat of a hostile takeover draws the attention of management away from long range planning and good business judgment. Further, these members believe that there are unseen social and economic implications to hostile takeovers.

A substantial majority of the Committee, however, is of the view that the economic data is problematic. They are unable to agree that substantial economic benefits or detriments of takeover activities have been conclusively established. Some question whether short term market price increases are the appropriate basis for concluding that takeovers provide economic benefits of such substance as to justify regulation adopted to promote such transactions. These members suggest that the principal basis for determining the macro-economic issue of whether takeovers are beneficial involves a long term evaluation of the economic soundness of the acquisition, as measured by the operations, conditions and productivity of the combined enterprises.[8] Others take issue with the general harm perceived by those opposed to

---

7. These members distinguish between defensive charter or by-law provisions and actions taken in response to a specific bid. They would limit the latter, but not necessarily the former, as the market would already have valued the target company's shares in the former case.

8. In addition to those taking issue with the basic premise that a short term increase in market price demonstrates eco-

nomic benefits, others have challenged the analysis of the available data or methodology of research. Some suggest that the data have been overstated. Others argue that there likewise have been increases in market price for shares of target companies that have successfully defended against hostile bids.

hostile offers; these members question the proposition that the method of acquisition affects its merits.

The Committee found that while in certain cases takeovers have served as a discipline on inefficient management, in other cases there is little to suggest that inefficiency of target company management is a factor. Similarly, while the threat of takeover may cause certain managements to emphasize short-term results at the expense of long-term growth, the Committee found little evidence that this is generally true. As with other capital transactions, the Committee believes the fact that some takeovers prove beneficial while others prove disappointing is less attributable to the method of acquisition and more to the business judgment reflected in combining the specific enterprises involved.

On the strength of the evidence presented, the Committee does not believe that there is sufficient basis for determining that takeovers are per se either beneficial or detrimental to the economy or the securities markets in general, or to issuers or their shareholders, specifically.

* * *

ADVISORY COMMITTEE REPORT, SEPARATE STATEMENT OF FRANK H. EASTERBROOK AND GREGG A. JARRELL
(pp. 71–73, 79–84).

* * *

We start from the position, backed up by evidence detailed in the Appendix, that tender offers benefit shareholders of both bidders and targets. The premiums paid to targets do not just come out of the hide of bidders' stockholders; there is a gain when the bidders and targets are evaluated as a unit. Moreover, the evidence also shows that both the regulation of bids and the targets' defensive tactics make initial tender offers more costly to mount, and thus there will be fewer of them. As the price of anything goes up, the number purchased decreases. Regulation increases the cost (including the cost of uncertainty and risk) in making offers. Fewer offers mean fewer occasions when shareholders collect premiums, which also means that all corporations trade for less in the market because their value as future acquisitions is less.

The premiums reflect real gains to society as well as to investors. Stock prices reflect the anticipated future dividends of the stock (including profits distributed in any "final" dividend, such as the payment accompanying a merger). Profits and dividends, in turn, increase when a firm becomes more efficient or better at producing what consumers want to buy. Higher stock prices thus are based on social as well as private gains. Perhaps the gains observed in tender offers come from the fact that bidders' managers make more efficient use of the targets' resources than the targets' managers do. Resurrecting a declining business is no less productive than building a new one. The threat of tender offers also induces managers to take more care in their work, so that there are fewer declining businesses to resurrect. Perhaps the gains come from the combination of the bidders' and targets' assets, including their production, sales, and distribution networks, into more efficient units. The exact source of the gain does not matter much, so long as it is real. The market evidence tells us it is real and large. Unless the market systematically (not just occasionally) is irrational, this evidence is compelling. Thus when tender offers are not made because of regulation or defense, real value is lost.

The gains from tender offers are important for new businesses as well as existing ones. The prospective investors in a new firm want some assurance that people will be looking over the managers' shoulders, ready to step in if the managers falter badly or if there is a better use for the firm's assets. When shareholdings are diversified, it is important to find ways, such as the employment market, the tender offer, and the proxy contest, to control the agency costs of management, which scattered shareholders cannot do for themselves. (Agency costs are the full costs, in both monitoring and lost profits, that investors incur in inducing managers to act completely in the investors' interests rather than the managers' own. Agency costs are apt to rise as managers' stake in the firms' profits falls, for the smaller the managers' stake, the less they will sacrifice at the margin to obtain gains that accrue to other people.) Investors pay more for new stock with better safeguards against agency costs built in. Another way to put this is that new investments are more attractive (and hence society will invest more, increasing productivity) when tender offers are available.

Much of this seems accepted by the Committee, although the report does not say so explicitly.

* * *

The Advisory Committee apparently saw its task as "balancing" fairness and deterrence. It wanted to obtain more fairness—more equality in the distribution of gains, given the existence of an offer—without unduly reducing the number of gain-creating offers. The regulation of bidders is designed with this fairness goal in mind. If the only objective of regulation is "more gains to shareholders, given an offer", then it also makes sense to permit targets to engage in defensive tactics that create auctions, although not to try to defeat offers altogether. Perhaps this explains the Advisory Committee's treatment of defensive tactics; it tries to balance auctioneering against offer-defeating strategies.

The critical assumptions underlying the Advisory Committee's work is that the target's shareholders want "equal" or "fair" distribution of gains, given that an offer has occurred, and that regulation is concerned almost exclusively with these shareholders. The Advisory Committee's recommendations systematically ignore the interests of bidders' and bystanders' shareholders. The focus is exclusively targets' shareholders, the perspective ex post (that is, it assumes that an offer is on the table). The recommendations recognize the effect of regulations on the number of future offers only incidentally, as part of the "balanc-ing" procedure. The shareholders of bidders get precious little recogni-tion. Yet the shareholders of bidders and the shareholders of targets are, or can easily be, the same people, who want to maximize the value of their whole portfolios, not just to get the best price they can given that an offer has landed on the table. This suggests that it is fallacious to assume that shareholders want "fair" treatment in the first place.

* * *

The definition of unfairness with unequal returns, given that an offer has occurred, is an unusual one. Most of us think of a game as fair when it is conducted in accordance with rules laid down in advance. A roulette game is fair if there are no unknown magnets under the table; it need not pay off on every number every time in order to be fair, and it need not give the players even odds with the house. If there are *known* magnets (so that red pays off twice as often as white), the game is still perfectly fair. There will be an adjustment in the odds. Similarly, insurance is fair if the premium reflects the chance of loss and the cost of administering the program. Many policyholders will never collect, and the total premiums may well exceed the total payout, yet the system is fair nonetheless.

Buying stock in new companies is risky business; many people will lose a bundle. We do not think of this as unfair, however, because shareholders go in with their eyes open. Shareholding is *actuarially* fair, the sense relevant here. The whole premise of the Securities Act of 1933 is that shareholders should be allowed to make choices—to take risks—if they have access to the information or advice necessary to act intelligently. People either demand compensation for the risks they take or shift to less risky investments.

Moreover, the equation of unfairness and abuse with unequal division assumes that shareholders *want* equal divisions. There is no evidence that they do. It is more appropriate to assume that share-holders want to maximize the expected value of their shares, not to concentrate on how the gains are divided in a given case. Almost all shareholders are repeat players in the market. If they do not get cut in on the gains today, they will tomorrow.

A shareholder who owns a share of stock in a randomly-selected firm (that is, one that could be either a bidder, a target, or a bystander) would not want equitable division of gains at the expense of a reduction in the number of offers. Investors unanimously prefer to maximize the total gains of shareholdings, even at the risk of unequal division, unless they are significantly risk-averse.[3] The holder of a more-valuable share can sell it and realize the gains.

Thus there are two questions. Does equal distribution of gains reduce value? Are investors risk-averse (in a way they cannot over-

3. Harry DeAngelo, Competition and Unanimity, 71 Am.Econ.Rev. 18 (1981); Louis Makowski, Competition and Una-nimity Revisited, 73 Am.Econ.Rev. 329 (1983).

come)? On the first question the answer is straightforward. Unequal division of gains may be very important in creating incentives to produce gains. The people who take active roles in gain production (the bidders and market professionals) incur substantial costs in searching for targets and bearing risk. They need more compensation than passive investors get to make this worthwhile.[4] Passive investors would like to get more, given an offer, but they know that if there is a rule of equal divisions, then it pays to be passive rather than active. An incentive to be passive is a formula for economic slumber.

Those who bring opportunities into being also need to differentiate among the passive investors. If the passive shareholders know that all will be treated equally—if, for example, those who do not tender are guaranteed returns equal to or better than those who do—why should any passive investor take the time and risk necessary to tender his shares? Better to sit back and watch, getting the gains without the costs. If more than a few investors reason this way, though, tender offers again become harder and costlier to mount, to everyone's detriment. "Unequal" treatment of shareholders thus is beneficial to shareholders, because it encourages them to cooperate in the creation of economic gains. When they do not cooperate, offers are deterred. There is a reduction in the expected value of each share, whereas a reshuffling of the gains when an offer does occur would not affect the expected value of the share at all. An investor interested in total returns thus would gleefully permit extra payoffs to some—what the Advisory Committee calls "abuses" or "coercive" (Report at 25)—whenever they increased the number of offers.

These arguments about unequal divisions may appear to overlook the fact that small shareholders are likely to be risk averse, and that such shareholders also may not play the game often enough to get their cut of the gains. This brings us to the second problem in the Advisory Committee's approach: these small, risk-averse shareholders can protect themselves very easily, at costs far lower than those entailed by the proposed regulations.[5] As a practical matter, they are not risk-averse.

Self-protection is simple. The small, risk-averse shareholder may simply sell his shares in the market—getting the enhanced price available in a world of easy takeovers—and buy something else. One option is to buy debt. Bonds and bond funds are not affected very much by tender offers, and the investor seeking security and identical treatment with the pros can get it through debt. Money market funds and banks are not affected at all by tender offers. Neither are the stocks of the very largest companies, which may be too big to take over.

---

4. Just consider the "unequal" treatment of managers, who get stock options and bonuses denied to ordinary, small shareholders. Is this unfair, reprehensible treatment, or is it an incentive necessary to induce managers to create the gains the small shareholders enjoy? Tender offerors and active shareholders need similar compensation.

5. This point is made in greater detail in Frank H. Easterbrook & Daniel R. Fischel, Corporate Control Transactions, 91 Yale L.J. 698, 711–14 (1982); Frank H. Easterbrook & Daniel R. Fischel, Auctions and Sunk Costs in Tender Offers, 35 Stan. L.Rev. 1, 7–9 (1982).

The other option is to buy a mutual fund or some other diversified portfolio. Then the investor is sure to hold bidders as well as targets and bystanders. More to the point, the "small" investor holding a mutual fund, pooled trust certificate, pension plan, or other diversified portfolio—the way "small" investors hold more than 90% of their investments—is delighted by any rule that enables market professionals to improve their position. Professionals manage these funds and trusts. There is no problem of timing when a mutual fund or pension trust hears about a tender offer. The money manager can move with dispatch.

We thus find it ironic that the Advisory Committee should express great concern for the plight of the small investor, unable to take advantage of a tender offer or open market purchase program. The risk-averse small investor is the one whose funds are under professional management or in instruments (debt or very large firms) that assure equal payouts. The person who needs to read the tender offer forms and decide for himself is generally the investor with a goodly stake in the market, $100,000 of investment and up, who can well afford to hold a diversified portfolio if he wants and is not likely to be baffled by the complexities of an offer. If he finds himself unsure, he can sell in the market, where professional investors, competing among themselves, have set a price fairly reflecting the probabilities of success of the various options open at the time.

Doubtless these forms of self-protection are imperfect. Not all small investors diversify their holdings or place them under professional management. But those who do not do so have reasons of their own. As things are (or were before the Williams Act in 1968) they are free to choose. They can protect themselves or take risks. If regulation is put into place for the purpose of ensuring equal payouts to all shareholders in each offer, all shareholders lose this option. It is difficult to see how we help shareholders by denying them an option (taking risk in pursuit of larger gains) they now have, while not creating any new option that they now lack. Regulation seems wholly destructive here.

The self-protection mechanisms discussed here have costs, no doubt of that. All of us, though, should be willing to compare these costs—small by any count—with the costs of new regulation. The costs of regulation are unlikely to be smaller than the costs of self-protection.

* * *

HERMAN AND LOWENSTEIN, THE EFFICIENCY EFFECTS OF HOSTILE TAKE-OVERS

In Coffee, Lowenstein and Rose–Ackerman (Eds.) Knights, Raiders and Targets: The Impact of the Hostile Takeover 211 (1988); pp. 213 to 216.

* * *

SOME FUNDAMENTAL POSTULATES OF EFFICIENCY–
ENHANCEMENT MODELS

Analyses that feature takeovers as efficiency-enhancing start with the premise that the acquiring firms' managements are striving to maximize shareholder wealth. In their search for ways of improving shareholder wealth, these managements observe that other firms are badly run or fail to put their resources to best use. These managers are thereby induced to acquire such badly managed firms, to take advantage of the Manne opportunity value. They frequently and regrettably encounter target managements who go to great pains to prevent takeovers that would provide large stockholder windfalls. It would appear, then, that the *defending* managements are not striving to maximize shareholder benefits. This dichotomous treatment of the motivation of the managers of bidding and acquired firms is partially bridged by the concession that there exists one dimension—the evaluation and hiring of management services—in which managerial and stockholder interests may deviate seriously. There may be "agency costs" as the agents fail to police themselves adequately; hence the service of takeovers in keeping such agency costs under control.

The flaw in this argument is that it opens a Pandora's box and gives no reason for closing it with only "defenses against takeovers" and "agency costs" removed. If managements can so egregiously waste opportunities where stockholder wealth could be quickly and obviously increased by more than 50 percent, it will not suffice to make this an exception to management loyalty by mere assertion or reference to stock option plans.[17] If managers can openly ignore stockholder interests in the one case—an obvious and public one—the reasonable presumption to be rebutted is that they may pursue non-stockholder interests in other cases, most relevantly here, in *acquiring* other companies. Efficiency enhancement may be only a partial and special case explanation of takeovers.

If managements defending against takeovers can pursue their private ends in serious violation of shareholder interests, this also raises questions about the meaning of the "agency" relationship and the parallel asymmetry of *its* applications. If the "agent" (management) is not subject to the control of his principals in the one case, why should we assume control in other cases? If the agent himself controls or substantially influences the board of directors, the control that the board then imposes on his activities may be largely nominal. The gearing of managerial and shareholder interests via executive compensation arrangements, for example, may be illusory if the fixing of the salaries and bonuses is under the control of the agent (who may adjust

---

17. An important alternative strand of "reductionist" analysis stresses an active managerial labor market and a labor market for directors to discipline managers. Fama, for example, elevates managerial-directorial labor markets to primacy, leaving the market for corporate control as a "last resort"; Agency Problems and the Theory of the Firm, 88 J.Pol.Econ. 288, 295 [1980]. Among its other weaknesses, the institutional premises of this alternative line of analysis seem to us far-fetched. See below, notes * * * 18 and 19 and associated text.

them ex post facto to accomplish his goals).[19]   The agreement of the
board to a new acquisition program may be as compelling an illustration of the control by the agent as board approval of management's
compensation arrangements.

The recent literature in defense of takeovers treats too lightly the
role of the board and the dynamics of power within the corporation.
Sometimes, on occasions when the virtues of the market for corporate
control are being extolled, the thoroughgoing domination of the organization by the management is stressed.   At other times, when it is
desired to show that the managerial interest may still be kept in line
with that of the shareholders by devices such as stock option plans,
reference is made to the independent directors who, according to Fama,
act "as professional referees [and have the] task * * * to stimulate and
oversee the competition among the firm's top managers * * *.   [The]
outside directors are in their turn disciplined by the market for their
services which *prices* them according to their performance as referees."[21]   If the board is dominated by the management and the management dominates the proxy machinery, however, the "price" will be a
function of service to the controlling management.   And there would
seem to be no independent source of power to contract that would
effectively limit the actions of the "agent."   The ability of the agent to
resist value enhancing takeover bids points up the fact that the agency
contract is an elusive construct, which permits an evasion of the
realities of corporate control and power.

The new defenses of takeovers as efficiency-enhancing also rest
their case heavily on stock prices as providing reliable measures of
asset and managerial worth.   Efficient markets digest all available
information and yield prices that show the only true valuation of the
assets of each company and their potential in the hands of existing
managements.   Takeover bid prices thus reflect the anticipated enhancement of values based on the perceived superiority of the new
management and its plans for redeployment, etc.   The efficient markets hypothesis denies that the stock market could undervalue corporate assets in any meaningful way.   There is, it is true, substantial
evidence of information-arbitrage market efficiency, meaning that
prices respond quickly to new information and "their correlations with
past histories are too weak to be exploited profitably."[23]   But this
technical efficiency is very different from the claimed ability of the
market to value stocks in accordance with the expected stream of

19. W. Lewellen, Recent Evidence on
Senior Executive Pay, Nat.Tax J. 161–64
[1975]; Herman, Corporate Control, Corporate Power 95–96.   In a 1982 study of 140
large corporations, Carol Loomis found
"some examples of consistency in which
pay and performance match.   But there
were many more examples of irrationality
and contradiction." Peter Grace, of W.R.
Grace, received, for example, a bonus of $1
million in 1981 in "recognition of his accomplishments during his 36–year tenure,"

a period in which the shareholders earned
an annual return of 7.4 percent. Loomis,
The Madness of Executive Compensation,
Fortune, July 12, 1982.

21. Fama, Agency Problems and the
Theory of the Firm, supra note 16, at 293–
94. Emphasis added.

23. Tobin, On the Efficiency of the Financial System, Hirsch Memorial Lecture,
May 15, 1984, at 6.

future earnings or dividends. On the contrary, there is substantial evidence that fundamental value equilibria are special cases. Traders and institutional investors, having extremely short time horizons, are influenced by their perceptions of what other market traders and the public will be thinking of stock prospects. This is not irrational. The stock market is almost entirely a secondary market, and the pricing of shares depends on extremely difficult projections of earnings and dividends on the one hand and an essentially subjective valuation process— fixing the price-earnings ratios—on the other. In the face of such uncertainty, it is not surprising that investors react by looking as much or more to each other—playing the "performance" game as it is currently called—than to the underlying fundamentals. What financial economists frequently characterize as quantifiable risks are in reality uncertainties of such large and incalculable proportions as to intimidate investors and send them scurrying to the seemingly safer ground of follow-the-leader. Such markets can be influenced by fads. The result is that stock prices do not move in any systematic relationship to changes in expected returns.[25]

There is good evidence, also, that investors who look at the value of corporate assets as a whole and as a producing entity value them differently than traders and passive investors.[26] No coherent explanation consistent with the efficient markets hypothesis has ever been given as to why acquiring firms will regularly pay large premia for companies whose managements they intend to retain and whose assets they have no plans to redeploy or recombine.

It may be argued, of course, that the acquisition which reduces undervaluation in trading markets is performing a valuable function, pushing market values closer to whole company values, and at the same time paying shareholders of the target firms sums reflecting those more valid market values. This may be true, but there are numerous costs involved in this rectification of prices, including both the transaction costs and, more importantly, a huge diversion of managerial effort into devising ways to reduce a vulnerability that did not grow out of managerial inefficiency. Some of the policies that may be employed to counter this threat, such as loading up on debt and "defensive acquisitions,"[28] may be seriously detrimental to the long-term interests of the shareholders. In short, it requires a giant leap to conclude that in order to correct market disequilibria we should encourage an active, day-to-day trading not merely of *shares* of firms but of the firms themselves. The main point, however, is that takeovers rooted in a market undervaluation of corporate assets are not designed to prune

25. See, e.g., Goodman and Peavy, Industry Relative Price–Earnings Ratios as Indicators of Investment Returns, Fin.Analysts J., July–Aug. 1983; R. Shiller, Do Stock Prices Move Too Much to be Justified by Subsequent Changes in Dividends?, 71 Am.Econ.Rev. 421 (1981); R. Shiller, Stock Prices and Social Dynamics, Cowles Found. Disc. Paper No. 719R [Oct.1984]; Wang, Some Arguments That the Stock Market Is Not Efficient, 19 U.C.Davis L.Rev. 341 (1986).

26. See M. Whitman & M. Shubik, The Aggressive Conservative Investor 51 [1979]; Shubik, Chapter 2 of this volume.

28. See, e.g., Panter v. Marshall Field & Co., 646 F.2d 271 [7th Cir.1981], cert. denied, 454 U.S. 1092 (1981).

dead managerial wood or improve asset utilization—on the contrary, they reflect a flaw in the market machinery and valuation process. Furthermore, an acquisitions route based on undervaluation can be pursued by bad as well as good managers. In fact, it may be the preferred path for those managers who can not perform well in their own productive domains.[29]

The efficiency-enhancement perspective also rests on a vision of a market for corporate control that gives only a very partial version of reality. There can be no doubt that Manne was pointing up a very significant development in formulating the idea of a market for corporate control. It is certainly important that by means of takeover bids outsiders can bypass managements and appeal directly to stockholders, a process that has made it possible to displace managements by operations and strategies in the financial markets. The former stability of corporate control and irrelevance of shareholder ownership and voting rights to corporate power has been badly shaken and weakened. Furthermore, the "market" has become quantitatively significant.

But several caveats are in order. The number of buyers who bid in particular takeover transactions is not large and does not meet a competitive standard. The assumption that these buyers are well informed is also implausible as a general rule, given the frequent lack of familiarity of the acquirer with the target's business, the lack of access to sometimes crucial inside knowledge, the great speed with which major decisions are frequently made, and the considerable evidence of unpleasant ex post surprises. We have also argued above that the Manne vision of the players in the market as competing managers seeking to control resources in order to manage them more efficiently is at best unproven. A substantial number of acquisitions are explained by the bidders themselves in terms of plans to enter fields with greater growth prospects, or to round out a product line, or to achieve some kind of advantage through vertical integration. Acquisitions made in connection with these strategic plans and efforts appear to be based only marginally on efficiency considerations.

The expansion of the takeover market has also brought with it numerous players who do not fit well the behavioral requirements of the efficiency-enhancement vision. There are now a substantial number of professional sharks in the business of putting companies "into play," not to acquire and manage these companies themselves, but to force bids and counterbids by unknown third parties. There are also "wolfpacks" of substantial investors now prepared to fund takeovers by

29. Analysts of the thrift crisis have stressed the problems of "moral hazard" and "adverse selection" that arise when financial institutions are insured and are permitted to survive with low or negative net worth. See J. Barth, R. Brumbaugh, G. Wang and D. Sauerhaft, Insolvency and Risk–Taking in the Thrift Industry: Implications for the Future, in *Contemporary Policy Issues,* Nov. 1985. Outsiders of dubious moral character may seek control to sell insured deposits to lend at high risk in a "go-for-broke" strategy, especially if minimal equity investment is required. Why should moral hazard and adverse selection factors not also impel inefficient managers with limited personal investment in their controlled companies to opt for rapid growth and trading in other companies as a preferred strategic option?

plausible bidders on high yield terms. The ability to mobilize in advance vast sums for bidding in takeover contests is a significant development. It has increased the size of potential targets and reduced the size and financial requirements of potential bidders. The risk to the lending syndicate is small, as the actual lending will occur simultaneously with the bidder's obtaining control, and the subsequent availability of the target's assets and income for payoff. The risk is greatly reduced by bidding with cash for only a bare majority of the target's shares, so that the lending syndicate is, in effect, assured of roughly $2 in purported value for each $1 invested in the takeover. (The target company's shareholders will then receive for their remaining interest new securities that are subordinated to the interests of the original lenders.) Whether the bidder's effort will "enhance efficiency" or allow him to dismantle and/or loot the acquired target would appear irrelevant to the calculations of the lenders, secured by the assets and short-term income flow of the captured prize.

The new institutional arrangements that are now in place are being steadily enlarged by the force of competitive pressure and short-run profitability calculations of investment bankers and investors, some of whom, such as thrifts urgently seeking short term earnings, are under heavy pressure to take a "piece" of each new offering in order to stay in good standing with the underwriter. These developments have already pushed us into a promotional environment in which the largest companies are now potentially "in play" and within the grasp of promotional interests.

* * *

NOTES

1. *Valuation.*

Can the debate over the purpose, effect and control of hostile takeovers be determined, as Easterbrook and Jarrell assert, by reference to objective evidence of value? Restating the question, should hostile tender offers be protected and encouraged because they produce "real" gains? If so, how do we know when we have a "real" gain? Reconsider the discussion of the sources of gains in mergers, supra pp. 654–669, and in particular, Kraakman's treatment of takeover premiums. Kraakman's discussion of value draws on both sides of the tender offer debate. What Kraakman terms the "misinvestment" theory of stock discounts is basic to the Easterbrook and Jarrell discussion. The "market" explanation informs Herman and Lowenstein's thinking.

Should both explanations be retained as alternatives, and perhaps, concomitants? If so, what follows for takeover policy? Does this complex view of valuation factors support the deregulatory program advocated by Easterbrook and Jarrell? If not, does it support validation of management defense tactics, state antitakeover legislation, or other law reform that would discourage takeovers? If not, where are we left?

2. *Antitakeover Reform Suggestions.*

Those who worry that unconstrained takeovers result in net social costs suggest legal constraints. Lowenstein, for example, would deter takeovers with a 100 percent tax on all gains from the sale of stock or derivative securities held for less than one year. L. Lowenstein, What's Wrong With Wall Street: Short Term Gain and the Absentee Shareholder 202–204 (1988). Lowenstein's suggestion would cause the time perspectives of investors to lengthen more toward the long term and would occasion greater investor participation in governance. Lipton and Rosenblum, A New System of Corporate Governance: The Quinquennial Election of Directors, 58 U.Chi.L.Rev. 187 (1991), make a more blunt (and arguably, more pro-management) proposal. They suggest that annual director elections be replaced with quinquennial elections and that nonconsensual changes of control between elections be barred, but that major stockholders have direct access to the proxy machinery at the time of the 5 year election.

———

(3) **The Market and Sole Owner Standards**

The inconclusive evidence on the existence and extent of net social gains attributable to hostile takeovers leads to uncertainties in the legal task of framing rules for their conduct. Moreover, so long as the bottom line matter of net social gain is debatable, the significance of the social costs of information asymmetries and institutional skews and consequent inequities in the allocation of takeover gain to stockholders also remains debatable.

Significantly, heated debate over these allocational problems continues within the group that subscribes to the view that takeovers produce net social gain. One side of this theoretical dispute over takeover gain shows up in the Easterbrook and Jarrell excerpt in the foregoing materials. They advocate a "market standard." Under this, shareholders and society together maximize in the long run if the market dominates the tender offer process and the law assists the market with a rule of management passivity. Their opponents advocate a "sole owner" standard. Under this, the appropriate price in a tender offer is measured by reference to the price that would be realized by a single owner of the assets in an arms' length negotiation.

Schwartz, "The Fairness of Tender Offer Prices in Utilitarian Theory," 17 J. Legal Studies 165, 165–167 (1988), offers a more complete description of the two positions:

"The current debate among legal commentators about tender offers has proved difficult and inconclusive. These troubles derive in part from disagreement over the appropriate standard by which to measure

the fairness of particular offers. The commentators rely, often implicitly, on two distinct standards of fairness: the 'market standard' and the
'single-owner standard.' * * *

"The market standard holds that any offer above the target's
prebid market price should succeed. According to the efficient-market
hypothesis the prebid market price is the present discounted value of
the target's future earnings under current management. A bid above
the market price implies that the bidder can increase these earnings, if
bidders are informed, rational, and maximize profits. An increase in
earnings from the same assets is an increase in welfare. Hence, any
bid price that induces tender is fair, if economic efficiency is the
standard by which the fairness of a transaction is measured.

"The single-owner standard holds that an efficient sale is one that
a willing buyer and seller would make were both parties free from
coercion. To understand the application of this standard here, suppose
the state were to appoint 'selling agents' just to represent target
shareholders in connection with takeovers. Each agent would be
charged with obtaining for its set of shareholders the highest price that
the traffic will bear. This charge would reflect shareholder preferences
because each shareholder too would bargain for the highest price were
he the sole owner of the target's business. Consequently, the measure
of an efficient—that is, fair—takeover price is its resemblance to the
price that would emerge from a hypothetical bargain between a potential acquirer and such a selling agent. This ideal price is referred to as
the 'single-owner price.'

"The concrete implications of a choice between these standards are
best introduced by an example. Let Company T have fifty shares
outstanding that sell for $2 each. A bidder B believes that it can
generate sufficient earnings from T's assets to give them a present
value of $200; B thereupon bids $2.35 a share—$117.50 in total—for all
T's shares. Let the direct costs to T's shareholders of tendering
(mailing shares, rebalancing portfolios) be $.05 per share. The market
standard holds that the bid should succeed because the acquisition is
probably value increasing, and T's shareholders have been more than
compensated for their "losses," which are only $2.05 per share. The
single-owner standard, on the other hand, is not necessarily satisfied on
these facts. According to it, T's actual or 'true' value is the reservation
price of a single owner of T's assets. If this true value exceeds $117.50,
as it well might, a transfer at $117.50 would be inefficient. Therefore,
some single-owner adherents claim, the state should require a target's
board to obtain the highest possible price. Other adherents, believing
that boards have a conflict of interest (they could want to block
acquisitions to retain their positions), urge the state to create institutions that would effectively bar transfers below single-owner prices."

The two competing approaches lead to markedly different prescriptions for regulatory policy. The market standard carries a norm of
management passivity in response to a hostile bid along with a recommendation for the repeal of all state antitakeover legislation and the

Williams Act. The sole owner standard implies approval of the Williams Act but not of state antitakeover legislation. It also prescribes strict scrutiny of management conduct of tender offer response but not a passivity rule. Actions that defeat takeovers in order to entrench managers should not be taken, but managers should take defensive steps that maximize shareholder return.

Professor Schwartz goes on to advocate the market standard. Like Easterbrook and Jarrell, he concludes that auctions by targets are inefficient. Since auctions increase sale prices, they decrease the incentive of potential bidders to search for mismanaged firms. And as less search occurs the takeover sanction becomes a less effective disciplinary force. Schwartz, Search Theory and the Tender Offer Auction, 2 J.L.Econs. & Org. 229 (1986). Although Schwartz recognizes that dispersed target shareholders in an unregulated environment face a hostile bid in a disadvantaged contracting position, he argues that they are not so disadvantaged as is commonly supposed. Schwartz, supra, 17 J.Legal Studies at 170–183. He contends, *inter alia,* that the possible appearance of competing bidders will encourage offerors to make high preemptive opening bids that benefit the shareholders, and that higher valuing bidders are more likely to make short-term take-it-or-leave-it offers than are lower valuing bidders. In any event, says Schwartz, id. pp. 184–185:

"The disadvantage that shareholders seemingly suffer stems from their relative inability to dissipate the bargaining power that the ability to make take it or leave it offers confers on bidders. This suggests that adherents to the single-owner standard should support reforms that are consistent with the management-passivity thesis that Easterbrook and Fischel derived from the market standard. The suggestion may seem surprising because the obvious way to make takeover prices more like single-owner prices is to empower target managers to bargain on their shareholders' behalf, but this reform has the equally obvious disadvantage that the managers may frustrate transfers that benefit shareholders in order to preserve their own positions. When managers do bargain for shareholders, they are effective largely insofar as they reduce entry costs for later bidders. These costs can be reduced by lengthening minimum-offer periods and increasing the disclosure obligations of initial offerors, reforms that do not require the participation of target managers. Because involving target management creates the risk of blocking efficient transfers, the single-owner standard is best implemented by reforms that promise to raise takeover prices without involving target managers in the takeover process.
* * *"

Professor Bebchuk, responding to Schwartz, in Bebchuk, The Sole Owner Standard for Takeover Policy, 17 J.Legal Studies 197 (1988), makes the following challenge to the basic assumptions of the market standard, id. pp. 203–204, 206–207:

"In advocating the market standard, Schwartz's analysis concentrates on the effect that takeover policy has on the outcome of bids and thus on the allocation of target assets. From the perspective of efficiency, it is desirable that a bid succeed if and only if the acquisition would put the target's assets to a more efficient, valuable use. Let us denote by W the value of the target's assets in the bidder's hands, and by V the value of the target's assets under independent existence. From the perspective of efficiency, the acquisition is desirable if and only if $V < W$.

"Thus, it follows that to ensure efficient outcome of bids, a takeover policy should accomplish two things. First, the policy should prevent any inefficient acquisition—that is, any acquisition where $V > W$. Second, the policy should facilitate any efficient acquisition—that is, any acquisition where $V < W$.

"The problem with the sole owner standard, and the reason why Schwartz objects to it, is that it might sometimes prevent an efficient acquisition. Consider a situation in which $V < W$ and in which an acquisition would thus be efficient. The buyer offers some acquisition price P, where presumably $P < W$. Even though the acquisition would be efficient, the owner(s) might reject the price P, insist on receiving a larger fraction of the acquisition gains, and hope that the buyer will raise its offer. While the buyer might indeed raise its offer, it might also walk away because of strategic or transaction cost considerations. Thus, the potential acquisition gains of $(W - V)$ might be lost because of such "bargaining failure." Such a possibility exists whenever owners have the power to reject offers—whether in the corporate context or in the sole owner context.

* * *

"The point Schwartz misses is that the market standard is significantly inferior to the sole owner standard in preventing inefficient acquisitions—that is, acquisitions where $V > W$. Schwartz incorrectly believes that the market standard would prevent all such inefficient acquisitions. This belief is based on Schwartz's claim that V is best represented by the prebid market price of the target's shares. Given this proposition, whenever the offered acquisition price exceeds the prebid market price, the acquisition price—and hence also W, as the bidder will presumably offer to pay less than W—will exceed V, and the acquisition would be efficient.

"Schwartz justifies his critical proposition—that, for the purpose of identifying the efficient outcome of a bid, V is best represented by the prebid market price of the target's shares—by asserting that it follows from the semistrong version of the efficient market hypothesis. As explained below, however, this justification is inadequate because (i) Schwartz's proposition does not follow from semistrong efficiency of the capital markets, and (ii) in any event, relying on the hypothesis of semistrong efficiency in designing takeover policy is risky.

* * *

"* * * [I]t is perfectly consistent with semistrong market efficiency that, between the last prebid trading time and the time of shareholders' tender decisions, the target's shareholders would receive a substantial amount of novel information about V, the target's independent value. Because most of this novel information is likely to be in the nature of "good news," the estimate of V that shareholders have at the time of their tender decisions is likely to be higher than the prebid market price. Therefore, the fact that the offered acquisition price exceeds the prebid price in no way implies that the offered price also exceeds the best estimate of V available when the outcome of the bid is determined. It follows that the market standard would enable some inefficient acquisitions that the sole owner standard would prevent."

* * *

Bebchuk adds, id. p. 209:

"[T]he existing evidence does not establish, certainly not with a significant degree of confidence, the proposition that the prebid price of all takeover targets fully reflects all information publicly available at the time, hard and soft. The evidence does not rule out this proposition, and some observers might even view the evidence as supportive. But the evidence does leave us with the nontrivial chance that the proposition does not hold or holds only with important exceptions and qualifications. This possibility should not be ignored in designing takeover policy."

Bebchuk goes on to insert a competing policy concern and to question the market side's emphasis on encouraging investment in the search for targets, id. pp. 210, 212–213:

"The sole owner standard would perform better than the market standard not only in attaining efficient outcome of bids, but also in providing incentives to investment decisions. This superior effect on investment decisions is due to the fact that the sole owner standard, by providing target shareholders with a substantial fraction of the produced acquisition gains, enables investors to capture social gains that result from their investment. * * *

"* * * The gains that result from an acquisition are attributable not only to the bidder's actions; they are also attributable to individuals' prior decisions to establish, and invest in, the target. Thus, for such decisions to be socially optimal, the target's shareholders must capture the social benefits produced by their investment. Unlike the market standard, the sole owner standard would provide shareholders with a substantial fraction of the acquisition gains that are attributable to the target's existence. Thus, the sole owner standard would move us closer to attaining optimal levels of investment in given companies."

Finally Bebchuk asserts that by focusing on shareholder choice as a primary objective, the problem of managerial misconduct can be solved without leaving the shareholders defenseless. He suggests a reform that removes management from the center of the process and assists the realization of maximum tender offer prices. Tender offers would be presented to the shareholders as yes/no ballots. Shareholders would mark either their approval or disapproval of the offer depending on their satisfaction with its terms, and only offers meeting a stated approval threshold would succeed. In the alternative, the tender offer would proceed only approval by a separate vote of the target shareholders. Id. pp. 222–223.

Advocates of the sole owner standard also attack the search costs point from another angle. They point out that a first bidder that does not win the contest can recoup its search costs by tendering the block of shares it accumulates before making the bid, or by selling those shares on the market in the midst of the contest. Since search costs are not excessive in the first instance, auctions do not significantly reduce takeover activity. Furthermore, assets should go to the highest valuing user, here the bidder with the largest potential synergistic gain. Auctions facilitate that process. See Romano, A Guide to Takeovers: Theory, Evidence, and Regulation, 9 Yale J. On Reg. 119, 157–158 (1992). Professor Schwartz, in turn, rebuts this line of argument by reference to the economic theory of auctions in Cramton and Schwartz, Using Auction Theory to Inform Takeover Regulation, 7 J.L.Econs. & Org. 27, 27–30, 45–46 (1991).

Which side, market or sole owner, has the better of the argument? With respect to the market position, is it clear that, as a practical matter, the legal regime respecting tender offers should be cast into a means/ends relationship with the economics of the search for targets? Does the valuation picture, viewed as a whole, support a simple division between synergy and management discipline as takeover objectives? Return again to Kraakman's discussion, supra pp. 654–665. To the extent that market failure has a legitimate place alongside the misinvestment explanation of price discounts, a single-minded adherence to the objective of encouraging search and disciplinary takeovers makes no sense. It is not clear that these "searchers" unlock "real" value. On the other hand, what are the ultimate normative implications of the sole owner standard and its heavy emphasis on shareholder choice? Does it imply that management has a duty to auction the company in order to realize maximum shareholder value, (a) whenever a transfer of control or corporate combination is proposed, (b) whenever 51 percent of the shareholders communicate an auction request to management, (c) every five years, or (d) not at all? Why should maximization of shareholder value have to be conditioned on action external to the firm?

On two points all would agree. First, governing federal and state law sometimes follows the sole owner standard but in many cases follows neither standard and favors management. Second, this debate has been exhaustively recorded in the journals. In addition to the articles mentioned above, a limited list includes, on the market standard side, F. Easterbrook and D. Fischel, The Economic Structure of Corporate Law 162–211 (1991); Schwartz, Defensive Tactics and Optimal Search, 5 J.L.Econs. & Org. 413 (1989); Easterbrook & Fischel, The Proper Role of the Target's Management in Responding to a Tender Offer, 94 Harv.L.Rev. 1161 (1981). On the sole owner side, a limited list includes Berkovitch, Bradley and Khanna, Tender Offer Auctions,

Resistance Strategies and Social Welfare, 5 J.L.Econs. & Org. 395 (1989); Bebchuk, Toward Undistorted Choice and Equal Treatment in Corporate Takeovers, 98 Harv.L.Rev. 69 (1985); Coffee, Regulating the Market for Corporate Control: A Critical Assessment of the Tender Offer's Role in Corporate Governance, 84 Colum.L.Rev. 1145 (1984); Lowenstein, Pruning Deadwood in Hostile Takeovers: A Proposal for Legislation, 83 Colum.L.Rev. 249 (1983); Gilson, The Case Against Shark Repellant Amendments: Structural Limitations on the Enabling Concept, 34 Stan.L.Rev. 775 (1982); Gilson, A Structural Approach to Corporations: The Case Against Defensive Tactics in Tender Offers, 33 Stan.L.Rev. 819 (1981).

NOTE: TENDER OFFERS AS STEPS TOWARD FRIENDLY MERGERS

It is easy to overemphasize the distinction between "hostile" and "friendly" acquisitions. From a social welfare point of view, the bottom line question is whether combinations create value, a question which need not turn on the means to the end of combination. As the earlier materials on the sources of value in mergers show, supra pp. 654–669, hostile and friendly transactions have collapsed into a unitary valuation discussion. This unitary treatment in part reflects the institutional developments of the 1980s. During the course of the decade, lines between "hostile" and "friendly" transactions became less and less distinct, both in a technical sense and a value-laden sense. Many hostile bids resulted in auctions of control in which managers participated as bidders along with outside contestants. Managers not only competed with hostile outsiders as bidders, but, with their MBO proposals, they often initiated the control contests. When attention focused on extracting maximum value for the shareholders, the "hostile" or "friendly" origins of the contestant began to lose relevance. Most shareholders cared only about the amount of consideration and not the source. Market actors that formerly played only "friendly" roles came to compete with managers, most famously when the Kohlberg, Kravis firm entered the management-initiated contest for RJR Nabisco. Hostile bidders, once described in pejorative terms, came to occupy a more respectable place in the business world, at least for a time. If restructurings were a good thing, as many argued then and continue to argue, then the initiating party had a plausible claim to the status of a good person.

The hostile/friendly distinction was by no means entirely eradicated, however. The decade's last great contest was a struggle to preserve the friendly transaction's claim to primacy over a hostile alternative. See Paramount Communications, Inc. v. Time Inc., 571 A.2d 1140 (Del.1989). Furthermore, state antitakeover legislation, enacted as a negative response to the proliferation of auctions of control, enhanced the position of defending managers, and thereby reinforced distinctions between friendly and hostile transactions.

Thus, tender offers can be more neutral than hostile. Furthermore, some tender offers occur as steps toward the accomplishment of negotiated arms-length mergers, for the very purpose of discouraging hostile activity. For a description of this usage, see Green and Freund, Substance Over Form—S14: A Proposal to Reform SEC Regulation of Negotiated Acquisitions, 36 Bus.Law. at 1499–1505 (1981):

"*The Traditional Approach*

"The traditional approach to a negotiated acquisition was a single merger-type transaction that, if successful, garnered 100 percent control of the seller. It was commenced by an agreement in principle on the main terms—principally, price—which the parties usually reduced to a signed letter of intent that spelled out where they were headed, but had no binding effect. Upon reaching agreement in principle—whether or not it was reduced to writing—the parties would typically issue a press release announcing the major terms of the deal.

"Then there would be a period of threefold activity: first, an intense investigation of the seller's affairs by the purchaser; second, negotiation of the terms of a definitive merger agreement with appropriate exhibits, schedules and lists; and third, preparation of a bulky proxy statement for the seller's shareholders. The merger proxy statements would contain a full description of the deal, a prospectus-like description of each company, and complete financial statements, including *pro formas*. If the parties moved diligently, this could all be accomplished in about a month, at which point the merger agreement was signed and the preliminary proxy statement filed with the Commission.

"After several weeks of Commission processing, the parties would receive the staff comments and respond. The rule of thumb was that the materials would be mailed to stockholders a month after filing. Another month was necessary for solicitation of votes. The stockholders' meeting was then held, the deal approved, and the merger took place the next day. From the agreement in principle to the closing, a period of roughly three months elapsed under the best of conditions.

"But the problem with this approach (and the reason why we have used the past tense to describe this method of accomplishing public acquisitions—particularly where cash is involved) is that in recent years there has been intense competition among suitors for desirable acquisition candidates. During this three-month acquisition period, the purchaser under the classic acquisition mold is very much at risk as to whether the deal can be accomplished. For the first month, the seller is not even contractually bound. Yet the press release issued at the time of agreement in principle has signaled the business and investment banking communities that the seller is for sale and that the knowledgeable purchaser is willing to pay a hefty premium for the shares. Uninvited third parties can be expected to enter the picture.

"If a better offer is made to the seller, whether on a friendly or unfriendly basis, the seller's board will have to consider it seriously, even where a merger agreement has been signed. And a spurned third party always has the option of making an unfriendly tender offer over the heads of the seller's board, directly to its stockholders.*

"Emergence of Multistep Transaction

"For these and other reasons, the multistep transaction has emerged as a highly practical alternative to the conventional one-step merger transaction for negotiated acquisitions of public companies— utilizing various tools of the acquisition trade formerly considered appropriate only in hostile or overreaching situations.

"For example, a first step often consists of a negotiated private purchase by the purchaser, usually for cash, of a substantial block of stock of the seller from a controlling shareholder or group if one exists, or from a large but noncontrolling holder (often institutional). The agreement for the block may contain the purchaser's undertaking to make a cash offer to all other shareholders of the seller, for any and all shares tendered, at the same price the blockholder is receiving. Upon signing of the agreement, a press release is issued—the first notice of the deal—announcing that the purchaser has acquired (or, if the closing is not simultaneous, has signed a binding agreement to acquire) the block and has undertaken to make an immediate tender offer on comparable terms to all other shareholders.

"The key to most multistep acquisitions is the 'friendly' tender offer directed to shareholders of the seller. Under present law, and assuming that reference to the number of shares sought and price is made in the public announcement (as should be the case, if these terms are contained in any block purchase agreement or have otherwise been agreed upon at the time of announcement), the tender offer must commence within five days after the announcement. Ideally, the seller's board of directors should recommend acceptance of the offer to shareholders—or at least not oppose it—and cooperate in its implementation.

---

* [Ed. Note] The duties—and rights—of management which has signed a merger agreement and is then confronted with a "better offer" before the stockholders vote on the merger have been the subject of litigation, which in some jurisdictions teaches that Boards can preclude themselves from undoing, or seeking to undo, the merger agreement by "no shop" commitments (Jewel Companies, Inc. v. Pay Less Drug Stores Northwest, Inc., 741 F.2d 1555 (9th Cir.1984)), or draw on the merger agreement as a justification for refusing to remove a defensive device, such as a poison pill, that obstructs the tender offer (Paramount Communications, Inc. v. Time Inc., 571 A.2d 1140 (Del.1989)). In other jurisdictions, the courts permit (but do not require) management to seek to undo the merger. (Great Western Producers Cooperative v. Great Western United Corporation, 200 Colo. 180, 613 P.2d 873 (1980); ConAgra, Inc. v. Cargill, Inc., 222 Neb. 92, 388 N.W.2d 458 (1986); cf. Revlon, Inc. v. MacAndrews & Forbes Holdings, infra p. 939.) Whether one potential merger partner can challenge a third party for making a better bid to the other merger partner raises problems in the law of tortious interference with prospective advantage. Belden Corp. v. InterNorth, Inc., 413 N.E.2d 98 (Ill.1980); cf. Texaco, Inc. v. Pennzoil Co., 729 S.W.2d 768 (Tex.Ct.App.1987), writ of error refused, 748 S.W.2d 631 (Tex.), cert. dism'd, 485 U.S. 994 (1988).

"The final step is generally a merger transaction between the seller and the purchaser (or more commonly, between the seller and a subsidiary of the purchaser), as a result of which the purchaser ends up owning 100 percent of the seller. In this transaction, once the requisite shareholder vote is cast (with the presumption being that the purchaser has acquired sufficient shares through the tender offer and any prior block purchase to approve the merger), the seller's remaining shareholders are involuntarily eliminated. In exchange for their shares, they receive a cash payment, which is generally equal to that received by the tendering shareholders (and probably, although not invariably, by the blockholder too). In almost all cases, they have appraisal rights. Depending on the percentage of outstanding seller shares owned by the purchaser upon completion of the tender offer, a so-called short-form merger under applicable state corporate law may be utilized; if not, regular statutory merger procedures apply, but with little suspense over the ultimate vote.

* * *

"In many cases, the purchaser and the seller enter into the final-step merger agreement before the purchaser commences its tender offer. In these instances, the merger agreement obligates the purchaser to make the tender offer (subject to certain conditions) and further conditions the purchaser's obligation to consummate the merger on completion of the tender offer. This sequence, particularly where no initial change of control has occurred through a block purchase, can help get the merger over the 'going private' hump, since it emphasizes the arm's-length dealings of the parties at the time the merger agreement is signed. This tends to be a fairly stripped-down merger agreement, however, with few of the usual detailed representations and schedules—since the parties are generally anxious to avoid the delays inherent in negotiating such a two-party document."

How would Schwartz view this practice? How would Bebchuk view it? Note that hostile offerors also tend to buy a substantial block of target shares before commencing an offer, whether in a negotiated transaction or on market, and the Williams Act requires public disclosure of such purchases once a five percent threshold is reached.

(B) TACTICS IN TENDER OFFERS

---

(1) Bidders and Target Shareholders

(a) Short Duration

The economics of a tender offer impel the tender offeror to initiate the transaction with as little notice as possible and to consummate it as

quickly as possible. The bidder wishes to preclude incumbent management from preparing resistance. The incentive for prompt completion
derives in part from market uncertainties and in part from business
necessities. Time affords the opportunity for the market price of the
target shares to move above the offering price, so as to negate the
premium offered, either because of market conditions generally or
because a competing tender offer, stimulated by the target's management or otherwise, might be made at a higher price. Similarly,
fluctuation in interest rates for offerors which must borrow to obtain
the purchase price poses a difficulty which increases with the length of
the offering period. And delay increases acquisition expenses for the
services of the dealer-manager, the depositary bank and others. Finally, any tie-up of the offeror's capital argues for a brief offering period.
In short, enforced delay in consummating the offer can, and has been
effective to, cause the offeror to terminate the offer.

A short timetable also can have a coercive effect on target shareholders, particularly when combined with an offer for less than all the
target stock outstanding. Bebchuk, The Sole Owner Standard for
Takeover Policy, 17 J.Legal Studies 197, 217–218 (1988) describes this
situation:

" * * * Facing no restrictions, bidders would generally make offers
of the Saturday Night Special type: partial offers that are open for a
very brief period on a first-come, first-served basis.[36] In the face of such
an offer, shareholders' situation would be pretty weak relative to that
of a sole owner engaged in bargaining with the bidder.

"To start with, the brevity of the offer's period would practically
rule out the possibility that a rival offer would be made before shareholders must make their tender decisions with respect to the present
offer. Thus, when shareholders make their decisions, only one offer
would be on the table.

"The brevity of the time a given offer is open, and the resulting
absence of rival offers, would not have a devastating effect on a sole
owner's position because the owner would be able to exercise an
undistorted choice, and would thus accept the offer only if he concludes
that acceptance is indeed his value-maximizing course of action. In
reaching his decision, he would take into account the expected value of
other offers that might be made later were he to reject the present
offer.

"In contrast, in the face of a Saturday Night Special offer, the
absence of the threat of rival offers would hurt the target's shareholders greatly. For the dispersed shareholders might be unable to reject
the offer even if rejection would constitute their value-maximizing
course of action—even if, for instance, they expect that rejection would

---

36. Bidders are at present prohibited
from making offers that are open for a
brief period or that are on a first-come,
first-served basis. While bidders are free
to use partial offers, they do not use them
all that often * * *. This is because partial offers become more coercive than offers for all shares only when combined
with a first-come, first-served structure.

lead to receiving much higher offers later on. As long as the expected post-takeover value of minority shares is lower than the bid price (which, under existing law, might well be the case even if the bid's premium is quite modest), the shareholders' decisions would be distorted in favor of tendering.

"The gap between the bid price and the expected value of minority shares would present shareholders with a "carrot" and a "stick," both pushing the shareholders toward tendering. The carrot is the prospect that, since the offer is partial and on a first-come, first-served basis, tendering early would enable a shareholder to have all of his shares acquired for the bid price and thus to end up with more than his pro rata fraction of the acquisition price. The stick is the prospect that, if the shareholder does not tender or does not tender early enough, he might end up with all of his shares becoming minority shares and thus with less than his pro rata fraction of the acquisition price."

The "two-step front-end loaded" tender offer leads to similar pressures to tender. Suppose a bidder wants to acquire a target for $52 per share. The stock is trading for $42, but each of the target's shareholders value the target at $60 per share. The bidder structures the tender offer as follows: $60 cash for 60 percent of the shares, and an announced intention to follow the tender offer with a second step merger in which the remaining 40 percent of the target's shares are exchanged for debt securities worth $40. The weighted average value of the offer is $52 per share. The shareholders are likely to find it rational to tender. The calculation is as follows: tendering results in the realization of at least $52; failing to tender holds open the possibility of realizing $60 only if this offer does not succeed and a higher offer materializes; failing to tender results in the realization of $40 in the second step merger if the offer succeeds. Absent an ability to coordinate with the other shareholders, the rational shareholder will tender.

(b) Limited Information

The target shareholder, confronted with an offer, faces a complex decision—whether to tender, not tender, or sell the shares on the open market to an arbitrageur for a lesser premium.[m] The decision entails a

---

m. "Arbitrageurs are market professionals who provide an alternative market for offerees. They purchase the shares of the target in the market in order to tender to the bidder, thereby narrowing the spread between the preoffer market price and the offer price and providing market liquidity at or near the offer price during the tender period for those who do not wish to incur the red tape or delay of a tender or take the risk of the non-consummation of the tender offer or of purchase of only some of his shares. Since the arbitrageur can pay as much as the offer price plus a portion of the soliciting dealer fee he can provide a stable market at prices close to the tender price. He will set the price he is willing to pay on the basis of his assessment of the probability that the tender will be consummated. If he believes that the tender is likely to fail or that due to proration he will not have 100% of his tenders purchased, he will take such risks into account and the price he offers will be substantially below the tender offer price. If, on the other hand, he believes that the original offer will be topped or that management of the target will be friendly and negotiate an increased offer price in consideration of management endorsement of the takeover, he will pay more than the original offer price. In exchange offers, arbitrageurs function by buying the shares of the target and selling short the securities of the offeror." Lipton, Corporate Takeovers: Tender Offers and Freeze–Outs (1976) pp. 5–6.

comparison of the offer price (P), a projected value of the target in the event that the offer fails (T), and a projected value of the untendered shares if the offer succeeds (S).

The projection of T is a daunting task. It includes everything that goes into an *ex ante* fundamental valuation of the target and goes on to add variables. For example, once a bid is made and the firm is in play, the bidder's private valuation of the target becomes a critical piece of information. If that valuation is high, compared to P, a higher bid can be expected in the event of target shareholder resistance. A decision not to tender is indicated. If that valuation is close to P, no more can be expected from this bidder. But it does not follow that the shareholder will decide that this offer should succeed. The shareholder's willingness to accept the offer also will depend on an estimate of, first, the likelihood of the appearance of a competing bid, and, second, an estimate of the value of the company in the event that the incumbent managers stay in control. In addition, to make an estimate of S, the shareholder needs to know what the bidder plans to with the target and the remaining shares in the event of success. See Schwartz, supra, 17 J.Legal Studies at 174–175.

A target shareholder with an informed basis for making these projections plus complete information on the terms and conditions of the offer still faces a significant information problem. It may have no way of knowing what action the other shareholders plan to take. If S is less than P, and P is less than T, then the shareholder should hold out—but only if all the other shareholders hold out. Since S is the low figure, if all the other shareholders tender the shareholder should do likewise. Id.

Thus the bidder's interest in prompt consummation is coupled with an interest in minimum disclosure. The less the target shareholders and potential competing bidders know about the bidder, its valuation of the target, and its post-offer plans for the target, the greater the likelihood that the bidder can win control of the target for a low price.

(2) Management Defenses

The efforts of managers to thwart takeover attempts, either in advance or in response to a bid, appear to be limited only by the ingenuity of counsel.

(a) Defenses Requiring Amendment of the Corporate Charter

A variety of "shark-repellent" charter amendments are designed to delay or complicate a successful bidder's accession to operating control. These include provisions (1) staggering the election of directors, (2) requiring "cause" for removal of directors, (3) requiring special qualifications for election to the board of directors (residence, occupation, etc.), (4) curtailing the availability of written consent action by stockholders (e.g., Del.Gen.Corp.Law, Section 228), (5) requiring super-majority (and disinterested majority) votes for removal of directors or sale of assets or merger, or for second tier mergers at prices lower than the first tier bid,[n] (6) limiting the voting power per share of holders of blocks of stock of specified size.   Other amendments contemplate the creation of a class of voting stock with greater voting power per share or special veto power on mergers.   Occasionally, too, mandatory requirements of offering to buy all the stock are sought to be imposed upon owners or acquirers of a specified percentage, such as 20 percent.

Such provisions are very common.   By 1986, over 40 percent of the Fortune 500 and over 700 NYSE companies had some form of shark repellent charter amendment.   See Pound, The Effects of Antitakeover Amendments on Takeover Activity: Some Direct Evidence, 30 J.L. & Econs. 353 (1987).

(b) Defenses Not Requiring Amendment of the Corporate Charter

Some of the procedures described above may be instituted by means of by law amendment.   But the most effective and widespread advance defense that management can employ without resort to the charter amendment process is the "poison pill."   This denomination covers an array of mechanisms.   The first poison pill plans were issued as dividends on common stock in the form of preferred stock.   Later plans were issued as rights to acquire preferred stock or rights to acquire notes.   The key takeover impediments in the plans are (1) "flip-over" or conversion provisions (as in the *Moran* case, infra p. 1080) under which shareholders of the target obtain rights to purchase the stock of the acquirer at bargain prices in connection with any merger that follows a tender offer, and (2) "flip-in" provisions (as with the notes in the *Revlon* case, infra p. 1095) under which target shareholders can put the poison pill security back to the target at a high principal amount in the wake of a successful tender offer.   Pill plans also may include extraordinary voting or other deterrent provisions.   The barrier they effect is substantial.   Flip overs and even more lethal flip ins make the consummation of a tender offer uneconomic from the bidder's point of view.   But the barrier is not absolute.   Plans customarily provide for redemption for a trivial price at the instance of the target board.   Thus, once a plan is in place, final decisionmaking authority in a takeover contest tends to lie in the target's boardroom rather than in the marketplace because no combination goes forward unless the board decides to redeem the pill.   Decisions not to redeem result in judicial review of the decision under applicable fiduciary law.

There are many other devices in management's arsenal.   Management can issue stock (with or without special voting power) into friendly hands, sometimes those of the trustees of an Employee Stock Ownership Plan organized for the occasion.   As discussed in Part IV, Subsection C, supra, management also sometimes repurchases the cor-

---

n. Such so called "fair price" provisions in charters, which are embodied in many state anti-takeover statutes (see p. 1145 infra), effectively preclude two-tier tender offers and raise the price for 100% offers, and pro-tanto discourage many offers.

poration's shares to reduce both corporate cash and the number of shares outstanding, and in the case of greenmail payments, to assure the disappearance of a particular hostile bidder. Settlements reached with particular bidders or potential bidders in these and other cases entail the execution of standstill agreements that freeze the stockholding status of the bidder at or about the number of shares held at the date of the contract. "Golden parachutes" and "tin parachutes"— contracts for generous payments to management and employees, respectively, if control of the corporation changes—do not block takeovers. But they do make them more expensive.

Managers in the midst of takeover battles can make moves directed at particular bidders (1) by granting options to purchase valuable target property ("lock ups") or target stock to preferred bidders or partners ("white knights" or "white squires"), (2) by entering into "scorched earth" sales of attractive properties, (3) by making a "pac man" counter tender offer against the bidder, or (4) by creating incompatibility between the target and the bidder by acquiring assets that would entail regulatory approval or antitrust clearance for the bidder.

None of the above actions amount to *per se* violations of state law fiduciary duties. But any of them can generate plausible allegations of breach of fiduciary duty or a state or federal claim of inadequate disclosure. Takeover litigation involves constant questions as to which, if any, of the above tactics is consistent with the duties—and rights—of a management faced with a tender offer. On what grounds can management legitimately use corporate assets thus to oppose a bidder (a) if the bid is for less than all the target's stock? (b) if the bid is a cash offer for all the target's stock by a bidder which proposes a cash-out merger if it obtains a majority of the stock? In the latter case, should management be forbidden from taking any "defensive" steps other than disclosing its position and the reasons therefor? Or does management have a duty to oppose two-step takeovers which contemplate, or create a likelihood of, a cash-out after a successful acquisition of control? In any event, does (should) management have a duty to consider, or to seek out, "better" bids or overtures, and therefore, at least when doing so, a right to oppose a tender offer? The cases and materials below illustrate underlying patterns and responses under state law and under the Williams Act.

A brief historical note should be appended to this survey of the tactical back-and-forth between hostile bidders and defending targets. The takeover movement of the 1980s proceeded in phases. In the early years of the decade, the bidders stepped up the attack. They were spurred in the first instance by relaxed enforcement of the antitrust laws, and then fueled forward by junk bond financing after 1983. Poison pill plans proliferated in response. The plans, combined with state antitakeover statutes drafted so as to pass constitutional scrutiny, caused the balance of power to shift back in management's direction during the latter years of the decade. After 1989 liberal and inexpensive debt financing also disappeared. As a result, hostile tender offers became a less desirable means of acquiring control, and the proxy contest reemerged as a major component in control contests. See Hamermesh, Defensive Techniques in Proxy Contests, 23 Rev.Sec. & Commod.Reg. 93 (1990).

(c) Empirical Studies of Defensive Tactics and Shareholder Value

Does management deploy its arsenal of defensive weaponry so effectively that it has a "show-stopping" effect—decreasing the number of takeovers and reducing the overall amount of premiums realized by shareholders in the long run? Or do defensive tactics cause more delay than deter hostile bidders, so as to assist the shareholders in surmounting their collective action problem, cause bids to go up, and increase the overall amount of premiums realized? An impressive body of empirical studies addresses these questions, but reaches inconclusive results. Qualified yes answers to *both* of the foregoing questions find support. It seems that some defensive devices adopted by some firms have a positive or neutral stock price effect, while other devices adopted by other firms have negative price effects. For a survey of the literature see Jarrell, Brickley and Netter, The Market for Corporate Control: The Empirical Evidence Since 1980, 2 J.Econ.Perspectives 49 (1988).

Jarrell and Poulsen, Stock Repellents and Stock Prices: The Effects of Antitakeover Amendments Since 1980, 19 J.Financial Econs. 127 (1987) is the touchstone study. It looks at the stock price effects of the adoption of two types of charter amendments: (1) supermajority voting provisions applying to all mergers following tender offers, and (2) fair price amendments, which are supermajority voting provisions that apply only to follow up mergers that pay the remaining shareholders less than the highest price paid by the bidder for target shares during a specified period. The study finds (1) that blanket supermajority provisions have significant negative stock price effects of around 3 percent at the time of introduction but that fair price amendments cause a statistically insignificant price reduction of 0.73 percent, and (2) that firms adopting blanket supermajority provisions have low institutional shareholdings (19 percent average) and high insider holdings (18 percent average), where firms adopting fair price amendments had more normal levels of institutional holdings (30 percent average) and insider holdings (12 percent average). The findings on stockholdings are interpreted as showing that the requirement of a shareholder vote retards the presentation of defensive amendments more harmful to shareholder interests. Compare DeAngelo and Rice, Antitakeover Charter Amendments and Shareholder Wealth, 11 J.Financial Econs. 329 (1983) (statistically insignificant negative abnormal returns); Linn and McConnell, An Empirical Investigation of the Effect of Antitakeover Amendments on Stock Prices, 11 J.Financial Econs. 361 (1983) (statistically significant positive abnormal returns).

Some studies subsequent to Jarrell and Poulsen accentuate the negative effects of shark repellents, while others reinforce the possibility of wealth neutral or positive results in some cases. Pound, The Effects of Antitakeover Amendments on Takeover Activity: Some Direct Evidence, 30 J.L. & Econs. 353 (1987), tests the effect of blanket supermajority provisions and classified board provisions, both thought to have negative wealth effects, and confirms that they dampen the frequency of subsequent takeovers. More significantly, the study shows (1) that once a takeover does occur, shareholders "protected" by shark repellents are not rewarded with higher premiums, and (2) that shark repellents do not seem to deter the incidence of front end loaded/two-step offers—the proportion of "any and all shares" offers is lower for targets with shark repellents. Pound concludes that, in practice, any increase in management bargaining power does not result in shareholder wealth increases in practice. McWilliams, Managerial Share Ownership and the Stock Price Effects of Antitakeover Amendment Proposals, 45 J.Finance 1627 (1990), makes for an interesting comparison. Like the Jarrell and Poulsen work, this is a stock price study. McWilliams' sample covers NYSE firms adopting the range of shark repellent amendments during the period 1980–1984. She finds that where the firm has a low level of managerial share ownership (10 percent or less), the shark repellent has significant positive price effect. The inference is that the dispersed shareholders of these firms rely on their managers to extract higher bids. She also finds that with higher levels of managerial share ownership, amendments have negative price effects, but that the positive effect with low ownership firms is larger than the negative effect with higher ownership firms. She concludes that on average shark repellents do not harm shareholders.

Studies of poison pills are more consistently condemnatory, but even here a contra signal shows up. Ryngaert, Effects of Poison Pills on Shareholder Wealth, 20 J.Financial Econs. 377 (1988), reports that where the adopting firm is not the subject of takeover speculation a statistically significant negative stock price effect of .34 percent results from the adoption of a pill. With takeover speculation the negative effect is a larger 1.51 percent. On the other hand, Ryngaert reports that the least potent pills cause stock price increases. In addition, pill-adopting firms have a low average managerial ownership of 3 percent, and in the event of litigation over the pill, a pro-target decision is likely to have a negative price effect (15 of 18 cases) and a pro-bidder decision a positive effect (6 of 11). Choi, Kamma and Weintrop, The Delaware Courts, Poison Pills, and Shareholder Wealth, 5 J.L.Econs. & Org. 375 (1989), and Malatesta and Walkling, Poison Pill Securities: Stockholder Wealth, Profitability and ownership Structure, 20 J.Financial Econs. 347 (1988), also report significant negative price effects. See also A Study On the Economics of Poison Pills, SEC Office of Chief Economist, CCH Fed.Sec.L.Rep. ¶ 83,971 (1987).

Studies of other devices extend this ambiguous picture. Litigation by the target has been reported to have shareholder-beneficial effects, due to delay and resulting auctions. But, of course, where the litigation succeeds absolutely and the bidder departs, the shareholders suffer a loss. Jarrell, The Wealth Effect of Litigation by Targets: Do Interests Diverge in a Merge? 28 J.L. & Econs. 151 (1985). Jarrell concludes that litigation may on average be consistent with shareholder wealth maximization. But cf. Netter, * * * (1987) (litigation based on claim of false 13D filing is detrimental to shareholders). Golden parachutes are said to benefit shareholders by making management less resistant to takeovers. Knoeber, Golden Parachutes, Shark Repellents and Hostile Takeovers, 76 Amer.Econ.Rev. 155 (1986). For a formal model to the effect that defenses that decrease the value of a target to a particular bidder, such as lock ups, litigation and crown jewel sales, can produce higher bids, see Berkovitch and Khanna, How Target Shareholders Benefit from Value–Reducing Defensive Strategies in Takeovers, 45 J.Finance 137 (1990).

What implications do these studies hold for policymaking? Should we conclude that defensive tactics injure shareholders? That they do not injure shareholders? That the matter tends to be determined by variables particular to each case? The studies do not seem to foreclose the case for intervention against management maneuvering. Stock price studies only reflect the choices of traders acting under uncertainty. To say that, on balance, those trading at the time a device is adopted project that it may have a slight positive result in the long run provides no basis for concluding that the device objectively maximizes shareholder wealth. As Pound, supra, points out, the shareholders may be guessing incorrectly. And, as the proponents of the sole owner standard tell us, techniques deployed within management's discretion hardly offer the best possible remedies for the collective action problem of shareholders facing a bid. The problem can be addressed directly by providing a structural assurance that the shareholders get an opportunity for uncoerced choice based on full information.

Those who tend toward the view that takeovers do not benefit overall social welfare may incline toward a more positive view of management defenses on the theory that the end justifies the means. But this initial response may have difficulty surviving extended inspection, unless sustained by a deep reservoir of sympathy for managers and their desires for status and security. After all, the empirical results go in both directions. Clearly, in many cases defensive devices only increase the stakes, so as to transfer wealth between the target and bidder equityholders. This effect presumably exacerbates the social welfare problems of lost investment opportunity and job loss. Where the devices serve their intended purpose, we are left with entrenched managers and a different set of social problems. Finally, defending managers often choose to take to the takeover field as players, participating in preemptive or responsive MBOs. By hypothesis, they thereby jeopardize social welfare for job security and the chance of a bonanza payoff. A basic and time-honored question arises: If significant social welfare is at stake, why should the legal system accord management groups the discretion to make the critical choices?

(3) Dual Class Common Recapitalizations

The dual class common recapitalization is a management defensive maneuver that merits separate discussion. Unlike "devices" that managers adopt and then hold in reserve until the day of attack, it presently and substantially alters the corporation's capital structure. It also bears a familial resemblance to the management buyout: it is a permanent alteration of the firm's organizational economics that bars a takeover absolutely.

(a) Description

Dual class common recapitalizations usually involve the creation of a new class of supervoting common stock and the alignment of the supervoting stock with insiders and the regular voting stock with the public shareholders. In the alternative, they involve the creation of a new class of limited voting common stock and its alignment with the public holders. The result is a new capital structure, with the public class holding a diminished control interest and in many cases an enhanced financial interest, and the inside class holding primary voting rights and in many cases a diminished financial interest.

Supervoting rights can be attached by adding more votes per share to the supervoting class or by attaching a majority of the seats on the board to the supervoting class. Once such stock has been distributed to the inside group, the publicly held class becomes a limited voting class automatically. Other means to the same end can be employed. For instance, a scheme can place a class of full voting stock carrying no financial rights with the insiders while transforming the existing stock into nonvoting stock. The insiders retain a financial interest to the extent of their prior holdings of the public class. The bottom line is the same. The insiders get unassailable power to elect a majority of the board. In many cases, the public shareholders get a step up in the dividend payout on the limited voting common in exchange.

The transformation from a single class, publicly held capital structure to a dual class division of voting and economic rights can be accomplished in a number of ways. In an exchange offer recapitalization, the shareholders approve a charter amendment providing for a class of common carrying, for example, 10 votes per share but receiving a 10 percent lower dividend. The supervoting common carries severe restrictions on transfer, violation of which causes the stock to be transformed into common of the low voting class. Then a one-time one-to-one exchange offer is made to the entire body of shareholders. The public shareholders have no reason to exchange, due to the payment stream incentive attached to the old common and the transfer disincentive attached to the new. Gordon, Ties That Bond: Dual Class Common Stock and the Problem of Shareholder Choice, 76 Cal.L.Rev. 3, 40–41 (1988), sets out this scenario and shows that given a 10 vote per share supervoting class, an insider group holding 9.091 percent of the common can gain majority voting power, provided that it exchanges all its shares and none of the public holders exchange theirs. In the alternative, the recapitalization can be effected by means of a dividend. Here again the charter is amended to authorize a new supervoting class of common again carrying strict restrictions providing for automatic conversion to low voting common in the event of a transfer. It may or may not carry a diminished dividend. The stock is distributed upon a one-to-one dividend declaration. No automatic change in voting power results since each public holder holds a share of supervoting stock. Control shifts as the public shareholders at the time of the dividend gradually trade their stock. Each trade causes conversion into lowvoting stock, causing the proportion of lowvoting stock held publicly to rise over time. In addition, the transfer restriction on the supervoting stock makes its acquisition by a hostile offeror impossible. Gordon, supra at pp. 41–42. See also Jarrell and Poulsen, Dual–Class Recapitalizations as Antitakeover Mechanisms: The Recent Evidence, 20 J. Financial Econs. 129, 135–136 (1988). Note that under either approach, this mode of defense presupposes an inside group holding a substantial, but less than majority block of common. Management groups controlling well under 10 percent blocks but desiring absolute security from attack tend to sponsor MBOs.

Dual class recapitalizations have their supporters. They point out that shareholder consent is required to effect the necessary charter amendment. The exchange offer mode gives the shareholders a second opportunity to exercise choice. At another level, the dual class recapitalizations are compared to management buyouts, see Gilson, Evaluating Dual Class Common Stock: The Relevance of Substitutes, 73 Va. L.Rev. 807, 811–823 (1987), and a productivity defense is articulated. The subject firms tend to be high growth enterprises dependent on the energies and skills of the inside group, in contrast to the mature, low growth subjects of MBOs. Absent the reorganization, the insiders would be less willing to accept the best investment opportunities. The announcement of the recapitalization is thus a positive signal. Since the public shareholders retain a substantial financial interest, they gain. See Partch, The Creation of a Class of Limited Voting Common Stock and Shareholders' Wealth, 18 J. Financial Econs. 313 (1987). See also Fischel, Organized Exchanges and the Regulation of Dual Class Common Stock, 54 U.Chi.L.Rev. 119 (1987).

The many detractors of dual class recapitalizations focus on the fact that the result is classic management entrenchment with all attendant agency costs. They also allege a wealth transfer. Voting control has a well-documented value, see Lease, McConnell and Mikkelson, The Market Value of Control in Publicly Traded Corporations, 11 J. Financial Econs. 439 (1983), and here the insiders acquire it for a suspect consideration. The shareholders' consent to the transfer is not effectively given. The first step charter amendment suffers the infirmities of all corporate governance provisions procured through proxy solicitation—the managers have agenda control, and no individual shareholder has an economic incentive to mount a counter attack. See Gordon, supra pp. 42–47. Furthermore, subsequent exchange offers are coercive. The dividend advantage attached to the lowvoting stock puts the public holders in an awkward position. If a given public holder accepts the offer and takes the high voting stock but the other public holders refuse the offer, the accepting holder in effect grants a dividend subsidy to the others. Ruback, Coercive Dual–Class Exchange Offers,

20 J. Financial Econs. 153 (1988). Lured by the carrot and hit with the stick, the rational holder declines the offer, even though exchange by all the holders would eliminate the dividend subsidy and at least delay any control transfer. See also Seligman, Equal Protection in Shareholder Voting Rights: The One Common Share, One Vote Controversy, 54 Geo.Wash.L.Rev. 687 (1987).

Question. Suppose you represent a shareholder who has just received a dual class exchange offer. You seek to obtain an injunction against the offer on the theory of breach of fiduciary duty. Would any of the following cases assist you in articulating a persuasive claim: *Katz v. Oak Industries,* supra p. 238? *Eisenberg v. Chicago, Milwaukee,* supra p. 378? *Kahn v. United States Sugar,* supra p. 618? *Perlman v. Feldmann,* supra p. 915? *Jones v. Ahmanson,* supra p. 928?

(b) Empirical Studies

Do dual class recapitalizations transfer value from public shareholders to insiders? As with other takeover defense maneuvers, a collection of empirical studies offers conflicting results. Partch, supra, studied 44 recapitalizations conducted between 1962 and 1984 and found nonnegative abnormal price returns (average gain of 2 percent; median effect of 0). Partch also found an average level of insider ownership of 48.6 percent. Gordon, supra at 28, studied 19 NYSE firms that recapitalized between 1984 and 1986 and found no significant wealth effects for the sample as a whole. In contrast, Jarrell and Poulsen, supra, cover 94 recapitalizations between 1976 and 1987 and find significant negative abnormal returns, with the negative returns increasing after 1984, the year the NYSE announced a moratorium on the delisting of issuers with classes of limited voting common. Gordon, supra at 39, surveys the conflicting evidence and concludes that these transactions on balance have negative wealth effects. He explains the wealth neutral statistical results in terms of a trade off: the recapitalization signals positive investment opportunities, but detracts from the value of the public stock. The shareholders thus are deprived of an upside opportunity.

(c) Regulatory Follies

For many years, the New York Stock Exchange maintained and enforced a "one share, one vote" rule. Thus a dual class recapitalization would come at the cost of delisting from the NYSE. Neither the American Stock Exchange nor the National Association of Securities Dealers imposed a similarly strict requirement. In 1984, the NYSE declared a moratorium on enforcement of its rule in the wake of a dispute with General Motors, one of its larger issuers. GM desired to issue a class of stock with lower voting rights in connection with the acquisition of a data services firm controlled by a Mr. Ross Perot. The NYSE, in turn, desired to hold onto its base of issuers, for whom AMEX or OTC trading had become a viable alternative. The NYSE proposed a dilution of its rule. But this needed SEC approval. The SEC attempted to mediate a uniform one share, one vote rule among the NYSE, AMEX and NASD. See Gordon, supra at 6–8. When these negotiations failed, the SEC commenced a rule-making proceeding of its own. The result was Exchange Act Rule 19c–4, which bars all national securities exchanges and the NASDQ from listing stock of a firm that takes action that nullifies, restricts, or disparately reduces the voting rights of existing shareholders. See Exchange Act Rel. Nos. 25,891, 25,891A, CCH Fed.Sec.L.Rep. ¶ 84,247 (1988); Lowenstein, Shareholder Voting Rights: A Response to the SEC Rule 19c–4 and to Professor Gilson, 89 Colum.L.Rev. 979 (1989). Each of the NYSE, AMEX and NASD was compelled to adopt the rule.

But the story continues. The SEC's rulemaking authority was challenged successfully in Business Roundtable v. SEC, 905 F.2d 406 (D.C.Cir.1990). The court took the position that section 19(c) of the 1934 Act, on which the SEC relied for rulemaking authority, does not provide a sufficiently broad delegation of corporate governance rule-making power. The SEC rule thus lost its mandatory force. The AMEX and NASD thereafter withdrew the SEC rule from their books, although not required to do so.

No agreement among the NYSE, AMEX and NASD is in sight as yet. In 1991, the AMEX filed a rule proposal with the SEC that would allow AMEX-listed companies to issue high vote stock provided a supermajority of shareholders approved. 23 BNA Sec.Reg. & L.Rep. 908 (1991). In 1992, the NYSE circulated a draft proposal on voting rights with a view to a uniform result. Under the NYSE proposal, *inter alia,* (a) all shares would be freely transferable, (b) a decision to issue shares with disparate voting rights or to change the voting rights of outstanding shares would require approval by a committee of independent directors and a majority of disinterested shareholders, and (c) if a change in voting rights left a control group with a majority of voting power, the company would have to have a board with an independent majority. 24 BNA Sec.Reg. & L.Rep. 1444 (1992).

Is there a moral to the story?

(4) The Sole Owner Standard and Tender Offer Tactics

As we have seen, a tender offer, if friendly, but particularly if hostile, differs from a negotiated transaction in significant part because the sellers of control are not a single knowledgeable person who can bargain about the transaction; instead they are dispersed offerees who cannot function coherently either to inquire about the facts and discover the relevant information or to negotiate the terms. If dispersed offerees should, in the interests of efficiency and equity, have an undistorted choice comparable to (albeit not identical with) that of a sole seller about responding to the tender offer, certain bargaining disadvantages—both of information and of power—should be mitigated or eliminated. By that test, offerees need protection against (a) the bidder from undue pressure or, in certain cases, lack of information, (b) their management's failure to proffer relevant information in timely fashion, improper rejection of the take-over bid and efforts to thwart the take-over attempt, and (c) market professionals who may manipulate the tender offer process.

The following materials address the legal responses (both under state law and under the federal securities laws) to the perceived needs of target offerees for disclosure and for regulatory protection to facilitate their undistorted choice.

The legal rules which govern the game involved in the takeover contest are primarily (1) the disclosure, anti-fraud and market manipulation rules of the federal securities legislation, (2) common law teaching on the fiduciary duties (both restrictions and disclosure obligations) of the management of the target company to its stockholders and of the management of the takeover company to its own stockholders, and (3) state statutes adopted to impede the takeover effort in the name of protecting local interests and the target company's stockholders.[o]

2. THE WILLIAMS ACT

(A) INTRODUCTION

Special obligations are imposed upon bidders, competing bidders, and target companies by the portions of §§ 13 and 14 of the Securities Exchange Act, known as the Williams Act. These sections, which were first adopted in 1968, were stated to be designed to protect investors, and *not* to regulate takeovers as an economic phenomenon or to favor either incumbent management or takeover bidders. They impose two kinds of requirements—regulatory restrictions and disclosure obligations. The former, together with implementing regulations, are designed to prohibit (a) time pressure or whipsaw constraints on investors to tender (by requiring a tolerable period for the offer and prescribing minimum withdrawal rights), (b) discrimination among tendering investors, and (c) maneuvers for favorable purchase prices before or after the tender offer or short tendering. The disclosure rules are designed to enable the public investors to make intelligent investment (or disinvestment) decisions.

The following excerpts from an Address by SEC Chairman Cohen summarizes, from the SEC perspective, the concerns that prompted and shaped the Williams Act.

---

o. Two other types of federal regulation impinge upon the takeover process—the notification and waiting period requirements of the Hart–Scott–Rodino Anti-Trust Improvements Act of 1976 (15 U.S.C. Section 18A)—and the FRB interpretation of its margin rules that subjects debt of a shell company used to absorb a target to those rules (see p. 498 supra). Is the impact of that interpretation to reduce the usefulness of borrowed funds to the bidder in seeking a takeover, but not to the target in resisting one?

COHEN, ADDRESS ON PROPOSED LEGISLATION
TO REGULATE TENDER OFFERS

Chairman, Securities and Exchange Commission Before
American Society of Corporate Secretaries, Inc.
Colorado Springs, Colorado
June 28, 1966

It is interesting to contrast the regulatory requirements applicable to cash tender offers with those which apply when an offer is made by one company to exchange its shares for shares of another. The exchange offer, as you know, requires registration under the Securities Act of 1933. The law recognizes that the shareholder whose stock is sought by means of the exchange offer is in the position both of a seller and a buyer; that is, he is selling the security he presently owns, and buying the security offered to him. The shareholder therefore gets a prospectus, explaining all material facts about the offer, he knows who the purchaser is, what plans have been made for the company, and is in a position to make an informed decision either to hold his original security or exchange it for the other. The disclosures, as in the case of a proxy contest, are filed with the Commission and are subject to statutory requirements and sanctions, which operate for the protection of the opposing parties as well as the shareholder.

Now look at the situation when the tender offer is solely for cash. The investment decision is similar—the choice whether to retain the original security or sell it is, in substance, little different from the decision made on an original purchase of a security, or on an offer to exchange one security for another. In many cases of cash tender offers, however, the public investor does not even know the identity of the purchaser, much less what the purchaser plans to do with the company if the takeover bid is successful. * * *

Investors should be informed of the identity, background, future plans and other material information about anyone seeking to acquire control of their company before they sell securities to that person. This is necessary if public investors are to stand on an equal footing with the acquiring person in assessing the future of the company and the value of its shares. Further, * * * the need of investors for full and complete information in arriving at a decision to sell securities is just as great as when they are arriving at a decision to buy securities—a concept which is inherent in the Exchange Act.

The proposed legislation would, of course, subject a new class of persons to the reporting requirements of the Exchange Act; that is, persons not yet in control.

But it would not represent a change in the fundamental policy underlying the federal securities laws that investors should be fully informed of all material facts before reaching an investment decision. I believe you will agree that information about control, or a potential change in control, which is so clearly essential to an informed decision to *buy* securities, is equally important in reaching an informed decision to *sell* securities—whether for cash, or in exchange for other securities.

Information about a potential change in control can be particularly essential to an informed decision. A change in control brings with it the possibility of different operating results and different investment results, or perhaps the possibility of realizing on a company's liquidation value. This may be either good, or bad, depending on the facts and circumstances involved. But no investor can reach a conclusion on the possible effects of a change in control until the facts are available to him.

It is argued by some that the basic factor which influences shareholders to accept a tender offer is the adequacy of the price. But, I might ask, how can an investor evaluate the adequacy of the price if he cannot assess the possible impact of a change in control? Certainly without such information he cannot judge its adequacy by the current market price. That price presumably reflects the assumption that the company's present business, control and management will continue. If that assumption is changed, is it not likely that the market price might change? An example will show why. Assume that a company's stock sells for $5 per share—its going concern value as assessed by investors. Its earnings are poor; its prospects dim; its management uninspired. Is a cash tender offer of $6 per share adequate? Or do we need more information? Suppose a person believes that with control he can liquidate the company and realize $15 per share, or maybe more. Certainly the company's shareholders would want to know about liquidation plans. Indeed, it is the plan to liquidate which makes the bidder willing to pay more than $5 per share. Whether or not the company's liquidation value is generally known is not important, for without someone to carry out the liquidation, this value is unobtainable. If the company's shareholders, at the time of the tender offer, know of the plan to liquidate, would they consider $6 per share adequate? I think a reasonable question arises.

I do not need to make the example so dramatic. Assume simply that the offeror has a proven record of accomplishment in the company's field, as opposed to a present management which has not done well. This factor alone would undoubtedly affect investors' assessments of the future worth of the company's securities. While the disclosure required by the bills might discourage some tender offers, it is perhaps a small price to pay for an informed choice by shareholders.

The importance of a potential change of control illustrates why the shareholder to whom even a cash tender offer is made is, in a sense, a purchaser as well as a seller of a security. A change in control can result in what amounts to a new, or at least vastly changed, company. A decision not to accept the offer amounts to a decision to buy into that new company. It is anomalous, therefore, to treat the cash tender offer differently from the exchange offer, and require as we do now—full disclosure for one, but not the other. Another relevant factor which should be considered is that when management is opposed to the takeover bid, in fairness to the shareholders it should have a real opportunity to make its case, either in opposition to the proposed change in control or with respect to any aspect of the bid, whether it is the price or any other pertinent consideration.   * * *

* * * It was originally proposed that a statement describing the offer be filed with the Commission and mailed to the offeree company at least 20 days before the solicitation commenced. This would have given shareholders 20 days to evaluate a tender offer.   * * * [W]e believed this might give management an unwarranted advantage when the offer is opposed. However, since time for careful consideration of the offer by shareholders is desirable and management should have a reasonable opportunity to present its case, we suggested that shareholders be allowed seven days after the offer is made to withdraw any shares they may have tendered.

For similar and additional reasons we also wanted to avoid having shareholders rush to accept an offer. To accomplish this, we suggested that where the person making the offer takes less than all the shares tendered, he should be required to take them on a pro rata basis. Further, we recommended that where a tender offer price is increased, that all persons having tendered shares, whether or not already taken up, be given the increased offering price. In this way we intended to remove a purely fortuitous factor from the calculation of the amount shareholders should receive for their shares, and to avoid the discriminatory effect of paying some holders more than others.

(B) TENDER OFFER LEGISLATION

Sections 13(d), 13(e) and 14(d), 14(e) and 14(f) provide in part (15 U.S.C. §§ 78m–(d), 78m–(e), 78n–(d), 78n–(e), 78n–(f)):

13(d)(1) Any person who, after acquiring directly or indirectly the beneficial ownership of any equity security of a class which is registered pursuant to section 12 of this title, or any equity security of an insurance company which would have been required to be so registered except for the exemption contained in section 12(g)(2)(G) of this title, or any equity security issued by a closed-end investment company registered under the Investment Company Act of 1940 or any equity security issued by a Native Corporation pursuant to Section 37(d)(6) of the Alaska Native Claims Settlement Act, is directly or indirectly the beneficial owner of more than 5 per centum of such class shall, within ten days after such acquisition, send to the issuer of the security at its principal executive office, by registered or certified mail, send to each exchange where the security is traded, and file with the Commission, a statement containing such of the following information, and such additional information, as the Commission may by rules and regulations prescribe as necessary or appropriate in the public interest or for the protection of investors—

(A) the background, and identity, residence, and citizenship of, and nature of such beneficial ownership by, such person and all other persons by whom or on whose behalf the purchases have been or are to be effected;

(B) the source and amount of the funds or other consideration used or to be used in making the purchases, and if any part of the purchase price or proposed purchase price is represented or is to be represented by funds or other consideration borrowed or otherwise obtained for the purpose of acquiring, holding, or trading such security, a description of the transaction and the names of the parties thereto, except that where a source of funds is a loan made in the ordinary course of business by a bank, as defined in section 3(a)(6) of this title, if the person filing such statement so requests, the name of the bank shall not be made available to the public;

(C) if the purpose of the purchases or prospective purchases is to acquire control of the business of the issuer of the securities, any plans or proposals which such persons may have to liquidate such issuer, to sell its assets to or merge it with any other persons, or to make any other major change in its business or corporate structure;

(D) the number of shares of such security which are beneficially owned, and the number of shares concerning which there is a right to acquire, directly or indirectly, by (i) such person, and (ii) by each associate of such person, giving the background, identity, residence, and citizenship of each such associate; and

(E) information as to any contracts, arrangements, or understandings with any person with respect to any securities of the issuer, including but not limited to transfer of any of the securities, joint ventures, loan or option arrangements, puts or calls, guaranties of loans, guaranties against loss or guaranties of profits, division of losses or profits, or the giving or withholding of proxies, naming the persons with whom such contracts, arrangements, or understandings have been entered into, and giving the details thereof.

* * *

13(d)(3) When two or more persons act as a partnership, limited partnership, syndicate, or other group for the purpose of acquiring, holding, or disposing of securities of an issuer, such syndicate or group shall be deemed a "person" for the purposes of this subsection.

* * *

13(d)(6) The provisions of this subsection shall not apply to—

(A) any acquisition or offer to acquire securities made or proposed to be made by means of a registration statement under the Securities Act of 1933;

(B) any acquisition of the beneficial ownership of a security which, together with all other acquisitions by the same person of securities of the same class during the preceding twelve months, does not exceed 2 per centum of that class;

(C) any acquisition of an equity security by the issuer of such security;

(D) any acquisition or proposed acquisition of a security which the Commission, by rules or regulations or by order, shall exempt from the provisions of this subsection as not entered into for the purpose of, and not having the effect of, changing or influencing the control of the issuer or otherwise as not comprehended within the purposes of this subsection.

13(e)(1) It shall be unlawful for an issuer which has a class of equity securities registered pursuant to section 12 of this title, or which is a closed-end investment company registered under the Investment Company Act of 1940, to purchase any equity security issued by it if such purchase is in contravention of such rules and regulations as the Commission, in the public interest or for the protection of investors, may adopt (A) to define acts and practices which are fraudulent, deceptive, or manipulative, and (B) to prescribe means reasonably designed to prevent such acts and practices. Such rules and regulations may require such issuer to provide holders of equity securities of such class with such information relating to the reasons for such purchase, the source of funds, the number of shares to be purchased, the price to be paid for such securities, the method of purchase, and such additional information, as the Commission deems necessary or appropriate in the public interest or for the protection of investors, or which the Commission deems to be material to a determination whether such security should be sold.

* * *

14(d)(1) It shall be unlawful for any person, directly or indirectly, by use of the mails or by any means or instrumentality of interstate commerce or of any facility of a national securities exchange or otherwise, to make a tender offer for, or a request or invitation for tenders of, any class of any equity security which is registered pursuant to section 12 of this title, or any equity security of an insurance company which would have been required to be so registered except for the exemption contained in section 12(g)(2)(G) of this title, or any equity security issued by a closed-end investment company registered under the Investment Company Act of 1940, if, after consummation thereof, such person would, directly or indirectly, be the beneficial owner of more than 5 per centum of such class, unless at the time copies of the offer or request or invitation are first published or sent or given to security holders such person has filed with the Commission a statement containing such of the information specified in section 13(d) of this title, and such additional information as the Commission may by rules and regulations prescribe as necessary or appropriate in the public interest or for the protection of investors. All requests or invitations for tenders or advertisements making a tender offer or requesting or inviting tenders of such a security shall be filed as a part of such statement and shall contain such of the information contained in such statement as the Commission may by rules and regulations prescribe.

Copies of any additional material soliciting or requesting such tender offers subsequent to the initial solicitation or request shall contain such information as the Commission may by rules and regulations prescribe as necessary or appropriate in the public interest or for the protection of investors, and shall be filed with the Commission not later than the time copies of such material are first published or sent or given to security holders. Copies of all statements, in the form in which such material is furnished to security holders and the Commission, shall be sent to the issuer not later than the date such material is first published or sent or given to any security holders.

14(d)(2) When two or more persons act as a partnership, limited partnership, syndicate, or other group for the purpose of acquiring, holding, or disposing of securities of an issuer, such syndicate or group shall be deemed a "person" for purposes of this subsection.

* * *

14(d)(5) Securities deposited pursuant to a tender offer or request or invitation for tenders may be withdrawn by or on behalf of the depositor at any time until the expiration of seven days after the time definitive copies of the offer or request or invitation are first published or sent or given to security holders, and at any time after sixty days from the date of the original tender offer or request or invitation, except as the Commission may otherwise prescribe by rules, regulations, or order as necessary or appropriate in the public interest or for the protection of investors.*

14(d)(6) Where any person makes a tender offer, or request or invitation for tenders, for less than all the outstanding equity securities of a class, and where a greater number of securities is deposited pursuant thereto within ten days after copies of the offer or request or invitation are first published or sent or given to security holders than such person is bound or willing to take up and pay for, the securities taken up shall be taken up as nearly as may be pro rata, disregarding fractions, according to the number of securities deposited by each depositor. The provisions of this subsection shall also apply to securities deposited within ten days after notice of an increase in the consideration offered to security holders, as described in paragraph (7), is first published or sent or given to security holders.

14(d)(7) Where any person varies the terms of a tender offer or request or invitation for tenders before the expiration thereof by increasing the consideration offered to holders of such securities, such person shall pay the increased consideration to each security holder whose securities are taken up and paid for pursuant to the tender offer or request or invitation for tenders whether or not such securities have been taken up by such person before the variation of the tender offer or request or invitation.

14(d)(8) The provisions of this subsection shall not apply to any offer for, or request or invitation for tenders of, any security—

---

* [Ed. Note] See Rule 14d–7, infra p. 981.

(A) if the acquisition of such security, together with all other acquisitions by the same person of securities of the same class during the preceding twelve months, would not exceed 2 per centum of that class;

(B) by the issuer of such security; or

(C) which the Commission, by rules or regulations or by order, shall exempt from the provisions of this subsection as not entered into for the purpose of, and not having the effect of, changing or influencing the control of the issuer or otherwise as not comprehended within the purposes of this subsection.

14(e) It shall be unlawful for any person to make any untrue statement of a material fact or omit to state any material fact necessary in order to make the statements made, in the light of the circumstances under which they are made, not misleading, or to engage in any fraudulent, deceptive, or manipulative acts or practices, in connection with any tender offer or request or invitation for tenders, or any solicitation of security holders in opposition to or in favor of any such offer, request, or invitation. The Commission shall, for the purposes of this subsection, by rules and regulations define, and prescribe means reasonably designed to prevent, such acts and practices as are fraudulent, deceptive, or manipulative.

14(f) If, pursuant to any arrangement or understanding with the person or persons acquiring securities in a transaction subject to subsection (d) of this section or subsection (d) of section 13 of this title, any persons are to be elected or designated as directors of the issuer, otherwise than at a meeting of security holders, and the persons so elected or designated will constitute a majority of the directors of the issuer, then, prior to the time any such person takes office as a director, and in accordance with rules and regulations prescribed by the Commission, the issuer shall file with the Commission, and transmit to all holders of record of securities of the issuer who would be entitled to vote at a meeting for election of directors, information substantially equivalent to the information which would be required by subsection (a) or (c) of this section to be transmitted if such person or persons were nominees for election as directors at a meeting of such security holders.

———

The Commission issued Regulations and disclosure schedules for third party bidders under Section 14(d) which it described as follows in Exchange Act Rel. No. 16,384 (Nov. 8, 1979):

* * *

The rules regulating the person making the tender offer (the "bidder") may be divided into four categories: filing requirements; dissemination provisions; disclosure requirements; and substantive provisions. Before discussing these categories, it should be noted that the operation of these rules is triggered by the date of commencement of the tender offer, which is defined by Rule 14d–2 as essentially equivalent to the date the tender offer is first published or sent or given to security holders.

The filing of Schedule 14D–1 with the Commission is governed by Rule 14d–3. In addition, a bidder is required to make hand delivery of the initial filing and any amendments to the company whose securities are being sought (the "subject company"), and under certain conditions to give telephonic notice of certain information and to mail copies to national securities exchanges and to the NASD. A competing bidder is also required to hand deliver the initial filing to any previous bidder whose tender offer for the same class of securities has not yet expired.

Rule 14d–4 establishes three alternative methods of disseminating a cash tender offer to security holders: long-form publication; summary publication; and the use of shareholder lists and security position listings ("stockholder lists"). The dissemination process includes both the initial and subsequent soliciting materials published or sent or given to security holders during the tender offer. While tender offers may be disseminated by methods other than those specified in Rule 14d–4, summary publication and the use of stockholder lists and security position listings pursuant to Rule 14d–5 must comply with Rules 14d–4(a)(2) and (a)(3), respectively. The dissemination of an exchange tender offer is governed by the provisions of the Securities Act if the transaction is subject to the registration requirements of that Act.

Rule 14d–5 allows a bidder to disseminate its tender offer materials in a manner substantially similar to that permitted under present Rule 14a–7 [17 CFR 240 14d–7], which relates to proxy contests. The tender offer materials would be disseminated to security holders pursuant to the stockholder lists. The subject company would determine whether to retain the stockholder lists, in which case the subject company would distribute the bidder's tender offer materials, or to furnish the stockholder lists to the bidder, in which case the bidder would distribute them.

While the dissemination provisions of Rule 14d–4 apply only to tender offers in which the consideration consists solely of cash and/or securities exempt from registration under Section 3 of the Securities Act and are not mandatory, the disclosure requirements of Rule 14d–6 apply to any tender offer subject to Section 14(d). The specific disclosure requirements generally depend on whether the tender offer is published or sent or given to security holders by means of summary publication pursuant to Rule 14d–4(a)(2) or the use of stockholder lists and security position listings pursuant to Rule 14d–5. The summary advertisement which is required to be published in connection with either of these means of dissemination must contain the disclosure called for by Rule 14d–6(e)(2). Tender offers which are disseminated other than by such means, such as cash tender offers which are published by means of long-form publication, registered exchange offers or unconventional tender offers, are subject to the disclosure requirements prescribed by Rule 14d–6(e)(1).

With respect to a tender offer in which the consideration consists solely of cash and/or securities exempt from registration under Section 3 of the Securities Act, Rules 14d–4, 14d–5 and 14d–6 are designed to operate in concert. This interrelationship may be demonstrated by the following brief description of the chronological operation of a cash tender offer by the use of stockholder lists: (1) the bidder requests the use of the stockholder lists pursuant to Rule 14d–5(a); (2) on or prior to the date of the request the bidder makes adequate publication of either a summary advertisement or long-form publication commencing the tender offer under Rule 14d–2; (3) the subject company makes its election either to disseminate the tender offer materials or to furnish the stockholder lists; (4) if the subject company conducts the dissemination, Rule 14d–5(b) governs the subject company's conduct and Rule 14d–5(f)(3) applies to the bidder; (5) if the subject company furnishes the stockholder lists to the bidder, Rule 14d–5(c) applies to the subject company and Rule 14d–5(f)(4) prescribes the method by which the bidder disseminates its tender offer materials; (6) under either option, the bidder's tender offer materials must include the disclosure required by Rule 14d–6(e)(1); and (7) a similar sequence will be followed with respect to material changes in the bidder's tender offer materials.

Substantive provisions concerning tender offer subject to Section 14(d) of the Exchange Act are set forth in Rules 14e–1, 14d–7, and 14d–8. Rule 14e–1 regulates the minimum length of a tender offer. Any tender offer (other than certain issuer tender offers) is required to remain open for a minimum of twenty business days from the date of commencement and for ten business days from the date of [any increase or decrease in the percentage of the class being sought,] any notice of increase in the offered consideration or the dealer's soliciting fee. These time periods are designed to operate concurrently. Thus, if a tender offer commences on business day 1 and the bidder increases the consideration on business day 8, the ten business day period will expire during the minimum twenty business day period.

[Rules 14d–7 and 14d–8 also relate to the terms under which the tender offer may be conducted. Under Rule 14d–7 a shareholder has the right to withdraw any securities tendered for the entire period the offer remains open. Rule 14d–8 enables a bidder for less than all securities of a class to vary the pro rata acceptance provisions of Section 14(d)(6) and take and pay for pro rata portions of all securities deposited during the period of the offer according to the number of securities deposited by each depositor.]

(C) DISCLOSURE BY THE BIDDER

The disclosure required of a third party buyer or bidder under Section 13(d) and Schedule 13D and Section 14(d) and Schedule 14D–1 is addressed in part to the identity and funding of the bidder and its relationship to the target and to the target's affiliates or associates; but the more significant substantive requirements are addressed to the bidder's "purpose or purposes" in making the acquisition of securities and to "any plan or proposal" the bidder may have which relates to acquiring or disposing of additional securities (in the case of disclosure under Section 13(d)) and to causing any extraordinary transactions such as sale of the target's assets or merger or liquidation of the target, or change in its Board or capital structure or dividend policy.[p] In addition, Schedule 14D–1 requires the bidder to furnish financial statements if "the bidder is other than a natural person and the bidder's financial condition is material" to the offeree's decision.

(1) There is a body of litigation in connection with the efforts of bidders filing Schedules 13D and 14D–1 to set forth as many possible alternatives for its future relationship to, or dealing with, the target as it can envision, so that it retains options to deal with the target as it chooses in the future and remains unconfined to particular alternatives. Another tactic to achieve similar freedom of action is to make bland statements of possibilities allegedly because the bidder is unable to be more definite (see e.g., Revlon, Inc. v. Pantry Pride, 621 F.Supp. 804 (D.Del.1985)). Comparable ambiguity attends discussion on disclosure of merger negotiations. See supra p. 871. Such statements invite a finding of inaccuracy only if the bidder takes particular action with respect to the target (e.g., merger) very shortly after the statement is made. See Maiwurm and Tobin, Beachhead Acquisitions: Creating Waves in the Market Place and Uncertainty in the Regulatory Framework, 38 Bus.Law. 419, 445–452. The large tolerance of courts for bland or ambiguous statements of purpose, at least under Schedule 14D–1, is suggested by cases like Electronic Specialty Co., infra p. 985 and Susquehanna Co., infra p. 1051.

[p] Item 4 of Schedule 13D requires:

Item 4. Purpose of Transaction

State the purpose or purposes of the acquisition of securities of the issuer. Describe any plans or proposals which the reporting persons may have which relate to or would result in:

(a) The acquisition by any person of additional securities of the issuer, or the disposition of securities of the issuer;

(b) An extraordinary corporate transaction, such as a merger, reorganization or liquidation, involving the issuer or any of its subsidiaries;

(c) A sale or transfer of a material amount of assets of the issuer or of any of its subsidiaries;

(d) Any change in the present board of directors or management of the issuer, including any plans or proposals to change the number or term of directors or to fill any existing vacancies on the board;

(e) Any material change in the present capitalization or dividend policy of the issuer;

(f) Any other material change in the issuer's business or corporate structure, including but not limited to, if the issuer is a registered closed-end investment company, any plans or proposals to make any changes in its investment policy for which a vote is required by section 13 of the Investment Company Act of 1940;

(g) Changes in the issuer's charter, bylaws or instruments corresponding thereto or other actions which may impede the acquisition of control of the issuer by any person;

(h) Causing a class of securities of the issuer to be delisted from a national securities exchange or to cease to be authorized to be quoted in an inter-dealer quotation system of a registered national securities association;

(i) A class of equity securities of the issuer becoming eligible for termination of registration pursuant to Section 12(g)(4) of the Act; or

(j) Any action similar to any of those enumerated above.

See also Item 5 of Schedule 14D–1.

(2) What information should a recipient of a tender offer seek in order to be able intelligently to make the decision whether to tender or not? If the information required by the statute with respect to the bidder's background or associates or sources of financing or future plans for the target company appeal to the offeree, should he tender any or all of his shares, or hold on to them? Should the answer be the same if the bidder is seeking only control of the target as if the bidder is seeking 100% of the target's stock and announces an intention (if it should acquire 51% or more) to cash out those who decline to tender?

Do the SEC filing requirements under §§ 13(d) and 14(d) prescribe too costly a disclosure program for the benefits provided? For example, in the case of a bidder seeking 100% control for cash, is any disclosure necessary or appropriate about the bidder, its finances or its plans?

Borden and Weiner, An Investment Decision Analysis of Cash Tender Offers, 23 NYLS L.Rev. 553 (1978), suggests that the SEC rules under the Williams Act impose disclosure costs which are greater than any benefits they can possibly confer, in fair part because no distinction is made with respect to the scope of required disclosure among various kinds of tender offers—e.g., the offer which is certain to result in a cash-out if it is successful, the offer which is likely to result in a cash-out within a year after it is successful, and the offer which suggests that the bidder is likely not to effect a complete cash-out, so that a substantial portion of the target's stock will remain outstanding for some indeterminate period after control of the target has passed to the successful bidder, and the holders of that stock will end up holding what the authors call "a New Security". In the last case, there is good reason to require considerably more extensive disclosure than in the first two, and possibly than in the case of an effort by a controlling stockholder merely to strengthen its control of the target. The authors conclude (at p. 644):

"Consideration should therefore be given to reassessing the rules in light of the realities. In the absence of such a reassessment, courts should adjudicate alleged disclosure delicts on the basis of their materiality to the investment decision which is posed to the Offeree by the particular form of offer and, where relevant, by the bidder's averment of his take-out intentions."

(3) If the bid is made without prior negotiations, must the bidder disclose theretofore undisclosed values of the target which its diligence has produced? If the bid is made with the cooperation of the target's management, is the disclosure obligation more demanding? See e.g. Plaine v. McCabe, 797 F.2d 713 (9th Cir.1986). In any event, must the bidder reveal the gains which it expects to follow from its combination with the target? Is the analogy to information required in a proxy or registration statement apposite? The two cases that follow deal with these questions.

What is the likely impact on potential take-over attempts of the requirement that the bidder disclose future merger or liquidation plans or other major changes (or discovery values) with respect to the target company (§ 13(d)(1)(C)), which the latter's management may thereupon be free to appropriate? Is it appropriate for the bidder to formulate its future plans for merger so ambiguously that offerees will not know whether, if they decline to tender at the bid price, they will later be under pressure to accept securities of lesser value in a merger forced by the successful bidder?

Courts, in enforcing those provisions, are under conflicting pressures to cause bidders to furnish information about their plans, particularly if they seek less than all the target's stock. If all offered stock will not, or cannot, be taken by the bidder, the investor is interested in learning as much, and as explicitly, as possible about those plans. But the bidder is fearful of too much specificity, both because it may not have enough knowledge about the target to make firm commitments or precise statements which increase the risk of its liability, and because it is not anxious to educate the target's management or potential competing bidders about unexploited opportunities.

(4) The context of a contest imposes other pressures on courts in enforcing the disclosure requirements of the Williams Act. The fact that offers must be responded to within a limited period may induce a court which is solicitous that offerees have adequate information to require more disclosure (for example, of alternatives, see e.g., Valente v. PepsiCo, Inc., 454 F.Supp. 1228 (D.Del.1978) (appraisal rights)) and clearer exposition than it would require in a less demanding situation. On the other hand, the fact of a contest puts time pressure on the parties (reducing their ability to formulate communications) and offers rebuttal opportunities which may mitigate the strictness of a requirement of "full" disclosure which would be applicable if only one party's communications were available to investors.

(5) Academic discussions of the Williams Act have not provided the courts with a unitary framework for answering these questions. The continuing debate between advocates of the market and sole owner standards, see supra pp. 950–956, provides bases for arguing both sides of many of the foregoing questions.

Assume, for the moment, a decision to adhere to the sole owner standard. Does the Williams Act, as drafted, provide the best possible framework for realizing shareholder value? Booth, The Problem With Federal Tender Offer Law, 77 Cal.L.Rev. 707, 713–715, 738–743 (1989), suggests that the Act, by offering the target shareholders too much in the way of procedural protection, inadvertently diminishes their returns. According to Booth, the Act's assurances of withdrawal rights, proration, and receipt of the highest price offered by a given bidder lull the shareholders into tendering. Pressure to hold out and force a higher price is dissipated. Given stair-step offers (forbidden by the Act) and absent withdrawal rights (provided by the Act), the shareholders would be forced to act defensively. Assured adequate information and time to think by the Act, the shareholders should be able to defend themselves. To guard against the possibility that such a regime would overly increase the pressure to tender, Professor Booth would require the bidder to pay the highest price to all shareholders after the point at which control is obtained. Would the target shareholders do better if the decision respecting the transfer of control were removed from the market context entirely? Compare Professor Bebchuk's suggestions, described supra p. 954.

Compare some modifications proposed in the unenacted Tender Offer Disclosure and Fairness Act of 1987, S. 1323, 100th Cong., 1st Sess. (1987): (a) section 13(d)'s 10 day window between purchase and filing would be reduced to 5 days and additional purchases prior to filing would be prohibited, and (b) a waiting period of sixty days would be imposed on a bidder commencing an offer after an earlier declaration of an investment intent. How would these changes cause the target shareholders' bargaining position to improve?

On the market side, see, e.g., Macey and Netter, Regulation 13D and the Regulatory Process, 65 Wash. U.L.Q. 131 (1987).

ELECTRONIC SPECIALTY CO. v. INTERNATIONAL CONTROLS CORP.

United States Court of Appeals, Second Circuit, 1969.
409 F.2d 937.

[The bidder, International Controls Corp. (ICC), owned between 40,000 and 50,000 (of 1,800,000 outstanding) shares of the target, Electronic Specialty Co. (ELS). ICC sought an additional 500,000 shares in a tender offer at $39 per share, including in the 500,000 limit all shares obtainable through tender of convertible debentures. During the period of the offer, which was opposed by the target's management (including its President, Burgess), ICC extended the time and offered to take all shares and debentures tendered. When the target's management was denied a preliminary injunction against the offer, it announced that it was tendering and, possibly as a result of its action, many more shares were tendered than had been expected. By the end of the offer, the equivalent of 1,200,000 shares of the target's stock (including shares to be obtained on conversion of the debentures) had been tendered, and ICC (headed by Robert Vesco) paid out some $48,000,000. After completion of the offer, the price of the target's stock dropped, possibly as the result of the announcement by the outgoing management of a drop in the target's earnings during the first half year (as compared with the prior year) from $1.11 per share to $.74 per share.

[An action to enjoin the offer on the ground, inter alia, that it was materially misleading in violation of the federal securities laws was brought by the target's management (individually as stockholders (non-tendering) and on behalf of the target) during the period of the offer and was tried after completion of the offer. The District Court found that the bidder had made false and misleading statements in violation of Rule 10b–5 and § 14(e). But the Court declined to require the bidder either to refrain from voting at the target's stockholders meeting or to divest itself of the target's stock. The Court of Appeals reversed the District Court's finding of violations of the securities laws, and ordered the complaint dismissed. It stated in the course of its opinion (Friendly, C.J.):]

I.

Defendant contends that the target corporation lacks standing to complain of a violation of § 14(d) or (e) since it can suffer no injury from a change in the ownership of its stock; it contends also that ELS is without standing to complain of violation of Rule 10b–5, an issue we left open in General Time Corp. v. Talley Industries, Inc., 403 F.2d 159, 164 (2 Cir.1968), certiorari denied, 393 U.S. 1026 (1969). At one point ICC argued that a nontendering stockholder lacked standing on similar grounds, but later abandoned this broad position in favor of a claim that Burgess' conduct disqualified him as a plaintiff. While not disputing that a tendering stockholder would usually have standing, it argues that Fitzpatrick did not have this since he tendered at Burgess' request and without reliance on any statement by ICC, and that even if he had standing, he lost any position when he failed to avail himself of the opportunity for withdrawal. While our holding on the merits makes it unnecessary for us to discuss the issue with respect to Fitzpatrick and indeed might allow us to pretermit the entire question of standing, the issues raised about the standing of the target corporation and nontendering stockholders have such general importance in the enforcement of § 14(d) and (e) as to make an expression of our views desirable.

The district court held, in accordance with a memorandum filed by the SEC as *amicus curiae,* that the target corporation had standing to complain of violations of § 14(d) and (e); since the latter largely tracks the substantive provisions of Rule 10b–5, the court found it unnecessary to determine the standing of the target corporation under that Rule. The decision rested in considerable part on an analogy to § 14(a), which makes it unlawful to solicit proxies "in contravention of such rules and regulations as the Commission may prescribe as necessary or appropriate in the public interest or for the protection of investors," and under which, as we held in Studebaker Corp. v. Gittlin, 360 F.2d 692 (2 Cir.1966), a corporation has standing to seek an injunction against violation by a group attempting to gain control. The district judge and the SEC pointed to the fact that the amendment with respect to tender offers took the form of an addition to § 14, and also to language in the House report on the amendment which stated "the cash tender offer is similar to a proxy contest" and emphasized the anomaly of "the present gap in the Federal securities laws which leaves the cash tender offer exempt from disclosure provisions" whereas the proxy contest was not. See H.R.Rep. No. 1711, 90th Cong., 2d Sess. 3, U.S.Code Cong. & Adm.News pp. 2997, 2999 (1968). Reverting to *Studebaker,* supra, they then stressed what we said with respect to § 14(a):

But the legislative history shows that Congress anticipated protection from "irresponsible outsiders seeking to wrest control of a corporation away from honest and conscientious corporation officials," S.Rep. No. 1455, 73d Cong., 2d Sess. 77 (1934), quoted in 2 Loss, supra at 950, and the Proxy Rules are shot through with provisions recognizing that in contests for control the management has a role to play as such and not merely insofar as the managers are stockholders.

Mere statement is enough to show that while the analogy is persuasive, it is not perfect. The legislative history of the 1968 amendment demonstrates that the focus of legislative interest was on the public shareholder; Congress wanted to ensure that he had the benefit of a full statement from the offeror, with a chance for "incumbent management" to "explain its position publicly," if so disposed, H.R.Rep. No. 1711, supra, at 2, U.S.Code Cong. & Adm.News at p. 2998. In a proxy contest the management is almost inevitably a party; indeed § 14(c), added in 1964, mandates that if management does not solicit proxies, it must furnish information equivalent to what would have had to be transmitted if a solicitation were made on its behalf. Furthermore if a holding of standing in the target corporation would mean that a nontendering stockholder would lack this unless he could satisfy the rather cumbersome requirements of F.R.Civ.P. 23.1 concerning derivative actions, the evil would be considerably more serious than under § 14(a). Management can generally be counted on to oppose a mere attempt to dislodge it in a proxy contest, whereas, it may well wish to accept a tender offer and the remedy of the individual stockholder might thus be postponed until too late for effective action. If recognition of standing on the part of the target corporation would require us to condition the standing of nontenderers on compliance with Rule 23.1, we thus might very well deny it.

We do not believe, however, that this choice is forced upon us. In determining who has standing to enforce duties created by statute, a court's quest must be for what will best accomplish the purposes of the legislature. In the instant context the proper solution is not necessarily determined by the rules developed in equity to delimit the circumstances under which a stockholder may assert a claim on his corporation's behalf. When we decided the *Studebaker* case as we did, we had no intention of discrediting an earlier holding that recognized the standing of a non-signing stockholder in a corporation which was the object of proxy solicitation even though there was no allegation that the corporation was in cahoots with the offender. Union Pacific R.R. v. Chicago & N.W. Ry., 226 F.Supp. 400, 406 (N.D.Ill.1961). While a nontenderer suffers no immediate injury from inadequacy of price in the sense that he retains his stock, such inadequacy is likely to have a depressing effect on the market for some time and thus may hurt him if, for one reason or another, he should later find it necessary or desirable to sell. Such depression may also harm the target corporation if it should wish to engage in financing or acquisitions, and a still different potential for harm to the corporation will exist where it is claimed that the offeror has evil designs on its treasury or business plans. The rights of the nontendering stockholder and the corporation thus seem sufficiently independent to give standing to both under all the provisions added to § 14. Cf. Symington Wayne Corp. v. Dresser Industries, Inc., supra, 383 F.2d at 812; Moore v. Greatamerica Corp., 274 F.Supp. 490 (N.D.Ohio 1967). The hidden question is one of policy with respect to suit by the corporation: Should management be allowed to spend the stockholders' money in resisting a tender offer that may well be advantageous and acceptable to a large majority when a stockholder is free to act in his own behalf and the managers will almost inevitably hold stock on their own account? Militating in favor of an affirmative answer is the very fact of the superior resources of the corporation, which can be vital in this context where remedial action must be speedy and forceful.* With the considerations thus in balance we would be reluctant to deny standing when Congress, had it considered the problem, would very likely have thought the rule already recognized under § 14(a) would apply. Moreover, in cases where management causes the corporation to bring a suit motivated by its own interests and contrary to the best interests of the true owners, shareholders have their usual remedies for waste. Cf. Rosenfeld v. Fairchild Engine & Airplane Corp., 309 N.Y. 168, 171 (1955).

* * *

III.

* * *

The likeness of tender offers to proxy contests is not limited to the issue of standing. They are alike in the fundamental feature that they generally are contests. This means that the participants on both sides act, not "in the peace of a quiet chamber," Hellenic Lines Ltd. v. Brown & Williamson Tobacco Corp., 277 F.2d 9, 13 (4 Cir.), certiorari denied, 364 U.S. 879 (1960), but under the stresses of the market place. They act quickly, sometimes impulsively, often in angry response to what they consider, whether rightly or wrongly, to be low blows by the other side. Probably there will no more be a perfect tender offer than a perfect trial. Congress intended to assure basic honesty and fair dealing, not to impose an unrealistic requirement of laboratory conditions that might make the new statute a potent tool for incumbent management to protect its own interests against the desires and welfare of the stockholders. These considerations bear on the kind of judgment to be applied in testing conduct—of both sides—and also on the issue of materiality. As to this we reaffirm the test announced in Symington Wayne, supra, 383 F.2d at 843, whether "any of the stockholders who tendered their shares would probably not have tendered their shares" if the alleged violations had not occurred. See also General Time Corp. v. Talley Industries, Inc., supra, 403 F.2d at 161–162.

---

* [Ed. Note] Compare Piper v. Chris Craft Industries, Inc., infra p. 1045.

We shall deal first with the point as to which Judge McLean thought there was a violation but Judge Lasker thought there was not—the statements with respect to merger. As previously noted, the regulations issued by the SEC require the maker of a tender offer to "describe any plans or proposals which such persons may have to * * * merge it [the target corporation] with any other persons." SEC Rule 14d–1(c) & Schedule 13D. It would be as serious an infringement of these regulations to overstate the definiteness of the plans as to understate them. As we read the record, ICC put forward merger early in the game as an alternative that, perhaps because of tax considerations to the stockholders, might be more acceptable to ELS than a tender offer, which ICC's directors then insisted could be made only if ELS agreed. Nothing in this committed ICC to propose a merger as a consequence of a successful "overhead" tender offer or evidenced a firm intention that it would. If ICC acquired control as a result of a tender offer, the circumstances might or might not suggest a merger—an issue that could and presumably would be explored with the deliberation then possible. The statement in the August 19 offer that ICC would "give consideration" to a merger in the event of success thus seems entirely accurate and the subsequent elaboration unnecessary. No one suggests, however, that the revised statement that any merger would be "on the basis of the relative market prices of the common stock of the respective companies during a representative period" was any less satisfactory.

* * *

[The Court went on to find no violation of the disclosure requirements by ICC and concluded:]

On plaintiffs' appeal the denial of the requested relief is affirmed; on defendant's appeal the order granting an injunction is reversed with directions to dismiss the complaint. In light of the imminence of the ELS stockholders' meeting, the mandate will issue forthwith.

FLYNN v. BASS BROS. ENTERPRISES, INC.

United States Court of Appeals, Third Circuit, 1984.
744 F.2d 978.

ADAMS, Circuit Judge.

This appeal concerns the adequacy under federal securities law of disclosure in a tender offer by defendant Bass Brothers Enterprises, Inc. (Bass Brothers) for the outstanding shares of defendant National Alfalfa Dehydrating and Milling Company (National Alfalfa) and the propriety of subsequent merger under Delaware law.

Plaintiffs, former minority shareholders of National Alfalfa, charge in a class action that Bass Brothers and the management of National Alfalfa violated sections 10(b) and 14(e) of the Securities Exchange Act of 1934 (1934 Act), as well as Delaware common law by failing to disclose material information in conjunction with the tender offer. At the conclusion of plaintiffs' case the district court directed a verdict for defendants. As to the federal claims, the judge ruled that plaintiffs had failed to produce sufficient evidence of fraudulent nondisclosure to raise a question of fact for the jury. Regarding the state claim, the judge found the subsequent merger had a proper business purpose. This appeal followed.

I.

The essential facts of the case are undisputed. Bass Brothers is a closely held Texas corporation. At the time of the tender offer its principal business was oil exploration with subsidiary interests in hydrocarbon production, radio, television, ranching and cattle-raising. In 1974 Bass Brothers was approached by the president of Prochemco, Inc. (Prochemco), a Texas corporation engaged in ranching and cattle-feeding, as a possible source of financing for a purchase by Prochemco of a large block of National Alfalfa's stock. National Alfalfa, a Delaware corporation whose stock was traded on the American Stock Exchange, was engaged in farming, farm supply operations and the sale of animal feed. Its former president, Charles Peterson, was seeking to sell his controlling interest in the company in order to raise sufficient capital to repay a large personal debt. To present its proposal to Bass Brothers and other potential sources of funding, Prochemco prepared two reports on National Alfalfa's history and operations, including an appraisal of its assets based on alternative hypothetical valuations.

Although Bass Brothers declined to finance such a purchase by Prochemco, it indicated that it might consider proceeding as a principal should Prochemco fail to obtain the necessary funding. In late 1975 Prochemco informed Bass Brothers that it had been unable to obtain financing and that Peterson's block of National Alfalfa stock was still available. In return for providing the detailed information about National Alfalfa contained in the Prochemco reports and for assistance in analyzing National Alfalfa's current and potential performance, Bass Brothers agreed to pay Prochemco a $130,000 finders fee.

In December 1975 Bass Brothers entered into an option agreement for the purchase of Peterson's 52% share of National Alfalfa's outstanding common stock. Thereafter, Bass Brothers exercised its option and bought the approximately 1.3 million shares from Peterson for a price of $8.44 million or $6.47 per share. A short time later, in a private sale, Bass Brothers was able to acquire an additional 226,673 shares of National Alfalfa, representing 9.1% of the outstanding shares, at $6.45 per share. This acquisition increased Bass Brothers' holding to 61.2% of the outstanding shares of National Alfalfa.

On March 2, 1976, Bass Brothers made public its tender offer for "any and all" outstanding shares of National Alfalfa at $6.45 per share. The reports prepared by Prochemco for Bass Brothers were not appended to the tender offer, nor did the tender offer refer to Prochemco's appraisal of the overall values per share of National Alfalfa which stated that:

$6.40 could be realized through "liquidation [of National Alfalfa] under stress conditions";

$12.40 could be realized through "liquidation in an orderly fashion over a reasonable period of time";

$16.40 represented National Alfalfa's value "as [an] ongoing venture."

The tender offer also did not refer to a second report prepared by Prochemco which gave two additional valuations: $17.28 representing the "Value per Peterson"; $7.60 representing the "Value per Prochemco." App. at 928a. To the contrary, the tender offer stated in bold letters that "Offeror did not receive any material non-public information from [National Alfalfa] with respect to its prior acquisitions of shares nor * * * does it believe it presently possesses any such information. Offeror has not been able to verify independently the accuracy or completeness of the information contained in Appendices A through E [furnished by National Alfalfa] and assumes no responsibility therefor."

On March 15, 1976, Bass Brothers did, however, issue a supplement to the tender offer describing the book value of "certain land owned or leased by" National Alfalfa and advising the shareholders that:

> While the Offeror has made no independent appraisal of the value of the Company's land and makes no representation with respect thereto, in view of the foregoing factors the aggregate current fair market value of the Company's agricultural land may be substantially higher than its original cost as reflected on the books of the Company. Depending upon the respective market values for such land, stockholders could receive, upon liquidation of the Company, an amount per share significantly higher than the current book value and possibly higher than the price of $6.45 per Share offered by Offeror in the Offer. The amount received by stockholders upon liquidation of the Company would also be dependent upon, among other things, the market value of the Company's other assets and the length of time allowed for such liquidation. The Offeror has no reason to believe that the Company's management has any present intention of liquidating the Company. As noted on page 8 of the Offer to Purchase under "Purpose of This Offer: Present Relationship of Company and Offeror", Offeror does not currently intend to liquidate the Company.

The supplement also extended the duration of the offer by one week "to afford stockholders an opportunity to evaluate" the new information. While the offer was in effect, the named plaintiffs tendered their shares to Bass Brothers for $6.45 per share. At the expiration of the extended offer, Bass Brothers owned more than 92% of the outstanding shares of National Alfalfa and took control of the company by removing the board of directors and electing a new board of directors. Shortly thereafter, a Delaware "short-form merger" was effected between National Alfalfa and Bass Brothers Farming Company, a wholly owned subsidiary of Bass Brothers. Emerging as the surviving entity, National Alfalfa became a wholly owned subsidiary of Bass Brothers.

On June 21, 1976, a group of former shareholders of National Alfalfa filed this class action for damages in the district court charging that the information disclosed in the tender offer was insufficient under federal and state securities law. Cross motions for summary judgment were denied. Flynn v. Bass Brothers Enterprises, Inc., 456 F.Supp. 484 (E.D.Pa.1978). A jury trial commenced on September 13, 1983. On September 15, 1983, at the close of plaintiffs' case, defendants moved for a directed verdict. The district judge concluded that "the information that was provided by the tender offeror was not materially misleading in any way" particularly because "the information that was contained in the Prochemco report is the kind that is not permitted to be disclosed to shareholders because it is not based on sufficient information * * * [T]he people who prepared it were interested in whatever transaction they were preparing it for at that time." * * *

The district judge, determining that plaintiffs had not presented sufficient evidence under federal or state law to warrant sending the case to the jury, granted defendants' motion for a directed verdict.

> * * *

III.

Plaintiffs allege that Bass Brothers and the management of National Alfalfa violated sections 10(b) and 14(e) of the 1934 Act and rule 10b–5 of the Securities and Exchange Commission (SEC) by not disclosing certain information with the tender offer. Specifically, plaintiffs maintain that defendants had a duty to disclose certain asset appraisal values because such information would have aided National Alfalfa's shareholders in deciding whether or not to accept Bass Brothers' tender offer. We must determine whether the district judge committed reversible error when he ruled that defendants had no duty to disclose the asset appraisal values they possessed.

> * * *

Where a "duty to speak" exists, therefore, federal securities law requires the disclosure of any "material fact" in connection with the purchase or sale of a security under rule 10b–5 or the tendering of an offer under section 14(e). See Chiarella v. United States, 445 U.S. 222, 235, 100 S.Ct. 1108, 1118, 63 L.Ed.2d 348 (1980); see also Staffin v. Greenberg, 672 F.2d 1196, 1202, 1205 (3d Cir.1982).[5] Bass Brothers does not deny that at the time of the tender offer it was under a duty to

---

5. Because we hold that at the time in question National Alfalfa had no duty to disclose the report prepared by Carl Schweitzer, a vice president of the company, we need not reach plaintiff's allegation that Bass Brothers, as the majority shareholder of National Alfalfa, had a duty to disclose the report. There is evidence in the record that Bass Brothers, although the majority shareholder of the target company, purposely distanced itself from the target management. App. at 323a. While not central to our decision in the present case, we note that a policy of conscious ignorance cannot eliminate the fiduciary duty a majority shareholder owes to the minority shareholders.

make certain disclosures in its capacity as a majority shareholder of National Alfalfa as well as in its capacity as a tender offeror. Similarly, the management of National Alfalfa does not deny that it owed a duty of disclosure to its shareholders. Our task, then, is to determine whether the alleged nondisclosures were material omissions, and thus breached the duty to disclose.

This Court has previously noted that section 14(e) of the Williams Act makes unlawful the failure to disclose any "material fact" in connection with a tender offer. See *Staffin,* 672 F.2d at 1205. Rule 10b–5 similarly prohibits such omissions with regard to the purchase or sale of a security. The Supreme Court defined materiality in the context of an alleged violation of rule 14a–9, which governs disclosure requirements for proxy statements, in * * * TSC Industries, Inc. v. Northway, Inc., 426 U.S. 438, 449, 96 S.Ct. 2126, 2132, 48 L.Ed.2d 757 (1976). This definition of "material" has been adopted for cases involving rule 10b–5 and we see no reason not to utilize the same formulation for evaluating materiality in the context of a tender offer.

* * *

As a matter of public policy, the SEC and the courts generally have not required the inclusion of appraised asset valuations, projections, and other "soft" information in proxy materials or tender offers. * * * The reasons underpinning the SEC's longstanding policy against disclosure of soft information stem from its concern about the reliability of appraisals, its fear that investors might give greater credence to the appraisals or projections than would be warranted, and the impracticability of the SEC's examining such appraisals on a case by case basis to determine whether they are sufficiently reliable to merit disclosure. * * *

Although the disclosure of soft information has not been prohibited as a matter of law, this Court in the past has followed the "general rule" that "presentations of future earnings, appraised asset valuations and other hypothetical data" are to be discouraged. *Kohn,* 458 F.2d at 265. In failing to require disclosure, courts have relied on a perceived SEC policy favoring nondisclosure of soft information, the lack of reliability of such information, and the reluctance to impose potentially huge liability for nondisclosure, even if desirable as a matter of public policy, because the law discouraged nondisclosure at the time of the alleged violation.

In assessing the need to disclose an appraised asset valuation courts have considered several indicia of reliability: the qualifications of those who prepared or compiled the appraisal; the degree of certainty of the data on which it was based; the purpose for which it was prepared; and evidence of reliance on the appraisal.

* * *

At the time Bass Brothers was making its tender offer, although courts did not generally require the disclosure of asset valuations, such disclosure was not prohibited. In *Alaska Interstate,* the acquiring company, over the objection of the target management, included, with proper cautionary remarks, a range of hypothetic liquidation values made by the target management. The court approved the release of the valuations in spite of the "general rule" discouraging such disclosure which this Court announced in *Kohn. Alaska Interstate,* 402 F.Supp. at 572.

Recently, there have been indications that the law, in response to developing corporate trends, such as the increase in mergers, has begun to favor more disclosure of soft information. In this regard, we note that SEC policy—a primary reason courts in the past have not required the disclosure of soft information—has begun to change. With respect to disclosure of projections of future earnings, the SEC in 1976 deleted future earnings from the list of examples of potentially misleading disclosures in the note which follows rule 14a–9.

More importantly, in 1978 the SEC issued a safe harbor rule for "forward-looking" statements, such as future earnings, made in good faith. And with respect to asset valuations, the SEC in 1980 authorized disclosure of good faith appraisals made on a reasonable basis in proxy contests in which a principal issue is the liquidation of all or a portion of a target company's assets. See SEC Release No. 34–16833, Fed.Sec. L.Rep. (CCH) ¶ 24,117 (May 23, 1980), codified at 17 C.F.R. § 241.16833 (1983). While SEC policy has not yet explicitly approved the disclosure of appraisal values when the target is to continue as a going concern rather than being liquidated, recent SEC promulgations herald a new view, more favorably disposed towards disclosure.

Part of the reason for this shift in policy is recognition of shareholders' need for such information. One rationale for the initial prohibition of soft information was the fear that potential *purchasers* of securities would be misled by overly optimistic claims by management. See *Gerstle,* 428 F.2d at 1294. An unintended by-product of such concern, however, was to keep valuable information from those shareholders who had to decide, within the context of a tender offer or merger, whether or not to *sell* their securities. See Kripke, Rule 10b–5 Liability and "Material Facts," 46 N.Y.U.L.Rev. 1061, 1071 (1971). The present spate of proxy contests and tender offers was not anticipated when the SEC initially formulated its policy of nondisclosure of soft information.

* * *

In order to give full effect to the evolution in the law of disclosure, and to avoid in the future, at least in the Third Circuit, the problem caused by the time lag between challenged acts and judicial resolution, today we set forth the law for disclosure of soft information as it is to be applied from this date on. Henceforth, the law is not that asset appraisals are, as a matter of law, immaterial. Rather, in appropriate cases, such information must be disclosed. Courts should ascertain the duty to disclose asset valuations and other soft information on a case by case basis, by weighing the potential aid such information will give a shareholder against the potential harm, such as undue reliance, if the information is released with a proper cautionary note.

The factors a court must consider in making such a determination are: the facts upon which the information is based; the qualifications of those who prepared or compiled it; the purpose for which the information was originally intended; its relevance to the stockholders' impending decision; the degree of subjectivity or bias reflected in its preparation; the degree to which the information is unique; and the availability to the investor of other more reliable sources of information. Cf. *Alaska Interstate Co.,* 402 F.Supp. at 567.[18]

IV.

It is against the background set forth in Part III, supra, that we must determine whether the trial judge erred in ruling that Bass Brothers and the management of National Alfalfa had no duty to disclose the asset valuations at issue in this case. We note that despite our formulation of the current law applicable to corporate disclosure, we are constrained by the significant development in disclosure law since 1976 not to apply the announced standard retroactively,[19] but to evaluate defendants' conduct by the standards which prevailed in 1976.

Plaintiffs point to three sources of information that they believe should have been disclosed in the tender offer; the Prochemco reports; a report allegedly commissioned by Bass Brothers to corroborate the appraisals in the Prochemco reports; and an internal valuation prepared by National Alfalfa's accountant and vice-president, Carl Schweitzer.

A.

The shareholders contend that the Prochemco reports were material and should have been disclosed. However, employing the approach commonly followed by courts when Bass Brothers made its tender offer in early 1976, we do not find the Prochemco reports had sufficient indicia of reliability to require disclosure. Plaintiffs did not adequately establish that the reports were prepared by experts. * * * Moreover, plaintiffs did not establish that the reports had sufficient basis in fact to be reliable. * * *

The purpose for which the Prochemco reports were prepared—to attract financing for its proposed purchase of Peterson's controlling block of National Alfalfa shares—also diminishes the reliability of the reports. Further, at the time of the tender offer the valuations in the Prochemco reports were outdated.

---

18. For the SEC's views, as of 1980, on factors to be considered when releasing appraisal valuations, see SEC Release No. 34–16833. Interpretive Release Relating to Proxy Rules, Fed.Sec.L.Rep. (CCH) ¶ 24.-117 (May 23, 1980).

19. Our reluctance to apply the new standard for disclosure retroactively is confined to the facts of this case. We do not intend to imply that in other cases based on actions occurring before the date of this opinion, the new standard necessarily is inapplicable.

Plaintiffs assert that the reliability of the reports was amply demonstrated by Bass Brothers' reliance on them and by the payment of $130,000 to Prochemco for them. The shareholders reason that "if the Prochemco reports were reliable and accurate enough for Bass Brothers to use * * * in deciding to [purchase Peterson's stock] then the existence of and valuations in the Prochemco reports were material and should have been shared with National Alfalfa's shareholders" through the tender offer. To bolster their argument, the shareholders note that after buying Peterson's stock, Bass Brothers chose not to examine any of National Alfalfa's internal asset valuations before making the tender offer.

Although it is not inconceivable that Bass Brothers may have relied on the Prochemco valuations, plaintiffs did not advance sufficient evidence to establish the point. Moreover, even if there had been some reliance on the reports, that alone would be insufficient to mandate disclosure in this case. The reports were not prepared by experts, had no adequately demonstrated basis in fact and were prepared to encourage financing to purchase Peterson's share. In light of the record before us, we cannot say that the district court erred in concluding that at the time of the tender offer Bass Brothers had no duty to disclose the Prochemco reports.

B.

Plaintiffs assert that Bass Brothers also should have disclosed its own internal valuations. To substantiate their belief that Bass Brothers commissioned a report to corroborate the information in the Prochemco report, the shareholders point to an informal typewritten list of "Items for Investigation" drawn up by Rusty Rose, a Bass Brothers consultant. The list sets forth a number of assignments to be performed by Rose. Item 2(a) states: "Have expert appraise farm land and equipment." A handwritten notation after this item states "Done— values confirmed." * * * The shareholders contend that this cryptic notation, without more, "confirms that Bass Brothers had obtained an 'expert' appraisal." Plaintiffs had ample opportunity during discovery to pursue this lead yet failed to turn up any additional evidence of a corroborating study. Presentation of this handwritten notation, alone, to the jury simply could not support a finding of fraudulent and material nondisclosure of information.

C.

The third piece of information that the shareholders claim should have been disclosed was a study prepared by Carl Schweitzer, a vice president of National Alfalfa, using various assumptions, such as the projected appreciation of National Alfalfa's land holdings, to arrive at a value per share of $12.95. At trial, Schweitzer's unrefuted testimony indicated that such a figure was, in fact, hypothetical because of the nature of the assumptions used in the calculation. Schweitzer stated that he used land values supplied by Peterson and some "unnamed people within or without of the company." Thus, plaintiffs have not established a sufficient factual basis for the valuations. Moreover, the purpose of some of these calculations was to help Peterson find a buyer for his stock. Schweitzer testified that the land values were inflated, or optimistic, so as to present the company in the best possible light to future investors. Moreover, Schweitzer admitted that neither he nor members of National Alfalfa's accounting staff had expertise with regard to land appraisal. Thus, plaintiffs were unable to produce evidence that the Schweitzer reports were sufficiently reliable to be material for shareholders confronted with the tender offer.

* * *

VII.

After carefully examining the evidence presented by the shareholders in the light most favorable to them, we are persuaded that the district court's grant of a directed verdict for defendants was not error; therefore it will be affirmed.

NOTE: LOCAL LAW

In **Joseph v. Shell Oil Co.,** 482 A.2d 335 (Del.Ch.1984), affirmed, 607 A.2d 1213 (Del.1992), the Delaware Vice–Chancellor enjoined a parent's tender offer for its subsidiary's stock because the fiduciary obligation of the parent to make adequate disclosure of "all germane facts with complete candor"—i.e., the subsidiary's probable oil reserves—to the stockholders of the subsidiary was not met. See also Shell Petroleum, Inc. v. Smith, 606 A.2d 112 (Del.1992); Rand v. Western Airlines, Inc., CCH Fed.Sec.L.Rep. ¶ 94,751 (Del.Ch.1989); Weinberger v. UOP supra; but cf. Rosenblatt v. Getty Oil Co., supra. Similarly, in Kahn v. U.S. Sugar Company, supra p. 618, a corporation making a tender offer for its own stock was faulted for failing to disclose material facts "with complete candor." Compare **Roberts v. General Instrument Corp.,** CCH Fed.Sec.L.Rep. ¶ 95,465 (Del.Ch. 1990), in which Chancellor Allen addressed a claim by a shareholder seeking to enjoin the closing of a friendly tender offer leading to an MBO on the ground, *inter alia,* that the bidder failed to disclose financial projections for various divisions of the target, although it had insisted upon receiving, and had received them, from the target. In denying the obligation to disclose those projections to the target's stockholders because, under Delaware law, they were not "material," Chancellor Allen said:

> With respect to his claim that financial projections for various divisions of the company are required, plaintiff's argument chiefly is that both Forstmann and the Board's banker had and needed access to such data to properly evaluate the value of the company. How then, plaintiff asks, can that same breakdown not be material to shareholders asked to tender their stock?
>
> To this Forstmann replies that its offer did include the consolidated projections for the company with which it had been fur-

nished. This further level of detail is not material to shareholders it says and, in all events, it contains confidential information the disclosure of which would injure the company.

The last assertion is supported in this record. I make no judgment on its legal significance, however. Instead I rest my decision on this point, on the conclusion that plaintiff has not shown a reasonable likelihood that this level of detailed projection is material to a selling shareholder in this instance, even though it was presumably material to a buyer of the corporation.

Projections that are of interest to an acquiror seeking control of a company are not necessarily material to the decision of a minority shareholder to sell or hold stock. A potential acquiror typically seeks great detail about the operations of a company. If it succeeds in its bid, it will have power over the organization and structure of the company's assets. It will have to determine which assets to sell, which to retain, and how to deploy those assets it retains. Indeed, acquirors often bid with such a plan in mind.

By contrast, a minority shareholder deciding whether to tender need not, and equally importantly will not as a practical matter, contemplate alternate management scenarios; will not consider alternative organizational plans for the company; will not consider which, if any, of the corporations assets should be sold or redeployed, or where in the organization expenses might be reduced, etc. The decision of a shareholder in a tender offer is more limited than the decision of a would-be acquiror (or lender) and the information material to her decision is different and not as extensive. It may in some instances be material to the shareholder's decision to know what the company's projections of earnings, etc. are, but the question of the necessity to disclose company projections is itself often not an easy one (see Flynn v. Bass Brothers Enterprises, Inc., 744 F.2d 978 (3d Cir.1984)). It may even be material in some instances in which company projections are given to know how they break down into line of business projections. But what seems clear to me, for the reasons set forth above, is that a shareholder does not show such a breakdown is material to his decision simply by showing that a buyer of the corporation, a banker lending to the acquiror or one opining on the fairness of the price, required such a breakdown. Cf. In re Genentech, Inc., Shareholders Litigation, Del.Ch., C.A. No. 11377, Chandler, V.C. (June 6, 1990) slip op. at 17–21.

In this instance plaintiff has shown, after discovery, no circumstances that make such a breakdown material, as that term is defined, to the shareholders' choices.

Plaintiff also argues that assumptions underlying divisional forecasts should have been disclosed. Because I find the divisional forecasts themselves not to be material, any assumptions underlying the divisional forecasts also are not material.

(D) DISCLOSURE BY THE TARGET

Rule 14e–2. Position of Subject Company With Respect to a Tender Offer

(a) *Position of subject company.* As a means reasonably designed to prevent fraudulent, deceptive or manipulative acts or practices within the meaning of section 14(e) of the Act, the subject company, no later than 10 business days from the date the tender offer is first published or sent or given, shall publish, send or give to security holders a statement disclosing that the subject company:

(1) Recommends acceptance or rejection of the bidder's tender offer;

(2) Expresses no opinion and is remaining neutral toward the bidder's tender offer; or

(3) Is unable to take a position with respect to the bidder's tender offer.

Such statement shall also include the reason(s) for the position (including the inability to take a position) disclosed therein.

(b) *Material change.* If any material change occurs in the disclosure required by paragraph (a) of this section, the subject company shall promptly publish, send or give a statement disclosing such material change to security holders.

In SEA Rel. No. 16,384 (Nov. 29, 1979) the Commission explained the promulgation of Rule 14e–2 as follows:

Rule 14e–2 implements this specific inquiry by requiring the subject company to publish or send or give to security holders a statement disclosing its position with respect to the tender offer within ten business days of the commencement of a tender offer by a person other than the issuer. The statement of position would take one of three forms: (1) the subject company recommends acceptance or rejection of a tender offer; (2) the subject company expresses no opinion and will remain neutral toward the tender offer; or (3) the subject company is unable to take a position with respect to the tender offer. In addition, the subject company is required to include the reason(s) for its position with respect to the tender offer, including the inability to take a position. If a subject company changes its position or other material changes occur in the disclosure required by the rule, the subject company is required to promptly publish or send or give to security holders a statement disclosing such material change.

As noted previously, a statement of position pursuant to Rule 14e–2 with respect to a tender offer which is subject to Section 14(d)(1) of the Act is deemed by Rule 14d–9(f) to constitute a solicitation or recommendation within the meaning of Rule 14d–9 and Section 14(d)(4) of the Act. In such case, a subject company is required to comply with the requirements of Rule 14d–9. Thus, among other things, a subject company is required to file a Schedule 14D–9 with the Commission and include the information required by certain items thereof in the information disseminated to security holders. Item 4 of the Schedule is among the items of information which is required to be communicated to security holders and is intended to serve as the vehicle by which the subject company will satisfy its disclosure obligation under Rule 14e–2 with respect to tender offers subject to Section 14(d)(1).*

RADOL v. THOMAS

United States Court of Appeals, Sixth Circuit, 1985.

772 F.2d 244, cert. denied 477 U.S. 903, 106 S.Ct. 3272, 91 L.Ed.2d 562 (1986).

MERRITT, Circuit Judge.

This class action suit arises out of the fall, 1981 contest for control of Marathon Oil Company which ended in a two-stage merger of Marathon into United States Steel (Steel), one of the largest mergers in United States history. * * * This suit is the consolidation of 13 separate actions challenging the two-step acquisition of Marathon by Steel as violative of the federal securities laws and state common law and fiduciary duty obligations. * * *

This action was heard before Judge Rubin in the Southern District of Ohio, and all issues were decided in favor of the defendants, some on summary judgment and others after trial before a jury. * * * [W]e affirm the District Court's decision in all respects.

I. FACTUAL BACKGROUND

[For presentation of the valuation background and the early stages of the contest for control of Marathon, consult part I of the opinion in Starkman v. Marathon Oil Co., supra p. 872.]

* [Ed. Note] from SEA Rel. No. 16384.

"Item 4 [of Schedule 14D–9] pertains to the solicitation or recommendation itself. Paragraph (a) of Item 4 requires the person filing the statement to state the nature of the solicitation/recommendation and to specify whether the person is advising security holders to accept, reject or take other action with respect to the tender offer. In order to accommodate new Rule 14e–2, a new requirement has been added to paragraph (a) which requires a subject company which is not making a recommendation to state whether it is expressing no opinion and is remaining neutral toward the tender offer or is unable to take a position with respect to the tender offer. Thus, Item 4 is intended to serve as the vehicle for the subject company to satisfy the disclosure obligation imposed by Rule 14e–2

with respect to a tender offer subject to Section 14(d). Item 4(b) has also been revised to account for Rule 14e–2. A subject company will therefore be required under this sub-item to state the reasons for its position with respect to the tender offer. It should be noted that the instruction to Item 4(b) indicates that conclusory statements will not be considered sufficient disclosure of the reasons stated in response thereto.

In 1989, members of the SEC staff expressed dissatisfaction with the quality of target disclosures elicited under the rule. Target managers tend to state that the bid is inadequate and leave it at that. The staff, accordingly, has considered a requirement that management disclose a justification for the position taken. See 21 BNA Sec.Reg. & L.Rep. 1719 (1989).

[The market price of Marathon's stock was $63.75 on October 29, 1981, far below the per share portion of the appraised values of Marathon's assets. On October 30, Mobil Oil Corp. made a tender offer for approximately 68 percent of Marathon's stock at $85 per share, to be followed by a freezeout merger of the remaining Marathon shares by payment of a debenture having an estimated market value of $85 per share.]

On November 1, 1981, Marathon filed its antitrust suit against Mobil, Marathon Oil Co. v. Mobil Corp., 530 F.Supp. 315 (N.D.Ohio 1981), and secured a temporary restraining order prohibiting Mobil from purchasing any additional Marathon shares. Marathon's board and senior management meanwhile speedily contacted all of the thirty to forty companies who were considered reasonable merger candidates, while simultaneously advising shareholders by letter to reject Mobil's bid as "grossly inadequate." Both the Strong and First Boston reports were presented to potential merger partners in an attempt to kindle interest in Marathon.

Representatives of Steel and Marathon first met on November 10, 1981, at which time Hoopman gave Steel president David Roderick a copy of the asset valuation reports. On November 12, board member Elmer Graham, Marathon's vice president for finance, delivered financial information, including five-year earnings and cash flow projections to Steel in Pittsburgh. Negotiations between Hoopman and Roderick ended on November 17 in an offer by Steel to purchase up to 30 million shares (about 51%) of Marathon stock for $125 per share in cash, to be followed by a merger proposal in which each remaining Marathon shareholder would receive one $100 face value, 12 year, 12½% guaranteed note per share of common stock.

On November 18, a formal meeting of Marathon's board was held to consider Steel's offer in light of competing, but more tentative, proposals from Allied Corporation and Gulf Oil Corporation. * * * First Boston estimated that since current market interest rates were then in the 18 to 20% range, the second stage notes offered in Steel's proposal would sell for approximately $86 per share, yielding an average price, with the first stage tender offer at $125 per share, of $106 per share. First Boston then compared the 76.6% premium over market offered by Steel with other recent takeover premiums, showing that the premium offered by Steel greatly exceeded the average premium in recent control transactions. First Boston recommended that the board accept Steel's bid.

Steel's offer was communicated by Roderick over a conference telephone call to the entire Marathon board, and was offered on a take-it-or-leave-it basis, to remain open for one day. After Roderick's call, the board discussed Steel's offer, and outside director Land asked if there were any severance agreements or "golden parachutes" granted to Marathon's senior management in a side agreement. Hoopman answered that Steel had agreed only to cash out Marathon employee stock options held by the officers and upper level management at the expected average price offered by Steel to other Marathon shareholders of $106 per share, and that Steel had requested that the present Marathon board be kept intact. After this brief discussion, the directors were polled individually, and voted unanimously in favor of recommending that the shareholders accept Steel's offer.[2]

* * *

After Steel's tender offer was announced, the market price of Marathon stock rose, and fluctuated between $100 and $105 per share from November 19 until December 7. * * * Mobil modified its offer in response to Steel's competing bid to provide for the purchase of 30 million shares at $126 per share, to be followed by a transaction in which the remaining shares would be exchanged for various securities to be valued at about $90 per share, and Mobil's offer remained open until enjoined on November 30 on the ground that it entailed probable antitrust violations. Marathon Oil Co. v. Mobil Corp., 530 F.Supp. 315 (N.D.Ohio), aff'd, 669 F.2d 378 (6th Cir.1981), cert. denied, 455 U.S. 982, 102 S.Ct. 1490, 71 L.Ed.2d 691 (1982). After this court invalidated both the stock and Yates Field options originally promised to Steel as manipulative devices under Section 14(e) of the Williams Act in Mobil Corp. v. Marathon Oil Co., 669 F.2d 366 (6th Cir.1981), the withdrawal date on Steel's tender offer was set at January 6, 1982. Between the original withdrawal deadline of December 7 and January 6, 1982, Marathon stock traded at between $88 and $82 per share. * * * By this latter date, a total of over 53 million shares, or 91.18% of the total outstanding had been tendered to Steel, and Steel purchased the promised 30 million shares on a pro rata basis on January 7.

On February 8, 1982, a proxy statement was sent to the remaining Marathon shareholders announcing a March 11, 1982 shareholder meeting at which the merger with Steel would be consummated if approved by two-thirds of the Marathon stockholders, as required by Ohio law. The proxy statement discussed the Strong and First Boston appraisals at some length, as is required in freezeout mergers by Rule 13e–3, 17 C.F.R. § 240–13e–3, warning, however, that the First Boston Report "should not be regarded as an independent evaluation or appraisal of Marathon's assets," and that the two reports were not "viewed by Marathon's Board of Directors as being reflective of * * * per share values that could realistically be expected to be received by

---

2. * * *

In the final agreement, Marathon also granted U.S. Steel an option to purchase up to 10,000 shares of Marathon common stock for $90 per share, and an option to purchase Marathon's interest in the Yates oil field for $2.8 billion if U.S. Steel's tender offer failed and another corporation succeeded in acquiring a majority interest in Marathon. On November 24, 1981, Mobil sued Marathon, U.S. Steel and directors of Marathon, seeking to enjoin the U.S. Steel tender offer. On December 23, 1981,

this court invalidated both the stock and Yates Field options as "manipulative devices" under 14(e) of the 1934 Exchange Act, 15 U.S.C. § 78n(e), and ordered that the U.S. Steel tender offer be kept open for a reasonable time. On remand, the District Court set a withdrawal deadline for the U.S. Steel offer of midnight, January 6, 1982 (the original withdrawal date stated in the offer was December 17, 1981). Mobil Corp. v. Marathon Oil Co., 669 F.2d 366 (6th Cir.1981).

Marathon or its shareholders in a negotiated sale of the Company as a going concern or through liquidation of the Company's assets." * * *

On March 11, 1982, the special shareholder meeting was held, and the shareholders approved the merger, with approximately 55% of the non-Steel Marathon shareholders voting for the merger, 20% voting against the merger, and 25% abstaining or not voting. A. 3525, Doc. 147. Marathon stock had traded at between $76 and $73 from the January 6 purchase date to the date of the shareholder meeting, indicating that the market eventually valued the bonds received in the merger at roughly $10 per share less than was forecast by First Boston.

II. SUMMARY OF PROCEEDINGS BELOW

The present class action suit represents the consolidation of thirteen separate actions by former Marathon shareholders asserting claims against Marathon, Steel, their directors (as of November, 1981) and investment bankers. The plaintiff class consists of two subclasses: Marathon shareholders who owned stock on November 19, 1981 and did not tender to Steel; and those who did tender to Steel. The plaintiffs presented claims under the federal securities laws and alleged state common law fraud and breach of fiduciary duty.

* * *

III. DISCUSSION: FEDERAL SECURITIES ISSUES

A. Duty to Disclose the Strong and First Boston Appraisal

Rule 13e–3(e) * * * requires the disclosure of certain information set forth in Schedule 13E–3, 17 C.F.R. § 240.13e–100, in freezeout merger proxy statements. Item 9 of Schedule 13E–3 requires that a summary of any asset appraisal prepared in connection with such a merger must be furnished, and the summary must describe the methods, results and underlying assumptions of the appraisal. Steel complied with this rule by describing the Strong and First Boston reports in the second stage merger proxy statement. Plaintiffs contend, however, that such disclosure should also have been made in the tender offer materials distributed to shareholders by Marathon and Steel, and that the failure to disclose these reports violated Section 10(b) of the Exchange Act, Rule 10b–5, and Section 14(e) of the Williams Act because it constituted an omission of material facts necessary to make not misleading other affirmative statements made in the tender offer materials.

On appeal, plaintiffs particularly challenge the trial court's jury instructions on materiality and the duty to disclose these reports. The disputed instructions state:

> An omitted fact is material if there is a substantial likelihood that a reasonable person would consider it important in deciding whether to tender his stock.

> Only disclosure of existing material facts is required. Economic forecasts are not.

A failure to make known a projection of future earnings is not a violation of the Federal Securities law. * * *

In Starkman v. Marathon Oil Co., 772 F.2d 231 (6th Cir.1985), we have reaffirmed our adherence to the basic rule established by our prior decisions that tender offer materials must disclose soft information, such as these asset appraisals based upon predictions regarding future economic and corporate events, only if the predictions underlying the appraisal are substantially certain to hold. The Supreme Court's test for materiality as set forth in TSC Industries, Inc. v. Northway, Inc., 426 U.S. 438, 450, 96 S.Ct. 2126, 2132, 48 L.Ed.2d 757 (1976), is whether there is a "substantial likelihood that, under all the circumstances, the omitted fact would have assumed actual significance in the deliberations of the reasonable shareholder." The District Court's instructions to the jury accurately stated this general test for materiality and the specific rule in this circuit governing the duty to disclose asset appraisals, and we have, in any event, held in *Starkman* that there was no duty to disclose the asset appraisals at issue here.

Indeed, if there was an error below on this issue, it was in allowing it to reach the jury. There is no other reported decision sending the materiality of an asset appraisal to the jury; every such decision involving an asset appraisal has held that there was no duty to disclose the appraisal.[6] Judge Rubin ruled that the Strong and First Boston reports were not immaterial as a matter of law because "[i]t is *conceivable* that a 'reasonable shareholder' would have accorded the valuations 'actual significance' in his deliberations, even if disclosure would not have altered his decision." Radol v. Thomas, 556 F.Supp. 586, 594 (S.D. Ohio 1983) (emphasis supplied). But the Supreme Court in TSC Industries v. Northway, 426 U.S. at 445–48, 96 S.Ct. at 2130–32, specifically reversed the court of appeals' definition in that case of material facts as all those which a reasonable shareholder *might* consider important, a definition which is essentially identical to Judge Rubin's ruling that the Strong and First Boston reports could be found to be material because a reasonable shareholder *conceivably* could consider them important.
* * *

B. Failure to Comply With the Proxy Rules

Plaintiffs claim that since the tender offer and the merger were viewed and represented by Steel and Marathon as a "unitary transaction," Marathon and Steel's tender offer materials constituted solicitations of shareholder consent to the proposed merger and should have contained all the information required to be included in a proxy statement under Section 14(a) of the Exchange Act. Relying on recent law review commentary,[7] plaintiffs argue that the two-tier tender offer

---

6. See the discussion in Starkman v. Marathon Oil Co., 772 F.2d 231 (6th Cir. 1985), and the compilation of cases in Flynn v. Bass Brothers Enterprises, Inc., 744 F.2d 978, 986, 988 (3d Cir.1984).

7. Plaintiffs rely on Brudney and Chirelstein, Fair Shares in Corporate Mergers and Takeovers, 88 Harv.L.Rev. 297, 330–40 (1974), and Brudney and Chirelstein, A Restatement of Corporate Freezeouts, 87 Yale L.J. 1354, 1361–62 (1978), where the au-

put the typical Marathon shareholder in a position where he had to assume that if he tendered, he would virtually assure Steel's ability to consummate the merger, and that shareholders thus should have received all the information needed to evaluate the merger prior to the deadline tendering. The only judicial authority adduced in support of the plaintiffs' position is Judge Learned Hand's ruling in SEC v. Okin, 132 F.2d 784, 786 (2d Cir.1943), that "writings which are part of a continuous plan ending in solicitation and which prepare the way for its success" are subject to the SEC's power to regulate proxy solicitations.

In rejecting this claim on the defendants' summary judgment motion, Judge Rubin correctly ruled that "a tender offer and subsequent merger are distinct acts with separate concerns toward which the securities laws and SEC rules are directed in their regulatory schemes," and that it was "entirely appropriate to consider each step in such a transaction separately." Radol v. Thomas, 556 F.Supp. 586, 591 (S.D. Ohio 1983). Steel complied with Rule 14d–3 * * * by filing a Schedule 14D–1 with the Commission which disclosed the basic terms of the proposed merger with Marathon, as required by Item 5(a) of 17 C.F.R. § 240.14d–100. As the target, Marathon complied with Rule 14e–2, 17 C.F.R. § 240.14e–2, by sending a letter to its shareholders recommending acceptance of Steel's offer and describing the two-stage plan, and Marathon also complied with Rule 14d–9, 17 C.F.R. § 240.14d–9 by filing a Schedule 14D–9 with the Commission which described the basic terms of the merger. Both Steel and Marathon therefore complied with the specific disclosure requirements which apply to tender offers.

Requiring compliance with the proxy rules, in particular Rule 14a–9, or the specific freezeout merger proxy disclosure requirements in Rule 13e–3, 17 C.F.R. § 240.13e–3, in the tender offer stage of a two-tier transaction of this sort would be unfair because it would subject the tender offeror and target to the risk of liability for violating Section 5 of the Securities Act of 1933, 15 U.S.C. § 77e, by making an "offer to sell" securities prior to filing a registration statement for the securities.[8] In Securities Act Release No. 33–5927, reprinted in 3 Fed.Sec.L.Rep. (CCH) ¶ 24,284H (April 24, 1978), the Commission stated that the Section 5 "jumping the gun" prohibition would not apply to disclosure of a proposed second stage merger in tender offer materials as required by Schedule 14D–1, because to rule that such disclosure constituted an offer to sell would not further the policies of the 1933 Act and would be inconsistent with the Williams Act policy of requiring such information in order to provide full disclosure to investors confronted with an investment decision in the context of a tender offer. However, the Commission also warned that disclosure at the tender offer stage should not go beyond that specifically required by the Williams Act and the

thors argue that two-tier tender offers involving a second stage merger at a lower price than the front end tender offer are inherently coercive and should be prohibited.

8. The securities involved here are the bonds to be exchanged for remaining Marathon shares in the second stage merger.

tender offer rules, and that "statements which are not required by the Williams Act may constitute an 'offer to sell' the securities to be exchanged in the subsequent merger and, in the absence of a registration statement filed with the Commission at the commencement of the tender offer, may constitute a violation of Section 5 of the 1933 Act." 3 Fed.Sec.L.Rep. at 17,754. The plaintiffs' proposed extension of the comprehensive proxy statement disclosure requirements to the tender offer stage of a two-tier transaction thus risks placing the board in a completely untenable position in which liability attaches under the proxy rules for too little disclosure and under the 1933 Act for too much disclosure, a result we are unwilling to endorse.   * * *

In addition, unlike SEC v. Okin, 132 F.2d at 786, where Judge Hand found that the Commission "would be powerless to protect shareholders" from misleading letters concerning an ongoing proxy solicitation sent in preparation for a soon-to-follow competing solicitation unless the letters were themselves held to be proxy solicitations, the Commission has set forth disclosure requirements for tender offers, and there are sound policy reasons for treating tender offers differently, with respect to the volume and content of required disclosure, than proxy statements.

Contrary to the plaintiffs' assumption, an individual shareholder does not assure the success of the second stage merger by choosing to tender in the first stage. Rather, the merger occurs only if the tender offer succeeds, and the success of the tender offer is determined by shareholders' collective valuation of the premium offered in relation to other competing offers (here, Mobil's outstanding tender offer). In the tender offer context, the market plays an important role in providing shareholders with information regarding the value of the target firm, and target management has an incentive to broker the best deal for shareholders and provide favorable, optimistic information to prospective bidders—precisely the kind of information the plaintiffs say was contained in the Strong and First Boston reports and precisely that which majority shareholders have an incentive to keep from the minority in an unfair freezeout merger. The more extensive legal disclosure requirements which apply to freezeout merger proxy statements are therefore justified by the fact that the law has given the majority the power to foreclose the ownership rights of the minority and has thereby eliminated the market as a correcting mechanism, leaving minority shareholders with only the option of dissent and appraisal, an option which cannot rationally be exercised unless the majority is compelled to make full disclosure regarding appraisals, earnings projections and other information that sheds light on the value of the firm. Cf. Toms, Compensating Shareholders Frozen Out in Two–Step Mergers, 78 Colum.L.Rev. 548, 554–60 (1978) (observing how the negotiating position of management in a unitary merger differs fundamentally from that of the corporation's individual shareholders in a tender offer).

For these reasons, neither Steel nor Marathon had a duty to comply with the proxy rules in their tender offer statements.

[The court also rejected the plaintiffs' claim that Marathon's two-tier, front end-loaded offer was a manipulative device in violation of sections 10(b) and 14(e), making reference to Santa Fe v. Green, 430 U.S. 462 (1977), and Schreiber v. Burlington Northern, Inc., 472 U.S. 1 (1985).]

* * *

Accordingly, the judgment of the District Court is affirmed.

NOTE: THE WILLIAMS ACT AND TARGET DEFENSIVE TACTICS

1. *Disclosure of Defensive Negotiations.*

The *Radol* court's treatment of Marathon's asset appraisals presumably should be reconsidered in light of Basic v. Levinson, supra p. 885. What should result from such a reconsideration? Does the context of a tender offer make a significant difference in the materiality determination in respect of asset appraisals? Compare the discussion of context in *Basic* with the discussion supra p. 961, of the target shareholders' information disadvantages.

The SEC's posture respecting disclosure of negotiations looking toward target asset sales or defensive mergers provides a striking comparison. The Commission long has insisted that the existence of such negotiations be disclosed promptly. The Commission set out its position in Exchange Act Rel. No. 16,384 (Nov. 29, 1979):

"Item 7 of Schedule 14D–9 requires disclosure with respect to certain negotiations and transactions by the subject company. As proposed for comment, Item 7 would have required disclosure of any negotiation or transaction being undertaken in response to the tender offer by the subject company which related to or would have resulted in any of the following: (1) an extraordinary transaction, such as a merger or reorganization, involving the subject company or any subsidiary of the subject company; (2) a sale or transfer of a material amount of assets of the subject company or any of its subsidiaries; (3) a tender offer for or other acquisition of subject company securities; or (4) any material change in the subject company's present capitalization or dividend policy. The proposal was criticized by commentators who were concerned that it would elicit premature disclosure of negotiations with competing bidders which could dissuade them from making an offer. It was noted that this would be harmful to security holders since they would be prevented from obtaining the highest price for their securities. In addition, concern was expressed that such disclosure may, either innocently or fraudulently, induce security holders to reject a tender offer on the basis of an unjustified inference that a competing bid is imminent.

"The Commission recognizes that premature disclosure of the matters contemplated by the proposal may be detrimental to the interests of security holders. The effective representation of the interests of security holders may at times require management to maintain confidentiality during the formative stages of negotiations. On the other hand, the major developments referred to in Item 7 can be one of the most material items of information received by security holders.

"The Commission has addressed these competing concerns by approaching disclosure of these matters at two levels. While the proposal would have required the subject company to describe negotiations in response to a tender offer which related to or would result in the specified events, new Item 7(a) requires a statement as to whether negotiations are being undertaken or are underway with respect to such events without requiring detailed disclosure. An instruction has also been added to Item 7(a) which clarifies the extent of the disclosure required with respect to negotiations. The instruction provides that, if an agreement in principle has not been reached, the possible terms of any transaction or the parties thereto need not be disclosed if in the opinion of the Board of Directors of the subject company such disclosure would jeopardize continuation of such negotiations. In such event, disclosure that negotiations are being undertaken or are underway and are in the preliminary stages will be sufficient. Thus, security holders will be apprised that such negotiations are being held without the subject company's having to furnish disclosure which would discourage further negotiations."

The SEC has been notably aggressive in its enforcement of the requirement that targets keep Item 7 current. In In re Revlon, CCH Fed.Sec.L.Rep. ¶ 84,006 (1986), the Commission ruled that Revlon violated the Act in failing to amend its Schedule 14D–9 to note the existence of negotiations with a group interested in purchasing its cosmetic producing assets, even though terms on price and structure were far from concluded. The fact that discussions on price and structure were under way and an initial offer on the table were enough. In In re The Lionel Corp., 1191 SEC LEXIS 2922 (Dec. 30, 1991), the Commission made a similar ruling in respect of the failure to disclose the commencement of settlement negotiations with a hostile bidder. In re Kern, CCH Fed.Sec.L.Rep. ¶ 84,342 (1988), a similar enforcement proceeding, extends the duty to outside counsel for the target where the lawyer, here the head of the mergers and acquisitions group at Sullivan & Cromwell, held all responsibility for compliance decisions.

2. *Defenses That Pretermit Actions for Inadequate Disclosure.*

In **Panter v. Marshall Field & Co.**, 646 F.2d 271 (7th Cir.1981), cert. denied, 454 U.S. 1092 (1981), target shareholders unsuccessfully brought an action under section 14(e) in respect of management defensive actions that caused a prospective hostile bid to fail to materialize. The management of Marshall Field brought an antitrust action against a merger proposed by the hostile suitor, Carter Hawley Hale (CHH). It simultaneously proceeded to expand Field's business into new geographic markets in which CHH had a significant presence. The court disposed of the 14(e) claim as follows, 646 F.2d at 283–284, 285–286:

"By denying the plaintiffs the opportunity to tender their shares to CHH, the plaintiffs claim the defendants deprived them of the difference between $42.00, the amount of the CHH offer, and $19.76, the amount at which Field's shares traded in the market after withdrawal of the CHH proposal. Total damages under this theory would exceed $200,000,000.00.

"Because § 14(e) is intended to protect shareholders from making a tender offer decision on inaccurate or inadequate information, among the elements of § 14(e) plaintiff must establish is 'that there was a misrepresentation upon which the target corporation shareholders relied * * *.' Chris–Craft Industries, Inc. v. Piper Aircraft Corp., 480 F.2d 341, 373 (2d Cir.), cert. denied, 414 U.S. 910, 94 S.Ct. 231, 38 L.Ed.2d 148 (1973). Because the CHH tender offer was withdrawn before the plaintiffs had the opportunity to decide whether or not to tender their shares, it was impossible for the plaintiffs to rely on any alleged deception in making the decision to tender or not. Because the plaintiffs were never presented with that critical decision and therefore never relied on the defendants' alleged misrepresentations, they fail to establish a vital element of a § 14(e) claim as regards the CHH $42.00 offer.

* * *

"The plaintiffs also contend that defendants' misrepresentations or omissions of material fact caused the plaintiffs not to dispose of their shares in the market, which was rising on the news of CHH's takeover attempt. Because we hold that a damages remedy for investors who determine not to sell in the marketplace when no tender offer ever takes place was not intended to be covered by § 14(e) of the statute, we are not swayed by the surface appeal of this argument.

* * *

"Courts seeking to construe the provisions of the Williams Act have also noted that its protections are required by the peculiar nature of a tender offer, which forces a shareholder to decide whether to dispose of his shares at some premium over the market, or retain them with knowledge that the offeror may alter the management of the target company to its detriment. See Piper v. Chris–Craft Industries, Inc., 430 U.S. at 35, 97 S.Ct. at 946; Bucher v. Shumway, 452 F.Supp. 1288, 1294 (S.D.N.Y.1978). * * * Here there was no deadline by which shareholders were forced to tender, and by hypothesis when we are discussing market transactions, no premium over the market. Therefore Field's shareholders were simply not subjected to the proscribed pressures the Williams Act was designed to alleviate. * * *"

(E) UNDISTORTED CHOICE FOR TARGET SHAREHOLDERS

Consult Sections 14(d)(5)–14(d)(7) of the Securities Exchange Act of 1934, supra p. 978.

(1) Withdrawal and Proration

Rule 14d–7.   Additional Withdrawal Rights

(a) *Rights.*   In addition to the provisions of section 14(d)(5) of the Act, any person who has deposited securities pursuant to a tender offer has the right to withdraw any such securities during the periods such offer request or invitation remains open.

* * *

Rule 14d–8.   Exemption From Statutory Pro Rata Requirements

Notwithstanding the pro rata provisions of Section 14(d)(6) of the Act, if any person makes a tender offer or request or invitation for tenders, for less than all of the outstanding equity securities of a class, and if a greater number of securities are deposited pursuant thereto than such person is bound or willing to take up and pay for, the securities taken up and paid for shall be taken up and paid for as nearly as may be pro rata, disregarding fractions, according to the number of securities deposited by each depositor during the period such offer, request or invitation remains open.*

PRYOR v. UNITED STATES STEEL CORP.
United States Court of Appeals, Second Circuit, 1986.
794 F.2d 52, cert. denied 479 U.S. 954, 107 S.Ct. 445, 93 L.Ed.2d 393 (1986).

[This case presents the question whether a bidder can be liable in a private action for damages for extending the pro-ration period (beyond the ten day period required by Section 14(d)(6) and which it prescribed

---

* [Ed. Note] In SEA Rel. No. 19,336 (12/15/82) revising Rule 14d–8 the Commission pointed out that "extension of pro-ration rights throughout the term of the offer is essential to assure security holders the time necessary to consider the merits of an offer and to obtain sufficient information upon which to base their investment decisions and to minimize the potential security holder confusion and misunderstanding generated by changing proration periods and multiple proration pools.

"A number of commentators related specific experiences in which they had problems receiving tender offer materials and effecting their investment decisions within the ten calendar day proration period. These experiences included receiving tender offer materials after the expiration of a bidder's proration period or so close to the end of the period that they could not tender before the expiration of the proration period. As a result, these commentators stated that they were foreclosed from participating in the offer and were likely to receive a lesser amount for their securities in a proposed second-step merger. In addition, these commentators highlighted the problems that individual security holders experience trying to understand the varying legal consequences of the deadlines contained in a partial tender offer, appreciating the importance of deciding before the expiration of the proration period whether to tender, sell or hold their stock, and comprehending the effect of multiple proration pools."

in its oversubscribed tender offer) and thereby diluting the receipts of those who had tendered within the original period. In answering the question in the affirmative, the court said:]

WINTER, Circuit Judge.

1. *Section 14(d)(6)*

Section 14(d)(6) requires that offers for less than an entire class of equity securities be subject to a ten-day proration period. The district court rejected Pryor's Section 14(d)(6) claim on the grounds that the statute simply creates a mandatory minimum proration period and that an offeror might, after the proration, delivery, and expiration dates, extend the proration period. In its view, U.S. Steel's offer thus complied with Section 14(d)(6) and the extension of the proration period specified in the tender offer was actionable, if at all, only in a state law breach of contract action. 591 F.Supp. 949. The district court found support for its view, that the statute merely creates a mandatory minimum proration period, in two SEC Rules. Rule 14d–8,[5] * * * at the time of this offer exempted from Section 14(d)(6) offers that provided for proration periods of longer than ten days. Rule 14d–6(e)(vi), * * * required offerors to disclose in their offering materials their intentions with respect to proration. Since these rules contemplated proration periods of more than ten days, the district court reasoned, Section 14(d)(6) is implicated only in situations in which an offeror fails to provide the ten-day minimum period.

We disagree. We believe that by failing to enforce the ten-day deadline required by Section 14(d)(6) and provided in the offer, U.S. Steel failed to purchase shares on a pro rata basis and thereby violated the statute. Section 14(d)(6) has dual purposes: (i) it ensures that shareholders have time to consider a tender offer carefully and yet share in any control premium paid; and (ii) it deprives the offeror of any discretion to select among shareholders in paying the control premium.

* * *

* * * Prior to Section 14(d)(6), first-come, first-serve offers were often employed in two-step takeovers. Offerors placed a premium on shares amounting to a control bloc, and tender offers for less than 100% of a company's common stock were believed by Congress to confront shareholders with a difficult and time-pressured decision. Congress reasoned that shareholders might be tempted to tender without carefully weighing the offer so as to avoid missing out on a piece of the control premium. * * * Section 14(d)(6)'s mandatory minimum proration period thus affords shareholders a period of time in which to consider the offer and also to share in the control premium if a decision to tender is made. It is clear therefore that the ten-day period is a mandatory minimum.

---

5. Rule 14d–8 now requires that all partial offers provide proration rights during the entire length of the offer. We express no view on the validity of this regulation.

In addition, Section 14(d)(6) requires equal treatment of holders who tender within the proration period and thus has a non-discrimination component. Had U.S. Steel purchased a greater than pro rata share of timely-tendered shares from a particular shareholder, it would have violated Section 14(d)(6). This is evident not only in the very use of the term pro rata, but also in Section 14(d)(6)'s requirement that "an increase in the consideration offered to security holders" automatically extends the proration period for an additional ten days. For better or for worse, Congress desired to spread any premium for control among all shareholders tendering within the proration period. This purpose cannot be achieved unless offerors are forbidden to purchase a greater than pro rata share from particular holders.

It also follows that offerors are not free to extend the proration deadline after it has expired where the effect is to diminish the numbers of shares purchased from those who tendered before the deadline. It cannot be determined whether U.S. Steel extended the proration period for the purpose of benefitting particular shareholders. However, the result of its increasing the size of the pool after expiration of the offer is the same as if it had. The discretionary power to extend selectively the proration date after the offer has been oversubscribed entails the power to alter the size and make-up of the proration pool, which in turn enables the offeror to favor certain holders to the detriment of others. Inclusion of shares that were not timely tendered obviously increases the amount purchased from late-tendering shareholders in the first step of the offer. Moreover, it allows an offeror to extend proration selectively so as to include particular shareholders the offeror may choose to favor. The cost of this discretionary, preferential treatment is, of course, borne not by the offeror but by those who have timely tendered their shares. The latter suffer from a reduced proration factor and a smaller share of the control premium.

Neither of the SEC regulations relied upon by the district court and in effect at the time of U.S. Steel's offer are inconsistent with our holding. The critical fact in the instant case is that U.S. Steel extended the proration period after the offer had been oversubscribed within the ten days specified by the offer and required by Section 14(d)(6), and after the proration deadlines had passed. The extension thus favored some shareholders at the expense of those who had tendered within the proration period. We need not, therefore, address the very different question of whether an offeror, when making the offer, may specify a proration period of longer than ten days. An offer that provides for a proration period of more than ten days does not, in and of itself, create a danger that an offeror may at its discretion select some shares for proration no matter when they were tendered. To the extent that the provision of the offer empowering U.S. Steel to determine the validity of a tender of shares or to waive the offer's conditions relating to tender purports to allow it to do what Section 14(d)(6) forbids, it is invalid.

2. *Private Right of Action Under Section 14(d)(6)*

Having dismissed Pryor's Section 14(d)(6) claim for failure to state a claim, the district court did not reach the question whether there is a private right of action under that section. Since we have reinstated that part of the complaint, we must decide whether Congress intended to provide such a cause of action. We conclude that it did.

* * *

[Viewing "the Cort factors * * * as proxies for congressional intent," the Court examined them and found that they supported the conclusion that Congress intended to provide such a cause of action under Section 14(d)(6).]

3. Claims Against Bankers Trust

Since neither Section 14(d)(6) nor Rule 10b–13 imposes any duties on a depositary, we affirm the district court's dismissal of Pryor's claims against Bankers Trust.

* * *

The judgment of the district court is affirmed in part and reversed in part.

LUMBARD, Circuit Judge, concurring and dissenting:

I agree that plaintiff has failed to state a cause of action against Bankers Trust, the depositary for the tendered stocks. I disagree, however, with the majority's holding that plaintiff has stated a claim against the tender offeror U.S. Steel.

* * *

Section 14(d)(6) is designed to eliminate the pressure on shareholders to respond to a tender offer immediately, out of fear that they will be shut out if the offer becomes oversubscribed. This is done by requiring the tender offeror to accept shares tendered within the first ten days of the offer and to buy a pro rata percentage of each tendering shareholder's shares if the offer does in fact become oversubscribed in that time. Shareholders are thus accorded an opportunity to reflect on the merits of the bid without risking their chance to participate in the offer.

U.S. Steel's alleged acceptance of late-tendered shares for proration did not interfere with these goals. U.S. Steel simply allowed more shareholders to participate in the bid than would otherwise have been able to had it been strict about the 10–day deadline. There is no indication that such conduct is actionable under § 14(d)(6) and I see no good reason why it should be. Indeed, SEC Rules 14d–8 * * * and 14d–6(e)(vi) * * * in force at the time of U.S. Steel's offer, stated that the proration deadline was left to the terms of the tender offer, so long as it met the 10–day statutory minimum. The SEC's interpretation of § 14(d)(6) suggests that enforcement of the proration deadline is a matter of contract law, not a matter cognizable under federal securities law.

As the majority points out, § 14(d)(6) also has a nondiscrimination component that prohibits an offeror from treating tendering shareholders unequally. I do not believe, however, that U.S. Steel discriminated among shareholders in a way that violated that section. During the legislative debates over the Williams Act, then SEC Chairman Cohen expressed concern over using 10 days as a minimum proration period because he felt that the tender offeror would favor sophisticated investors by waiting until the eleventh day in order to buy up *all* their shares rather than just a percentage. * * * In response to Chairman Cohen's concerns, proponents of the 10–day rule emphasized that a tender offeror would not be permitted to accept more shares than were originally sought without first accepting all the shares tendered within the proration period. * * *

In this case, U.S. Steel has not purchased any more shares than it had originally sought. Plaintiff is not complaining that U.S. Steel bought additional *non-prorated* shares, but that U.S. Steel allowed late shares *to be prorated*. I believe that the distinction is important because in the former case, the tender offeror treats tendering shareholders unequally: some shareholders have their shares prorated while others get all their shares taken up. In the latter case which is the case at bar, all tendering shareholders are treated equally: everyone's shares are prorated.

Moreover, in this latter case, there should be little concern that the tender offeror will favor one group of shareholders over another. Because the tender offeror is committed to accepting a fixed number of shares, it gains nothing from allowing late tendering shareholders into the proration pool. Indeed, it is usually in the tender offeror's best interest to close the proration pool as quickly as possible in a hostile takeover battle against target management or a competing tender offeror.[2]

One plausible explanation of why a tender offeror might wish to accept late tendered shares for proration is that it hopes to avoid complaints from and possible lawsuits brought by the late tenderers. I imagine that whenever a tender offeror fixes the proration date there will be shareholders who straggle in late because of the mails, excusable neglect, or other reasons. By accommodating these shareholders, the tender offeror has liberally construed the precise terms of the offer, but I see little reason why this is of federal concern.

This is not to say that U.S. Steel is necessarily free from any liability. The Marathon shareholders who tendered on time are harmed if U.S. Steel did in fact include late-tendered shares in the

---

2. This explains, in part, why Congress adopted a short mandatory proration period of 10 days. When the Williams Act was first under consideration, the SEC endorsed a Senate bill which would have made the proration period co-extensive with the entire length of the offer. This suggestion was rejected in favor of the 10–day proration period used by the New York Stock Exchange because if pro rata acceptance were made mandatory for the entire period of the offer, it would allow shareholders to delay their decision to tender and give target management an unfair time advantage in a takeover battle. Congress believed that the 10–day rule both provided sufficient time for shareholders to assess the merits of a tender offer and recognized the tender offeror's desire to move quickly. See S.Rep. No. 550, 90th Cong., 1st Sess. 4–5 (1967).

proration pool because fewer of their shares were taken up. I do not believe, however, that U.S. Steel's actions violated § 14(d)(6). If anything, its actions promoted the purposes of that section by allowing more shareholders to participate in the bid and by treating all tendering shareholders equally. If timely tendering shareholders are entitled to a preference over those who tender late, the entitlement derives from the terms of the tender offer and state contract law, not from § 14(d)(6).

I would also affirm the dismissal of the plaintiff's claim under SEC Rule 10b–13, * * * which prohibits a tender offeror from making any purchases otherwise than pursuant to the offer while the offer is in effect. Plaintiff contends that by including late-tendered shares in the proration pool, U.S. Steel purchased those shares "otherwise than pursuant to" the offer. I disagree.

The purpose of the Rule is to prevent a tender offeror from making "outside" purchases on different terms, especially different price terms, from those offered to shareholders who have already tendered. But, as Judge Lowe noted, plaintiff's complaint is very different. "Plaintiff is not really claiming that purchases from the late-tendering shareholders were made outside of the tender offer, but rather that the "late-tendering shareholders were wrongfully allowed to *participate* in the offer as if they had made a valid tender.' " * * *

Because I would hold that U.S. Steel's actions did not violate § 14(d)(6) or Rule 10b–13, I would not reach the question of an implied damage remedy.

———

SCHREIBER v. BURLINGTON NORTHERN, INC.

Supreme Court of the United States, 1985.
472 U.S. 1, 105 S.Ct. 2458, 86 L.Ed.2d 1.

Chief Justice BURGER delivered the opinion of the Court.

We granted certiorari to resolve a conflict in the Circuits over whether misrepresentation or nondisclosure is a necessary element of a violation of § 14(e) of the Securities Exchange Act of 1934, 15 U.S.C. § 78n(e).

I

On December 21, 1982, Burlington Northern, Inc., made a hostile tender offer for El Paso Gas Co. Through a wholly owned subsidiary, Burlington proposed to purchase 25.1 million El Paso shares at $24 per share. Burlington reserved the right to terminate the offer if any of several specified events occurred. El Paso management initially opposed the takeover, but its shareholders responded favorably, fully subscribing the offer by the December 30, 1982 deadline.

Burlington did not accept those tendered shares; instead, after negotiations with El Paso management, Burlington announced on January 10, 1983, the terms of a new and friendly takeover agreement. Pursuant to the new agreement, Burlington undertook, *inter alia*, to (1) rescind the December tender offer, (2) purchase 4,166,667 shares from El Paso at $24 per share, (3) substitute a new tender offer for only 21 million shares at $24 per share, (4) provide procedural protections against a squeeze-out merger of the remaining El Paso shareholders, and (5) recognize "golden parachute" contracts between El Paso and four of its senior officers. By February 8, more than 40 million shares were tendered in response to Burlington's January offer, and the takeover was completed.

The rescission of the first tender offer caused a diminished payment to those shareholders who had tendered during the first offer. The January offer was greatly oversubscribed and consequently those shareholders who retendered were subject to substantial proration. Petitioner Barbara Schreiber filed suit on behalf of herself and similarly situated shareholders, alleging that Burlington, El Paso, and members of El Paso's board violated § 14(e)'s prohibition of "fraudulent, deceptive or manipulative acts or practices * * * in connection with any tender offer." 15 U.S.C. § 78n(e). She claimed that Burlington's withdrawal of the December tender offer coupled with the substitution of the January tender offer was a "manipulative" distortion of the market for El Paso stock. Schreiber also alleged that Burlington violated § 14(e) by failing in the January offer to disclose the "golden parachutes" offered to four of El Paso's managers. She claims that this January nondisclosure was a deceptive act forbidden by § 14(e).

The District Court dismissed the suit for failure to state a claim. 568 F.Supp. 197 (Del.1983). The District Court reasoned that the alleged manipulation did not involve a misrepresentation, and so did not violate § 14(e). The District Court relied on the fact that in cases involving alleged violations of § 10(b) of the Securities Exchange Act, 15 U.S.C. § 78j(b), this Court has required misrepresentation for there to be a "manipulative" violation of the section. 568 F.Supp., at 202.

The Court of Appeals for the Third Circuit affirmed. 731 F.2d 163 (1984). The Court of Appeals held that the acts alleged did not violate the Williams Act, because "§ 14(e) was not intended to create a federal cause of action for all harms suffered because of the proffering or the withdrawal of tender offers." Id., at 165. The Court of Appeals reasoned that § 14(e) was "enacted principally as a disclosure statute, designed to insure that fully-informed investors could intelligently decide how to respond to a tender offer." Id., at 165–166. It concluded that the "arguable breach of contract" alleged by petitioner was not a "manipulative act" under § 14(e).

We granted certiorari to resolve the conflict,[3] 469 U.S. 815 (1984). We affirm.

---

3. The Court of Appeals for the Sixth Circuit has held that manipulation does not always require an element of misrepresentation or nondisclosure. Mobil Corp. v. Marathon Oil Co., 669 F.2d 366 (1981), cert. denied, 455 U.S. 982, 102 S.Ct. 1490, 71 L.Ed.2d 691 (1982). The Court of Appeals for the Second and Eighth Circuits have

II

A

We are asked in this case to interpret § 14(e) of the Securities Exchange Act, 48 Stat. 895, as amended, 15 U.S.C. § 78n(e). The starting point is the language of the statute. Section 14(e) provides:

"It shall be unlawful for any person to make any untrue statement of a material fact or omit to state any material fact necessary in order to make the statements made, in the light of the circumstances under which they are made, not misleading, or to engage in any fraudulent, deceptive or manipulative acts or practices, in connection with any tender offer or request or invitation for tenders, or any solicitation of security holders in opposition to or in favor of any such offer, request, or invitation. The Commission shall, for the purposes of this subsection, by rules and regulations define, and prescribe means reasonably designed to prevent, such acts and practices as are fraudulent, deceptive, or manipulative." 15 U.S.C. § 78n(e).

Petitioner relies on a construction of the phrase, "fraudulent, deceptive or manipulative acts or practices." Petitioner reads the phrase "fraudulent, deceptive or manipulative acts or practices" to include acts which, although fully disclosed, "artificially" affect the price of the takeover target's stock. Petitioner's interpretation relies on the belief that § 14(e) is directed at purposes broader than providing full and true information to investors.

Petitioner's reading of the term "manipulative" conflicts with the normal meaning of the term. We have held in the context of an alleged violation of § 10(b) of the Securities Exchange Act:

"Use of the word 'manipulative' is especially significant. It is and was virtually a term of art when used in connection with the securities markets. It connotes intentional or willful conduct *designed to deceive or defraud* investors by controlling or artificially affecting the price of securities." Ernst & Ernst v. Hochfelder, 425 U.S. 185, 199, 96 S.Ct. 1375, 1384, 47 L.Ed.2d 668 (1976) (emphasis added).

Other cases interpreting the term reflect its use as a general term comprising a range of misleading practices:

"The term refers generally to practices, such as wash sales, matched orders, or rigged prices, that are intended to mislead investors by artificially affecting market activity * * *. Section 10(b)'s general prohibition of practices deemed by the SEC to be 'manipulative'—in this technical sense of artificially affecting market activity in order to mislead investors—is fully consistent with

applied an analysis consistent with the one we apply today. Feldbaum v. Avon Products, Inc., 741 F.2d 234 (CA8 1984); Buffalo Forge Co. v. Ogden Corp., 717 F.2d 757 (CA2), cert. denied, 464 U.S. 1018, 104 S.Ct. 550, 78 L.Ed.2d 724 (1983); Data Probe Acquisition Corp. v. Datatab, Inc., 722 F.2d 1 (CA2 1983), cert. denied 465 U.S. 1052, 104 S.Ct. 1326, 79 L.Ed.2d 722 (1984).

the fundamental purpose of the 1934 Act ' "to substitute a philosophy of full disclosure for the philosophy of *caveat emptor* * * *." ' * * * Indeed, nondisclosure is usually essential to the success of a manipulative scheme * * *. No doubt Congress meant to prohibit the full range of ingenious devices that might be used to manipulate securities prices. But we do not think it would have chosen this 'term of art' if it had meant to bring within the scope of § 10(b) instances of corporate mismanagement such as this, in which the essence of the complaint is that shareholders were treated unfairly by a fiduciary." Santa Fe Industries, Inc. v. Green, 430 U.S. 462, 476–477, 97 S.Ct. 1292, 1302–1303, 51 L.Ed.2d 480 (1977).

The meaning the Court has given the term "manipulative" is consistent with the use of the term at common law,[4] and with its traditional dictionary definition.[5]

She argues, however, that the term manipulative takes on a meaning in § 14(e) that is different from the meaning it has in § 10(b). Petitioner claims that the use of the disjunctive "or" in § 14(e) implies that acts need not be deceptive or fraudulent to be manipulative. But Congress used the phrase "manipulative or deceptive" in § 10(b) as well, and we have interpreted "manipulative" in that context to require misrepresentation. Moreover, it is a " 'familiar principle of statutory construction that words grouped in a list should be given related meaning.' " Securities Indus. Assn. v. Board of Governors, 468 U.S. ___, ___, 104 S.Ct. 3003, 3010, 82 L.Ed.2d 158 (1984). All three species of misconduct, i.e., "fraudulent, deceptive or manipulative," listed by Congress are directed at failures to disclose. The use of the term "manipulative" provides emphasis and guidance to those who must determine which types of acts are reached by the statute; it does not suggest a deviation from the section's facial and primary concern with disclosure or Congressional concern with disclosure which is the core of the Act.

B

Our conclusion that "manipulative" acts under § 14(e) require misrepresentation or nondisclosure is buttressed by the purpose and legislative history of the provision. Section 14(e) was originally added to the Securities Exchange Act as part of the Williams Act, 82 Stat. 457. "The purpose of the Williams Act is to insure that public shareholders who are confronted by a cash tender offer for their stock will not be required to respond without adequate information." Ron-

---

4. See generally, L. Loss, Securities Regulation 984–989 (3d ed. 1983). For example, the seminal English case of Scott v. Brown, Doering, McNab & Co., [1892] 2 Q.B. 724, 724 (C.A.), which broke new ground in recognizing that manipulation could occur without the dissemination of false statements, nonetheless placed emphasis on the presence of deception. As Lord Lopes stated in that case, "I can see no substantial distinction between false rumours and false and fictitious acts." Id.,

at 730. See also, United States v. Brown, 5 F.Supp. 81, 85 (SDNY 1933) ("[E]ven a speculator is entitled not to have any present fact involving the subject matter of his speculative purchase or the price thereof misrepresented by word or act").

5. See Webster's Third New International Dictionary 1376 (1971) (Manipulation is "management with use of unfair, scheming, or underhanded methods").

deau v. Mosinee Paper Corp., 422 U.S. 49, 58, 95 S.Ct. 2069, 2075, 45 L.Ed.2d 12 (1975).

It is clear that Congress relied primarily on disclosure to implement the purpose of the Williams Act. Senator Williams, the Bill's Senate sponsor, stated in the debate:

"Today, the public shareholder in deciding whether to accept or reject a tender offer possesses limited information. No matter what he does, he acts without adequate knowledge to enable him to decide rationally what is the best course of action. This is precisely the dilemma which our securities laws are designed to prevent."

113 Cong.Rec. 24664 (1967) (Remarks of Sen. Williams).

The expressed legislative intent was to preserve a neutral setting in which the contenders could fully present their arguments.[8] The Senate sponsor went on to say:

"We have taken extreme care to avoid tipping the scales either in favor of management or in favor of the person making the takeover bids. S. 510 is designed solely to require full and fair disclosure for the benefit of investors. The bill will at the same time provide the offeror and management equal opportunity to present their case." Ibid.

To implement this objective, the Williams Act added §§ 13(d), 13(e), 14(d), 14(e), and 14(f) to the Securities Exchange Act. Some relate to disclosure; §§ 13(d), 14(d) and 14(f) all add specific registration and disclosure provisions. Others—§§ 13(e) and 14(d)—require or prohibit certain acts so that investors will possess additional time within which to take advantage of the disclosed information.

Section 14(e) adds a "broad antifraud prohibition," Piper v. Chris–Craft Industries, 430 U.S. 1, 24, 97 S.Ct. 926, 940, 51 L.Ed.2d 124 (1977), modeled on the antifraud provisions of § 10(b) of the Act and Rule 10b–5, 17 CFR § 240.10b–5 (1984).[10] It supplements the more precise

---

8. The process through which Congress developed the Williams Act also suggests a calculated reliance on disclosure, rather than court-imposed principles of "fairness" or "artificiality," as the preferred method of market regulation. For example, as the bill progressed through hearings, both Houses of Congress became concerned that corporate stock repurchases could be used to distort the market for corporate control. Congress addressed this problem with § 13(e), which imposes specific disclosure duties on corporations purchasing stock and grants broad regulatory power to the Securities Exchange Commission to regulate such repurchases. Congress stopped short, however, of imposing specific substantive requirements forbidding corporations to trade in their own stock for the purpose of maintaining its price. The specific regulatory scheme set forth in § 13(e) would be unnecessary if Congress at the

same time had endowed the term "manipulative" in § 14(e) with broad substantive significance.

10. Section 10(b) provides:

"It shall be unlawful for any person, directly or indirectly, * * *

"(b) To use or employ, in connection with the purchase or sale of any security registered on a national securities exchange or any security not so registered, any manipulative or deceptive device or contrivance in contravention of such rules and regulations as the Commission may prescribe as necessary or appropriate in the public interest or for the protection of investors." 15 U.S.C. § 78j.

Rule 10b–5 provides:

"It shall be unlawful for any person, directly or indirectly, by the use of any

disclosure provisions found elsewhere in the Williams Act, while requiring disclosure more explicitly addressed to the tender offer context than that required by § 10(b).

While legislative history specifically concerning § 14(e) is sparse, the House and Senate Reports discuss the role of § 14(e). Describing § 14(e) as regulating "fraudulent transactions," and stating the thrust of the section:

> "This provision would affirm the fact that persons engaged in making or opposing tender offers or otherwise seeking to influence the decision of investors or the outcome of the tender offer are under an obligation to make *full disclosure* of material information to those with whom they deal." H.R.Rep. No. 1711, 90th Cong., 2d Sess., 11 (1968), U.S.Code Cong. & Admin.News 1968, pp. 2811, 2821 (emphasis added); S.Rep. No. 550, 90th Cong., 1st Sess., 11 (1967) (emphasis added).

Nowhere in the legislative history is there the slightest suggestion that § 14(e) serves any purpose other than disclosure,[11] or that the term "manipulative" should be read as an invitation to the courts to oversee the substantive fairness of tender offers; the quality of any offer is a matter for the marketplace.

To adopt the reading of the term "manipulative" urged by petitioner would not only be unwarranted in light of the legislative purpose but would be at odds with it. Inviting judges to read the term "manipulative" with their own sense of what constitutes "unfair" or "artificial"

means or instrumentality of interstate commerce, or of the mails or of any facility of any national securities exchange,

(a) To employ any device, scheme, or artifice to defraud,

(b) To make any untrue statement of a material fact or to omit to state a fact necessary in order to make the statements made, in the light of the circumstances under which they were made, not misleading, or

(c) To engage in any act, practice or course of business which operates or would operate as a fraud or deceit upon any person, in connection with the purchase or sale of any security." 17 CFR § 240.10b–5 (1984).

Because of the textual similarities, it is often assumed that § 14(e) was modeled on § 10(b) and Rule 10b–5. See, e.g., Panter v. Marshall Field & Co., 646 F.2d 271, 283 (CA7), cert. denied, 454 U.S. 1092, 102 S.Ct. 658, 70 L.Ed.2d 631 (1981). For the purpose of interpreting the term "manipulative," the most significant changes from the language of § 10(b) were the addition of the term "fraudulent," and the reference to "acts" rather than "devices." Nei-

ther change bears in any obvious way on the meaning to be given to "manipulative."

Similar terminology is also found in § 15(c) of the Securities Exchange Act, 15 U.S.C. § 780(c); § 17(a) of the Securities Act of 1933, 15 U.S.C. § 77q, and § 206 of the Investment Advisers Act of 1940, 15 U.S.C. § 80b–6.

11. The Act was amended in 1970, and Congress added to § 14(e) the sentence, "The Commission shall, for the purposes of this subsection, by rules and regulations define, and prescribe means reasonably designed to prevent, such acts and practices as are fraudulent, deceptive, or manipulative." Petitioner argues that this phrase would be pointless if § 14(e) was concerned with disclosure only.

We disagree. In adding the 1970 amendment, Congress simply provided a mechanism for defining and guarding against those acts and practices which involve material misrepresentation or nondisclosure. The amendment gives the Securities and Exchange Commission latitude to regulate nondeceptive activities as a "reasonably designed" means of preventing manipulative acts, without suggesting any change in the meaning of the term "manipulative" itself.

conduct would inject uncertainty into the tender offer process. An essential piece of information—whether the court would deem the fully disclosed actions of one side or the other to be "manipulative"—would not be available until after the tender offer had closed. This uncertainty would directly contradict the expressed Congressional desire to give investors full information.

Congress' consistent emphasis on disclosure persuades us that it intended takeover contests to be addressed to shareholders. In pursuit of this goal, Congress, consistent with the core mechanism of the Securities Exchange Act, created sweeping disclosure requirements and narrow substantive safeguards. The same Congress that placed such emphasis on shareholder choice would not at the same time have required judges to oversee tender offers for substantive fairness. It is even less likely that a Congress implementing that intention would express it only through the use of a single word placed in the middle of a provision otherwise devoted to disclosure.

C

We hold that the term "manipulative" as used in § 14(e) requires misrepresentation or nondisclosure. It connotes "conduct designed to deceive or defraud investors by controlling or artificially affecting the price of securities." Ernst & Ernst v. Hochfelder, 425 U.S., at 199, 96 S.Ct., at 1384. Without misrepresentation or nondisclosure, § 14(e) has not been violated.*

Applying that definition to this case, we hold that the actions of respondents were not manipulative. The amended complaint fails to allege that the cancellation of the first tender offer was accompanied by any misrepresentation, nondisclosure or deception. The District Court correctly found, "All activity of the defendants that could have conceivably affected the price of El Paso shares was done openly." 568 F.Supp., at 203.

Petitioner also alleges that El Paso management and Burlington entered into certain undisclosed and deceptive agreements during the making of the second tender offer. The substance of the allegations is that, in return for certain undisclosed benefits, El Paso managers agreed to support the second tender offer. But both courts noted that petitioner's complaint seeks redress only for injuries related to the cancellation of the first tender offer. Since the deceptive and misleading acts alleged by the petitioner all occurred with reference to the making of the second tender offer—when the injuries suffered by petitioner had already been sustained—these acts bear no possible causal relationship to petitioner's alleged injuries. The Court of Appeals dealt correctly with this claim.

---

* [Ed. Note] See Abella v. Universal Leaf Tobacco Co., 546 F.Supp. 795 (E.D.Va.1982) holding Section 14(e) inapplicable to simple payment of "greenmail." That Section 14(e) does not include standstill agreements, as such, in the manipulative category is the suggestion of Biechele v. Cedar Point, Inc., 747 F.2d 209, 215–216 (6th Cir. 1984).

III

The judgment of the Court of Appeals is Affirmed.

Justice POWELL took no part in the decision of this case. Justice O'CONNOR took no part in the consideration or decision of this case.

―――――

For additional discussion of the possible import of Section 14(e) see Junewicz, The Appropriate Limits of Section 14(e) of the Securities Exchange Act of 1934, 62 Texas L.Rev. 1171 (1984); Poser, Stock Market Manipulation and Corporate Control Transactions, 40 U. of Miami L.Rev. 671 (1986). There have been suggestions of broader scope for the power of the Commission in prohibiting behavior under Section 14(e) (and Section 13(e)) than under Section 10(b), e.g., the power to proscribe negligent, not merely knowledgeable, behavior. See Caleb & Co. v. E.I. DuPont de Nemours & Co., 599 F.Supp. 1468 (S.D.N.Y.1984); Loewenstein, Section 14(e) of the Williams Act and Rule 10b–5 Comparisons, 71 Geo.L.J. 1311 (1983). But see Fiflis, Of Lollipops and Law * * *, 19 U.C. Davis L.Rev. 303, 322 (1986).

(2) Equal Treatment

Rule 14d–10. Equal Treatment of Security Holders

(a) No bidder shall make a tender offer unless:

(1) The tender offer is open to all security holders of the class of securities subject to the tender offer; and

(2) The consideration paid to any security holder pursuant to the tender offer is the highest consideration paid to any other security holder during such tender offer.

(b) Paragraph (a)(1) of this section shall not:

(1) Affect dissemination under Rule 14d–4 (§ 240.14d–4); or

(2) Prohibit a bidder from making a tender offer excluding all security holders in a state where the bidder is prohibited from making the tender offer by administrative or judicial action pursuant to a state statute after a good faith effort by the bidder to comply with such statute.

(c) Paragraph (a)(2) of this section shall not prohibit the offer of more than one type of consideration in a tender offer, provided that:

(1) Security holders are afforded equal right to elect among each of the types of consideration offered; and

(2) The highest consideration of each type paid to any security holder is paid to any other security holder receiving that type of consideration.

* * *

(e) This section shall not apply to any tender offer with respect to which the Commission, upon written request or upon its own motion, either unconditionally or on specified terms and conditions, determines that compliance with this section is not necessary or appropriate in the public interest or for the protection of investors.

Provisions similar to those in Rule 14d–10 are contained in Rule 13e–4(f)(8)–(11) governing issuer tender offers.

NOTE: THE ALL HOLDERS RULE AND THE SEC'S RULEMAKING AUTHORITY

Securities Act Rel. No. 6653 (July 11, 1986), published as Part II, No. 1186, CCH Fed.Sec.L.Rep. (July 16, 1986), discusses the bases on which the Commission relied in promulgating Rule 14d–10 and related provisions. See also Securities Act Rel. No. 6595 (July 1, 1985), CCH Fed.Sec.L.Rep. ¶ 83,797; Securities Act Rel. No. 6596 (July 1, 1985), CCH Fed.Sec.L.Rep. ¶ 83,798; Exchange Act Rel. No. 16,385 (Nov. 11, 1979), CCH Fed.Sec.L.Rep. ¶ 82,374. The Release intimates that the principles underlying the Williams Act contemplate equal treatment of stockholders.

If equality of treatment of stockholders is contemplated by the Williams Act, is it only as an instrument for facilitating a purpose of undistorted choice by the target stockholders? At what point does undistorted choice dictate equal treatment? In any event, in the case of an issuer tender offer is there a state law basis for a goal of equality of treatment which is lacking under both federal and state law for a third party bid? See Brudney, Equal Treatment of Shareholders in Distributions and Reorganizations, 71 Cal.L.Rev. 1073 (1983).

Does the Act support the All Holders Rule at all? Note that prior to the promulgation of the rule it was held in Unocal Corp. v. Pickens, 608 F.Supp. 1081 (C.D.Cal.1985), that the Act permits tender offers to be made to less than all stockholders. Note also that in Schreiber v. Burlington Northern, supra, the Supreme Court limited the Act's coverage of "manipulative" conduct.

The validity of the All Holders Rule was confirmed in **Polaroid Corp. v. Disney**, 862 F.2d 987 (3d Cir.1989):

> Section 14(e) of the Williams Act proscribes "fraudulent, deceptive, or manipulative acts * * * in connection with any tender offer." 15 U.S.C. § 78n(e). A unanimous Court in Schreiber v. Burlington Northern, Inc., 472 U.S. 1 (1985), held that section 14(e) does not prohibit manipulative conduct unless there has been some element of deception through a material misrepresentation or omission. The Court held that "[i]t is clear that Congress relied primarily on disclosure to implement the purpose of the Williams Act" and characterized all of the Williams Act provisions as disclo-

sure provisions. *Id.* at 8–9. *Schreiber* characterizes even section 14(d)(6), which mandates the proration of share purchases when the number of shares tendered exceeds the number of shares sought, and section 14(d)(7), which mandates the payment of the same price to all those whose shares are purchased, as "requir[ing] or prohibit[ing] certain acts so that investors will possess additional time within which to take advantage of the disclosed information." *Id.* at 9. It is thus possible to read *Schreiber* to imply that the All Holders Rule is beyond the SEC's authority under the Williams Act, for the Rule's purpose seems to be neither to ensure full disclosure nor to provide for an adequate time period for investors to comprehend disclosed information.

Although *Schreiber* categorizes the proration and best price provisions of the Williams Act as relating to disclosure, these provisions are only tangentially related to ensuring that investors make fully informed decisions. While the All Holders Rule thus has little to do with ensuring complete disclosure, it is no less related to disclosure than are the proration and best price provisions. Moreover, the SEC has articulated a disclosure justification for the Rule:

> [t]he all-holders requirement would realize the disclosure purposes of the Williams Act by ensuring that all members of the class subject to the tender offer receive information necessary to make an informed decision regarding the merits of the tender offer. If tender offer disclosure is given to all holders, but some are barred from participating in the offer, the Williams Act disclosure objectives would be ineffective.

51 Fed.Reg. at 25,875 (footnote omitted). In light of the loose definition that *Schreiber* itself ascribes to the meaning of a "disclosure" provision, the emphasis in *Schreiber* on characterizing the Williams Act as a disclosure statute *simpliciter* is of small force in an effort to invalidate the All Holders Rule. For the foregoing reasons, we are satisfied that the SEC was acting within its authority in promulgating the All Holders Rule. This conclusion is buttressed by the deference due the agency's interpretation of its enabling statute, the statute being ambiguous on the issue and the agency's interpretation being a permissible one. Chevron, U.S.A., Inc. v. Natural Resources Defense Council, Inc., 467 U.S. 837, 843 (1984).

The holding of *Schreiber*—that misrepresentation or nondisclosure is a necessary element of a violation of section 14(e)—is not compromised by a determination that the All Holders Rule is a valid exercise of SEC rulemaking authority. The All Holders Rule is not an attempt to proscribe manipulative practices so much as an attempt to ensure that all holders of a class of securities subject to a tender offer receive fair and equal treatment. And, as explained in the SEC's release, this attempt to ensure fair and equal treatment is the purpose behind both the proration and best price provisions. 51 Fed.Reg. at 25,876.

NOTE: CONTRACT AS A REGULATORY ALTERNATIVE

Notwithstanding the Commission's promulgation of the "all holders" rules on July 11, 1986, on July 31, 1986 it asked for comments on a proposal to permit corporations to "contract out" of the rules by a process which the Commission labels "self-governance." SEA Rel. No. 23,486 (July 31, 1986). As the Commission explained it:

"The Commission seeks public comment on the advisability of a rule whereby stockholders and directors would be permitted to decide for themselves whether they require certain protections of the Williams Act. The Commission seeks public comment on this concept in two contexts: (1) as applied to the 'all holders' rule, and (2) as applied to other provisions of the tender offer rules.

"A. *The 'All Holders' Requirement*

　　　* * *

"As applied to the 'all holders' rule, a self-governance provision could, for example, provide that corporations may exempt themselves from the rule if their charters are amended, in accordance with state law, expressly to authorize exclusionary tender offers. A charter provision authorizing such an exemption could cover either issuer or third-party tender offers for such issuer, or it could apply to both issuer and third-party tender offers. The charter provision could also define particular circumstances under which issuer or third-party exclusionary offers would continue to be prohibited.

"The Williams Act and the Commission's tender offer rules currently operate as rules of general applicability with no provision for exemptions or modifications by stockholder or director action. Tender offers are thus conducted in accordance with uniform rules, and all participants are equally subject to regulations that Congress and the Commission have determined to be in the public interest.

"A self-governance exemption would alter the current structure of the Commission's tender offer rules by allowing individual corporations, within bounds set by the Commission, to modify the protections of the rules to suit their particular circumstances. The Commission requests comment on whether the public interest would be well served if stockholders and directors of individual corporations are permitted, under certain circumstances, to craft safeguards designed to suit the specific circumstances of individual corporations. A body of recent research suggests that self-determination in matters related to corporate governance yields benefits that may not be as readily attainable under rules of general applicability. Thus, without a self-governance exemption, there is a possibility that the 'all holders' rule might impose protections on certain corporate investors who neither desire nor benefit from safeguards that might be reasonable for investors in other corporations that are subject to the 'all holders' rule. A self-governance exemption might thus help minimize whatever ancillary burdens are imposed by an 'all holders' rule without diminishing the rule's general protections.

* * *

"B. *Self-Governance Provisions Applied to Other Tender Offer Regulations*

"The Commission also seeks comment on the concept of adopting self-governance exemptions to tender offer rules other than the 'all holders' provision. The Commission has not determined which, if any, tender offer rules are appropriate candidates for self-governance exemptions, and seeks comment identifying rules that are either particularly appropriate or inappropriate candidates for self-governance exemptions. The Commission requests that comments address the costs and benefits of providing self-governance exemptions to specific tender offer rules and, as in the case of the 'all holders' rule, address: (1) relevant analogues and empirical evidence; (2) specific language for suggested exemptions; and (3) whether the exemption should rely on the charter amendment provisions of the issuer's domicile, or on some other rule of corporate self-governance.

"In connection with such proposals, the Commission observes that members of Congress have introduced numerous amendments to the Williams Act. Some of these proposals suggest congressional support for time deadlines and thresholds different than those currently found in the statute. Corporate self-governance exemptions could allow issuers to elect deadlines and thresholds within ranges defined by currently pending legislation. In addition, some business organizations and academics have proposed takeover rules that are incompatible with the Williams Act, but that could potentially be adopted in the form of self-governance exemptions.[54] The Commission invites comment regarding the advisability of adopting or recommending to Congress self-governance exemptions that would permit corporations to adopt these or other takeover rules to govern contests for corporate control."

---

54. See, e.g., Bebchuck, Toward an Undistorted Choice and Equal Treatment in Corporate Takeovers, 98 Harv.L.Rev. 1695 (1985) (proposing that the fate of all offers aimed at acquiring a controlling interest (e.g., above 20 percent) be decided upon a poll of shareholders, regardless of whether they tender their shares, and that nontendering shareholders be given certain immediate takeout or redemption rights); Business Roundtable, Statement of Principles on Hostile Takeover Abuses (undated) (proposing that no one may purchase more than 15 percent of the voting securities of a company without board or shareholder approval and that all purchasers of more than 15 percent must offer to purchase all voting securities in a tender offer).

NOTE: RULE 10B–13

Rule 10b–13. Prohibiting Other Purchases During Tender Offer or Exchange Offer

(a) No person who makes a cash tender offer or exchange offer for any equity security shall, directly or indirectly, purchase, or make any arrangement to purchase, any such security (or any other security which is immediately convertible into or exchangeable for such security), otherwise than pursuant to such tender offer or exchange offer, from the time such tender offer or exchange offer is publicly announced or otherwise made known by such person to holders of the security to be acquired until the expiration of the period, including any extensions thereof, during which securities tendered pursuant to such tender offer or exchange offer may by the terms of such offer be accepted or rejected; *provided, however,* that if such person is the owner of another security which is immediately convertible into or exchangeable for the security which is the subject of the offer, his subsequent exercise of his right of conversion or exchange with respect to such other security shall not be prohibited by this rule.

(b) The term "exchange offer" as used in this rule shall include a tender offer for, or request or invitation for tenders of, any security in exchange for any consideration other than for all cash.

* * *

SECURITIES EXCHANGE ACT RELEASE NO. 8712

Securities and Exchange Commission.
October 8, 1969.

* * *

Where securities are purchased for a consideration greater than that of the tender offer price, this operates to the disadvantage of the security holders who have already deposited their securities and who are unable to withdraw them in order to obtain the advantage of possible resulting higher market prices. Additionally, irrespective of the price at which such purchases are made, they are often fraudulent or manipulative in nature and they can deceive the investing public as to the true state of affairs. Their consequences can be various, depending upon conditions in the market and the nature of the purchases. They could defeat the tender offer, either by driving the market price above the offer price or by otherwise reducing the number of shares tendered below the stated minimum. Alternatively, they could further the tender offer by raising the market price to the point where ordinary investors sell in the market to arbitrageurs, who in turn tender. Accordingly, by prohibiting a person who makes a cash tender offer or exchange offer from purchasing equity securities of the same class during the tender offer period otherwise than pursuant to the offer itself, the rule accomplishes the objective of safeguarding the interests of the persons who have tendered their securities in response to a cash tender offer or exchange offer; moreover once the offer has been made, the rule removes any incentive on the part of holders of substantial blocks of securities to demand from the person making a tender offer or exchange offer a consideration greater than or different from that currently offered to public investors.

* * *

The rule deals with purchases or arrangements to purchase, directly or indirectly, which are made from the time of public announcement or initiation of the tender offer or exchange offer, until the person making the offer is required either to accept or reject the tendered securities. As used in the rule an offer could be publicly announced or otherwise made known to the holders of the target security through a published advertisement, a news release, or other communication by or for the person making the offer to holders of the security being sought for cash tender or exchange. Moreover, any understanding or arrangement during the tender offer period, whether or not the terms and conditions thereof have been agreed upon, to make or negotiate such a purchase after the expiration of that period would be prohibited by the rule. Purchases made prior to the inception of that period are not specifically prohibited under the rule, although disclosure of such purchases within a specific prior period is required to be filed in schedules filed under Sections 13(d) and 14(d) of the Act. Of course, the general anti-fraud and anti-manipulation provisions could apply to such pre-tender purchases. The prohibition of Rule 10b–13 applies to exchange offers when publicly announced even though they cannot be made until the happening of a future event, such as the effectiveness of a registration statement under the Securities Act of 1933. As the Commission explained in Securities Exchange Act Release No. 8595, as applied to the offer by one company of its own securities in exchange for the securities of another issuer, the application of Rule 10b–13 to exchange offers is essentially a codification of existing interpretations under Rule 10b–6, which among other things, prohibits a person making a distribution from bidding for or purchasing the security being distributed or any right to acquire that security. These interpretations have pointed out that the security to be acquired in the exchange offer is, in substance, either a right to acquire the security being distributed or is brought within the rule under paragraph (b) thereof; and Rule 10b–6 prohibits the purchase of such security during the distribution except through the exchange offer, unless an exemption is available.

Since Rule 10b–13 applies to a cash tender offer or an offer of an exchange by an issuer to its own security holders of one class of its securities for another, if repurchase of the other security is subject to the prohibitions of Rule 10b–6, the issuer would have to obtain an exemption under paragraph (f) of that rule. * * *

The variety of practices at which Rule 10b–13 is aimed, and the reach of the rule, are suggested by the circumstances involved in **Swanson v. Wabash, Inc.,** 577 F.Supp. 1308 (N.D.Ill.1983). In that case a target's stockholders charged that the acquiring company purchased stock options from the target's executives and stock from selected stockholders on terms that differed from the tender offer terms. The difference in terms resulted from (1) the payment by the acquiring company of 50% tax bonuses to the executives in order to compensate them for the tax consequences sustained on the sale of their options, and (2) arrangements between the acquirer and special stockholders to postpone the acceptance of their stock beyond expiration of the term of the tender offer until six months had elapsed from the time they had purchased it, so that they would receive long term capital gains, a postponement which was not available for the bulk of the tendering stockholders. The Court held that both the alleged transactions violated section 10b–13, which prohibits both direct and indirect purchases of securities outside the tender offer terms, and declined to dismiss the complaint.

The requirement of scienter as a condition of liability under Rule 10b–13 (SEC v. Mick Stack Assoc., 675 F.2d 1148 (10th Cir.1982)) will doubtless dilute the import of the Rule.

The effort by tenderers to avoid the pro-rata limitations by short tenders and hedged tenders is addressed in Rule 14e–4.[q] Merrill Lynch, Pierce, Fenner & Smith v. Bobker, 808 F.2d 930 (2d Cir.1986) intimated that an earlier version of Rule 14e–4 exceeded the Commission's powers under Section 10 of the '34 Act with respect to regulation of manipulative or deceptive devices, at least insofar as it required tenderers to maintain a "net long" position. The Commission, in revising the Rule in response to *Bobker*, retained but clarified the "net long" requirement. See 22 BNA Sec.Reg. & L.Rep. 1653 (11/30/90).

q. Rule 14e–4 is a revision of Rule 10b–4, originally promulgated in 1968. In SA Rel. No. 8321 (May 28, 1968), the Commission pointed out the following:

"By prohibiting short tendering, Rule 10b–4 was designed to promote equality of opportunity and risk for all tendering securityholders. In the years since the Rule's adoption, it has become apparent that simply requiring a tendering person to tender from a long position does not reach certain conduct that has the same purpose and effect as short tendering. Under the Rule, arbitrageurs are able to tender to an offer involving prorationing or selection by lot and then sell into a market that reflects the offer the portion of shares that they estimate will be returned unaccepted by the bidder. The shares sold may, in turn, be bought and tendered by another arbitrageur who may also hedge his tender by selling a portion of the shares. As a result, the same shares are effectively tendered by two (or more) shareholders and those shareholders who tender and do not engage in any hedging continue to experience the same dilution of their *pro rata* acceptance that occurred before the Rule was adopted."

(3) Coverage Problems
FIELD v. TRUMP

United States Court of Appeals, Second Circuit, 1988.
850 F.2d 938.

[Samuel Stroum, Stuart Sloan, and members of their families (the "Stroums") were the dissatisfied holders of 18.4 percent of the stock of Pay'n Save Corp. They had acquired the stock in early 1984 in connection with the acquisition by Pay'n Save of a corporation they controlled. Under a subsequent standstill agreement, they had agreed to neither sell their Pay'n Save shares, nor offer to purchase additional shares in exchange for two seats on the board.

[In August 1984, Pay'n Save's managers arranged for a friendly acquisition of the company by Eddie Trump and his Trump Group, Ltd. (the "Trumps"). On August 31, the Trumps proposed to the Pay'n Save board a cash tender offer at $22 per share for two thirds of the stock, to be followed by a cash out merger at the same price. One week later, the Trumps increased the offer to $22.50 but warned that it would be withdrawn if not approved. Upon receiving a favorable opinion as to the offer's fairness from an investment banker, the board approved the offer in the middle of the night of September 6. The deal was announced in a press release the next day. The Stroums had dissented, however. They issued a statement of their own, calling the offer "skimpy" and accusing management of "unseemly haste."

[Meetings between the Stroums and Eddie Trump occurred during the following few days. At 5:10 P.M. on September 12, the Trumps told the Pay'n Save board that the tender offer would be withdrawn in order to "facilitate the negotiations with Messrs. Stroum and Sloan." The Trumps issued a press release both as to the withdrawal and as to the negotiations. Later that night, the Trumps and the Stroums entered into a Settlement Agreement. Under this the Trumps paid the Stroums $3.3 million for an option to purchase the Stroums' shares for $23.50 per share, and paid $900,000 for the Stroums' "fees and expenses," on condition that the Pay'n Save board approved an amendment to the merger agreement increasing the price per share in the tender offer and merger to $23.50. The board approved the amendment the next day. (The plaintiff's complaint alleged that the September 12 press release announcing the withdrawal of the offer and the release announcing the new price reached the public simultaneously.)

[Plaintiff brought an action against Pay'n Save, its officers and directors, the Stroums and the Trumps, alleging, *inter alia*, that the total of $4.2 million received by the Stroums constituted a premium of $1.50 per share above the price received by the other shareholders in violation of Section 14(d)(7) and Rule 10b–13.]

Plaintiff's principal claim arises under Section 14(d)(7) of the Williams Act. * * * The purpose of this provision is to prevent a tender offeror from discriminating in price among tendering shareholders. The position taken by the SEC thus is that:

(i) a tender offer must be extended to all holders of the class of securities which is the subject of the offer (the "all-holders requirement"); and (ii) all such holders must be paid the highest consideration offered under the tender offer (the "best-price rule").

Proposed Amendments to Tender Offer Rules, Securities Act Release No. 6595 [1984–1985 Transfer Binder] Fed.Sec.L.Rep. (CCH) ¶ 83,797 (July 1, 1985). To codify the "all-holders requirement" and "best-price rule," the SEC has adopted Rule 14d–10, 17 C.F.R. § 240.14d–10 (1987). * * * To the same end, the SEC has promulgated a rule prohibiting side transactions involving purchases of securities subject to a tender offer. Rule 10b–13 * * *. The essence of plaintiff's claim is that the $4,200,-000 paid to the Stroums during the brief "withdrawal" of the offer was in law and fact a payment of a $1.50 per share premium intended to induce the Stroums to accept the tender offer. The failure to pay this premium to the other tendering shareholders, plaintiff argues, violated the "best-price rule."

No party disputes the proposition that payment of a premium to one shareholder and not others during a tender offer is illegal. The issue rather is whether the purported withdrawal effectively ended the offer so that the $4,200,000 payment was not during or part of a tender offer. In dismissing the Section 14(d)(7) claim, the district court relied upon SEC rules governing the commencement of a tender offer, specifically Rule 14d–2(b), which provides that:

[a] public announcement by a bidder through a press release, newspaper advertisement or public statement which includes the information in paragraph (c) of this section [namely, the identity of the bidder and the target, the amount and class of the securities sought, and the price to be paid] with respect to a tender offer * * * shall be deemed to constitute the commencement of a tender offer [for the purposes of Section 14(d) and rules promulgated thereunder] *Except,* That such tender offer shall not be deemed to [have commenced under this section] on the date of such public announcement *if within five business days of such public announcement, the bidder * * * [m]akes a subsequent public announcement stating that the bidder has determined not to continue with such tender offer * * *.*

17 C.F.R. § 240.14d–2(b) (1987) (emphasis added). Thus, while the public announcement of the essential terms of a tender offer results in the technical "commencement" of a tender offer, the offer will nevertheless be legally deemed not to have commenced if its withdrawal is announced within five business days. In the instant case, the initial announcement of the Trumps' tender offer came on the morning of Friday, September 7, 1984, and the purported withdrawal was announced on the afternoon of Wednesday, September 12, four business days later. Based on these facts, the district court concluded that, for purposes of Section 14(d)(7), "there was no tender offer in place at the time of the Settlement Agreement, and thus, as a matter of law, no violation of [that] Section." 661 F.Supp. at 532. We disagree, however,

and believe that the allegations of the complaint state a claim under the Williams Act.

The Williams Act does not define "tender offer." Courts faced with the question of whether purchases of a corporation's shares are privately negotiated or are part of a tender offer have applied a functional test that scrutinizes such purchases in the context of various salient characteristics of tender offers and the purposes of the Williams Act. SEC v. Carter Hawley Hale Stores, 760 F.2d 945, 950 (9th Cir.1985); Hanson Trust PLC v. SCM Corp., 774 F.2d 47, 56–57 (2d Cir.1985) (eight factor "test"; balancing of factors in particular case determined in light of Act's policy to protect ill-informed solicitees). Whether the acquisition of shares in a corporation is part of a tender offer for purposes of the Act cannot be determined by rubber-stamping the label used by the acquiror. Wellman v. Dickinson, 475 F.Supp. 783, 823–25 (S.D.N.Y. 1979) (so-called "privately negotiated" purchases of shares constitute tender offer for purposes of Williams Act); aff'd on other grounds, 682 F.2d 355 (2d Cir.1982), cert. denied, 460 U.S. 1069 (1983). * * *

Similarly, giving effect to every purported withdrawal that allows a discriminatory premium to be paid to large shareholders would completely undermine the "best-price rule." For example, plaintiff has alleged that the purported withdrawal of the original tender offer was intended solely to allow the Trumps to pay a premium of $1.50 per share to the Strouns that was not offered to shareholders who tendered pursuant to the "new" tender offer announced immediately thereafter.[1] The "best-price rule" of Section 14(d)(7) and Rule 14d–10 is completely unenforceable if offerors may announce periodic "withdrawals" during which purchases at a premium are made and thereafter followed by "new" tender offers. Unless successive tender offers interrupted by withdrawals can in appropriate circumstances be viewed as a single tender offer for purposes of the Williams Act, the "best-price rule" is meaningless.

Whether the purchase of the Stroum shares was a private purchase or part of a continuing tender offer is not determined simply by the Trumps' use of the labels "withdrawal" and "new" offer. Cf. McDermott, Inc. v. Wheelabrator–Frye, Inc., 649 F.2d 489 (7th Cir.1980) (announcement of increase in number of shares sought not new tender offer). Indeed, we have explicitly recognized that purchases after a purported withdrawal of a tender offer may constitute a continuation of the offer in light of the surrounding circumstances. *Hanson Trust,* 774 F.2d at 58–59. Finally, Section 14(d)(7) itself explicitly treats a material change in the terms of a tender offer in the form of an increased price as a continuation of the original offer rather than as a new tender offer. Clearly, therefore, purchases of shares by an offeror after a

---

1. Whether the "fees and expenses" for which the Trumps paid $900,000 to the Strouns were actually incurred is irrelevant under the "best-price rule." Some or all of those sums were expended in order to obtain a premium for the Strouns, and it would thwart the purposes of Section 14(d)(7) to allow reimbursement. Moreover, we believe the "best-price rule" would be unworkable if offerors were permitted to discriminate among shareholders according to expenses that were not uniformly incurred, such as broker's or attorney's fees.

purported withdrawal of a tender offer may constitute a continuation of the original tender offer.

Rule 14d–2(b) is not to the contrary. That Rule merely creates a window of time during which a genuine withdrawal leaves matters for all legal purposes as though a tender offer had never been commenced. The Rule does nothing to alter the principle that the mere announcement of a withdrawal may not be effective if followed by purchases of shares and other conduct inconsistent with a genuine intent to withdraw. The Rule is also irrelevant because a bidder is always free to withdraw a tender offer. The argument advanced by defendants, if correct, would thus apply even in cases in which the provisions of Rule 14d–2(b) governing withdrawal announcements did not.[2]

For purposes of the "best-price rule," therefore, an announcement of a withdrawal is effective when the offeror genuinely intends to abandon the goal of the original offer. See id. (termination of tender offer effective in light of evidence that goal of obtaining control of target corporation was abandoned). The complaint here alleges that the Trumps' Offer to Purchase explicitly stated that the purported withdrawal was intended to allow negotiations with the Stroums. Such negotiations indicate a continuing intent to obtain control of Pay'n Save.

Moreover, the complaint alleges conduct from which inferences might be drawn that the Trumps had not abandoned the goal of the original offer. In determining the most appropriate analysis for evaluating the conduct of an offeror surrounding a purported withdrawal, we draw upon a suggestion of Professor Loss. He has noted that the determination of whether formally separate offerings of securities should be "integrated," and thus considered a single offering, for the purposes of the various registration exemptions, is closely analogous to the question of whether single or multiple tender offers have been made. L. Loss, Fundamentals of Securities Regulation 577 n. 33 (1983) (suggesting comparison of " 'integration' problem with respect to certain exemptions under the 1933 Act" with Section 202(166)(B) of the ALI's proposed Federal Securities Code, which "treats [tender] offers as separate if they are for different classes of securities or are 'substantially distinct on the basis of such factors as manner, time, purpose, price and kind of consideration' ").

---

2. Defendants have emphasized that "the public shareholders of Pay'n Save ultimately received $23.50 per share, or approximately $5.00 per share in excess of the market value of their shares on the last full trading date prior to the announcement of the proposed tender offer and merger." Appellees' Joint Brief at 2–3. They apparently wish to stress that application of the "best-price rule" where a payment of a premium above the offer to a large shareholder is necessary to consummate the transaction will ultimately work to the detriment of shareholders generally by decreasing such transactions. This point, however, can be made about the Williams Act generally, see, e.g., Dynamics Corp. of Am. v. CTS Corp., 794 F.2d 250, 262 (7th Cir.1986) rev'd on other grounds, ___ U.S. ___, 107 S.Ct. 1637, 95 L.Ed.2d 67 (1987), (citing Jarrell & Bradley, The Economic Effects of Federal and State Regulations of Cash Tender Offers, 23 J.Law & Econ. 371 (1980)), and thus must be addressed to Congress.

In establishing criteria to govern the integration of formally separate offerings, the SEC has identified the following factors, *inter alia,* as relevant: "(1) are the offerings part of a single of financing; (2) do the offerings involve issuance of the same class of security; (3) are the offerings made at or about the same time * * * ?" Section 3(a)(11) Exemption for Local Offerings, Securities Act Release No. 4434 (Dec. 6, 1961). Analogous factors may thus point to "integration" in the context of formally separate tender offers: (1) are the offers part of a single plan of acquisition; (2) do the offers involve the purchase of the same class of security; and (3) are the offers made at or about the same time? These factors are useful in determining the ultimate fact of whether an offeror has abandoned the goal of an initial tender offer in announcing a withdrawal of that offer. As previously noted, where the goal has not been abandoned, a purported withdrawal followed by a "new" offer must be treated as a single continuing offer for purposes of the "best-price rule."

Accepting as true the facts alleged in plaintiff's complaint, all of the listed factors weigh in favor of treating the Trumps' acquisition of Pay'n Save shares as a single tender offer. If the allegations are proven, the alleged $1.50 premium to the Strouns would violate Section 14(d)(7).

The parties and the district court have correctly assumed that Section 14(d)(7) impliedly affords a private right of action to shareholders. In Pryor v. United States Steel Corp., 794 F.2d 52, 57–58 (2d Cir.), cert. denied, ___ U.S. ___, 107 S.Ct. 445 (1986), we held that the best-price provision's statutory neighbor, Section 14(d)(6) of the '34 Act, 15 U.S.C. § 78n(d)(6) (1982), which requires pro rata acceptance of tendered shares in oversubscribed offers, could be privately enforced. Section 14(d)(7) certainly provides at least as strong a basis for the implication of a private remedy as does Section 14(d)(6). As in *Pryor,* the plaintiff here is "surely [one of] the primary intended beneficiaries of [the statute], since 'the sole purpose of the Williams Act was the protection of investors who are confronted with a tender offer.'" 794 F.2d at 57 (quoting Piper v. Chris–Craft Indus., 430 U.S. 1, 35 (1977)). Moreover, Section 14(d)(7), like Section 14(d)(6) and "unlike the bulk of federal securities regulation, confers a substantive right on [its] beneficiaries," thereby "suggest[ing] that Congress intended to create a private right of action." Id. In addition, as is true of the proration provision, a private damage action provides a particularly effective means of enforcing the strictures of the "best-price rule." When a premium is paid to one shareholder in violation of Section 14(d)(7), "the injury is easy to calculate, the victims are easy to locate, and the likelihood of litigation by such victims is high if a private right of action exists." Id. at 58. Finally, a cause of action under Section 14(d)(7) is not one "traditionally relegated to state law." Id. (quoting Cort v. Ash, 422 U.S. 66, 78, 95 S.Ct. 2080, 2088, 45 L.Ed.2d 26 (1975)). Accordingly, we hold that Section 14(d)(7) affords private plaintiffs an implied right of action, and we therefore reverse the dismissal of the Section 14(d)(7) claim.[3]

NOTE: DEFINING (AND NOT DEFINING) "TENDER OFFER"

1. *Rule 14d–2.*

The Securities Exchange Commission has declined to define the term "tender offer" by rule, taking the position that a bright-line definition would invite evasion by resourceful bidders. But, as the *Field v. Trump* court's reference to Rule 14d–2 makes clear, the Commission has addressed the problem of defining when a tender offer commences.

In SEA Rel. No. 16,384 (Nov. 29, 1979) the Commission discussed the problem of commencement of a tender offer as follows:

"In view of the importance of the concept of 'commencement' of a tender offer to the operation of the Williams Act as well as the need to provide content and clarity to the term, the Commission has determined to adopt Rule 14d–2, which follows closely proposed Rule 14d–6. The provisions of Rule 14d–2(a)(1) through (3) are related to the methods by which tender offer materials may be disseminated under Rule 14d–4. Hence, a tender offer using long-form publication commences on the date of the newspaper publication. A tender offer disseminated by means of summary publication commences on the date the summary advertisement appears in the newspapers. If stockholder lists and security position listings are used pursuant to Rule 14d–5 to disseminate the tender offer, the bidder is also required to make either long-form or summary publication of the tender offer on or prior to the date of the bidder's request pursuant to Rule 14d–5(a). Publication of the long-form publication or the summary advertisement commences the tender offer under Rule 14d–2(a)(3). Tender offers in which the consideration offered consists of securities registered pursuant to the Securities Act commence when the bidder's registration statement becomes effective thereunder. A tender offer which is not disseminated by any of these means commences on the date it is first published or sent or given.

"Rule 14d–2(a) has been revised to clarify that a tender offer which is disseminated by a combination of methods commences on the date that the first method is used. It has also been revised to specify that the tender offer commences on 12:01 a.m. on that date. Accordingly, the date of commencement will be included as a full day in computing any applicable time periods.

"* * * Rule 14d–2(b) is intended to prevent public announcements by a bidder of the material terms of its tender offer in advance of the

---

3. Because full relief is available to plaintiff under Section 14(d)(7), we need not address the claim asserted under Rule 10b–13. Cf. Pryor, 794 F.2d at 53; see also Beaumont v. American Can Co., 797 F.2d 79, 83–84 (2d Cir.1986) (expressing doubt that private right of action exists under Rule 10b–13).

offer's formal commencement. The Commission believes that this practice is detrimental to the interests of investors and results in many of the abuses the Williams Act was enacted to prevent. Such pre-commencement public announcements cause security holders to make investment decisions with respect to a tender offer on the basis of incomplete information and trigger market activity normally attendant to a tender offer, such as arbitrageur activity. Since they constitute the practical commencement of a tender offer, such pre-commencement public announcements cause the contest for control of the subject company to occur prior to the application of the Williams Act and therefore deny security holders the protections which that Act was intended by Congress to provide.

"Under Rule 14d–2(b) a bidder's public announcement through a press release, newspaper advertisement or public statement of certain material terms of a cash tender offer causes the bidder's tender offer to commence under Section 14(d) of the Exchange Act. In order to provide certainty to bidders, the information which will trigger Rule 14d–2(b) is set forth in Rule 14d–2(c). Generally, this information relates to: the identity of the bidder and the subject company; a statement of the class and amount of securities being sought; and disclosure of the price or range of prices being offered therefor. Safe harbor provisions for public announcements which will not trigger the operation of Rule 14d–2(b) are set forth in Rules 14d–2(d) and (e).

* * *

"Some commentators noted that there is a direct conflict between Rule 14d–2(b) and state anti-takeover statutes with the effect that such statutes are preempted. These statutes typically require a publication of or a public filing which includes the material terms of the tender offer prior to the time the offer may be commenced. These requirements of the state statutes will trigger the commencement of the tender offer under Rule 14d–2(b) despite the fact that the state statutes do not permit the offer to commence until the conclusion of any applicable waiting period and hearing process. * * *

"Thus, the conflict between Rule 14d–2(b) and such state statutes is so direct and substantial as to make it impossible to comply with both sets of requirements as they presently exist. While recognizing its long and beneficial partnership with the states in the regulation of securities transactions, the Commission nevertheless believes that the state take-over statutes presently in effect frustrate the operation and purposes of the Williams Act and that, based upon the abuses in current tender offer practice discussed above, Rule 14d–2(b) is necessary for the protection of investors and to achieve the purposes of the Williams Act."

Do you agree with the *Field v. Trump* court that the Rule 14d–2's provision respecting withdrawal should not be read to determine the question as to when a tender offer ends? The Commission's "solution" certainly has not avoided the necessity for courts to determine whether the behavior of the bidder is a tender offer. Nor does the rule aim at, or cover, negotiated purchases of control from a controlling person.

2. *Street Sweeps.*

Compare the facts of *Field v. Trump* with those of **Hanson Trust PLC v. SCM Corp.,** 774 F.2d 47 (2d Cir.1985). Hanson Trust had made a $72 per share cash tender offer for shares of SCM. SCM responded by announcing a $74 per share two-step acquisition with Merrill Lynch, a white knight. This defensive proposal depended on the acquisition of two thirds of SCM's stock by Merrill. It included a lock up option under which Merrill had the right to purchase SCM's two most profitable divisions. Hanson Trust withdrew its offer in response to the lock up. The withdrawal was announced on the Dow Jones tape at 12:38 P.M. on September 11. Either immediately before or immediately after the announcement, Hanson Trust decided to make open market purchases of SCM stock with the objective of acquiring enough shares to block the defensive merger. Within two hours, on the same afternoon, Hanson Trust concluded five separately negotiated cash purchases of SCM and one open market purchase, purchasing a total of 3.1 million shares or 25 percent. All five negotiated purchases were concluded at $73.50 per share; the market price ranged between $72.50 and $73.50 during the afternoon. The sellers were arbitrageurs, who had accumulated large positions. One of the five negotiated purchases was solicited by Hanson, the others were not.

Such a program of quick and substantial post-withdrawal negotiated purchases is termed a "street sweep." Street sweeps occurred frequently during the mid 1980s.

Should street sweeps be deemed to constitute tender offers? In *Hanson Trust,* the Second Circuit ruled that the street sweep was not a tender offer. In so doing it declined to bring to bear an eight part test that had been approved by the SEC and employed by other courts, 774 F.2d at 56–57:

"* * * The borderline between public solicitations and privately negotiated stock purchases is not bright and it is frequently difficult to determine whether transactions falling close to the line or in a type of 'no man's land' are 'tender offers' or private deals. This has led some to advocate a broader interpretation of the term 'tender offer' than that followed by us in Kennecott Copper Corp. v. Curtiss–Wright Corp., supra, 584 F.2d at 1207, and to adopt the eight-factor "test" of what is a tender offer, which was recommended by the SEC and applied by the district court in Wellman v. Dickinson, 475 F.Supp. 783, 823–24 (S.D.N.Y.1979), aff'd on other grounds, 682 F.2d 355 (2d Cir.1982), cert. denied, 460 U.S. 1069, 103 S.Ct. 1522, 75 L.Ed.2d 946 (1983), and by the Ninth Circuit in SEC v. Carter Hawley Hale Stores, Inc., supra. The eight factors are:

'(1) active and widespread solicitation of public shareholders for the shares of an issuer;

(2) solicitation made for a substantial percentage of the issuer's stock;

(3) offer to purchase made at a premium over the prevailing market price;

(4) terms of the offer are firm rather than negotiable;

(5) offer contingent on the tender of a fixed number of shares, often subject to a fixed maximum number to be purchased;

(6) offer open only for a limited period of time;

(7) offeree subjected to pressure to sell his stock;

* * *

[(8)] public announcements of a purchasing program concerning the target company precede or accompany rapid accumulation of large amounts of the target company's securities.' (475 F.Supp. at 823–24).

Although many of the above-listed factors are relevant for purposes of determining whether a given solicitation amounts to a tender offer, the elevation of such a list to a mandatory 'litmus test' appears to be both unwise and unnecessary. * * *

"We prefer to be guided by the principle followed by the Supreme Court in deciding what transactions fall within the private offering exemption provided by § 4(1) of the Securities Act of 1933, and by ourselves in *Kennecott Copper* in determining whether the Williams Act applies to private transactions. That principle is simply to look to the statutory purpose. * * * [T]he question of whether a solicitation constitutes a "tender offer" within the meaning of § 14(d) turns on whether, viewing the transaction in the light of the totality of circumstances, there appears to be a likelihood that unless the pre-acquisition filing strictures of that statute are followed there will be a substantial risk that solicitees will lack information needed to make a carefully considered appraisal of the proposal put before them."

SEC v. Carter Hawley Hale Stores, Inc., 760 F.2d 945 (9th Cir.1985), cited by the *Hanson Trust* court, applied the eight part test to reach the same result with respect to a target's repurchase of over 50 percent of its own shares on the open market.

What result does the "sole owner" standard for forming tender offer rules counsel in these situations? Should the SEC have defined "tender offer" so as to pick up these transactions and thereby extend the protection of section 14(d) to unsophisticated investors? For criticism of the SEC's approach, see Oesterle, The Rise and Fall of Street Sweep Takeovers, 1989 Duke L.J. 202.

The SEC proposed but never promulgated a rule that would have prohibited street sweeps. Even so, street sweeps did cease during the last years of the 1980s. The proliferation of poison pills and state antitakeover statutes had made piecemeal acquisitions of large blocks of target stock disadvantageous to bidders. See Oesterle, supra p. 239–241.

3. *Reform Proposals.*

In 1980, in connection with Congressional concern about the operation of the Williams Act, the Commission submitted a comprehensive memorandum discussing the problems and proposing solutions. Among other things it suggested altering the triggering apparatus invoking section 14(d) disclosure so that instead of being tripped by a "tender offer" it was tripped by a "statutory offer." A "statutory offer" was defined to mean (with certain exceptions, including one for privately negotiated transactions) any offer by a person who would, upon consummation of the offer, become the owner of more than 10% of the relevant class of securities (see Securities Regulation and Law Report (BNA) No. 542 (special Supp.) Feb. 27, 1980, pp. 21–22).

Is that solution appropriate? How early in the process of acquisition should (1) an acquirer be obliged to incur the cost (and delay) of compliance with section 14, and (2) the public stockholders be entitled to the protection of section 14? See Fogelson, Wenig and Friedman, Changing the Takeover Game: The Securities & Exchange Commission's Proposed Amendments to the Williams Act, 17 Harv.J. on Legisl. 409 (1980); Note, Wurczinger, Toward A Definition of "Tender Offer," 19 Harv.J. on Legisl. 191 (1982).

Later, in an effort to deal with the problems generated by the Hanson and Carter Hawley Hale cases, the Commission proposed a new Rule 14d–11 requiring that upon commencement of a tender offer by any person (and until the expiration of 30 days after the termination of that offer in the case of bidders and 10 days after termination in the case of other persons) all persons seeking to acquire a substantial amount of the target company securities (10 percent) effect that acquisition only through a conventional tender offer. (SEA Rel. No. 24,976 (Oct. 1, 1987)). The establishment of a "cooling off" period after termination of the tender offer (compare Rule 13e–4(f)(6) providing a ten business day period for issuer tender offers) "would ensure that neither the initial bidder nor any other person could take advantage of the market activity generated by an offer to effect a rapid acquisition of securities."

Does this approach avoid all or most problems which are unsolved by the 1980 proposal?

4. *Problems.*

Suppose a bidder makes a $25 any and all offer providing, in accordance with the Act, for expiration of withdrawal rights on a stated date in advance of the expiration of the offer. The offer is conditioned on receipt of 51 percent of the shares, but also provides for waiver of the condition in the bidder's discretion. A competing $27 offer for 70 percent of the shares is made before the expiration of the first offer but after the expiration of withdrawal rights. Thereafter, on the first offer's expiration date, the bidder accepts all shares tendered, even though less than 51 percent, waiving the condition. One week later, the bidder starts a new $30 tender offer, later raising the price to $32. Can *Field v. Trump* be applied so as to collapse the two offers and create a violation of the best price rule? See Feder v. MacFadden Holdings, Inc., 698 F.Supp. 47 (S.D.N.Y.1988).

Suppose the target of a friendly tender offer decides to modify the provisions of its top executives' stock option plan during the course of the bid. The plan has a provision for the resale of the optioned stock to the target. The target's board amends the plan to raise the resale price to keep it in line with the tender offer price. The amendment provides for an increase in the resale price to $70, to be paid in cash in exchange for surrender of the rights in connection with the second step merger contemplated under the tender offer. Meanwhile, the target's other shareholders are receiving a securities package worth $61.75. Has the best price rule been violated? See Kramer v. Time Warner Inc., 937 F.2d 767 (2d Cir.1991).

NOTE: DEFINING "PERSONS," "GROUPS," AND "BIDDERS"

These three statutory concepts give rise to endless questions of interpretation. When is a "person," including a "group," far enough along in a takeover attempt to be required to file under section 13(d), or far enough along in a tender offer to be required to file under section 14(d)? For example, if a group of stockholders, each of whom owns 2 percent of the stock, enters into initial discussion of arrangements for a possible takeover, does the discussion come within section 13(d)? Suppose an actor in the market for corporate control, owning 4.99 percent or less of a target, calls a brokerage firm and suggests that if the firm buys up to 4.99 percent of the target stock, the actor will pay a commission and purchase the stock, and in any event reimburse the broker for any interim decline in the stock's value. Does this arrangement, called "parking," trigger a Section 13(d) disclosure duty? See SEC v. First City Financial Corp., 890 F.2d 1215 (D.C.Cir.1989). Suppose an actor in the market for corporate control informs selected institutional investors, investment bankers or other parties disposed to sell in the event of a tender offer, of an "interest" in a particular firm. Does such an informal encouragement, entailing no promise to purchase but known as "warehousing," for the purchase and holding or perhaps voting of stock, trigger compliance or disclosure duties under sections 13(d), 14(d) and 14(e)? See, e.g., GAF Corp. v. Milstein, 453 F.2d 709 (2d Cir.1971), cert. denied, 406 U.S. 910 (1972); Bath Indus. v. Blot, 427 F.2d 97 (7th Cir.1970); Champion Parts Rebuilders, Inc. v. Cormier Corp., 661 F.Supp. 825 (N.D.Ill.1987) (formation of a "group" triggering disclosure requirements). Finally, at what point does the investment banking firm advising the bidder become so involved in the transaction, whether due to present or contingent equity participations, fees or otherwise, that it becomes a member of the bidding "group," triggering additional disclosure obligations?

The latter question came up during the late 1980s, more than once in respect of the transactions of the Drexel Burnham firm. Consider its participation in the tender offer at issue in **MAI Basic Four, Inc. v. Prime Computer, Inc.**, 871 F.2d 212 (1st Cir.1989). A group of firms made an any and all cash offer for the shares of Prime Computer, Inc. ("Prime"). The bidding group included three entities, MAI Basic Four,

Inc., Choice Corp., and Brooke Partners, L.P. (collectively, "Basic"), controlled by Bennett LeBow and William Weksel. LeBow and Weksel had done two previous acquisitions in association with Drexel Burnham Lambert.

Drexel had complex ties to the bidding group. It held (a) 5 percent of the equity of MAI Basic Four, Inc. with a right to purchase an additional 9 percent at half price, (b) a one third equity interest in the parent corporation of the sole general partner of Brooke Partners, L.P., with the right to name three board members and veto power over some corporate action, and (c) a further 17 percent equity interest in Brooke Partners itself.

The tender offer was to be financed as follows: (a) $20 million cash from Brooke Partners, L.P., (b) $650 million bank financing, (c) $875 million of junk bonds placed by Drexel in exchange for a $65 million fee. Drexel had issued a "highly confident" letter in respect of the projected sale of the junk bonds. Weksel testified to an understanding that the "highly confident" letter meant that Drexel would come up with the $875 million even if it failed to sell the entire issue of junk bonds through its "road show" sales effort. In the event of failure of the offer, Drexel was entitled to 15 percent of any profit realized on the group's prior holdings of Prime stock.

The District Court enjoined the tender offer, holding that Drexel was a "bidder" within the meaning of the applicable regulation and requiring extensive disclosure of its current capital conditions. Drexel's ability to arrange financing depended on its capital. Questions respecting its capital had arisen because of its recent expressed willingness to plead guilty to six felony counts in a proceeding in the Southern District of New York.

The Court of Appeals affirmed. It recognized the desirability of a bright line rule to determine when an investment banker is a bidder, but decided to follow a different approach advanced by Judge Weis, dissenting in City Capital Assocs. Ltd. Partnership v. Interco, Inc., 860 F.2d 60 (3d Cir.1988). Said the Court, 871 F.2d at 219–221:

" * * * The more flexible, fact-based approach advocated by Judge Weis is consistent with our reading of the Williams Act.[5]

" * * * Section 14(d)(1) * * * defines 'person':

"When two or more persons act as a partnership, limited partnership, syndicate, or other group for the purpose of acquiring, holding, or disposing of securities of an issuer, such syndicate or group shall be deemed a 'person' for purposes of this subsection.

"Williams Act § 14(d)(2), 15 U.S.C. § 78n(d)(2).

"The SEC Rule, 14d–1(b)(1), 17 C.F.R. § 240.24d–1(b)(1), uses the word 'bidder' in place of 'person' in the statute. It defines a bidder as

---

5. The appellant in *Interco* disavowed that Drexel was part of a "group," and the majority therefore declined to reach this issue. 860 F.2d at 65 n. 6. In view of our interpretation and application of the group concept, infra, our analysis may not ultimately contradict that of the Third Circuit.

'any person who makes a tender offer or on whose behalf a tender offer is made.' Id. The SEC, in a 1979 Release, stated that bidder was a 'short-hand reference[ ] to [a] principal participant[ ] in a tender offer.' Exchange Act Release No. 15,548 [1979 Transfer Binder] Fed.Sec.L.Rep. (CCH) ¶ 81,935, at 81,216 (Feb. 5, 1979). We read the 'on whose behalf' language of Rule 14d–1(b)(1) to incorporate the 'group' concept of sections 13(d) and 14(d) of the Williams Act. As pointed out by Judge Weis in *Interco,* the statute authorizes the SEC to require 'additional information,' but does not appear to grant the Commission discretion to narrow the definition of 'person' explicitly defined in the Act.

" * * * The definition of 'person' in § 14(d)(2) is identical to the formulation found in § 13(d)(3). The legislative history of the latter section contradicts an exclusive focus on control, a factor provisionally raised in Schedule 14D–1, General Instruction G, Item 9, in determining who is a bidder under the regulation.[6] * * *

"We distill from these guides, which use the words 'directly or indirectly,' 'on whose behalf,' 'principal participant[ ],' and 'any contract, understanding, relationship, agreement or other arrangement' that there is no bright, hard-line test for bidder under the regulation. We empathize with the Third Circuit when it said in *Interco,* '[t]his is an area of law in which predictability is of crucial importance.' 860 F.2d at 64. But we are skeptical. We suspect that any bright-line test, separating those who are subject to the Williams Act from those who are not, would merely invite the ingenuity of resourceful counsel to place their client formally on the desired side of the line, whatever the underlying reality may be.

"In this case we cannot say that, as a matter of law, an active advisor-broker-financier-participant who owns less than a majority interest in the surviving entity is not a bidder where, as here, there has been a history of close association, equity sharing, board representation and involvement from the beginning of the present offer, and where there is the possibility of the advisor-broker being the indispensable key to the offer's success. Nor can we say that while a 46 percent stockholder qualifies as a bidder, a 14 percent direct stockholder with other indirect equity interests cannot qualify. At a minimum it is evident that Drexel has 'act[ed] as a partnership, limited partnership, * * * or other group for the purpose of acquiring, holding, or disposing of securities of an issuer.' 15 U.S.C. § 78n(d)(2). We are not convinced that the district court erred in determining that Prime demonstrated a likelihood of success on the merits, and therefore affirm the court's ruling that Drexel is a bidder."

---

6. The instruction provides:

Where the bidder is other than a natural person and the bidder's financial condition is material to a decision by a security holder of the subject company whether to sell, tender or hold securities being sought in the tender offer, furnish current, adequate financial information concerning the bidder; *Provided,* That if the bidder is controlled by another entity which is not a natural person and has been formed for the purpose of making the tender offer, furnish current, adequate financial information concerning such parent.

17 C.F.R. § 240.14d–100.

The court went on to hold that information respecting Drexel's capital was material. Suppose the issue respecting Drexel's status as a bidder had come up a year or two earlier, well before Drexel's $650 million plea bargain? Would diminished concerns respecting the firm's financial abilities have caused the same participation in the bidding group to have a different legal effect under the court's flexible approach?

(F) STANDING, RELIEF, AND THE PROBLEMS OF WILLIAMS ACT LITIGATION

Whatever may be the value to investors of compliance by either target or bidder with applicable disclosure obligations, the existence of those obligations furnishes each with the opportunity to litigate over the adequacy of the other's disclosure, and thus to obtain the benefits of impeding or delaying the effectiveness of the other's moves in the contest. Thus, the target may seek to delay the bidder or prevent the bidder from acquiring more stock or voting the stock it has acquired until defective disclosure is corrected—which may be long enough to discourage the bidder or enable the target to prepare its defenses. And the bidder may seek to impede a defensive merger proposed by the target. In either case, the information gains to the investors may well be trivial (e.g. the financial condition of a cash bidder offering to take 100% of the target as in Copperweld Corp. v. Imetal, 403 F.Supp. 579 (W.D.Pa.1975); a description of "questionable payments" by such a bidder as in Berman v. Gerber Products Co., 454 F.Supp. 1310 (W.D.Mich.1978); or a description by the *bidder* of potential environmental liabilities of the *target* as in Koppers Co., Inc. v. American Express Co., 689 F.Supp. 1371 (W.D.Pa.1988)), and in any event may be offset by the loss of the opportunity to use the information because of discontinuance of the contest.[r]

The tactical value of the process of litigation in seeking and resisting takeovers makes litigation an almost inevitable response to a take-over bid.[s] As a result, the courts are confronted with the problems

r. To what extent are the bidder's financing plans material to target shareholders? The courts tend to be firm in enforcing requirements that these be disclosed. See, e.g., SEC v. Levy, 706 F.Supp. 61 (D.D.C.1989) (failure to disclose bank loans); A.P. Green Indus., Inc. v. East Rock Partners, Inc., 726 F.Supp. 757 (E.D.Mo. 1989) (failure to disclose plan to encumber target assets). But the Act does not require that firm financing commitments be in place before the offer's commencement. Two cases confirm this point, sanctioning offers proceeding on "highly confident" letters from Drexel Burnham Lambert respecting projected junk bond sales. See IU Int'l Corp. v. NX Acquisition Corp., 840 F.2d 220 (4th Cir.1988); Newmont Mining Corp. v. Pickens, 831 F.2d 1448 (9th Cir. 1987). If the creditworthiness of individuals in the bidding group figures into the economics of the bid, then disclosure of their financial condition may be required. Compare Pabst Brewing Co. v. Kalmanovitz, 551 F.Supp. 882 (D.Del.1982), aff'd, 707 F.2d 1392 (3d Cir.1982), with Arkansas Best Corp. v. Pearlman, 688 F.Supp. 976 (D.Del.1988).

s. In suits by targets' managements to enjoin bidders (from consummating the bid, from buying more stock, from retaining or voting stock already acquired, etc.) complaints often have been filled with boiler plate which may have been prepared in advance to resist any conceivable take-over attempt. It rests on charges which may

of whether to limit standing to invoke judicial aid, and how to fashion relief which protects public investors who are rarely parties to the litigation.

(1) Standing

If, for example, a filing required by the statute, is not made, or false statements or omissions to state material facts are attributable to either contestant, what parties are entitled to seek relief?

When the acquirer or bidder violates the disclosure requirements, do the target company, individual stockholders of the target company (who are not deceived) or competing bidders have standing to seek injunctive relief? damages? rescission? When the target company or a competing bidder violates the disclosure obligations do the target's stockholders, the bidder, or competing bidders have such standing?

The case law is not uniform, but at least in the Courts of Appeal, since Electronics Specialty Co., supra p. 985, the teaching is that stockholders of target companies, whether tendering or not and whether deceived or not, have standing under §§ 14(d) and 14(e) to seek injunctive relief, corrective disclosure (Florida Commercial Banks v. Culverhouse, 772 F.2d 1513 (11th Cir.1985) and possibly other relief including money damages. Plaine v. McCabe, 797 F.2d 713 (9th Cir. 1986); Pryor v. United States Steel Corp., 794 F.2d 52 (2d Cir.1986). There also are suggestions that target stockholders have standing to bring derivative suits against their directors for violating § 14(e). See Abella v. Universal Leaf Tobacco Co., 546 F.Supp. 795 (E.D.Va.1982). In addition, implied actions by targets for a variety of relief except possibly divestiture by the errant bidder have been upheld under § 13(d) (Indiana National Corp. v. Rich, 712 F.2d 1180 (7th Cir.1983); cf. Liberty National Insurance Holding Co. v. Charter Co., 734 F.2d 545 (11th Cir.1984)). On the other hand, in **Polaroid Corp. v. Disney,** 862 F.2d 987 (3d Cir.1988), the Court denied the target standing to bring an action on its shareholders' behalf to enforce the All Holders Rule, 14d–10, against a bid that excluded shares recently issued by the target to its Employee Stock Ownership Plan. But the Court also held that the target did have standing to protect its shareholders against the bidder's violation of section 14(e). Is this distinction valid? Compare the discussion in Judge Cowan's dissenting opinion and Judge Friendly's opinion in *Electronic Specialty,* supra.

range from claims of inadequate disclosure, principally of the bidder's plans or purposes or its financial condition or of its "questionable payments" (notwithstanding that only a cash bid is involved), to violation of any conceivable collateral statute or regulations which the draftsman can think of, such as the margin regulations, the anti-trust laws, the Federal Communica-tions Act or other regulatory or licensing laws if the target is subject to them. And a count under local take-over statutes is also now generally available. The bidder generally counterclaims, at least for violation of the disclosure provisions of the securities laws, and often charges the target's management with violation of its fiduciary duties under local law.

The leading case on the standing of bidders is **Piper v. Chris–Craft Industries, Inc.,** 430 U.S. 1 (1977). There the Supreme Court ruled that Chris–Craft, a bidder for control of Piper Aircraft lacked standing to bring a private suit for money damages (against Piper or a competitive bidder (Bangor Punta) or the target's banker) for failure to obtain control caused by the defendants' false statements made in violation of § 14(e) and by violation of Rule 10b–6, as a result of which enough Piper stock was diverted from plaintiff to defendant competitive bidder to cause the former to lose the battle for control.

Proceeding on the premise that the Williams Act was designed to protect public investors but not bidders, the Court found that the goal of investor protection did not require a bidder to be authorized to recover damages for failure to succeed resulting from the target's or a competing bidder's violation of the Exchange Act, and declined to fashion such a cause of action.

In the course of its opinion the Court (Burger, C.J.) said:

Section 14(e), like § 10(b), makes no provision whatever for a private cause of action, such as those explicitly provided in other sections of the 1933 and 1934 Acts. E.g., §§ 11, 12, 15 of the 1933 Act, 15 U.S.C. §§ 77k, 77*l*, 77 *o;* §§ 9, 16, 18, 20 of the 1934 Act, 15 U.S.C. §§ 78i, 78p, 78r, 78t. This court has nonetheless held that in some circumstances a private cause of action can be implied with respect to the 1934 Act's antifraud provisions, even though the relevant provisions are silent as to remedies. J.I. Case Co. v. Borak, 377 U.S. 426 (1964) (§ 14(a)); Superintendent of Insurance v. Bankers Life & Cas. Co., 404 U.S. 6, 13 n. 9 (1971) (§ 10(b)).

The reasoning of these holdings is that, where congressional purposes are likely to be undermined absent private enforcement, private remedies may be implied in favor of the particular class intended to be protected by the statute.

* * *

Against this background we must consider whether § 14(e), which is entirely silent as to private remedies, permits this Court to read into the statute a damages remedy for unsuccessful tender offerors. To resolve that question we turn to the legislative history to discern the congressional purpose underlying the specific statutory prohibition in § 14(e). Once we identify the legislative purpose, we must then determine whether the creation by judicial interpretation of the implied cause of action asserted by Chris–Craft is necessary to effectuate Congress' goals.

* * *

A

* * *

The legislative history thus shows that the sole purpose of the Williams Act was the protection of investors who are confronted with a tender offer. As we stated in Rondeau v. Mosinee Paper Corp., 422 U.S., at 58, "[t]he purpose of the Williams Act is to insure that public shareholders who are confronted by a cash tender offer for their stock will not be required to respond without adequate information * * *." We find no hint in the legislative history, on which respondent so heavily relies, that Congress contemplated a private cause of action for damages by one of several contending offerors against a successful bidder or by a losing contender against the target corporation.

* * *

B

Our conclusion as to the legislative history is confirmed by the analysis in Cort v. Ash, 422 U.S. 66 (1975). There, the Court identified four factors as "relevant" in determining whether a private remedy is implicit in a statute not expressly providing one. The first is whether the plaintiff is " 'one of the class for whose *especial* benefit the statute was enacted * * *.' " Id., at 78. (Emphasis in original.) As previously indicated, examination of the statute and its genesis shows that Chris–Craft is not an intended beneficiary of the Williams Act, and surely is not one "for whose *especial* benefit the statute was enacted." Id., at 78. To the contrary, Chris–Craft is a member of the class whose activities Congress intended to regulate for the protection and benefit of an entirely distinct class, shareholders-offerees. As a party whose previously unregulated conduct was purposefully brought under federal control by the statute, Chris–Craft can scarcely lay claim to the status of "beneficiary" whom Congress considered in need of protection.

Second, in Cort v. Ash we inquired whether there is "any indication of legislative intent, explicit or implicit, either to create such a remedy or to deny one?" Id., at 78. Although the historical materials are barren of any express intent to deny a damages remedy to tender offerors as a class, there is, as we have noted, no indication that Congress intended to create a damages remedy in favor of the loser in a contest for control. Fairly read, we think the legislative documents evince the narrow intent to curb the unregulated activities of tender offerors. The expression of this purpose, which pervades the legislative history, negates the claim that tender offerors were intended to have additional weapons in the form of an implied cause of action for damages, particularly if a private damages action confers no advantage on the expressly protected class of shareholders-offerees, a matter we discuss later.

Chris–Craft argues, however, that Congress intended standing under § 14(e) to encompass tender offerors since the statute, unlike § 10(b), does not contain the limiting language, "in connection with the purchase or sale" of securities. Instead, in § 14(e), Congress broadly proscribed fraudulent activities "in connection with any tender offer * * * or any solicitation * * * in opposition to or in favor of any such offer * * *."

The omission of the purchaser-seller requirement does not mean, however, that Chris–Craft has standing to sue for damages under § 14(e) in its capacity as a takeover bidder. It may well be that Congress desired to protect, among others, shareholders-offerees who decided not to tender their stock due to fraudulent misrepresentations by persons opposed to a takeover attempt. See generally 1 A. Bromberg, supra, § 6.3(101b), at 122.17. See also Senate Report, at 2; House Report, at 3. These shareholders, who might not enjoy the protection of § 10(b) under Blue Chip Stamps v. Manor Drug Stores, supra, could perhaps state a claim under § 14(e), even though they did not tender their securities.[25] But increased protection, if any, conferred upon the class of shareholders-offerees by the elimination of the purchaser-seller restriction can scarcely be interpreted as giving protection to the entirely separate and unrelated class of persons whose conduct the statute is designed to regulate.

Third, Cort v. Ash tells us that we must ascertain whether it is "consistent with the underlying purposes of the legislative scheme to imply such a remedy for the plaintiff." Ibid. We conclude that it is not. As a disclosure mechanism aimed especially at protecting shareholders of target corporations, the Williams Act cannot consistently be interpreted as conferring a monetary remedy upon regulated parties, particularly where the award would not redound to the direct benefit of the protected class. Although it is correct to say that the $36 million damage award indirectly benefits those Piper shareholders who became Chris–Craft shareholders when they accepted Chris–Craft's exchange offer, it is equally true that the damage award injures those Piper shareholders who exchanged their shares for Bangor Punta's stock and who, as Bangor Punta shareholders, would necessarily bear a large part of the burden of any judgment against Bangor Punta. The class sought to be protected by the Williams Act are the shareholders of the *target* corporation; hence it can hardly be said that their interests as a class are served by a judgment in favor of Chris–Craft and against Bangor Punta. Moreover, the damages are awarded to the very party whose activities Congress intended to curb; Chris–Craft did not sue in the capacity of an injured Piper shareholder, but as a defeated tender offeror.

Nor can we agree that an ever-present threat of damages against a successful contestant in a battle for control will provide significant additional protection for shareholders in general. The deterrent value, if any, of such awards can never be ascertained with precision. More likely, however, is the prospect that shareholders may be prejudiced because some tender offers may never be made if there is a possibility of massive damages claims for what courts subsequently hold to be an actionable violation of § 14(e). Even a contestant who "wins the battle" for control may well wind up exposed to a costly "war" in a later and successful defense of its victory. Or at worst—on Chris–

---

25. This case, of course, does not present that issue, and we express no view on it.

Craft's damage theory—the victorious tender offeror or the target corporation might be subject to a large substantive judgment, plus high costs of litigation.

In short, we conclude that shareholder protection, if enhanced at all by damages awards such as Chris–Craft contends for, can more directly be achieved with other less drastic means more closely tailored to the precise congressional goal underlying the Williams Act.

Fourth, under the Cort v. Ash analysis, we must decide whether "the cause of action [is] one traditionally relegated to state law * * *." Ibid. Despite the pervasiveness of federal securities regulation, the Court of Appeals concluded in this case that Chris–Craft's complaint would give rise to a cause of action under common-law principles of interference with a prospective commercial advantage. Although Congress is, of course, free to create a remedial scheme in favor of contestants in tender offers, we conclude, as we did in Cort v. Ash, that "it is entirely appropriate in this instance to relegate [the offeror-bidder] and others in [that] situation to whatever remedy is created by state law," at least to the extent that the offeror seeks damages for having been wrongfully denied a "fair opportunity" to compete for control of another corporation.

C

What we have said thus far suggests that, unlike J.I. Case v. Borak, supra, judicially creating a damages action in favor of Chris–Craft is unnecessary to ensure the fulfillment of Congress' purposes in adopting the Williams Act. Even though the SEC operates in this context under the same practical restraints recognized by the Court in *Borak,* institutional limitations alone do not lead to the conclusion that any party interested in a tender offer should have a cause of action for damages against a competing bidder. First, as Judge Friendly observed in Electronic Specialty Co. v. International Controls Corp., 409 F.2d 937, 947 (2d Cir.1969), in corporate control contests the stage of preliminary injunctive relief, rather than post-contest lawsuits, "is the time when relief can best be given." Furthermore, awarding damages to parties other than the protected class of shareholders has only a remote, if any, bearing upon implementing the congressional policy of protecting shareholders who must decide whether to tender or retain their stock.[28] Indeed, as we suggested earlier, a damages award of this nature may well be inconsistent with the interests of many members of the protected class and of only indirect value to shareholders who accepted the exchange offer of the defeated takeover contestant.

28. Our holding is a limited one. Whether shareholders-offerees, the class protected by § 14(e), have an implied cause of action under § 14(e) is not before us, and we intimate no view on the matter. Nor is the target corporation's standing to sue in issue in this case. We hold only that a tender offeror, suing in its capacity as a takeover bidder, does not have standing to sue for damages under the Williams Act.

Our precise holding disposes of many observations made in dissent. Thus, the argument with respect to the "exclusion" from standing for "persons most interested in effective enforcement," * * * is simply unwarranted in light of today's narrow holding.

We therefore conclude that Chris–Craft, as a defeated tender offeror, has no implied cause of action for damages under § 14(e).

* * *

The decision in Chris–Craft apparently does not foreclose standing to request injunctive relief against targets by bidders in their efforts to acquire control. See e.g., Crane Co. v. Harsco Corp., 511 F.Supp. 294 (D.Del.1981); Marathon Oil Co. v. Mobil Corp., 669 F.2d 378 (6th Cir.1981), cert. denied, 455 U.S. 982 (1982). Does it leave bidders, in their capacity as stockholders, free to seek money damages as well as injunctive relief against the target company or its management or other bidders for violation of the Securities Exchange Act?

Does the decision imply that a take-over bidder (1) which is frustrated by the joint activities of the target and a competing bidder in violation of § 9(a) and Rule 10b–5 under the Exchange Act and (2) which becomes a "forced" seller, has no cause of action for damages under Rule 10b–5 or § 9? Crane v. American Standard, Inc., 603 F.2d 244 (2d Cir.1979) refuses the bidder standing under the other two sections.

(2) **Relief**

Apart from the question of standing to seek judicial aid when there has been a violation of the disclosure or anti-manipulation obligations, questions arise as to whether the violation is curable and, if so, what relief should be granted to sterilize its consequences until it is cured, and then after it is cured. Certainly, the target of a fraudulent offer may seek equitable relief. See Diceon Electronics, Inc. v. Calvary Partners, Inc., 772 F.Supp. 859 (D.Del.1991). But, if the violation is cured, should the bidder be enjoined from future efforts to acquire stock or from voting stock already acquired for some period? See Rondeau v. Mosinee Paper Corp., 422 U.S. 49 (1975), which upheld a District Court's refusal to issue a permanent injunction after the bidder had cured a failure to make a filing under § 13(d) upon acquiring more than five percent of the target's stock. Extension of depositors' withdrawal rights may be a feasible remedy in enforcing § 14(d); but formidable difficulties are encountered in imposing more effective remedies, such as ordering divestiture or restraining voting by the errant bidder, as the Electronic Specialty case (supra p. 985) suggests. In that case, the Court of Appeals (Friendly, J.) pointed out:

"Plaintiffs assert that the decision under review is infected by a fatal flaw. The court, they say, has found a number of violations on the part of ICC but has done nothing more than administer a slap on the wrist. They argue that the opportunity afforded by ICC for withdrawal was insufficient, both because the court has now held there were inequities beyond those found by Judge McLean whose opinion was the only one sent to shareholders, and because the sole option afforded an individual stockholder was to withdraw under circumstances wherein, because of the inaction of others, ICC might be left in control of ELS. They say that approval on our part of the pattern here displayed—denial of interlocutory relief because divestiture or prohibition of voting may be later available, followed by denial of these remedies on final hearing because they are too severe—would frustrate the plain intention of Congress to do something effective when it added § 14(d) and (e).

"We agree with plaintiffs to the extent of believing that the application for a preliminary injunction is the time when relief can best be given. * * * [W]e think that in administering § 14(d) and (e), district judges would do well to ponder whether, if a violation has been sufficiently proved on an application for a temporary injunction, the opportunity for doing equity is not considerably better then than it will be later on. The court will have a variety of tools usable at that stage. If the filings are defective or the tender offer misleading, the court can require correction, along, of course, with an opportunity to withdraw and an injunction against further solicitation until the period for withdrawal has expired. Since the amount of stock tendered is likely to be smaller at that time, the difficulties with respect to withdrawal described by plaintiffs will at least be less acute than after the offer has been concluded. If the court believes the offeror has improperly depressed the price of the stock before making the offer, it can require rescission and enjoin further solicitation for a period, or allow the offeror the alternative of raising the price for both past and future deposits. We cite these merely as examples; other techniques will doubtless suggest themselves to resourceful judges. On the other hand, we do not mean at all that interlocutory relief should be given lightly. To the contrary, district judges must be vigilant against resort to the courts on trumped-up or trivial grounds as a means for delaying and thereby defeating legitimate tender offers. Recognizing the heavy burden all this entails on district judges, particularly in the Southern District of New York where so much of this litigation occurs, and to a lesser extent on this court as well, we think the need for prompt and judicious handling of applications for temporary injunctions in cases arising under § 14(d) and (e) is an inevitable consequence of the new statute.

"On the other hand we must agree with defendant that even if it had violated § 14(e) in the manner found by the district court, the judge was well within the bounds of discretion in denying divestiture or sterilization. Courts cannot too often recall the statement in Hecht Co. v. Bowles, 321 U.S. 321, 329–330 (1944):

'The historic injunctive process was designed to deter, not to punish. The essence of equity jurisdiction has been the power of the Chancellor to do equity and to mould each decree to the necessities of the particular case. Flexibility rather than rigidity has distinguished it. The qualities of mercy and practicality have made equity the instrument for nice adjustment and reconciliation between the public interest and private needs as well as between competing private claims.'

"It is not irreverent to cite also the admonition of an equally exalted authority whose 'object all sublime' was to 'let the punishment fit the crime.'

"To afford an opportunity for withdrawal would be the idlest of gestures now, since the ELS stock purchased by ICC at $39 is selling around $26–$27, and compulsory rescission is out of the question. Divestiture of 1,200,000 shares of ELS probably would involve certain and huge loss. Even if ICC could find a purchaser at the present market, the amount of loss would approach $15,000,000. If the stock had to be sold in small quantities over a period, ICC would likely suffer still greater loss and the prospect would hang heavy over the nontendering stockholders of ELS. Permanent deprivation of voting rights and an injunction against the solicitation of proxies would be just as detrimental. This would simply be a disguised method of forcing divestiture, and it would be decidedly unhealthy to leave the direction of an enterprise to 45% of the stock, especially when the management has sold out. There is also the seeming inequity in administering such strong medicine to an offeror when no such remedy would be available against management for violations in opposing the offer.[7] Moreover, none of these remedies would get the tendering stockholders the higher price on which ELS claims they would have insisted if ICC had not depressed the market. Yet no one has had the temerity to suggest that ICC now be required to raise the price to a figure it was never willing to pay."

———

The task is not made easier by the variety of tribunals to which the same question of violation may be submitted and the resulting possibility of conflict. For an illustration, compare Susquehanna Corp. v. Pan American Sulphur Co., 423 F.2d 1075 (5th Cir.1970), with In re Susquehanna Corp., Rel. No. 34–8933, CCH ¶ 77,842 (July 17, 1970), in which an injunctive proceeding in the federal courts and an SEC enforcement proceeding reach different conclusions on the question whether a bidder's 13D statement was deficient.

The Act also provides for SEC administrative proceedings leading to cease-and-desist orders. Such an order can include a provision for the disgorgement of profits. See section 21C(e) of the Act. In addition, the Commission can bring an action in federal district court for the imposition of a civil penalty for each violation of up to $100,000 for a natural person and $500,000 for a firm. See section 21(d). The leading case involving the calculation of the profits to be disgorged in respect of a Williams Act violation is **SEC v. First City Financial Corp., Ltd.,**

---

7. Although the "dirty hands" defense might be available to the offeror, the innocent stockholder would find cold comfort in a result that because both the offeror and the management had violated the statute all relief should be denied.

890 F.2d 1215 (D.C.Cir.1989). The defendant had engaged in "parking" in violation of section 13(d). It had purchased 4.9 percent of the target's stock on the open market and then arranged for a friendly brokerage firm to make continued purchases for its own account. Under the arrangement, the brokerage firm accumulated a block of stock in a rising market, and then sold it to the defendant at a substantial discount from the market price. The court required the defendant, which had resold the entire block of target stock it accumulated (between 8 and 9 percent total of the total outstanding) back to the target, to disgorge all profits realized on stock purchased after the latest date on which it might have filed a complying disclosure statement under section 13(d). The theory was that had the disclosure been made, the stock would have been purchased in a different and more expensive market. The defendant offered more complex hypothetical pictures of both its own behavior and that of the markets based on the assumption of timely disclosure. Under one of the defendant's scenarios there would have been no profits to disgorge because the defendant would have taken the rational step of front-loading its purchases over the 5 percent level during the 10 day statutory period between accumulation and filing. The court rejected all of the defendant's scenarios, however plausible, taking the enforcement-minded view that "disgorgement need only be a reasonable approximation of profits causally connected to the violation:"

> "If exact information were obtainable at negligible cost, we would not hesitate to impose upon the government a strict burden to produce the data to measure the precise amount of the ill-gotten gains. Unfortunately, we encounter imprecision and imperfect information. Despite sophisticated econometric modelling, predicting stock market responses to alternative variables is, as the district court found, at best speculative. Rules for calculating disgorgement must recognize that separating legal from illegal profits exactly may at times be a near-impossible task." 890 F.2d at 1231.

Is the court's approach impermissibly punitive, as the defendant argued?

3. FEDERAL INSIDER TRADING RESTRICTIONS
INTRODUCTION

1. *The Debate Over the Insider Trading Ban.*

Easterbrook and Fischel, in an article excerpted in Appendix B, Section 2, make an efficiency case for federal mandatory disclosure system in terms of the quantity and quality of information circulated, but assume that the timing takes care of itself. In the efficient market picture, the first market actor to learn the information profits from trading. Thereafter the price contains the news. Does it follow that the securities laws should encourage insider trading in order to speed the reception of news into the market price of securities? A market price justification for insider trading has been articulated. It tends to appear together with the assertion that insider trading profits are a legitimate form of management compensation that rewards entrepreneurship. These points are posed in opposition to the traditional assertion that the ban on insider trading promotes investor confidence and therefore is beneficial.

Henry Manne was the first to advance the market price/executive compensation justification of insider trading. Manne, Insider Trading and The Stock Market (1966).[t] Building on Manne's work, Carlton and Fischel have argued that insider trading fine tunes the firm's public disclosures so as to benefit the shareholders as a group. In some cases, they note, complete disclosure is not optimal, as where a confidential study shows the location of valuable mineral ore deposits that the firm has not yet purchased. Here, they argue, insider trading causes "the share price [to] move closer to what it would have been had the information been disclosed. How close will depend on the amount of noise surrounding the trade. * * * Conversely, firms also could use insider trading to limit the amount of information to be reflected in price. Controlling the number of traders who have access to information may be easier than controlling how much information gets announced over time." Carlton and Fischel, The Regulation of Insider Trading, 35 Stan.L.Rev. 857, 868 (1983). See also Kahan, Securities Laws and the Social Costs of "Inaccurate" Stock Prices, 41 Duke L.J. 977, 1001–1005 (1992); Haddock and Macey, A Coasian Model of Insider Trading, 80 Nw.U.L.Rev. 1449 (1987); Easterbrook, Insider Trading as an Agency Problem, in Principals and Agents: The Structure of Business (J. Pratt and R. Zeckhauser, eds. 1985); Macey, From Fairness to Contract: The New Direction of the Rules Against Insider Trading, 13 Hofstra L.Rev. 9 (1984).

There is a large body of responsive commentary. Many argue that the securities laws' "disclose or abstain" rule for insiders in fact promotes allocative efficiency. These arguments tend[u] to build on the assertion that the information asymmetry that separates insiders from outsiders prevents a situation of free contract between insiders and outsiders from operating effectively in this context. Under one version

---

t. For responses to Manne see, e.g., O.E. Williamson, Corporate Control and Business Behavior 93–96 (1970); Schotland, Unsafe at any Price: A Reply to Manne, Insider Trading and the Stock market, 53 Va.L.Rev. 1425 (1967).

u. An exception is Haft, The Effect of Insider Trading Rules on the Internal Efficiency of the Large Corporation, 80 Mich. L.Rev. 1051 (1982), which draws on learning about organizational behavior to justify the insider trading prohibition from the point of view of internal corporate operations.

Defects in the role of insider trading profits as an optimal mode of compensation or as a stimulus to entrepreneurial efforts by salaried managers are examined by Schotland and by Williamson, supra note t. Quite apart from compensation techniques other than insider trading that can offer managers appropriate entrepreneurial incentives, insider trading profits are counter productive if, as is likely, they will go to some executives whose activities cannot be connected with stock price increases, or indeed caused stock price decreases.

of this argument, the trading insider is seen as the potential provider of information that would change and correct the marketplace's extant impression of the corporate affairs. The costs of nondisclosure of this information are seen as outweighing the benefits of insider trading, including partial market price adjustments. See Brudney, Insiders, Outsiders, and Informational Advantages under the Federal Securities Laws, 93 Harv.L.Rev. 322, 345–346 (1979). A related version of this argument emphasizes the preference of investors for a market structured so as to discourage delayed disclosure. See Seligman, The Reformation of Federal Securities Law Concerning Nonpublic Information, 73 Geo.L.J. 1083, 1115–20 (1985). Cox recasts the investor preference point in a hypothetical contract model. Under this, insider trading profits are shown to be a suboptimal form of executive compensation from a shareholder point of view. Insider trading is based on informational asymmetries; shareholders, who want to know what their managers are being paid, rationally will prefer a more open compensation arrangement. The law thus replicates the contract that rational shareholders and managers would enter into anyway. Cox, Insider Trading and Contracting: A Critical Response to the "Chicago School," 1986 Duke L.J. 628, 655–657.

Consonance between the insider trading ban and investor expectations is asserted more broadly in Ausubel, Insider trading In a Rational Expectations Economy, 80 Amer.Econ.Rev. 1022 (1990). In Ausubel's model, abolition of insider trading improves the expected return on investment of outsiders. Increased expected return leads to increased investment by outsiders, which in turn benefits insiders. The "confidence" that the insider trading ban instills therefore is optimal for all participants.

A different line of justificatory argument approaches the objective of "investor confidence" from another perspective, emphasizing that insider trading is unfair. See Brudney, supra p. 346. Again the informational asymmetry lies at the argument's base. The insider has access to the information that the outsider cannot lawfully acquire. "The unfairness is not a function merely of possessing more information—outsiders may possess more information than other outsiders by reason of their diligence or zeal—but of the fact that it is an advantage that cannot be competed away since it depends upon a lawful privilege which an outsider cannot acquire." Id. See also Bromberg, 2 Securities Law: Fraud—SEC Rule 10b–5, sec. 8.7(2) (1972) ("the market should not produce windfalls for some at the expense of others through control of information").

2. *Insider Trading in Connection With Mergers and Takeovers.*

Whatever may be the pros and cons of the doctrine that governs trading by corporate insiders who make use of conventional insider information about corporate affairs, a different set of problems arises in the context of mergers and takeovers. These problems are generated by a somewhat different cast of players—lawyers, investment bankers, security analysts, accountants, public relations consultants, proxy solicitors, printers, etc.—and implicate a different set of economic and social values.[v] The incidence of "insider" trading in connection with mergers and takeovers increased substantially during the 1970s and 1980s as the number of both transactions and players grew significantly. The stock prices of target companies almost invariably shot up in the days before the transactions were announced publicly.

The SEC promulgated a rule directed to insider trading in connection with mergers and takeovers under Section 14(e) in 1980. It took this step to offset the Supreme Court's narrowing of scope of Section 10(b) and Rule 10b–5 in Chiarella v. United States, 445 U.S. 222 (1980).

Rule 14e–3. Transactions in Securities on the Basis of Material, Nonpublic Information in the Context of Tender Offers

(a) If any person has taken a substantial step or steps to commence, or has commenced, a tender offer (the "offering person"), it shall constitute a fraudulent, deceptive or manipulative act or practice within the meaning of section 14(e) of the Act for any other person who is in possession of material information relating to such tender offer which information he knows or has reason to know is nonpublic and which he knows or has reason to know has been acquired directly or indirectly from (1) the offering person, (2) the issuer of the securities sought or to be sought by such tender offer, or (3) any officer, director, partner or employee or any other person acting on behalf of the offering person or such issuer, to purchase or sell or cause to be purchased or sold any of such securities or any securities convertible into or exchangeable for any such securities or any option or right to obtain or to dispose of any of the foregoing securities, unless within a reasonable time prior to any purchase or sale such information and its source are publicly disclosed by press release or otherwise.

(b) A person other than a natural person shall not violate paragraph (a) of this section if such person shows that:

(1) The individual(s) making the investment decision on behalf of such person to purchase or sell any security described in paragraph (a) or to cause any such security to be purchased or sold by or on behalf of others did not know the material, nonpublic information; and

(2) Such person had implemented one or a combination of policies and procedures, reasonable under the circumstances,

---

v. This is not to deny that the more conventional disclosure problems under Rule 10b–5 also arise in the context of mergers, as when a negotiator for an acquirer receives information about the target "in confidence" and later, after the proposed merger aborts, uses the information to trade for itself. See, e.g., Walton v. Morgan Stanley & Co., 623 F.2d 796 (2d Cir.1980), and compare Frigitemp Corp. v. Financial Dynamics Fund, 524 F.2d 275 (2d Cir.1975). Contractual solutions to this type of problem are suggested in Mann and Schwartzbaum, Negotiating Confidentiality Agreements: Issues for the Bidder's Counsel, 6 Insights, No. 8, p. 18 (August 1992).

taking into consideration the nature of the person's business, to ensure that individual(s) making investment decision(s) would not violate paragraph (a), which policies and procedures may include, but are not limited to, (i) those which restrict any purchase, sale and causing any purchase and sale of any such security or (ii) those which prevent such individual(s) from knowing such information.

(c) Notwithstanding anything in paragraph (a) to the contrary, the following transactions shall not be violations of paragraph (a) of this section:

(1) Purchase(s) of any security described in paragraph (a) by a broker or by another agent on behalf of an offering person; or

(2) Sale(s) by any person of any security described in paragraph (a) to the offering person.

(d)(1) As a means reasonably designed to prevent fraudulent, deceptive or manipulative acts or practices within the meaning of section 14(e) of the Act, it shall be unlawful for any person described in paragraph (d)(2) of this section to communicate material, nonpublic information relating to a tender offer to any other person under circumstances in which it is reasonably foreseeable that such communication is likely to result in a violation of this section except that this paragraph shall not apply to a communication made in good faith.

(i) To the officers, directors, partners or employees of the offering person, to its advisors or to other persons, involved in the planning, financing, preparation or execution of such tender offer;

(ii) To the issuer whose securities are sought or to be sought by such tender offer, to its officers, directors, partners, employees or advisors or to other persons, involved in the planning, financing, preparation or execution of the activities of the issuer with respect to such tender offer; or

(iii) To any person pursuant to a requirement of any statute or rule or regulation promulgated thereunder.

(d)(2) The persons referred to in paragraph (d)(1) of this section are:

(i) The offering person or its officers, directors, partners, employees or advisors;

(ii) The issuer of the securities sought or to be sought by such tender offer or its officers, directors, partners, employees or advisors;

(iii) Anyone acting on behalf of the persons in paragraph (d)(2)(i) or the issuer or persons in paragraph (d)(2)(ii); and

(iv) Any person in possession of material information relating to a tender offer which information he knows or has reason to know is nonpublic and which he knows or has reason to know has been acquired directly or indirectly from any of the above.

SECURITIES EXCHANGE ACT RELEASE NO. 17120
September 4, 1980.

* * *

Rule 14e–3(a) establishes a "disclose or abstain from trading" rule under the Williams Act. A person who is in possession of material information that relates to a tender offer by another person which information he knows or has reason to know is nonpublic and which he also knows or has reason to know was acquired directly or indirectly from a person who has taken a substantial step or steps to commence or has commenced a tender offer (hereinafter also referred to as the "offering person"), the issuer whose securities are subject to the tender offer or any officer, director, partner or employee or any other person acting on behalf of the offering person or the issuer would be subject to the restrictions of the new rule. Any person subject to the rule would be prohibited from purchasing or selling or causing the purchase or sale of the securities to be sought or being sought in the tender offer unless within a reasonable period of time prior to the purchase or sale, the information and its source are publicly disclosed.

Rule 14e–3(b) provides that certain transactions by multi-service financial institutions under certain circumstances which would otherwise be proscribed will not violate Rule 14e–3(a). This exception is available for purchases or sales by multi-service institutions where the institution can show that the individuals making the investment decision did not know the information and that the institution has established policies and procedures reasonable under the circumstances to ensure that individual decision maker(s) would not violate Rule 14e–3(a).

Rule 14e–3(c) provides that certain transactions which would otherwise be proscribed will not violate Rule 14e–3(a). These exceptions include: (1) the execution by a broker or another agent on behalf of the offering person, and (2) sales by any person to the offering person.

Rule 14e–3(d) is designed to prevent leaks of material, nonpublic information relating to a tender offer. Rule 14e–3(d) provides that, as a means reasonably designed to prevent fraudulent, deceptive or manipulative acts or practices within the meaning of Section 14(e), it shall be unlawful for certain specified persons to communicate such information to persons under circumstances in which it is reasonably foreseeable that such communication is likely to result in a violation of Rule 14e–3. An exception to the rule provides that a communication made in good faith to certain other persons involved in the planning, financing, preparation or execution of the tender offer, to the issuer and certain affiliated persons or to any person pursuant to applicable statute will not violate Rule 14e–3(d).

Rule 14e–3(a) does not proscribe purchases or sales of securities to be sought or sought in a tender offer by the person who has taken a substantial step or steps to commence or has commenced the tender offer. The offering person will be subject to liability however, under Rule 14e–3(d) if he tips, i.e., communicates material, nonpublic information relating to a tender offer to someone under circumstances in which it is reasonably foreseeable that he may violate Rule 14e–3. Persons other than the offering person will also be subject to liability for tipping under Rule 14e–3(d).

* * *

1. *Operation of Rule 14e–3(a)*

The "disclose or abstain from trading" duty of Rule 14e–3(a) will arise if the following elements are present:

(a) If any person has taken a substantial step or steps to commence or has commenced a tender offer and another person is in possession of material information relating to such tender offer;

(b) which information the other person knows or has reason to know is nonpublic;

(c) which information the other person knows or has reason to know has been acquired directly or indirectly from the offering person, from the issuer of the securities sought or to be sought in such tender offer or from an officer, director, partner or employee or any other person acting on behalf of the offering person or the issuer; and

(d) the other person purchases or sells or causes the purchase or sale of any security to be sought or sought in such tender offer, or any other security convertible into or exchangeable for such security or any option or right to obtain or to dispose of such securities.

As adopted, the information which will trigger the operation of the Rule (1) must be material, (2) must relate to a tender offer, (3) must be nonpublic and (4) must have been acquired directly or indirectly from the offering person, from the issuer or from another specified person. For the last two requisites, there is a "knows or has reason to know" standard by the person who has possession of the information. For the first two requisites, i.e., materiality and relation to a tender offer, there is no "knows or has reason to know" standard.

In addition, Rule 14e–3(a) applies prior to the commencement of a tender offer as well as after an offer has commenced. Trading while in possession of material, nonpublic information prior to the commencement of a tender offer results in the same abuses and causes the same detrimental effects as trading during a tender offer. Since the scope of Section 14(e) applies to acts or practices "in connection with any tender offer," it was, in the Commission's judgment, intended that conduct prior to the date of commencement as well as during a tender offer be covered.

The operation of Rule 14e–3(a) may be illustrated by examples. It should be emphasized that these examples are not exclusive and do not constitute the only situations in which the duty under Rule 14e–3(a) would arise.

(1) If an offering person tells another person that the offering person will make a tender offer which information is nonpublic, the other person has acquired material, nonpublic information directly from the offering person and has a duty under Rule 14e–3(a).

(2) If an offering person delegates the authority to determine whether such offering person should take a substantial step or steps to commence or should commence a tender offer to an officer, employee, director or partner and such person decides to implement the tender offer, such person will be deemed to have acquired information relating to the tender offer from the offering person and therefore will have a duty under Rule 14e–3(a) to disclose or abstain from trading.

(3) If the offering person sends a nonpublic letter to a subject company notifying the subject company of a proposed tender offer at a specified price and upon specified terms and the management of the subject company learns the contents of the letter, the management of the subject company has acquired material, nonpublic information directly from the offering person. An individual member of such management will violate Rule 14e–3(a) if he purchases or sells or causes the purchase or sale of the securities to be sought in the tender offer.

(4) If, under the facts in the preceding example, the management of the subject company also tells other persons not affiliated with management of the letter, then those other persons have acquired material, nonpublic information indirectly from the offering person and are under a duty to disclose or abstain from trading under Rule 14e–3(a).

(5) If a person receives material information from the subject company relating to its response to another person's tender offer for the subject company's securities, such person will be under a duty to disclose or abstain from trading provided that such person knows or has reason to know the information is nonpublic.

(6) If a person steals, converts or otherwise misappropriates material, nonpublic information relating to a tender offer from an offering person, such person will have acquired the information directly from the offering person and has a duty under Rule 14e–3(a).

(7) If an offering person tells another person of his intention to make a tender offer, and such other person subsequently tells a third person that a tender offer will be made and this third person knows or has reason to know that this non-public information came indirectly from the offering person, then this third person has a duty under Rule 14e–3(a).

* * *

QUESTIONS

1. Is the market information about pending mergers and takeovers at which Rule 14e–3 is directed the same kind of efficiency enhancing information whose flow the Court sought to encourage in order to facilitate the analysts' function in bringing the market price of securities into line with "real" value in Dirks v. SEC, 463 U.S. 646 (1983)? Does the imminence of a merger offer a greater temptation for "insider" trading than information about expected corporate earnings?

2. Do the considerations supporting (and opposing) a requirement of "disclose or abstain" with respect to information about a pending merger or takeover by the assorted troops involved in the transaction differ from those supporting (and opposing) a similar requirement for corporate insiders with respect to expected corporate earnings or assets or other kinds of corporate developments?

(a) Should the same criteria determine who should be beneficiaries of such disclosure requirements and who should be denied trading advantages in each case?

(b) Should the answers to the above questions differ if the issue in suit is civil liability of the possessor of the information to persons with whom he may have traded than if it is whether he has violated the law?

3. Are Sections 13(e) and 14(e) subject to the same narrowing strictures derived from the concept of fiduciary duty to particular transactors which underlie the Supreme Court's interpretation of Section 10b and Rule 10b–5?

4. Can (does) the "in connection with" requirement of Section 14(e) cover use of information in anticipation of a tender offer that is considered but is aborted? Compare Applied Digital Data Systems, Inc. v. Milgo Electronic Corp., 425 F.Supp. 1145 (S.D.N.Y.1977), 425 F.Supp. 1163 (S.D.N.Y.1977) and Hanna Mining Co. v. Norcen Energy Resources Ltd., 574 F.Supp. 1172 (N.D.Ohio 1982) with Lewis v. McGraw, 619 F.2d 192 (2d Cir.1980), cert. denied, 449 U.S. 951 (1980) and Panter v. Marshall Field & Co., 646 F.2d 271 (7th Cir.1981), cert. denied, 454 U.S. 1092 (1981); compare Sanders v. Thrall Car Manufacturing Co., 582 F.Supp. 945 (S.D.N.Y.1983), aff'd, 730 F.2d 910 (2d Cir.1984).

UNITED STATES v. CHESTMAN

United States Court of Appeals, Second Circuit (en banc), 1991.
947 F.2d 551.

MESKILL, Circuit Judge, joined by CARDAMONE, PRATT, MIN-ER and ALTIMARI, Circuit Judges:

* * *

Robert Chestman is a stockbroker. Keith Loeb first sought Chestman's services in 1982, when Loeb decided to consolidate his and his wife's holdings in Waldbaum, Inc. (Waldbaum), a publicly traded company that owned a large supermarket chain. During their initial meeting, Loeb told Chestman that his wife was a granddaughter of Julia Waldbaum, a member of the board of directors of Waldbaum and the wife of its founder. Julia Waldbaum also was the mother of Ira Waldbaum, the president and controlling shareholder of Waldbaum. From 1982 to 1986, Chestman executed several transactions involving Waldbaum restricted and common stock for Keith Loeb. To facilitate some of these trades, Loeb sent Chestman a copy of his wife's birth certificate, which indicated that his wife's mother was Shirley Waldbaum Witkin.

On November 21, 1986, Ira Waldbaum agreed to sell Waldbaum to the Great Atlantic and Pacific Tea Company (A & P). The resulting stock purchase agreement required Ira to tender a controlling block of Waldbaum shares to A & P at a price of $50 per share. Ira told three of his children, all employees of Waldbaum, about the pending sale two days later, admonishing them to keep the news quiet until a public announcement. He also told his sister, Shirley Witkin, and nephew, Robert Karin, about the sale, and offered to tender their shares along with his controlling block of shares to enable them to avoid the administrative difficulty of tendering after the public announcement. He cautioned them "that [the sale was] not to be discussed," that it was to remain confidential.

In spite of Ira's counsel, Shirley told her daughter, Susan Loeb, on November 24 that Ira was selling the company. Shirley warned Susan not to tell anyone except her husband, Keith Loeb, because disclosure could ruin the sale. The next day, Susan told her husband about the pending tender offer and cautioned him not to tell anyone because "it could possibly ruin the sale."

The following day, November 26, Keith Loeb telephoned Robert Chestman at 8:59 a.m. Unable to reach Chestman, Loeb left a message asking Chestman to call him "ASAP." According to Loeb, he later spoke with Chestman between 9:00 a.m. and 10:30 a.m. that morning and told Chestman that he had "some definite, some accurate information" that Waldbaum was about to be sold at a "substantially higher" price than its market value. Loeb asked Chestman several times what he thought Loeb should do. Chestman responded that he could not advise Loeb what to do "in a situation like this" and that Loeb would have to make up his own mind.

That morning Chestman executed several purchases of Waldbaum stock. At 9:49 a.m., he bought 3,000 shares for his own account at $24.65 per share. Between 11:31 a.m. and 12:35 p.m., he purchased an additional 8,000 shares for his clients' discretionary accounts at prices ranging from $25.75 to $26.00 per share. One of the discretionary accounts was the Loeb account, for which Chestman bought 1,000 shares.

Before the market closed at 4:00 p.m., Loeb claims that he tele-phoned Chestman a second time. During their conversation Loeb again pressed Chestman for advice. Chestman repeated that he could not advise Loeb "in a situation like this," but then said that, based on his research, Waldbaum was a "buy." Loeb subsequently ordered 1,000 shares of Waldbaum stock. * * *

[On November 26, the tender offer was made, and Waldbaum stock rose to $49 per share.]

* * *

A grand jury returned an indictment on July 20, 1988, charging Chestman with the following counts of insider trading and perjury: ten counts of fraudulent trading in connection with a tender offer in violation of Rule 14e–3(a), ten counts of securities fraud in violation of Rule 10b–5, ten counts of mail fraud, and one count of perjury in connection with his testimony before the SEC. * * * After a jury trial, Chestman was found guilty on all counts.

* * *

DISCUSSION

A. *Rule 14e–3(a)*

     * * *

Chestman's first challenge concerns the validity of a rule pre-scribed by the SEC pursuant to a congressional delegation of rulemak-ing authority. The question presented is whether Rule 14e–3(a) repre-sents a proper exercise of the SEC's statutory authority. * * *

     * * *

One violates Rule 14e–3(a) if he trades on the basis of material nonpublic information concerning a pending tender offer that he knows or has reason to know has been acquired "directly or indirectly" from an insider of the offeror or issuer, or someone working on their behalf. Rule 14e–3(a) is a disclosure provision. It creates a duty in those traders who fall within its ambit to abstain or disclose, without regard to whether the trader owes a pre-existing fiduciary duty to respect the confidentiality of the information. Chestman claims that the SEC exceeded its authority in drafting Rule 14e–3(a)—more specifically, in drafting a rule that dispenses with one of the common law elements of fraud, breach of a fiduciary duty.

* * *

The plain language of section 14(e) represents a broad delegation of rulemaking authority. The statute explicitly directs the SEC to "define" fraudulent practices and to "prescribe means reasonably designed to prevent" such practices. It is difficult to see how the power to "define" fraud could mean anything less than the power to "set forth the meaning of" fraud in the tender offer context. See Webster's Third New International Dictionary 592 (1971). This delegation of rulemaking responsibility becomes a hollow gesture if we cabin the SEC's rulemaking authority, as Chestman urges we should, by common law definitions of fraud. Under Chestman's construction of the statute, the separate grant of rulemaking power would be rendered superfluous because the SEC could never define as fraud anything not already prohibited by the self-operative provision. Such a narrow construction of the congressional grant of authority would cramp the SEC's ability to define fraud flexibly in the context of the discrete and highly sensitive area of tender offers. And such a delegation of "power," paradoxically, would allow the SEC to limit, but not extend, a trader's duty to disclose.

Even if we were to accept the argument that the SEC's definitional authority is circumscribed by common law fraud, which we do not, the SEC's power to "prescribe means reasonably designed to prevent" fraud extends the agency's rulemaking authority further. The language of this portion of section 14(e) is clear. The verb "prevent" has a plain meaning: "[T]o keep from happening or existing esp[ecially] by precautionary measures." Webster's New Third International Dictionary 1798 (1971). A delegation of authority to enact rules "reasonably designed to prevent" fraud, then, necessarily encompasses the power to proscribe conduct outside the purview of fraud, be it common law or SEC-defined fraud. Because the operative words of the statute, "define" and "prevent," have clear connotations, the language of the statute is sufficiently clear to be dispositive here. *Chevron,* 467 U.S. at 842–43, 104 S.Ct. at 2781–82. We note, however, other factors that bolster our interpretation.

Nothing in the legislative history of section 14(e) indicates that the SEC frustrated congressional intent by enacting Rule 14e–3(a). To the contrary, what legislative history there is suggests that Congress intended to grant broad rulemaking authority to the SEC in this instance.

* * *

The legislative history of the 1970 amendment to section 14(e), the rulemaking provision, likewise suggests a broad grant of congressional authority. Senator Williams, the bill's sponsor, asserted the "utmost necessity" of granting "full rulemaking powers" to the SEC in the area of tender offers. 116 Cong.Rec. 3024 (Feb. 10, 1970). The amendment "would add to the Commission's rulemaking power," Senator Williams explained, "and enable it to deal promptly and * * * flexib[ly]" with problems in that area. Hearings on S.3431 before the Subcom. on Securities of the Senate Comm. on Banking and Currency, 91st Cong., 2nd Sess. 2 (1970) [hereinafter S.3431 Hearings]; see also H.R.Rep. No. 1655, 91st Cong., 2nd Sess. 4, reprinted in 1970 U.S.Code Cong. & Admin.News 5025, 5028. During hearings on the 1970 Amendment, moreover, Senator Williams asked the SEC chairman for "examples of the fraudulent, deceptive, or manipulative practices used in tender offers which the proposed [SEC] rulemaking powers would prevent," noting that the information "would be most helpful to the committee as we continue developing this legislation." S.3431 Hearings, at 11. Responding to the Senator's request, the SEC identified one such "problem" that the SEC's proposed rulemaking authority would be used to prevent:

> The person who has become aware that a tender bid is to be made, or has reason to believe that such bid will be made, may fail to disclose material facts with respect thereto to persons who sell to him securities for which the tender bid is to be made.

Id. at 12. Notably, this hypothetical does not contain any requirement that the trader breach a fiduciary duty. All told, the legislative history indicates that Congress intended to grant broad rulemaking power to the SEC under section 14(e). This delegation of authority was aimed at promoting full disclosure in the tender offer context and, in so doing, contributing to informed decisionmaking by shareholders.

In promulgating Rule 14e–3(a), the SEC acted well within the letter and spirit of section 14(e). Recognizing the highly sensitive nature of tender offer information, its susceptibility to misuse, and the often difficult task of ferreting out and proving fraud, Congress sensibly delegated to the SEC broad authority to delineate a penumbra around the fuzzy subject of tender offer fraud. See generally Loewenstein, Section 14(e) of the Williams Act and the Rule 10b–5 Comparisons, 71 Geo.L.J. 1311, 1356 (1983) ("It is difficult to see why Congress would grant such broad powers to the SEC if the SEC was not expected to have some leeway in utilizing its powers."). To be certain, the SEC's rulemaking power under this broad grant of authority is not unlimited. The rule must still be "reasonably related to the purposes of the enabling legislation." Mourning v. Family Publications Service, Inc., 411 U.S. 356, 369 (1973) (quoting Thorpe v. Housing Authority of the City of Durham, 393 U.S. 268, 280–81 (1969)). The SEC, however, in adopting Rule 14e–3(a), acted consistently with this authority. While dispensing with the subtle problems of proof associated with demonstrating fiduciary breach in the problematic area of tender offer insider trading, the Rule retains a close nexus between the prohibited conduct and the statutory aims.

Legislative activity since the SEC promulgated Rule 14e–3(a) further supports the Rule's validity. * * *

[The] * * * references to Rule 14e–3 during debates on proposed insider trading legislation may not amount to congressional ratification of the Rule, see Red Lion Broadcasting Co. v. FCC, 395 U.S. 367, 381–82, 89 S.Ct. 1794, 1801–03, 23 L.Ed.2d 371 (1969), but they do support the Rule's validity. Congressional silence in the face of administrative construction of a statute lends support to the validity of that interpretation. * * *

In sum, the language and legislative history of section 14(e), as well as congressional inactivity toward it since the SEC promulgated Rule 14e–3(a), all support the view that Congress empowered the SEC to prescribe a rule that extends beyond the common law.

Chestman points to nothing in the language or legislative history of section 14(e) to refute our construction of the statute. Instead he relies principally on Chiarella v. United States, 445 U.S. 222 (1980), and *Schreiber,* 472 U.S. 1, to advance his argument that section 14(e) parallels common law fraud. That reliance is misplaced.

Chiarella considered whether trading stock on the basis of material nonpublic information in the absence of a fiduciary breach constitutes fraud under section 10(b). Confronted with both congressional and SEC silence on the issue, see section 10(b) and Rule 10b–5, the Court applied common law principles of fraud. It concluded, based on those principles, that liability under section 10(b) requires a fiduciary breach.

Several factors limit *Chiarella's* precedential value in this case. First, *Chiarella* of course concerns section 10(b), not section 14(e). Section 10(b) is a general antifraud statute, while section 14(e) is an antifraud provision specifically tailored to the field of tender offers, an area of the securities industry that, the Williams Act makes clear, deserves special regulation.

Second, section 14(e) evinces a clear indication of congressional intent, while section 10(b) does not. * * * Section 10(b) speaks in terms of the use "in connection with the purchase or sale of any security" of "any manipulative or deceptive device or contrivance in contravention of such rules and regulations as the [SEC] may prescribe as necessary or appropriate in the public interest or for the protection of investors." 15 U.S.C. § 78j(b). Section 14(e) directly proscribes, in self-operative fashion, "any fraudulent, deceptive, or manipulative acts or practices" in connection with a tender offer. Then, in a separate sentence, the statute directs the SEC to draft rules to define these practices and to prevent them: "The [SEC] shall, for the purposes of this subsection, by rules and regulations define, and prescribe means reasonably designed to prevent, such acts and practices as are fraudulent, deceptive, or manipulative." The contrast in statutory language is telling. It underscores, first of all, the dubious premise of Chestman's argument—that section 14(e) was modeled after section 10(b). The two provisions are hardly identical in scope. The language of section 14(e)'s rulemaking provision, instead of tracking section 10(b), in fact mirrors section 15(c)(2), 15 U.S.C. § 78o(c)(2), which concerns broker-dealer relations. "The language of the addition to section 14(e) is identical to that contained in section 15(c)(2) of the Securities Exchange Act concerning practices of brokers and dealers in securities transactions in the over-the-counter markets." H.R.Rep. No. 1655, 91st Cong., 2nd Sess. 4, reprinted in 1970 U.S.Code Cong. & Admin.News 5025, 5028. The contrast also illustrates that section 14(e) provides a more compelling legislative delegation to the SEC to prescribe rules than does section 10(b). While section 10(b) refers to such rules as the SEC "may prescribe as necessary or appropriate," section 14(e) commands the SEC to prescribe rules that will "define" and "prevent" fraud. See Loewenstein, supra, 71 Geo.L.J. at 1356 ("By comparison, the Commission's rulemaking authority under section 10(b) does not include the power to define manipulative or deceptive" acts or to adopt prophylatic measures.).

* * *

Finally, *Chiarella* faced not only statutory silence on the issue before it but also administrative reticence. Neither the language of Rule 10b–5, SEC discussions of the rule, nor administrative interpretations of the rule offered any evidence that the SEC, in drafting Rule 10b–5, intended the rule to go beyond common law fraud. See Rule 10b–5 (referring to "artifice to defraud" and to "fraud * * * upon any person"); see also *Chiarella,* 445 U.S. at 226 ("When Rule 10b–5 was promulgated in 1942, the SEC did not discuss the possibility that failure to provide information might run afoul of § 10(b).") (footnote omitted); id. at 230; id. 445 U.S. at 233 ("neither the Congress nor the Commission ever has adopted a parity-of-information rule"). The language of Rule 14e–3(a), on the other hand, reveals express SEC intent to proscribe conduct not covered by common law fraud. And "[p]resumably the SEC perceived Rule 14e–3 as a valid exercise of its statutory authority." United States v. Marcus Schloss & Co., Inc., 710 F.Supp. 944, 956 (S.D.N.Y.1989).

Thus, the question presented here differs markedly from that presented in *Chiarella.* It is not whether section 14(e), standing alone, prohibits insider trading in the absence of a fiduciary breach. It is whether section 14(e)'s broad rulemaking provision, together with SEC action under that authority in the form of Rule 14e–3(a), represent a valid exercise of administrative rulemaking. In *Chiarella,* the Court refused to recognize "a general duty between all participants in market transactions to forgo actions based on material nonpublic information * * * absent some explicit evidence of congressional intent." 445 U.S. at 233. Our task is easier. Rule 14e–3(a) creates a narrower duty than that once proposed for Rule 10b–5—a parity of information rule—and, as the language and legislative history of section 14(e) make clear, the rule has Congress' blessing.

Equally unavailing is Chestman's reliance on *Schreiber.* * * *

Chestman claims that *Schreiber* demonstrates that section 14(e), like section 10(b), projects no further than common law fraud. To support this argument, he points to a statement in *Schreiber* indicating that section 14(e) is "modeled on the antifraud provisions of § 10(b)." Id. at 10, 105 S.Ct. at 2463. What Chestman ignores, however, is that *Schreiber* contrasted as well as compared the two statutes. Following the language Chestman quotes, the Court stated that section 14(e) "supplements" the other disclosure provisions in the Williams Act and requires "disclosure more explicitly addressed to the tender offer context than that required by § 10(b)." Id. at 10–11. In addition, the Court's reference to the similarity between sections 10(b) and 14(e) only refers to section 14(e)'s substantive provision. Section 10(b), as we have emphasized, lacks a separate rulemaking grant akin to section 14(e). Moreover, even to the extent section 10(b) may be accurately described as the father of section 14(e), as well as all later antifraud provisions under the 1934 Act, we cannot agree that section 10(b) therefore confines section 14(e), and its other antifraud progeny, to an identical reach.

Chestman also attempts to draw support from footnote 11 in *Schreiber*. There, in rejecting petitioner's argument that the 1970 amendment to section 14(e), the rulemaking provision, would be meaningless if section 14(e) concerned disclosure only, the Court observed:

> In adding the 1970 amendment, Congress simply provided a mechanism for defining and guarding against those acts and practices which involve material misrepresentation or nondisclosure. The amendment gives the [SEC] latitude to regulate nondeceptive activities as a "reasonably designed" means of preventing manipulative acts, without suggesting any change in the meaning of the term "manipulative" itself.

Id. at 11 n. 11. Whatever may be gleaned from the footnote on the SEC's definitional authority under section 14(e), the footnote plainly endorses the SEC's authority to draft prophylactic rules under section 14(e). It states that the rulemaking provision "gives the [SEC] latitude to regulate *nondeceptive* activities as a 'reasonably designed' means of preventing manipulative acts." Id. (emphasis added). Chestman offers no persuasive explanation why the authority "to regulate nondeceptive activities" would not also allow the SEC to regulate *nonfraudulent* conduct.

As for the SEC's authority to define the operative words of section 14(e), *Schreiber* seems to be saying only that section 14(e)'s rulemaking provision does not itself change the common law meaning of "manipulative." The Court was not confronted with the question raised here— whether SEC action pursuant to the rulemaking delegation exceeds statutory authority—because the petitioner did not point to any SEC rules drafted under section 14(e) that covered Burlington's activities. Moreover, even if we were to agree with Chestman that, under *Schreiber*, the common law confines the SEC in defining "manipulative," we would still uphold the validity of Rule 14e–3(a). In *Schreiber*, the definition of "manipulative" proffered by the plaintiff would have eliminated a requirement that there be a nondisclosure or material misrepresentation, the primary evils at which section 14(e) took aim. Rule 14e–3(a), in contrast, does not stray from congressional intent; it remains a disclosure provision.

* * *

B. *Rule 10b–5*

* * * With respect to the shares Chestman purchased on behalf of Keith Loeb, Chestman was convicted of aiding and abetting Loeb's misappropriation of nonpublic information in breach of a duty Loeb owed to the Waldbaum family and to his wife Susan. As to the shares Chestman purchased for himself and his other clients, Chestman was convicted as a "tippee" of that same misappropriated information. Thus, while Chestman is the defendant in this case, the alleged misappropriator was Keith Loeb. The government agrees that Chestman's convictions cannot be sustained unless there was sufficient evidence to show that (1) Keith Loeb breached a duty owed to the Waldbaum family or Susan Loeb based on a fiduciary or similar relationship of trust and confidence, and (2) Chestman knew that Loeb had done so. We have heretofore never applied the misappropriation theory—and its predicate requirement of a fiduciary breach—in the context of family relationships. As a prologue to that analysis, we canvass past Rule 10b–5 jurisprudence.

1. Traditional Theory of Rule 10b–5 Liability

The traditional theory of insider trader liability derives principally from the Supreme Court's holdings in *Chiarella*, 445 U.S. 222, and *Dirks v. SEC*, 463 U.S. 646 (1983). A securities trader commits Rule 10b–5 fraud, the *Chiarella* Court held, only if he "fails to disclose material information prior to the consummation of a transaction * * * when he is under a duty to do so." *Chiarella*, 445 U.S. at 228. The *Chiarella* Court then delineated when a person possessing material nonpublic information owes such a duty—what it called "[t]he obligation to disclose or abstain" from trading. Id. at 227. It held that this duty "does not arise from the mere possession of nonpublic market information." Id. at 235. That is, the duty inquiry does not turn on whether the parties to the transaction have "equal information." *Dirks*, 463 U.S. at 657 (construing *Chiarella*). Rather, a duty to disclose or abstain arises only from " 'a fiduciary or other similar relation of trust and confidence between [the parties to the transaction].' " *Chiarella*, 445 U.S. at 228 (quoting Restatement (Second) of Torts § 551(2)(a) (1976)).

In *Dirks*, an action concerning the liability of a tippee of material nonpublic information, the Court built on its holding in *Chiarella*. *Dirks* again rejected a parity of information theory of Rule 10b–5 liability, reiterating the "requirement of a specific relationship between the shareholders and the individual trading on inside information." *Dirks*, 463 U.S. at 655. It then examined when a tippee inherits a fiduciary duty to the corporation's shareholders to disclose or refrain from trading. Noting the "derivative" nature of tippee liability, id. at 659, the Court held that tippee liability attaches only when an "insider has breached his fiduciary duty to the shareholders by disclosing the information to the tippee and the tippee knows or should know that there has been a breach." Id. at 660.

Dirks established, in *dictum,* an additional means by which erstwhile outsiders become fiduciaries of a corporation's shareholders. Justice Powell explained:

> Under certain circumstances, such as where corporate information is revealed legitimately to an underwriter, accountant, lawyer, or consultant working for the corporation, these outsiders may become fiduciaries of the shareholders. The basis for recognizing this fiduciary duty is not simply that such persons acquired nonpublic corporate information, but rather that they have entered into a special confidential relationship in the conduct of the business of the enterprise and are given access to information solely for corporate purposes * * *. For such a duty to be imposed, however, the corporation must expect the outsider to keep the disclosed nonpublic information confidential, and the relationship at least must imply such a duty.

Id. at 655 n. 14, 103 S.Ct. at 3262 n. 14 (citations omitted). This theory clothes an outsider with temporary insider status when the outsider obtains access to confidential information solely for corporate purposes in the context of "a special confidential relationship." The temporary insider thereby acquires a correlative fiduciary duty to the corporation's shareholders.

Binding these strands of Rule 10b–5 liability are two principles— one, the predicate act of fraud must be traceable to a breach of duty to the purchasers or sellers of securities, two, a fiduciary duty does not run to the purchasers or sellers solely as a result of one's possession of material nonpublic information.

2. Misappropriation Theory

The second general theory of Rule 10b–5 liability, the misappropriation theory, has not yet been the subject of a Supreme Court holding, but has been adopted in the Second, Third, Seventh and Ninth Circuits. See, e.g., SEC v. Cherif, 933 F.2d 403 (7th Cir.1991); SEC v. Clark, 915 F.2d 439 (9th Cir.1990); Rothberg v. Rosenbloom, 771 F.2d 818 (3d Cir.1985), rev'd on other grounds after remand, 808 F.2d 252 (3d Cir.1986), cert. denied, 481 U.S. 1017 (1987); United States v. Newman, 664 F.2d 12 (2d Cir.1981), aff'd after remand, 722 F.2d 729 (2d Cir.1983), cert. denied, 464 U.S. 863, 104 S.Ct. 193 (1983). Under this theory, a person violates Rule 10b–5 when he misappropriates material nonpublic information in breach of a fiduciary duty or similar relationship of trust and confidence and uses that information in a securities transaction. See, e.g., *Carpenter,* 791 F.2d at 1028–29; *Materia,* 745 F.2d at 201; *Newman,* 664 F.2d at 17–18. In contrast to *Chiarella* and *Dirks,* the misappropriation theory does not require that the buyer or seller of securities be defrauded. *Newman,* 664 F.2d at 17. Focusing on the language "fraud or deceit upon *any* person" (emphasis added), we have held that the predicate act of fraud may be perpetrated on the source of the nonpublic information, even though the source may be unaffiliated with the buyer or seller of securities. See *Carpenter,* 791 F.2d at 1032. To date we have applied the theory only in the context of employment relationships. See *Carpenter,* 791 F.2d at 1032 (financial columnist breached duty to his newspaper); *Materia,* 745 F.2d at 202 (copyholder breached duty to his printing company); *Newman,* 664 F.2d at 17 (investment banker breached duty to his firm). District courts in this Circuit have applied the theory in other settings as well as in the employment context. See, e.g., United States v. Willis, 737 F.Supp. 269 (S.D.N.Y.1990) (denying motion to dismiss indictment of psychiatrist who traded on the basis of information obtained from patient, in breach of duty arising from relationship of trust and confidence); United States v. Reed, 601 F.Supp. 685 (S.D.N.Y.), rev'd on other grounds, 773 F.2d 477 (2d Cir.1985) (allegation that son breached fiduciary duty to father, a corporate director, withstood motion to dismiss indictment); SEC v. Musella, 578 F.Supp. 425 (S.D.N.Y.1984) (office services manager of law firm breached duty to law firm and its clients by trading on the basis of material nonpublic information acquired in the course of his employment).

* * *

* * * In *Carpenter* none of the prongs of liability under the traditional theory applied. That is, the defendants did not owe the people with whom they traded a duty to disclose or abstain from trading— absent resurrection of the twice-rejected parity of information theory. *Carpenter,* then, represents the first fact pattern we have considered that is clearly beyond the pale of the traditional theory of insider trading.

After *Carpenter,* the fiduciary relationship question takes on special importance. This is because a fraud-on-the-source theory of liability extends the focus of Rule 10b–5 beyond the confined sphere of fiduciary/shareholder relations to fiduciary breaches of any sort, a particularly broad expansion of 10b–5 liability if the add-on, a "similar relationship of trust and confidence," is construed liberally. One concern triggered by this broadened inquiry is that fiduciary duties are circumscribed with some clarity in the context of shareholder relations but lack definition in other contexts. * * * Tethered to the field of shareholder relations, fiduciary obligations arise within a narrow, principled sphere. The existence of fiduciary duties in other common law settings, however, is anything but clear. Our Rule 10b–5 precedents under the misappropriation theory, moreover, provide little guidance with respect to the question of fiduciary breach, because they involved egregious fiduciary breaches arising solely in the context of employer/employee associations. See *Carpenter,* 791 F.2d at 1028 ("It is clear that defendant Winans * * * breached a duty of confidentiality to his employer"); *Newman,* 664 F.2d at 17 ("we need spend little time on the issue of fraud and deceit"); *Materia,* 745 F.2d at 201 (same). For these reasons we tread cautiously in extending the misappropriation theory to new relationships, lest our efforts to construe Rule 10b–5 lose method and predictability, taking over "the whole corporate universe." United States v. Chiarella, 588 F.2d 1358, 1377 (2d Cir.1978) (Meskill, J., dissenting) (quoting Santa Fe Industries, Inc. v. Green, 430 U.S. 462, 480 (1977)), rev'd, 445 U.S. 222 (1980).

3. Fiduciary Duties and Their Functional Equivalent

Against this backdrop, we turn to our central inquiry—what constitutes a fiduciary or similar relationship of trust and confidence in the context of Rule 10b–5 criminal liability? We begin by noting two factors that do not themselves create the necessary relationship.

First, a fiduciary duty cannot be imposed unilaterally by entrusting a person with confidential information. * * * Second, marriage does not, without more, create a fiduciary relationship. * * * In sum, more than the gratuitous reposal of a secret to another who happens to be a family member is required to establish a fiduciary or similar relationship of trust and confidence.

We take our cues as to what is required to create the requisite relationship from the securities fraud precedents and the common law. See *Chiarella,* 445 U.S. at 227–30. The common law has recognized that some associations are inherently fiduciary. Counted among these hornbook fiduciary relations are those existing between attorney and client, executor and heir, guardian and ward, principal and agent, trustee and trust beneficiary, and senior corporate official and shareholder. * * * [I]t is clear that the relationships involved in this case— those between Keith and Susan Loeb and between Keith Loeb and the Waldbaum family—were not traditional fiduciary relationships.

That does not end our inquiry, however. The misappropriation theory requires us to consider not only whether there exists a fiduciary relationship but also whether there exists a "similar relationship of trust and confidence." As the term "similar" implies, a "relationship of trust and confidence" must share the essential characteristics of a fiduciary association. * * * A fiduciary relationship involves discretionary authority and dependency: One person depends on another— the fiduciary—to serve his interests. In relying on a fiduciary to act for his benefit, the beneficiary of the relation may entrust the fiduciary with custody over property of one sort or another. Because the fiduciary obtains access to this property to serve the ends of the fiduciary relationship, he becomes duty-bound not to appropriate the property for his own use. What has been said of an agent's duty of confidentiality applies with equal force to other fiduciary relations: "an agent is subject to a duty to the principal not to use or to communicate information confidentially given him by the principal or acquired by him during the course of or on account of his agency." Restatement (Second) of Agency § 395 (1958). These characteristics represent the measure of the paradigmatic fiduciary relationship. A similar relationship of trust and confidence consequently must share these qualities.

* * *

We recognize, as *Reed* did, that equity has occasionally established a less rigorous threshold for a fiduciary-like relationship in order to right civil wrongs arising from non-compliance with the statute of frauds, statute of wills and parol evidence rule.   * * * Commenting on the boundless nature of relations of trust and confidence, one scholar observed:

> Equity has never bound itself by any hard and fast definition of the phrase "confidential relation" and has not listed all the necessary elements of such a relation, but has reserved discretion to apply the doctrine whenever it believes that a suitable occasion has arisen.

Reed, 601 F.Supp. at 712 n. 38 (quoting G.G. Bogert, The Law of Trusts and Trustees § 482, at 284–86 (Rev. 2d ed. 1978)). Useful as such an elastic and expedient definition of confidential relations, i.e., relations of trust and confidence, may be in the civil context, it has no place in the criminal law. A "suitable occasion" test for determining the presence of criminal fraud would offend not only the rule of lenity but due process as well. * * *

4. Application of the Law of Fiduciary Duties

* * *

We have little trouble finding the evidence insufficient to establish a fiduciary relationship or its functional equivalent between Keith Loeb and the Waldbaum family. The government presented only two pieces of evidence on this point. The first was that Keith was an extended member of the Waldbaum family, specifically the family patriarch's (Ira Waldbaum's) "nephew-in-law." The second piece of evidence concerned Ira's discussions of the business with family members. "My children," Ira Waldbaum testified, "have always been involved with me and my family and they know we never speak about business outside of the family." His earlier testimony indicates that the "family" to which he referred were his "three children who were involved in the business."

[This evidence] falls short of establishing the relationship necessary for fiduciary obligations. Kinship alone does not create the necessary relationship. The government proffered nothing more to establish a fiduciary-like association. It did not show that Keith Loeb had been brought into the family's inner circle, whose members, it appears, discussed confidential business information either because they were kin or because they worked together with Ira Waldbaum. Keith was not an employee of Waldbaum and there was no showing that he participated in confidential communications regarding the business. The critical information was gratuitously communicated to him. The disclosure did not serve the interests of Ira Waldbaum, his children or the Waldbaum company. Nor was there any evidence that the alleged relationship was characterized by influence or reliance of any sort. * * *

The government's theory that Keith breached a fiduciary duty of confidentiality to Susan suffers from similar defects. The evidence showed: Keith and Susan were married; Susan admonished Keith not to disclose that Waldbaum was the target of a tender offer; and the two had shared and maintained confidences in the past.

Keith's status as Susan's husband could not itself establish fiduciary status. Nor, absent a pre-existing fiduciary relation or an express agreement of confidentiality, could the coda—"Don't tell." That leaves the unremarkable testimony that Keith and Susan had shared and maintained generic confidences before. The jury was not told the nature of these past disclosures and therefore it could not reasonably find a relationship that inspired fiduciary, rather than normal marital, obligations.

In the absence of evidence of an explicit acceptance by Keith of a duty of confidentiality, the context of the disclosure takes on special import. While acceptance may be implied, it must be implied from a pre-existing fiduciary-like relationship between the parties. Here the government presented the jury with insufficient evidence from which to draw a rational inference of implied acceptance. Susan's disclosure of the information to Keith served no purpose, business or otherwise. The disclosure also was unprompted. Keith did not induce her to convey the information through misrepresentation or subterfuge. Superiority and reliance, moreover, did not mark this relationship either before or after the disclosure of the confidential information. Nor did Susan's dependence on Keith to act in her interests for some purpose inspire the disclosure. The government failed even to establish a pattern of sharing business confidences between the couple. The government, therefore, failed to offer sufficient evidence to establish the functional equivalent of a fiduciary relation.

In sum, because Keith owed neither Susan nor the Waldbaum family a fiduciary duty or its functional equivalent, he did not defraud them by disclosing news of the pending tender offer to Chestman. Absent a predicate act of fraud by Keith Loeb, the alleged misappropriator, Chestman could not be derivatively liable as Loeb's tippee or as an aider and abettor. Therefore, Chestman's Rule 10b–5 convictions must be reversed.

* * *

[Opinion of Winter, J. (joined by Oakes, C.J., and Newman, Kearse, and McLaughlin, J.J.) dissenting on Rule 10b–5 omitted.]

———

See also SEC v. Peters, 978 F.2d 1162, CCH Fed.Sec.L.Rep. ¶ 97,045 (10th Cir.1992) (in accord with *Chestman* on the matter of SEC authority to promulgate Rule 14e–3).

———

4. MANAGEMENT DEFENSIVE TACTICS AND MANAGEMENT DUTIES UNDER STATE CORPORATE LAW

(A) DEFENSIVE TACTICS AND STRUCTURAL PROVISIONS OF CORPORATE LAW

(1) Shareholder Voting

Defensive provisions such as shark repellent charter amendments require shareholder approval. The determination of the validity of such amendments can raise questions as to whether (a) adequate disclosure is made to the shareholders, and (b) the shareholders have free choice in approving the amendment. The operation of the proxy system is more likely to satisfy these two conditions in the context of a defensive action taken in anticipation of bids than of action that management seeks from shareholders in other contexts. Shareholders, and particularly institutional holders, tend to be more alert to their interests and more likely to vote against management with respect to anti-takeover amendments than in normal election contests. Schrager, Corporate Conflicts: Proxy Fights in the '80s (1986). If an amendment is sought *after* a bid is made, there is an even larger likelihood of free choice by stockholders, cf. Asarco Inc. v. MRH Holmes A Court, 611 F.Supp. 468 (D.N.J.1985), if not larger likelihood of adequate disclosure by management. In any event, courts appear to be unlikely to find inadequate disclosure to, or inadequate freedom of choice for, stockholders when such amendments are adopted, whether before or after a bid.

Sometimes, particularly in recent years, hostile actors mount direct assaults on incumbents by soliciting proxies for their own slates of directors or restructuring proposals. The combination of a poison pill plan and a state antitakeover statute makes a frontal assault on control by means of the purchase of shares disadvantageous. The purchase of large blocks of shares triggers the rights under the pill, putting the bidder in the awkward position of demanding redemption of the rights by the target board. Antitakeover statutes disable purchasers of substantial blocks of stock from making subsequent mergers. Delaware's statute, Del.Gen.Corp.L. section 203, for example, provides that the acquisition of a block of target stock greater than 15 percent but less than 85 percent triggers a three year freeze on a subsequent merger with the target subject to release only by action of the defending board or a supermajority vote of the disinterested shareholders. These barriers caused proxy fights to reappear on the front lines of corporate control battles. The hostile party either states an intention to effect a restructuring that creates shareholder value, or announces a heavily conditioned tender offer. Then the hostile party attempts to elect a majority of the board, or, in the case of a staggered board, to combine the election of a slate with the removal of incumbents. See NCR Corp. v. American Telephone & Telegraph Co., 761 F.Supp. 475 (S.D.Ohio

1991). A proxy fight ensues, with the merits of the restructuring or tender offer on the table as the issue for discussion. Victory for the hostile challenger's slate means board action to redeem the rights under the pill and make the necessary waivers of application of the antitakeover statute.

Procedural maneuvers by defending managers that have the effect of forestalling such exercises of the shareholder franchise occasionally have been subjected to special judicial scrutiny. Over all, however, courts have done little to restrain directors' actions to manipulate the terms of stockholder access to (or use of) the voting process in order to thwart or impede stockholder choice.

In **Blasius Industries, Inc. v. Atlas Corp.**, 564 A.2d 651 (Del.Ch. 1988), the Delaware Chancellor purported to require "compelling justification" for such Board action instead of testing it under the permissive business judgment standard. There Blasius, a holder of 9.1 percent of Atlas stock, delivered to the Board a form of stockholder consent to increase the size of the board from 7 to 15 (its maximum permissible size under the Atlas charter) and elect 8 new members. The board thwarted Blasius by amending the by-laws to increase the size of the board by 2 and electing 2 new directors before the stockholder consent could be acted upon. Chancellor Allen was unable to find "compelling justification" for the board action, notwithstanding his conclusion that the board acted with appropriate care and in good faith. Concluding that the primary purpose of the board action was to prevent or impede the desires of an unaffiliated majority of the stock, he set aside the board action.

Soon after *Blasius,* the Chancellor receded from this stated concern for the protection of stockholder suffrage and reverted to a more characteristic concern for board power to protect stockholders from their own imprudent choices. In **Stahl v. Apple Bancorp, Inc.**, 579 A.2d 1115 (Del.Ch.1990), he declined to cancel a board's defensive postponement of the annual stockholders' meeting. The postponement obstructed the effort of Stahl, a 30 percent stockholder, to conduct a proxy fight and tender offer. The board asserted that postponement would give the stockholders time to consider alternatives to Stahl's proposals—alternatives for which the board was searching at the time. The Chancellor retreated from his previously announced requirement of the need for a "compelling justification" of the board's obstruction of stockholder suffrage to a much less demanding standard. He also was unable to find that the board had acted "for the primary purpose of impairing or impeding the effective exercise of the corporate franchise." See also Stahl v. Apple Bancorp Inc., CCH Fed.Sec.L.Rep. ¶ 95,412 (Del.Ch.1990); Stroud v. Grace, 606 A.2d 75 (Del.1992). Compare American Hardware Corp. v. Savage Arms Corp., 37 Del. 59, 136 A.2d 690 (1957) (upholding management maneuver denying stockholder choice), with Condec v. Lunkenheimer Co., 43 Del.Ch. 353, 230 A.2d 769 (1967) (preventing management from thwarting majority). But cf. Schnell v. Chris–Craft Industries, 285 A.2d 437 (Del.Sup.1971) (enjoining management from thwarting stockholder vote in circumstances comparable to *Stahl*).

(2) Structural Limits

The legality of antitakeover defenses involving charter or by law amendments depends in the first instance on enabling statutory provisions. The courts, informed by Delaware's tradition of "independent" reading of the separate provisions of state corporation law, tend to read these liberally. The validation of poison pill plans in Moran v. Household International, Inc., infra p. 1080, demonstrates this. The *Moran* court could, consistently with the language and origins of blank check preferred stock, have interpreted the provision in question to preclude its being fashioned into a poison pill. But the tradition of reading corporate statutes as broadly enabling has led even those courts that have invalidated poison pills to confirm the sufficiency of the blank check. See Asarco v. MRH Holmes A Court, 611 F.Supp. 468 (D.N.J. 1985).

Statutory technicalities have been successfully invoked to invalidate defensive provisions only on isolated occasions. **Georgia–Pacific Corp. v. Great Northern Nekoosa Corp.,** 731 F.Supp. 38 (D.Me.1990), presents a rare instance in which a court reaches out for a narrow reading of a corporation statute's enabling scope. The court there invalidated a shareholder-approved charter provision requiring a 75 percent shareholder vote for the removal of a director. It made reference to the Maine statute's specific provision for removal by a two-thirds shareholder vote. In the court's view, the "specific" provision for two thirds removal took interpretive precedence over the statute's "general" allowance of supermajority voting provisions by charter or by law amendment.

Bank of New York Co. v. Irving Bank Corp., 139 Misc.2d 665, 528 N.Y.S.2d 482 (1988), aff'd, 143 A.D.2d 1070, 533 N.Y.S.2d 411 (1988), which invalidates a poison pill, bears comparison. The pill in question provided the rights could be redeemed only by a majority of class of "continuing directors," defined as incumbents as of the date of distribution of the rights and successors elected by a two-thirds vote. The court construed this provision as a limitation of the power of the board to manage the business of the corporation, which under NYBCL section 620 required a certificate amendment and 100 percent shareholder vote. In addition, the supermajority requirement for the status of "qualifying director" was construed to conflict with NYBCL section 614's requirement of a full-blown certificate amendment. Does the New York court's characterization of these pill provisions entail a more defensible interpretive leap than the *Georgia–Pacific* court's interpretation of the Maine statute? The interpretation in *Bank of New York* can be defended on an additional ground. It advances an underlying statutory norm—that major changes in structure and voting rights should be approved by the shareholders. See also Minstar Acquiring Corp. v. AMF, Inc., 621 F.Supp. 1252 (S.D.N.Y.1985). New York's legislature, however, was unimpressed and responded with provisions sanctioning pill plans explicitly.   See NYBCL sections 4603(a) and 912(a)(10).

Other cases invalidate defensive provisions for noncompliance with other overarching norms deemed part of the substance of state corporation laws.   A few successful attacks have been based on the ground that rights plans discriminate among holders of the same class of stock. Here a leading case is **Asarco, Inc. v. MRH Holmes A Court**, 611 F.Supp. 468 (D.N.J.1985), applying New Jersey law.   The rights plan in question provided for a new series of preferred stock carrying no voting rights unless acquired by a holder of 20 percent of either the issuer's common stock or the preferred issue itself.   In that event, each holder of the preferred other than the 20 percent holder received five votes on all matters.   The plan was invalidated on the ground that the state statute permitted voting differentials only as among classes or series of stock.   See also Minstar Acquiring Corp. v. AMF, Inc., 621 F.Supp. 1252 (S.D.N.Y.1985) (nontransferable rights issue improperly discriminates against shareholders purchasing stock after record date); Amalgamated Sugar Co. v. NL Industries, Inc., 644 F.Supp. 1229 (S.D.N.Y.1986).   The Delaware courts, in contrast, accept the proposition that the vote per share attached to homogenized shares of a single class may be reduced as the number of shares of a particular owner increases.   See Providence & Worcester Co. v. Baker, 378 A.2d 121 (Del.1977).   See also Dynamics Corp. of America v. CTS Corp., 805 F.2d 705, 717–718 (7th Cir.1986) affirmed, 481 U.S. 69 (1987).

Finally, charter restrictions that restrict the transfer of rights have been successfully attacked as prohibited restraints on alienation.   See Unilever Acquisition Corp. v. Richardson–Vicks, Inc., 618 F.Supp. 407 (S.D.N.Y.1985) (invoking Del.Gen.Corp.L. section 202(b) requirement of shareholder approval of transfer restriction);   Minstar Acquiring Corp. v. AMF, Inc., supra.   On the other hand, Revlon, Inc. v. MacAndrews & Forbes Holdings, Inc., infra p. 1095, confirms the validity of rights that cannot be transferred to a later acquirer under Delaware law.

(B) THE DUTY OF LOYALTY

---

(1) Introduction: Defensive Tactics and Business Judgment— The Evolution of the Delaware Rule

Two opposing possibilities present themselves when managers defend themselves and their firms from takeovers.   At one pole, these actions could be promoting management's interest in entrenching itself. At the other pole, these actions could be taken to facilitate higher values for the benefit of the shareholders.   If, at the one pole, management can be found to seek *only* to perpetuate its own hold on office or to bargain for side payments or advantageous purchases for itself, the defensive action and any related use of corporate assets violates elementary notions of fiduciary obligation. If, at the other pole, management can be found to seek *only* to protect or enhance stockholder wealth, the action and any related use of corporate assets should be regulated only by conceptions of waste and the business judgment rule. Since both possibilities usually are present, both intrinsic fairness scrutiny and the business judgment rule come to bear as the duty of loyalty is articulated in the context of takeover defense.

The triggers that govern the business judgment rule's application in this context have been set and reset as the Delaware courts have negotiated a route between the two poles. The first version of their test was formulated in **Cheff v. Mathes,** 41 Del.Ch. 494, 199 A.2d 548 (1964), an early greenmail case. The *Cheff* rule made a variant of the business judgment shield available to defending managers. The plaintiff had an initial burden to show that management had a personal interest in the defense of the corporation. This was not a difficult showing for a plaintiff to make, since managers defend their own corporate positions by virtue of defending the firm. Once the plaintiff made a showing of self interest, the burden shifted to the managers to show a "reasonable ground to believe a danger to corporate policy and effectiveness existed" by the presence of the proposed threat. That burden could be met "by showing good faith and reasonable investigation; the directors will not be penalized for an honest mistake of judgment, if the judgment appeared reasonable at the time the decision was made."

On the facts of *Cheff,* a board (only a minority of which had an express financial interest in entrenchment) that used corporate funds to repurchase a substantial block of stock held by a potential bidder, was held to have made an adequate showing. The board established that the potential bidder had a reputation for liquidating companies and thus constituted "a reasonable threat to the continued existence" of the corporation in its present form. This "danger" went to the integrity of the business plan and employee welfare—*corporate* as opposed to *shareholder* concerns. Any shareholder value concerns at the other pole went unmentioned.

Business judgment treatment under *Cheff* did not quite guarantee judicial sanction of any and all defensive tactics. In theory, once management made its showing of a threat and a "good faith, "reasonable investigation," the burden shifted back to the plaintiff to show that an improper purpose to stay in control was management's sole or predominant motive. But, the cases that followed *Cheff* showed that this burden was extremely difficult to surmount. See, e.g., Panter v. Marshall Field & Co., 646 F.2d 271 (7th Cir.1981), cert. denied, 454 U.S. 1092 (1981); Johnson v. Trueblood, 629 F.2d 287 (3d Cir.1980). The plaintiff had to make out a picture of management self-aggrandizing behavior from which it was virtually impossible for the court to avert its gaze. In *Panter,* for example, defending management successfully used a combination of antitrust litigation and selective expansion into markets occupied by the potential bidder. The case stood for the proposition that, as applied, *Cheff* permitted the "business plan," and as a result management self-interest (not to mention federal antitrust policy), to take precedence over shareholder value.

Under *Cheff,* a modicum of boardroom diligence usually was sufficient to secure the protection of the business judgment shield. Outside counsel were adept at engineering the final shift in the burden to the plaintiff by documenting a "reasonable investigation" keyed to a corporate policy and bolstering the case for "good faith" through the use of independent directors.

The resulting deference to boardroom processes was puzzling in view of the structural significance and self-dealing import of anti-takeover defenses. The rule permitted decisionmaking power in respect of the disposition of shares to be shifted from stockholders and markets to the management-controlled venue of the boardroom. Courts under *Cheff* paid small attention to (1) the difference between the justification for the business judgment rule in validating exercises of managerial decisionmaking power over normal corporate operations and its limited relevance to the interests of stockholders in the disposition of their stock in takeover bids, and (2) the incongruity of relying upon business judgment as the predicate for managerial behavior which frustrates the function of takeovers in policing management's normal exercise of business judgment.

The Delaware Supreme Court restated the *Cheff* rule in **Unocal Corp. v. Mesa Petroleum Co.,** 493 A.2d 946 (Del.1985). A new element was added:

> "If a defensive measure is to come within the ambit of the business judgment rule, it must be reasonable in relation to the threat posed. This entails an analysis by the directors of the nature of the takeover bid and its effect on the corporate enterprise. Examples of such concerns may include: inadequacy of the price offered, nature and timing of the offer, questions of illegality, the impact on 'constituencies' other than shareholders (i.e., creditors, customers, employees, and perhaps even the community generally), the risk of nonconsummation, and the quality of securities being offered in exchange.   * * * "

The restated test reflected dissatisfaction with *Cheff's* close to absolute business judgment shield and held out the possibility of more searching judicial scrutiny of defensive tactics.

The application of the new rule on the facts of *Unocal* itself did little to signal a shift to more searching scrutiny. There Unocal's management devised a very effective response to a $54 two-tier, front-end loaded tender offer. The offeror, Boone Pickens' Mesa Petroleum, already owned 13 percent of Unocal's stock, and tendered for an additional 37 percent. Unocal made a cash exchange offer for 49 percent of its stock outstanding conditioned on the acquisition by Mesa of the 37 percent for which it had tendered. Borrowing was to provide the source of funds for the cash consideration. The upshot would be that Mesa, upon succeeding with its tender offer, would be deprived of the borrowing base it needed for financing. Moreover, the Unocal exchange offer excluded Mesa from participation. Applying its new test, the court validated the tactic. The threat posed was a "grossly inadequate two-tier coercive tender offer coupled with the threat of greenmail." The selective exchange offer reasonably responded to the threat because it was keyed to shares left in the back-end of Mesa's proposed transaction; the exclusion of Mesa prevented Pickens from drawing down any of the funds thus designated for those shares.

The cases that follow pose the question as to the degree to which the possibility of searching scrutiny of defensive tactics under the *Unocal* rule has been realized. First, what is a cognizable "threat" within the rule? Will proposed disruption to an established business plan suffice? Or must the threat be directed to the shareholders' interest, as in the case of a coercive two-tier front-end loaded offer? If "corporate" and "constituency" interests as well as shareholder interests can be taken into account in defining the threat, how is the balance between them to be set? Second, how is a "reasonable" response defined? Is a judicially controlled rule of proportionality contemplated? Or will the establishment of a "threat" simply bring in the business judgment shield provided management employs the right procedures? Finally, to what extent does deference to management's business judgment affect the identification of a "threat" and the determination of the reasonable response?

---

(2) The Operation of the *Unocal* Standard

(a) Poison Pills

MORAN v. HOUSEHOLD INTERNATIONAL, INC.

Supreme Court of Delaware, 1985.
500 A.2d 1346.

[This case involved the legality of the adoption by Household International, Inc. (Household) of a Rights Plan "as a preventative mechanism to ward off future" raiders. The Plan was described as follows by the Delaware Supreme Court (McNeilly, J.):]

* * *

The intricacies of the Rights Plan are contained in a 48-page document entitled "Rights Agreement". Basically, the Plan provides that Household common stockholders are entitled to the issuance of one Right per common share under certain triggering conditions. There are two triggering events that can activate the Rights. The first is the announcement of a tender offer for 30 percent of Household's shares ("30% trigger") and the second is the acquisition of 20 percent of Household's shares by any single entity or group ("20% trigger").

If an announcement of a tender offer for 30 percent of Household's shares is made, the Rights are issued and are immediately exercisable to purchase $1/100$ share of new preferred stock for $100 and are redeemable by the Board for $.50 per Right. If 20 percent of Household's shares are acquired by anyone, the Rights are issued and become nonredeemable and are exercisable to purchase $1/100$ of a share of preferred. If a Right is not exercised for preferred, and thereafter, a merger or consolidation occurs, the Rights holder can exercise each Right to purchase $200 of the common stock of the tender offeror for $100. This "flip-over" provision of the Rights Plan is at the heart of this controversy.

* * *

The primary issue here is the applicability of the business judgment rule as the standard by which the adoption of the Rights Plan should be reviewed. Much of this issue has been decided by our recent decision in Unocal Corp. v. Mesa Petroleum Co., Del.Supr., 493 A.2d 946 (1985). In *Unocal*, we applied the business judgment rule to analyze Unocal's discriminatory self-tender. We explained:

> When a board addresses a pending takeover bid it has an obligation to determine whether the offer is in the best interests of the corporation and its shareholders. In that respect a board's duty is no different from any other responsibility it shoulders, and its decisions should be no less entitled to the respect they otherwise would be accorded in the realm of business judgment.

Id. at 954 (citation and footnote omitted).

[Before testing management's behavior by the business judgment rule, however, the Court examined whether there existed sufficient authority to permit management to adopt the Rights Plan, because if the Board lacked that authority, no issue of business judgment remained in the case.]

Appellants vehemently contend that the Board of Directors was unauthorized to adopt the Rights Plan. First, appellants contend that no provision of the Delaware General Corporation Law authorizes the issuance of such Rights. Secondly, appellants, along with the SEC, contend that the Board is unauthorized to usurp stockholders' rights to receive hostile tender offers. Third, appellants and the SEC also contend that the Board is unauthorized to fundamentally restrict stockholders' rights to conduct a proxy contest. We address each of these contentions in turn.

[With respect to the first contention, the Court replied that the language of Sections 151(g) and 157 of the General Corporation Law of Delaware contained sufficient authority. Section 157 authorized the issuance of rights generally, and did not forbid the issuance of rights of the kind here at issue. Presumably similar logic dictated the implicit conclusion of the Court that Section 151(g) authorized the issuance of blank check preferred stock generally and did not forbid the variety of blank check preferred stock here involved. And Section 141(a) conferring power on the Board to manage "the business and affairs" of the corporation adds to the authority to issue the poison pill. The flavor of the Court's logic is revealed in its observation, quoting from its Unocal opinion: "[O]ur corporate law is not static. It must grow and develop in response to, indeed in anticipating of, evolving concepts and needs. Merely because the General Corporation Law is silent as to a specific matter does not mean that it is prohibited."]

[With respect to appellants' contention that "the Board is unauthorized to usurp stockholders' rights to receive tender offers by changing Household's fundamental structure," the Court concluded "that the Rights Plan does not prevent stockholders from receiving tender offers, and that the change of Household's structure was less than that which results from the implementation of other defensive mechanisms upheld by various courts." It went on to say:]

The fallacy of that contention is apparent when we look at the recent takeover of Crown Zellerbach, which has a similar Rights Plan, by Sir James Goldsmith. Wall Street Journal, July 26, 1985, at 3, 12. The evidence at trial also evidenced many methods around the Plan ranging from tendering with a condition that the Board redeem the Rights, tendering with a high minimum condition of shares and Rights, tendering and soliciting consents to remove the Board and redeem the Rights, to acquiring 50% of the shares and causing Household to self-tender for the Rights. One could also form a group of up to 19.9% and solicit proxies for consents to remove the Board and redeem the Rights. These are but a few of the methods by which Household can still be acquired by a hostile tender offer.*

In addition, the Rights Plan is not absolute. When the Household Board of Directors is faced with a tender offer and a request to redeem the Rights, they will not be able to arbitrarily reject the offer. They will be held to the same fiduciary standards any other board of directors would be held to in deciding to adopt a defensive mechanism, the same standard as they were held to in originally approving the Rights Plan. See *Unocal*, 493 A.2d at 954–55, 958.

In addition, appellants contend that the deterrence of tender offers will be accomplished by what they label "a fundamental transfer of

---

* [Ed. Note] In contrast to the view of the Delaware Supreme Court the trial court observed, 490 A.2d at 1077–1078:

Household * * * does concede, and the evidence so indicates, that the Plan will virtually eliminate hostile two-tiered offers for Household. Unsolicited or non-management-endorsed tender offers which are not front-end loaded or conditioned by high minimum acquisition or the surrender of rights to avoid the dilution effect of the flip-over provision have little hope of succeeding. The market professionals on both sides agree that a high minimum offer for a company of

Household's size has never been attempted and it is questionable that such would succeed * * * It clearly would not attract the interest of arbitrageurs or large institutional investors without whose support a hostile tender offer cannot succeed. Even a high minimum-partial offer which leaves a 5% unacquired residual may be deterred. There is apparent agreement that the primary goal of a potential acquiror is to achieve 100% ownership both for tax purposes and in order to operate the company without concern for the interests of minority shareholders.

power from the stockholders to the directors." They contend that this transfer of power, in itself, is unauthorized.

The Rights Plan will result in no more of a structural change than any other defensive mechanism adopted by a board of directors. The Rights Plan does not destroy the assets of the corporation. The implementation of the Plan neither results in any outflow of money from the corporation nor impairs its financial flexibility. It does not dilute earnings per share and does not have any adverse tax consequences for the corporation or its stockholders. The Plan has not adversely affected the market price of Household's stock.

Comparing the Rights Plan with other defensive mechanisms, it does less harm to the value structure of the corporation than do the other mechanisms. Other mechanisms result in increased debt of the corporation. See Whittaker Corp. v. Edgar, supra (sale of "prize asset"), Cheff v. Mathes, supra, (paying greenmail to eliminate a threat), Unocal Corp. v. Mesa Petroleum Co., supra, (discriminatory self-tender).

There is little change in the governance structure as a result of the adoption of the Rights Plan. The Board does not now have unfettered discretion in refusing to redeem the Rights. The Board has no more discretion in refusing to redeem the Rights than it does in enacting any defensive mechanism.

The contention that the Rights Plan alters the structure more than do other defensive mechanisms because it is so effective as to make the corporation completely safe from hostile tender offers is likewise without merit. As explained above, there are numerous methods to successfully launch a hostile tender offer.

[With respect to the third contention, that the Board was "unauthorized to fundamentally restrict stockholders' rights to conduct a proxy contest," the Court said:]

The issue, then, is whether the restriction upon individuals or groups from first acquiring 20% of shares before waging a proxy contest fundamentally restricts stockholders' right to conduct a proxy contest. Regarding this issue the Court of Chancery found:

> Thus, while the Rights Plan does deter the formation of proxy efforts of a certain magnitude, it does not limit the voting power of individual shares. On the evidence presented it is highly conjectural to assume that a particular effort to assert shareholder views in the election of directors or revisions of corporate policy will be frustrated by the proxy feature of the Plan. Household's witnesses, Troubh and Higgins described recent corporate takeover battles in which insurgents holding less than 10% stock ownership were able to secure corporate control through a proxy contest or the threat of one.

Moran, 490 A.2d at 1080.

We conclude that there was sufficient evidence at trial to support the Vice–Chancellor's finding that the effect upon proxy contests will be minimal. Evidence at trial established that many proxy contests are won with an insurgent ownership of less than 20%, and that very large holdings are no guarantee of success. There was also testimony that the key variable in proxy contest success is the merit of an insurgent's issues, not the size of his holdings.

* * *

Having concluded that the adoption of the Rights Plan was within the authority of the Directors, we now look to whether the Directors have met their burden under the business judgment rule.

The business judgment rule is a "presumption that in making a business decision the directors of a corporation acted on an informed basis, in good faith and in the honest belief that the action taken was in the best interests of the company." Aronson v. Lewis, Del.Supr., 473 A.2d 805, 812 (1984) (citations omitted). Notwithstanding, in *Unocal* we held that when the business judgment rule applies to adoption of a defensive mechanism, the initial burden will lie with the directors. The "directors must show that they had reasonable grounds for believing that a danger to corporate policy and effectiveness existed. * * * [T]hey satisfy that burden 'by showing good faith and reasonable investigation. * * *' " *Unocal*, 493 A.2d at 955 (citing Cheff v. Mathes, 199 A.2d at 554–55). In addition, the directors must show that the defensive mechanism was "reasonable in relation to the threat posed." *Unocal*, 493 A.2d at 955. Moreover, that proof is materially enhanced, as we noted in *Unocal*, where, as here, a majority of the board favoring the proposal consisted of outside independent directors who have acted in accordance with the foregoing standards. *Unocal*, 493 A.2d at 955; *Aronson*, 473 A.2d at 815. Then, the burden shifts back to the plaintiffs who have the ultimate burden of persuasion to show a breach of the directors' fiduciary duties. *Unocal*, 493 A.2d at 958.

There are no allegations here of any bad faith on the part of the Directors' action in the adoption of the Rights Plan. There is no allegation that the Directors' action was taken for entrenchment purposes. Household has adequately demonstrated, as explained above, that the adoption of the Rights Plan was in reaction to what it perceived to be the threat in the market place of coercive two-tier tender offers. Appellants do contend, however, that the Board did not exercise informed business judgment in its adoption of the Plan.

* * *

To determine whether a business judgment reached by a board of directors was an informed one, we determine whether the directors were grossly negligent. Smith v. Van Gorkom, Del.Supr., 488 A.2d 858, 873 (1985). Upon a review of this record, we conclude the Directors were not grossly negligent. The information supplied to the Board on August 14 provided the essentials of the Plan. The Directors were given beforehand a notebook which included a three-page summary of the Plan along with articles on the current takeover environment. The extended discussion between the Board and representatives of Wachtell, Lipton and Goldman, Sachs before approval of the Plan reflected a full and candid evaluation of the Plan. Moran's expression of his views at the meeting served to place before the Board a knowledgeable critique of the Plan. The factual happenings here are clearly distinguishable from the actions of the directors of Trans Union Corporation who displayed gross negligence in approving a cash-out merger. Id.

In addition, to meet their burden, the Directors must show that the defensive mechanism was "reasonable in relation to the threat posed". The record reflects a concern on the part of the Directors over the increasing frequency in the financial services industry of "boot-strap" and "bust-up" takeovers. The Directors were also concerned that such takeovers may take the form of two-tier offers.[14] In addition, on August 14, the Household Board was aware of Moran's overture on behalf of D–K–M. In sum, the Directors reasonably believed Household was vulnerable to coercive acquisition techniques and adopted a reasonable defensive mechanism to protect itself.

* * *

While we conclude for present purposes that the Household Directors are protected by the business judgment rule, that does not end the matter. The ultimate response to an actual takeover bid must be judged by the Directors' actions at that time, and nothing we say here relieves them of their basic fundamental duties to the corporation and its stockholders. *Unocal,* 493 A.2d at 954–55, 958; Smith v. Van Gorkom, 488 A.2d at 872–73; *Aronson,* 473 A.2d at 812–13; Pogostin v. Rice, Del.Supr., 480 A.2d 619, 627 (1984). Their use of the Plan will be evaluated when and if the issue arises.

* * *

Affirmed.

NOTE: POISON PILLS AND SHAREHOLDER CHOICE

Suppose Coercive Co. is looking over two potential targets, Sitting Duck Co., and Porcupine Co. Both Sitting Duck and Porcupine have 10,000 widely dispersed shares outstanding and all the shareholders of both value their shares at $100. The shares are trading for a considerably lower price, however.

Sitting Duck has no takeover defenses in place. Coercive would like to acquire it for $94. To do so, it would structure a two-tier, front-end loaded offer as follows: $100 per share cash for 60 percent of the stock in a tender offer; $85 per share in senior securities in a second-step merger.

Porcupine, in contrast, has a poison pill that contains flip-over and flip-in provisions with a $250 exercise price. Yablon, Poison Pills and

---

14. We have discussed the coercive nature of two-tier tender offers in *Unocal,* 493 A.2d at 956, n. 12. We explained in *Unocal* that a discriminatory self-tender was reasonably related to the threat of two-tier tender offers and possible greenmail.

Litigation Uncertainty, 1989 Duke L.J. 54, 64, explains that the poison pill creates a new problem of distorted choice:

"Clearly, Coercive's bidding strategy for Sitting Duck would not work in a bid for Porcupine. In the first place, the strategy would involve considerably more expense when applied to Porcupine. In addition to offering $100 per share for the 60% taken in the first step and $85 per share for the remaining 40%, Coercive would trigger the flip-over rights of the 40% minority, which would require payment of $1,000,000 (4000 $\times$ $250) over and above the $940,000 that Coercive expects to pay for Porcupine's common stock. Coercive attempts to solve this problem by abandoning its two-step strategy, tendering for *all* of Porcupine's shares, and requiring, as a condition of its offer, that at least 90% of the outstanding shares (along with their accompanying Rights) be tendered. In doing so, Coercive is offering a deal with an aggregate value of $1,235,000 ((9000 $\times$ $100) + (1000 $\times$ $85) + (1000 $\times$ $250)), considerably more than the amount at which Porcupine shareholders value their stock. If the shareholders could coordinate their responses, their most rational strategy would be to tender the 90% on a pro rata basis, thus giving each share a blended value of $123.50.

"Without such coordination, however, shareholders' individual decisions result in a distorted choice that is the mirror image of the non-poison-pill scenario. In this case, if you tender and the offer succeeds, you receive $100 per share. But if you do not tender and the offer succeeds, you receive $355 per share ($85 for the share and $250 from the flip-over Right). If the offer does not succeed, it makes no difference whether you tendered or not. Accordingly, in this scenario, you reluctantly refrain from tendering, and the offer fails, even though it exceeds your and the other shareholders' valuation of Porcupine's shares.

"One important factor, however, distinguishes the two scenarios. In the poison pill scenario, Porcupine's board has the power to solve the shareholder-coordination problem by offering to redeem the pill in a negotiated transaction in which Coercive pays $123.50 for each share. Presumably, Coercive would have no objection to such a deal, since it has already offered to pay the same aggregate value for the Porcupine shares. The question, of course, is whether Porcupine's directors would have any incentive to make such a deal."

Suppose we change the facts so that $123.50 is more than any bidder is likely to pay. Does an overly high reservation price make a pill subject to challenge? In Dynamics Corp. v. CTS Corp., 805 F.2d 705 (7th Cir.1986), the court, per Judge Posner, announced that "the reservation price must be reasonably related to the value of the corporation, and the decision to establish such a price and do so by means of a poison pill must be made in good faith after proper consideration." The conflicting valuation evidence on the record caused the court to remand on the question, after expressing "serious doubt" as to whether the target had satisfied the standard.

(b) All Cash All Shares Tender Offers

Unocal's modification of the business judgment approach to take-over defenses held out a possibility of strict scrutiny of defenses toward the end of maximization of shareholder value. Application of the two-step test on the facts of *Moran* and *Unocal* itself heralded no steps toward the realization of this potential. But a few such steps were taken in a subsequent series of Delaware Chancery decisions respecting all cash, all shares offers.

(1) *Chancery Decisions Taking a Shareholder Choice Perspective*

(a) *Anderson, Clayton*

In **AC Acquisitions Corp. v. Anderson, Clayton & Co.,** 519 A.2d 103 (Del.Ch.1986), the bidder made an any and all shares offer of $56 and announced its intention to conduct a second-step merger at the same $56 consideration upon acquiring a majority of the target stock. The target responded by (a) commencing a self tender for 65 percent of its outstanding shares at $60, and (b) announcing an intention to sell an amount of its stock equal to 25 percent of all stock outstanding to a newly formed ESOP. Chancellor Allen ruled that this defense did not pass the *Unocal* test. The bidder had made a noncoercive offer at a fair price. Given this, the first leg of the test allowed the Board the leeway to respond to the offer by proposing an alternative restructuring plan. But the response here was not reasonable in relation to the "threat" posed. The only threat presented by this offer lay in the possibility that a majority of the shareholders might prefer an alternative to the $56 any and all offer. The response went beyond the provision of a choice, and, due to its timing, had the effect of coercively precluding the shareholders from accepting the bidder's offer. Because the $56 offer was subject to conditions, no shareholder tendering into it had an assurance of an eventual acceptance. By tendering, the shareholder precluded itself from participating in the "fat" end of the target's $60 offer. Further, a shareholder not tendering into the target's offer would run a substantial risk of having the value of its stock decline sharply, down to a $22–$31 range, if the restructuring succeeded. Given the downside, a rational shareholder would tender into the target's offer even if it thought the bidder's $56 offer to be preferable. All management had to do in order to eliminate the coercive element of its offer, said the court, was change the timing. It might, for example, have put its proposal on the table for inspection, and then waited to see whether or not 51 percent of the shareholders tendered into the hostile $56 offer.

(b) *Interco*

In **City Capital Associates v. Interco Inc.,** 551 A.2d 787 (Del.Ch. 1988), Chancellor Allen brought the shareholder choice theme of *Anderson, Clayton* to a poison pill defense. The bidder made a $70 any and all shares cash offer, later raised to $74. The offer was conditioned on receipt of 75 percent of the shares and the board's redemption of a poison pill plan. The plan contained a "flip in" right to purchase target stock on a 2 for 1 basis triggered by a stockholder reaching a 30 percent ownership threshold, and a "flip over" right to purchase stock of the acquirer on a 2 for 1 basis on a subsequent merger. The target's management responded by (a) proposing a complex restructuring plan valued by its investment banker at $76 (but discounted to a figure well below $74 by the bidder's investment banker), and (b) refusing to redeem the poison pill.

Chancellor Allen took the occasion to explicate the first leg of the *Unocal* test:

" * * * [I]n the special case of a tender offer for all shares, the threat posed, if any, is not importantly to corporate policies * * * but rather the threat, if any, is most directly to shareholder interests. Broadly speaking, threats to shareholders in that context may be of two types: threats to the voluntariness of the choice offered by the offer, and threats to the substantive economic interest represented by stock-holding.

" * * * It is now universally acknowledged that the structure of an offer can render mandatory in substance that which is voluntary in form. The so-called 'front-end' loaded partial offer—already a largely vanished breed—is the most extreme example of this phenomenon. * * *

" * * * Even where an offer is noncoercive, it may represent a 'threat' to shareholder interests in the special sense that an active negotiator with power, in effect, to refuse the proposal may be able to arrange an alternative transaction or a modified business plan that will present a more valuable option to shareholders. * * * Our cases, however, also indicate that in the setting of a noncoercive offer, absent unusual facts, there may come a time when a board's fiduciary duty will require it to redeem the rights and to permit shareholders to choose. * * * "

Thus, concluded Chancellor Allen, given a noncoercive offer, a target board could use a poison pill to create a window of time in which to arrange an alternative value maximizing transaction. At some point, however, the time would run out. Then the pill's only function was to prevent the shareholders from making an open choice between the two alternatives. The Chancellor ruled that the time had expired in this target's case, and its board's decision not to redeem the pill did not satisfy the *Unocal* test. In so doing, the Chancellor refused the target board's invitation to rule that its action was reasonable because its restructuring proposal was worth $2 more than the hostile bid. The values were debatable, he said, and the choice should be the shareholders'.

(c) *Pillsbury*

Grand Metropolitan PLC v. Pillsbury Co., 558 A.2d 1049 (Del. Ch.1988), also decreed the redemption of poison pill rights. Here the bidder made a $63 any and all cash offer for Pillsbury, representing a 60 percent premium over market value. Management, refusing to redeem the pill, announced a restructuring centered on a spin off of the company's Burger King subsidiary. This, said management would result in value of $68 per share, after four or five years. The court ordered the pill's redemption, noting that no threat was posed to the shareholders or any other corporate constituency, 87 percent of the shares had been tendered, a reasonable shareholder very well might take $63 in 1988 instead of waiting for $68 in 1992, and, finally, two months had elapsed and no competing offers had emerged.

(2) *Cases for Comparison*

The foregoing opinions provide a basis for concluding that, at least in the case of an any or all shares cash offer, target management may have extraordinary difficulty persuading the Delaware courts that potent defensive measures are reasonable in relation to the threat posed. But, before drawing that conclusion, the observer should inspect a few comparison cases.

(a) *Ivanhoe*

Consider first the Delaware Supreme Court's decision in **Ivanhoe Partners v. Newmont Mining Corp.**, 535 A.2d 1334 (Del.1987). Newmont had already disposed of a first takeover attempt when Ivanhoe Partners, controlled by Boone Pickens, came along. The first potential bidder, Consolidated Gold Fields, had acquired 26 percent of Newmont's stock. It held this subject to a standstill agreement that provided, among other things, a right of first refusal to Newmont if Gold Fields should sell its stake. But it also provided for termination of the standstill at Gold Fields' option if any other party acquired 9.9 percent or more of Newmont's stock. Ivanhoe acquired 9.95 percent of Newmont's stock, giving Gold Fields the option of going forward with a takeover of Newmont. Ivanhoe made overtures to Gold Fields. Ivanhoe also made a $95 offer for 42 percent of Newmont's stock, stating an intention to pay $95 cash in a second step merger, but not specifying a committed source of financing.

Gold Fields opted to continue to cooperate with Newmont's managers. The Newmont board declared the Ivanhoe offer to be inadequate. It also approved a restructuring under which some assets were to be sold and the proceeds devoted to a dividend of $33 per share. At the same time, Newmont and Gold Fields revised their agreement to allow Gold Fields to purchase up to 49.9 percent of Newmont's stock, but to be limited to 40 percent of the seats on the board. Gold Fields, upon receiving the $33 dividend on its block of Newmont shares, took the proceeds and, in a street sweep, purchased 15.8 million Newmont shares at an average of $98 per share and increased its holdings to 49.7 percent.

The Delaware Supreme Court validated Newmont's defensive program under *Unocal*. It identified two *Unocal* threats. First, Ivanhoe's offer was coercive because it had two tiers. Second, since Ivanhoe's stock acquisition released Gold Fields from the first standstill agreement, the possibility existed that Gold Fields would attempt a two-tier acquisition, whether or not in concert with Ivanhoe, leaving a substantial number of shareholders in the back end. The defensive measures were reasonable in relation to the threat. The $33 dividend gave all the shareholders a means of participating in the value of the assets sold at an adequate price and facilitated the Gold Fields street sweep. The street sweep itself was reasonable and noncoercive. And the new standstill agreement protected Newmont's public shareholders from being squeezed out by a majority shareholder.[w]

(b) *Polaroid*

Compare also **Shamrock Holdings, Inc. v. Polaroid Corp.**, 559 A.2d 278 (Del.Ch.1989), in which Polaroid's defense against an all shares, all cash offer included a $1.1 billion stock repurchase program along with the placement of an issue convertible preferred into friendly hands. The court ruled that a threat did exist on the facts of the case. Although the offer was non-coercive, the shareholders were not in a position to appraise its adequacy. Polaroid had obtained a judgment as to liability in a billion-dollar patent infringement action against Kodak. Said the court, 559 A.2d at 290:

> "Although the stock market has 'valued' the Kodak judgment and analysts have made estimates, Polaroid's stockholders really have very little way of assessing the present worth of this extremely valuable asset. Under these circumstances, there is a real possibility that the Polaroid stockholders will undervalue the Kodak judgment and it does not appear that the mere dissemination of information will cure this problem. Thus, I am satisfied that the Polaroid directors were entitled to treat the Shamrock offer as a threat."

(c) *ESOPs*

Placing a block of stock in friendly hands can be very a effective defense when combined with a shark repellent provision or state antitakeover statute that conditions a corporate action, such as the approval of a second step merger, on a supermajority shareholder vote. The defending managers can place the block of stock with a friendly blocking minority. Employee Stock Ownership Plans are an attractive means to this end because they can be created by unilateral issuer action, funded with borrowed money, and justified as a component of the issuer's overall compensation policy. Bidder challenges have produced mixed results, as the following descriptions of the two leading cases show.

Shamrock Holdings, Inc. v. Polaroid Corp., 559 A.2d 257 (Del. Ch.1989), another phase of the *Polaroid* case, sustained an ESOP. The

---

w. Nor, said the court, did *Revlon* apply. Newmont had never been offered for sale. The board pursued the goal of independence through the entire course of events. Newmont was the only bidder. Gold Fields bought its additional stock from third party sellers; it did not purchase the firm from the board.

board had been considering setting up an ESOP for some time. When Shamrock revealed a substantial stockholding holding, management finally and hastily got around to shaping a final plan and secured prompt board approval. Under the plan, a new issue of stock amounting to 14 percent of Polaroid's stock outstanding was issued to the ESOP—enough stock to create a potential problem for an acquirer under Del.Gen.Corp.L. section 203(a)(2), Delaware's antitakeover statute. The consideration was $300 million, funded by a $15 million contribution by the issuer and a $285 million bank borrowing. The stock placed in the ESOP was to be allocated to the participating employees over a 10 year period, with an initial retroactive allocation of a small portion. The plan provided for mirrored voting and tendering; that is, the trustee was to follow the confidential directions of the holders of the accounts to which the plan's stock was allocated. In addition, voting or tendering of unallocated stock was to be proportioned in accordance with the confidential shareholder directions. Employee pay cuts and other givebacks were to provide the source of funds to carry the costs of the debt incurred to pay for the stock placed in the plan.

The board approved the plan so hastily that the court ruled that the *Unocal* business judgment test did not apply at all—no reasonable investigation by the board had been shown. Hence the plan was inspected under an intrinsic fairness standard. But the plan passed the inspection. On the positive side, the plan promoted employee productivity, and permitted secret voting by its beneficiaries. Moreover, no tender offer had been made at the time the plan was adopted. Indeed, the plaintiff did not contend that the plan of itself would block a takeover. It would, said the plaintiff, cause it to offer $40 rather than $42 and had already caused dilution of the shareholders' equity interest. The court, balancing productivity advantages against these objections, found the plan fair.

NCR Corp. v. American Telephone & Telegraph Co., 761 F.Supp. 475 (S.D.Ohio 1991), invalidates a defensive ESOP. AT & T had mounted a $90 all shares cash offer, into which more than 70 percent of the shares had been tendered. The board opposed the offer, taking the position that NCR was worth $125 per share. AT & T, which needed to gain control of the board prior to closing on its tender offer, began a concomitant proxy contest to remove the incumbent board. This required an 80 percent supermajority vote.

Nine days before the record date for the shareholders' meeting, the NCR board approved an ESOP and placed 5.5 million voting preferred shares in the plan. Each share was convertible into eight tenths of a common share at a conversion price of $113. This plan preferred stock carried 8 percent of the voting power. Like the plan in *Polaroid,* this plan involved a present allocation of a small portion of the stock to employees, with allocation of the remaining stock over time (here, 25 years) and mirrored voting of the entire block in accord with the directions of the employee participants. The numbers worked so that at the time of the meeting each plan participant would in effect have

229 votes for each allocated share. The plan differed from the *Polaroid* plan in a number of respects. First, it was inside funded. NCR loaned the purchase money to the plan in exchange for a $500 million nonrecourse note of the plan trustee. NCR, in turn, promised to pay the trustee funds to service the debt. No compensating employee givebacks were required. Second, the terms of the plan were structured to give the voting employees an economic incentive to defeat the AT & T proposal. The plan contained a redemption provision under which holders could receive the value of the common into which the plan preferred could be converted or $90, whichever was greater. This protected the participants from a stock drop in the event of defeat of the tender offer. In addition, the redemption rights provided for a 25 percent "redemption premium" over the price of common subject to a ceiling of $123. This operated so that the plan participants would be indifferent to increases in the tender offer price up to the $123 ceiling. Finally, to provide additional protection against the disappearance of the offer, the conversion price of the plan stock could be reset downward if the price of the common dropped for a period of fourteen months. The combination of the redemption rights and the reset provision meant that the plan stock would be most valuable in the long run in the event of a substantial decrease in the stock price during the fourteen month reset period followed by eventual recovery in the price.

The federal district court applied a two-step Maryland law test. First, the approving directors had to act in the manner they reasonably believed to be in the corporation's best interests. The court, focussing on the limited information set made available to the board and a lack of outside opinions, found that the board did not meet the standard. Second, the primary purpose had to be a legitimate corporate purpose rather than a self-interested one. Here the court balanced the corporate purpose of compensating the employees against the plan's entrenching effect. Given the timing of the plan, the disproportion between small amount of present compensation and the large present voting impact, and the inclusion of incentives to vote against the AT & T proposal, the court found the entrenching effect to weigh more heavily and invalidated the plan.

Certainly the entrenching effects of the *NCR* plan were greater than those of the *Polaroid* plan. Does it follow that the *Polaroid* court reached the right result?

(d) A Comment on Unocal as Applied

Decisions applying the *Unocal* rule do not successfully teach us how to measure the dimensions or import of either the requisite threat or the appropriate response so as to be able to tell whether the latter is reasonable in relation to, or proportionate to, the former. Commentators have tried to cabin the open-ended judicial discretion embodied in the formulae by categorization of threatened harms and proportionate responses. See Gilson and Kraakman, Delaware's Intermediate Standard for Defensive Tactics: Is There Substance to Proportionality

Review? 44 Bus.Law. 247 (1989). But the courts rarely follow even the limited constraints they suggest.

(1) *Substantive Standards*

As cases like *Anderson Clayton* and *Interco* suggest, the *Unocal* proportionality test could derive content by an emphasis on the distinction between harm that results from bids that are structurally coercive on shareholders (e.g., two-tier front-end loaded bids) and the harm embodied in bids that are not coercive but otherwise conceivably objectionable (e.g., an all shares bid at an inadequate cash price or a price paid in currency of dubious value). That difference is said to justify different measures of proportionality in evaluating management responses. See Gilson and Kraakman, supra. Does this mean that the "harm" from the fact that the bid is "structurally" coercive should be sufficient to justify a structurally coercive or preclusive response that effectively denies the target shareholders any opportunity to accept the bid? *Unocal* intimates this result. If not, and if some kinds of "coercive" responses should be permitted sometimes and others not in the face of a "structurally" coercive bid, what criteria should define the difference? Cf. Buckhorn, Inc. v. Ropak Corp., 656 F.Supp. 209, 229–235 (S.D.Ohio 1987).

Similarly, if the threat of harm consists only of inadequacy of price, questions arise as to the criteria courts should use to measure either the adequacy of the price or the appropriately proportional response. Sometimes management has been upheld and sometimes it has not been upheld when responding with a preclusive defense that would effectively deny the target's stockholders an opportunity to choose the bid. *Anderson, Clayton,* supra, and Robert M. Bass Group v. Evans, 552 A.2d 1227 (Del.Ch.1988) go against management. Compare the approval of the defenses in the *Polaroid* cases, supra, and of the preclusive merger in *Time,* infra p. 1115. Less uncertainty seems to attend cases where the "just say no" defense does not preclude the 100 percent cash offer. Management provides no immediate alternative for the stockholders but insists that the offer is inadequate, and obstructs but does not entirely block the bid by poison pill or another device.[x] Courts decline to direct elimination of such obstacles to shareholder choice if, clairvoyantly, they see bidding being stimulated by continuing them in force.[y]

---

x. See, e.g., Torchmark Corp. v. Bixby, 708 F.Supp. 1070 (W.D.Mo.1988); BNS, Inc. v. Koppers Co., Inc., 683 F.Supp. 458 (D.Del.1988); TW Services, Inc. v. SWT Acquisition Co., CCH Fed.Sec.L.Rep. ¶ 94,334 (Del.Ch.1989).

y. See, e.g., MAI Basic Four, Inc. v. Prime Computer, Inc., 1988 WL 140221 (Del.Ch.1988); Nomad Acquisition Corp. v. Damon Corp., 1988 WL 96192 (Del.Ch. 1988); Southdown, Inc. v. Moore McCormack Resources, Inc., 686 F.Supp. 595 (S.D.Tex.1988).

What sort of showing should management be required to make to establish its view that present operational plans for the company will produce value for the stockholder that will eventually exceed the bid price? See Gilson and Kraakman, supra. A similar problem is entailed in the assessment of a management claim that the corporation is worth more than the bid by reason of its break-up or restructuring potential or a management claim that it can negotiate a better price from the bidder or

The same seems true if management, rather than "just saying no," offers the stockholders an alternative, such as a restructuring or a leveraged buyout, which is not totally preclusive. In these cases it is often hard to decipher criteria for determining whether management's alternative meets its proportionality (or *Revlon* auction) obligations [z]— except where the alternative is a visibly disadvantageous management buyout.[a]

Presumably, a court decision that correctly sees that management's response permits or encourages "the market" to determine whether the bidder prevails, leaves the stockholders better off than a court decision that paternalistically favors either management or bidder. But suppose the court that decides that the defense benefits the stockholders by prompting a "market" decision makes a mistake, either because of judicial myopia or because the "market" envisioned is sticky or otherwise obstructed. In that case the stockholders are unlikely to have any effective alternative to management's "just say no" stance or other proposal. The judge pursuing a possible market solution envisioned through a lens focussed by management in the end favors management and deprives stockholders of an opportunity to accept an acceptable bid.

Can a better solution to this and the foregoing problems be devised than *ad hoc* judicial intervention under the *Unocal* rule? Consider the materials on the market and sole owner standards, supra p. 950 and the *Revlon* case that follows.

(2) *The Business Judgment Factor*

The role accorded to the board's business judgment in implementing its "enhanced duties" under *Unocal* further widens the range of discretion the rule leaves to the courts.[b] If the court must itself first

---

find a third party who will make a higher bid.

z. See, e.g., Citron v. Fairchild Camera and Instrument Co., 569 A.2d 53 (Del.1989); West Point Pepperell, Inc. v. J.P. Stevens & Co., 542 A.2d 770 (Del.Ch.1988); In re Fort Howard Corp. Shareholders Litigation, 1988 WL 83147 (Del.Ch.1988); Doskocil Cos. Inc. v. Griggy, 1988 WL 81267 (Del.Ch.1988); Nomad Acquisition Corp. v. Damon Corp., supra; Cottle v. Storer Communications, Inc., 849 F.2d 570 (11th Cir. 1988); In re RJR Nabisco, Inc. Shareholders Litigation, 1989 WL 7036 (Del.Ch.1989).

a. See, e.g., Black & Decker Corp. v. American Standard, Inc., 682 F.Supp. 772 (D.Del.1988); Robert M. Bass Group, Inc. v. Evans, 552 A.2d 1227 (Del.Ch.1988). But cf. Caruana v. Saligman, 1990 WL 212340 (Del.Ch.1990).

b. See, e.g., In re Fort Howard Corp. Shareholders Litigation, 1988 WL 83147 (Del.Ch.1988); Gelco Corp. v. Coniston Partners, 652 F.Supp. 829 (D.Minn.1986); BNS v. Koppers Co., Inc., 683 F.Supp. 458 (D.Del.1988); CRTF v. Federated Dept.

Stores, 683 F.Supp. 422 (S.D.N.Y.1988); Tate & Lyle PLC v. Staley Continental, Inc., CCH Fed.Sec.L.Rep. ¶ 93,764 (Del.Ch. 1988); Cottle v. Storer Communications, Inc., 849 F.2d 570 (11th Cir.1988); TW Services v. SWT Acquisition Co., CCH Fed.Sec. L.Rep. ¶ 94,334 (Del.Ch.1989). Compare Blasius Industries, Inc. v. Altas Corp., 564 A.2d 651 (Del.Ch.1988), with Stahl v. Apple Bancorp, Inc., 579 A.2d 1115 (Del.Ch.1990).

Should a court assess management's justification for its belief and blocking behavior with deference to the board's business judgment (whether the board acts only by, or with the concurrence of, its outside directors?) or should it examine the matter more critically? Should the customary or usual fees and perquisites that outside directors receive cast a sufficient shadow on their independence to preclude the judicial deference to their acts in takeover situations that the business judgment rule otherwise dictates? Compare Samuel M. Feinberg Testamentary Trust v. Carter, 652 F.Supp. 1066, 1072–1075 (S.D.N.Y. 1987), with Grobow v. Perot, 539 A.2d 180 (Del.1988).

decide whether the nature of the proposed response to an unsolicited bid is justified by the magnitude of the threatened harm, the weight (if any) to be accorded to the board's business judgment by a court which has decided that question seems rather light. On the other hand, if the board's business judgment is to affect the court's determination of whether the board's response is proportionate to the threatened harm it claims to see, the court's scrutiny is apt to occur through the wrong end of the telescope. In either case, the ambiguity in the role assigned by the court to the board's business judgment is reflected in the somewhat confusing results reached in the lower court decisions. It is not reduced by the Delaware Supreme Court's repeated discourses on the subject. Thus in Gilbert v. The El Paso Co., 575 A.2d 1131 (1990), the Delaware Supreme Court admonished the lower court for erroneously relying upon the business judgment test of the propriety of the defendants' behavior, but vindicated that behavior by applying the *Unocal* test to the recorded events. The Court noted, 575 A.2d at 1145, fn. 29: "In arguing against the application of the *Unocal* standard to these circumstances, defendants apparently fear that the conduct of the El Paso board might somehow wither under enhanced judicial scrutiny. Like the traditional business judgment analysis, however, *Unocal* also implicitly acknowledges that courts should not impose their own business judgment upon independent directors who reasonably respond to a threat to the corporate enterprise in good faith and on an informed basis." Both the result and the opinion raise the question of the significance of the difference between "ordinary" business judgment and the "enhanced" duty under *Unocal,* or between the judicial role when the former is invoked and when the latter is called for.

---

(3) The *Revlon* Auction Duty

REVLON, INC. v. MacANDREWS & FORBES HOLDINGS, INC.

Supreme Court of Delaware, 1985.
506 A.2d 173.

[The opinion in this case addressed three defenses by the management of Revlon, Inc. (Revlon) against an ultimately successful takeover attempt by Pantry Pride, Inc. (Pantry Pride). The first two defenses entailed (a) the issuance by Revlon as a dividend to its stockholders of redeemable poison pill Rights (to acquire upon tender of a share of common stock a one year Note for $65 bearing interest at 12 percent) exercisable when anyone acquired 20% or more of Revlon stock (other than an acquisition of all Revlon stock for cash at not less than $65 per share) by all stockholders other than the acquiror, and (b) acquisition by Revlon of ten million shares of its common stock in exchange for its subordinated Notes and preferred stock. The last defense was a lock-up and "no-shop" agreement (including an escrowed $25 million cancellation fee) which the management of Revlon made with its white knight,

Forstmann, Little, & Co. (Forstmann), in order to fend off Pantry Pride's increased bids for control.

The Delaware Supreme Court, affirming the issuance by the trial court of a preliminary injunction against the Forstmann, Little transaction, rejected the attacks on the poison pill defense and on the repurchase of stock for Notes. Its decision rested on the ground that neither the discriminatory rights offering nor the repurchase was objectionable per se as a tactic, and that in the circumstances of this case each constituted a reasonable exercise of directorial business judgment in response to Pantry Pride's initial bid for control, which the Board on advice of its bankers thought (apparently correctly) to be inadequate. With respect to the third defense, it reached a different conclusion.

The Notes issued on the repurchase of the Revlon common stock "contained covenants which limited Revlon's ability to incur additional debt, sell assets, or pay dividends unless otherwise approved by the 'independent' (non-management) members of the board." In connection with its efforts to induce Forstmann to become the white knight, Revlon indicated that its outside directors would waive those covenants and would redeem the poison pill Rights. As a result of the suggestion of waiver of the covenants, the price of those Notes began to fall in the market, and there were threats of litigation by Noteholders and of director personal liability which the directors appear to have taken seriously. In the course of the ensuing bidding war between Pantry Pride and Forstmann, in which Pantry Pride raised its price substantially, Forstmann offered to outbid slightly Pantry Pride's then highest bid, and undertook to support the par value of the falling Notes—but only on the condition that it be given a lock-up on the assets of two of Revlon's divisions at a substantial discount from their value, and that Revlon enter into a no-shop agreement.

The Delaware Supreme Court, after noting that the directors of Revlon had acted appropriately and within the limits of business judgment with respect to the first two defenses, observed that circumstances were altered by the time of the Forstmann lock-up and no-shop agreement, and went on to say (Moore, J.):]

However, when Pantry Pride increased its offer to $50 per share, and then to $53, it became apparent to all that the break-up of the company was inevitable. The Revlon board's authorization permitting management to negotiate a merger or buyout with a third party was a recognition that the company was for sale. The duty of the board had thus changed from the preservation of Revlon as a corporate entity to the maximization of the company's value at a sale for the stockholders' benefit. This significantly altered the board's responsibilities under the *Unocal* standards. It no longer faced threats to corporate policy and effectiveness, or to the stockholders' interests, from a grossly inadequate bid. The whole question of defensive measures became moot. The directors' role changed from defenders of the corporate bastion to auctioneers charged with getting the best price for the stockholders at a sale of the company.

This brings us to the lock-up with Forstmann and its emphasis on shoring up the sagging market value of the Notes in the face of threatened litigation by their holders. Such a focus was inconsistent with the changed concept of the directors' responsibilities at this stage of the developments. The impending waiver of the Notes covenants had caused the value of the Notes to fall, and the board was aware of the noteholders' ire as well as their subsequent threats of suit. The directors thus made support of the Notes an integral part of the company's dealings with Forstmann, even though their primary responsibility at this stage was to the equity owners.

The original threat posed by Pantry Pride—the break-up of the company—had become a reality which even the directors embraced. Selective dealing to fend off a hostile but determined bidder was no longer a proper objective. Instead, obtaining the highest price for the benefit of the stockholders should have been the central theme guiding director action. Thus, the Revlon board could not make the requisite showing of good faith by preferring the noteholders and ignoring its duty of loyalty to the shareholders. The rights of the former already were fixed by contract. Wolfensohn v. Madison Fund, Inc., Del.Supr., 253 A.2d 72, 75 (1969); Harff v. Kerkorian, Del.Ch., 324 A.2d 215 (1974). The noteholders required no further protection, and when the Revlon board entered into an auction-ending lock-up agreement with Forstmann on the basis of impermissible considerations at the expense of the shareholders, the directors breached their primary duty of loyalty.

The Revlon board argued that it acted in good faith in protecting the noteholders because *Unocal* permits consideration of other corporate constituencies. Although such considerations may be permissible, there are fundamental limitations upon that prerogative. A board may have regard for various constituencies in discharging its responsibilities, provided there are rationally related benefits accruing to the stockholders. *Unocal,* 493 A.2d at 955. However, such concern for non-stockholder interests is inappropriate when an auction among active bidders is in progress, and the object no longer is to protect or maintain the corporate enterprise but to sell it to the highest bidder.

Revlon also contended that by Gilbert v. El Paso Co., Del.Ch., 490 A.2d 1050, 1054–55 (1984), it had contractual and good faith obligations to consider the noteholders. However, any such duties are limited to the principle that one may not interfere with contractual relationships by improper actions. Here, the rights of the noteholders were fixed by agreement, and there is nothing of substance to suggest that any of those terms were violated. The Notes covenants specifically contemplated a waiver to permit sale of the company at a fair price. The Notes were accepted by the holders on that basis, including the risk of an adverse market effect stemming from a waiver. Thus, nothing remained for Revlon to legitimately protect, and no rationally related benefit thereby accrued to the stockholders. Under such circumstances we must conclude that the merger agreement with Forstmann was unreasonable in relation to the threat posed.

A lock-up is not *per se* illegal under Delaware law. Its use has been approved in an earlier case. Thompson v. Enstar Corp., Del.Ch. (1984). Such options can entice other bidders to enter a contest for control of the corporation, creating an auction for the company and maximizing shareholder profit. Current economic conditions in the takeover market are such that a "white knight" like Forstmann might only enter the bidding for the target company if it receives some form of compensation to cover the risks and costs involved. Note, Corporations–Mergers— "Lock-up" Enjoined Under Section 14(e) of Securities Exchange Act— Mobil Corp. v. Marathon Oil Co., 669 F.2d 366 (6th Cir.1981), 12 Seton Hall L.Rev. 881, 892 (1982). However, while those lock-ups which draw bidders into the battle benefit shareholders, similar measures which end an active auction and foreclose further bidding operate to the shareholders' detriment. Note, Lock-up Options: Toward a State Law Standard, 96 Harv.L.Rev. 1068, 1081 (1983).[14]

Recently, the United States Court of Appeals for the Second Circuit invalidated a lock-up on fiduciary duty grounds similar to those here.[15] Hanson Trust PLC, et al. v. ML SCM Acquisition Inc., et al., 781 F.2d 264 (2nd Cir.1986). Citing Thompson v. Enstar Corp., supra, with approval, the court stated:

> In this regard, we are especially mindful that some lock-up options may be beneficial to the shareholders, such as those that induce a bidder to compete for control of a corporation, while others may be harmful, such as those that effectively preclude bidders from competing with the optionee bidder. 781 F.2d at 274.

In *Hanson Trust,* the bidder, Hanson, sought control of SCM by a hostile cash tender offer. SCM management joined with Merrill Lynch to propose a leveraged buy-out of the company at a higher price, and Hanson in turn increased its offer. Then, despite very little improvement in its subsequent bid, the management group sought a lock-up option to purchase SCM's two main assets at a substantial discount. The SCM directors granted the lock-up without adequate information as to the size of the discount or the effect the transaction would have on the company. Their action effectively ended a competitive bidding situation. The Hanson Court invalidated the lock-up because the directors failed to fully inform themselves about the value of a transaction in which management had a strong self-interest. "In short, the Board appears to have failed to ensure that negotiations for alternative

---

14. For further discussion of the benefits and detriments of lock-up options, also see: Nelson, Mobil Corp. v. Marathon Oil Co.—The Decision and Its Implications for Future Tender Offers, 7 Corp.L.Rev. 233, 265–68 (1984); Note, Swallowing the Key to Lock-up Options: Mobil Corp. v. Marathon Oil Co., 14 U.Tol.L.Rev. 1055, 1081–83 (1983).

15. The federal courts generally have declined to enjoin lock-up options despite arguments that lock-ups constitute impermissible "manipulative" conduct forbidden by Section 14(e) of the Williams Act [15 U.S.C. § 78n(e)]. See Buffalo Forge Co. v. Ogden Corp., 717 F.2d 757 (2nd Cir.1983), cert. denied, 464 U.S. 1018, 104 S.Ct. 550, 78 L.Ed.2d 724 (1983); Data Probe Acquisition Corp. v. Datatab, Inc., 722 F.2d 1 (2nd Cir.1983); cert. denied 465 U.S. 1052, 104 S.Ct. 1326, 79 L.Ed.2d 722 (1984); but see Mobil Corp. v. Marathon Oil Co., 669 F.2d 366 (6th Cir.1981). The cases are all federal in nature and were not decided on state law grounds.

bids were conducted by those whose only loyalty was to the shareholders." Id. at 277.

The Forstmann option had a similar destructive effect on the auction process. Forstmann had already been drawn into the contest on a preferred basis, so the result of the lock-up was not to foster bidding, but to destroy it. The board's stated reasons for approving the transactions were: (1) better financing, (2) noteholder protection, and (3) higher price. As the Court of Chancery found, and we agree, any distinctions between the rival bidders' methods of financing the proposal were nominal at best, and such a consideration has little or no significance in a cash offer for any and all shares. The principal object, contrary to the board's duty of care, appears to have been protection of the noteholders over the shareholders' interests.

While Forstmann's $57.25 offer was objectively higher than Pantry Pride's $56.25 bid, the margin of superiority is less when the Forstmann price is adjusted for the time value of money. In reality, the Revlon board ended the auction in return for very little actual improvement in the final bid. The principal benefit went to the directors, who avoided personal liability to a class of creditors to whom the board owed no further duty under the circumstances. Thus, when a board ends an intense bidding contest on an insubstantial basis, and where a significant by-product of that action is to protect the directors against a perceived threat of personal liability for consequences stemming from the adoption of previous defensive measures, the action cannot withstand the enhanced scrutiny which *Unocal* requires of director conduct. See *Unocal,* 493 A.2d at 954–55.

In addition to the lock-up option, the Court of Chancery enjoined the no-shop provision as part of the attempt to foreclose further bidding by Pantry Pride. MacAndrews & Forbes Holdings, Inc. v. Revlon, Inc., 501 A.2d at 1251. The no-shop provision, like the lock-up option, while not *per se* illegal, is impermissible under the *Unocal* standards when a board's primary duty becomes that of an auctioneer responsible for selling the company to the highest bidder. The agreement to negotiate only with Forstmann ended rather than intensified the board's involvement in the bidding contest.

It is ironic that the parties even considered a no-shop agreement when Revlon had dealt preferentially, and almost exclusively, with Forstmann throughout the contest. After the directors authorized management to negotiate with other parties, Forstmann was given every negotiating advantage that Pantry Pride had been denied: cooperation from management, access to financial data, and the exclusive opportunity to present merger proposals directly to the board of directors. Favoritism for a white knight to the total exclusion of a hostile bidder might be justifiable when the latter's offer adversely affects shareholder interests, but when bidders make relatively similar offers, or dissolution of the company becomes inevitable, the directors cannot fulfill their enhanced *Unocal* duties by playing favorites with the contending factions. Market forces must be allowed to operate freely to bring the target's shareholders the best price available for their equity.[16] Thus, as the trial court ruled, the shareholders' interests necessitated that the board remain free to negotiate in the fulfillment of that duty.

* * *

In conclusion, the Revlon board was confronted with a situation not uncommon in the current wave of corporate takeovers. A hostile and determined bidder sought the company at a price the board was convinced was inadequate. The initial defensive tactics worked to the benefit of the shareholders, and thus the board was able to sustain its *Unocal* burdens in justifying those measures. However, in granting an asset option lock-up to Forstmann, we must conclude that under all the circumstances the directors allowed considerations other than the maximization of shareholder profit to affect their judgment, and followed a course that ended the auction for Revlon, absent court intervention, to the ultimate detriment of its shareholders. No such defensive measure can be sustained when it represents a breach of the directors' fundamental duty of care. See Smith v. Van Gorkom, Del.Supr., 488 A.2d 858, 874 (1985). In that context the board's action is not entitled to the deference accorded it by the business judgment rule. The measures were properly enjoined. The decision of the Court of Chancery, therefore, is affirmed.

NOTE: CONSTITUENCIES

Given *Unocal*, the cases that apply it, and now the *Revlon* case, what can be concluded about the legitimacy of defensive actions taken to protect constituencies other than stockholders? Assessing the "threat" under *Unocal* entails answering the question whether and how harm to the "enterprise" or to its nonstockholder stakeholders should be considered in determining whether any defensive response is justified, let alone proportional. In this connection, some opinions, such as *Unocal* itself, *Time*, infra p. 1115, and *Pillsbury*, supra p. 1088, suggest that a broader constituency than the target's stockholders is to be protected. Others, like *Revlon*, and *Interco*, supra p. 1087, suggest a focus exclusively on stockholders. To the extent that constituency interests may be considered, do the opinions offer criteria by which to measure an acceptable balance among competing stakeholders? Consider the suggestion in the *MacMillan* case, infra p. 1101 at footnote 29, that although the interests of other constituencies may be considered, vindication of those interests must bear "some reasonable relationship to general shareholder interests." But the courts have not offered criteria by which to measure an acceptable balance among the compet-

---

16. By this we do not embrace the "passivity" thesis rejected in *Unocal*. See 493 A.2d at 954–55, nn. 8–10. The directors' role remains an active one, changed only in the respect that they are charged with the duty of selling the company at the highest price attainable for the stock holders' benefit.

ing stakeholders.   How, given that advancing the interests of some requires scanting the interests of others, can this suggestion be applied?

Delaware does not have express statutory provisions, such as do many other states, authorizing a board to consider the interests of non-stockholders in reaching decisions.   These statutes vary in the signal they give as to the appropriate balance to be struck among competing constituencies—sometimes leaving uncertain whether stockholder interests can be sacrificed if claims conflict, see N.Y.B.C.L. sec. 717(b), and other times expressly leaving the board with discretion to choose among the constituencies.   See Ind.Gen.Corp.Act. sec. 23–1–35(1).

MILLS ACQUISITION CO. v. MACMILLAN, INC.

Supreme Court of Delaware, 1989.
559 A.2d 1261.

[Macmillan Inc., (Macmillan), a large publishing, educational and informational services company, was the target of a takeover effort by the Robert M. Bass Group, Inc. and affiliates (Bass) in October, 1987. The Bass overtures were resisted by Macmillan's management (led by Evans, the CEO, and Reilly, the chief operating officer) which proposed a restructuring of the enterprise under which management, particularly Evans and Reilly, would have an immensely larger equity than they had at the outset, would acquire it "on extremely favorable terms" at the expense of the public stockholders, and would end up in control of the enterprise.   The board of Macmillan and a Special Committee of the board (composed of nominal outsiders who were "hand picked" by management) seem to have relied largely on management to select and deal with the Committee's legal (Wachtell, Lipton, Rosen & Katz) and financial advisors (Lazard Freres & Co.) and to constitute the board's principal source of information of the virtues and vices of the Bass Group and their proposal.   Macmillan's financial advisors valued the proposed restructuring of the enterprise as producing the equivalent of $64.15 per share for Macmillan's public common stockholders; the Special Committee's financial advisors valued the enterprise at $72.57 per share on a pre-tax basis, possibly as high as $80.00 per share, but found the restructuring at $64.15 per share to be "fair".   Wasserstein, Perella and Co. Inc., the special advisors to Macmillan's management, valued the enterprise at between $63.00 and $68.00 per share but possibly as high as $80.00 per share.   All concurred in recommending to the board that the Bass offers (of $64.00 per shares at first and $73.00 per share later) were inadequate, and that the restructuring was preferable to either of the Bass offers.

[On July 14, 1988, the Macmillan restructuring was enjoined preliminarily on the ground that the Bass offers were "clearly superior to the restructuring".   As the Supreme Court (Moore, J.) pointed out, 559 A.2d 1271:]

On July 14, 1988, the Vice Chancellor preliminarily enjoined the Evans designed restructuring, and held that both of the revised Bass offers were "clearly superior to the restructuring." The Court further inferred that the only real "threat" posed by the Bass offers was to the incumbency of the board "or to the management group's expectation of garnering a 39% ownership interest in Information on extremely favorable terms." Id. at 1241 & n. 34.

Thus, *Macmillan I* essentially ended on July 14, 1988. However, it only set the stage for the saga of *Macmillan II* to begin that same day. It opened with Macmillan's senior management holding extensive discussions with KKR* in an attempt to develop defensive measures to thwart the Bass Group offer. This included a management-sponsored buyout of the company by KKR. There is nothing in the record to suggest that this was done pursuant to board action. If anything, it was Evans acting alone in his own personal interest.

Within a few hours after the Court of Chancery issued its preliminary injunction, Evans and Reilly formally authorized Macmillan's investment advisors to explore a possible sale of the entire company. This procedure eventually identified six potential bidders.[17] That search process appears to have been motivated by two primary objectives: (1) to repel any third party suitors unacceptable to Evans and Reilly, and (2) to transfer an enhanced equity position in a restructured Macmillan to Evans and his management group. * * *

On July 20, a most significant development occurred when Maxwell** intervened in the Bass–Macmillan bidding contest by proposing to Evans a consensual merger between Macmillan and Maxwell at an all-cash price of $80 per share. This was $5.00 higher than any other outstanding offer for the company.[18] Maxwell further stated his intention to retain the company's management, and additionally, to negotiate appropriate programs of executive incentives and compensation.

Macmillan did not respond to Maxwell's overture for five weeks. Instead, during this period, Macmillan's management intensified their discussions with KKR concerning a buyout in which senior management, particularly Evans and Reilly, would have a substantial ownership interest in the new company. Upon execution of a confidentiality agreement, KKR was given detailed internal, non-public, financial information of Macmillan, culminating in a series of formal "due diligence" presentations to KKR representatives by Macmillan senior management on August 4 and 5, 1988.

On August 12, 1988, after more than three weeks of silence from the company, Maxwell made an $80 per share, all-cash tender offer for

---

* [Ed. Note] Kohlberg, Kravis, Roberts & Co., an investment firm specializing in leveraged buy outs.

17. These entities were the Bass Group, Maxwell, KKR, Gulf & Western, McGraw–Hill and News–America Corp.

** [Ed. Note] The Late Robert Maxwell and enterprises he controlled.

18. Two days before the initial Maxwll bid, the Bass Group had raised its offer for the company to $75.00 per share. Although this final Bass offer remained open into September, the entry of Maxwell into the fray, for all practical purposes, rendered the Bass bid academic.

Macmillan, conditioned solely upon receiving the same nonpublic information which Macmillan had given to KKR three weeks earlier. * * *

[Macmillan's management, acting without any significant board supervision, conducted an "auction" between Maxwell and KKR in a manner that the court found significantly favored the latter and disfavored the former. Among the "tilts" which management was found to have injected into the auction process were a tipping of KKR about the content of Maxwell's bid so that KKR could offer a better bid, and later misleading Maxwell into believing that there was no need for him to respond to the opportunity held out to him to increase his bid because his bid was then the higher of the two pending bids. According to the Delaware Supreme Court, management not only kept the Macmillan board in significant ignorance of events and relevant information, occasionally actually deceiving the board, but the board itself was culpably negligent in its participation in the "auction" process, at least to the extent of making voidable the transaction with KKR which it approved. On October 4, 1988, the board accepted the offer of KKR (consisting of cash and securities which had a "face value" of $90.05 per share) in preference to a Maxwell offer of $90.25 per share all cash, but conditioned on invalidation of lock up and no shop agreements that Macmillan had made with KKR in connection with KKR's submission.]

After a hearing on Maxwell's motion for a preliminary injunction, on October 17, the Court of Chancery denied Maxwell's request to enjoin the lockup agreement, the break-up fees and expenses granted by the Macmillan board to KKR. In ruling for Macmillan, the trial court found that although KKR was consistently and deliberately favored throughout the auction process, Maxwell was not prevented from, or otherwise misled to refrain from, submitting a higher bid for the company. However, the court found that Macmillan's shareholders should have the opportunity to consider an alternative offer for the company, and therefore enjoined the operation of Macmillan's "poison pill" shareholder rights plan as a defensive measure to Maxwell's still open tender offer. In this appeal neither party has challenged that limited injunction. Thus, the sole issue before us is the validity, under all of the foregoing circumstances, of the asset lock-up option granted pursuant to the KKR–Macmillan merger agreement with its attendant breakup fees and expenses.

II.

* * *

A.

* * *

While it is apparent that the Court of Chancery seemingly attempted to evaluate this case under the relatively broad parameters of the business judgment rule, it nevertheless held that the relevant inquiry must focus upon the "fairness" of the auction process in light of promoting the maximum shareholder value as mandated by this Court in *Revlon.* In denying Maxwell's motion for an injunction, the Vice–Chancellor concluded that the auction-related deficiencies could be deemed "material" only upon a showing that they actually deterred a higher bid from Maxwell.

* * * [J]udicial reluctance to assess the merits of a business decision ends in the face of illicit manipulation of a board's deliberative processes by self-interested corporate fiduciaries. Here, not only was there such deception, but the board's own lack of oversight in structuring and directing the auction afforded management the opportunity to indulge in the misconduct which occurred. In such a context, the challenged transaction must withstand rigorous judicial scrutiny under the exacting standards of entire fairness. Weinberger v. UOP, Inc., Del.Supr., 457 A.2d 701, 710 (1983); Gottlieb v. Heyden Chemical Corp., Del.Supr., 33 Del.Ch. 177, 91 A.2d 57, 58 (1952). Compare Rosenblatt v. Getty Oil Co., Del.Supr., 493 A.2d 929, 937–40 (1985). What occurred here cannot survive that analysis.[27]

The Vice Chancellor correctly found that Evans and Reilly, as participants in the leveraged buyout, had significant self-interest in ensuring the success of a KKR bid. Given this finding, Evans' and Reilly's deliberate concealment of material information from the Macmillan board must necessarily have been motivated by an interest adverse to Macmillan's shareholders. Evans' and Reilly's conduct throughout was resolutely intended to deliver the company to themselves in *Macmillan I,* and to their favored bidder, KKR, and thus themselves, in *Macmillan II.* The board was torpid, if not supine, in its efforts to establish a truly independent auction, free of Evans' interference and access to confidential data. By placing the entire process in the hands of Evans, through his own chosen financial advisors, with little or no board oversight, the board materially contributed to the unprincipled conduct of those upon whom it looked with a blind eye.

B.

* * *

[D]irectors are required to demonstrate both their utmost good faith and the most scrupulous inherent fairness of transactions in which they possess a financial, business or other personal interest which does not devolve upon the corporation or all stockholders generally. *Aronson,* 473 A.2d at 812; *Pogostin,* 480 A.2d at 624; *Weinberger,* 457 A.2d at 710. When faced with such divided loyalties, directors have the burden of establishing the entire fairness of the transaction to survive careful scrutiny by the courts.

---

27. See AC Acquisitions v. Anderson, Clayton & Co., Del.Ch., 519 A.2d 103, 111 (1986) wherein the court correctly noted that "where a self-interested corporate fiduciary has set the terms of a transaction and caused its effectuation, it will be required to establish the entire fairness of the transaction to a reviewing court's satisfaction." Id. [citing Weinberger v. UOP, Inc., Del.Supr., 457 A.2d 701 (1983); Sterling v. Mayflower Hotel Corp., Del.Supr., 33 Del.Ch. 293, 93 A.2d 107 (1952); Guth v. Loft, Del.Supr., 23 Del.Ch. 255, 5 A.2d 503 (1939)]. We could conceive no clearer instance of the proper application of this most basic rule of law than the present case.

Under Delaware law this concept of fairness has two aspects: fair dealing and fair price. *Weinberger,* 457 A.2d at 711. "Fair dealing" focuses upon the actual conduct of corporate fiduciaries in effecting a transaction, such as its initiation, structure, and negotiation. This element also embraces the duty of candor owed by corporate fiduciaries to disclose all material information relevant to corporate decisions from which they may derive a personal benefit. See 8 *Del.C.* § 144. "Fair price," in the context of an auction for corporate control, mandates that directors commit themselves, inexorably, to obtaining the highest value reasonably available to the shareholders under all the circumstances. *Weinberger,* 457 A.2d at 711.

III.

The voluminous record in this case discloses conduct that fails all basic standards of fairness. While any one of the identifiable breaches of fiduciary duty, standing alone, should easily foretell the outcome, what occurred here, including the lack of oversight by the directors, irremediably taints the design and execution of the transaction.

It is clear that on July 14, 1988, the day that the Court of Chancery enjoined the management-induced reorganization, and with Bass' $73 offer outstanding, Macmillan's management met with KKR to discuss a management sponsored buyout. This was done without prior board approval. By early September, Macmillan's financial and legal advisors, originally chosen by Evans, independently constructed and managed the process by which bids for the company were solicited. Although the Macmillan board was fully aware of its ultimate responsibility for ensuring the integrity of the auction, the directors wholly delegated the creation and administration of the auction to an array of Evans' hand-picked investment advisors. It is undisputed that Wasserstein, who was originally retained as an investment advisor to Macmillan's senior management, was a principal, if not the primary, "auctioneer" of the company. While it is unnecessary to hold that Wasserstein lacked independence, or was necessarily "beholden" to management, it appears that Lazard Freres, allegedly the investment advisor to the independent directors, was a far more appropriate candidate to conduct this process on behalf of the board. Yet, both the board and Lazard acceded to Wasserstein's, and through him Evans', primacy.

While a board of directors may rely in good faith upon "information, opinions, reports or statements presented" by corporate officers, employees and experts "selected with reasonable care," 8 *Del.C.* § 141(e), it may not avoid its active and direct duty of oversight in a matter as significant as the sale of corporate control. That would seem particularly obvious where insiders are among the bidders. This failure of the Macmillan board significantly contributed to the resulting mismanagement of the bidding process. When presumably well-intentioned outside directors remove themselves from the design and execution of an auction, then what occurred here, given the human temptations left unchecked, was virtually inevitable.

Clearly, this auction was clandestinely and impermissibly skewed in favor of KKR. The record amply demonstrates that KKR repeatedly received significant material advantages to the exclusion and detriment of Maxwell to stymie, rather than enhance, the bidding process.

As for any "negotiations" between Macmillan and Maxwell, they are noteworthy only for the peremptory and curt attitude of Macmillan, through its self-interested chief executive officer Evans, to reject every overture from Maxwell. In Robert Maxwell's initial letter to Evans of July 21, he proposed an $80 all-cash offer for the company. This represented a substantial increase over any other outstanding offer. Indeed, it equalled the highest per share price, which both Wasserstein, Perella and Lazard had previously ascribed to the value of the company on June 7, when the Evans' sponsored restructuring was before the board. Now, not only was Maxwell ignored, but Evans convinced Wasserstein, Perella and Lazard, contrary to their June 7 opinions, ascribing a maximum value to the company of $80 per share, to declare Maxwell's August 12 bid of $80 inadequate.[28] Not only did Macmillan's financial advisors dismiss all Maxwell offers for negotiations, but they also deliberately misled Maxwell in the final stage of the auction by perpetuating the mistaken belief that Maxwell had the high bid. Additionally, Maxwell was subjected to a series of short bid deadlines in a seeming effort to prevent the submission of a meaningful bid. The defendants have totally failed to justify this calculated campaign of resistance and misinformation, despite the strict duties of care and loyalty demanded of them. See *Revlon*, 506 A.2d at 181.

* * *

This continuing hostility toward Maxwell cannot be justified after the Macmillan board actually decided on September 10–11 to abandon any further restructuring attempts, and to sell the entire company. Although Evans had begun negotiations with KKR on July 14, the board's action in September formally initiated the auction process. Further discriminatory treatment of a bidder, without any rational benefit to the shareholders, was unwarranted. The proper objective of Macmillan's fiduciaries was to obtain the highest price reasonably available for the company, provided it was offered by a reputable and responsible bidder.[29] *Revlon*, 506 A.2d at 182, 184. At this point, there was no justification for denying Maxwell the same courtesies and access to information as had been extended to KKR. Id. at 184. Without

---

28. Yet, on May 30 these same advisors had found management's $64.15 restructuring to be fair.

29. In assessing the bid and the bidder's responsibility, a board may consider, among various proper factors, the adequacy and terms of the offer; its fairness and feasibility; the proposed or actual financing for the offer, and the consequences of that financing; questions of illegality; the impact of both the bid and the potential acquisition on other constituencies, provid-ed that it bears some reasonable relationship to general shareholder interests; the risk of nonconsummation; the basic stockholder interests at stake; the bidder's identity, prior background and other business venture experiences; and the bidder's business plans for the corporation and their effects on stockholder interests. Cf. Ivanhoe, 535 A.2d at 1341–42; Unocal, 493 A.2d at 955–56; Revlon, 506 A.2d at 182–83.

board planning and oversight to insulate the self-interested management from improper access to the bidding process, and to ensure the proper conduct of the auction by truly independent advisors selected by, and answerable only to, the independent directors, the legal complications which a challenged transaction faces under *Revlon* are unnecessarily intensified. See *Weinberger,* 457 A.2d at 709 n. 7. Compare *Rosenblatt,* 493 A.2d at 937–40, where an authentic independent negotiating structure had been established.

IV.

In examining the actual conduct of this auction, there can be no justification for the telephonic "tip" to KKR of Maxwell's $89 all-cash offer following the first round of bidding held on September 26th. Although the defendants contend that this tip was made "innocently" and under the impression that the auction process had already ended, this assertion is refuted by the record. The recipient of the "tip", KKR, immediately recognized its impropriety.[30] Evans' and Reilly's knowing concealment of the tip at the critical board meeting of September 27th utterly destroys their credibility. Given their duty of disclosure under the circumstances, this silence is an explicit acknowledgment of their culpability. * * *

* * * [F]iduciaries, corporate or otherwise, may not use superior information or knowledge to mislead others in the performance of their own fiduciary obligations. The actions of those who join in such misconduct are equally tainted. * * *

Defendants maintain that the Evans–Reilly tip was immaterial, because it did not prevent Maxwell from submitting a higher bid in the second and final round of the auction on September 26th. However, this "immaterial" tip revealed both the price and form of Maxwell's first round bid, which constituted the two principal strategic components of their otherwise unconditional offer. With this information, KKR knew every crucial element of Maxwell's initial bid. The unfair tactical advantage this gave KKR, since no aspect of its own bid could be shopped, becomes manifest in light of the situation created by Maxwell's belief that it had submitted the higher offer.[31] Absent an

---

30. Although the KKR representative initially was unaware of the unauthorized nature of the tip, it is revealing that he abruptly terminated the call when he realized that Evans and Reilly were acting improperly. At the least, it stands in stark contrast to the later efforts of KKR, Evans and other defendants to trivialize this extraordinary act of misconduct.

31. Although KKR maintains that it considered this disclosure of Maxwell's initial bid to be "immaterial", counsel for KKR at oral argument asserted that KKR would have held an analogous disclosure of any aspect of its bid to Maxwell to be material. See 1 Mergers & Acquisitions L.Rep. at 902–05. In short, if the same

"immaterial" disclosure had been made of KKR's bid, it would have "walked". Id. at 905. An example of KKR's incongruous position is demonstrated by the following colloquy:

* * *

JUSTICE HOLLAND: Well, Maxwell's question, realizing they had a cash bid, was, "Do you have a higher bid?" Now, would it have violated your client's no-shop provision to say, "Yes, we do"?

MR. KOOB (counsel for KKR): Your Honor, my client's position is that had that been told to Mr. Maxwell and we found out about it, we would have withdrawn publicly.

Id. at 907.

unprompted and unexpected improvement in Maxwell's bid, the tip provided vital information to enable KKR to prevail in the auction.

Similarly, the defendants argue that the subsequent Wasserstein "long script"—in reality another form of tip—was an immaterial and "appropriate response" to questions by KKR, providing no tactical information useful to KKR. As to this claim, the eventual auction results demonstrate that Wasserstein's tip relayed crucial information to KKR: the methods by which KKR should tailor its bid in order to satisfy Macmillan's financial advisors. It is highly significant that both aspects of the advice conveyed by the tip—to "focus on price" and to amend the terms of its lockup agreement—were adopted by KKR. They were the very improvements upon which the board subsequently accepted the KKR bid on Wasserstein's recommendation. Nothing could have been more material under the circumstances. It violated every principle of fair dealing, and of the exacting role demanded of those entrusted with the conduct of an auction for the sale of corporate control. *Weinberger,* 457 A.2d at 710–711; *Revlon,* 506 A.2d at 182, 184.

V.

Given the materiality of these tips, and the silence of Evans, Reilly and Wasserstein in the face of their rigorous affirmative duty of disclosure at the September 27 board meeting, there can be no dispute but that such silence was misleading and deceptive. In short, it was a fraud upon the board. * * *

Under 8 Del.C. § 141(e), when corporate directors rely in good faith upon opinions or reports of officers and other experts "selected with reasonable care", they necessarily do so on the presumption that the information provided is both accurate and complete. * * * However, when a board is deceived by those who will gain from such misconduct, the protections girding the decision itself vanish. Decisions made on such a basis are voidable at the behest of innocent parties to whom a fiduciary duty was owed and breached, and whose interests were thereby materially and adversely affected.[32] This rule is based on the unyielding principle that corporate fiduciaries shall abjure every temp-

---

32. In this context we speak only of the traditional concept of protecting the decision itself, sometimes referred to as the business judgment doctrine. *Revlon,* 506 A.2d at 180 n. 10. The question of the independent directors' personal liability for these challenged decisions, reached under circumstances born of the board's lack of oversight, is not the issue here. However, we entertain no doubt that this board's virtual abandonment of its oversight functions in the face of Evans' and Reilly's patent self-interest was a breach of its fun-

damental duties of loyalty and care in the conduct of this auction. More than anything else it created the atmosphere in which Evans, Reilly and others could act so freely and improperly. Given these facts, a board can take little comfort in what was said under far different circumstances in *Graham v. Allis Chalmers Mfg. Co.,* Del. Supr., 41 Del.Ch. 78, 188 A.2d 125, 130–31 (1963). See *Smith,* 488 A.2d at 872; *Lutz v. Boas,* 39 Del.Ch. 585, 171 A.2d 381 (1961). Nor can decisions reached under such circumstances be sustained.

tation for personal profit at the expense of those they serve.[33] *Guth,* 5 A.2d at 510.

VI.

In *Revlon,* we addressed for the first time the parameters of a board of directors' fiduciary duties in a sale of corporate control. There, we affirmed the Court of Chancery's decision to enjoin the lockup and no-shop provisions accepted by the Revlon directors, holding that the board had breached its fiduciary duties of care and loyalty.[34]

Although we have held that such agreements are not *per se* illegal, we recognized that like measures often foreclose further bidding to the detriment of shareholders, and end active auctions prematurely. * * * If the grant of an auction-ending provision is appropriate, it must confer a substantial benefit upon the stockholders in order to withstand exacting scrutiny by the courts. * * * Moreover, where the decision of the directors, granting the lockup option, was not informed or was induced by breaches of fiduciary duties, such as those here, they cannot survive. * * *

A.

Perhaps the most significant aspect of *Revlon* was our holding that when the Revlon board authorized its management to negotiate a sale of the company:

> [t]he duty of the board had thus changed from the preservation of Revlon as a corporate entity to the maximization of the company's value at a sale for the stockholders benefit * * *. [The board] no longer faced threats to corporate policy and effectiveness, or to the stockholders' interests, from a grossly inadequate bid. The whole question of defensive measures became moot. The directors' role changed from defenders of the corporate bastion to auctioneers charged with getting the best price for the stockholders at a sale of the company.

Revlon, 506 A.2d at 182.

This case does not require a judicial determination of *when* Macmillan was "for sale."[35] By any standards this company was for sale

33. Although Wasserstein was not a Macmillan officer or director, it is bedrock law that the conduct of one who knowingly joins with a fiduciary, including corporate officials, in breaching a fiduciary obligation, is equally culpable. Thus, decisions based on the advice of such persons share the same defects as those discussed in n. 32, supra. *Ivanhoe,* 535 A.2d at 1344; *Penn Mart Realty,* 298 A.2d at 351.

34. Following *Revlon,* there appeared to be a degree of "scholarly" debate about the particular fiduciary duty that had been breached in that case, i.e. the duty of care or the duty of loyalty. In *Ivanhoe,* 535 A.2d at 1345, we made it abundantly clear that *both* duties were involved in *Revlon,* and that both had been breached.

35. This Court has been required to determine on other occasions since our decision in *Revlon,* whether a company is "for sale". See *Ivanhoe,* 535 A.2d at 1345; *Bershad v. Curtiss–Wright Corp.,* Del.Supr., 535 A.2d 840, 845 (1987). Clearly not every offer or transaction affecting the corporate structure invokes the *Revlon* duties. A refusal to entertain offers may comport with a valid exercise of business judgment. See *Bershad; Ivanhoe,* 535 A.2d at 1341–42; *Pogostin,* 480 A.2d at 627; *Aronson,* 473 A.2d at 812–16. Circumstances may dictate that an offer be rebuffed, given the

both in *Macmillan I* and *II*. In any event, the board of directors formally concluded on September 11 that it would be in the best interests of the stockholders to sell the company. Evidently, they reached this decision with the prospect of a KKR—management sponsored buyout in mind. * * *

What we are required to determine here is the scope of the board's responsibility in an active bidding contest once their role as auctioneer has been invoked under *Revlon*. Particularly, we are concerned with the use of lockup and no-shop clauses.

* * *

The Macmillan directors argue that a "blind auction" is a desirable means to fulfill their primary duty to the shareholders. That may be so, but it did not happen here. Only Maxwell was blind.

B.

Turning to the lockup option, * * * it has escaped some that in *Revlon* we distinguished the potentially valid uses of a lockup from those that are impermissible:

> "[W]hile those lockups which draw bidders into a battle benefit shareholders, similar measures which end an active auction and foreclose further bidding operate to the shareholders detriment."

Id. at 183. See also *Hanson Trust*, 781 F.2d at 272.

In this case, a lockup agreement was not necessary to draw any of the bidders into the contest. Macmillan cannot seriously contend that they received a final bid from KKR that materially enhanced general stockholder interests. By all rational indications it was intended to have a directly opposite effect. As the record clearly shows, on numerous occasions Maxwell requested opportunities to further negotiate the price and structure of his proposal. When he learned of KKR's higher offer, he increased his bid to $90.25 per share. * * * Further, KKR's "enhanced" bid, being nominal at best, was a *de minimis* justification for the lockup. When one compares what KKR received for the lockup, in contrast to its inconsiderable offer, the invalidity of the agreement becomes patent. * * *

nature and timing of the offer; its legality, feasibility and effect on the corporation and the stockholders; the alternatives available and their effect on the various constituencies, particularly the stockholders; the company's long term strategic plans; and any special factors bearing on stockholder and public interests. *Unocal*, 493 A.2d at 954–56. See also *Smith*, 488 A.2d 872–78. In *Ivanhoe* we recognized that a change in corporate structure under the special facts and circumstances of that case did not invoke *Revlon*, 535 A.2d at 1345. Specifically, Newmont's management faced two potentially coercive offers.

In responding to such threats management's efforts were viewed as reasonable decisions intended to guide the corporation through the minefield of dangers directly posed by one bidder, and potentially by another. Id. at 1342–45. While it was argued that the transaction benefited management by strengthening its position, at most this was a secondary effect. There was no proof of self-dealing, and the evidence clearly sustained the conclusion that the board of Newmont punctiliously met its fiduciary obligations to the stockholders in the face of two major threats.

Here, the assets covered by the lockup agreement were some of Macmillan's most valued properties, its "crown jewels." Even if the lockup is permissible, when it involves "crown jewel" assets careful board scrutiny attends the decision. When the intended effect is to end an active auction, at the very least the independent members of the board must attempt to negotiate alternative bids before granting such a significant concession. See *Revlon,* 506 A.2d at 183; *Hanson Trust,* 781 F.2d at 277. Maxwell invited negotiations for a purchase of the same four divisions, which KKR originally sought to buy for $775 million. Maxwell was prepared to pay $900 million. Instead of serious negotiations with Maxwell, there were only concessions to KKR by giving it a lockup of seven divisions for $865 million.

Thus, when directors in a *Revlon* bidding contest grant a crown jewel lockup, serious questions are raised, particularly where, as here, there is little or no improvement in the final bid. * * *

C.

As for the no-shop clause, *Revlon* teaches that the use of such a device is even more limited than a lockup agreement. Absent a material advantage to the stockholders from the terms or structure of a bid that is contingent on a no-shop clause, a successful bidder imposing such a condition must be prepared to survive the careful scrutiny which that concession demands. *Revlon,* 506 A.2d at 184.

VII.

A.

Directors are not required by Delaware law to conduct an auction according to some standard formula, only that they observe the significant requirement of fairness for the purpose of enhancing general shareholder interests. That does not preclude differing treatment of bidders when necessary to advance those interests. Variables may occur which necessitate such treatment.[38] However, the board's primary objective, and essential purpose, must remain the enhancement of the bidding process for the benefit of the stockholders.

We recognize that the conduct of a corporate auction is a complex undertaking both in its design and execution. See e.g. McAfee & Macmillan, Auctions and Bidding, 25 J.Econ.Lit. 699 (1987); Milgrom, The Economics of Competitive Bidding: A Selected Survey, in Social Goals and Social Organization 261 (Hurwitz, Schneidler & Sonnenschein eds. 1985.) We do not intend to limit the broad negotiating authority of the directors to achieve the best price available to the stockholders. To properly secure that end may require the board to invoke a panoply of devices, and the giving or receiving of concessions that may benefit one bidder over another. See e.g., In re J.P. Stevens & Co., Inc. Shareholders Litigation, Del.Ch., 542 A.2d 770, 781–784 (1988); appeal refused, 540 A.2d 1088 (1988). But when that happens, there

---

38. For example, this Court has upheld actions of directors when a board is confronted with a coercive "two-tiered" bust-up tender offer. See *Unocal,* 493 A.2d at 956; *Ivanhoe,* 535 A.2d at 1342. Compare *Revlon,* 506 A.2d at 184.

must be a rational basis for the action such that the interests of the stockholders are manifestly the board's paramount objective.

B.

In the absence of self-interest, and upon meeting the enhanced duty mandated by *Unocal,* the actions of an independent board of directors in designing and conducting a corporate auction are protected by the business judgment rule. * * *

However, as we recognized in *Unocal,* where issues of corporate control are at stake, there exists "the omnipresent specter that a board may be acting primarily in its own interests, rather than those of the corporation and its shareholders." *Unocal,* 493 A.2d at 954. For that reason, an "enhanced duty" must be met at the threshold before the board receives the normal protections of the business judgment rule. * * *

As we held in *Revlon,* when management of a target company determines that the company is for sale, the board's *responsibilities* under the enhanced *Unocal* standards are significantly altered. *Revlon,* 506 A.2d at 182. Although the board's *responsibilities* under *Unocal* are far different, the enhanced *duties* of the directors in responding to a potential shift in control, recognized in *Unocal,* remain unchanged. This principle pervades *Revlon,* and when directors conclude that an auction is appropriate, the standard by which their ensuing actions will be judged continues to be the enhanced duty imposed by this Court in *Unocal.*

* * *

When *Revlon* duties devolve upon directors, this Court will continue to exact an enhanced judicial scrutiny at the threshold, as in *Unocal,* before the normal presumptions of the business judgment rule will apply. However, as we recognized in *Revlon,* the two part threshold test, of necessity, is slightly different. *Revlon,* 506 A.2d at 182.

At the outset, the plaintiff must show, and the trial court must find, that the directors of the target company treated one or more of the respective bidders on unequal terms. It is only then that the two-part threshold requirement of *Unocal* is truly invoked, for in *Revlon* we held that "[f]avoritism for a white knight to the total exclusion of a hostile bidder might be justifiable when the latter's offer adversely affects shareholder interests, but * * * the directors cannot fulfill their enhanced *Unocal* duties by playing favorites with the contending factions." Id. 506 A.2d at 184.

In the face of disparate treatment, the trial court must first examine whether the directors properly perceived that shareholder interests were enhanced. In any event the board's action must be reasonable in relation to the advantage sought to be achieved, or conversely, to the threat which a particular bid allegedly poses to stockholder interests. *Unocal,* 493 A.2d at 955.

If on the basis of this enhanced *Unocal* scrutiny the trial court is satisfied that the test has been met, then the directors' actions necessarily are entitled to the protections of the business judgment rule. The latitude a board will have in responding to differing bids will vary according to the degree of benefit or detriment to the shareholders' general interests that the amount or terms of the bids pose. We stated in *Revlon,* and again here, that in a sale of corporate control the responsibility of the directors is to get the highest value reasonably attainable for the shareholders. *Revlon,* 506 A.2d at 182. Beyond that, there are no special and distinct "Revlon duties". Once a finding has been made by a court that the directors have fulfilled their fundamental duties of care and loyalty under the foregoing standards, there is no further judicial inquiry into the matter. * * *

For the foregoing reasons, the judgment of the Court of Chancery, denying Maxwell's motion for a preliminary injunction, is reversed.

NOTE: THE *REVLON* AUCTION

1. *The Trigger.*

When is the corporation deemed to be "for sale" so as to change the directors' role from that of defender of the corporate bastion to that of an auctioneer charged with getting the best price for the stockholders? The *Revlon* formula, as modified in *Macmillan,* contains significant ambiguous components.

Is the company "for sale," so that management must conduct an auction:

a. If, and only if, management contemplates a bust-up and sale of all or most of its assets? See *Time,* infra.

b. If, and only if, management has proposed a transaction that results in a new management or new controlling stockholder group?

c. If management has begun negotiations for a friendly merger but no unfriendly bid has been made? Rand v. Western Airlines, Inc., 1989 WL 104933 (Del.Ch. 1989). If an unfriendly, competing bid is made thereafter?

d. If a third party is sought for a friendly merger after an unsolicited bid has been made?

e. If management proposes to effect a restructuring after a hostile bid has been made?

f. If management seeks effect a restructuring and then an unsolicited bid is made? Barkan v. Amsted Indus., Inc., 567 A.2d 1279 (Del.1989).

Should a proposed change of control result in the company being "for sale"? If so, is the relevant change of control a change of managerial control or a change of controlling stock ownership or both? Should it be the acquisition of an actual majority of the shares or only of enough shares to give effective control? *Time,* infra, suggests that a merging enterprise is not for sale even though the old managers remain effectively entrenched in operating control, because the resulting company's widely dispersed public stockholdings keep open the technical possibility of a takeover. Is this a persuasive suggestion? See Gilson & Kraakman, What Triggers Revlon? 25 Wake Forest L.Rev. 37 (1990).

2. *The Duty.*

If the corporation is found to be for sale, will management's behavior be constrained and assessed more rigorously than under *Unocal* proportionality? The answer to this question depends in part on the determination of the permissible objective of the auction process. Should the object be the highest immediate price for stockholders? Or should some other concept of value "enhancement" be admitted, such as long term imputed value? Must the objective be stockholder gain, or can some conception of maximum return for all stakeholders be admitted?

Whatever the objective of the auction, *Revlon* is said to require that management conduct it "fairly." But, of course, the operational meaning of fairness will vary in accord with the choice of objective. Possibly, uncertainty as to the object of the auction explains why the Delaware courts sometimes find the process to be "fair" only if the board does not procedurally favor any bidder, and at other times find "fairness" to be satisfied notwithstanding that the board thus favors the successful bidder (by way of lock-ups, no shops, special fees, or confidential information), who is often a management affiliate or sponsor.[c] Possibly the explanation is to be found in inquiry as to how the *Unocal* standard would apply to the favoring acts.

Lower court decisions on occasion seem to respect the board's business judgment with little review of its conclusion to tilt the auction, at least if the court believes that the board reasonably thinks that doing so will favor some conception of a market process, or, more vaguely, the best interests of the stockholders.[d] The Delaware Supreme Court's language in *Revlon* suggests that more demanding standards of judicial review are to be invoked and more rigorous standards of fidelity are to be required of the board in the conduct of an auction than are involved in connection with other defensive maneuvers. But Part VI of *Macmillan* suggests that the same "standard" or duty or level of constraint appears in both circumstances. Perhaps both *Revlon* and *Macmillan* can be distinguished on their facts. Both involve obvious managerial self-dealing and suggestions of board failure ade-

---

c. Compare *Macmillan* and Black & Decker Corp. v. American Standard Inc., 682 F.Supp. 772 (D.Del.1988), with West Point Pepperell, Inc. v. J.P. Stevens & Co., 542 A.2d 770, 782 (Del.Ch.1988); Fort Howard Corp. Shareholders Litigation, supra note i; Dockocil Cos., Inc. v. Griggy, supra note z; In re Holly Farms Corp. Litigation, 1989 WL 25810 (Del.Ch.1989); CRTF v. Federated Dept. Stores, Inc., 683 F.Supp. 422 (S.D.N.Y.1988).

d. See, e.g., West Point–Pepperell, Inc. v. J.P. Stevens & Co., supra note c; Samjens Partners v. Burlington Industries, Inc., 663 F.Supp. 614 (S.D.N.Y.1987); In re Holly Farms Corp. Litigation, supra note c; CRTF Corp. v. Federated Dept. Stores, Inc., supra note c.

quately to supervise.　Strict review follows where such facts obtain; where self-dealing is less self evident, scrutiny is less strict.[e]

If there probably "will no more be a perfect tender offer than a perfect trial," [f] there is not likely to be a perfect *Revlon* auction.　These events do not occur in the "peace of a quiet chamber" or with the gentility thought to attend art sales at Southeby's.　Moreover, uncertainty as to the object to be attained and a broad range of process variables leave management with considerable discretion and courts with few operating guidelines in deciding particular cases under *Revlon.*

---

(4) Retrenchment

PARAMOUNT COMMUNICATIONS, INC. v. TIME INC.

Supreme Court of Delaware, 1989.
571 A.2d 1140.

HORSEY, Justice:

Paramount Communications, Inc. ("Paramount") and two other groups of plaintiffs ("Shareholder Plaintiffs"), shareholders of Time Incorporated ("Time"), a Delaware corporation, separately filed suits in the Delaware Court of Chancery seeking a preliminary injunction to halt Time's tender offer for 51% of Warner Communication, Inc.'s ("Warner") outstanding shares at $70 cash per share.　The court below consolidated the cases and, following the development of an extensive record, after discovery and an evidentiary hearing, denied plaintiffs' motion.　In a 50–page unreported opinion and order entered July 14, 1989, the Chancellor refused to enjoin Time's consummation of its tender offer, concluding that the plaintiffs were unlikely to prevail on the merits.　In re Time Incorporated Shareholder Litigation, Del.Ch., C.A. No. 10670, Allen, C., 1989 WL 79880 (July 14, 1989).

* * *

Applying our standard of review, we affirm the Chancellor's ultimate finding and conclusion under *Unocal.*　We find that Paramount's tender offer was reasonably perceived by Time's board to pose a threat to Time and that the Time board's "response" to that threat was, under the circumstances, reasonable and proportionate.　Applying *Unocal,* we reject the argument that the only corporate threat posed by an all-shares, all-cash tender offer is the possibility of inadequate value.

We also find that Time's board did not by entering into its initial merger agreement with Warner come under a *Revlon* duty either to auction the company or to maximize short-term shareholder value,

---

e.　See Chancery cases cited in note c supra.

f.　Electronic Specialty Co. v. International Controls Co., 409 F.2d 937, 948 (2d Cir.1969).

notwithstanding the unequal share exchange. Therefore, the Time board's original plan of merger with Warner was subject only to a business judgment rule analysis. See Smith v. Van Gorkom, Del.Supr., 488 A.2d 858, 873–74 (1985).

I

Time is a Delaware corporation with its principal offices in New York City. Time's traditional business is publication of magazines and books; however, Time also provides pay television programming through its Home Box Office, Inc. and Cinemax subsidiaries. In addition, Time owns and operates cable television franchises through its subsidiary, American Television and Communication Corporation. During the relevant time period, Time's board consisted of sixteen directors. Twelve of the directors were "outside," nonemployee directors. Four of the directors were also officers of the company. * * *

As early as 1983 and 1984, Time's executive board began considering expanding Time's operations into the entertainment industry. In 1987, Time established a special committee of executives to consider and propose corporate strategies for the 1990s. The consensus of the committee was that Time should move ahead in the area of ownership and creation of video programming. This expansion, as the Chancellor noted, was predicated upon two considerations: first, Time's desire to have greater control, in terms of quality and price, over the film products delivered by way of its cable network and franchises; and second, Time's concern over the increasing globalization of the world economy. Some of Time's outside directors, especially Luce and Temple, had opposed this move as a threat to the editorial integrity and journalistic focus of Time.[4] Despite this concern, the board recognized that a vertically integrated video enterprise to complement Time's existing HBO and cable networks would better enable it to compete on a global basis.

[In 1987, presumably stimulated by the above considerations, representatives of Time entered into negotiations with representatives of Warner Brothers for a consolidation of the two enterprises. The negotiations were complicated and protracted.]

From the outset, Time's board favored an all-cash or cash and securities acquisition of Warner as the basis for consolidation. Bruce Wasserstein, Time's financial advisor, also favored an outright purchase of Warner. However, Steve Ross, Warner's CEO, was adamant that a business combination was only practicable on a stock-for-stock basis. Warner insisted on a stock swap in order to preserve its shareholders' equity in the resulting corporation. Time's officers, on the other hand, made it abundantly clear that Time would be the

---

4. The primary concern of Time's outside directors was the preservation of the "Time Culture." They believed that Time had become recognized in this country as an institution built upon a foundation of journalistic integrity. Time's management made a studious effort to refrain from involvement in Time's editorial policy. Several of Time's outside directors feared that a merger with an entertainment company would divert Time's focus from news journalism and threaten the Time Culture.

acquiring corporation and that Time would control the resulting board. Time refused to permit itself to be cast as the "acquired" company.

Eventually Time acquiesced in Warner's insistence on a stock-for-stock deal, but talks broke down over corporate governance issues. Time wanted Ross' position as a co-CEO to be temporary and wanted Ross to retire in five years. Ross, however, refused to set a time for his retirement and viewed Time's proposal as indicating a lack of confidence in his leadership. Warner considered it vital that their executives and creative staff not perceive Warner as selling out to Time. Time's request of a guarantee that Time would dominate the CEO succession was objected to as inconsistent with the concept of a Time–Warner merger "of equals." Negotiations ended when the parties reached an impasse. Time's board refused to compromise on its position on corporate governance. Time, and particularly its outside directors, viewed the corporate governance provisions as critical for preserving the "Time Culture" through a pro-Time management at the top. See supra note 4.

Throughout the fall of 1988 Time pursued its plan of expansion into the entertainment field; Time held informal discussions with several companies, including Paramount. Capital Cities/ABC approached Time to propose a merger. Talks terminated, however, when Capital Cities/ABC suggested that it was interested in purchasing Time or in controlling the resulting board. Time steadfastly maintained it was not placing itself up for sale.

Warner and Time resumed negotiations in January 1989. The catalyst for the resumption of talks was a private dinner between Steve Ross and Time outside director, Michael Dingman. Dingman was able to convince Ross that the transitional nature of the proposed co-CEO arrangement did not reflect a lack of confidence in Ross. Ross agreed that this course was best for the company and a meeting between Ross and Munro resulted. Ross agreed to retire in five years and let Nicholas succeed him. Negotiations resumed and many of the details of the original stock-for-stock exchange agreement remained intact. In addition, Time's senior management agreed to long-term contracts.

Time insider directors Levin and Nicholas met with Warner's financial advisors to decide upon a stock exchange ratio. Time's board had recognized the potential need to pay a premium in the stock ratio in exchange for dictating the governing arrangement of the new Time–Warner. Levin and outside director Finkelstein were the primary proponents of paying a premium to protect the "Time Culture." The board discussed premium rates of 10%, 15% and 20%. Wasserstein also suggested paying a premium for Warner due to Warner's rapid growth rate. The market exchange ratio of Time stock for Warner stock was .38 in favor of Warner. Warner's financial advisors informed its board that any exchange rate over .400 was a fair deal and any exchange rate over .450 was "one hell of a deal." The parties ultimately agreed upon an exchange rate favoring Warner of .465. On that basis, Warner stockholders would have owned approximately 62% [7] of the common stock of Time–Warner.

On March 3, 1989, Time's board, with all but one director in attendance, met and unanimously approved the stock-for-stock merger with Warner. Warner's board likewise approved the merger. The agreement called for Warner to be merged into a wholly-owned Time subsidiary with Warner becoming the surviving corporation. The common stock of Warner would then be converted into common stock of Time at the agreed upon ratio. Thereafter, the name of Time would be changed to Time–Warner, Inc.

The rules of the New York Stock Exchange required that Time's issuance of shares to effectuate the merger be approved by a vote of Time's stockholders. The Delaware General Corporation Law required approval of the merger by a majority of the Warner stockholders. Delaware law did not require any vote by Time stockholders. The Chancellor concluded that the agreement was the product of "an arms-length negotiation between two parties seeking individual advantage through mutual action."

The resulting company would have a 24–member board, with 12 members representing each corporation. The company would have co-CEO's, at first Ross and Munro, then Ross and Nicholas, and finally, after Ross' retirement, by Nicholas alone. The board would create an editorial committee with a majority of members representing Time. A similar entertainment committee would be controlled by Warner board members. A two-thirds supermajority vote was required to alter CEO successions but an earlier proposal to have supermajority protection for the editorial committee was abandoned. Warner's board suggested raising the compensation levels for Time's senior management under the new corporation. Warner's management, as with most entertainment executives, received higher salaries than comparable executives in news journalism. Time's board, however, rejected Warner's proposal to equalize the salaries of the two management teams.

At its March 3, 1989 meeting, Time's board adopted several defensive tactics.[*] Time entered an automatic share exchange agreement with Warner. Time would receive 17,292,747 shares of Warner's outstanding common stock (9.4%) and Warner would receive 7,080,016 shares of Time's outstanding common stock (11.1%). Either party could trigger the exchange. Time sought out and paid for "confidence" letters from various banks with which it did business. In these letters, the banks promised not to finance any third-party attempt to acquire Time. Time argues these agreements served only to preserve the confidential relationship between itself and the banks. The Chancellor

---

7. As was noted in the briefs and at oral argument, this figure is somewhat misleading because it does not take into consideration the number of individuals who owned stock in both companies.

*[Court's footnote 5.] Time had in place a panoply of defensive devices, including a staggered board, a "poison pill" * * * triggered by an acquisition of 15% of the company, a fifty-day notice period for shareholder motions, and restrictions on shareholders' ability to call a meeting or act by consent.

found these agreements to be inconsequential and futile attempts to "dry up" money for a hostile takeover. Time also agreed to a "no-shop" clause, preventing Time from considering any other consolidation proposal, thus relinquishing its power to consider other proposals, regardless of their merits. Time did so at Warner's insistence. Warner did not want to be left "on the auction block" for an unfriendly suitor, if Time were to withdraw from the deal.

Time's board simultaneously established a special committee of outside directors, Finkelstein, Kearns, and Opel, to oversee the merger. The committee's assignment was to resolve any impediments that might arise in the course of working out the details of the merger and its consummation.

Time representatives lauded the lack of debt to the United States Senate and to the President of the United States. Public reaction to the announcement of the merger was positive. Time–Warner would be a media colossus with international scope. The board scheduled the stockholder vote for June 23; and a May 1 record date was set. On May 24, 1989, Time sent out extensive proxy statements to the stockholders regarding the approval vote on the merger. In the meantime, with the merger proceeding without impediment, the special committee had concluded, shortly after its creation, that it was not necessary either to retain independent consultants, legal or financial, or even to meet. Time's board was unanimously in favor of the proposed merger with Warner; and, by the end of May, the Time–Warner merger appeared to be an accomplished fact.

On June 7, 1989, these wishful assumptions were shattered by Paramount's surprising announcement of its all-cash offer to purchase all outstanding shares of Time for $175 per share. The following day, June 8, the trading price of Time's stock rose from $126 to $170 per share. Paramount's offer was said to be "fully negotiable."[8]

Time found Paramount's "fully negotiable" offer to be in fact subject to at least three conditions. First, Time had to terminate its merger agreement and stock exchange agreement with Warner, and remove certain other of its defensive devices, including the redemption of Time's shareholder rights. Second, Paramount had to obtain the required cable franchise transfers from Time in a fashion acceptable to Paramount in its sole discretion. Finally, the offer depended upon a judicial determination that section 203 of the General Corporate Law of Delaware (The Delaware Anti–Takeover Statute) was inapplicable to any Time–Paramount merger. While Paramount's board had been privately advised that it could take months, perhaps over a year, to forge and consummate the deal, Paramount's board publicly proclaimed its ability to close the offer by July 5, 1989. Paramount executives

---

8. Subsequently, it was established that Paramount's board had decided as early as March 1989 to move to acquire Time. However, Paramount management intentionally delayed publicizing its proposal until Time had mailed to its stockholders its Time–Warner merger proposal along with the required proxy statements.

later conceded that none of its directors believed that July 5th was a realistic date to close the transaction.

Over the following eight days, Time's board met three times to discuss Paramount's $175 offer. The board viewed Paramount's offer as inadequate and concluded that its proposed merger with Warner was the better course of action. Therefore, the board declined to open any negotiations with Paramount and held steady its course toward a merger with Warner.

[C]ertain Time directors expressed their concern that Time stockholders would not comprehend the long-term benefits of the Warner merger. Large quantities of Time shares were held by institutional investors. The board feared that even though there appeared to be wide support for the Warner transaction, Paramount's cash premium would be a tempting prospect to these investors. In mid-June, Time sought permission from the New York Stock Exchange to alter its rules and allow the Time–Warner merger to proceed without stockholder approval. Time did so at Warner's insistence. The New York Stock Exchange rejected Time's request on June 15; and on that day, the value of Time stock reached $182 per share.

The following day, June 16, Time's board met to take up Paramount's offer. The board's prevailing belief was that Paramount's bid posed a threat to Time's control of its own destiny and retention of the "Time Culture." The board determined to retain its same advisors even in light of the changed circumstances. The board rescinded its agreement to pay its advisors a bonus based on the consummation of the Time–Warner merger and agreed to pay a flat fee for any advice rendered. Finally, Time's board formally rejected Paramount's offer.[11]

At the same meeting, Time's board decided to recast its consolidation with Warner into an outright cash and securities acquisition of Warner by Time; and Time so informed Warner. Time accordingly restructured its proposal to acquire Warner as follows: Time would make an immediate all-cash offer for 51% of Warner's outstanding stock at $70 per share. The remaining 49% would be purchased at some later date for a mixture of cash and securities worth $70 per share. To provide the funds required for its outright acquisition of Warner, Time would assume 7–10 billion dollars worth of debt, thus eliminating one of the principal transaction-related benefits of the original merger agreement. Nine billion dollars of the total purchase price would be allocated to the purchase of Warner's goodwill.

Warner agreed but insisted on certain terms. Warner sought a control premium and guarantees that the governance provisions found in the original merger agreement would remain intact. Warner further sought agreements that Time would not employ its poison pill against Warner and that, unless enjoined, Time would be legally bound to complete the transaction. Time's board agreed to these last mea-

---

11. Meanwhile, Time had already begun erecting impediments to Paramount's offer. Time encouraged local cable franchises to sue Paramount to prevent it from easily obtaining the franchises.

sures only at the insistence of Warner. For its part, Time was assured of its ability to extend its efforts into production areas and international markets, all the while maintaining the Time identity and culture. The Chancellor found the initial Time–Warner transaction to have been negotiated at arms length and the restructured Time–Warner transaction to have resulted from Paramount's offer and its expected effect on a Time shareholder vote.

On June 23, 1989, Paramount raised its all-cash offer to buy Time's outstanding stock to $200 per share. Paramount still professed that all aspects of the offer were negotiable. Time's board met on June 26, 1989 and formally rejected Paramount's $200 per share second offer. The board reiterated its belief that, despite the $25 increase, the offer was still inadequate. The Time board maintained that the Warner transaction offered a greater long-term value for the stockholders and, unlike Paramount's offer, did not pose a threat to Time's survival and its "culture." Paramount then filed this action in the Court of Chancery.

II

The Shareholder Plaintiffs first assert a *Revlon* claim. They contend that the March 4 Time–Warner agreement effectively put Time up for sale, triggering *Revlon* duties, requiring Time's board to enhance short-term shareholder value and to treat all other interested acquirors on an equal basis. The Shareholder Plaintiffs base this argument on two facts: (i) the ultimate Time–Warner exchange ratio of .465 favoring Warner, resulting in Warner shareholders' receipt of 62% of the combined company; and (ii) the subjective intent of Time's directors as evidenced in their statements that the market might perceive the Time–Warner merger as putting Time up "for sale" and their adoption of various defensive measures.

The Shareholder Plaintiffs further contend that Time's directors, in structuring the original merger transaction to be "take-over-proof," triggered *Revlon* duties by foreclosing their shareholders from any prospect of obtaining a control premium. In short, plaintiffs argue that Time's board's decision to merge with Warner imposed a fiduciary duty to maximize immediate share value and not erect unreasonable barriers to further bids. Therefore, they argue, the Chancellor erred in finding: that Paramount's bid for Time did not place Time "for sale"; that Time's transaction with Warner did not result in any transfer of control; and that the combined Time–Warner was not so large as to preclude the possibility of the stockholders of Time–Warner receiving a future control premium.

Paramount asserts only a *Unocal* claim in which the shareholder plaintiffs join. Paramount contends that the Chancellor, in applying the first part of the *Unocal* test, erred in finding that Time's board had reasonable grounds to believe that Paramount posed both a legally cognizable threat to Time shareholders and a danger to Time's corporate policy and effectiveness. Paramount also contests the court's finding that Time's board made a reasonable and objective investigation of Paramount's offer so as to be informed before rejecting it. Paramount further claims that the court erred in applying *Unocal*'s second part in finding Time's response to be "reasonable." Paramount points primarily to the preclusive effect of the revised agreement which denied Time shareholders the opportunity both to vote on the agreement and to respond to Paramount's tender offer. Paramount argues that the underlying motivation of Time's board in adopting these defensive measures was management's desire to perpetuate itself in office.

The Court of Chancery posed the pivotal question presented by this case to be: Under what circumstances must a board of directors abandon an in-place plan of corporate development in order to provide its shareholders with the option to elect and realize an immediate control premium? As applied to this case, the question becomes: Did Time's board, having developed a strategic plan of global expansion to be launched through a business combination with Warner, come under a fiduciary duty to jettison its plan and put the corporation's future in the hands of its shareholders?

While we affirm the result reached by the Chancellor, we think it unwise to place undue emphasis upon long-term versus short-term corporate strategy. Two key predicates underpin our analysis. First, Delaware law imposes on a board of directors the duty to manage the business and affairs of the corporation. 8 Del.C. § 141(a). This broad mandate includes a conferred authority to set a corporate course of action, including time frame, designed to enhance corporate profitability. Thus, the question of "long-term" versus "short-term" values is largely irrelevant because directors, generally, are obliged to chart a course for a corporation which is in its best interests without regard to a fixed investment horizon. Second, absent a limited set of circumstances as defined under *Revlon*, a board of directors, while always required to act in an informed manner, is not under any *per se* duty to maximize shareholder value in the short term, even in the context of a takeover.[12] In our view, the pivotal question presented by this case is: "Did Time, by entering into the proposed merger with Warner, put itself up for sale?" A resolution of that issue through application of *Revlon* has a significant bearing upon the resolution of the derivative *Unocal* issue.

A.

We first take up plaintiffs' principal *Revlon* argument, summarized above. In rejecting this argument, the Chancellor found the original Time–Warner merger agreement not to constitute a "change of control" and concluded that the transaction did not trigger *Revlon* duties. The Chancellor's conclusion is premised on a finding that "[b]efore the

---

12. Thus, we endorse the Chancellor's conclusion that it is not a breach of faith for directors to determine that the present stock market price of shares is not representative of true value or that there may indeed be several market values for any corporation's stock. We have so held in another context. See *Van Gorkom*, 488 A.2d at 876.

merger agreement was signed, control of the corporation existed in a fluid aggregation of unaffiliated shareholders representing a voting majority—in other words, in the market." The Chancellor's findings of fact are supported by the record and his conclusion is correct as a matter of law. However, we premise our rejection of plaintiffs' *Revlon* claim on different grounds, namely, the absence of any substantial evidence to conclude that Time's board, in negotiating with Warner, made the dissolution or break-up of the corporate entity inevitable, as was the case in *Revlon.*

Under Delaware law there are, generally speaking and without excluding other possibilities, two circumstances which may implicate *Revlon* duties. The first, and clearer one, is when a corporation initiates an active bidding process seeking to sell itself or to effect a business reorganization involving a clear break-up of the company. See, e.g., Mills Acquisition Co. v. Macmillan, Inc., Del.Supr., 559 A.2d 1261 (1988). However, *Revlon* duties may also be triggered where, in response to a bidder's offer, a target abandons its long-term strategy and seeks an alternative transaction involving the breakup of the company. Thus, in *Revlon,* when the board responded to Pantry Pride's offer by contemplating a "bust-up" sale of assets in a leveraged acquisition, we imposed upon the board a duty to maximize immediate shareholder value and an obligation to auction the company fairly. If, however, the board's reaction to a hostile tender offer is found to constitute only a defensive response and not an abandonment of the corporation's continued existence, *Revlon* duties are not triggered, though *Unocal* duties attach.[14] See, e.g., Ivanhoe Partners v. Newmont Mining Corp., Del.Supr., 535 A.2d 1334, 1345 (1987).

The plaintiffs insist that even though the original Time–Warner agreement may not have worked "an objective change of control," the transaction made a "sale" of Time inevitable. Plaintiffs rely on the subjective intent of Time's board of directors and principally upon certain board members' expressions of concern that the Warner transaction *might* be viewed as effectively putting Time up for sale. Plaintiffs argue that the use of a lock-up agreement, a no-shop clause, and so-called "dry-up" agreements prevented shareholders from obtaining a control premium in the immediate future and thus violated *Revlon.*

We agree with the Chancellor that such evidence is entirely insufficient to invoke *Revlon* duties; and we decline to extend *Revlon*'s application to corporate transactions simply because they might be construed as putting a corporation either "in play" or "up for sale." See Citron v. Fairchild Camera, Del.Supr., 569 A.2d 53, (1989); *Macmillan,* 559 A.2d at 1285 n. 35. The adoption of structural safety devices

---

14. Within the auction process, any action taken by the board must be reasonably related to the threat posed or reasonable in relation to the advantage sought, see Mills Acquisition Co. v. Macmillan, Inc., Del.Supr., 559 A.2d 1261, 1288 (1988). Thus, a *Unocal* analysis may be appropriate when a corporation is in a *Revlon* situation and *Revlon* duties may be triggered by a defensive action taken in response to a hostile offer. Since *Revlon,* we have stated that differing treatment of various bidders is not actionable when such action reasonably relates to achieving the best price available for the stockholders. *Macmillan,* 559 A.2d at 1286–87.

alone does not trigger *Revlon.*[15] Rather, as the Chancellor stated, such devices are properly subject to a *Unocal* analysis.

Finally, we do not find in Time's recasting of its merger agreement with Warner from a share exchange to a share purchase a basis to conclude that Time had either abandoned its strategic plan or made a sale of Time inevitable. The Chancellor found that although the merged Time–Warner company would be large (with a value approaching approximately $30 billion), recent takeover cases have proven that acquisition of the combined company might nonetheless be possible. In re Time Incorporated Shareholder Litigation, Del.Ch., C.A. No. 10670, Allen, C. (July 14, 1989), slip op. at 56. The legal consequence is that *Unocal* alone applies to determine whether the business judgment rule attaches to the revised agreement. Plaintiffs' analogy to *Macmillan* thus collapses and plaintiffs' reliance on *Macmillan* is misplaced.

B.

We turn now to plaintiffs' *Unocal* claim. We begin by noting, as did the Chancellor, that our decision does not require us to pass on the wisdom of the board's decision to enter into the original Time–Warner agreement. That is not a court's task. Our task is simply to review the record to determine whether there is sufficient evidence to support the Chancellor's conclusion that the initial Time–Warner agreement was the product of a proper exercise of business judgment. *Macmillan,* 559 A.2d at 1288.

* * * Time's decision in 1988 to combine with Warner was made only after what could be fairly characterized as an exhaustive appraisal of Time's future as a corporation. After concluding in 1983–84 that the corporation must expand to survive, and beyond journalism into entertainment, the board combed the field of available entertainment companies. By 1987 Time had focused upon Warner; by late July 1988 Time's board was convinced that Warner would provide the best "fit" for Time to achieve its strategic objectives. The record attests to the zealousness of Time's executives, fully supported by their directors, in seeing to the preservation of Time's "culture," i.e., its perceived editorial integrity in journalism. We find ample evidence in the record to support the Chancellor's conclusion that the Time board's decision to expand the business of the company through its March 3 merger with Warner was entitled to the protection of the business judgment rule. See Aronson v. Lewis, Del.Supr., 473 A.2d 805, 812 (1984).

---

15. Although the legality of the various safety devices adopted to protect the original agreement is not a central issue, there is substantial evidence to support each of the trial court's related conclusions. Thus, the court found that the concept of the Share Exchange Agreement predated any takeover threat by Paramount and had been adopted for a rational business purpose: to deter Time and Warner from being "put in play" by their March 4 Agreement. The court further found that Time had adopted the "no-shop" clause at Warner's insistence and for Warner's protection. Finally, although certain aspects of the "dry-up" agreements were suspect on their face, we concur in the Chancellor's view that in this case they were inconsequential.

The Chancellor reached a different conclusion in addressing the Time–Warner transaction as revised three months later. He found that the revised agreement was defense-motivated and designed to avoid the potentially disruptive effect that Paramount's offer would have had on consummation of the proposed merger were it put to a shareholder vote. Thus, the court declined to apply the traditional business judgment rule to the revised transaction and instead analyzed the Time board's June 16 decision under *Unocal*. The court ruled that *Unocal* applied to all director actions taken, following receipt of Paramount's hostile tender offer, that were reasonably determined to be defensive. Clearly that was a correct ruling and no party disputes that ruling.

In *Unocal*, we held that before the business judgment rule is applied to a board's adoption of a defensive measure, the burden will lie with the board to prove (a) reasonable grounds for believing that a danger to corporate policy and effectiveness existed; and (b) that the defensive measure adopted was reasonable in relation to the threat posed. *Unocal*, 493 A.2d 946. Directors satisfy the first part of the *Unocal* test by demonstrating good faith and reasonable investigation. We have repeatedly stated that the refusal to entertain an offer may comport with a valid exercise of a board's business judgment. See, e.g., *Macmillan*, 559 A.2d at 1285 n. 35; *Van Gorkom*, 488 A.2d at 881; Pogostin v. Rice, Del.Supr., 480 A.2d 619, 627 (1984).

Unocal involved a two-tier, highly coercive tender offer. In such a case, the threat is obvious: shareholders may be compelled to tender to avoid being treated adversely in the second stage of the transaction. Accord *Ivanhoe*, 535 at 1344. In subsequent cases, the Court of Chancery has suggested that an all-cash, all-shares offer, falling within a range of values that a shareholder might reasonably prefer, cannot constitute a legally recognized "threat" to shareholder interests sufficient to withstand a *Unocal* analysis. AC Acquisitions Corp. v. Anderson, Clayton & Co., Del.Ch., 519 A.2d 103 (1986); see Grand Metropolitan, PLC v. Pillsbury Co., Del.Ch., 558 A.2d 1049 (1988); City Capital Associates v. Interco, Inc., Del.Ch., 551 A.2d 787 (1988). In those cases, the Court of Chancery determined that whatever threat existed related only to the shareholders and only to price and not to the corporation.

From those decisions by our Court of Chancery, Paramount and the individual plaintiffs extrapolate a rule of law that an all-cash, all-shares offer with values reasonably in the range of acceptable price cannot pose any objective threat to a corporation or its shareholders. Thus, Paramount would have us hold that only if the value of Paramount's offer were determined to be clearly inferior to the value created by management's plan to merge with Warner could the offer be viewed—objectively—as a threat.

Implicit in the plaintiffs' argument is the view that a hostile tender offer can pose only two types of threats: the threat of coercion that results from a two-tier offer promising unequal treatment for nontendering shareholders; and the threat of inadequate value from an all-shares, all-cash offer at a price below what a target board in good faith deems to be the present value of its shares. See, e.g., *Interco,* 551 A.2d at 797; see also BNS, Inc. v. Koppers, D.Del., 683 F.Supp. 458 (1988). Since Paramount's offer was all-cash, the only conceivable "threat," plaintiffs argue, was inadequate value.[17]   We disapprove of such a narrow and rigid construction of *Unocal,* for the reasons which follow.

Plaintiffs' position represents a fundamental misconception of our standard of review under *Unocal* principally because it would involve the court in substituting its judgment as to what is a "better" deal for that of a corporation's board of directors.   To the extent that the Court of Chancery has recently done so in certain of its opinions, we hereby reject such approach as not in keeping with a proper *Unocal* analysis. See, e.g., *Interco,* 551 A.2d 787, and its progeny; but see TW Services, Inc. v. SWT Acquisition Corp., Del.Ch., C.A. No. 1047, Allen, C., 1989 WL 20290 (March 2, 1989).

The usefulness of *Unocal* as an analytical tool is precisely its flexibility in the face of a variety of fact scenarios.   *Unocal* is not intended as an abstract standard; neither is it a structured and mechanistic procedure of appraisal.   Thus, we have said that directors may consider, when evaluating the threat posed by a takeover bid, the "inadequacy of the price offered, nature and timing of the offer, questions of illegality, the impact on 'constituencies' other than share-holders * * * the risk of nonconsummation, and the quality of securi-ties being offered in the exchange."   493 A.2d at 955.   The open-ended analysis mandated by *Unocal* is not intended to lead to a simple mathematical exercise: that is, of comparing the discounted value of Time–Warner's expected trading price at some future date with Para-mount's offer and determining which is the higher.   Indeed, in our view, precepts underlying the business judgment rule militate against a court's engaging in the process of attempting to appraise and evaluate the relative merits of a long-term versus a short-term investment goal for shareholders.   To engage in such an exercise is a distortion of the *Unocal* process and, in particular, the application of the second part of *Unocal*'s test, discussed below.

In this case, the Time board reasonably determined that inade-quate value was not the only legally cognizable threat that Para-mount's all-cash, all-shares offer could present.   Time's board concluded that Paramount's eleventh hour offer posed other threats.   One con-

---

17. Some commentators have suggested that the threats posed by hostile offers be categorized into not two but three types: "(i) *opportunity loss* * * * [where] a hostile offer might deprive target shareholders of the opportunity to select a superior alter-native offered by target management [or, we would add, offered by another bidder]; (ii) *structural coercion,* * * * the risk that disparate treatment of non-tendering shareholders might distort shareholders' tender decisions; and * * * (iii) *substantive*

coercion, * * * the risk that shareholders will mistakenly accept an underpriced of-fer because they disbelieve management's representations of intrinsic value."   The recognition of substantive coercion, the au-thors suggest, would help guarantee that the *Unocal* standard becomes an effective intermediate standard of review.   Gilson & Kraakman, Delaware's Intermediate Stan-dard for Defensive Tactics: Is There Sub-stance to Proportionality Review?, 44 The Business Lawyer, 247, 267 (1989).

cern was that Time shareholders might elect to tender into Paramount's cash offer in ignorance or a mistaken belief of the strategic benefit which a business combination with Warner might produce. Moreover, Time viewed the conditions attached to Paramount's offer as introducing a degree of uncertainty that skewed a comparative analysis. Further, the timing of Paramount's offer to follow issuance of Time's proxy notice was viewed as arguably designed to upset, if not confuse, the Time stockholders' vote. Given this record evidence, we cannot conclude that the Time board's decision of June 6 that Paramount's offer posed a threat to corporate policy and effectiveness was lacking in good faith or dominated by motives of either entrenchment or self-interest.

Paramount also contends that the Time board had not duly investigated Paramount's offer. Therefore, Paramount argues, Time was unable to make an informed decision that the offer posed a threat to Time's corporate policy. Although the Chancellor did not address this issue directly, his findings of fact do detail Time's exploration of the available entertainment companies, including Paramount, before determining that Warner provided the best strategic "fit." In addition, the court found that Time's board rejected Paramount's offer because Paramount did not serve Time's objectives or meet Time's needs. Thus, the record does, in our judgment, demonstrate that Time's board was adequately informed of the potential benefits of a transaction with Paramount. We agree with the Chancellor that the Time board's lengthy pre-June investigation of potential merger candidates, including Paramount, mooted any obligation on Time's part to halt its merger process with Warner to reconsider Paramount. Time's board was under no obligation to negotiate with Paramount. *Unocal,* 493 A.2d at 954–55; see also *Macmillan,* 559 A.2d at 1285 n. 35. Time's failure to negotiate cannot be fairly found to have been uninformed. The evidence supporting this finding is materially enhanced by the fact that twelve of Time's sixteen board members were outside independent directors. *Unocal,* 493 A.2d at 955; Moran v. Household Intern., Inc., Del.Supr., 500 A.2d 1346, 1356 (1985).

We turn to the second part of the *Unocal* analysis. The obvious requisite to determining the reasonableness of a defensive action is a clear identification of the nature of the threat. As the Chancellor correctly noted, this "requires an evaluation of the importance of the corporate objective threatened; alternative methods of protecting that objective; impacts of the 'defensive' action, and other relevant factors." In Re: Time Incorporated Shareholder Litigation, Del.Ch., 1989 WL 79880 (July 14, 1989). It is not until both parts of the *Unocal* inquiry have been satisfied that the business judgment rule attaches to defensive actions of a board of directors. *Unocal,* 493 A.2d at 954.[18] As

---

18. Some commentators have criticized *Unocal* by arguing that once the board's deliberative process has been analyzed and found not to be wanting in objectivity, good faith or deliberateness, the so-called "en- hanced" business judgment rule has been satisfied and no further inquiry is undertaken. See generally Johnson & Siegel, Corporate Mergers: Redefining the Role of

applied to the facts of this case, the question is whether the record evidence supports the Court of Chancery's conclusion that the restructuring of the Time–Warner transaction, including the adoption of several preclusive defensive measures, was a *reasonable response* in relation to a perceived threat.

Paramount argues that, assuming its tender offer posed a threat, Time's response was unreasonable in precluding Time's shareholders from accepting the tender offer or receiving a control premium in the immediately foreseeable future. Once again, the contention stems, we believe, from a fundamental misunderstanding of where the power of corporate governance lies. Delaware law confers the management of the corporate enterprise to the stockholders' duly elected board representatives. 8 Del.C. § 141(a). The fiduciary duty to manage a corporate enterprise includes the selection of a time frame for achievement of corporate goals. That duty may not be delegated to the stockholders. *Van Gorkom*, 488 A.2d at 873. Directors are not obliged to abandon a deliberately conceived corporate plan for a short-term shareholder profit unless there is clearly no basis to sustain the corporate strategy. See, e.g., *Revlon*, 506 A.2d 173.

Although the Chancellor blurred somewhat the discrete analyses required under *Unocal*, he did conclude that Time's board reasonably perceived Paramount's offer to be a significant threat to the planned Time–Warner merger and that Time's response was not "overly broad." We have found that even in light of a valid threat, management actions that are coercive in nature or force upon shareholders a management-sponsored alternative to a hostile offer may be struck down as unreasonable and non-proportionate responses. *Macmillan*, 559 A.2d 1261; *AC Acquisitions Corp.*, 519 A.2d 103.

Here, on the record facts, the Chancellor found that Time's responsive action to Paramount's tender offer was not aimed at "cramming down" on its shareholders a management-sponsored alternative, but rather had as its goal the carrying forward of a pre-existing transaction in an altered form.[19] Thus, the response was reasonably related to the threat. The Chancellor noted that the revised agreement and its accompanying safety devices did not preclude Paramount from making an offer for the combined Time–Warner company or from changing the conditions of its offer so as not to make the offer dependent upon the nullification of the Time–Warner agreement. Thus, the response was proportionate. We affirm the Chancellor's rulings as clearly supported by the record. Finally, we note that although Time was required, as a result of Paramount's hostile offer, to incur a heavy debt to finance its

Target Directors, 136 U.Pa.L.Rev. 315 (1987). We reject such views.

19. The Chancellor cited Shamrock Holdings, Inc. v. Polaroid Corp., Del.Ch., 559 A.2d 257 (1989), as a closely analogous case. In that case, the Court of Chancery upheld, in the face of a takeover bid, the establishment of an employee stock ownership plan that had a significant anti-take-over effect. The Court of Chancery upheld the board's action largely because the ESOP had been adopted *prior* to any contest for control and was reasonably determined to increase productivity and enhance profits. The ESOP did not appear to be primarily a device to affect or secure corporate control.

acquisition of Warner, that fact alone does not render the board's decision unreasonable so long as the directors could reasonably perceive the debt load not to be so injurious to the corporation as to jeopardize its well being.

C.

Conclusion

Applying the test for grant or denial of preliminary injunctive relief, we find plaintiffs failed to establish a reasonable likelihood of ultimate success on the merits. Therefore, we affirm.

NOTE: LEGAL UNCERTAINTY AND CORPORATE POLITICS

Perhaps inevitably, the opinions of Delaware (and other) courts do not go much distance in articulating workable substantive or procedural standards for judicial review of the propriety of defensive actions. The cases teach that a transactional configuration that appears to put a corporation "in play" and to be a "fair" auction, or a defensive maneuver that appears to be a proportionate response to a threatened harm in one case, need not do so in another that is formally distinguishable but functionally similar. The Delaware Supreme Court has taken no advantage of its many opportunities to fashion intelligible subsidiary rules to channel the application of the expansive formulae of *Unocal* and *Revlon*. It has declined to draw on the formulations of either Chancellor Allen in cases like *Anderson, Clayton* and *Interco,* or of the commentators. See Gilson and Kraakman, Delaware's Intermediate Standard for Defensive Tactics: Is There Substance to Proportionality Review? 44 Bus.Law. 247 (1989); Gilson and Kraakman, What Triggers Revlon? 25 Wake Forest L.Rev. 37 (1990). Instead it has opted for unpredictable, if not wholly limitless, judicial discretion to give the formulae whatever content the court sees fit at any particular time. If there is a pattern, it is that norms that restrain management impediments to stockholder choice are articulated only to be diluted in favor of management discretion in subsequent cases (except occasionally in cases of a management buy-out in response to a hostile bidder).

These uncertain rules follow to some extent from the very complexity of the cases.[f] As pointed out in Yablon, Poison Pills and Litigation Uncertainty, 1989 Duke L.J. 54, 74, the governing standards permit Delaware courts to "engage in wide-ranging factual enquiries to test the 'reasonableness' and 'proportionality' of managers' conduct. Wary of any attempt to legislate in this area, the Delaware courts do not even try to enunciate a more specific 'test' or limit the factors relevant to the issue of poison pill redemption. Rather, each decision tends to provide a detailed factual description of the transaction at issue, followed by a

---

f. For expositions of the complexity of the judicial task in litigation spawned by takeover efforts and the need for judicial discretion in assessing the propriety of one or more particular defensive maneuvers in particular contexts, see CRTF Corp. v. Federated Dept. Stores, 683 F.Supp. 422 (S.D.N.Y.1988); In re Holly Farms Shareholder Litigation, CCH Fed.Sec.L.Rep., ¶ 94,443 (Del.Ch.1989).

determination that management's response does or does not meet the proportionality test. Since every case involves a different transaction, case outcomes cannot logically conflict in such a situation. Any attempt, however, to identify one or two dispositive factors in one case is rebuttable by another case in which the same factors were present and lacked dispositive effect." Yablon goes on to analyze the advantages and disadvantages for participants and for society of the condition of legal uncertainty that thus results. That uncertainty is not without its costs to bidders (at least in contrast to rules that more or less expressly limit management's freedom to adopt self-serving defensive maneuvers) or benefits to the Delaware bar.

Under the umbrella of ambiguity that covers both substantive standards and the standard for judicial review, courts are able to sprinkle opinions with admonitory remarks (either addressed to specific defensive maneuvers in the cases before them or of more general piety) formally designed to benefit stockholders' or possibly other stakeholders' interests.[b] But at the same time they are able to issue rulings in the case at hand that impede stockholders' opportunity to accept "better," if not the conceivably "best" offers. Here judicial uncertainty as to the objectives of restricting managerial power is combined with an equivocal use of the business judgment concept. As a result, actions taken at the stockholders' expense are upheld with a frequency that is difficult to attribute to either the expected or the random distribution of "threatened harm" or "proportionate" responses or "fair" auctions or the workings of a meaningful "market."

The jurisprudence of takeovers, at least in Delaware, thus seems to be premised on two notions—(1) it is desirable *not* to prevent management from taking many kinds of defensive actions against third party bids or threats of such bids, and (2) it is undesirable (or impossible) for common law courts to fashion rules that will assure stockholders the "best" price or other stakeholders of substantively "fair" treatment. Instead, it is thought desirable to fashion norms that allow management to determine in the first instance what is "best" for stockholders and possibly other stakeholders. But if the courts do not (or cannot) quantify the concept of "best" in measuring stockholders' interests or define it in measuring the proper balance among the conflicting claims of stakeholders, then judicial review will not often check managerial discretion to favor its own interests at others' expense. Is there a systemic flaw in society's effort to allow management to resort to some (or indeed to any) kinds of defensive maneuvers, but to monitor them by a cumbersome judicial process that nominally encourages a "market decision" or stockholder choice as the mechanism for achieving the "best" result?

This combination of a rhetorical nod toward market and stockholder interests in the statement of the rules and a bottom line preference

---

b. Possibly, these remarks benefit public stockholders by signalling to the bar steps to advise management to take in order to avoid adverse rulings—such as examining the market for the corporation or shopping it before shaping the alternative management offers to its stockholders.

the management-favorable results invites explanation in political terms. For "political" discussions of the cases, see Johnson, The Delaware Judiciary and the Meaning of Corporate Life and Law, 68 Texas L.Rev. 865 (1990); Gordon, Corporations, Markets, and Courts, 91 Colum.L.Rev. 1931 (1991). Can the cases be read as a result of the Delaware courts' performance of the job of defending the state's institutional primacy as a corporate forum in the volatile world of takeovers? Under this view, the courts shift from an initial stance upholding management's defensive power against takeovers to a stance critical of management's power and then shift back to a stance upholding management, as they interpret the shifting preferences of (and equilibria between) capital and management in the markets and board rooms. Or is their indecision instead a reflection of the normative indecision of the academic literature respecting the "best" available legal framework?

(C) THE DUTY OF CARE

The emphasis in the cash-out merger cases on compliance by the board with appropriate procedure in considering the terms of the merger and in informing stockholders is replicated in assessing challenges to management's defensive maneuvers in tender offers. Thus, at least where the self-serving character of the target management's behavior is visible, one recurring focus of judicial review under *Unocal* is the extent to which the board has informed itself about the transaction—the character of the board's inquiry into and deliberation about the bid and the bidder, about the "value" of the target apart from the bid, and about the quality and thoroughness of the report and recommendations of the investment banker or other "independent" financial expert. Another theme emphasizes the extent to which the financial experts can be deemed "independent," and the virtue of using outside counsel rather than management's counsel. A detailed study is required, however, to determine how the procedure in those cases in which management's defensive maneuvers were found flawed differed from the procedure in the cases in which management's defensive maneuvers were approved, if indeed any principled distinctions are to be derived.

The focus on the duty of care in this area begins with **Smith v. Van Gorkom,** 488 A.2d 858 (Del.1985), a case not involving any apparent conflict of interest and thus not entailing an application of the *Unocal* standard. That case was an action by dissident stockholders of Trans Union Corporation (Trans Union) for rescission and damages on account of the merger of Trans Union with a wholly owned subsidiary of the Marmon Group Inc. (Marmon), resulting in the cashout of Trans Union stockholders at $55 per share of stock that had never traded at more than $39\frac{1}{2}$. The case turned on (1) whether the Trans Union board, in the exercise of its duty of care in approving the merger, had sufficiently informed itself of the "intrinsic value" of the company and of the terms and conditions of the merger to pass the test of exercise of informed business judgment in approving the merger, and

(2) whether the board had complied with its fiduciary obligations under Delaware law to disclose in the proxy material which it circulated soliciting stockholder approval of the merger, "all facts germane to the transaction at issue in an atmosphere of complete candor."

The Delaware Supreme Court, reversing the Chancellor, ruled (1) that "gross negligence" is the test of propriety of Board action, (2) that the Board, which did not include an investment banker or a financial analyst, acting at a hastily called meeting on September 20, 1980 which lasted about two hours, had not sufficiently informed itself of the intrinsic value of the company or the "fairness" of the merger price (e.g., it had not obtained an outside banker's opinion or examined documentation on value) or the terms of the merger agreement; nor did it, by the time of its later meeting on January 26 formally approving the merger, cure those deficiencies; and (3) that the resulting avoidability of the merger was not cured by stockholder ratification because the proxy material soliciting stockholder approval was defective, in that among other things (a) it failed to disclose to the stockholders the board's ignorance of the intrinsic value of the company, (b) in characterizing $55 as a "substantial" premium it failed to disclose the Board's failure to assess the premium in terms of other relevant valuation techniques, and (c) in supplying material additional information in support of the merger in a supplementary Proxy Statement dated January 27, it failed to disclose that the Board had learned of that additional information only on January 26 when it formally approved the merger.

The decision appears to focus primarily on the propriety of the Board's procedure (cf. Weinberger v. UOP, supra p. 766; Rosenblatt v. Getty Oil Co., supra p. 802) in approving the merger. For a list of procedural defects that may infect Board action, and possible corrections see Manning, Reflections and Practical Tips on Life in the Boardroom After Van Gorkom, 41 Bus.Law. 1, 8–14 (1985).

An agreement was ultimately reached to settle the litigation "by payment of $23.5 million to the plaintiff class. Of that amount, a reported $10 million, the policy limit, is to be provided by Trans Union's directors and officers liability insurance carrier. Although the group which acquired Trans Union in the disputed acquisition was not a defendant, according to newspaper account nearly all of the $13.5 million balance will be paid by the acquiring group on behalf of the Trans Union defendant directors." See 41 Business Lawyer 1, (footnote) (1985).

The focus on process and the duty of care appears to be attractive to courts dealing with "outside" directors in transactions involving more obvious conflicts of interest among target managers, as in the Hanson case, infra, and as in the Polaroid case, supra p. 1090. What considerations support (or oppose) a judicial preference for instructing outside directors on how to proceed in form, rather than testing their actions by substantive standards that implicate their integrity, and may entail measurements of "fairness" or the reasonableness of the business judgment as to the need for, and propriety of, the defensive maneuver?

HANSON TRUST PLC v. ML SCM ACQUISITION, INC.

United States Court of Appeals, Second Circuit, 1986.
781 F.2d 264.

[The case was an effort by a bidder, Hanson Trust PLC (Hanson), to enjoin defensive maneuvers by a target (SCM) and the financier for a leveraged buyout of the target, Merrill Lynch, Pierce, Fenner & Smith Incorporated (and a related entity formed for the purpose, ML–SCM Acquisition Co., hereafter together called "Merrill"). The particular maneuver at which the suit was aimed was "an asset purchase option (hereinafter sometimes referred to as a 'lock-up option') pursuant to an Asset Option Agreement and a Merger Agreement between those corporate entities. Under those Agreements, in the event that by March 1, 1986, any third party acquires one third or more of SCM's outstanding common stock or rights to acquire such stock, Merrill would have the right to purchase SCM's Pigments and Consumer Foods Divisions for $350 million and $80 million, respectively." The trial court denied the request for injunction "principally because it found that under New York law approval of the lock-up option by the SCM directors (hereinafter sometimes referred to as the 'Board'), and the lock-up option itself, were, in the exercise of business judgment, 'part of a viable business strategy, as the law currently defines those terms,' and because 'Hanson failed to adduce sufficient credible proof to the contrary.'"

The Court of Appeals reversed and remanded. It regarded as crucial the magnitude of the possible disparity between the value of the two divisions and the option price at which Merrill was permitted to buy them. It addressed principally the process of the board (containing nine "outside" and three "inside" directors) in agreeing to the lock-up in the course of a hectic effort to thwart Hanson's bids to SCM stockholders. Hanson announced its intention to make a $60 per share cash tender offer on August 21, 1985; SCM management met with its lawyers (Wachtell, Lipton, Rosen & Katz) and bankers (Goldman Sachs & Co.) on August 22, and discussed possible responses, including leveraged buyouts; the SCM board met on August 25 and focussed principally on seeking a white knight or a leveraged buyout. The conglomerate character of SCM made it unlikely that a white knight would be found quickly. After shopping for five days, SCM found that only Merrill showed an interest in participating in a leveraged buyout. The SCM board, at a meeting on September 3, approved an LBO agreement with Merrill entailing a $70 bid for SCM shares. Hanson thereupon announced that it would raise its bid to $72 per share, making the Merrill LBO agreement ineffectual, so that it was terminated on September 6. To induce Merrill to raise its bid to top Hanson (by offering a nominal $74 per share) a new LBO agreement was negotiated, in which, at Merrill's insistence, SCM gave Merrill the challenged Asset–Option lock-up, a $6 million "hello again" fee and a $9 million break-up fee (in escrow) against a third party's acquisition of one third or more SCM stock. That agreement was first shown and explained to (and approved by) the SCM board on September 10, at a meeting which lasted approximately three hours from 9 p.m.

In assessing the propriety of the board's actions (and of the District Court in denying the requested injunction), the court (Pierce, J.) said:]

SCM is a New York corporation, and no party disputes that the acts of its directors are to be considered in light of New York law.

* * *

Thus, in duty of care analysis, a presumption of propriety inures to the benefit of directors; absent a prima facie showing to the contrary, directors enjoy "wide latitude in devising strategies to resist unfriendly [takeover] advances" under the business judgment rule. See *Norlin*, supra, 744 F.2d at 264–65 (citing Treadway v. Care Corp., 638 F.2d 357, 380–84 (2d Cir.1980); Crouse–Hinds Co. v. Internorth, Inc., 634 F.2d 690, 701–04 (2d Cir.1980)). However, even if a board concludes that a takeover attempt is not in the best interests of the company, it does not hold a blank check to use all possible strategies to forestall the acquisition moves. *Norlin*, 744 F.2d at 265–66.

Although in other jurisdictions, directors may not enjoy the same presumptions per the business judgment rule, at least in a takeover context, see, e.g., Unocal Corp. v. Mesa Petroleum Co., 493 A.2d 946, 954–55 (Del.Sup.1985) (initial burden on directors in takeover to show reasonable grounds for believing that takeover would endanger corporate policy; satisfied by directors' showing good faith and reasonable investigation), under New York law, the initial burden of proving directors' breach of fiduciary duty rests with the plaintiff. See Crouse–Hinds, 634 F.2d at 702; see also Auerbach, 419 N.Y.S.2d at 926–27, 393 N.E. at 1000–01.

In the present case, the challenged acts of the directors concern the grant of the lock-up option. This takeover defensive tactic is not per se illegal.

* * * In this regard, we are especially mindful that some lock-up options may be beneficial to the shareholders, such as those that induce a bidder to compete for control of a corporation, while others may be harmful, such as those that effectively preclude bidders from competing with the optionee bidder. See Thompson v. Enstar Corp., Nos. 7641, 7643 at 7–13 (Del.Ch. June 20, 1984), at 7–13 revised, Aug. 16, 1984 (distinguishing options that attract or foreclose competing bids); see also Note, Lock–Up Options: Towards a State Law Standard, 96 Harv. L.Rev. 1068, 1076–82 (1983).

II

Under the circumstances presented in this case, the business judgment doctrine is misapplied when it is extended to provide protection to corporate board members where there is an abundance of evidence strongly suggesting breach of fiduciary duty, as we develop below. See generally, Arsht, The Business Judgment Rule Revisited, 8 Hofstra L.Rev. 93 (1979) (noting limits of business judgment rule).

* * *

The law is settled that, particularly where directors make decisions likely to affect shareholder welfare, the duty of due care requires that a director's decision be made on the basis of "reasonable diligence" in gathering and considering material information. In short, a director's decision must be an informed one. * * *

Directors may be liable to shareholders for failing reasonably to obtain material information or to make a reasonable inquiry into material matters.

* * * Thus, while directors are protected to the extent that their actions evidence their business *judgment,* such protection assumes that courts must not reflexively decline to consider the content of their "judgment" and the extent of the information on which it is based.

The actions of the SCM Board do not rise to that level of gross negligence found in Smith v. Van Gorkom, 488 A.2d 858, 874–78 & n. 19 (Del.Sup.1985). There, in making its decision after only two hours of consideration, the board relied primarily on a twenty-minute presentation by the chief executive officer who had arranged the proposed merger without informing other Board members and despite the advice of senior management that the merger price was inadequate. On the other hand, the SCM directors failed to take many of the affirmative directorial steps that underlie the finding of due care in *Treadway,* supra, on which the district court herein relied. In *Treadway,* the directors "armed" their bankers with financial questions to evaluate; they requested balance sheets; they adjourned deliberations for one week to consider the requisitioned advice; and they conditioned approval of the deal on the securing of a fairness opinion from their bankers. See *Treadway,* 638 F.2d at 384. By contrast, the SCM directors, in a three-hour late-night meeting, apparently contented themselves with their financial advisor's conclusory opinion that the option prices were "within the range of fair value," although had the directors inquired, they would have learned that Goldman Sachs had not calculated a range of fairness. There was not even a written opinion from Goldman Sachs as to the value of the two optioned businesses. Tr. 1070. Moreover, the Board never asked what the top value was or why two businesses that generated half of SCM's income were being sold for one third of the total purchase price of the company under the second LBO merger agreement, or what the company would look like if the options were exercised. * * * There was little or no discussion of how likely it was that the option "trigger" would be pulled, or who would make that decision—Merrill, the Board, or management. Also, as was noted in *Van Gorkom,* the directors can hardly substantiate their claim that Hanson's efforts created an emergency need for a hasty decision, given that Hanson would not acquire shares under the tender offer until September 17. * * * The directors manifestly declined to use "time available for obtaining information" that might be critical, given "the importance of the business judgment to be made." See ALI supra, § 4.01 at 66. In short, the SCM directors' paucity of information and their swiftness of decision-making strongly suggest a breach of the duty of due care.

Nor is SCM's argument that it was entitled to rely on advice of Wachtell Lipton and Goldman Sachs dispositive of Hanson's claim that the SCM directors failed adequately to inform themselves under the duty of care. In general, directors have some oversight obligations to become reasonably familiar with an opinion, report, or other source of advice before becoming entitled to rely on it. In our view, the test of reasonableness should suffice with respect to the area of expertise relied upon, whether that area be legal or financial. * * *

The district court in the present case notes that the Board failed to read or review carefully the various offers and agreements and instead relied on the advisers' descriptions. In particular, the district court found that at the September 10 Board meeting, the directors accepted Goldman Sachs' conclusion that the prices of the optioned assets were fair, without ever inquiring about the range of fair value.

* * *

We find unpersuasive SCM's defense that this "working board" was already familiar with SCM, and hence was capable of making the swift decisions that it made. Given this "working board's" considerable familiarity with SCM, we must question why it did not find the option prices troublesome in light of the considerable evidence—from Overlock, its own investment banker, and others, and from valuations made by SCM's management and Merrill—that the optioned assets were worth considerably more than their option prices. Indeed, given that the very purpose of an asset option in a takeover context is to give the optionee a bargain as an incentive to bid and an assured benefit should its bid fail, see Fraidin & Franco, Lock–Up Arrangements, 14 Rev.Sec. Reg. 821, 823, 827 (1981), one again might have expected under such circumstances a *heightened* duty of care. The price may be low enough to entice a reluctant potential bidder, but no lower than "reasonable pessimism will allow." Cf. Brudney & Chirelstein, Fair Shares in Corporate Mergers and Takeovers, 88 Harv.L.Rev. 297, 298 (1974). To ascertain that management's proposal has not crossed this critical line, the Board certainly should have subjected the proposal to some substantial analysis. Instead, we view the board as only minimally fulfilling, if not abdicating, its role.

* * *

In the context of a self-interested management proposing a defensive LBO, the independent directors have an important duty to protect shareholder interests, as it would be unreasonable to expect management, with financial expectancies in an LBO, fully to represent the shareholders. Cf. Longstreth, Fairness of Management Buyouts Needs Evaluation, Legal Times, Oct. 10, 1983, at 15 (noting that independent directors, even without evidencing "wrongdoing, venality or antisocial behavior," may improperly defer to management at the expense of shareholders).   See also Cox & Munsinger, Bias in the Boardroom: Psychological Foundations and Legal Implications of Corporate Cohesion, 48 Law & Contemp.Probs. 83 (1985).   We do not say that the independent directors of SCM were required to appoint an independent negotiating committee of outside directors to negotiate with Merrill, as the court suggested in Weinberger v. UOP, Inc., 457 A.2d 701, 709 n. 7 (Del.Sup.1983), though that certainly would have constituted one appropriate procedure under the circumstances.   But in approving *post hoc* the LBO negotiated and proposed by management directors with a not insubstantial potential 15% equity interest in the arrangement, the independent directors should have taken at least some of the prophylactic steps that were identified as constituting due care in *Treadway*, 638 F.2d at 384.

SCM's board delegated to management broad authority to work directly with Merrill to structure an LBO proposal, * * * and then appears to have swiftly approved management's proposals.   Such broad delegations of authority are not uncommon and generally are quite proper as conforming to the way that a Board acts in generating proposals for its own consideration.   However, when management has a self-interest in consummating an LBO, standard *post hoc* review procedures may be insufficient.

* * *

[The Board knew or should have known that the effect of the Asset Option Agreement] * * * was to preclude shareholders from achieving any value higher than that agreed upon by SCM management and Merrill.   In short, the Board appears to have failed to ensure that alternative bids were negotiated or scrutinized by those whose only loyalty was to the shareholders.

III

Having determined that the synergies of evidence showing a prima facie case of breach of the duty of care effectively shifted the burden of justification to SCM, we now consider SCM's claims of justification. First, SCM argues that it presented evidence to rebut Hanson's extensive evidence that the option prices were undervalued.   A director's obligation to protect the financial interests of the corporation, and thereby the shareholders, see, e.g., *Data Probe*, No. 92138–1983 at 8, may not be compromised by a competing interest in other legitimate corporate purposes, such as fending off a hostile takeover bid.   When engaging in defensive maneuvers, such as a lock-up option, a director's primary obligation is to ensure the overall fairness, including a fair option price, to the shareholders.   * * * The inquiry is not whether the asset option prices represented fair value as a factual matter, but whether SCM met its burden of justifying the fairness of the lock-up option by adducing legally sufficient evidence to render inappropriate the remedy of a preliminary injunction.

* * *

Hanson produced substantial evidence at the eight-day hearing that the optioning of the "crown jewels" demonstrates that the directors failed to meet their duty of inquiry and had an inadequate basis for concluding one way or the other that the prices were "within the range of fair value." First, as to Pigments, optioned at $350 million, Overlock, SCM's own investment banker at Goldman Sachs, testified that, using Goldman Sachs' own valuation charts, * * * and applying thereto price-earnings ratios that Overlock accepted as appropriate, the value of that division is between $420 and $544 million.

* * *

* * * The *lowest* of all of * * * [the] estimates of value, $420 million, suggests a $70 million undervaluation in the optioned price as to Pigments, a differential that would suggest serious undervaluation. See *Revlon,* No. 8126 at 1248–1249 (questioning shareholder benefit where, to secure additional $1 per share, Board optioned certain divisions at price $75 million below Revlon's own investment banker's lowest estimate of fair value).[9]

Regarding Consumer Foods, Hanson again adduced considerable evidence that the business was optioned at a considerably undervalued price.

9. We note that a prima facie showing of lack of due care is distinct from a prima facie showing of corporate waste, which may constitute a cause of action against directors separate and distinct from breach of the duty of loyalty or due care. See Ludlum v. Riverhead Bond & Mortgage Corp., 244 A.D. 113, 278 N.Y.S. 487 (2d Dep't 1935). It might well be that Hanson's evidence was sufficient to establish a prima facie case of waste, even given the considerable burden of proof required under that cause of action. See Cohen v. Ayers, 596 F.2d 733, 739 (7th Cir.1979) (applying New York law) (plaintiff must show that "no reasonable businessman could find that adequate consideration had been supplied"); accord, Aronoff v. Albanese, 85 A.D.2d 3, 5, 446 N.Y.S.2d 368, 371 (2d Dep't 1982) ("The objecting stockholder must demonstrate that no person of ordinary sound business judgment would say that the corporation received fair benefit."). However, we need not reach the issue of waste given the sufficient grounds presented herein in support of a preliminary injunction. See *Revlon,* No. 8126 (enjoining lock-up option without specifically noting waste); *Data Probe,* No. 92138–1983 (same).

We find unpersuasive the district court's efforts to distinguish *Revlon.* See Op. at 858. First, although Revlon's fourteen-member board included six directors who held prominent management positions, and while most of the remaining directors had associations with entities that did business with Revlon, *Revlon,* No. 8126 at 1243 n. 2, the absence in the present case of such indicia of disloyalty does not limit the likelihood of a breach of the duty of due care. Second, although the hostile bidder in *Revlon* expressly intended to outbid every offer by the "white knight," id. at 1245, here the district court expressly found that the SCM directors "knew or should have known" that the lock-up would foreclose additional bidding—by Hanson or any other bidder. Op. at 855. Third, while the *Revlon* court noted that the option price was $75,000,-000.00 below the lowest fair value placed upon it by Revlon's own investment banker (Goldman Sachs), *Revlon,* No. 8126 at 1249, here the option price of Pigments *alone* was $70,000,000.00 below the lowest fair value placed upon it in any of the testimony specifying a purported fair value—and this differential represents a *greater proportion* of the option price than that represented by the differential in *Revlon.* Finally, while the Revlon board acted to protect note or debtholders instead of shareholders, *Revlon,* No. 8126 at 1249–1250, here the SCM board appears to have failed to protect steadfastly shareholders interests in the face of a management-interested LBO, and, through junk bond financing, to have subordinated in significant part the equity of existing SCM shareholders to the future debt of the acquired company.

* * *

We conclude that the district court erred in declining to consider evidence, which the court admittedly found troublesome, which was importantly related to the critical issue of the value of the optioned assets. The court erred in failing to recognize that Hanson had presented a prima facie case of breach of fiduciary duty, and thus should have considered the extensive evidence on whether the option prices were indeed "within the range of fair value."

* * * SCM's second attempt at justification is to argue that the purpose of the lock-up option is to achieve a better bid for the shareholders. Primary purpose analysis is undoubtedly a sound theory of lock-up option justification, and is tested in pertinent part according to whether the lock-up option objectively benefits shareholders. Cf. N.Y.Bus.Corp.L. § 717 ("ordinarily prudent person" standard); see also *Revlon*, No. 8126 at 1250 ("objective needs of shareholders"); Bennett v. Propp, 41 Del.Ch. 14, 22, 187 A.2d 405, 409 (Del.Sup.1962) (directors may justify stock purchase as "in the corporate interest"); *Norlin*, 744 F.2d at 265–66. Whatever good intentions the directors might have had, they have pointed to little or no evidence to rebut the evidence discussed above that suggested that they failed to ensure that their acts would redound to the benefit of SCM and its shareholders. Indeed, the district court found that the directors "knew or should have known" that the lock-up option would end the bidding. * * * The directors thus face the difficult task of justifying a lock-up option that is suspect for foreclosing bidding, see Thompson v. Enstar, Nos. 7641, 7643 and for thereby impinging upon shareholder decisional rights regarding corporate governance, see *Norlin*, 744 F.2d at 258.

Viewing the LBO proposal in its entirety, we cannot see how the deal redounds to the benefit of SCM and its shareholders. For the benefit of an offer superior to Hanson's $72 cash bid by at best one dollar and change, and which arbitrageurs would value at no more than $.75 to $1.00 higher than Hanson's $72 bid, according to Overlock,[11] the Board approved immediate release of a $6 million "hello again" fee, and approved management's transfer into escrow of the $9 million "break-up" fee payable upon a third party's acquisition of one-third of SCM's common stock. The Board additionally optioned 50 percent of SCM's operating income from two prime businesses at conceivably well below fair value, according to the abundant evidence before the district court. Cf. *Revlon*, No. 8126 at 1249 (noting costs of securing additional $1 per share). Of course, the tendering shareholders would appear to get the benefits but not pay the costs of this arrangement if the LBO were to be consummated and the new entity were a financial success.

---

11. According to Overlock, arbitrageurs, who are among the most sophisticated investors, would value the $74 LBO offer at about $72.50 in view of not just the cost of money but the "risk" involved in connection with the use of the "junk bonds." Tr. 1180–81. Precisely what risk or risks he was referring to was not developed in the record, although such risk or risks might involve the collapse of the "junk bond" market or the failure of the new corporate entity due to an unserviceable debt resulting from the LBO. According to Overlock, arbitrageurs would also value Hanson's $72 cash offer between $71.50 and $71.75. Tr. 1181.

However, serious questions are presented as to whether the shareholders would be economically harmed by effectively being forced to tender if the lock-up option is not enjoined. Those who do not tender will either become remaining twenty percent holders with appraisal rights which may be valued less because of the lock-up options, and who will be forced out in the second-step of the merger, or, if the requisite two thirds do not tender to Merrill, will be left facing the prospect of the transfer of effectively half the company for inadequate consideration, in addition to the already effected diminution of the corporate treasury resulting from the considerable fees paid by SCM in the course of its defensive tactics.[12] Thus, the SCM–Merrill LBO appears to benefit shareholders, if at all, only so long as it succeeds all the way through the merger stage and the new entity is a financial success. But if the buyout falls short of its ultimate goal, non-tendering shareholders may bear all of the potential risks of an aborted effort, including the risk of significant undervaluation. Indeed, it is the prospect of inadequate consideration that coerces shareholders to tender, and thereby serves as the means by which SCM's managers and directors could wrest from the shareholders the power to make the *independent* ownership choices that Judge Kaufman saw as the prerogative of shareholders alone, "in accordance with democratic procedures." See *Norlin,* 744 F.2d at 258.

SCM argues that the above concerns notwithstanding, its offer must be upheld as *facilitating* competition in the market for control of SCM. The argument is flawed because it assumes that a competing bidder is not handicapped by the existence of the option. This is not a case where only in hindsight could the directors have known that the terms of their offer could ultimately harm shareholders. Cf. Thompson v. Enstar, Nos. 7641, 7643 at 9–10. Here, as the district court found, the directors knew or should have known that the lock-up option would foreclose any better offers. Op. at 855. Since the option threatens inadequate consideration, a competing bidder is deterred from making a tender offer, unless conditioned on the withdrawal or invalidation of the subject lock-up, for substantially the same reasons that shareholders are deterred from resisting the SCM–Merrill offer. Both Hanson and other SCM shareholders must be concerned that if the SCM–Merrill deal is consummated through the merger stage, then to be left holding shares is to bear the risk of undervaluation.

Indeed, the deterrence to Hanson is even greater than to a small shareholder who does not have or expect to have a blocking position. For, assuming SCM and Merrill achieve a two-thirds majority, the small shareholder most likely risks only being forced to tender under the 20% debenture provision in the SCM–Merrill $74 offer or resorting to appraisal rights. By contrast, hypothetically, Hanson, as the likely largest minority shareholder, holds enough shares to thwart not only the merger but also the 20% freeze-out, and consequently risks holding over one third of a denuded company, a risk that it concededly took in acquiring the additional shares involved in *Hanson I.* Thus, if the lock-

---

12. The $16.5 million in fees to Merrill represents a diminution in value equal to approximately $1.25 per share if the $74 LBO does not succeed.

up option is not invalidated, and if it indeed threatens to dissipate the company for inadequate consideration, then Hanson's only rational move is to tender into the SCM–Merrill offer, thereby ending the bidding. In sum, we think the offer forecloses rather than facilitates, competitive bidding. Cf. Thompson v. Enstar, Nos. 7641, 7643.

The foregoing compels us to ask the question that the district court failed to consider, but that the court in *Revlon* wisely raised: "What motivated the directors to end the auction with so little objective improvement?" *Revlon,* No. 8126 at 1249. In *Revlon,* the inescapable conclusion was that the Board seemed to want the LBO partner "in the picture at all costs." Id. at 1249. In the present case, the SCM Board, by its lack of due care, appears to have achieved the same questionable result.

*   *   *

The order of the district court is reversed, and the case is remanded for prompt issuance of a preliminary injunction enjoining SCM, Merrill, and any other parties acting in concert with or on behalf of SCM or Merrill from exercising or purporting to or seeking to exercise the lock-up option considered herein. Judgment to be entered in accordance with this opinion.

It is so ordered.

[Concurring opinion of OAKES and dissenting opinion of KEARSE omitted.]

NOTES

1. For the view that inadequate inquiry made the business judgment rule inapplicable to a board decision to approve golden parachutes at the time of a merger, where four of the five executive beneficiaries resigned so as to avail themselves of the parachutes' benefits shortly thereafter, see Gaillard v. Natomas Co., 208 Cal.App.3d 1250, 256 Cal.Rptr. 702 (1989). Under the circumstances, said the court, usual justifications of golden parachutes, such as the promotion of executive objectivity and attraction of top management did not apply. For a more favorable description of golden parachutes, see International Insurance v. Johns, 874 F.2d 1447 (11th Cir.1989).

2. To the extent that courts may be deemed to be narrowing the protection offered by the business judgment rule to target management and directors, consider a new wave of protective legislation. Delaware Corp. Law 102(b)(7) now provides that a corporate charter may include:

> A provision eliminating or limiting the personal liability of a director to the corporation or its stockholders for monetary damages for breach of fiduciary duty as a director, provided that such provision shall not eliminate or limit the ability of a director (i) for

any breach of the director's duty of loyalty to the corporation or its stockholders, (ii) for acts or omissions not in good faith or which involve intentional misconduct or a knowing violation of law, (iii) under section 174 of this Title, or (iv) for any transaction from which the director derived an improper personal benefit. No such provision shall eliminate or limit the liability of a director for any act or omission occurring prior to the date when such provision becomes effective. All references in this subsection to a director shall also be deemed to refer to a member of the governing body of a corporation which is not authorized to issue capital stock.

Comparable provisions have been adopted in most other states. For commentary, see Romano, Corporate Governance in the Aftermath of the Insurance Crisis, 39 Emory L.J. 1155 (1990).

Does the Delaware statute expand or narrow the protection of a target's outside directors?

5. STATE ANTI–TAKEOVER LEGISLATION

During the past two decades shark repellent provisions have found their way into the business corporation laws of at least 35 states. By now these statutes have undergone three, and by some counts, four stages of evolution. They come in a variety of shapes and sizes, and lack the uniform aspect of other state corporation and Blue Sky law provisions. Management lobbying provides the motive force for this law reform movement. See, e.g., Romano, The Political Economy of Takeover Statutes, 73 Va.L.Rev. 111 (1987).

(A) FIRST GENERATION STATUTES

The first generation of antitakeover statutes followed the regulatory pattern of some Blue Sky laws and accorded a state securities administrator the power to review the adequacy of tender offer disclosure and, in some cases, the merits of the bid. The schemes thus involved a time-consuming administrative hearing process. Some of the statutes also inserted waiting periods between the time of the filing of the offer and its effectiveness—an administrative control the Williams Act avoids. The Supreme Court struck down these statutes in **Edgar v. MITE,** 457 U.S. 624 (1982). Goelzer and Cohen, The Empire Strikes Back—Post MITE Developments in State–Anti–Takeover Legislation, in Steinberg (ed.), Tender Offers: Developments and Commentaries 51–53 (1984), discuss the case:

The Illinois Business Takeover Act, the statute at issue in *MITE,* required a tender offeror to notify the secretary of the state of Illinois twenty business days before commencement of a tender offer. The secretary of state was empowered to convene a hearing, and the tender offer could not proceed until that hearing was completed. One function of the hearing was to permit the secretary of state to review the substantive fairness of the tender offer; were an offer found "unfair," it could be permanently blocked.

MITE Corp. initiated a tender offer for Chicago Rivet & Machine Co., by filing a Schedule 14D with the Securities and Exchange Commission pursuant to the Williams Act. MITE Corp. made no effort to comply with the Illinois Business Takeover Act; rather, it commenced an action in federal court challenging the constitutionality of the statute and obtained a permanent injunction against its enforcement. The Court of Appeals for the Seventh Circuit affirmed, and the Supreme Court accepted, the case for review.

Justice White's opinion, in which only the chief justice joined entirely, held (1) that the Illinois statute unduly favored incumbent management and thus contravened the Supremacy Clause of the U.S. Constitution, because it upset the neutrality policy which is the object of federal tender offer regulation, as embodied in the Williams Act, and (2) that the statute directly restrained interstate commerce in violation of the Commerce Clause. Five justices joined in part, but not all, of the Commerce Clause holding; thus, a majority of the Court held that the Illinois statute was void, because it imposed burdens on interstate commerce that were excessive in light of Illinois' interests.

Justice White's Commerce Clause opinion had two branches. In the first (in which only three other justices joined), he noted that the statute regulated interstate transactions taking place wholly outside of Illinois (in this case purchases by a Delaware corporation of shares owned by non-Illinois residents). Thus, the statute constituted a "direct" restraint on interstate commerce and was, therefore, void, even without an inquiry into the state interests involved. The second branch of Justice White's Commerce Clause opinion, in which five justices concurred and which stands as the opinion of the Court, was based on Pike v. Bruce Church, Inc. In that 1970 case, the Court held that a statute which has only an incidental effect on interstate commerce is valid "unless the burden imposed on such commerce is clearly excessive in relation to the putative local benefits." As the Court stated in *MITE:*

> While protecting local investors is plainly a legitimate state objective, the state has no legitimate interest in protecting nonresident shareholders. Insofar as the Illinois law burdens out-of-state transactions, there is nothing to be weighed in the balance to sustain the law.

Five of the six justices reaching the merits in *MITE* expressly held that the Act was invalid on Commerce Clause grounds, because it placed a substantial burden on interstate commerce which outweighed any local benefits.

* * *

Several courts, both state and federal, have applied the Supreme Court's Commerce Clause holding in *MITE* to particular state takeover statutes. These decisions, dealing with both tender offers and open market purchase programs, have been uniformly adverse to state regulation. As *MITE* has been applied to various state antitakeover statutes, it has become increasingly clear that minor variations on the Illinois theme * do not change the ultimate result.

(B) SECOND GENERATION STATUTES

----

(1) Legislation

The states responded to *MITE* with a new set of antitakeover statutes designed to circumvent the factors the case identified as objectionable. Sargent, Do the Second Generation State Takeover Statutes Violate the Commerce Clause? A Preliminary Inquiry, in Steinberg (ed.), Tender Offers: Development and Commentaries 76–83 (1984), describes the new legislation:

* * * [I]t is almost certain that the state attempts to regulate the takeover process through Williams Act-type regulation of tender offers are unconstitutional. In other words, the first-generation state takeover statutes are probably dead.

Some of the state legislatures, however, have not allowed the demise of these statutes to divert them from their goal of somehow regulating corporate takeovers. In fact, the repudiation of the first-generation statutes has led to the adoption of some very different forms of takeover regulation. The difference between these second-generation takeover statutes and the unconstitutional first-generation statutes reflects the distinction between state tender offer regulation and traditional state corporation law. That is, the second-generation statutes do not directly condition or restrain the tender offer or the consequent tender of shares; instead, they readjust the target's internal ordering mechanism in a way that will have a substantial impact on what can happen after the tender offer is completed. In essence, the new direction shifts the focus from *securities regulation to corporate law;* the new statutes attempt to regulate the takeover process through regulation of the internal affairs of corporations organized under the laws of the state.

* * *

A. Ohio

In November 1982, the Ohio legislature enacted a bill requiring all acquisitions of controlling stock interests to be approved by the share-

----

* [Ed. Note] E.g., elimination of requirement of a preliminary filing before commencement of an offer.

holders. This requirement applies to all control acquisitions, whether accomplished by tender offer or not, and it applies to all Ohio corporations, unless a corporation's charter excludes the corporation from the coverage of the statute.

Under this statute, the directors of the subject corporation must call a special shareholders' meeting within ten days of receipt of an acquirer's statement of intention to acquire shares sufficient to move the acquirer into a control position or from one level of control to another. At this meeting, which must be held within fifty days of receipt of the acquirer's statement of intention, the shareholders are to vote on the proposed acquisition. In order for the acquisition to proceed, it must be approved by both a majority of the voting power present at the meeting and a majority of the voting power excluding "interested shares" (primarily those owned by the acquirer and its affiliates).

The new Ohio statute thus differs from the first-generation statutes insofar as it does not regulate or otherwise condition either the tender offer itself or the tendering of shares. It shifts the focus of regulation from those phases of the takeover process to the point immediately precedent to any second-step transaction—the actual purchase of the control bloc of shares. The technique of regulation applied at this point is also quite different from those applied under the first-generation statutes to the tender offer; there are no administrative hearings, no proration or withdrawal provisions, no review of the fairness of the offering, indeed no role whatsoever for the state securities administrator. Instead, the Ohio statute draws upon the principle of shareholder approval of organic transactions to regulate this form of control transaction.

The Ohio statute does not represent, however, a complete departure from the first-generation statutes. The new approach is a form of internal affairs regulation, but by imposing conditions upon the offeror's purchase of the tendered shares, the statute will still directly affect transactions between the shareholders and the offeror. The new Maryland statute, in contrast, confines itself to the second-step transaction and has no direct effect on the tender offer. * * *

B. Maryland

The Maryland legislature enacted, in June 1983, a quite different form of takeover statute. This legislation shifted the regulatory focus entirely to the second-step transaction. It requires the successful tender offeror intending a post-tender offer "business combination" to either obtain super-majority approval from all the shareholders and from the disinterested shareholders or pay a "fair price" to all those nontendering shareholders who are forced to sell in the course of the business combination. In essence, the statute is designed to inhibit front-end—loaded, two-step takeovers, on the ground that such takeover bids are inherently coercive and unfair to nontendering shareholders.

The act is drafted very tightly to cover almost every conceivable form of business combination and to ensure that a truly "fair" price is paid to shareholders bought out in the second-step transaction. The result of this approach is the potential applicability of the fair-price/supermajority provisions to negotiated business combinations and other transactions that have nothing to do with hostile takeovers. The Maryland Act attempts to avoid this problem by granting the board of directors substantial control over when and to whom these provisions will apply. The Act thus operates something like a shark repellant, which the board, rather than the shareholders, has the authority to implement or abandon.

While the Maryland Act represents an abandonment of any attempt to regulate tender offers, it may prevent at least some partial tender offers from being made and may even reduce the aggregate number of takeover bids for Maryland corporations. This raises novel Commerce Clause questions, because these results would be achieved not through a form of securities regulation restraining the tender offeror's acquisition of shares but through corporate internal affairs regulation restricting what can be done with the shares once they have been acquired.

C. Pennsylvania

A Pennsylvania statute enacted in December 1983 represents an even more thorough exploitation of the internal affairs provisions of the general corporation law. First, the Act provides that corporate fiduciaries "may, in considering the best interests of the corporation, consider the effects of any action upon employers, suppliers and customers of the corporation, communities in which offices and other establishments of the corporation are located and all other pertinent factors." As one commentator has already noted, this language may further expand the presumption of the business judgment rule, making it nearly impossible for a shareholder complaining of management defensive tactics to overcome that presumption. This effect could strengthen management's hand, thereby inhibiting takeover bids for Pennsylvania corporations.

Second, the Act contains provisions similar to the fair-price/supermajority provisions of the Maryland Act and is designed to have similar effects on front-end—loaded, two-step takeovers. The Act also grants the target board substantial leverage over these provisions; second-step transactions are exempted if a majority of the board approves the transactions. Accordingly, these provisions will end up being applied only to hostile takeovers.

Third, the Act requires "controlling shareholders" (persons or groups owning thirty percent of a class of voting stock) to provide notice to the other shareholders that they may obtain an appraisal—"fair" value for their shares—from the controlling shareholder. This provision should seriously inhibit partial bids for the shares of corporations subject to the Act, since it will come into play even if the bidder does not plan a second-step transaction. The board of directors also has substantial leverage over this provision, since timely adoption of an amendment to the bylaws can exempt a particular bidder from its coverage.

[D. New York (Business Corporation Law, section 912, Appendix G)

The New York statute takes a slightly different tack than the other second generation state laws. In principal part, it addresses the internal affairs of resident New York corporations (i.e., a corporation with its principal executive office and significant business operations in New York and with 10% of its voting stock owned by New Yorkers) by allocating more power to the board of directors than do conventional corporation laws. It effects that result by requiring bidders who seek to acquire ownership of 20% or more of the outstanding voting shares of a target to receive the prior approval of the target's board of directors for their purchase (or for the merger they contemplate), and failing such approval to be precluded from combining the target with the bidder's enterprise(s) for 5 years; moreover, the ultimate combination must either be approved by disinterested target stockholders or the bidder must pay a "fair" price, generally the highest price it has previously paid for such shares. The 5 year restriction may be waived by vote of disinterested shareholders to amend the target's by-laws to opt out of the statutory restriction; but even then, 18 months after its adoption must elapse before the amendment is effective. The statute also seeks to limit greenmail payments by requiring stockholder approval of them. And finally it requires more extensive disclosure (than previously required by state law) by a person who seeks to acquire more than 5% of any class of stock to be made to offerees, the target and the Attorney General at the time of, or before, the bid. The new disclosure provisions are said to produce conformity with "recent federal court decisions."]

Five states adopted statutes along the lines of the Ohio "control share" model. Only two states adopted a "redemption rights" statute like Pennsylvania's. Maryland's "fair price" provisions proved the most popular, finding their way into the statutes of thirteen other states within a few years. See Romano, supra at 117–118. The New York statute, with its "business combination" prohibition, became a model for other jurisdictions later on, in the "third generation."

(2) Constitutionality

The second round in the adjudication of the statutes' constitutionality centered on a "control share" provision adopted in Indiana. The Supreme Court sustained the statute into **CTS Corp. v. Dynamics Corp. of America,** 481 U.S. 69 (1987). The Indiana statute, like the Ohio statute, applied only to corporations incorporated in the state, and contained a provision for opting out by certificate or by law amendment or board resolution. Under the statute, an entity acquiring more than 20 percent of a corporation's stock acquired the right to vote the stock only upon the resolution of a majority of the disinterested shareholders. The necessary meeting was to be held within fifty days of the acquirer's filing of a statement with the corporation. In the event the shareholders decided against the restoration of the vote to the shares of the "control" holder, the corporation had a right to redeem the shares at fair value.

The Seventh Circuit, following *MITE*, found the statute to be unconstitutional on Commerce Clause grounds due its potential to hinder tender offers. It also, with reservations, applied the preemption rationale set out in Justice White's plurality opinion. The Supreme Court, in an opinion by Justice Powell, reversed on both grounds.

As to preemption, the Supreme Court adopted *MITE's* "broad interpretation" of the field occupied by the Williams Act only for the sake of argument. It found the Indiana statute to be consistent with the Williams Act, thus described. Unlike the Illinois statute, which favored management at the expense of bidders and therefore shareholders, the Indiana statute protected the shareholder against both parties, and thus furthered the Williams Act purpose of placing investors on an equal footing with the bidder. Said the court, 481 U.S. at 82–83:

"The Indiana Act operates on the assumption, implicit in the Williams Act, that independent shareholders faced with tender offers often are at a disadvantage. By allowing such shareholders to vote as a group, the Act protects them from the coercive aspects of some tender offers. If, for example, shareholders believe that a successful tender offer will be followed by a purchase of nontendering shares at a depressed price, individual shareholders may tender their shares—even if they doubt the tender offer is in the corporation's best interest—to protect themselves from being forced to sell their shares at a depressed price. * * * In such a situation under the Indiana Act, the shareholders as a group, acting in the corporation's best interest, could reject the offer, although individual shareholders might be inclined to accept it. The desire of the Indiana Legislature to protect shareholders of Indiana corporations from this type of coercive offer does not conflict with the Williams Act. Rather, it furthers the federal policy of investor protection."

The court dealt with the contention that the Indiana statute conflicted with the Williams Act as follows, 481 U.S. at 84–85:

"The Act does not impose an absolute 50–day delay on tender offers, nor does it preclude an offeror from purchasing shares as soon as federal law permits. If the offeror fears an adverse shareholder vote under the Act, it can make a conditional tender offer, offering to accept shares on the condition that the shares receive voting rights within a certain period of time. The Williams Act permits tender offers to be conditioned on the offeror's subsequently obtaining regulatory approval. * * *

"Even assuming that the Indiana Act imposes some additional delay, nothing in *MITE* suggested that *any* delay imposed by state regulation, however short, would create a conflict with the Williams Act. The plurality argued only that the offeror should 'be free to go forward without *unreasonable* delay.' 457 U.S., at 639 (emphasis added). In that case, the Court was confronted with the potential for indefinite delay and presented with no persuasive reason why some deadline could not be established. By contrast, the Indiana Act provides that full voting rights will be vested—if this eventually is to occur—within 50 days after commencement of the offer. This period is within the 60–day period Congress established for reinstitution of withdrawal rights in 15 U.S.C. § 78n(d)(5). We cannot say that a delay within that congressionally determined period is unreasonable."

Finally, the court asserted that if this state voting statute were preempted, then any state statutory provision that limited the free exercise power of a successful bidder, such as provisions enabling staggered boards and cumulative voting, also would be preempted.

As to the Commerce Clause, the court noted that no problem of inconsistent regulation was presented because the statute applied only to Indiana corporations. The court, going on to review the balance of benefits and burdens, emphasized that the role of the states in creating corporations, prescribing their powers, and defining the rights attached to shares, was a long-accepted part of the business landscape. "A State," said the court, 481 U.S. at 91, "has an interest in promoting stable relationships among parties involved in the corporations it charters, as well as in ensuring that investors in such corporations have an effective voice in corporate affairs." The Indiana statute, with its purpose to protect shareholders from coercive offers by enhancing their autonomy, fell into this historical zone of state interest and activity. The court then addressed the economic argument that the concern with shareholder coercion was "illusory," and that tender offers should be favored because they move assets into the most productive hands. The court responded by noting that both scholars and the SEC had recognized the coercion problem, and added, 481 U.S. at 92: "The Constitution does not require the States to subscribe to any particular economic theory." The state's interest might become attenuated if, like the statute in *MITE*, the statute applied to nonresident shareholders of nonresident corporations. But such was not the case. The court concluded by addressing the bidder's bottom line claim, 481 U.S. at 93–94:

"Dynamics' argument that the Act is unconstitutional ultimately rests on its contention that the Act will limit the number of successful tender offers. There is little evidence that this will occur. But even if true, this result would not substantially affect our Commerce Clause analysis. We reiterate that this Act does not prohibit any entity—resident or nonresident—from offering to purchase, or from purchasing, shares in Indiana corporations, or from attempting thereby to gain control. It only provides regulatory procedures designed for the better protection of the corporations' shareholders. We have rejected the "notion that the Commerce Clause protects the particular structure or methods of operation in a * * * market." Exxon Corp. v. Governor of Maryland, 437 U.S., at 127. The very commodity that is traded in the securities market is one whose characteristics are defined by state law. Similarly, the very commodity that is traded in the "market for corporate control"—the corporation—is one that owes its existence and attributes to state law. Indiana need not define these commodities as other States do; it need only provide that residents and nonresidents have equal access to them. This Indiana has done. Accordingly, even if the Act should decrease the number of successful tender offers for Indiana corporations, this would not offend the Commerce Clause."

Justice White, joined by Justices Blackmun and Stevens, dissented on the Commerce Clause ground. Only Justice White took the position that the Williams Act preempted the Indiana statute.

If the issue is ever joined, will the "broad interpretation" of the Williams Act set out in *MITE* but employed in *CTS* only for the sake of argument be adopted? How would a narrower interpretation of the Williams Act affect the preemption analysis? See Amanda Acquisition v. Universal Foods, infra p. 1152. How much room does *CTS* leave open for the argument that an antitakeover statute unconstitutionally burdens interstate commerce? Would a state corporate law provision requiring a 100 percent vote in a second step merger amount to such a burden? Would a provision forbidding second step mergers entirely? Would a corporate law provision forbidding public tenders for shares?

(C) THIRD GENERATION STATUTES

---

(1) The Delaware Statute

After the *CTS* decision, Delaware lawmakers went to work on the formulation of an antitakeover statute. They found a model in the "business combination" model devised in New York during the second generation. NYBCL sec. 912. Under this version, the rights attached to the tendered stock are not impaired, but substantial barriers are placed in the way of the consummation of the back end transaction that concludes a two-step acquisition. By now at least 27 states have adopted business combination statutes.

Del.Gen.Corp.L., section 203, Appendix G

PROBLEM

If section 203 had been on the books, how would the contest in each of the following cases have been affected?

1. Hanson Trust PLC v. SCM Corp.
2. Unocal v. Mesa Petroleum

3. Revlon v. MacAndrews & Forbes Holdings

4. AC Acquisitions v. Anderson Clayton

5. City Capital v. Interco

6. Ivanhoe Partners v. Newmont Mining

---

(2) Pennsylvania and Massachusetts

The innovative drafting of antitakeover statutes continues. Pennsylvania, which already had control share and redemption provisions in effect, created a stir in 1990 when it added a new "profit disgorgement" provision to its statute. Under this, unsuccessful suitors are locked into the ownership of any stock they acquire. More particularly, those holding 20 percent of the stock who dispose of the stock within 18 months of becoming 20 percent holders must disgorge to the corporation any profit realized upon the disposition. 15 Pa.Cons.Stat.Ann. sec. 2575. Corporations subject to the provision were given a limited time to opt out by means of a by-law amendment approved by the board. 15 Pa.Cons.Stat.Ann. sec. 2571(b). In 1990 Pennsylvania also added a business combination provision carrying a five year merger prohibition. This cumulation of provisions makes those Pennsylvania corporations not choosing to opt out as close to invulnerable to hostile attack as American corporations can be.

Massachusetts amended its statute in 1990 to mandate classified boards and staggered shareholder voting for board seats, subject to opting out by board resolution or a two thirds shareholder vote. Mass. Gen.Laws Ann., ch. 149, sec. 184.

---

(3) Constitutionality

CTS did not offer clear guidance for testing the constitutionality of "business combination" statutes such as Delaware's, or for that matter, all features of other second generation statutes. For discussion of the open-ended aspects of the court's analysis, see, e.g., Weiss, What Lawyers Do When the Emperor Has No Clothes: Evaluating *CTS Corp. v. Dynamics Corp. of America* and Its Progeny—Part I, 78 Geo.L.J. 1655 (1990); Pinto, The Constitution and the Market for Corporate Control: State Antitakeover Statutes After *CTS Corp.*, 29 Wm. & Mary L.Rev. 699 (1988). The question is whether *CTS* stands for the proposition that the Commerce Clause and the Williams Act allow only narrowly drafted statutes keyed to protection of carefully articulated shareholder interests, or whether they allow virtually any takeover block so long as it applies only to domestic corporations and does not interfere directly with the operation of the Williams Act.

The constitutionality of Delaware section 203 has been confirmed on several occasions by courts reading *CTS* to contemplate scrutiny for consonance with the Williams Act's shareholder protective purpose and going through the motions of Commerce Clause balancing. See BNS, Inc. v. Koppers Co., Inc., 683 F.Supp. 458 (D.Del.1988); RP Acquisitions Corp. v. Staley Continental, Inc., 686 F.Supp. 476 (D.Del.1988); City Capital Associates v. Interco, Inc., 696 F.Supp. 1551 (D.Del.1988). But cf. Hyde Park Partners, L.P. v. Connolly, 839 F.2d 837 (1st Cir.1988) (Massachusetts statute creating one year moratorium on takeover attempts as sanction for disclosure violations preempted). Provisions applying to nonresident corporations have fared less well. See Tyson Foods, Inc. v. McReynolds, 865 F.2d 99 (6th Cir.1989); TLX Acquisition Corp. v. Telex Corp., 679 F.Supp. 1022 (W.D.Okl.1987).

AMANDA ACQUISITION CORP. v. UNIVERSAL FOODS CORP.

United States Court of Appeals, Seventh Circuit, 1989.
877 F.2d 496, cert. denied, 493 U.S. 955, 110 S.Ct. 367, 107 L.Ed.2d 353 (1989).

EASTERBROOK, Circuit Judge.

* * *

I

Amanda Acquisition Corporation is a shell with a single purpose: to acquire Universal Foods Corporation, a diversified firm incorporated in Wisconsin and traded on the New York Stock Exchange. Universal is covered by Wisconsin's anti-takeover law. * * *

In mid-November 1988 Universal's stock was trading for about $25 per share. On December 1 Amanda commenced a tender offer at $30.50, to be effective if at least 75% of the stock should be tendered. This all-cash, all-shares offer has been increased by stages to $38.00. Amanda's financing is contingent on a prompt merger with Universal if the offer succeeds, so the offer is conditional on a judicial declaration that the law is invalid.

No firm incorporated in Wisconsin and having its headquarters, substantial operations, or 10% of its shares or shareholders there may "engage in a business combination with an interested stockholder * * * for 3 years after the interested stockholder's stock acquisition date unless the board of directors of the [Wisconsin] corporation has approved, before the interested stockholder's stock acquisition date, that business combination or the purchase of stock", Wis.Stat. § 180.726(2). An "interested stockholder" is one owning 10% of the voting stock, directly or through associates (anyone acting in concert with it), § 180.-726(1)(j). A "business combination" is a merger with the bidder or any of its affiliates, sale of more than 5% of the assets to bidder or affiliate, liquidation of the target, or a transaction by which the target guarantees the bidder's or affiliates debts or passes tax benefits to the bidder or affiliate, § 180.726(1)(e). The law, in other words, provides for almost hermetic separation of bidder and target for three years after the bidder obtains 10% of the stock—unless the target's board consented before then. No matter how popular the offer, the ban applies: obtaining 85% (even 100%) of the stock held by non-management shareholders won't allow the bidder to engage in a business combination, as it would under Delaware law. * * * Wisconsin firms cannot opt out of the law, as may corporations subject to almost all other state takeover statutes. In Wisconsin it is management's approval in advance, or wait three years. Even when the time is up, the bidder needs the approval of a majority of the remaining investors, without any provision disqualifying shares still held by the managers who resisted the transaction, § 180.726(3)(b). * * * As a practical matter, Wisconsin prohibits any offer contingent on a merger between bidder and target, a condition attached to about 90% of contemporary tender offers.

Amanda filed this suit seeking a declaration that this law is preempted by the Williams Act and inconsistent with the Commerce Clause. * * *

II

* * *

A

If our views of the wisdom of state law mattered, Wisconsin's takeover statute would not survive. Like our colleagues who decided *MITE* and *CTS*, we believe that antitakeover legislation injures shareholders.[5]

[The court then describes the benefits to shareholders of takeover premiums and the governance benefits of takeovers. It refutes management claims that successful takeover defense promotes long term investment gain by reference to stock price studies proving gain.]

Although a takeover-*proof* firm leaves investors at the mercy of incumbent managers (who may be mistaken about the wisdom of their business plan even when they act in the best of faith), a takeover-*resistant* firm may be able to assist its investors. An auction may run

---

5. Because both the district court and the parties—like the Williams Act—examine tender offers from the perspective of equity investors, we employ the same approach. States could choose to protect "constituencies" other than stockholders. Creditors, managers, and workers invest human rather than financial capital. But the limitation of our inquiry to equity investors does not affect the analysis, because no evidence of which we are aware suggests that bidders confiscate workers' and other participants' investments to any greater degree than do incumbents—who may (and frequently do) close or move plants to follow the prospect of profit. Jo- seph A. Grundfest, a Commissioner of the SEC, showed in Job Loss and Takeovers, address to University of Toledo College of Law, Mar. 11, 1988, that acquisitions have no logical (or demonstrable) effect on employment. See also Brown & Medoff, The Impact of Firm Acquisitions on Labor, in Corporate Takeovers: Causes and Consequences 9 (A. Auerbach ed. 1988); Roberta Romano, The Future of Hostile Takeovers: Legislation and Public Opinion, 57 U.Cin. L.Rev. 457 (1988); C. Steven Bradford, Protecting Shareholders from Themselves? A Policy and Constitutional Review of a State Takeover Statute, 67 Neb.L.Rev. 459, 529–34 (1988).

up the price, and delay may be essential to an auction. * * * Devices giving managers some ability to orchestrate investors' responses, in order to avoid panic tenders in response to front-end-loaded offers, also could be beneficial, as the Supreme Court emphasized in *CTS*, 481 U.S. at 92–93, 107 S.Ct. at 1651–52. ("Could be" is an important qualifier; even from a perspective limited to targets' shareholders given a bid on the table, it is important to know whether managers use this power to augment bids or to stifle them, and whether courts can tell the two apart.)

State anti-takeover laws do not serve these ends well, however. Investors who prefer to give managers the discretion to orchestrate responses to bids may do so through "fair-price" clauses in the articles of incorporation and other consensual devices. Other firms may choose different strategies. A law such as Wisconsin's does not add options to firms that would like to give more discretion to their managers; instead it destroys the possibility of divergent choices. Wisconsin's law applies even when the investors prefer to leave their managers under the gun, to allow the market full sway. Karpoff and Malatesta found that state anti-takeover laws have little or no effect on the price of shares if the firm already has poison pills (or related devices) in place, but strongly negative effects on price when firms have no such contractual devices. To put this differently, state laws have bite only when investors, given the choice, would deny managers the power to interfere with tender offers (maybe already *have* denied managers that power). See also Roberta Romano, The Political Economy of Takeover Statutes, 73 Va.L.Rev. 111, 128–31 (1987).

B

Skepticism about the wisdom of a state's law does not lead to the conclusion that the law is beyond the state's power, however. * * * Unless a federal statute or the Constitution bars the way, Wisconsin's choice must be respected.

Preemption has not won easy acceptance among the Justices for several reasons. First there is § 28(a) of the '34 Act, 15 U.S.C. § 78bb(a), which provides that "[n]othing in this chapter shall affect the jurisdiction of the securities commission * * * of any State over any security or any person insofar as it does not conflict with the provisions of this chapter or the rules and regulations thereunder." Although some of the SEC's regulations (particularly the one defining the commencement of an offer) conflict with some state takeover laws, the SEC has not drafted regulations concerning mergers with controlling shareholders, and the Act itself does not address the subject. States have used the leeway afforded by § 28(a) to carry out "merit regulation" of securities—"blue sky" laws that allow securities commissioners to forbid sales altogether, in contrast with the federal regimen emphasizing disclosure. So § 28(a) allows states to stop some transactions federal law would permit, in pursuit of an approach at odds with a system emphasizing disclosure and investors' choice. Then there is the traditional reluctance of federal courts to infer preemption of "state law in areas traditionally regulated by the States" * * *. States have regulated corporate affairs, including mergers and sales of assets, since before the beginning of the nation.

Because Justice White's views of the Williams Act did not garner the support of a majority of the Court in *MITE,* we reexamined that subject in *CTS* and observed that the best argument for preemption is the Williams Act's "neutrality" between bidder and management, a balance designed to leave investors free to choose. This is not a confident jumping-off point, though: "Of course it is a big leap from saying that the Williams Act does not itself exhibit much hostility to tender offers to saying that it implicitly forbids states to adopt more hostile regulations, but this leap was taken by the Supreme Court plurality and us in *MITE* and by every court to consider the question since * * *. [W]hatever doubts of the Williams' Act preemptive intent we might entertain as an original matter are stifled by the weight of precedent." 794 F.2d at 262. The rough treatment our views received from the Court—only Justice White supported the holding on preemption—lifts the "weight of precedent".

There is a big difference between what Congress *enacts* and what it *supposes* will ensue. Expectations about the consequences of a law are not themselves law. To say that Congress wanted to be neutral between bidder and target—a conclusion reached in many of the Court's opinions, e.g., Piper v. Chris–Craft Industries, Inc., 430 U.S. 1, 97 S.Ct. 926, 51 L.Ed.2d 124 (1977)—is not to say that it also forbade the states to favor one of these sides. Every law has a stopping point, likely one selected because of a belief that it would be unwise (for now, maybe forever) to do more. * * * Nothing in the Williams Act says that the federal compromise among bidders, targets' managers, and investors is the only permissible one. * * *

The Williams Act regulates the *process* of tender offers: timing, disclosure, proration if tenders exceed what the bidder is willing to buy, best-price rules. It slows things down, allowing investors to evaluate the offer and management's response. Best-price, proration, and short-tender rules ensure that investors who decide at the end of the offer get the same treatment as those who decide immediately, reducing pressure to leap before looking. After complying with the disclosure and delay requirements, the bidder is free to take the shares. *MITE* held invalid a state law that increased the delay and, by authorizing a regulator to nix the offer, created a distinct possibility that the bidder would be unable to buy the stock (and the holders to sell it) despite compliance with federal law. Illinois tried to regulate the process of tender offers, contradicting in some respects the federal rules. Indiana, by contrast, allowed the tender offer to take its course as the Williams Act specified but "sterilized" the acquired shares until the remaining investors restored their voting rights. Congress said nothing about the voting power of shares acquired in tender offers. Indiana's law reduced the benefits the bidder anticipated from the acquisition but left the process alone. So the Court, although accepting Justice White's views for the purpose of argument, held that Indiana's rules do not conflict with the federal norms.

CTS observed that laws affecting the voting power of acquired shares do not differ in principle from many other rules governing the internal affairs of corporations. Laws requiring staggered or classified boards of directors delay the transfer of control to the bidder; laws requiring supermajority vote for a merger may make a transaction less attractive or impossible. 481 U.S. at 85–86, 107 S.Ct. at 1647–48. Yet these are not preempted by the Williams Act, any more than state laws concerning the *effect* of investors' votes are preempted by the portions of the Exchange Act, 15 U.S.C. § 78n(a)–(c), regulating the process of soliciting proxies. Federal securities laws frequently regulate process while state corporate law regulates substance. Federal proxy rules demand that firms disclose many things, in order to promote informed voting. Yet states may permit or compel a supermajority rule (even a unanimity rule) rendering it all but impossible for a particular side to prevail in the voting. See Robert Charles Clark, *Corporate Law* § 9.1.3 (1986). Are the state laws therefore preempted? How about state laws that allow many firms to organize without traded shares? Universities, hospitals, and other charities have self-perpetuating boards and cannot be acquired by tender offer. Insurance companies may be organized as mutuals, without traded shares; retailers often organize as co-operatives, without traded stock; some decently large companies (large enough to be "reporting companies" under the '34 Act) issue stock subject to buy-sell agreements under which the investors cannot sell to strangers without offering stock to the firm at a formula price; Ford Motor Co. issued non-voting stock to outside investors while reserving voting stock for the family, thus preventing outsiders from gaining control (dual-class stock is becoming more common); firms issue and state law enforces poison pills. All of these devices make tender offers unattractive (even impossible) and greatly diminish the power of proxy fights, success in which often depends on buying votes by acquiring the equity to which the vote is attached. See Douglas H. Blair, Devra L. Golbe & James M. Gerard, *Unbundling the Voting Rights and Profit Claims of Common Shares*, 97 J.Pol.Econ. 420 (1989). None of these devices could be thought preempted by the Williams Act or the proxy rules. If they are not preempted, neither is Wis.Stat. § 180.726.

Any bidder complying with federal law is free to acquire shares of Wisconsin firms on schedule. Delay in completing a second-stage merger may make the target less attractive, and thus depress the price offered or even lead to an absence of bids; it does not, however, alter any of the procedures governed by federal regulation. Indeed Wisconsin's law does not depend in any way on how the acquiring firm came by its stock: open-market purchases, private acquisitions of blocs, and acquisitions via tender offers are treated identically. Wisconsin's law is no different in effect from one saying that for the three years after a person acquires 10% of a firm's stock, a unanimous vote is required to merge. Corporate law once had a generally-applicable unanimity rule in major transactions, a rule discarded because giving every investor the power to block every reorganization stopped many desirable changes. (Many investors could use their "hold-up" power to try to engross a larger portion of the gains, creating a complex bargaining problem that often could not be solved.) Wisconsin's more restrained version of unanimity also may block beneficial transactions, but not by tinkering with any of the procedures established in federal law.

Only if the Williams Act gives investors a right to be the beneficiary of offers could Wisconsin's law run afoul of the federal rule. No such entitlement can be mined out of the Williams Act, however. *Schreiber v. Burlington Northern, Inc.,* 472 U.S. 1, 105 S.Ct. 2458, 86 L.Ed.2d 1 (1985), holds that the cancellation of a pending offer because of machinations between bidder and target does not deprive investors of their due under the Williams Act. The Court treated § 14(e) as a disclosure law, so that investors could make informed decisions; it follows that events leading bidders to cease their quest do not conflict with the Williams Act any more than a state law leading a firm not to issue new securities could conflict with the Securities Act of 1933. * * * Investors have no right to receive tender offers. More to the point—since Amanda sues as bidder rather than as investor seeking to sell—the Williams Act does not create a right to profit from the business of making tender offers. It is not attractive to put bids on the table for Wisconsin corporations, but because Wisconsin leaves the process alone once a bidder appears, its law may co-exist with the Williams Act.

C

The Commerce Clause, Art. I, § 8 cl. 3 of the Constitution, grants Congress the power "[t]o regulate Commerce * * * among the several States". * * *

When state law discriminates against interstate commerce expressly—for example, when Wisconsin closes its border to butter from Minnesota—the negative Commerce Clause steps in. The law before us is not of this type: it is neutral between inter-state and intra-state commerce. Amanda therefore presses on us the broader, all-weather, be-reasonable vision of the Constitution. Wisconsin has passed a law that unreasonably injures investors, most of whom live outside of Wisconsin, and therefore it *has* to be unconstitutional, as Amanda sees things. Although Pike v. Bruce Church, Inc., 397 U.S. 137, 90 S.Ct. 844, 25 L.Ed.2d 174 (1970), sometimes is understood to authorize such general-purpose balancing, a closer examination of the cases may support the conclusion that the Court has looked for discrimination rather than for baleful effects. * * * At all events, although *MITE* employed the balancing process described in *Pike* to deal with a statute that regulated all firms having "contacts" with the state, *CTS* did not even cite that case when dealing with a statute regulating only the affairs of a firm incorporated in the state, and Justice Scalia's concurring opinion questioned its application. 481 U.S. at 95–96, 107 S.Ct. at 1652–53. The Court took a decidedly confined view of the judicial role: "We are not inclined 'to second-guess the empirical judgments of lawmakers concerning the utility of legislation,' Kassel v. Consolidated Freightways Corp., 450 U.S. [662] at 679 [101 S.Ct. 1309, 1320, 67 L.Ed.2d 580 (1981)] (BRENNAN, J., concurring in judgment)." 481 U.S. at 92, 107 S.Ct. at 1651. Although * * * scholars * * * conclude that laws such as Wisconsin's injure investors, Wisconsin is entitled to give a different answer to this empirical question—or to decide that investors' interests should be sacrificed to protect managers' interests or promote the stability of corporate arrangements.

Illinois's law, held invalid in *MITE,* regulated sales of stock elsewhere. Illinois tried to tell a Texas owner of stock in a Delaware corporation that he could not sell to a buyer in California. By contrast, Wisconsin's law, like the Indiana statute sustained by *CTS,* regulates the internal affairs of firms incorporated there. Investors may buy or sell stock as they please. Wisconsin's law differs in this respect not only from that of Illinois but also from that of Massachusetts, which forbade any transfer of shares for one year after the failure to disclose any material fact, a flaw that led the First Circuit to condemn it. Hyde Park Partners, L.P. v. Connolly, 839 F.2d 837, 847–48 (1st Cir.1988).

Buyers of stock in Wisconsin firms may exercise full rights as investors, taking immediate control. No interstate transaction is regulated or forbidden. True, Wisconsin's law makes a potential buyer less willing to buy (or depresses the bid), but this is equally true of Indiana's rule. Many other rules of corporate law—supermajority voting requirements, staggered and classified boards, and so on—have similar or greater effects on some persons' willingness to purchase stock. *CTS,* 481 U.S. at 89–90, 107 S.Ct. at 1649–50. States could ban mergers outright, with even more powerful consequences. * * * Wisconsin did not allow mergers among firms chartered there until 1947. We doubt that it was violating the Commerce Clause all those years. * * * Every rule of corporate law affects investors who live outside the state of incorporation, yet this has never been thought sufficient to authorize a form of cost-benefit inquiry through the medium of the Commerce Clause.

Wisconsin, like Indiana, is indifferent to the domicile of the bidder. A putative bidder located in Wisconsin enjoys no privilege over a firm located in New York. So too with investors: all are treated identically, regardless of residence. Doubtless most bidders (and investors) are located outside Wisconsin, but unless the law discriminates according to residence this alone does not matter. *CTS,* 481 U.S. at 87–88, 107 S.Ct. at 1648–49; Lewis v. BT Investment Managers, Inc., 447 U.S. 27, 36–37, 100 S.Ct. 2009, 2015–16, 64 L.Ed.2d 702 (1980); Exxon Corp. v. Governor of Maryland, 437 U.S. 117, 98 S.Ct. 2207, 57 L.Ed.2d 91 (1978). Every state's regulation of domestic trade (potentially) affects those who live elsewhere but wish to sell their wares within the state. A law making suppliers of drugs absolutely liable for defects will affect the conduct (and wealth) of Eli Lilly & Co., an Indiana firm, and the many other pharmaceutical houses, all located in other states, yet Wisconsin has no less power to set and change tort law than do states with domestic drug manufacturers. "Because nothing in the [Wisconsin] Act imposes a greater burden on out-of-state offerors than it does on similarly situated [Wisconsin] offerors, we reject the contention that the Act discriminates against interstate commerce." *CTS,* 481 U.S. at 88, 107 S.Ct. at 1649. For the same reason, the Court long ago held that state blue sky laws comport with the Commerce Clause. Hall v. Geiger–Jones Co., 242 U.S. 539, 37 S.Ct. 217, 61 L.Ed. 480 (1917); Caldwell v. Sioux Falls Stock Yards Co., 242 U.S. 559, 37 S.Ct. 224, 61 L.Ed. 493 (1917); Merrick v. N.W. Halsey & Co., 242 U.S. 568, 37 S.Ct. 227, 61 L.Ed. 498 (1917). Blue sky laws may bar Texans from selling stock in Wisconsin, but they apply equally to local residents' attempts to sell. That their application blocks a form of commerce altogether does not strip the states of power.

* * * This leaves only the argument that Wisconsin's law hinders the flow of interstate trade "too much". *CTS* dispatched this concern by declaring it inapplicable to laws that apply only to the internal affairs of firms incorporated in the regulating state. 481 U.S. at 89–94, 107 S.Ct. at 1649–52. States may regulate corporate transactions as they choose without having to demonstrate under an unfocused balancing test that the benefits are "enough" to justify the consequences.

To say that states have the power to enact laws whose costs exceed their benefits is not to say that investors should kiss their wallets goodbye. States compete to offer corporate codes attractive to firms. Managers who want to raise money incorporate their firms in the states that offer the combination of rules investors prefer. Ralph K. Winter, Jr., State Law, Shareholder Protection, and the Theory of the Corporation, 6 J. Legal Studies 251 (1977) * * *. Laws that in the short run injure investors and protect managers will in the longer run make the state less attractive to firms that need to raise new capital. If the law is "protectionist", the protected class is the existing body of managers (and other workers), suppliers, and so on, which bears no necessary relation to state boundaries. States regulating the affairs of domestic corporations cannot in the long run injure anyone but themselves. * * *

The long run takes time to arrive, and it is tempting to suppose that courts could contribute to investors' welfare by eliminating laws that impose costs in the short run. * * * The price of such warfare, however, is a reduction in the power of competition among states. Courts seeking to impose "good" rules on the states diminish the differences among corporate codes and dampen competitive forces. Too, courts may fail in their quest. How do judges know which rules are best? Often only the slow forces of competition reveal that information. Early economic studies may mislead, or judges (not trained as social scientists) may misinterpret the available data or act precipitously. Our Constitution allows the states to act as laboratories; slow migration (or national law on the authority of the Commerce Clause) grinds the failures under. No such process weeds out judicial errors, or decisions that, although astute when rendered, have become anachronistic in light of changes in the economy. Judges must hesitate for these practical reasons—and not only because of limits on their constitutional competence—before trying to "perfect" corporate codes.

The three district judges who have considered and sustained Delaware's law delaying mergers did so in large measure because they believed that the law left hostile offers "a meaningful opportunity for success". BNS, Inc. v. Koppers Co., 683 F.Supp. at 469. See also RP Acquisition Corp., 686 F.Supp. at 482–84, 488; *City Capital Associates,* 696 F.Supp. at 1555. Delaware allows a merger to occur forthwith if the bidder obtains 85% of the shares other than those held by management and employee stock plans. If the bid is attractive to the bulk of the unaffiliated investors, it succeeds. Wisconsin offers no such opportunity, which Amanda believes is fatal.

Even in Wisconsin, though, options remain. Defenses impenetrable to the naked eye may have cracks. Poison pills are less fatal in practice than in name (some have been swallowed willingly), and corporate law contains self-defense mechanisms. Investors concerned about stock-watering often arranged for firms to issue pre-emptive rights, entitlements for existing investors to buy stock at the same price offered to newcomers (often before the newcomers had a chance to buy in). Poison pills are dilution devices, and so pre-emptive rights ought to be handy countermeasures.[11] So too there are countermeasures to statutes deferring mergers. The cheapest is to lower the bid to reflect the costs of delay. Because every potential bidder labors under the same drawback, the firm placing the highest value on the target still should win. Or a bidder might take down the stock and pledge it (or its dividends) as security for any loans. That is, the bidder could operate the target as a subsidiary for three years. The corporate world is full of partially owned subsidiaries. If there is gain to be had from changing the debt-equity ratio of the target, that can be done consistent with Wisconsin law. The prospect of being locked into place as holders of illiquid minority positions would cause many persons to sell out, and the threat of being locked in would cause many managers to give assent in advance, as Wisconsin allows. (Or bidders might demand that directors waive the protections of state law, just as Amanda believes that the directors' fiduciary duties compel them to redeem the poison pill rights.) Many bidders would find lock-in unattractive because of the potential for litigation by minority investors, and the need to operate the firm as a subsidiary might foreclose savings or synergies from merger. So none of these options is a perfect substitute for immediate merger, but each is a crack in the defensive wall allowing some value-increasing bids to proceed.

11. Imagine a series of Antidote rights, issued by would-be bidding firms, that detach if anyone exercises flip-over rights to purchase the bidder's stock at a discount. Antidote rights would entitle the bidder's investors, *other than those who exercise flip-over rights,* to purchase the bidder's stock at the same discount available to investors exercising flip-over rights. Antidotes for flip-in rights also could be issued. In general, whenever one firm can issue rights allowing the purchase of cheap stock, another firm can issue the equivalent series of contingent preemptive rights that offsets the dilution.

At the end of the day, however, it does not matter whether these countermeasures are "enough". The Commerce Clause does not demand that states leave bidders a "meaningful opportunity for success". Maryland enacted a law that absolutely banned vertical integration in the oil business. No opportunities, "meaningful" or otherwise, remained to firms wanting to own retail outlets. Exxon Corp. v. Governor of Maryland held that the law is consistent with the Commerce Clause, even on the assumption that it injures consumers and investors alike. A state with the power to forbid mergers has the power to defer them for three years. Investors can turn to firms incorporated in states committed to the dominance of market forces, or they can turn on legislators who enact unwise laws. The Constitution has room for many economic policies. "[A] law can be both economic folly and constitutional." CTS, 481 U.S. at 96–97, 107 S.Ct. at 1653–54 (Scalia, J., concurring). Wisconsin's law may well be folly; we are confident that it is constitutional.

Affirmed.

NOTE: ANTITAKEOVER STATUTES AND SHAREHOLDER VALUE

1. *Empirical Studies.*

Economists have produced a series of studies of the stock price effects of the announcement and enactment of antitakeover statutes. The results follow the ambiguous pattern of the results of similar studies of shark repellent charter provisions and dual class recapitalizations. See supra pp. 965 and 976. That is, some studies support the hypothesis that defensive provisions entrench managers and increase the cost of takeovers and thus reduce the wealth of shareholders. See Ryngaert and Netter, Shareholder Wealth Effects of the Ohio Antitakeover Law, 4 J.L. Econ. & Org. 373 (1988) (passage of Ohio second generation statute causes 3.24 percent stock price decrease for firms with less than 30 percent inside ownership); Schumann, State Regulation of Takeovers and Shareholder Wealth: The Case of New York's 1985 Takeover Statute, 19 Rand J. Econ. 557 (1989) (1 percent price decrease on announcement and passage); Sidak and Woodward, Corporate Takeovers, The Commerce Clause, and the Efficient Anonymity of Shareholders, 84 Nw.U.L.Rev. 1092 (1990) (New York and Indiana; significant negative effect). See also Note, Second Generation State Takeover Statutes and Shareholder Wealth: An Empirical Study, 97 Yale L.J. 1193 (1988). Other studies support the hypothesis that defenses increase premiums, even while deterring some bids, and thereby enhance shareholder wealth. See Romano, The Political Economy of Takeover Statutes, 73 Va.L.Rev. 111 (1987) (Connecticut, Missouri, Pennsylvania; no significant effect on prices); Margotta, McWilliams & McWilliams, An Analysis of the Stock Price Effect of the 1986 Ohio Takeover Legislation, 6 J.L.Econ. & Org. 235 (1990) (no significant effect). See also Jarrell and Bradley, The Economic Effects of Federal and State Regulation of Cash Tender Offers, 23 J.L. & Econ. 371 (1980) (first generation statutes increase premiums).

Surveying some of this material, Karpoff and Malatesta, The Wealth Effects of Second–Generation State Takeover Legislation, 25 J.Fin.Econ. 291, 293 (1989), conclude that the discrepancies can be accounted for in major part by reference to the fact that "estimates of any single law's effect are heavily influenced by idiosyncratic characteristics of the researcher's event window and sample affected firms." Karpoff and Malatesta's study purports to circumvent these problems by studying the stock price effect of all new second generation statutes covered in the press through 1987, and controlling for antecedent poison pills and shark repellent charter provisions in the corporations studied. The study finds a small but statistically significant stock price decline for affected firms without antecedent pills or defensive charter provisions. Stock prices of firms with preexisting defenses experienced no significant affects.

2. *Legal Commentaries.*

How should the history of state antitakeover legislation be rated as an exercise in the evolution of economic regulation in the federal system? Some commentators take the position that the system is not working well here because this is interest group legislation enacted in disregard of the broader public interest. See, e.g., Macey, State and Federal Regulation of Corporate Takeovers: A View From the Demand Side, 69 Wash.U.L.Q. 383 (1991); Romano, The Future of Hostile Takeovers: Public Opinion and Prospects for Legislation, 57 U.Cinn. L.Rev. 457 (1988); Romano, The Political Economy of Takeover Statutes, supra. Other commentators find aspects to approve in this federal-state back and forth. See Booth, Federalism and the Market for Corporate Control, 69 Wash.U.L.Q. 411 (1991); Shipman, The Case for A Reasonable State Regulation of Corporate Takeovers: Some Observations Concerning the Ohio Experience, 57 U.Cinn.L.Rev. 507 (1988). On the preemption question, see Johnson and Millon, Misreading the Williams Act, 87 Mich.L.Rev. 1862 (1989). For the view that the statutes should be struck down under the Contract Clause, see Butler and Ribstein, State Anti–Takeover Statutes and the Contract Clause, 57 U.Cinn.L.Rev. 612 (1988).

NOTE: THE CONSTITUENCY STATUTES

One variety of antitakeover legislation, now adopted in 28 states, modifies the statutory statement of the duty of loyalty by authorizing, or in some instances requiring, management in a control transfer situation to consider the interests of constituencies other than shareholders. According to their critics, these statutes provide management with much more additional power than is needed or appropriate to meet takeover threats. See, e.g., New York Bus.Corp.L. section 717(b), Appendix G; Indiana Code, section 23–1–35–1 et seq. For an overview of the issues, see Symposium, Corporate Malaise—Stakeholder Statutes: Cause or Cure?, 21 Stetson L.Rev. 1 (1991). For economic analyses of the constituency question, see Macey, Externalities, Firm Specific Capital Investments, and the Legal Treatment of Fundamental Corporate Changes, 1989 Duke L.J. 173; Carney, Does Defining Constituencies Matter?, 59 U.Cinn.L.Rev. 385 (1990).

Constituency statutes accord management authority to depart from the norm of shareholder value maximization and recognize the interests of other parties, such as bondholders and employees. In so doing, they implicate a debate over corporate objectives that has been conducted many times in the past. See Dodd, For Whom Are Corporate Managers Trustees?, 45 Harv.L.Rev. 1145 (1932), and Berle, For Whom Corporate Managers Are Trustees: A Note, 45 Harv.L.Rev. 1365 (1932). Other protagonists later continued the debate in E. Mason (ed.), The Corporation in Modern Society (1959). For a discussion of the contemporary significance of the Berle/Dodd debate, see Millon, Theories of the Corporation, 1990 Duke L.J. 201.

The import of the statutes for the takeover movement lies in the virtually untrammeled discretion they vest in management, as pointed out in Hanks, Non–Stockholder Constituency Statutes, 3 Insights 20 (December 1989):

"Even if it were possible to identify the nature and extent of non-stockholders constituencies' interests, none of the statutes offers any guidance as to how much weight should be given to the interests of one constituency versus another or the weight to be given to one claim of a constituency versus other possible claims of the same constituency. Proponents of these statutes have not articulated any standard for determining "how much" of the stockholders' wealth the directors should be permitted to allocate to other groups. Do they think, for example, that under a non-stockholder constituency statute a board could cause all of the stockholders' equity (or all of the premium in a takeover) to be paid out to the employees as a special bonus? It is evident that these statutes, especially those with open-ended language such as "any other factors the director considers pertinent," result in virtually standardless discretion. This absence of standards is likely to lead not only to greater uncertainty and unpredictability in the boardroom but also to difficulty in judicial review."

But see Ryan, Calculating the "Stakes" for Corporate Stakeholders as Part of Business Decision–Making, 44 Rutgers L.Rev. 555 (1992) which takes a first step toward a response to the standards question, proposing an analytical framework for balancing constituency conflicts. See also Millon, Redefining Corporate Law, 24 Ind.L.Rev. 223 (1991), which argues in favor of a constituent right (and right of action) at least to have its interests considered by management.

The corporate governance implications of the sweeping discretion that these statutes vest in management are indeed large—so large as to present problems well beyond those necessary or appropriate for a casebook on corporate finance.

APPENDIX A

MATERIALS ON ACCOUNTING

SECTION 1. VALUATION AND ACCOUNTING EARNINGS

(a) Accounting Income as a Predicate for Estimating Future Value per Share

Today's value per share is said to be set by the relative likelihood of various time series of *future* distributions.[a] Estimation of future events must, according to the usual theory of prediction, be derived from (a) past and current data about the complex reality of the firm and the external environment in which the "firm" functions, and (b) a theory (or model) which defines the relevance of the data to that which is to be predicted.

How useful is the trend of annual earnings per share, stated according to generally accepted accounting principles, in deriving value per share? The issuance of an income statement is often preceded or followed by increased market activity in the company's shares. Persons thus reacting must have something in mind, and we could impute to them the simplest of all prediction theories, viz., "the past persists." It could then be supposed that their reaction to the latest income statement is, whether they know it or not, simply extrapolative: the past series of income statements increased 10% per year during each of the past 10 years; the prediction is made that next year again will see a 10% increase. Hence each new income statement is important because it continues the trend line, and thus the extrapolated future.

But anyone who believes "the past persists" ought not bother extrapolating the time series of *accounting income* per share. He could, if his theory is right, predict share price directly from the time series trend of *share prices* itself. Hence our extrapolator apparently believes not that *all* the past persists (some of course does, some doesn't), but rather that movements of the accounting-income-per-share series capture some important management quality: a management with good past results will be able to squeeze success out of the Protean future.

Whichever prediction theory is assumed, the extrapolation operations must be more precisely stated to justify actual buy-sell decisions at actual price quantities. To state that the accounting past—even if suitably represented—can be used to predict the distributions future

---

a. This ignores the possibility that short or long term movements in share *prices* are a function of market behavior disconnected from the theory of share *values*.

A–1

involves two propositions: (a) a past direction and rate of change of accounting earnings will persist, and (b) there is an invariant relationship between changes in the series *accounting net income per share* and the series *distributions per share*.[b] However, the premises and conventions of current accounting practice are such that year to year changes in accounting net income are unlikely to reflect, in timing and amount, those improvements and declines in company fortunes which do seem (a) likely to persist and (b) likely to find reflection in future distributions.

(1) *The Cost Principle: The Special Case of Inflation*

Suppose between one year and the next there is a currency inflation which raises every price 10%. The obvious effect on the money value of the firm is an increase of 10%—not that this will do anyone any good. The effect will be experienced via a 10% increase in the firm's prospective cash inflow and expenses and needs to be compensated for in provision for future capital expenditures. The year to year change in the firm's accounting net income, however, will be an increase of more than 10% if the firm has fixed assets on which it calculated depreciation expense by accepted accounting principles.

	19X1	19X2
Sales	$2,000,000	$2,200,000
Operating Expenses	600,000	660,000
Depreciation	600,000	600,000
Net Income	$ 800,000	$ 940,000

General monetary inflation of 10% has produced an accounting income increase of considerably more than 10%. This is caused by the flat original cost depreciation charge required under the accountant's cost principle. The effect here noted will increase in magnitude in the degree that the enterprise being described is capital intensive.

No matter how the dollar volume of sales is altered, whether by price level changes, or by other economic events, the convention of amortizing past costs will always produce a leverage effect: the percentage of net income change will be greater than the percentage of sales dollar volume change.

We have already learned from (Blum & Katz, supra p. 43) that serious errors are introduced into valuation if predicted future gross receipts are netted by a standard accounting depreciation charge rather than by a charge reflecting the timing and amount of future replacement expenditures. Perhaps that alone is a sufficient reason for

b. It may be noted that the two propositions lack sufficient content to be operational. As to the first, rates of change cannot continue indefinitely, but we can suppose that the extrapolation will hold only within some undefined range. Further, the question remains whether to derive our extrapolative series from the past two years (or quarters) or ten, or other period. And, as to the second proposition, the problem remains to define the formula which relates the two time series.

rejecting past trends in accounting income as predictors and substituting some sort of cash flow trending. Here we simply make the further point that accounting income trends are further infected by price level changes.

Accountants have for decades debated whether a depreciation allowance based on original cost is truly appropriate during an era of inflation, with many contending that a supplemental allowance is necessary in view of the higher prices at which worn-out equipment must ultimately be replaced. Depreciation based on replacement cost continues to be regarded as not within accepted accounting practice. During the 1970s, however, both the Financial Accounting Standards Board (FASB) and the Securities and Exchange Commission (SEC) required certain large, publicly held corporations to include financial statements adjusted for changing prices due to both general inflation and increases in specific prices (current cost basis) as supplementary information in published annual reports. See FASB, Statement of Financial Accounting Standards No. 33: Financial Reporting and Changing Prices (1979); SEC, Accounting Series Release No. 190 (1976). The FASB reduced these disclosure requirements as inflation declined during the 1980s. Finally, it dropped the requirement of disclosure of the effects of inflation entirely, while encouraging corporations to make voluntary disclosures. FASB Statement of Financial Accounting Standards No. 89, Financial Reporting and Changing Prices (1986). For discussion of this shift toward the provision of a richer set of accounting information, see W. Beaver, Financial Reporting: An Accounting Revolution (1981).

Accounting theorists are suggesting a new measure of depreciation—"annuity" depreciation. Under this, depreciation charges would be calculated in the same way that periodic loan payments are divided into principal and interest, with depreciation taking the place of principal. McFarland, Alternative Methods of Depreciation and the Reliability of Accounting Measures of Economic Profits, 72 Rev.Econs. & Statistics 521 (1990), concludes that this technique would significantly improve the accuracy of accounting rates of return but would have little effect on the ratio or market value to replacement cost.

(2) *The Realization Principle: Delayed Recognition of Economic Changes*

Suppose highly successful 1990 selling efforts produced a 50% increase in the company's unfilled order book which permitted it to operate in 1991 for the first time at full capacity. 1990 accounts show no item for these happenings except perhaps a high selling expense and correspondingly lower income. 1991 income receives the full benefit of the higher volume produced at efficient capacity levels.

What will 1992 be like? If this prediction is derived solely from trending accounting net income, there is a nice earnings gain from 1990 to 1991, which makes 1992 look promising. But the figures are also consistent with the proposition that 1991's "success" was the result of realizations on 1990 activity, and that 1991 was pretty dead on its own account (and in its implications for 1992). Moreover, if an estimate were to have been made in 1990, consider what predictions would have been made for 1991 if the prediction base were simply trends in net income per share:

	Orders Index (1988 = 100)	Income Index (1989 = 100)
1988	100	—
1989	100	100
1990	150	95
1991	125	160

A priori, at least, the income trend does not seem too useful; [c] the order trend appears the better predictor of net income. It is not presently part of an *accountant's duty* to present data on unfilled orders or future contracts (whether or not such information should or may be supplied by the company direct to the public). Indeed a central premise of accounting is that happy prospects for 1992 which become visible in 1991, even if confirmed by executory contract, are not relevant in the measurement of 1991 income.

But even if such backlog figures were deemed to be relevant, the question would still remain whether any or all of the aggregates of financial reporting furnish a timely and accurate reflection of past success. Those aggregates are not set up to enable one to relate change within the company with changes in supply and demand and in macrofactors affecting each of the myriad of buying and selling transactions (classified by product, geography, type of buyer, time, etc.) in which even a single product enterprise must function. Its relation to these markets will significantly affect the firm's future prosperity, and even if the future is hinted at by extrapolation of internal data in some or another relation with the movement of external time series, the internal data relevant to the several markets are not to be found by examining only the financial aggregates. In short, the past success which is to be used as a predicate for future success cannot be measured solely by reference to data internal to the company.

The FASB is proposing a modification of the realization principle. Under this, firms would report gains and losses on unrealized appreciation or depreciation in respect of investment securities. Under a tentatively approved standard, all companies will be required to dis-

---

c. Criticism of the realization principle has pointed not merely to its failure adequately to relate time sequences with increments in value, but to defects in its operation which are independent of that deficiency in its major premise—e.g., failure to insist upon enforceable, qualitative distinctions among items treated as realized (among receivables or installment paper); failure to preclude management from advancing or delaying "sales" (and receipts) on a non-functional basis, solely for the purpose of affecting reported income.

close the estimated current value of financial instruments, whether assets or liabilities; firms would continue to book their debt at face value but would include a footnote to their financials disclosing the "fair value" of their debt securities, which would in some circumstances be the market value.

(b) Alternative Accounting Principles and Problems of Inter-company Comparison

The problem of annualizing costs incurred in one period over periods during which they do, or are expected to, generate returns also is accentuated because large corporations generally use the accrual method in reporting earnings under generally accepted accounting principles. The result is to vest large discretion in management to recognize revenue as services or goods are provided and to expense costs as assets are utilized, rather than when cash is received and paid. There is a range of permissible variations in the timing and selection of items of revenue and expense (in addition to depreciation) which affect the computation of the relevant annual returns. For example, decisions as to when to recognize revenue or how to account for inventory, pensions, fixed assets or mergers can cause variations in annual accounting earnings which distort comparisons of annual earnings of the same firm over time, or of otherwise similar firms for identical periods.

This reserve of management discretion creates difficulties for investors and security analysts who use accounting data to rate one company against another. The decision to buy or sell *A* implies a judgment that *A*'s prospects are better or worse than the prospects of other companies. The operations and premises on which inter-company comparisons are based involve measuring past returns in terms of the relative rate of increase of the company's accounting income as against income trends of similar companies, and translating accounting income into distribution potential.

If Company *A* has used "conservative" accounting and Company *B* in the same industry "radical," the ability to make comparisons would depend upon each company's giving enough information in its reports to show how it would have done under the other's accounting technique. As to some accounting choices, e.g. treatment of extraordinary items (see below), financial statements do give enough information to permit recasting of the net income figure under whatever theory of income measurement; as to other choices, e.g. rate of write-off of assets (see below), often the premises may not be disclosed and more often the data required for recasting are not given.

(1) *Rate of Write–Off of Past Costs*

Suppose that a good part of the dollar difference between the reported income of two Companies, A and B, results from A's using a non-straight line write-off of costs. Thus, at A depreciation is taken on an accelerated, rather than straight-line basis, and costs of developing trademarks, franchises, organization and plant rearrangement costs, and costs of formulas and processes are written off immediately. At B, depreciation is taken on a straight line basis, and the other costs are amortized over periods of years.[d]

Assume that each of A and B has been in operation for five years, each spending $1,000,000 per year for an amortizable item which each conceives to have a five-year useful life. A writes off the expenditure immediately; B amortizes it over the five-year period. Beginning in the 6th year and thereafter, each company will show the same amount for the item. A will show the year's expenditure as an expense, but none from past years; the second company will show ⅕th of the year's expenditure, and also ⅕th from each of the past four years.

The only years in which the two systems will reflect a difference are those in which the expenditure for the item changes; but those are the interesting years. At any point where the cost of the item is going up (from whatever cause) or down, income will reflect the full immediate cost consequence of the change under the full write-off system. However, suppose that each company increases its expenditure for the item 10% per year simply because of a 10% annual inflation which equally affects all its expenses and receipts. The fast write-off company will then show year to year money income increases of 10%; but the income of the other will reflect a larger annual increase, since only ⅕ of the year's increased expenditure will be reflected in the year's income. Two generalizations or truisms can thus be stated for the fast write-off problem, applicable, as we have seen, to depreciation and to other capital asset charges:

1. The faster the write-off of the expenditure, the greater the year to year variation in the series *per share* during years of change;

2. The faster the write-off, the less year to year variation in the series *net income per share* during years in which earnings net of all expenses except for that item are changing in the same direction as the item.

A fast write-off, in other words, damps the effects on income of business cycles and produces less steep income trend lines in years of inflation or other secular movement. In appropriate measure, then, a fast write-off diminishes the distortive effect of the cost principle during inflation.

The difference between lifo and fifo inventory accounting has a similar effect. Lifo shows greater year to year variations in Cost of

d. Under FASB Statement No. 2, Accounting for Research and Development Costs (1974), both A and B would expense research and development costs when incurred.

Goods Sold, but damps cycles and inflationary trends as reflected in net income per share.

(2) *Treatment of Extraordinary Items*

There is an old struggle in the accounting literature between two competing conceptions of income—the "all-inclusive" and the "current operating performance." For discussion of the two conceptions, see Accounting Research Bulletin No. 32, A.I.C.P.A., 1947. The major difference between the two views was whether the special nonrecurring items, such as proceeds derived from the sale of fixed assets should be called "income." But each agreed:

(1) that the special item should be specially disclosed;

(2) that whether it should be called "income" is to be resolved in terms of the interest of the statement user; and

(3) that the statement user will be influenced by whether the special item *is* named "income." e

Under the prevailing rule enunciated in Accounting Principles Board Opinion No. 9 (1966), the income statement ought to contain three items:

Income before extraordinary items

Extraordinary items

Net Income

But dispute continues over the concept "extraordinary." In theory, "extraordinary" items are rare—they are material in amount, unusual in nature and not expected to recur in the foreseeable future. Other "unusual" gains and losses, such as losses incurred due to a strike, are not extraordinary, and are listed as items of revenue or expense. See Meigs & Meigs, Accounting: The Basis for Business Decisions 559–60 (8th ed. 1990).

Now, suppose Corporation *A* treats $1,000,000 realized on the sale of obsolete plant as an "extraordinary" item, while Corporation *B* treats a comparable $1,000,000 as merely "unusual." Does the choice really matter for valuation purposes? Where a difference in income figures is solely attributable to a choice among *descriptive* techniques, and where the choice of description has no substantive (e.g., tax) consequence, is it conceivable that the difference would produce different market values per share? Certainly no investor who jerks to the urgings of the invisible hand would apply the same multiplier to a

---

e. With reference to point 3, accounting literature is full of hypothetical actors who might as well be known as "reasonably unsophisticated statement users." It is hard to imagine who such persons are, but apparently they are conceived to be incapable of paying attention to any figure other than the one called "net income." Or perhaps they get their earnings data from the financial pages of the Beaver Rapids Weekly Intelligencer, a newspaper notoriously casual with accounting footnotes such as "Before special credit of $150,000 from sale of plant."

company's earnings "conservatively" determined as to those more "liberally" stated.

(c) Market Pricing, Empirical Studies, and Legal Policy

The schoolmen have been justly criticized for attempting to answer the question "How many angels can dance on the head of a pin?" through cloistered *a priori* discussion rather than direct observation.[f] Happily, such excesses do not recur in the study of accounting. A large body of studies looks into the question whether stock prices are affected by such events as earnings announcements, changes in accounting practices within a given firm, or changes in Generally Accepted Accounting Principles themselves.

The first generation of these studies, see, e.g., Ball & Brown, An Empirical Evaluation of Accounting Income Numbers, 6 J. Accounting Research 157 (1968), was conducted during the heyday of the efficient market hypothesis. Thus Ball and Brown found that while accounting information was part of the information determining stock prices, they suggested that the market anticipated the bulk of the annual accounting numbers. Other studies suggested accounting decisions might be irrelevant to valuation in some instances. For example, Comiskey, Market Response to Changes in Depreciation Accounting, 46 Accounting Rev. 279 (1971), studied a change of accounting technique from accelerated to straight line depreciation in the steel industry. There resulted an industry wide showing of higher income per share, but *no* perceptible change in stock prices. Such results gave rise to staggering questions. If the market is so penetrating in pricing securities notwithstanding (a) differences between accountants' and economists' measures of "value" and "income", and (b) obscurities generated by the range of permissible choices of accounting techniques, questions arise as to why, and to what extent, management and courts behave as though market penetration does not always occur—i.e., why does management prefer to select one accounting technique rather than another? And why do courts predicate findings of fraud on accounting presentations which are not entirely false and which are consistent with generally accepted accounting principles?

Subsequent empirical studies took the edge off of these questions, however. Results were not conclusive. See Watts and Zimmerman, Positive Accounting Theory (1986). Some studies show that accounting alternatives do affect business decisions, Wyatt, Efficient Market Theory: Its Impact on Accounting, 2 J. Accountancy 56 (1983), and the behavior of market actors. Elliott and Philbrick, Accounting Changes and Earnings Predictability, 65 Accounting Rev. 157 (1990) (concluding that earnings forecasts are more dispersed and less accurate in a year with an accounting change). There is also considerable anecdotage about dramatic short term price movements produced by recasting income figures.

---

f. We owe this observation to Professor Alan Axelrod.

Participants in these discussions express disappointment in the lack of progress made in articulating the relationship between accounting and valuation. Methodological problems are still being identified. Brennan, A Perspective on Accounting and Stock Prices, 66 Accounting Review 67, 73, 77 (1991). A recent survey of the studies does conclude that accounting earnings has indeed made a poor showing on the utility chart—the correlation between stock returns and earnings is weak and unstable. Lev, On the Usefulness of Earnings and Earnings Research: Lessons and Directions from Two Decades of Empirical Research, 27 J. Accounting Research, 1989 Supp. 153, 185–86 (1989). But, according to Lev, a range of explanations can be offered for the result. It could be due to methodological shortcomings in the empirical paradigm employed in the studies, or due to irrationality on the part of investors. And, as Lev stresses, it could also be due to the low information content of earnings figures, due to biases induced by accounting principles in some cases, and by manipulation of reported data by managers in other cases. Id. at 185. (For discussion of problems attending the rules governing accounting for mergers, see pp. A–10–A–36 infra.)

What implications do these mixed results have for disclosure policy? It would seem that in many cases where the use of accounting techniques that differ from those "the market" considers most useful for pricing a security or an enterprise is flagged plainly enough in financial statements, the off-statement information necessary for the market to make the relevant adjustments will be found and applied. But, in other cases, the failure of a financial statement in conformity to GAAP to indicate adequately the extent of its departure from the relevant pricing information can result in advantaging insiders and misleading "the market"—both analysts and public investors. Indeed, that result has been produced on more than one occasion, as is suggested by Gerstle v. Gamble–Skogmo, Inc., 478 F.2d 1281 (2d Cir.1973), and other cases—whether the relevant accounting principles or the permissible choice among them is a matter of individual judgment, of custom of the profession, or even of explicit rule by an institutional authority. Hence, reports going beyond—if not indeed departing from—statements prescribed by accounting principles may be required in order fairly to disclose material facts to persons seeking to make an investment decision. Yet according to the Securities and Exchange Commission (see e.g., A.S.R. No. 4 (1938); A.S.R. No. 150 (12/73)) failure to follow generally accepted accounting principles—i.e., preparing statements for which there is no substantial authoritative support—will result in a presumption of inaccurate or misleading disclosure.

The apparent incongruity results because accounting reports serve many other purposes than that of setting forth statements of earnings and assets in order to guide investors' buy-sell decisions. Regulatory (or, more broadly, "political") and tax considerations may induce (and the regulatory and tax authorities may tolerate) modes of reporting that produce earnings and asset figures designed to minimize the cost to the enterprise and its investors of regulation or taxes, but not necessarily to result in, or reflect, maximum earnings for market valuation purposes. "Flexibility" in the statements permitted by generally accepted accounting principles is necessary in order to effect reports which produce such selective minimization. Accounting data also are designed to assist management in keeping control over business activities and over the operating processes of the enterprise. Their utility for the resulting business decisions does not depend upon their validity in measuring the economic value with which the securities market is concerned. Moreover, management may have more sectarian interests in seeking, and making the choices permitted by, such "flexibility" in reporting earnings and assets, such as debt-asset ratio prescriptions in bond covenants which make straight line depreciation preferable to accelerated depreciation, or executive bonus entitlements dependent upon defined "earnings." See e.g., Holthausen, Evidence on the Effect of Bond Covenants and Management Compensation Contracts on Choice of Accounting Techniques, 3 J. Accounting & Econs. 73 (1981); Holthausen and Leftwich, The Economic Implications of Accounting Choice: Implications of Costly Contracting and Monitoring, 5 J. Accounting and Econs. 77, 108–109 (1983); see also Kamin v. American Express Co., 86 Misc.2d 809, 383 N.Y.S.2d 807 (1976); aff'd on opinion below, 54 A.D.2d 654, 387 N.Y.S.2d 993 (1st Dept.1976). For thoughtful analysis, discussion and survey of studies of the roles of management's accounting choices in varied contexts including monitoring agency costs, see Watts and Zimmerman, Positive Accounting Theory chs. 8–11 (1986).

SECTION 2. ACCOUNTING FOR MERGERS— PURCHASE OR POOLING

Subject to the limitations described at pp. A–25–A–30, infra, accounting for business combinations admits of two alternative procedures when the combination is affected by an exchange of voting stock.

Under the "purchase" method, the assets and liabilities of the acquired company are recorded on the books of the acquiring company at their fair values as of the date of the combination. Any difference between the total value of the consideration paid by the acquiring company and the fair value of the tangible and identifiable intangible assets of the acquired firm is recorded as good will. If good will is recognized to have a limited useful life, then, like any other asset whose value disappears over time, its cost is amortized year-by-year against the income of the combined enterprise.

Under the "pooling" method, the combination is treated not as a purchase but as a joining or "marriage" of two previously separated entities. The amounts (roughly, historical cost) at which assets and liabilities are recorded on the books of the acquired company are carried forward without change in the accounts of the acquiring company. Neither the fair value of the acquired company's assets nor the value of its good will, is recognized. As a consequence, the income of the combined enterprise is not changed by the increased depreciation allowance that would result from a revaluation of tangible assets nor by amortization of an amount attributable to the acquired company's good will.

The following are examples of the "Pooling" and "Purchase" techniques of accounting for mergers. They focus on the activities of merger-minded Bigco, Inc., a description of which follows. Which treatment would APB Opinion No. 16, infra pp. A–25–A–30, require?

(A)

In early 19X1 Bigco, Inc. learned that Litco–1 was interested in a merger with a larger company. Litco–1 was owned by the Smith brothers and had enjoyed spectacular growth within a short period. While the Smiths were optimistic about the future of their company, they wanted to insure their pot of gold by merging with a larger company whose stock was traded on a national securities exchange.

Shortly after Bigco, Inc.'s team of merger makers had descended on the Smith brothers, a preliminary deal was worked out. Thereafter, Bigco, Inc.'s seasoned attorneys put all the paper work in order, and the deal was consummated on September 1, 19X1.

The balance sheets of both Bigco, Inc. and Litco–1 as of August 31, 19X1 are shown in EXHIBIT 1. In early 19X1 Litco–1's plant and equipment had been appraised at $5,500,000 for insurance purposes. The Smith brothers believed this amount was approximately the fair market value of the property at the time of the merger. The book value of Litco–1's other assets approximated its fair market value. Income statements for both Bigco, Inc. and Litco–1 for the first eight months of 19X1 are shown in EXHIBIT 2. Both companies use a calendar fiscal year.

The merger agreement stated that Bigco, Inc. would exchange 400,000 shares of its common stock for all of Litco–1's common stock. On August 31, 19X1 the closing price of Bigco, Inc.'s common stock was $30. There were 4,000,000 shares of Bigco, Inc.'s $5 par value common issued and outstanding as of the date of the merger. A total of 10,000,000 shares were authorized. The Smith brothers and their families held all 500 shares of Litco–1's no par common stock.

A ruling from the Internal Revenue Service had been obtained which stated that the merger constituted a tax free transaction. Bigco, Inc. assumed the tax basis of Litco–1's assets.

A–11

EXHIBIT 1

BALANCE SHEETS OF BIGCO, INC. AND LITCO–1 AS OF CLOSE OF BUSINESS ON AUGUST 31, 19X1

(000 omitted)

	BIGCO, INC.	LITCO–1
ASSETS:		
Current Assets	$ 65,000	$4,000
Plant and Equipment (net)	60,000	3,000
Other	10,000	1,000
TOTAL ASSETS	$135,000	$8,000
LIABILITIES AND STOCKHOLDERS EQUITY		
Current Liabilities	$ 19,000	$1,000
Long-term Liabilities	41,000	2,000
Stockholders' Equity:		
Capital Stock, Par Value $5	20,000	—
Capital Stock, No Par Value	—	1,000
Capital Surplus	15,000	—
Retained Earnings	40,000	4,000
Total Stockholders' Equity	75,000	5,000
TOTAL LIABILITIES AND STOCK– HOLDERS' EQUITY	$135,000	$8,000

EXHIBIT 2

INCOME STATEMENTS FOR BIGCO, INC. AND LITCO–1 EIGHT MONTHS ENDED AUGUST 31, 19X1

(000 omitted)

	BIGCO, INC.	LITCO–1
Net Sales	$200,000	$15,000
Cost of Goods Sold	150,000	8,000
Gross Margin	50,000	7,000
Sales and Administrative Expenses	35,000	4,000
Earnings Before Taxes	15,000	3,000
Taxes	7,500	1,500
Net Earnings	$ 7,500	$ 1,500

400,000 shares
$5 par value
$30 MV

2,000,000 par value
12,000,000 MV

A–12

EXHIBIT 3

COMPARISON OF CONSOLIDATED BALANCE SHEETS OF BIGCO, INC. AT YEAR–END PREPARED UNDER BOTH "PURCHASE" AND "POOLING" TREATMENTS

(000 omitted)

	PURCHASE	POOLING
ASSETS:		
Current Assets	$ 69,000	$ 69,000
Plant and Equipment	65,500(1) *FMV*	63,000
Other	11,000	11,000
Goodwill Arising From Excess Of Cost Over Book Value of Purchased Assets	4,500(2) *goodwill*	
TOTAL ASSETS	$150,000	$143,000
LIABILITIES AND STOCKHOLDERS' EQUITY		
Current Liabilities	$ 20,000	$ 20,000
Long-term Liabilities	43,000	43,000
Stockholders' Equity		
Capital Stock, Par Value $5	22,000(3)	22,000(3)
Capital Surplus	25,000(4)	14,000(5)
Retained Earnings	40,000	44,000(6)
Total Stockholders' Equity	87,000	80,000
TOTAL LIABILITIES AND STOCKHOLDERS' EQUITY	$150,000	$143,000

FOOTNOTES TO EXHIBIT 3

(1) Consists of $60,000,000 + $5,500,000. The estimated fair market value of Litco–1's plant and equipment, $5,500,000, exceeds book value by $2,500,000.

(2) Total consideration = 400,000 shares × $30/share = $12,000,000. This exceeds Litco–1's equity of $5,000,000 by $7,000,000. Of this excess, $2,500,000 is assigned to plant and equipment, leaving $4,500,000 assigned to Goodwill.

(3) Consists of $20,000,000 + $2,000,000 (400,000 shares at $5 Par Value = $2,000,000.)

(4) Consists of $15,000,000 + $10,000,000 (total consideration of $12,000,000 less par value of shares exchanged, $2,000,-000, which was added to Capital Stock account.)

(5) Unlike Purchase treatment, Pooling views the merger as a joining together of ongoing enterprises and therefore dictates that book values be cross-added. However, as happened here, it is often the case that the stated capital of the consolidated corporations will be more (or less) than the total of the stated capitals of the constituent corporations. In such a case ARB # 48 states that "the excess may be deducted first from the total of any other contributed capital (capital surplus), and next from the total of any earned surplus, of the constituent corporations."

Here, the new stated capital for the 4,400,-000 shares outstanding after the merger = $5 Par Value × 4,400,000 shares = $22,-000,000. Since the combined stated capitals of Bigco, Inc. and Litco–1 only equalled $21,000,000, the excess of $1,000,000 was deducted from the total capital surplus ($15,000,000 − $1,000,000 = $14,000,000).

(6) Combination of earned surpluses in the consolidated balance sheet is proper under Pooling.

EXHIBIT 3 shows a comparison of consolidated balance sheets for Bigco, Inc. as of December 31, 19X1, prepared under Pooling and Purchase treatments.

EXHIBIT 4 shows a comparison of consolidated income statements for Bigco, Inc. for the year ending December 31, 19X1 prepared under Purchase and Pooling approaches.

EXHIBIT 5 sets forth a 10 year comparison of the net income and earnings per share figures given in EXHIBIT 4, assuming net sales and costs will remain constant.

EXHIBIT 6 shows ten year comparisons of net income and earnings per share under the assumption that Bigco, Inc. acquires another company, Litco–2, on January 1, 19X2 and still another company, Litco–3, on January 1, 19X3.

EXHIBIT 4

COMPARISON OF CONSOLIDATED INCOME STATEMENTS OF BIGCO, INC. FOR YEAR ENDED 19X1 PREPARED UNDER BOTH "PURCHASE" AND "POOLING" TREATMENTS

(000 omitted)

	PURCHASE	POOLING
Net Sales	$307,500(1)	$322,500(1)
Cost of Goods Sold	229,000	237,000
Gross Margin	78,500	85,500
Selling and Administrative Expenses	54,500	58,500
Earnings Before Additional Amortization and Depreciation	24,000	27,000
Amortization	225(2)	—
Depreciation	250(3)	—
Earnings Before Taxes	23,525	27,000
Taxes	12,000(4)	13,500
Net Earnings	$ 11,525	$13,500

(handwritten annotations: "½ yr. (reduction) longer" and "-50%")

COMPARISON:

There is a $1,975,000 difference in reported net income between the two methods. This represents almost a 17% variation, which is certainly material.

Earnings Per Share (EPS) results would be:

Purchase — EPS = $2.79
Pooling — EPS = $3.07.

This represents a difference of $.28, or about 10%. (The difference is smaller in % terms on an EPS basis because under a Purchase treatment the EPS is determined by dividing the net earnings by the weighted average number of shares outstanding in 19X1. This is done because the results of Litco–1 are only relevant from the date of purchase, and the added shares are considered outstanding only from that date.)

FOOTNOTES TO EXHIBIT 4

(1) Under Purchase treatment, only sales and costs from the date of the acquisition are included. Bigco, Inc.'s eight-month figures are multiplied by $\frac{3}{2}$ to get the year's results. Those for Litco–1 are multiplied by ½ to get the results for the last four months of the year. The resulting figures for Bigco, Inc. and Litco–1 are added together to give the data for the income statement. Under Pooling, sales and costs for the full year are included. Hence eight-month figures of both companies are multiplied by $\frac{3}{2}$ to get the year's results.

(2) The Goodwill arising from the excess of cost over book value is amortized over 10 years. ($\frac{1}{10}$ × $4,500,000 = $450,000/yr.)* As with depreciation, ½ of a year's amortization expense is charged to 19X1. (½ × $450,000 = $225,000.)

(3) The estimated useful remaining life of the plant and equipment is 5 years. Therefore the excess $2,500,000 of fair market value over book value is depreciated over 5 years. ($\frac{1}{5} \times$ $2,500,000 = $500,000.) In accordance with a generally accepted practice $\frac{1}{2}$ of a year's depreciation is recorded for 19X1, the year of purchase, even though only 4 months of use expired by December 31, 19X1. ($\frac{1}{2} \times$ $500,000 = $250,000.)

(4) Based on $24,000,000 of taxable income. Amortization of Goodwill and additional depreciation are not tax deductible. Though treated as a Purchase for accounting purposes, the exchange remains tax-free to the sellers.

* APB Opinion No. 17 requires amortization by charges to earnings over a period not to exceed 40 years.

EXHIBIT 5

10 YEAR COMPARISON OF NET EARNINGS UNDER POOLING AND PURCHASE

Year	PURCHASE Net Earnings	EPS	POOLING Net Earnings	EPS
19X1	$11,525,000	$2.79	$13,500,000	$3.07
19X2	12,550,000	2.84	" "	"
19X3	" "	"	" "	"
19X4	" "	"	" "	"
19X5	" "	"	" "	"
19X6	12,800,000	2.91	" "	"
19X7	13,050,000	2.96	" "	"
19X8	" "	"	" "	"
19X9	" "	"	" "	"
19Y0	" "	"	" "	"

3

EXHIBIT 6

10 YEAR COMPARISON OF NET EARNINGS UNDER POOLING AND PURCHASE AFTER ACQUISITION OF LITCO–2

	PURCHASE		POOLING	
Year	Net Earnings	EPS	Net Earnings	EPS (1)
19X2	$13,850,000	$2.89	$15,750,000	$3.31
19X3	" "	"	" "	"
19X4	" "	"	" "	"
19X5	" "	"	" "	"
19X6	$14,100,000	2.94	" "	"
19X7	$14,850,000	3.10	" "	"
19X8	" "	"	" "	"
19X9	" "	"	" "	"
19Y0	" "	"	" "	"

8 YEAR COMPARISON OF NET EARNINGS UNDER POOLING AND PURCHASE AFTER ACQUISITION OF LITCO–3

Year	Net Earnings	EPS	Net Earnings	EPS (2)
19X3	$15,150,000	$2.90	$18,000,000	$3.53
19X4	" "	"	" "	"
19X5	" "	"	" "	"
19X6	15,400,000	2.96	" "	"
19X7	16,150,000	3.11	" "	"
19X8	16,650,000	3.20	" "	"
19X9	" "	"	" "	"
19Y0	" "	"	" "	"

FOOTNOTES TO EXHIBIT 6

(1) EPS here is based on only 4,765,000 shares. It is assumed that the market price for both Litco–2 and Litco–3 is exactly $12,000,000. Further it is assumed that the stock market will value Bigco, Inc.'s shares at a constant multiple. (Constant multiple = Price of Stock on August 31, 19X1, $30, divided by EPS at that date, $2.80 = 10.7 times). Since EPS at end of 19X1 under Pooling are $3.07, market price per share is assumed to be 10.7 × 3.107 = $32.85. This means that only 365,000 shares are required to be exchanged by Bigco, Inc. to cover the $12,000,000 price tag on Litco–2.

(2) See (1) above. (10.7 × EPS on January 1, 19X3, $3.31 = $35.40). This means that only about 339,000 shares are needed to reach the $12,000,000 price of Litco–3.

(B)

Problems comparable to those illustrated in Example (A) also arise in a "bargain purchase" situation. Such a situation exists when an acquiring corporation pays less than book value for the acquired corporation, as, for example, if Bigco, Inc. had only exchanged 100,000 shares of its common stock for all of Litco–1's common shares. EXHIBIT 7 presents consolidated balance sheets and income statements prepared

under Purchase and Pooling for such an example.   In that exhibit it is
assumed that the transaction took place on January 1, 19X1.

EXHIBIT 7

COMPARISON OF CONSOLIDATED BALANCE SHEETS AND INCOME STATEMENTS UNDER POOLING AND PURCHASE TREATMENT IN "BARGAIN PURCHASE" CASE

Bigco, Inc. Balance Sheet—December 31, 19X1

(000 omitted)

	PURCHASE	POOLING
ASSETS:		
Current Assets	$ 69,000	$ 69,000
Plant and Equipment	63,000(1)	63,000
Other	11,000	11,000
TOTAL ASSETS	$143,000	$143,000
LIABILITIES AND STOCKHOLDERS' EQUITY		
Current Liabilities	$ 20,000	$ 20,000
Long-term Liabilities	43,000	43,000
Excess of Book Value of Assets Purchased Over Cost	2,000	—
Stockholders' Equity		
Capital Stock	20,500(2)	20,500(4)
Capital Surplus	17,500(3)	15,500(5)
Retained Earnings	40,000	44,000
TOTAL LIABILITIES AND STOCK-HOLDERS' EQUITY	$143,000	$143,000

Bigco, Inc. Income Statement—Year Ended Dec. 31, 19X1

(000 omitted)

	PURCHASE	POOLING
Net Sales	$322,500	$322,500
Cost of Goods Sold	237,000	237,000
Gross Margin	85,500	85,500
Sales and Administrative	58,500	58,500
Earnings Before Tax and Amortization of Credit Excess	27,000	27,000
Amortization	200(6)	—
Earnings before Taxes	27,200	27,000
Taxes	13,500	13,500
Net Earnings	$ 13,700	$ 13,500

COMPARISON:
Purchase − EPS = $3.12
Pooling − EPS = $3.07

FOOTNOTES TO EXHIBIT 7

(1) Consists of $60,000,000 + $3,000,000. Fair market value of plant and equipment is assumed to equal book value here, not $5,500,000 as in EXHIBIT 1.

(2) Consists of $20,000,000 + $500,000. (100,000 shares × $5 Par Value = $500,000.)

(3) Consists of $15,000,000 + $2,500,000. (100,000 shs. × $30 market value =

$3,000,000 total consideration. $3,000,-000 less the $500,000 addition to stated capital = $2,500,000.)

(4) Consists of $20,000,000 + $500,000. (4,100,000 shs. outstanding × $5 Par Value = $20,500,000.)

(5) Consists of $15,000,000 + $500,000. ARB # 48 states that "when the stated capital of the surviving corporation is less than the combined stated capitals of the constituent corporations, the difference should appear in the balance sheet of the surviving corporation as other contributed capital (capital sur-plus), analogous to that created by a reduction in stated capital where no combination is involved." Therefore since the stated capital of Bigco, Inc. ($20,500,000) is less than the sum of the stated capitals before the merger ($20,-000,000 and $1,000,000), the difference ($500,000) appears as capital surplus.

(6) The Excess of Book Value of Assets Purchased Over Cost ($5,000,000 − $3,000,000, the consideration given) is amortized over 10 years. ($\frac{1}{10}$ × $2,000,000 = $200,000.) Again, the tax law takes no account of this item.

HACKNEY, ACCOUNTING FOR MERGERS AND ACQUISITIONS UNDER THE NEW JERSEY BUSINESS CORPORATION ACT

23 Rutgers Law Review 689, 702–713 (1969).

The essence of the accounting treatment of a "pooling" is that "[w]hen a combination is deemed to be a pooling of interest, *a new basis of accountability does not arise.*" This provision contradicted the more fundamental principle that all acquired assets must be carried at cost and thus created a salient exception to cost theory.   * * *   This approach is based on the theory that the stockholders of each constituent obtain relatively smaller interests in the larger combined entity. In the resultant "marriage," neither constituent has "acquired" the other, so that there has been no "cost" to either and, therefore, no new basis of accountability has arisen, meaning that no new "values" need be brought into the accounts.

　　　* * *

In an earlier analysis of accounting principles for valuation of assets, it was indicated that the method of valuation to be followed could be thought of as ultimately dependent upon the objective sought in the determination of income, whether income be conceived of: (1) as increase in wealth, or worth-value, remaining *after provision for maintenance of economic capital,* or (2) as money revenue remaining *after recovery of original costs.* Expressed another way, the difference in viewpoint regarding asset valuation arises from different conceptions of the nature of capital: If the capital of a business is conceived of as its tools of production—the capital assets themselves—then the value thereof must be recovered in order to maintain capital and before income can be reported. But, if capital is deemed to be the number of dollars expended in acquiring the tools of production, then only the same number of dollars as were expended needs to be recovered from revenue and all surplus over this amount is income.

The asset-capital approach implies that there can be no real income without prior provision for maintenance of economic capital, e.g., plant, equipment, and working capital. Under this approach, exhaustion charges would be based upon current values. The money-capital approach, on the other hand, assumes that net income over a period of years is the excess of money taken in over the amount paid out, and that periodic net income is the excess of revenue for the period in question over the allocable portion of prior, current and expected future expenditures attributable to such period. From this concept it follows that periodic revenues should be charged with allocable portions of original costs only. If the asset-capital approach is adopted, then assets on the balance sheet would consist of "worth-values" of all assets or property rights, in order for the balance sheet to be a vehicle for charging current revenues with exhaustion charges on a current value basis. Under the money-capital approach, assets would simply be unexpired costs, i.e., those portions of prior outlays not previously charged against prior revenues.

It is submitted that accounting principles today are founded upon the money-capital concept of income.

* * *

"Cost" Where Assets Are Acquired in a Purchase for Equity Securities

There was the fellow who boasted he had just sold his dog for $50,000. "In cash?" asked his friend. "Of course not," he replied. "The guy gave me two $25,000 cats."

In an acquisition for cash, the historical "cost" seems clear: One asset is removed from the balance sheet, and another takes its place; the cost of the second is the amount deducted when the first was removed. In an acquisition for stock that is accounted for as a "purchase" however, the "cost" is not as readily determined. The longstanding accounting rule is that where assets are acquired for stock, the assets should be recorded at the *fair value of the consideration given,* or at the *fair value of the property acquired, whichever is more clearly evident.* The self-contradiction involved in the rule is evident when tested in the light of the two varying objectives of income accounting previously described. "Fair value of the consideration given" exemplifies accountability based on cost, while "fair value of the property acquired" implies a disregard of cost or what was foregone, placing emphasis upon exhaustion charges based on fair value.

In practice, however, the accounting principle is invariably interpreted today, at least for securities listed or traded, to mean that assets acquired (including goodwill) are to be valued, in the aggregate, at the *total market value* of all the securities issued in exchange. This total market value approach is apparently based on the assumption that the equity securities issued could have been sold for cash at their current market value, this being "more clearly evident" than the fair value of the assets acquired. * * *

* * * [I]t is questionable whether stock is just a substitute for cash, so that the market value of the stock issued should be deemed equivalent to a cash "cost" of the acquired assets. Kripke argues persuasively that a few sales cannot be any assurance that a large block could be marketed successfully at anything like the same price, and extraneous factors may make a public issue or a cash purchase impractical in any event.

* * * [I]t is doubtful whether the market value of the stock issued should be considered the measure of the "accountability" of the management issuing such stock, with the concomitant requirement that the net assets (including goodwill) be recorded at such aggregate market value. If the assets being acquired are inflated in value through optimistic expectations and an inflationary psychology, it should be equally recognized that the stock being issued is "a medium of exchange inflated by the same factors which inflate the value of the acquired company." It seems somewhat inconsistent to make an exchange transaction a reason to hold management accountable for the inflated values of the acquired business while ignoring the values of the acquiring business which gave rise to the inflated currency used as the measure of the other's value.

* * * [I]n revaluing the acquired assets on the basis of the inflated currency being used, as required by purchase accounting, one must recognize that the net earnings of the acquired company are the prime indicator of its over-all value to the potential purchaser, and that injecting new values which require greater exhaustion charges will remove much of the income and hence the value. Kripke touched the heart of the matter when he stated: "In modern corporate affairs an acquisition is negotiated in terms of acquiring earnings, and *the result of purchase accounting is to destroy what is being acquired.*"

* * * [P]roblems relating to goodwill present major difficulty. Much of the trouble is in definition. When assets are purchased for cash at a purchase price clearly in excess of their fair value, such excess is an intangible asset, a garden-variety type of goodwill, and should, of course, be booked and amortized against income. The notion that a value ascribed to a company's outstanding securities by an investor can give rise to an asset on the company's books is a far different matter. Yet, that is precisely the definition of goodwill proposed in *Accounting Research Study No. 10.* When so defined, the conclusion that self-developed goodwill should not be booked and that purchased goodwill should be immediately written off against an equity account seems justifiable only as an expression of belief that such a concept of goodwill should not have been booked in the first place.

Finally, if, in a purchase, the market value of the securities issued to acquire certain assets is deemed the amount for which management should be accountable and therefore should be recorded as the "cost" thereof, the principle may prove too much. It would appear that logic would require a number of changes in accounting theory to follow: (1) Any time a company issues any stock (whether or not in a purchase transaction), the entire value of all the net assets of the company should be recomputed as equivalent to the aggregate market value of all the outstanding stock. The value should be extrapolated from the same price as the shares so sold, and the new values should be substituted in the books for the old; (2) the same result should follow any time a company purchases a block of treasury stock; (3) assuming a fair transaction between two independent parties, the same result should follow upon any sale of a block of shares of outstanding stock from one person to another; (4) the assets should be revalued every day, based upon market value of the outstanding shares traded that day.

* * *

Asset Valuation in a Pooling

In a pooling, asset values on the books of both companies are carried forward intact, and no new costs are entered. Although the problems of overvaluation and goodwill arising from accounting on the basis of market values of securities are eliminated, a number of new problems, difficult and disturbing both to the accountant and to the lawyer, nevertheless arise:

Although the central question in accounting is the choice between "cost" and "value," the carry-forward of historic prior costs from the books of a predecessor company seems to offer a third choice, far removed from the notion of "cost" to the surviving entity and even further removed from current value. As stated by a committee of the American Accounting Association, pooling accounting "is perhaps the classic case of quantifiability and verifiability warring with relevance."

Carry-forward of prior book values means that future revenues will not be burdened with charges based in any way upon the number of shares issued in the acquisition. In other words, additional "cost," i.e., additional shares issued, would in no way affect future reported net income. If two purchasers paid different amounts for the same assets and, all other things being equal, thereafter reported the same profits, accounting does not seem to be performing its function of reporting results on a basis which will enable investors to evaluate the performance of management.

Earnings per share after a business combination, if management is in any sense to be accountable for the transaction, should be burdened with two diluent effects based upon the number of shares issued: (1) the more shares, the greater the "cost," the more the exhaustion charges, and the lower the income, and (2) the more shares, the less net income per share. Pooling eliminates the first diluent effect; and frequently, in the past, the second has been avoided by the use of a convertible preferred stock with an aggregate annual dividend preference less than the acquired company's expected annual earnings, in which event (no matter how many shares were issued) the result had to be an increase in earnings per share on common stock. If the bidding must be increased above the magic number of shares, the conversion rate could be increased, or warrants to purchase common stock could be attached, to increase the value of the consideration paid, without affecting earnings per share. The "chain-letter effect" of increasing earnings per share, by acquisition of companies with shares selling at a lower price-earnings ratio than the acquiring company, has been decisively commented upon.

The purpose of requiring full value to be received for stock is to avoid watering the stock, but the effect of allowing assets to be entered on the books at less than full value is, through depreciation and amortization based upon such lowered values, to allow the stock to become "watered" over the life of the assets. Both existing shareholders and purchasers of the newly issued stock may have grounds for complaint. Existing shareholders have a right to expect that additional shares will not be sold to others for less than their current fair value, in order to prevent a dilution of the current holder's economic interest. They would seem to have an equal right to demand that exhaustion charges used in the determination of future income be sufficient (a) to maintain the cushion represented as originally obtained, and (b) to prevent a return of capital from being reported as income available for distribution as dividends. Likewise, new shareholders, particularly if they are preferred shareholders with an assets preference, may have a right to expect that the actual value of their contribution will be maintained before income is reported and dividends are paid therefrom.

To enter the acquired assets at prior book values, lower than current costs, seems similar to writing off a "cost," at moment of acquisition, to paid-in surplus, thus avoiding one of the oldest and most fundamental of all accounting rules—that capital surplus "should not be used to relieve the income account of the current or future years of charges which would otherwise fail to be made there-against."

If exhaustion charges are based on book values less than the value of the paid-in capital, not only will future reported net income be, in effect, a return of capital, but also, in a pooling, acquired earned surplus may be carried forward so that the acquired assets themselves might be paid out to the shareholders of the acquiring company the very next day as though they were out of retained earnings.

* * *

Pooling accounting was originally conceived as appropriate in a situation where neither company was "acquiring" the other but where the two were "marrying" and there was a pervasive continuity of management, business and shareholders. Because of pressures favoring pooling as against purchase accounting, however, the criteria distinguishing a pooling from a purchase have evaporated to the point where, today, virtually any acquisition in exchange for equity securities may be accounted for as a pooling. The criteria have deteriorated to the point where an essentially cash purchase—either of treasury stock, later used for the acquisition, or of the acquired company's stock, followed by a downstream merger—can be accounted for as a pooling.

Pressures for Pooling

The pressures against accounting for business combinations as purchases, and in favor of pooling accounting wherever possible, are enormous and all-pervasive. For example, where equity securities are issued in the acquisition, it is likely to be tax free. Without a capital gains tax to pay, the shareholders of the selling corporation are much more amenable to a stock than a cash transaction, and presumably would be willing to take securities having a market value less than the amount of cash they would require. Additionally, the acquiring company, if able to carry forward prior book values (which are today ordinarily far less than "cost"), tends to be willing to issue shares having a greater market value than the equivalent amount of cash it would be willing to pay, since cash would result in a write-up of the assets (plus goodwill) to the cash price and a consequent lowering of future earnings. Stock, in other words, through the vagaries of the tax law relating to tax-free reorganizations, and the accounting principles applicable to a pooling, is a medium of exchange worth a great deal more to both buyer and seller than its equivalent cash value.

Moreover, accounting for the transaction as a "purchase" in a tax-free reorganization ordinarily requires booking goodwill and other asset values which cannot be deducted or amortized for tax purposes. Management ordinarily seeks to avoid goodwill, because: (a) it is not fashionable as an asset on the balance sheet, and accounting principles will sooner or later require it to be written off or, more likely, amortized against income; (b) it is paradoxical to carry goodwill without amortization when earnings are good and then be forced to amortize it against income at the very moment such income declines; and (c) when being amortized it reduces net income substantially while it produces no related tax benefit to partially offset its expense character. The consequences of "purchase" accounting are simply deemed unacceptable by the business community and pooling principles have been extended to fill the gap.

Furthermore, the differences in valuation of assets between a "purchase" and a "pooling" are often enormous; in some cases they are far greater than the amount of the acquisition itself, if accounted for as a pooling. The avoidance of enormous asset write-ups, none of which provide a tax benefit, makes it literally true that mergers or acquisitions which would result in future *losses,* if accounted for as a purchase, will result in *increased earnings,* if accounted for as a pooling. The simple fact is that a business combination which might be very attractive as a pooling might have to be abandoned if it had to be accounted for as a purchase.

* * *

Lack of Consensus Among Accountants

The state of confusion in the accounting profession over the matter of accounting for business combinations is readily apparent.   * * *

* * *

[I]t appears that the horns of the accounting dilemma are alternative methods of accounting for business combinations, neither of which is generally acceptable either to accountants or to businessmen: (1) Purchase accounting results in excess valuation of assets and consequent goodwill (attributable to the "inflated currency" used as the measure of value), and consequent destruction of the earnings upon which the valuation of the acquired company was based. (2) Pooling accounting requires the use of historic book values which overstate future income and fail to make management accountable for the actual consideration paid (or values of assets acquired). The pooling concept, applied narrowly at first, has gained widespread acceptance and, indeed, preference. Although the criteria for its applicability have deteriorated and the reasons for its use have become distorted, nevertheless, the pressures for its increasing use have become irresistible, and the number of business combinations has so increased that a point of crisis has now been reached.*

NOTE: APB OPINIONS NO. 16 AND NO. 17

In Accounting Research Bulletin No. 48 (1957), the American Institute of Certified Public Accountants (AICPA) adopted criteria for identifying when a corporate combination should be treated as a pooling-of-interests and when as a purchase. As Hackney indicates, however, those criteria were totally ineffectual to separate the circumstances requiring pooling from those requiring purchase treatment. As a result, only in rare instances were enterprises engaged in amalgamations precluded from selecting freely either purchase or pooling accounting.

This virtually unrestrained option caused considerable distress in accounting circles and elsewhere. As a consequence, after much debate, the AICPA in 1970 adopted APB Opinions No. 16 and No. 17 which are described in the following excerpt.

---

* [Ed. Note] As Exhibit 7, supra pp. A–18–A–19 discloses, the preferability of "pooling" to "purchase" accounting is reversed in the case of a "bargain purchase"—i.e. when the purchase price is less than the carrying value of assets.

OLSON, ACCOUNTING FOR MERGERS
3 Rev.Sec.Reg. 867–871 (1970).

The Accounting Principles Board (APB) of the AICPA, its members deeply divided in their views, has finally issued its new rules for accounting for business combinations and goodwill. Spelled out in APB Opinions No. 16, Business Combinations and No. 17, Intangible Assets, the rules establish multiple criteria designed to restrict the availability of pooling of interests accounting. In addition, Opinion No. 17 mandates that when mergers are accounted for as purchases, goodwill must be amortized by charges to earnings. The new rules, which are not retroactive, will apply to business combinations initiated after October 31, 1970.

* * *

POOLING CRITERIA

Pooling of interest accounting views certain business combinations not as purchases of one company by another but as transactions occurring outside the corporate entity being accounted for—a mere pooling or sharing of risks among shareholders. Opinion No. 16 limits pooling of interests accounting to those combinations effected by issuance of voting common stock. In addition, it lays down an intricate set of rules aimed at prohibiting gimmicks or merger terms which would tend to negate the fragile, "sharing-of-risks" concept upon which pooling accounting is based.

Use of 90% voting common stock. To qualify for pooling accounting a business combination must be effected by the issuance of voting common stock in exchange for at least 90% of the voting common stock interests of another company or for all of its net assets. Having acquired 90% of the voting common stock, the entire transaction would be treated as a pooling. The remaining 10% may continue outstanding as a minority interest or be acquired for cash or other consideration. No pro rata distribution of cash or other consideration to the holders of the 90% may be made. * * *

A number of specific criteria attempt to ensure the essential stock-for-stock nature of the transaction. They are as follows:

1. The combining companies may not change the equity interests of the voting common stock (by distributions to stockholders, exchanges or retirements) in contemplation of a combination within the two years preceding initiation of the plan of combination, or after initiation of the plan.

2. Each combining company may acquire its own voting common stock only for purposes other than business combinations. No more than the normal number of shares may be acquired after the date the plan of combination is initiated.

3. The relative interests of individual common stockholders in each of the constituents to the combination must not be realigned by the exchange of securities effecting the combination.

4. The stockholders in the continuing enterprise must not be deprived of, nor restricted in exercising, their voting rights for any period. The voting rights to which common stock ownership interests in the combined corporation are entitled must be exercisable only by the stockholders. Thus, common stock received in a pooling may not be transferred to a voting trust.

5. The combined corporation must not agree, directly or indirectly, to retire or reacquire all or a part of the common stock issued to effect the merger. The merger plan cannot contain any financial arrangements for the benefit of former stockholders of a combining company—such as guaranteeing of loans secured by the stock issued.

Qualifying transactions. To qualify for pooling, each of the combining companies must be autonomous, and must not have been a subsidiary or division of any other corporation within two years before the plan of combination is initiated. A wholly owned subsidiary which effects a combination by issuance of its parent company's shares may use pooling accounting provided the other criteria are met.

The combination must be effected in a single transaction or be completed according to a specific plan within one year, unless delayed by the proceedings of a governmental authority or by litigation. This condition, together with the requirement that the combining companies must be independent of each other, will make it difficult to obtain the advantages of poolings in business combinations resulting from take-overs. "Independent" for this purpose means that at the outset, a combining company must not hold an investment of more than 10% of the outstanding voting common stock of another combining company. An unsuccessful take-over where a company winds up holding 11% of another company's stock would appear to preclude subsequent pooling of those companies unless an additional 79% of stock could later be acquired on the same terms as part of the same plan within the year.

Prohibition of contingent payments. The merger plan may not provide for any future issue of additional shares or payment of other consideration on the basis of some contingency. The popular "earn-out" provisions, under which the terms of the combination are tied to earnings performance for a given number of years, would disqualify a transaction as a pooling. By the same token, selling stockholders cannot be given protection by provisions for the issuance of additional shares in the event of a subsequent decline in the market price of the issuing company's stock.

The no-contingency criteria may prove to be a substantial obstacle to pooling accounting. Contingency provisions in merger plans help eliminate some of the immediate risks of combination to both buyers and sellers. In the case of acquisitions of small stockholder-managed companies, earn-out provisions have provided an effective means of assuring the continuation of competent management in the selling company. Presumably, the theory of the no-contingency criteria is that the "sharing-of-risks" would be negated during the period of contingency. But it borders on the absurd to permit contingency arrangements to decide the whole basis for the valuation of assets and the determination of earnings in a business combination.

Disposition of assets. If pooling accounting is to apply, there must be no intent or plan for the surviving company to dispose of a significant part of the assets of the combining companies within two years after the combination, except to sell (a) duplicate facilities, (b) excess capacity, and (c) assets that would have been disposed of in the ordinary course of business of the separate company. Further, where any such disposition takes place, the gain must be clearly segregated and labeled in the income statement as an extraordinary item. These provisions are meant to minimize the impact of "instant earnings" from the sale of valuable assets at substantial amounts in excess of their book values immediately after a pooling takes place. * * *

POOLING ACCOUNTING

If a combination meets the new qualifying conditions for pooling of interests accounting, the procedures to be followed, with a few exceptions, are substantially those which have existed for some time.

While a company can combine with another company on a pooling basis late in the year and include in its earnings the income of the absorbed company for the complete year, Opinion No. 16 prohibits the practice of padding earnings by retroactively combining the financial statements of companies pooled after the end of a fiscal year but before financial statements are issued. Whether this prohibition will eliminate an abuse or create more confusion is debatable. The effect on financial statements of post year-end poolings must be disclosed and the statements of such pooled companies must be restated and combined in all subsequent interim and annual reports issued by the combined company.

* * *

PURCHASE ACCOUNTING

Business combinations that do not meet the new pooling criteria must be accounted for as purchases. Under the purchase accounting procedures, the tangible assets, identifiable intangible assets, and liabilities of the acquired company are to be recorded on the books of the acquiring company at their fair values at the date of the combination. The excess of the consideration given above the net amount of these fair values is considered goodwill and must be amortized against net earnings over a period not to exceed forty years. While the quoted market price of an equity security issued to effect a business combination may usually be used to approximate the fair value of the consideration given, Opinion No. 16 warns against blind acceptance of a market price where there is a thin market or prices are extremely volatile.

Earnings of the acquired company are to be reported only from the date of acquisition in the financial statements of the combined company. However, the Opinion requires the presentation of supplemental pro forma information as to the combined earnings of the companies for the year in which the merger occurs and for the immediately preceding year, where comparative statements are presented.   * * *

The general requirement for amortization of *all* intangibles in purchase accounting will reduce future reported earnings. The cost of acquiring "unlimited-life" rights such as sport franchises, broadcasting licenses, and highway-trucking routes must be amortized against the earnings they produce, even when the values of these properties may be rising.

But goodwill remains the most difficult problem in business combinations. Where purchase accounting is required by the new rules, the difference between the fair values assigned to the net separable resources and identifiable intangibles and the consideration given (merely a stock market speculative value) must be recorded as an asset and amortized by charges to earnings over a period not to exceed 40 years. The new rules are likely to produce strenuous efforts to structure merger plans to meet the pooling criteria and to devise ingenious schemes to avoid the rigid and arguably improper requirements for accounting for goodwill. That disputes over goodwill are likely to continue unabated is evidenced by the dissents to Opinion No. 17.

In addition, difficult encounters are foreseeable between the accounting profession and certain regulatory agencies, notably those with jurisdiction over financial reporting by banks, whose regulations prohibit the recording of goodwill in the balance sheet.

DISCLOSURE

The opinions require extensive disclosure of financial effects and other data related to business combinations. The nature of the rules, together with the mixture of old and new procedures, including the special rules applicable to the five-year transitional period, will render such disclosures very difficult for even the most sophisticated investor to interpret. The desirability of a fair presentation of financial position and earnings without the need for resort to complex footnotes cannot be overemphasized. Complex footnote disclosures may only magnify the "information gap" between the sophisticated and the unsophisticated reader, and reinforce the disadvantage of those investors most in need of protection.

For comments on APB 16 see Accounting Principles for Pooling of Interests: A Panel Discussion, 25 Tax Law Rev. 29 (1971); Scruggins,

Business Combinations, 27 Bus.Law 1245 (1972).[g] The issues addressed by APB Opinions No. 16 and 17 have not been resolved by the opinions, and as a result the FASB has continued the debate with a Discussion Memorandum dated Aug. 19, 1976 on which hearings have been held but no conclusions reached. For an explanation of the differences between purchase and pooling accounting and the criteria for invoking pooling when one corporation combines with another and acquires some or all of the assets and liabilities of the other see Fiflis, Accounting for Mergers, Acquisitions and Investments, in a Nutshell: The Interrelationships of, and Criteria for, Purchase or Pooling, The Equity Method, and Parent–Company–Only and Consolidated Statements, 37 Bus.Law. 89 (1981). As the title indicates, Fiflis also explains the accounting treatment possibilities when both corporations continue as legal entities and one controls the other, and when one does not acquire enough stock to control the other—the equity method and the cost method.

The accepted, if not welcome, status of the norms established by APB 16 is reflected in the responses of practitioners and academics to a questionnaire on the subject, reported in Hermanson and Hughes, Pooling v. Purchase and Goodwill: A Longstanding Controversy Abates 15 Mergers and Acquisitions 15 (Fall 1980). The controversy never seems to die down completely. Recently, a Securities and Exchange Commissioner made a bid to reopen the debate, complaining that APB 16 has not effectively controlled the practice of disguising purchase transactions as poolings, and suggesting that the FASB reconsider its policies. See 23 BNA Sec.Reg. & L.Rep. 1659 (11/15/91).

To what extent does the purchase-pooling dilemma derive from anomalies in the requirements of cost accounting, quite apart from any issue of choice between pooling and purchase?

NOTE: THE LEGAL FRAMEWORK

Whatever may be the requirements of the AICPA with respect to the circumstances under which pooling-of-interest is required or permitted, do the local corporation laws prescribe the same (or any) conditions for pooling accounting? Consider pre–1980 MBCA §§ 2(*l*) and 21, and NYBCL § 517(a)(1)(B) which deal with earned surplus (or deficit) carryovers, and pre–1980 MBCA §§ 18, 19; NYBCL § 504; Del.Corp.Law §§ 152, 153 which deal with valuation of the acquired assets. The revised MBCA is even less constraining. See Appendix F, infra.

---

g. For flexible interpretations of the tests in APB Opinion No. 16 to distinguish purchase from pooling transactions (i.e. techniques for effecting one method or the other at the cost (or loss) of an expendable attribute of the transaction), see pamphlet published by AICPA, Accounting Standards—Original Pronouncements. The SEC has interpreted APB No. 16 somewhat more restrictively, to limit the opportunity to resort to pooling accounting (by requiring stock issued in a merger to be held for a minimum period and presuming stock repurchased by a merger partner within two years prior to the merger to have been acquired in contemplation of merger). See ASR No. 135 (1/5/73) CCH Fed.Sec.L.Rep. ¶ 72,152; ASR No. 146A (4/11/74) CCH Fed.Sec.L.Rep. ¶ 72,168A; see also CCH Fed.Sec.Law Reg. ¶ 39,028 (Nov. 5, 1986).

Would pooling-of-interest accounting in circumstances which are subsequently determined to have failed to meet the conditions for pooling-of-interest accounting prescribed in APB Opinion No. 16 be deemed, for that failure alone, to be misleading in violation of the federal securities acts? Even if pooling is permitted by generally accepted accounting principles, can the SEC, by rule, proclaim it to be misleading generally, or must its misleading character be determined on a case by case basis? See Note, 23 Stanford L.Rev. 330 (1971).

SECURITIES ACT RELEASE NO. 4910

Securities and Exchange Commission, June 18, 1968.

The Securities and Exchange Commission today called attention to two positions taken recently in matters of interest to issuers and others who file, or participate in the filing of, registration statements, proxy material and reports with the Commission. * * *

Issuers and underwriters generally request acceleration of the effective date of a registration statement to a specified date as soon as practicable after the filing of an appropriate correcting or completing amendment.[1] The acceleration procedure enables issuers and underwriters to set the terms of the offering on the anticipated effective date in view of conditions then existing in the securities market and the granting of acceleration by the Commission on that date permits the sale in that same market of the securities subject to registration.

It has been the long standing policy of the Commission to cooperate with registrants requesting acceleration, giving due consideration to the standards set forth in Section 8(a). However, each acceleration request is considered on the basis of the facts and circumstances relevant to it and in certain situations the Commission may deny acceleration. * * * There are set out below the circumstances relating to a recent case in which the Commission indicated it would not consider favorably a request for acceleration.

a. Comparison of "Pooled" and "Unpooled" Figures

A company with a registration statement on file at the Commission issued its Annual Report to Shareholders for fiscal year 1967. Page 1 of that report included a comparative summary purporting to indicate the amounts of sales, net income, and earnings per share for the years 1966 and 1967, together with figures showing substantial "percentage

---

1. Section 8(a) of the Securities Act of 1933, as amended, provides that a registration statement shall become effective on the twentieth day after it is filed (or on the twentieth day after the filing of any amendment thereto) or such earlier date as the Commission may determine "having due regard to the adequacy of the informa- tion respecting the issuer theretofore avail- able to the public, to the facility with which the nature of the securities to be registered, their relationship to the capital structure of the issuer and the rights of holders thereof can be understood, and to the public interest and the protection of investors."

increases" in 1967 based on the amounts shown.   References to these
percentage increases were also made elsewhere in the report to shareholders.

Paid advertisements in magazines and newspapers also showed
similar percentage increases in sales and net income of the company for
the year 1967 when compared to 1966.

The figures used in the table (and in the advertisements) as a basis
for determining the percentage increases were taken from the company's 1967 consolidated income statement which included the accounts of
a significant company acquired in that year in a "pooling of interests"
transaction and from the Company's 1966 consolidated income statement "as previously reported" without giving effect to retroactive
inclusion of the related amounts of the acquired company.

The substantial percentage increases in sales, net income and
earnings per share obtained by such comparisons are misleading as a
measure of the growth of the company in 1967.   If the comparisons had
been made with 1966 figures restated to include the accounts of the
acquired company, there would have been reported for 1967 percentage
declines in net income and earnings per share and only a nominal
percentage increase in sales.

In the opinion of the Commission, it is misleading to make comparisons such as were made in this instance or to invite or draw conclusions
as to improvement in a company's operations by comparing pooled
figures for a particular year with unpooled figures for the prior year.
Comparisons in such case should be made with financial data for the
prior period restated on a combined (pooled) basis.

b.   *Earnings Per Share Determination*

The company had outstanding a class of convertible preferred
shares, all held by the company's parent.   These shares of stock were
convertible into a substantially larger number of shares of common
stock.   This preferred stock is a "residual security" since it derived the
major portion of its value from its conversion rights.

In the present case, the earnings per share figures for 1966 and
1967 in the table on page 1 of the annual report to shareholders for
fiscal year 1967 were presented both on the basis of average common
shares outstanding, including residual securities, i.e., including common
shares issuable upon conversion of the preferred stock (as in the
registration statement and in the financial statement section of the
shareholders' report), and also on the basis of average common shares
"actually outstanding," without giving effect to inclusion of residual
securities.   The latter determination resulted in higher per share
figures and it was only these higher figures which were commented on
later in the annual report to shareholders.

In the opinion of the Commission, companies having only common
stock and other residual securities outstanding should present earnings

per share figures solely on the basis of equivalent outstanding common shares, including residual securities. In such circumstances the presentation of a second earnings per share figure based on outstanding common shares, excluding residual securities, is misleading. Where there are also outstanding options, warrants or convertible senior securities which may result in material dilution of earnings per share in the future, earnings per share figures should be presented on the basis of outstanding common shares including residual securities, and on a supplementary basis assuming exercise of the options or warrants and conversion of the senior securities.

* * *

———

NOTE: ACCOUNTING FOR LEVERAGED BUYOUTS

How should the assets of the target firm in a leveraged buyout be accounted for upon the merger of the target and the shell corporation that acquires it? In theory, either the target's assets could be booked at fair value, the book values of the target firm's assets could carry over, or some weighted average of the two values could be employed. The choice of fair value leaves the post buyout firm with a larger asset base. This carries the tax benefit of larger depreciation deductions, the cosmetic benefit of a higher shareholders' equity figure and a lower debt-asset ratio, and perhaps the legal benefit of diminished risk of fraudulent conveyance scrutiny in the event of subsequent financial distress. The choice of continuing the target's book values carries the cosmetic benefit of higher annual earnings results (due to lower depreciation figures) accompanied by the cosmetic detriment of a minimal or negative shareholders' equity figure (since the acquisition indebtedness is booked against the lower historical asset figures).

Under FASB Emerging Issues Task Force, Basis in Leveraged Buyout Transactions, Issue No. 88–16 (1989), the post LBO firm may have to adopt a mixed basis of historical and fair values. If the acquiring corporation has no significant business operations and there is overlapping ownership between the shareholders of the acquisition shell and the group of target shareholders, 100 percent purchase accounting may not be employed and a complex "part purchase" formula applies. The higher the percentage of shareholders taken out, the heavier the weight of fair value in the calculation. Debate about this approach continues. See Ginsburg and Levin, Mergers, Acquisitions and Leveraged Buyouts, ¶ 1503 (1991); Gorman, How Accounting Rules Shook Up LBO Deal Making, Mergers & Acquisitions July–August 1990, p. 45; Gorman, LBO Frontiers in the 1990s: Can Accounting Keep Pace? 169 J. Accountancy, June 1990, p. 100.

NOTE: HOW MUCH DOES IT MATTER

The debate over pooling versus purchase assumes that investors really *will* value the shares of a given company differently if it uses one method rather than the other to account for a merger, even though the choice of an accounting method may have no effect on the firm's economic status as such or on its real worth. Although seemingly no great effort is required for a skilled analyst to convert pooled earnings per share into purchased earnings per share, the reformers and counter-reformers whose views are set out above must have thought that such a conversion operation was beyond the capability of investors and their advisers and that the market really was taken in by the inflated representations of earnings and growth that arose from the use of pooling.[i] In a sense, of course, accountants *must* believe this in order to feel that accounting information is important to investors in the first place. If investors were unaffected by the choice between pooling and purchase and would pay the same price for the firm's shares whichever method was used, the implication might be that the market sees through accounting data in many instances and is able to reprocess and standardize that data no matter what method of reporting is employed. Still another possibility would be that the market makes its stock appraisals on the basis of other kinds of information than that traditionally supplied by the accountant, and that it views the accounting product as irrelevant.

In Hong, Kaplan and Mandelker, Pooling v. Purchase: The Effects of Accounting for Mergers on Stock Prices, 53 Accounting Rev. 31 (1978), the authors made a statistical analysis of the market behavior of the shares of acquiring companies that reported higher earnings as a result of "pooling" than would have been reported under the "purchase" method. Did the use of pooling lead to an increase in share values at the time, or during the year in which the acquisitions took place? The answer was entirely negative:

> "There is a clear lack of evidence to support the hypothesis that using the pooling-of-interests method raises the stock prices of acquiring firms around the time or in the year after the merger. Investors do not seem to have been fooled by this accounting convention into paying higher stock prices even though firms in our sample using pooling-of-interests accounting report higher earnings than if they had used the purchase method * * *.

> "People who wish to continue to believe that 'dirty pooling' raises the stock prices of acquiring firms may raise the following

i. If past earnings or (increasing) earnings trends are deemed to persist (absent reasons for doubt in particular cases), then the acquiring company is constantly increasing its earnings per share if its stock (used as currency in the merger) sells at a higher P/E than does the acquired company's stock. The question is whether an increase in *reported* earnings per share by pooling accounting should mask the fact that there was no comparable increase in real earnings per share.

objections to our study.   * * * [O]ne could [also] argue that while
for many firms the income difference between pooling and purchase is minimal, there are a few mergers in which the difference
is highly significant.   Our procedure of aggregating all firms together regardless of the magnitude of the income effect, therefore
depresses significant findings by averaging many small effects
along with potentially significant accounting impacts.   This is a
reasonable criticism which also applies to previous studies of the
effects of accounting changes * * *.

"No single empirical study is ever completely convincing on
settling a controversy.   Problems in sample selection, financial and
statistical models, and interpretation of results are inherent in all
empirical work.   We believe, however, the effect of this study is to
shift the burden of proof to those who claim that the stock price of
acquiring firms is raised when the pooling-of-interests method is
used in a merger.   We have looked at a large sample of mergers
and have been unable to find any evidence that the selection of an
accounting method affects the valuation of the acquiring firm.   In
the absence of future studies that would demonstrate such an
effect, we must believe that fully disclosed accounting policies are
properly reflected in the stock prices of firms."

Whatever may be the limitations of the above study or of the authors'
interpretation of its results, a comparable conclusion—with respect to
the insignificant impact of announced regulatory changes embodied in
APB 16 and 17 was reached in Schipper and Thompson, The Impact of
Merger–Related Regulations on the Shareholders of Acquiring Firms,
21 J.Acct. Research 184 (1983).   See also, Davis, Differential Market
Reaction to Pooling and Purchase Methods, 65 Accounting Rev. 696
(1990) (replicating results of Hong, Kaplan and Mandelker study).
That the matter of determining the stock price effects of accounting
changes is more complicated and the answers less clear than intimated,
however, is the teaching of the Leftwich study of the effects of APB
opinions No. 16 and 17 on the stock prices of active acquiring companies (Evidence of the Impact of Mandatory Changes in Accounting
Principles on Corporate Loan Agreements, 3 J. of Accounting and
Economics (March 1981) pp. 3–36), which is discussed in Watts and
Zimmerman, Positive Accounting Theory (1986), Ch. 12.

Finally, it should be noted that significance of a particular accounting choice may depend on the identity of the party in interest.   The
studies just mentioned concern the responses of investors acting in
trading markets.   The responses of managers making choices respecting mergers and acquisitions may be more open to influence by the
differences between purchase and pooling.   Robinson and Shane, Acquisition Accounting Method and Bid Premia for Target Firms, 65 Accounting Rev. 25 (1990), finds that acquisitions accounted for as pool-

ings involved higher average bid premia than did acquisitions accounted for as purchases, and suggests this may reflect an additional amount that bidders are willing to pay for the benefits of pooling. But see Nathan, Do Firms Pay to Pool?: Some Empirical Evidence, 7 J. Accounting & Pub.Pol. 185 (1988), finding that pooling treatment did not result in higher acquisition prices.

APPENDIX B

CAPITAL MARKETS AND SECURITIES REGULATION

SECTION 1. THE CAPITAL MARKETS

(a) Overview

ROSS, WESTERFIELD AND JORDAN, FUNDAMENTALS OF CORPORATE FINANCE
17–20, 386–388 (1991).

The financial market, like any market, is just a way of bringing buyers and sellers together. In financial markets, it is debt and equity securities that are bought and sold. Financial markets differ in detail, however. The most important differences concern the types of securities that are traded, how trading is conducted, and who the buyers and sellers are.   * * *

Money versus Capital Markets

Financial markets can be classified as either **money markets** or **capital markets.** Short-term debt securities of many varieties are bought and sold in money markets. These short-term debt securities are often called money market "instruments" and are essentially IOUs. For example, *commercial paper* represents short-term borrowing by large corporations and is a money market instrument. Capital markets are the markets for long-term debt and shares of stock, so the New York Stock Exchange, for example, is a capital market.

The money market is a *dealer market.* Generally speaking, dealers buy and sell something for themselves, at their own risk. A car dealer, for example, buys and sells automobiles. In contrast, brokers and agents match buyers and sellers, but they do not actually own the commodity. A real estate agent or broker, for example, does not normally buy and sell houses.

The largest money market dealers are the so-called money market banks, which are primarily large New York City banks. These banks, along with other market participants, are connected electronically via telephone and computer, so the money market has no actual physical location.

Primary versus Secondary Markets

Financial markets function as both primary and secondary markets for debt and equity securities. The term *primary market* refers to the

original sale of securities by governments and corporations. The *secondary markets* are where these securities are bought and sold after the original sale. Equities are, of course, issued solely by corporations. Debt securities are issued by both governments and corporations.
* * *

Primary Markets. In a primary market transaction, the corporation is the seller, and the transaction raises money for the corporation. Corporations engage in two types of primary market transactions: public offerings and private placements. A public offering, as the name suggests, involves selling securities to the general public, while a private placement is a negotiated sale involving a specific buyer. * * *

Most publicly offered debt and equity securities are "underwritten." *Underwriters,* or *investment banks,* are firms that specialize in marketing securities. Merrill Lynch, Goldman Sachs, and Payne Weber [sic] are three examples of such investment banks.

When a public offering is underwritten, an investment bank or a group of investment banks (called a *syndicate*) typically purchases the securities from the firm and markets them to the public. The underwriters hope to profit by reselling the securities to investors at a higher price than they pay the firm.
* * *

Partly to avoid the various regulatory requirements and the expense of public offerings, debt and equity are often sold privately to large financial institutions such as life insurance companies or mutual funds. Such private placements do not have to be registered with the SEC and do not require the involvement of underwriters.

Secondary Markets. A secondary market transaction involves one owner or creditor selling to another. It is therefore the secondary markets that provide the means for transferring ownership of corporate securities. There are two kinds of secondary markets: *auction* markets and *dealer* markets.

Dealer markets in stocks and long-term debt are called *over-the-counter* (OTC) markets. Most trading in debt securities takes place over the counter. The expression "over the counter" refers to days of old when securities were literally bought and sold at counters in offices around the country. Today, like the money market, a significant fraction of the market for stocks and almost all of the market for long-term debt have no central location; the many dealers are connected electronically.

The equity shares of most of the large firms in the United States trade in organized auction markets. The largest such market is the New York Stock Exchange (NYSE, pronounced "ny-see") which accounts for more than 85 percent of all the shares traded in auction markets. Other auction exchanges include the American Stock Exchange (AMEX) and regional exchanges such as the Midwest Stock Exchange.

Auction markets differ from dealer markets in two ways. First, an auction market or exchange, unlike a dealer market, has a physical location (like Wall Street), and all trading in a particular security takes place at a designated spot on the floor of the exchange. Second, in a dealer market most of the buying and selling is done by the dealer. The primary purpose of an auction market, on the other hand, is to match those who wish to sell with those who wish to buy. Dealers play a limited role.

In addition to the stock exchanges, there is a large OTC * * * market for stocks. In 1971, the National Association of Securities Dealers (NASD) made available to dealers and brokers an electronic quotation system called NASDAQ (NASD Automated Quotation system, pronounced "naz-dak"). There are roughly three times as many companies on NASDAQ as there are on NYSE, but they tend to be much smaller in size and trade less actively. There are exceptions, of course. Both Apple Computer and MCI trade OTC, for example. Nonetheless, the total value of NASDAQ stocks was about 20 percent of the value of NYSE stocks at the end of 1986.

Stocks that trade on an organized exchange are said to be *listed* on that exchange. In order to be listed, firms must meet certain minimum criteria concerning, for example, asset size and number of shareholders. These criteria differ for different exchanges.

NYSE has the most stringent requirements of the exchanges in the United States. For example, to be listed on NYSE, a company is expected to have a market value for its publicly held shares of at least $18 million and a total of at least 2,000 shareholders with at least 100 shares each. There are additional minimums on earnings, assets, and number of shares outstanding.

> * * *

PATTERNS OF LONG–TERM FINANCING

* * * Table 12.2 summarizes the sources and uses of long-term financing for U.S. industrial firms from the decade just ended in dollar and percentage terms.

In Table 12.2, under sources of financing, we have internally generated financing and external sources. The internal financing is defined here as net income plus depreciation less dividends, and it is a measure of the internally generated cash flow from operations that is reinvested in the firm.

The external financing consists of net new long-term borrowing, short-term borrowing, and common stock. One striking trend in recent years is the tendency for net new equity issues to be *negative*, meaning that more equity is bought back than sold. Long-term debt has become correspondingly more important as a source of financing. For example, in 1988, corporations borrowed $138.2 billion long-term. New equity sales where—$130.5, meaning that repurchases of stock exceeded sales of stock by this amount.

TABLE 12.2 Patterns of corporate financing 1980–1989 (billions of dollars)

	1980	1981	1982	1983	1984	1985	1986	1987	1988	1989
Uses of funds										
Capital spending	$237.5	$269.4	$269.1	$261.5	$308.4	$329.1	$318.2	$318.4	$350.9	$361.9
Short-term uses										
Inventory	− $43.2	$35.9	− $10.8	$11.5	$57.5	$8.1	$− 3.3	$45.8	$51.3	$− 9.7
Liquid assets	25.7	23.9	46.3	35.1	24.1	27.6	75.7	7.7	35.0	17.2
Accounts receivable	48.8	25.4	− 14.0	56.7	52.9	47.9	19.5	70.9	17.0	27.3
Other	29.3	52.9	23.6	39.2	38.7	8.9	34.5	31.9	42.0	77.4
	$60.6	$138.1	$45.1	$142.5	$173.2	$92.5	$126.4	$156.3	$145.3	$112.2
Total uses	$298.1	$407.5	$314.2	$404.0	$481.6	$421.6	$444.6	$474.7	$496.2	$474.1
Sources of funds										
Internally generated funds	$156.2	$263.7	$252.7	$296.6	$342.1	$354.0	$338.1	$371.5	$397.5	$345.4
External financing										
New equity sales	$12.9	− $11.5	$6.4	$23.5	− $74.5	− $81.5	− $80.8	$76.5	− $130.5	− $93.0
Other equity	15.3	25.3	13.8	11.5	25.6	20.5	36.1	47.3	57.6	46.2
Long-term debt	17.7	36.9	− 8.2	21.0	65.3	78.5	139.7	114.6	138.2	121.2
Short-term debt	37.5	56.3	48.2	31.5	89.9	55.1	51.5	28.9	59.4	45.7
Accounts payable	38.0	28.6	4.9	37.0	33.7	34.0	3.1	18.0	3.2	19.3
Other financing	2.0	2.2	− 4.5	8.9	18.6	− 1.5	16.2	7.0	8.1	4.8
	$123.4	$137.8	$60.6	$133.4	$158.6	$105.1	$165.8	$139.3	$136.0	$144.2
Discrepancy	18.5	6.0	0.9	− 26.0	− 19.1	− 37.5	− 59.3	− 36.1	− 37.3	− 15.5
Total sources	$298.1	$407.5	$314.2	$404.0	$481.6	$421.6	$444.6	$474.7	$496.2	$474.1

TABLE 12.2 (concluded) Patterns of corporate financing: 1980–1989 (percentage of total uses).

	1980	1981	1982	1983	1984	1985	1986	1987	1988	1989
Uses of funds:										
Capital spending	0.80	0.66	0.86	0.65	0.64	0.78	0.72	0.67	0.71	.76
Short-term uses										
Inventory	− 0.14	0.09	− 0.03	0.03	0.12	0.02	− 0.01	0.10	0.10	− .02
Liquid assets	0.09	0.06	0.15	0.09	0.05	0.07	0.17	0.02	0.07	.04
Accounts receivable	0.16	0.06	− 0.04	0.14	0.11	0.11	0.04	0.15	0.03	.06
Other	0.10	0.13	0.08	0.10	0.08	0.02	0.08	0.07	0.08	.16
	0.20	0.34	0.14	0.35	0.36	0.22	0.28	0.33	0.29	.24
Total uses	1.00	1.00	1.00	1.00	1.00	1.00	1.00	1.00	1.00	1.00
Sources of funds										
Internally generated funds *	0.52	0.65	0.80	0.73	0.71	0.84	0.76	0.78	0.80	.73
External financing										
New equity sales	0.04	− 0.03	0.02	0.06	− 0.15	− 0.19	− 0.18	− 0.16	− 0.26	− .20
Other equity	0.05	0.06	0.04	0.03	0.05	0.05	0.08	0.10	0.12	.10
Long-term debt	0.06	0.09	− 0.03	0.05	0.14	0.19	0.31	0.24	0.28	.26
Short-term debt	0.13	0.14	0.15	0.08	0.19	0.13	0.12	0.06	0.12	.10
Accounts payable	0.13	0.07	0.02	0.09	0.07	0.08	0.01	0.04	0.01	.04
Other financing	0.01	0.01	− 0.01	0.02	0.04	0.00	0.04	0.01	0.02	.01
	0.42	0.34	0.20	0.33	0.33	0.25	0.37	0.30	0.28	.30
Discrepancy †	0.06	0.01	0.00	− 0.06	− 0.04	− 0.09	− 0.13	− 0.08	− 0.08	− .03
Total sources	1.00	1.00	1.00	1.00	1.00	1.00	1.00	1.00	1.00	1.00

Note: Column totals may be inexact because of rounding errors.
* Internally generated funds is net income plus depreciation less dividends.
† Discrepancy refers to the statistical error in the flow of funds accounts.
Source: Derived from various issues of Board of Governors of the Federal Reserve System. *Flow of Funds Accounts.*

Several other features of long-term financing are apparent in Table 12.2:

1. Internally generated cash flow has dominated as a source of funds. Between 50 percent and 85 percent of long-term financing comes from cash flow generated by operations and "plowed back." Typically, internally generated funds provide about 70 percent to 80 percent of total sources.

2. The primary use of long-term financing is capital spending, which regularly accounts for about 70 percent to 80 percent of all uses. Capital spending and internally generated cash flow are thus roughly equal.

3.   A financial "deficit" is created by the difference between uses of
     long-term financing and internally generated sources, and corpora-
     tions have been net issuers of securities. For example, in 1982, 80
     percent of long-term financing came from internal cash flow, leav-
     ing a deficit of 20 percent. In this particular year, the shortfall was
     financed mostly with short-term debt (15 percent).

   * * * [T]he financial deficit averages about 30 percent. In general,
the deficit is covered by borrowing and new equity. However, as we
have seen, one of the most prominent aspects of external financing is
that new issues of equity seem to be less and less important, at least in
aggregate.

   While debt issues dominate the primary or new issue market when
compared to equities, the reverse is the case in the secondary or resale
market. The New York Stock Exchange (NYSE) is the country's most
active and sophisticated securities market. In 1992, the par value of all
bonds traded on the NYSE was $11.6 billion, while the value of all
stocks traded in 1992 amounted to $1,745.5 billion. Part of the relative
attractiveness of equity ownership is the liquidity of the trading market
for stocks: because the secondary market has both breadth and depth,
it is usually very easy to sell any number of shares of a particular issue
at prices reflective of market forces without disturbing the market.
Several commentators have noted that junk bonds possess potential
price appreciation and liquidity characteristics more akin to stocks
than to conventional corporate bonds. This factor undoubtedly contributed to the popularity of high yield bonds in recent years. (A liquid
security can be quickly bought or sold in quantity without affecting its
price.)

(b) Institutional and Individual Investors

   The so-called institutionalization of the stock market is reflected in
the increase in the value of New York Stock Exchange listed stocks
held by financial institutions from 15% of the total in 1955 to 35.4% in
1980 and an estimated 45% by 1988. In 1990, institutional ownership
of the largest 100 companies (in terms of market value) was 53%.
Institutional participation in the volume of trading on the Exchange
rose from approximately 25% in 1955 to approximately 65% by the end
of 1980 and to more than 80% by the late 1980s. The talent of the
institutions' personnel and their financial ability to fund research
presumably have an impact on the pursuit and digestion of relevant
information in effecting investment decisions, and on the so-called
efficiency of the market. Notwithstanding such institutionalization,
large numbers of individual shareholders of apparently modest means
have remained participants. In mid–1990 (as in mid–1970) one in four
adult Americans held stock in a publicly traded company. Of this
group, 47 percent (20,910,000) held portfolios valued at less than $10,-
000. Moreover 6 percent had household incomes of less than $10,000
and almost 16 percent had household incomes under $25,000.

SECTION 2. THE FEDERAL MANDATORY DISCLOSURE SYSTEM

INTRODUCTION

Valuations are based on information about the performance of business enterprises. Presumably, the better the quality of the information base, the better the quality of the projection of future performance, and the more accurate the calculation of present value. And, presumably, the cheaper and more accurate the valuation process, the more risky investments become attractive to risk averse investors, and the lower the cost of capital.

Does it follow from this that the law should assure the availability of high quality information to investors? And, does it also follow that the law should assure that securities markets function so that trading prices come as close as possible to identity with fundamental value? And, if legal regulation is a desirable means to the end of accurate market valuations, to what extent do the precepts of financial economics give us correct, coherent instructions for shaping the law?

These questions come up with respect to the Federal Securities Laws. These lie at the base of a regulatory system that, as implemented by the Securities and Exchange Commission and the courts, compels the disclosure of information thought to be relevant to the valuation of publicly issued and traded securities and forbids the purveying of false or incomplete information respecting them. The Securities Act of 1933 and the Securities Exchange Act of 1934 (supplemented by the Investment Company Act of 1940, the Public Utility Holding Company Act of 1935 and the Investment Advisors Act of 1940) directly prescribe the disclosure of information by requiring the filing and/or distribution of specified financial statements and operating information, and indirectly compel disclosure by prohibiting transactions which in the absence of disclosure would be held to constitute one or another variety of "fraud".

The basic outline of this regulatory system has remained constant for more than a half century. Even so, the policy concepts that explain and shape the system have changed markedly. Today, different reasons tend to be offered to justify the presence of disclosure rules and to define their appropriate scope than were offered twenty years ago. This shift tracks the appearance of modern finance theory in legal discussions and the changes it has brought to the operative model of valuation.

In the earlier, now seemingly outmoded picture of the securities markets, a population of individual small investors selected stocks on the basis of fundamental analysis, performed personally or by a professional advisor. Emphasis was placed on the fact that both the investor and advisor stood outside the issuer and therefore lacked access to basic valuation information. Financial economic models reshaped this picture. The capital asset pricing model instructs us that investors can diversify firm-specific risk cheaply. The efficient capital market hypothesis instructs us that market prices already reflect company specific information. Together, these make the individual investor's lack of access to company-specific information seem less of a problem.

What are the regulatory implications of this displacement of the old small investor/fundamental analysis model of the securities markets? Is deregulation in the federal securities context implied? Or does this in the end merely reconfirm the validity of decades-old regulations? And, assuming the latter case, how should these concepts figure into the ongoing evolution of this body of law?

This Appendix explores these questions. It does not purport to offer a working introduction to the federal securities laws, however. The focus instead is on the theoretical question whether, in light of the precepts of financial economics, we need a mandatory disclosure system at all. Securities law policy is thus discussed as basis for exploring the legal implications of modern finance economics and the problems that come up when the law and finance economics become intertwined.

(A) BACKGROUND: THE LEGAL FRAMEWORK

The federal securities laws mandate disclosure of material information (1) by compelling the filing with the Securities Exchange Commission and the dissemination to the public of information which the statutes authorize the Commission to request (on specific occasions as well as periodically on a continuing basis), and (2) by policing failures to make required filings accurately, and entirely apart from required filings, by forbidding misstatements of, and omissions to state, material facts in a variety of circumstances.

(1) *Registration Requirements of the Securities Act of 1933.*

With exceptions not here important, the Securities Act of 1933 requires information to be filed with the Commission and disseminated to potential investors whenever a public distribution of securities is being made by issuers or controlling persons of issuers. In general, any effort by an enterprise—whether newly formed or established and, whether previously publicly held or not—to obtain capital by selling or offering to sell securities to public investors requires registration of the securities with the Commission.

The Securities Act effects its informational mandate through an intricate scheme. Under Section 5, securities must be registered (i.e., information about the issuer and the offering must be filed on specified forms with the Commission), and the information must be disseminated

Brudney & Chirelstein Corp. Fin. 4th Ed. UCS—27

B–7

by prospectus before any person may make offers or sales of the securities. The requirement of prior registration is limited to issuers and controlling persons who are making distributions. Accordingly, exemptions from registration are provided for (a) offerings by the issuer which are not "public"—i.e., offerings generally to persons, or limited numbers of persons who presumably can bargain cohesively and comprehendingly for the information—or which are limited in amount (see Sections 3(b), 4(2) and 4(6) and Regulation D), and (b) non-distributional sales—i.e., trading—by controlling persons and others (see Sections 4(1), 4(3) and 4(4) and Rule 144).

The registration provisions of the 1933 Act are enforced directly by the Commission, and may also be enforced indirectly by private action. Section 11 imposes civil liability at the suit of "any person acquiring such security," upon the signatories of the registration statement (including the issuer, directors of the issuer, underwriters, and other specified persons) for defects in the registration statement: Section 12(1) imposes civil liability upon any person who offers or sells a security in violation of Section 5 to the "person purchasing such security from him." Sections 12(2) and 17(a) proscribe fraudulent offers and sales.

Sections 11 and 12 of the Act furnish a special goad to full disclosure in registration statements and in sales efforts in distributions of securities. Since the threshold of culpability they prescribe for liability is low, the in terrorem effect is great.

(2) *Registration and Other Disclosure Requirements Under the Securities Exchange Act.*

The Securities Exchange Act of 1934 requires issuer disclosure (1) on a continuing basis, in order to facilitate trading in securities on the basis of current information, and (2) on the occasion of particular transactions which both constitute and reflect special facts about which an investor should be specially notified and informed.

(a) *Registration Requirements.* Section 12 of the Exchange Act requires the registration of securities with the securities exchange on which they are traded. In addition, corporations having assets in excess of $1 million (increased to $5 million by regulation) and a class of equity security held by 500 persons or more, must register securities of each such class with the Commission. The information to be supplied in a registration statement under Section 12 includes a description of the registrant's organization, its financial structure, and the nature of its business, the terms of its outstanding securities, the identity of its directors, officers and controlling stockholders and their remuneration and emoluments, along with its earnings statements and balance sheets. Under Section 13, as implemented by Commission rules, the information filed under Section 12 is to be kept current and key developments are to be reported currently. Finally, under Section 15(d), corporations which register securities for sale under the '33 Act and retain a substantial number of securityholders but which do not fall within the parameters of Section 12 must file current reports under Section 13.

(b) *Other Exchange Act Disclosure Provisions.* (1) Rules promulgated by the Commission pursuant to Section 14 to govern the solicitation of proxies also require information to be provided—both regularly in connection with annual meetings and episodically in connection with special stockholder meetings—e.g., to pass on mergers.

(2) Another source of mandated disclosure comes from sections 13(d), 13(c) and 14(d) of the Exchange Act and implementing regulations. These govern tender offer and potential tender offer activity and certain purchases by a corporation of its own equity securities.

(3) Under Section 16(a), information must be filed monthly with respect to insiders' changes of ownership of equity securities of their corporations.

(4) The anti-fraud provisions of the Exchange Act, particularly Sections 10(b) and 14(c), police the filing requirements and independently prohibit misstatements and compel disclosure of information not required in the filings.

(3) *Integration of '33 and '34 Act Schemes.*

Historically, neither the Commission nor the corporations making "current" filings under Sections 12 and 13 of the 1934 Act regarded those provisions as imposing the same extensive disclosure obligations as did registration under the 1933 Act. The '34 Act registration and the current information forms developed by the Commission requested less information than did the '33 Act forms. The Commission's staff did not process the filings with the attention and care used in examining '33 Act registration statements. Personal liability in civil actions was (and continues to be) less clear under the '34 Act. Moreover, '34 Act filings lacked the critical examination of underwriters. And, unlike a '33 Act registration, a filing under the '34 Act's Section 13 was not a condition to selling securities. Hence neither the functional pressure to obtain funds, the time pressure to "catch the market," nor a liability risk operated to induce those making '34 Act reports to be complete and fully responsive. Finally, so-called current filings under Section 13 were not required to be filed until so long after the period for which they constituted reports that much of their import was lost. See Cohen, "Truth in Securities" Revisited, 79 Harv.L.Rev. 1340 (1966), the article that inspired the effort to integrate the disclosure scheme.

In 1982, the Commission promulgated an extensive revision designed to integrate the '33 and '34 Act registration systems. Securities Act Release No. 6383 (March 2, 1982). As already noted, this reform stemmed from dissatisfaction with the level of disclosure mandated under the '34 Act's continuous systems. An additional and different reservoir of dissatisfaction also came to bear. This went to the "registration costs and administrative obstacles incurred by industrial users [whose securities were already public] in raising [added] capital" from new issues under the '33 Act. Report of the Advisory Committee on Corporate Disclosure to the Securities and Exchange Commission (Committee Print 95–29, Nov. 3, 1977, 95th Cong. 1st Sess.) pp. 3–7 (hereafter, 1977 Advisory Committee Report). According to Gilson and Kraakman, The Mechanisms of Market Efficiency, supra, 70 Va.L.Rev. at 550, the efficient capital market hypothesis provided the "intellectual premise" for this latter reform. That is, the reformers assumed that where the issuer's stock already is publicly traded, its market price already has responded to the existing store of public information; the marketplace, accordingly, can function just as well with a less costly compliance process for a new issue.

The reform minimized the differential between the two disclosure schemes largely by permitting the information requested under '34 Act sections 12 and 13 to do duty under the '33 Act. At the same time, according to Milton Cohen, under the reform "the continuous disclosure effort of the 1934 Act has been greatly strengthened in coverage and quality. For thousands of companies we now have continuously updated reservoirs of information comparable in scope to what we used to get from a relatively small number of companies on the occasion of a public offering." Cohen, The Integrated Disclosure System—Unfinished Business, 40 Bus.Law. 987–988 (1985). But questions still came up as to whether the quality of '34 Act continuous disclosures—now the foundation for '33 Act public offerings—had risen to a sufficiently high level so as to prevent deterioration of the quality of disclosures under the '33 Act. Cohen thought not. He questioned the effectiveness of the principal integration technique—incorporating the '33 Act issuer's latest '34 Act disclosures into its '33 Act registration statement by reference. This imposes obligations under section 11 of the '33 Act on parties, such as underwriters, who played no part in the earlier '34 Act disclosure, or who, even though involved with the earlier disclosure process, did not feel "the in terrorem breath of section 11" at the time the disclosures were made. The upshot, according to Cohen, is a system in which the quality of disclosures accompanying new issues has deteriorated: "Most registrants are understandably reluctant to reconsider and rewrite at the time of a public offering what they have previously filed for purposes of the continuous disclosure system; and most underwriters feel unable, within the time frame of a modern offering, to exercise due diligence in the old-fashioned sense." Id. at 992–93.

(B) POLICY JUSTIFICATIONS FOR THE MANDATORY DISCLOSURE SYSTEM

(1) *The Traditional Approach.*

Traditionally, the federal securities laws' affirmative disclosure requirements and broad extensions of the "fraud" concept in securities transactions are thought to perform two functions—a bargaining and informational role and an inhibiting role. In performing these two functions the securities laws assertedly affect investors so as to induce a lower cost of capital for the enterprise.

(a) The bargaining role is thought to be necessary because of the nature of the commodity being bought and sold and the difficulties in obtaining access to relevant and accurate information about it. Sales of securities tend to involve greater inequality of access to information between buyers and sellers than is likely to be encountered in transactions in other commodities. To the extent that a buyer or a seller has legitimate, effectively monopolistic, access to material non-public information from the corporation which is not similarly available to the other party to the transaction, that party has a bargaining advantage. The federal securities laws offset the advantage by requiring disclosure of such information. Thus the "bargaining role" is in substance informational. Although bargaining disadvantages are not redressed structurally, the system is designed to fill the needs of investors for information in order to make intelligent investment decisions.

But should not buyers of securities avoid this problem without the necessity of legal intervention by simply insisting that pertinent information be disclosed before completing their purchases? The traditional answer is that securities sales in public trading markets, unlike other sales contracts, present no realistic opportunity for the purchaser to get the facts. Take the case of a public offering of a new issue. While a single offeree or a cohesive group of offerees might be able to press the issuer for the needed information and explanation, the dispersed public is thought to be unable effectively to do so. The issuer is tempted to view its prospects more optimistically than would a potential buyer of securities. In the absence of mandated information, the issuer's selling efforts are not likely to be accompanied by full disclosure of the risks affecting, and the premises underlying (and presumably qualifying) the description of the issuer, its assets and its earnings. Nor, in the traditional picture, does the presence of financial intermediaries cure the problem. The intermediaries (underwriters and broker-dealers) buy the block of securities from the issuer for resale or act as selling agents. They are paid for thus distributing the securities to the public, and in any event do not wish to be left holding the issue. The inducement to these intermediaries to facilitate distribution is thus not likely to encourage a less than optimistic sales pitch. By the same token, nothing in the distribution process diminishes the offeree's need for the mandated information.

(b) The disclosure system's inhibiting function is a by product of its bargaining function. The disclosure requirements are designed to shed light on the behavior of corporate insiders and in that way to have the disinfecting qualities of sunlight. The assumption is that people will refrain from engaging in, or that it will be impossible to consummate, many kinds of unlawful or otherwise undesirable transactions (e.g., diversion of assets or opportunities to insiders) if they are required to disclose what they are doing.

(2) *Protective and Informational Models.*

The system's bargaining function presupposes investors in need of assistance. Yet no single model of needy investors and their trading situation ever gained undisputed ascendancy in the world of securities law policymaking. Instead, two models of bargaining assistance have competed over time. One is a protective model focused on small individual investors. The other is an informational model focused on investment professionals. The protective model is firm oriented and centers on cost accounting. The informational model has a broader focus, extending to information on the product markets and industries in which individual firms operate. It also is more open to the influence of financial economics.

The protective model tended to determine the shape of SEC disclosure rules until around 1980, when growing criticism prompted reform. Problems resulting from the Commission's adherence to the protective model were described in the 1977 Advisory Report on Corporate Disclosure, pp. 347–349:

"Disclosure was intended by the framers of the Securities Act and Exchange Act to serve two primary, and correlative, functions. It was believed that disclosure (1) would provide investors with a sound basis for making informed and rational investment decisions; and (2) would deter those in control of public business enterprises from fraudulent and unethical conduct.

"Although it is at least arguable that the statutory disclosure system created by the 1933 and 1934 Acts was perceived by Congress and commentators as being particularly suited to the interests of sophisticated investors and securities professionals, for many years the disclosure policy of the Commission was based on the belief that the relevant constituency was the unsophisticated investor.

"The disclosure objective of providing meaningful information to the investment community has, in cases of perceived conflict, been subordinated to the objective of protecting unsophisticated investors from their own ignorance. Thus, for example, the Commission has excluded certain types of information from SEC filings for fear that such information, although useful and important to knowledgeable constituents of the investment community, might be misunderstood and unduly relied on by unsophisticated investors.

"Critics of the exclusionary policy have contended that the Commission has subverted the statutory mandate and the underlying Congressional objectives of disclosure. These critics believe that the interests of all would be better served by a disclosure policy that had as its predominant objective the disclosure of meaningful information to the investment community. It would indirectly benefit unsophisticated investors by promoting the development of more informed investment advisory services and market prices that more accurately and reliably reflect the intrinsic value of securities.

"The Commission has exhibited an increasing awareness of the importance of disclosure for informational purposes as opposed to protectionist purposes. Most notable were its 1973 statement that projections of future economic performance would be permitted in company filings under certain conditions * * * and its 1976 proposed guides for disclosures of projections of future economic performance. Such information was, until recently, regarded as not sufficiently 'hard' to be disclosed in Commission filings."

(3) *Law Reform and the System's Evolution From a Protective to an Informational Model—Disclosure of Projections and Other Soft Information.*

The SEC, operating under the protective model, built its mandatory disclosure system around cost accounting results. The cost accounting mandate had two aspects. First, the figures had to be produced and disclosed. Second, the disclosure of other "soft" or "future oriented" information was impermissible. Thus documents filed with the SEC could not include either (1) internal estimates of a corporation's future performance, such as projections of earnings, sales or stock prices, (2) appraisals of the present salable value of illiquid assets, or (3) information about merger negotiations in which the corporation was involved.

The new learning on valuation and abandonment of the strict protective model led the SEC to relax the second leg of the mandate. Room for disclosure of projections and other "soft" information has been worked into the system.

(a) *Cost versus Value Accounting.* The single most important substantive element in protective disclosure scheme was (and in fact continues to be) accounting data—balance sheets, income statements and changes in financial position, all required to be prepared in accordance with generally accepted accounting principles. The problem with the protective system, thus grounded, was that its exclusive focus on cost accounting results could not easily be defended as a means to the end of the stated objective of protecting small investors. First, it was not clear that small investors could understand or interpret the technical data disclosed in a way that was useful to them. Second, accounting results are largely historical; investors, in contrast, are interested in the future. Presumably, they may be misled if they use past history as a basis for making predictions about what is to come— unless there is good reason to suppose that the past will repeat itself and that simple extrapolation is a sound way to proceed. Third, accounting data, past or projected, are incomplete. Under the strict protective model, "information on unfilled orders, the current and expected market price of inventories (when greater than cost), valuable research findings, and other 'favorable' data not reflected in the ordinary accounting records need not be reported to the investor. Nor are statements about the ability and health of management, public acceptability of products, subtle changes of labor-management relations, effect of political events on the company, and other vital activities required by SEC regulations. (That these may not be objectively determinable does not deny their 'usefulness to investors')." Bentson, The Effectiveness and Effects of the SEC's Accounting Disclosure Requirements, in Economic Policy and The Regulation of Corporate Securities 29–30 (Manne ed. 1969). By the 1970s it was widely held that the cost accounting mandate was outliving its usefulness. See Kripke, The SEC, the Accountants, Some Myths and Some Realities, 45 N.Y.U.L.Rev. 1151 (1970).

(b) *Projections.* The protective model led the SEC not only to limit the disclosure mandate to past information, but to prohibit the formal use of profit projections in materials required to be filed with it. The ground was that such projections were, or might be, misleading and subject to manipulation. In the effort to sell securities to the public, the temptation is to predict a bright future. See, e.g., In re Thomas Bond, 5 S.E.C. 60 (1939). Under the traditional SEC view, "the inclusion of soft information in filings would clothe such information with an unduly high aura of credibility. Investors assume, with a great deal of justification, that information appearing in SEC filings has been prepared with considerable care, tending to assure its accuracy. Therefore, under the SEC's approach, if soft information appeared in a prospectus, the public would incorrectly assume an unwarranted degree of reliability—that a prediction or projection would almost certainly be fulfilled, or that any statement made is subject to verification by objective evidence." Schneider, Nits, Grits And Soft Information in SEC Filings, 121 U.Pa.L.Rev. 254, 258 (1972). See also Hiler, The SEC and the Courts' Approach to the Disclosure of Earnings Projections, Asset Appraisals and Other Soft Information: Old Problems, Changing Views, 46 Md.L.Rev. 1114 (1987).

Arguments against the traditional SEC policy and in favor of published projections rested in part on the value of projections for the investment decision making process and for policing management, and in part on the fact that they were in any event being offered to analysts at regular meetings and otherwise, but not directly to public investors. A two-tiered market in information was said to have been created to the disadvantage of public investors. It was argued that if such data were publicly filed, it would be equally available to all—and precisely because it was filed it would be made more carefully and therefore would be more reliable.

The investment community, particularly investment analysts and financial intermediaries, pressured for authorization of published profit projections. Managers (and their counsel and accountants), on the other hand, were less than enthusiastic about having the privilege of announcing internal projections in SEC filings, let alone the obligation to do so. According to the 1977 Advisory Committee Report (pp. 20–23), management often appeared to consider its projections to be "so unreliable that disclosure would only harm the firm's credibility. * * * The concern was voiced that if a requirement for earning forecasts were imposed, management would alter its behavior by projecting an earnings figure it was confident of obtaining and avoid riskier projects rather than disappoint analysts' and investors' expectations." See also Skousen, Sharp and Tolman, Corporate Disclosure of Budgetary Data, J. Accountancy 50 (May, 1972). Fears of liability also were expressed on the theory that if management's projections turned out to be incorrect, a jury trial long after events made the projections "wrong" would expose it to liability notwithstanding rules of law which make it liable only for misstatements made with scienter. See Marsh, Symposium, Bus.Lawyer 505–535 (1973); Dean, Public Discussion of Projected Earnings—Pros and Cons., 25 Mercer L.Rev. 511 (1974).[a]

(c) *Revised Rules.* The SEC reformed its rules to allow projections in SEC documents in 1979. The new rules do not mandate disclosure. Instead they construct a safe harbor from the securities laws' liability provisions for a defined class of forward looking statements made in "good faith" and with a "reasonable basis." Securities Act.Rel. No. 6084 (1979).

(C) FINANCIAL ECONOMIC CONCEPTS AND THE MANDATORY DISCLOSURE SYSTEM

Since 1980, a critique of the mandatory disclosure system and traditional securities law policies has been articulated in financial economic terms.

(1) *Protective Model.*

The traditional investor protection norm has lost vitality with acceptance of the CAPM's lesson of cheap diversification of firm specific risk and the ECMH's promise of reasonably accurate market pricing. The basic arguments against the investor protection norm are set out in the following comments of Professor Jeffrey Gordon, addressed to the question whether corporate charter terms appropriately can be legally

---

a. Studies have reported, more or less consistently, that management's earnings projections, although generally skewed toward optimistic results, are more "accurate" (i.e., turn out to offer smaller disparities between estimate and result) than securities analysts' projections. But more than a trivial portion of the former turn out to be significantly "inaccurate". See Cox, Insider Trading Regulation and the Production of Information: Theory and Evidence, 64 Wash.U.L.Q. 475, 481–482 (1986).

mandated, in Gordon, The Mandatory Structure of Corporate Law, 89 Colum.L.Rev. 1549, 1557 (1989):

> " * * * It is a mistake to assume that investors can obtain information only through independent research, i.e., to isolate individuals from markets. Well-functioning securities markets aggregate information from all active market participants, embody that information in a single fact—price—and make the fact available for free. There are nevertheless significant gains from having information first, of course, and some investors will find it profitable to spend resources to become specifically informed. In equilibrium, we would expect to see a pattern in which some investors choose to become specifically informed, others choose to remain uninformed, acting as price takers in the market, and still others choose to follow a mixed strategy. Let us assume that unsophisticated investors are likely to be uninformed (or underinformed), either because they have undertaken no (or too little) securities research or because they are unable accurately to process information if received. The uninformed investors will pay too high a price only if the market is not efficient, that is only if there are too few sophisticated market participants who choose to become specifically informed. It therefore seems unlikely that investors who buy shares in secondary market trading on the highly efficient national securities markets could be systematically victimized by unexpected charter terms."

Does the noise trading approach, discussed supra pp. 136–143, give rise to a contrary implication—that investors are hopelessly naive and need constant regulatory protection? According to Shliefer and Summers, supra at 30: "Investors who trade on noise or on popular models are worse off than they would be if their expectations were rational * * *." Should we legislate to protect noise traders from themselves? What would such a regulatory regime look like? Does the case resemble, as Shliefer and Summers suggest, the case for prohibiting casinos, horse races and state lotteries? Or, are there significant differences between the securities markets, on the one hand, and casinos and race tracks, on the other, that are relevant to the selection of the appropriate regulatory regime?

(2) *Informational Model.*

Even if market processes adequately protect small, uninformed investors, it does not follow that a mandatory disclosure system is unnecessary. It still may be needed to backstop the protective "market processes." Indeed, the more stress placed on the efficient markets point, the stronger the inference that all securities market participants rely on high quality disclosure by market participants and that the mandatory system enhances market efficiency.

But an economic case that supplements this "market reliance" justification of mandatory disclosure has been articulated. As the following commentary shows, this argument draws heavily on the "agency" theory of corporate organization.

EASTERBROOK AND FISCHEL, MANDATORY DISCLOSURE AND THE PROTECTION OF INVESTORS

70 Virginia Law Review 669 (1984).
680–687, 696–699.

* * *

II. Mandatory Disclosure

A. *Disclosure and the Public Goods Aspect of Information*

In a world with an anti-fraud rule but no mandatory disclosure system, firms could remain silent with impunity.[18] If they disclosed, they could do so in any way they wished, provided they did not lie. They could attempt to sell securities with ads in glossy magazines and on television featuring sexy models or herds of bulls, as sellers of other products (including brokerage services) do.

A mandatory disclosure system substantially limits firms' ability to remain silent. Just as importantly, it controls the time, place, and manner of disclosure.

* * *

What does a mandatory disclosure system add to the prohibition of fraud? The implicit public-interest justification for disclosure rules is that markets produce "too little" information about securities when the only rule is one against fraud. One often hears the assertion that information is a "public good," meaning that it can be used without being used up and that the producer of information cannot exclude others from receiving the benefits. If the producer of information cannot obtain all of its value, too little will be produced. It seems to follow that there are virtues in a rule requiring production of all information that would be forthcoming were gains fully appropriable.

This rationale gets us only so far. For one thing, it proves too much. No one can fully appropriate the value of information about

---

18. This is something of an overstatement, because the distinction between failure to inform and misrepresentation is not always clear. Failure to speak may be viewed as an implied representation that "nothing has changed." The securities laws recognize this by penalizing the omission of material facts necessary to make the actual disclosures not misleading.

toothpaste, but there is no federal rule about disclosing the efficacy of toothpaste in preventing cavities. Why are securities different? We leave the other products to competitive markets because of a conclusion that people who make or use a product (or test it as Consumers' Union does) will obtain enough of the gains from information to make the markets reasonably efficient.

Similarly, those who learn about a security may profit from their information. They cannot obtain all of the benefits, because others in the market will infer the news, and the price of the securities will adjust. The new price will "contain" the news, preventing the person who first learned it from taking further gains. This also means, however, that the value of news decays very quickly in securities markets; the information is "used up" as subsequent people see things, and these people then have their own incentives to go out and find information.

The more sophisticated version of the public goods explanation is that although investors produce information, they produce both too much and too little. They produce too little because the benefits are imperfectly appropriable. If information is worth one hundred dollars to investors as a group, but no one can capture more than ten dollars of gains, then no one will obtain more than ten dollars worth of information. Investors produce too much information, though, if several create because investors always assume the worst. It must disclose the bad with the good, lest investors assume that the bad is even worse than it is. And the firm cannot stand on its say-so alone. Mere disclosure would be enough if the rule against fraud were perfectly enforced, but it is not. Thus the firm uses * * * verification and certification devices* * * *. Given these devices, a rule compelling disclosure seems redundant, and if the fraud penalty and verification devices do not work, a rule compelling disclosure is not apt to be enforceable either.

The principle of self-induced disclosure as a solution to the lack of property rights in information applies to trading in the secondary market as well as to the initial issuance of stock. The firm's investors always want to be able to sell their stock in the aftermarket for the highest price. Their ability to do so depends on a flow of believable information (otherwise potential buyers reduce the bid prices, assuming the worst). For most information about a firm, the firm itself can create and distribute the knowledge at less cost than the shareholders, and the firm's decision, because it reflects the value to all shareholders, will be correct at the margin. A firm that wants the highest possible price when it issues stock must take all cost-justified steps to make the stock valuable in the aftermarket, so it must make a believable pledge to continue disclosing.

     * * *

---

* [Ed. Note] E.g., independent auditors,   underwriters, stock options to executives.

Disclosure for the purpose of stilling investors' doubts also reduces (to the appropriate degree) investors' incentives to search too much for trading information. The problem, as we described it above, is that knowing the future creates profit opportunities without making investors as a group better off. Because searching out such information is costly, investors as a group gain if firms disclose so as to minimize the opportunities and thus the incentives to search. The net return on a security is its gross return (dividends plus any liquidating distribution) less the cost of information and transactions in holding the security. A firm can increase this net return as easily by reducing the cost of holding the stock as well as by increasing its business profits. Firms that promise to make disclosures for this purpose will prosper relative to others, because their investors incur relatively lower costs and can be more passive with safety. The more convincing the promise, the more investors will pay for the stock.

B. *Limitations on the Self–Interest Model of Disclosure*

That information is a "public good" means that investors acting independently do the wrong amount of information-gathering, but for reasons we have explained, the self-interest of firms' managers lead them to supply roughly the amount of information investors as a group desire. This amount is "rough," however, because of the certification and verification costs in the supply of information. If disclosure rules, like fraud rules, could reduce the costs, then firms' disclosure would be improved. * * * There is one other reason why firms' disclosures may not be optimal: third party effects.

The information produced by one firm for its investors may be valuable to investors in other firms. Firm A's statements may reveal something about the industry in which Firm A operates—if only the size of Firm A's anticipated production—that other participants in the industry can use in planning their own operations. There may be other collateral benefits to investors in rival firms. Yet Firm A cannot charge the investors in these other firms for the benefits, although they would be willing to pay for them. Because they cannot be charged, the information will be underproduced.

The problem is related to the prisoners' dilemma. The firms and investors, acting as a group, would want the firms to disclose information with both firm and industry-specific components. Each firm acting individually will not do so, in part because the others would get a free ride and in part because some of the information (such as that pertaining to new products) may give a competitive advantage to rivals. Each firm would be willing to disclose, but only if all others were required to do likewise. Then the costs and any business risks would be distributed more evenly. In the absence of some requirement or strong inducement to disclose, each firm will want to be a holdout.

There is a similar free riding problem in the disclosure of information that facilitates comparisons among firms. Firm C may know something that makes it attractive relative to D. It cannot convey this information effectively, however, without conveying information about D's plans and prospects. The information about D will redound partly to the benefit of present or prospective investors in D, and Firm C cannot obtain compensation. Firm C could appropriate part of the gain by buying or selling D's stock, but this is a costly transaction, and Firm C could not appropriate the full gain without owning D, E, F, G, and so on, outright. An increase in the size of firms to allow greater internalization of information has other costs, including monopoly and a reduction in investors' ability to diversify their holdings.

Firm C also encounters difficulty in appropriating the value of information affecting risk-return characteristics. The less the degree of difference among firms, the more spillover the disclosures of one firm will have, and the poorer this firm's incentives to disclose. Many firms will have similar risk-return characteristics. Some form of collective action (whether or not through the government) could be beneficial in principle here. Which method of tackling the collective action problem has the lowest net costs is an empirical problem.

Or suppose there is an optimal format for communicating information to investors. Some disclosures are easier to understand, verify, etc., than others, while some disclosures tend more to hide than to reveal information. If contracts among all investors in society could be written costlessly, the investors would require all firms to identify and use the optimal format of disclosure. The costs may be too high, though, for one firm acting on its own. The optimal form of disclosure may entail use of some specialized language (one can think of accounting principles, with their detailed definitions, as a specialized disclosure language), yet no one firm can obtain a large share of the benefits of inventing and employing this language; others will be able to use the format without charge. Sometimes, too, the case of using a given method of disclosure will depend on other firms adopting the same format, so as to facilitate comparisons across investments. Other firms may not be anxious to cooperate.

Mandatory disclosure rules promulgated by the government are one means to achieve standardization, but it does not follow that mandatory disclosure is necessary. Markets frequently devise ingenious solutions to problems of information. Indeed, the problems faced by sellers of securities are not much different from those involved in bringing new products to market. Mass sale of records and stereo systems was facilitated by the development of standard record speeds. Color television was not feasible until manufacturers and broadcasters agreed on a standard method of transmission. The new laser compact disk players are greatly aided in competing against tapes and records by the standard promulgated by Phillips, the holder of an important patent. Sometimes trade associations may devise such standards, as the electronics industry and, in part, the accounting industry have done. Whether standardization may be achieved more cheaply by private or governmental responses is an empirical question.

* * *

III. The Disclosure Rules as a Response to Third Party Effects, Legal Error, and Rent Seeking

Although the rationales usually advanced for the disclosure provisions of the securities acts are unconvincing,* we believe that there is a more plausible line of argument, which (to our knowledge) has not previously been advanced. We sketch this argument below.

* * *

1. *Controlling Third–Party Effects*

We discussed in Part II.B. three reasons why the self-interest model of disclosure might not lead to optimal release of information: (1) some data would concern the industry as well as the firm, and firms would underproduce this data both because they could not charge for benefits conferred on others and because they would want to learn the plans of others without disclosing their own; (2) comparative data would be underproduced because of the inability to charge for it; (3) no firm would have the appropriate incentives to create the least-cost formula for disclosure. We discussed private and state methods by which these may be addressed, but the solutions will be incomplete (at least when compared with a world of no transactions costs). Private organizations cannot compel adherence, so there will be holdout problems. Competition among the states cannot obtain all benefits because of the interstate nature of some of these effects; if being a holdout is in the interest of some firms, it could pay states to be havens to the holdouts.

* * *

V. Conclusion

A variety of private and public responses to the problem of asymetric information establish powerful incentives for firms to disclose what investors want to know. Mandatory national disclosure legislation may well improve the incentives, but if it does this the improvement comes about for reasons other than a need to deal with fraud or any systematic tendency to hide.

* * *

* * * No satisfactory data suggest that the SEC's rules are beneficial. Perhaps problems in implementation prevent realization of whatever savings are available in principle. There is less reason to regulate securities than, say, the funeral industry, which also lacks standardized transactions and in which shopping by informed traders may not lead

---

* [Ed. Note] The authors reject the notions that mandatory disclosure increases public confidence in the markets or protects unsophisticated investors or increases the supply of truthful information sufficiently to be worth their costs.

to efficient prices. We have not constructed a compelling case for regulation of any sort, let alone for the particular regulations the SEC uses.

There is nonetheless a case for mandatory disclosure, and it is a far different case from that usually advanced by those who endorse the securities laws. Our approach suggests that the telling blows that can be struck against the usual case are not fatal.

NOTES

1. How do the assumptions undergirding traditional justifications of the mandatory disclosure system differ from the assumptions undergirding Easterbrook and Fischel's more equivocal evaluation? Which approach draws on the more plausible picture of the operations of the securities markets and the behavior of investors and insiders?

Note the assertion, critical to Easterbrook and Fischel's analysis, that market forces will induce the self-serving securities issuer to disclose bad news as well as good—because investors always assume the worst. With this vision of the rational actor's self-protective skepticism, compare the following description from the March 22, 1844 number of the London *Times:* [b]

> "The merchant, the humbler tradesman, the small shopkeeper, and the servant—these are the people whose little all is sacrificed to the impudent impostures of our modern joint stock companies. * * * A system of falsehood marks them from the moment of their birth. They are born and cradled in falsehood. To give them an introduction into society, they are fathered upon unconscious peers and non-existent commoners. By the aid of a Blue Book, some dozen merchants and lawyers are appended to the senatorial list, and when this has been done, a miscellaneous body of Tomkinses and Jenkinses is tacked on, in order that no plebeian idealist may be deterred from taking a share by the array of noble names. * * *
>
> " * * * Then do imaginary dividends dance before the gloating eyes—then do gratuitous mines of copper and tin open in soils unconscious of a grain of ore;—then does one hundred per cent arise from ideal slate quarries, or visionary canals;— then do streams of wealth irrigate the long sterility of Irish bogs, and every miracle is born which avarice can beget upon credulity. Then are the hoardings of years and the pittances

b. *As quoted by* Hunt, B.C., The Development of the Business Corporation in England, 1800–1867, Cambridge, Mass. (Harvard) 1936, pp. 90–92.

of poverty carried to the bourne from which they never can return."

The Easterbrook and Fischel picture of a securities offering differs from this Victorian picture because Easterbrook and Fischel, like the proponents of the intrinsic value version of the EMH, assume the presence of rational actors who act only on the basis of information on fundamental value. Those taking a traditional approach assume that market participants are as likely to trade securities in a posture of hopeful ignorance as in one of self-protected rationality.

How would a proponent of the "noise trading" approach to finance, discussed supra pp. 136–143 react to the traditional justifications for the mandatory disclosure system?

2. Loss and Seligman argue that the management incentive picture set out by Easterbrook and Fischel " * * * helps explain why firms might voluntarily disclose information material to investors. However * * * it is not sufficiently consistent with available empirical evidence to be regarded as wholly satisfactory. Among other points, it does not account for the incidence of securities fraud throughout this century, or explain why the incidence of securities fraud seems to increase dramatically during certain periods. It does not adequately explain why small firms not subject to the SEC's mandatory corporate disclosure system seem to have been responsible for a majority of the fraud cases brought by the Commission. Nor does it adequately explain why so many firms have employed practices such as 'income smoothing' to obscure bad economic news." L. Loss and J. Seligman, 1 Securities Regulation 191–192 (1989).

3. Compare the comments of Coffee, "Market Failure and the Economic Case for a Mandatory Disclosure System," 70 Va.L.Rev. 717, 722–723 (1984):

"[B]ecause information has many characteristics of a public good, securities research tends to be underprovided. This underprovision means both that information provided by corporate issuers will not be optimally verified and that insufficient efforts will be made to search for material information from non-issuer sources. A mandatory disclosure system can thus be seen as a desirable cost reduction strategy through which society, in effect, subsidizes search costs to secure both a greater quantity of information and a better testing of its accuracy. Although the end result of such increased efforts may not significantly affect the balance of advantage between buyers and sellers, or even the more general goal of distributive fairness, it does improve the allocative efficiency of the capital market—and this improvement in turn implies a more productive economy.

        *   *   *

"[T]he theory of self-induced disclosure, now popular among theorists of the firm and relied upon by Professors Easterbrook and Fischel, has only a limited validity. A particular flaw in this theory is that it overlooks the significance of corporate control transactions and assumes much too facilely that manager and shareholder interests can be perfectly aligned. In fact, the very preconditions specified by these theorists as being necessary for an effective voluntary disclosure system do not seem to be satisfied. Although management can be induced through incentive contracting devices to identify its self-interest with the maximization of share value, it will still have an interest in acquiring the shareholders' ownership at a discounted price, at least so long as it can engage in insider trading or leveraged buyouts. Because the incentives for both seem likely to remain strong, instances will arise in which management can profit by giving a false signal to the market."

4. Professor Ian Ayres offers still another approach. He places the whole matter into a hypothetical contract model and makes disclosure rules gap-fillers, subject to opting out by particular corporations in their certificates of incorporation. Thus he supports disclosure rules but not strictly *mandatory* disclosure rules. As between a default rule of no disclosure and a default rule pursuant to which corporations warrant truthful statements, he posits that the latter would be the less costly. Ayres, Back to *Basics:* Regulating How Corporations Speak to the Market, 77 Va.L.Rev. 945, 952–53 (1991).

5. Is the foregoing commentary of academic interest only? When, if ever, would facility with this sort of discussion, be useful to a securities lawyer?

APPENDIX C

ADDITIONAL MATERIALS ON DEBT SECURITIES

SECTION 1. MARKET INSTABILITY AND INNOVATION

Historically, most debt was issued and sold in a primary market. The prevailing philosophy was "buy and hold." Most bonds were held to maturity; interim sales occurred only occasionally. Bond buyers looked only for maximum yields within "acceptable" quality ranges. See Leibowitz, The Bond Investing Environment, in Cottle, Murray & Block, Graham and Dodd's Security Analysis 403–407 (5th ed. 1988). Economic changes after 1970 disrupted this pattern. The greatest shock came from the high inflation of the 1970s and early 1980s. Its effect on those following the traditional buy and hold strategy was discussed in the following excerpts from Van Horne, Financial Management and Policy (6th Ed.1983), pp. 507–509, 513–515:

"*Anticipated* (or expected) inflation is presently recognized by financial market participants and embodied in expected security returns. In this regard, we assume that a single index effectively portrays the general price level at various moments in time. The anticipated rate of inflation is defined in terms of the expected annual rate of change in this index. If the inflation that actually occurs over the life of a security is exactly that which was anticipated when its terms were set, neither borrowers nor lenders gain (or lose) because of inflation. Lenders receive the real returns they expected when they made loans, and borrowers pay the real returns they expected to pay.

"An *unanticipated* (or unexpected) change in inflation is an unforeseen change in the rate of expected inflation. If the present rate of inflation is 8 percent, and it shifts upward to 11 percent in a way that market participants did not anticipate, we would say that there was a 3 percent unanticipated increase in inflation.

* * *

"In perhaps the most extensive study of actual nominal and real returns, Roger G. Ibbotson and Rex A. Sinquefield analyzed Treasury bills, long-term government bonds, long-term corporate bonds, and common stocks over the 1926–78 period.[7] The authors found that over the entire period, Treasury bills provided a zero real return. In other words, on average the nominal return matched inflation. Of course, for

7. Stocks, Bonds, Bills, and Inflation (Charlottesville, Va.: Financial Analysts Research Foundation, 1979).

C–1

the taxable investor, the real after-tax return was negative. Other real before-tax returns were positive, and the overall results were

	Inflation adjusted average return (before tax)	Standard deviation of nominal returns
Treasury bills	0.0%	2.2%
Long-term government bonds	0.6	5.7
Long-term corporate bonds	1.3	5.6
Common stocks	6.1	22.2

Year-to-year and month-to-month differences in real and nominal returns occurred. As evidenced by the standard deviation column, the fluctuations were smallest for Treasury bills and largest for common stocks, all of which is in keeping with the notion of risk and return.

* * *

"The high and unstable inflation in the 1970s and early 1980s was unsettling to financial markets. During 1980, there was almost a 10 percent decline in short-term interest rates from March to June and over a 10 percent rise from July to December. Financial institutions that make fixed-rate, long-term loans are unable to live with such volatility. On the one hand, their return on assets is locked in, while usually their cost of funds is more directly related to current interest rates in the market. This relationship is due to liabilities being of typically shorter maturity than that of assets. With unanticipated increases in inflation, nominal rates of interest for all maturities rise; and those who "lend long and borrow short" are hurt.

* * *

"This phenomenon, coupled with considerable uncertainty, was untenable for many financial institutions. Having little control over their costs of funds during the life of the loan, they could no longer afford to make fixed-rate, long-term loans. Many came to the conclusion that they had to adapt and learn to live with variability. One means for doing so was to shorten the maturity of loans to conform more nearly with the maturity structure of their liabilities."

Inflation was not the only cause of changes in the debt markets during the past two decades. We can note, among other things, the growth of the federal deficit, which, in turn, caused substantial growth in the treasury securities market. In addition, both the credit and capital markets have became internationalized. And, as always, some transaction forms have come and gone as the tax laws have changed.

The attitudes and practices of financial institutions also have been reshaped by deregulation of interest rates within the financial system. This has resulted in increased competition. During the 1980s, institutions such as banks and insurance companies were thus forced to offer higher returns to investors. Their demand for investments offering higher returns intensified accordingly. In line with this, bond portfolio management became a more active endeavor—many institutions that once had been primary debt investors became wholesalers and repackagers of debt securities. At the same time, negative attitudes of debt issuers toward financial leverage began to change. Issuers also ceased the conservative practice of linking capital investment lifetimes to the maturity of the debt used to fund the projects. See Liebowitz, supra at 408.

The 1980s began with primary debt markets and conservative attitudes. They ended with a mix of primary and trading markets, and a range of risk strategies. The appearance of the junk bond market figured prominently in the new picture. Many other innovations also played a part. A short list follows.

1. *Floating Rate Debt.*

A floating interest rate reduces the risk of interest rate volatility. Such a rate is adjusted periodically to keep current with changes in the lender's short term cost of funds. Coupon payments are determined as a function of the value of a stated interest rate index, such as the Treasury bill interest rate or 30–year treasury bond rate, at the time the payment is due. The floating rate also usually is subject to a floor or a ceiling. There are many variations on the theme. See Van Horne, Financial Management and Policy 559, 569–570 (9th ed. 1992).

2. *Interest Rate Swaps.*

Liebowitz, supra at 434–35 describes these:

"Another phenomenon of the 1980s has been the quiet marketplace explosion of interest rate swaps. An interest rate swap is basically a contract in which one party agrees to pay a series of fixed-rate coupon payments in exchange for the receipt of floating-rate coupon payments from a second party. There is no exchange of principal payments. Thus, in an interest rate swap, an investor who holds a fixed-rate instrument can agree to swap its coupon flows for the flows that would be received from a floating-rate instrument.

"Interest rate swaps can be used either for investors such as thrifts and insurance companies (asset-based swaps) or for issuers (liability-based swaps). Interest rate swaps can be struck across many maturities and with a wide range of counterparties. They are powerful weapons in the battle for greater flexibility for both investors and issuers, and they have a very wide range of applications: The swap market grew from a standing start in 1982 to over $200 billion by 1986!

"Issuers can use interest rate swaps to achieve important savings in financing costs. For example, suppose a given issuer wishes to obtain floating-rate financing, but the issuer represents a more attractive credit to investors as a long-term issuer in certain markets. The issuer can proceed to issue long-term debt at the preferential rates, then execute an interest rate swap with a counterparty into a more attractive floating-rate exposure than could have been obtained by going directly to the floating-rate market. As another example of a liability-based application, suppose an issuer of outstanding long-term debt feels that rates may be heading lower. Participation in that decline can be achieved by swapping the currently outstanding long-term payments for floating-rate payments.

"On the investment side, interest rate swaps can be used to transform the cash flow of a fixed-payment portfolio to that of a floating-rate portfolio or vice-versa. Moreover, since the floating rate component acts as a proxy for future short-term rates, the floating-rate side can be used as a hedge against arbitrage financing costs or against the costs of future cash borrowings. By entering into an interest rate swap that substitutes floating-rate payments for a series of fixed payments, investors also significantly lower the duration of an existing component of their portfolios. Note that interest rate swaps can often have accounting advantages. For example, by acting as a counterhedge to an existing investment position, swaps can reduce the interest rate exposure of existing bond holdings. The use of swaps can materially alter the interest rate sensitivity and cash flow characteristics of a portfolio without incurring the adverse tax and accounting consequences of an outright sale.

"In today's world, the drive for flexibility has become paramount, and the interest rate swap is indeed a powerful tool. From this brief sampling of its many applications, one can see why the interest rate swap market has so quickly grown to its current size.

"The corporate borrower who issues floating-rate obligations or engages in interest rate swaps makes life difficult for the security analyst seeking to project borrowing costs. There is no practical alternative to selecting some arbitrary but reasonable average rate."

3. *Futures and Options.*

Bond market participants now use interest rate futures as hedging devices. A financial institution establishes a futures position so that movements in the value of the position offset the movements of either the securities it holds outright or the movements of the financial liabilities it has outstanding. The hedge protects the institution against changes in interest rates. Van Horne, Financial Management and Policy 591–593 (9th ed. 1992).

The Chicago Mercantile Exchange and Chicago Board of Trade introduced the first treasury bill futures contract in the late 1970s. This became the most successful contract in the history of exchange-traded futures. Futures contracts in certificates of deposit, treasury notes, treasury bonds, municipals and other financial instruments now are available. Options on treasury bond futures were introduced in 1982. These protect investors who want to lock in a current interest rate for a span of time and are willing to pay a premium for the privilege. See Liebowitz, The Bonds Investing Environment, supra at 431–432.

4. *Zero Coupon Bonds.*

These are bonds that pay a lump sum at maturity and no interest at all. They therefore are offered at very deep discounts. "Original issue discount bonds," are similar. These bonds are issued at a very low rate of interest and hence also sell at a deep discount at original issue.

A flurry of zero coupon issues appeared in 1981 due to a mistake in tax treatment by the Internal Revenue Service. The Service recognized that the issuer of such a bond incurs an imputed interest cost, and should be able to deduct a portion of the original issue discount each year of the life of the bond as the functional equivalent of interest. But the IRS used simple rather than compound interest in setting the imputed rate for deduction purposes. The issuer thus deducted a level amount during the life of the issue—the discount divided by the number of years. Meanwhile, the bond's path of appreciation was, in the early years of its life, lower per year than the amount of the interest being deducted. The IRS straightened this out in 1982, removing the issuer's tax incentive. Brealey & Myers, Principles of Corporate Finanace 607 (4th ed. 1991). Thereafter, corporate zeroes continued to be issued, but at a slower rate. Attention turned to the treasury markets. According to Liebowitz, supra, at 433–434:

"Since the zero-coupon bond provided no interim payments until maturity, the credit of the issuing entity was emphasized. This naturally led to a strong interest in obtaining zero-coupon instruments based on U.S. Treasury securities. By "stripping" the coupons from a U.S. Treasury bond, one could obtain individual coupon payments (and of course one maturity payment) that would act as such single-payment instruments. These so called "stripped treasuries" were available from time to time, but the supply was limited because U.S. Treasury regulations discouraged their formation.

"In 1982, in conjunction with changes in tax rules that rationalized their tax treatment, the U.S. Treasury lifted these restrictions. Investment dealers immediately began to create various forms of single-payment instruments derived from stripped Treasury bonds. These instruments were immensely popular, and large proportions of certain Treasury issues were transformed into these specialized securities. These instruments were given an amusing set of acronyms, all depicting different species of the feline family: *TIGERS* (Treasury Investment Grade Receipts), *CATS* (Certificates of Accrual for Treasury Securities), etc. These new securities developed into a relatively liquid market with pure single-payment instruments that spanned the entire yield curve. At long last, the academic's dream of having market-determined discount rates for virtually every point in the future was now at hand (subject to a few mild distortions that always seem inevitable in any real capital market). Any fixed income security could—in theory—be decomposed into its individual cash flows, and then these flows could be valued relative to the corresponding maturity point on the "spot rate" yield curve.

"In practice, these single-payment vehicles were used in a host of applications in the new high interest rate environment. For the investor who wished to lock up yield over a specified period, they provided the ideal vehicle. For the rate-of-return investor who wished to obtain a precise duration instrument, these single-payment bonds provided the answer. For the dedicated portfolio that needed to fit additional dollar flows into precise periods in the future, the single-payment bond was the perfect 'plug.'

"The various packagers of such securities waged a considerable battle until the U.S. Treasury decided to get directly into the act in 1985. * * * In essence, the U.S. government would perform the role of stripping dealer by dismembering a Treasury security into its component cash flows and registering each of the components separately. This "strips" market continued to flourish on this new basis until the appetite for single-payment instruments abated during the lower interest rate periods that followed the great rallies of 1984 and 1985 to 1986."

5. Junk Bonds.

The rise and fall of the junk bond market is the great financial story of the 1980s. It has been chronicled in popular form more than once. See, e.g., Anders, KKR and the Mortgaging of American Business (1992); Bruck, The Predators' Ball: The Junk Bond Raiders and the Man Who Stalked Them (1988). The following summary of events from Ross, Westerfield and Jordan, Fundamentals of Corporate Finance 374 (1991), was contributed by Professor Edward I. Altman, a leading financial academic writer on the subject of debt:

> One of the most important developments in corporate finance over the last decade has been the re-emergence of publicly owned and traded low-rated corporate debt. Originally offered to the public in the early 1900s to help finance some of our emerging growth industries, these high yield/high risk bonds virtually disappeared after the rash of bond defaults during the depression. In the last 12 years, however, the junk bond market has been catapulted from an insignificant element in the corporate fixed income market to one of the fastest growing and most controversial types of financing mechanisms.
>
> The term *junk* emanates from the dominant type of low-rated bond issues outstanding prior to 1977 when the "market" consisted

almost exclusively of original issue investment grade bonds that fell from their lofty status to a higher default risk, speculative grade level. These so-called "fallen angels" amounted to about $8.5 billion in 1977. At the beginning of 1990, fallen angels comprised about 20 percent of the $200 billion publicly owned junk bond market.

Beginning in 1977, issuers began to go directly to the public to raise capital for growth purposes. Early users of junk bonds were energy-related firms, cable TV companies, airlines, and assorted other industrial companies. This type of financing is a form of securitization of what heretofore was the sole province of private placements financed by banks and insurance companies. The emerging growth company rationale coupled with relatively high returns to early investors helped legitimize this sector. Most investment banks ignored junk bonds until 1983–1984, when their merits and profit potential became more evident.

Synonymous with the market's growth was the emergence of the investment banking firm, Drexel Burnham Lambert, and its junk bond wizard, Michael Milken. Drexel established a potent network of issuers and investors and rode the wave of new financing and the consequent surge in secondary trading to become one of the powerful investment banks in the late 1980s. The incredible rise in power of this firm was followed by an equally incredible fall resulting first in a government civil indictment and huge fine for various misdealings and finally the firm's total collapse and bankruptcy in February 1990. In April 1990, Milken pleaded guilty to various violations of the securities law.

By far the most important and controversial aspect of junk bond financing was its role in the corporate restructuring movement from 1985–1989. High leverage transactions and acquisitions, such as leveraged buyouts (LBOs), which occur when a firm is taken private, and leveraged recapitalizations (debt for equity swaps) transformed the face of corporate America leading to a heated debate as to the economic and social consequences of firms being transformed from public to private enterprises with debt/equity ratios of at least 6:1.

These transactions involved increasingly large companies and the multibillion dollar takeover became fairly common, finally capped by the huge $25+ billion RJR Nabisco LBO in 1989. LBOs were typically financed with about 60 percent senior bank debt, about 25–30 percent subordinated public debt (junk bonds) and 10–15 percent equity. The junk bond segment is sometimes referred to as "mezzanine" financing because it lies between the "balcony" senior debt and the "basement" equity.

These restructurings resulted in huge fees to advisors and underwriters and huge premiums to the old shareholders who were bought out, and they continued as long as the market was willing to buy these new debt offerings at what appeared to be a favorable risk/return tradeoff. The bottom fell out of the market in the last six months of 1989 due to a number of factors including a marked increase in defaults, government regulation against S & Ls holding junk bonds, fears of higher interest rates and a recession, and, finally, the growing realization of the leverage excesses of certain ill-conceived restructurings. The default rate in 1989 jumped from about 2 percent to 4 percent, involving over $8 billion of debt. The pendulum of growth and returns swung dramatically in the opposite direction as junk bond prices plummeted, yields skyrocketed, and new issues dried up. The leverage boom of the 1980s appeared to be over.

Will the junk bond market survive? Yes, it probably will, but the growth will almost certainly slow dramatically, and the new offerings will revert back to more soundly financed capital structures. Restructurings will also continue with the mezzanine debt increasingly of the private placement variety.

Studies of junk bond default rates have reached a series of different conclusions that track the rise and fall of the market. A famous mid–1980s study sponsored by Drexel Burnham Lambert compared bonds in default to the total amount of junk bonds outstanding and found a default rate of 2 percent for the years 1970 through 1985. But it was later pointed out that the steady 2 percent rate was due primarily to constant increases in the number of junk bonds outstanding. See Henriques, "Debunking the 'Junk Bomb' Theory," New York Times, March 22, 1992, p. D15. A later study, covering junk bonds issued between 1977 and 1982 found that almost one third had defaulted by the end of 1988. Asquith, Mullins & Wolff, Original Issue High Yield Bonds: Aging Analysis of Defaults, Exchanges and Calls, 44 J. Finance 923 (1989). See also Altman, Measuring Corporate Bond Mortality and Performance, 44 J. Finance 909 (1989). These studies gave rise to the "time bomb" theory of default: the default rate inevitably would escalate each year. In 1991, the rule of thumb was that 10 to 15 percent of outstanding junk bonds could be expected to default in a given year. The Economist, Oct. 5, 1991, p. 103. A less alarming theory of junk bond default rates accompanied a recovery in the junk bond market in 1992. Under the new view, the junk default curve is bell-shaped, and given the fall off in new junk issues after 1988, the worst was over by 1992. See Henriques, supra.

A report published by Lipper Analytical Services compared the performance of junk bonds with those of other investments for the ten years ended September 30, 1990. According to the report, money invested in junk bonds during the period would have returned 145%, where stocks would have returned 207%, rated corporates 202% and treasury bonds 177%.

Junk bonds still have their defenders. Rosengren, The Case for Junk Bonds, N.E.Econ.Rev., May/June 1990, p. 40, restates the case for junk bonds as a low cost alternative to bank loans for smaller firms.

6. *Pay-in-Kind Bonds.*

These "PIKs" make regular interest payments, but in the earlier years of the bond's life the issuer can choose to make the payment in either cash or more bonds with the equivalent face value. These bonds were widely employed in the high leverage restructurings of the 1980s, and were created to deal with projections that the cash flows of the restructured firm would not be sufficient to meet debt interest charges during the first period after closing. They gave the issuer a valuable source of flexibility in a distress situation, but amounted to very speculative pieces of paper. See Goodman & Cohen, Pay–In–Kind Debentures: An Innovation, J. Portfolio Management, Winter 1989, p. 9; Brealey & Myers, Principles of Corporate Finance 604–605 (4th ed. 1991).[a]

SECTION 2. THE LEVERAGED RESTRUCTURINGS OF THE 1980s

There follows a description of leveraged buyout activity at the crest of the 1980s' wave of restructurings, from Leveraged Buyouts and the Pot of Gold: Trends, Public Policy, and Case Studies, A Report Prepared by the Economics Division of the Congressional Research Service pp. 5–7 (1987):

1. *Types of Leveraged Buyout Transactions*

There are numerous variations on the basic leveraged buyout format, which generally involves the purchase of assets of a company or subsidiary with borrowed funds, using the assets of that acquired company or subsidiary as collateral for the loan. The major types of leveraged buyout transactions generally involve either: (1) large public corporations; (2) divestitures or spinoffs of divisions of public or private companies; or (3) closely held private companies.

When a company undergoes a leveraged buyout, its purchaser uses mostly debt and little or no equity capital. Often, when a publicly owned firm is involved, the public stockholders are bought out, and the company is "taken private." This creates a large scale substitution of debt for equity. It is frequently intended that this

a. Liquid Yield Option Notes, or "LYONs" are another innovative debt security issued in recent years. They are a callable, putable, convertible, retractable, zero coupon note created by the Merrill Lynch firm. See McConnell & Schwartz, Taming LYONS, 41 J. Finance 561 (1986).

debt be retired in a few years. This may be accomplished either by applying the cash flow of the operations of the company or, as is increasingly common, through the sale of company assets.

When management is either exclusively or substantially involved as the purchaser in any of these three types of deals, the deal is generally referred to as a *management buyout* (MBO), a subset of the generic *leveraged buyout* (LBO) transaction. Management may join with pools of investors, banks and/or insurance companies to lend money for the transaction.

A relatively new phenomenon is the *non-management involved LBO deal* which can result from a hostile attempt to take over a publicly-traded target company. In this case, management is not part of the buyout group.

When the entire outstanding stock of a publicly traded company is repurchased by management, by an outside group of investors, or by some combination of both, so that ownership is no longer public, the transaction is referred to as a *going-private deal. In some cases not all the stock is repurchased and a stub* of shares may continue to trade.

Another subset of leveraged and/or management buyout transactions involves *divestitures* of subsidiaries or portions of a company. Divestitures involve the outright sale of the assets to management or an investing group. These may be contrasted with *spin-offs* which are internalized divestitures where a subsidiary is set up and ownership shares are issued to the original stockholders.

In a recent wave of *"reverse" LBO deals,* corporations have come full circle. Thus, some companies which have been taken private in LBO/MBO transactions are now *going public* again, with their shares being sold in a new public offering to shareholders.

2. *Principal Features of Current LBO's— The "Liquefying" of America*

The size and character of the leveraged buyout market has changed dramatically within the past few years. Leveraged buyout transactions have grown explosively and are now counted among the country's top "megadeal" merger transactions. In 1984, former Securities and Exchange Commission Chairman, John Shad, warned of the consequences of the "leveraging" of America. Now, however, there is not only rapid growth in LBO's, but rapid cycling of assets sold to retire LBO debt. This has resulted in an unprecedented liquidity of corporate plant and equipment assets in the post-War era. In view of this trend, one might update Shad's "leveraging" of America and instead refer now to the "liquefying" of America.

The 1987 LBO market is considerably different from its early stages. Prior to about 1984, small and medium sized companies went private with the expectation that solid cash flow from continuing manager-owned operations would repay initial debt in about 5 years. After retiring this debt, a company could be taken public again, and the resultant influx of cash from the sale of stock to the public would afford the principals a solid, but not necessarily exorbitant, profit.

In the past 3 years, however, there has been an explosion in LBO's, fueled by several factors. First, there has been a rapid cycling of reverse LBO's, whereby a company taken private is taken public again, well before the traditional 5-year debt retirement period. This has enabled investors to reap unprecedented profits, in turn attracting a battery of financial participants ready to pay increasingly higher prices for LBO candidates. Formerly, the banks were the principal providers of funds, but investment bankers have entered the market in a large scale, not only by directing the proceeds of large quantities of high yield "junk" bond offerings to this market, but also by taking equity positions themselves.

In addition, pools of LBO investors, including large pension funds, have provided unprecedented liquidity to the market, spurring on larger and larger deals in an increasingly hostile atmosphere. Finally, the size of transactions and level of debt have increased to such an extent that cash flow alone is rarely enough to retire the debt. Thus, it has become virtually certain that assets will have to be sold to repay the debt, a generally profitable undertaking for the investors, but with more uncertain advantages for the economy at large. This whole process has produced a "liquefying" of the asset base for corporate plant and equipment, essentially changing the nature of modern corporate America.

* * * In comparison to the LBO deals prior to about 1984, the current LBO transactions generally have the following characteristics. They:

—Are often bigger and more complex;

—Involve more liquid financing not merely through banks but by investment bankers who use "highly confident letters," and commit an increasingly large amount of equity or "bridge" capital themselves;

—Depend on pools of capital from LBO funds and from an increasingly large and highly liquid network of insurance companies and pension fund investors;

—Depend on larger amounts of lower quality debt, frequently with debt of such low quality as to carry deferred interest payments (and, because of the increased liquidity in the market, even these lowest quality debt instruments can be floated or refinanced);

—Are more often rapidly done restructurings or "white knight" deals done either in anticipation of, or to ward off, a hostile takeover situation;

—May involve groups other than management, such as employee stock ownerships plans (ESOP's) or third party investment firms;

—Cannot service debt solely from the cash flow of continuing operations but require divesting and sale of assets to repay debt to banks and bridge loans made by investment bankers (this essentially means that corporate plant and equipment assets have become "liquid");

—Involve a much more rapid cycle from going private to going public again, with increased criticism of the substantially larger profits reaped by management and/or initial equity investors; and

—Continue to enjoy tax benefits of the deductibility of interest (although certain tax advantages have been diminished through tax reform).

The high leverage restructuring movement stalled four years later at the onset of an economic downturn. The excerpt that follows describes the situation at that time.

CRABBE, PICKERING, AND PROWSE, RECENT DEVELOPMENTS IN CORPORATE FINANCE

76 Federal Reserve Bulletin 593, 594–600 (1990)

RESTRUCTURINGS AND CORPORATE FINANCIAL DEVELOPMENTS

Merger and acquisition activity, which was instrumental in shaping corporate financial patterns, was strong throughout the decade * * *. The number of transactions rose moderately through 1983 and then accelerated between 1984 and 1986. Although the number fell over the remainder of the decade, it remained high by past standards. More important, the dollar value of the transactions continued to climb rapidly until 1989, easing only briefly in 1987, after the October stock market break. Acquisitions of U.S. firms by foreign companies since 1987 have added significantly to the volume of merger activity. Divestitures rose at a strong pace throughout the 1980s, accounting in the last five years for nearly one-third of the dollar value of all mergers and acquisitions.

* * *

Corporate Balance Sheets and Profitability

Whatever their cause, corporate restructurings have resulted in an unprecedented retirement of outstanding equity shares, which far outstripped the moderate level of new equity issuance * * *. Overall, retirements of nonfinancial corporate stock have exceeded new issues by about $600 billion since 1983, in sharp contrast to the rest of the postwar period, when retirements of shares exceeded new issues in only a handful of years, and then by very small amounts. Even the stock market break in 1987 had little effect on retirements because a pickup in stock repurchases by many corporations largely offset the brief pause in merger activity.

Unlike the mergers of the 1960s, which were financed largely by an exchange of securities, acquisitions in the 1980s relied heavily on borrowed funds to pay cash to selling shareholders. Leveraged buyouts (LBOs), the most highly leveraged acquisitions, mushroomed from less than $5 billion in 1983 to more than $60 billion in 1989, the year that included the $25 billion RJR–Nabisco transaction. LBOs served to transfer assets from publicly held corporations to closely held partnerships and private corporations. Some were structured with as little as 10 percent equity, provided largely by buyout pools that takeover specialists assembled. To finance the remainder, the new firm effectively pledged the assets of the acquired company as collateral for new debt obligations. The LBO firms then sought to lower the debt burden through improved cash flow and sales of some operations. Many of these divestitures were themselves structured as LBOs.

In addition to financing LBOs and other mergers and acquisitions, debt commonly was used to finance defensive measures such as leveraged recapitalizations undertaken to discourage unsolicited or "hostile" takeovers. As a result of all these restructuring activities, the indebtedness of nonfinancial corporations grew rapidly, as illustrated by a sharp increase in the ratio of the market value of debt to the gross domestic product of nonfinancial corporations.

The rapid buildup of debt in the nonfinancial corporate sector was accompanied by rising net interest payments that absorbed a growing share of corporate gross product * * *. The interest share expanded even though interest rates were lower, on balance, during the last half of the 1980s, and that expansion was one factor acting to depress corporate profitability. Before-tax profits slipped from roughly 9 percent of corporate output in 1987 to about $7\frac{3}{4}$ percent in 1989. Over the same period, net interest payments rose from about $4\frac{1}{4}$ percent to more than 5 percent of corporate gross product, accounting for more than half of the drop in the profits share.

 * * *

Merger Financing and the Junk Bond Market

 * * *

* * * [S]ecurities firms, led by Drexel Burnham Lambert, began actively promoting public offerings of high-yield bonds in the early 1980s. At the same time, institutional investors in the public market became convinced that the bonds' higher yields more than compensated for their greater risks, especially when the bonds were held in a diversified portfolio. The economic expansion also provided a favorable environment by seeming to mitigate risk.

These developments interacted with the growth of financing needs arising from mergers and restructurings to spur a dramatic increase in the issuance of junk bonds. Between 1983 and 1989, nonfinancial corporations issued $160 billion of junk bonds to the public; that sum accounted for more than 35 percent of public bond offerings by the sector. About two-thirds of the high-yield bonds offered during this period were associated with restructurings—leveraged buyouts, other mergers and acquisitions, divestitures, stock repurchases, leveraged recapitalizations, or other restructuring activities * * *. In most cases, junk bonds provided permanent financing for cash buyouts, which replaced part or all of the funds supplied initially by commercial or investment banks.

As the high-yield market matured, new instruments that offered issuers greater leeway in managing the timing of their interest payments were introduced. These instruments grew out of the need to minimize interest payments until cash flow improved or until debt loads could be reduced with the proceeds from sales of assets. The deferred-cash-payment bond and the reset note were commonly used for these purposes.

* * *

Corporate Credit Quality

The increase in the use of debt finance has been associated with a deterioration in many indicators of corporate financial health. Interest payments in the aggregate have claimed an increasing proportion of the cash flow of nonfinancial corporations since 1983 * * *. Furthermore, the number of firms whose interest expense exceeded cash flow rose significantly between 1983 and 1988, despite favorable economic conditions and falling interest rates. In these circumstances, concerns have arisen about the ability of highly leveraged firms to service their debt, especially in light of the slowing of the economy in 1989.

The secular erosion in corporate credit quality accelerated in the last half of the 1980s, an erosion evidenced by the increase in downgradings of corporate bonds relative to upgradings. The growth in new issues by lower-rated firms, which are more prone to downgradings, has meant that more frequent changes in credit ratings are likely. Nonetheless, the general deterioration in creditworthiness is noteworthy because it occurred while the economy was expanding.

As a result of these changes in ratings, the median rating that Standard and Poor's assigned to industrial bonds dropped from an investment-grade A in the early 1980s to a below-investment-grade BB at the close of the decade * * *. One-third of the estimated $600 billion of rated nonfinancial corporate bonds outstanding at the end of 1989 was rated as noninvestment grade. In the early 1980s, before the recent wave of restructurings, these low-grade bonds accounted for less than one-tenth of the total outstanding.

Some of the growth in below-investment-grade debt stemmed from the downgrading of outstanding debt to speculative grade because of events related to restructuring. More important, that growth was boosted by new debt issues of these downgraded companies. Furthermore, in the late 1980s, many new issues carried ratings at the lower end of the credit spectrum—B and Caa on Moody's scale. In the past these ratings generally appeared only when corporations on the edge of default were downgraded. The relative importance of the other component of speculative issuers, those companies downgraded to noninvestment grade because of a long-term decline in business fundamentals, has changed little over the past ten years.

Default rates on corporate bonds of below-investment grade, while still low, have risen, from 1.4 percent of outstanding bonds in 1987 to 4 percent in 1989 * * *. Moreover, many market analysts expect much higher default rates over the next few years, both because the overall quality of the noninvestment grade bonds has declined and because defaults tend to rise as bonds age. Indeed, several recent studies have found cumulative default rates for particular cohorts of bonds to be as high as 30 percent over the first ten years after issue.

Other measures of the condition of corporate balance sheets suggest that stockholders have not been overly concerned with the growing indebtedness of corporations. In particular, the ratio of debt to equity, both measured at market values, has increased only slightly since 1982, as rising equity prices have largely countered the rise in corporate indebtedness * * *. Nevertheless, the deterioration in other indicators of corporate financial condition, especially the ratio of interest expense to cash flow, indicates that the financial health of the business sector may be vulnerable to a significant slowing in economic activity.

     * * *

RECENT DEVELOPMENTS IN MERGER AND RESTRUCTURING ACTIVITY

Early in 1989, the hectic pace of debt-financed restructuring began to subside. The amount of stock-for-stock exchanges in merger transactions rebounded in 1989 from the extremely low levels of 1987 and 1988. This rebound largely reflected the increase in emphasis last year on friendly strategic corporate acquisitions in which the new, combined company issued new common shares to stockholders of the two original companies. Then, late in the year, the deepening difficulties in the market for below-investment-grade bonds further encouraged combination offers of cash and securities, particularly preferred stock, to shareholders of the acquired company.

The acquisition market was jolted last fall when a few companies involved in highly leveraged transactions failed to perform up to expectations, defaulted on bond issues, and sought bankruptcy protection. Others, seeking to prevent default, have reached agreement with bondholders to reschedule debt or are attempting to do so. These "distressed" exchanges typically replace existing debt with securities carrying a longer maturity, lower interest rate, some substitution of equity, or a combination of these features; and they must be approved by a predetermined share of bondholders specified in the original bond's covenant. Whereas such exchanges are still few, these unravelings of acquisitions and the general vulnerability of highly leveraged firms to adverse economic developments have heightened concerns in the financial markets; and thus they have made investors much more cautious in extending funds to highly leveraged borrowers.

Uneasiness about rising bond defaults contributed to chaotic conditions in the market for speculative-grade bonds early this year as prices of restructuring-related issues dropped precipitously. The withdrawal of the savings and loan associations from the junk bond market and outflows from high-yield mutual funds further curtailed demand for these issues. The liquidation of Drexel Burnham Lambert early this year was another negative factor for the market to absorb, even though Drexel's participation had already dwindled.

New merger proposals dropped off noticeably during the first part of 1990 as a consequence of the virtual unavailability of funds for new financing in the low-grade bond market; the more cautious attitude of commercial banks, both domestic and foreign; and the weakening in the market for asset sales. Nevertheless, although restructuring activity is considerably less than it was in 1988 and 1989, it remains substantial. Despite the disarray in the junk bond market and investor caution, well-structured acquisition proposals, especially those aimed at enhancing a firm's competitiveness within its own lines of business, have been well received by investors.

SECTION 3. DEBT CONTRACT FORMS

MODEL SIMPLIFIED INDENTURE

This model form was drafted by the American Bar Association Section of Corporation, Banking and Business Law from a predecessor form prepared by Morey W. McDaniel. It was published in 38 Bus.Law. 741 (1983).

INDENTURE dated as of _____, between UNIVERSAL BUSINESS CORPORATION, a Delaware corporation ("Company"), and GREATER BANK AND TRUST COMPANY, a New York corporation ("Trustee").

Each party agrees as follows for the benefit of the other party and for the equal and ratable benefit of the Holders of the Company's __% Convertible Subordinated Debentures Due _____ ("Securities"):

ARTICLE 1

DEFINITIONS AND INCORPORATION BY REFERENCE

Section 1.01. *Definitions.*

"*Affiliate*" means any person directly or indirectly controlling or controlled by or under direct or indirect common control with the Company.

"*Agent*" means any Registrar, Paying Agent, Conversion Agent or co-registrar.

"*Board of Directors*" means the Board of Directors of the Company or any authorized committee of the Board.

"*Company*" means the party named as such above until a successor replaces it and thereafter means the successor.

"*Default*" means any event which is, or after notice or passage of time would be, an Event of Default.

"*Holder*" or "*Securityholder*" means a person in whose name a Security is registered.

"*Indenture*" means this Indenture as amended from time to time.

"*Officers' Certificate*" means a certificate signed by two Officers, one of whom must be the President, the Treasurer or a Vice–President of the Company. See Sections 12.04 and 12.05.

"*Opinion of Counsel*" means a written opinion from legal counsel who is acceptable to the Trustee. The counsel may be an employee of or counsel to the Company or the Trustee. See Sections 12.04 and 12.05.

"*Principal*" of a debt security means the principal of the security plus the premium, if any, on the security.

"*SEC*" means the Securities and Exchange Commission.

"*Securities*" means the Securities described above issued under this Indenture.

"*TIA*" means the Trust Indenture Act of 1939 (15 U.S.Code §§ 77aaa–77bbbb) as in effect on the date shown above.

"*Trustee*" means the party named as such above until a successor replaces it and thereafter means the successor.

"*Trust Officer*" means the Chairman of the Board, the President or any other officer or assistant officer of the Trustee assigned by the Trustee to administer its corporate trust matters.

* * *

Section 1.03. *Incorporation by Reference of Trust Indenture Act.* Whenever this Indenture refers to a provision of the TIA, the provision is incorporated by reference in and made a part of this Indenture.

The following TIA terms used in this Indenture have the following meanings:

"*indenture securities*" means the Securities;

"*indenture security holder*" means a Securityholder;

"*indenture to be qualified*" means this Indenture;

"*indenture trustee*" or "*institutional trustee*" means the Trustee;

"*obligor*" on the indenture securities means the Company.

All other terms used in this Indenture that are defined by the TIA, defined by TIA reference to another statute or defined by SEC rule under the TIA have the meanings assigned to them.

* * *

ARTICLE 3

REDEMPTION

Section 3.01. *Notices to Trustee.* If the Company wants to redeem Securities pursuant to paragraph 5 of the Securities, it shall notify the Trustee of the redemption date and the principal amount of Securities to be redeemed. If the Company wants to redeem Securities pursuant to paragraph 7 of the Securities, it shall notify the Trustee of the principal amount of Securities to be redeemed. The Company's notice shall specify the paragraph of the Securities pursuant to which it wants to redeem Securities.

If the Company wants to reduce the principal amount of Securities to be redeemed pursuant to paragraph 6 of the Securities, it shall notify the Trustee of the amount of the reduction and the basis for it. If the Company wants to credit against any such redemption Securities it has not previously delivered to the Trustee for cancellation, it shall deliver the Securities with the notice.

The Company shall give each notice provided for in this Section at least 50 days before the redemption date.

Section 3.02. *Selection of Securities to Be Redeemed.* If less than all the Securities are to be redeemed, the Trustee shall select the Securities to be redeemed pro rata or by lot. The Trustee shall make the selection not more than 75 days before the redemption date from Securities outstanding not previously called for redemption. The Trustee may select for redemption portions of the principal of Securities that have denominations larger than $1000. Securities and portions of them it selects shall be in amounts of $1000 or whole multiples of $1000. Provisions of this Indenture that apply to Securities called for redemption also apply to portions of Securities called for redemption.

Section 3.03. *Notice of Redemption.* At least 30 days but not more than 60 days before a redemption date, the Company shall mail a notice of redemption to each Holder whose Securities are to be redeemed.

The notice shall identify the Securities to be redeemed and shall state:

(1) the redemption date;

(2) the redemption price;

(3) the conversion price;

(4) the name and address of the Paying Agent and Conversion Agent;

(5) that Securities called for redemption may be converted at any time before the close of business on the redemption date;

(6) that Holders who want to convert Securities must satisfy the requirements in paragraph 9 of the Securities;

(7) that Securities called for redemption must be surrendered to the Paying Agent to collect the redemption price; and

(8) that interest on Securities called for redemption ceases to accrue on and after the redemption date.

At the Company's request, the Trustee shall give the notice of redemption in the Company's name and at its expense.

Section 3.04. *Effect of Notice of Redemption.* Once notice of redemption is mailed, Securities called for redemption become due and payable on the redemption date at the redemption price.

Section 3.05. *Deposit of Redemption Price.* On or before the redemption date, the Company shall deposit with the Paying Agent money sufficient to pay the redemption price of and accrued interest on all Securities to be redeemed on that date. The Paying Agent shall return to the Company any money not required for that purpose because of conversion of Securities.

Section 3.06. *Securities Redeemed in Part.* Upon surrender of a Security that is redeemed in part, the Trustee shall authenticate for the Holder a new Security equal in principal amount to the unredeemed portion of the Security surrendered.

ARTICLE 6

DEFAULTS AND REMEDIES

Section 6.01. *Events of Default.* An "Event of Default" occurs if:

(1) the Company defaults in the payment of interest on any Security when the same becomes due and payable and the Default continues for a period of 30 days;

(2) the Company defaults in the payment of the principal of any Security when the same becomes due and payable at maturity, upon redemption or otherwise;

(3) the Company fails to comply with any of its other agreements in the Securities or this Indenture and the Default continues for the period and after the notice specified below;

(4) the Company pursuant to or within the meaning of any Bankruptcy Law:

(A) commences a voluntary case,

(B) consents to the entry of an order for relief against it in an involuntary case,

(C) consents to the appointment of a Custodian of it or for all or substantially all of its property, or

(D) makes a general assignment for the benefit of its creditors; or

(5) a court of competent jurisdiction enters an order or decree under any Bankruptcy Law that:

(A) is for relief against the Company in an involuntary case,

(B) appoints a Custodian of the Company or for all or substantially all of its property, or

(C) orders the liquidation of the Company,

and the order or decree remains unstayed and in effect for 60 days.

The term "Bankruptcy Law" means title 11, U.S.Code or any similar Federal or State law for the relief of debtors. The term "Custodian" means any receiver, trustee, assignee, liquidator or similar official under any Bankruptcy Law.

A Default under clause (3) is not an Event of Default until the Trustee or the Holders of at least 25% in principal amount of the Securities notify the Company of the Default and the Company does not cure the Default within 60 days after receipt of the notice. The notice must specify the Default, demand that it be remedied and state that the notice is a "Notice of Default."

Section 6.02. *Acceleration.* If an Event of Default occurs and is continuing, the Trustee by notice to the Company, or the Holders of at least 25% in principal amount of the Securities by notice to the Company and the Trustee, may declare the principal of and accrued interest on all the Securities to be due and payable. Upon such declaration the principal and interest shall be due and payable immediately. The Holders of a majority in principal amount of the Securities by notice to the Trustee may rescind an acceleration and its consequences if the rescission would not conflict with any judgment or decree and if all existing Events of Default have been cured or waived except nonpayment of principal or interest that has become due solely because of the acceleration.

Section 6.03. *Other Remedies.* If an Event of Default occurs and is continuing, the Trustee may pursue any available remedy to collect the payment of principal or interest on the Securities or to enforce the performance of any provision of the Securities or this Indenture.

The Trustee may maintain a proceeding even if it does not possess any of the Securities or does not produce any of them in the proceeding. A delay or omission by the Trustee or any Securityholder in exercising any right or remedy accruing upon an Event of Default shall not impair the right or remedy or constitute a waiver of or acquiescence in the Event of Default. All remedies are cumulative to the extent permitted by law.

Section 6.04. *Waiver of Past Defaults.* The Holders of a majority in principal amount of the Securities by notice to the Trustee may waive an existing Default and its consequences except a Default in the payment of the principal of or interest on any Security or a Default under Article 10.

Section 6.05. *Control by Majority.* The Holders of a majority in principal amount of the Securities may direct the time, method and place of conducting any proceeding for any remedy available to the Trustee or exercising any trust or power conferred on it. However, the Trustee may refuse to follow any direction that conflicts with law or this Indenture, is unduly prejudicial to the rights of other Securityholders, or would involve the Trustee in personal liability.

Section 6.06. *Limitation on Suits.* A Securityholder may pursue a remedy with respect to this Indenture or the Securities only if:

(1) the Holder gives to the Trustee notice of a continuing Event of Default;

(2) the Holders of at least 25% in principal amount of the Securities make a request to the Trustee to pursue the remedy;

(3) such Holder or Holders offer to the Trustee indemnity satisfactory to the Trustee against any loss, liability or expense;

(4) the Trustee does not comply with the request within 60 days after receipt of the request and the offer of indemnity; and

(5) during such 60–day period the Holders of a majority in principal amount of the Securities do not give the Trustee a direction inconsistent with the request.

A Securityholder may not use this Indenture to prejudice the rights of another Securityholder or to obtain a preference or priority over another Securityholder.

Section 6.07. *Rights of Holders to Receive Payment.* Notwithstanding any other provision of this Indenture, the right of any Holder of a Security to receive payment of principal and interest on the Security, on or after the respective due dates expressed in the Security, or to bring suit for the enforcement of any such payment on or after such respective dates, shall not be impaired or affected without the consent of the Holder.

Notwithstanding any other provision of this Indenture, the right of any Holder of a Security to bring suit for the enforcement of the right to convert the Security shall not be impaired or affected without the consent of the Holder.

Section 6.08. *Collection Suit by Trustee.* If an Event of Default specified in Section 6.01(1) or (2) occurs and is continuing, the Trustee may recover judgment in its own name and as trustee of an express trust against the Company for the whole amount of principal and interest remaining unpaid.

Section 6.09. *Trustee May File Proofs of Claim.* The Trustee may file such proofs of claim and other papers or documents as may be necessary or advisable in order to have the claims of the Trustee and the Securityholders allowed in any judicial proceedings relative to the Company, its creditors or its property.

Section 6.10. *Priorities.* If the Trustee collects any money pursuant to this Article, it shall pay out the money in the following order:

First: to the Trustee for amounts due under Section 7.07;

Second: to holders of Senior Debt to the extent required by Article 11;

Third: to Securityholders for amounts due and unpaid on the Securities for principal and interest, ratably, without preference or priority of any kind, according to the amounts due and payable on the Securities for principal and interest, respectively; and

Fourth: to the Company.

The Trustee may fix a record date and payment date for any payment to Securityholders.

Section 6.11. *Undertaking for Costs.* In any suit for the enforcement of any right or remedy under this Indenture or in any suit against the Trustee for any action taken or omitted by it as Trustee, a court in its discretion may require the filing by any party litigant in the suit of an undertaking to pay the costs of the suit, and the court in its discretion may assess reasonable costs, including reasonable attorneys' fees, against any party litigant in the suit, having due regard to the merits and good faith of the claims or defenses made by the party litigant. This Section does not apply to a suit by the Trustee, a suit by a Holder pursuant to Section 6.07, or a suit by Holders of more than 10% in principal amount of the Securities.

ARTICLE 7

TRUSTEE

Section 7.01. *Duties of Trustee.*

(a) If an Event of Default has occurred and is continuing, the Trustee shall exercise such of the rights and powers vested in it by this Indenture, and use the same degree of care and skill in their exercise, as a prudent man would exercise or use under the circumstances in the conduct of his own affairs.

(b) Except during the continuance of an Event of Default:

(1) The Trustee need perform only those duties that are specifically set forth in this Indenture and no others.

(2) In the absence of bad faith on its part, the Trustee may conclusively rely, as to the truth of the statements and the correctness of the opinions expressed therein, upon certificates or opinions furnished to the Trustee and conforming to the requirements of this Indenture. However, the Trustee shall examine the certificates and opinions to determine whether or not they conform to the requirements of this Indenture.

(c) The Trustee may not be relieved from liability for its own negligent action, its own negligent failure to act, or its own wilful misconduct, except that:

(1) This paragraph does not limit the effect of paragraph (b) of this Section.

(2) The Trustee shall not be liable for any error of judgment made in good faith by a Trust Officer, unless it is proved that the Trustee was negligent in ascertaining the pertinent facts.

(3) The Trustee shall not be liable with respect to any action it takes or omits to take in good faith in accordance with a direction received by it pursuant to Section 6.05.

(d) Every provision of this Indenture that in any way relates to the Trustee is subject to paragraphs (a), (b) and (c) of this Section.

(e) The Trustee may refuse to perform any duty or exercise any right or power unless it receives indemnity satisfactory to it against any loss, liability or expense.

(f) The Trustee shall not be liable for interest on any money received by it except as the Trustee may agree with the Company. Money held in trust by the Trustee need not be segregated from other funds except to the extent required by law.

Section 7.02. *Rights of Trustee.*

(a) The Trustee may rely on any document believed by it to be genuine and to have been signed or presented by the proper person. The Trustee need not investigate any fact or matter stated in the document.

(b) Before the Trustee acts or refrains from acting, it may require an Officers' Certificate or an Opinion of Counsel. The Trustee shall not be liable for any action it takes or omits to take in good faith in reliance on the Certificate or Opinion.

(c) The Trustee may act through agents and shall not be responsible for the misconduct or negligence of any agent appointed with due care.

(d) The Trustee shall not be liable for any action it takes or omits to take in good faith which it believes to be authorized or within its rights or powers.

Section 7.03. *Individual Rights of Trustee.* The Trustee in its individual or any other capacity may become the owner or pledgee of Securities and may otherwise deal with the Company or an Affiliate with the same rights it would have if it were not Trustee. Any Agent may do the same with like rights. However, the Trustee is subject to Sections 7.10 and 7.11.

Section 7.04. *Trustee's Disclaimer.* The Trustee makes no representation as to the validity or adequacy of this Indenture or the Securities, it shall not be accountable for the Company's use of the proceeds from the Securities, and it shall not be responsible for any statement in the Securities other than its authentication.

Section 7.05. *Notice of Defaults.* If a Default occurs and is continuing and if it is known to the Trustee, the Trustee shall mail to Securityholders a notice of the Default within 90 days after it occurs. Except in the case of a Default in payment on any Security, the Trustee may withhold the notice if and so long as a committee of its Trust Officers in good faith determines that withholding the notice is in the interests of Securityholders.

Section 7.06. *Reports by Trustee to Holders.* Within 60 days after the reporting date stated in Section 12.10, the Trustee shall mail to Securityholders a brief report dated as of such reporting date that complies with TIA § 313(a). The Trustee also shall comply with TIA § 313(b)(2).

A copy of each report at the time of its mailing to Securityholders shall be filed with the SEC and each stock exchange on which the Securities are listed. The Company shall notify the Trustee when the Securities are listed on any stock exchange.

Section 7.07. *Compensation and Indemnity.* The Company shall pay to the Trustee from time to time reasonable compensation for its services. The Trustee's compensation shall not be limited by any law on compensation of a trustee of an express trust. The Company shall reimburse the Trustee upon request for all reasonable out-of-pocket expenses incurred by it. Such expenses shall include the reasonable compensation and out-of-pocket expenses of the Trustee's agents and counsel.

The Company shall indemnify the Trustee against any loss or liability incurred by it. The Trustee shall notify the Company promptly of any claim for which it may seek indemnity. The Company shall defend the claim and the Trustee shall cooperate in the defense. The Trustee may have separate counsel and the Company shall pay the reasonable fees and expenses of such counsel. The Company need not pay for any settlement made without its consent.

The Company need not reimburse any expense or indemnify against any loss or liability incurred by the Trustee through negligence or bad faith.

To secure the Company's payment obligations in this Section, the Trustee shall have a lien prior to the Securities on all money or property held or collected by the Trustee, except that held in trust to pay principal and interest on particular Securities.

When the Trustee incurs expenses or renders services after an Event of Default specified in Section 6.01(4) or (5) occurs, the expenses and the compensation for the services are intended to constitute expenses of administration under any Bankruptcy Law.

Section 7.08. *Replacement of Trustee.* A resignation or removal of the Trustee and appointment of a successor Trustee shall become effective only upon the successor Trustee's acceptance of appointment as provided in this Section.

The Trustee may resign by so notifying the Company. The Holders of a majority in principal amount of the Securities may remove the Trustee by so notifying the Trustee and the Company. The Company may remove the Trustee if:

(1) the Trustee fails to comply with Section 7.10;

(2) the Trustee is adjudged a bankrupt or an insolvent;

(3) a receiver or public officer takes charge of the Trustee or its property; or

(4) the Trustee becomes incapable of acting.

If the Trustee resigns or is removed or if a vacancy exists in the office of Trustee for any reason, the Company shall promptly appoint a successor Trustee. Within one year after the successor Trustee takes office, the Holders of a majority in principal amount of the Securities may appoint a successor Trustee to replace the successor Trustee appointed by the Company.

If a successor Trustee does not take office within 60 days after the retiring Trustee resigns or is removed, the retiring Trustee, the Company or the Holders of at least 10% in principal amount of the Securities may petition any court of competent jurisdiction for the appointment of a successor Trustee.

If the Trustee fails to comply with Section 7.10, any Securityholder may petition any court of competent jurisdiction for the removal of the Trustee and the appointment of a successor Trustee.

A successor Trustee shall deliver a written acceptance of its appointment to the retiring Trustee and to the Company. Thereupon the resignation or removal of the retiring Trustee shall become effective, and the successor Trustee shall have all the rights, powers and duties of the Trustee under this Indenture. The successor Trustee shall mail a notice of its succession to Securityholders. The retiring Trustee shall promptly transfer all property held by it as Trustee to the successor Trustee, subject to the lien provided for in Section 7.07.

Section 7.09. *Successor Trustee by Merger, etc.* If the Trustee consolidates, merges or converts into, or transfers all or substantially all of its corporate trust business to, another corporation, the successor corporation without any further act shall be the successor Trustee.

Section 7.10. *Eligibility; Disqualification.* This Indenture shall always have a Trustee who satisfies the requirements of TIA § 310(a)(1). The Trustee shall always have a combined capital and surplus as stated in § 12.10. The Trustee is subject to TIA § 310(b), including the optional provision permitted by the second sentence of TIA § 310(b)(9). § 12.10 lists any excluded indenture or trust agreement.

Section 7.11. *Preferential Collection of Claims Against Company.* The Trustee is subject to TIA § 311(a), excluding any creditor relationship listed in TIA § 311(b). A Trustee who has resigned or been removed is subject to TIA § 311(a) to the extent indicated.

ARTICLE 9

AMENDMENTS

Section 9.01. *Without Consent of Holders.* The Company and the Trustee may amend this Indenture or the Securities without the consent of any Securityholder:

(1) to cure any ambiguity, defect or inconsistency;

(2) to comply with Sections 5.01 and 10.15;

(3) to provide for uncertificated Securities in addition to certificated Securities; or

(4) to make any change that does not adversely affect the rights of any Securityholder.

Section 9.02. *With Consent of Holders.* The Company and the Trustee may amend this Indenture or the Securities with the written consent of the Holders of at least 66⅔% in principal amount of the Securities. However, without the consent of each Securityholder affected, an amendment under this Section may not:

(1) reduce the amount of Securities whose Holders must consent to an amendment;

(2) reduce the rate of or change the time for payment of interest on any Security;

(3) reduce the principal of or change the fixed maturity of any Security;

(4) make any Security payable in money other than that stated in the Security;

(5) make any change in Section 6.04, 6.07 or 9.02 (second sentence);

(6) make any change that adversely affects the right to convert any Security; or

(7) make any change in Article 11 that adversely affects the rights of any Securityholder.

An amendment under this Section may not make any change that adversely affects the rights under Article 11 of any holder of an issue of Senior Debt unless the holders of the issue pursuant to its terms consent to the change.

After an amendment under this Section becomes effective, the Company shall mail to Securityholders a notice briefly describing the amendment.

Section 9.03. *Compliance With Trust Indenture Act.* Every amendment to this Indenture or the Securities shall be set forth in a supplemental indenture that complies with the TIA as then in effect.

Section 9.04. *Revocation and Effect of Consents.* Until an amendment or waiver becomes effective, a consent to it by a Holder of a Security is a continuing consent by the Holder and every subsequent Holder of a Security or portion of a Security that evidences the same debt as the consenting Holder's Security, even if notation of the consent is not made on any Security. However, any such Holder or subsequent Holder may revoke the consent as to his Security or portion of a Security if the Trustee receives the notice of revocation before the date the amendment or waiver becomes effective. An amendment or waiver becomes effective in accordance with its terms and thereafter binds every Securityholder.

Section 9.05. *Notation on or Exchange of Securities.* The Trustee may place an appropriate notation about an amendment or waiver on any Security thereafter authenticated. The Company in exchange for all Securities may issue and the Trustee shall authenticate new Securities that reflect the amendment or waiver.

Section 9.06. *Trustee Protected.* The Trustee need not sign any supplemental indenture that adversely affects its rights.

ARTICLE 11

SUBORDINATION

Section 11.01. *Agreement to Subordinate.* The Company agrees, and each Securityholder by accepting a Security agrees, that the indebtedness evidenced by the Securities is subordinated in right of payment, to the extent and in the manner provided in this Article, to the prior payment in full of all Senior Debt, and that the subordination is for the benefit of the holders of Senior Debt.

Section 11.02. *Certain Definitions.*

"*Debt*" means any indebtedness for borrowed money or any guarantee of such indebtedness.

"*Representative*" means the indenture trustee or other trustee, agent or representative for an issue of Senior Debt.

"*Senior Debt*" means Debt of the Company outstanding at any time except Debt that by its terms is not senior in right of payment to the Securities. Senior Debt may be further defined in Section 12.10.

A distribution may consist of cash, securities or other property.

Section 11.03. *Liquidation; Dissolution; Bankruptcy.* Upon any distribution to creditors of the Company in a liquidation or dissolution of the Company or in a bankruptcy, reorganization, insolvency, receivership or similar proceeding relating to the Company or its property:

(1) holders of Senior Debt shall be entitled to receive payment in full in cash of the principal of and interest (including interest accruing after the commencement of any such proceeding) to the date of payment on the Senior Debt before Securityholders shall be entitled to receive any payment of principal of or interest on Securities; and

(2) until the Senior Debt is paid in full in cash, any distribution to which Securityholders would be entitled but for this Article shall be made to holders of Senior Debt as their interests may appear, except that Securityholders may receive securities that are subordinated to Senior Debt to at least the same extent as the Securities.

Section 11.04. *Default on Senior Debt.* The Company may not pay principal of or interest on the Securities and may not acquire any Securities for cash or property other than capital stock of the Company if:

(1) a default on Senior Debt occurs and is continuing that permits holders of such Senior Debt to accelerate its maturity, and

(2) the default is the subject of judicial proceedings or the Company receives a notice of the default from a person who may give it pursuant to Section 11.12. If the Company receives any such notice, a similar notice received within nine months thereafter relating to the same default on the same issue of Senior Debt shall not be effective for purposes of this Section.

The Company may resume payments on the Securities and may acquire them when:

(a) the default is cured or waived, or

(b) 120 days pass after the notice is given if the default is not the subject of judicial proceedings,

if this Article otherwise permits the payment or acquisition at that time.

Section 11.05. *Acceleration of Securities.* If payment of the Securities is accelerated because of an Event of Default, the Company shall promptly notify holders of Senior Debt of the acceleration. The Company may pay the Securities when 120 days pass after the acceleration occurs if this Article permits the payment at that time.

Section 11.06. *When Distribution Must Be Paid Over.* If a distribution is made to Securityholders that because of this Article should not have been made to them, the Securityholders who receive the distribution shall hold it in trust for holders of Senior Debt and pay it over to them as their interests may appear.

Section 11.07. *Notice by Company.* The Company shall promptly notify the Trustee and the Paying Agent of any facts known to the Company that would cause a payment of principal of or interest on the Securities to violate this Article.

Section 11.08. *Subrogation.* After all Senior Debt is paid in full and until the Securities are paid in full, Securityholders shall be subrogated to the rights of holders of Senior Debt to receive distributions applicable to Senior Debt to the extent that distributions otherwise payable to the Securityholders have been applied to the payment of Senior Debt. A distribution made under this Article to holders of Senior Debt which otherwise would have been made to Securityholders is not, as between the Company and Securityholders, a payment by the Company on Senior Debt.

Section 11.09. *Relative Rights.* This Article defines the relative rights of Securityholders and holders of Senior Debt. Nothing in this Indenture shall:

(1) impair, as between the Company and Securityholders, the obligation of the Company, which is absolute and unconditional, to pay principal of and interest on the Securities in accordance with their terms;

(2) affect the relative rights of Securityholders and creditors of the Company other than holders of Senior Debt; or

(3) prevent the Trustee or any Securityholder from exercising its available remedies upon a Default, subject to the rights of holders of Senior Debt to receive distributions otherwise payable to Securityholders.

If the Company fails because of this Article to pay principal of or interest on a Security on the due date, the failure is still a Default.

Section 11.10. *Subordination May Not Be Impaired by Company.* No right of any holder of Senior Debt to enforce the subordination of the indebtedness evidenced by the Securities shall be impaired by any act or failure to act by the Company or by its failure to comply with this Indenture.

Section 11.11. *Distribution or Notice to Representative.* Whenever a distribution is to be made or a notice given to holders of Senior Debt, the distribution may be made and the notice given to their Representative.

Section 11.12. *Rights of Trustee and Paying Agent.* The Trustee or Paying Agent may continue to make payments on the Securities until it receives notice of facts that would cause a payment of principal of or interest on the Securities to violate this Article. Only the Company, a Representative or a holder of an issue of Senior Debt that has no Representative may give the notice.

The Trustee in its individual or any other capacity may hold Senior Debt with the same rights it would have if it were not Trustee. Any Agent may do the same with like rights.

EXHIBIT A

(Face of Security)

No. $

UNIVERSAL BUSINESS CORPORATION

promises to pay to

or registered assigns, the principal sum of   Dollars on

% Convertible Subordinated Debenture Due

Interest Payment Dates:

Record Dates:

Dated:

Authenticated:

GREATER BANK AND TRUST   UNIVERSAL BUSINESS
  COMPANY as Trustee   CORPORATION

By   By
       Authorized Officer

OR   By

NATIONAL BANK AND TRUST
  COMPANY, as Authenticating
  Agent

By
      Authorized Officer   (SEAL)

(Back of Security)

UNIVERSAL BUSINESS CORPORATION

% Convertible Subordinated Debenture Due

1. *Interest.* Universal Business Corporation ("Company"), a Delaware corporation, promises to pay interest on the principal amount of this Security at the rate per annum shown above. The Company will pay interest semiannually on _____ and _____ of each year. Interest on the Securities will accrue from the most recent date to which interest has been paid or, if no interest has been paid, from _____. Interest will be computed on the basis of a 360–day year of twelve 30–day months.

2. *Method of Payment.* The Company will pay interest on the Securities (except defaulted interest) to the persons who are registered holders of Securities at the close of business on the record date for the next interest payment date even though Securities are cancelled after the record date and on or before the interest payment date. Holders must surrender Securities to a Paying Agent to collect principal pay-

Brudney & Chirelstein Corp. Fin. 4th Ed. UCS—28

C–31

ments. The Company will pay principal and interest in money of the United States that at the time of payment is legal tender for payment of public and private debts. However, the Company may pay principal and interest by check payable in such money. It may mail an interest check to a holder's registered address.

3. *Paying Agent, Registrar, Conversion Agent.* Initially, Greater Bank and Trust Company ("Trustee"), 500 Wall Street, New York, NY 10015, will act as Paying Agent, Registrar and Conversion Agent. The Company may change any Paying Agent, Registrar, Conversion Agent or co-registrar without notice. The Company may act in any such capacity.

4. *Indenture.* The Company issued the Securities under an Indenture dated as of _____ ("Indenture") between the Company and the Trustee. The terms of the Securities include those stated in the Indenture and those made part of the Indenture by reference to the Trust Indenture Act of 1939 (15 U.S.Code §§ 77aaa–77bbbb) as in effect on the date of the Indenture. The Securities are subject to all such terms, and Securityholders are referred to the Indenture and the Act for a statement of such terms. The Securities are unsecured general obligations of the Company limited to $_____ in aggregate principal amount.

5. *Optional Redemption.* The Company may redeem all the Securities at any time or some of them from time to time at the following redemption prices (expressed in percentages of principal amount), plus accrued interest to the redemption date:

If redeemed during the 12–month period beginning _____ 1,

Year	Percentage	Year	Percentage

6. *Mandatory Redemption.* The Company will redeem $_____ principal amount of Securities on _____ and on each _____ thereafter through _____ at a redemption price of 100% of principal amount, plus accrued interest to the redemption date. The Company may reduce the principal amount of Securities to be redeemed pursuant to this paragraph 6 by subtracting 100% of the principal amount (excluding premium) of any Securities that Securityholders have converted (other than Securities converted after being called for mandatory redemption), that the Company has delivered to the Trustee for cancellation or that the Company has redeemed other than pursuant to this paragraph 6. The Company may so subtract the same Security only once.

7. *Additional Optional Redemption.* In addition to redemptions pursuant to paragraph 6, the Company may redeem not more than

$_____ principal amount of Securities on _____ and on each _____ thereafter through _____ at a redemption price of 100% of principal amount, plus accrued interest to the redemption date.

8. *Notice of Redemption.* Notice of redemption will be mailed at least 30 days but not more than 60 days before the redemption date to each holder of Securities to be redeemed at his registered address. Securities in denominations larger than $1000 may be redeemed in part but only in whole multiples of $1000. On and after the redemption date interest ceases to accrue on Securities or portions of them called for redemption.

9. *Conversion.* A holder of a Security may convert it into Common Stock of the Company at any time before the close of business on _____. If the Security is called for redemption, the holder may convert it at any time before the close of business on the redemption date. The initial conversion price is $_____ per share, subject to adjustment in certain events. To determine the number of shares issuable upon conversion of a Security, divide the principal amount to be converted by the conversion price in effect on the conversion date. On conversion no payment or adjustment for interest will be made. The Company will deliver a check for any fractional share.

To convert a Security a holder must (1) complete and sign the conversion notice on the back of the Security, (2) surrender the Security to a Conversion Agent, (3) furnish appropriate endorsements and transfer documents if required by the Registrar or Conversion Agent, and (4) pay any transfer or similar tax if required. A holder may convert a portion of a Security if the portion is $1000 or a whole multiple of $1000.

The conversion price will be adjusted for dividends or distributions on Common Stock payable in Company stock; subdivisions, combinations or certain reclassifications of Common Stock; distributions to all holders of Common Stock of certain rights to purchase Common Stock at less than the current market price at the time; distributions to such holders of assets or debt securities of the Company or certain rights to purchase securities of the Company (excluding cash dividends or distributions from current or retained earnings). However, no adjustment need be made if Securityholders may participate in the transaction or in certain other cases. The Company from time to time may voluntarily reduce the conversion price for a period of time.

If the Company is a party to a consolidation or merger or a transfer or lease of all or substantially all of its assets, the right to convert a Security into Common Stock may be changed into a right to convert it into securities, cash or other assets of the Company or another.

10. *Subordination.* The Securities are subordinated to Senior Debt, which is any Debt of the Company except subordinated Debt specified in the Indenture and Debt that by its terms is not senior in right of payment to the Securities. A Debt is any indebtedness for

borrowed money or any guarantee of such indebtedness. To the extent provided in the Indenture, Senior Debt must be paid before the Securities may be paid. The Company agrees, and each Securityholder by accepting a Security agrees, to the subordination and authorizes the Trustee to give it effect.

11. *Denominations, Transfer, Exchange.* The Securities are in registered form without coupons in denominations of $1000 and whole multiples of $1000. The transfer of Securities may be registered and Securities may be exchanged as provided in the Indenture. The Registrar may require a holder, among other things, to furnish appropriate endorsements and transfer documents and to pay any taxes and fees required by law or permitted by the Indenture. The Registrar need not exchange or register the transfer of any Security or portion of a Security selected for redemption. Also, it need not exchange or register the transfer of any Securities for a period of 15 days before a selection of Securities to be redeemed.

12. *Persons Deemed Owners.* The registered holder of a Security may be treated as its owner for all purposes.

13. *Amendments and Waivers.* Subject to certain exceptions, the Indenture or the Securities may be amended with the consent of the holders of at least $66\frac{2}{3}\%$ in principal amount of the Securities, and any existing default may be waived with the consent of the holders of a majority in principal amount of the Securities. Without the consent of any Securityholder, the Indenture or the Securities may be amended to cure any ambiguity, defect or inconsistency, to provide for assumption of Company obligations to Securityholders or to make any change that does not adversely affect the rights of any Securityholder.

14. *Defaults and Remedies.* An Event of Default is: default for 30 days in payment of interest on the Securities; default in payment of principal on them; failure by the Company for 60 days after notice to it to comply with any of its other agreements in the Indenture or the Securities; and certain events of bankruptcy or insolvency. If an Event of Default occurs and is continuing, the Trustee or the holders of at least 25% in principal amount of the Securities may declare all the Securities to be due and payable immediately. Securityholders may not enforce the Indenture or the Securities except as provided in the Indenture. The Trustee may require indemnity satisfactory to it before it enforces the Indenture or the Securities. Subject to certain limitations, holders of a majority in principal amount of the Securities may direct the Trustee in its exercise of any trust or power. The Trustee may withhold from Securityholders notice of any continuing default (except a default in payment of principal or interest) if it determines that withholding notice is in their interests. The Company must furnish an annual compliance certificate to the Trustee.

15. *Trustee Dealings With Company.* Greater Bank and Trust Company, the Trustee under the Indenture, in its individual or any

other capacity, may make loans to, accept deposits from, and perform services for the Company or its Affiliates, and may otherwise deal with the Company or its Affiliates, as if it were not Trustee.

16. *No Recourse Against Others.* A director, officer, employee or stockholder, as such, of the Company shall not have any liability for any obligations of the Company under the Securities or the Indenture or for any claim based on, in respect of or by reason of such obligations or their creation. Each Securityholder by accepting a Security waives and releases all such liability. The waiver and release are part of the consideration for the issue of the Securities.

17. *Authentication.* This Security shall not be valid until authenticated by the manual signature of the Trustee or an authenticating agent.

18. *Abbreviations.* Customary abbreviations may be used in the name of a Securityholder or an assignee, such as: TEN COM (= tenants in common), TEN ENT (= tenants by the entireties), JT TEN (= joint tenants with right of survivorship and not as tenants in common), CUST (= Custodian), and U/G/M/A (= Uniform Gifts to Minors Act).

The Company will furnish to any Securityholder upon written request and without charge a copy of the Indenture, which has in it the text of this Security in larger type. Requests may be made to: Secretary, Universal Business Corporation, 1 Commerce Plaza, New York, NY 10099.

AMERICAN BAR FOUNDATION, COMMENTARIES ON INDENTURES

1971

Article 13, Conversion—Sample Provision

[Alternate Form Combining Provisions of §§ 13–
1 through 13–5; § 13–6 (Alternate 3)]

§ 13–1. Right of Conversion, Manner of Exercise, Issuance of Common Stock on Conversion, Conversion Price[s] and Rate of Conversion.

The Holder of any Debenture, at his option, at any time and from time to time up to the close of business on _____ (or as to any Debenture called for redemption, then not later than the close of business on [the _____ day next preceding] the day fixed for redemption), may convert all or any portion of any Debenture held by him into shares of the Common Stock of the Company, at the conversion price and rate, and upon the other terms, hereinafter set forth in this Section.

In each case, the Debentureholder shall deliver written notice of his election to convert said Debenture or a specified principal amount thereof (a multiple of $_____), and shall surrender the same (properly endorsed or assigned for transfer, if the Board of Directors [the Company] shall so require) with all unmatured coupons, if any, thereto appertaining, to the Company at its office or agency in the City of _____ maintained pursuant to § 10–2. If the last day for the exercise of the conversion right [or the last day of any conversion period] shall be, in the City of _____, a legal holiday or a day on which banking institutions are authorized by law to close, then such conversion right may be exercised[, or such conversion period shall be extended,] up to the close of business on the next succeeding day not, in the City of _____, a legal holiday or a day on which banking institutions are authorized by law to close.

For all purposes of this Indenture, unless the context otherwise requires, all provisions relating to the conversion of Debentures shall relate, in the case of any Debenture converted or to be converted only in part, to the portion of the principal of such Debenture which has been or is to be converted.

In the case of any Debenture which is surrendered for conversion only in part, the Company shall execute and the Trustee shall authenticate and deliver to the Holder of such Debenture, without service charge, a new Debenture or Debentures of any authorized denomination or denominations as requested by such Holder in aggregate principal amount equal to the unconverted portion of the principal of the Debenture so surrendered.

For all purposes of this Section, the *"date of conversion"* of any Debenture shall be deemed to be the day on which, at or prior to the close of business, delivery of such notice or the surrender of the Debenture (whichever shall last occur) shall be made, and notwithstanding that the stock transfer books are at the time closed; and for all purposes the rights of a converting Holder of a Debenture as such Holder shall cease, and the Person or Persons in whose name or names the certificates for the shares of Common Stock issuable upon such conversion are to be issued shall be deemed to have become the record holder or holders of such shares of Common Stock, at the close of business on the date of conversion, and such shares shall then be deemed to be "issued shares" for the purposes of this Section.

"Common Stock", when used in this Section with reference to the Common Stock into which Debentures are convertible, shall mean only Common Stock of the class existing on [issue date of Debentures] and any stock into which such Common Stock may thereafter have been changed, and, when otherwise used in this Section, shall include also stock of the Company of any other class, whether now or hereafter

authorized, which ranks, or is entitled to a participation, as to assets or dividends, substantially on a parity with such existing Common Stock or other class of stock into which such Common Stock may have been changed.

Upon receipt by the Company of any such notice by a Holder of a Debenture of his election to convert any such Debenture, and upon the surrender of the Debenture, the Company shall, as soon as may be, and in any event within _____ full business days after the date of conversion, execute and deliver to such Holder a certificate or certificates for the number of full shares of Common Stock sufficient for the conversion of said Debenture. The stock certificates so delivered shall be in the name of the record Holder, if any, of the Debenture so surrendered for conversion, or in such other name or names as the person surrendering said Debenture may direct. The Company shall pay the amount of any and all taxes which may be imposed in respect of any issue or delivery of stock certificates under this Section, except that, in case such stock certificates shall be issued in a name or names other than the name of the registered Holder of the Debenture so surrendered, all stock transfer taxes that may be payable in respect thereof shall be paid by the person surrendering said Debenture for conversion.

The Company shall not be required to deliver certificates for shares of Common Stock upon conversion while its stock transfer books are closed, but the stock transfer books shall never be closed at any time for a period longer than _____ days, and such certificates shall be delivered as soon as the stock transfer books shall be opened.

The Company shall not be required upon any such conversion to issue a certificate representing any fraction of a share of Common Stock, but, in lieu thereof, may either pay cash for such fraction of a share at the fair value thereof as determined by the Board of Directors from time to time in its absolute discretion or issue a non-dividend bearing and non-voting instrument, in form approved by the Board of Directors, evidencing a fractional right to receive a certificate for one share of Common Stock when presented with other like certificates together representing rights to at least one such share. Such instrument may contain such terms as shall be fixed by the Board of Directors and may become void after a reasonable period, not less than three years from the date of issuance, to be specified in such instrument. For the purposes of this Section, all shares of Common Stock issuable under the terms of any such instrument shall be treated as "issued" shares.

All shares of Common Stock issuable upon conversion of any Debenture pursuant to this Section shall be full paid and nonassessable.

For the purpose of any conversion under this Section, each Debenture shall be treated as the equivalent of its principal amount. The number of shares of Common Stock issuable in respect of any Debenture upon any conversion (the "*rate of conversion*") shall be computed (to the nearest one one-hundredth of one share of Common Stock) by dividing the aggregate dollar equivalent of all Debentures at any one time surrendered for conversion by any one Holder thereof, by the conversion price in effect at the date of conversion.

The price[s] per share at which shares of Common Stock are to be issuable upon any conversion under this Section (the "*conversion price[s]*"), shall be $_____ (hereinafter called the "*basic conversion price*") [shall be $_____ if the date of conversion is in the period ending _____, $_____ if the date of conversion is in the period _____ to _____, inclusive, and $_____ if the date of conversion is in the period _____ to _____, inclusive (each of said periods being hereinafter called a "*conversion period*", and the conversion prices above specified being hereinafter called the "*basic conversion prices*", and each increase in the conversion price brought about by the arrival of a subsequent conversion period being hereinafter called a "*step-up*")]. The conversion price[s] shall be subject to adjustment from time to time in certain instances as provided in *Subsections* _____ of this Section.

The term "conversion price in effect" at any time shall mean the basic conversion price [for the relevant conversion period] until the same has been so adjusted, and after any such adjustment, the conversion price resulting from the most recent adjustment.

[If and whenever the conversion price in effect in any conversion period shall have been adjusted pursuant to the provisions of the following *Subsection* _____ of this Section, the respective conversion prices which would become effective (except for such adjustment) for each of the subsequent conversion periods, if any, shall be adjusted so that the conversion price to be in effect for each such subsequent period, instead of being the relevant basic conversion price, shall be a price which shall bear the same ratio to the conversion price in effect at the end of the next preceding conversion period as the basic conversion price for such subsequent period bears to the basic conversion price for such next preceding period.]

§ 13–6. Adjustment of Conversion Price.

[Alternate 3—Market Price Formula]

The Conversion Price shall be subject to adjustment as follows:

A. In case the Company shall issue rights or warrants to all holders of its Common Stock entitling them (for a period expiring within _____ days after the record date mentioned below) to subscribe for or purchase shares of Common Stock at a price per share less than the current market price per share of Common Stock (as determined pursuant to Subsection D of this § 13–6) on the record date mentioned below, the Conversion Price shall be adjusted so that the same shall equal the price determined by multiplying the Conversion Price in effect immediately prior to the date of issuance of such rights or warrants by a fraction whose *numerator* shall be the number of shares of Common Stock outstanding on the date of issuance of such rights or warrants plus the number of shares which the aggregate exercise price of the shares of Common Stock called for by all such rights or warrants would purchase at such current market price, and whose *denominator* shall be the number of shares of Common Stock outstanding on the date of issuance of such rights or warrants plus the number of additional shares of Common Stock called for by all such rights or warrants. Subject to Subsection D of this § 13–6, such adjustment shall be made whenever such rights or warrants are issued and shall be retroactively effective as of immediately after the record date for the determination of stockholders entitled to receive such rights or warrants. No adjustment of the Conversion Price shall be made unless such adjustment would require an increase or decrease of at least ... cents in such price; *provided, however,* that any adjustments which by reason of this sentence are not required to be made shall be carried forward and taken into account in any subsequent adjustment.

B. In case the Company shall (1) pay a dividend or make a distribution in shares of its capital stock (whether shares of Common Stock or of capital stock of any other class), (2) subdivide its outstanding shares of Common Stock into a greater number of shares, (3) combine its outstanding shares of Common Stock into a smaller number of shares, or (4) issue by reclassification of its shares of Common Stock any shares of capital stock of the Company (other than a change in par value, or from par value to no par value, or from no par value to par value), the Conversion Price in effect immediately prior thereto shall be adjusted so that the holder of any Debenture thereafter surrendered for conversion shall be entitled to receive the number of shares of capital stock of the Company which he would have owned or have been entitled to receive immediately following the happening of any of the events described above, had such Debenture been converted immediately prior thereto. An adjustment made pursuant to this Subsection shall become effective immediately after the record date in the case of a dividend or distribution in shares of the Company's capital stock and shall become effective immediately after the effective date in the case of a subdivision, combination or reclassification. If, as a result of an adjustment made pursuant to this Subsection, the Holder of any Debenture thereafter surrendered for conversion shall become entitled to receive shares of two or more classes of capital stock of the Company, the Board of Directors (whose determination shall be conclusive and shall be evidenced by a Board Resolution filed with the Trustee and the conversion agent) shall determine the allocation of the adjusted conversion price between or among shares of such classes of capital stock.

C. In case the Company shall distribute to all holders of its Common Stock evidences of its indebtedness or assets (excluding any cash dividend or distribution which is permitted by § _____ [27]) or rights to subscribe for or warrants to purchase (excluding those referred to in Subsection A of this § 13–6) shares of Common Stock, then in each such case the Conversion Price shall be adjusted so that the same shall equal the price determined by multiplying the Conversion Price in effect immediately prior to the date of such distribution by a fraction whose *numerator* shall be the current market price per share of Common Stock (determined as provided in Subsection D of this § 13–6) on the effective date of distribution less the then fair market value (as determined by the Board of Directors, whose determination shall be conclusive and evidenced by a Board Resolution filed with the Trustee) of the portion of the assets or evidences of indebtedness so distributed or of such subscription rights or warrants applicable to one share of Common Stock, and whose *denominator* shall be such current market price per share of the Common Stock. Subject to Subsection D of this § 13–6, such adjustment shall be made whenever any such distribution is made and shall be retroactively effective as of immediately after the record date for the determination of stockholders entitled to receive such distribution.

D. For the purpose of any computation under Subsections A and C of this § 13–6, the current market price per share of Common Stock on any date shall be deemed to be the average of the daily closing prices for the _____ consecutive business days commencing _____ business days before the day in question. The closing price for each day shall be the last reported sales price regular way or, in case no such reported sale takes place on such day, the average of the reported closing bid and asked prices regular way, in either case on the New York Stock Exchange, or, if the Common Stock is not listed or admitted to trading on such Exchange, on the principal national securities exchange on which the Common Stock is listed or admitted to trading, or, if not listed or admitted to trading on any national securities exchange, the average of the closing bid and asked prices in the over-the-counter market, as furnished by any New York Stock Exchange firm selected from time to time by the Company for that purpose. For purposes of this Subsection the term business day shall not include any day on which securities are not traded on such exchange or in such market.

---

27. The exclusion in the parentheses of cash dividends or distributions which, for example, are paid out of earned surplus and might otherwise be permitted under provisions similar to those found in the Sample Covenants in § 10–12 (Restrictions on Dividends and Other Distributions) may or may not be included in an indenture.

[E]. If any capital reorganization or reclassification of the capital stock of the Company, or consolidation or merger of the Company with another corporation, or the sale of all or substantially all of its assets to another corporation, shall be effected in such a way that holders of Common Stock shall be entitled to receive stock, securities or assets with respect to or in exchange for Common Stock, then, as a condition of such reorganization, reclassification, consolidation, merger or sale, the Company or such successor or purchasing corporation, as the case may be, shall execute with the Trustee a supplemental indenture providing that the Holder of each Debenture then Outstanding shall have the right thereafter and until the expiration of the period of convertibility to convert such Debenture into the kind and amount of stock, securities or assets receivable upon such reorganization, reclassification, consolidation, merger or sale by a holder of the number of shares of Common Stock into which such Debenture might have been converted immediately prior to such reorganization, reclassification, consolidation, merger or sale, subject to adjustments which shall be as nearly equivalent as may be practicable to the adjustments provided for in this Article Thirteen.

§ 13–7. Covenant to Reserve Shares for Conversion.

A. The Company covenants that it will at all times reserve and keep available out of its authorized Common Stock and/or shares of its Common Stock then owned or held by or for the account of the Company, solely for the purpose of delivery upon conversion of Debentures as herein provided, such number of shares of Common Stock as shall then be deliverable upon the conversion of all Outstanding Debentures. All shares of Common Stock which shall be so deliverable shall be duly and validly issued and fully paid and nonassessable.

B. Before taking any action which would cause an adjustment reducing the Current Conversion Price at any time in effect below the then par value of the shares of Common Stock issuable upon conversion of the Debentures, the Company shall take any corporate action which may, in the Opinion of Counsel, be necessary in order that the Company may validly and legally issue fully paid and nonassessable shares of such Common Stock at such Current Conversion Price as so adjusted.

§ 13–8. Compliance With Governmental Requirements.

If any shares of Common Stock required to be reserved for purposes of conversion of Debentures hereunder require registration with or approval of any governmental authority under any Federal or State law, or listing upon any national securities exchange, before such shares may be issued upon conversion, the Company will in good faith and as expeditiously as possible endeavor to cause such shares to be duly registered, approved or listed, as the case may be.

§ 13–9. Notice of Change of Conversion Price.

Whenever the Conversion Price is adjusted, as herein provided, the Company shall promptly file with the Trustee a certificate of a firm of

Independent public accountants (who may be the accountants regularly employed by the Company) selected by the Board of Directors setting forth the Conversion Price after such adjustment and setting forth a brief statement of the facts requiring such adjustment. Such certificate shall be conclusive evidence of the correctness of such adjustment. Notice of an adjustment in the Conversion Price shall be given by publication by the Company at least once in an Authorized Newspaper, such publication to be made as soon as practicable after the filing with the Trustee of the certificate required by this Section.[33]

§ 13–10. Notice of Taking of Certain Actions.

In case:

A.   the Company shall declare a dividend (or any other distribution) on its Common Stock payable otherwise than out of its earned surplus; or

B.   the Company shall authorize the granting to holders of Common Stock of rights to subscribe for or purchase any shares of capital stock of any class or of any other rights; or

C.   of any capital reorganization or reclassification of the capital stock of the Company or of any consolidation or merger of the Company with another corporation, or of the sale of all or substantially all of its assets to another corporation which is to be effected in such a way that holders of Common Stock shall be entitled to receive stock, securities or other assets with respect to or in exchange for Common Stock; or

D.   of the voluntary or involuntary dissolution, liquidation or winding up of the Company;

then the Company shall promptly file with the Trustee and cause to be mailed to the Holders of Debentures at their last addresses as they shall appear on the register provided for in the Indenture, at least 14 days prior to the applicable record date hereinafter specified, a notice stating (1) the date on which a record is to be taken for the purpose of such dividend or distribution of rights, or, if a record is not to be taken, the date as of which the holders of Common Stock of record would be entitled to such dividend or distribution of rights, or (2) the date on which such capital reorganization, reclassification, consolidation, merger, sale, dissolution, liquidation or winding up is expected to become effective, and the date as of which it is expected that the holders of Common Stock of record shall be entitled to exchange their shares of Common Stock for securities or other assets deliverable upon such reorganization, reclassification, consolidation, merger, sale, dissolution, liquidation or winding up. Such notice shall also be published not later than the aforesaid mailing date at least once in an Authorized Newspaper.

---

33. In any particular case, the method of giving the notice referred to in this section will depend upon whether the debentures are in coupon form or registered form or both.

APPENDIX D

THE BANKRUPTCY CODE

1. SELECTED PROVISIONS

§ 361. Adequate protection

When adequate protection is required under section 362, 363, or 364 of this title of an interest of an entity in property, such adequate protection may be provided by—

(1) requiring the trustee to make a cash payment or periodic cash payments to such entity, to the extent that the stay under section 362 of this title, use, sale, or lease under section 363 of this title, or any grant of a lien under section 364 of this title results in a decrease in the value of such entity's interest in such property;

(2) providing to such entity an additional or replacement lien to the extent that such stay, use, sale, lease, or grant results in a decrease in the value of such entity's interest in such property; or

(3) granting such other relief, other than entitling such entity to compensation allowable under section 503(b)(1) of this title as an administrative expense, as will result in the realization by such entity of the indubitable equivalent of such entity's interest in such property.

§ 362. Automatic stay

(a) Except as provided in subsection (b) of this section, a petition filed under section 301, 302, or 303 of this title, or an application filed under section 5(a)(3) of the Securities Investor Protection Act of 1970 (15 U.S.C. 78eee(a)(3)), operates as a stay, applicable to all entities, of—

(1) the commencement or continuation, including the issuance or employment of process, of a judicial, administrative, or other action or proceeding against the debtor that was or could have been commenced before the commencement of the case under this title, or to recover a claim against the debtor that arose before the commencement of the case under this title;

(2) the enforcement, against the debtor or against property of the estate, of a judgment obtained before the commencement of the case under this title;

(3) any act to obtain possession of property of the estate or of property from the estate or to exercise control over property of the estate;

(4) any act to create, perfect, or enforce any lien against property of the estate;

(5) any act to create, perfect, or enforce against property of the debtor any lien to the extent that such lien secures a claim that arose before the commencement of the case under this title;

(6) any act to collect, assess, or recover a claim against the debtor that arose before the commencement of the case under this title;

(7) the setoff of any debt owing to the debtor that arose before the commencement of the case under this title against any claim against the debtor; and

(8) the commencement or continuation of a proceeding before the United States Tax Court concerning the debtor.

* * *

(d) On request of a party in interest and after notice and a hearing, the court shall grant relief from the stay provided under subsection (a) of this section, such as by terminating, annulling, modifying, or conditioning such stay—

(1) for cause, including the lack of adequate protection of an interest in property of such party in interest; or

(2) with respect to a stay of an act against property under subsection (a) of this section, if—

(A) the debtor does not have an equity in such property; and

(B) such property is not necessary to an effective reorganization.

(e) Thirty days after a request under subsection (d) of this section for relief from the stay of any act against property of the estate under subsection (a) of this section, such stay is terminated with respect to the party in interest making such request, unless the court, after notice and a hearing, orders such stay continued in effect pending the conclusion of, or as a result of, a final hearing and determination under subsection (d) of this section. A hearing under this subsection may be a preliminary hearing, or may be consolidated with the final hearing under subsection (d) of this section. The court shall order such stay continued in effect pending the conclusion of the final hearing under subsection (d) of this section if there is a reasonable likelihood that the party opposing relief from such stay will prevail at the conclusion of such final hearing. If the hearing under this subsection is a preliminary hearing, then such final hearing shall be commenced not later than thirty days after the conclusion of such preliminary hearing.

(f) Upon request of a party in interest, the court, with or without a hearing, shall grant such relief from the stay provided under subsection (a) of this section as is necessary to prevent irreparable damage to the interest of an entity in property, if such interest will suffer such damage before there is an opportunity for notice and a hearing under subsection (d) or (e) of this section.

(g) In any hearing under subsection (d) or (e) of this section concerning relief from the stay of any act under subsection (a) of this section—

(1) the party requesting such relief has the burden of proof on the issue of the debtor's equity in property; and

(2) the party opposing such relief has the burden of proof on all other issues.

* * *

§ 1101. Definitions for this chapter

In this chapter—

(1) "debtor in possession" means debtor except when a person that has qualified under section 322 of this title is serving as trustee in the case;

(2) "substantial consummation" means—

(A) transfer of all or substantially all of the property proposed by the plan to be transferred;

(B) assumption by the debtor or by the successor to the debtor under the plan of the business or of the management of all or substantially all of the property dealt with by the plan; and

(C) commencement of distribution under the plan.

§ 1102. Creditors' and equity security holders' committees

(a)(1) As soon as practicable after the order for relief under chapter 11 of this title, the United States trustee shall appoint a committee of creditors holding unsecured claims and may appoint additional committees of creditors or of equity security holders as the United States trustee deems appropriate.

(2) On request of a party in interest, the court may order the appointment of additional committees of creditors or of equity security holders if necessary to assure adequate representation of creditors or of equity security holders. The United States trustee shall appoint any such committee.

(b)(1) A committee of creditors appointed under subsection (a) of this section shall ordinarily consist of the persons, willing to serve, that hold the seven largest claims against the debtor of the kinds represented on such committee, or of the members of a committee organized by creditors before the commencement of the case under this chapter, if such committee was fairly chosen and is representative of the different kinds of claims to be represented.

(2) A committee of equity security holders appointed under subsection (a)(2) of this section shall ordinarily consist of the persons, willing to serve, that hold the seven largest amounts of equity securities of the debtor of the kinds represented on such committee.

§ 1103. Powers and duties of committees

(a) At a scheduled meeting of a committee appointed under section 1102 of this title, at which a majority of the members of such committee are present, and with the court's approval, such committee may select and authorize the employment by such committee of one or more attorneys, accountants, or other agents, to represent or perform services for such committee.

(b) An attorney or accountant employed to represent a committee appointed under section 1102 of this title may not, while employed by such committee, represent any other entity having an adverse interest in connection with the case. Representation of one or more creditors of the same class as represented by the committee shall not per se constitute the representation of an adverse interest.

(c) A committee appointed under section 1102 of this title may—

(1) consult with the trustee or debtor in possession concerning the administration of the case;

(2) investigate the acts, conduct, assets, liabilities, and financial condition of the debtor, the operation of the debtor's business and the desirability of the continuance of such business, and any other matter relevant to the case or to the formulation of a plan;

(3) participate in the formulation of a plan, advise those represented by such committee of such committee's determinations as to any plan formulated, and collect and file with the court acceptances or rejections of a plan;

(4) request the appointment of a trustee or examiner under section 1104 of this title; and

(5) perform such other services as are in the interest of those represented.

(d) As soon as practicable after the appointment of a committee under section 1102 of this title, the trustee shall meet with such committee to transact such business as may be necessary and proper.

§ 1104. Appointment of trustee or examiner

(a) At any time after the commencement of the case but before confirmation of a plan, on request of a party in interest or the United States trustee, and after notice and a hearing, the court shall order the appointment of a trustee—

(1) for cause, including fraud, dishonesty, incompetence, or gross mismanagement of the affairs of the debtor by current management, either before or after the commencement of the case, or similar cause, but not including the number of holders of securities of the debtor or the amount of assets or liabilities of the debtor; or

(2) if such appointment is in the interests of creditors, any equity security holders, and other interests of the estate, without regard to the number of holders of securities of the debtor or the amount of assets or liabilities of the debtor.

* * *

§ 1111. Claims and interests

(a) A proof of claim or interest is deemed filed under section 501 of this title for any claim or interest that appears in the schedules filed under section 521(1) or 1106(a)(2) of this title, except a claim or interest that is scheduled as disputed, contingent, or unliquidated.

(b)(1)(A) A claim secured by a lien on property of the estate shall be allowed or disallowed under section 502 of this title the same as if the holder of such claim had recourse against the debtor on account of such claim, whether or not such holder has such recourse, unless—

(i) the class of which such claim is a part elects, by at least two-thirds in amount and more than half in number of allowed claims of such class, application of paragraph (2) of this subsection; or

(ii) such holder does not have such recourse and such property is sold under section 363 of this title or is to be sold under the plan.

(B) A class of claims may not elect application of paragraph (2) of this subsection if—

(i) the interest on account of such claims of the holders of such claims in such property is of inconsequential value; or

(ii) the holder of a claim of such class has recourse against the debtor on account of such claim and such property is sold under section 363 of this title or is to be sold under the plan.

(2) If such an election is made, then notwithstanding section 506(a) of this title, such claim is a secured claim to the extent that such claim is allowed.

§ 1121. Who may file a plan

(a) The debtor may file a plan with a petition commencing a voluntary case, or at any time in a voluntary case or an involuntary case.

(b) Except as otherwise provided in this section, only the debtor may file a plan until after 120 days after the date of the order for relief under this chapter.

(c) Any party in interest, including the debtor, the trustee, a creditors' committee, an equity security holders' committee, a creditor, an equity security holder, or any indenture trustee, may file a plan if and only if—

(1) a trustee has been appointed under this chapter;

(2) the debtor has not filed a plan before 120 days after the date of the order for relief under this chapter; or

(3) the debtor has not filed a plan that has been accepted, before 180 days after the date of the order for relief under this chapter, by each class of claims or interests that is impaired under the plan.

(d) On request of a party in interest made within the respective periods specified in subsections (b) and (c) of this section and after notice and a hearing, the court may for cause reduce or increase the 120–day period or the 180–day period referred to in this section.

§ 1122. Classification of claims or interests

(a) Except as provided in subsection (b) of this section, a plan may place a claim or an interest in a particular class only if such claim or interest is substantially similar to the other claims or interests of such class.

(b) A plan may designate a separate class of claims consisting only of every unsecured claim that is less than or reduced to an amount that the court approves as reasonable and necessary for administrative convenience.

§ 1123. Contents of plan

(a) Notwithstanding any otherwise applicable nonbankruptcy law, a plan shall—

(1) designate, subject to section 1122 of this title, classes of claims, other than claims of a kind specified in section 507(a)(1), 507(a)(2), or 507(a)(7) of this title, and classes of interests;

(2) specify any class of claims or interests that is not impaired under the plan;

(3) specify the treatment of any class of claims or interests that is impaired under the plan;

(4) provide the same treatment for each claim or interest of a particular class, unless the holder of a particular claim or interest agrees to a less favorable treatment of such particular claim or interest;

(5) provide adequate means for the plan's implementation, such as—

    (A) retention by the debtor of all or any part of the property of the estate;

    (B) transfer of all or any part of the property of the estate to one or more entities, whether organized before or after the confirmation of such plan;

    (C) merger or consolidation of the debtor with one or more persons;

    (D) sale of all or any part of the property of the estate, either subject to or free of any lien, or the distribution of all or any part of the property of the estate among those having an interest in such property of the estate;

    (E) satisfaction or modification of any lien;

    (F) cancellation or modification of any indenture or similar instrument;

    (G) curing or waiving of any default;

    (H) extension of a maturity date or a change in an interest rate or other term of outstanding securities;

    (I) amendment of the debtor's charter; or

    (J) issuance of securities of the debtor, or of any entity referred to in subparagraph (B) or (C) of this paragraph, for cash, for property, for existing securities, or in exchange for claims or interests, or for any other appropriate purpose;

(6) provide for the inclusion in the charter of the debtor, if the debtor is a corporation, or of any corporation referred to in paragraph (5)(B) or (5)(C) of this subsection, of a provision prohibiting the issuance of nonvoting equity securities, and providing, as to the several classes of securities possessing voting power, an appropriate distribution of such power among such classes, including, in the case of any class of equity securities having a preference over another class of equity securities with respect to dividends, adequate provisions for the election of directors representing such preferred class in the event of default in the payment of such dividends; and

(7) contain only provisions that are consistent with the interests of creditors and equity security holders and with public policy with respect to the manner of selection of any officer, director, or trustee under the plan and any successor to such officer, director, or trustee.

(b) Subject to subsection (a) of this section, a plan may—

(1) impair or leave unimpaired any class of claims, secured or unsecured, or of interests;

(2) subject to section 365 of this title, provide for the assumption, rejection, or assignment of any executory contract or unexpired lease of the debtor not previously rejected under such section;

(3) provide for—

(A) the settlement or adjustment of any claim or interest belonging to the debtor or to the estate; or

(B) the retention and enforcement by the debtor, by the trustee, or by a representative of the estate appointed for such purpose, of any such claim or interest;

(4) provide for the sale of all or substantially all of the property of the estate, and the distribution of the proceeds of such sale among holders of claims or interests; and

(5) include any other appropriate provision not inconsistent with the applicable provisions of this title.

(c) In a case concerning an individual, a plan proposed by an entity other than the debtor may not provide for the use, sale, or lease of property exempted under section 522 of this title, unless the debtor consents to such use, sale, or lease.

§ 1124. Impairment of claims or interests

Except as provided in section 1123(a)(4) of this title, a class of claims or interests is impaired under a plan unless, with respect to each claim or interest of such class, the plan—

(1) leaves unaltered the legal, equitable, and contractual rights to which such claim or interest entitles the holder of such claim or interest;

(2) notwithstanding any contractual provision or applicable law that entitles the holder of such claim or interest to demand or receive accelerated payment of such claim or interest after the occurrence of a default—

(A) cures any such default that occurred before or after the commencement of the case under this title, other than a default of a kind specified in section 365(b)(2) of this title;

(B) reinstates the maturity of such claim or interest as such maturity existed before such default;

(C) compensates the holder of such claim or interest for any damages incurred as a result of any reasonable reliance by such holder on such contractual provision or such applicable law; and

(D) does not otherwise alter the legal, equitable, or contractual rights to which such claim or interest entitles the holder of such claim or interest; or

(3) provides that, on the effective date of the plan, the holder of such claim or interest receives, on account of such claim or interest, cash equal to—

(A) with respect to a claim, the allowed amount of such claim; or

(B) with respect to an interest, if applicable, the greater of—

(i) any fixed liquidation preference to which the terms of any security representing such interest entitle the holder of such interest; or

(ii) any fixed price at which the debtor, under the terms of such security, may redeem such security from such holder.

§ 1125. Postpetition disclosure and solicitation

(a) In this section—

(1) "adequate information" means information of a kind, and in sufficient detail, as far as is reasonably practicable in light of the nature and history of the debtor and the condition of the debtor's books and records, that would enable a hypothetical reasonable investor typical of holders of claims or interests of the relevant class to make an informed judgment about the plan, but adequate information need not include such information about any other possible or proposed plan; and

(2) "investor typical of holders of claims or interests of the relevant class" means investor having—

(A) a claim or interest of the relevant class;

(B) such a relationship with the debtor as the holders of other claims or interests of such class generally have; and

(C) such ability to obtain such information from sources other than the disclosure required by this section as holders of claims or interest in such class generally have.

(b) An acceptance or rejection of a plan may not be solicited after the commencement of the case under this title from a holder of a claim or interest with respect to such claim or interest, unless, at the time of or before such solicitation, there is transmitted to such holder the plan or a summary of the plan, and a written disclosure statement approved, after notice and a hearing, by the court as containing adequate information. The court may approve a disclosure statement without a valuation of the debtor or an appraisal of the debtor's assets.

(c) The same disclosure statement shall be transmitted to each holder of a claim or interest of a particular class, but there may be transmitted different disclosure statements, differing in amount, detail, or kind of information, as between classes.

(d) Whether a disclosure statement required under subsection (b) of this section contains adequate information is not governed by any otherwise applicable nonbankruptcy law, rule, or regulation, but an agency or official whose duty is to administer or enforce such a law, rule, or regulation may be heard on the issue of whether a disclosure statement contains adequate information. Such an agency or official may not appeal from, or otherwise seek review of, an order approving a disclosure statement.

(e) A person that solicits acceptance or rejection of a plan, in good faith and in compliance with the applicable provisions of this title, or that participates, in good faith and in compliance with the applicable provisions of this title, in the offer, issuance, sale, or purchase of a security, offered or sold under the plan, of the debtor, of an affiliate participating in a joint plan with the debtor, or of a newly organized successor to the debtor under the plan, is not liable, on account of such solicitation or participation, for violation of any applicable law, rule, or regulation governing solicitation of acceptance or rejection of a plan or the offer, issuance, sale, or purchase of securities.

§ 1126. Acceptance of plan

(a) The holder of a claim or interest allowed under section 502 of this title may accept or reject a plan. If the United States is a creditor or equity security holder, the Secretary of the Treasury may accept or reject the plan on behalf of the United States.

(b) For the purposes of subsections (c) and (d) of this section, a holder of a claim or interest that has accepted or rejected the plan before the commencement of the case under this title is deemed to have accepted or rejected such plan, as the case may be, if—

    (1) the solicitation of such acceptance or rejection was in compliance with any applicable nonbankruptcy law, rule, or regulation governing the adequacy of disclosure in connection with such solicitation; or

    (2) if there is not any such law, rule, or regulation, such acceptance or rejection was solicited after disclosure to such holder of adequate information, as defined in section 1125(a) of this title.

(c) A class of claims has accepted a plan if such plan has been accepted by creditors, other than any entity designated under subsection (e) of this section, that hold at least two-thirds in amount and more than one-half in number of the allowed claims of such class held by creditors, other than any entity designated under subsection (e) of this section, that have accepted or rejected such plan.

(d) A class of interests has accepted a plan if such plan has been accepted by holders of such interests, other than any entity designated under subsection (e) of this section, that hold at least two-thirds in amount of the allowed interests of such class held by holders of such interests, other than any entity designated under subsection (e) of this section, that have accepted or rejected such plan.

(e) On request of a party in interest, and after notice and a hearing, the court may designate any entity whose acceptance or rejection of such plan was not in good faith, or was not solicited or procured in good faith or in accordance with the provisions of this title.*

(f) Notwithstanding any other provision of this section, a class that is not impaired under a plan, and each holder of a claim or interest of such class, are conclusively presumed to have accepted the plan, and solicitation of acceptances with respect to such class from the holders of claims or interests of such class is not required.

(g) Notwithstanding any other provision of this section, a class is deemed not to have accepted a plan if such plan provides that the claims or interests of such class do not entitle the holders of such claims or interests to receive or retain any property under the plan on account of such claims or interests.

§ 1128. Confirmation hearing

(a) After notice, the court shall hold a hearing on confirmation of a plan.

(b) A party in interest may object to confirmation of a plan.

§ 1129. Confirmation of plan

(a) The court shall confirm a plan only if all of the following requirements are met:

(1) The plan complies with the applicable provisions of this title.

(2) The proponent of the plan complies with the applicable provisions of this title.

(3) The plan has been proposed in good faith and not by any means forbidden by law.

---

* [Ed. Note]

Is it of any significance that a previous version of subsection (e) permitted exclusion of the votes of any person who, with respect to the class, had such a conflict of interest "as would justify exclusion" for calculating the amounts and numbers of the class required to accept? According to H.R.Rep. No. 95–595 at 411, "A person might have such a conflict, for example, where he held a claim or interest in more than one class. Exclusion from one class for voting purposes would not require his exclusion from the other class as well.

The result is to overrule cases such as Aladdin Hotel Corp. v. Bloom, 200 F.2d 627 (8th Cir.1953), which though not in the bankruptcy context, would appear to count votes for a reorganization plan motivated by an attempt to squeeze out a minority of a class. In that case, the conflict interest of those voting for the plan was clear, but the court permitted the votes." The provision was said to be unnecessary in view of the Bankruptcy Court's general powers to issue appropriate orders under § 105. See 124 Cong.Rec. 103 (Daily Ed. 10/28/78) Cong. Edwards.

(4) Any payment made or to be made by the proponent, by the debtor, or by a person issuing securities or acquiring property under the plan, for services or for costs and expenses in or in connection with the case, or in connection with the plan and incident to the case, has been approved by, or is subject to the approval of, the court as reasonable;

(5)(A)(i) The proponent of the plan has disclosed the identity and affiliations of any individual proposed to serve, after confirmation of the plan, as a director, officer, or voting trustee of the debtor, an affiliate of the debtor participating in a joint plan with the debtor, or a successor to the debtor under the plan; and

(ii) the appointment to, or continuance in, such office of such individual, is consistent with the interests of creditors and equity security holders and with public policy; and

(B) the proponent of the plan has disclosed the identity of any insider that will be employed or retained by the reorganized debtor, and the nature of any compensation for such insider.

(6) Any governmental regulatory commission with jurisdiction, after confirmation of the plan, over the rates of the debtor has approved any rate change provided for in the plan, or such rate change is expressly conditioned on such approval.

(7) With respect to each impaired class of claims or interests—

(A) each holder of a claim or interest of such class—

(i) has accepted the plan; or

(ii) will receive or retain under the plan on account of such claim or interest property of a value, as of the effective date of the plan, that is not less than the amount that such holder would so receive or retain if the debtor were liquidated under chapter 7 of this title on such date; or

(B) if section 1111(b)(2) of this title applies to the claims of such class, each holder of a claim of such class will receive or retain under the plan on account of such claim property of a value, as of the effective date of the plan, that is not less than the value of such holder's interest in the estate's interest in the property that secures such claims.

(8) With respect to each class of claims or interests—

(A) such class has accepted the plan; or

(B) such class is not impaired under the plan.

(9) Except to the extent that the holder of a particular claim has agreed to a different treatment of such claim, the plan provides that—

(A) with respect to a claim of a kind specified in section 507(a)(1) or 507(a)(2) of this title, on the effective date of the plan, the holder of such claim will receive on account of such claim cash equal to the allowed amount of such claim;

(B) with respect to a class of claims of a kind specified in section 507(a)(3), 507(a)(4), 507(a)(5) or 507(a)(6) of this title, each holder of a claim of such class will receive—

(i) if such class has accepted the plan, deferred cash payments of a value, as of the effective date of the plan, equal to the allowed amount of such claim; or

(ii) if such class has not accepted the plan, cash on the effective date of the plan equal to the allowed amount of such claim; and

(C) with respect to a claim of a kind specified in section 507(a)(7) of this title, the holder of such claim will receive on account of such claim deferred cash payments, over a period not exceeding six years after the date of assessment of such claim, of a value, as of the effective date of the plan, equal to the allowed amount of such claim.

(10) If a class of claims is impaired under the plan, at least one class of claims that is impaired under the plan has accepted the plan, determined without including any acceptance of the plan by any insider.

(11) Confirmation of the plan is not likely to be followed by the liquidation, or the need for further financial reorganization, of the debtor or any successor to the debtor under the plan, unless such liquidation or reorganization is proposed in the plan.

(12) All fees payable under section 1930, as determined by the court at the hearing on confirmation of the plan, have been paid or the plan provides for the payment of all such fees on the effective date of the plan.

(13) The plan provides for the continuation after its effective date of payment of all retiree benefits, as that term is defined in section 1114 of this title, at the level established pursuant to subsection (e)(1)(B) or (g) of section 1114 of this title, at any time prior to confirmation of the plan, for the duration of the period the debtor has obligated itself to provide such benefits.

(b)(1) Notwithstanding section 510(a) of this title, if all of the applicable requirements of subsection (a) of this section other than paragraph (8) are met with respect to a plan, the court, on request of the proponent of the plan, shall confirm the plan notwithstanding the requirements of such paragraph if the plan does not discriminate unfairly, and is fair and equitable, with respect to each class of claims or interests that is impaired under, and has not accepted, the plan.

(2) For the purpose of this subsection, the condition that a plan be fair and equitable with respect to a class includes the following requirements:

 (A) With respect to a class of secured claims, the plan provides—

  (i)(I) that the holders of such claims retain the liens securing such claims, whether the property subject to such liens is retained by the debtor or transferred to another entity, to the extent of the allowed amount of such claims; and

  (II) that each holder of a claim of such class receive on account of such claim deferred cash payments totaling at least the allowed amount of such claim, of a value, as of the effective date of the plan, of at least the value of such holder's interest in the estate's interest in such property;

  (ii) for the sale, subject to section 363(k) of this title, of any property that is subject to the liens securing such claims, free and clear of such liens, with such liens to attach to the proceeds of such sale, and the treatment of such liens on proceeds under clause (i) or (iii) of this subparagraph; or

  (iii) for the realization by such holders of the indubitable equivalent of such claims.

 (B) With respect to a class of unsecured claims—

  (i) the plan provides that each holder of a claim of such class receive or retain on account of such claim property of a value, as of the effective date of the plan, equal to the allowed amount of such claim; or

  (ii) the holder of any claim or interest that is junior to the claims of such class will not receive or retain under the plan on account of such junior claim or interest any property.

 (C) With respect to a class of interests—

  (i) the plan provides that each holder of an interest of such class receive or retain on account of such interest property of a value, as of the effective date of the plan, equal to the greatest of the allowed amount of any fixed liquidation preference to which such holder is entitled, any fixed redemption price to which such holder is entitled, or the value of such interest; or

  (ii) the holder of any interest that is junior to the interests of such class will not receive or retain under the plan on account of such junior interest any property.

(c) Notwithstanding subsections (a) and (b) of this section and except as provided in section 1127(b) of this title, the court may confirm only one plan, unless the order of confirmation in the case has been revoked under section 1144 of this title. If the requirements of subsections (a) and (b) of this section are met with respect to more than one plan, the court shall consider the preferences of creditors and equity security holders in determining which plan to confirm.

(d) Notwithstanding any other provision of this section, on request of a party in interest that is a governmental unit, the court may not confirm a plan if the principal purpose of the plan is the avoidance of taxes or the avoidance of the application of section 5 of the Securities Act of 1933 (15 U.S.C. 77e). In any hearing under this subsection, the governmental unit has the burden of proof on the issue of avoidance.

§ 1173. Confirmation of Plan [Railroad Reorganizations]

(a) The court shall confirm a plan if—

(1) the applicable requirements of section 1129 of this title have been met;

(2) each creditor or equity security holder will receive or retain under the plan property of a value, as of the effective date of the plan, that is not less than the value of property that each such creditor or equity security holder would so receive or retain if all of the operating railroad lines of the debtor were sold, and the proceeds of such sale, and the other property of the estate, were distributed under chapter 7 of this title on such date;

(3) in light of the debtor's past earnings and the probable prospective earnings of the reorganized debtor, there will be adequate coverage by such prospective earnings of any fixed charges, such as interest on debt, amortization of funded debt, and rent for leased railroads, provided for by the plan; and

(4) the plan is compatible with the public interest.

(b) If the requirements of subsection (a) of this section are met with respect to more than one plan, the court shall confirm the plan that is most likely to maintain adequate rail service in the public interest.

2. EXCERPTS FROM THE HOUSE REPORT

THE HOUSE REPORT
(H.R.Rep. No. 95–595 (95th Cong. 1st Sess.1977), pp. 408–418, 425).

§ 1124. Impairment of Claims or Interests

This section is new. It is designed to indicate when contractual rights of creditors or interest holders are not materially affected. The section specifies three ways in which the plan may leave a claim or interest unimpaired.

First, the plan may propose not to alter the legal, equitable, or contractual rights to which the claim or interest entitled its holder.

Second, the plan is permitted to reinstate a claim or interest and thus leave it unimpaired. Reinstatement consists of curing any default (other than a default under an ipso facto or bankruptcy clause) and reinstatement of the maturity of the claim or interest. Further, the plan may not otherwise alter any legal, equitable, or contractual right to which the claim or interest entitles its holder.

Third, the plan may leave a claim or interest unimpaired by paying its amount in full other than in securities of the debtor, an affiliate of the debtor participating in a joint plan, or a successor to the debtor. These securities are excluded because determination of their value would require a valuation of the business being reorganized. Use of them to pay a creditor or equity security holder without his consent may be done only under section 1129(b) and only after a valuation of the debtor. Under this paragraph, the plan must pay the allowed amount of the claim in full, in cash or other property, or, in the case of an equity security, must pay the greatest of any fixed liquidation preference to which the terms of the equity security entitle its holder, any fixed price at which the debtor, under the terms of the equity security may redeem such equity security, and the value, as of the effective date of the plan, of the holder's interest in the debtor. The value of the holder's interest need not be determined precisely by valuing the debtor's business if such value is clearly below redemption or liquidation preference values. If such value would require a full-scale valuation of the business, then such interest should be treated as impaired. But, if the debtor corporation is clearly insolvent, then the value of the common stock holder's interest in the debtor is zero, and offering them nothing under the plan of reorganization will not impair their rights.

"Value, as of the effective date of the plan," as used in paragraph (3) and in proposed 11 U.S.C. 1179(a)(7)(B), 1129(a)(9), 1129(b), 1172(2), 1325(a)(4), 1325(a)(5)(B), and 1328(b), indicates that the promised payment under the plan must be discounted to present value as of the effective date of the plan. The discounting should be based only on the unpaid balance of the amount due under the plan, until that amount, including interest, is paid in full.

§ 1125. Postpetition Disclosure and Solicitation

This section is new. It is the heart of the consolidation of the various reorganization chapters found in current law. It requires disclosure before solicitation of acceptances of a plan of reorganization.

Subsection (a) contains two definitions. First, "adequate information" is defined to mean information of a kind, and in sufficient detail, as far as is reasonably practical in light of the nature and history of the debtor and the condition of the debtor's books and records, that would enable a hypothetical reasonable investor typical of holders of claims or interests of the relevant class to make an informed judgment about the plan. Second, "investor typical of holders of claims or interests of the relevant class" is defined to mean an investor having a claim or interest of the relevant class, having such a relationship with the debtor as the holders of other claims or interests of the relevant class have, and having such ability to obtain information from sources other than the disclosure statement as holders of claims or interests of the relevant class have, and having such ability to obtain information from sources other tha[n] the disclosure statement as holders of claims or interests of the relevant class have. That is, the hypothetical investor against which the disclosure is measured must not be an insider if other members of the class are not insiders, and so on. In other words, the adequacy of disclosure is measured against the typical investor, not an extraordinary one.

The Supreme Court's rulemaking power will not extend to rule-making that will prescribe what constitutes adequate information. That standard is a substantive standard. Precisely what constitutes adequate information in any particular instance will develop on a case-by-case basis. Courts will take a practical approach as to what is necessary under the circumstances of each case, such as the cost of preparation of the statements, the need for relative speed in solicitation and confirmation, and, of course, the need for investor protection. There will be a balancing of interests in each case. In reorganization cases, there is frequently great uncertainty. Therefore the need for flexibility is greatest.

Subsection (b) is the operative subsection. It prohibits solicitation of acceptances or rejections of a plan after the commencement of the case unless, at the time of the solicitation or before, there is transmitted to the solicitee the plan or a summary of the plan, and a written disclosure statement approved by the court as containing adequate information. The subsection permits approval of the statement without the necessity of a valuation of the debtor or an appraisal of the debtor's assets. However, in some cases, a valuation or appraisal will be necessary to develop adequate information. The court will be able to determine what is necessary in light of the facts and circumstances of each particular case.

Subsection (c) requires that the same disclosure statement go to all members of a particular class, but permits different disclosure to different classes.

Subsection (d) excepts the disclosure statements from the requirements of the securities laws (such as section 14 of the 1934 Act and section 5 of the 1933 Act), and from similar State securities laws (blue sky laws, for example). The subsection permits an agency or official whose duty is to administer or enforce such laws (such as the Securities and Exchange Commission or State Corporation Commissioners) to appear and be heard on the issue of whether a disclosure statement contains adequate information, but the agencies and officials are not granted the right of appeal from an adverse determination in any capacity. They may join in an appeal by a true party in interest, however.

Subsection (e) is a safe harbor provision, and is necessary to make the exemption provided by subsection (d) effective. Without it, a creditor that solicited an acceptance or rejection in reliance on the court's approval of a disclosure statement would be potentially liable under antifraud sections designed to enforce the very sections of the securities laws from which subsection (d) excuses compliance. The subsection protects only persons that solicit in good faith and in compliance with the applicable provisions of the reorganization chapter. It provides protection from legal liability as well as from equitable liability based on an injunctive action by the SEC or other agency or official.

* * *

§ 1129. Confirmation of Plan

Subsection (a) enumerates the requirement governing confirmation of a plan. The court is required to confirm a plan if and only if all of the requirements are met.

* * *

Paragraph (7) incorporates the former "best interest of creditors" test found in chapter 11, but spells out precisely what is intended. With respect to each class, the holders of the claims or interests of that class must receive or retain under the plan on account of those claims or interest property of a value, as of the effective date of the plan, that is not less than the amount that they would so receive or retain if the debtor were liquidated under chapter 7 on the effective date of the plan.

In order to determine the hypothetical distribution in a liquidation, the court will have to consider the various subordination provisions of proposed 11 U.S.C. 510, 726(a)(3), 726(a)(4), and the postponement provisions of proposed 11 U.S.C. 724. Also applicable in appropriate cases will be the rules governing partnership distributions under proposed 11 U.S.C. 723, and distributions of community property under proposed 11 U.S.C. 726(c).

* * *

Property under subparagraph (B) may include securities of the debtor. Thus, the provision will apply in cases in which the plan is confirmed under proposed 11 U.S.C. 1129(b).

Paragraph (8) is central to the confirmation standards. It requires that each class either have accepted the plan or be unimpaired.

* * *

Paragraph * * * [11] contains the feasibility standards. It requires that the court find that confirmation of the plan is not likely to be followed by the liquidation or need for further financial reorganization of the debtor or any successor to the debtor, unless the plan so contemplates (such as under a liquidating plan).

[The House Report's discussion of section 1129(b) is set out in the text supra at 313–315.]

APPENDIX E

SECURED CREDITORS UNDER THE BANKRUPTCY CODE

(1) Problem

Ineptco is a manufacturing concern which has fallen upon hard times. Its debt/capital structure is as follows: 10,000 $1,000 principal amount, 10% yield first mortgage bonds secured by its plant; unsecured debt in the amount of $5,000,000, and 10,000 shares of common stock. Its balance sheet is presented below:

Ineptco—Balance Sheet

January 1, 199x

(000 omitted)

Cash	500	First Mortgage Bonds	10,000
Accounts Receivable....	1,500	Unsecured Debt..........	5,000
Inventory.............	3,000	Common Stock Equity....	(3,000)
Plant.................	7,000		12,000
	12,000		

The "fairly" determined [a] going concern value of Ineptco equals 115% of the book value of its assets: $13.8 million, $8.8 million of which is attributable to its plant. The plant would command $6 million and inventory $2 million if disposed of on a forced sale basis while Ineptco's accounts receivable can be liquidated for $1 million, making the liquidation value of the firm's assets $9 million.

Ineptco has defaulted on its bond payments, interest arrears of $1 million, and on its unsecured debt obligations, interest arrears of $100,000. Its management has decided to petition for reorganization under Chapter 11 of the Bankruptcy Code. The following are questions which may arise during the proceedings. Assume that all proposed plans meet the good faith requirement of section 1129(a)(3) and the feasibility requirement of section 1129(a)(11).

Questions

1. What type of valuation proceeding does Chapter 11 require if all impaired classes accept Ineptco's reorganization plan, with at least one individual creditor or shareholder dissenting? If all classes and members within each class approve? If an impaired class does not accept? What was the requirement under Chapter X? What difference does it make?

a. As used in Brudney, The Bankruptcy Commission's Proposed "Modifications" of the Absolute Priority Rule, 48 Am.Bankr. L.J. 305, 321–323 (1974).

2.   Determine the classes and the allowed amounts of claims of the bondholders and unsecured creditors.

In answering, consider that the first mortgage bondholders have claims totalling $11 million. Since the valuations of the property securing the bonds range from $8.8 million (going concern) to $6 million (forced sale), will the first mortgage bondholders have both secured and unsecured claims? Section 506(a) provides that the bondholders have a secured claim "to the extent of the value of [their] interest" in the debtor's property. Which valuation of the plant should be used to determine the amount of the bondholder's secured claim? See the discussion infra pp. E–21 – E–22. Collier states that liquidation valuation is inappropriate when the debtor proposes to use the secured property after reorganization and suggests that going concern valuation is appropriate, especially when the court finds that the prospects of success of the reorganized debtor are good. 3 Collier on Bankruptcy ¶ 506.04, 506–24, 27. On this authority, the bondholder's allowed secured claim is $8.8 million. Thus, the bondholders have two claims: a secured claim of $8.8 million and an unsecured claim of $2.2 million, if they do not make the section 1111(b) election.[b] Would the bondholders' two claims be placed in separate classes which would vote separately? The unsecured creditors have claims totalling $5.1 million. Should the claims of the trade creditors, debenture holders, and the unsecured deficiency claims of the bondholders constitute a single class? Can some of the claims be subordinated under section 510? (Question 7 also concerns the classification of the unsecured claims into classes.)

3.   Using the claim values derived in question 1, would the absolute priority rule be satisfied by the following allocations?

The going concern value of the reorganized enterprise is $13.8 million. Absolute priority requires that the bondholders receive $8.8 million for their secured claims. The difference between these amounts, $5 million, is to be divided between the unsecured claims of the bondholders ($2.2 million) and the unsecured creditors ($5.1 million) in proportion to the size of their claims. Thus,

---

b. Section 1111(b)(2) allows secured creditors to elect to have their entire claim treated as secured, thus giving them an interest in any increase in the value of the liened assets after reorganization. The cost of such election (which offers a kind of second bite to secured creditors) is loss of their right to be treated as unsecured for the balance of their allowed claim, with the accompanying loss of a claim against the unsecured assets and of voting power as an unsecured creditor in the reorganization.

Bondholders Unsecured = $\frac{2.2}{7.3}$ × (5 million) = \$1.5 million*
Claims

Unsecured Creditors = $\frac{5.1}{7.3}$ × (5 million) = \$3.5 million*
Claims

* Approximately.

[313a]

Old common will receive nothing, unless, of course, every senior class unanimously approved its participation.

4.   Again using the claim values derived in question 1, what is the smallest amount a majority of each class of creditors could consent to receive under Chapter 11? If each class of creditors so consents, what would be the participation of old common in the reorganized enterprise?

Consider that section 1129(a)(7) provides that the secured class may agree to accept any amount above \$6 million, the liquidation value of its security interest. If the secured class agrees to this, the remaining \$3 million of the \$9 million liquidation value of the assets could be divided between the unsecured classes. From question 1, recall that the bondholders' unsecured claims amount to \$2.2 million, while the remaining unsecured creditors have claims of \$5.1 million. Thus,

Bondholders Unsecured = $\frac{2.2}{7.3}$ × (3 million) = \$0.9 million*
Claims

Unsecured Creditors = $\frac{5.1}{7.3}$ × (3 million) = \$2.1 million*
Claims

* Approximately.

[314a]

The going concern value of the reorganized enterprise is \$13.8 million. Under Chapter 11, it is possible that the old common could receive up to \$4.8 million (35% of the value) of the tickets of the new enterprise, if two-thirds in amount and a majority in number of those voting of each class of senior claims consent to receiving the minimum amount allowed by statute.

The following is a table comparing the results obtained under the absolute priority rule and the most favorable equity treatment possible under Chapter 11.

E–3

COMPARISON OF ABSOLUTE PRIORITY AND MOST FAVORABLE EQUITY TREATMENT UNDER CHAPTER 11

	Allowed Amount	Absolute Priority	Chapter 11
Bondholders:			
Secured Claims:	8.8	8.8	6.0
Unsecured Claims:	2.2	1.5	0.9
Unsecured Debt:			
Unsecured Claims:	5.1	3.5	2.1
Equity:	—	0.0	4.8

5. Ineptco proposes a plan which offers the secured class of claims common stock of the reorganized enterprise with a value equalling the allowed amount of their claims. If the plan is not approved by the requisite majority of the class, can it be "crammed down" on them?

On the one hand, section 1129(b)(2)(a)(i)(II) requires that any new paper of the debtor issued to a dissenting class of secured creditors be in the nature of an indebtedness. See Blum, Treatment of Interest on Debtor Obligations in Reorganizations Under the Bankruptcy Code, 50 U.Chi.L.Rev. 430, 445 (1983). On the other hand, section 1129(b)(2)(A)(iii) provides that, in the alternative, absolute priority is satisfied if the holders receive the "indubitable equivalent" of their claims. May this provision be employed so as to give the secured class common stock of the reorganized enterprise with a value equaling the allowed amount of their claims along with something extra for the loss of senior rights? There are statements in 124 Cong.Rec. 32407 and 34007 that "Unsecured notes as to the secured claim or equity securities of the debtor would not be the indubitable equivalent" within the meaning of section 1129(b)(2)(A)(iii). See also 5 Collier on Bankruptcy ¶ 1129.03[4][c] (15th ed. 1991). Does this mean that a corporate debtor can never be reorganized where all assets are encumbered and worth less than the secured debt, or when considerations of feasibility dictate an all-stock plan?

6. Another plan proposes that the bondholders retain their security interest in the plant and receive 20 annual cash payments of $1.4 million [c] on account of their secured claims, the first payment commencing 1 year after confirmation of the plan. The court finds that a discount rate of 15% is appropriate for discounting the cash payments to present value. The secured class does not approve the plan and brings forth an expert witness who testifies that the cash value of the tickets issued is $6 million dollars. The proponents of the plan do not

c. The present value of these payments discounted at 15% is $8.75 million (approximately $8.8 million).

dispute this testimony yet still move to have the plan "crammed down" on the secured class. What result?

Section 1129(b)(2)(a)(i)(II) provides that holders of secured claims are to receive on account of such claims deferred cash payments which have a value on the effective date of the plan equal to at least the value of their interest in the debtor's property. This rule says pay 100% of the claim and take into account the time value of money, but does not address the question of the valuation of tickets—nominal or cash value—which is precisely the issue in dispute. From question 1, we know that the value of the secured interest in the debtor's property is $8.8 million. If nominal value is the standard used, will the plan pass muster, because the present value of the cash payments is approximately $8.8 million? If the standard is cash value, will the plan fail?

7. The unsecured creditors consist of debenture holders and trade creditors. In addition, the secured debt has an unsecured claim equal to its deficiency claim, if it does not make the section 1111(b) election. At the time the Chapter 11 petition was filed, the outstanding principal amounts and interest arrears of the trade notes and debentures were equal. The debentures and the trade debt have the same claim priority. If the debenture holders and trade creditors are considered separate classes, can they be treated differently? If they are aggregated into a single class? Should they be treated differently? Might they have different interests?

8. Ineptco proposed the following plan: the bondholders are to retain their liens and receive 20 annual cash payments of $1.25 million on account of their secured claims, the first payment to be received one year after adoption of the plan, and 30% of the new common on account of their unsecured claims; the unsecured creditors are to receive 60% of the new common; and the old common shareholders are to receive the remaining 10% of the new common. The court finds that 15% is the appropriate discount rate to apply to the cash payments. Does the plan meet Chapter 11 standards if the requisite majority of each class approves the plan? If the class of unsecured claims dissents, what will be the result?

Consider that the present discounted value of the 20 annual cash payments is $7.8 million, which exceeds the liquidation value of the collateral. Since the going concern value is $13.8 million, the value of the new common should be equal to the difference, $6 million, if the court chose the proper discount rate for the cash payments. 30% of $6 million is $1.8 million, the value of the common received by the bondholders on account of their unsecured claims; 60% of $6 million is $3.6 million, the value of the common received by the general unsecured creditors on account of their unsecured claims; and 10% of $6 million is $0.6 million, the value of the new common the old common receives on account of its nuisance value. Since the claims receive more than liquidation value, should the plan be approved, if the other requirements of section 1129 are met?

If the class of unsecured claims dissents section 1129(b)(1) requires that the fair and equitable standard be applied to the dissenting class. Since the unsecured debt class has a claim with an allowed amount of $5.1 million, and has received only $3.6 million on account of this claim, does absolute priority dictate that old common not participate in the reorganized enterprise and that cram down of the plan not be allowed?

(2) Valuation

IN RE PULLMAN CONSTRUCTION INDUSTRIES INC.

United States Bankruptcy Court, Northern District of Illinois, 1989.
107 B.R. 909.

JACK B. SCHMETTERER, Bankruptcy Judge.

[Pullman Construction Industries Inc. and three wholly-owned subsidiaries ("Pullman" or "Debtors"), a sheet metal and mechanical contracting firm, filed a chapter 11 petition on May 1, 1987. Inside the chapter, Pullman managed its own affairs as debtor-in-possession.

[Pullman was deeply insolvent in a balance sheet sense. As of June 30, 1989, its total assets were $5,901,000 and its total liabilities were in excess of $14,000,000. But, once inside the chapter, it consolidated its operations, and, but for its outstanding obligations, returned to profitability. It proposed a Plan premised on $2.08 million of new financing, $1 million of which was to be provided by a new secured bank loan. The remaining $1,080,000 was to come from Lester and Norma Goldwyn, the holders of all of Pullman's common stock, John Goldwyn, their son, and three employees. This contribution was to be made as follows: Lester and John would make a subordinated loan of $330,000; the common stock of the reorganized firm would be distributed to the Goldwyns and the employees in exchange for $390,000 from Lester, $225,000 from John, $60,000 from Norma, and $75,000 from the employees. Lester and John Goldwyn also were to execute personal guaranties of the bank loan. Pullman had $1.4 million cash on hand, which included the proceeds of the settlement of an outstanding claim (the "Sheraton settlement").

[Pullman's largest creditor was the Wells Fargo Bank (the "Bank"), which had a secured claim amounting to $8,038,000. The Bank had a first priority, properly perfected security interest in and to all assets of Pullman, including, without limitation, accounts, accounts receivable, contracts, contract rights, inventory, goods, raw materials, work in process, machinery and equipment, vehicles, general intangibles and the proceeds thereof. It also had a first priority lien on all shares of stock issued by the corporations in the Pullman group. The Bank was, nevertheless, undersecured. Because the Bank did not make the section 1111(b) election to have its undersecured claim treated as though fully secured, under section 506(a) its $8 million claim was divided into secured (the "Class 4 Claim") and unsecured (the "Class 5 Claim") portions.]

Debtors contend that the value of the Bank's Class 4 Claim as of the Plan's Effective Date, without regard to the value of the Contract Claims or Preference Claims, is $3,274,000, derived as follows [Pullman Ex. 49 and 50]:

Aggregate Value

Most Likely Net Present Value of Free Cash Flows	$3,411,000
Excess Cash Excluding Proceeds of Sheraton Claim Settlement Before Reorganization Adjustments	717,000
Sheraton Claim Settlement Proceeds	687,000
Payments/Transfers to Bank During Chapter 11 Case as Adequate Protection	732,000
Most Likely Aggregate Value of Pullman Estate as of the Plan's Effective Date	5,547,000
Less "Costs to Reorganize" and Priority Lien Claim of Robertshaw	(2,273,000)
Net Value Offered by Plan to the Bank	$3,274,000

Debtors' Plan proposes to pay that sum to the Bank as follows:

Payments/Transfers heretofore made to Bank During Chapter 11 Case as Adequate Protection	$ 732,000
Sheraton Claim Settlement Proceeds	687,000
Cash at Confirmation	1,855,000
	$3,274,000

Under the Plan the Bank would receive, in full satisfaction of its Class 4 Claim, cash in an amount equal to the value of the Bank's lien interest in Pullman's property, less the value of all Pullman's property transferred to the Bank during the Chapter 11 case ($732,000). That net amount is $2,542,000, including the Sheraton Claim settlement proceeds.

The Bank has voted its Class 4 Claim to reject the Plan. Consequently § 1129(b)(2)(A) must be applied for the Plan to be confirmed.

* * *

[T]he amount of Bank's Class 5 Claim computed by Debtors is $4,764,138, [Pullman Ex. 61] derived as follows:

Bank's Aggregate Pre–Petition Claim	$8,038,138
Less the amount offered on Bank's Class 4 Claim (without regard to value of Preference and Contract Claims)	(3,274,000)
Bank's Provisional Class 5 Claim	$4,764,138

The Plan proposes to satisfy the Bank's Class 5 Claim by payment of $131,000 on the Effective Date. This represents an immediate cash dividend of approximately three percent (3%) on account of the Bank's Class 5 Claim. * * *

The Bank has voted its Class 5 Claim to reject the Plan. Consequently, application of § 1129(b)(2)(B)(ii) is necessary for the Plan to be confirmed.

* * *

[Pullman's other general creditors (the "Committee") had claims totalling at least $6 million, and voted to accept the Plan. The Plan provided for the payment to this class of six tenths of one percent of Pullman's earned revenues over a five year period. The Court estimated the net present value of these payments to be $336,000—a 5.6 percent payout on the claims. The Plan provided that the outstanding equity interests be canceled. An additional $655,000 of claims filed by Pullman's insiders were canceled in exchange for the waiver of a $56,000 preference claim against them.

[The cram down against the Bank presented the following issue, among others: What is the allowed amount of the Bank's secured claim, and does the Plan provide the Bank with a present value equal to the allowed amount of the secured claim?]

The Dispute as to Going Concern Value

17. Debtors and Wells Fargo cannot agree upon the going concern value of Wells Fargo's collateral for purposes of establishing the secured portion of Wells Fargo's allowed claim under 11 U.S.C. § 506(a). Since Wells Fargo has a lien on all of Debtors' assets, Wells Fargo's allowed secured claim is equal to the going concern value of Debtors' assets or estate. The Plan must provide Wells Fargo, on account of its Class 4 secured claim, with payments having a present value equal to the going concern value of Wells Fargo's collateral.

* * *

The factual issue to be resolved is this: Whether the Debtors' proposed $1,855,000 cash payment at confirmation, or the lesser amount suggested by the Committee, is equal to the going concern value of Wells Fargo's presently existing collateral? For reasons stated below, the Court finds that the answer is no.

19. This Court previously has found as of the Petition Date that the forced liquidation value of Debtors' cash, accounts receivable, machinery and equipment and inventory was $3,182,500. * * *

Theories and Evidence as to Valuation

21. Pullman's going concern valuation expert witnesses relied primarily upon a discounted cash flow analysis and have concluded that

the appropriate discount rate for Pullman is 18 percent. * * * [A]n 18 percent discount rate * * *, when applied to the anticipated future cash flows set forth in Pullman's Business Plan, produces what they found to be the most likely net present value of Pullman's future cash flows. This is one component of Pullman's aggregate reorganization value, the other being excess cash or non-operative assets.[6]

22. Pullman's expert witnesses on this issue were Harold W. Sullivan, Jr. of Ernst & Whinney and Dr. Robert S. Hamada. Mr. Sullivan utilized the CAPM as well as several other valuation methodologies discussed hereinbelow, while Dr. Hamada used only his refinement of the CAPM approach to validate and corroborate Ernst & Whinney's conclusion that Pullman's cost of capital, or the property discount rate, is eighteen percent (18%).

    * * *

25. Professor Alfred Rappaport defines "corporate value" as the sum of "present value of cash flow from operations during the forecast period plus residual value plus marketable securities." This definition was essentially followed by experts for both sides. Debtors claim corporate value of $5,547,000 comports with this definition as follows: (a) present value of cash flow from operations during the forecast period—$1,354,000, (present value of free cash flows 1989 through 1993); plus, (b) residual value—$2,057,000, (present value of free cash flows after forecast period); plus, (c) marketable securities—$2,136,000 (non-operating items). Mr. Sullivan testified that these items have a strong or identical correlation to Professor Rappaport's definition of corporate value.

26. The following is a discussion of each of the valuation approaches utilized by Debtors' witnesses to determine the most likely value of Pullman's Aggregate Estate.

a. *Discounted Cash Flow*

The discounted cash flow method presents value as the sum of a stream of free cash flows from the Plan's Effective Date into perpetuity. The present value of the cash flows is dependent on the time value of money and the risk of producing the projected cash flows. The projected cash flows are based on Pullman's Business Plan. Those cash flows include both the projection period through 1993 and the perpetuity period beginning in 1994. Pullman's experts prepared detailed projec-

---

6. "Pullman's Aggregate Estate" was said to mean the combined value of: (i) Pullman's net future cash flows; (ii) property transferred to the Bank during the Chapter 11 cases; and (iii) Pullman's excess cash on the Effective Date, including the Sheraton settlement proceeds. The most likely aggregate value of Pullman's estate is said by Debtor's to be $5,547,000, calculated as follows:

Net Future Value of Cash Flows	$3,411,000
Value Transferred to Bank During Ch. 11	732,000
Excess Cash ($717,000 plus $687,000)	1,404,000
	$5,547,000

tions through 1993 because they assumed that by that time Pullman would regain its historical market share and achieve its growth projections. It is found below that if Debtor were reorganized in 1989, they would gain their maximum market share by 1993. After that, they will be unable to grow further in value because of the competitive nature of the construction industry and the historical inverse relationship between Debtors' revenues and margins. The evidence does not demonstrate that Pullman can make additional investments after 1993 that will generate returns in excess of its cost of capital.

After gaining its maximum market share, Pullman will not experience further economic growth, even though it may grow in size. The addition of years of projections after 1993 does not demonstrate any real value for purposes of a present valuation. Instead, the residual value of Pullman's cash flows from 1994 into perpetuity can be determined by the perpetuity method. As Dr. Rappaport explained it.

Using the perpetuity method, the present value (at the end of the forecast period) is therefore calculated by dividing a "perpetuity cash flow" by the cost of capital:

$$\text{Residual value} = \frac{\text{Perpetuity cash flow}}{\text{Cost of capital}}$$

Keep in mind that the perpetuity method for estimating residual value is not based on the assumption that all future cash flows will actually be identical. It simply reflects the fact that the cash flows resulting from future investments will not affect the value of the firm because the overall rate of return earned on those investments is equal to the cost of capital.

Pullman's value is properly calculated discounting each projected annual cash flow through 1993 by the cost of capital and calculating the value of the cash flows thereafter by the perpetuity method as described by Dr. Rappaport.

Once the annual cash flows have been projected, the other important component to be determined is Pullman's cost of capital or discount rate. Pullman's experts utilized several methodologies in forming their opinion as to the appropriate discount rate. These methods, which rely in varying degrees upon analyses of publicly-held companies in the construction industry are:

Arbitrage Pricing Theory ("APT")—This is a multi-variable model which estimates cost of capital based on the performance of identified stocks relative to the market as a whole and to selected other stock portfolios. The APT formulation uses the following portfolios in addition to the market portfolio.

—Large Capitalization Stocks

—Small Capitalization Stocks

—High Cash Flow/Price Stocks

—Low Cash Flow/Price Stocks

Capital Asset Pricing Model ("CAPM")—The CAPM methodology measures a company's risk relative to the stock market as a whole. Risk is measured as the variability of a stock price relative to a market portfolio. The average historical annual premium of an investment in the market portfolio relative to an investment in an estimated risk-free instrument is adjusted by the variability of the individual stock price relative to the market portfolio (*i.e.,* an estimate of the riskiness of the particular stock or its "beta"). This estimate is added to the current risk-free rate to estimate the rate of return an investor would require on such an investment.

Here, an equally weighted New York Stock Exchange portfolio was analyzed as the "market portfolio" in order better to reflect the performance of both smaller and larger publicly-held companies. A value weighted portfolio (the S & P 500) was also analyzed and adjusted for a small stock premium. The use of CAPM methodology is described below.

Weighted Average Cost of Capital ("WACC")—WACC is the weighted average of the after-tax cost of debt (*i.e.,* the marginal rate at which a company can borrow funds) and the company's cost of equity. The cost of debt is tax-effected because of the tax deductions associated with interest payments. Cost of equity has been based on analysis of potential peer companies. The costs are weighted respectively by the ratios of the market values of debt and equity to the market value of total capital (debt plus equity) to derive a weighted average. The results were very similar to those obtained using CAPM methodology.

Survey of Alternative Investments—A survey of alternative investments currently available in today's market, evidencing rates of return currently expected by investors, was also made to determine Pullman's cost of capital.

b. *Peer Group Multiple Analyses*

In order to confirm their discounted cash flow valuation findings, Pullman's experts analyzed certain multiples of financial data for other companies. Although this analysis was not performed in the same depth as the discounted cash flow analysis, and it is not entitled to the same weight because of its reliance on accounting-based numbers, it serves to corroborate results of the cash flow analysis. This multiple analysis, which was performed on publicly-held companies in the construction industry, included:

Price–Earnings Multiple ("P/E")—"Earnings" is defined as operating earnings after taxes. The respective median P/E multiples for the Peer Group were estimated to be 11.79 and 9.86. These multiples were applied to Pullman's actual 1988 and projected 1989 operating earnings to calculate a range of potential values.

EBIT Multiple—"EBIT" is earnings before interest and taxes. The median Peer Group EBIT multiple was estimated to be 6.06. This multiple was applied to PCI's 1988 actual earnings before interest and taxes to calculate a potential value.

EBDIT Multiple—"EBDIT" is earnings before depreciation, interest and taxes. The median EBDIT multiple for the Peer Group was 5.03. This multiple was applied to PCI's 1988 earnings before depreciation, interest and taxes to calculate a potential value.

Book Value Multiple—Book value is the excess of the net book value of the assets over the net book value of the liabilities (i.e., stockholder's equity). The Peer Group companies' median book value multiple was estimated to be 1.38. Pullman's net book value was calculated both before and after the new equity investments, and those figures were multiplied by the median book value multiple to estimate potential values.

All of these multiple analyses were adjusted by reconciling items to make estimates of Pullman's gross reorganization value.

c. *Dividend Capitalization*

Another confirming technique employed was the dividend capitalization model, which assumes that dividends are a constant stream of cash flows to equity investors. The present value of a stream of equal cash flows, or an annuity, is the cash flow divided by the discount rate. The discount rate is calculated as described above in the Discounted Cash Flow Approach Summary. Items were added to this calculated value to reconcile to the reorganization value.

d. *The Synthesis of the Various Techniques Used*

In addition to these confirming techniques, Pullman's experts considered certain other factors, including the following: (i) Pullman is privately-held and does not have access to public capital markets; (ii) achieving the Business Plan's objectives is dependent on the continued involvement of a few key managers; (iii) Pullman has been in bankruptcy; (iv) the construction industry is very dependent upon personal relationships and a substantial portion of Pullman's good will and value resides in the Goldwyns; and (v) Pullman operates in a single localized market, not a regional or national market. Finally, Pullman's experts weighed the strengths and weaknesses of each of the methodologies employed in forming their opinions that 18% is the appropriate discount rate and that the most likely gross value of Pullman's aggregate estate is $5,547,000.

Application of the various confirming techniques produced the following range of values of Pullman's Aggregate Estate:

Price/Earnings Multiple on Forecasted 1989 Earnings	$4,490,000
Book Value Multiple Before New Equity Investment	$4,693,000
Dividend Capitalization Model	$4,803,000

Price/Earnings Multiple on EBIT	$4,815,000
Price/Earnings Multiple on EBDIT	$4,882,000
Book Value Multiple After New Equity Investment	$5,390,000
Price/Earnings Multiple on Pre–Confirmation 1988 Earnings	$5,663,000

CAPM Methodology

The principal technique employed by both Ernst & Whinney and Dr. Hamada * to determine the discount rate was CAPM. CAPM methodology recognizes that different investments have different levels of risk and, therefore, should produce different returns to investors. The CAPM method measures the risk associated with a specific investment relative to the risk of a portfolio of investments, and prices or values that investment relative to the return on the portfolio. The general CAPM cost of capital equation is summarized as follows:

$$R(c) = R(f) + B(a) \times [R(m) - R(f)]$$

where

$R(c)$ = the CAPM cost of capital
$R(f)$ = the after-tax risk-free rate of return
$B(a)$ = the beta, or risk, of the asset
$R(m)$ = the return on the market portfolio
$R(m) - R(f)$ = the market risk premium

The derivation of each of the components of the CAPM equation used in calculating Pullman's cost of capital is as follows:

The after-tax risk-free rate of return is first calculated. This is the rate of return an investor could expect to receive by investing in a risk-free asset, after paying taxes on the investor's return. One year Treasury Bills, backed by the full faith and credit of the United States Government, are generally considered to be the best proxy for the risk-free rate. Pullman's before-tax risk-free rate was assumed to be equal to the yield, as of April 11, 1989, on one-year Treasury Bills due April 12, 1990. That rate is 9.72 percent. Using the same forty percent (40%) assumed corporate tax rate that was used in developing the "free cash flows" in Pullman's Business Plan and Projected Financial Statements, the after-tax risk-free rate was calculated as follows:

Before-tax risk-free rate	9.72%
Less: Taxes at 40%	(3.89%)
After-tax risk-free rate	5.83%

The "beta" coefficient measures the risk of an investment in Pullman's business relative to the risk of the market as a whole. See In re Jartran, Inc., 44 B.R. 331, 370 (Bankr.N.D.Ill.1984), citing In re The Valuation Proceedings Under Sections 303(c) and 306 of the Re-

---

* [Ed. note] A second expert retained by the Debtor.

gional Rail Reorganization Act of 1973, 531 F.Supp. 1191, 1233 (Regional Rail Reorg.Ct.1981) ("Valuation Proceedings"). Since Pullman is not publicly traded, it is impossible to measure changes in the return on Pullman's common stock over time against a portfolio of market securities. Accordingly, a group of publicly-traded companies in the construction industry was selected in order to measure the risk of the special trade contracting industry against the risk of the entire market. This group of companies was used as Pullman's "Peer Group." These comparable publicly-traded companies were selected through an analysis of publicly-traded companies in the special trade contracting and non-residential general contracting business.

Using the Alcar database and the COMPACT Disclosure database, Ernst & Whinney initially identified 108 publicly-traded companies having either primary or secondary business lines within Standard Industrial Codes in the 1,700 series ("Special Trade Contractors") or 1,540 series ("Non–Residential Building Contractors"). Ninety of these companies were excluded as potential peers because they were not deemed to be comparable to Pullman. The reasons for exclusion were as follows:

— Certain companies were excluded because their primary SIC Code was not in the 1,540 or 1,700 series;

— Certain companies were excluded because their lines of business are not comparable to Pullman's business;

— Certain companies were excluded because they were in bankruptcy proceedings at sometime during 1985–1987;

— Certain companies were excluded because they operate primarily outside of the United States;

— One company was excluded because it was privately held until August, 1987;

— Certain companies were excluded because of thin trading of their securities on regional stock markets; and

— Certain companies were excluded because their beta coefficient was not statistically significant.

After these exclusions * * * eighteen companies formed Pullman's "Peer Group" * * *.

The eighteen companies making up the Peer Group were then further analyzed and divided into three separate "Cases." Case I includes all eighteen companies in the Peer Group; Case II includes only eleven companies in the Peer Group; and Case III includes sixteen of the original eighteen companies in the Peer Group. Two deletions were made from the Case I companies to arrive at the Case III group of companies. One company was deleted because it provided maintenance services only, a business line markedly different than Pullman's. The other company was excluded because it had significant units in the business of manufacturing and distributing auto parts, auto paints and industrial supplies.

Beta statistics for each company in the Peer Group were calculated by Ernst & Whinney, utilizing a linear regression technique. The linear regression methodology calculates the relationship between monthly returns on the peer company stock and monthly returns on a weighted New York Stock Exchange portfolio of stocks during the period January, 1983 through December, 1987. A calculated beta of 1.0 generally indicates that the volatility or risk of an investment in a stock is equal to the volatility or risk of the market as a whole; that is, a one percent change in the value of the market portfolio is accompanied by a one percent change in the value of the stock. Betas above 1.0 indicate stocks that are more volatile (risky) than the market, while betas less than 1.0 indicate stocks that are less volatile (risky).

The betas calculated by this linear regression method for all Peer Group companies are equity or stock betas, which measure the risk of an investment in the equity of a company. Such equity returns are affected by the level of debt, or leverage, that the company carries. In order to estimate the risk of the *business* rather than the risk of an investment in the *equity* of the business, an asset beta is calculated which adjusts to eliminate the financial risk of leverage. The asset beta for each Peer Group company was calculated from its equity beta, using the following formula (referred to as "unlevering the beta"):

$$beta(a) = [beta(d) \times (1 - Tc) \times (D/V)] = [beta(e) \times (E/V)] *$$

where

        beta(a) = asset beta
        beta(e) = beta of the company's equity, as calculated
        beta(d) = beta of the company's debt, assumed to be .195
        E   = Market value of equity
        D   = Market value of debt
        V   = Market value of capital (i.e., D + E)

———

The appropriate market values of debt and equity for the above equation were estimated as follows:

— The market value of debt was derived from an analysis of the 10–K annual reports filed by each Peer Group company and a

---

* [Ed. Note] There seems to be a typographical error in the statement of the formula. Beta (a) is the weighted average of the betas of the firm's debt and equity securities. The formula should read:

  beta(a) = [beta(d) × (1 − Tc) × (D/V)] + [beta(e) × (E/V)] "Tc" presumably represents the marginal tax rate of the firm, so that the cost of debt in the weighted average is calculated on an after-tax basis. See Brigham and Gapenski, Financial Management: Theory and Practice 296, 408–409 (1991).

survey of Moody's Bond Record to obtain prices on publicly traded debt.

— The market value of equity was derived by extending the number of shares outstanding by the share price derived from the Wall Street Journal and/or public databases.

— The debt/capital and equity/capital ratios were calculated for each of the peer company's three fiscal years ending before June 39, 1988 (where market information for all three years was available).

— The average of the debt/capital and debt/equity ratios calculated for each year was used in the equation to "unlever" the beta.

Once the asset betas were calculated for each Peer Group company, the Peer Group asset beta was calculated as the average of the asset betas for each company in the Peer Group.

Next, the market risk premium was calculated. This is defined as the premium which investors demand over the risk-free rate in order to compensate them for investments in common stock. The market risk premium for the stock market as a whole was calculated as follows:

— The Center for Research in Security Prices ("CRSP") calculates a monthly equal-weighted market return on the New York Stock Exchange portfolio of securities for each month from 1926 through 1987. These monthly NYSE portfolio returns were downloaded from CRSP by Ernst & Whinney, and comparable annual returns were calculated from these monthly returns.

— The average monthly return on Treasury Bills was also downloaded from the CRSP database. Comparable annual returns were calculated from these monthly returns. The top marginal tax rate in each year from 1926 through 1987 was applied to the calculated annual Treasury Bill returns to determine the after-tax return on Treasury Bills, i.e., the after-tax risk-free rate.

— The market risk premium between the equal weighted NYSE portfolio and the after-tax risk-free rate was calculated by Ernst & Whinney for each year from 1926 to 1987. The average of these annual premiums, 14.98% was used as the market risk premium in the CAPM equation.

The CAPM cost of capital for each of the three Cases was calculated using the risk-free rate (5.83%), the market risk-premium (14.98%) and the applicable asset betas (.80 for Case I, .85 for Case II, and .82 for Case III) as follows:

	CASE I	CASE II	CASE III
After–Tax Market Risk Premium	14.98%	14.98%	14.98%
Peer Group Asset Beta	0.80	0.85	0.82
	11.94%	12.72%	12.24%
Add: After–Tax Risk–Free Rate	5.83%	5.83%	5.83%
Derived Discount Rate	17.77%	18.55%	18.07%

Pullman and Wells Fargo experts concluded that 18% is the proper rate applicable here.

The Creditors Committee Argument as to Discount Rate

The Creditor's Committee offered no expert witnesses of its own. However, from the evidence it argued that the 18% discount rate used in calculations by the experts of Cash Flow Value is overly optimistic, asserting that they failed to account for particular risks unique to an investment in Pullman. * * * Accordingly, the Committee asks this Court to find the discount rate to be 20% so as to account for these special risks.

* * * While there is some weight to [this] argument, the weight of evidence supports a finding of an 18% rate. The evidence also establishes that the actual insider investors in this case are expecting to receive a rate of return on their investment substantially below 18%. Debtors contend that the actual rate of return on the new equity investment is 8.42%. * * *

The Evidence and Theories of Wells Fargo

27.   Richard P. Bail, a principal with the firm of Houlihan, Lokey, Howard & Zukin, Inc. ("Houlihan, Lokey"), testified on behalf of Wells Fargo regarding the going concern value of Debtors' existing estate. * * *

* * *

35. Analysis of the Bank's Arguments on Valuation

The Bank argued that selected assumptions in Pullman's Business Plan should be modified so that Pullman's value, and thus the value of the Bank's Class 4 Claim, should be increased. Its argument is, however, flawed.

(a) The Bank's Lack of In–Depth Analysis

First, neither the Bank nor its expert offered any independent analysis of the value of Pullman's business. Instead, the Bank had its expert rely heavily upon Ernst & Whinney's work but selectively alter certain Business Plan assumptions. Neither the Bank nor its expert spent any time with Pullman's management discussing the assumptions underlying the Business Plan.

(b) The Unsupported Infinite Growth Assumption

* * *

The Bank's use of the Gordon Growth model is also inappropriate to project growth for Pullman. This model, also referred to as the Dividend Discount Model, was formulated to forecast the prices of publicly traded stocks assuming that dividends grew at a constant rate into perpetuity. Not only is the model subject to several restrictive assumptions which are not satisfied by Pullman, but it also ignores the highly competitive nature of Pullman's business and fails to identify any source of growth for Pullman after 1993.

Well-recognized authority on corporate finance also indicates that the Bank's infinite growth assumption is inappropriate and that Pullman's experts' view of Pullman's residual value is correct:

> The perpetuity method for estimating residual value is based on the foregoing competitive dynamics. It is essentially based on the assumption that a company that is able to generate returns above the cost of capital (i.e., achieve excess returns) will eventually attract competitors, whose entry into the business will drive returns down to the minimum acceptable or cost of capital rate. Specifically, the perpetuity method assumes that after the forecast period, the business will earn, on average, the cost of capital on new investments. Another way of expressing this idea is to say that after the forecast period, the business will invest, on average, in strategies whose net present value is zero.

Rappaport, supra, at 60–61.

* * *

(e) *The Bank's Valuation is Unrealistic*

The Bank's valuation of Pullman is unrealistically high when viewed against Pullman's projected cash flows. Pullman has neither the capacity to borrow an additional $1 million to satisfy the Bank's inflated valuation nor the available cash flow to service the resulting increased debt level. If Pullman were required to undertake additional borrowing, the drain on its cash flows for interest expense would prevent it from growing to regain its market share, and hence from achieving the cash flow levels which form the basis of both Pullman's and the Bank's valuations. * * *

(g) *Optimistic Business Assumptions by Pullman*

[The Court identified a number of "overly optimistic" assumptions in the business plan.]

36. *The Courts Conclusions as to Value From All the Evidence*

Considering the foregoing evidence and arguments, the Court concludes that Debtors' approach and computation as to valuation was correct in the main and generally adequate to enable this Court to find the appropriate value. As many other judges have found, this Court recognizes that all valuations of going business value are only educated estimates in the absence of one or more buyers ready, willing and able to purchase the business. Given the two years of bankruptcy wherein no buyer appeared, the closely held nature of a business in which its president is a key and perhaps irreplaceable leader, and the inherent uncertainties of future business in the construction industry, an arms length outside buyer is not foreseeable and was not obtained. Consequently, based on expert evidence and historic results, this Court must fix a value through the use of imperfect theories, formulas, and assumptions. Some of the assumptions are uncertain (e.g. use of the "Peer Group" of companies to formulate a capitalization rate despite many differences between those companies and the Debtors.) However, use of uncertain assumptions are inherent in this process. While this underlines the inherently uncertain quality of the analysis, economic assumptions that all experts agreed on provide persuasive evidence even where they are uncertain.

However, the Court need not and does not accept one assumption that came from the Debtors and is more a wild leap of faith than a reasoned but uncertain assumption. That is the projection by Debtors of future "large commercial construction" business to be obtained by it in the years following its hoped-for confirmation.

Debtors project that revenue from that source will rise from $6,964,000 in 1988 to $7,268,000 in 1989, and then jump to a whopping $10,037,000 in 1990 after confirmation. That projects an increase of more than one-third in one year. This projection is a major component in the valuation of cash flow. However, it is based almost entirely on an anticipated "bounce" from the hoped-for reorganization. No firm evidence of actual specific new jobs and customers support this projection which is therefore a mere hope.

Wells Fargo sought a finding of value even higher than that proposed by Debtors, so it did not question the projection by Debtors for large commercial projects. The Committee and this Court does. Based on historic data (and Debtors' prior shortfalls in revenues predicted in prior hearings before this Court), it is doubtful that revenues from large commercial construction will be as high as projected. The Debtors' exaggerated projection inflates its computation of value. A five percent shortfall from Debtors' projections is likely. This reduces the Debtor's total valuation computation of $5,547,000 by $516,000.

Rounding off the result recognizes that valuation here is only an informed approximation. The Court finds the going concern value of Debtors to be $5,000,000.

[The court rejected additional arguments made by the general creditors committee.

[The court found that upon liquidation under chapter 7, Pullman's creditors would recover $2,579,750. The largest components of the total were cash on hand of $1,117,000, and accounts receivable of $812,500 (assuming a 25 percent rate of collection). The $2.5 million liquidation figure exceeded the cash amount offered to the Bank upon confirmation under the Plan.

Brudney & Chirelstein Corp. Fin. 4th Ed. UCS—29

[The court also found that the Plan's scheme for new equity financing by members of the Goldwyn family did not meet the standards of the "new value" exception to the absolute priority rule.]

* * *

CONCLUSIONS OF LAW

* * *

Valuation

* * *

7. The Plan cannot be confirmed because Wells Fargo will not receive payments equal to the full going concern value of its collateral.

[C]reditors are entitled to have the full value of the property, whether "present or prospective, for dividends or only for purposes of control", first appropriated to payment of their claims.

Consolidated Rock Products Co. v. DuBois, 312 U.S. 510 (1941) (citation omitted). * * *

8. In valuing the allowed amount of Wells Fargo's secured claim for purposes of the Plan, "[v]alue should be determined by the purpose of the valuation and the proposed disposition or use of the property." Barash v. Public Finance Corp., 658 F.2d 504, 512 (7th Cir.1981). Here, Debtors propose to retain and use Wells Fargo's collateral (accounts receivable, contracts, contract rights, machinery, equipment, inventory, etc.) in the ongoing operations of the reorganized entity, and to pledge the collateral as security for $1,330,000 of new loans from South Chicago Savings Bank and Lester and John Goldwyn. A forced-sale or liquidation value of Wells Fargo's collateral, for purposes of determining the allowed amount of its Class 4 secured claim for Plan purposes, is improper.

A going concern analysis is the appropriate approach for establishing the allowed amount of Wells Fargo's secured claim. See, e.g., In re Fiberglass Industries, Inc., 74 B.R. 738 (Bankr.N.D.N.Y.1987).

* * *

Cramdown Requirements

10. Since Wells Fargo voted its Class 4 secured claim and Class 5 unsecured claim to reject the Plan, the Plan fails to meet the requirements of Section 1129(a)(8). The Plan may, however, be confirmed if it meets the requirements of Section 1129(b). * * *

12. Debtor's Plan does not comply with the requirements of § 1129(b)(2). * * *

13. The Plan is not fair and equitable. Compared to the $3,274,-000 offered to Wells Fargo, under the proposed Plan and in light of the history of this case Pullman would have paid: a) over $2,000,000 to its

attorneys, consultants and accountants; b) over $2,500,000 to pre-petition trade creditors; c) over $800,000 on account of pre-petition, unsecured union claims; d) over $1,500,000 to pre-petition, unsecured tax claims; and, e) over $300,000 (projected) to unsecured trade creditors. The Plan, in effect, attempts to take value that should be distributed to Wells Fargo, and distributes that value to junior claimants "to protect" those junior claimants. Because certain junior claimants have potential personal claims against the Goldwyns, and the Goldwyns would obtain a release from the estate from potential avoidance actions, the Plan truly "protects" the Goldwyns at Wells Fargo's expense.

* * *

The Plan Cannot Be Crammed Down Because It Fails to Pay Wells Fargo the Going Concern Value of Its Collateral

35. The Plan cannot be confirmed under 11 U.S.C. § 1129(b) because it does not provide Wells Fargo with payments having a present value equal to the going concern value of Wells Fargo's collateral. This Court found that the going concern value of Wells Fargo's collateral is $5,000,000. The Plan proposes payments totalling $3,274,-000.

* * *

73. The Plan cannot be confirmed because * * * it is not fair and equitable, it violates the absolute priority rule, and does not meet requirements of the new capital exception to that rule.

* * *

The Automatic Stay Must Be Lifted

76. This case is over two years old. The present proposed Plan cannot be confirmed. It appears clear that a non-consensual cramdown plan is not feasible. There is not an effective reorganization in process. Because the instant proposed Plan has been represented to be the best offer Debtors' will make, and parties have been unable to agree on a consensual Plan, there is no "reasonable possibility of a successful reorganization within a reasonable time." In re 8th Street Village Ltd. Partnership, 94 B.R. 993, 995 (N.D.Ill.1988), citing *Timbers*, 108 S.Ct. at 632.

NOTE: BANKRUPTCY VALUATION

1. *Valuation Methodology.*

With *Pullman*, we see a technically sophisticated, contemporary valuation proceeding. Under the state of the art practice, experts in financial economics come to court and make available a range of techniques. The fact finder, recognizing that no one technique has an exclusive hold on the future, reviews a range of results. Can we conclude, based on *Pullman's* demonstration of the practice, that the normative problems of valuation have been solved and that we now have technical guarantees against manipulation of the valuation process for the benefit of one or another party in the litigation? Recall that the historic problem of valuation in bankruptcy proceedings is the systematic overstatement of expected earnings—due to undue optimism about the future and an inability to take into account adequately the traumatic effects of changes brought about by the reorganization on the near term earning ability of the enterprise. See Blum, Corporate Reorganization Doctrine as Recently Applied by the Securities Exchange Commission, 40 U.Chi.L.Rev. 96 (1972). Can we conclude, based on the analysis in *Pullman* that these problems have been surmounted? If so, can we go a step farther and conclude that, given state of the art methodology, judicial valuation is now cheap as well as reliable? If we can, does it follow that the reorganization system is in no need of reform? Or, if reform is needed, it should take the form of a return to the mandatory absolute priority of Chapter X?

A few points to the opposite effect should be noted. First, in *Pullman,* the expert worked with data prepared by the debtor—a set of projections informed by optimistic assumptions. None of the critical weapons introduced by the experts obviated reliance on that data. Moreover, under the approach taken by the court, the party making a root and branch objection to the business plan had the cost burden to present a competing business plan. Absent control of the enterprise, this is a burden which a class of claimants is unlikely to meet as a practical matter. Second, it does not seem likely that concern for methodological correctness will control the litigation strategies of competing claimants. Suppose in *Pullman,* that all the claims, including the Bank's, had been unsecured. What would you expect the insiders' expert to contend in that case? Would it have been arguing for a greater or lesser going concern value?

2. *Valuation of Collateral.*

The court in *Pullman* values the collateral securing the Bank on a going concern basis, due to the fact that the debtor is retaining the property to produce cash flows in the future. In so doing, it follows the approach of most bankruptcy courts. The practice in valuing collateral is to make reference to going concern value in reorganization cases and liquidation value in liquidation cases. See Carlson, Secured Creditors and the Eely Character of Bankruptcy Valuations, 41 Am.U.L.Rev. 63, 76–77 (1991), noting that this rule has the "dubious virtue of associational logic." The rule also has the property of coming at the expense of the general creditors, if it is safe to assume that the liquidation measure would result in a lower value attaching to the property under the lien.

The court might instead have measured the value of the property under the lien by reference to the proceeds that would be realized in a hypothetical foreclosure proceeding in which the property is sold off in commercially reasonable units. For the argument that bankruptcy judges always should use the measure of a hypothetical sale by the secured party, see Queenan, Standards for Valuation of Security Interests in Chapter 11, 92 Com.L.J. 18, 32–34 (1987).

Why does the court choose the greater, going concern measure? A number of arguments can be articulated against it. The property subject to the lien does not by itself produce future cash flows. It takes a "firm"—a combination of property, people and organization—to do that. No matter how many separate items of property are aggregated under the bank's lien, they do not add up to a "firm." Furthermore, viewed before the fact as an item for purchase, the "firm" no doubt costs considerably more than does the lien. Of course, the absolute priority rule does, in fact, accord the creditors a right to succeed to ownership of the "firm," as against the equity. The question here is whether a similar effect follows as between classes of creditors by virtue of the priority status that follows from the taking of security. See Baird and Jackson, Bargaining After the Fall and the Contours of the Absolute Priority Rule, 55 U.Chi.L.Rev. 738, 781 (1988).

Carried to its logical conclusion, the going concern measure leads to a somewhat awkward result. Consider, in contrast to the omnibus lien held by the bank in *Pullman,* a security interest in a single piece of equipment or a mortgage on a particular facility. Going concern valuation of these secured claims presumably requires, first, calculation of the liquidation value of the firm, then, calculation of the firm's going concern value, and finally calculation of the liquidation value of the particular property and the ascription of a pro rata portion of going concern value to it. The simple appraisal of the property's value upon foreclosure sale certainly would be cheaper from an administrative point of view, and also would seem unlikely to frustrate the expectations of the secured party. Baird and Jackson, supra, at 782, add that the portion of going concern value allocated to the property stems from the expertise of the manager, and therefore should not automatically be allocated to the property. Carlson, supra pp. 88–89, rejoins that while the attribution of going concern value to a specific piece of collateral requires the imposition of some "accounting fictions," it should not be ruled out as a general proposition. Management, Carlson notes, often is replaceable and is not always causally necessary for future profits.

There also is the matter of the expectations of the parties. When a bank takes an omnibus lien, does it ordinarily formulate a legitimate expectation of going concern treatment of its claim's priority in a subsequent bankruptcy? It may very well do so in the context of today's credit markets. Certainly, as Baird and Jackson note, supra at 785, borrowers and lenders should be permitted to contract explicitly for going concern treatment in a subsequent reorganization. Absent such a specific provision, the question of expectations is, in theory, subject to an empirical answer. A determination would be made respecting the spread between interest rates on secured and unsecured loans and the spread's sensitivity to the valuation treatment applied in reorganization. Absent such a showing (one way or the other), the question of expectations as to the degree of priority treatment is a conventional one of contract interpretation. Like many such questions, it could be decided either way with plausibility. In arguing for a liquidation valuation, we would point to the security document itself. This specifies foreclosure in the event of default. By implication, we should attach a liquidation measure, determined by reference to the proceeding specified. On the other hand, in the case of a perfected, floating lien on all of the property of the debtor, including the intangible financial proceeds doing business as a going concern, the inference of an expectation of a going concern priority arises from the scope of the lien.

Finally, we might view the question from the point of view of bankruptcy law and policy. The language of the Bankruptcy Code is pertinent. Section 506(a) describes valuations of collateral and specifies that "[s]uch value shall be determined in light of the purpose of the valuation and of the proposed disposition or use of such property * * *." The reference to "use" implies a preference for valuation by reference to the going concern actually projected rather than to a hypothetical foreclosure. See Carlson, supra p. 77; In re Frost, 47 B.R. 961, 963–964 (D.Kan.1985) (citing legislative history in noting provision's preference for going concern standard). But see In re Robbins, 119 Bankr. 1 (D.Mass.1990) (Queenan, J.), arguing that, since the creditor's lien is being valued and not the collateral itself, there is no requirement that reference be made to the actual or intended use of the collateral.

If reference to the language of the statute does not conclude the matter, then the question is whether the grant of the larger measure of going concern value to the secured claimant makes for a fairer or more efficient proceeding. Here it would seem that both fairness and efficiency follow the *ex ante* expectations of the parties—if they could be determined reliably. If not, as between the secured and unsecured creditors, what principle should determine this particular pie slicing contest? Says Carlson, supra at 79: "In the end, the choice between liquidation and going concern value is based on whether you think the secured parties or general creditors should own the bonus that adheres to the idea of a going concern. Who deserves what property is a question on which we can all have intuitions, but logic alone cannot settle such questions in an uncontroversial manner."

NOTE: ADEQUATE PROTECTION AND
POST PETITION INTEREST

The Bankruptcy Code strikes a complicated balance between the secured party's right to repossess on default and the estate's need to use the collateral in connection with the reorganization. The automatic stay extends to collateral given by the debtor. 11 U.S.C. § 362(a). The stay may not be lifted if the debtor has an equity in the collateral or the collateral is necessary for an effective reorganization. 11 U.S.C. § 362(d)(2). In other words, the stay can be lifted only if the creditor's claim is greater than the value of the property and there is no prospect of an effective reorganization. **United Savings Ass'n v. Timbers of Inwood Forest Ass'n,** 484 U.S. 365 (1988).[g] But the stay is subject to a qualification. The estate is privileged to keep the collateral only if it provides "adequate protection" for the collateral itself or its value. If the secured party can show a lack of "adequate protection" of its "interest in [the] property," the court must lift the stay. 11 U.S.C. § 362(d)(1). This "adequate protection" must extend to the value of the collateral. If, for example, the value of the collateral is depreciating during the term of the stay, the secured party is entitled to compensation. This can come in the form of additional security or cash payments. 11 U.S.C. § 362(1), (2). Where the debtor has a substantial equity cushion, however, that equity is deemed adequate to protect the secured party. In re Mellor, 734 F.2d 1396, 1400 (9th Cir.1984). The automatic stay will be lifted only if the creditor can show that its claim is greater than the value of the property and that provision of substitute security or other relief will be inadequate. See 11 U.S.C. § 361.

Does the "adequate protection" requirement imply an award of post-petition interest to the secured party to compensate for lost use of the property during the term of the stay? A unanimous Supreme Court held that it does not in United Savings Ass'n v. Timbers of Inwood Forest Associates, supra. There, an undersecured claimant argued that the phrase "interest in property" in section 362 includes the secured party's right to take immediate repossession of the defaulted security and apply it to repayment of the debt. Adequate protection of that right is reimbursement for the use of the foregone proceeds—in effect, interest. The Court rebutted the argument by reference to section 506(b) of the Code, which provides explicitly for post-petition interest, but only for *over* secured creditors "to the extent that an allowed secured claim is secured by property the value of which * * * is greater than the amount of such claim." Said the court, 484 U.S. at 373:

"If the Code had meant to give the undersecured creditor, who is thus denied interest on his *claim,* interest on the value of his *collateral,*

---

g. Baird and Picker, A Simple Non-cooperative Bargaining Model of Corporate Reorganization, 20 J. Legal Studies 311 (1991), makes a powerful challenge to the automatic stay from the perspective of game theory.

surely this is where that disposition would have been set forth, and not obscured within the "adequate protection" provision of § 362(d)(1). Instead of the intricate phraseology set forth above, § 506(b) would simply have said that the secured creditor is entitled to interest "on his allowed claim, or on the value of the property securing his allowed claim, whichever is lesser." Petitioner's interpretation of § 362(d)(1) must be regarded as contradicting the carefully drawn disposition of § 506(b).

"Petitioner seeks to avoid this conclusion by characterizing § 506(b) as merely an alternative method for compensating oversecured creditors, which does not imply that no compensation is available to undersecured creditors. This theory of duplicate protection for oversecured creditors is implausible even in the abstract, but even more so in light of the historical principles of bankruptcy law. Section 506(b)'s denial of postpetition interest to undersecured creditors merely codified pre-Code bankruptcy law, in which that denial was part of the conscious allocation of reorganization benefits and losses between undersecured and unsecured creditors. 'To allow a secured creditor interest where his security was worth less than the value of his debt was thought to be inequitable to unsecured creditors.' Vanston Bondholders Protective Committee v. Green, 329 U.S. 156, 164 (1946). It was considered unfair to allow an undersecured creditor to recover interest from the estate's unencumbered assets before unsecured creditors had recovered any principal. See id., at 164, 166; Ticonic Nat. Bank v. Sprague, 303 U.S. 406, 412 (1938). We think it unlikely that § 506(b) codified the pre-Code rule with the intent, not of achieving the principal purpose and function of that rule, but of providing oversecured creditors an alternative method of compensation. Moreover, it is incomprehensible why Congress would want to favor undersecured creditors with interest if they move for it under § 362(d)(1) at the inception of the reorganization process—thereby probably pushing the estate into liquidation—but not if they forbear and seek it only at the completion of the reorganization."

For criticism of the Court's analysis on the theory that section 361 was intended to protect "value," see Carlson, Postpetition Interest Under the Bankruptcy Code, 43 Miami L.Rev. 577 (1989).

Note that application of section 362 entails the valuation of the collateral. As of what time should the value be calculated? Courts have employed each of (1) the date of the bankruptcy petition, (2) a later date fixed as the time at which the secured creditor would have realized value in the foreclosure that would have proceeded absent bankruptcy, and (3) the time of the determination. Carlson, Time, Value, and the Rights of Secured Creditors in Bankruptcy, or When Does Adequate Protection Begin? 1 J.Bankr.L. & Practice 113 (1991). *Timbers of Inwood Forest* implies that the time should be the time of the petition. 484 U.S. at 374. Carlson, supra at 148–149, argues the time of the hypothetical foreclosure better accords with the notion of adequate protection.

APPENDIX F

REVISED MODEL BUSINESS CORPORATION ACT

Contents

CHAPTER 1. GENERAL PROVISIONS

Subchapter A. Short Title and Reservation of Power

* * *

Subchapter D. Definitions

CHAPTER 2. INCORPORATION

* * *

CHAPTER 3. PURPOSES AND POWERS

* * *

* * *

* * *

CHAPTER 6. SHARES AND DISTRIBUTIONS

Subchapter A. Shares

* * *

Subchapter B. Issuance of Shares

* * *

CHAPTER 1.   GENERAL PROVISIONS
SUBCHAPTER A.   SHORT TITLE AND RESERVATION OF POWER

§ 1.02   Reservation of Power to Amend or Repeal

The [name of state legislature] has power to amend or repeal all or part of this Act at any time and all domestic and foreign corporations subject to this Act are governed by the amendment or repeal.

SUBCHAPTER D.   DEFINITIONS

§ 1.40   Act Definitions

In this Act:

(1) "Articles of incorporation" include amended and restated articles of incorporation and articles of merger.

(2) "Authorized shares" means the shares of all classes a domestic or foreign corporation is authorized to issue.

* * *

(6) "Distribution" means a direct or indirect transfer of money or other property (except its own shares) or incurrence of indebtedness by a corporation to or for the benefit of its shareholders in respect of any of its shares. A distribution may be in the form of a declaration or payment of a dividend; a purchase, redemption, or other acquisition of shares; a distribution of indebtedness; or otherwise.

F–4

* * *

(8) "Employee" includes an officer but not a director. A director may accept duties that make him also an employee.

* * *

(21) "Shares" means the units into which the proprietary interests in a corporation are divided.

(22) "Shareholder" means the person in whose name shares are registered in the records of a corporation or the beneficial owner of shares to the extent of the rights granted by a nominee certificate on file with a corporation.

* * *

(24) "Subscriber" means a person who subscribes for shares in a corporation, whether before or after incorporation.

* * *

(26) "Voting group" means all shares of one or more classes or series that under the articles of incorporation or this Act are entitled to vote and be counted together collectively on a matter at a meeting of shareholders. All shares entitled by the articles of incorporation or this Act to vote generally on the matter are for that purpose a single voting group.

* * *

§ 1.42 Number of Shareholders

(a) For purposes of this Act, the following identified as a shareholder in a corporation's current record of shareholders constitutes one shareholder:

(1) three or fewer co-owners;

(2) a corporation, partnership, trust, estate, or other entity;

(3) the trustees, guardians, custodians, or other fiduciaries of a single trust, estate, or account.

(b) For purposes of this Act, shareholdings registered in substantially similar names constitute one shareholder if it is reasonable to believe that the names represent the same person.

CHAPTER 2. INCORPORATION

* * *

§ 2.02 Articles of Incorporation

(a) The articles of incorporation must set forth:

(1) a corporate name for the corporation that satisfies the requirements of section 4.01;

(2) the number of shares the corporation is authorized to issue;

(3) the street address of the corporation's initial registered office and the name of its initial registered agent at that office; and

(4) the name and address of each incorporator.

(b) The articles of incorporation may set forth:

(1) the names and addresses of the individuals who are to serve as the initial directors;

(2) provisions not inconsistent with law regarding:

(i) the purpose or purposes for which the corporation is organized;

(ii) managing the business and regulating the affairs of the corporation;

(iii) defining, limiting, and regulating the powers of the corporation, its board of directors, and shareholders;

(iv) a par value for authorized shares or classes of shares;

(v) the imposition of personal liability on shareholders for the debts of the corporation to a specified extent and upon specified conditions; and

(3) any provision that under this Act is required or permitted to be set forth in the bylaws.

(c) The articles of incorporation need not set forth any of the corporate powers enumerated in this Act.

* * *

CHAPTER 3.   PURPOSES AND POWERS

* * *

§ 3.02   General Powers

Unless its articles of incorporation provide otherwise, every corporation has perpetual duration and succession in its corporate name and has the same powers as an individual to do all things necessary or convenient to carry out its business and affairs, including without limitation power:

(1) to sue and be sued, complain and defend in its corporate name;

(2) to have a corporate seal, which may be altered at will, and to use it, or a facsimile of it, by impressing or affixing it or in any other manner reproducing it;

(3) to make and amend bylaws, not inconsistent with its articles of incorporation or with the laws of this state, for managing the business and regulating the affairs of the corporation;

(4) to purchase, receive, lease, or otherwise acquire, and own, hold, improve, use, and otherwise deal with, real or personal property, or any legal or equitable interest in property, wherever located;

(5) to sell, convey, mortgage, pledge, lease, exchange, and otherwise dispose of all or any part of its property;

(6) to purchase, receive, subscribe for, or otherwise acquire; own, hold, vote, use, sell, mortgage, lend, pledge, or otherwise dispose of; and deal in and with shares or other interests in, or obligations of, any other entity;

(7) to make contracts and guarantees, incur liabilities, borrow money, issue its notes, bonds, and other obligations, (which may be convertible into or include the option to purchase other securities of the corporation), and secure any of its obligations by mortgage or pledge of any of its property, franchises, or income;

(8) to lend money, invest and reinvest its funds, and receive and hold real and personal property as security for repayment;

(9) to be a promoter, partner, member, associate, or manager of any partnership, joint venture, trust, or other entity;

(10) to conduct its business, locate offices, and exercise the powers granted by this Act within or without this state;

(11) to elect directors and appoint officers, employees, and agents of the corporation, define their duties, fix their compensation, and lend them money and credit;

(12) to pay pensions and establish pension plans, pension trusts, profit sharing plans, share bonus plans, share option plans, and benefit or incentive plans for any or all of its current or former directors, officers, employees, and agents;

(13) to make donations for the public welfare or for charitable, scientific, or educational purposes;

(14) to transact any lawful business that will aid governmental policy;

(15) to make payments or donations, or do any other act, not inconsistent with law, that furthers the business and affairs of the corporation.

* * *

CHAPTER 6. SHARES AND DISTRIBUTIONS
SUBCHAPTER A. SHARES

§ 6.01 Authorized Shares

(a) The articles of incorporation must prescribe the classes of shares and the number of shares of each class that the corporation is authorized to issue. If more than one class of shares is authorized, the articles of incorporation must prescribe a distinguishing designation for each class, and prior to the issuance of shares of a class the preferences, limitations, and relative rights of that class must be described in the articles of incorporation. All shares of a class must have preferences, limitations, and relative rights identical with those of other shares of the same class except to the extent otherwise permitted by section 6.02.

(b) The articles of incorporation must authorize (1) one or more classes of shares that together have unlimited voting rights, and (2) one or more classes of shares (which may be the same class or classes as those with voting rights) that together are entitled to receive the net assets of the corporation upon dissolution.

(c) The articles of incorporation may authorize one or more classes of shares that:

(1) have special, conditional, or limited voting rights, or no right to vote, except to the extent prohibited by this Act;

(2) are redeemable or convertible as specified in the articles of incorporation (i) at the option of the corporation, the shareholder, or another person or upon the occurrence of a designated event; (ii) for cash, indebtedness, securities, or other property; (iii) in a designated amount or in an amount determined in accordance with a designated formula or by reference to extrinsic data or events;

(3) entitle the holders to distributions calculated in any manner, including dividends that may be cumulative, noncumulative, or partially cumulative;

(4) have preference over any other class of shares with respect to distributions, including dividends and distributions upon the dissolution of the corporation.

(d) The description of the designations, preferences, limitations, and relative rights of share classes in subsection (c) is not exhaustive.

§ 6.02   Terms of Class or Series Determined by Board of Directors

(a) If the articles of incorporation so provide, the board of directors may determine, in whole or part, the preferences, limitations, and relative rights (within the limits set forth in section 6.01) of (1) any class of shares before the issuance of any shares of that class or (2) one or more series within a class before the issuance of any shares of that series.

(b) Each series of a class must be given a distinguishing designation.

(c) All shares of a series must have preferences, limitations, and relative rights identical with those of other shares of the same series and, except to the extent otherwise provided in the description of the series, of those of other series of the same class.

(d) Before issuing any shares of a class or series created under this section, the corporation must deliver to the secretary of state for filing articles of amendment, which are effective without shareholder action, that set forth:

(1) the name of the corporation;

(2) the text of the amendment determining the terms of the class or series of shares;

(3) the date it was adopted; and

(4) a statement that the amendment was duly adopted by the board of directors.

§ 6.03 Issued and Outstanding Shares

(a) A corporation may issue the number of shares of each class or series authorized by the articles of incorporation. Shares that are issued are outstanding shares until they are reacquired, redeemed, converted, or cancelled.

(b) The reacquisition, redemption, or conversion of outstanding shares is subject to the limitations of subsection (c) of this section and to section 6.40.

(c) At all times that shares of the corporation are outstanding, one or more shares that together have unlimited voting rights and one or more shares that together are entitled to receive the net assets of the corporation upon dissolution must be outstanding.

* * *

SUBCHAPTER B. ISSUANCE OF SHARES

§ 6.20 Subscription for Shares Before Incorporation

(a) A subscription for shares entered into before incorporation is irrevocable for six months unless the subscription agreement provides a longer or shorter period or all the subscribers agree to revocation.

(b) The board of directors may determine the payment terms of subscriptions for shares that were entered into before incorporation, unless the subscription agreement specifies them. A call for payment by the board of directors must be uniform so far as practicable as to all shares of the same class or series, unless the subscription agreement specifies otherwise.

(c) Shares issued pursuant to subscriptions entered into before incorporation are fully paid and nonassessable when the corporation receives the consideration specified in the subscription agreement.

(d) If a subscriber defaults in payment of money or property under a subscription agreement entered into before incorporation, the corporation may collect the amount owed as any other debt. Alternatively, unless the subscription agreement provides otherwise, the corporation may rescind the agreement and may sell the shares if the debt remains unpaid more than 20 days after the corporation sends written demand for payment to the subscriber.

(e) A subscription agreement entered into after incorporation is a contract between the subscriber and the corporation subject to section 6.21.

§ 6.21 Issuance of Shares

(a) The powers granted in this section to the board of directors may be reserved to the shareholders by the articles of incorporation.

(b) The board of directors may authorize shares to be issued for consideration consisting of any tangible or intangible property or benefit to the corporation, including cash, promissory notes, services performed, contracts for services to be performed, or other securities of the corporation.

(c) Before the corporation issues shares, the board of directors must determine that the consideration received or to be received for shares to be issued is adequate. That determination by the board of directors is conclusive insofar as the adequacy of consideration for the issuance of shares relates to whether the shares are validly issued, fully paid, and nonassessable.

(d) When the corporation receives the consideration for which the board of directors authorized the issuance of shares, the shares issued therefor are fully paid and nonassessable.

(e) The corporation may place in escrow shares issued for a contract for future services or benefits or a promissory note, or make other arrangements to restrict the transfer of the shares, and may credit distributions in respect of the shares against their purchase price, until the services are performed, the note is paid, or the benefits received. If the services are not performed, the note is not paid, or the benefits are not received, the shares escrowed or restricted and the distributions credited may be cancelled in whole or part.

§ 6.22 Liability of Shareholders

(a) A purchaser from a corporation of its own shares is not liable to the corporation or its creditors with respect to the shares except to pay the consideration for which the shares were authorized to be issued (section 6.21) or specified in the subscription agreement (section 6.20).

(b) Unless otherwise provided in the articles of incorporation, a shareholder of a corporation is not personally liable for the acts or debts of the corporation except that he may become personally liable by reason of his own acts or conduct.

§ 6.23 Share Dividends

(a) Unless the articles of incorporation provide otherwise, shares may be issued pro rata and without consideration to the corporation's shareholders or to the shareholders of one or more classes or series. An issuance of shares under this subsection is a share dividend.

(b) Shares of one class or series may not be issued as a share dividend in respect of shares of another class or series unless (1) the articles of incorporation so authorize, (2) a majority of the votes entitled to be cast by the class or series to be issued approve the issue, or (3) there are no outstanding shares of the class or series to be issued.

(c) If the board of directors does not fix the record date for determining shareholders entitled to a share dividend, it is the date the board of directors authorizes the share dividend.

§ 6.24 Share Options

A corporation may issue rights, options, or warrants for the purchase of shares of the corporation. The board of directors shall determine the terms upon which the rights, options, or warrants are issued, their form and content, and the consideration for which the shares are to be issued.

§ 6.25 Form and Content of Certificates

(a) Shares may but need not be represented by certificates. Unless this Act or another statute expressly provides otherwise, the rights and obligations of shareholders are identical whether or not their shares are represented by certificates.

(b) At a minimum each share certificate must state on its face:

(1) the name of the issuing corporation and that it is organized under the law of this state;

(2) the name of the person to whom issued; and

(3) the number and class of shares and the designation of the series, if any, the certificate represents.

* * *

(d) Each share certificate (1) must be signed (either manually or in facsimile) by two officers designated in the bylaws or by the board of directors and (2) may bear the corporate seal or its facsimile.

(e) If the person who signed (either manually or in facsimile) a share certificate no longer holds office when the certificate is issued, the certificate is nevertheless valid.

§ 6.26 Shares Without Certificates

(a) Unless the articles of incorporation or bylaws provide otherwise, the board of directors of a corporation may authorize the issue of some or all of the shares of any or all of its classes or series without certificates. The authorization does not affect shares already represented by certificates until they are surrendered to the corporation.

(b) Within a reasonable time after the issue or transfer of shares without certificates, the corporation shall send the shareholder a written statement of the information required on certificates by section 6.25(b) and (c), and, if applicable, section 6.27.

* * *

§ 6.28 Expense of Issue

A corporation may pay the expenses of selling or underwriting its shares, and of organizing or reorganizing the corporation, from the consideration received for shares.

SUBCHAPTER C. SUBSEQUENT ACQUISITION OF SHARES BY SHAREHOLDERS AND CORPORATION

§ 6.30 Shareholders' Preemptive Rights

(a) The shareholders of a corporation do not have a preemptive right to acquire the corporation's unissued shares except to the extent the articles of incorporation so provide.

* * *

§ 6.31 Corporation's Acquisition of Its Own Shares

(a) A corporation may acquire its own shares and shares so acquired constitute authorized but unissued shares.

(b) If the articles of incorporation prohibit the reissue of acquired shares, the number of authorized shares is reduced by the number of shares acquired, effective upon amendment of the articles of incorporation.

(c) The board of directors may adopt articles of amendment under this section without shareholder action and deliver them to the secretary of state for filing. The articles must set forth:

(1) the name of the corporation;

(2) the reduction in the number of authorized shares, itemized by class and series; and

(3) the total number of authorized shares, itemized by class and series, remaining after reduction of the shares.

SUBCHAPTER D. DISTRIBUTIONS

§ 6.40 Distributions to Shareholders

(a) A board of directors may authorize and the corporation may make distributions to its shareholders subject to restriction by the articles of incorporation and the limitation in subsection (c).

(b) If the board of directors does not fix the record date for determining shareholders entitled to a distribution (other than one involving a purchase, redemption, or other acquisition of the corporation's shares), it is the date the board of directors authorizes the distribution.

(c) No distribution may be made if, after giving it effect:

(1) the corporation would not be able to pay its debts as they become due in the usual course of business; or

(2) the corporation's total assets would be less than the sum of its total liabilities plus (unless the articles of incorporation permit otherwise) the amount that would be needed, if the corporation were to be dissolved at the time of the distribution, to satisfy the preferential rights upon dissolution of shareholders whose preferential rights are superior to those receiving the distribution.

(d) The board of directors may base a determination that a distribution is not prohibited under subsection (c) either on financial statements prepared on the basis of accounting practices and principles that are reasonable in the circumstances or on a fair valuation or other method that is reasonable in the circumstances.

(e) Except as provided in subsection (g), the effect of a distribution under subsection (c) is measured:

(1) in the case of distribution by purchase, redemption, or other acquisition of the corporation's shares, as of the earlier of (i) the date money or other property is transferred or debt incurred by the corporation or (ii) the date the shareholder ceases to be a shareholder with respect to the acquired shares;

(2) in the case of any other distribution of indebtedness, as of the date the indebtedness is distributed; and

(3) in all other cases, as of (i) the date the distribution is authorized if the payment occurs within 120 days after the date of authorization or (ii) the date the payment is made if it occurs more than 120 days after the date of authorization.

(f) A corporation's indebtedness to a shareholder incurred by reason of a distribution made in accordance with this section is at parity with the corporation's indebtedness to its general, unsecured creditors except to the extent subordinated by agreement.

(g) Indebtedness of a corporation, including indebtedness issued as a distribution, is not considered a liability for purposes of determinations under subsection (c) if its terms provide that payment of principal and interest are made only if and to the extent that payment of a distribution to shareholders could then be made under this section. If the indebtedness is issued as a distribution, each payment of principal or interest is treated as a distribution, the effect of which is measured on the date the payment is actually made.

* * *

CHAPTER 7. SHAREHOLDERS

* * *

SUBCHAPTER B. VOTING

* * *

§ 7.21 Voting Entitlement of Shares

(a) Except as provided in subsections (b) and (c) or unless the articles of incorporation provide otherwise, each outstanding share, regardless of class, is entitled to one vote on each matter voted on at a shareholders' meeting. Only shares are entitled to vote.

(b) Absent special circumstances, the shares of a corporation are not entitled to vote if they are owned, directly or indirectly, by a second corporation, domestic or foreign, and the first corporation owns, directly or indirectly, a majority of the shares entitled to vote for directors of the second corporation.

(c) Subsection (b) does not limit the power of a corporation to vote any shares, including its own shares, held by it in a fiduciary capacity.

(d) Redeemable shares are not entitled to vote after notice of redemption is mailed to the holders and a sum sufficient to redeem the shares has been deposited with a bank, trust company, or other financial institution under an irrevocable obligation to pay the holders the redemption price on surrender of the shares.

* * *

§ 7.25 Quorum and Voting Requirements for Voting Groups

(a) Shares entitled to vote as a separate voting group may take action on a matter at a meeting only if a quorum of those shares exists with respect to that matter. Unless the articles of incorporation or this Act provide otherwise, a majority of the votes entitled to be cast on the matter by the voting group constitutes a quorum of that voting group for action on that matter.

(b) Once a share is represented for any purpose at a meeting, it is deemed present for quorum purposes for the remainder of the meeting and for any adjournment of that meeting unless a new record date is or must be set for that adjourned meeting.

(c) If a quorum exists, action on a matter (other than the election of directors) by a voting group is approved if the votes cast within the voting group favoring the action exceed the votes cast opposing the action, unless the articles of incorporation or this Act require a greater number of affirmative votes.

(d) An amendment of articles of incorporation adding, changing, or deleting a quorum or voting requirement for a voting group greater than specified in subsection (b) or (c) is governed by section 7.27.

(e) The election of directors is governed by section 7.28.

§ 7.26 Action by Single and Multiple Voting Groups

(a) If the articles of incorporation or this Act provide for voting by a single voting group on a matter, action on that matter is taken when voted upon by that voting group as provided in section 7.25.

(b) If the articles of incorporation or this Act provide for voting by two or more voting groups on a matter, action on that matter is taken only when voted upon by each of those voting groups counted separately as provided in section 7.25. Action may be taken by one voting group on a matter even though no action is taken by another voting group entitled to vote on the matter.

§ 7.27 Greater Quorum or Voting Requirements

(a) The articles of incorporation may provide for a greater quorum or voting requirement for shareholders (or voting groups of shareholders) than is provided for by this Act.

(b) An amendment to the articles of incorporation that adds, changes, or deletes a greater quorum or voting requirement must meet the same quorum requirement and be adopted by the same vote and voting groups required to take action under the quorum and voting requirements then in effect or proposed to be adopted, whichever is greater.

§ 7.28 Voting for Directors; Cumulative Voting

(a) Unless otherwise provided in the articles of incorporation, directors are elected by a plurality of the votes cast by the shares entitled to vote in the election at a meeting at which a quorum is present.

(b) Shareholders do not have a right to cumulate their votes for directors unless the articles of incorporation so provide.

* * *

Section 7.31(b) provides that voting agreements may be specifically enforceable. A voting agreement may provide its own enforcement mechanism, as by the appointment of a proxy to vote all shares subject to the agreement; the appointment may be made irrevocable under section 7.22. If no enforcement mechanism is provided, a court may order specific enforcement of the agreement and order the votes cast as the agreement contemplates. This section recognizes that damages are not likely to be an appropriate remedy for breach of a voting agreement, and also avoids the result reached in Ringling Bros. Barnum & Bailey Combined Shows v. Ringling, 53 A.2d 441 (Del.1947), where the court held that the appropriate remedy to enforce a pooling agreement was to refuse to permit any voting of the breaching party's shares.

§ 7.32 Shareholder Agreements

(a) An agreement among the shareholders of a corporation that complies with this section is effective among the shareholders and the corporation even though it is inconsistent with one or more other provisions of this Act in that it:

    (1) eliminates the board of directors or restricts the discretion or powers of the board of directors;

    * * *

(d) An agreement authorized by this section shall cease to be effective when shares of the corporation are listed on a national securities exchange or regularly traded in a market maintained by one or more members of a national or affiliated securities association. If the agreement ceases to be effective for any reason, the board of directors may, if the agreement is contained or referred to in the corporation's articles of incorporation or bylaws, adopt an amendment to the articles of incorporation or bylaws, without shareholder action, to delete the agreement and any references to it.

    * * *

CHAPTER 8. DIRECTORS AND OFFICERS
SUBCHAPTER A. BOARD OF DIRECTORS

§ 8.01 Requirement For And Duties Of Board Of Directors

(a) Except as provided in section 7.32, each corporation must have a board of directors.

(b) All corporate powers shall be exercised by or under the authority of, and the business and affairs of the corporation managed under the direction of, its board of directors, subject to any limitation set forth in the articles of incorporation or in an agreement authorized under section 7.32.

    * * *

§ 8.04 Election of Directors by Certain Classes of Shareholders

If the articles of incorporation authorize dividing the shares into classes, the articles may also authorize the election of all or a specified number of directors by the holders of one or more authorized classes of shares. Each class (or classes) of shares entitled to elect one or more directors is a separate voting group for purposes of the election of directors.

    * * *

SUBCHAPTER C. STANDARDS OF CONDUCT

§ 8.30 General Standards for Directors

(a) A director shall discharge his duties as a director, including his duties as a member of a committee:

(1) in good faith;

(2) with the care an ordinarily prudent person in a like position would exercise under similar circumstances; and

(3) in a manner he reasonably believes to be in the best interests of the corporation.

(b) In discharging his duties a director is entitled to rely on information, opinions, reports, or statements, including financial statements and other financial data, if prepared or presented by:

(1) one or more officers or employees of the corporation whom the director reasonably believes to be reliable and competent in the matters presented;

(2) legal counsel, public accountants, or other persons as to matters the director reasonably believes are within the person's professional or expert competence; or

(3) a committee of the board of directors of which he is not a member if the director reasonably believes the committee merits confidence.

(c) A director is not acting in good faith if he has knowledge concerning the matter in question that makes reliance otherwise permitted by subsection (b) unwarranted.

(d) A director is not liable for any action taken as a director, or any failure to take any action, if he performed the duties of his office in compliance with this section.

§ 8.33 Liability for Unlawful Distributions

(a) A director who votes for or assents to a distribution made in violation of section 6.40 or the articles of incorporation is personally liable to the corporation for the amount of the distribution that exceeds what could have been distributed without violating section 6.40 or the articles of incorporation if it is established that he did not perform his duties in compliance with section 8.30. In any proceeding commenced under this section, a director has all of the defenses ordinarily available to a director.

(b) A director held liable under subsection (a) for an unlawful distribution is entitled to contribution:

(1) from every other director who could be held liable under subsection (a) for the unlawful distribution; and

(2) from each shareholder for the amount the shareholder accepted knowing the distribution was made in violation of section 6.40 or the articles of incorporation.

(c) A proceeding under this section is barred unless it is commenced within two years after the date on which the effect of the distribution was measured under section 6.40(e) or (g).

SUBCHAPTER D. OFFICERS

§ 8.40 Required Officers

(a) A corporation has the officers described in its bylaws or appointed by the board of directors in accordance with the bylaws.

(b) A duly appointed officer may appoint one or more officers or assistant officers if authorized by the bylaws or the board of directors.

* * *

§ 8.42 Standards of Conduct for Officers

(a) An officer with discretionary authority shall discharge his duties under that authority:

(1) in good faith;

(2) with the care an ordinarily prudent person in a like position would exercise under similar circumstances; and

(3) in a manner he reasonably believes to be in the best interests of the corporation.

(b) In discharging his duties an officer is entitled to rely on information, opinions, reports, or statements, including financial statements and other financial data, if prepared or presented by:

(1) one or more officers or employees of the corporation whom the officer reasonably believes to be reliable and competent in the matters presented; or

(2) legal counsel, public accountants, or other persons as to matters the officer reasonably believes are within the person's professional or expert competence.

(c) An officer is not acting in good faith if he has knowledge concerning the matter in question that makes reliance otherwise permitted by subsection (b) unwarranted.

(d) An officer is not liable for any action taken as an officer, or any failure to take any action, if he performed the duties of his office in compliance with this section.

* * *

CHAPTER 10. AMENDMENT OF ARTICLES OF INCORPORATION AND BYLAWS

SUBCHAPTER A. AMENDMENT OF ARTICLES OF INCORPORATION

§ 10.01 Authority to Amend

(a) A corporation may amend its articles of incorporation at any time to add or change a provision that is required or permitted in the articles of incorporation or to delete a provision not required in the articles of incorporation. Whether a provision is required or permitted in the articles of incorporation is determined as of the effective date of the amendment.

(b) A shareholder of the corporation does not have a vested property right resulting from any provision in the articles of incorporation, including provisions relating to management, control, capital structure, dividend entitlement, or purpose or duration of the corporation.

§ 10.02 Amendment by Board of Directors

Unless the articles of incorporation provide otherwise, a corporation's board of directors may adopt one or more amendments to the corporation's articles of incorporation without shareholder action:

(1) to extend the duration of the corporation if it was incorporated at a time when limited duration was required by law;

(2) to delete the names and addresses of the initial directors;

(3) to delete the name and address of the initial registered agent or registered office, if a statement of change is on file with the secretary of state;

(4) to change each issued and unissued authorized share of an outstanding class into a greater number of whole shares if the corporation has only shares of that class outstanding;

(5) to change the corporate name by substituting the word "corporation," "incorporated," "company," "limited," or the abbreviation "corp.," "inc.," "co.," or "ltd.," for a similar word or abbreviation in the name, or by adding, deleting, or changing a geographical attribution for the name; or

(6) to make any other change expressly permitted by this Act to be made without shareholder action.

§ 10.03 Amendment by Board of Directors and Shareholders

(a) A corporation's board of directors may propose one or more amendments to the articles of incorporation for submission to the shareholders.

(b) For the amendment to be adopted:

(1) the board of directors must recommend the amendment to the shareholders unless the board of directors determines that because of conflict of interest or other special circumstances it should make no recommendation and communicates the basis for its determination to the shareholders with the amendment; and

(2) the shareholders entitled to vote on the amendment must approve the amendment as provided in subsection (e).

(c) The board of directors may condition its submission of the proposed amendment on any basis.

(d) The corporation shall notify each shareholder, whether or not entitled to vote, of the proposed shareholders' meeting in accordance with section 7.05. The notice of meeting must also state that the purpose, or one of the purposes, of the meeting is to consider the proposed amendment and contain or be accompanied by a copy or summary of the amendment.

(e) Unless this Act, the articles of incorporation, or the board of directors (acting pursuant to subsection (c)) require a greater vote or a vote by voting groups, the amendment to be adopted must be approved by:

> (1) a majority of the votes entitled to be cast on the amendment by any voting group with respect to which the amendment would create dissenters' rights; and

> (2) the votes required by sections 7.25 and 7.26 by every other voting group entitled to vote on the amendment.

§ 10.04 Voting on Amendments by Voting Groups

(a) The holders of the outstanding shares of a class are entitled to vote as a separate voting group (if shareholder voting is otherwise required by this Act) on a proposed amendment if the amendment would:

> (1) increase or decrease the aggregate number of authorized shares of the class;

> (2) effect an exchange or reclassification of all or part of the shares of the class into shares of another class;

> (3) effect an exchange or reclassification, or create the right of exchange, of all or part of the shares of another class into shares of the class;

> (4) change the designation, rights, preferences, or limitations of all or part of the shares of the class;

> (5) change the shares of all or part of the class into a different number of shares of the same class;

> (6) create a new class of shares having rights or preferences with respect to distributions or to dissolution that are prior, superior, or substantially equal to the shares of the class;

> (7) increase the rights, preferences, or number of authorized shares of any class that, after giving effect to the amendment, have rights or preferences with respect to distributions or to dissolution that are prior, superior, or substantially equal to the shares of the class;

> (8) limit or deny an existing preemptive right of all or part of the shares of the class; or

> (9) cancel or otherwise affect rights to distributions or dividends that have accumulated but not yet been declared on all or part of the shares of the class.

(b) If a proposed amendment would affect a series of a class of shares in one or more of the ways described in subsection (a), the shares of that series are entitled to vote as a separate voting group on the proposed amendment.

(c) If a proposed amendment that entitles two or more series of shares to vote as separate voting groups under this section would affect those two or more series in the same or a substantially similar way, the shares of all the series so affected must vote together as a single voting group on the proposed amendment.

(d) A class or series of shares is entitled to the voting rights granted by this section although the articles of incorporation provide that the shares are nonvoting shares.

§ 10.05 Amendment Before Issuance of Shares

If a corporation has not yet issued shares, its incorporators or board of directors may adopt one or more amendments to the corporation's articles of incorporation.

§ 10.06 Articles of Amendment

A corporation amending its articles of incorporation shall deliver to the secretary of state for filing articles of amendment setting forth:

(1) the name of the corporation;

(2) the text of each amendment adopted;

(3) if an amendment provides for an exchange, reclassification, or cancellation of issued shares, provisions for implementing the amendment if not contained in the amendment itself;

(4) the date of each amendment's adoption;

(5) if an amendment was adopted by the incorporators or board of directors without shareholder action, a statement to that effect and that shareholder action was not required;

(6) if an amendment was approved by the shareholders:

(i) the designation, number of outstanding shares, number of votes entitled to be cast by each voting group entitled to vote separately on the amendment, and number of votes of each voting group indisputably represented at the meeting;

(ii) either the total number of votes cast for and against the amendment by each voting group entitled to vote separately on the amendment or the total number of undisputed votes cast for the amendment by each voting group and a statement that the number cast for the amendment by each voting group was sufficient for approval by that voting group.

§ 10.07 Restated Articles of Incorporation

(a) A corporation's board of directors may restate its articles of incorporation at any time with or without shareholder action.

(b) The restatement may include one or more amendments to the articles. If the restatement includes an amendment requiring shareholder approval, it must be adopted as provided in section 10.03.

(c) If the board of directors submits a restatement for shareholder action, the corporation shall notify each shareholder, whether or not entitled to vote, of the proposed shareholders' meeting in accordance with section 7.05. The notice must also state that the purpose, or one of the purposes, of the meeting is to consider the proposed restatement and contain or be accompanied by a copy of the restatement that identifies any amendment or other change it would make in the articles.

(d) A corporation restating its articles of incorporation shall deliver to the secretary of state for filing articles of restatement setting forth the name of the corporation and the text of the restated articles of incorporation together with a certificate setting forth:

(1) whether the restatement contains an amendment to the articles requiring shareholder approval and, if it does not, that the board of directors adopted the restatement; or

(2) if the restatement contains an amendment to the articles requiring shareholder approval, the information required by section 10.06.

(e) Duly adopted restated articles of incorporation supersede the original articles of incorporation and all amendments to them.

(f) The secretary of state may certify restated articles of incorporation, as the articles of incorporation currently in effect, without including the certificate information required by subsection (d).

§ 10.08 Amendment Pursuant to Reorganization

(a) A corporation's articles of incorporation may be amended without action by the board of directors or shareholders to carry out a plan of reorganization ordered or decreed by a court of competent jurisdiction under federal statute if the articles of incorporation after amendment contain only provisions required or permitted by section 2.02.

(b) The individual or individuals designated by the court shall deliver to the secretary of state for filing articles of amendment setting forth:

(1) the name of the corporation;

(2) the text of each amendment approved by the court;

(3) the date of the court's order or decree approving the articles of amendment;

(4) the title of the reorganization proceeding in which the order or decree was entered; and

(5) a statement that the court had jurisdiction of the proceeding under federal statute.

(c) Shareholders of a corporation undergoing reorganization do not have dissenters' rights except as and to the extent provided in the reorganization plan.

(d) This section does not apply after entry of a final decree in the reorganization proceeding even though the court retains jurisdiction of the proceeding for limited purposes unrelated to consummation of the reorganization plan.

§ 10.09 Effect of Amendment

An amendment to articles of incorporation does not affect a cause of action existing against or in favor of the corporation, a proceeding to which the corporation is a party, or the existing rights of persons other than shareholders of the corporation. An amendment changing a corporation's name does not abate a proceeding brought by or against the corporation in its former name.

SUBCHAPTER B. AMENDMENT OF BYLAWS

§ 10.20 Amendment by Board of Directors or Shareholders

(a) A corporation's board of directors may amend or repeal the corporation's bylaws unless:

(1) the articles of incorporation or this Act reserve this power exclusively to the shareholders in whole or part; or

(2) the shareholders in amending or repealing a particular bylaw provide expressly that the board of directors may not amend or repeal that bylaw.

(b) A corporation's shareholders may amend or repeal the corporation's bylaws even though the bylaws may also be amended or repealed by its board of directors.

§ 10.21 Bylaw Increasing Quorum or Voting Requirement for Shareholders

(a) If expressly authorized by the articles of incorporation, the shareholders may adopt or amend a bylaw that fixes a greater quorum or voting requirement for shareholders (or voting groups of shareholders) than is required by this Act. The adoption or amendment of a bylaw that adds, changes, or deletes a greater quorum or voting requirement for shareholders must meet the same quorum requirement and be adopted by the same vote and voting groups required to take action under the quorum and voting requirement then in effect or proposed to be adopted, whichever is greater.

(b) A bylaw that fixes a greater quorum or voting requirement for shareholders under subsection (a) may not be adopted, amended, or repealed by the board of directors.

§ 10.22 Bylaw Increasing Quorum or Voting Requirement for Directors

(a) A bylaw that fixes a greater quorum or voting requirement for the board of directors may be amended or repealed:

(1) if originally adopted by the shareholders, only by the shareholders;

(2) if originally adopted by the board of directors, either by the shareholders or by the board of directors.

(b) A bylaw adopted or amended by the shareholders that fixes a greater quorum or voting requirement for the board of directors may provide that it may be amended or repealed only by a specified vote of either the shareholders or the board of directors.

(c) Action by the board of directors under subsection (a)(2) to adopt or amend a bylaw that changes the quorum or voting requirement for the board of directors must meet the same quorum requirement and be adopted by the same vote required to take action under the quorum and voting requirement then in effect or proposed to be adopted, whichever is greater.

CHAPTER 11. MERGER AND SHARE EXCHANGE

§ 11.01 Merger

(a) One or more corporations may merge into another corporation if the board of directors of each corporation adopts and its shareholders (if required by section 11.03) approve a plan of merger.

(b) The plan of merger must set forth:

(1) the name of each corporation planning to merge and the name of the surviving corporation into which each other corporation plans to merge;

(2) the terms and conditions of the merger; and

(3) the manner and basis of converting the shares of each corporation into shares, obligations, or other securities of the surviving or any other corporation or into cash or other property in whole or part.

(c) The plan of merger may set forth:

(1) amendments to the articles of incorporation of the surviving corporation; and

(2) other provisions relating to the merger.

§ 11.02 Share Exchange

(a) A corporation may acquire all of the outstanding shares of one or more classes or series of another corporation if the board of directors of each corporation adopts and its shareholders (if required by section 11.03) approve the exchange.

(b) The plan of exchange must set forth:

(1) the name of the corporation whose shares will be acquired and the name of the acquiring corporation;

(2) the terms and conditions of the exchange;

(3) the manner and basis of exchanging the shares to be acquired for shares, obligations, or other securities of the acquiring or any other corporation or for cash or other property in whole or part.

(c) The plan of exchange may set forth other provisions relating to the exchange.

(d) This section does not limit the power of a corporation to acquire all or part of the shares of one or more classes or series of another corporation through a voluntary exchange or otherwise.

§ 11.03 Action on Plan

(a) After adopting a plan of merger or share exchange, the board of directors of each corporation party to the merger, and the board of directors of the corporation whose shares will be acquired in the share exchange, shall submit the plan of merger (except as provided in subsection (g)) or share exchange for approval by its shareholders.

(b) For a plan of merger or share exchange to be approved:

(1) the board of directors must recommend the plan of merger or share exchange to the shareholders, unless the board of directors determines that because of conflict of interest or other special circumstances it should make no recommendation and communicates the basis for its determination to the shareholders with the plan; and

(2) the shareholders entitled to vote must approve the plan.

(c) The board of directors may condition its submission of the proposed merger or share exchange on any basis.

(d) The corporation shall notify each shareholder, whether or not entitled to vote, of the proposed shareholders' meeting in accordance with section 7.05. The notice must also state that the purpose, or one of the purposes, of the meeting is to consider the plan of merger or share exchange and contain or be accompanied by a copy or summary of the plan.

(e) Unless this Act, the articles of incorporation, or the board of directors (acting pursuant to subsection (c)) require a greater vote or a

Brudney & Chirelstein Corp. Fin. 4th Ed. UCS—30

F–25

vote by voting groups, the plan of merger or share exchange to be authorized must be approved by each voting group entitled to vote separately on the plan by a majority of all the votes entitled to be cast on the plan by that voting group.

(f) Separate voting by voting groups is required:

(1) on a plan of merger if the plan contains a provision that, if contained in a proposed amendment to articles of incorporation, would require action by one or more separate voting groups on the proposed amendment under section 10.04;

(2) on a plan of share exchange by each class or series of shares included in the exchange, with each class or series constituting a separate voting group.

(g) Action by the shareholders of the surviving corporation on a plan of merger is not required if:

(1) the articles of incorporation of the surviving corporation will not differ (except for amendments enumerated in section 10.02) from its articles before the merger;

(2) each shareholder of the surviving corporation whose shares were outstanding immediately before the effective date of the merger will hold the same number of shares, with identical designations, preferences, limitations, and relative rights, immediately after;

(3) the number of voting shares outstanding immediately after the merger, plus the number of voting shares issuable as a result of the merger (either by the conversion of securities issued pursuant to the merger or the exercise of rights and warrants issued pursuant to the merger), will not exceed by more than 20 percent the total number of voting shares of the surviving corporation outstanding immediately before the merger; and

(4) the number of participating shares outstanding immediately after the merger, plus the number of participating shares issuable as a result of the merger (either by the conversion of securities issued pursuant to the merger or the exercise of rights and warrants issued pursuant to the merger), will not exceed by more than 20 percent the total number of participating shares outstanding immediately before the merger.

(h) As used in subsection (g):

(1) "Participating shares" means shares that entitle their holders to participate without limitation in distributions.

(2) "Voting shares" means shares that entitle their holders to vote unconditionally in elections of directors.

(i) After a merger or share exchange is authorized, and at any time before articles of merger or share exchange are filed, the planned merger or share exchange may be abandoned (subject to any contractual rights), without further shareholder action, in accordance with the procedure set forth in the plan of merger or share exchange or, if none is set forth, in the manner determined by the board of directors.

§ 11.04 Merger of Subsidiary

(a) A parent corporation owning at least 90 percent of the outstanding shares of each class of a subsidiary corporation may merge the subsidiary into itself without approval of the shareholders of the parent or subsidiary.

(b) The board of directors of the parent shall adopt a plan of merger that sets forth:

(1) the names of the parent and subsidiary; and

(2) the manner and basis of converting the shares of the subsidiary into shares, obligations, or other securities of the parent or any other corporation or into cash or other property in whole or part.

(c) The parent shall mail a copy or summary of the plan of merger to each shareholder of the subsidiary who does not waive the mailing requirement in writing.

(d) The parent may not deliver articles of merger to the secretary of state for filing until at least 30 days after the date it mailed a copy of the plan of merger to each shareholder of the subsidiary who did not waive the mailing requirement.

(e) Articles of merger under this section may not contain amendments to the articles of incorporation of the parent corporation (except for amendments enumerated in section 10.02).

§ 11.05 Articles of Merger or Share Exchange

(a) After a plan of merger or share exchange is approved by the shareholders, or adopted by the board of directors if shareholder approval is not required, the surviving or acquiring corporation shall deliver to the secretary of state for filing articles of merger or share exchange setting forth:

(1) the plan of merger or share exchange;

(2) if shareholder approval was not required, a statement to that effect;

(3) if approval of the shareholders of one or more corporations party to the merger or share exchange was required:

(i) the designation, number of outstanding shares, and number of votes entitled to be cast by each voting group entitled to vote separately on the plan as to each corporation; and

(ii) either the total number of votes cast for and against the plan by each voting group entitled to vote separately on the plan or the total number of undisputed votes cast for the plan separately by each voting group and a statement that the number cast for the plan by each voting group was sufficient for approval by that voting group.

(b) A merger or share exchange takes effect upon the effective date of the articles of merger or share exchange.

§ 11.06 Effect of Merger or Share Exchange

(a) When a merger takes effect:

(1) every other corporation party to the merger merges into the surviving corporation and the separate existence of every corporation except the surviving corporation ceases;

(2) the title to all real estate and other property owned by each corporation party to the merger is vested in the surviving corporation without reversion or impairment;

(3) the surviving corporation has all liabilities of each corporation party to the merger;

(4) a proceeding pending against any corporation party to the merger may be continued as if the merger did not occur or the surviving corporation may be substituted in the proceeding for the corporation whose existence ceased;

(5) the articles of incorporation of the surviving corporation are amended to the extent provided in the plan of merger; and

(6) the shares of each corporation party to the merger that are to be converted into shares, obligations, or other securities of the surviving or any other corporation or into cash or other property are converted and the former holders of the shares are entitled only to the rights provided in the articles of merger or to their rights under chapter 13.

(b) When a share exchange takes effect, the shares of each acquired corporation are exchanged as provided in the plan, and the former holders of the shares are entitled only to the exchange rights provided in the articles of share exchange or to their rights under chapter 13.

* * *

CHAPTER 12. SALE OF ASSETS

§ 12.01 Sale of Assets in Regular Course of Business and Mortgage of Assets

(a) A corporation may, on the terms and conditions and for the consideration determined by the board of directors:

(1) sell, lease, exchange, or otherwise dispose of all, or substantially all, of its property in the usual and regular course of business,

(2) mortgage, pledge, dedicate to the repayment of indebtedness (whether with or without recourse), or otherwise encumber any or all of its property whether or not in the usual and regular course of business, or

(3) transfer any or all of its property to a corporation all the shares of which are owned by the corporation.

(b) Unless the articles of incorporation require it, approval by the shareholders of a transaction described in subsection (a) is not required.

§ 12.02 Sale of Assets Other Than in Regular Course of Business

(a) A corporation may sell, lease, exchange, or otherwise dispose of all, or substantially all, of its property (with or without the good will), otherwise than in the usual and regular course of business, on the terms and conditions and for the consideration determined by the corporation's board of directors, if the board of directors proposes and its shareholders approve the proposed transaction.

(b) For a transaction to be authorized:

(1) the board of directors must recommend the proposed transaction to the shareholders unless the board of directors determines that because of conflict of interest or other special circumstances it should make no recommendation and communicates the basis for its determination to the shareholders with the submission of the proposed transaction; and

(2) the shareholders entitled to vote must approve the transaction.

(c) The board of directors may condition its submission of the proposed transaction on any basis.

(d) The corporation shall notify each shareholder, whether or not entitled to vote, of the proposed shareholders' meeting in accordance with section 7.05. The notice must also state that the purpose, or one of the purposes, of the meeting is to consider the sale, lease, exchange, or other disposition of all, or substantially all, the property of the corporation and contain or be accompanied by a description of the transaction.

(e) Unless the articles of incorporation or the board of directors (acting pursuant to subsection (c)) require a greater vote or a vote by voting groups, the transaction to be authorized must be approved by a majority of all the votes entitled to be cast on the transaction.

(f) After a sale, lease, exchange, or other disposition of property is authorized, the transaction may be abandoned (subject to any contractual rights) without further shareholder action.

(g) A transaction that constitutes a distribution is governed by section 6.40 and not by this section.

CHAPTER 13.   DISSENTERS' RIGHTS
SUBCHAPTER A.   RIGHT TO DISSENT AND OBTAIN PAYMENT FOR SHARES

§ 13.01   Definitions

In this chapter:

(1) "Corporation" means the issuer of the shares held by a dissenter before the corporate action, or the surviving or acquiring corporation by merger or share exchange of that issuer.

(2) "Dissenter" means a shareholder who is entitled to dissent from corporate action under section 13.02 and who exercises that right when and in the manner required by sections 13.20 through 13.28.

(3) "Fair value," with respect to a dissenter's shares, means the value of the shares immediately before the effectuation of the corporate action to which the dissenter objects, excluding any appreciation or depreciation in anticipation of the corporate action unless exclusion would be inequitable.

(4) "Interest" means interest from the effective date of the corporate action until the date of payment, at the average rate currently paid by the corporation on its principal bank loans or, if none, at a rate that is fair and equitable under all the circumstances.

(5) "Record shareholder" means the person in whose name shares are registered in the records of a corporation or the beneficial owner of shares to the extent of the rights granted by a nominee certificate on file with a corporation.

(6) "Beneficial shareholder" means the person who is a beneficial owner of shares held by a nominee as the record shareholder.

(7) "Shareholder" means the record shareholder or the beneficial shareholder.

§ 13.02   Right to Dissent

(a) A shareholder is entitled to dissent from, and obtain payment of the fair value of his shares in the event of, any of the following corporate actions:

(1) consummation of a plan of merger to which the corporation is a party (i) if shareholder approval is required for the merger by section 11.03 or the articles of incorporation and the shareholder is entitled to vote on the merger or (ii) if the corporation is a subsidiary that is merged with its parent under section 11.04;

(2) consummation of a plan of share exchange to which the corporation is a party as the corporation whose shares will be acquired, if the shareholder is entitled to vote on the plan;

(3) consummation of a sale or exchange of all, or substantially all, of the property of the corporation other than in the usual and

regular course of business, if the shareholder is entitled to vote on the sale or exchange, including a sale in dissolution, but not including a sale pursuant to court order or a sale for cash pursuant to a plan by which all or substantially all of the net proceeds of the sale will be distributed to the shareholders within one year after the date of sale;

(4) an amendment of the articles of incorporation that materially and adversely affects rights in respect of a dissenter's shares because it:

(i) alters or abolishes a preferential right of the shares;

(ii) creates, alters, or abolishes a right in respect of redemption, including a provision respecting a sinking fund for the redemption or repurchase, of the shares;

(iii) alters or abolishes a preemptive right of the holder of the shares to acquire shares or other securities;

(iv) excludes or limits the right of the shares to vote on any matter, or to cumulate votes, other than a limitation by dilution through issuance of shares or other securities with similar voting rights; or

(v) reduces the number of shares owned by the shareholder to a fraction of a share if the fractional share so created is to be acquired for cash under section 6.04; or

(5) any corporate action taken pursuant to a shareholder vote to the extent the articles of incorporation, bylaws, or a resolution of the board of directors provides that voting or nonvoting shareholders are entitled to dissent and obtain payment for their shares.

(b) A shareholder entitled to dissent and obtain payment for his shares under this chapter may not challenge the corporate action creating his entitlement unless the action is unlawful or fraudulent with respect to the shareholder or the corporation.

§ 13.03 Dissent by Nominees and Beneficial Owners

(a) A record shareholder may assert dissenters' rights as to fewer than all the shares registered in his name only if he dissents with respect to all shares beneficially owned by any one person and notifies the corporation in writing of the name and address of each person on whose behalf he asserts dissenters' rights. The rights of a partial dissenter under this subsection are determined as if the shares as to which he dissents and his other shares were registered in the names of different shareholders.

(b) A beneficial shareholder may assert dissenters' rights as to shares held on his behalf only if:

(1) he submits to the corporation the record shareholder's written consent to the dissent not later than the time the beneficial shareholder asserts dissenters' rights; and

(2) he does so with respect to all shares of which he is the beneficial shareholder or over which he has power to direct the vote.

SUBCHAPTER B. PROCEDURE FOR EXERCISE OF DISSENTERS' RIGHTS

§ 13.20 Notice of Dissenters' Rights

(a) If proposed corporate action creating dissenters' rights under section 13.02 is submitted to a vote at a shareholders' meeting, the meeting notice must state that shareholders are or may be entitled to assert dissenters' rights under this chapter and be accompanied by a copy of this chapter.

(b) If corporate action creating dissenters' rights under section 13.02 is taken without a vote of shareholders, the corporation shall notify in writing all shareholders entitled to assert dissenters' rights that the action was taken and send them the dissenters' notice described in section 13.22.

§ 13.21 Notice of Intent to Demand Payment

(a) If proposed corporate action creating dissenters' rights under section 13.02 is submitted to a vote at a shareholders' meeting, a shareholder who wishes to assert dissenters' rights (1) must deliver to the corporation before the vote is taken written notice of his intent to demand payment for his shares if the proposed action is effectuated and (2) must not vote his shares in favor of the proposed action.

(b) A shareholder who does not satisfy the requirements of subsection (a) is not entitled to payment for his shares under this chapter.

§ 13.22 Dissenters' Notice

(a) If proposed corporate action creating dissenters' rights under section 13.02 is authorized at a shareholders' meeting, the corporation shall deliver a written dissenters' notice to all shareholders who satisfied the requirements of section 13.21.

(b) The dissenters' notice must be sent no later than 10 days after the corporate action was taken, and must:

(1) state where the payment demand must be sent and where and when certificates for certificated shares must be deposited;

(2) inform holders of uncertificated shares to what extent transfer of the shares will be restricted after the payment demand is received;

(3) supply a form for demanding payment that includes the date of the first announcement to news media or to shareholders of

the terms of the proposed corporate action and requires that the person asserting dissenters' rights certify whether or not he acquired beneficial ownership of the shares before that date;

(4) set a date by which the corporation must receive the payment demand, which date may not be fewer than 30 nor more than 60 days after the date the subsection (a) notice is delivered; and

(5) be accompanied by a copy of this chapter.

§ 13.23 Duty to Demand Payment

(a) A shareholder sent a dissenters' notice described in section 13.22 must demand payment, certify whether he acquired beneficial ownership of the shares before the date required to be set forth in the dissenters' notice pursuant to section 13.22(b)(3), and deposit his certificates in accordance with the terms of the notice.

(b) The shareholder who demands payment and deposits his shares under section (a) retains all other rights of a shareholder until these rights are cancelled or modified by the taking of the proposed corporate action.

(c) A shareholder who does not demand payment or deposit his share certificates where required, each by the date set in the dissenters' notice, is not entitled to payment for his shares under this chapter.

§ 13.24 Share Restrictions

(a) The corporation may restrict the transfer of uncertificated shares from the date the demand for their payment is received until the proposed corporate action is taken or the restrictions released under section 13.26.

(b) The person for whom dissenters' rights are asserted as to uncertificated shares retains all other rights of a shareholder until these rights are cancelled or modified by the taking of the proposed corporate action.

§ 13.25 Payment

(a) Except as provided in section 13.27, as soon as the proposed corporate action is taken, or upon receipt of a payment demand, the corporation shall pay each dissenter who complied with section 13.23 the amount the corporation estimates to be the fair value of his shares, plus accrued interest.

(b) The payment must be accompanied by:

(1) the corporation's balance sheet as of the end of a fiscal year ending not more than 16 months before the date of payment, an income statement for that year, a statement of changes in shareholders' equity for that year, and the latest available interim financial statements, if any;

(2) a statement of the corporation's estimate of the fair value of the shares;

(3) an explanation of how the interest was calculated;

(4) a statement of the dissenter's right to demand payment under section 13.28; and

(5) a copy of this chapter.

§ 13.26 Failure to Take Action

(a) If the corporation does not take the proposed action within 60 days after the date set for demanding payment and depositing share certificates, the corporation shall return the deposited certificates and release the transfer restrictions imposed on uncertificated shares.

(b) If after returning deposited certificates and releasing transfer restrictions, the corporation takes the proposed action, it must send a new dissenters' notice under section 13.22 and repeat the payment demand procedure.

§ 13.27 After–Acquired Shares

(a) A corporation may elect to withhold payment required by section 13.25 from a dissenter unless he was the beneficial owner of the shares before the date set forth in the dissenters' notice as the date of the first announcement to news media or to shareholders of the terms of the proposed corporate action.

(b) To the extent the corporation elects to withhold payment under subsection (a), after taking the proposed corporate action, it shall estimate the fair value of the shares, plus accrued interest, and shall pay this amount to each dissenter who agrees to accept it in full satisfaction of his demand. The corporation shall send with its offer a statement of its estimate of the fair value of the shares, an explanation of how the interest was calculated, and a statement of the dissenter's right to demand payment under section 13.28.

§ 13.28 Procedure if Shareholder Dissatisfied With Payment or Offer

(a) A dissenter may notify the corporation in writing of his own estimate of the fair value of his shares and amount of interest due, and demand payment of his estimate (less any payment under section 13.25), or reject the corporation's offer under section 13.27 and demand payment of the fair value of his shares and interest due, if:

(1) the dissenter believes that the amount paid under section 13.25 or offered under section 13.27 is less than the fair value of his shares or that the interest due is incorrectly calculated;

(2) the corporation fails to make payment under section 13.25 within 60 days after the date set for demanding payment; or

(3) the corporation, having failed to take the proposed action, does not return the deposited certificates or release the transfer restrictions imposed on uncertificated shares within 60 days after the date set for demanding payment.

(b) A dissenter waives his right to demand payment under this section unless he notifies the corporation of his demand in writing under subsection (a) within 30 days after the corporation made or offered payment for his shares.

SUBCHAPTER C. JUDICIAL APPRAISAL OF SHARES

§ 13.30 Court Action

(a) If a demand for payment under section 13.28 remains unsettled, the corporation shall commence a proceeding within 60 days after receiving the payment demand and petition the court to determine the fair value of the shares and accrued interest. If the corporation does not commence the proceeding within the 60–day period, it shall pay each dissenter whose demand remains unsettled the amount demanded.

(b) The corporation shall commence the proceeding in the [name or describe] court of the county where a corporation's principal office (or, if none in this state, its registered office) is located. If the corporation is a foreign corporation without a registered office in this state, it shall commence the proceeding in the county in this state where the registered office of the domestic corporation merged with or whose shares were acquired by the foreign corporation was located.

(c) The corporation shall make all dissenters (whether or not residents of this state) whose demands remain unsettled parties to the proceeding as in an action against their shares and all parties must be served with a copy of the petition. Nonresidents may be served by registered or certified mail or by publication as provided by law.

(d) The jurisdiction of the court in which the proceeding is commenced under subsection (b) is plenary and exclusive. The court may appoint one or more persons as appraisers to receive evidence and recommend decision on the question of fair value. The appraisers have the powers described in the order appointing them, or in any amendment to it. The dissenters are entitled to the same discovery rights as parties in other civil proceedings.

(e) Each dissenter made a party to the proceeding is entitled to judgment (1) for the amount, if any, by which the court finds the fair value of his shares, plus interest, exceeds the amount paid by the corporation or (2) for the fair value, plus accrued interest, of his after-acquired shares for which the corporation elected to withhold payment under section 13.27.

§ 13.31 Court Costs and Counsel Fees

(a) The court in an appraisal proceeding commenced under section 13.30 shall determine all costs of the proceeding, including the reasonable compensation and expenses of appraisers appointed by the court. The court shall assess the costs against the corporation, except that the court may assess costs against all or some of the dissenters, in amounts the court finds equitable, to the extent the court finds the dissenters acted arbitrarily, vexatiously, or not in good faith in demanding payment under section 13.28.

(b) The court may also assess the fees and expenses of counsel and experts for the respective parties, in amounts the court finds equitable:

(1) against the corporation and in favor of any or all dissenters if the court finds the corporation did not substantially comply with the requirements of sections 13.20 through 13.28; or

(2) against either the corporation or a dissenter, in favor of any other party, if the court finds that the party against whom the fees and expenses are assessed acted arbitrarily, vexatiously, or not in good faith with respect to the rights provided by this chapter.

(c) If the court finds that the services of counsel for any dissenter were of substantial benefit to other dissenters similarly situated, and that the fees for those services should not be assessed against the corporation, the court may award to these counsel reasonable fees to be paid out of the amounts awarded the dissenters who were benefited.

CHAPTER 14. DISSOLUTION
SUBCHAPTER A. VOLUNTARY DISSOLUTION

* * *

§ 14.02 Dissolution by Board of Directors and Shareholders

(a) A corporation's board of directors may propose dissolution for submission to the shareholders.

(b) For a proposal to dissolve to be adopted:

(1) the board of directors must recommend dissolution to the shareholders unless the board of directors determines that because of conflict of interest or other special circumstances it should make no recommendation and communicates the basis for its determination to the shareholders; and

(2) the shareholders entitled to vote must approve the proposal to dissolve as provided in subsection (e).

(c) The board of directors may condition its submission of the proposal for dissolution on any basis.

(d) The corporation shall notify each shareholder, whether or not entitled to vote, of the proposed shareholders' meeting in accordance with section 7.05. The notice must also state that the purpose, or one of the purposes, of the meeting is to consider dissolving the corporation.

(e) Unless the articles of incorporation or the board of directors (acting pursuant to subsection (c)) require a greater vote or a vote by voting groups, the proposal to dissolve to be adopted must be approved by a majority of all the votes entitled to be cast on that proposal.

§ 14.03 Articles of Dissolution

(a) At any time after dissolution is authorized, the corporation may dissolve by delivering to the secretary of state for filing articles of dissolution setting forth:

(1) the name of the corporation;

(2) the date dissolution was authorized;

(3) if dissolution was approved by the shareholders:

(i) the number of votes entitled to be cast on the proposal to dissolve; and

(ii) either the total number of votes cast for and against dissolution or the total number of undisputed votes cast for dissolution and a statement that the number cast for dissolution was sufficient for approval.

(4) If voting by voting groups is required, the information required by subparagraph (3) shall be separately provided for each voting group entitled to vote separately on the plan to dissolve.

(b) A corporation is dissolved upon the effective date of its articles of dissolution.

* * *

§ 14.05 Effect of Dissolution

(a) A dissolved corporation continues its corporate existence but may not carry on any business except that appropriate to wind up and liquidate its business and affairs, including:

(1) collecting its assets;

(2) disposing of its properties that will not be distributed in kind to its shareholders;

(3) discharging or making provision for discharging its liabilities;

(4) distributing its remaining property among its shareholders according to their interests; and

(5) doing every other act necessary to wind up and liquidate its business and affairs.

(b) Dissolution of a corporation does not:

(1) transfer title to the corporation's property;

(2) prevent transfer of its shares or securities, although the authorization to dissolve may provide for closing the corporation's share transfer records;

(3) subject its directors or officers to standards of conduct different from those prescribed in chapter 8;

(4) change quorum or voting requirements for its board of directors or shareholders; change provisions for selection, resignation, or removal of its directors or officers or both; or change provisions for amending its bylaws;

(5) prevent commencement of a proceeding by or against the corporation in its corporate name;

(6) abate or suspend a proceeding pending by or against the corporation on the effective date of dissolution; or

(7) terminate the authority of the registered agent of the corporation.

§ 14.06 Known Claims Against Dissolved Corporation

(a) A dissolved corporation may dispose of the known claims against it by following the procedure described in this section.

(b) The dissolved corporation shall notify its known claimants in writing of the dissolution at any time after its effective date. The written notice must:

(1) describe information that must be included in a claim;

(2) provide a mailing address where a claim may be sent;

(3) state the deadline, which may not be fewer than 120 days from the effective date of the written notice, by which the dissolved corporation must receive the claim; and

(4) state that the claim will be barred if not received by the deadline.

(c) A claim against the dissolved corporation is barred:

(1) if a claimant who was given written notice under subsection (b) does not deliver the claim to the dissolved corporation by the deadline;

(2) if a claimant whose claim was rejected by the dissolved corporation does not commence a proceeding to enforce the claim within 90 days from the effective date of the rejection notice.

(d) For purposes of this section, "claim" does not include a contingent liability or a claim based on an event occurring after the effective date of dissolution.

§ 14.07 Unknown Claims Against Dissolved Corporation

(a) A dissolved corporation may also publish notice of its dissolution and request that persons with claims against the corporation present them in accordance with the notice.

(b) The notice must:

(1) be published one time in a newspaper of general circulation in the county where the dissolved corporation's principal office (or, if none in this state, its registered office) is or was last located;

(2) describe the information that must be included in a claim and provide a mailing address where the claim may be sent; and

(3) state that a claim against the corporation will be barred unless a proceeding to enforce the claim is commenced within five years after the publication of the notice.

(c) If the dissolved corporation publishes a newspaper notice in accordance with subsection (b), the claim of each of the following claimants is barred unless the claimant commences a proceeding to enforce the claim against the dissolved corporation within five years after the publication date of the newspaper notice:

(1) a claimant who did not receive written notice under section 14.06;

(2) a claimant whose claim was timely sent to the dissolved corporation but not acted on;

(3) a claimant whose claim is contingent or based on an event occurring after the effective date of dissolution.

(d) A claim may be enforced under this section:

(1) against the dissolved corporation, to the extent of its undistributed assets; or

(2) if the assets have been distributed in liquidation, against a shareholder of the dissolved corporation to the extent of his pro rata share of the claim or the corporate assets distributed to him in liquidation, whichever is less, but a shareholder's total liability for all claims under this section may not exceed the total amount of assets distributed to him.

* * *

CHAPTER 16. RECORDS AND REPORTS

* * *

SUBCHAPTER B. REPORTS

§ 16.20 Financial Statements for Shareholders

(a) A corporation shall furnish its shareholders annual financial statements, which may be consolidated or combined statements of the corporation and one or more of its subsidiaries, as appropriate, that include a balance sheet as of the end of the fiscal year, an income statement for that year, and a statement of changes in shareholders' equity for the year unless that information appears elsewhere in the financial statements. If financial statements are prepared for the corporation on the basis of generally accepted accounting principles, the annual financial statements must also be prepared on that basis.

(b) If the annual financial statements are reported upon by a public accountant, his report must accompany them. If not, the statements must be accompanied by a statement of the president or the person responsible for the corporation's accounting records:

(1) stating his reasonable belief whether the statements were prepared on the basis of generally accepted accounting principles and, if not, describing the basis of preparation; and

(2) describing any respects in which the statements were not prepared on a basis of accounting consistent with the statements prepared for the preceding year.

(c) A corporation shall mail the annual financial statements to each shareholder within 120 days after the close of each fiscal year. Thereafter, on written request from a shareholder who was not mailed the statements, the corporation shall mail him the latest financial statements.

§ 16.21 Other Reports to Shareholders

(a) If a corporation indemnifies or advances expenses to a director under section 8.51, 8.52, 8.53, or 8.54 in connection with a proceeding by or in the right of the corporation, the corporation shall report the indemnification or advance in writing to the shareholders with or before the notice of the next shareholders' meeting.

(b) If a corporation issues or authorizes the issuance of shares for promissory notes or for promises to render services in the future, the corporation shall report in writing to the shareholders the number of shares authorized or issued, and the consideration received by the corporation, with or before the notice of the next shareholders' meeting.

§ 16.22 Annual Report for Secretary of State

(a) Each domestic corporation, and each foreign corporation authorized to transact business in this state, shall deliver to the secretary of state for filing an annual report that sets forth:

(1) the name of the corporation and the state or country under whose law it is incorporated;

(2) the address of its registered office and the name of its registered agent at that office in this state;

(3) the address of its principal office;

(4) the names and business addresses of its directors and principal officers;

(5) a brief description of the nature of its business;

(6) the total number of authorized shares, itemized by class and series, if any, within each class; and

(7) the total number of issued and outstanding shares, itemized by class and series, if any, within each class.

(b) Information in the annual report must be current as of the date the annual report is executed on behalf of the corporation.

(c) The first annual report must be delivered to the secretary of state between January 1 and April 1 of the year following the calendar year in which a domestic corporation was incorporated or a foreign corporation was authorized to transact business. Subsequent annual reports must be delivered to the secretary of state between January 1 and April 1 of the following calendar years.

(d) If an annual report does not contain the information required by this section, the secretary of state shall promptly notify the reporting domestic or foreign corporation in writing and return the report to it for correction. If the report is corrected to contain the information required by this section and delivered to the secretary of state within 30 days after the effective date of notice, it is deemed to be timely filed.

* * *

APPENDIX G

PROVISIONS OF THE DELAWARE AND NEW YORK STATUTES CONCERNING SENIOR SECURITIES, MERGERS, SALES OF ASSETS, AND APPRAISAL

SECTIONS OF DELAWARE GENERAL CORPORATION LAW

§ 151. Classes and Series of Stock; Rights, etc.

(a) Every corporation may issue one or more classes of stock or one or more series of stock within any class thereof, any or all of which

G–1

classes may be of stock with par value or stock without par value and which classes or series may have such voting powers, full or limited, or no voting powers, and such designations, preferences and relative, participating, optional or other special rights, and qualifications, limitations or restrictions thereof, as shall be stated and expressed in the certificate of incorporation or of any amendment thereto, or in the resolution or resolutions providing for the issue of such stock adopted by the board of directors pursuant to authority expressly vested in it by the provisions of its certificate of incorporation. Any of the voting powers, designations, preferences, rights and qualifications, limitations or restrictions of any such class or series of stock may be made dependent upon facts ascertainable outside the certificate of incorporation or of any amendment thereto, or outside the resolution or resolutions providing for the issue of such stock adopted by the board of directors pursuant to authority expressly vested in it by the provisions of its certificate of incorporation, provided that the manner in which such facts shall operate upon the voting powers, designations, preferences, rights and qualifications, limitations or restrictions of such class or series of stock is clearly and expressly set forth in the certificate of incorporation or in the resolution or resolutions providing for the issue of such stock adopted by the board of directors. The power to increase or decrease or otherwise adjust the capital stock as provided in this chapter shall apply to all or any such classes of stock.

(b) The stock of any class or series may be made subject to redemption by the corporation at its option or at the option of the holders of such stock or upon the happening of a specified event; provided however, that at the time of such redemption the corporation shall have outstanding shares of at least 1 class or series of stock with full voting powers which shall not be subject to redemption. Notwithstanding the limitation stated in the foregoing proviso:

(1) Any stock of a regulated investment company registered under the Investment Company Act of 1940, as heretofore or hereafter amended, may be made subject to redemption by the corporation at its option or at the option of the holders of such stock.

(2) Any stock of a corporation which holds (directly or indirectly) a license or franchise from a governmental agency to conduct its business or is a member of a national securities exchange, which license, franchise or membership is conditioned upon some or all of the holders of its stock possessing prescribed qualifications, may be made subject to redemption by the corporation to the extent necessary to prevent the loss of such license, franchise or membership or to reinstate it.

Any stock which may be made redeemable under this section may be redeemed for cash, property or rights, including securities of the same or another corporation, at such time or times, price or prices, or rate or rates, and with such adjustments, as shall be stated in the certificate of incorporation or in the resolution or resolutions providing for the issue of such stock adopted by the board of directors pursuant to subsection (a) of this section.

(c) The holders of preferred or special stock of any class or of any series thereof shall be entitled to receive dividends at such rates, on such conditions and at such times as shall be stated in the certificate of incorporation or in the resolution or resolutions providing for the issue of such stock adopted by the board of directors as hereinabove provided, payable in preference to, or in such relation to, the dividends payable on any other class or classes or of any other series of stock, and cumulative or non-cumulative as shall be so stated and expressed. When dividends upon the preferred and special stocks, if any, to the extent of the preference to which such stocks are entitled, shall have been paid or declared and set apart for payment, a dividend on the remaining class or classes or series of stock may then be paid out of the remaining assets of the corporation available for dividends as elsewhere in this chapter provided.

(d) The holders of the preferred or special stock of any class or of any series thereof shall be entitled to such rights upon the dissolution of, or upon any distribution of the assets of, the corporation as shall be stated in the certificate of incorporation or in the resolution or resolutions providing for the issue of such stock adopted by the board of directors as hereinabove provided.

(e) Any stock of any class or of any series thereof may be made convertible into, or exchangeable for, at the option of either the holder or the corporation or upon the happening of a specified event, shares of any other class or classes or any other series of the same or any other class or classes of stock of the corporation, at such price or prices or at such rate or rates of exchange and with such adjustments as shall be stated in the certificate of incorporation or in the resolution or resolutions providing for the issue of such stock adopted by the board of directors as hereinabove provided.

(f) If any corporation shall be authorized to issue more than one class of stock or more than one series of any class, the powers, designations, preferences and relative, participating, optional or other special rights of each class of stock or series thereof and the qualifications, limitations or restrictions of such preferences and/or rights shall be set forth in full or summarized on the face or back of the certificate which the corporation shall issue to represent such class or series of stock, provided that, except as otherwise provided in section 202 of this title, in lieu of the foregoing requirements, there may be set forth on the face or back of the certificate which the corporation shall issue to represent such class or series of stock, a statement that the corporation will furnish without charge to each stockholder who so requests the powers, designations, preferences and relative, participating, optional or other special rights of each class of stock or series thereof and the qualifications, limitations or restrictions of such preferences and/or rights. Within a reasonable time after the issuance or transfer of uncertificated stock, the corporation shall send to the registered owner thereof a written notice containing the information required to be set forth or stated on certificates pursuant to this Section or Sections 156, 202(a) or 218(a) or with respect to this Section a statement that the corporation will furnish without charge to each stockholder who so requests the powers, designations, preferences and relative participating, optional or other special rights of each class of stock or series thereof and the qualifications, limitations or restrictions of such preferences and/or rights. Except as otherwise expressly provided by law, the rights and obligations of the holders of uncertificated stock and the rights and obligations of the holders of certificates representing stock of the same class and series shall be identical.

(g) When any corporation desires to issue any shares of stock of any class or of any series of any class of which the powers, designations, preferences and relative, participating, optional or other rights, if any, or the qualifications, limitations or restrictions thereof, if any, shall not have been set forth in the certificate of incorporation or in any amendment thereto but shall be provided for in a resolution or resolutions adopted by the board of directors pursuant to authority expressly vested in it by the provisions of the certificate of incorporation or any amendment thereto, a certificate of designations setting forth a copy of such resolution or resolutions and the number of shares of stock of such class or series as to which the resolution or resolutions apply shall be executed, acknowledged, filed, recorded, and shall become effective, in accordance with § 103 of this Title. Unless otherwise provided in any such resolution or resolutions, the number of shares of stock of any such series to which such resolution or resolutions apply may be increased (but not above the total number of authorized shares of the class) or decreased (but not below the number of shares thereof then outstanding) by a certificate likewise executed, acknowledged, filed and recorded setting forth a statement that a specified increase or decrease therein had been authorized and directed by a resolution or resolutions likewise adopted by the board of directors. In case the number of such shares shall be decreased the number of shares so specified in the certificate shall resume the status which they had prior to the adoption of the first resolution or resolutions. Unless otherwise provided in the certificate of incorporation, if no shares of stock have been issued of a class or series of stock established by a resolution of the board of directors, the voting powers, designations, preferences and relative, participating, optional or other rights, if any, or the qualifications, limitations or restrictions thereof, may be amended by a resolution or resolutions adopted by the board of directors. A certificate which (1) states that no shares of the class or series have been issued, (2) sets forth a copy of the resolution or resolutions and (3) if the designation of the class or series is being changed, indicates the original designation and the new designation, shall be executed, acknowledged, filed, recorded [and] shall become effective, in accordance with § 103 of this title. When no shares of any such class or series are outstanding, either because none were issued or because no issued shares of any such class or series remain outstanding, a certificate setting forth a resolution or resolutions adopted by the board of directors that none of the authorized shares of such class or series are outstanding, and that none will be issued subject to the certificate of designations previously filed with respect to such class or series, may be executed, acknowledged, filed and recorded in accordance with § 103 of this Title and, when such certificate becomes effective, it shall have the effect of eliminating from the certificate of incorporation all matters set forth in the certificate of designations with respect to such class or series of stock.

When any certificate filed under this subsection becomes effective, it shall have the effect of amending the certificate of incorporation; except that neither the filing of such certificate nor the filing of a restated certificate of incorporation pursuant to § 245 of this Title shall prohibit the board of directors from subsequently adopting such resolutions as authorized by this subsection.

§ 157. Rights and Options Respecting Stock

Subject to any provisions in the certificate of incorporation, every corporation may create and issue, whether or not in connection with the issue and sale of any shares of stock or other securities of the corporation, rights or options entitling the holders thereof to purchase from the corporation any shares of its capital stock of any class or classes, such rights or options to be evidenced by or in such instrument or instruments as shall be approved by the board of directors. The terms upon which, including the time or times, which may be limited or unlimited in duration, at or within which, and the price or prices at which any such shares may be purchased from the corporation upon the exercise of any such right or option, shall be such as shall be stated in the certificate of incorporation, or in a resolution adopted by the board of directors providing for the creation and issue of such rights or options, and, in every case, shall be set forth or incorporated by reference in the instrument or instruments evidencing such rights or options. In the absence of actual fraud in the transaction, the judgment of the directors as to the consideration for the issuance of such rights or options and the sufficiency thereof shall be conclusive. In case the shares of stock of the corporation to be issued upon the exercise of such rights or options shall be shares having a par value, the price or prices so to be received therefor shall not be less than the par value thereof. In case the shares of stock so to be issued shall be shares of stock without par value, the consideration therefor shall be determined in the manner provided in section 153 of this title.

§ 203. Business Combinations With Interested Stockholders

(a) Notwithstanding any other provisions of this chapter, a corporation shall not engage in any business combination with any interested stockholder for a period of 3 years following the date that such stockholder became an interested stockholder, unless (1) prior to such date the board of directors of the corporation approved either the business combination or the transaction which resulted in the stockholder becoming an interested stockholder, or (2) upon consummation of the transaction which resulted in the stockholder becoming an interested stockholder, the interested stockholder owned at least 85% of the voting stock of the corporation outstanding at the time the transaction commenced, excluding for purposes of determining the number of shares outstanding those shares owned (i) by persons who are directors and also officers and (ii) employee stock plans in which employee participants do not have the right to determine confidentially whether shares held subject to the plan will be tendered in a tender or exchange offer, or (3) on or subsequent to such date the business combination is approved by the board of directors and authorized at an annual or special meeting of stockholders, and not by written consent, by the affirmative vote of at least 66⅔ of the outstanding voting stock which is not owned by the interested stockholder.

(b) The restrictions contained in this section shall not apply if:

(1) the corporation's original certificate of incorporation contains a provision expressly electing not to be governed by this section;

(2) the corporation, by action of its board of directors, adopts an amendment to its bylaws within 90 days of the effective date of this section, expressly electing not to be governed by this section, which amendment shall not be further amended by the board of directors;

(3) the corporation, by action of its stockholders, adopts an amendment to its certificate of incorporation or bylaws expressly electing not to be governed by this section, provided that, in addition to any other vote required by law, such amendment to the certificate of incorporation or bylaws must be approved by the affirmative vote of a majority of the shares entitled to vote. An amendment adopted pursuant to this paragraph shall not be effective until 12 months after the adoption of such amendment and shall not apply to any business combination between such corporation and any person who became an interested stockholder of such corporation on or prior to such adoption. A bylaw amendment adopted pursuant to this paragraph shall not be further amended by the board of directors;

(4) the corporation does not have a class of voting stock that is (i) listed on a national securities exchange, (ii) authorized for quotation on an inter-dealer quotation system of a registered na-

tional securities association or (iii) held of record by more than 2,000 stockholders, unless any of the foregoing results from action taken, directly or indirectly, by an interested stockholder or from a transaction in which a person becomes an interested stockholder;

(5) a stockholder becomes an interested stockholder inadvertently and (i) as soon as practicable divests sufficient shares so that the stockholder ceases to be an interested stockholder and (ii) would not, at any time within the 3 year period immediately prior to a business combination between the corporation and such stockholder, have been an interested stockholder but for the inadvertent acquisition; or

(6) the business combination is proposed prior to the consummation or abandonment of and subsequent to the earlier of the public announcement or the notice required hereunder of a proposed transaction which (i) constitutes one of the transactions described in the second sentence of this paragraph; (ii) is with or by a person who either was not an interested stockholder during the previous 3 years or who became an interested stockholder with the approval of the corporation's board of directors; and (iii) is approved or not opposed by a majority of the members of the board of directors then in office (but not less than 1) who were directors prior to any person becoming an interested stockholder during the previous 3 years or were recommended for election or elected to succeed such directors by a majority of such directors. The proposed transactions referred to in the preceding sentence are limited to (x) a merger or consolidation of the corporation (except for a merger in respect of which, pursuant to section 251(f) of the chapter, no vote of the stockholders of the corporation is required); (y) a sale, lease, exchange, mortgage, pledge, transfer or other disposition (in one transaction or a series of transactions), whether as part of a dissolution or otherwise, of assets of the corporation or of any direct or indirect majority-owned subsidiary of the corporation (other than to any direct or indirect wholly-owned subsidiary or to the corporation) having an aggregate market value equal to 50% or more of either [the] aggregate market value of all of the assets of the corporation determined on a consolidated basis or the aggregate market value of all the outstanding stock of the corporation; or (z) a proposed tender or exchange offer for 50% or more of the outstanding voting stock of the corporation. The corporation shall give not less than 20 days notice to all interested stockholders prior to the consummation of any of the transactions described in clauses (x) or (y) of the second sentence of this paragraph. Notwithstanding paragraphs (1), (2), (3) and (4) of this subsection, a corporation may elect by a provision of its original certificate of incorporation or any amendment thereto to be governed by this section, provided that any such amendment to the certificate of incorporation shall not apply to restrict a business combination

between the corporation and an interested stockholder of the corporation if the interested stockholder became such prior to the effective date of the amendment.

(c) As used in this section only, the term:

(1) "affiliate" means a person that directly, or indirectly through one or more intermediaries, controls, or is controlled by, or is under common control with, another person.

(2) "associate," when used to indicate a relationship with any person, means (i) any corporation or organization of which such person is a director, officer or partner or is, directly or indirectly, the owner of 20% or more of any class of voting stock, (ii) any trust or other estate in which such person has at least a 20% beneficial interest or as to which such person serves as trustee or in a similar fiduciary capacity, and (iii) any relative or spouse of such person, or any relative of such spouse, who has the same residence as such person.

(3) "business combination," when used in reference to any corporation and any interested stockholder of such corporation, means:

(i) any merger or consolidation of the corporation or any direct or indirect majority-owned subsidiary of the corporation with (A) the interested stockholder, or (B) with any other corporation if the merger or consolidation is caused by the interested stockholder and as a result of such merger or consolidation subsection (a) of this section is not applicable to the surviving corporation;

(ii) any sale, lease, exchange, mortgage, pledge, transfer or other disposition (in one transaction or a series of transactions), except proportionately as a stockholder of such corporation, to or with the interested stockholder, whether as part of a dissolution or otherwise, of assets of the corporation or of any direct or indirect majority-owned subsidiary of the corporation which assets have an aggregate market value equal to 10% or more of either the aggregate market value of all the assets of the corporation determined on a consolidated basis or the aggregate market value of all the outstanding stock of the corporation;

(iii) any transaction which results in the issuance or transfer by the corporation or by any direct or indirect majority-owned subsidiary of the corporation of any stock of the corporation or of such subsidiary to the interested stockholder, except (A) pursuant to the exercise, exchange or conversion of securities exercisable for, exchangeable for or convertible into stock of such corporation or any such subsidiary which securities were outstanding prior to the time that the interested stockholder became such, (B) pursuant to a dividend or distribution paid or made, or the exercise, exchange or conversion of securities exercisable for, exchangeable for or convertible into stock of such corporation or any such subsidiary which security is distributed, pro rata to all holders of a class or series of stock of such corporation subsequent to the time the interested stockholder became such, (C) pursuant to an exchange offer by the corporation to purchase stock made on the same terms to all holders of said stock, or (D) any issuance or transfer of stock by the corporation, provided however, that in no case under (B)–(D) above shall there be an increase in the interested stockholder's proportionate share of the stock of any class or series of the corporation or of the voting stock of the corporation;

(iv) any transaction involving the corporation or any direct or indirect majority-owned subsidiary of the corporation which has the effect, directly or indirectly, of increasing the proportionate share of the stock of any class or series, or securities convertible into the stock of any class or series, of the corporation or of any such subsidiary which is owned by the interested stockholder, except as a result of immaterial changes due to fractional share adjustments or as a result of any purchase or redemption of any shares of stock not caused, directly or indirectly, by the interested stockholder; or

(v) any receipt by the interested stockholder of the benefit, directly or indirectly (except proportionately as a stockholder of such corporation) of any loans, advances, guarantees, pledges or other financial benefits (other than those expressly permitted in subparagraphs (i)–(iv) above) provided by or through the corporation or any direct or indirect majority-owned subsidiary.

(4) "control," including the term "controlling," "controlled by" and "under common control with," means the possession, directly or indirectly, of the power to direct or cause the direction of the management and policies of a person, whether through the ownership of voting stock, by contract, or otherwise. A person who is the owner of 20% or more of a corporation's outstanding voting stock shall be presumed to have control of such corporation, in the absence of proof by a preponderance of the evidence to the contrary. Notwithstanding the foregoing, a presumption of control shall not apply where such person holds voting stock, in good faith and not for the purpose of circumventing this section, as an agent, bank, broker, nominee, custodian or trustee for one or more owners who do not individually or as a group have control of such corporation.

(5) "interested stockholder" means any person (other than the corporation and any direct or indirect majority-owned subsidiary of the corporation) that (i) is the owner of 15% or more of the outstanding voting stock of the corporation, or (ii) is an affiliate or associate of the corporation and was the owner of 15% or more of the outstanding voting stock of the corporation at any time within the 3–year period immediately prior to the date on which it is sought to be determined whether such person is an interested stockholder; and the affiliates and associates of such person; provided, however, that the term "interested stockholder" shall not include (x) any person who (A) owned shares in excess of the 15% limitation set forth herein as of, or acquired such shares pursuant to a tender offer commenced prior to, December 23, 1987 or pursuant to an exchange offer announced prior to the aforesaid date and commenced within 90 days thereafter and continued to own shares in excess of such 15% limitation or would have but for action by the corporation or (B) acquired said shares from a person described in (A) above by gift, inheritance or in a transaction in which no consideration was exchanged; or (y) any person whose ownership of shares in excess of the 15% limitation set forth herein [is] the result of action taken solely by the corporation provided that such person shall be an interested stockholder if thereafter he acquires additional shares of voting stock of the corporation, except as a result of further corporate action not caused, directly or indirectly, by such person. For the purpose of determining whether a person is an interested stockholder, the voting stock of the corporation deemed to be outstanding shall include stock deemed to be owned by the person through application of paragraph (8) of this subsection but shall not include any other unissued stock of such corporation which may be issuable pursuant to any agreement, arrangement or understanding, or upon exercise of conversion rights, warrants or options, or otherwise.

(6) "person" means any individual, corporation, partnership, unincorporated association or other entity.

(7) "voting stock" means stock of any class or series entitled to vote generally in the election of directors.

(8) "owner" including the terms "own" and "owned" when used with respect to any stock means a person that individually or with or through any of its affiliates or associates:

(i) beneficially owns such stock, directly or indirectly; or

(ii) has (A) the right to acquire such stock (whether such right is exercisable immediately or only after the passage of time) pursuant to any agreement, arrangement or understanding, or upon the exercise of conversion rights, exchange rights, warrants or options, or otherwise; provided, however, that a person shall not be deemed the owner of stock tendered pursuant to a tender or exchange offer made by such person or any of such person's affiliates or associates until such tendered stock is accepted for purchase or exchange; or (B) the right to vote such stock pursuant to any agreement, arrangement or understanding; provided, however, that a person shall not be deemed the owner of any stock because of such person's right to vote such stock if the agreement, arrangement or understanding to vote such stock arises solely from a revocable proxy or consent given in response to a proxy or consent solicitation made to 10 or more persons; or

(iii) has any agreement, arrangement or understanding for the purpose of acquiring, holding, voting (except voting pursuant to a revocable proxy or consent as described in item (B) of clause (ii) of this paragraph), or disposing of such stock with any other person that beneficially owns, or whose affiliates or associates beneficially own, directly or indirectly, such stock.

(d) No provision of a certificate of incorporation or bylaw shall require, for any vote of stockholders required by this section a greater vote of stockholders than that specified in this section.

(e) The Court of Chancery is hereby vested with exclusive jurisdiction to hear and determine all matters with respect to this section.

§ 221. Voting, Inspection and Other Rights of Bondholders and Debenture Holders

Every corporation may in its certificate of incorporation confer upon the holders of any bonds, debentures, or other obligations issued or to be issued by the corporation the power to vote in respect to the corporate affairs and management of the corporation to the extent and in the manner provided in the certificate of incorporation, and may confer upon such holders of bonds, debentures or other obligations the same right of inspection of its books, accounts and other records, and also any other rights, which the stockholders of the corporation have or may have by reason of the provisions of this chapter or of its certificate of incorporation. If the certificate of incorporation so provides, such holders of bonds, debentures or other obligations shall be deemed to be stockholders, and their bonds, debentures or other obligations shall be deemed to be shares of stock, for the purpose of any provision of this chapter which requires the vote of stockholders as a prerequisite to any corporate action and the certificate of incorporation may divest the holders of capital stock, in whole or in part, of their right to vote on any corporate matter whatsoever, except as set forth in § 242(b)(2) of this chapter.

§ 242. Amendment of Certificate of Incorporation After Receipt of Payment for Stock ...

(a) After a corporation has received payment for any of its capital stock, it may amend its certificate of incorporation, from time to time, in any and as many respects as may be desired, so long as its certificate of incorporation as amended would contain only such provisions as it would be lawful and proper to insert in an original certificate of incorporation filed at the time of the filing of the amendment; and, if a change in stock or the rights of stockholders, or an exchange, reclassification or cancellation of stock or rights of stockholders is to be made, such provisions as may be necessary to effect such change, exchange, reclassification or cancellation. In particular, and without limitation upon such general power of amendment, a corporation may amend its certificate of incorporation, from time to time, so as:

(1) To change its corporate name; or

(2) To change, substitute, enlarge or diminish the nature of its business or its corporate powers and purposes; or

(3) To increase or decrease its authorized capital stock or to reclassify the same, by changing the number, par value, designations, preferences, or relative, participating, optional, or other special rights of the shares, or the qualifications, limitations or restrictions of such rights, or by changing shares with par value into shares without par value, or shares without par value into shares with par value either with or without increasing or decreasing the number of shares; or

(4) To cancel or otherwise affect the right of the holders of the shares of any class to receive dividends which have accrued but have not been declared; or

(5) To create new classes of stock having rights and preferences either prior and superior or subordinate and inferior to the stock of any class then authorized, whether issued or unissued; or

(6) To change the period of its duration.

Any or all such changes or alterations may be effected by one certificate of amendment.

(b) Every amendment authorized by subsection (a) of this section shall be made and effected in the following manner—

(1) If the corporation has capital stock, its board of directors shall adopt a resolution setting forth the amendment proposed, declaring its advisability, and either calling a special meeting of the stockholders entitled to vote in respect thereof for the consideration of such amendment or directing that the amendment proposed be considered at the next annual meeting of the stockholders. Such special or annual meeting shall be called and held upon notice in accordance with section 222 of this title. The notice shall set forth such amendment in full or a brief summary of the changes to be effected thereby, as the directors shall deem advisable. At the meeting a vote of the stockholders entitled to vote thereon shall be taken for and against the proposed amendment. If a majority of the outstanding stock of each class entitled to vote

thereon as a class has been voted in favor of the amendment, a certificate setting forth the amendment and certifying that such amendment has been duly adopted in accordance with the provisions of this section shall be executed, acknowledged, filed, and recorded, and shall become effective in accordance with section 103 of this title.

(2) The holders of the outstanding shares of a class shall be entitled to vote as a class upon a proposed amendment, whether or not entitled to vote thereon by the provisions of the certificate of incorporation, if the amendment would increase or decrease the aggregate number of authorized shares of such class, increase or decrease the par value of the shares of such class, or alter or change the powers, preferences or special rights of the shares of such class so as to affect them adversely. If any proposed amendment would alter or change the powers, preferences, or special rights of one or more series of any class so as to affect them adversely, but shall not so affect the entire class, then only the shares of the series so affected by the amendment shall be considered a separate class for the purposes of this paragraph. The number of authorized shares of any such class or classes of stock may be increased or decreased (but not below the number of shares thereof then outstanding) by the affirmative vote of the holders of a majority of the stock of the corporation entitled to vote irrespective of the provisions of this paragraph (b)(2), if so provided in the original certificate of incorporation, in any amendment thereto which created such class or classes of stock or which was adopted prior to the issuance of any shares of such class or classes of stock, or in any amendment thereto which was authorized by a resolution or resolutions adopted by the affirmative vote of the holders of a majority of such class or classes of stock * * *.

(4) Whenever the certificate of incorporation shall require for action by the board of directors, by the holders of any class or series of shares or by the holders of any other securities having voting power the vote of a greater number or proportion than is required by any section of this title, the provision of the certificate of incorporation requiring such greater vote shall not be altered, amended or repealed except by such greater vote.

* * *

§ 251. Merger or Consolidation of Domestic Corporations

(a) Any two or more corporations existing under the laws of this State may merge into a single corporation, which may be any one of the constituent corporations or may consolidate into a new corporation formed by the consolidation, pursuant to an agreement of merger or consolidation, as the case may be, complying and approved in accordance with this section.

(b) The board of directors of each corporation which desires to merge or consolidate shall adopt a resolution approving an agreement of merger or consolidation. The agreement shall state: (1) the terms and conditions of the merger or consolidation; (2) the mode of carrying the same into effect; (3) in the case of a merger, such amendments or changes in the certificate of incorporation of the surviving corporation as are desired to be effected by the merger, or, if no such amendments or changes are desired, a statement that the certificate of incorporation of the surviving corporation shall be its certificate of incorporation; (4) in the case of a consolidation, that the certificate of incorporation of the resulting corporation shall be as set forth in an attachment to the agreement; (5) the manner of converting the shares of each of the constituent corporations into shares or other securities of the corporation surviving or resulting from the merger or consolidation, and, if any shares of any of the constituent corporations are not to be converted solely into shares or other securities of the surviving or resulting corporation, the cash, property, rights or securities of any other corporation which the holders of such shares are to receive in exchange for, or upon conversion of such shares and the surrender of any certificates evidencing them, which cash, property, rights or securities of any other corporation may be in addition to or in lieu of shares or other securities of the surviving or resulting corporation; and (6) such other details or provisions as are deemed desirable, including, without limiting the generality of the foregoing, a provision for the payment of cash in lieu of the issuance or recognition of fractional shares, interests or rights, or for any other arrangement with respect thereto, consistent with the provisions of section 155 of this title. The agreement so adopted shall be executed and acknowledged in accordance with section 103 of this title. Any of the terms of the agreement of merger or consolidation may be made dependent upon facts ascertainable outside of such agreement, provided that the manner in which such facts shall operate upon the terms of the agreement is clearly and expressly set forth in the agreement of merger or consolidation.

(c) The agreement required by subsection (b) shall be submitted to the stockholders of each constituent corporation at an annual or special meeting thereof for the purpose of acting on the agreement. Due notice of the time, place and purpose of the meeting shall be mailed to each holder of stock, whether voting or non-voting, of the corporation at his address as it appears on the records of the corporation, at least 20 days prior to the date of the meeting. The notice shall contain a copy of the agreement or a brief summary thereof, as the directors shall deem advisable. At the meeting the agreement shall be considered and a vote taken for its adoption or rejection. If a majority of the outstanding stock of the corporation entitled to vote thereon shall be voted for the adoption of the agreement, that fact shall be certified on the agreement by the secretary or assistant secretary of the corporation. If the agreement shall be so adopted and certified by each constituent corporation, it shall then be filed, and shall become effective, in accordance with section 103 of this title. It shall be recorded in the office of the Recorder of the County of this State in which the registered office of each such constituent corporation is located; or if any of the constituent corporations shall have been specially created by a public act of the Legislature, then the agreement shall be recorded in the County where such corporation had its principal place of business in this State. In lieu of filing and recording the agreement of merger or consolidation required by this Section, the surviving or resulting corporation may file a certificate of merger or consolidation, executed in accordance with section 103 of this title, which states (1) the name and state of incorporation of each of the constituent corporations, (2) that an agreement of merger or consolidation has been approved, adopted, certified, executed and acknowledged by each of the constituent corporations in accordance with this Section, (3) the name of the surviving or resulting corporation, (4) in the case of a merger, such amendments or changes in the certificate of incorporation of the surviving corporation as are desired to be effected by the merger, or, if no such amendments or changes are desired, a statement that the certificate of incorporation of the surviving corporation shall be its certificate of incorporation, (5) in the case of a consolidation, that the certificate of incorporation of the resulting corporation shall be as is set forth in an attachment to the certificate, (6) that the executed agreement of consolidation or merger is on file at the principal place of business of the surviving corporation, stating the address thereof and (7) that a copy of the agreement of consolidation or merger will be furnished by the surviving corporation, on request and without cost, to any stockholder of any constituent corporation.

(d) Any agreement of merger or consolidation may contain a provision that at any time prior to the filing of the agreement (or a certificate in lieu thereof) with the Secretary of State, the agreement may be terminated by the board of directors of any constituent corporation notwithstanding approval of the agreement by the stockholders of all or any of the constituent corporations. Any agreement of merger or consolidation may contain a provision that the boards of directors of the constituent corporations may amend the agreement at any time prior to the filing of the agreement (or a certificate in lieu thereof) with the Secretary of State, provided that an amendment made subsequent to the adoption of the agreement by the stockholders of any constituent corporation shall not (1) alter or change the amount or kind of shares, securities, cash, property and/or rights to be received in exchange for or on conversion of all or any of the shares of any class or series thereof of such constituent corporation, (2) alter or change any term of the certificate of incorporation of the surviving corporation to be effected by the merger or consolidation, or (3) alter or change any of the terms and conditions of the agreement if such alteration or change would

Brudney & Chirelstein Corp. Fin. 4th Ed. UCS—31

G–15

adversely affect the holders of any class or series thereof of such constituent corporation.

(e) In the case of a merger, the certificate of incorporation of the surviving corporation shall automatically be amended to the extent, if any, that changes in the certificate of incorporation are set forth in the agreement of merger.

(f) Notwithstanding the requirements of subsection (c), unless required by its certificate of incorporation, no vote of stockholders of a constituent corporation surviving a merger shall be necessary to authorize a merger if (1) the agreement of merger does not amend in any respect the certificate of incorporation of such constituent corporation, (2) each share of stock of such constituent corporation outstanding immediately prior to the effective date of the merger is to be an identical outstanding or treasury share of the surviving corporation after the effective date of the merger, and (3) either no shares of common stock of the surviving corporation and no shares, securities or obligations convertible into such stock are to be issued or delivered under the plan of merger, or the authorized unissued shares or the treasury shares of common stock of the surviving corporation to be issued or delivered under the plan of merger plus those initially issuable upon conversion of any other shares, securities or obligations to be issued or delivered under such plan do not exceed 20 percent of the shares of common stock of such constituent corporation outstanding immediately prior to the effective date of the merger. No vote of stockholders of a constituent corporation shall be necessary to authorize a merger or consolidation if no shares of the stock of such corporation shall have been issued prior to the adoption by the board of directors of the resolution approving the agreement of merger or consolidation. If an agreement of merger is adopted by the constituent corporation surviving the merger, by action of its board of directors and without any vote of its stockholders pursuant to this subsection, the secretary or assistant secretary of that corporation shall certify on the agreement that the agreement has been adopted pursuant to this subsection and, (1) if it has been adopted pursuant to the first sentence of this subsection, that the conditions specified in that sentence have been satisfied, or (2) if it has been adopted pursuant to the second sentence of this subsection, that no shares of stock of such corporation were issued prior to the adoption by the board of directors of the resolution approving the agreement of merger or consolidation. The agreement so adopted and certified shall then be filed and shall become effective, in accordance with section 103 of this title. Such filing shall constitute a representation by the person who executes the agreement that the facts stated in the certificate remain true immediately prior to such filing.

§ 253. Merger of Parent Corporation and Subsidiary or Subsidiaries

(a) In any case in which at least 90 percent of the outstanding shares of each class of the stock of a corporation or corporations is owned by another corporation and one of such corporations is a corporation of this State and the other or others are corporations of this State or of any other state or states or of the District of Columbia and the laws of such other state or states or of the District permit a corporation of such jurisdiction to merge with a corporation of another jurisdiction, the corporation having such stock ownership may either merge such other corporation or corporations into itself and assume all of its or their obligations, or merge itself, or itself and one or more of such other corporations, into one of such other corporations by executing, acknowledging and filing, in accordance with section 103 of this title, a certificate of such ownership and merger setting forth a copy of the resolution of its board of directors to so merge and the date of the adoption thereof; provided, however, that in case the parent corporation shall not own all the outstanding stock of all the subsidiary corporations, parties to a merger as aforesaid, the resolution of the board of directors of the parent corporation shall state the terms and conditions of the merger, including the securities, cash, property, or rights to be issued, paid, delivered or granted by the surviving corporation upon surrender of each share of the subsidiary corporation or corporations not owned by the parent corporation. If the parent corporation be not the surviving corporation, the resolution shall include provision for the pro rata issuance of stock of the surviving corporation to the holders of the stock of the parent corporation on surrender of any certificates therefor, and the certificate of ownership and merger shall state that the proposed merger has been approved by a majority of the outstanding stock of the parent corporation entitled to vote thereon at a meeting thereof duly called and held after 20 days' notice of the purpose of the meeting mailed to each such stockholder at his address as it appears on the records of the corporation if the parent corporation is a corporation of this State or state that the proposed merger has been adopted, approved, certified, executed and acknowledged by the parent corporation in accordance with the laws under which it is organized if the parent corporation is not a corporation of this State. A certified copy of the certificate shall be recorded in the office of the Recorder of the County in this State in which the registered office of each constituent corporation which is a corporation of this State is located. If the surviving corporation exists under the laws of the District of Columbia or any state other than this State, the provisions of section 252(d) of this title shall also apply to a merger under this section.

(b) If the surviving corporation is a Delaware corporation, it may change its corporate name by the inclusion of a provision to that effect in the resolution of merger adopted by the directors of the parent corporation and set forth in the certificate of ownership and merger, and upon the effective date of the merger, the name of the corporation shall be so changed.

(c) The provisions of Section 251(d) of this title shall apply to a merger under this section, and the provisions of Section 251(e) shall apply to a merger under this section in which the surviving corporation is the subsidiary corporation and is a corporation of this State. References to "agreement of merger" in Sections 251(d) and 251(e) of this title shall mean for purposes of this Section 253(c) the resolution of merger adopted by the board of directors of the parent corporation. Any merger which effects any changes other than those authorized by this section or made applicable by this subsection shall be accomplished under the provisions of Section 251 or Section 252 of this title. The provisions of Section 262 of this title shall not apply to any merger effected under this section, except as provided in subsection (d) of this section.

(d) In the event all of the stock of a subsidiary Delaware corporation party to a merger effected under this Section is not owned by the parent corporation immediately prior to the merger, the stockholders of the subsidiary Delaware corporation party to the merger shall have appraisal rights as set forth in Section 262 of this Title.

(e) A merger may be effected under this section although one or more of the corporations parties to the merger is a corporation organized under the laws of a jurisdiction other than one of the United States; provided that the laws of such jurisdiction permit a corporation of such jurisdiction to merge with a corporation of another jurisdiction; and provided further that the surviving or resulting corporation shall be a corporation of this State.

§ 262. Appraisal Rights

(a) Any stockholder of a corporation of this State who holds shares of stock on the date of the making of a demand pursuant to the provisions of subsection (d) of this section with respect to such shares, who continuously holds such shares through the effective date of the merger or consolidation, who has otherwise complied with the provisions of subsection (d) of this Section and who has neither voted in favor of the merger or consolidation nor consented thereto in writing pursuant to § 228 of this Chapter shall be entitled to an appraisal by the Court of Chancery of the fair value of his shares of stock under the circumstances described in subsections (b) and (c) of this Section. As used in this Section, the word "stockholder" means a holder of record of stock in a stock corporation and also a member of record of a non-stock corporation; the words "stock" and "share" mean and include what is ordinarily meant by those words and also membership or membership interest of a member of a non-stock corporation.

(b) Appraisal rights shall be available for the shares of any class or series of stock of a constituent corporation in a merger or consolidation to be effected pursuant to Sections 251, 252, 254, 257, 258 or 263 of this Chapter;

(1) provided, however, that no appraisal rights under this Section shall be available for the shares of any class or series of stock which, at the record date fixed to determine the stockholders entitled to receive notice of and to vote at the meeting of stockholders to act upon the agreement of merger or consolidation, were either (i) listed on a national securities exchange or (ii) held of record by more than 2,000 stockholders; and further provided that no appraisal rights shall be available for any shares of stock of the constituent corporation surviving a merger if the merger did not require for its approval the vote of the stockholders of the surviving corporation as provided in subsection (f) of Section 251 of this Chapter.

(2) Notwithstanding the provisions of subsection (b)(1) of this Section, appraisal rights under this Section shall be available for the shares of any class or series of stock of a constituent corporation if the holders thereof are required by the terms of an agreement of merger or consolidation pursuant to Sections 251, 252, 254, 257 and 258 of this Chapter to accept for such stock anything except (i) shares of stock of the corporation surviving or resulting from such merger or consolidation; (ii) shares of stock of any other corporation which at the effective date of the merger or consolidation will be either listed on a national securities exchange or held of record by more than 2,000 stockholders; (iii) cash in lieu of fractional shares of the corporations described in the foregoing clauses (i) and (ii); or (iv) any combination of the shares of stock and cash in lieu of fractional shares described in the foregoing clauses (i), (ii) and (iii) of this subsection.

(3) In the event all of the stock of a subsidiary Delaware corporation party to a merger effected under Section 253 of this chapter is not owned by the parent corporation immediately prior to the merger, appraisal rights shall be available for the shares of the subsidiary Delaware corporation.

(c) Any corporation may provide in its certificate of incorporation that appraisal rights under this Section shall be available for the shares of any class or series of its stock as a result of an amendment to its certificate of incorporation, any merger or consolidation in which the corporation is a constituent corporation or the sale of all or substantially all of the assets of the corporation. If the certificate of incorporation contains such a provision, the procedures of this Section, including those set forth in subsections (d) and (e), shall apply as nearly as is practicable.

(d) Appraisal rights shall be perfected as follows:

(1) If a proposed merger or consolidation for which appraisal rights are provided under this Section is to be submitted for approval at a meeting of stockholders, the corporation, not less than 20 days prior to the meeting, shall notify each of its stockhold-

ers who was such on the record date for such meeting with respect to shares for which appraisal rights are available pursuant to subsections (b) or (c) hereof that appraisal rights are available for any or all of the shares of the constituent corporations, and shall include in such notice a copy of this Section. Each stockholder electing to demand the appraisal of his shares shall deliver to the corporation, before the taking of the vote on the merger or consolidation, a written demand for appraisal of his shares. Such demand will be sufficient if it reasonably informs the corporation of the identity of the stockholder and that the stockholder intends thereby to demand the appraisal of his shares. A proxy or vote against the merger or consolidation shall not constitute such a demand. A stockholder electing to take such action must do so by a separate written demand as herein provided. Within 10 days after the effective date of such merger or consolidation, the surviving or resulting corporation shall notify each stockholder of each constituent corporation who has complied with the provisions of this subsection and has not voted in favor of or consented to the merger or consolidation of the date that the merger or consolidation has become effective; or

(2) If the merger or consolidation was approved pursuant to Section 228 or Section 253 of this Chapter, the surviving or resulting corporation, either before the effective date of the merger or consolidation or within 10 days thereafter, shall notify each of the stockholders entitled to appraisal rights of the effective date of the merger or consolidation and that appraisal rights are available for any or all of the shares of the constituent corporation, and shall include in such notice a copy of this Section. The notice shall be sent by certified or registered mail, return receipt requested, addressed to the stockholder at his address as it appears on the records of the corporation. Any stockholder entitled to appraisal rights may, within 20 days after the date of mailing of the notice, demand in writing from the surviving or resulting corporation the appraisal of his shares. Such demand will be sufficient if it reasonably informs the corporation of the identity of the stockholder and that the stockholder intends thereby to demand the appraisal of his shares.

(e) Within 120 days after the effective date of the merger or consolidation, the surviving or resulting corporation or any stockholder who has complied with the provisions of subsections (a) and (d) hereof and who is otherwise entitled to appraisal rights, may file a petition in the Court of Chancery demanding a determination of the value of the stock of all such stockholders. Notwithstanding the foregoing, at any time within 60 days after the effective date of the merger or consolidation, any stockholder shall have the right to withdraw his demand for appraisal and to accept the terms offered upon the merger or consolidation. Within 120 days after the effective date of the merger or consolidation, any stockholder who has complied with the requirements of subsections (a) and (d) hereof, upon written request, shall be entitled to receive from the corporation surviving the merger or resulting from the consolidation a statement setting forth the aggregate number of shares not voted in favor of the merger or consolidation and with respect to which demands for appraisal have been received and the aggregate number of holders of such shares. Such written statement shall be mailed to the stockholder within 10 days after his written request for such a statement is received by the surviving or resulting corporation or within 10 days after expiration of the period for delivery of demands for appraisal under subsection (d) hereof, whichever is later.

(f) Upon the filing of any such petition by a stockholder, service of a copy thereof shall be made upon the surviving or resulting corporation, which shall within 20 days after such service file in the office of the Register in Chancery in which the petition was filed a duly verified list containing the names and addresses of all stockholders who have demanded payment for their shares and with whom agreements as to the value of their shares have not been reached by the surviving or resulting corporation. If the petition shall be filed by the surviving or resulting corporation, the petition shall be accompanied by such a duly verified list. The Register in Chancery, if so ordered by the Court, shall give notice of the time and place fixed for the hearing of such petition by registered or certified mail to the surviving or resulting corporation and to the stockholders shown on the list at the addresses therein stated. Such notice shall also be given by one or more publications at least one week before the day of the hearing, in a newspaper of general circulation published in the City of Wilmington, Delaware or such publication as the Court deems advisable. The forms of the notices by mail and by publication shall be approved by the Court, and the costs thereof shall be borne by the surviving or resulting corporation.

(g) At the hearing on such petition, the Court shall determine the stockholders who have complied with the provisions of this Section and who have become entitled to appraisal rights. The Court may require the stockholders who have demanded an appraisal for their shares and who hold stock represented by certificates to submit their certificates of stock to the Register in Chancery for notation thereon of the pendency of the appraisal proceedings; and if any stockholder fails to comply with such direction, the Court may dismiss the proceedings as to such stockholder.

(h) After determining the stockholders entitled to an appraisal, the Court shall appraise the shares, determining their fair value exclusive of any element of value arising from the accomplishment or expectation of the merger or consolidation, together with a fair rate of interest, if any, to be paid upon the amount determined to be the fair value. In determining such fair value, the Court shall take into account all relevant factors. In determining the fair rate of interest, the Court may consider all relevant factors, including the rate of interest which the surviving or resulting corporation would have had to pay to borrow money during the pendency of the proceeding. Upon application by the surviving or resulting corporation or by any stockholder entitled to participate in the appraisal proceeding, the Court may, in its discretion, permit discovery or other pretrial proceedings and may proceed to trial upon the appraisal prior to the final determination of the stockholder entitled to an appraisal. Any stockholder whose name appears on the list filed by the surviving or resulting corporation pursuant to subsection (f) of this Section and who has submitted his certificates of stock to the Register in Chancery, if such is required, may participate fully in all proceedings until it is finally determined that he is not entitled to appraisal rights under this Section.

(i) The Court shall direct the payment of the fair value of the shares, together with interest, if any, by the surviving or resulting corporation to the stockholders entitled thereto. Interest may be simple or compound, as the Court may direct. Payment shall be so made to each such stockholder, in the case of holders of uncertificated stock forthwith, and in the case of holders of shares represented by certificates upon the surrender to the corporation of the certificates representing such stock. The Court's decree may be enforced as other decrees in the Court of Chancery may be enforced, whether such surviving or resulting corporation be a corporation of this State or of any other state.

(j) The costs of the proceeding may be determined by the Court and taxed upon the parties as the Court deems equitable in the circumstances. Upon application of a stockholder, the Court may order all or a portion of the expenses incurred by any stockholder in connection with the appraisal proceeding, including, without limitation, reasonable attorney's fees and the fees and expenses of experts, to be charged pro rata against the value of all of the shares entitled to an appraisal.

(k) From and after the effective date of the merger or consolidation, no stockholder who has demanded his appraisal rights as provided in subsection (d) of this Section shall be entitled to vote such stock for any purpose or to receive payment of dividends or other distributions on the stock (except dividends or other distributions payable to stockholders of record at a date which is prior to the effective date of the merger or consolidation); provided, however, that if no petition for an appraisal shall be filed within the time provided in subsection (e) of this Section, or if such stockholder shall deliver to the surviving or resulting corporation a written withdrawal of his demand for an appraisal and an acceptance of the merger or consolidation, either within 60 days after the effective date of the merger or consolidation as provided in subsection (e) of this Section or thereafter with the written approval of the corporation, then the right of such stockholder to an appraisal shall cease. Notwithstanding the foregoing, no appraisal proceeding in the Court of Chancery shall be dismissed as to any stockholder without the approval of the Court, and such approval may be conditioned upon such terms as the Court deems just.

(*l*) The shares of the surviving or resulting corporation into which the shares of such objecting stockholders would have been converted had they assented to the merger or consolidation shall have the status of authorized and unissued shares of the surviving or resulting corporation.

§ 271. Sale, Lease or Exchange of Assets; Consideration; Procedure

(a) Every corporation may at any meeting of its board of directors or governing body sell, lease, or exchange all or substantially all of its property and assets, including its goodwill and its corporate franchises, upon such terms and conditions and for such consideration, which may consist in whole or in part of money or other property, including shares of stock in, and/or other securities of, any other corporation or corporations, as its board of directors or governing body deems expedient and for the best interests of the corporation, when and as authorized by a resolution adopted by the holders of a majority of the outstanding stock of the corporation entitled to vote thereon or, if the corporation is a non-stock corporation, by a majority of the members having the right to vote for the election of the members of the governing body, at a meeting duly called upon at least 20 days notice. The notice of the meeting shall state that such a resolution will be considered.

(b) Notwithstanding authorization or consent to a proposed sale, lease or exchange of a corporation's property and assets by the stockholders or members, the board of directors or governing body may abandon such proposed sale, lease or exchange without further action by the stockholders or members, subject to the rights, if any, of third parties under any contract relating thereto.

SECTIONS OF NEW YORK BUSINESS CORPORATION LAW

§ 501. Authorized Shares

(a) Every corporation shall have power to create and issue the number of shares stated in its certificate of incorporation. Such shares may be all of one class or may be divided into two or more classes. Each class shall consist of either shares with par value or shares without par value, having such designation and such relative voting, dividend, liquidation and other rights, preferences and limitations, consistent with this chapter, as shall be stated in the certificate of incorporation. The certificate of incorporation may deny, limit or otherwise define the voting rights and may limit or otherwise define the dividend or liquidation rights of shares of any class, but no such denial, limitation or definition of voting rights shall be effective unless at the time one or more classes of outstanding shares or bonds, singly or in the aggregate, are entitled to full voting rights, and no such limitation or definition of dividend or liquidation rights shall be effective unless at the time one or more classes of outstanding shares, singly or in the aggregate, are entitled to unlimited dividend and liquidation rights.

(b) If the shares are divided into two or more classes, the shares of each class shall be designated to distinguish them from the shares of all other classes. Shares which are entitled to preference in the distribution of dividends or assets shall not be designated as common shares. Shares which are not entitled to preference in the distribution of dividends or assets shall be common shares, even if identified by a class or other designation, and shall not be designated as preferred shares.

(c) Subject to the designations, relative rights, preferences and limitations applicable to separate series and except as otherwise permitted by subparagraph two of paragraph (a) of section five hundred five of this article, each share shall be equal to every other share of the same class * * *.*

§ 502. Issue of Any Class of Preferred Shares in Series

(a) If the certificate of incorporation so provides, a corporation may issue any class of preferred shares in series. Shares of each such series when issued, shall be designated to distinguish them from shares of all other series.

(b) The number of shares included in any or all series of any classes of preferred shares and any or all of the designations, relative rights, preferences and limitations of any or all such series may be fixed in the certificate of incorporation, subject to the limitation that, if the stated dividends and amounts payable on liquidation are not paid in full, the shares of all series of the same class shall share ratably in the payment of dividends including accumulations, if any, in accordance with the sums which would be payable on such shares if all dividends were declared and paid in full, and in any distribution of assets other than by way of dividends in accordance with the sums which would be payable on such distribution if all sums payable were discharged in full.

(c) If any such number of shares or any such designation, relative right, preference or limitation of the shares of any series is not fixed in the certificate of incorporation, it may be fixed by the board, to the extent authorized by the certificate of incorporation.

(d) Before the issue of any shares of a series established by the board, a certificate of amendment under section 805 (Certificate of amendment; contents) shall be delivered to the department of state. Such certificate shall set forth:

(1) The name of the corporation, and, if it has been changed, the name under which it was formed.

---

* Effective July 1, 1993 (c) will no longer contain "and except as otherwise permit- ted by subparagraph two of paragraph (a) of section five hundred five of this article."

(2) The date the certificate of incorporation was filed by the department of state.

(3) That the certificate of incorporation is thereby amended by the addition of a provision stating the number, designation, relative rights, preferences, and limitations of the shares of the series as fixed by the board, setting forth in full the text of such provision.

§ 505. Rights and Options to Purchase Shares; Issue of Rights and Options to Directors, Officers and Employees

(a)(1) Except as otherwise provided in this section or in the certificate of incorporation, a corporation may create and issue, whether or not in connection with the issue and sale of any of its shares or bonds, rights or options entitling the holders thereof to purchase from the corporation, upon such consideration, terms and conditions as may be fixed by the board, shares of any class or series, whether authorized but unissued shares, treasury shares or shares to be purchased or acquired or assets of the corporation.

(2)(i) In the case of a resident domestic corporation that has a class of voting stock registered with the Securities and Exchange Commission pursuant to section twelve of the Exchange Act, the terms and conditions of such rights or options may include, without limitation, restrictions or conditions that preclude or limit the exercise, transfer or receipt of such rights or options by an interested shareholder or any transferee of any such interested shareholder or that invalidate or void such rights or options held by any such interested shareholder or any such transferee. For the purposes of this subparagraph, the terms "resident domestic corporation," "voting stock," "Exchange Act" and "interested shareholder" shall have the same meanings as set forth in section nine hundred twelve of this chapter.

(ii) Determinations of the board of directors whether to impose, enforce or waive or otherwise render ineffective such limitations or conditions as are permitted by clause (i) of this subparagraph shall be subject to judicial review in an appropriate proceeding in which the courts formulate or apply appropriate standards in order to insure that such limitations or conditions are imposed, enforced or waived in the best long-term interests and short-term interests of the corporation and its shareholders considering, without limitation, the prospects for potential growth, development, productivity and profitability of the corporation.* * * *

§ 518. Corporate Bonds

(a) No corporation shall issue bonds except for money or other property, tangible or intangible, or labor or services actually received by or performed for the corporation or for its benefit or in its formation or reorganization, or a combination thereof. In the absence of fraud in

---

* Effective July 1, 1993, (a)(2)(i) and (ii) will no longer be part of § 505.

the transaction, the judgment of the board as to the value of the consideration received shall be conclusive.

(b) If a distribution of its own bonds is made by a corporation to holders of any class or series of its outstanding shares, there shall be concurrently transferred to the liabilities of the corporation in respect of such bonds an amount of surplus equal to the principal amount of, and any accrued interest on, such bonds. The amount of the surplus so transferred shall be the consideration for the issue of such bonds.

(c) A corporation may, in its certificate of incorporation, confer upon the holders of any bonds issued or to be issued by the corporation, rights to inspect the corporate books and records and to vote in the election of directors and on any other matters on which shareholders of the corporation may vote.

§ 519. Convertible Shares and Bonds

(a) When so provided in the certificate of incorporation, and subject to the restrictions in paragraph (d), a corporation may issue shares convertible,

(1) at the option of the holder only, into shares of any class or into shares of any series of any class, except into a class of shares having rights or preferences as to dividends or distribution of assets upon liquidation which are prior to superior in rank to those of the shares being converted, and

(2) if a member corporation of a national securities exchange registered under a statute of the United States such as the Securities Exchange Act of 1934,[1] at the option of the corporation or upon the happening of a specified event, into shares of any class or into shares of any series of any class or into any other security of the corporation. Authorized shares, whether issued or unissued, may be made so convertible within such period and upon such terms and conditions as are stated in the certificate of incorporation.

(b) Unless otherwise provided in the certificate of incorporation, and subject to the restrictions of paragraph (d), a corporation may issue its bonds convertible into other bonds or into shares of the corporation within such period and upon such terms and conditions as are fixed by the board.

(c) If there is shareholder approval for the issue of bonds or shares convertible into shares of the corporation, such approval may provide that the board is authorized by certificate of amendment under section 805 (Certificate of amendment; contents) to increase the authorized shares of any class or series to such number as will be sufficient, when added to the previously authorized but unissued shares of such class or series, to satisfy the conversion privileges of any such bonds or shares convertible into shares of such class or series.

(d) No issue of bonds or shares convertible into shares of the corporation shall be made unless:

(1) A sufficient number of authorized but unissued shares of the appropriate class or series are reserved by the board to be issued only in satisfaction of the conversion privileges of such convertible bonds or shares when issued; or

(2) The aggregate conversion privileges of such convertible bonds or shares when issued do not exceed the aggregate of any shares reserved under subparagraph (1) and any additional shares which may be authorized by the board under paragraph (c).

(e) No conversion of shares shall result in a reduction of stated capital. No privilege of conversion may be conferred upon, or altered in respect to, any shares or bonds that would result in the receipt by the corporation of less than the minimum consideration required to be received upon the issue of new shares. The consideration for shares issued upon the exercise of a conversion privilege shall be that provided in paragraph (g) of section 504 (Consideration and payment for shares).

(f) When shares have been converted, they shall be cancelled and disclosure of the conversion of shares during a stated period of time and its effect, if any, upon stated capital shall be made in the next financial statement covering such period that is furnished by the corporation to all its shareholders or, if practicable, in the first notice of dividend or share distribution that is furnished to the holders of each class or series of its shares between the end of such period and the next such financial statement, and in any event to all its shareholders within six months of the date of the conversion of shares. When bonds have been converted, they shall be cancelled and not reissued except upon compliance with the provisions governing the issue of convertible bonds.

§ 623. Procedure to Enforce Shareholder's Right to Receive Payment for Shares.—

* * *

(d) A shareholder may not dissent as to less than all of the shares, as to which he has a right to dissent held by him of record, that he owns beneficially. A nominee or fiduciary may not dissent on behalf of any beneficial owner as to less than all of the shares of such owner, as to which such nominee or fiduciary has a right to dissent, held of record by such nominee or fiduciary.

(e) Upon consummation of the corporate action, the shareholder shall cease to have any of the rights of a shareholder except the right to be paid the fair value of his shares and any other rights under this section.

* * *

(g) Within fifteen days after the expiration of the period within which shareholders may file their notices of election to dissent, or within fifteen days after the proposed corporate action is consummated, whichever is later (but in no case later than ninety days from the shareholders' authorization date), the corporation or, in the case of a merger or consolidation, the surviving or new corporation, shall make a written offer by registered mail to each shareholder who has filed such notice of election to pay for his shares at a specified price which the corporation considers to be their fair value. Such offer shall be accompanied by a statement setting forth the aggregate number of shares with respect to which notices of election to dissent have been received and the aggregate number of holders of such shares. If the corporate action has been consummated, such offer shall also be accompanied by (1) advance payment to each such shareholder who has submitted the certificates representing his shares to the corporation, as provided in paragraph (f), of an amount equal to eighty percent of the amount of such offer, or (2) as to each shareholder who has not yet submitted his certificates a statement that advance payment to him of an amount equal to eighty percent of the amount of such offer will be made by the corporation promptly upon submission of his certificates. If the corporate action has not been consummated at the time of the making of the offer, such advance payment or statement as to advance payment shall be sent to each shareholder entitled thereto forthwith upon consummation of the corporate action. Every advance payment or statement as to advance payment shall include advice to the shareholder to the effect that acceptance of such payment does not constitute a waiver of any dissenters' rights. If the corporate action has not been consummated upon the expiration of the ninety day period after the shareholders' authorization date, the offer may be conditioned upon the consummation of such action. Such offer shall be made at the same price per share to all dissenting shareholders of the same class, or if divided into series, of the same series. * * *

(h) The following procedure shall apply if the corporation fails to make such offer [to pay fair value] * * * or if it makes the offer and any dissenting shareholder or shareholders fail to agree with it * * * upon the price to be paid for their shares:

        * * *

(4) The court shall determine whether each dissenting shareholder, as to whom the corporation requests the court to make such determination, is entitled to receive payment for his shares. If the corporation does not request any such determination or if the court finds that any dissenting shareholder is so entitled, it shall proceed to fix the value of the shares, which, for the purposes of this section, shall be the fair value as of the close of business on the day prior to the shareholders' authorization date. In fixing the fair value of the shares, the court shall consider the nature of the transaction giving rise to the shareholder's right to receive payment for shares and its effects on the corporation and its shareholders, the concepts and methods then customary in the relevant

securities and financial markets for determining fair value of shares of a corporation engaging in a similar transaction under comparable circumstances and all other relevant factors. The court shall determine the fair value of the shares without a jury and without referral to an appraiser or referee.* * * *

* * *

(6) The final order shall include an allowance for interest at such rate as the court finds to be equitable, from the date the corporate action was consummated to the date of payment. In determining the rate of interest, the court shall consider all relevant factors, including the rate of interest which the corporation would have had to pay to borrow money during the pendency of the proceeding. If the court finds that the refusal of any shareholder to accept the corporate offer of payment for his shares was arbitrary, vexatious or otherwise not in good faith, no interest shall be allowed to him.

(7) Each party to such proceeding shall bear its own costs and expenses, including the fees and expenses of its counsel and of any experts employed by it. Notwithstanding the foregoing, the court may in its discretion, apportion and assess all or any part of the costs, expenses and fees incurred by the corporation against any or all of the dissenting shareholders who are parties to the proceeding, including any who have withdrawn their notices of election as provided in paragraph (e), if the court finds that their refusal to accept the corporate offer was arbitrary, vexatious or otherwise not in good faith. The court may, in its discretion, apportion and assess all or any part of the costs, expenses and fees incurred by any or all of the dissenting shareholders who are parties to the

---

* Legislative Finding for 1982 Amendment. Section 1 of L.1982, c. 202, provided: "Legislative declaration. A shareholder's right to dissent from certain corporate actions and to receive payment of fair value for his shares is a basic right of share ownership and, except where the corporate action is unlawful or fraudulent as to the shareholder, it is exclusive. Consequently, it is important that the right be made effective. Procedures for the exercise of the right should be as simple as possible, and dissenting shareholders should be entitled to receive payment for their shares on an expedited basis. Resolution, without judicial proceedings, of disagreements between dissenting shareholders and the corporation regarding fair value should be encouraged. Courts should determine fair value by reference to the nature and effects of the transaction giving rise to the shareholder's right to dissent, to the concepts and methods then customary in the relevant securities and financial markets and to all other relevant factors. The case law interpretation of fair value has not always reflected the reality of corporate business combinations. These transactions involve the sale of the corporation as a whole, and the corporation's value as an entirety may be substantially in excess of the actual or hypothetical market price for shares trading among investors. Thus, experience has demonstrated that large premiums over market price are commonplace in mergers and in asset acquisitions. In cases where the transaction involves a restructuring of the shareholders' relative interests in the corporation by amendment of the certificate of incorporation, courts may find it appropriate to determine only the fair value of the dissenters' shares, rather than the value of the corporation as a whole, employing traditional valuation concepts."

proceeding against the corporation if the court finds any of the following: (A) that the fair value of the shares as determined materially exceeds the amount which the corporation offered to pay; (B) that no offer or required advance payment was made by the corporation; (C) that the corporation failed to institute the special proceeding within the period specified therefor; or (D) that the action of the corporation in complying with its obligations as provided in this section was arbitrary, vexatious or otherwise not in good faith. In making any determination as provided in clause (A), the court may consider the dollar amount or the percentage, or both, by which the fair value of the shares as determined exceeds the corporate offer.

* * *

(k) The enforcement by a shareholder of his right to receive payment for his shares in the manner provided herein shall exclude the enforcement by such shareholder of any other right to which he might otherwise be entitled by virtue of share ownership, except as provided in paragraph (e), and except that this section shall not exclude the right of such shareholder to bring or maintain an appropriate action to obtain relief on the ground that such corporate action will be or is unlawful or fraudulent as to him.*

* * *

§ 717. Duty of Directors.

(a) A director shall perform his duties as a director, including his duties as a member of any committee of the board upon which he may serve, in good faith and with that degree of care which an ordinarily prudent person in a like position would use under similar circumstances. * * *

* * *

(b) In taking action, including, without limitation, action which may involve or relate to a change or potential change in the control of the corporation, a director shall be entitled to consider, without limitation, (1) both the long-term and the short-term interests of the corpora-

---

* [Ed. Note] The revisers' notes state, with respect to Section 623(k):

"The principle that the right of appraisal, if duly consummated in accordance with the statutes, is the exclusive right of the shareholder (see, Beloff v. Consolidated Edison Company, 300 N.Y. 11, 87 N.E.2d 561 (1949); Anderson v. International Mineral & Chemical Corp., 295 N.Y. 343, 67 N.E.2d 573 (1946)) has been codified, subject to the well recognized exception that this principle does not apply where the statutory procedures for appraisal are disregarded (Matter of Drosnes, 187 App.Div. 425, 175 N.Y.S. 628 (1st Dep't.1919)), or where the transaction involved fraud or overreaching (see, Eisenberg v. Central Zone Property Corp., 306 N.Y. 58, 115 N.E.2d 652 (1953))." In 1984 the New York Court of Appeals (Walter J. Schlors Associates v. Arkwin Industries, 61 N.Y.2d 700, 460 N.E.2d 1090 (1984)) implied that although § 623(K) is effective to preclude an action for damages by a complaining shareholder, it does not preclude a shareholder who alleges grounds for which a court of equity would recognize a cause of action (e.g. fraud or breach of fiduciary duty) and makes a "primary request for equitable relief."

tion and its shareholders and (2) the effects that the corporation's actions may have in the short-term or in the long-term upon any of the following:

(i) the prospects for potential growth, development, productivity and profitability of the corporation;

(ii) the corporation's current employees;

(iii) the corporation's retired employees and other beneficiaries receiving or entitled to receive retirement, welfare or similar benefits from or pursuant to any plan sponsored, or agreement entered into, by the corporation;

(iv) the corporation's customers and creditors; and

(v) the ability of the corporation to provide, as a going concern, goods, services, employment opportunities and employment benefits and otherwise to contribute to the communities in which it does business.

Nothing in this paragraph shall create any duties owed by any director to any person or entity to consider or afford any particular weight to any of the foregoing or abrogate any duty of the directors, either statutory or recognized by common law or court decisions.

For purposes of this paragraph, "control" shall mean the possession, directly or indirectly, of the power to direct or cause the direction of the management and policies of the corporation, whether through the ownership of voting stock, by contract, or otherwise.

§ 801. Right to Amend Certificate of Incorporation

(a) A corporation may amend its certificate of incorporation, from time to time, in any and as many respects as may be desired, if such amendment contains only such provisions as might be lawfully contained in an original certificate of incorporation filed at the time of making such amendment.

(b) In particular, and without limitation upon such general power of amendment, a corporation may amend its certificate of incorporation, from time to time, so as:

(1) To change its corporate name.

(2) To enlarge, limit or otherwise change its corporate purposes.

(3) To specify or change the location of the office of the corporation.

(4) To specify or change the post office address to which the secretary of state shall mail a copy of any process against the corporation served upon him.

(5) To make, revoke or change the designation of a registered agent, or to specify or change the address of its registered agent.

(6) To extend the duration of the corporation or, if the corporation ceased to exist because of the expiration of the duration specified in its certificate of incorporation, to revive its existence.

(7) To increase or decrease the aggregate number of shares, or shares of any class or series, with or without par value, which the corporation shall have authority to issue.

(8) To remove from authorized shares any class of shares, or any shares of any class, whether issued or unissued.

(9) To increase the par value of any authorized shares of any class with par value, whether issued or unissued.

(10) To reduce the par value of any authorized shares of any class with par value, whether issued or unissued.

(11) To change any authorized shares, with or without par value, whether issued or unissued, into a different number of shares of the same class or into the same or a different number of shares of any one or more classes or any series thereof, either with or without par value.

(12) To fix, change or abolish the designation of any authorized class or any series thereof or any of the relative rights, preferences and limitations of any shares of any authorized class or any series thereof, whether issued or unissued, including any provisions in respect of any undeclared dividends, whether or not cumulative or accrued, or the redemption of any shares, or any sinking fund for the redemption or purchase of any shares, or any preemptive right to acquire shares or other securities.

(13) As to the shares of any preferred class, then or theretofore authorized, which may be issued in series, to grant authority to the board or to change or revoke the authority of the board to establish and designate series and to fix the number of shares and the relative rights, preferences and limitation as between series.

(14) To strike out, change or add any provision, not inconsistent with this chapter or any other statute, relating to the business of the corporation, its affairs, its rights or powers, or the rights or powers of its shareholders, directors or officers, including any provision which under this chapter is required or permitted to be set forth in the by-laws, except that a certificate of amendment may not be filed wherein the duration of the corporation shall be reduced.

(c) A corporation created by special act may accomplish any or all amendments permitted in this article, in the manner and subject to the conditions provided in this article.

§ 803. Authorization of Amendment or Change

(a) Amendment or change of the certificate of incorporation may be authorized by vote of the board, followed by vote of the holders of a majority of all outstanding shares entitled to vote thereon at a meeting of shareholders.

(b) Alternatively, any one or more of the following changes may be authorized by or pursuant to authorization of the board:

(1) To specify or change the location of the corporation's office.

(2) To specify or change the post office address to which the secretary of state shall mail a copy of any process against the corporation served upon him.

(3) To make, revoke or change the designation of a registered agent, or to specify or change the address of its registered agent.

(c) This section shall not alter the vote required under any other section for the authorization of an amendment referred to therein, nor alter the authority of the board to authorize amendments under any other section.

(d) Amendment or change of the certificate of incorporation of a corporation which has no shareholders of record, no subscribers for shares whose subscriptions have been accepted and no directors may be authorized by the sole incorporator or a majority of the incorporators.

§ 804. Class Voting on Amendment

(a) Notwithstanding any provision in the certificate of incorporation, the holders of shares of a class or series shall be entitled to vote and to vote as a class upon the authorization of an amendment and, in addition to the authorization of the amendment by vote of the holders of a majority of all outstanding shares entitled to vote thereon, the amendment shall be authorized by vote of the holders of a majority of all outstanding shares of the class or series when a proposed amendment would:

(1) Exclude or limit their right to vote on any matter, except as such right may be limited by voting rights given to new shares then being authorized of any existing or new class or series.

(2) Change their shares under subparagraphs (b)(10), (11) or (12) of section 801 (Right to amend certificate of incorporation) or provide that their shares may be converted into shares of any other class or into shares of any other series of the same class, or alter the terms or conditions upon which their shares are convertible or change the shares issuable upon conversion of their shares, if such action would adversely affect such holders, or

(3) Subordinate their rights, by authorizing shares having preferences which would be in any respect superior to their rights.

(b) If any proposed amendment referred to in paragraph (a) would adversely affect or subordinate the rights of the holders of shares of only one or more series of any class, but not the entire class, then only the holders of each series whose rights would be adversely affected or subordinated shall be considered a separate class for the purposes of this section.

§ 902. Plan of Merger or Consolidation

(a) The board of each corporation proposing to participate in a merger or consolidation under section 901 (Power of merger or consolidation) shall adopt a plan of merger or consolidation, setting forth:

(1) The name of each constituent corporation and, if the name of any of them has been changed, the name under which it was formed; and the name of the surviving corporation, or the name, or the method of determining it, of the consolidated corporation.

(2) As to each constituent corporation, the designation and number of outstanding shares of each class and series, specifying the classes and series entitled to vote and further specifying each class and series, if any, entitled to vote as a class; and, if the number of any such shares is subject to change prior to the effective date of the merger or consolidation, the manner in which such change may occur.

(3) The terms and conditions of the proposed merger or consolidation, including the manner and basis of converting the shares of each constituent corporation into shares, bonds or other securities of the surviving or consolidated corporation, or the cash or other consideration to be paid or delivered in exchange for shares of each constituent corporation, or a combination thereof.

(4) In case of merger, a statement of any amendments or changes in the certificate of incorporation of the surviving corporation to be effected by such merger; in case of consolidation, all statements required to be included in a certificate of incorporation for a corporation formed under this chapter, except statements as to facts not available at the time the plan of consolidation is adopted by the board.

(5) Such other provisions with respect to the proposed merger or consolidation as the board considers necessary or desirable.

§ 903. Authorization by Shareholders

(a) The board of each constituent corporation, upon adopting such plan of merger or consolidation, shall submit such plan to a vote of shareholders in accordance with the following:

(1) Notice of meeting shall be given to each shareholder of record, * * * whether or not entitled to vote. A copy of the plan of merger or consolidation or an outline of the material features of the plan shall accompany such notice.

(2) The plan of merger or consolidation shall be adopted at a meeting of shareholders by vote of the holders of two-thirds of all outstanding shares entitled to vote thereon. Notwithstanding any

provision in the certificate of incorporation, the holders of shares of a class or series shall be entitled to vote and to vote as a class if the plan of merger or consolidation contains any provision which, if contained in an amendment to the certificate of incorporation, would entitle the holders of shares of such class or series to vote and to vote as a class thereon. In such case, in addition to the authorization of the merger or consolidation by vote of the holders of two-thirds of all outstanding shares entitled to vote thereon, the merger or consolidation shall be authorized by vote of the holders of two-thirds of all outstanding shares of each such class or series.

(b) Notwithstanding shareholder authorization and at any time prior to the filing of the certificate of merger or consolidation, the plan of merger or consolidation may be abandoned pursuant to a provision for such abandonment, if any, contained in the plan of merger or consolidation.

§ 909. Sale, Lease, Exchange or Other Disposition of Assets

(a) A sale, lease, exchange or other disposition of all or substantially all the assets of a corporation, if not made in the usual or regular course of the business actually conducted by such corporation, shall be authorized only in accordance with the following procedure:

(1) The board shall authorize the proposed sale, lease, exchange or other disposition and direct its submission to a vote of shareholders.

(2) Notice of meeting shall be given to each shareholder of record, whether or not entitled to vote.

(3) The shareholders shall approve such sale, lease, exchange or other disposition and may fix, or may authorize the board to fix, any of the terms and conditions thereof and the consideration to be received by the corporation therefor, which may consist in whole or in part of cash or other property, real or personal, including shares, bonds or other securities of any other domestic or foreign corporation or corporations, by vote at a meeting of shareholders of the holders of two-thirds of all outstanding shares entitled to vote thereon.

* * *

(d) Whenever a transaction of the character described in paragraph (a) involves a sale, lease, exchange or other disposition of all or substantially all the assets of the corporation, including its name, to a new corporation formed under the same name as the existing corporation, upon the expiration of thirty days from the filing of the certificate of incorporation of the new corporation, with the consent of the state tax commission attached, the existing corporation shall be automatically dissolved, unless, before the end of such thirty-day period, such corporation has changed its name. The adjustment and winding up of the affairs of such dissolved corporation shall proceed in accordance with the provisions of article 10 (Non-judicial dissolution).

* * *

(f) Notwithstanding shareholder approval, the board may abandon the proposed sale, lease, exchange or other disposition without further action by the shareholders, subject to the rights, if any, of third parties under any contract relating thereto.

* * *

§ 910. Right of Shareholder to Receive Payment for Shares Upon Merger, Consolidation or Sale, Lease, Exchange or Other Disposition of Assets

(a) A shareholder of a domestic corporation shall, subject to and by complying with section 623 (Procedure to enforce shareholder's right to receive payment for shares), have the right to receive payment of the fair value of his shares and the other rights and benefits provided by such section, in the following cases:

(1) Any shareholder entitled to vote who does not assent to the taking of an action specified in subparagraphs (A), (B) and (C).

(A) Any plan of merger or consolidation to which the corporation is a party; except that the right to receive payment of the fair value of his shares shall not be available:

(i) To a shareholder of the surviving corporation in a merger authorized by section 905 (Merger of subsidiary corporation), * * *; and

(ii) To a shareholder of the surviving corporation in a merger authorized by this article, other than a merger specified in subparagraph (i), unless such merger effects one or more of the changes specified in subparagraph (b)(6) of section 806 * (Provisions as to certain proceedings) in the rights of the shares held by such shareholder.

* [Ed. Note] § 806 provides in relevant part:

(b) The following provisions shall apply to amendments and changes under this article, except under section 808 (Reorganization under act of congress):

* * *

(6) A holder of any adversely affected shares who does not vote for or consent in writing to the taking of such action shall, subject to and by complying with the provisions of section 623 (Procedure to enforce shareholder's right to receive payment for shares), have the right to dissent and to receive payment for such shares, if the certificate of amendment (A) alters or abolishes any preferential right of any outstanding shares having preferences; or (B) creates, alters or abolishes any provision or right in respect of the redemption of such shares or any sinking fund for the redemption or purchase of such shares; or (C) alters or abolishes any preemptive right of such holder to acquire shares or other securities; or (D) excludes or limits the right of such holder to vote on any matter, except as such right may be limited by the voting rights given to new shares then being authorized of any existing or new class.

(B) Any sale, lease, exchange or other disposition of all or substantially all of the assets of a corporation which requires shareholder approval under section 909 (Sale, lease, exchange or other disposition of assets) other than a transaction wholly for cash where the shareholders' approval thereof is conditioned upon the dissolution of the corporation and the distribution of substantially all of its net assets to the shareholders in accordance with their respective interests within one year after the date of such transaction.

* * *

(C) Any share exchange authorized by section 913 in which the corporation is participating as a subject corporation [i.e. not an acquiring corporation]; except that the right to receive payment of the fair value of his shares shall not be available to a shareholder whose shares have not been acquired in the exchange.

(2) Any shareholder of the subsidiary corporation in a merger authorized by section 905 or paragraph (c) of section 907, or in a share exchange authorized by paragraph (g) of section 913, who files with the corporation a written notice of election to dissent as provided in paragraph (c) of section 623.

* * *

§ 912. Requirements Relating to Certain Business Combinations

(a) For the purposes of this section:

(1) "Affiliate" means a person that directly, or indirectly through one or more intermediaries, controls, or is controlled by, or is under common control with, a specified person.

(2) "Announcement date", when used in reference to any business combination, means the date of the first public announcement of the final, definitive proposal for such business combination.

(3) "Associate", when used to indicate a relationship with any person, means (A) any corporation or organization of which such person is an officer or partner or is, directly or indirectly, the beneficial owner of ten percent or more of any class of voting stock, (B) any trust or other estate in which such person has a substantial beneficial interest or as to which such person serves as trustee or in a similar fiduciary capacity, and (C) any relative or spouse of such person, or any relative of such spouse, who has the same home as such person.

(4) "Beneficial owner", when used with respect to any stock, means a person:

(A) that, individually or with or through any of its affiliates or associates, beneficially owns such stock, directly or indirectly; or

(B) that, individually or with or through any of its affiliates or associates, has (i) the right to acquire such stock (whether such right is exercisable immediately or only after the passage of time), pursuant to any agreement, arrangement or understanding (whether or not in writing), or upon the exercise of conversion rights, exchange rights, warrants or options, or otherwise; provided, however, that a person shall not be deemed the beneficial owner of stock tendered pursuant to a tender or exchange offer made by such person or any of such person's affiliates or associates until such tendered stock is accepted for purchase or exchange; or (ii) the right to vote such stock pursuant to any agreement, arrangement or understanding (whether or not in writing); provided, however, that a person shall not be deemed the beneficial owner of any stock under this item if the agreement, arrangement or understanding to vote such stock (X) arises solely from a revocable proxy or consent given in response to a proxy or consent solicitation made in accordance with the applicable rules and regulations under the Exchange Act and (Y) is not then reportable on a Schedule 13D under the Exchange Act (or any comparable or successor report); or

(C) that has any agreement, arrangement or understanding (whether or not in writing), for the purpose of acquiring, holding, voting (except voting pursuant to a revocable proxy or consent as described in item (ii) of clause (B) of this subparagraph), or disposing of such stock with any other person that beneficially owns, or whose affiliates or associates beneficially own, directly or indirectly, such stock.

(5) "Business combination", when used in reference to any resident domestic corporation and any interested shareholder of such resident domestic corporation, means:

(A) any merger or consolidation of such resident domestic corporation or any subsidiary of such resident domestic corporation with (i) such interested shareholder or (ii) any other corporation (whether or not itself an interested shareholder of such resident domestic corporation) which is, or after such merger or consolidation would be, an affiliate or associate of such interested shareholder;

(B) any sale, lease, exchange, mortgage, pledge, transfer or other disposition (in one transaction or a series of transactions) to or with such interested shareholder or any affiliate or associate of such interested shareholder of assets of such resident domestic corporation or any subsidiary of such resident domestic corporation (i) having an aggregate market value equal to ten percent or more of the aggregate market value of all the assets, determined on a consolidated basis, of such resident domestic corporation, (ii) having an aggregate market value equal to ten percent or more of the aggregate market value of all the outstanding stock of such resident domestic corporation, or (iii) representing ten percent or more of the earning power or net income, determined on a consolidated basis, of such resident domestic corporation;

(C) the issuance or transfer by such resident domestic corporation or any subsidiary of such resident domestic corporation (in one transaction or a series of transactions) of any stock of such resident domestic corporation or any subsidiary of such resident domestic corporation which has an aggregate market value equal to five percent or more of the aggregate market value of all the outstanding stock of such resident domestic corporation to such interested shareholder or any affiliate or associate of such interested shareholder except pursuant to the exercise of warrants or rights to purchase stock offered, or a dividend or distribution paid or made, pro rata to all shareholders of such resident domestic corporation;

(D) the adoption of any plan or proposal for the liquidation or dissolution of such resident domestic corporation proposed by, or pursuant to any agreement, arrangement or understanding (whether or not in writing) with, such interested shareholder or any affiliate or associate of such interested shareholder;

(E) any reclassification of securities (including, without limitation, any stock split, stock dividend, or other distribution of stock in respect of stock, or any reverse stock split), or recapitalization of such resident domestic corporation, or any merger or consolidation of such resident domestic corporation with any subsidiary of such resident domestic corporation, or any other transaction (whether or not with or into or otherwise involving such interested shareholder), proposed by, or pursuant to any agreement, arrangement or understanding (whether or not in writing) with, such interested shareholder or any affiliate or associate of such interested shareholder, which has the effect, directly or indirectly, of increasing the proportionate share of the outstanding shares of any class or series of voting stock or securities convertible into voting stock of such resident domestic corporation or any subsidiary of such resident domestic corporation which is directly or indirectly owned by such interested shareholder or any affiliate or associate of such interested shareholder, except as a result of immaterial changes due to fractional share adjustments; or

(F) any receipt by such interested shareholder or any affiliate or associate of such interested shareholder of the benefit, directly or indirectly (except proportionately as a shareholder of such resident domestic corporation) of any loans, advances, guarantees, pledges or other financial assistance or any tax credits or other tax advantages provided by or through such resident domestic corporation.

(6) "Common stock" means any stock other than preferred stock.

(7) "Consummation date", with respect to any business combination, means the date of consummation of such business combination, or, in the case of a business combination as to which a shareholder vote is taken, the later of the business day prior to the vote or twenty days prior to the date of consummation of such business combination.

(8) "Control", including the terms "controlling", "controlled by" and "under common control with", means the possession, directly or indirectly, of the power to direct or cause the direction of the management and policies of a person, whether through the ownership of voting stock, by contract, or otherwise. A person's beneficial ownership of ten percent or more of a corporation's outstanding voting stock shall create a presumption that such person has control of such corporation. Notwithstanding the foregoing, a person shall not be deemed to have control of a corporation if such person holds voting stock, in good faith and not for the purpose of circumventing this section, as an agent, bank, broker, nominee, custodian or trustee for one or more beneficial owners who do not individually or as a group have control of such corporation.

(9) "Exchange Act" means the Act of Congress known as the Securities Exchange Act of 1934, as the same has been or hereafter may be amended from time to time.

(10) "Interested shareholder", when used in reference to any resident domestic corporation, means any person (other than such resident domestic corporation or any subsidiary of such resident domestic corporation) that

(A)(i) is the beneficial owner, directly or indirectly, of twenty percent or more of the outstanding voting stock of such resident domestic corporation; or

(ii) is an affiliate or associate of such resident domestic corporation and at any time within the five-year period immediately prior to the date in question was the beneficial owner, directly or indirectly, of twenty percent or more of the then outstanding voting stock of such resident domestic corporation; provided that

(B) for the purpose of determining whether a person is an interested shareholder, the number of shares of voting stock of such resident domestic corporation deemed to be outstanding shall include shares deemed to be beneficially owned by the person through application of subparagraph four of this paragraph but shall not include any other unissued shares of voting stock of such resident domestic corporation which may be issuable pursuant to any agreement, arrangement or understanding, or upon exercise of conversion rights, warrants or options, or otherwise.

(11) "Market value", when used in reference to stock or property of any resident domestic corporation, means:

(A) in the case of stock, the highest closing sale price during the thirty-day period immediately preceding the date in question of a share of such stock on the composite tape for New York stock exchange-listed stocks, or, if such stock is not quoted on such composite tape or if such stock is not listed on such exchange, on the principal United States securities exchange registered under the Exchange Act on which such stock is listed, or, if such stock is not listed on any such exchange, the highest closing bid quotation with respect to a share of such stock during the thirty-day period preceding the date in question on the National Association of Securities Dealers, Inc. Automated Quotations System or any system then in use, or if no such quotations are available, the fair market value on the date in question of a share of such stock as determined by the board of directors of such resident domestic corporation in good faith; and

(B) in the case of property other than cash or stock, the fair market value of such property on the date in question as determined by the board of directors of such resident domestic corporation in good faith.

(12) "Preferred stock" means any class or series of stock of a resident domestic corporation which under the by-laws or certificate of incorporation of such resident domestic corporation is entitled to receive payment of dividends prior to any payment of dividends on some other class or series of stock, or is entitled in the event of any voluntary liquidation, dissolution or winding up of the resident domestic corporation to receive payment or distribution of a preferential amount before any payments or distributions are received by some other class or series of stock.

(13) "Resident domestic corporation" means an issuer of voting stock which:

(A) is organized under the laws of this state; and

(B) either (i) has its principal executive offices and significant business operations located in this state; or (ii) has, along or in combination with one or more of its subsidiaries of which it owns at least eighty percent of the voting stock, at least two hundred fifty employees or twenty-five percent of the total number of all employees of itself and such subsidiaries employed primarily within the state; and

(C) has at least ten percent of its voting stock owned beneficially by residents of this state. For purposes of this section, the residence of a partnership, unincorporated association, trust or similar organization shall be the principal office of such organization.

No resident domestic corporation, which is organized under the laws of this state, shall cease to be a resident domestic corporation by reason of events occurring or actions taken while such resident domestic corporation is subject to the provisions of this section.

(14) "Stock" means:

(A) any stock or similar security, any certificate of interest, any participation in any profit sharing agreement, any voting trust certificate, or any certificate of deposit for stock; and

(B) any security convertible, with or without consideration, into stock, or any warrant, call or other option or privilege of buying stock without being bound to do so, or any other security carrying any right to acquire, subscribe to or purchase stock.

(15) "Stock acquisition date", with respect to any person and any resident domestic corporation, means the date that such person first becomes an interested shareholder of such resident domestic corporation.

(16) "Subsidiary" of any person means any other corporation of which a majority of the voting stock is owned, directly or indirectly, by such person.

(17) "Voting stock" means shares of capital stock of a corporation entitled to vote generally in the election of directors.

(b) Notwithstanding anything to the contrary contained in this chapter (except the provisions of paragraph (d) of this section), no resident domestic corporation shall engage in any business combination with any interested shareholder of such resident domestic corporation for a period of five years following such interested shareholder's stock acquisition date unless such business combination or the purchase of stock made by such interested shareholder on such interested shareholder's stock acquisition date is approved by the board of directors of such resident domestic corporation prior to such interested shareholder's stock acquisition date. If a good faith proposal is made in writing to the board of directors of such resident domestic corporation regarding a business combination, the board of directors shall respond, in writing, within thirty days or such shorter period, if any, as may be required by the Exchange Act, setting forth its reasons for its decision regarding such proposal. If a good faith proposal to purchase stock is made in writing to the board of directors of such resident domestic corporation, the board of directors, unless it responds affirmatively in writing within thirty days or such shorter period, if any, as may be required by the Exchange Act, shall be deemed to have disapproved such stock purchase.

(c) Notwithstanding anything to the contrary contained in this chapter (except the provisions of paragraphs (b) and (d) of this section), no resident domestic corporation shall engage at any time in any business combination with any interested shareholder of such resident domestic corporation other than a business combination specified in any one of subparagraph (1), (2) or (3):

(1) A business combination approved by the board of directors of such resident domestic corporation prior to such interested shareholder's stock acquisition date, or where the purchase of stock made by such interested shareholder on such interested shareholder's stock acquisition date had been approved by the board of directors of such resident domestic corporation prior to such interested shareholder's stock acquisition date.

(2) A business combination approved by the affirmative vote of the holders of a majority of the outstanding voting stock not beneficially owned by such interested shareholder or any affiliate or associate of such interested shareholder at a meeting called for such purpose no earlier than five years after such interested shareholder's stock acquisition date.

(3) A business combination that meets all of the following conditions:

(A) The aggregate amount of the cash and the market value as of the consummation date of consideration other than cash to be received per share by holders of outstanding shares of common stock of such resident domestic corporation in such business combination is [at] least equal to the higher of the following:

(i) the highest per share price paid by such interested shareholder at a time when he was the beneficial owner, directly or indirectly, of five percent or more of the outstanding voting stock of such resident domestic corporation, for any shares of common stock of the same class or series acquired by it (X) within the five-year period immediately prior to the announcement date with respect to such business combination, or (Y) within the five-year period immediately prior to, or in, the transaction in which such interested shareholder became an interested shareholder, whichever is higher; plus, in either case, interest compounded annually from the earliest date on which such highest per share acquisition price was paid through the consummation date at the rate for one-year United States treasury obligations from time to time in effect; less the aggregate amount of any cash dividends paid, and the market value of any dividends paid other than in cash, per share of common stock since such earliest date, up to the amount of such interest; and

(ii) the market value per share of common stock on the announcement date with respect to such business combination or on such interested shareholder's stock acquisition date, whichever is higher; plus interest compounded annually from such date through the consummation date at the rate for one-year United States treasury obligations from time to time in effect; less the aggregate amount of any cash dividends paid, and the market value of any dividends paid other than in cash, per share of common stock since such date, up to the amount of such interest.

(B) The aggregate amount of the cash and the market value as of the consummation date of consideration other than cash to be received per share by holders of outstanding shares of any class or series of stock, other than common stock, of such resident domestic corporation is at least equal to the highest of the following (whether or not such interested shareholder has previously acquired any shares of such class or series of stock):

(i) the highest per share price paid by such interested shareholder at a time when he was the beneficial owner, directly or indirectly, of five percent or more of the outstanding voting stock of such resident domestic corporation, for any shares of such class or series of stock acquired by it (X) within the five-year period immediately prior to the announcement date with respect to such business combination, or (Y) within the five-year period immediately prior to, or in, the transaction in which such interested shareholder became an interested shareholder, whichever is higher; plus, in either case, interest compounded annually from the earliest date on which such highest per share acquisition price was paid through the consummation date at the rate for one-year United States treasury obligations from time to time in effect; less the aggregate amount of any cash dividends paid, and the market value of any dividends paid other than in cash, per share of such class or series of stock since such earliest date, up to the amount of such interest;

(ii) the highest preferential amount per share to which the holders of shares of such class or series of stock are entitled in the event of any voluntary liquidation, dissolution or winding up of such resident domestic corporation, plus the aggregate amount of any dividends declared or due as to which such holders are entitled prior to payment of dividends on some other class or series of stock (unless the aggregate amount of such dividends is included in such preferential amount); and

(iii) the market value per share of such class or series of stock on the announcement date with respect to such business combination or on such interested shareholder's stock acquisition date, whichever is higher; plus interest compounded annually from such date through the consummation date at the rate for one-year United States treasury obligations from time to time in effect; less the aggregate amount of any cash dividends paid, and the market value of any dividends paid other than in cash, per share of such class or series of stock since such date, up to the amount of such interest.

(C) The consideration to be received by holders of a particular class or series of outstanding stock (including common stock) of such resident domestic corporation in such business combination is in cash or in the same form as the interested shareholder has used to acquire the largest number of shares of such class or series of stock previously acquired by it, and such consideration shall be distributed promptly.

(D) The holders of all outstanding shares of stock of such resident domestic corporation not beneficially owned by such interested shareholder immediately prior to the consummation of such business combination are entitled to receive in such business combination cash or other consideration for such shares in compliance with clauses (A), (B) and (C) of this subparagraph.

(E) After such interested shareholder's stock acquisition date and prior to the consummation date with respect to such business combination, such interested shareholder has not become the beneficial owner of any additional shares of voting stock of such resident domestic corporation except:

(i) as part of the transaction which resulted in such interested shareholder becoming an interested shareholder;

(ii) by virtue of proportionate stock splits, stock dividends or other distributions of stock in respect of stock not constituting a business combination under clause (E) of subparagraph five of paragraph (a) of this section;

(iii) through a business combination meeting all of the conditions of paragraph (b) of this section and this paragraph; or

(iv) through purchase by such interested shareholder at any price which, if such price had been paid in an otherwise permissible business combination the announcement date and consummation date of which were the date of such purchase, would have satisfied the requirements of clauses (A), (B) and (C) of this subparagraph.

(d) The provisions of this section shall not apply:

(1) to any business combination of a resident domestic corporation that does not have a class of voting stock registered with the Securities and Exchange Commission pursuant to section twelve of the Exchange Act, unless the certificate of incorporation provides otherwise; or

(2) to any business combination of a resident domestic corporation whose certificate of incorporation has been amended to provide that such resident domestic corporation shall be subject to the provisions of this section, which did not have a class of voting stock registered with the Securities and Exchange Commission pursuant to section twelve of the Exchange Act on the effective date of such amendment, and which is a business combination with an interested shareholder whose stock acquisition date is prior to the effective date of such amendment; or

(3) to any business combination of a resident domestic corporation (i) the original certificate of incorporation of which contains a provision expressly electing not to be governed by this section, or (ii) which adopts an amendment to such resident domestic corporation's by-laws prior to March thirty-first, nineteen hundred eighty-six, expressly electing not to be governed by this section, or (iii) which adopts an amendment to such resident domestic corporation's by-laws, approved by the affirmative vote of the holders, other than interested shareholders and their affiliates and associates, of a majority of the outstanding voting stock of such resident domestic corporation, excluding the voting stock of interested shareholders and their affiliates and associates, expressly electing not to be governed by this section, provided that such amendment to the by-laws shall not be effective until eighteen months after such vote of such resident domestic corporation's shareholders and shall not apply to any business combination of such resident domestic corporation with an interested shareholder whose stock acquisition date is on or prior to the effective date of such amendment; or

(4) to any business combination of a resident domestic corporation with an interested shareholder of such resident domestic corporation which became an interested shareholder inadvertently,

if such interested shareholder (i) as soon as practicable, divests itself of a sufficient amount of the voting stock of such resident domestic corporation so that it no longer is the beneficial owner, directly or indirectly, of twenty percent or more of the outstanding voting stock of such resident domestic corporation, and (ii) would not at any time within the five-year period preceding the announcement date with respect to such business combination have been an interested shareholder but for such inadvertent acquisition.

(5) to any business combination with an interested shareholder who was the beneficial owner, directly or indirectly, of five per cent or more of the outstanding voting stock of such resident domestic corporation on October thirtieth, nineteen hundred eighty-five, and remained so to such interested shareholder's stock acquisition date.

§ 913. Share Exchanges

(a)(1) Two domestic corporations may, as provided in this section, participate in the consummation of a plan for binding share exchanges.

(2) Whenever used in this article:

(A) "Acquiring corporation" means a corporation that is participating in a procedure pursuant to which such corporation is acquiring all of the outstanding shares of one or more classes of a subject corporation.

(B) "Subject corporation" means a corporation that is participating in a procedure pursuant to which all of the outstanding shares of one or more classes of such corporation are being acquired by an acquiring corporation.

(b) The board of the acquiring corporation and the board of the subject corporation shall adopt a plan of exchange, setting forth:

(1) The name of the acquiring corporation and the name of the subject corporation, and, if the name of either of them has been changed, the name under which it was formed;

(2) As to the acquiring corporation and the subject corporation, the designation and number of outstanding shares of each class and series, specifying the classes and series entitled to vote and further specifying each class and series, if any, entitled to vote as a class; and, if the number of any such shares is subject to change prior to the effective date of the exchange, the manner in which such change may occur;

(3) The terms and conditions of the proposed exchange, including the manner and basis of exchanging the shares to be acquired for shares, bonds or other securities of the acquiring corporation, or the cash or other consideration to be paid or delivered in exchange for such shares to be acquired, or a combination thereof; and

(4) Such other provisions with respect to the proposed exchange as the board considers necessary or desirable.

(c) The board of the subject corporation, upon adopting the plan of exchange, shall submit such plan, except as provided in paragraph (g) of this section, to a vote of shareholders in accordance with the following:

(1) Notice of meeting shall be given to each shareholder of record, as of the record date fixed pursuant to section 604 (Fixing record date), whether or not entitled to vote. A copy of the plan of exchange or an outline of the material features of the plan shall accompany such notice.

(2) The plan of exchange shall be adopted at a meeting of shareholders by vote of the holders of two-thirds of all outstanding shares entitled to vote thereon. Notwithstanding any provision in the certificate of incorporation, the holders of shares of a class or series shall be entitled to vote and to vote as a class if the plan of exchange contains any provision which, if contained in an amendment to the certificate of incorporation, would entitle the holders of shares of such class or series to vote and to vote as a class thereon, or if the shares of such class or series are to be exchanged pursuant to the plan of exchange. In such case, in addition to the authorization of the exchange by vote of the holders of two-thirds of all outstanding shares entitled to vote thereon, the exchange shall be authorized by vote of the holders of a majority of all outstanding shares of each such class or series. Notwithstanding shareholder authorization and at any time prior to the filing of the certificate of exchange, the plan of exchange may be abandoned pursuant to a provision for such abandonment, if any, contained in the plan of exchange.

(d) After adoption of the plan of exchange by the board of the acquiring corporation and the board of the subject corporation and by the shareholders of the subject corporation entitled to vote thereon, unless the exchange is abandoned in accordance with paragraph (c), a certificate of exchange, entitled "Certificate of exchange of shares of _____, subject corporation, for shares of _____, acquiring corporation, or other consideration, under section 913 of the Business Corporation Law", shall be signed and verified on behalf of each corporation and delivered to the department of state. * * *

(e) Upon the filing of the certificate of exchange by the department of state or on such date subsequent thereto, not to exceed thirty days, as shall be set forth in such certificate, the exchange shall be effected. When such exchange has been effected, ownership of the shares to be acquired pursuant to the plan of exchange shall vest in the acquiring corporation, whether or not the certificates for such shares have been surrendered for exchange, and the acquiring corporation shall be entitled to have new certificates registered in its name or at its direction. Shareholders whose shares have been so acquired shall become entitled to the shares, bonds or other securities of the acquiring corporation, or the cash or other consideration, required to be paid or delivered in exchange for such shares pursuant to the plan. Subject to any terms of the plan regarding surrender of certificates theretofore evidencing the shares so acquired and regarding whether such certificates shall thereafter evidence securities of the acquiring corporation, such certificates shall thereafter evidence only the right to receive the consideration required to be paid or delivered in exchange for such shares pursuant to the plan or, in the case of dissenting shareholders, their rights under section 910 (Right of shareholder to receive payment for shares upon merger or consolidation, or sale, lease, exchange or other disposition of assets, or share exchange) and section 623 (Procedure to enforce shareholder's right to receive payment for shares).

(f)(1) A foreign corporation and a domestic corporation may participate in a share exchange, but, if the subject corporation is a foreign corporation, only if such exchange is permitted by the laws of the jurisdiction under which such foreign corporation is incorporated. With respect to such exchange, any reference in subparagraph (2) of paragraph (a) of this section to a corporation shall, unless the context otherwise requires, include both domestic and foreign corporations, and the provisions of paragraphs (b), (c), (d) and (e) of this section shall apply, except to the extent otherwise provided in this paragraph.

    * * *

(g)(1) Any corporation owning at least ninety percent of the outstanding common shares, having full voting rights, of another corporation may acquire by exchange the remainder of such outstanding common shares, without the authorization of the shareholders of any such corporation and with the effect provided for in paragraph (e) of this section. The board of the acquiring corporation shall adopt a plan of exchange, setting forth the matters specified in paragraph (b) of this section. A copy of such plan of exchange or an outline of the material features thereof shall be given, personally or by mail, to all holders of shares of the subject corporation that are not owned by the acquiring corporation, unless the giving of such copy or outline has been waived by such holders.

(2) A certificate of exchange, entitled "Certificate of exchange of shares of _____, subject corporation, for shares of _____, acquiring corporation, or other consideration, under paragraph (g) of section 913 of the Business Corporation Law" * * * shall be signed, verified and delivered to the department of state by the acquiring corporation, but not less than thirty days after the giving of a copy or outline of the material features of the plan of exchange to shareholders of the subject corporation, or at any time after the waiving thereof by the holders of all the outstanding shares of the subject corporation not owned by the acquiring corporation.

(3) The right of exchange of shares granted by this paragraph to certain corporations shall not preclude the exercise by such corporations of any other right of exchange under this article.

(4) The procedure for the exchange of shares of a subject corporation under this paragraph (g) of this section shall be available where either the subject corporation or the acquiring corporation is a foreign corporation, and, in case the subject corporation is a foreign corporation, where such exchange is permitted by the laws of the jurisdiction under which such foreign corporation is incorporated.

(h) This section does not limit the power of a domestic or foreign corporation to acquire all or part of the shares of one or more classes of another domestic or foreign corporation by means of a voluntary exchange or otherwise.

(i)(1) A binding share exchange pursuant to this section shall constitute a "business combination" pursuant to section nine hundred twelve of this chapter (Requirements relating to certain business combinations) if the subject corporation is a "resident domestic corporation" and the acquiring corporation is an "interested shareholder" of the subject corporation, as such terms are defined in section nine hundred twelve of this chapter.

(2) With respect to convertible securities and other securities evidencing a right to acquire shares of a subject corporation, a binding share exchange pursuant to this section shall have the same effect on the rights of the holders of such securities as a merger of the subject corporation.

INDEX

References are to pages

I-1

†